New Perspectives on

Microsoft® Windows Vista™ for Power Users

Power Users

Harry L. Phillips
Santa Rosa Junior College

Australia • Brazil • Japan • Korea • Mexico • Singapore • Spain • United Kingdom • United States

COURSE TECHNOLOGY
CENGAGE Learning™

New Perspectives on Microsoft Windows Vista for Power Users

Executive Editor: Marie L. Lee
Senior Product Manager: Kathy Finnegan
Product Manager: Erik Herman
Associate Acquisitions Editor: Brandi Henson
Associate Product Manager: Leigh Robbins
Editorial Assistant: Patrick Frank
Director of Marketing: Cheryl Costantini
Marketing Manager: Ryan DeGrote
Marketing Specialist: Jennifer Hankin
Developmental Editor: Lisa Ruffolo
Content Project Manager: Erin Dowler
Composition: GEX Publishing Services
Text Designer: Steve Deschene
Art Director: Marissa Falco
Cover Designer: Elizabeth Paquin
Cover Art: Bill Brown
Copyeditor: Judi Silver
Proofreader: Kathy Orrino
Indexer: Rich Carlson

ISBN-13: 978-1-4239-0603-2

ISBN-10: 1-4239-0603-9

Course Technology
25 Thomson Place
Boston, Massachusetts 02210
USA

Cengage Learning is a leading provider of customized learning solutions with office locations around the globe, including Singapore, the United Kingdom, Australia, Mexico, Brazil, and Japan. Locate your local office at: **international.cengage.com/region**

Cengage Learning products are represented in Canada by Nelson Education, Ltd.

For your lifelong learning solutions, visit **course.cengage.com**

Visit our corporate website at **cengage.com**

Purchase any of our products at your local college store or at our preferred online store **www.ichapters.com**

Printed in Canada
1 2 3 4 5 6 7 8 9 12 11 10 09 08

Preface

The New Perspectives Series' critical-thinking, problem-solving approach is the ideal way to prepare students to transcend point-and-click skills and take advantage of all that Microsoft Windows Vista has to offer.

Our goal in developing the New Perspectives Series was to create books that give students the software concepts and practical skills they need to succeed beyond the classroom. With this new edition, we've updated our proven case-based pedagogy with more practical content to make learning skills more meaningful to students.

With the New Perspectives Series, students understand *why* they are learning *what* they are learning, and are fully prepared to apply their skills to real-life situations.

"This text is one book my students don't sell at the end of the semester. They find it an invaluable resource for their higher level courses as well as their work outside the classroom."
—Debra Geoghan
Bucks County
Community College

About This Book

This book provides extensive coverage of the Windows Vista operating system, and includes the following:

- Complete coverage of Windows Vista basics, guiding students to manage folders and files, enhance the security of their computers, and troubleshoot problems so they quickly learn to work independently
- Thorough explanations of the concepts, techniques, and advanced skills students need to become power users of Windows Vista in particular and operating systems in general
- Expanded and in-depth coverage of features new to Windows Vista, including Instant Search, power plans, Windows Aero, Windows ReadyBoost, system diagnostic tools, and more
- Appealing, clear instructions for novices and comprehensive, thoughtful details for knowledgeable users to create an enriched learning experience for all students

System Requirements

This book assumes a standard installation of Microsoft Windows Vista Ultimate on a networked or standalone computer with the Windows Aero color scheme enabled. Most tasks in this text can also be completed with a standard installation of the Windows Vista Business, Home Premium, and Enterprise editions. Users with Windows Vista Home Basic can perform some of the basic types of Windows Vista operations covered in the textbook. The book also examines security and privacy features of the Windows Internet Explorer 7 Web browser and, therefore, assumes a standard installation of that Web browser.

"The New Perspectives case-based approach lays out a methodology that makes the instructional process relevant to students and enables them to apply what they have learned in a meaningful way."
—Richard Pollak
Minneapolis Community and Technical College

The New Perspectives Approach

Context
Each tutorial begins with a problem presented in a "real-world" case that is meaningful to students. The case sets the scene to help students understand what they will do in the tutorial.

Hands-on Approach
Each tutorial is divided into manageable sessions that combine reading and hands-on, step-by-step work. Numerous screenshots help guide students through the steps. **Trouble?** tips anticipate common mistakes or problems to help students stay on track and continue with the tutorial.

InSight

InSight Boxes
New for this edition! InSight boxes offer expert advice and best practices to help students better understand how to work with the Windows Vista operating system. With the information provided in the InSight boxes, students achieve a deeper understanding of the concepts behind the features and skills presented.

Tip

Margin Tips
New for this edition! Margin Tips provide helpful hints and shortcuts for more efficient use of Windows Vista. The Tips appear in the margin at key points throughout each tutorial, giving students extra information when and where they need it.

Reality Check

Reality Check
New for this edition! A capstone, open-ended Reality Check exercise gives students the opportunity to complete practical, real-world tasks, such as customizing their desktops and personalizing security settings.

Review

In New Perspectives, retention is a key component to learning. At the end of each session, a series of Quick Check questions helps students test their understanding of the concepts before moving on. Each tutorial also contains an end-of-tutorial summary and a list of key terms for further reinforcement.

Apply

Assessment
Engaging and challenging Review Assignments and Case Problems have always been a hallmark feature of the New Perspectives Series. Instructive labels and brief descriptions accompany the exercises, making it easy to understand, at a glance, both the goal and level of challenge a particular assignment holds.

Reference Window

Task Reference

Reference
While contextual learning is excellent for retention, there are times when students will want a high-level understanding of how to accomplish a task. Within each tutorial, Reference Windows appear before a set of steps to provide a succinct summary and preview of how to perform a task. In addition, a complete Task Reference at the back of the book provides quick access to information on how to carry out common tasks. Finally, each book includes a combination Glossary/Index to promote easy reference of material.

Our Complete System of Instruction

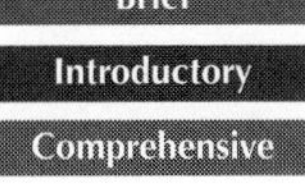

Coverage To Meet Your Needs

Whether you're looking for just a small amount of coverage or enough to fill a semester-long class, we can provide you with a textbook that meets your needs.

- Brief books typically cover the essential skills in just 2 to 4 tutorials.
- Introductory books build and expand on those skills and contain an average of 5 to 8 tutorials.
- Comprehensive books are great for a full-semester class, and contain 9 to 12+ tutorials.

So if the book you're holding does not provide the right amount of coverage for you, there's probably another offering available. Visit our Web site or contact your Course Technology sales representative to find out what else we offer.

CourseCasts – Learning on the Go. Always available...always relevant.

Want to keep up with the latest technology trends relevant to you? Visit our site to find a library of podcasts, CourseCasts, featuring a "CourseCast of the Week," and download them to your mp3 player at http://coursecasts.course.com.

Ken Baldauf, host of CourseCasts, is a faculty member of the Florida State University Computer Science Department where he is responsible for teaching technology classes to thousands of FSU students each year. Ken is an expert in the latest technology trends; he gathers and sorts through the most pertinent news and information for CourseCasts so your students can spend their time enjoying technology, rather than trying to figure it out. Open or close your lecture with a discussion based on the latest CourseCast.

Visit us at http://coursecasts.course.com to learn on the go!

Instructor Resources

We offer more than just a book. We have all the tools you need to enhance your lectures, check students' work, and generate exams in a new, easier-to-use and completely revised package. This book's Instructor's Manual, ExamView testbank, PowerPoint presentations, data files, solution files, figure files, and a sample syllabus are all available on a single CD-ROM or for downloading at www.course.com.

Online Content

Blackboard is the leading distance learning solution provider and class-management platform today. Course Technology has partnered with Blackboard to bring you premium online content. Blackboard test banks for use with *New Perspectives on Microsoft Windows Vista for Power Users* are available online. Course Technology also has solutions for several other learning management systems. Please visit http://www.course.com today to see what's available for this title.

Skills Assessment and Training
SAM 2007 helps bridge the gap between the classroom and the real world by allowing students to train and test on important computer skills in an active, hands-on environment. SAM 2007's easy-to-use system includes powerful interactive exams, training or projects on critical applications such as Word, Excel, Access, PowerPoint, Outlook, Windows, the Internet, and much more. SAM simulates the application environment, allowing students to demonstrate their knowledge and think through the skills by performing real-world tasks. Powerful administrative options allow instructors to schedule exams and assignments, secure tests, and run reports with almost limitless flexibility.

Acknowledgments

Many dedicated individuals at Course Technology actively participated in the planning, development, writing, review, editing, testing, and production of this book. Their efforts reflect Cengage Learning's strong commitment to the highest quality college textbooks for instructors and students, and to all of them I owe many thanks. I extend my sincere thanks to all the members of the New Perspectives team who assisted with the development and production of this textbook.

Once again, special thanks go to Lisa Ruffolo of The Software Resource, who as Developmental Editor, successfully guided this textbook project and contributed her invaluable insight and experience as an author to the development and scope of the textbook. Kathy Finnegan, Senior Product Manager, also deserves special thanks for planning, coordinating, and contributing her expertise and ideas to this textbook. I thank Marie Lee, Executive Editor; Leigh Robbins, Associate Product Manager; Patrick Frank, Editorial Assistant; Erin Dowler, Content Project Manager; Christian Kunciw, Manuscript Quality Assurance Supervisor; and Nicole Ashton, John Freitas, Serge Palladino, Danielle Shaw, Teresa Storch, and Ashlee Welz Smith, Quality Assurance Testers.

I especially thank the following reviewers, whose invaluable comments and insight helped shape and improve the focus of this textbook: John Blackwood, Umpqua Community College; Debra Geoghan, Bucks County Community College; Gralan Gilliam, Kaplan Career Institute; and Richard Pollak, Minneapolis Community and Technical College.

– Harry L. Phillips

Brief Contents

Windows

Table of Contents

Objectives

Session 1.1
- Learn about operating system software
- Examine PC operating systems and operating environments
- Examine the Windows operating systems

Session 1.2
- Work with features of the Windows Vista desktop
- Learn about the importance of Windows Aero
- Find Help in Windows Help and Support

Session 1.3
- Navigate your computer's disk and folder structure
- View properties of your computer system
- Evaluate your computer's Windows Experience Index

Introducing the Windows Vista Operating System

Evaluating Windows Vista

Case | Deep Earth GeoThermal Systems, Ltd.

Deep Earth GeoThermal Systems, Ltd. is a rapidly growing Seattle-based company that locates and develops new sources of geothermal energy stretching along the west coasts of North America, Latin America, and South America in a part of the Pacific Rim called the Ring of Fire. Juliann Chapin, a network specialist at Deep Earth GeoThermal Systems, is supervising the upgrade of company computers to Windows Vista. Many of the company's employees are also ready to upgrade their home computers to Windows Vista so that they can take advantage of new features that allow them to work more efficiently and productively. Juliann works with you and other employees to explore some new and fundamental features of Windows Vista, provide you with important information on how to properly assess the performance of Windows Vista, and identify what types of hardware and software work with your edition of Windows Vista.

In this tutorial, you will examine the importance, role, and basic functions of operating system software, and then look at specific PC operating systems and their features. This overview will provide a historical perspective on the development of the Windows operating system. You will also explore the Windows Vista desktop, Windows Aero, and Windows Help and Support. Finally, you will navigate your computer, view its properties, and learn how to interpret its Windows Experience Index, and then apply that information to the purchase of new hardware and software.

Starting Data Files

There are no starting Data Files needed for this tutorial.

Session 1.1

The Importance of Operating System Software

After working with you to install Windows Vista on the computers at Deep Earth GeoThermal Systems, Juliann announces an upcoming hands-on workshop to demonstrate the important role that operating system software plays in the proper functioning of an employee's computer system and its resources. She also wants to touch on new features of Windows Vista that meet the specific needs of Deep Earth GeoThermal Systems.

An **operating system (OS)** is software that manages all the operations on your computer from the time that you power on your computer until you shut it down. In this role, the operating system manages the interaction of hardware and software so that all the hardware and software work together. It also provides support to other software that you use on your computer, including application software, Web browsers, email programs, utilities, and games.

Operating system software has evolved and become increasingly complex over the years to adapt to newer types of hardware and software and to support the ever-changing needs of users. As the complexity of operating system software increases, computer users must become more savvy and knowledgeable about the use of the operating system on their computers.

Operating system software, or OS software, is responsible for the following types of operations:

- **Booting a computer** The operating system plays a role in booting a computer. **Booting** refers to the initial startup operations that get your computer up and running. When you press the power button to start your computer, you are performing a **cold boot** and starting your computer from scratch. During the initial stages of a cold boot, **routines** (or small programs) stored on a special type of computer chip called the **BIOS** (**basic input/output system**) on the motherboard perform a series of important startup operations to make sure that your computer hardware is working and to load the operating system. One specific routine locates the operating system software on the hard disk and starts loading the operating system. **Loading** refers to copying software from the hard disk into RAM (or memory) so that you have a working copy of that software in addition to the permanent copy stored on disk. **RAM** (**random access memory**), also referred to as **system memory**, is the predominant type of memory within a computer. RAM (or system memory) stores currently used programs, documents, and data, and thereby provides a temporary workspace for your use.

  After the startup routine loads core operating system files into memory, the operating system takes control of the computer, loads and configures the remainder of the operating system software, allocates system resources to hardware **devices** (hardware components in a computer), and completes the booting of the computer. If you encounter an error while working on the computer, you can perform a **warm boot** to restart your computer without shutting down power to the hardware devices. A warm boot is therefore faster than a cold boot.

  Current computer systems require the BIOS to start your computer because the operating system is not yet active when you first turn it on. Therefore, the BIOS plays an essential role in booting your computer because it provides access to a set of specific routines needed for the initial boot process, and it loads whatever operating system is installed on a computer.

- **Configuring a computer** During the early stages of booting, the operating system detects the hardware in your computer and **configures** (or modifies) itself to support that hardware by loading the appropriate device drivers. A **device driver** is a file containing software that enables the operating system to communicate with, and manage the use of, a specific hardware device. To support each hardware device, the operating system must load one or more device drivers. If you attach a new hardware device to your computer, the operating system automatically detects that hardware device during the early stages of booting, locates and loads the device drivers for the hardware device, and then configures the hardware so that it is ready to use when you see the desktop. If the operating system cannot locate the device drivers for a hardware device, it prompts you to insert a disk with the device drivers and other software for that hardware device, and then it installs that software, loads the device drivers, and configures the hardware so that you can use it when booting is complete.
- **Customizing a computer** Near the end of the booting process, the operating system loads optional programs that you want to use on your computer. For example, many people use **antivirus software** to protect their computer system from computer viruses and other types of malicious software. **Computer viruses** are programs designed to interfere with the performance of, or even damage, your computer or other computers to which you are connected. The operating system loads your antivirus software as early as possible during booting so that the antivirus software can check your computer for viruses and remove them before they become active. After your computer boots, your antivirus software monitors your computer while you work and checks each disk you access and each program and file you open. Configuring a computer is therefore designed to prepare the computer for use by the operating system, while customizing a computer is designed to meet your specific needs and preferences.
- **Displaying a user interface** After your computer boots, the operating system displays a **user interface** that enables you to interact with your computer. Although most people think of the interface as the desktop or the view displayed on their computer by the operating system, the user interface also includes hardware, such as the monitor, keyboard, and mouse you use to interact with the operating system. The user interface also consists of software (i.e., Windows) that allows you to interact with your computer. The user interface presented by the operating system has become increasingly important to users because they rely on it to simplify the tasks they perform. The first PC operating systems featured a command-line interface, whereas present-day operating systems have a graphical user interface. As a result, most computer users today are familiar with the graphical user interface included in Windows, but not necessarily with a command-line interface. As you will see later, in a **command-line interface**, you interact with the operating system by entering and executing commands.
- **Providing support services to applications** The operating system provides important support services to software applications and other programs that you use. Since almost every program provides you with an option for saving and retrieving files from disk, the operating system handles these tasks. If you need to create a document, such as a report, you open a program, such as Microsoft Office Word, and then you create the document. At some point, you instruct the program to save your document. The program prompts you for the disk where you want to store the document, the folder where you want to place the document, and the filename for the document. The operating system then locates storage space on the disk for the file and mediates the transfer of a copy of the document from RAM or memory to the disk, folder, and file you designated. If you want to make changes to that document several days later, you open the same program and instruct it to open the file by identifying the disk and folder where the file is stored and then by selecting the file that contains the document. The

operating system then manages the transfer of a copy of that file from disk into RAM so that you can change that document. Because RAM is **volatile** (dependent on the availability of power), you need to periodically save your documents and data to disk in case of a power failure or computer problem; otherwise, you run the risk of losing all or part of your work. Since almost every program needs to provide you with an option for saving and retrieving documents stored in files, it makes sense to delegate this task to the operating system rather than include the same program code for saving and retrieving files in every program. This approach also provides consistency across different applications. Furthermore, it is a security feature that protects the file system on your computer from harmful changes by malicious software that might gain access to your computer.

- **Handling input and output** The operating system manages all input and output. **Input** refers to data that you provide to a program, and **output** refers to the results produced by a program. Saving a newly created document to a file is an example of storing the output of a program (i.e., your final document). Retrieving a document for revision is an example of input. Printing is another example of output. When you print a document, the operating system uses a process called **spooling** to store the processed document in a temporary file on disk (a **spool file**) and to transmit the spool file to the printer in the background so that you can continue to work in your application or perform other tasks, such as checking your email. Also, by spooling documents to disk, the operating system can print a set of documents one after the other while you continue to work. The operating system stores the documents in a **print queue** (a list of print jobs) and prints the documents in the order in which they were received. Without spooling, you would have to wait until each document printed before you could do anything else. Windows Vista deletes spool files when printing is complete.
- **Managing the file system** Your computer's **file system** consists of the operating system components and data structures that the operating system uses to keep track of all the folders and files on your computer. The operating system manages all the disks, drives, folders, subfolders, and files on a computer. These file system components are organized into a **hierarchy**, or file system structure, that starts with disks at the top of the hierarchy and works its way down through the individual drives and folders to the files at the bottom of the hierarchy. Although your computer might have only one physical hard disk, that disk might be subdivided into one or more partitions that are treated as **logical drives**, each with a different drive name. A **partition** is a subdivision of a physical hard disk, and each partition appears as a separate hard disk that is identified by a drive name. For example, you might have one physical hard disk in your computer, but it might be partitioned, or subdivided, into two drives named C: (for drive C) and D: (for drive D). In this configuration, your computer's operating system and other software are stored on drive C, and you might use drive D to store only your personal files. If your computer has only one physical hard disk, and if it is not partitioned, then you have one drive (most likely identified as drive C) that stores your computer's operating system, other software, and your personal files.
- **Working with folders and files** The operating system provides features and tools for organizing, locating, and using programs, folders, and files on your computer quickly and easily. For example, you can search for all files that contain information on a specific topic within the file itself so that you can locate the files you need for a specific project. You can create **shortcuts**, or links, to programs, folders, files, and Web sites so that you can open them with a single click.

Tip

You can customize elements of the graphical user interface, such as a folder, to simplify file management tasks.

- **Managing system resources** The operating system manages all the hardware and software on your computer so that everything works together properly—a major feat because of the wide spectrum of hardware and software products and the constant introduction of newer types of hardware and software. One especially important resource managed by the operating system is memory. When you open an application, utility, or game, the operating system loads or copies that program from disk into RAM and, in the process, allocates a certain amount of memory to that program so that you can use the program. When you exit an application, utility, or game, the operating system reclaims the memory used by that program so it can make that memory available to the next program you use. Furthermore, Windows supports **multitasking** so you can open more than one program or folder window at a time. If your computer does not have enough RAM for multitasking and the programs you use, the operating system can set aside unused storage space on your hard disk for use as additional memory (called **virtual memory**), thereby increasing the total amount of memory available to the operating system and programs.
- **Resolving system errors and problems** The operating system must handle and, if possible, resolve errors as they occur on a computer. The errors can range from simple to very complex. The operating system will attempt to identify the error, correct the error, or request that you correct the problem. The operating system also provides specific troubleshooting utilities, or tools, for identifying the cause of a problem and for correcting the problem. For example, you might use a utility to check the hard disk for errors and, where possible, to repair those errors.
- **Optimizing system performance** Operating systems also include a variety of tools for analyzing, evaluating, and optimizing the performance of your computer. For example, you might use a utility to improve the speed of accessing data on a disk by rearranging how programs, folders, and your document files are stored on that disk. You might use another utility that evaluates memory usage on your computer and helps you decide whether you need to add more RAM. Your operating system can also automatically perform preventive maintenance on your computer to optimize its performance.
- **Backing up your computer** In addition to troubleshooting and performance tools, operating systems provide utilities for backing up your entire computer system or just your important personal files. **Backing up** refers to storing a duplicate copy of files on another disk. If you lose an important file, or if your hard disk fails, you can restore copies of important files or your entire hard disk from a backup. To further protect your computer, the operating system can restore your computer to an earlier point in time when it was working properly, and it can keep copies of all previous versions of folders and files so that you can revert to an earlier version.
- **Power management** The operating system manages power to all the hardware devices in a computer. It can reduce power consumption to devices when they are not in use and then restore power to those devices when you need to use them. The operating system can also place your entire computer into a low-power state when you are not using your computer, and then restore it to a full working state when you need to use it. These power management features not only conserve power but also extend the useful lifetime of your computer and save energy.

Tip

If you do not already have a password for your user account, you should create one to enhance the security and privacy of your computer.

- **Computer and Internet security** The operating system provides access to a computer via user accounts. A **user account** provides you with access to specific programs, folders, and files on your computer, enables you to create your own folders for storing personal files, and allows you to specify custom settings for using the computer. Furthermore, it determines what types of operations you can perform on your computer. To gain access to your user account, you provide your user name and password. The operating system then uses that information to verify that you are authorized to use the computer. If more than one person wants to use the same computer, the operating system allows each user to set up and customize their own account. Each user's files and settings are kept separate from each other. Also, the operating system prevents changes to important operating system files and folders to protect the integrity of your computer. When you are connected to the Internet or another network, the operating system includes features that prevent malicious software, Web sites, and hackers from gaining access to your computer and makes sure that malicious or questionable software already installed on your computer does not attempt to access a Web site without your knowledge. You can also set up your computer so that the operating system automatically checks for and installs important updates to the operating system, including updates that enhance the security of your computer.
- **Providing networking support** The operating system detects, sets up, configures, and enables security on computers connected together via a wired or wireless network. The operating system also enables users to access other computers and hardware on a network, share hardware, folders, and files, modify network settings, monitor network performance, and troubleshoot network problems.
- **Providing Help** Operating systems typically include a Help system that provides you with information about the use of the operating system and its features. The Help system replaces the use of printed manuals and incorporates the content typically found in those manuals for ease of access while you're working. Help systems provide links to explanations of specific features as well as wizards, demos, and online Help. These various features identify the steps you need to perform an operation, troubleshoot a problem, or locate the Help you need. A **wizard** is a tool that asks you a series of questions about what you want to do and what settings or features you want to use, and then completes the operation for you. A **demo** is a video clip that explains a feature or shows you how to complete an operation. Links found in a Help system are identical to links that you use on a Web site to jump to another Web page**. Online Help** is Help information provided at a Web site by the manufacturer of the software you are using on your computer.

The operating system is an indispensable component of your computer. You cannot use a computer without an operating system. As you work with applications or other types of software, such as utilities and games, the operating system manages the moment-to-moment operation of your computer in the background, from when you initially power on the computer until you shut it down. Furthermore, since the operating system handles important operations, such as disk, drive, folder, and file management, as well as all input/output functions, application software can focus on what it is designed to do best, and the operating system can focus on core functions required of all programs. As you examine desktop operating systems in general and Windows Vista in particular, you will learn about other ways the operating system manages your computer and provides you with the tools you need to work effectively and productively.

PC Operating Systems

The predominant operating systems used on PCs today are ones developed by Microsoft Corporation, so they share a common history and common features. Features, concepts, and techniques introduced with earlier operating systems remain important to the effective use of later operating systems. Therefore, you should be familiar not only with the operating system used on your computer, which might be one of the editions of Windows Vista, for example, but also with other editions of Windows Vista and other versions of the operating systems that preceded Windows Vista.

The DOS Operating System

In 1981, IBM contracted with Microsoft Corporation, then a small company in Washington State, to provide the operating system for its first IBM PC. Microsoft developed DOS 1.0, the first version of DOS, for use on these IBM PCs. **DOS**, an abbreviation for **disk operating system**, eventually referred to three related operating systems: PC-DOS, IBM-DOS, and MS-DOS. Over the years, Microsoft and IBM worked cooperatively to develop different versions of PC-DOS or IBM-DOS for use on IBM PCs, while Microsoft developed different versions of MS-DOS for use on IBM-compatible computers. An IBM-compatible was a personal computer that adhered to standards established by IBM for the IBM PC. IBM-compatible computers contained similar or identical hardware, functioned like an IBM PC, and provided support for the same types of software. Eventually, IBM developed its own versions of IBM-DOS for its IBM computers. Although there were subtle differences between PC-DOS, IBM-DOS, and MS-DOS, all managed the hardware and software resources within a computer in similar ways, provided access to similar types of features, and included similar utilities for enhancing the performance of a system. Once you knew how to use MS-DOS, you also knew how to use IBM-DOS, and vice-versa.

The DOS operating system and present-day operating systems, such as UNIX and Linux, use a command-line interface that enables you to communicate with the operating system by typing a command after an **operating system prompt**, or **command prompt**. After you powered on a computer that used the DOS operating system, it displayed an operating system prompt (usually C:\>) on the screen unless someone had already customized the startup process to make the computer easier to use. See Figure 1-1.

Figure 1-1 DOS command-line user interface

The operating system prompt indicated that the computer booted successfully from C: (the hard disk drive), that the operating system loaded into memory, and that it used a specific drive and folder as a reference point (namely, C:\, the top level folder of drive C). The screen provided no other clues to help you figure out what to do next. You had to know what command to use, and you also had to know the proper format for entering each command. Furthermore, you had to know what options were available for modifying how each command worked. For example Figure 1-2, illustrates how you used the DOS CHKDSK command to check a disk for errors. After you entered the command with the proper syntax, the operating system located and loaded the program for that command. Then that program performed a specific action; in this example, checking a disk for problems. In this case, it found no problems. When the program completed its operation, the operating system redisplayed the command prompt so that you could enter another command to start another program. **Syntax** refers to the proper format for entering a command, including the spelling of the command and any optional parameters or switches. A **parameter** is additional information needed by the command, such as the name of a drive. A **switch** is an optional parameter that changes the way the command works. In Figure 1-2, the /F switch for the CHKDSK command specifies that it repair disk errors as it checks the disk. (*Note*: In Figure 1-2, MS-DOS 6.22 is running in a Virtual PC environment and window on the Windows Vista desktop.)

Figure 1-2 **DOS CHDSK command**

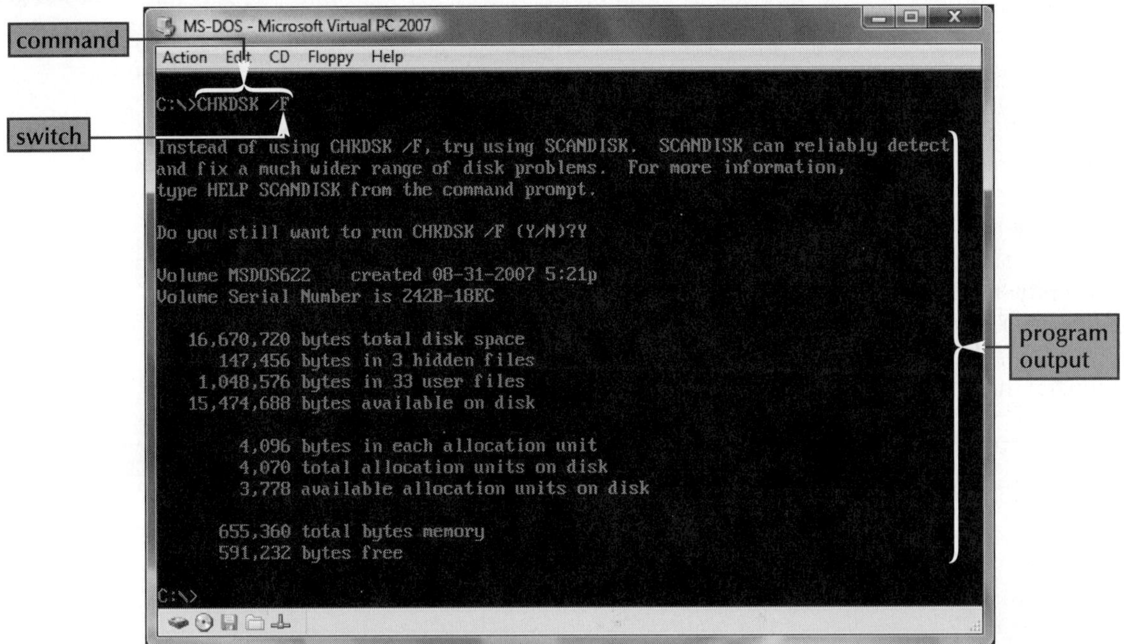

Microsoft included the CHKDSK command in every version of the DOS operating system and in every version of Windows, including Windows Vista. You will examine the use of this important command-line utility in Tutorial 6.

Not surprisingly, because of the simplicity of the user interface and the need to know the names of the operating system commands and their proper syntax, users found it difficult to use DOS. They relied on computer technicians to customize their computers so that DOS automatically loaded a graphical user interface, such as Windows 3.1, or displayed a custom menu that listed installed applications or common tasks, such as **formatting**, or preparing, a disk for use on a computer. In some cases, a computer was customized to automatically start Windows 3.1 (for example) after the operating system booted the computer so that the user did not realize that the underlying operating system was DOS.

Another important feature of command-line interface operating systems is that they operate in text mode. In **text mode**, the operating system displays only text, numbers, symbols, and a small set of graphics characters, such as ╦╔, using white, amber, or green characters on a black background, or perhaps, black characters on a white background. Because text mode does not need to display a user interface with complex graphics, the DOS operating system and present-day command-line operating system are fast and require far less memory and other system resources than contemporary computers that rely on a graphical user interface.

Tip

The user interface in a command-line operating system is also called a Text User Interface (or TUI, pronounced "tooey").

Command-line concepts and skills that derive from using the DOS operating system are still important today, especially for network administrators, network specialists, network technicians, telecommunication specialists, computer and network troubleshooters, computer consultants, tweakers (people who specialize in fine-tuning and optimizing computers), and trainers, to name a few professions. All of these professionals find command-line skills an invaluable resource in their jobs. In some cases, command-line tools enable you to perform operations that are not possible in the Windows graphical user interface (even in Windows Vista).

The Windows Operating Environments

In 1985, Microsoft introduced Windows 1.0, the first in a series of Windows operating environments, and seven years later, Windows 3.1 became the most common version of the Windows operating environment. An **operating environment** is software that performs the same functions as an operating system except for configuring and customizing a computer system during booting and handling the storage and retrieval of files on a disk. The Windows operating environments therefore required a version of the DOS operating system on the computer to handle booting and basic file functions. More importantly, the Windows operating environments were the first versions of Windows to use a graphical user interface that was originally derived from the one used on Apple computers and similar to today's Windows graphical user interface.

Although DOS was the predominant PC operating system for 14 years from 1981-1995, the Windows operating environments were important because they eventually led to the development of the Windows operating system. In fact, Microsoft referred to the Windows operating environment as an operating system, anticipating the day when Windows would be a full-fledged operating system that no longer required the DOS operating system and that in turn would mark a major change in the way that people used computers.

The Windows Operating Systems

The first Windows operating system was Windows 95, and it marked a revolutionary change in operating system technology. The following list describes some Windows 95 features that are still important in current Windows operating systems:

- **Graphical user interface** The Windows operating systems all rely on a graphical user interface. A **graphical user interface**, or **GUI** (pronounced "gooey"), uses a combination of features and screen elements to provide a visually rich working environment as well as on-screen clues that simplify interaction with the operating system. The graphical user interface in different versions of Windows uses colors, **fonts** (different character styles), special screen design elements (such as shading, shadows, and **translucency** or transparency), and animation to provide a more interesting working environment.

  Windows displays **icons**, or pictures, to represent hardware and software components, as well as system tools, that you can open and use. Although the icons are designed to identify their purpose, it is not always obvious to users what feature is associated with a specific icon, so icons typically have **icon titles** or labels that describe their purpose.

Tip

You can point to an icon to display its ToolTip, which identifies its function.

The Windows graphical user interface relies on the use of **windows**, or work areas on the screen (usually defined by borders) that are designed to organize your view of applications and documents. Every time you open a program, it appears within a program or **application window**. If you open more than one program, then each program is displayed within its own window. Likewise, for many applications, each document you open in an application appears within its own **document window**. Windows also uses **menus** to list options for performing different types of command operations. Like a restaurant menu, you know what your choices are, and you can easily select them from a list displayed on the menu. When you select a menu option, Windows may display a **dialog box** that includes options for completing that operation. In a graphical user interface, the mouse plays an important role and is a required hardware component. You use it to point to and select icons, as well as options, in windows, on menus, and in dialog boxes, and to open programs.

Unlike a command-line operating system, Windows operates in graphics mode rather than text mode. In **graphics mode**, Windows can display text in a variety of fonts and colors, as well as graphic images and animation; however, the use of graphics mode requires far more memory and system resources than text mode.

- **Document-oriented approach** The redesigned graphical user interface in the Windows operating systems makes it easier to use a document-oriented approach, rather than an application-oriented approach, to open files that contain documents that you want to use. When using an **application-oriented approach**, you first open the software application, and then you locate and open the document you want to use. This approach was the only one available with the DOS operating system, and the predominant approach used with the Windows operating environments. In contrast, when using a **document-oriented approach**, you double-click a file icon in a folder window to open the document contained within the file. The operating system opens both the application associated with that type of file and the document at the same time. This approach is useful if you are working in a folder containing files that you open to copy data from one file to another or to create new files. You don't need to use the Start menu and All Programs menu to locate and start the program for each type of file in the folder or perform the steps of opening a file from within a program. The document-oriented approach is a faster and smarter way to work with files. Although this approach was available with the Windows operating environments, it did not come into its own right until the release of Windows 95.
- **Object-oriented interface** The Windows operating systems treat components of the graphical user interface and the computer as **objects**. Hardware and software components, such as disks, drives, folders, files, and programs, are all objects. Objects have actions and properties. **Actions** are operations you can perform on an object. For example, you can open and explore the contents of your hard disk drive, search its contents, share the drive on your network, create a shortcut to the drive, and change the **volume label** (the electronic name) assigned to the drive. Each object has a **default action**, such as Open, which is the action that Windows takes when you double-click the object. You can view a list of other actions for an object by right-clicking the object and displaying its **shortcut menu**, or **context menu**.
- **Properties**, on the other hand, are characteristics of an object. You can view and, in many cases, change an object's settings by right-clicking the object and selecting Properties on its shortcut menu. An object can therefore be defined as an element of the user interface that you can right-click. Because every object is associated with a shortcut menu, you can use the same approach for performing actions and examining properties, whether the object is a drive, a piece of clip art pasted into a document, an icon in the notification area on the taskbar, a desktop shortcut, a Web page, or the desktop

Tip

A good way to learn about unfamiliar objects is to right-click the object, and then examine the options on the shortcut menu.

itself. Shortcut menus provide a consistent way to work with different types of objects and clearly identify the actions available for an object.

- **Long filenames** Under the DOS operating system, folder and filenames were limited to eight characters and an optional three characters separated from the main part of the filename by a period (called an **extension** or **file extension**). For example, if you created an Annual Report, you might have stored it in a file named ANNRPT, ANN_RPT, or ANNUAL.RPT. (DOS used only uppercase characters.) Since you could not include spaces in the filename, you had to use an underscore or dash between parts of the filename to make it easier to read. The limitations on naming files under DOS meant that you had to be creative and develop a naming scheme so that you could later identify the file you needed. Under Windows XP and previous versions of the Windows operating system, filenames could have up to 255 characters, including spaces and certain types of symbols and a file extension separated from the main part of the filename by a period. The same options apply to Windows Vista, though it supports filenames up to 260 characters. However, in both cases, Windows must keep track of the location of the file, so the actual number of characters allowed for a filename is less than 255 or 260 characters. Later in this tutorial, you will examine filenames in more detail. The Insight at the end of this section focuses on the importance of file extensions.
- **Shortcuts** Under any version of the Windows operating system you can create shortcuts (or links) to programs, folders, files, Web sites, and components of the graphical user interface so that you can quickly open and access these objects.
- **Multitasking, task-switching, and multithreading** As noted earlier, the Windows operating systems support multitasking and allow you to open multiple programs and folders, each of which appears in a different window. The Windows operating systems also support task switching and multithreading. When you switch from one open task to another, such as from one program window to another program window, from one folder window to another folder window, or from a program window to a folder window (or vice-versa), you are **task switching**. **Multithreading** refers to the ability of the Windows operating systems to **execute**, or carry out, the instructions contained within units of program code (called **threads**) within a program. For example, Windows can handle two threads in two different programs almost simultaneously. Windows can also handle two different threads within the same program, or two of the same threads in the same program. A **process** is an open and running program that consists of one or more threads and associated data structures.

  Multitasking, task switching, and multithreading improve the performance of your computer and allow you to be more productive. In contrast, the DOS operating system supported only **single tasking**. You could perform only one task at a time, so you had to wait until that task was complete before you could perform another task. For example, you could open only one program at a time. If you wanted to use another program, you had to close your current program first. Also, you could print only one document at a time, and you could not perform any other computer tasks until printing was complete.

- **Backward compatibility** The ability of the Windows operating systems to work with older hardware, as well as software designed for earlier versions of the Windows operating system, is called **backward compatibility**. While not perfect, this capability improves the chances that you can keep your current computer system and its hardware and software without having to purchase a new computer system or upgrade your hardware and software when you install a new version of Windows. At the same time, backward compatibility has hindered the development of the Windows operating system by requiring it to support outdated hardware and software technologies.

- **Plug and Play** The Windows operating systems support Plug and Play hardware. **Plug and Play** (**PnP**) refers to a set of specifications for automatically detecting and configuring hardware. When you add a new Plug and Play hardware device to your computer, the operating system automatically detects and configures the hardware device either during booting or when the computer is already on, with little or no intervention on your part. In contrast, **legacy** or **non-Plug and Play devices** are older types of hardware components that do not meet the Plug and Play specifications and therefore require manual installation. Plug and Play hardware is the standard today.

InSight | **Understanding the Importance of File Extensions**

Under Windows, the file extension is important because it identifies the application you use to open the file. For example, if you create an Annual Report, you might store it in a file named "Annual Report.docx". Unlike DOS, the filename clearly identifies the content contained in the file (i.e., an Annual Report), and the file extension ("docx") identifies it as a document file that was most likely created by Microsoft Word. The DOS file-naming conventions are still used today in assigning names to program files and many of the other files included with a software product, even the Windows operating system, so that problems do not arise when a Windows computer is connected to a network.

The Windows 95, Windows 98, and Windows ME Operating Systems

In the summer of 1995, Microsoft released Windows 95, the first Windows operating system for home users. After installing Windows 95 on a computer that already had an installed version of the DOS operating system, Windows 95 replaced DOS as the operating system. If the computer also included an installed version of a Windows operating environment, such as Windows 3.1, Windows 95 replaced that as well. Microsoft later introduced four other versions of Windows 95 that added support for newer types of hardware devices, included new or updated components, and provided fixes that corrected problems in earlier versions of Windows 95. For example, an update to Windows 95B added support for **USB** (**Universal Serial Bus**), a technology for the high-speed transfer of data between hardware devices. Over the years, USB became the standard for newer types of hardware devices, including flash drives. Rapid changes in hardware and software technologies are an important driving force in producing new versions of the Windows operating system.

Windows 95 was the first Internet-oriented operating system because it enabled millions of users to access the Internet and its benefits for the first time, and those users did not need to know the details of how their computers and Windows operated. Windows 95 users were therefore among the first to access resources available on Internet and Web servers around the world and to exchange e-mail. If you examine statistics on the growth of the Internet and World Wide Web at Hobbe's Internet Timeline (*www.zakon.org/robert/internet/timeline/#Growth*), you will discover that the rapid increase in Internet use occurred right after the introduction of Windows 95. The line charts in Figure 1-3, Figure 1-4, and Figure 1-5 were created by plotting information derived from that Web site. The chart in Figure 1-3 shows the growth of the Internet by plotting the number of computers on the Internet over time. As you can see, the sharp rise in the curve occurred right after Microsoft released Windows 95 and marked increase use and rapid development of the Internet. The chart in Figure 1-4 shows the growth of the World Wide Web, a component of the Internet, by plotting the number of Web sites over time. The dramatic increase in number of Web sites started to occur after Microsoft released Windows 98. This rise peaked during the first half of 2002; after that, the number of Web sites declined. The period from early 2000 to late 2003 was referred to as the "Dot-Com Crash." Many Internet companies went out of business because they were overvalued and not showing a profit. By the end of 2002 and the beginning of 2003, the growth of the World Wide Web improved and has continued to experience rapid growth. If you examine the same data plotted on one chart using the same scale, as shown in Figure 1-5, the increase in number of Web sites is not as remarkable as the increase in the number of computers on the Internet. Furthermore, as you would expect, growth in Web sites only started to occur about four years after Internet growth accelerated. However, if you plot the increase in computers on the Internet and the increase in Web sites on different scales, the growth patterns are comparable.

Growth of the Internet

Figure 1-3

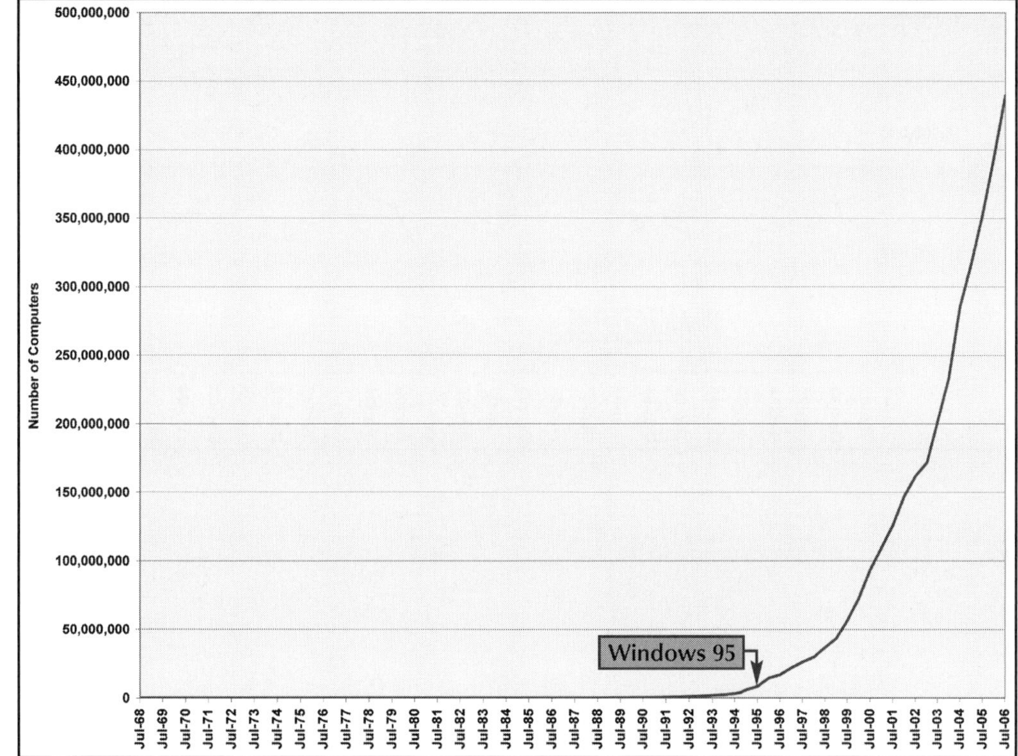

Figure 1-4 Growth of the World Wide Web

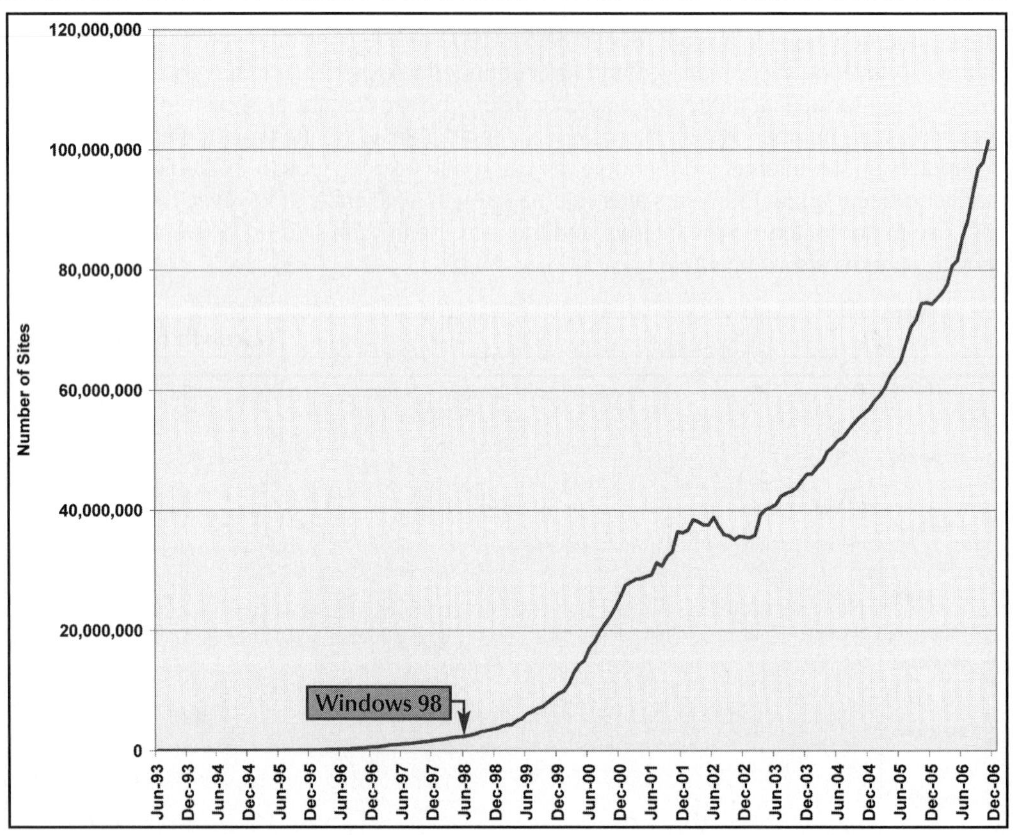

Figure 1-5 Growth of the Internet and World Wide Web

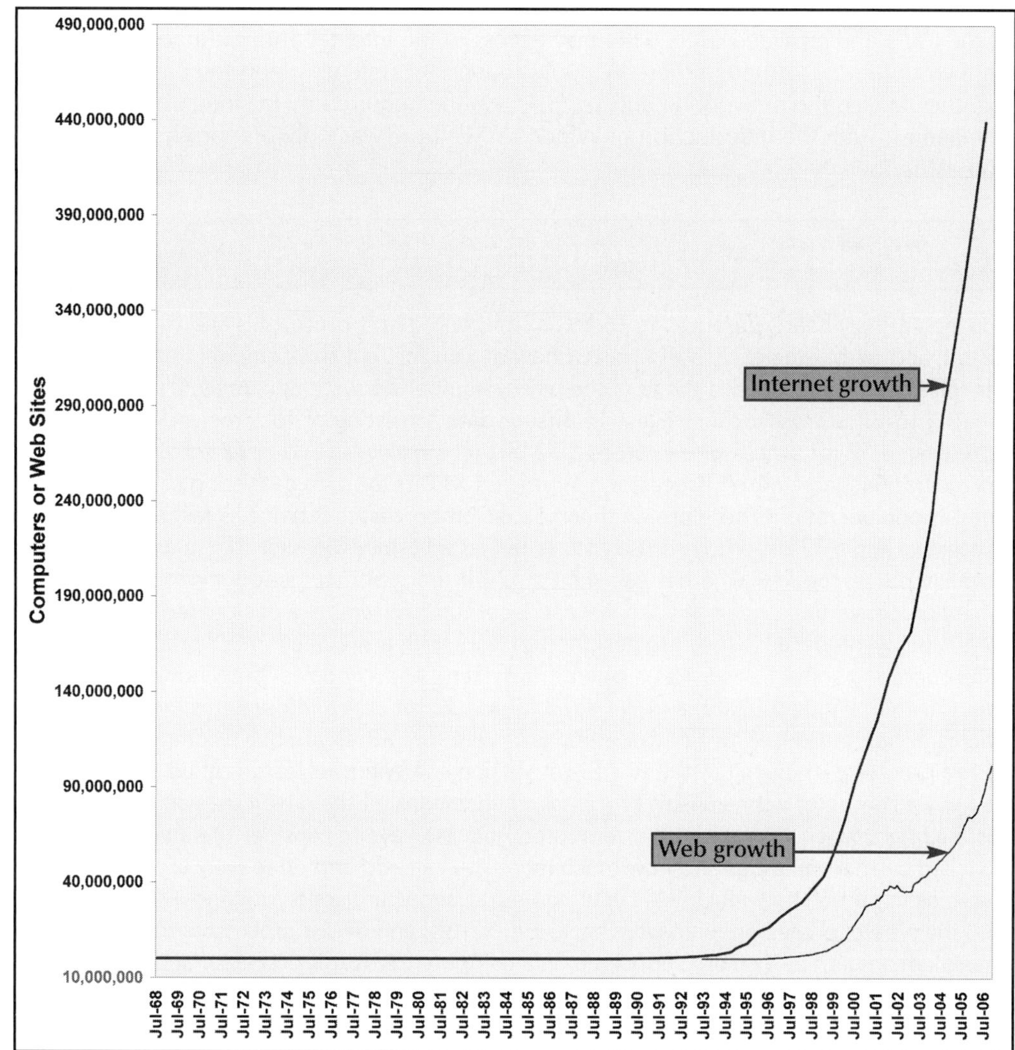

In the summer of 1998, Microsoft released Windows 98 for home users. Like Windows 95, Windows 98 included support for newer types of hardware, such as DVD drives, and new Windows components and features, including tools for optimizing and troubleshooting your computer. Microsoft later released an improved version of Windows 98 known as Windows SE (for "Second Edition") that enabled Windows 98 to manage power to hardware devices.

In late 2000, Microsoft introduced the Windows ME operating system, or Windows Millennium Edition, for home users. One of the important new features introduced in Windows ME was the System Restore utility. This utility periodically saved changes to system files, device drivers, and system settings on your computer system so that if you installed new software or made a change to your computer that created a problem, you could "roll back" your computer to the point just before you made these changes, and restore a previous configuration that worked without any problems, essentially undoing the changes you made. This feature was designed so that the average user could easily resolve a problem that occurred from a change to the computer system. Microsoft has retained the System Restore utility in Windows XP and Windows Vista.

Windows 95, Windows 98, and Windows ME fell into a Microsoft product line called the **Windows 9x product line**. These Windows operating systems were designed for home users and provided users with easy access to the Internet and multimedia content on their computer. Although these Windows operating systems supported basic networking, they lacked the networking and security features required by businesses and companies. With the introduction of Windows XP, there was only one product line—Windows NT.

InSight | **Understanding Processors and Operating Systems**

You increasingly hear references to 16-bit, 32-bit, and 64-bit processors and to 16-bit, 32-bit, and 64-bit operating systems, but how do you sort out this complex topic? The term **bit** refers to each of the two digits in the binary numbering system; namely, 0 (zero) and 1 (one). A 16-bit processor can process 16 bits (or data consisting of 16 zeros and ones) in one operation, a 32-bit processor can process 32 bits (or data consisting of 32 zeros and ones) in one operation, and a 64-bit processor can process 64 bits (or data consisting of 64 zeros and ones) in one operation. Therefore, in theory, a 64-bit processor is twice as fast as a 32-bit processor, and a 32-bit processor is twice as fast as a 16-bit processor. If you are buying a new computer, consider whether you want a 32-bit processor (current generation) or a 64-bit processor (next generation). Likewise, operating systems are designated as 16-bit, 32-bit, or 64-bit because they are designed to work with a specific type of processor. The DOS operating system was a 16-bit operating system, and Windows 95, Windows 98, Windows ME, Windows 2000, and Windows XP are 32-bit operating systems; however, Microsoft has introduced two 64-bit editions of Windows XP. If you buy a computer with a 32-bit processor, then you install the 32-bit version of a Windows Vista edition. Likewise, if you buy a computer with a 64-bit processor, then you install the 64-bit version of a Windows Vista edition. When you purchase a computer, you also have to consider the amount of RAM installed on that computer and how much more you can add and effectively use. That depends in part on how much RAM your computer and your version of Windows supports, and the type of processor you have. The 16-bit, 32-bit, and 64-bit processors determine the maximum amount of memory supported on a computer. A 16-bit processor supports up to 1 MB (megabyte) of RAM, a 32-bit processor supports up to 4 GB of RAM, and a 64-bit processor supports up to 16 EB (exabytes) (or 16 billion gigabytes) of RAM.

The Windows NT Workstation 4.0, Windows 2000, and Windows XP Operating Systems

In 1993, Microsoft introduced an advanced network operating system named Windows NT (for "New Technology") that was primarily used by companies and businesses. Over the years, Windows NT gained a reputation in corporate and industrial circles for its networking and security features and its stability. In the summer of 1996, a year after the release of Windows 95, Microsoft released the Windows NT Workstation 4.0 network operating system for use on desktop computers. Microsoft adapted part of the Windows 95 interface and included many Windows 95 features in Windows NT Workstation 4.0. This version of the Windows operating system did not support Plug and Play, had limited multimedia support, and did not support as many hardware devices as Windows 95. However, its release was important because it introduced a network operating system for use on desktop computers and, furthermore, it served as the precursor to the Windows 2000 Professional operating system.

In early 2000, Microsoft introduced the Windows 2000 Professional operating system. Microsoft had planned to call it Windows NT Workstation 5.0, an upgrade to Windows NT Workstation 4.0, but because of delays in the development of this operating system, Microsoft changed its name to Windows 2000 Professional Edition. The final Windows 2000 Professional operating system proved to be a powerful, reliable, and stable desktop network operating system, and many of its features are found in Windows XP and Windows Vista.

The Windows XP (for "Experience") operating system marked another important and major change in the development of the Windows operating system. Like all previous versions of the Windows operating system, Windows XP supported and enhanced many features found in earlier versions of Windows and introduced other new features. Over a five-year period, Microsoft released seven editions of Windows XP:

- **Windows XP Professional Edition**, designed for business use and advanced users
- **Windows XP Home Edition**, designed for home users
- **Windows XP 64-Bit Edition**, designed for scientific, engineering, and business uses that required resource-intensive applications, such as those required for handling special digital effects in movies and 3D animation
- **Windows XP Media Center Edition**, which enabled home users to access and use their home-based entertainment technologies and their computer with a single remote control
- **Windows XP Tablet PC Edition**, designed for mobile users who needed a notebook computer for note-taking at meetings or while traveling
- **Windows XP Professional x64 Edition**, which was designed for a new generation of 64-bit processors
- **Windows XP Starter Edition**, a scaled-down version of the Windows XP operating system designed and customized for individuals in certain developing countries

Microsoft also released slightly modified editions of Windows XP for use in Europe that did not contain Windows Media Player. An **edition** is a different version of the same Windows operating system.

Windows NT Workstation 4.0 and Windows 2000 Professional fall into a Microsoft product line called the **Windows NT product line**. These Windows network operating systems were commonly used in companies and businesses that needed a secure network operating system. Over the years, Microsoft tried to combine the Windows 9x and Windows NT product lines into one product line, and they finally succeeded with Windows XP. Windows XP and its successor, Windows Vista, are part of the NT product line and therefore are secure network operating systems.

Two competitors to the Windows operating system are Linux and the Mac OS. Linux is a free or low-cost PC operating system similar to the UNIX operating system. Like Windows, Linux has a graphical user interface with a desktop and an underlying powerful command-line interface. UNIX is a multiuser, multitasking operating system that has played an important role in the development of the Internet. The Mac OS is a graphical user interface operating system designed for Apple computers and containing features similar to those found in the Windows operating system. The Mac OS X also contains a command-line operating system based on the UNIX operating system.

Review | Session 1.1 Quick Check

1. A(n) ________________ is a software product that manages all the operations that occur in a computer from the time you start your computer until you shut it down.
2. What type of software does the operating system load to provide support for hardware devices and to enable the operating system to communicate with and manage those devices?
3. What type of user interface requires you to interact with the operating system by entering and executing commands at a command prompt?
4. True or False. When you print a document, the operating system uses a process called spooling to store the processed document in a temporary file on disk and to transmit the spool file to the printer in the background.
5. Your computer's ________________ consists of the operating system components and data structures that the operating system uses to keep track of all the folders and files on your computer.
6. What Windows feature enables you to open more than one program and folder window at the same time?
7. Objects have ________________ and ________________ .
8. A file's ________________ is important to Windows because it identifies the type of file and the application you use to open the file.

Session 1.2

The Windows Vista Operating System

In January 2007, Microsoft introduced six editions of the Windows Vista operating system:

- **Windows Vista Home Basic** for basic home use, such as creating Office documents, browsing the Web, and using email, and for use on older computers
- **Windows Vista Home Premium** for home computing and entertainment and for newer types of computers
- **Windows Vista Business** for small and mid-sized businesses
- **Windows Vista Ultimate**, the most complete edition of Windows Vista with all the features found in all the other editions of Windows Vista as well as many new features not available in those editions
- **Windows Vista Enterprise** for large, global companies, businesses, and organizations
- **Windows Vista Starter Edition**, a scaled-down version of the Windows Vista operating system for emerging markets

The edition of Windows Vista that you choose depends on what you want to do on your computer, what features you want, and the hardware capabilities of your computer. You can examine the features of different Windows Vista editions at Microsoft's Windows Vista Web site (*www.microsoft.com/windows/products/windowsvista*). You can also download and install a free copy of the Windows Upgrade Advisor and then use that program to determine which Windows Vista edition will work best on your computer. The Upgrade Advisor also identifies hardware and software problems as well as system settings and other drawbacks, such as the amount of available hard disk storage space, that determine whether you can upgrade from a previous version of Windows or from one Windows Vista edition to another.

Windows Vista retains many of the important features found in earlier versions of Windows, but improves on them. Windows Vista also contains many new features that you will explore as you work with Windows Vista in the tutorials in this book.

Logging on to Windows

Now that Juliann has installed Windows Vista on your computer, you are ready to log on and examine the Windows Vista desktop and graphical user interface.

The figures in this book are derived from a computer that uses Windows Vista Ultimate. If you are using another edition of Windows Vista, then you may not have all the features covered in this textbook. If a feature is not available in another edition of Windows Vista, then the tutorial instructions note this fact. Also, you may notice differences between your screen views and the figures. Even if your edition of Windows Vista does not have all the features described in this textbook, and even if your computer hardware does not support certain Windows Vista features, you should still know about those features so that you can make an informed decision when you upgrade your computer or purchase a new one.

In the next set of steps, you log on your computer. If you are working in a computer lab at your college, your instructor or technical support staff will explain how to log on a computer in your computer lab.

To log on to Windows:

1. If your computer is turned off, power on your computer. During booting, your computer might briefly display information about startup operations and technical specifications of your computer, or you might see a splash logo for your computer's manufacturer. Then you will briefly see a progress indicator. The next screen displays the Microsoft Windows Vista logo. Then, depending on how your computer is set up, Windows Vista may display a Welcome screen so you can select or enter your user account and enter your password, or Windows Vista may boot directly to the desktop shown in Figure 1-6.

   Your Windows Vista desktop might differ from the one shown in this figure if you or your computer dealer has already customized the Windows Vista desktop. Also, if you upgraded your computer from a previous version of Windows, your Windows Vista desktop will differ. If you've just purchased a new computer, Windows Vista may display a Welcome Center window on the desktop.

   Trouble? If you are working in a computer lab at your college, your instructor and technical support staff will tell you what user account and password you should use.

2. If Windows Vista displays a Welcome screen, click your **user account icon** (if necessary), enter your **password** (if necessary), and then click the **Next** button with a white arrow. You may also see a Switch User button if more than one user has an account on the computer. Windows Vista then displays the desktop. See Figure 1-6. Your Windows Vista desktop might differ from that shown in this figure if you or your computer dealer has already customized the Windows Vista desktop. Also, if you upgraded your computer from a previous version of Windows, your Windows Vista desktop will differ. If you've just purchased a new computer, Windows Vista may display a Welcome Center window on the desktop.

   Trouble? If you do not use a password, Windows Vista displays the Windows Vista desktop.

Trouble? If you type an incorrect password or mistype the password, Windows Vista informs you that your user name or password is incorrect. Click the OK button to continue. Windows Vista then displays the Password box again so that you can re-enter your password. It also displays your password hint under the Password text box and includes a link for resetting your password. Type your password correctly, and then click the Next button.

Trouble? If you are working in a computer lab and are unsure as to how to log on a computer, ask your instructor or technical support staff for assistance.

Figure 1-6 Windows Vista desktop

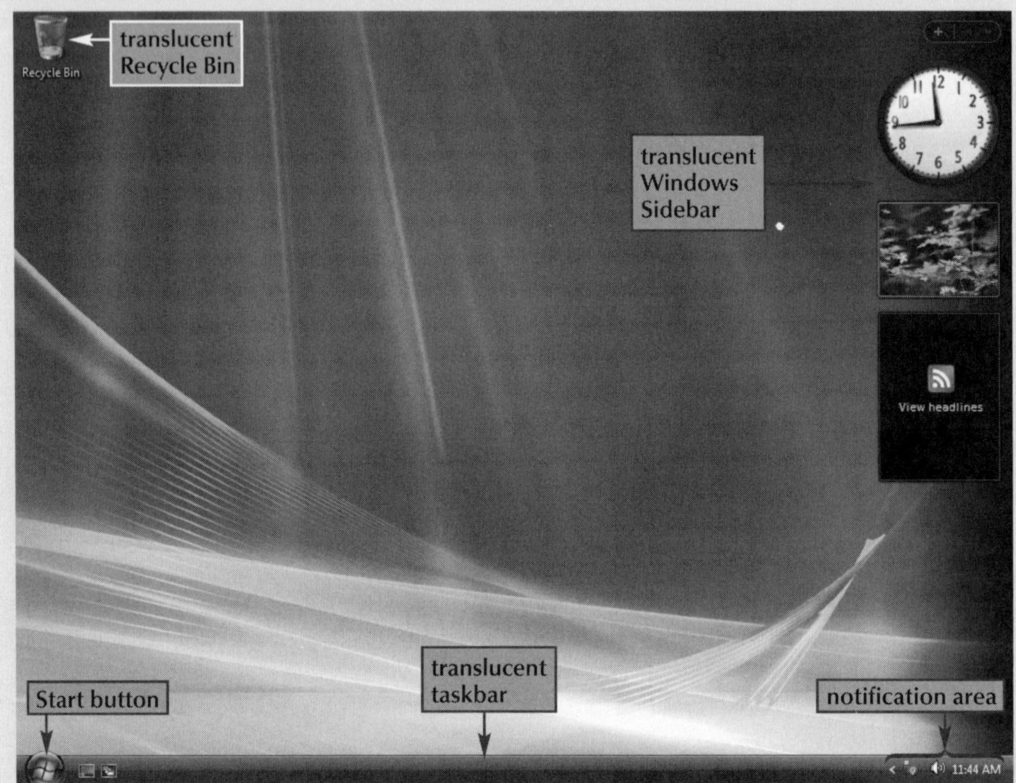

3. If Windows Vista displays a Welcome Center window on the desktop, click the **Run at startup** check box located in the lower-left corner of the window to remove the check mark from the check box. Then click the red **Close** button in the upper-right corner of the window to close this window. Windows Vista will then no longer display the Welcome Center window after you start your computer and log on your user account.

Now you're ready to examine Windows Vista and its features, starting with the Windows Vista desktop.

Touring the Windows Vista Desktop

Like all other versions of the Windows operating system, the Windows Vista desktop is your starting point for accessing the resources and tools on your computer. The **desktop background** (also called **wallpaper**) contains an image that you can change. Depending on the version of Windows Vista that you use and depending on the capabilities of the hardware on your computer, you can display live video on the desktop background instead of an image. In Tutorial 2 you will examine how to change the desktop background and use live video on the desktop.

The icons that you see on the desktop depend on how you installed Windows Vista. If you upgraded from a previous version of Windows, such as Windows XP, then your desktop should contain the same icons. If you purchased a new computer with Windows Vista, then the Recycle Bin is the only icon on the desktop unless the manufacturer of that computer customized the desktop. Likewise, if you performed what's called a **clean install** and erased everything on your computer before you installed Windows Vista, then the only icon on the desktop is the Recycle Bin. As you install software and hardware, icons for opening those programs or for opening documentation on those products might also be placed on the desktop. On the computer used for Figure 1-6, the Recycle Bin is **translucent**, or partially transparent. That means that you can see the desktop background under portions of the Recycle Bin icon.

By default, desktop icons are set to a size called Medium Icons; however, you can change this setting. Like every other software product that you use, Windows Vista uses predefined settings, or **default settings**, which the vast majority of people are likely to use, and which the majority of businesses are likely to prefer, and that in turn saves time and effort because these settings do not have to be changed. However, Juliann suggests that you might want to change certain settings like desktop icon size to make it easier for you to see the content on your monitor and to use your computer.

To change desktop icon sizes:

1. Right-click the **desktop background** and then point to **View** on the shortcut menu. The first three options on the cascading View menu—Large Icons, Medium Icons, and Classic Icons—determine icon sizes.
2. Click **Large Icons**. Windows Vista increases the size of the desktop icons. See Figure 1-7. On computers that support this feature, the translucency of desktop icons is more evident at this larger size.

Figure 1-7 Desktop icon changed to Large Icons size

3. Right-click the **desktop background**, point to **View** on the shortcut menu, and then click **Medium Icons**. Windows Vista restores the default size of the desktop icons. The other View menu option, Classic Icons, reduces the desktop icons to a very small size.

You can also use your mouse scroll wheel to adjust icon sizes along a continuum, or range, of sizes.

To adjust icon sizes with your mouse:

1. Hold down the **Ctrl** key (also called the Control key) on the left side of the keyboard, and then move the mouse wheel one notch at a time *away* from you. Windows Vista gradually increases the size of the desktop icons. See Figure 1-8.

Figure 1-8 **Desktop icon sizes adjusted with Ctrl key and mouse wheel**

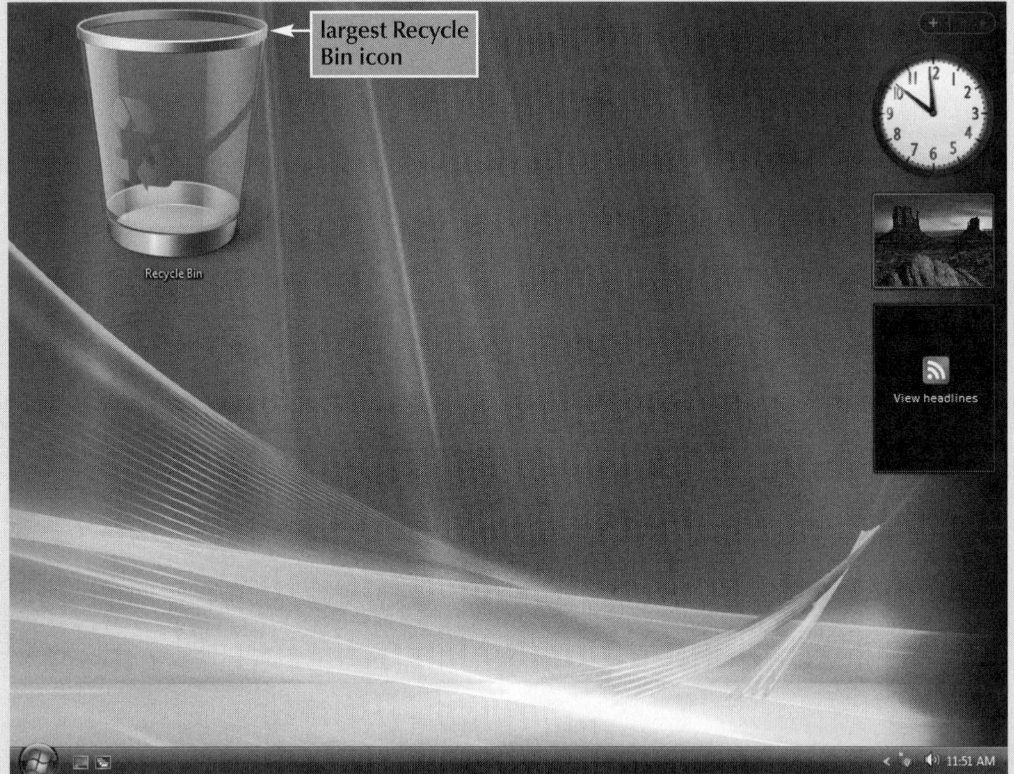

2. Hold down the **Ctrl** key and then move the mouse wheel one notch at a time *towards* you. Windows Vista gradually decreases the size of the desktop icons.
3. To restore your default icon size, right-click the **desktop background**, point to **View** on the shortcut menu, and then click **Medium Icons**.

You can use the "Show Desktop Icons" option on the View menu to turn off the display of all desktop icons so that you can view the desktop background or background video, and you can use this menu option to redisplay hidden desktop icons.

Changing and Restoring Desktop Icon Sizes

| Reference Window

- Right-click the desktop background, point to View on the shortcut menu, and click Large Icons or Classic Icons.

or

- Hold down the Ctrl key and move the mouse wheel one notch at a time away from you to increase icon sizes or towards you to decrease icon sizes.
- To restore desktop icon sizes, right-click the desktop background, point to View on the shortcut menu, and then click Medium Icons.

Windows Vista automatically aligns icons to an invisible desktop grid so that icons are arranged evenly in columns and rows on the desktop. You can turn off the "Align to Grid" option on the View menu, and then you can place icons anywhere you want on the desktop. You can also use this same menu option to automatically realign desktop icons to the invisible desktop grid. If you enable the "Auto Arrange" option on the View menu, Windows Vista arranges icons in columns starting on the left side of the desktop, and you cannot move desktop icons to another location. If you try, the icons automatically snap back to the left side of the desktop. If you turn off this option by choosing it again, then you can reposition icons wherever you want on the desktop.

Exploring Windows Aero

If your version of Windows Vista and your hardware support **Windows Aero**, a new user interface enhancement available in certain Windows Vista editions that operate on higher performance computers, then elements of the graphical user interface, such as the taskbar, Start menu, window frames, windows, dialog boxes, some toolbars, and some toolbar buttons are translucent. Furthermore, if you have multiple overlapping windows, and if portions of those windows are translucent, you can view the desktop background through multiple windows. Windows Aero is also called **Aero Glass** because the translucency effects take on the appearance of translucent (or frosted) glass.

Windows Aero is responsible for displaying a shadow around windows and dialog boxes, animation effects (such as a window zooming out to a taskbar button as you minimize it), smooth scaling of icon sizes on the desktop (as you saw earlier when you used the Ctrl key and mouse to resize desktop icons), a glowing effect when you point to a window's or dialog box's resizing buttons, and smooth visual refreshing (updating your view) of the Windows desktop.

Windows Aero also supports the following new Windows Vista features (provided the computer's hardware also supports these features):

- **Windows Flip** If you press the Alt+Tab keyboard shortcut, Windows Vista displays a pane with thumbnails of open windows so that you can pick the window in which you want to work. Figure 1-9 illustrates an example of using Windows Flip to view thumbnails of minimized Computer, Sample Pictures folder, and Sample Music folder windows. Windows Flip also displays a thumbnail of the desktop window on the pane so that you can minimize all open windows and return to the desktop. A **keyboard shortcut** consists of one or more keys that provide an alternate method for performing a task. People who are proficient at using a keyboard often prefer to use keyboard shortcuts rather than move their right (or left) hand from the keyboard to the mouse and then back to the keyboard. To use the Alt+Tab keyboard shortcut, press and hold down the Alt key, and then press and release the Tab key while still pressing the Alt key. You can then click one of the Windows Flip thumbnails and restore (and display) that window. You can also hold down the Alt key and repeatedly press the Tab key until Windows Vista highlights the desired thumbnail or icon.

Tip

In all previous versions of Windows, the Alt+Tab keyboard shortcut was called the CoolSwitch.

Figure 1-9 Enabling Windows Flip with the Alt+Tab keys

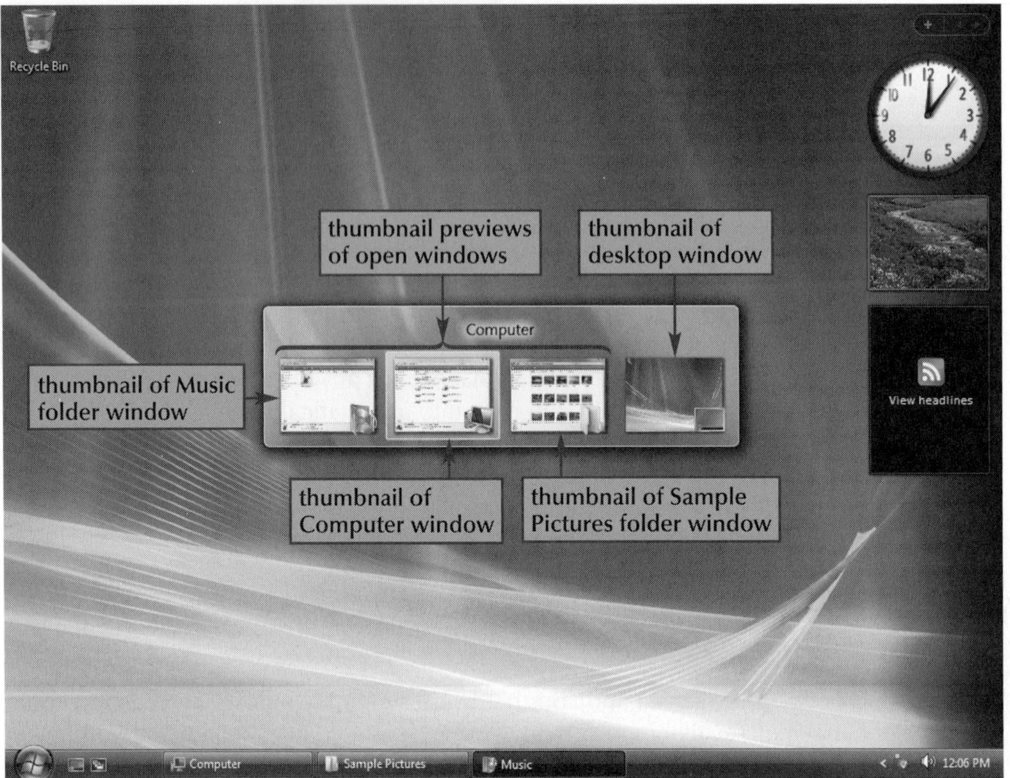

- **Windows Flip 3D** stacks all open windows at a 3D angle on the desktop so that you can see more of the content of the windows and select the window in which you want to work. In Figure 1-10, Windows Vista displays 3D-stacked views of a Sample Pictures folder, Sample Music folder, and Computer window as well as the desktop window. The translucency of the windows allows you to see through one window onto part of the next window, improving your view of all the windows. Furthermore, you can use your mouse scroll wheel to advance the windows forwards or backwards in the stack.

  To activate Windows Flip 3D, you click the "Switch between windows" button on the Quick Launch toolbar. You can also press and hold the Windows Logo key and then press the Tab key. To scroll forward through the stacked windows, you can use the mouse wheel, the Windows Logo+Tab keyboard shortcut, the right arrow key, or the down arrow key. To use the mouse wheel, roll the mouse wheel one notch towards you to advance the stacked windows to the front of the stack, one by one. To scroll backward through the stacked windows, you can use the mouse wheel, left arrow key, or the up arrow key. To use the mouse wheel, roll the mouse wheel one notch away from you to roll back the stacked windows to the rear of the stack, one by one. To use the Windows Logo+Tab keyboard shortcut, you hold down the Windows Logo key and repeatedly press the Tab key to flip the windows.

Figure 1-10 Windows Flip 3D

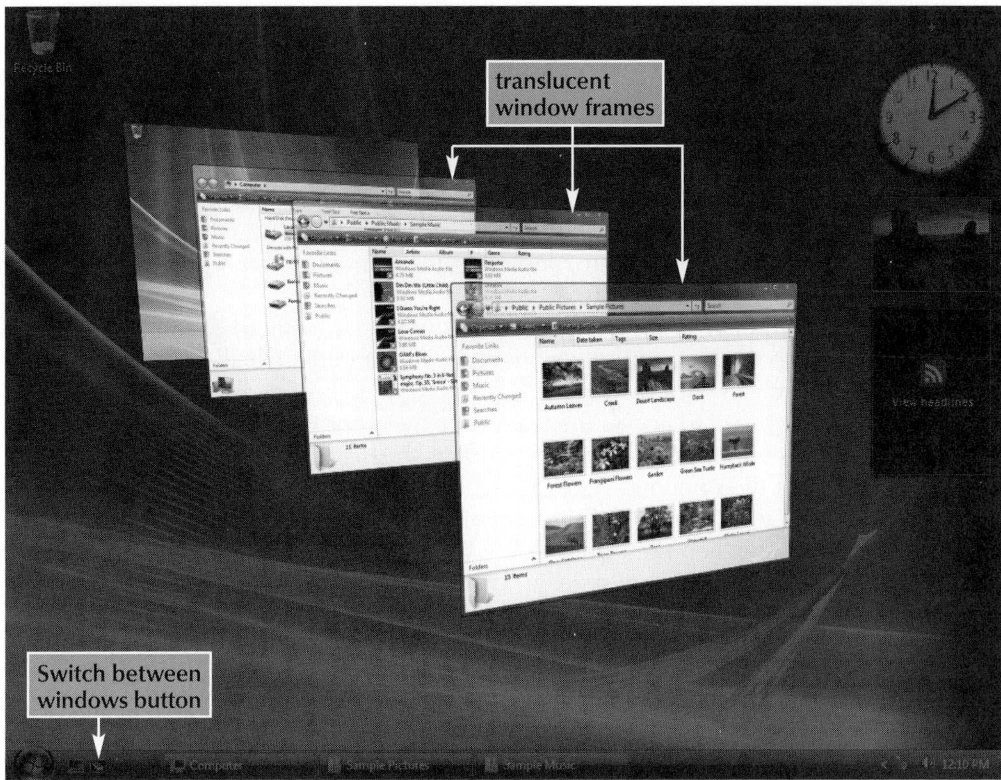

- **Live Taskbar Thumbnails** If you minimize a window, you can point to the taskbar button for that window, and Windows Vista will display a pop-up thumbnail of the window's contents with a pop-up label above the thumbnail that contains the name of the window. The pop-up thumbnail is called a **Live Taskbar Thumbnail,** and the pop-label is called a **ToolTip**. In Figure 1-11, Windows Vista displays a Live Taskbar Thumbnail and ToolTip for a minimized Sample Pictures folder window. If the window contains live content, such as video, Windows Vista plays the video in the Live Taskbar Thumbnail. If you open multiple documents with the same application and then point to the minimized taskbar button for all the documents (called a **grouped taskbar button**), you will see a stack of thumbnails, one for each open document window, but only the content of the top thumbnail will be visible.

Tip

The same types of pop-up labels displayed in an application window are called ScreenTips.

Figure 1-11 Live Taskbar Thumbnail

Windows Aero is not available in Windows Vista Home Basic, but it is available in the other editions of Windows Vista if your hardware supports Windows Aero. The Windows component that manages Windows Aero is called the **Desktop Window Manager** (**DWM**), which Windows Vista Home Basic does not contain. If you are using another edition of Windows Vista and do not see the Windows Aero effects, then Windows Aero may be turned off on that computer. You will learn how to check and change this setting in Tutorial 2. If you see some of the Windows Aero effects, but not others, then your computer's hardware probably supports only some of the Windows Aero effects. Also, Windows Vista automatically adjusts itself to the capabilities of each computer system.

The Windows Taskbar

At the bottom of the desktop is the Windows taskbar with a redesigned Start button and a notification area on the right side of the taskbar. If your edition of Windows Vista and your hardware support Windows Aero, and assuming Windows Aero is enabled, the Windows taskbar appears translucent.

The Quick Launch toolbar has a redesigned Show Desktop button for minimizing all open windows so that you can see the desktop. If you minimize all open windows with this button, you can click the button a second time to restore all your windows. You can also use the keyboard to access the features of the icons on the Quick Launch toolbar. For example, if the Show Desktop button is the first button on the Quick Launch toolbar, you can use the Windows Logo+1 keyboard shortcut to minimize all open windows and then later to restore the minimized windows. (Press and hold down the Windows Logo key and then press and release the 1 key to perform these operations.)

The Quick Launch toolbar also has a "Switch between windows" button that enables Windows Flip 3D on computers that support Windows Aero. If the "Switch between windows" button is the second button on the Quick Launch toolbar, you can use the Windows Logo+2 keyboard shortcut to enable Windows Flip 3D. This feature of selecting Quick Launch toolbar options by using the keyboard applies to the first ten items in the Quick Launch toolbar. You use the keys 1 through 9 for the first nine items on the Quick Launch toolbar and the 0 (zero) key for the tenth item on the Quick Launch toolbar.

Windows Vista uses the notification area on the right side of the taskbar to display the time and the icons for programs that were loaded during booting and are currently running in the background. In Tutorial 8, you will examine how to control the loading of these background programs during booting. Windows Vista also uses the notification area to display alerts to potential problems on your computer (hence its name).

The Windows Sidebar

On the right side of the Windows Vista desktop is a new Windows Vista feature called the Windows Sidebar. The **Windows Sidebar** is a pane that contains miniprograms called **gadgets**. These gadgets provide easily accessible information and tools. If you have closed the Windows Sidebar, you can display it again by clicking the Windows Sidebar icon in the notification area or by clicking the Windows Sidebar option in the Accessories group on the All Programs menu. If the Windows Sidebar is hidden behind a maximized window, you can click the Windows Sidebar icon in the notification area or use the Windows Logo+Spacebar keyboard shortcut to display it in front of the open window.

By default, the Windows Sidebar contains three gadgets—a Clock gadget, a Slide Show gadget, and a Feed Headlines gadget. With a single glance at the Clock gadget, you know the current time. You can pick one of eight different styles for the appearance of the Clock gadget, specify a clock name that appears on the clock, add a second hand, and change the time zone.

The Slide Show gadget displays a different image from the Sample Pictures folder every 15 seconds. You can select images from another folder, change the setting for how long each image is displayed, and specify a transition effect. A **transition effect** determines the way the Slide Show gadget changes from one image to another. For example, you might have each image fade to the next image.

The Feed Headlines gadget displays updated news or headlines from Web sites that support this feature. Feeds are also called **RSS Feeds** (**Really Simple Syndication Feeds**). You can use the Internet Explorer Feeds button to choose one or more feeds from a Web site that provides them. Then you can use the Feed Headlines gadget to display feeds from that and other Web sites.

You can add more gadgets to the Windows Sidebar, and you can add the same gadget more than once and customize each one in different ways. For example, you can add a second Clock gadget and change the time zone so that the Clock shows the time in a locale where you frequently contact friends, co-workers, or clients. At the top of the Windows Sidebar is a Gadgets button bar. The Add Gadget button with the plus sign opens the Gadget Gallery dialog box, where you can double-click a gadget to add it to the Windows Sidebar. After that, you can customize the gadget. You can also download additional gadgets from the Microsoft Gadgets Web site and use them on the Windows Sidebar.

If you point to a gadget, a vertical Gadget button bar for that gadget appears to the right of the gadget. You can use the Close button to remove the gadget from the Windows Sidebar, and you can use the Options button to customize the gadget. You can point to a gadget and drag it to another location on the Windows Sidebar (or you can use the Move button on the verical Gadget button bar to drag the gadget to another location on the Windows Sidebar). You can also drag gadgets off the Windows Sidebar and place them on the desktop. After you place a gadget on the desktop, you can drag it back onto the Windows Sidebar.

Because the Windows Sidebar is an object, you can view its properties by right-clicking it and selecting Properties. Then, you can choose whether to display the Windows Sidebar when your computer boots to the desktop, whether the Windows Sidebar should always appear on top of other windows, and whether the Windows Sidebar appears on the right or left side of the desktop.

Juliann recommends that you examine the types of available gadgets so that you can decide whether there are other useful gadgets that you want to add to your Windows Sidebar.

To add a gadget to the Windows Sidebar:

1. If your Windows Sidebar contains a Feed Headlines gadget, point to the **Feed Headlines** gadget, then click the **Close** button on this Gadget's button bar.
2. Click the **Add Gadget** button on the Gadgets button bar at the top of the Windows Sidebar. Windows opens the Gadget Gallery dialog box and shows you various gadgets that you can add to the Windows Sidebar. See Figure 1-12. If your computer supports Windows Aero, the top and bottom window frames and the background of the window background appear translucent, and a shadow is visible around the entire dialog box.

Figure 1-12 Gadget Gallery

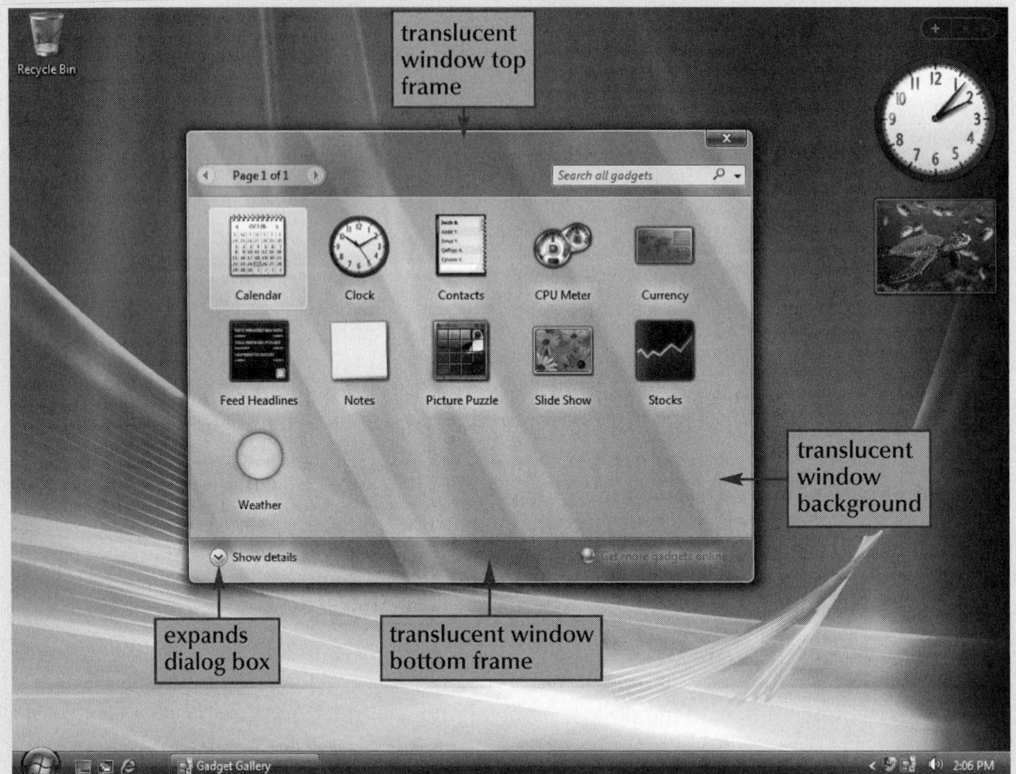

3. Click the **Show details** button in the lower-left corner of the Gadget Gallery dialog box. Windows expands the Gadget Gallery dialog box and displays information about the selected gadget. The "Get more gadgets online" link takes you to the Microsoft Gadgets Gallery Web site where you can download more gadgets.
4. Click **CPU Meter**. In the Details area of the Gadget Gallery dialog box, Windows Vista notes that this gadget provides information about your computer's CPU and RAM (also called system memory).
5. Double-click **CPU Meter**. Windows Vista adds a CPU Meter gadget to the top of your Windows Sidebar.
6. Point to the **Close** button in the upper-right corner of the Gadget Gallery dialog box and note that it glows red if your computer supports Windows Aero, then click the **Close** button to close the Gadget Gallery dialog box.
7. Point to the **CPU Meter** on the Windows Sidebar and drag it below the Slide Show gadget. Windows Vista moves the CPU Meter under the Slide Show gadget. See Figure 1-13.

Figure 1-13 Moving the CPU Meter

The left meter shows you the percentage of time that the processor is busy, and the right meter shows you the percentage of RAM in use on your computer.

Adding Gadgets to the Windows Sidebar | Reference Window

- Click the Add Gadget button on the Gadgets button bar at the top of the Windows Sidebar.
- Click the Show details button in the lower-left corner of the Gadget Gallery dialog box, and then click the gadget icon to display information about the gadget in the Details area of the Gadget Gallery dialog box.
- Double-click the gadget you want to add to the Windows Sidebar.
- Close the Gadget Gallery dialog box.
- If you want to move a gadget, drag it to a new location on the Windows Sidebar.

You can also customize Windows Sidebar gadgets, such as the CPU Meter. The options that are available depend on the type of gadget. In the case of the CPU Meter, you can change its **opacity**, or its level of transparency.

To change the CPU Meter's opacity:

1. Right-click the **CPU Meter** gadget on the Windows Sidebar and note the options on the shortcut menu. You can add Gadgets to the Windows Sidebar, detach the CPU Meter from the Windows Sidebar, move the CPU Meter, change the CPU Meter's opacity, or close the CPU Meter gadget. If you detach the CPU Meter, Windows Vista places it in the upper-left corner of the desktop and increases its size. If you close the CPU Meter, Windows Vista removes it from the Windows Sidebar.
2. Point to **Opacity** on the shortcut menu. The default setting is 100%, which means that the CPU meter is opaque or not transparent.
3. Click **20%** on the Opacity menu. The CPU Meter's opacity decreases, and its transparency increases. See Figure 1-14. You can also choose a value between 20% and 100% so that the CPU Meter is more opaque and less translucent.

Figure 1-14 Adjusting the opacity of the CPU Meter

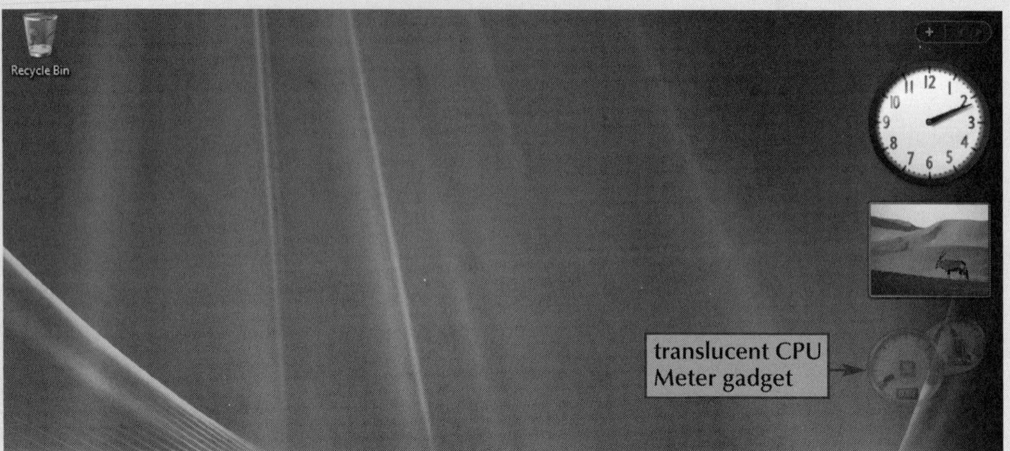

4. Point to the **CPU Meter** on the Windows Sidebar. Windows Vista displays the CPU Meter at 100% opacity.
5. Move your mouse pointer to the middle of the desktop. Windows Vista switches back to 20% opacity for the CPU Meter on the Windows Sidebar.
6. Right-click the **CPU Meter**, point to **Opacity**, and then click **100%** to restore the CPU Meter to its original opacity.

InSight | **Using the CPU Meter**

As you perform operations on your computer and open programs, you can quickly monitor changes using the CPU Meter and determine how different operations and programs affect the performance of your computer. You can monitor changes in the right meter that shows RAM usage to determine whether you need to purchase more RAM for your computer. If the level of RAM usage is high and stays high, then you would benefit from adding more RAM to your computer. You can monitor changes in the left meter that shows processor usage. If the processor usage remains high while you're using certain applications, then you're using a resource-intensive application that is affecting the performance of your computer, and you would benefit from replacing your current computer with one that has a newer high-performance processor.

The Windows Vista Start Menu

The Windows Vista Start menu contains two panels, each separated into groups. See Figure 1-15. The left panel of the Start menu contains two groups: the pinned items list and the most recently opened programs list. The **pinned items list** at the top of the left pane contains an Internet link and an email link. On the computer used for this figure, Internet Explorer and Microsoft Outlook are listed above the separator line in the pinned items list. Items in this area always remain on the Start menu. Under the separator line, Windows Vista lists your most recently used programs in an area called the **recently opened programs list** so that you can quickly open a program you recently used.

Figure 1-15 Start menu

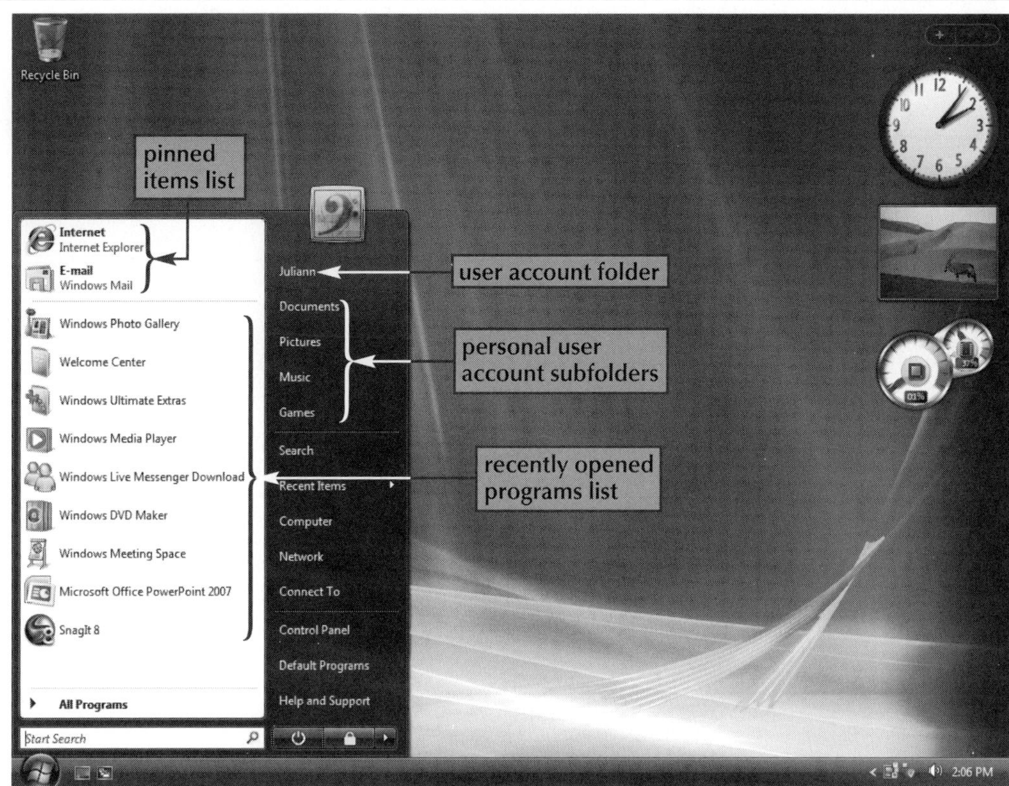

The right panel of the Start menu contains three groups of options. In the upper-right area, Windows Vista displays options for opening your personal folders. The first option is the name of your user account folder. If you click your user account name, Windows Vista opens your user account folder and displays within that folder all your personal user account folders—Contacts, Desktop, Documents, Downloads, Favorites, Links, Music, Pictures, Saved Games, Searches, and Videos. See Figure 1-16. The Documents folder contains all your personal documents, the Downloads folder contains files that you download from the Internet, the Favorites folder contains Internet shortcuts to Web sites, and the Desktop folder contains whatever you place on your desktop.

Figure 1-16 User account folders

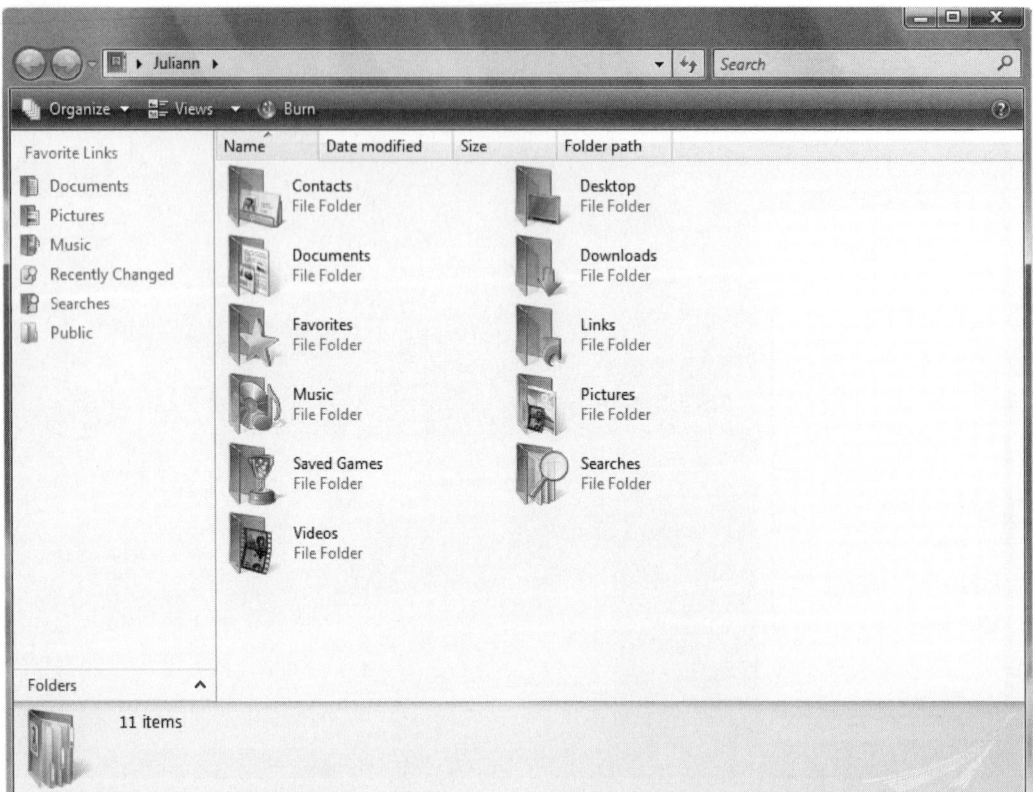

One important new Windows Vista folder is the Contacts folder. You use the Contacts folder to manage your professional and personal contacts. In the Contacts folder, you can create a **contact**, which consists of information about a business or person. For each contact, you can specify one or more email addresses, phone numbers, the street address, Web site addresses, family information, notes about a contact, and even a picture. You can also create **contact groups**, which consist of multiple contacts, such as business contacts and family contacts.

When you point to All Programs at the bottom of the left panel, Windows Vista changes the left panel of the Start menu to display a list of programs in alphabetical order followed by **group folders** that contain one or more programs for each software product you install on your computer. Unlike previous versions of Windows, you do not see menus cascade to the right (or in some cases, to the left) as you point to options on the All Programs menu. If you click a group folder for a specific software product, such as Microsoft Office, then Windows Vista expands the group and displays the programs included with that software product. See Figure 1-17. Again, you do not see cascading menus as in previous versions of Windows.

Figure 1-17 All Programs menu

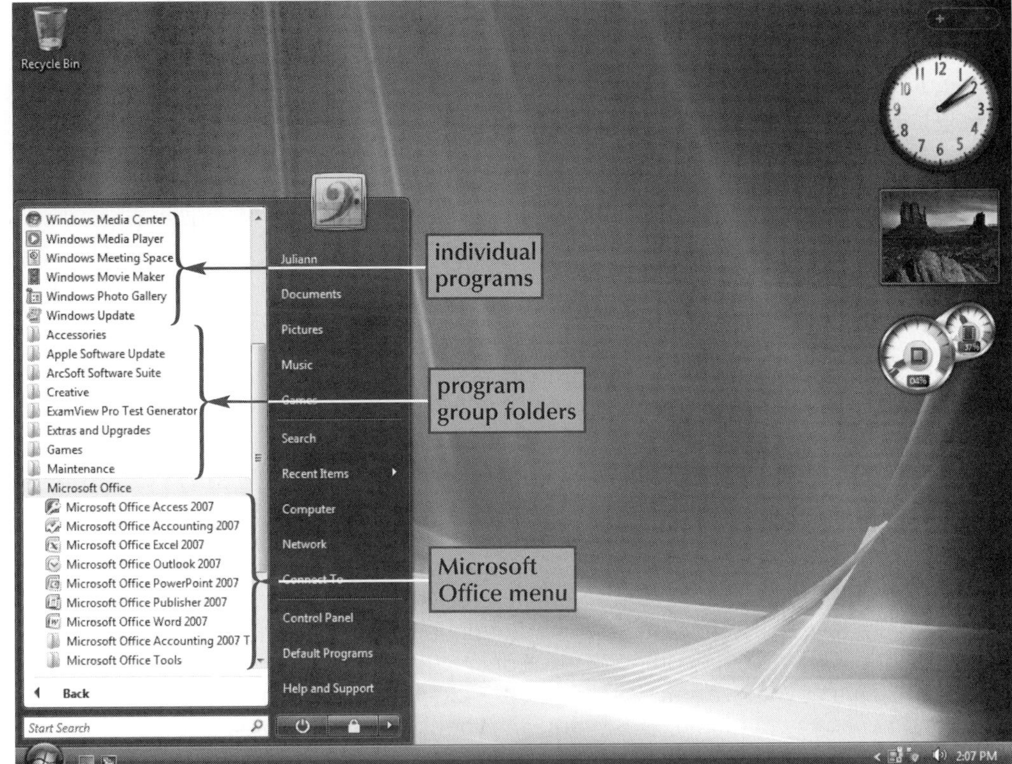

At the bottom of the Start menu is a Start Search text box for locating programs, folders, and files on your computer, using a feature called **Instant Search**, which you will examine in more detail in Tutorial 3.

If you prefer, you can use the Start menu to put a Computer icon on your desktop so that you do not have to open the Computer window from the Start menu. The Computer window is an important resource because it displays a list of your hard disk drives and your removable disk drives and allows you to access those drives. If no Computer icon appears on your desktop, complete the following steps to add the icon to your desktop. If you already have a Computer icon on the desktop, skip the following steps.

To place a Computer icon on the desktop:

1. Click the **Start** button on the taskbar, and then right-click **Computer** on the Start menu. Windows Vista displays a shortcut menu for this object.
2. Click **Show on Desktop**, and then click the **Start** button a second time to close the Start menu. Windows Vista now displays a Computer icon on the desktop.

Tip

You can also use the Windows Logo key to open the Start menu. Press this key a second time to close the Start menu.

If you later want to remove the Computer icon from the desktop, repeat the same steps to turn off this feature. The "Show on Desktop" option on the Computer's shortcut menu allows you to **toggle**, or switch, between displaying and not displaying the Computer icon. If you enable the option for displaying the Computer icon, and then display the Computer icon shortcut menu again, you'll notice that the option has a check mark next to it, indicating that it is enabled. If you turn off this feature, and then display the Computer icon shortcut menu, no check mark appears next to "Show on Desktop," indicating that this feature is turned off.

Using Single-Click Activation

By default, Windows Vista and all previous versions of Windows are set up so that if you want to open a desktop object, folder, or file, you have to double-click the icon for the object. In contrast, if you single-click a desktop object, folder, or file, then Windows Vista selects that object. After you select an object, you can perform an operation on the object, such as moving, copying, renaming, or deleting the object. This way of using the mouse is the classic way most people use a mouse on their local computer system (it is therefore referred to as **Classic Style**), but it's not the way they use the mouse when they browse the Web. On the Web, if you want to go to a new Web page, you single-click the link to that Web page. You don't have to double-click the link. Many people immediately ask, "Why can't I work with the objects on a local computer in the same way that I browse the Web? Why do I have to use two different ways of working with the mouse?" As it turns out, Windows Vista, as well as previous versions of Windows, has an option called **single-click activation** that enables you to browse your local computer in the same way you browse the Web. After you enable this feature, you can use the same set of skills on your local computer that you use on the Web. If you want to open a desktop object, folder, or file, you single-click the object, folder, or file. If you want to select an object, folder, or file, you point to the object, folder, or file. By using this feature, you eliminate almost all double-clicking, which some users find difficult anyway. You also eliminate all the single-clicking that you used to do when you selected an object. Most people do not realize the inordinate amount of double-clicking and single-clicking they perform while working on a computer. By reducing the amount of double-clicking and single-clicking that you perform, you can save a lot of wear-and-tear on the muscles, tendons, and nerves in your hand, wrist, arm, and shoulder. Since single-click activation is similar to the way in which you browse the Web, it's referred to as **Web Style**. Single-click activation makes navigating your computer simple and easy.

You can use Folder Options in the Control Panel to enable single-activation on your computer. The Control Panel is a commonly used Windows tool for changing Windows settings. The Folder Options dialog box has three tabs for three different groups of settings—General, View, and Search. Each tab displays a group of related settings on what's called a **property sheet**. The General tab displays the General property sheet with the option for enabling single-click activation. Under the "Click items as follows" section, an option labeled "Double-click to open (single-click to select)" is enabled by default for all versions of Windows. Juliann suggests that you change this setting now.

To enable single-click activation:

1. Click the **Start** button on the taskbar, and then click **Control Panel**. Windows Vista opens the Control Panel window.
2. Click the **Appearance and Personalization** link. Windows Vista opens the Appearance and Personalization window.
3. Under Folder Options, click the **Specify single- or double-click to open** link. Windows Vista opens the Folder Options dialog box and displays the contents of the General property sheet. See Figure 1-18.

Figure 1-18 Folder Options dialog box

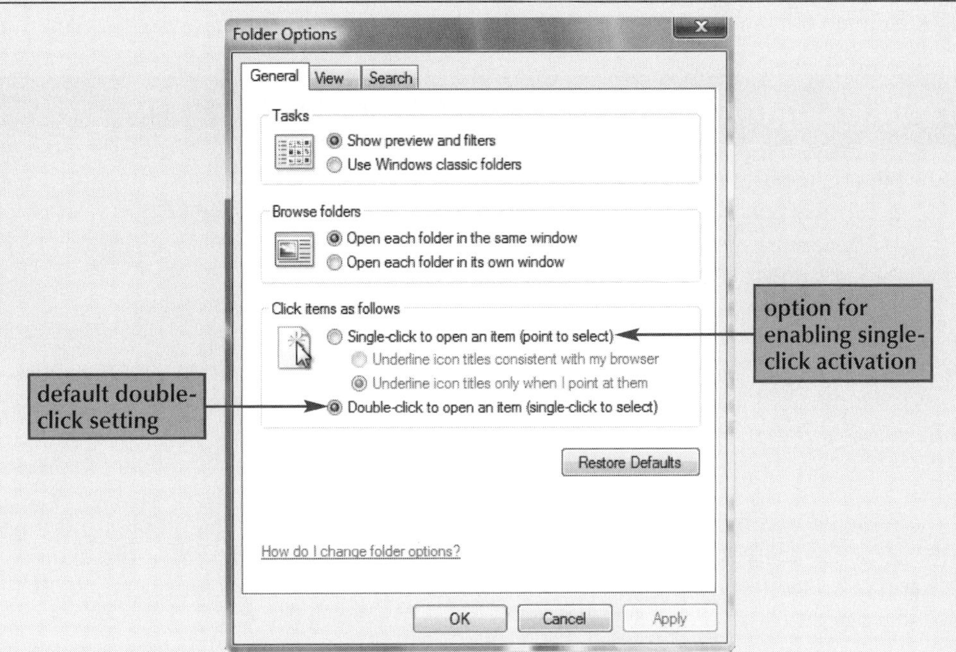

4. Under "Click items as follows" on the General property sheet, click the **Single-click to open an item (point to select)** option button if it is not already selected. As soon as you enable this option, two additional options under this setting become available. If you enable the option labeled "Underline icon titles consistent with my browser," then the icon titles for all desktop objects, folder icons, and file icons are underlined, similar to links on a Web page. The second option, labeled "Underline icon titles only when I point to them," only displays the underline when you point to a desktop object, folder icon, or file icon, and therefore does not change your view of your computer.
5. Click the **Underline icon titles only when I point at them** option button if it is not already selected, and then click the **OK** button.
6. Close the Appearance and Personalization window.
7. Point to, and rest the mouse pointer, on the **Computer** icon on the desktop. Windows Vista selects and highlights the Computer icon and then displays an underline under the icon title. See Figure 1-19. Note that you did not need to click the icon to select it. Also note that the mouse pointer appears as a hand with a finger pointing to the link, just like it appears when you point to a link on a Web page.

Figure 1-19 Using Web style

8. Click the **Computer** icon. Windows Vista opens a Computer window with a single-click.
9. Close the Computer window.

Working in Web style with single-click activation is far easier than using the traditional Windows Classic Style. Furthermore, the content of your computer acts as Web pages so that you can navigate and open files in the same way you browse the Web.

Reference Window | Enabling Single-Click Activation

- Click the Start button, and then click Control Panel.
- In the Control Panel window, click the Appearance and Personalization link.
- In the Appearance and Personalization window, click the "Specify single- or double-click to open" link under Folder Options.
- On the General property sheet, click the "Single-click to open an item (point to select)" option.
- Click the "Underline icon titles only when I point at them" option button, and then click the OK button.
- Close the Appearance and Personalization window.

The remainder of the instructions and the figures in this tutorial and all other tutorials in the book assume you are using Web style with single-click activation. At the end of the tutorial, you will have the option to restore your original settings for opening and selecting objects if you prefer to work in Windows Classic style.

Using Windows Help and Support

In her Windows Vista orientation, Juliann explains to employees that they should first check Windows Help and Support for answers to their questions before contacting her tech support staff.

After you open Windows Help and Support, you can use the following techniques to locate information you need:

- **Browse Help** Right after you open Windows Help and Support, you can browse Help by first selecting a general Help category, such as "Windows Basics," locate a more-specific Help category, such as "Desktop fundamentals," and then choose a specific Help topic, such as "Windows Sidebar and gadgets (overview)."

  You can also browse Help using the Table of Contents. You select a topic from the Table of Contents similar to the way you locate information in a book. For example, you might use the Table of Contents to find information on techniques for working with a mobile PC by locating the Mobile PC Help chapter. Then you look for a specific Help topic. The Table of Contents is useful if you want to examine all the Help information related to a specific feature in an organized way, but it can take more time than other techniques to locate the Help you need because you might have to keep selecting one Help topic after another until you find what you want.
- **Search Help** Searching Windows Help and Support is the fastest way to find Help information. You use one or more descriptive words called **keywords**, such as "Windows Aero," to obtain a list of search results for all the Help topics that include the word or phrase you specified.
- **Windows Vista Demos** Windows Help and Support contains video clips called Windows Vista demos that provide an overview of Windows Vista features and how to use them. For example, you might want to view a video on understanding user accounts. You can view those demos with Windows Media Player. Most of the Windows Vista demos are close to three minutes in length.

In the next three sections, you use these three approaches for locating Help information.

Browsing Help

Now that you've added the CPU Meter gadget to your Windows Sidebar, Juliann recommends that you use Help and Support to become more familiar with how the Windows Sidebar works.

To open and browse Help and Support:

1. Click the **Start** button on the taskbar, click **Help and Support** on the Start menu, and then click the **Maximize** button if the Windows Help and Support window does not fill the desktop. See Figure 1-20. You can browse Help by starting with one of the six icons located under "Find an answer."

   Trouble? If you do not have an active Internet connection, Windows Vista prompts you to connect to the Internet. If you want to access Online Help, you need to connect to the Internet. Otherwise, you can use Help and Support offline.

   Trouble? If your view of the Help and Support window differs, your computer manufacturer probably customized Windows Vista's Help and Support. Continue with step 2.

Tip

To open Windows Help and Support quickly from the desktop, press the F1 key.

Figure 1-20 Windows Help and Support

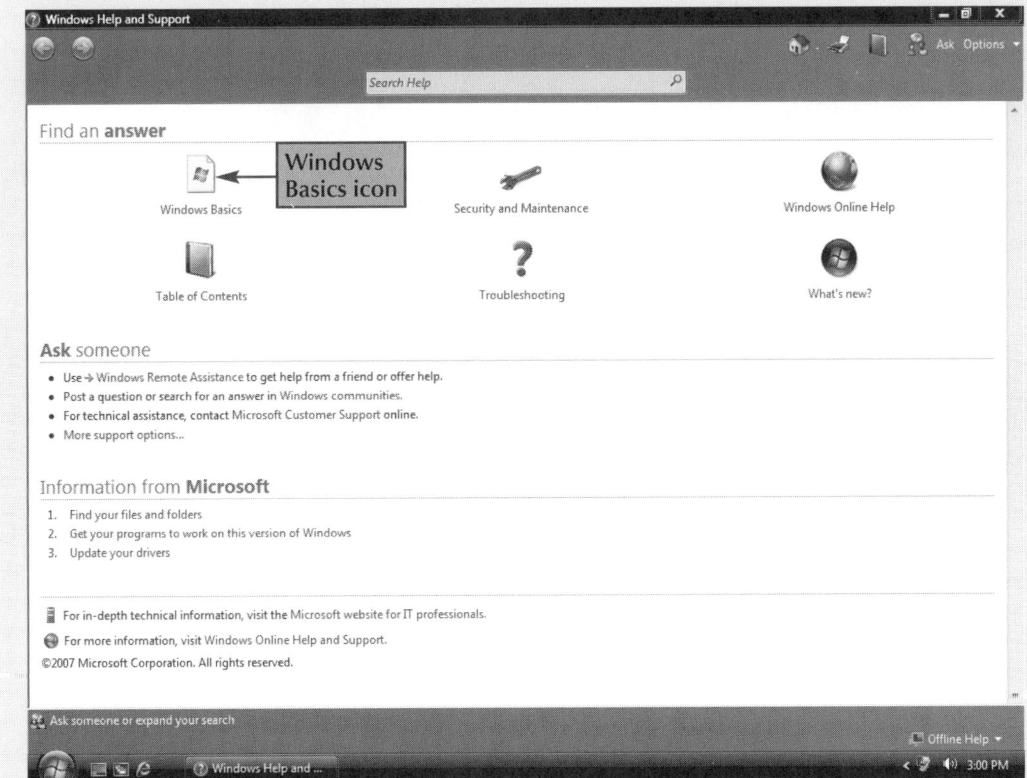

2. Click the **Windows Basics** icon. Windows Help and Support displays categories of Help topics about basic Windows features and, under each category, lists specific Help topics.

Trouble? If your Help and Support window does not include a "Find an answer" section or display a Windows Basic icon, click in the Search box, type Windows Basics, and then click the Search button.

3. Under Desktop fundamentals, click **Windows Sidebar and gadgets (overview)**. The "Windows Sidebar and gadgets (overview)" Help topic explains what the Sidebar is, why you use it, how it works, and the use of gadgets—including adding, removing, and organizing gadgets.
4. Under "In this article" on the right side of the window, click the **Organizing gadgets** link. This link takes you directly to the "Organizing gadgets" section in this Help topic so that you don't have to scroll. The Help information points out that you can place all or part of the gadgets on the desktop.
5. Click the **To place a gadget on the desktop** link. Windows Help and Support expands this Help topic and lists the steps for performing this operation. The Help information explains that you can detach a gadget from the Windows Sidebar by dragging it to the desktop, and if you want to place the gadget back on the Windows Sidebar, you drag it onto the Windows Sidebar.
6. Click the **Minimize** button to minimize the Windows Help and Support window.
7. Drag the **CPU Meter** to the middle of the desktop. Windows Vista moves the CPU Meter from the Windows Sidebar to the desktop. See Figure 1-21. Notice that the CPU Meter increases in size when you place it on the desktop.

Figure 1-21 Dragging the CPU Meter to the desktop from the Windows Sidebar

8. Drag the **CPU Meter** from the desktop to the Windows Sidebar and place it under the Slide Show gadget. Windows Vista moves the CPU Meter back to the Windows Sidebar, and the CPU Meter returns to its original size.

9. Click the **Windows Help and Support** taskbar button on the taskbar. Windows Vista restores the Windows Help and Support window.

The table in Figure 1-22 identifies and describes buttons on the Help and Support Window command bar.

Figure 1-22 Windows Help and Support window buttons

Button Name	Help Button	Description
Home		If you click the Home button, you return directly to the starting or opening Windows Help and Support page. This is particularly useful if you want to select one of the options under "Find an answer," such as Windows Basics, Security and Maintenance, Troubleshooting, Windows Online Help, and What's New?
Print		If you want to print a Help topic, click this button.
Browse Help		This button opens the Table of Contents.
Ask	 Ask	This button displays options for getting Help from someone else, a Windows community, Microsoft Customer Support, and Microsoft's Knowledge Base as well as locating in-depth technical information at Microsoft's Web site for IT professionals.
Options	 Options	This button displays a list with options for printing, browsing Help, changing the size of the text in Windows Help and Support, searching for information on a page, and changing Help settings.

Browsing Windows Help and Support | Reference Window

- Click the Start button, and then click Help and Support (or press the F1 key).
- Under "Find an answer," click one of the six Help topic icons, and then click a specific Help topic.
- If you want to quickly locate a section within a Help topic, click one of the links under "In this article" on the right side of the window.
- If necessary, click a Help link to display more information about a topic or to display the steps for performing a task.
- If you want to return to the initial opening page to select another Help topic, click the Home button in the Windows Help and Support window.

Next, you want to search for Help information on correcting red eye in digital images.

To search Windows Help and Support using keywords:

1. Click in the Search Help text box in the Windows Help and Support window, type **red eye**, and then click the **Search Help** button. Windows Help and Support displays a list of search results related to the keywords you specified. See Figure 1-23.

Figure 1-23 Search results

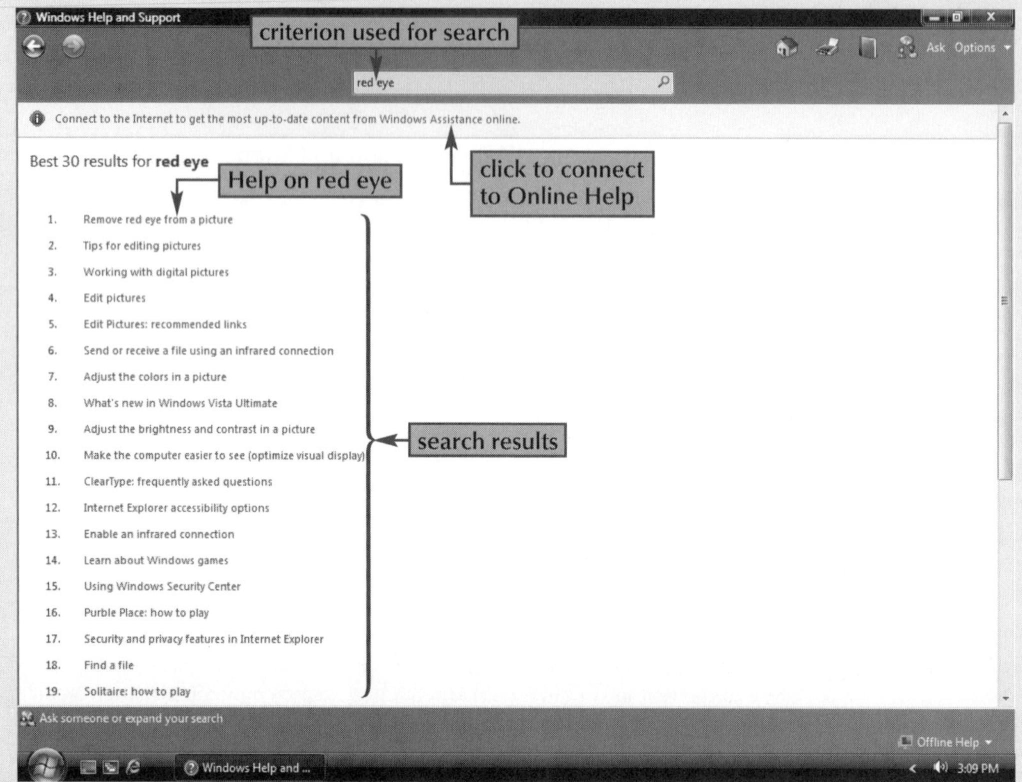

2. Click the **Remove red eye from a picture** link. Windows Help and Support displays Help information on this topic, which describes red eye and explains that you can correct this problem using your digital camera or by using the Windows Photo Gallery, a new Windows Vista feature for working with pictures and videos. The Help information also lists the steps for performing this operation.
3. Read the Help information on how to correct red eye with the Windows Photo Gallery and examine the figures in the Help and Support window.

You can use the same approach to search for help on other topics.

Reference Window | Searching Windows Help and Support

- Click the Start button, and then click Help and Support (or press the F1 key).
- Click in the Search Help text box in the Windows Help and Support window, type a keyword or phrase that identifies the type of Help you want to locate, and then click the Search Help button.
- In the list of Search results, click the Help topic you want to examine.

Juliann suggests that you search for a Windows Vista demo on understanding user accounts so that you are more familiar with why user accounts are important and how they affect your use of your computer.

If you are working in a computer lab, you will need to check out and use earphones so that you can hear the video on user accounts.

To locate and view a Windows demo on understanding user accounts:

1. Click in the Search Help text box, point to the first character in the Search Help text box, drag to select the remaining characters in the keywords you last entered, type **demos** in the Search Help text box, and then click the **Search Help** button. Windows Help and Support displays a set of search results.
2. Click **Windows Vista demos** in the Search results. Windows Help and Support lists Windows Vista demos available in Windows Help and Support and notes that you can access the complete collection of Windows Vista demos online.
3. Under the last category, "Security and maintenance," click **Demo: Understanding user accounts**. The introduction to this Windows Vista demo notes that several people can share the same computer system by creating separate user accounts. Then Windows Help and Support explains what the demo covers.

   Trouble? If your computer has been customized by the manufacturer, then your view in the Help and Support window may differ. Locate the "Understanding user accounts" topic and click the link for this topic.
4. Click the **Watch the demo** link. Windows Media Player opens and begins to play the Windows Vista demo.

   Trouble? If you haven't opened Windows Media Player before, you might need to first specify settings on how you want to use Windows Media Player on your computer.
5. After the Windows Vista demo is complete, close Windows Media Player, then close the Windows Help and Support window.

Windows Help and Support includes other videos, such as one for showing how to diagnose problems with your computer and one for working with files and folders.

Locating and Viewing Windows Vista Demos | Reference Window

- Click the Start button, and then click Help and Support (or press the F1 key).
- Click in the Search Help text box in the Windows Help and Support window, type "demos" (without the quotation marks), and then click the Search Help button.
- In the list of Search results, click the link for the Windows Vista demo that you want to watch.
- Click "Watch the demo."
- After the Windows Vista demo is complete, close Windows Media Player.

The Windows Help and Support Center can quickly provide you with information on how to complete a task or explain how to use new features. From the initial Windows Help and Support page, you can click the Windows Online Help link to get additional help from the Microsoft Windows Help and How-to Web site. On this Web site, you can find more information about basic and advanced Windows Vista features, view "how-to" videos, get help from other people in Windows Vista online discussion groups or Windows communities, read up-to-date articles on changes in Windows Vista, and get online support from Microsoft technical support staff. For more advanced users who want to locate in-depth technical information, there is a link to Microsoft's Web site for IT (Information Technology) professionals on the opening Windows Help and Support page.

InSight | Using Remote Assistance

Under "Ask someone" on the initial Windows Help and Support page, you can use a more advanced Windows Vista feature called Remote Assistance to obtain help from a friend or even offer help to someone. With Remote Assistance, you extend an invitation via e-mail or instant messaging for someone to help you on your computer. Using your invitation, that person connects to your computer via the Internet with Windows Vista's Remote Assistance tool. That person can view your computer screen, discuss your problem with you, and use your computer to correct the problem as you watch. You can search Help and Support for more information on using and setting up Remote Assistance on your computer.

Windows Help and Support provides Help information about programs that are part of Windows Vista, such as the Windows Photo Gallery, but it does not provide Help for other programs, such as Microsoft Office programs or programs developed by companies other than Microsoft. Each of those programs has its own Help system where you can find more detail about the use of that program. If you press the F1 key while using one of these programs, that program opens its Help system and, in some cases, provides **context-sensitive Help**, or Help directly related to the task at hand.

Review | Session 1.2 Quick Check

1. Windows uses predefined, or ________________, settings to simplify your use of a computer.
2. What user interface technology supports the new Windows Vista features, such as object translucency, smooth scaling of icon sizes, smooth visual refreshing of the desktop, Live Taskbar Thumbnails, Windows Flip, and Windows Flip 3D?
3. Windows Sidebar uses miniprograms called ________________ .
4. What personal user folder can you use to keep track of email addresses and other information about professional and work associates as well as friends?
5. In Windows Vista, what feature can you enable so that you can browse your local computer in the same way you browse the Web?
6. True or False. A group of related settings stored on a tab in a dialog box is called a property sheet.

Session 1.3

Navigating Your Computer

To more effectively use Windows Vista, you should be familiar with how Windows Vista organizes and provides access to resources, drives, folders, and files on your computer.

Computers typically have at least one hard disk drive and one or more removable drives, such as a DVD or CD drive. The hard disk drive contains the installed version of the Windows Vista operating system, all applications, utilities, and games installed on your computer, and your document files. Since software and hardware developers distribute software on DVDs and CDs, you need at least a DVD drive for installing software products, such as Microsoft Windows and Microsoft Office, and for installing software and device drivers for new hardware products you purchase. In the past, software was distributed on CDs, but that standard is changing. The software for Windows Vista does not fit on a CD, so it is now distributed on a DVD. DVD drives can read or access the information on both DVDs and CDs, but CD drives can read only CDs. When purchasing a new computer, consider purchasing a combination DVD-Rewritable/CD-Rewritable drive so that you can record multiple times to both DVDs and CDs.

The operating system assigns a unique drive name to each drive in your computer. The **drive name** consists of a letter of the alphabet followed by a colon (**:**). According to conventions set in 1981 by IBM for the first IBM PC, the first floppy disk drive (if present) is assigned the drive name A: and called drive A, and the second floppy disk drive (if present) is assigned the drive name B: and called drive B. The first hard disk drive is named C: and called drive C. Any additional disk drives are assigned drive names starting with the next available drive letter; however, you can change drive names on a computer. Although most people work on computers whose entire hard disk is assigned the drive name C: for drive C, you can partition, or subdivide, one physical hard disk into multiple logical drives. For example, your computer manufacturer or you might subdivide the storage space on a single hard disk into two drives, a drive C and a drive D, and install all software on drive C and use drive D for storing document files. Then you can back up all your personal files by selecting drive D when using backup software. Also, it is possible to have more than one physical hard disk in a computer; each hard disk would then have a different drive name.

USB flash drives (**UFDs**) are popular, portable drives for storing documents. These type of drives are also referred to as pen drives, jump drives, key drives, keychain drives, disk-on-key drives, memory keys, flash memory drives, USB keys, and USB sticks (to name a few). When you attach a USB flash drive to a computer, Windows Vista assigns it a drive name, which is visible in the Computer window. When you detach or safely remove a USB flash drive from a computer, Windows Vista removes its drive name from the Computer window. When you safely remove a USB flash drive, Windows Vista ensures that all data has been written to the disk before you remove it. To safely remove a USB flash drive, you click the Safely Remove Hardware icon in the notification area on the taskbar, and then choose the hardware device that you want to remove. Because there might be more than one hardware device that you can safely remove, you identify the one you want to remove by its drive name.

On hard disks, software and documents are organized into folders. A **folder** is a file that keeps track of a group of related objects, such as files and perhaps other subfolders. The term **subfolder** refers to a folder contained within another folder, and it keeps track of a smaller set of related files within a larger, related group of files. A **file** consists of a collection of data, such as a program or a document, stored on a disk under a unique filename and file extension (if specified). The operating system allocates a certain amount of disk storage space to each program and document, and associates each file's allocated space with the filename assigned to the file.

The primary function of folders is to organize related information so that you (and the operating system) can easily find that information. In a command-line operating system or a command-line environment, the terms **directory** and **subdirectory** are used instead of the terms folder and subfolder. If you open a Command Prompt window in Windows Vista and work in a command-line environment, you use the terms directory and subdirectory to refer to the folders and subfolders on the disks in your computer.

Although most people think of a folder as a container for objects, such as subfolders and files, the folder itself and the subfolders and files are all separate objects stored at different locations on the hard disk. The subfolders and files are not actually stored within that one folder. A folder is therefore a logical concept, not a physical reality. However, it is common practice to think of files as being stored within folders (and subfolders stored within other folders) so that it is easier to understand and work with folders and files. As noted earlier, the operating system uses a file system to keep track of and manage folders and files on a disk. Different operating systems support different types of file systems, which is the focus of Tutorial 5.

Using Long Filenames

Tip

Depending on how your computer is set up, you might or might not see the file extension with filenames when viewing files.

Another important operating system feature is the support that it provides for assigning names to files. Most filenames consist of three parts: the main part of the name (sometimes called the "root name"), a period (referred to as a **delimiter** or **separator**, and called a "dot" by computer-savvy individuals), and the file extension, which consists of the characters that follow the period. For example, the program that displays the desktop and the view that you see within a folder window is called Explorer, and it is stored in a file with the filename Explorer.exe under the Windows folder. "Explorer" is the main part of the filename and "exe" is the file extension. The "exe" file extension stands for "executable," and identifies this file as a program file whose program code can be loaded into memory and executed (or performed). The contents of an executable file are stored in a format that the processor can directly execute, and unlike the **source code** (or original program code) from which it was originally derived, you cannot read the contents of the file.

As noted earlier, you can use descriptive filenames. These filenames can include spaces, periods, and symbols; however, the following nine symbols are not allowed because they have special meaning to the operating system:

: / \ | < > * ? "

As you already know, the colon (**:**) is used as part of a drive name, so you cannot use it in a filename. If you try to use one of these **reserved symbols** in a filename, Windows will not accept the symbol you type. Figure 1-24 lists examples of valid and invalid filenames.

Figure 1-24 **Examples of valid and invalid filenames**

Valid Filenames	Valid Characters or Features
Five Year Sales Projection.xls	Spaces
PerformanceMeasurements.htm	Mixed case
NTFS vs. FAT Comparison.txt	Multiple periods
CASHFLOW.XLS	All uppercase characters
bootmgr	No file extension
Resume #1.doc	Pound sign (#) and numbers
Windows Vista's System Requirements.doc	Apostrophe
Windows XP 64-Bit Edition Overview.htm	Dash and numbers
Windows Vista Performance_Files	Underscore
Sales Commissions (1st Quarter).xls	Parentheses and numbers
Pilot Project Analysis & Summary.doc	Ampersand (&)
Multi-Booting with Windows XP, Windows 2000, & Windows 98.doc	Commas
@Backup Privacy Policy.doc	@ Symbol
Résumés	Accents and special symbols
Invalid Filenames	**Invalid Characters**
Drive C: Backup Report.txt	Reserved device name (C:) in filename
Analysis: First Quarter Performance.doc	Colon in filename
File Systems (NTFS/FAT32/FAT16).doc	Slashes (/)
Explorer\Advanced Registry Subkey.txt	Backslash (\ )
High Priority Projects.doc	Asterisks (*)
Potential Mergers?.doc	Question mark (?)
"Top-Notch" Sales Staff.doc	Quotation marks (" ")
< Client Mailing List>.mdb	Chevrons (< and >)
Level 1 | Level 2 | Level 3 Rating Systems.doc	Pipe symbol (|)

Since a filename might contain multiple periods, the last period in the filename is the one that separates the main part of the filename from the file extension. Although the file extension is not always required, Windows programs typically assign file extensions to files you produce with those programs, and Windows Vista uses those file extensions to determine which application to open when you click (or double-click) a file icon. Also, file extensions serve to organize files by function and type, and when you choose the option to open a file from an application, that application displays a filtered view of the files within a folder, showing you only those filenames that have a certain file extension. If you want to view other file types (in other words, files with a different file extension), you specify the file type. You can also specify that you want to view all files, regardless of their file extension. When you create and name a file, all you provide is the main part of the filename, and then the program adds a file extension.

You can also use these long filenames, as they are called, for folders, but a folder name usually does not have a file extension (except for temporary folders used to install software) and, in some cases, files (such as operating system files) do not have file extensions. Because some network operating systems do not recognize long filenames, Microsoft uses names for its program files and other supporting files that follow the DOS conventions or rules for naming files. DOS filenames are limited to eight characters for the main part of the filename, followed by a period, and then three characters for the file extension (called an **8.3 filename**). Furthermore, no spaces are allowed in a DOS filename, you can use only one period to separate the filename from the file extension, and the file extension cannot exceed three characters.

Juliann recommends that each employee take the time to explore and become familiar with the drives and personal folders on their new computer and examine how Windows Vista organizes their view of the computer.

Next, you are going to open your personal user account folder, navigate around your personal folder structure, and examine the features of folder windows and files.

To understand how Windows Vista organizes drives, folders, and files:

1. If you have already opened an application, drive, or folder window, close those windows.
2. Click the **Computer** icon on the desktop, and if necessary, maximize the Computer window. Windows Vista displays the Computer window. See Figure 1-25.

Tip

You can also use the Windows Logo+E (for Explorer) keyboard shortcut to open the Computer window.

Figure 1-25 **Viewing the contents of a Computer window**

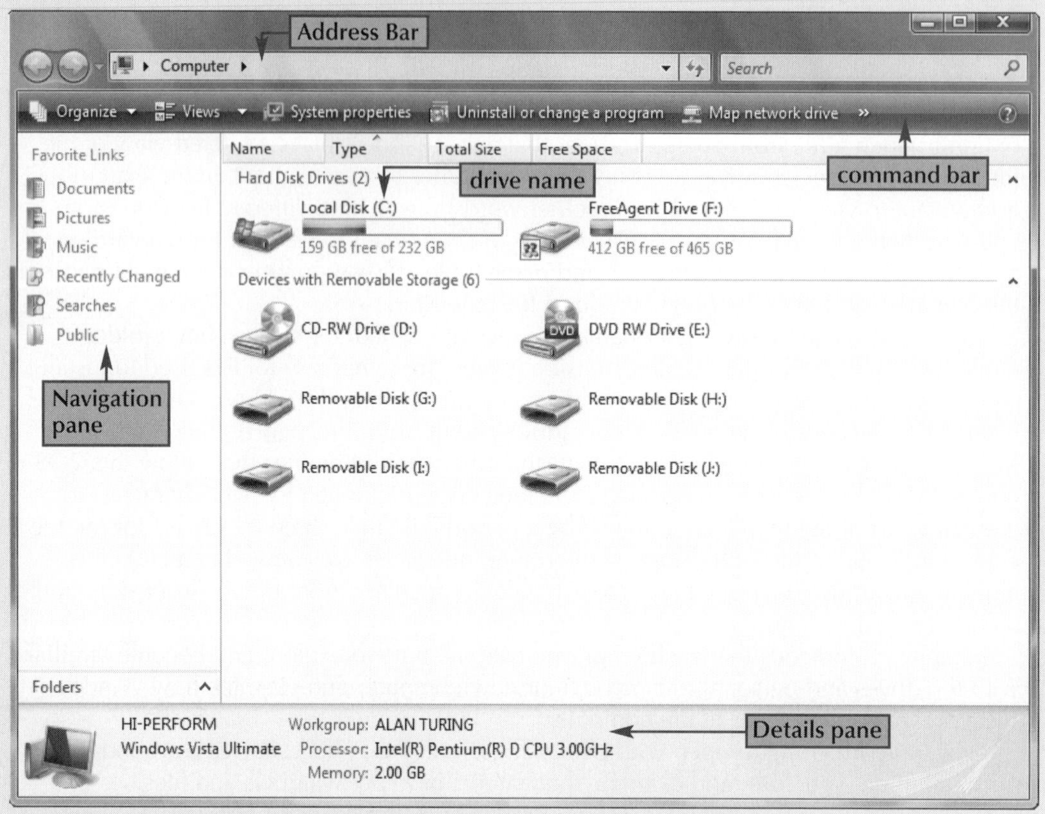

The Computer window, like every other type of window, contains an **Address Bar** at the top of the window that identifies your location on the computer and allows you to navigate your computer. **Resizing buttons** located in the upper-right corner of the window let you minimize, maximize, restore down, and close a window. To the left of the Address Bar are a Back button to back up to the previous window and a Forward button to undo moving back to a previous window. To the right of the Address Bar is a Search text box. Below the Address Bar is a command bar with a set of buttons for performing specific operations, such as changing your view in this window. The **command bar** is essentially a combination menu bar and toolbar that replaces the two separate menu bar and standard toolbars in previous versions of Windows. The pane on the left side of the Computer window is the **Navigation pane**, which contains links to other frequently used locations on your computer (called Favorite Links).

In the main part of the Computer window, Windows Vista lists hard disk drives and removable disk drives in two separate groups. On the computer shown in Figure 1-25, the hard disk drive is identified as Local Disk (C:), a common designation for drives (though the drive name itself can vary). Drive F (or F:) is an external USB hard disk drive assigned the name FreeAgent Drive by the manufacturer. The drive F icon contains a smaller picture of two individuals , indicating that the drive is a shared drive on a network. The bars beneath each drive visually show the amount of free (or available) storage space and the total storage space. Beneath the bars, Windows Vista notes the amount of free space and the total storage capacity in GB (gigabytes) for each disk. **GB** is an abbreviation for gigabytes. A **gigabyte** is equal to approximately one billion bytes of storage. A **byte** is the storage space on disk or in RAM for one character. Figure 1-26 lists storage capacity terms and their common abbreviations. The Power column shows the powers of 10 used to calculate the exact number of bytes. For example, 2^{10} equals 1,024 bytes.

Commonly used terms for measuring storage capacity

Figure 1-26

Term	Abbreviation	Equals	Bytes (Actual)	Power
Byte	B	1 character	1	2^{0}
Kilobyte	K or KB	1,024 bytes	1,024	2^{10}
Megabyte	M, MB, or megs	1,024 kilobytes	1,048,576	2^{20}
Gigabyte	G, GB, or gigs	1,024 megabytes	1,073,741,824	2^{30}
Terabyte	TB	1,024 gigabytes	1,099,511,627,776	2^{40}
Petabyte	PB	1,024 terabytes	1,125,899,906,842,624	2^{50}
Exabyte	EB	1,024 petabytes	1,152,921,504,606,846,976	2^{60}
Zettabyte	ZB	1,024 exabytes	1,180,591,620,717,411,303,424	2^{70}
Yottabyte	YB	1,024 zettabytes	1,208,925,819,614,629,174,706,176	2^{80}

Under Devices with Removable Storage, Windows Vista displays icons for removable devices on the computer used in the previous Figure 1-25. In addition to a DVD-RW (RW for Rewritable) and a CD-RW drive, this computer has four other drives for different types of memory card readers.

If you select a drive, then Windows Vista displays information about the drive in the **Details pane** at the bottom of the window.

To view details of your hard disk and then navigate to your personal user account folders:

1. Point to the **Local Disk (C:)** icon (or the icon for your hard disk), but do not click this drive icon. Windows Vista selects the drive. Once selected, Windows Vista displays a light blue border and light blue background around the drive as well as a ToolTip with free space and total size information in GB. See Figure 1-27. In the Details pane, Windows Vista displays the same information shown in the main part of the window, but also identifies the file system used on the hard disk. Your hard disk drive icon might have a different name, and other details of your hard disk might differ. The computer used for this figure has a hard disk that uses NTFS, a file system commonly used on disks with large storage capacities. (In Tutorial 5, you will examine file systems in more detail.)

Figure 1-27 Viewing information about the hard disk drive

Tip

To navigate to another drive, click the Address Bar arrow to the right of Computer in the Address Bar, and then click the drive.

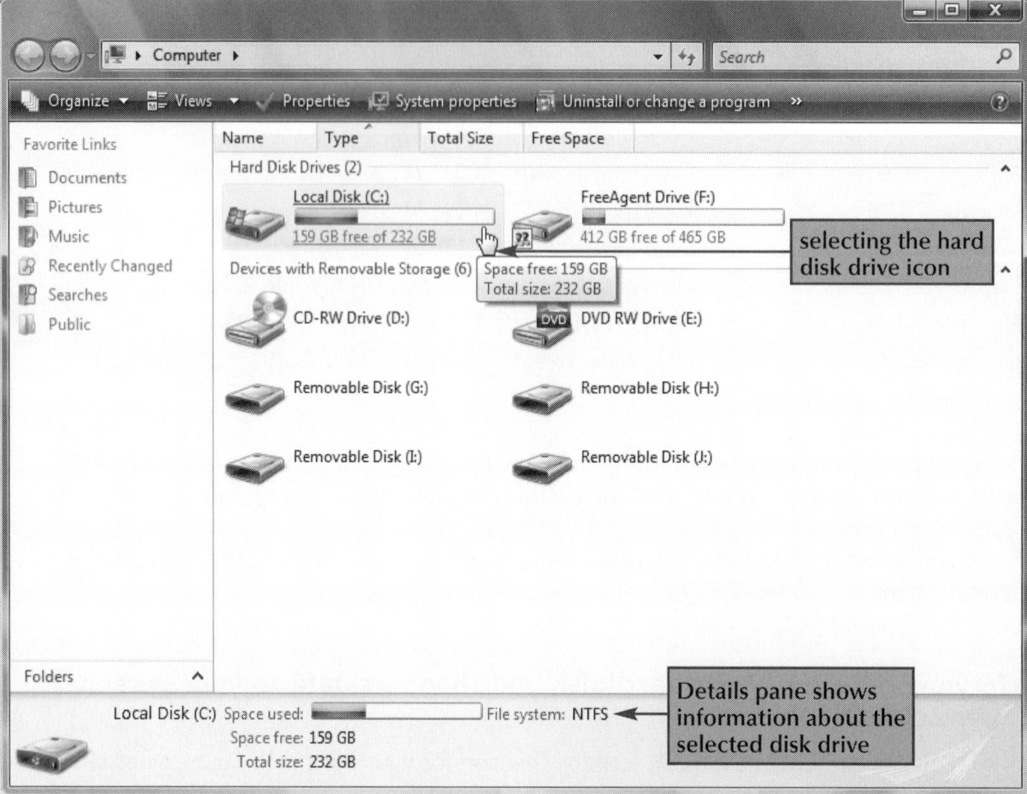

2. Click the **first Address Bar arrow** to the left of the Computer icon in the Address Bar. Windows Vista displays a list of locations to which you can navigate. See Figure 1-28. You can navigate to your personal Desktop folder, the Recycle Bin window, the Control Panel, the Public folder, your personal user account folder with your user account name, and to the Network folder.

Figure 1-28 Navigating with the Address Bar

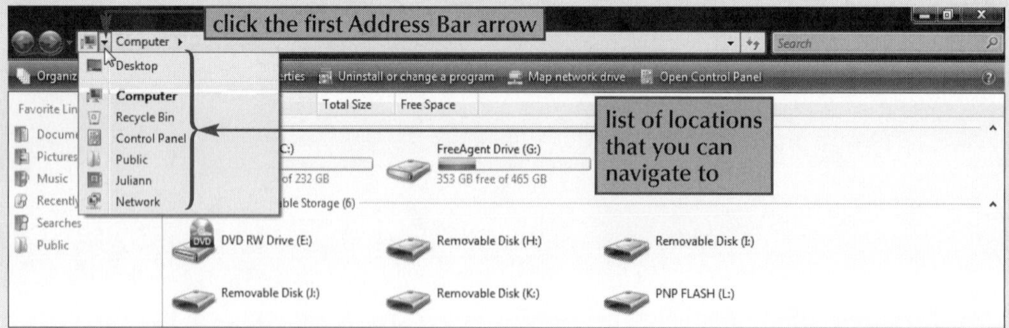

3. Click your **user account name** in the drop-down location list. Windows Vista switches to your user account folder and displays your user account subfolders. See Figure 1-29. Note that the Address Bar now shows that you are in your user account. Although you can access your Documents, Pictures, Music, and Searches folder from the Navigation pane, your user account folder allows you to access your other personal folders.

Locating the Videos folder

Figure 1-29

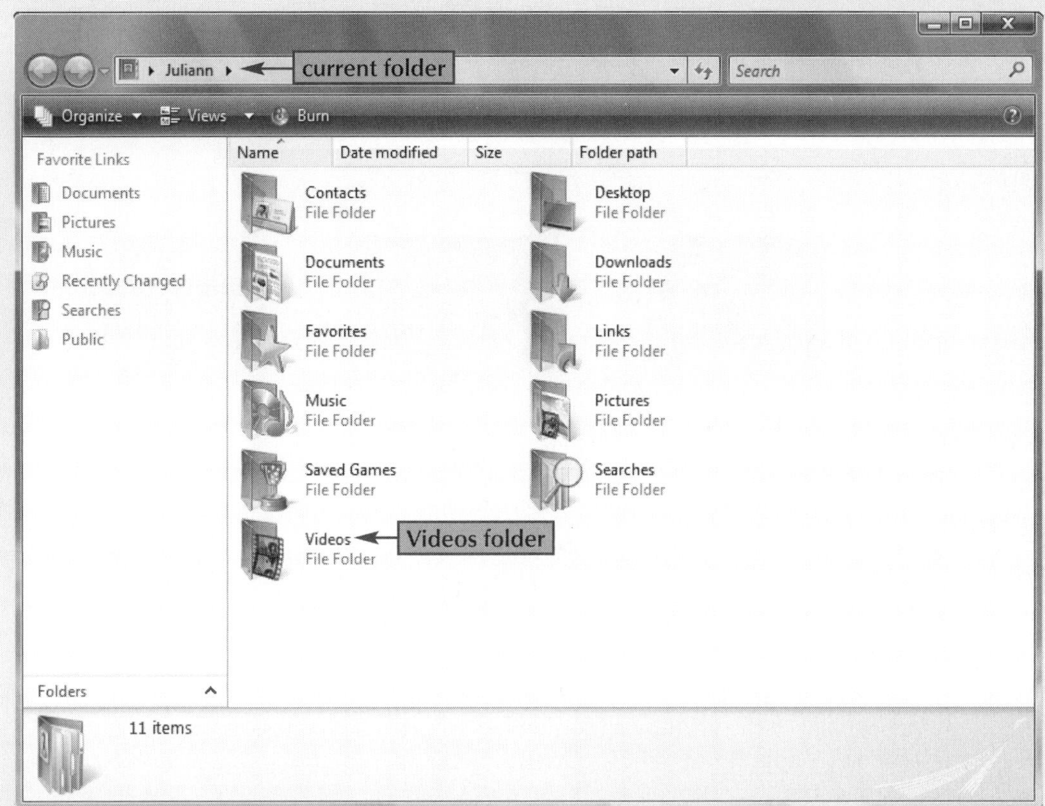

4. Click the **Videos** folder icon. Windows Vista opens the Videos folder, which includes a Sample Videos folder. The Address Bar now shows that the Videos folder is under your user account folder.

5. Click the **Sample Videos** folder icon. Windows Vista opens the Sample Videos folder, which contains three video files named Bear, Butterfly, and Lake. The Address Bar now shows that the Sample Videos folder is under the Public Videos folder, which is in turn under the Public folder.

6. Click the **Views button arrow** on the command bar, notice that the drop-down Views menu has a slider bar on the left, click **Extra Large Icons**, and then maximize the Sample Videos folder window. Windows Vista switches from Large Icons view to Extra Large Icons view. See Figure 1-30.

Figure 1-30 Extra Large Icons view of the Sample Videos folder

> **Tip**
>
> To permanently display the classic menu bar, click the Organize button on the command bar, point to Layout, and then click Menu Bar.

7. Press the **Alt** key. Above the command bar, Windows Vista displays the classic menu bar found in earlier versions of Windows.
8. Press the **Alt** key again. Windows Vista hides the classic menu bar. You can also use the F10 key to display the classic menu bar. If you are already familiar with the classic menu bar from earlier versions of Windows, this feature can save you time and effort.
9. Click the **Bear** video icon, and after Windows Media Player opens and begins to play the video, point to the **Windows Media Player** button on the taskbar (but do not click the Windows Media Player taskbar button). Windows Vista displays a Live Taskbar Thumbnail of the live video playing in Windows Media Player if your Windows Vista version and hardware support Windows Aero. You can also use the Slide Show button on the command bar to watch all the videos in this folder. See Figure 1-31.

   Trouble? If Windows Vista displays Windows Media Player and prompts you to choose the initial settings for the Windows Media Player, click the Express Settings (Recommended) option button if you want to configure Windows Media Player as described, or click the Custom Settings option button if you prefer to select your own settings.

Figure 1-31 Viewing a video

10. Close Windows Media Player, click the **Views button arrow** on the command bar, click **Large Icons**, and then close the Sample Videos folder window. You've just restored the default icon size to the Sample Videos folder window before you closed it.

When using the Views menu to select an icon size, you can also drag the tab on the slider bar to choose an icon size that is intermediate between one of the icon size options on the View menu, or as you did earlier with desktop icons, you can use the Ctrl key and your mouse wheel to adjust icon sizes in a folder window along a continuum (or range) of sizes.

Navigating Your Computer

Reference Window

- Click the Start button, and then click the name of your personal user account or click one of your personal user account folders, such as Documents, Pictures, or Music.
- Click one of the links in the Navigation pane, or click the Address Bar arrow before or after the name of any window in the Address Bar, and then click the location you want to access, or, if you want to view the contents of a specific subfolder within the current folder window, click the icon of that folder.
- Use the Views button, its menu options, and slider bar to adjust the sizes of icons in the folder window (or use the Ctrl key and your mouse wheel to scroll through a range of icon sizes).
- Press the Alt key or the F10 key to display the classic menu bar (or click Organize on the command bar, point to Layout, and then click Menu Bar to permanently display the classic menu bar).

As a power user, you will want to become familiar with how Windows organizes folders on your hard disk drive so that you can quickly access whatever resources, folders, and files you need and so that you can customize your folder structure and access to those resources, folders, and files.

Viewing Properties of Your Computer

Juliann notes that, whether you're a novice or power user, you should know how to find basic information about your computer, such as the operating system version and edition and the amount of RAM installed in your computer, especially if you need to evaluate the performance of your computer or troubleshoot your computer.

To locate this information, you view the properties of your computer system.

To view basic information about your computer:

1. Right-click the **Computer** icon on the desktop (or the Start menu), click **Properties** on the shortcut menu, and then, if necessary, maximize the System window. At the top of this window, Windows Vista displays the edition of Windows Vista used on your computer. See Figure 1-32. In the System section, Windows Vista displays information about the processor and RAM, two important hardware components in any computer system. Also, under System, note that this computer has a Windows Experience Index base score or rating of 4.8 (explained in the next section of the tutorial). Your computer's settings and Windows Experience Index will differ.

Figure 1-32 Viewing computer properties

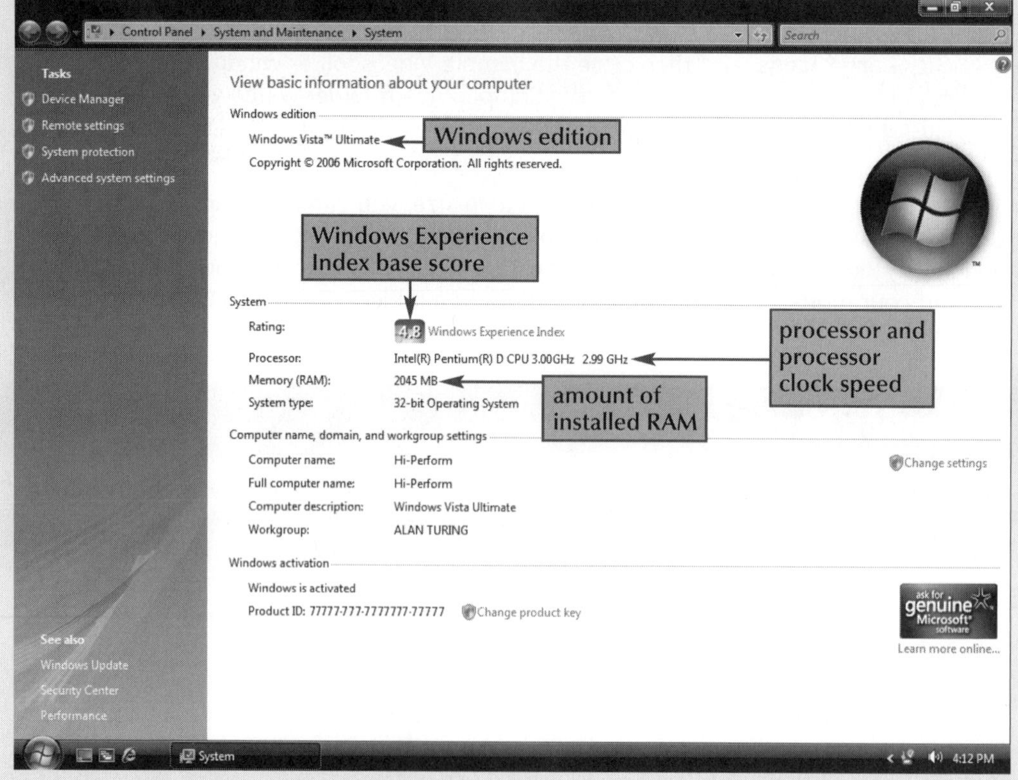

2. Keep the System window open for the next section of the tutorial.

As shown in Figure 1-32, Windows Vista Ultimate is installed on the computer used for the figure. This computer has an Intel Pentium D CPU that has a rated clock speed of 3.00 GHz, and it has 2045 MB (or 2 GB) of RAM. This processor is a **dual-core processor** that can process two sets of instructions from the same program or two different programs simultaneously. Windows Vista Ultimate, Windows Vista Business, Windows Vista Home Premium, and Windows Vista Home Basic require a 32-bit (or x86) or 64-bit (or x64) processor with a clock speed of 1 GHz. The **clock speed** refers to the pace at which operations are performed by the processor. The abbreviation **GHz** stands for GigaHertz. One **Hertz** is one cycle per second, and one **GigaHertz** is one billion cycles per second. The higher this value, the more operations the processor can perform in a given period of time.

When you display the System window for your computer, the amount of installed RAM is shown in MB, or megabytes, even if you have 1 or more GB of RAM. As noted in the table in the earlier Figure 1-26, a megabyte is approximately one million bytes of storage. Windows Vista Ultimate, Windows Vista Business, and Windows Vista Home Premium require at least 1 GB of RAM, while Windows Vista Home Basic requires 512 MB of RAM. When evaluating a new computer for purchase, examine the type of processor, the clock speed, and the amount of installed RAM.

Next, Juliann encourages you to examine the Windows Experience Index for your computer.

The Windows Experience Index

The **Windows Experience Index** is a rating that measures the overall capability and performance of your computer hardware and software. This rating is called your computer's **base score**. A higher score indicates that your computer will perform better and faster and support Windows Vista features such as Windows Aero.

From the System window, you can access more detailed information about the Windows Experience Index, including ratings, or **subscores**, for five separate hardware components in your computer: processor, memory (RAM), graphics, gaming graphics, and primary hard disk. The Memory (RAM) subscore measures the rate of transfer of data in megabytes to and from RAM and is dependent on the amount of installed RAM. The Gaming graphics subscore measures the ability of the video graphics card to handle textures. **Texture** refers to the detail applied to the surface of three-dimensional images. The Primary hard disk subscore is derived by measuring the number of megabytes of data transferred per second between the hard disk and RAM. The Windows Experience Index base score is not an average of the five subscores, but rather it is identical to the lowest subscore because the lowest subscore identifies the hardware component that limits the overall performance of the computer.

Using the Windows Experience Index | InSight

You can use the Windows Experience Index base score to evaluate the performance of your computer and determine whether, for example, you need to purchase more RAM or a higher performance video display card. When you do purchase new hardware or software for your computer, you can use this rating to make sure that you purchase hardware and software that will work with your version of Windows Vista and perform optimally on your computer. If you are purchasing a new computer, you can evaluate that new computer's capabilities by examining its Windows Experience Index to make sure the computer will meet your needs. In fact, if you are purchasing new hardware and software, the products you examine may list the minimum and recommended Windows Experience Index rating or base score that is needed on your computer for those products to work properly.

To view details on the Windows Experience Index:

1. Click the **Windows Experience Index** link. Windows Vista opens a Performance Information and Tools window with a table of subscores. See Figure 1-33. The table shows what hardware component is rated, how it is rated, and the subscore for that hardware component. On the computer used for this figure, the dual-core, high-performance processor is the limiting hardware component, and its rating determines the base score for the Windows Experience Index. Your base score and subscores will differ.

Figure 1-33 Viewing the Windows Experience Index subscores

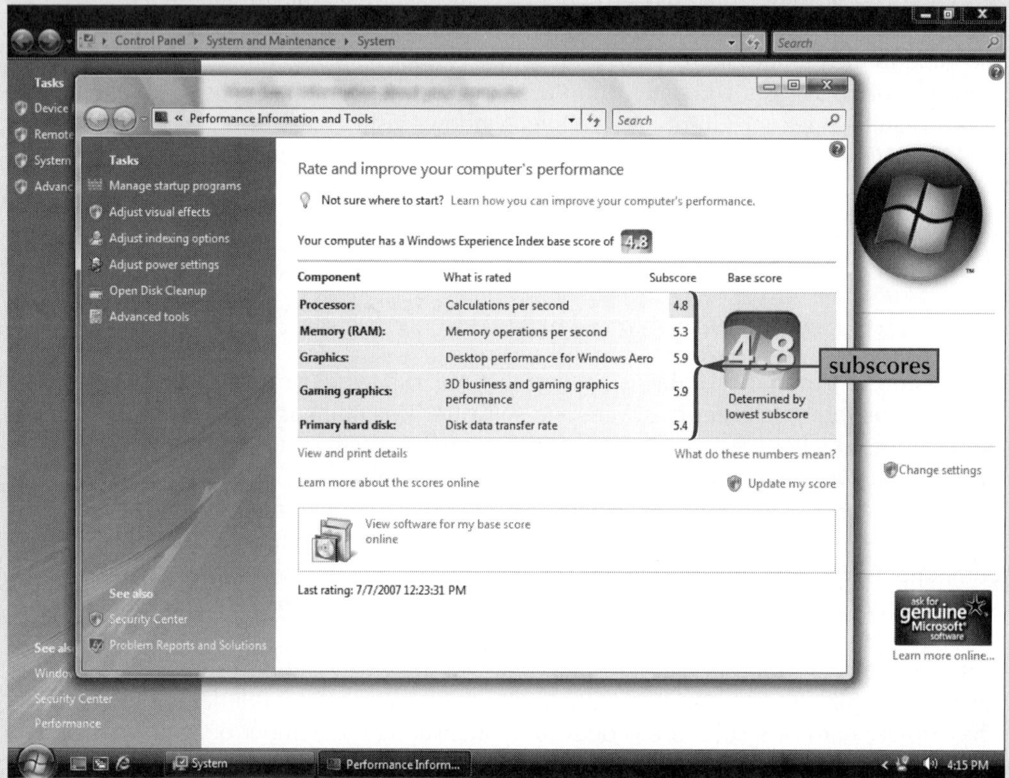

2. To understand the meaning of these subscores on your computer, click the **What do these numbers mean?** link and, if necessary, maximize the Windows Help and Support window. Windows Vista displays Help information on the Windows Experience Index.

3. After you read the initial explanation on the Windows Experience Index, scroll down and click the **About your computer's base score** link. Windows Vista expands this Help topic and provides detailed information about the kind of experience you can expect from your computer based on its base score. It notes that a computer with a base score of 1-2 can handle basic computing tasks, such as creating documents with applications, browsing the Web, and using email. It also notes this base score is too low to support Windows Aero. A computer with a base score of 3 supports Windows Aero and many new Windows Vista features, but only at a basic level. If a computer has a base score of 4 or 5, then it supports all new Windows Vista features with full functionality, and it supports high-end, graphics-intensive computing. Windows Help and Support also notes that the Windows Experience Index will support higher ratings as advances in computer hardware occur, but that the standards for existing base scores will stay the same. The computer in the earlier Figure 1-33 has a base score of 4.8, and therefore was a top-of-the-line system at the time of Windows Vista's release. Also, this computer's base score of 4.8 identifies this computer as a level 4 PC.

4. Click the **About your computer's base score** link to collapse this Help topic.
5. Click the **About your computer's subscore** link. Windows Vista expands this Help topic and explains how specific subscores affect your computer. It notes that high subscores for the Processor and Memory (RAM) are important if you use your computer for creating office documents, Web browsing, and email. Subscores of 2.0 or higher are usually sufficient for the other categories. If you use digital video editing applications or graphic-intensive games, then you need high subscores for the Memory (RAM), Graphics, and Gaming Graphics categories and subscores of 3 or higher for the other categories. If you use the Windows Media Center for more complex types of multimedia operations, such as HDTV (High Definition TV) programming, then you need high subscores for Processor, Primary hard disk, and Graphics, and subscores of 3 or higher for the other categories.
6. Close the Windows Help and Support window.

Juliann asks you to print a copy of your computer's Windows Experience Index base scores and its subscores, as well as general information about your computer system, so that you have a record of your computer's important components, capabilities, and performance.

To print a system summary report:

1. In the Performance Information and Tools window, click the **View and print details** link. Windows Vista displays another Performance Information and Tools window with a summary of your computer's Windows Experience Index base score and subscores as well as important specifications about your computer. See Figure 1-34 .

Figure 1-34 Viewing more details of a computer

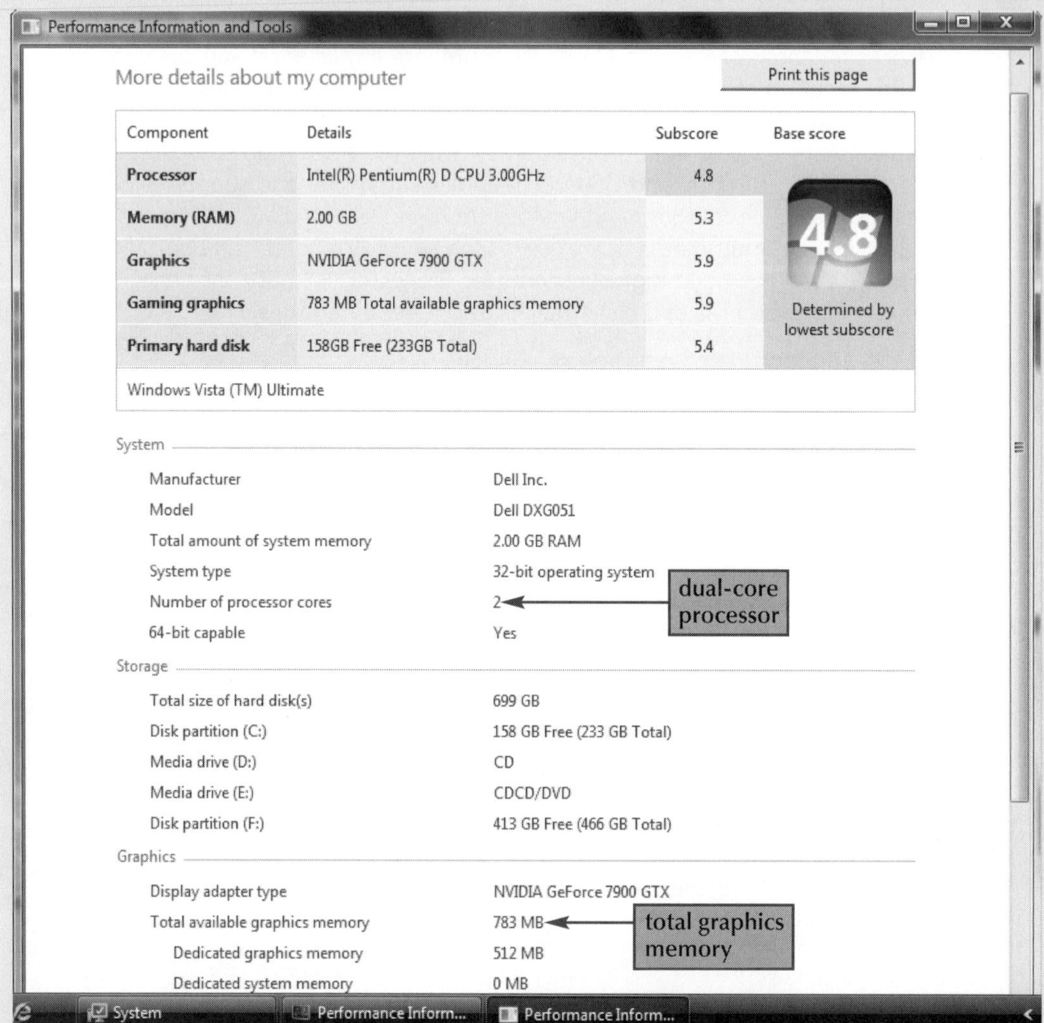

2. Click the **Print this page** button.
3. Close the Performance Information and Tools window, and then close the System window.

This report identifies the video graphics card for the Graphics subscore and the total graphics memory for the Gaming Graphics subscore, both of which are important in supporting the use of Windows Aero. In the System section, the report shows the computer's exact model, useful information when you need to download updates from a manufacturer's Web site. Also in the System section, the report identifies the number of processor cores. Dual-core computers like the one used for this report have two **processor cores**, each of which is equivalent to a separate processor and can process a set of instructions. The processor cores, or **execution cores**, are stored side by side on the same computer chip for faster processing.

The Graphics section of this report shows the total **dedicated graphics memory**, which consists of the memory available on the video display card itself or a portion of system memory dedicated exclusively for use by the Windows Vista graphics subsystem, and **shared system memory**, which consists of system memory (or RAM) that can be used by the graphics subsystem, but which is not dedicated exclusively to that use. Windows Vista Ultimate, Windows Vista Business, and Windows Vista Home Premium require 128 MB of graphics memory (but perform far better with more graphics memory), while Windows Vista Home Basic requires 32 MB. Both dedicated graphics memory and shared system memory are important in supporting the use of Windows Aero in the Windows Vista Ultimate, Windows Vista Business, and Windows Vista Home Premium Editions.

This section also shows the display adapter type and the DirectX version. Knowing your display adapter type is important in downloading updates for your video display adapter. **DirectX** refers to a set of Windows Vista technologies for handling multimedia software and content, including video, audio, 3D graphics, animation, and gaming. Windows Vista Ultimate, Windows Vista Business, Windows Vista Home Premium, and Windows Vista Home Basic require a video display adapter that supports at least DirectX 9 (or preferably DirectX 10), a WDDM driver, Pixel Shader 2.0, and 32 bits per pixel. **WDDM** (**Windows Display Driver Model**) refers to specifications for a new type of video display adapter device driver required by Windows Vista to deliver high-performance and high-quality graphics and video and thereby support Windows Aero. Furthermore, this type of device driver provides far better multitasking, rapid updating of windows without visual artifacts (or defects), and increased overall system stability. A **pixel shader** consists of software that renders (or generates) graphics effects on a pixel-by-pixel basis. A **pixel** (an abbreviation for "picture element") is the smallest logical unit on a monitor or in a graphic image that can be illuminated in a specific color formed by a blend of red, blue, and green (**RGB**). The video display adapter uses 32 bits per pixel as the **color depth setting**, which refers to the use of 32 **binary digits** (or bits), a combination of thirty-two 0's and 1's that define a unique code for one of almost 16.8 million possible colors that can be displayed on a monitor. You will examine this same information in more detail in later tutorials that focus on customizing your display (Tutorial 2) and upgrading to Windows Vista (Tutorial 11).

The Windows Experience Index is designed to make it easy for the average user to have a feeling for the overall performance of their computer and to act as an important guideline in purchasing a new computer, new computer hardware, and new software.

Restoring Your Computer

If you are working in a computer lab where you need to restore the computer to its original settings, or if you want to restore your computer to its original state (prior to starting this tutorial), complete the following steps.

To restore your computer:

1. If you want to remove the CPU Meter from the Windows Sidebar, right click the **CPU Meter gadget,** and then click **Close Gadget**.
2. If you want to remove the Computer icon from the desktop, click the **Start** button on the taskbar, right-click **Computer**, and then click **Show on Desktop** to remove the check mark.

3. If you want to turn off single-click activation, click the **Start** button on the taskbar, click **Control Panel**, click the **Appearance and Personalization** link, click the **Specify single- or double-click to open** link under Folder Options, click the **Double-click to open an item (single-click to select)** option button under "Click items as follows" on the General property sheet of the Folder Options dialog box, click the **OK** button, and then close the Appearance and Personalization window.

After restoring your computer, you can log off or turn it off.

Logging Off Windows and Turning Off Your Computer

After you have finished using your computer, Windows Vista provides you with the following options for shutting down your computer or logging off your user account:

- **Shut Down** Windows completely shuts down your computer, but you may need to manually shut the power off to your monitor and printer. If you are planning on installing or replacing hardware in your system unit, you want to completely shut down and unplug your computer before you open your system unit. If you are attaching a new hardware device to your computer, use the quick setup guides and other documentation for installing that hardware to determine whether you need to completely shut down your computer.
- **Log Off** Windows Vista closes all windows, programs, and documents. If you want to use your computer later, you must log on under your user account.
- **Restart** Windows shuts down your computer and then restarts it. This option is useful if you notice that your computer responds slowly or if you encounter a problem. You may also need to use this option after installing a new software product or software update.
- **Lock** Windows Vista locks your user account. You must re-enter your password to use your computer (assuming you use a password). This option is useful if you need to leave your computer for a while but want to make sure it is secure.
- **Sleep** Windows Vista saves your work, turns off the monitor, and then reduces power consumption to all hardware components in your computer. Your computer appears off, but Windows Vista has actually placed your computer and its hardware in a low power state called **Sleep**. When you are ready to use your computer again, you press a key on the keyboard or press the Power button on your computer. Windows Vista then restarts your computer and restores it to its previous state. It also opens any programs or files that you previously opened so that you are ready to work. Using this option is the fastest way to shut down your computer and the fastest way to restart it. Although Windows Vista saves any open documents, it's always a good idea to save your work manually in case you encounter an unexpected problem. You will examine Sleep in more detail shortly and in Tutorial 2.
- **Hibernate** If hibernation is enabled on your computer, then you will see this option on the Lock menu. If you choose this option, Windows Vista saves the contents of RAM to a **hibernation file** on disk and then shuts down your computer. When you next power on your computer, Windows Vista restores the contents of RAM from the hibernation file so that your computer returns to the state it was in before you implemented hibernation. You do not need to save your work; however, that is always a good precaution against problems you might not anticipate. You will examine Hibernation in more detail shortly and in Tutorial 2.

- **Switch User** If more than one person uses your computer and each person has a different user account, you will see this option on the Lock menu. If someone else with an account on the same computer wants to use the computer, you can choose this option to have Windows Vista lock your user account and display the Welcome screen so that another user can log on under their user account. Each user can set up their user account in different ways, use different Windows settings, keep their personal files separate from those of other users on the same computer, and, if required, use this option so that another person can quickly access their user account and complete a time-sensitive task and then log off so that you can log back on and pick up where you left off.

Windows Vista can implement one of two types of Sleep: Standard Sleep and Hybrid Sleep. When using **Standard Sleep**, which is similar to **Standby mode** in Windows XP, Windows Vista saves your computer's settings in memory, turns off your monitor and hard disk, and reduces the computer's power usage to a level where the computer appears off. If you press a key or move the mouse, the operating system resumes power to the monitor and hard disk. If your computer uses Standard Sleep, you have to manually save your work before your computer enters a Sleep state. If a power failure occurs during Standard Sleep, and if you have not saved your work, you will lose your work and the settings stored in RAM, which are needed to restore your computer to its previous operating state.

In **Hybrid Sleep**, Windows Vista saves your computer's settings in memory and in a hibernation file on disk, turns off your monitor and hard disk, and reduces your computer's power usage. If you press a key or move the mouse, Windows Vista resumes power to the monitor and hard disk and you are ready to use your computer. However, if a power failure occurs, Windows Vista uses the hibernation file on disk to restore your computer to its previous operating state. Hybrid Sleep is automatically enabled on desktop computers, but not on mobile PCs. In Tutorial 2, you will examine power management settings, including those for turning on and turning off hibernation and Hybrid Sleep.

The Power button on the Start menu enables Sleep, but you can also choose Sleep on the Lock button menu by clicking the Lock menu button . If Sleep is not available on your computer, or if you have specified that the Power button always shut down your computer, the Power button will display a different icon and will completely shut down your computer.

The Start menu also contains a Lock button , but you can also choose Lock on the Lock button menu. The Lock button menu contains Switch User (if applicable), Log Off, Lock, Restart, Sleep, and Shut Down.

If you are working in a computer lab, do not shut down your computer unless your instructor or technical support staff specifically requests you to shut it down. College computer labs can vary in their policies regarding shutting down computers, so if you are unsure as to what to do, check with your instructor or technical support staff.

To log off, or turn off, your computer:

1. If you want to log off your own computer, or if you are working in a computer lab and want to log off the computer you are using, click the **Start** button on the taskbar, point to the **Lock menu** button , and then click **Log Off**.
2. If you are using your own computer and want to place it into a Sleep state, click the **Start** button on the taskbar and then click the **Power** button .
3. If you are using your own computer and want to completely shut down your computer, click the **Start** button on the taskbar, point to the **Lock menu** button , and then click **Shut Down**.

You can also open the Shut Down Windows dialog box by clicking the desktop background and then pressing the Alt+F4 keys. The Shut Down Windows dialog box includes the Switch User (if applicable), Log Off, Restart, Sleep, and Shut Down options found on the Lock button menu.

If you are working on a company network, or even on your computer, it is a good idea to log off when you finish your work so that no one else will be able to access files under your user account.

Juliann's co-workers thank her for the information she has shared with them, and they ask her to set aside some time at weekly staff meetings to describe new features of interest to the staff, answer questions that might arise on the use of Windows Vista, and provide them with tips to help them become more productive.

Review | Session 1.3 Quick Check

1. The operating system assigns a unique ________________ to each drive in a computer.
2. True or False. You can use the colon symbol (:) in certain types of filenames.
3. Windows Vista uses a new type of combination menu bar and toolbar called a(n) ________________ in folder windows.
4. What two features can you use in a folder window to navigate your computer?
5. The ________________ , which is measured in GHz, refers to the pace at which operations are performed by the processor.
6. What is the name of the rating that Windows Vista uses to measure the overall capability and performance of your computer hardware and software?

Review | Tutorial Summary

In this tutorial, you learned about the importance of, and the essential functions performed by, operating system software. You examined PC operating systems and operating environments, and examined important features of the various Windows operating systems. You examined and worked with features of the Windows Vista desktop and Windows Aero. You used Windows Help and Support to browse and search for Help information and to watch a Windows Vista demo. You navigated the drive and folder structure, or hierarchy, of your computer, viewed properties of your computer system, and evaluated the Windows Experience Index for your computer. Finally, you reviewed different options for shutting down your computer.

Key Terms

8.3 filename
action
Address Bar
Aero Glass
antivirus software
application window
application-oriented approach
backing up
backward compatibility
base score
binary digit (bit)
basic input/output system (BIOS)
bit
boot
byte
Classic Style
clean install
clock speed
cold boot
color depth setting
command bar
command prompt
command-line interface
computer virus
configure
contact
contact group
context menu
context-sensitive Help
dedicated graphics memory
default action
default setting
delimiter
demo
desktop background
Desktop Window Manager (DWM)
Details pane
device
device driver
dialog box
directory
DirectX
document window
document-oriented approach
DOS
drive name
dual-core processor
edition
execute
execution core
extension
file
file extension
file system
folder
font
format
gadget
gigabyte (GB)
GigaHertz (GHz)
graphical user interface
graphics mode
group folder
grouped taskbar button
Hertz
hibernation file
hierarchy
Hybrid Sleep
icon
icon title
input
Instant Search
keyboard shortcut
keyword
legacy
Live Taskbar Thumbnails
loading
logical drive
long filename
menu
multitasking
multithreading
Navigation pane
non-Plug and Play devices
object
Online Help
opacity
operating environment
operating system prompt
operating system (OS)
output
parameter
partition
pinned items list
pixel
pixel shader
Plug and Play (PnP)
print queue
process
processor core
properties
property sheet
random access memory (RAM)
recently opened programs list
reserved symbol
resizing buttons
RGB
routine
Really Simple Syndication Feed (RSS Feed)
separator
shared system memory
shortcut
shortcut menu
single-click activation
single-tasking

Sleep
source code
spool file
spooling
Standard Sleep
Standby mode
subdirectory
subfolder
subscore
switch
syntax
system memory
task-switching
text mode
texture
thread
toggle
ToolTip
transition effect
translucency
translucent
Universal Serial Bus (USB)
USB flash drive (UFD)
user account
user interface
virtual memory
volatile
volume label
wallpaper
warm boot
Web Style
window
Windows 9x product line
Windows Aero
Windows Display Driver Model (WDDM)
Windows Experience Index
Windows NT product line
Windows Sidebar
wizard

Practice | Review Assignments

Practice the skills you learned in the tutorial.

There are no Data Files needed for the Review Assignments.

Juliann has just hired Chad Cottrill, a new summer intern, to assist her with a special project. Since he is familiar with the use of Windows XP on computers at his high school, she thinks he will adapt to Windows Vista quickly. While she is waiting for the go-ahead to implement the new project, she asks Chad to explore Windows Vista and become comfortable with the operating system. He is interested in animation, graphics, and music and wants to eventually design special effects for movies, so she recommends that he explore the new features found in Windows Vista's Pictures and Music folders.

As you complete each step, record your answers to questions so that you can submit them to your instructor. Use a word processing application such as Microsoft Word or the Windows WordPad accessory to prepare your answers to these questions. Also, if you change any settings on the computer you are using, make a note of the original settings so that you can restore them later. If you are working in a computer lab, you will need earphones so that you can listen to music. Complete the following steps:

1. If necessary, start Windows Vista and log on your computer under your user account. What is the process for logging on your computer? For example, does Windows Vista display a Welcome screen and, if not, what happens? Is there only one user account, or are there multiple user accounts on the computer? Do you have to select a user account, or does your computer automatically boot to the desktop? Do you have to enter a password?
2. From the Start menu, click in the Search Text box, type **folder options**, and then press the Enter key. What happens? Open Folder Options, and then enable the option for single-click activation, and apply this change to your computer.
3. Display the desktop View menu. Which options are enabled? Close the View menu.
4. Open the Gadget Gallery, double-click the Clock gadget in the Gadget Gallery dialog box, and then close the Gadget Gallery dialog box. What change did Windows Vista make to the Windows Sidebar? Close the Gadget Gallery dialog box.
5. Right-click the Clock Gadget at the top of the Windows Sidebar, and then choose Options. Click the Next button under the view of the clock in the Clock dialog box, examine each of the eight different styles for the clock, and then choose one of the eight styles. Click the "Show the second hand" check box to enable this option. Click the Time zone arrow button, choose a different time zone from the one in which you reside, and note the name of that time zone. In the Clock name text box, type the name of the time zone or the name of a city in that time zone. Click the OK button to apply these new Clock gadget settings. Briefly describe the appearance and features of your new Clock gadget and indicate whether you would benefit from having two or more clocks for different time zones on the Windows Sidebar and, if so, why?
6. If Windows Vista does not display a Computer icon on the desktop, use the Start menu to display the Computer icon on the desktop.
7. Open Windows Help and Support, and then use the Windows Basics icon to browse Help and find information that provides an overview of the taskbar. In the Help topic, locate information on how the taskbar groups similar items. Read the information on taskbar grouping, and then briefly describe how taskbar grouping works and how you can close all the items in a group.

8. Use the Windows Help and Support Search feature to locate Help information on keyboard shortcuts. Examine the "Windows Explorer keyboard shortcuts" Help topic. If you were in a folder window (and assuming you've already selected a file), what keyboard shortcut can you use to go directly to the last file in the window? What keyboard shortcut can you use to go to the very first file in the window?
9. Click the "Windows Explorer keyboard shortcuts" link to collapse or close this Help topic. Then examine the "General keyboard shortcuts" Help topic. What keyboard shortcut could you use to select everything in a document or all the folders and files in a window? What keyboard shortcut could you use to rename an icon? What keyboard shortcut could you use to undo an operation? What keyboard shortcut can you use to cancel the current action?
10. Use Windows Help and Support to search for demos. Choose the option for Windows Vista demos in the Search results, and under "Programs, files, and folders," watch the Windows Vista demo entitled "Working with files and folders." After you watch the video, close Windows Media Player, and then close the Windows Help and Support window. If you frequently open a folder that contains important files, what change can you make in a folder window so that you can quickly jump to that folder no matter which folder you are in?
11. Open the Computer window from the Computer desktop icon. List the names of the hard disk drive (or drives) on your computer, and list the names of your computers' devices with removable storage. What is the storage capacity of your hard disk drive? How much of your hard disk drive's storage space is free? How much of your hard disk drive's storage space is used?
12. Open the Pictures folder from the Navigation pane, and then open the Sample Pictures folder. Using the information in the Address Bar, explain where the Sample Pictures folder is located in the folder structure of your computer. What other panes are visible in the Sample Pictures window? What type of view does Windows Vista use for the contents of this folder? What options are available on the command bar?
13. Use the Views button to change the view to Extra Large Icons view. What advantage(s) does this view have?
14. Point to one of the thumbnails in the Sample Pictures folder and rest the mouse pointer on that thumbnail. Describe the two different ways in which Windows Vista displays information about the image in the file you selected.
15. Click one of the thumbnail images. What happens, and what program are you currently using? Close the program window.
16. Click the Address Bar button to the right of the Public folder, click Public Videos in the drop-down location list, and then click the Sample Videos folder. What options are available on the command bar?
17. Use the Slide Show button on the command bar to watch all the videos. After you have viewed the videos, use the Esc keyboard shortcut to cancel the current task and exit the slide show. Then close the Public Videos folder.
18. Use the Computer icon on the desktop to view properties of your computer. What edition of Windows Vista are you using? What type of processor does your computer use and what is its clock speed? How much RAM is installed in your computer? What is your Windows Experience Index base score?
19. Use the Windows Experience Index link to view the subscores for each of the five components that the Windows Experience Index is based on. What component is the most limiting factor in the performance of your computer?

20. Choose the option to view and print details. How many processor cores does your computer have? What is the total dedicated graphics memory on your computer? How much shared system memory does your computer use?
21. Close the Performance Information and Tools windows, and then close the System window.
22. Remove the second Clock gadget from the Windows Sidebar.
23. If you want to remove the Computer icon from the desktop, use the Start menu to turn off the display of the Computer icon on the desktop.
24. If you want to turn off single-click activation, open the Folder Options dialog box and choose the option "Double-click to open an item (single-click to select)," and then apply this setting and close the dialog box.
25. Submit your answers to the questions in this Review Assignment to your instructor either in printed or electronic form, as requested. Remember to include your name and any other information requested by your instructor on your assignment.

Apply | Case Problem 1

Use the skills you learned in the tutorial to justify a software upgrade.

There are no Data Files needed for this Case Problem.

Robotic Designs, Inc. Kent Claypool works as a robotic programmer for Robotic Designs, Inc., a Delaware firm. As part of his job responsibility, Kent prepares technical manuals on the design and use of robotic software. To produce these manuals, he must work with multiple applications and documents, and copy text, graphics, concept art, and illustrations from one document to another. The company's IT staff wants to upgrade the operating systems used on the company's computers so that Kent and other employees can work more efficiently on the company's intranet. Kent asks you to examine the features of Windows Vista and prepare a report that identifies features of the Windows Vista operating system that will enable him and other employees to work productively.

Use a word processing application such as Microsoft Word or WordPad to prepare a one to two-page report on your recommendations. Complete the following steps:

1. Identify five features of operating system software that would support and simplify the process that Kent Claypool and other employees use to produce training manuals at Robotic Designs.
2. Describe each of the five features and briefly explain in one paragraph what benefits employees at Robotic Designs might derive from using each of these features.
3. Submit your paper to your instructor either in printed or electronic form, as requested.

Apply | Case Problem 2

Use the skills you learned in the tutorial to recommend the best strategy for managing files.

There are no Data Files needed for this Case Problem.

Web Stats, Inc. You have recently been hired as an information engineer by Web Stats, a company specializing in mining and analyzing large volumes of data for information. Serena Tusing, your supervisor, asks you to come up with a list of recommendations for improving how she and her workgroup employees can more efficiently share computers, folders, and files and, at the same time, enable staff members to keep certain folders and files used by staff separate and secure. One feature that immediately comes to your mind is Fast User Switching.

To watch a Help and Support demo on user accounts in the following steps, you might need to specify settings on how you want to use Windows Media Player on your computer.

Use a word processing application such as Microsoft Word or WordPad to prepare a one-page report that lists a set of recommendations for using staff computers effectively. Complete the following steps:

1. Use Windows Help and Support to locate Help information on user accounts, sharing files with the Public folder, and Fast User Switching.
2. Review the "Demo: Understanding User Accounts." (*Note*: You can use the same Help topic link to read a transcript of the demo.)
3. EXPLORE Using Help and Support and what you've learned in this tutorial, prepare a one- to two-page report with a set of recommendations for managing access to the same computer by several employees and for sharing important folders and files on the same computer. Address the following questions in your report:
   - What is a user account, and how does each user open their user account?
   - What are the advantages or disadvantages of each employee having a separate user account or sharing the same user account?
   - Where can staff members store company files, software downloads, and other types of files needed by all staff members who use the same computer? How can you organize different types of files for easy access?
   - Where can these employees store business contacts, documents, downloads, and Internet shortcuts that only they need to access and use?
   - How can Fast User Switching enable several staff members to share the same computer and, at the same time, keep their folders and files separate from other staff members?

Apply | Case Problem 3

Use the skills you learned in the tutorial to prepare a workshop on editing digital pictures.

There are no Data Files needed for this Case Problem.

Equus Graphics, Inc. Equus Graphics is a small business in San Francisco that develops brochures and advertising for other small businesses who specialize in travel tours to exotic islands in the Pacific. Son Chiou, the owner, asks you to prepare an employee workshop on editing digital pictures used for client brochures and advertising as well as images used on the company's Web site. As a first step, he recommends that you start by examining the Windows Help and Support Center for information about editing digital photos.

Use a word processing application such as Word or WordPad to prepare your answers to these questions. Also, if you change any settings on the computer you are using, make a note of the original settings so that you can restore them later. Complete the following steps:

1. Open Windows Help and Support Center and search for information on tips for editing digital pictures.

2. Prepare a one to two-page report that identifies the Windows program that you can use to edit digital pictures and the types of digital editing tasks that you can perform with this program. Explain the concept of digital workflow, describe the recommended digital workflow for editing pictures, and explain why the digital workflow is important to follow. Also note what precaution you might want to take so that you have a copy of your original picture in case the editing changes you make do not produce the result you want.

EXPLORE

3. Make a copy of an image (preferably one with red eye), and then use the information and techniques you gleaned from the previous step to edit the image. Describe what type of image you used, what techniques you tried for editing the image, and what changes you made to the image. Also briefly describe what single change improved the overall quality of the image.
4. Submit your paper to your instructor either in printed or electronic form, as requested.

Challenge | Case Problem 4

Use the skills you learned in the tutorial to evaluate a computer upgrade.

There are no Data Files needed for this Case Problem.

Pixel Dynamics, Inc. Imogene Maynard, the owner of Pixel Dynamics, and her staff use resource-intensive applications to design 3D graphics, animation, video, and online presentations for the Web sites of the company's business clients. She asks you to examine the feasibility of upgrading the company's computers from Windows XP Professional to Windows Vista Business Edition. She further notes that their computers must support Windows Aero to more efficiently and effectively meet the needs of their clients and to attract new clients. She asks you to prepare a report that summarizes your analysis and evaluation of upgrading the company's computers.

Use a word processing application, such as Word or WordPad, to prepare a one to two-page report on your recommendations. Complete the following steps:

1. Locate and list the Windows Experience Index base score and the Processor, Memory (RAM), Graphics, Gaming graphics, and Primary hard disk subscores for your computer.

EXPLORE

2. Open Help and Support and locate information on the Windows Experience Index and examine the Help information on your computer's base score and subscore.

EXPLORE

3. Using your computer's base score, rate your computer's performance based on the information covered in this tutorial and in Help and Support.

EXPLORE

4. Examine the Windows Experience Index subscores and identify the component that limits the performance of your computer. How do these subscores affect the performance of your computer? In your analysis, identify and list any ways in which you can improve the performance of your computer by upgrading its hardware.
5. In what other ways might you use the Windows Experience Index base score and subscores?
6. Submit your paper to your instructor either in printed or electronic form, as requested.

Review | Quick Check Answers

Session 1.1

1. operating system
2. device driver
3. command-line interface
4. True
5. file system
6. multitasking
7. actions, properties
8. extension

Session 1.2

1. default
2. Windows Aero
3. gadgets
4. Contacts
5. single-click activation
6. True

Session 1.3

1. drive name
2. False
3. command bar
4. Navigation pane and Address Bar
5. clock speed
6. Windows Experience Index

Ending Data Files

There are no ending Data Files needed for this tutorial.

Objectives

Session 2.1
- Change the desktop theme and color scheme
- Adjust window frame, Start menu, and taskbar colors
- Customize elements of the graphical user interface
- Choose special visual effects
- Change your desktop background

Session 2.2
- Customize the Start menu, taskbar, and notification area
- Change the Quick Launch toolbar
- Create a desktop toolbar

Session 2.3
- Modify the resolution, color depth, and refresh rate
- Adjust DPI Scaling settings
- Examine power management features

Customizing Microsoft Windows Vista

Customizing Desktops

Case | Kimbrough & Co.

Kimbrough & Co. is a global company that develops and sells pharmaceuticals around the world. During the last 25 years, Kimbrough & Co. developed new drugs in its research labs in Great Britain, France, and Sweden. Recently, Kimbrough & Co. opened a research facility in the United States that uses DNA-splicing technology to accelerate the process for finding new classes of drugs. Furthermore, a new research group is exploring how to develop new pharmaceuticals from rain forests around the world. To increase the productivity of its staff, Kimbrough & Co. has purchased 100 top-of-the-line computers for its scientific, technical, office, and administrative support staff in its U.S. division. Over the next several weeks, you will work with Alejandro Castillo, a computer systems specialist at the new research facility, to help staff members customize their desktops. As Alejandro has discovered, employees are more productive if they can customize their working environment.

In this tutorial, you customize Windows Vista on your computer by changing the desktop theme and color scheme and by adjusting colors of window frames, the Start menu, and the taskbar. You also modify elements of the graphical user interface, choose special visual effects, and change the desktop background. You customize the Start menu, taskbar and notification area, and the Quick Launch toolbar, and then create a desktop toolbar. Next, you modify the resolution, color depth, and refresh rate of your monitor and examine the use of DPI Scaling. Finally, you examine power management features on your computer.

Starting Data Files

There are no starting Data Files needed for this tutorial.

Session 2.1

Customizing the Graphical User Interface

Like all earlier versions of Windows, Windows Vista provides a variety of options for customizing the graphical user interface. Also, as you saw in Tutorial 1, Windows Aero provides enhanced features and a new user interface design that is richer than previous versions of Windows. In the following sections, you examine different ways of customizing the Windows Vista graphical user interface and, if your computer supports Windows Aero, verify that it is properly enabled on your computer.

Setting Up Your Computer

To complete this tutorial, you must display the Computer icon on the desktop and switch your computer to single-click activation. In the following steps, you will check and, if necessary, change these settings.

To set up your computer:

1. If Windows Vista does not display a Computer icon on the desktop, click the **Start** button on the taskbar, right click **Computer**, click **Show on Desktop**, and then close the Start menu.
2. If you need to enable single-click activation, double-click the **Computer** icon on the desktop, click the **Organize** button on the command bar, click **Folder and Search Options**, and under "Click items as follows" on the General property sheet in the Folder Options dialog box, click the **Single-click to open an item (point to select)** option button, click the **Underline icon titles only when I point at them** option button, click the **OK** button to close the Folder and Options dialog box, and then close the Computer window.

Now you're ready to look at themes and color schemes.

Choosing a Theme and Color Scheme

Windows Vista provides two themes—Windows Vista and Window Classic. A **theme** consists of a set of visual elements, such as the background image on the desktop, as well as other elements, such as sound, that provide a unified look for your desktop and user interface. The default theme is Windows Vista and it enables the Windows Aero color scheme if your Windows Vista edition and your hardware support it. If you choose the Windows Classic theme, your desktop, windows, dialog boxes, Start menu, taskbar, and menus appear similar to how they appeared with the Windows Classic theme in Windows XP. Windows Vista also changes the color scheme setting to Windows Standard (described next).

In contrast, a **color scheme** is a combination of settings that determine the appearance of elements of the graphical user interface, such as the desktop, desktop icons, menus, message boxes, and ToolTips (to name a few). You can select and use one of the following color schemes:

- **Windows Aero** As noted in Tutorial 1, Windows Aero is available in the Windows Vista Home Premium, Business, Enterprise, and Ultimate Editions, though your computer's hardware must also support Windows Aero for you to use it. Windows Aero is not available in the Windows Vista Home Basic Edition. As you saw in Tutorial 1, Windows Aero features enhance the graphical user interface and are useful to power users and people interested in gaming, graphics and graphics design, video, music, animation, and multimedia in general.
- **Windows Vista Basic** The Windows Vista Basic color scheme is designed for computers that do not support Windows Aero. Under the Windows Vista Basic color scheme, windows, window frames, and window borders are not translucent; however, the background of the Windows Sidebar remains transparent. Furthermore, you do not have the option of specifying color settings for windows, the Start menu, and the taskbar (features you will examine later in this tutorial). When you point to a taskbar button, Windows Vista does not display a Live Taskbar Thumbnail, but only a ToolTip. When you invoke Windows Flip using the Alt+Tab keyboard shortcut, the Windows Flip pane is not translucent (but rather light blue) and Windows Vista displays icons on the pane rather than thumbnails for open windows, including the desktop. The "Switch between windows" button on the Quick Launch toolbar does not invoke Windows Flip 3D to display three-dimensional, stacked views of all open windows as it does in Windows Aero, but rather displays the Windows Flip pane as just described. When you point to a window resizing button, the button changes color but does not glow. You can, however, adjust the sizes of desktop and folder window icons over a range of sizes.
- **Windows Standard** Windows Standard is available in all Windows Vista Editions except Windows Vista Starter Edition. Like Windows Aero, the Windows Standard user interface requires graphics hardware that supports WDDM (Windows Driver Display Model). When you switch to the Windows Standard color scheme, your view of the desktop and other elements of the user interface are similar to what you see when you choose the Windows Classic theme. However, using Windows Standard, the Windows Sidebar is not translucent but has a gray background.
- **Windows Classic** All Windows Vista Editions support the Windows Classic user interface. When you switch to Windows Classic, your view of desktop and the user interface is very similar to that available with Windows Standard.

The theme and color scheme settings work with each other, so the actual effect you see depends on what combination of the two settings you specify. For example, if you change the theme to Windows Classic, Windows Vista switches to the Windows Standard color scheme and turns off Windows Aero features. Windows, dialog boxes, borders, the Start menu, and the taskbar are no longer translucent, but have a gray background. Furthermore, the background of the Windows Sidebar changes to a solid gray. Windows Flip no longer displays thumbnails for open windows, but instead displays a pane with icons for those open windows, and the pane's background is solid gray rather than translucent. Windows Vista no longer displays a "Switch between windows" button on the Quick Launch toolbar for Windows Flip 3D or Live Taskbar Thumbnails when you point to a taskbar button for an open window. Folder windows still retain the Navigation, Details, and Preview panes, and you can still adjust the sizes of desktop and folder window icons over a range of sizes.

Alejandro suggests that you check your computer's theme and color scheme setting.

To check the desktop theme setting:

Tip

You can also open the Theme Settings dialog box by right-clicking the desktop, clicking Personalize, and then clicking Theme in the Personalization window.

1. Click the **Start** button on the taskbar, click **Control Panel**, click the **Appearance and Personalization** link, and then click the **Change the theme** link in the Personalization category. Windows Vista opens the Theme Settings dialog box. See Figure 2-1. At the top of this dialog box, Windows Vista points out that a theme consists of a background and a set of sounds, icons, and other elements that you can select from this dialog box and apply with a single click. On the Theme list button, Windows Vista displays your current theme. On the computer used for Figure 2-1, the theme is Windows Vista. Yours may differ.

Figure 2-1 Viewing the current theme setting

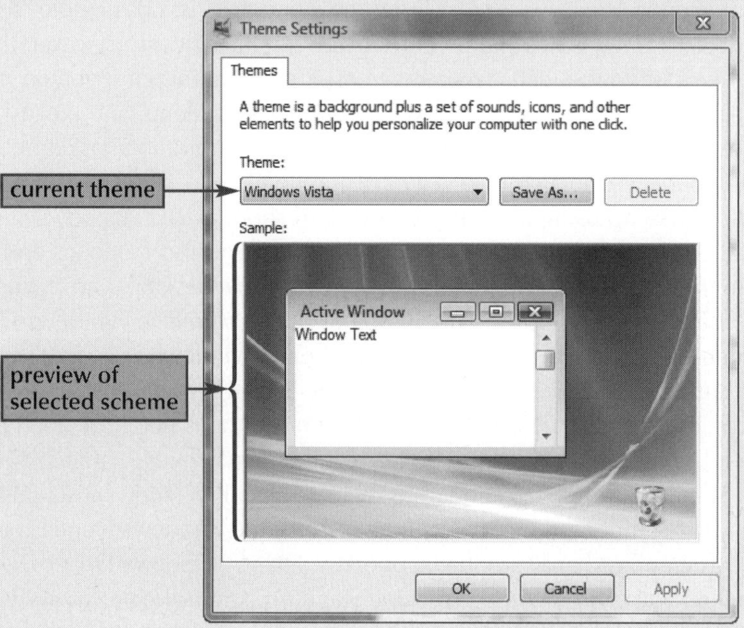

2. Click the **Theme** list button with the name of the current theme. Windows Vista displays a list of themes. See Figure 2-2.

Figure 2-2 List of available themes

Tip

If you choose Browse in the Theme list, you can browse your computer for other themes that you acquired.

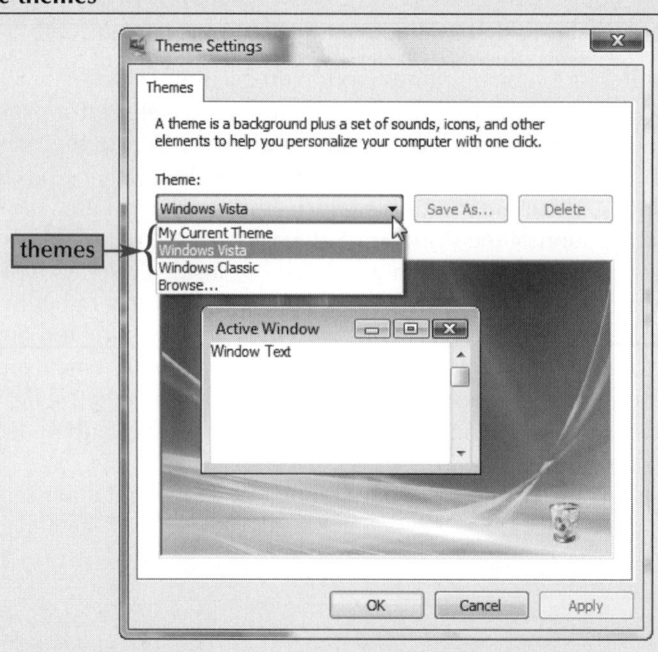

3. Click **Windows Classic**. In the preview area labeled Sample, Windows Vista updates the desktop view so that you can see how the graphical user interface will appear if you choose this theme.
4. Click the **Cancel** button to close the Theme Settings dialog box without making any changes to your computer.

You've just verified whether your computer uses the Windows Vista theme or the Windows Classic theme. If you change settings for specific components of the graphical user interface, such as choosing another background image for the desktop, Windows Vista updates your theme name to "Modified Theme." You can then use the Save As button in the Theme Settings dialog box to assign a new name to the theme settings you are using. Windows Vista stores those settings in a Windows Theme File with the "Theme" file extension in the Documents folder. The next time you examine the list of themes on your computer, you will see the name you specified for the new theme. You can create and name more custom themes and then choose the theme you want to use in the Theme Settings dialog box. If you delete a custom theme, Windows Vista keeps your current theme settings but refers to them as "My Current Theme."

Now you're ready to examine your computer's color scheme and verify whether your computer supports Windows Aero as Alejandro suggested.

To check your color scheme:

1. In the Appearance and Personalization window, click the **Customize colors** link in the Personalization category. Windows Vista opens the Window Color and Appearance window if your computer supports Windows Aero. See Figure 2-3. In this window, you can change and adjust the intensity of the color that Windows Vista uses for windows, the Start menu, and the taskbar, and you can enable transparency. Light blue (labeled Default) is the default color setting. The Enable transparency check box determines whether Windows Vista uses translucency. If you remove the check mark from this box, the Start menu, taskbar, windows, and dialog boxes are no longer partially translucent, though the background of the Windows Sidebar remains transparent. For some Live Taskbar Thumbnails, Windows Vista displays a folder or document icon rather than the actual contents of a window or document. Previews of thumbnails with pictures or videos are also not available.

   Trouble? If Windows Vista opens the Appearance Settings dialog box or if your Appearance and Personalization window includes a Change the color scheme link instead of a Customize colors link, your computer might not support Windows Aero, your theme might be set to Windows Classic, or your color scheme might not be set to Windows Aero. Read Step 2, and then continue with Step 3.

Tip

You can also open Window Color and Appearance by right-clicking the desktop, clicking Personalize, and then clicking Window Color and Appearance.

Figure 2-3 Viewing color options for windows, the Start menu, and the taskbar

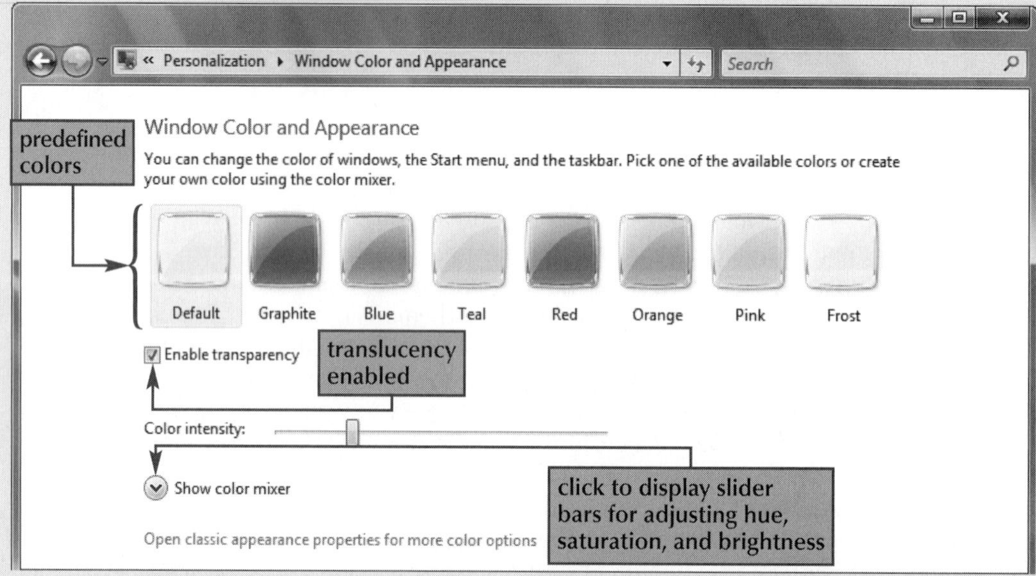

2. Click the **Open classic appearance properties for more color options** link. Windows Vista opens the Appearance Settings dialog box. See Figure 2-4. In the Color scheme list box, Windows Vista displays options for Windows Aero, Windows Vista Basic, Windows Standard, and Windows Classic as well as other options.

Figure 2-4 Viewing the color scheme setting

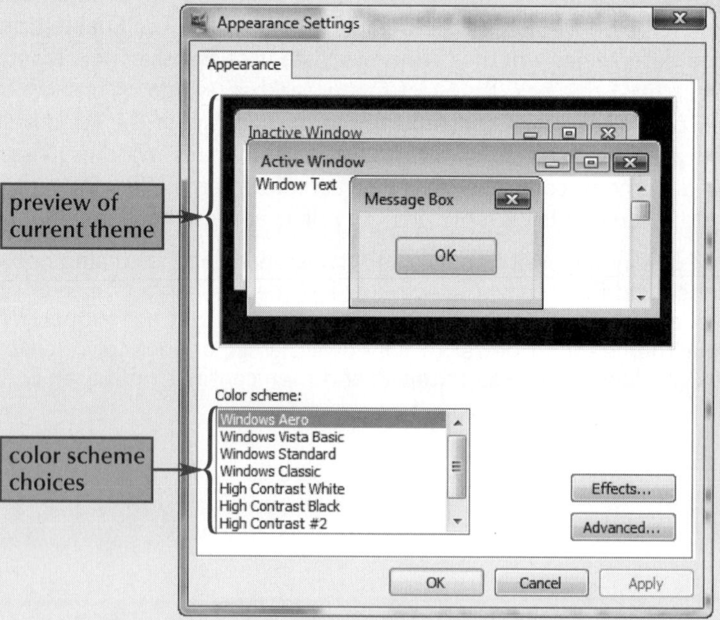

3. Click **Windows Standard**. In the preview area directly above the Color scheme list box, Windows Vista displays a preview of this user interface. Notice that this color scheme changes the appearance of desktop background, windows and window elements, and dialog boxes.

4. Click **Windows Classic**. As you can see from the preview area, although Windows Standard and Windows Classic have subtle differences, such as slightly different fonts and colors for title bars, they share many features.
5. Click **High Contrast White** and examine the preview area. The High Contrast options are designed to make it easier for people with visual disabilities to see more clearly what's displayed on the monitor.
6. Preview each of the remaining High Contrast Options in the Color scheme list box.
7. Click the **Cancel** button to close the Appearance Settings dialog box without making any changes to your computer.
8. Keep the Personalization window open for the next section of the tutorial.

Choosing a Theme and Color Scheme | Reference Window

- To change the theme, open the Control Panel from the Start menu, click the Appearance and Personalization link, and then click the "Change the theme" link under Personalization in the Appearance and Personalization window.
- To review a list of themes, click the Theme list button in the Theme Settings dialog box.
- To use another theme, click the theme you want to use, click the OK button to close the Theme Settings dialog box and apply your new theme choice, or click the Cancel button to close the Appearance and Personalization window if you do not want to change your theme.
- To select another color scheme, click the "Customize colors" link under Personalization in the Appearance and Personalization window.
- In the Window Color and Appearance window, click the "Open classic appearance properties for more color options" link (if necessary).
- In the Appearance Settings dialog box, choose the user interface setting you want to use from the Color scheme list box, and then click the OK button.
- Close the Appearance and Personalization window.

If you switch the color scheme from Windows Aero to Windows Vista Basic, Windows Standard, or Windows Classic, you no longer have access in the Control Panel to the Window Color and Appearance window where you change the color of windows, the Start menu, and taskbar or the option for enabling transparency. To restore these options, you must enable Windows Aero in the Appearance Settings dialog box first.

InSight | **Troubleshooting Windows Aero**

If your computer supports Windows Aero, it's a good idea to use it because it enhances your computing experience. To make sure you have access to the Windows Aero user interface and features, open the Appearance Settings dialog box and, if necessary, set the color scheme to Windows Aero if it is available. You might also have to open the Theme Settings dialog box and set the theme to Windows Vista. Even if your computer uses the Windows Vista theme, it might be set for the Windows Vista Basic color scheme, which does not provide you with full access to Windows Aero features. Other factors can interfere with the use of Windows Aero. If you run a program that is incompatible with the Windows Aero color scheme, Windows Vista turns off some or all Windows Aero features until you close the program. Likewise, if you are multitasking, your computer may not have enough memory to support all the open windows and programs while displaying the Windows Aero color scheme, so Windows Vista temporarily turns off Windows Aero features. If you make changes to your monitor's settings or if your hardware configuration changes, Windows Vista might also turn off Windows Aero features.

Adjusting Window Frame, Start Menu, and Taskbar Colors

You can choose different color settings for window frames and borders, the Start menu, and the taskbar. You can select a basic color and change the color intensity, which determines the richness of the window colors. You can also use a Color Mixer to adjust the hue, saturation, and brightness of a color. **Hue** refers to the position of a color in the color spectrum, or what is typically thought of as a specific color, such as red, yellow, green, or blue. **Saturation** refers to the amount of gray in the color and therefore helps to determine the purity of a color.

Alejandro recommends that you experiment with different color settings and personalize your work environment.

To complete this section, your computer must support Windows Aero. Your theme must be set to Windows Vista or a modified theme based on Windows Vista, and your color scheme must be set to Windows Aero. If your computer does not support Windows Aero, do not keystroke the following steps, but instead read the steps and examine the figures so that you are familiar with customizing window, Start menu, and taskbar colors.

To adjust window frame colors:

1. Click the **Window Color and Appearance** link in the Personalization window, and then examine the Window Color and Appearance window. At the top of this window are eight predefined colors from which you can choose. The Windows Vista default color is called Default.
2. Click **Red** and notice that Windows Vista applies this color to the frame and border of the Window Color and Appearance window. If you examine the taskbar or open the Start menu, you may also see the same color change in the background of the taskbar and the Start menu and in its borders.
3. Gradually drag the **Color intensity** slider tab to the right and then to the left and observe the change in the intensity of the color of the window frame and border. Windows Vista intensifies the richness of the color as you drag to the right and then softens the color as you drag to the left.
4. Click **Red**. Windows Vista restores the Color intensity setting.
5. Click the **Show color mixer** expand button. Windows Vista displays slider bars for adjusting Hue, Saturation, and Brightness. See Figure 2-5. Notice that each slider bar shows how the color of the window frame and borders will change as you drag the slider tab to the left or right.

Options for adjusting window color and appearance

Figure 2-5

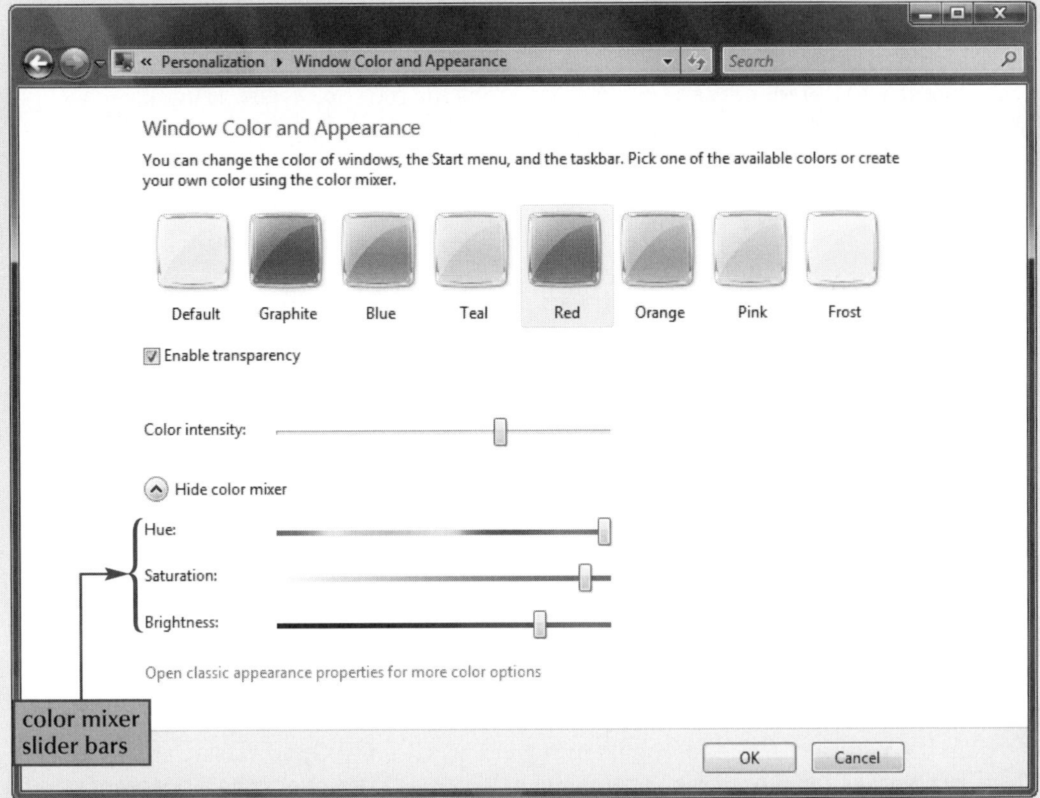

6. Gradually drag the **Hue** slider tab to the left and then to the right. Windows Vista changes the color of the window's frame and borders.
7. Click **Red** to restore the default Hue setting for this color, and then gradually drag the **Saturation** slider tab to the left and then to the right. The shade of red in the window frame and borders gradually becomes lighter as you drag to the left and darker as you drag to the right.
8. Click **Red** to restore the default Saturation setting for this color, and then gradually drag the **Brightness** slider tab to the left and then to the right. The window frame and borders gradually become darker red as you drag to the left and brighter as you drag to the right.
9. Click the **Default** icon to restore the default window color and appearance setting.
10. Keep the Window Color and Appearance window open for the next section of the tutorial.

Reference Window | Adjusting Window Frame, Start Menu, and Taskbar Colors

- Open the Control Panel from the Start menu, and under Appearance and Personalization, click the "Customize colors" link.
- Click one of the eight colors, and then drag the slider tab on the Color Intensity, Hue, Saturation, and Brightness slider bars to fine-tune the color you prefer to use for windows, the Start menu, and the taskbar.
- Click the OK button to close the Window Color and Appearance window and apply your new settings.

Customizing Elements of the Graphical User Interface

You can also customize individual elements of the graphical user interface, including 3D objects, active and inactive title bars, active and inactive window borders, the background of an application window, border padding, caption buttons, the desktop, desktop icons, horizontal and vertical icon spacing, disabled items, hyperlinks, menus and items that you select on menus, message boxes, scroll bars, ToolTips, and windows.

In preparation for an upcoming presentation at Kimbrough, you ask Alejandro for suggestions on how best to customize individual elements of the user interface so that you can make it easier for all participants in a large audience to clearly see desktop and window icons and icon titles on your laptop computer display.

To customize individual elements of the user interface:

1. In the Window Color and Appearance window, click the **Open classic appearance properties for more color options** link. Windows Vista opens the Appearance Settings dialog box.
2. Click the **Advanced** button on the Appearance property sheet. Windows Vista opens the Advanced Appearance dialog box. See Figure 2-6. Windows Vista notes that the settings you select here apply only if you are using the Windows Classic color scheme. If you use any other scheme, those colors and sizes may not appear.

Figure 2-6 Viewing options for customizing the graphical user interface

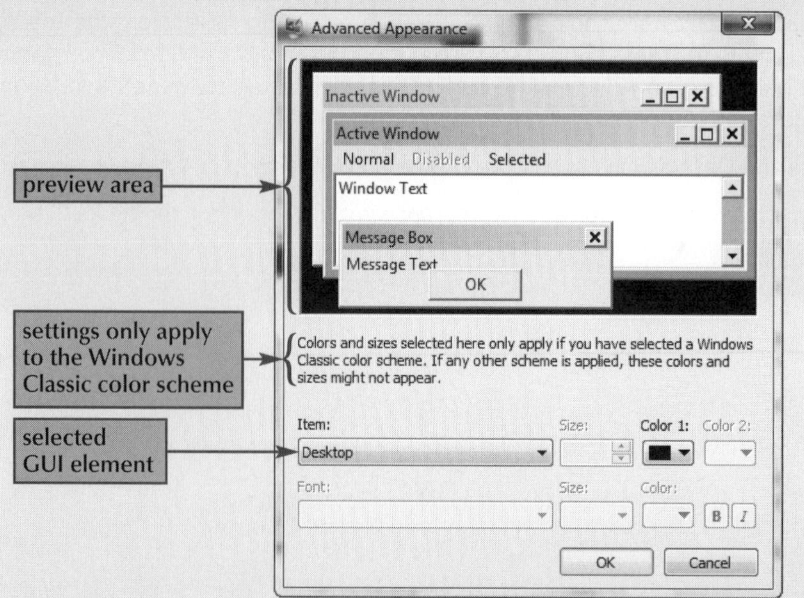

3. Click the **Item** list button. Windows Vista displays different elements of the user interface that you can customize. See Figure 2-7. Depending on which element you select, Windows Vista may display options for changing the element's size, color (and in some instances, combinations of colors that you can use), font, font size, and font color, and Bold and Italics buttons. If you click an element of the user interface in the preview area (such as the desktop), Windows Vista selects that item in the Item list box. However, not all items in the Item list box are shown in the preview area, such as ToolTip, so you must select some items from the Item list box.

Figure 2-7 GUI elements you can customize

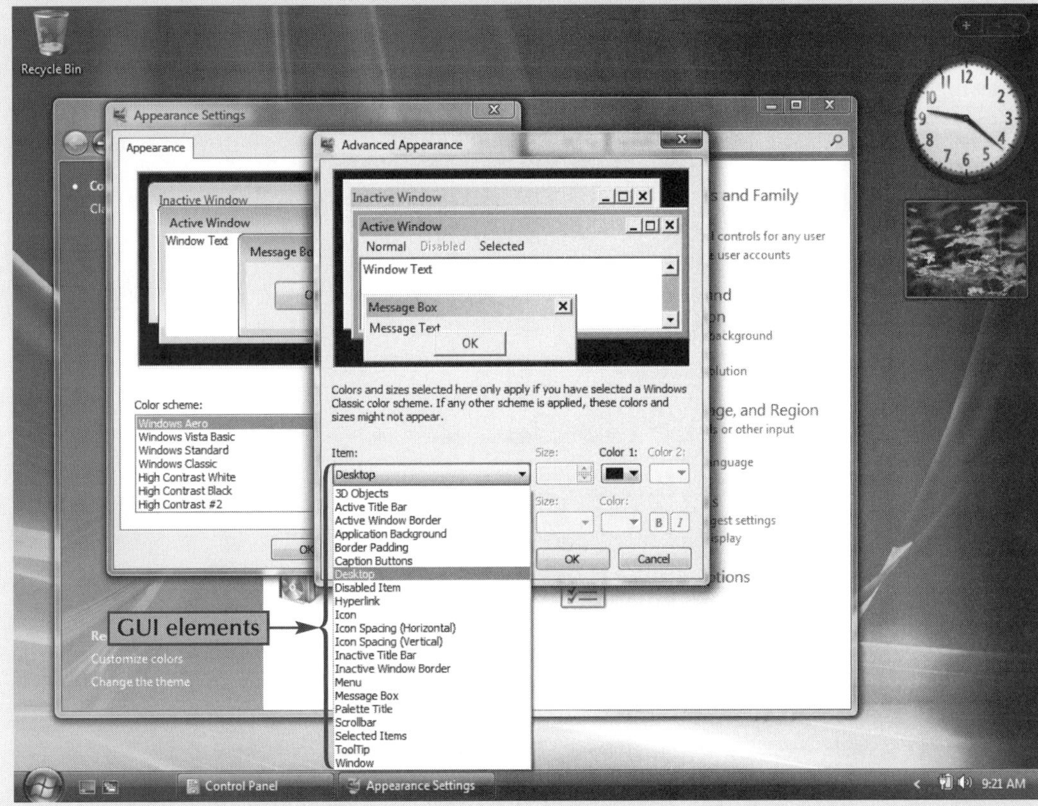

4. Click **Icon** in the Item list. Windows Vista now shows which features of desktop icons you can modify—the icon size (in pixels), the font, the font size, bold, and italics.

5. Click the **Bold** button [B].

6. Click the **Item** list button, click **Menu** in the Item list, and then click the **Bold** button [B].

7. Click the **Item** list button, click **Message Box** in the Item list, and then click the **Bold** button [B].

8. Click the **OK** button in the Advanced Appearance dialog box, click the **OK** button in the Appearance Settings dialog box, and then wait for Windows Vista to apply the settings.

9. Close the Appearance and Personalization window. Note that the icon titles for desktop icons are now shown in bold.

By applying bold to desktop icon titles, people sitting near the back of a room can more easily see icon titles. Next, you want to examine how these settings affected other parts of the user interface.

To examine other elements of the user interface:

1. Right-click the **Computer** icon on the desktop and examine the shortcut menu. Notice that the items on the shortcut menu are now shown in bold and are much easier to read.

   Trouble? If no Computer icon appears on your desktop, right-click Computer on the Start menu, click "Show on Desktop," and then repeat Step 1.

2. Click **Open** on the shortcut menu. After Windows Vista opens the Computer window, notice that the icon titles for all of the icons in this window are now shown in bold.
3. Click the **Views button arrow** (not the Views button itself). Note that the options on the Views button are shown in bold. See Figure 2-8.

Figure 2-8 Viewing changes to GUI elements

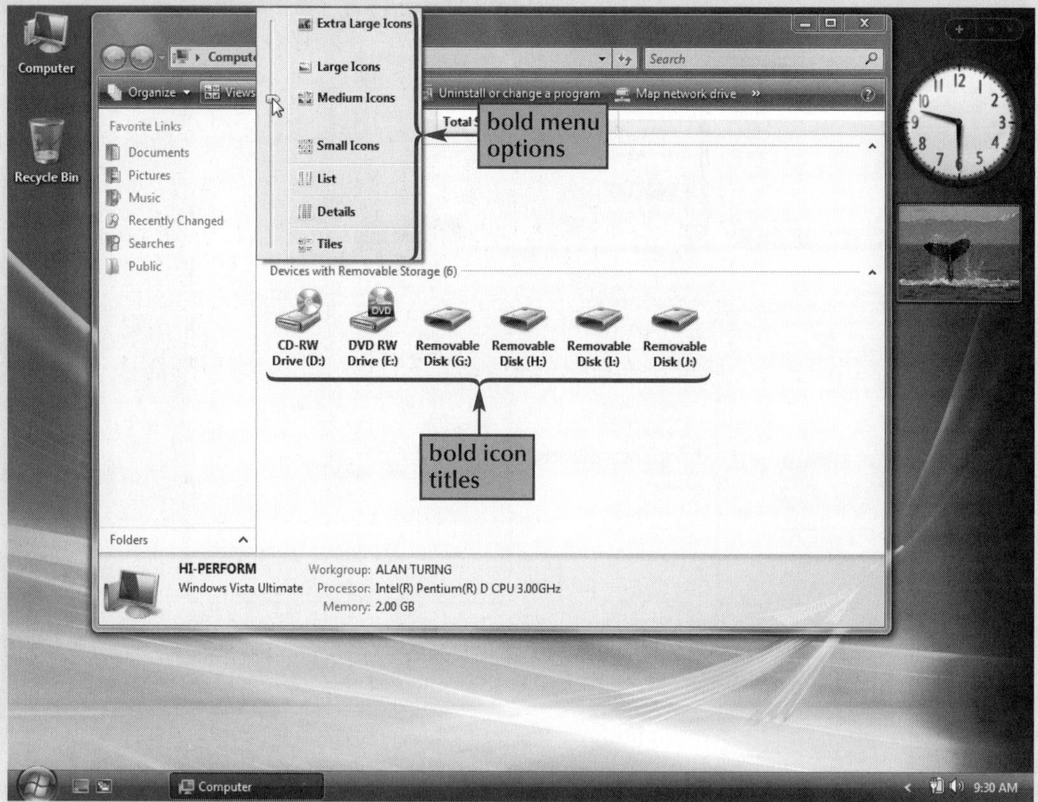

4. Press the **Esc** key to close the Views menu, and then close the Computer window.
5. Click the **Start** button, examine the left pane of the Start menu, point to **All Programs**, and then examine the All Programs menu. Menu options, programs, and group folders on the Start menu and All Programs menu are displayed in bold.

Recall that the Advanced Appearance dialog box noted that changes like the ones you just made and examined apply only if you use the Windows Classic color scheme. However, the computer used for these figures was set to the Windows Aero color scheme, and the changes that were made to items of the user interface in the Advanced Appearance dialog box also applied to the Windows Aero user interface.

Customizing Elements of the User Interface | Reference Window

- From the Start menu, open the Control Panel, click the "Customize colors link" in the Appearance and Personalization category, and then click the "Open classic appearance properties for more color options" link.
- In the Appearance Settings dialog box, click the Advanced button.
- In the Advanced Appearance dialog box, click the Item list button, click an element of the graphical user interface from the Item list (or click that element in the preview area), change settings of the element you selected, and then click the OK button.
- Repeat the previous step for every other item of the graphical user interface that you want to customize.
- In the Appearance Settings dialog box, click the OK button, and then close the Control Panel.

These options for customizing elements of the graphical user interface are useful not only in situations where you have to use a computer during a presentation before a large audience or a small work group, but also when you are working on your computer at home and work and want to see more easily what's on your monitor.

Choosing Special Display Effects

To further enhance your use of Windows Vista, you can choose from a variety of special visual display effects. One important option is the ability to smooth the edge of screen fonts. A **screen font** is a specific typeface that Windows Vista uses to display information on the monitor (or screen). A **typeface** consists of a set of characters that have the same design style. For example, the text of this paragraph uses the Optima typeface.

If you magnify what you see on the monitor, you will discover that the image consists of pixels that blend together smoothly at regular magnification to form the final image. A **pixel** is the smallest unit on a monitor for displaying a specific color. The images that you see on a monitor are composed of thousands of very small pixels arranged in columns and rows. However, even at regular magnification, an image or character on the monitor can appear uneven, as shown in Figure 2-9. Notice that the sides of the uppercase character A are uneven and exhibit what's called a **stairstep effect**. This type of problem occurs with diagonal and curved lines but not with straight lines. To create a perfectly even diagonal or curved line, your video display adapter would need to illuminate only a portion of each pixel that forms the edge of a line or curve. Even that would pose a problem because the video display adapter would need to illuminate a tiny portion of a pixel in some cases and a larger portion of a pixel in other cases. Since that's not yet possible, this stairstep effect, or what's also referred to as **jaggies**, occurs.

Figure 2-9 Stairstep effect

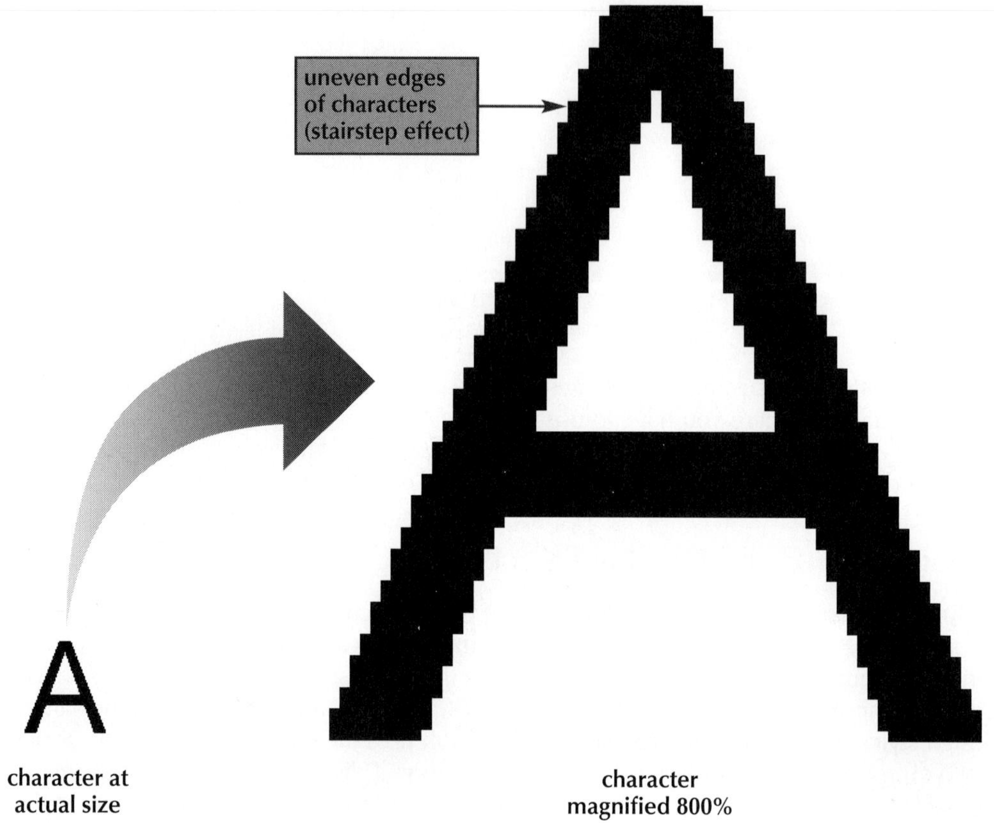

One way to handle the problem is for Windows Vista to use **font-smoothing**. If you enable the option for smoothing the edges of screen fonts, Windows Vista changes the appearance of characters so that they look smoother, as shown in Figure 2-10. Font-smoothing fills in pixels adjacent to a diagonal or curved line with colors that are intermediate between the color of the object and the color the background. For example, in the case of the uppercase character A that is rendered in black, Windows uses shades of dark brown, brown, and light yellow on the left edges of the two stems of the letter A and dark blue, blue, and light blue for pixels located on the right edges of the two stems of the letter A. The font-smoothing produces a more even look at actual size and reduces the stairstep effect or jaggies, as shown in Figure 2-10. This shading of adjacent pixels also produces a slight three-dimensional appearance.

Figure 2-10 Font-smoothing reduces stairstep effect

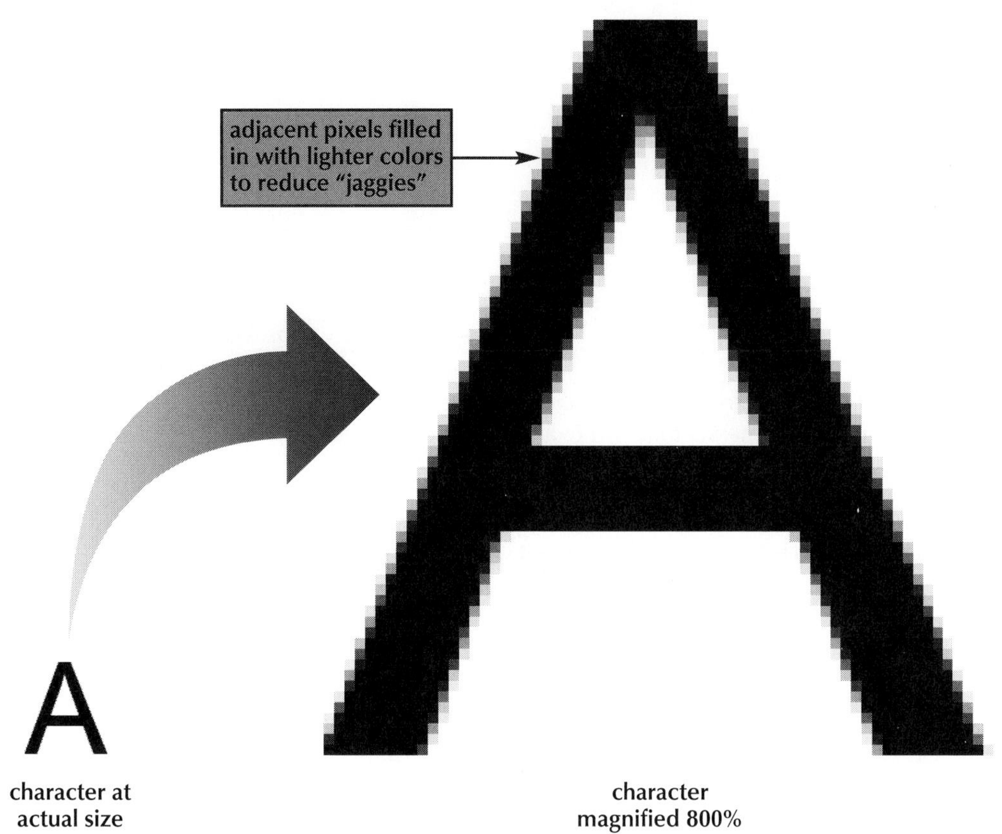

If you examine the "before" and "after" font-smoothing images, as shown in Figure 2-11, you can tell that the uppercase letter A on the right appears sharper because it has been rendered with font-smoothing.

Figure 2-11 How font-smoothing affects the sharpness of characters

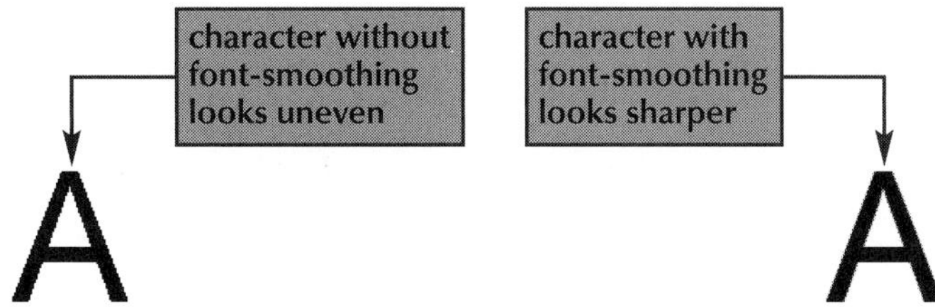

The font-smoothing approach used in Figure 2-10 and Figure 2-11 is called **ClearType**. Microsoft introduced this technology for LCD monitors in Windows XP. On LCD monitors, pixels are composed of three vertical **subpixels**—a red, green, and blue subpixel, as shown in Figure 2-12. Windows XP and Windows Vista can adjust the color of each subpixel so that characters appear more even and sharper on the monitor. ClearType is automatically enabled on LCD monitors.

Figure 2-12 Subpixels within an LCD pixel

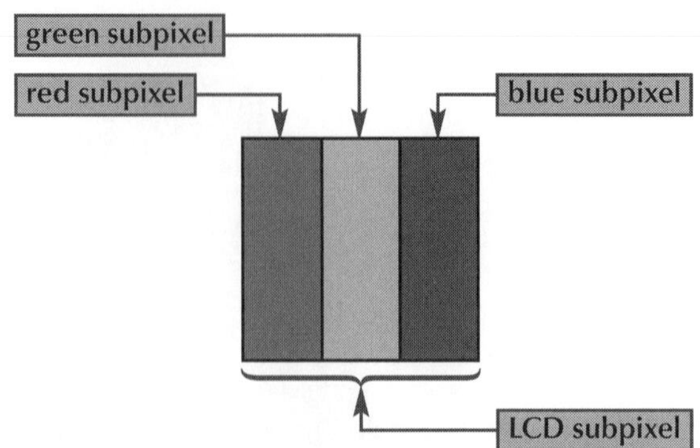

Alejandro describes some other special visual effects that you might find useful in your work and recommends that you examine these settings on your computer and, if necessary, adjust them to suit your needs.

To check the settings for special display effects:

1. Right-click the **desktop**, click **Personalize** on the shortcut menu, and in the Personalization window, click the **Window Color and Appearance** link. Windows Vista opens the Window Color and Appearance window.
2. Click the **Open classic appearance properties for more color options** link. Windows Vista opens the Appearance Settings dialog box.
3. Click the **Effects** button on the Appearance property sheet. Windows Vista opens the Effects dialog box. See Figure 2-13.

Figure 2-13 Viewing the font-smoothing setting

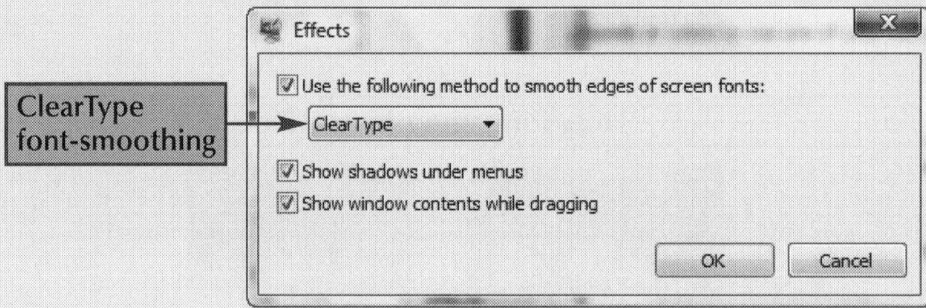

4. If the "Use the following method to smooth edges of screen fonts" check box does not contain a check mark, click this check box.
5. Click the **Use the following methods to smooth edges of screen fonts** list button. Windows Vista displays two options for smoothing the edges of screen fonts—Standard and ClearType. The Standard setting is designed for use with CRT monitors whereas the ClearType setting is designed for LCD monitors. However, Microsoft noted in Windows XP that some CRT monitors might benefit from the ClearType technology and display characters more sharply.
6. Click **ClearType**.
7. If the "Show shadows under menus" check box does not contain a check mark, click this check box. When enabled, Windows Vista displays a slight shadow behind menu options to create a three-dimensional look.

8. If the "Show window contents while dragging" check box does not contain a check mark, click this check box. When you drag a window or dialog box to another location on the desktop, Windows Vista displays the content within a window or dialog box. If you turn this option off, and then drag a window or dialog box, you see only an outline of the window or dialog box to indicate where Windows Vista will place the object once you release the left mouse button. While this latter option might boost the performance of your computer slightly, most new computers should have no difficulty showing the contents of a window or dialog as you drag these objects.
9. Click the **OK** button to close the Effects dialog box, click the **OK** button to close the Appearance Settings dialog box, and then close the Personalization window.

You can access the same visual effects shown in the Effects dialog box plus others that affect the appearance and performance of your computer by examining Advanced System Settings. When you perform certain operations that require Administrator privileges or credentials, Windows Vista switches to **Secure Desktop Mode**, which is a display mode under which Windows Vista can run only one program and perform only one operation.

Before you check these advanced visual display settings, determine whether you are logged on under an Administrator or Standard user account.

To determine whether your user account is an Administrator or Standard user account:

1. From the Start menu, open the Control Panel, and then click the **User Accounts and Family Safety** link.
2. In the User Accounts and Family Safety window, click the **User Accounts** link. Next to your user account icon and under your user name, Windows Vista identifies whether your account is an Administrator account or Standard user account. As shown in Figure 2-14, Alejandro's user account is a Standard user account. To the left of your user account icon are options for managing your user account and other user accounts. You can change your user account password and picture without Administrator credentials.

Figure 2-14 Viewing Alejandro's account type

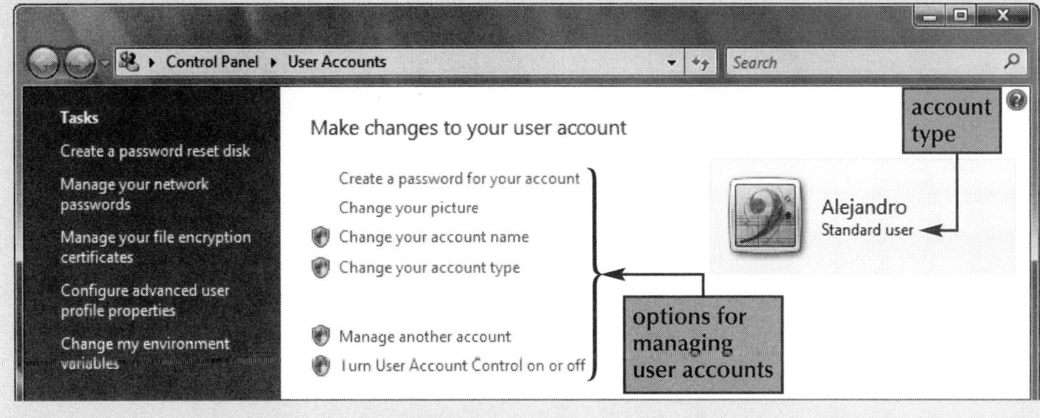

3. Close the User Accounts window.

If you are logged on under an Administrator account and initiate an operation that requires Administrator credentials, Windows Vista displays a User Account Control dialog box and notes that it needs your permission to continue. If you started this action, you can click the Continue button. If you are logged on under a Standard user account, Windows Vista displays a User Account Control dialog box where you must enter the password for an Administrator account before you can continue.

Now, you're ready to examine advanced system settings.

To complete the following steps, you must provide Administrator credentials. If you are not logged on under an Administrator account or do not know the password for an Administrator account, do not keystroke the following steps, but instead read the steps and examine the figures so that you are familiar with the use of this feature.

Tip

You can also press the Windows Logo+Break keys to open the System window.

To examine a more comprehensive list of special visual effects:

1. Right-click the **Computer** icon on the desktop, and then click **Properties**. Windows Vista opens the System window.
2. Under Tasks on the left side of the System window, click the **Advanced system settings** link. Windows Vista switches to Secure Desktop Mode and displays a User Account Control dialog box.
3. In the User Account Control dialog box, click the **Continue** button if you are logged on under an Administrator account, or if you are logged on under a Standard User account, enter the **password** for an Administrator account, and then click the **OK** button. Windows Vista opens the System Properties dialog box and displays the contents of the Advanced property sheet. See Figure 2-15.

Figure 2-15 **Viewing options for adjusting advanced system settings**

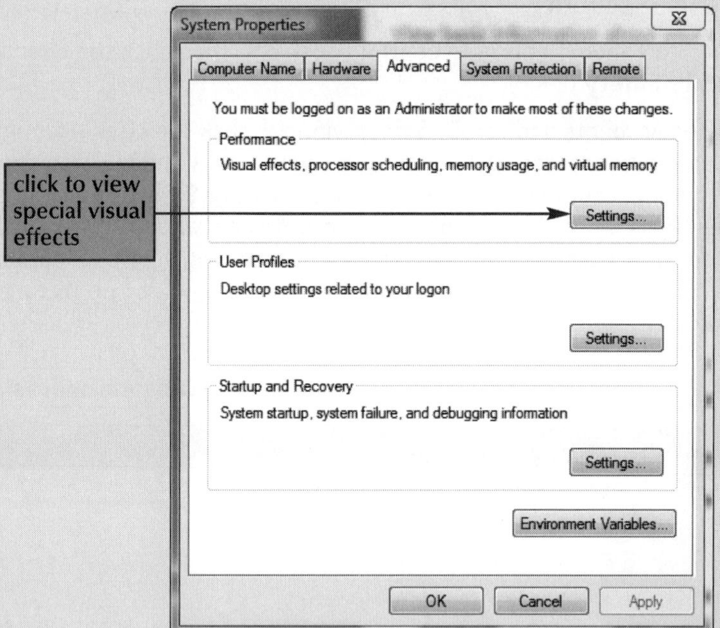

4. In the Performance section, click the **Settings** button. Windows opens the Performance Options dialog box and displays the contents of the Visual Effects property sheet. See Figure 2-16. From the Custom list box on this property sheet, you can adjust 20 different settings to improve the appearance of your computer or to optimize its performance.

Figure 2-16 Viewing options for selecting visual effects

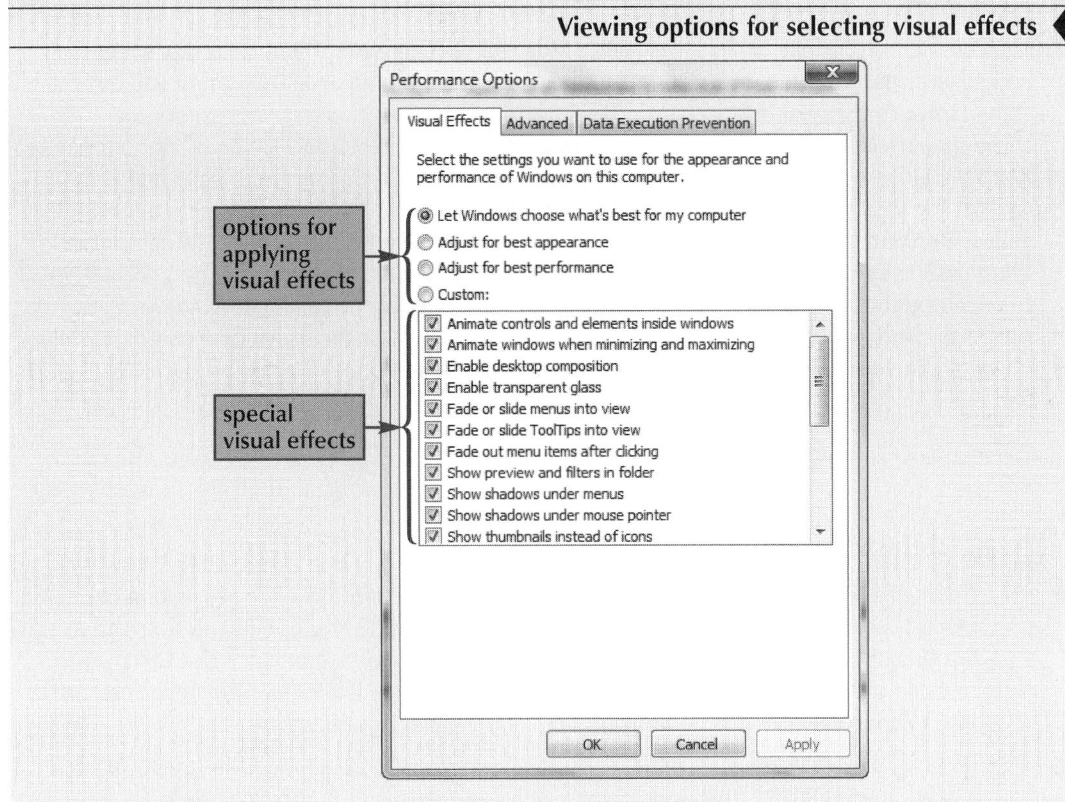

Most of the options shown in the Custom list box are also available in Windows XP. The following new options in the Custom list box relate to the use of Windows Aero:

- **Enable desktop composition** A feature found in those editions of Windows Vista that support Windows Aero, **desktop composition** refers to the new Windows Vista window-management technology for updating your view of the desktop and open windows and for supporting the use of Windows Aero. Desktop composition must be enabled to view translucent window borders, Live Taskbar Thumbnails, Windows Flip, and Windows Flip 3D.
- **Enable transparent glass** Like the "Enable transparency" option you examined earlier in the Window Color and Appearance window, this option enables or disables translucency. However, it requires that the color scheme be set to Windows Aero. Transparent glass is a term that's commonly used to describe the glass-like translucency feature in Windows Aero.

Included in the list of visual effects are "Smooth edges of screen fonts," "Show shadows under menus," and "Show window contents when dragging," which are also available from the Effects dialog box you examined in the previous section.

Three other useful visual effects include:

- **Show translucent selection rectangle** When enabled, Windows draws a translucent, or partially transparent, blue rectangle around folders or files in a window (or on the desktop) as you drag the mouse to select the folders or files.
- **Use drop shadows for icon labels on the desktop** When enabled, this feature further enhances the visibility and display of desktop icon titles or labels and also provides a three-dimensional perspective.
- **Show shadows under mouse pointer** When enabled, Windows Vista displays a shadow under the mouse pointer, providing a three-dimensional perspective and making it easier to see and locate the pointer.

InSight | Balancing Appearance and Performance

You can use one of the first three options at the top of the Visual Effects property sheet to adjust settings for all the visual effects in the Custom list box in one step. When you do, you should be sure that you balance settings that affect the appearance of your computer with those that affect performance. If you choose the "Adjust for best performance" option, Windows Vista turns off all the visual effects, which maximizes performance. If you choose the "Adjust for best appearance" option, Windows Vista enables all the visual effects but might reduce performance. If you choose the "Let Windows choose what's best for my computer," Windows Vista decides which visual effects to enable and which to turn off. The information provided by the latter option can help you determine the degree to which Windows Vista supports Windows Aero features and other features, such as showing window contents while dragging on your computer and their impact on the performance of your computer.

Next, you can examine the settings for visual effects.

To finish inspecting visual effects:

1. If you are working on your own computer and want to make changes to one or more of these visual effects, adjust these settings using the one of the first three options or by choosing specific options in the Custom list box, click the **OK** button to close the Performance Options dialog box, click the **OK** button to close the System Properties dialog box, and then close the System window.
2. If you are working in a computer lab, or if you are working on your own computer and do not want to change any of these visual effects, click the **Cancel** button to close the Performance Options dialog box, click the **Cancel** button to close the System Properties dialog box, and then close the System window.

So that your computer performs optimally, and so that you have access to the types of visual effects that you want to use, you should test each of these visual effect settings and observe whether and how they affect your computer's performance. In some cases, you might want to keep a visual effect because of its benefits even if it slightly affects the performance of your computer.

Choosing Special Display Effects | Reference Window

- Right-click the Computer icon on the desktop (or on the Start menu), and then click Properties.
- Under Tasks on the left side of the System window, click Advanced system settings.
- When Windows Vista displays a User Account Control dialog box, click the Continue button if you are logged on under an Administrator account. If you are logged on under a Standard User account, enter the password for an Administrator account, and then click the Continue button.
- In the Performance section of the System Properties dialog box, click the Settings button.
- If you want Windows Vista to adjust your computer's settings for best performance, click the "Adjust for best performance" option button.
- If you want Windows Vista to adjust your computer's setting for the best appearance, click the "Adjust for best appearance" option button.
- If you want Windows Vista to choose the best settings for your computer, click the "Let Windows choose what's best for my computer" option button.
- If you want to specify a setting for each visual setting, examine each visual setting in the Custom list box and add a check mark to the check box to enable the option or remove the check mark from the check box to turn off the option.
- Click the OK button to close the Performance Options dialog box, click the OK button to close the System Properties dialog box, and then close the System window.

Next, Alejandro suggests you consider changing your desktop background.

Changing Your Desktop Background

Using Windows Vista, you can place images and, in some cases, video on the desktop background. You can use images stored in files with the file extension "bmp" for **Bitmap Image**, "jpg" or "jpeg" for **Joint Photographic Experts Group**, and "dib" for **Device Independent Bitmap**. Each of these types of graphic file formats contains a bitmapped graphic. A **bitmapped graphic** is an image represented by a pattern of pixels, or picture elements, as shown in Figure 2-17. This figure shows the Windows logo on the Start button at actual size and magnified 800%. As you can see, the image consists of an array of pixels, each of which consists of a different color. Each pixel consists of one or more dots, or points, which are treated as one unit on the monitor. Each dot in turn is composed of Red, Green, and Blue (RGB) components that blend together to form a single color. At your computer's maximum resolution (covered in the next section of the tutorial), one pixel equals one dot. The number of bits used for each pixel determines the number of colors available for a pixel.

Example of a bitmapped graphic **Figure 2-17**

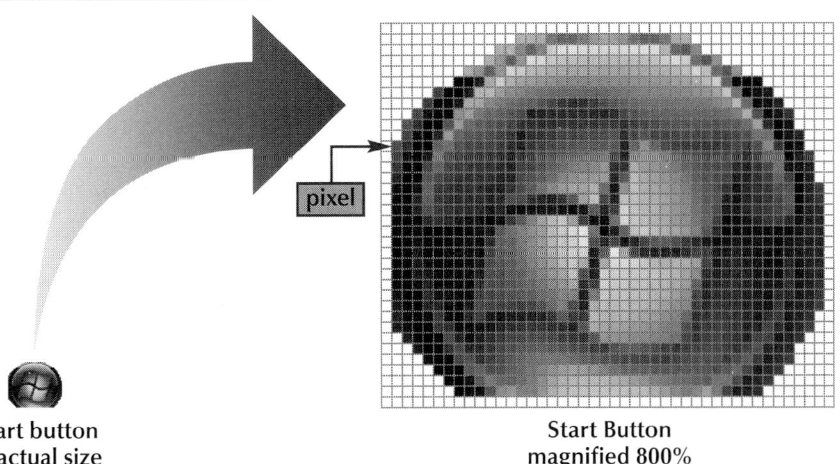

Bitmap Image files with the "bmp" file extension contain images with hundreds of thousands or millions of pixels in an uncompressed format, so file sizes can be quite large.

The JPG or JPEG (pronounced "jay peg") file format with the "jpg" or "jpeg" file extension stores images in a compressed format at a ratio of 10:1 or 20:1, or greater, by removing some of the detail in an image (changes that the human eye presumably cannot detect), and therefore is called **lossy compression**. Also, JPG file sizes are relatively small. Real-life images, such as images or photos of individuals or landscapes, are usually JPG files. Also, JPG images are commonly used on Web pages and, because of their small size, the amount of time required to transmit them over the Internet is far less than for uncompressed Bitmap Images.

Under Windows XP, you could use the **GIF** (for **Graphics Interchange Format** and pronounced "jiff" or "gif") file format and the **PNG** (for **Portable Network Graphics** and pronounced "ping") files as desktop backgrounds, but Windows Vista does not support these file formats for use as desktop backgrounds. The GIF file format stores a bitmap image at a compression of 1.5:1 to 2:1 without any loss of detail in the image (called **lossless compression**). The actual amount of compression depends on the degree to which the same colors are repeated within the image itself. The standard types of GIF files are limited to a palette of 256 colors or less. A **palette**, or **color palette**, is a set of available colors used either by an application or by the operating system. GIF files are well suited for cartoon or line art and relatively small images with few colors and clearly marked borders between different parts of an image. They are often used for buttons and small icons on Web pages. An **animated GIF** is a GIF file format that contains multiple images through which a Web browser can cycle to display animation. The PNG file format is similar to the GIF file format, although it does achieve a slightly greater compression. It may eventually replace the GIF file format since it is an improvement in several ways and is patent-free, therefore requiring no license for its use.

In Windows Vista, you can now use certain types of video files as a desktop background. Windows Vista supports two common video formats—**MPG** or **MPEG** (**Moving Pictures Experts Group**) and **WMV** (**Windows Media Audio/Video**). When you choose one of these video file formats for use as a desktop background, Windows Vista plays back the video in the file continuously (automatically restarting when the video clip ends). If the video contains sound, you hear the sound.

Windows Vista has five options for positioning an image or video on the desktop:

- **Fit to screen** Windows Vista stretches an image or video so that it fills the entire desktop. That may mean altering the ratio of its width to length and introducing distortion; however, the distortion may appear fine and just reflect another way to look at the same image. In fact, a small amount of distortion might not even be discernable. If the height of an image or video is greater than its width, the height of the image or video fits the height of the desktop, and the width of the image or video is stretched to fit across the desktop (and vice-versa).
- **Tile** Windows Vista repeats the image at actual size across the desktop, starting in the upper-left corner of the desktop. Windows Vista displays the image or video with no distortion; however, only portions of an image or video may be visible in the tiles on the right and bottom edges of the desktop. This option is useful for files that contain a small graphic image because you can create a collage effect on the desktop.
- **Center** Windows Vista centers an image or video at actual size on the desktop and maintains the ratio of its width to length with no distortion. In some cases, the image or video may not fill the entire desktop; however that can be useful because icons can be placed on the desktop outside the image or video. This option provides the sharpest view of an image or video.

- **Maintain aspect ratio** Windows Vista stretches the image or video to fill either the width or length of the desktop, but maintains the ratio of the width to the length so that there is no distortion. In some cases, the image or video may not fill the entire desktop, but as noted, that leaves desktop space for icons.
- **Crop to fit screen** Windows Vista resizes an image or video to fill the desktop but maintains the ratio of its width to length. However, Windows Vista crops that part of the image that does not fit on the desktop. For example, if the image's height is greater than the width, Windows Vista resizes the image so that the entire width of the image stretches across the desktop and crops the top and bottom of the image that does not fit on the desktop.

Alejandro mentions that you can also use graphic images and videos of your own creation on the desktop background. He suggests you examine the desktop backgrounds provided with Windows Vista.

To place an image on the desktop:

1. Right-click the **desktop**, click **Personalize** on the shortcut menu, and after Windows Vista opens the Personalization window, click **Desktop Background**. Windows opens the Desktop Background window and displays thumbnails of pictures or videos content from the group shown on the Location button.
2. Click the **Location** list button. Windows Vista lists locations on your computer, or content groups, which contain images and videos. See Figure 2-18. You can use Windows Wallpapers (pictures) or Solid Colors (a single color background with no image or video). You can locate images stored in your personal Pictures folder, the Sample Pictures folder, and the Public Pictures folder. In your edition of Windows Vista, you may also be able to select videos from your personal Videos folder, the Sample Videos folder, and the Public Videos folder.

   Trouble? If the Desktop Background window does not contain a Location list button, Windows Vista might identify your Location list button as Picture Location.

Figure 2-18 Viewing categories of desktop backgrounds

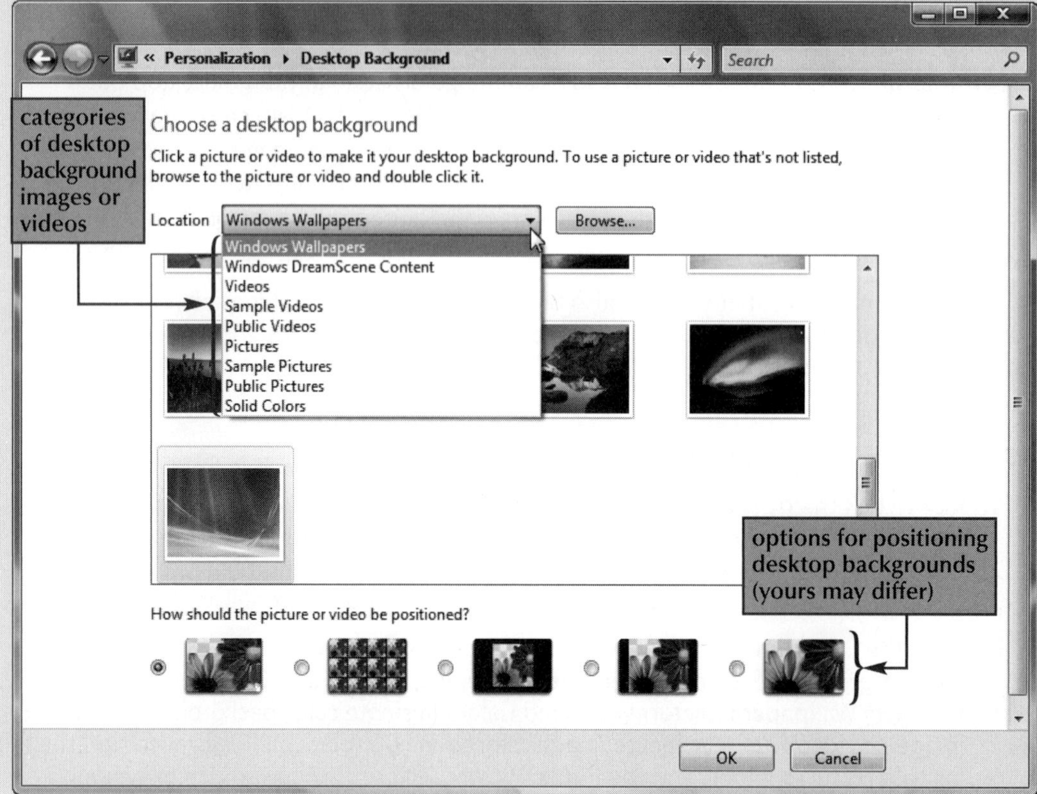

If you have Windows Vista Ultimate and have downloaded Windows DreamScene Content from Microsoft's Update Web site, that option will be listed in the Location list so that you can choose from continuously playing, high-quality videos for use as desktop backgrounds. If you access another image or video for use as a desktop background from another folder, the location of that folder is subsequently displayed in the Location list.

Tip

You can also use the Browse button to navigate to a folder and locate other images and videos.

3. If it is not already selected, click **Windows Wallpapers** in the Location list. Windows Wallpapers contain six categories of desktop backgrounds—Black and White, Light Auras, Paintings, Textures, Vistas, and Widescreen (designed for widescreen LCDs).
4. Under Textures, point to the third image, which contains a view of multicolored rocks. Windows Vista displays this image on the desktop background.
5. Under "How should the picture or video be positioned?" try each of the options for positioning a desktop background by clicking each of the icons that show how pictures or videos can be positioned on the desktop, and then examine the picture on your desktop (you may need to minimize, move, or resize the Desktop Background window for a better view).
6. From the Location list box, select and examine each of the other categories of options that contain desktop backgrounds and preview any of interest to you.
7. To restore the default desktop background used by Windows Vista, click the **Desktop Background** taskbar button to restore the Desktop Background window (if necessary), click the **Location** list button, click **Windows Wallpapers**, scroll to the **Vistas** category, click the last desktop background under this category, click the **OK** button, and then close the Personalization window.

If you have scanned images or digital photos of family, friends, vacation spots, landscapes, or videos in one of the file formats described earlier, you can place them into specific folders for use as desktop backgrounds.

Choosing Desktop Backgrounds | Reference Window

- Right-click the desktop, and then click Personalize on the shortcut menu.
- In the Personalization window, click Desktop Background.
- In the Desktop Background window, click the Location list button and select a category or folder that contains pictures or videos you want to use as desktop backgrounds.
- Select the picture or video you want to use as a desktop background, and under "How should the picture or video be positioned?", select the positioning option you want to use for placing the desktop background on the desktop, click the OK button, and then close the Personalization window.

If you are viewing an image or video in a folder and decide you want to use it as a desktop background, right-click the image or video, and choose "Set as Desktop Background." Windows Vista will then center the image or video on the desktop. Likewise, if you are browsing the Web with Internet Explorer and find an image without copyright restrictions that you want to use as a desktop background, you can right-click the image, and then choose "Set as Background."

Session 2.1 Quick Check | Review

1. A(n) ______________________ consists of a set of visual elements, as well as other elements, such as sound, that provide a unified look for your desktop and user interface, whereas a(n) ______________________ is a combination of settings for displaying individual elements of the user interface.
2. What are the four basic types of Windows Vista user interfaces available?
3. By using ______________________, you can improve the appearance of text that would otherwise exhibit a stair step effect on diagonal or curved lines.
4. What is the name of the Microsoft technology for improving the appearance and readability of text on LCD monitors?
5. ______________________ refers to the new Windows Vista window-management technology for updating your view of the desktop and open windows and for supporting Windows Aero.
6. True or False? A bitmapped graphic is an image represented by a pattern of pixels.

Session 2.2

Customizing the Start Menu

Since the Start menu remains the focal point for accessing the contents of a computer, you can customize it to simplify your access to Windows Vista tools and installed applications. For example, you can specify:

- **Start menu style** Windows Vista automatically uses a Start menu style similar to the one used in Windows XP, but you have the option of switching to a Classic Start menu style which is similar to the same option available in earlier versions of Windows.
- **Privacy options** By default, Windows Vista stores and displays a list of recently opened files and programs; however, you can turn off both these options. If you use different applications, utilities, and games, Windows Vista will display them on the most recently opened programs list when this feature is enabled so that you have quick access to these programs. Windows Vista updates this list as you open and use other programs. You can also adjust the number of programs it displays on the Start menu from a default value of 9 to whatever best suits your needs. With the option for displaying recently opened files enabled, Windows Vista displays a "Recent Items" option on the Start menu so that you can quickly select a document you've previously used.
- **Start menu items** You can specify whether Windows Vista displays Computer, Connect To, Control Panel, Default Programs, Documents, Favorites, Games, Help (for Help and Support), Music, Network, Pictures, Printers, Run command, Search, System Administrative Tools, and even your Personal (user account) folder on the Start menu. For some of these items, you can also specify whether Windows Vista displays the item as a link directly to the folder or as a menu of links. For example, when you click Documents on the Start menu, Windows Vista opens the Documents folder window so that you can work with your personal folders and files. If you display Documents as a menu, Windows Vista does not open the Documents folder, but instead displays a list of the folders and files in the Documents folder as items on a Documents menu. This same feature is available for the Computer, Control Panel, Games, Music, Pictures, and System Administration Tools folders as well as your Personal folder. If you display the Favorites menu on the Start menu, you have another method for locating and opening Web sites that you've bookmarked with Internet Explorer (only). If you've organized your bookmarks into folders, you will see those folders on the Favorites menu. If you are a member of the Administrators group, you can display Administrative Tools on the Programs menu. From the System Administrative Tools menu, you can open tools for managing your computer and monitoring its performance.
- **Pinned items list** You can specify which programs Windows Vista displays as links in the pinned items list for Internet access and for e-mail. If you use Internet Explorer and Mozilla Firefox, you can specify which of these options to display in the pinned items list. Also, you might have options for displaying Microsoft Office Outlook, Windows Live Mail, or Windows Mail (part of Windows Vista) on the pinned items list for your primary e-mail account. As noted in Tutorial 1, anything you place in the pinned items list stays there.
- **Sort All Programs menu by name** Unlike earlier versions of Windows, Windows Vista automatically sorts programs and group folders on the All Programs menu and lists newly installed programs in alphabetical order.

- **Icon sizes** By default, Windows Vista uses small icons to display the contents of the pinned items list and recently opened programs list. However, you can switch the icons in these two parts of the Start menu to Large Icons to make it easier to locate a program. Small icons are useful if you add more items to the Start menu.
- **Highlighting newly installed software** Windows Vista highlights newly installed programs on the Start menu in a different color so that you can quickly find them; however, you can turn off this feature.
- **Opening submenus when you pause on them with the mouse pointer** Windows Vista immediately displays the submenu for a menu option when you pause on that menu option; however, you can turn off this setting.
- **Enable context menus and dragging and dropping** If you can right-click a Start menu item, Windows Vista displays a shortcut menu, or context menu, with a list of options associated with that menu item. You can use drag and drop to rearrange some items on the Start menu. These options are automatically enabled; however, you can turn off these settings.

Alejandro points out that the Start menu is an important resource that you use every day, so you should take a few minutes to customize it to meet your needs.

To check and change Start menu settings:

1. Right-click the **Start** button on the taskbar, and then click **Properties**. Windows Vista opens the Taskbar and Start Menu Properties dialog box and displays the Start Menu property sheet in the foreground. See Figure 2-19. The "Start menu" option is the default Start menu style used by Windows Vista. The "Classic Start menu" style uses a Start menu style similar to that found in earlier versions of Windows. Under Privacy, you can specify whether you want Windows Vista to store and display a list of recently opened files and programs. These options are independent of the Start menu style you choose.

Figure 2-19 Start Menu property sheet

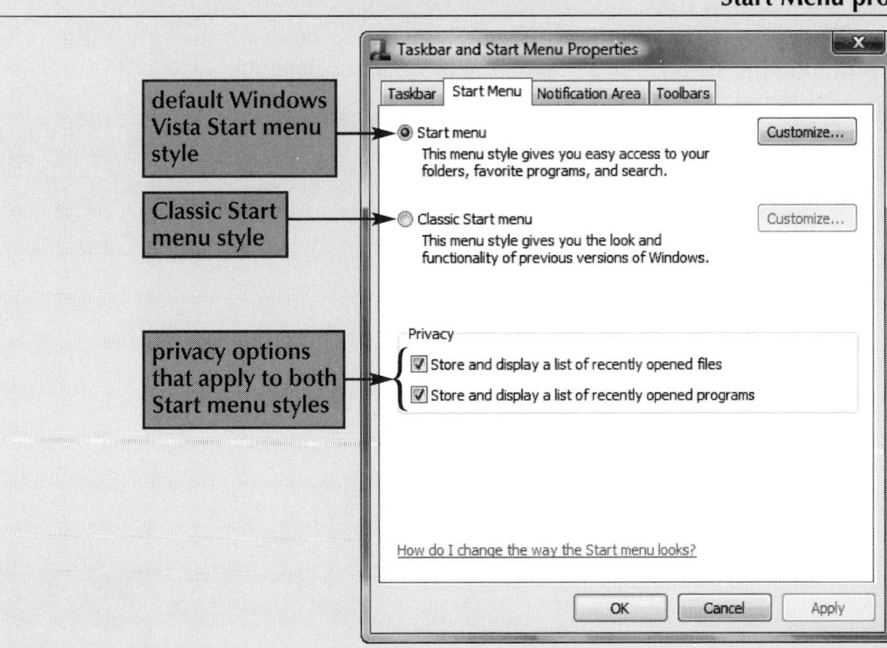

2. If Windows Vista is set to use the Classic Start menu style on your computer, click the **Start menu** option button, and then click the **Apply** button.

Tip

If you open the Start menu, and then realize that you want to change its properties, you can right-click the background of the Start menu, and then click Properties.

3. Click the **Customize** button next to the Start menu option button on the Start Menu property sheet. Windows Vista opens the Customize Start Menu dialog box and lists all the items described earlier for customizing the Start menu. See Figure 2-20. Under Start menu size, you can specify the number of recently used programs to display on the Start menu. Under "Show on Start menu," you can specify links for your Web browser and e-mail software (which may differ from that shown in the figure). You can use the "Use Default Settings" button to restore Windows Vista's default settings for the Start menu.

Figure 2-20 **Options for customizing the Start menu**

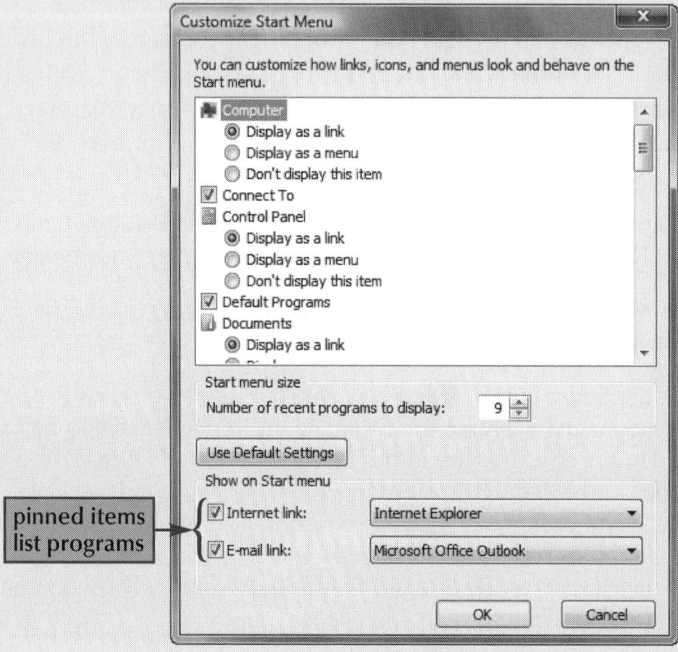

4. Under Control Panel in the list box, click the **Display as a menu** option button, click the **OK** button in the Customize Start Menu dialog box, and then click the **Apply** button in the Taskbar and Start Menu Properties dialog box.

5. Open the **Start menu,** and then point to **Control Panel**. Windows Vista displays a Control Panel menu that lists in alphabetical order all the options available from the Control Panel. See Figure 2-21. At the bottom of the Control Panel is a button for scrolling down the Control Panel menu and viewing other Control Panel options. This is particularly useful if you do not remember or can not find certain Control Panels tools.

Figure 2-21 Viewing the Control Panel menu

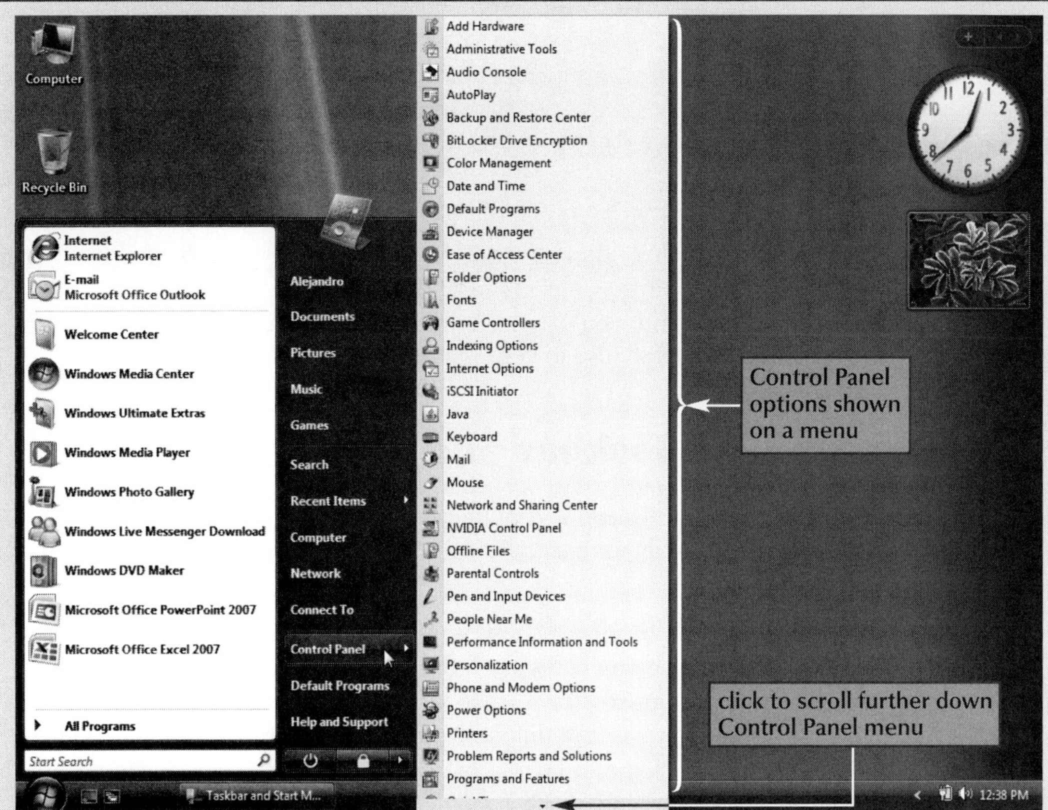

6. Click **Personalization** on the Control Panel menu. Windows Vista opens the Personalization window that you examined earlier (and ones you will examine in the next session). Menu links like this one can provide faster access to Windows tools and your personal folders and files.
7. Close the Personalization window.

The Windows Vista Start menu style also includes options for controlling how the new Windows Vista Instant Search feature works. By default, Instant Search searches for communications (such as e-mail messages and contacts), favorites and history, and programs. Also, it is set to search only your own user files, but you can change or adjust all these settings. You will explore the Instant Search feature in more detail in Tutorial 3.

If you prefer the Classic Start menu style, you will discover that although you do have access to some of the same options available for the default Windows Vista Start menu style, there are fewer options for customizing the Start menu. Also, some options are not available with the Start menu style, such as adding a Log Off option to the Start menu and using personalized menus. **Personalized menus** are menus that display only the most commonly used menu options or menu options that were previously used.

Reference Window | Customizing the Start Menu

- Right-click the Start button, and then click Properties.
- In the Taskbar and Start Menu Properties dialog box, choose your Start menu style by clicking the Start menu or Classic Start menu option button.
- Click the Customize button next to the Start menu style you selected, select the Start menu features you want to use and, if necessary, turn off features you do not want, and then click the OK button.
- Click the OK button in the Taskbar and Start Menu Properties dialog box to apply your changes.

By customizing your Start menu, you can make life easier and gain quick access to the options you need and frequently use in your line of work.

Customizing the Taskbar and Notification Area

Since the taskbar is an object, and since it's another important desktop resource that you rely on, you can also customize it. For example, you can specify the following properties or features of the taskbar:

- **Lock or unlock the toolbar** By default, the taskbar is locked so that you cannot move it or make changes to it; however, you can unlock the taskbar. When locked, you cannot change the size or position of any toolbar on the taskbar. If you need to move the taskbar or a toolbar on the taskbar, you can unlock the taskbar by right-clicking it and turning off the option labeled "Lock the Taskbar." If you unlock the taskbar, you can dock it on another edge of the desktop, and increase (or decrease) its height. Increasing the taskbar height is especially useful if you have added shortcuts to the Quick Launch toolbar and want to view all of those shortcut icons or if you open multiple windows and want to easily see their taskbar buttons.

Tip

The Auto-hide the taskbar option is also useful if you want to view more of a Web page.

- **Auto-hide the taskbar** Although the taskbar is always visible by default, you can hide the taskbar to display more of the window you are using. When you hide the taskbar, it resizes itself to a thin bar at the bottom of the desktop. When you point to this thin bar, Windows Vista immediately displays the taskbar so that you can select the Start button, a taskbar button, or an icon in the notification area, or view the time. Then it hides the taskbar when you move the mouse pointer away from the taskbar.
- **Keep the taskbar on top of other windows** By default, the taskbar appears on top of any other windows you open so that it's always visible and thereby provides you with quick access to the Start menu and open windows; however, you can turn off this option so that, for example, maximized windows cover the taskbar.
- **Group similar taskbar buttons** Like Windows XP, Windows Vista uses **taskbar grouping** to combine taskbar buttons for similar types of windows into one button, such as multiple folder windows or multiple document windows, if the taskbar buttons shrink below a certain size.
- **Show Quick Launch** From the Taskbar property sheet, you can turn off the display of the Quick Launch toolbar.
- **Show windows previews (thumbnails)** When enabled, Windows Vista displays a Live Taskbar Thumbnail when you point to the taskbar button for an open window whether it's maximized, minimized, or at its default size if your computer supports Windows Aero.

- **Hiding icons in the notification area** You can decide which icons you want to see in the notification area for programs that load during booting or startup. You can customize the notification area and decide whether you want to hide each icon only when it is inactive, always hide the icon, or always show the icon. Then, you always have access to those notification area icons that are important to how you work on your computer.
- **Displaying system icons in the notification area** You can choose whether you want to display the clock, the volume icon (for controlling the sound volume), the network icon for access to network connections and for displaying the status of network connections, and the power icon for quick access to power settings.
- **Displaying toolbars on the taskbar** You can determine whether to display the Address, Windows Media Player, Links, Tablet PC Input Panel (if available in your Windows Vista edition), Desktop, and Quick Launch toolbars on the taskbar. With the Tablet PC Input Panel, you can enter text without using a standard keyboard.

Alejandro recommends that you check your taskbar and notification area settings so that they are set properly and meet your daily needs. He also recommends that you enable the option for always showing the Windows Sidebar icon in the notification area so you have quick access to the Windows Sidebar any time you need it.

To check your taskbar settings:

1. Right-click the **taskbar**, and then click **Properties** on the taskbar shortcut menu. Windows Vista opens the Taskbar and Start Menu Properties dialog box and displays the Taskbar property sheet in the foreground. See Figure 2-22. By default, all the options, including taskbar grouping, are enabled except for Auto-hide. If Windows Vista does not display Live Taskbar Thumbnails on your computer, and if your computer supports Windows Aero, you can enable this feature on this property sheet.

Tip

You can lock and unlock the taskbar from the Taskbar shortcut menu or from the Taskbar property sheet.

Figure 2-22 Viewing taskbar settings

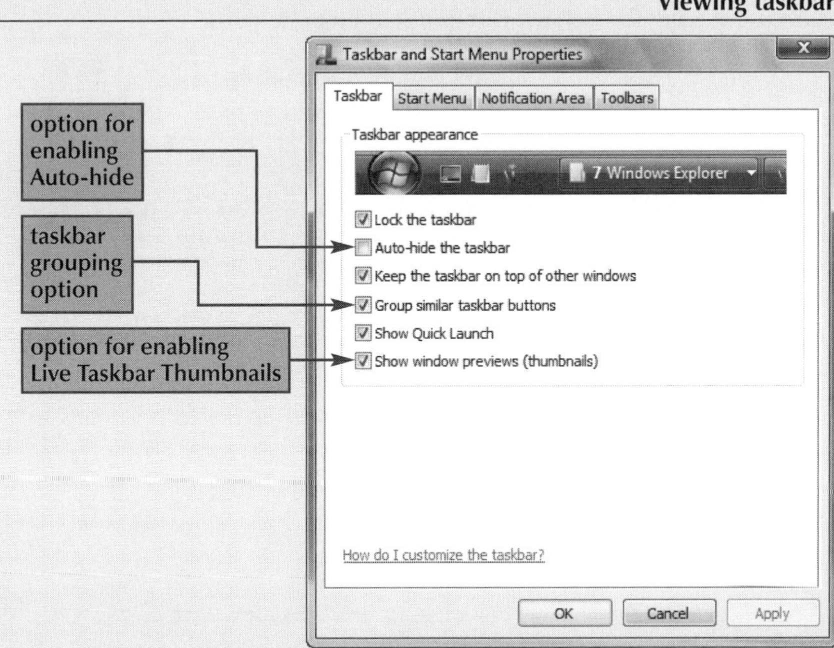

2. Click the **Notification Area** tab. From this property sheet, you can customize the display of icons in the notification area and decide which system icons you want to display in the notification area. See Figure 2-23.

Figure 2-23 Viewing notification area settings

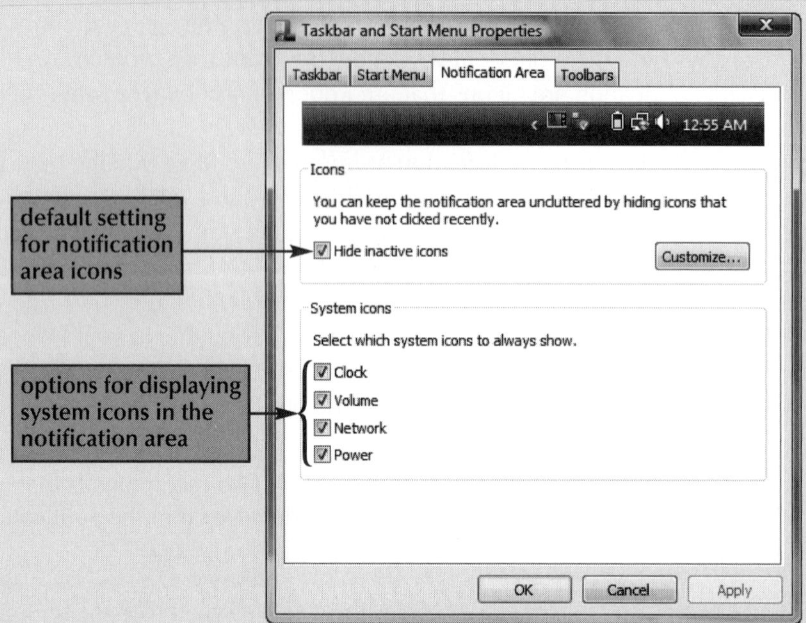

3. Click the **Customize** button. In the Customize Notification Icons dialog box, you can change the behavior of notification area icons. See Figure 2-24. Icons are grouped into two categories: Current Items and Past Items. The default behavior is to hide icons when inactive. If you want to change the behavior of an icon, you first select the icon by clicking it, you click the Icon Behavior button to its right and choose "Hide when inactive," Hide (to always hide the icon), or Show (to always show the icon).

Figure 2-24 Options for customizing the behavior of notification area icons

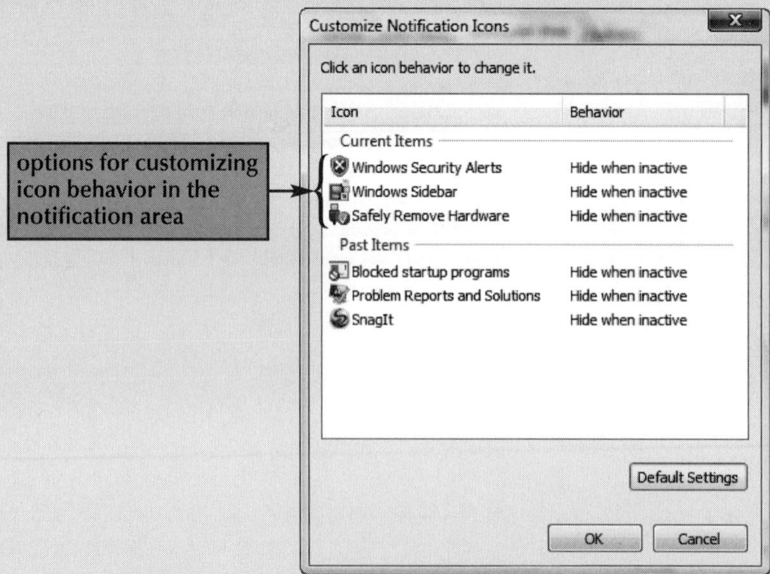

4. In the Current Items list, click **Windows Sidebar**, click the **Behavior** list button to its right, click **Show**, click the **OK** button in the Customize Notification Icons dialog box, and then click the **OK** button in the Taskbar and Start Menu Properties dialog box to apply this new setting.

5. Use the Computer desktop icon to open the Computer window, and then maximize the Computer window.
6. Click the **Windows Sidebar** icon in the notification area. Windows Vista displays the Windows Sidebar in front of the Computer window. See Figure 2-25. Now you have access to any of the gadgets available on the Windows Sidebar.

Figure 2-25 Displaying the Windows Sidebar in the foreground

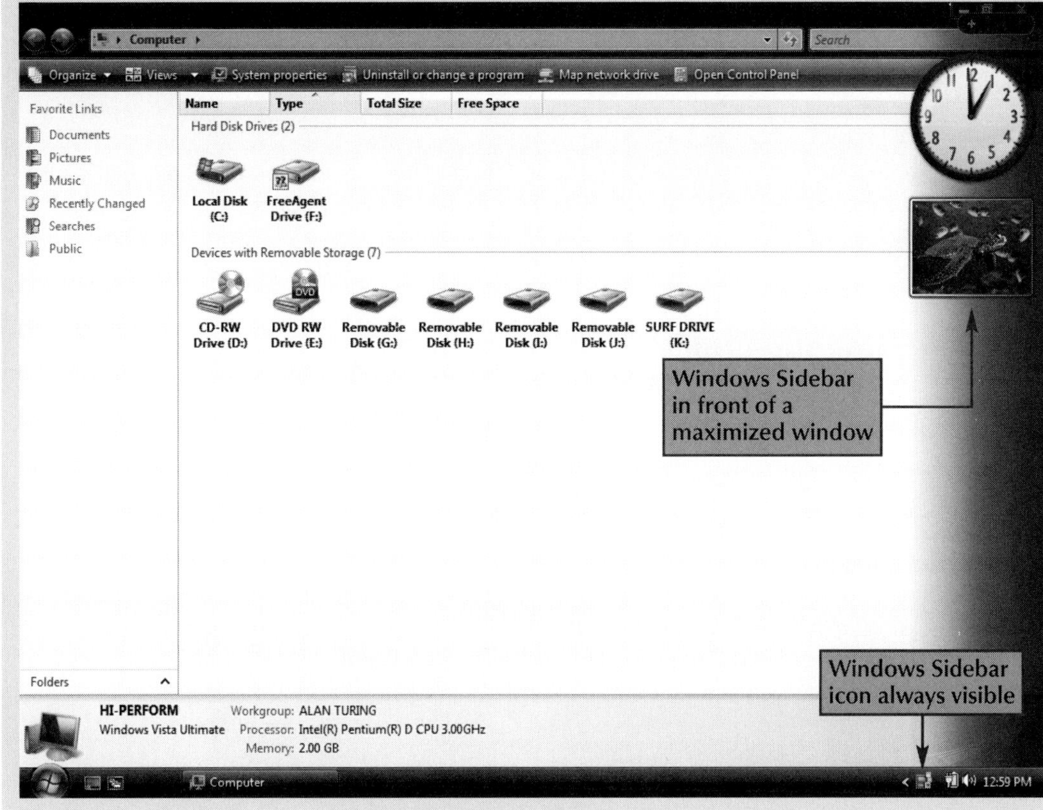

7. Click the **Computer** taskbar button to bring the Computer window to the foreground, and then close the Computer window.

Taking Advantage of the Notification Area | InSight

To view hidden notification area icons, you can click the "Show hidden icons" button on the left side of the notification area. The "Show hidden icons" button then changes to a Hide button. Switching between showing and hiding icons is useful if you only need to access a notification area icon on an occasional basis. However, if you access the same notification area icon frequently, changing its behavior so that it is always shown can save you time and effort. Plus, you may want to hide certain notification area icons you never use or that take up space on the taskbar.

Reference Window | Customizing the Taskbar and Notification Area

- Right-click the taskbar, click Properties on the Taskbar shortcut menu, examine and change any options for customizing the appearance of the taskbar on the Taskbar property sheet, and then click the Apply button to immediately apply the changes.
- Click the Notification Area tab and choose which system icons you want to display in the notification area.
- If you want to change the behavior of inactive icons in the notification area, make sure there is a check mark in the "Hide inactive icons" check box, click the Customize button, and in the Customize Notification Icons dialog box, select an icon in the Current Items list, click the Icon Behavior button to the right of the selected icon, click Hide when inactive, Hide (to always hide the icon), or Show (to always show the icon), and then repeat this same process for any other icon you want to customize.
- Click the OK button to close the Customized Notification Icons dialog box, and then click the OK button in the Taskbar and Start Menu Properties dialog box to apply the settings you have changed.

Customizing the Quick Launch Toolbar

The Quick Launch toolbar contains the Show desktop button for displaying the desktop and the "Switch between windows" button for switching to Windows Flip 3D view if your computer supports Windows Aero. You may also have a Launch Internet Explorer Browser button for opening Internet Explorer. You can use the Show Desktop button not only to minimize all open windows but also to reopen and restore all minimized windows.

Kenyetta Iverson, a staff scientist at Kimbrough & Co., wants to set up her computer so that she can quickly open the Documents and Pictures folders from the application window where she records and analyzes her scientific measurements. Alejandro recommends that you show Kenyetta how to customize her Quick Launch toolbar.

To customize the Quick Launch toolbar:

1. If the Quick Launch toolbar does not appear on the left side of the taskbar, right-click the **taskbar**, point to **Toolbars** on the taskbar shortcut menu, and then click **Quick Launch**. Windows Vista displays the Quick Launch toolbar on the left side of the taskbar to the right of the Start button.
2. Right-click the **taskbar**, and if you see a check mark next to "Lock the Taskbar," click **Lock the Taskbar** on the taskbar shortcut menu. If there is no check mark next to "Lock the Taskbar," press the **Esc** key to close the taskbar shortcut menu. After you unlock the taskbar, you can adjust the width of the Quick Launch toolbar.
3. Open the **Start menu** and drag **Documents** from the Start menu to the right side of the Quick Launch toolbar. Windows Vista creates a Documents shortcut on the Quick Launch toolbar. See Figure 2-26. Unlike other types of shortcuts, Windows Vista does not display the shortcut arrow as part of the icon because of its small size. (The same applies to shortcuts on the All Programs menus and menus for group folders.) If a toolbar is not wide enough to display all the available options on the toolbar, you may not see the Documents shortcut or other Quick Launch toolbar shortcuts. Under these conditions, Windows Vista displays a pop-up menu button on the right side of the toolbar. You can use the pop-up menu button to display the other options available on this toolbar, or you can complete the next step to widen your Quick Launch toolbar so that it shows all the options.

Tip

To add a shortcut to a program on the All Programs menu or recently open programs list, right-click the program and choose Add to Quick Launch.

Figure 2-26 Customizing the Quick Launch toolbar

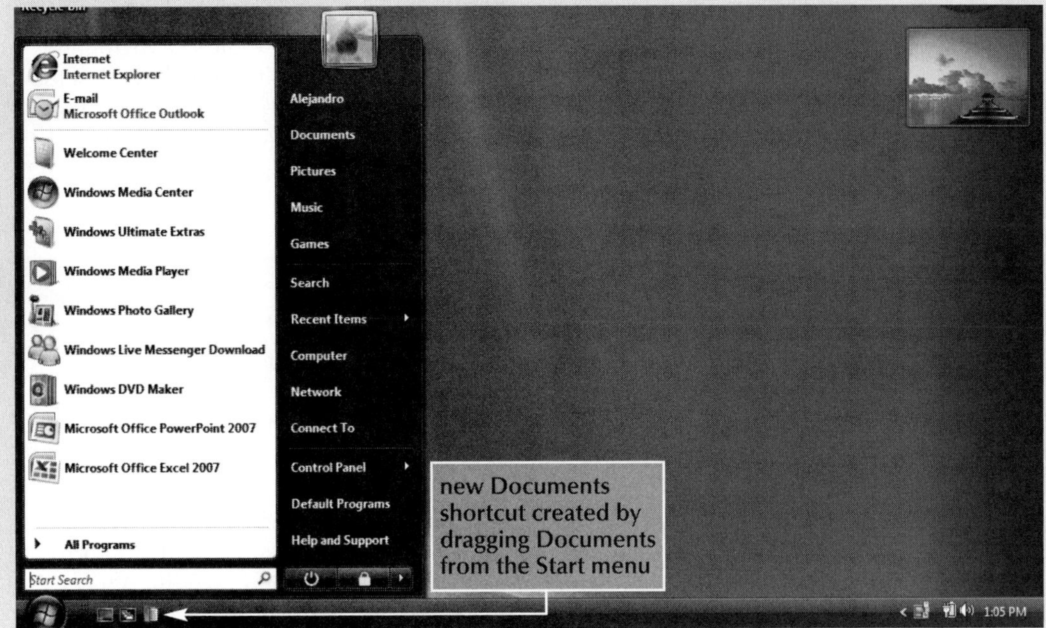

4. If the Quick Launch toolbar displays a pop-up menu button, point to the **right resizing border** of the Quick Launch toolbar, drag it to the right until Windows Vista displays all the icons on the Quick Launch toolbar, and then drag it slightly more to the right so that you have enough space to add other shortcuts.
5. Point to the **Documents** icon on the Quick Launch toolbar and let the mouse pointer rest on it until Windows Vista displays a ToolTip. The ToolTip shows the actual icon name: Documents – Shortcut
6. Open the **Start menu** and drag **Pictures** to the right of the Documents icon on the Quick Launch toolbar. Windows Vista adds a Pictures shortcut on the Quick Launch toolbar. After you place a shortcut on the Quick Launch toolbar, you can drag it to a more convenient position on this toolbar and rearrange shortcut icons to make it easier to locate them.
7. Drag the **Pictures — Shortcut** icon on the Quick Launch toolbar and drag it to the left of the Documents icon on the Quick Launch toolbar.

Now that you have placed these shortcuts on your Quick Launch toolbar, you can quickly open these windows from the Quick Launch toolbar.

To test the new shortcuts you placed on the Quick Launch toolbar:

1. Click the **Pictures — Shortcut** icon on the Quick Launch toolbar. Windows Vista opens the Pictures window.
2. Click the **Documents — Shortcut** icon on the Quick Launch toolbar. Windows Vista opens the Documents window.
3. Close the Documents and Pictures windows.

Like any other object, you can customize a toolbar using its shortcut menu. For example, you can right-click the background or left side of the Quick Launch toolbar to display a shortcut menu that contains options for showing large icons instead of small icons (the default), for showing the title of the toolbar (for example, Quick Launch), and for showing a text label of each icon (for example, "Show desktop" for the Show desktop icon). However, the latter two options take up too much horizontal space on the taskbar to be useful. From the Quick Launch toolbar shortcut menu, you can open the Quick Launch folder so that you work directly with the shortcuts on this toolbar. You can also close the Quick Launch toolbar.

Reference Window | Adding a Documents Shortcut to the Quick Launch Toolbar

- If there is no Quick Launch toolbar on the left side of the taskbar, right-click the taskbar, point to Toolbars, and then click Quick Launch.
- Right-click the taskbar, and if you see a check mark next to "Lock the Taskbar," then click Lock the Taskbar on the taskbar shortcut menu. If there is no check mark next to "Lock the Taskbar," press the Esc key to close the taskbar shortcut menu.
- Open the Start menu and drag Documents to a position on the Quick Launch toolbar.
- If the Quick Launch toolbar displays a pop-up menu button, point to the right resizing border of the Quick Launch toolbar and drag it to the right until Windows Vista displays all the icons on the Quick Launch toolbar.

InSight | Using the Quick Launch Toolbar to Work Smart

The Quick Launch toolbar is one of the most useful and easily accessible toolbars in Windows Vista. You can improve its usefulness by adding to the toolbar shortcuts to frequently used programs, folders, files, and Web sites. After you log on your user account and see the desktop, you can use the Quick Launch toolbar shortcuts to quickly access the programs, folders, documents, and Web sites that you use every day and to start your e-mail software to check your messages.

Creating a Desktop Toolbar

You can place a toolbar on the desktop that contains shortcuts to tools, programs, and folders that you frequently use on your computer. Windows Vista creates the desktop toolbar from a folder that contains shortcuts, actual folders, or actual files when you drag the folder to one side of the desktop.

Alejandro offers to step you through the process for creating and customizing this type of toolbar. He also recommends that you temporarily close the Windows Sidebar so that you can create the toolbar on the right side of the desktop where you have more space available.

To close the Windows Sidebar and create a desktop toolbar:

1. Right-click the **Windows Sidebar** icon in the notification area, click **Exit**, and in the Windows Sidebar dialog box, click the **Exit Sidebar** button. Windows Vista closes the Windows Sidebar.
2. Right-click the **desktop**, point to **New**, click **Folder**, and after Windows Vista creates the new folder, type **Shortcuts** for the folder name, and then press the **Enter** key. Windows Vista creates a new, empty desktop folder called Shortcuts.

Tip

You can also use this same technique to close the programs for other notification area icons.

3. Drag the **Shortcuts** folder icon to the far right side of the desktop, and then release the left mouse button. Windows Vista creates a Shortcuts toolbar. See Figure 2-27.

   Trouble? If you do not see a Shortcuts toolbar like the one shown in Figure 2-27, repeat this step but move your mouse pointer as far to the right as possible.

Figure 2-27 New Shortcuts desktop toolbar

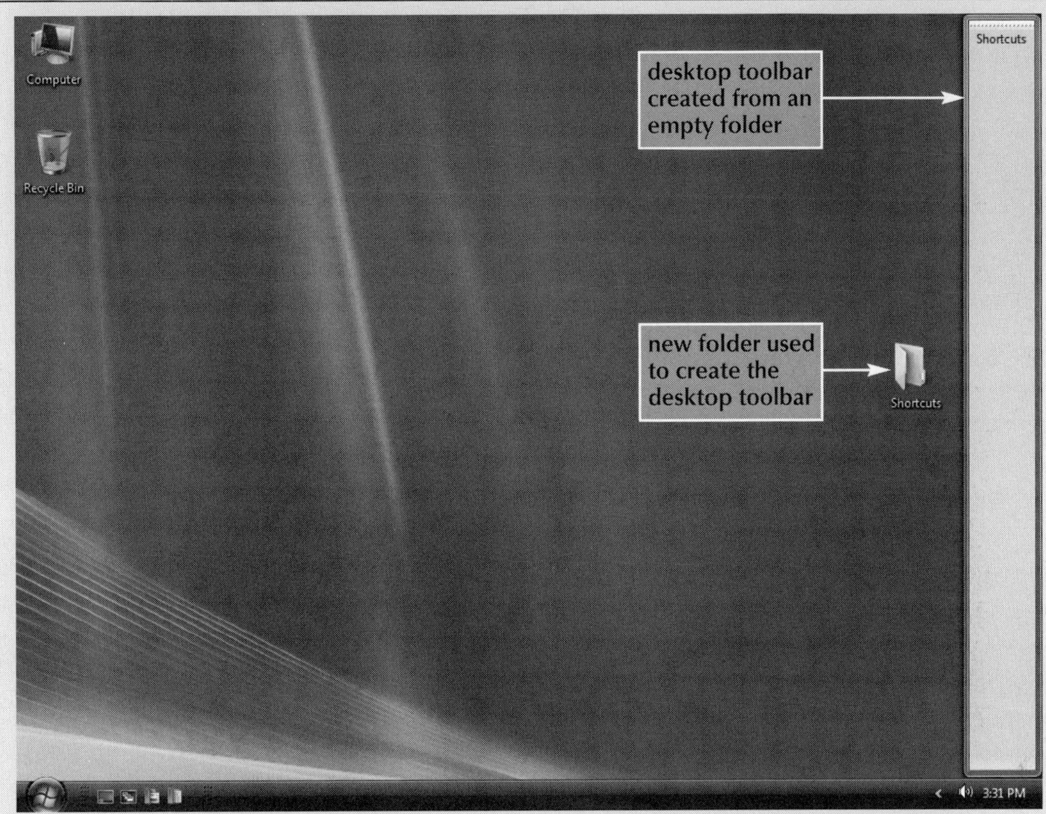

4. Open the **Start menu**, and then drag **Documents** from the Start menu to the Shortcuts toolbar. Windows Vista creates a Documents shortcut on the Shortcuts toolbar.

5. From the Start menu, drag **Pictures**, **Music**, **Recent Items**, **Control Panel**, and **Help and Support** to the Shortcuts toolbar. Windows Vista creates shortcuts to each of these Start menu items and adds them to the Shortcuts toolbar. See Figure 2-28. When you point to a shortcut on the toolbar, Windows Vista displays the option as a button on the toolbar.

   Trouble? If you find that you cannot drag Recent Items to the Shortcuts toolbar, close the Start menu, open the Start menu again, and quickly point to and drag Recent Items to the Shortcuts toolbar before Windows Vista displays a cascading submenu.

Figure 2-28 Customized Shortcuts desktop toolbar

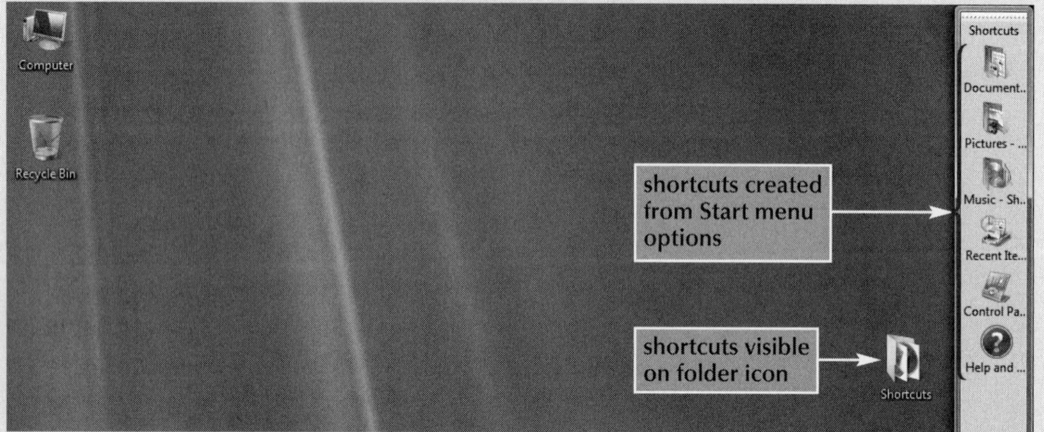

6. Click the **Help and Support** icon on the Shortcuts toolbar. Windows Vista opens Help and Support.
7. Close the Help and Support window, and then click the **Recent Items** icon on the Shortcuts toolbar. Windows Vista opens the Recent Items folder where Windows Vista stores shortcuts to all the folders and files you've recently opened. You can click one of these shortcuts to go directly to a folder or to open a file.
8. Close the Recent Items window.

You can right-click a shortcut on the toolbar and choose the option to rename or delete a shortcut. If you rename a shortcut, you can use a shorter name that is more easily visible on the Shortcuts toolbar. You can also close the Shortcuts folder bar, and then create the toolbar again later.

To close the Shortcuts toolbar and redisplay the Windows Sidebar:

1. Right-click **Shortcuts** at the top of the Shortcuts toolbar, and then click **Close Toolbar**.
2. In the Confirm Toolbar Close dialog box, click the **OK** button. Windows Vista closes the Shortcuts toolbar. However, the Shortcuts folder remains on the desktop. If you open it, you see all the shortcuts that you created for this toolbar. (It's a regular folder.) You can add more shortcuts directly to this folder, and the next time you display the Shortcuts toolbar, it includes any new shortcuts.
3. To remove the Shortcuts folder from your desktop, right-click the **Shortcuts** folder icon, click **Delete**, and in the Delete Folder dialog box, click the **Yes** button.
4. To restore your Windows Sidebar, click the **Start** button on the taskbar, point to **All Programs**, click **Accessories**, and then click **Windows Sidebar**.

If you already have a folder or a shortcut to a folder on the desktop, you can drag it to one side of the desktop to create a desktop toolbar for that folder, and then you have access to the contents of the folder from the toolbar. If you close a desktop toolbar, you can drag the folder icon for the desktop toolbar to one edge of the desktop and Windows Vista will create the desktop toolbar again.

Creating a Folder Toolbar | Reference Window

- Right-click the desktop, point to New, click Folder, and after Windows Vista creates a new folder, type a name for the folder, and then press the Enter key.
- Drag the new folder's icon to one side of the desktop, and then release the left mouse button to create a folder toolbar.
- Open the Start menu, and then drag icons for Windows tools (such as Help and Support), icons for programs (such as Microsoft Word), icons for folders (such as Documents), and file icons to the new desktop toolbar.
- To temporarily close a desktop toolbar, right-click the toolbar name, click Close Toolbar, and in the Confirm Toolbar Close dialog box, click the OK button.
- To redisplay the desktop toolbar, drag the folder icon on the desktop to one side of the desktop.

You can also create other toolbars for specific folders on your computer so that you can quickly access the subfolders and files within those folders. For example, you might create a toolbar for the Documents folder (or one of its subfolders that you frequently use), the Pictures folder, or the Videos folder, or you can create a toolbar for the Computer window so that you can access specific drives in your computer more quickly. To create these types of toolbars, right-click the taskbar, point to Toolbars, choose New Toolbar, and then choose a folder. For these types of toolbars, shortcuts to the contents of the folder window would easily exceed the amount of space available on your taskbar, so you would limit the size of the toolbar to just the toolbar's name (i.e., Documents or Computer), and then use the pop-up menu button » to quickly access a subfolder or file in the Documents folder or a drive in the Computer folder. If you point to a folder on the toolbar's pop-up menu, you access subfolders and specific files from cascading submenus. That means you do not have to open window after window as you navigate to locate a subfolder or file.

Session 2.2 Quick Check | Review

1. True or False? Windows Vista automatically sorts newly installed programs and group folders on the All Programs menu.
2. You can customize certain Start menu options, such as the Control Panel, as either ________________ or as ________________ .
3. Windows Vista uses ____ to combine taskbar buttons for similar types of windows into one button.
4. True or False? If your computer supports Windows Aero and you do not see Live Taskbar Thumbnails, you can enable this setting on the Taskbar property sheet.
5. True or False? You cannot change the behavior of icons in the notification area.
6. A(n) ________________ is a toolbar that appears on one side of the desktop and contains shortcuts to tools, programs, and folders that you frequently use on your computer.

Session 2.3

Adjusting the Resolution, Color Depth, and Refresh Rate

One of the important characteristics of your monitor is its **resolution**, or the sharpness of the image that appears on the monitor. Your monitor's resolution is expressed by a combination of two numbers, such as 1680 by 1050. The first number refers to the number of pixels displayed across the width of your monitor, and the second number refers to the number of pixels displayed down its length. Therefore, at a resolution of 1680 by 1050, the video display adapter displays 1680 pixels across the width of the screen and 1050 pixels down the screen. If you multiply 1680 by 1050, you'll find that an image displayed on the monitor at this resolution is composed of 1,764,000 pixels. Also, LCD (Liquid Crystal Display) monitors, or flat panel displays, have a preset resolution called the **native resolution** which is the best resolution for the monitor. The native resolution is set by the manufacturer, and it is typically the highest resolution available for a specific type of monitor.

You can increase or decrease the resolution of your video display. For example, you might set your video display to a lower resolution, such as 1024 by 768, and elements of the graphical user interface then appear larger and easier to see; however, the sharpness of the image on the monitor decreases because the video display adapter displays fewer pixels, and they are larger in size. Furthermore, the desktop appears smaller, and there's less room on the desktop for shortcuts and other objects, such as dialog boxes. If you set your video display to a higher resolution, such as 1680 by 1050, the sharpness of the image on the monitor increases because the video display adapter displays more pixels, and they are smaller in size. While the size of your desktop increases and there is more room on the desktop, elements of the graphical user interface become smaller and more difficult to see.

Another important feature of an image is its aspect ratio. The **aspect ratio** compares the width of an image displayed on a monitor to its height. Newer computer monitors and High Definition TVs (HDTV) in the United States (and certain other countries) use an aspect ratio of 16:9. A **16:9 aspect ratio** means that the image on the monitor is 1.78 times wider than it is tall (16 / 9 = 1.78), or almost twice as wide. In contrast, older TVs and older computer monitors displayed images using an aspect ratio of 4:3. With a **4:3 aspect ratio**, the image is only 1.33 times wider than it was high (4 / 3 = 1.33), closer to a square image in appearance. The resolution that you use determines whether the video display adapter displays the image at an aspect ratio of 16:9 or 4:3, examples of which are shown in Figure 2-29. If you switch to a resolution that changes to a different ratio of the number of pixels for the width and height of the monitor, certain desktop elements, such as the Windows Sidebar clocks, may exhibit distortion. Also, if you use an aspect ratio of 4:3 on a widescreen monitor, the image does not fill the width of the monitor. Instead, you see a black background on the left and right sides of a centered image. If you switch to a resolution that uses an aspect ratio of 16:9, the image fills the entire width of the widescreen monitor. (The computer used for figures in this book is set for a lower resolution of 1024 x 768 so that the details of the image are visible in the printed book.)

Examples of resolutions with total number of pixels and aspect ratios

Figure 2-29

Resolution	Number of Pixels	Aspect Ratio
800 x 600	480,000	4:3
1024 x 768	786,432	4:3
1088 x 612	665,856	16:9
1152 x 648	746,496	16:9
1152 x 684	787,968	16:9
1152 x 864	995,328	4:3
1176 x 664	780,864	16:9
1216 x 684	831,744	16:9
1280 x 720	921,600	16:9
1280 x 768	983,040	16:9
1280 x 800	1,024,000	16:9
1280 x 1024	1,310,720	4:3
1360 x 768	1,044,480	16:9
1680 x 1050	1,764,000	16:9

In addition to controlling resolution, you can typically set your video display adapter to use one of two **color depth** settings, each of which determines the maximum number of colors used to compose an onscreen image. A Medium (16 bit) color depth setting means that your video display adapter uses 16 bits to display 65,536 colors. The "16 bit" refers to the number of bits used by the video adapter to define individual colors. With 16 bits, there are a maximum of 2^{16} or 65,536 possible combinations of 0 (zero) and 1. As you may already know, the 0 (zero) and 1 are the only two digits used in the binary numbering system. By combining 16 of these 0s and 1s in different ways, you can produce 65,536 codes, each of which uniquely defines a color. With the Highest (32 bit) color depth setting, your video display adapter can use 24 bits to display 16,777,216 colors (or approximately 16.8 million colors). The other 8 bits (24 bits + 8 bits = 32 bits) supports transparency. Windows XP referred to the Medium (16 bit) color depth setting as **High Color** and the Highest (32 bit) color depth setting as **True Color** (whether it used just 24 bits or 32 bits). Windows Aero requires a color depth setting of 32 bits.

Peter Nuri, another staff scientist, analyzes models of the molecular structure and intermolecular forces of new chemical compounds on his computer and wants to improve the resolution and color of these models. Alejandro asks you to help Peter determine the best resolution and color setting for his work.

To view and adjust your computer's resolution:

1. Right-click the desktop, click **Personalize**, and when the Personalization window opens, click **Display Settings**. Windows Vista opens the Display Settings dialog box. See Figure 2-30. The computer used for this figure has a video adapter card that currently uses a nonnative screen resolution of 1024 by 768 and a color setting of Highest (32 bit) for True Color (for screen captures for this book). Yours will differ.

Tip

If you right-click the desktop, the shortcut menu may provide an option for customizing settings for your specific monitor model.

Figure 2-30 Viewing monitor display settings

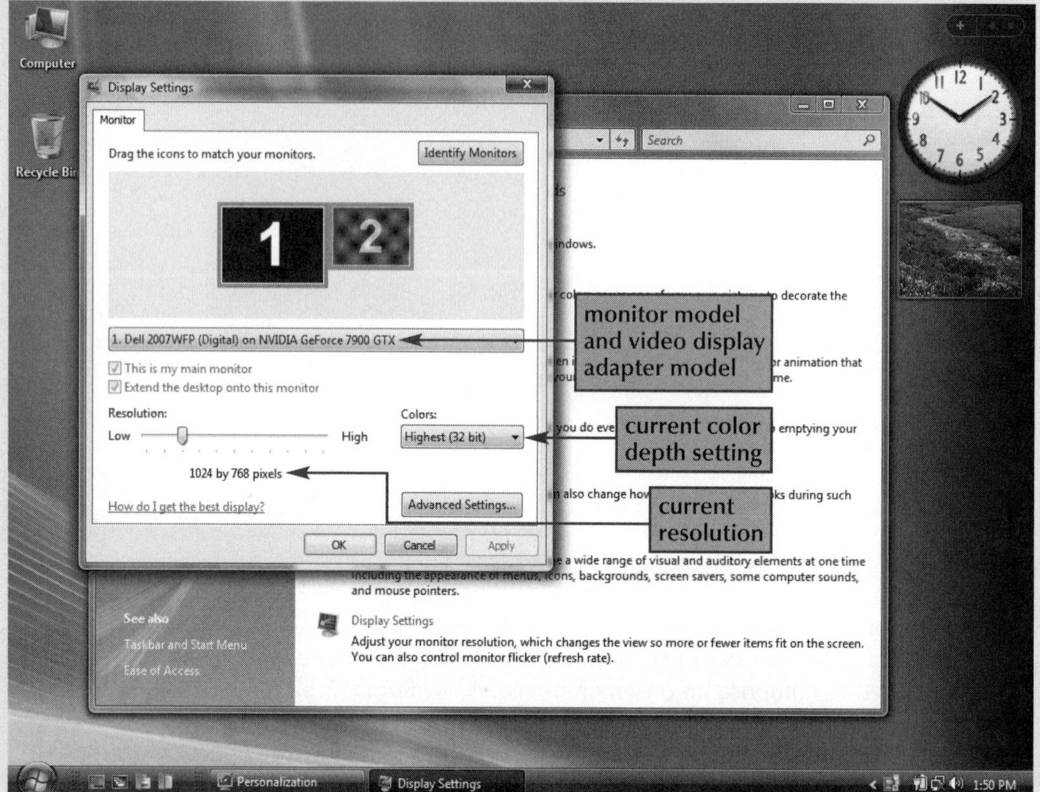

2. Note the current resolution and color depth setting on your computer so that you can restore these settings later.

3. Drag the **Resolution** slider tab right to the highest resolution.

   Trouble? If your monitor is already set to the highest resolution possible, drag the slider tab left one notch to the next lower resolution.

4. Click the **Apply** button. Windows Vista resizes the desktop and opens a Display Settings dialog box so that you can choose whether to keep the new setting. If you wait 15 seconds, Windows Vista will restore your previous resolution. This option is useful if you encounter an unexpected problem.

5. Click the **Yes** button in the Display Settings dialog box to apply your new resolution. On the computer used in Figure 2-31, the screen resolution increased to 1680 by 1050, the native resolution for this monitor. The desktop increased in size; however, desktop icons, taskbar buttons, notification area icons, Windows Sidebar gadgets, the dialog box, and the window decreased in size. Plus, the text shown for icon titles and taskbar buttons, as well as text in dialog boxes and windows, is smaller and more difficult to read. If you compare Figure 2-31 with Figure 2-30, it becomes immediately obvious how a change in resolution affects your desktop view.

Figure 2-31 Viewing the desktop at a higher resolution

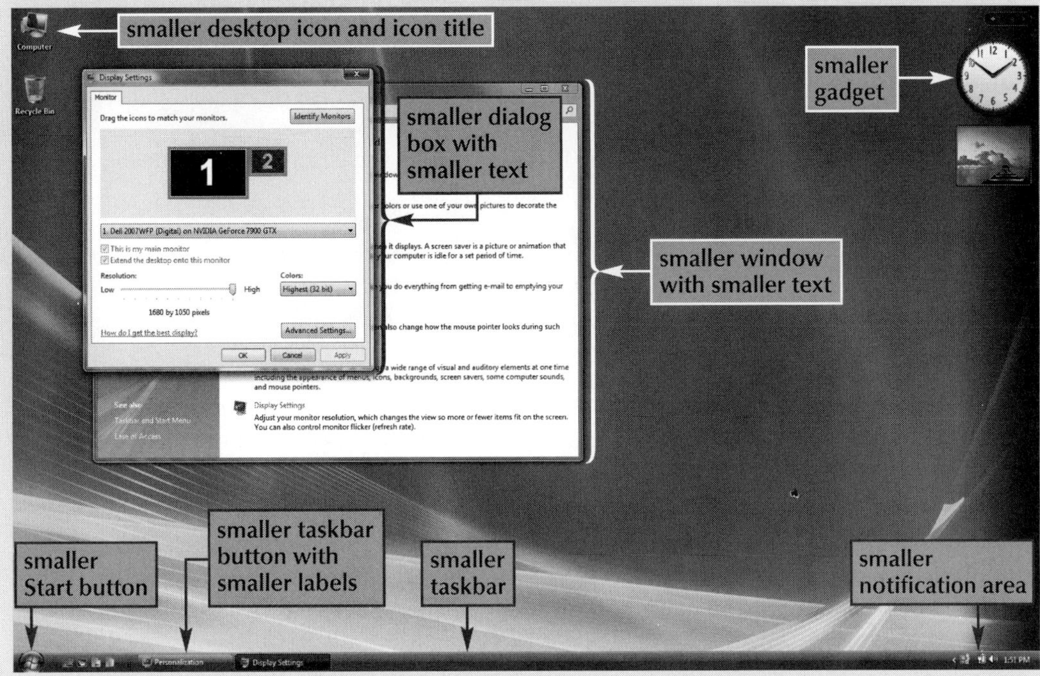

6. To restore your previous or native resolution, drag the **Resolution** slider tab back to your previous or native resolution, click the **Apply** button, and then click the **Yes** button in the Display Settings dialog box.
7. Keep the Display Settings dialog box open.

Using Your Monitor's Built-in Menu | InSight

For certain resolutions, you can use your monitor's built-in menu on the front of the monitor itself to further adjust your display settings and, if necessary, eliminate distortion. For example, your default monitor display setting might be Fill (the image fills the entire monitor), with two other options under a setting called Wide Mode, such as 4:3 (for a ratio of 1.33) and 1:1 (that keeps the same ratio of width to height), both of which can change the ratio of the image and reduce distortion; however, the image does not fill the complete monitor. You may also want to use your monitor's built-in menu to adjust brightness, color settings, image mode settings (for example, Desktop Mode, Multimedia Mode, and Gaming Mode), and other display settings and to specify the input source for the image.

You may want to experiment with the different resolutions available for your video display and perhaps also test different built-in display settings for your monitor with different resolutions to locate the best display settings for your work and play.

Reference Window | Changing the Resolution

- Right-click the desktop, click Personalize, and after the Personalization window opens, click Display Settings.
- Note the current resolution on your computer so that you can restore this setting.
- Drag the slider tab on the slider bar in the Resolution area to another resolution you want to try.
- Click the Apply button, and then click the Yes button in the Display Settings dialog box to apply this new setting.
- To restore your previous or native resolution, drag the slider tab on the slider bar in the Resolution area back to your previous or native resolution, click the Apply button, and then click the Yes button in the Display Settings dialog box.
- Close the Display Settings dialog box and Personalization window.

The color depth setting also determines the final quality of your monitor's image. You can change the color depth setting using the Colors button in the Display Settings dialog box.

To view and change the color setting:

1. Click the **Show desktop** button on the Quick Launch toolbar to minimize all windows and dialog boxes, and then examine the quality of the image displayed on the desktop.
2. Click the **Display Settings** taskbar button to restore the Display Settings dialog box.
3. Click the **Colors** list button. Windows Vista lists the color depth settings available for your video display adapter. See Figure 2-32. The computer used for this figure has two color depth settings: Medium (16 bit) for High Color and Highest (32 bit) for True Color. Yours may differ.

Figure 2-32 Viewing color depth options

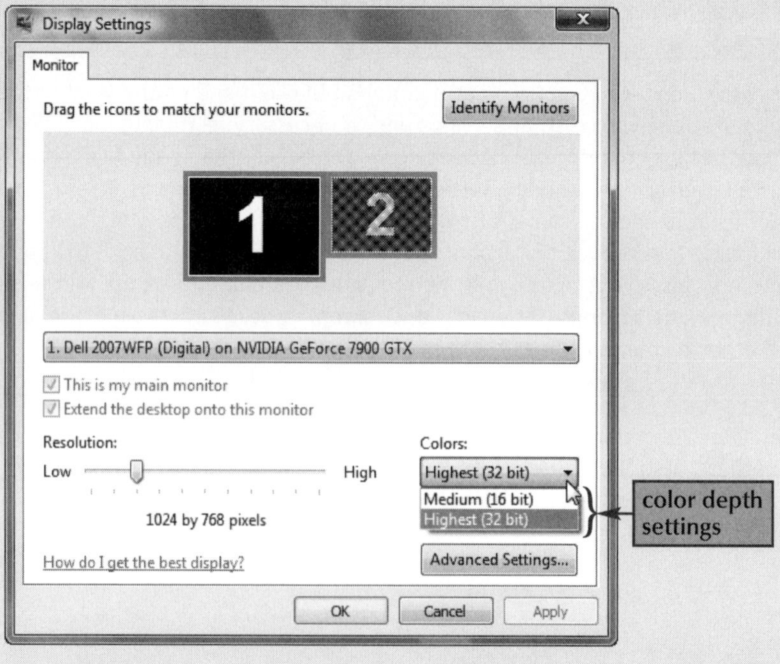

4. In the Colors list, click the next lower color depth setting (or next higher color depth setting) for your computer, click the **Apply** button, click the **Yes** button in the Display Settings dialog box, click the **Show desktop** button on the Quick Launch toolbar to minimize all windows and dialog boxes, and then examine the quality of the desktop background image, desktop icons, and the Display Settings dialog box itself. If you take a close look at the image, you should see a decrease in the quality of the image. On the computer used for Figure 2-33, the desktop background image appears "washed out." Also, desktop icons appear less sharp and exhibit a stair step effect, or jaggies, along the sides of desktop icons. On the computer used for this figure, Windows Vista switched from the Windows Aero color scheme to the Windows Vista Basic color scheme. Therefore, windows, dialog boxes, and the taskbar are no longer transparent. Also, other Windows Aero features, such as Live Taskbar Thumbnails, Windows Flip, and Windows Flip 3D no longer work at all or in the same way.

Figure 2-33 Desktop viewed at lower color depth setting

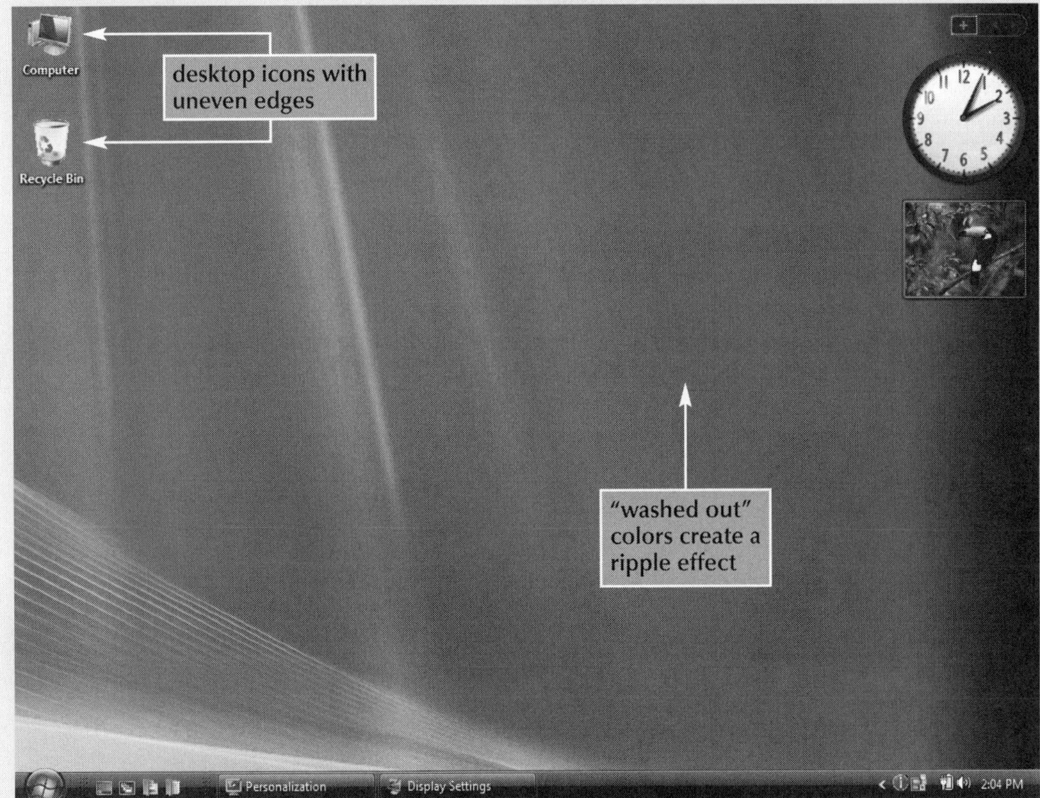

5. To restore your color depth setting, click the **Display Settings** taskbar button to restore the Display Settings dialog box, click the **Colors** list button in the Display Settings dialog box, click the original color depth setting for your computer, click the **Apply** button, and then click the **Yes** button in the Display Settings dialog box. On the computer used for the previous figure, Windows Vista switched from the Windows Vista Basic color scheme back to the Windows Aero color scheme. Then, Windows Aero features, such as Windows Flip, Windows Flip 3D, and live taskbar thumbnails, were immediately available.

6. Keep the Display Settings dialog box open for the next section of the tutorial.

If your computer supports Windows Aero, you will need to keep your color depth setting at 32 bits.

Reference Window | Changing the Color Depth Setting

- Right-click the desktop, click Personalize, and after the Personalization window opens, click Display Settings.
- Click the Colors list button, click the color depth setting that you want to use, click the OK button, and then click the Yes button in the Display Settings dialog box.

Another setting that you can control on a computer is the refresh rate. The **refresh rate** refers to the number of times per second that the image on the screen is redrawn by the video card. If you are using an older television-style **CRT** (**cathode-ray tube**) monitor and if the refresh rate is too low, the image on the monitor will flicker and that flicker will make it difficult to work with the monitor. In fact, it can create persistent headaches. It is generally recommended that you work with a refresh rate of 75 Hz (Hertz) or slightly higher on CRT monitors. Most people cannot detect flicker on CRT monitors at refresh rates above 75 Hz. However, because individuals differ in their ability to perceive flicker, it is a good idea to test settings in the range of 75 to 85 Hz. It serves no purpose to increase the refresh rate to very high values because it is not likely that your eyes can detect flicker at these rates. Also, a higher than needed refresh rate might result in a drop in resolution or color depth because the video display adapter might not support all combinations of resolutions, color depths, and refresh rates.

While the refresh rate is more important for users of CRT monitors and typically not a problem with LCD monitors, the refresh rate still remains important if your computer supports Windows Aero and you have an LCD monitor. Windows Aero requires that the refresh rate be above 10 Hz (a rather low value).

Before he leaves for his next appointment, Alejandro decides to show you how to check the refresh rate of your LCD monitor to make sure it meets the minimum standard required of Windows Aero. In the process, you will examine some other video display settings.

To examine other video display settings and check the refresh rate:

Tip

Your Advanced Settings dialog box may have a property sheet for customizing display settings for your particular video display adapter.

1. On the Monitor tab in the Display Settings dialog box, click the **Advanced Settings** button. Windows Vista opens the Properties dialog box for your monitor and video display adapter, with the Adapter property sheet in the foreground. See Figure 2-34. The Adapter property sheet has information about your video display adapter, including the total available graphics memory, dedicated video memory, system video memory, and shared system memory (all of which are important to the use of Windows Aero under Windows Vista). On the computer used for this figure, the dedicated video memory, or the total memory available on the video display card itself, is 512 MB.

Figure 2-34 Viewing video display adapter settings

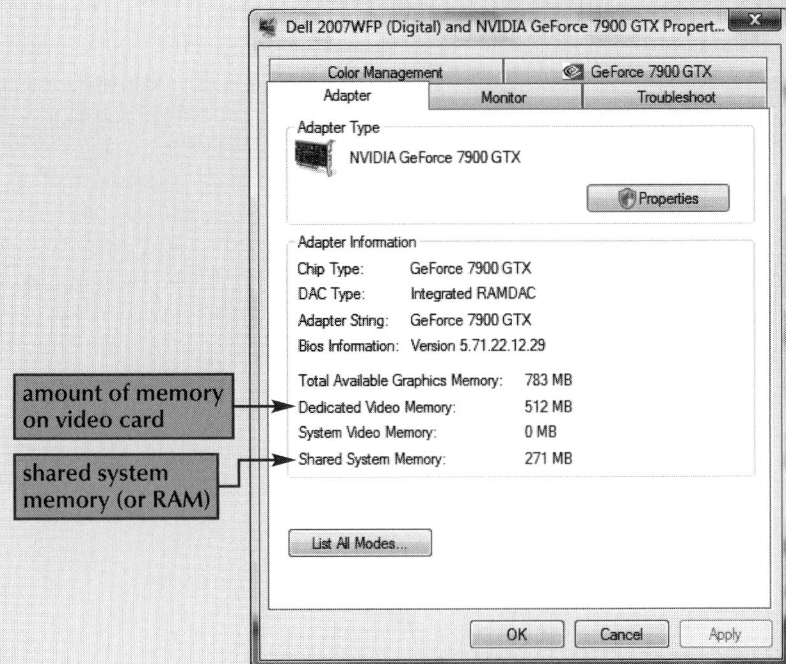

2. Click the **Monitor** tab. On the Monitor property sheet, Windows Vista identifies the monitor type and displays the current screen refresh rate in the Monitor Settings section. See Figure 2-35. On the computer used for this figure, the refresh rate is set to 75 Hertz, well above that required to support Windows Aero on this computer. In this same section, Windows Vista automatically enables the option for hiding refresh rates that are not supported by your monitor. Windows Vista warns you that if you turn off this option and choose a refresh rate that the monitor cannot support, you run the risk of an unusable display or damaged hardware.

Figure 2-35 Viewing the screen refresh rate setting

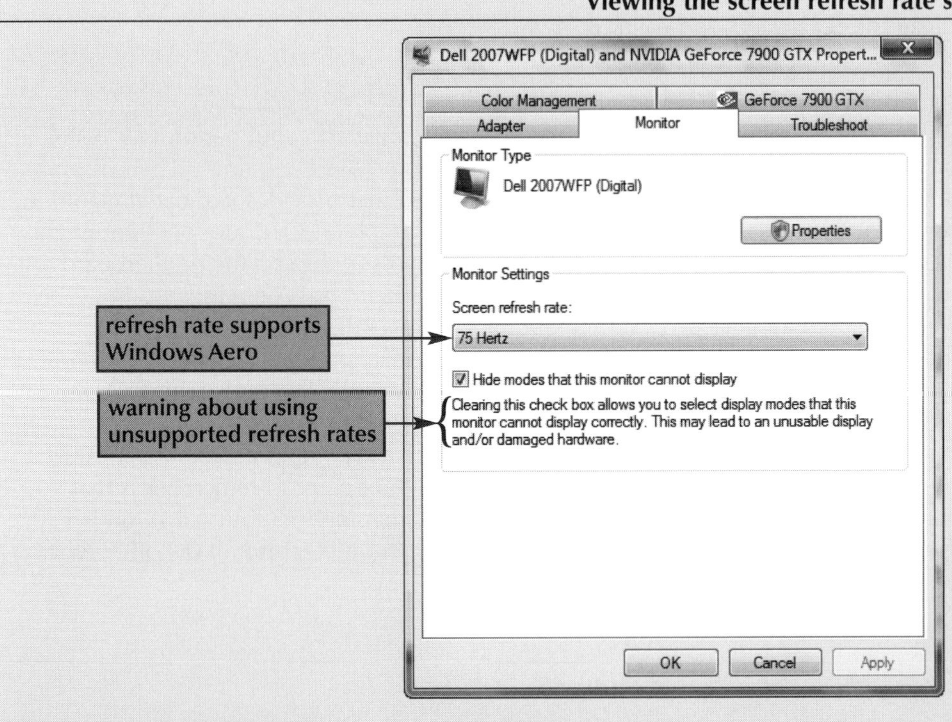

3. Click the **Screen refresh rate** list button to view other screen refresh rates supported by your monitor. On the computer used for the previous figure, only one other refresh rate is supported, namely, 60 Hertz.

4. Click the **Adapter** tab, and then click the **List All Modes** button. In the List All Modes dialog box, Windows Vista lists all combinations of resolutions, color settings, and refresh rates that are supported on your computer. See Figure 2-36. Your settings might differ. If you examine this list, you will discover screen resolutions lower than those available in the Display Settings dialog box, such as 640 × 480, 720 × 480, and 720 × 576, as well as intermediate resolutions, such as 848 × 480, which are also not available in the Display Settings dialog box. You will also find color depth settings, such as 256 colors, that are not available in the Colors list box. If you choose one of the modes in the List All Modes dialog box, Windows Vista will apply all three settings at once and adjust the resolution, color depth, and refresh rate in one step.

Figure 2-36 **Viewing a list of valid display modes**

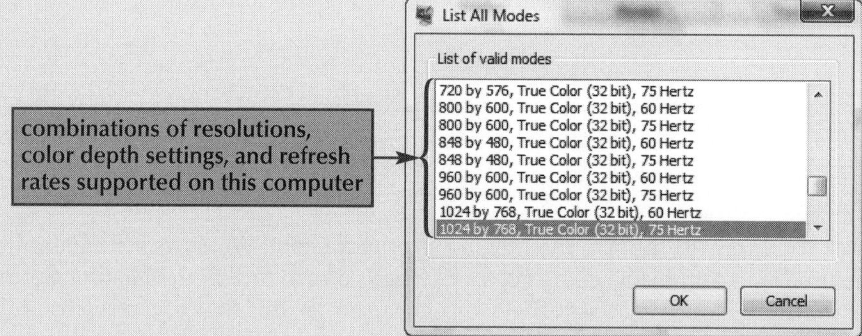

5. Click the **Cancel** button to close the List All Modes dialog box without making changes, click the **Cancel** button to close the Properties dialog box for your monitor and video display adapter without inadvertently making any changes that you might not want, and then click the **Cancel** button to close the Display Settings dialog box.

6. Close the Personalization window.

As noted in Tutorial 1, Windows Vista Ultimate, Windows Vista Business, and Windows Vista Home Premium require 128 MB of graphics memory (but perform far better with more graphics memory), while Windows Vista Home Basic requires 32 MB. To handle graphics, your computer might use a video card that provides dedicated graphics memory; in other words, RAM devoted exclusively to graphics. Or your computer might use integrated graphics and depend on a graphics processor chip on the motherboard to handle graphics. In the latter case, a portion of regular RAM or system memory must be used (or dedicated) for graphics, and that reduces the overall performance of your computer. The more dedicated graphics memory you have (preferably 512 MB or more), the better your computer performs and the more support you have for Windows Aero. Also, if you're into gaming, you want to use dedicated graphics memory for best performance. Dedicated graphics memory is more expensive than integrated graphics memory, but you obtain better performance. The important point to remember is that you want to purchase a video card with sufficient graphics memory not only for Windows Vista but for all the other applications you use on your computer and all the other type of tasks you require of your computer.

Checking Video Display Settings

| Reference Window

- Right-click the desktop, click Personalize, and after the Personalization window opens, click Display Settings.
- On the Monitor tab in the Display Settings dialog box, click the Advanced Settings button.
- In the Properties dialog box for your monitor and video display adapter, click the Monitor tab and verify that the refresh rate is set to 75 Hertz or higher if you use a CRT monitor, and that it meets the minimum value of 10 Hertz for Windows Aero.
- Click the Adapter tab and examine the information about the adapter, including the amount of total video memory to make sure that it meets the minimum requirement of 128 MB for Windows Vista Ultimate, Windows Vista Business, and Windows Vista Home Premium and the minimum requirement of 32 MB for Windows Vista Home Basic.
- Click the List All Modes button and examine the list of all combinations of resolutions, color settings, and refresh rates that are supported on your computer.
- If you do not want to inadvertently make any changes to these settings, click the Cancel button to close the List All Modes dialog box, click the Cancel button to close the Properties dialog box for your monitor and display adapter, and then click the Cancel button to close the Display Settings dialog box.
- Close the Personalization window.

When you are ready to purchase a new computer, make sure you purchase a high-performance video display adapter card with ample amounts of dedicated video memory.

Adjusting DPI Settings

As noted earlier, the native resolution of a flat panel display (or LCD monitor) is the highest resolution for that monitor, and you achieve the sharpest resolution and detail possible. The desktop appears larger, and you can fit more objects on the desktop. If you have two windows open, you can view more of the content of each window. You can also view a dialog box without it covering a portion of a window. However, desktop icons, the taskbar, the notification area, dialog boxes, and other elements of the graphical user interface are very small in size and may be difficult to see. Furthermore, you may find it difficult to read the text of icon titles, menus, dialog boxes, and windows. If you decrease the resolution, desktop objects and other elements of the graphical user interface become larger in size and are easier to see. Furthermore, the text of icon titles, menus, notification area, dialog boxes, and other elements of the graphical user interface are larger and therefore, easier to read. However, at a lower resolution, text and images are larger and less sharp. Also, since objects are larger, the desktop appears smaller, and windows and dialog box overlap each other.

If you want to use the native resolution of your monitor or set your monitor to another high resolution option, but at the same time want to more easily see desktop icons and the content of windows and dialog boxes, as well as the text of icon titles and menus, you can adjust the DPI Scaling setting for your computer. **DPI** stands for "dots per inch." By default, the DPI Scaling setting is 96 DPI. You can increase that value to 120 DPI to display text and icons 25% larger. You can also define a Custom DPI setting.

Alejandro recommends you examine these settings in the event you decide to adjust your resolution to an even higher value than you already have.

To complete the following steps, you must provide Administrator credentials. If you are not logged on under an Administrator account or do not know the password for an Administrator account, do not keystroke the following steps, but instead read the steps and examine the figures so that you are familiar with the use of this feature. Also, if you make a change to the DPI setting on a computer, Windows Vista must restart the computer to implement the change. If you are working in a computer lab, you may not have the option of restarting your computer and applying this change because the computers are set up to restore their original settings. This setup in turn guarantees that changes you make do not affect other users of the same computer. Your instructor can explain what options are available to you in your college's computer lab, or your instructor might just discuss and demonstrate this feature during lecture.

Tip

Click "Change desktop icons" under Tasks in the Personalization window to select which icons appear on the desktop, and then customize those icons.

To adjust font sizes with the DPI Scaling setting:

1. Right-click the desktop and then click **Personalize**. In the Personalization window, notice the options listed under Tasks in the upper-left corner of the window. "Adjust font size (DPI)" under Tasks has a security icon displayed to its left. That security icon identifies an operation that requires Administrator privileges. If your user account is an Administrator account, Windows Vista will verify that you want to continue with this operation. If your user account is a Standard User account, you must provide a password for an Administrator account on your computer. You will examine this security feature in more detail in Tutorial 7.
2. Click **Adjust font size (DPI)**. Windows Vista switches to Secure Desktop Mode and displays a User Account Control dialog box.
3. In the User Account Control dialog box, click the **Continue** button if you are logged on under an Administrator account, or if you are logged on under a Standard User account, enter the **password** for an Administrator account, and then click the **OK** button. Windows Vista then opens the DPI Scaling dialog box. See Figure 2-37. Windows Vista advises you to choose a smaller scale to fit more information on the screen or a larger scale to make text more readable. Windows Vista also shows you the difference between the Default scale (96 DPI) and the Larger scale (120 DPI) options. Notice how much easier it is to read text with the Larger scale (120 DPI) option.

Figure 2-37 Viewing DPI Scaling options

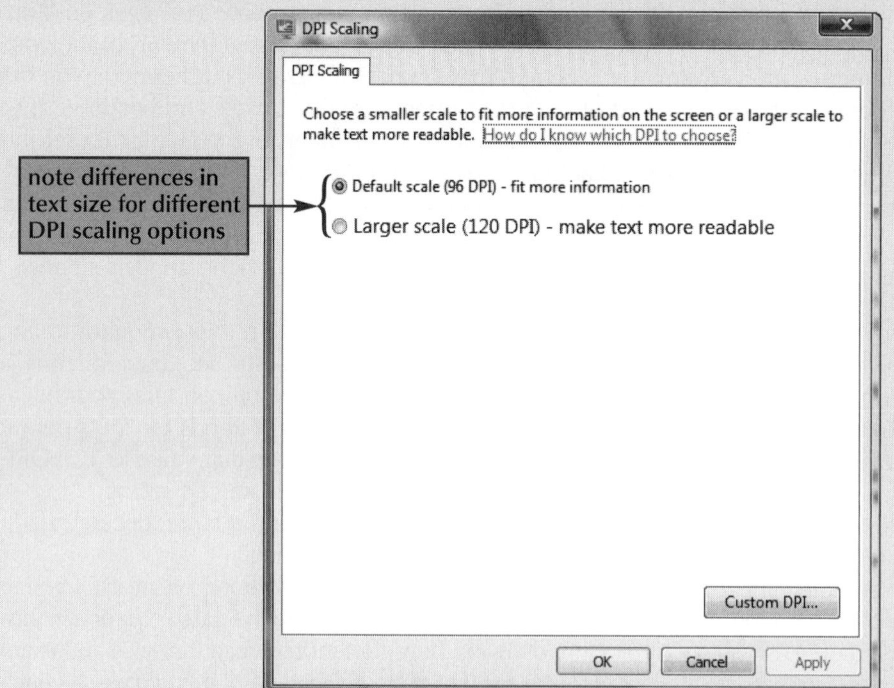

4. Click the **Custom DPI** button. In the Custom DPI Setting dialog box, Windows Vista shows you how the 9 point Segoe UI font looks at 96 pixels per inch with your current DPI setting of 100%. See Figure 2-38. You can change the current setting by selecting a DPI setting of 100%, 125%, 150%, or 200% from the "Scale to this percentage of normal use" list box. Or you can point to the 1-inch mark on the ruler and drag it to the right (or left) to manually adjust the scaling to another value not available in the "Scale to this percentage of normal use" list box. When you release the mouse pointer, the text below the ruler will change size, and Windows Vista will also list the number of pixels per inch at this new setting. If you do desktop publishing and want to view documents at the same size as they will appear when printed, you can place a real ruler on the monitor over the Custom DPI Scaling ruler and then drag and drop the 1-inch mark on the Custom DPI Scaling ruler so that it matches an inch on a physical ruler.

Figure 2-38 Viewing custom DPI Scaling options

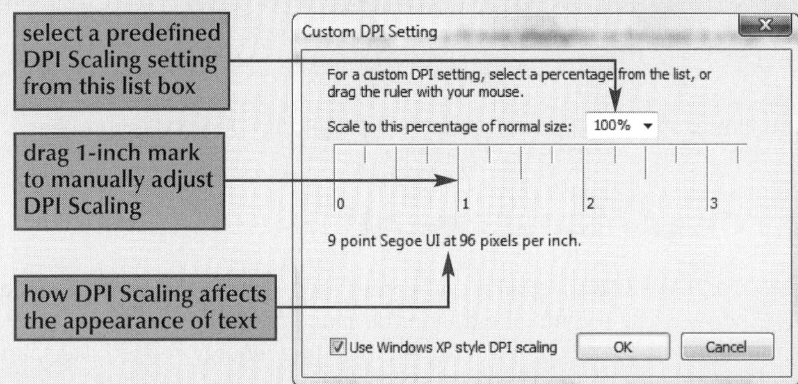

5. If you do not want to make a change to the DPI setting on the computer you are using, or if you are working in a computer lab, click the **Cancel** button to close the DPI Custom Setting dialog box, and then click the **Cancel** button in the DPI Scaling dialog box. If you do change this setting on your computer, you will need to restart your computer to see how it affects the use of your computer. Therefore, you must think about this course of action and save any documents you are currently using.

6. Close the Personalization window.

If you work in desktop publishing or graphics design, you may want to adjust the DPI setting so that what you see on the monitor exactly matches what you see when the document is printed.

Reference Window | **Checking the DPI Setting**

- Right-click the desktop, click Personalize, and in the Personalization window, click Adjust font size (DPI) under Tasks.
- In the User Account Control dialog box, click the Continue button if you are logged on under an Administrator account, or if you are logged on under a Standard User account, enter the password for an Administrator account, and then click the OK button.
- In the DPI Scaling dialog box, click the Custom DPI button.
- In the Custom DPI Setting dialog box, select a new DPI setting of 100%, 125%, 150%, or 200% from the "Scale to this percentage of normal use" list box, or point to the 1-inch mark on the ruler and drag it to the right (or left) to manually adjust the scaling to another value not available in the "Scale to this percentage of normal use" list box.
- If you do change this setting on your computer, restart your computer to see how it affects the use of your computer. If you do not want to make a change to the DPI setting on the computer you are using, click the Cancel button to close the DPI Custom Setting dialog box, and then click the Cancel button in the DPI Scaling dialog box.
- Close the Personalization window.

Next, you can examine the power management settings on your computer.

Using Power Management

Kimbrough & Co., like all other global companies, depends on the power management features of Windows Vista to enhance the performance of employee's computers while at the same time conserving energy, reducing skyrocketing, energy-related costs, and protecting the environment.

Windows Vista supports the **Advanced Configuration and Power Interface** (**ACPI**), a set of power-management specifications developed by Microsoft, Intel, and Toshiba that allow the operating system to control the amount of power that each device receives. Windows Vista monitors the power state of the computer, determines the power needs of applications and hardware devices, and increases or decreases the availability of power as needed.

If your desktop or mobile computer is idle for a certain period of time, Windows Vista can automatically perform both of the following tasks:

- Turn off your video display and hard disk
- Place your computer in one of three sleep states—Standard Sleep, Hibernation, or Hybrid Sleep

When using **Standard Sleep**, which is similar to **Standby mode** in Windows XP, Windows Vista saves your computer's settings in memory, turns off your monitor and hard disk, and reduces the computer's power usage. If your computer uses Standard Sleep, you have to manually save your work before your computer enters a Sleep state. If a power failure occurs during Standard Sleep, and if you have not saved your work, you will lose your work and the settings stored in RAM, which are needed to restore your computer to its previous operating state. A computer wakes up from Standard Sleep faster than it does from Hibernation (described next). Therefore, it's useful when you are away from your computer for a short while but want to return to work quickly.

When using **Hibernation**, Windows Vista saves the contents of RAM to a **hibernation file** on disk and then shuts down your computer. When you next power on your computer, Windows Vista restores the contents of RAM from the hibernation file so that your computer returns to the state it was in before you implemented Hibernation. You do not need to save your work; however, that is always a good precaution against problems you might not anticipate. Hibernation saves more power than Standard Sleep. Therefore, it's useful if you plan on being away from your computer for a longer period of time. It's also useful if you do not want to shut down your computer every night. However, your computer wakes up from Hibernation more slowly than when using Standard Sleep.

When using its new power management feature called **Hybrid Sleep**, Windows Vista saves your computer's settings in memory and also in a hibernation file on disk, turns off your monitor and hard disk, and reduces your computer's power usage. If you press a key or move the mouse, Windows Vista resumes power to the computer, and you are ready to use it almost immediately. If a power failure occurs, Windows Vista uses the hibernation file on disk instead to restore your computer to its previous operating state. Hybrid Sleep is automatically enabled on desktop computers but not on mobile PCs. Also, your video driver must support WDDM (Windows Display Driver Model), and your computer must be able to enter a sleep state for Hybrid Sleep to work. Hybrid Sleep is the more useful power management option for those computers that support Hybrid Sleep because it combines the advantages of both Standard Sleep and Hibernation. Your computer wakes up more quickly, and Windows Vista restores it to its previous working state. At the same time, if a power failure occurs, Windows Vista can still restore your computer to its previous state by using the hibernation file. In contrast, if your computer relies solely on Standard Sleep, you don't have the protection that a hibernation file provides for restoring your computer to its previous state after a power failure. Likewise, if your computer relies solely on Hibernation, it starts up more slowly.

Windows Vista automatically examines the hardware configuration of a computer and determines what types of power management settings to make available for a specific computer.

In Windows Vista, you can choose a **power plan**, or combination of settings that manages power usage on your computer, and if necessary, you can customize those settings. Windows Visa includes three basic power plans:

- **Balanced** for matching power usage to system needs and system performance
- **Power Save** for conserving power usage and maximizing battery life on mobile computers even if it results in reduced performance
- **High Performance** for maximizing power usage on mobile computers even if it means shorter battery life

Tip

Your computer's manufacturer may provide additional power plans.

Alejandro wants to show you how to locate, review, and adjust the power management settings on your computer.

To view Windows Vista power plans and power plan settings:

1. Click the **Start** button, point to **Control Panel**, and then click **Power Options**. In the Power Options window, Windows Vista displays the three basic power plans. See Figure 2-39. To the right of each power plan is a visual representation of how each plan balances power usage (or battery life) with performance.

Figure 2-39 Viewing power plan options for conserving battery life and improving performance

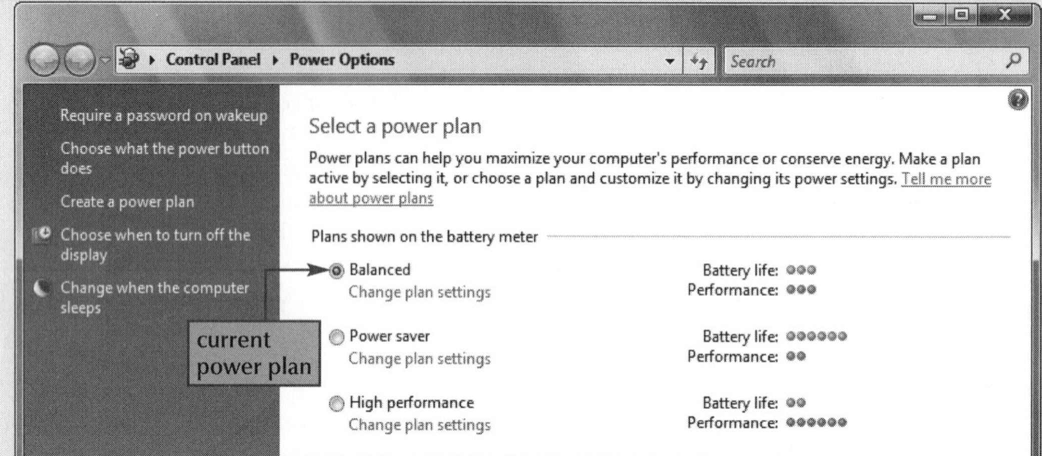

2. Under Balanced, click the **Change plan settings** link. In the Edit Plan Settings window, Windows Vista shows the settings for turning off the display and placing a computer in a Sleep state for this power plan. As shown in Figure 2-40, if the computer is plugged into a power outlet, Windows Vista will turn off the video display after 20 minutes of user and system inactivity and place that same computer in a Sleep state after 1 hour of user and system inactivity. If the computer is operating on battery, Windows Vista will turn off the video display after 5 minutes and place the computer in a Sleep state after 15 minutes. Your settings may differ. The computer used for this figure is a desktop computer plugged into a UPS (Uninterruptible Power Supply) unit. Notice that there is an option for restoring default settings of this plan if you have previously changed them.

   Trouble? The manufacturer of your computer might have customized it so that you see a custom power plan option, such as Dell Recommended, rather than Balanced. If this is the case, choose the recommended option. If you have modified your power management settings, the power plan name may be different. Use the first power plan to examine its power management settings in the remaining steps.

Figure 2-40 Viewing power management settings for turning off the display and Sleep

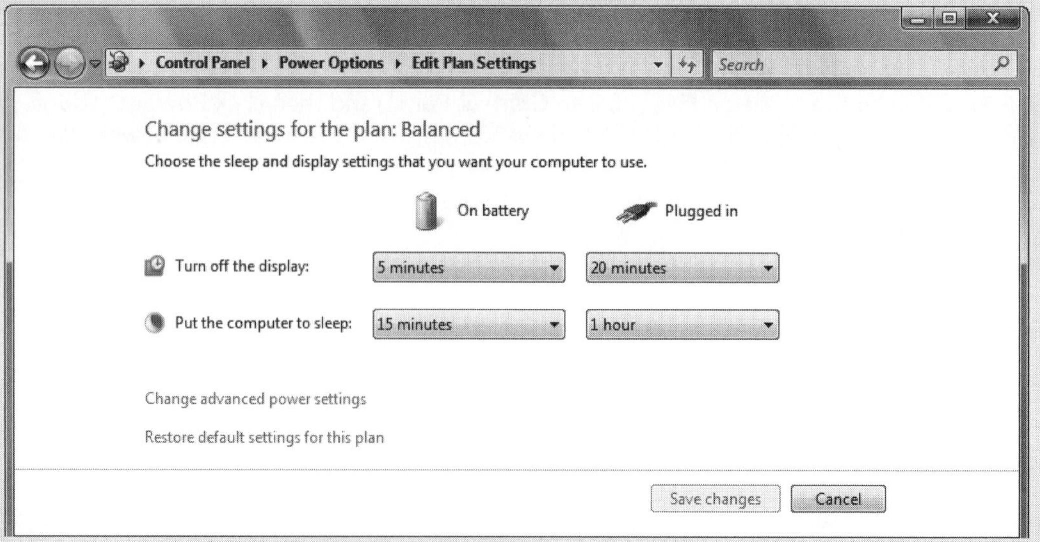

Control Panel ▸ Power Options ▸ Edit Plan Settings
Search
Change settings for the plan: Balanced
Choose the sleep and display settings that you want your computer to use.
On battery
Plugged in
Turn off the display: 5 minutes 20 minutes
Put the computer to sleep: 15 minutes 1 hour
Change advanced power settings
Restore default settings for this plan
Save changes
Cancel

3. Click the **Change advanced power settings** link. In the Power Options dialog box, you can review and, if necessary, change specific power settings on the Advanced settings property sheet. If you click the "Change settings that are currently unavailable" link and provide Administrator credentials, Windows Vista will not display any new items in the Advanced settings dialog box. Instead, you will be able to edit some options that you would not have otherwise been able to change.

4. Click the **Expand** button ⊞ to the left of Hard disk, and then click the **Expand** button ⊞ to the left of "Turn off hard disk after." On the computer used for this figure, Windows Vista turns off the hard disk after 10 minutes of user and system inactivity on battery power. When plugged in, the computer turns off the hard disk after 20 minutes. See Figure 2-41. Your settings may differ. If you want to adjust either or both of these settings, you click the setting, and then use an arrow button or list button for that setting to view and select another option.

Figure 2-41

Viewing power management settings for the hard disk

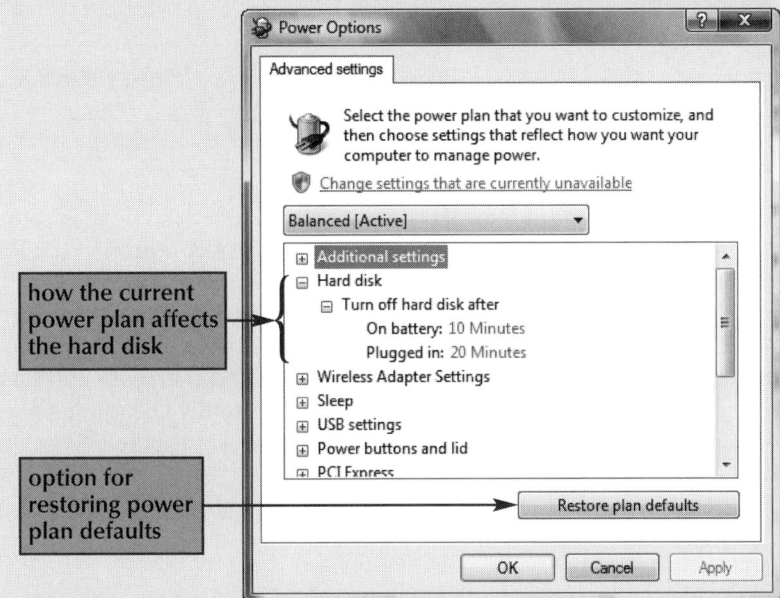

5. Click the **Expand** button ⊞ to the left of Sleep, and then click the **Expand** buttons ⊞ to the left of "Sleep after," "Allow hybrid sleep," and "Hibernate after." On the computer used for this figure, Windows Vista automatically enabled Hybrid Sleep when on battery and when plugged in. See Figure 2-42. Your settings may differ. By checking these settings for Sleep, you can determine whether Hybrid Sleep is enabled on your computer, you can also enable Hibernation, and you can adjust each of these settings manually. While the options in the Edit Plan Settings window that you previously examined allow you to select only certain intervals of time for Sleep and turning off the display, in the Power Options dialog box you can specify the exact number of minutes you want for a setting.

Figure 2-42 Viewing Sleep and Hibernation power management settings

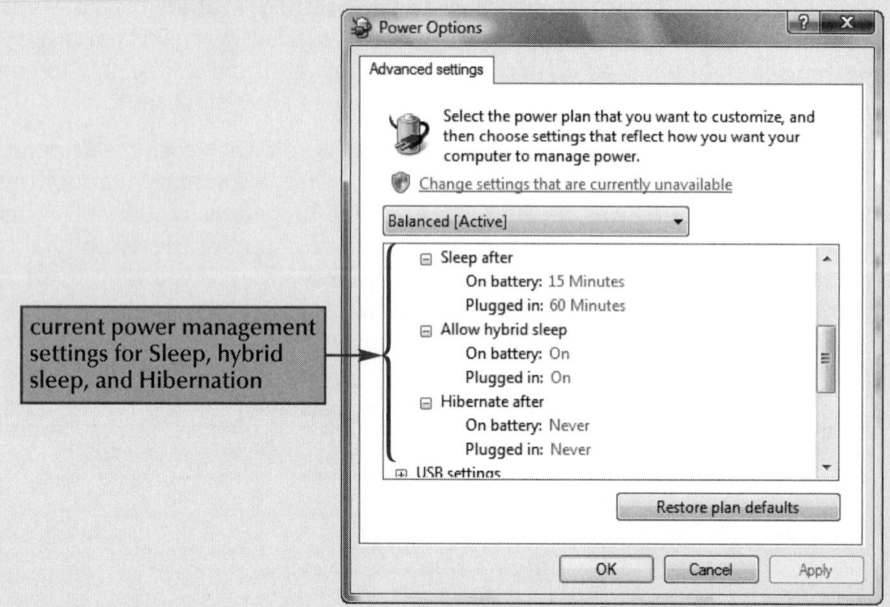

6. Examine other categories of interest to you, and if you make changes to power management settings that you want to keep, click the **OK** button in the Power Options dialog box, and then click the **Save Changes** button in the Edit Plan Settings window. If you have made changes to the power management settings that you do not want to keep, or if you are using a computer in a computer lab, click the **Cancel** button in the Power Options dialog box, and then click the **Cancel** button in the Edit Plan Settings window to avoid inadvertently changing any settings. Both the Cancel and the Save Changes buttons return you to the Power Options window.
7. Keep the Power Options window open for the next section of this tutorial.

The Power Saving Mode option for the Wireless Network Adapter setting on the Advanced settings property sheet is especially important for mobile computers because it determines whether the wireless adapter uses any power management features, and that in turn can determine the speed at which the wireless adapter communicates with a wireless access point.

The Power buttons and lid settings specify what Windows Vista does when you press the Power button on your computer, when you choose the Power button on the Start menu, and when you close the lid of a mobile computer.

The Multimedia settings on the Advanced settings property sheet apply to Media Center PCs that share media with other hardware devices. The "Allow the computer to enter Away Mode" option switches the PC to a state in which it appears off. The display is turned off, and sound is muted. However, the computer is still operational and can handle background tasks, such as recording TV broadcasts or streaming multimedia content to other devices, including other computers.

On the left side of the Power Options window, there are four options for adjusting power management settings. The "Require a password on wakeup" and the "Choose what the power button does" options open the System Settings window where you can change both settings. Likewise, the "Choose when to turn off the display" and the "Change when the computer sleeps" options are accessible here or by changing your current power plan's settings.

The "Create a power plan" option allows you to create a new power plan based on an existing power plan and then modify your new power plan's settings. Then, you can save your new power plan settings under a new power plan name of your own choosing, so you can keep all three of the original plans and add any additional custom power plans you want.

To view these additional power option settings:

1. In the left pane, click the **Require a password on wakeup** link. Under "Password protection on wakeup" in the System Settings window, Windows Vista is set to automatically require a password, and the options in this section are dimmed to prevent changes. See Figure 2-43. If you want to change these settings, you have to click "Change settings that are currently unavailable." To access these settings you must provide Administrator credentials.

Figure 2-43 Viewing Power button power management settings

You can also change the Power button settings in this window and specify what Windows should do when you press the Power button on your computer's system unit.

2. Click the **Plugged in** (or **On battery**) list button to the right of "When I press the power button." You can specify that Windows Vista do nothing, place your computer in a sleep state or in Hibernation, or shut down your computer (the default). By using Sleep, Hibernate, or Shut Down, you don't have to choose the option you most commonly use from the Start menu; instead, you just press the Power button on your computer, and Windows Vista shuts your computer down in the way you specified here.

3. Click the **Plugged in** (or **On Battery**) list button a second time to close the list, and then click the **Back** button.
4. Close the Power Options window.

Power management is particularly important in the case of portable computers because these features can double or triple the lifetime of the battery in the computer. Furthermore, the use of power-saving features on PCs, now commonplace in offices and homes, can not only significantly reduce the cost of electricity to both business and home users, but can also improve the quality of the environment.

Reference Window | Checking Power Management Settings

- From the Start menu, open the Control Panel, click System and Maintenance, and then click Power Options.
- In the Power Options window, click the "Change plan settings" link for the power plan you currently use, and then in the Edit Plan Settings window, review and, if necessary, change the settings for turning off the display and putting the computer to sleep, and then click the Save changes button if you have made changes you want to keep.
- Click the "Change advanced power settings" link, and in the Power Options dialog box, review and, if necessary, change specific power management settings on the Advanced settings property sheet. If you want to keep any changes you have made, click the OK button in the Power Options dialog box, and then click the Save Changes button in the Edit Plan Settings window. If you have made changes to the settings to power management settings that you do not want to keep, click the Cancel button in the Power Options dialog box, and then click the Cancel button in the Edit Plan Settings window to avoid inadvertently changing any settings.
- In the Power Options window, click the "Require a password on wakeup" link or the "Choose what the power button does" link to open the System Settings window, view your current password setting and the setting for what Windows Vista does when you press the Power button, and if necessary, change that setting. If you change one or both of these settings and want to keep those changes, click the Save changes button, otherwise click the Cancel button.
- To create a new power plan with your own custom settings, click the "Create a power plan" link in the Power Options window, choose an existing power plan as the basis for your new power plan, enter a name for your power plan, click the Next button, specify settings for turning off the display and placing your computer in a sleep state, and then click the Create button. Next, you can modify this new power plan in the same way as you modify other power plans.
- In the Power Options window, click the "Choose when to turn off the display" link or the "Change when the computer sleeps" link, and in the Edit Plan Settings window, examine and, if necessary, change one or both of these settings. If you want to keep any changes you have made, click the Save Changes button in the Edit Plan Settings window. If you have made changes to power management settings that you do not want to keep, click Cancel in the Edit Plan Settings window to avoid inadvertently changing any settings.
- Close the Power Options window.

Windows Vista provides many more options than Windows XP for fine-tuning the power management on your computer. Custom power management settings not only conserve power and optimize the performance of your computer, but also streamline your use of your computer and save you time and effort.

Restoring Your Computer's Settings

If you work in a computer lab, you will need to restore the original settings to the computer you used. If you used your own computer, you might want to restore some or all of the original settings.

To restore your computer's settings:

1. To restore your computer to its original Start menu style, right-click the **Start** button, and then click **Properties**. If your computer was originally set up for the Classic Start menu option, click the **Classic Start menu** option button, and then click the **OK** button to close the Taskbar and Start Menu Properties dialog box. If your computer was set up for the Start menu option, click the **Customize** button, click **Display as a link** under Control Panel, click the **OK** button to close the Customize Start Menu dialog box, and then click the **OK** button to close the Taskbar and Start Menu properties dialog box.
2. To restore the default behavior of the Windows Sidebar icon in the notification area, right-click the **taskbar**, click **Properties**, click the **Notification Area** tab, click the **Customize** button, click **Windows Sidebar** under Current Items in the Customize Notification Icons dialog box, click the Windows Sidebar **Behavior** button, click **Hide when active**, click the **OK** button to close the Customize Notification Icons dialog box, and then click the **OK** button to close the Taskbar and Start Menu Properties dialog box.
3. To restore the Quick Launch toolbar, right-click the **Documents — Shortcut** icon, click **Delete**, click the **Yes** button, right-click the **Pictures — Shortcut** icon, click **Delete**, and then click the **Yes** button.
4. To restore the original Windows Vista theme and the appearance of individual elements of the user interface, right-click the **desktop**, click **Personalize**, click **Theme**, click the **Theme** list button, click **Windows Vista**, and then click the **OK** button.
5. To restore Advanced Appearance settings, click **Window Color and Appearance** in the Personalization window, click **Open classic appearance properties for more color options**, click the **Advanced** button in the Appearance Settings dialog box, click the **Item** list button, click **Icon**, and then click the **Bold** button B.
6. Click the **Item** list box, click **Menu**, and then click the **Bold** button B.
7. Click the **Item** list box, click **Message Box**, and then click the **Bold** button B.
8. Click the **OK** button in the Advanced Appearance dialog box, click the **OK** button in the Appearance Settings dialog box, and then close the Personalization window.

Session 2.3 Quick Check | Review

1. ______________________ refers to the sharpness of the image on a monitor.
2. True or False. Color depth refers to the maximum number of colors used to compose an onscreen image.
3. Windows Aero requires a color depth setting of ______________ bits.

4. What setting can you adjust to set the number of times per second that the image on the screen is redrawn by the video card?
5. True or False. You can use the DPI setting to improve readability of text at higher resolutions.
6. What new type of Sleep state does Windows Vista support?

Review | Tutorial Summary

In this tutorial, you explored the use and importance of the Windows Vista and Windows Classic theme and the Windows Aero, Windows Basic, Windows Standard, Windows Classic, and high-contrast color schemes. You adjusted the hue, saturation, and brightness of colors used for window frames, the Start menu, and the taskbar. You customized individual elements of the graphical user interface to sharpen your view. You examined the importance and use of special visual effects, such as font-smoothing and Microsoft's ClearType technology. Prior to reviewing other visual effects that require Administrator credentials, you checked your user account to determine whether it is an Administrator or Standard user account. You examined the options for displaying different image formats and video on the desktop background, and then you changed your desktop background. You examined Start menu, taskbar, notification area, and Quick Launch toolbar taskbar, and then customized each of these components of the graphical user interface. You created a desktop toolbar and added shortcuts to the toolbar to quickly access components on your computer, such as Help and Support. You examined the concept and use of screen resolution, color depth, and refresh rate, and then changed your desktop view. You also examined DPI Scaling settings and how you might apply them to high-resolution monitors. Finally, you examined Windows Vista's power management capabilities and power plans and the use of Sleep, Hibernation, and Hybrid Sleep.

Key Terms

4:3 aspect ratio
16:9 aspect ratio
ACPI (Advanced Configuration and Power Interface)
animated GIF
aspect ratio
Bitmap Image (BMP)
bitmapped graphic
cathode-ray tube (CRT)
ClearType
color depth
color scheme
desktop composition
Device Independent Bitmap (DIB)
DPI
font-smoothing
Graphics Interchange Format (GIF)
Hibernation
hibernation file
High Color
hue
Hybrid Sleep
jaggie
Joint Photographic Experts Group (JPG or JPEG)
lossless compression
lossy compression
Moving Pictures Experts Group (MPG or MPEG)
native resolution
palette (or color palette)
personalized menus
Portable Network Graphics (PNG)
power plan
power scheme
refresh rate
resolution
saturation
screen font
Secure Desktop Mode
stairstep effect
Standard Sleep
Standby mode
subpixel
taskbar grouping
theme
True Color
typeface
Windows Media Audio/Video (WMV)

Practice | Review Assignments

Practice the skills you learned in the tutorial.

There are no Data Files needed for the Review Assignments.

Alejandro's supervisor at Kimbrough & Co. has asked him to assist employees in a new research division to customize their computers and provide the right type of working environment for their research efforts. To expedite this task, Alejandro asks for your assistance.

To view advanced system settings and DPI Scaling options, you must provide Administrator credentials. If you are logged on under a Standard user account and do not know the password for an Administrator account, skip those steps that require Administrator credentials and continue with the remaining steps.

As you complete the following steps, record your observations and answers to questions so that you can later prepare a one to two-page report that summarizes your findings. Use a word processing application, such as WordPad or Microsoft Word, to prepare that report. Also, if you change any settings on the computer you are using, note the original settings so that you can restore them later. Complete the following steps:

1. If necessary, switch to single-click activation so you can work in Web style.
2. Open the Personalization window, and then open the Theme Settings dialog box. What desktop theme does Windows Vista use on your computer? Close the Theme Settings dialog box without changing your current theme setting.
3. In the Personalization window, select Window Color and Appearance. If Windows opens the Appearance settings dialog box, skip the remainder of this step and continue with the next step. If Windows opens the Window Color and Appearance window, which one of the eight color options does Windows Vista use for windows, the Start menu, and the taskbar? Does Windows Vista use a custom color setting instead? If so, describe it. Is transparency enabled on your computer? Choose the option for opening classic appearance properties for more color options.
4. What color scheme does Windows Vista use on your computer? Does your computer support Windows Aero?
5. Open the Effects dialog box. Does Windows Vista use ClearType or Standard font-smoothing on your computer? Close the Effects dialog box.
6. Open the Advanced Appearance dialog box from the Appearance Settings dialog box. In the Item list box, choose Hyperlink. What color does Windows Vista use for hyperlinks in the graphical user interface? Close the Advanced Appearance dialog box without changing the color setting for hyperlinks and close the Appearance Settings dialog box.
7. In the Personalization window, choose the option for changing desktop icons. In the Desktop Icon Settings dialog box, choose the option for placing an icon on the desktop for your user (account) files, the Control Panel, and Network, and then apply the setting.
8. Use the Show Desktop button on the Quick Launch toolbar to minimize all open windows so that you can view the new desktop icons. Then use the Show Desktop button to restore all open windows. In the Desktop Icon Settings dialog box, turn off the option for displaying your user account files, the Control Panel, and the Network, or restore your computer's original desktop icon settings.

9. If you are logged on under an Administrator account, or know the password of an Administrator account, choose the option for adjusting font size (DPI) in the Personalization window. What DPI Scaling setting does your computer use? Is that DPI setting high enough so that you find it easy to work on your computer, or could you benefit from a higher DPI setting? Close the DPI Scaling dialog box without changing your current DPI Scaling setting.
10. Close the Personalization window.
11. If necessary, add the Quick Launch toolbar to the taskbar.
12. If you are logged on under an Administrator account or know the password of an Administrator account, open the System window, choose the option for viewing Advanced system settings, and in the System Properties dialog box, choose the option for viewing Performance settings. On the Visual Effects property sheet in the Performance Options dialog box, what option does Windows Vista use for determining the appearance and the performance of your computer? Does Windows Vista use all of the visual effects in the Custom list box, or only certain ones? Is your computer set for the visual effects you prefer to use and, if not, would you prefer only those visual effects that produce the best appearance or those for best performance? List up to three visual effects that you think are the most important to you. Close the Performance Options dialog box, the System Properties dialog box, and the System window.
13. Open the Personalization window, and then select Desktop Background. In the Location list, choose Sample Pictures, and then point to and view each of the images as they are displayed on your desktop background. After you select each image, click the Desktop Background taskbar button to minimize the Desktop Background window so you can see the desktop background, and then click it again to restore the Desktop Background window so you can choose another desktop background.
14. Choose the desktop background option that you like most from this group, and then try each of the different options for positioning the desktop background and examine the effect of each option. Restore the original desktop background on your computer and its original positioning option, close the Desktop Background window, and then close the Personalization window.
15. Right-click the Start button and choose the option for viewing Start menu properties. Does your computer use the default Start menu style or the Classic Start menu style? If necessary, choose the Start menu style option and then click its Customize button.
16. Use the Customize Start Menu dialog box to display the Music and Pictures folders as menus. Enable the Favorites menu option so it will appear on the Start menu. Apply the setting as you close the Customize Start Menu dialog box, and then choose the option to apply the change in the Taskbar and Start Menu Properties dialog box.
17. Open the Start menu and point to Pictures. What does Windows Vista display on the Pictures menu? Point to Music on the Start menu. What does Windows Vista display on the Music menu? Point to Favorites on the Start menu. What does Windows Vista display? Would these options prove useful to you?
18. Open the Customize Start menu dialog box and restore the default settings for the Favorites menu, Music, and Pictures. Then close the Customize Start Menu dialog box and Taskbar and Start Menu Properties dialog box.
19. If necessary, unlock the taskbar, and then view properties of the taskbar. Is the option for showing window previews (or thumbnails) enabled in your Taskbar and Start Menu Properties dialog box?

20. Enable the option for auto-hiding the taskbar, and then apply this setting. What happens to the taskbar? Move your mouse pointer to the bottom and then to the middle of the desktop. What happens as you perform these two steps? Turn off the option for auto-hiding the taskbar, and then apply this setting. What happens next? If necessary, restore and apply your computer's original setting for "Auto-hide the taskbar."
21. Select the Notification Area tab. Which system icons does Windows Vista display in the notification area? Is the Power system icon available, or is it dimmed (and therefore not available)?
22. If necessary, enable the option for Hiding inactive icons, and then choose the option for customizing notification area icons. What is the Behavior setting for the Safely Remove Hardware and Windows Sidebar items? Close the Customize Notification Icons dialog box and the Taskbar and Start Menu Properties dialog box.
23. Add the Control Panel, Network, and your user account folder icons to the Quick Launch toolbar. What does Windows Vista do? (If necessary, adjust the width of the Quick Launch toolbar.) Describe what happens when you click each of these Quick Launch toolbar icons. Is there any advantage to placing these objects on the Quick Launch toolbar? If so, explain.
24. Open the Personalization window, and then open Display Settings dialog box. What is your current resolution? Change your screen resolution to the highest or lowest resolution on your computer, and then view the desktop. What resolution setting did you choose, and how did this change your view of the desktop and its contents? If necessary, open the Display Settings dialog box and restore your original resolution.
25. According to the Display Settings dialog box, what is your current color depth setting? Change your color depth setting to the next lower or higher setting on your computer. What color depth setting did you choose, and how did this change your view of the desktop and its contents? Restore your original color depth setting.
26. In the Display Settings dialog box, choose Advanced Settings to view information about your video display adapter and monitor. What type of adapter does your computer have? How much dedicated video memory does it have? Is this enough to support Windows Aero on your computer? How much shared system memory does your video display adapter use? What is the total available amount of graphics memory?
27. Select the monitor property sheet. What type of monitor does your computer have, and what is its refresh rate? Close your monitor and video display adapter properties dialog box without making any changes to your monitor and video display adapter settings, and then close the Display Settings dialog box. Close the Personalization window.
28. To restore your computer:
    - If your taskbar did not originally contain the Quick Launch toolbar, right-click the taskbar, point to Toolbars, and then choose the option for removing the Quick Launch toolbar from the taskbar.
    - If your taskbar was originally locked, right-click the taskbar, and then click "Lock the Taskbar."
    - If necessary, turn off single-click activation.
29. Prepare a one- to two-page summary that concisely summarizes your findings in a bulleted list. Submit your answers to the questions in the Review Assignments to your instructor, either in printed or electronic form, as requested.

Apply | Case Problem 1

Use the skills you learned in the tutorial to customize display settings for an e-book publishing firm.

There are no Data Files needed for this Case Problem.

ePsionics Li-ying Yiu, the owner of ePsionics, a firm that publishes online science fiction and fantasy books, recently purchased several new Windows Vista Ultimate computers for new employees to meet the increased demand for books in this genre. She asks you to set up these computers for her new employees and customize display settings on these computers so that employees have full access to all Windows Aero features.

Use a word processing application, such as Microsoft Word or WordPad, to prepare your answers to these questions. Complete the following steps:

1. What edition of Windows Vista does your computer use? How much RAM does your computer have? How much video RAM does the video display adapter have? How much dedicated video memory, shared system memory, system video memory, and total available graphics memory does your computer use? Does your computer support Windows Aero?
2. Open the Desktop Background dialog box, select the Windows Wallpapers location, and then choose one of the desktop backgrounds under Textures and apply it to your computer desktop.
3. Open the Display Settings dialog box. What is the native resolution of your computer, and what is its current resolution? What color depth setting does your computer use?
4. Test each of the screen resolutions available on your computer, using your current color depth setting. Start with the lowest resolution and increase the resolution one step at a time until you reach the highest resolution available on your computer. List the screen resolutions available on your computer, note the default screen resolution on your computer and its aspect ratio, and then briefly describe how the quality of the desktop wallpaper and the aspect ratio changes with each change in the screen resolution. Briefly describe what you think is the best resolution and note any other Windows Vista options that you might use to enhance the view of the content on your desktop.
5. Switch back to your original or native screen resolution. Test each of the color depth settings available on your computer, using your current screen resolution. At each color depth setting, examine the image on the monitor and notice how the color depth setting affects the image. Prepare a list of each color depth setting that you tested, note the resolution that you used and the original color depth setting on your computer, note the current color scheme, and then briefly describe how the quality of the image changed with each change in the color depth setting and whether you noticed any distortion of the shapes of desktop objects. If your computer supports Windows Aero, comment on how the color depth setting affected access to Windows Aero features.
6. Briefly explain what you think is the best resolution and color depth setting for your computer and for Windows Aero (if your computer supports Windows Aero).
7. Restore your computer to its original desktop resolution, color depth setting, and desktop background.
8. Submit your document to your instructor, either in printed or electronic form, as requested.

Apply | Case Problem 2

Use the skills you learned in the tutorial to support employees at a community college.

There are no Data Files needed for this Case Problem.

Evan Gates Community College Buster McFadden works for the Computer Help Desk at Evans Gate Community College in Wisconsin and provides technical computer support to employees all over campus. Employees work on computers with different types of hardware and software, including different Windows Vista editions. As Buster works with users to customize their computers and resolve problems, he adds the question or problem to a database, along with information on how to resolve an issue or problem so that college employees can check online for answers to their questions.

Use a word processing application, such as Microsoft Word or WordPad, to prepare your answers to these questions. Complete the following:

1. A new employee discovers that his computer only displays a Recycle Bin on the desktop. List the steps that he needs to perform to display the Computer, Control Panel, and his user files icons on the desktop.
2. Another employee has added the Quick Launch toolbar to the taskbar and then customized it by adding icons for the Documents, Pictures, Computer, and Recent Items folder as well as a Help and Support icon. However, Windows Vista does not display buttons for all the items on the toolbar. Although Windows Vista does display a pop-up menu button from which she can access all the options on the Quick Launch toolbar, she would prefer to view all the icons on the toolbar instead. Also, she wants to rearrange the icons so that she can more easily locate the icons she needs. What would you recommend she do to correct these problems?
3. Another employee who works in Applied Graphics wants to customize his Start menu so that he can open a file from his user account folder and from his Documents folder without opening a window for each of these folders. He also wants to be able to quickly access a drive without opening the Computer window. List the steps this employee should follow to customize the Start menu on his computer.
4. An employee who does desktop publishing for her department complains that the desktop background images she places on the desktop are not sharp and that they also seem "washed out." What two ways can this employee improve the quality of the image on her computer desktop?
5. An employee in the Life Sciences department notices that Windows Vista Basic on her computer does not display translucent windows and dialog boxes and a translucent taskbar and Start menu. Plus, she does not have access to Live Taskbar Thumbnails, Windows Flip, and Windows Flip 3D. What is the cause of this problem, and what would she have to do so that she can use these Windows Aero features?
6. An intern working on a computer in Admissions and Records complains that his computer is unusually slow. After watching him work on the computer, you notice that his computer uses a variety of special visual effects. What would you recommend that the intern do to improve the performance of his computer?

7. An employee in Health Services complains that his monitor "goes blank" periodically. Although the image on the monitor reappears when he touches the keyboard or mouse, he wants to know if there is a problem with the monitor and, if so, what he can do to correct this problem. After examining his computer, you discover that he is not using a screen saver. What is the probable cause, and what would you recommend that he do?
8. An instructor in the Graphics department has a computer that supports Windows Aero. She notices that she does not have access to certain Windows Aero features, such as Live Taskbar Thumbnails. Prepare a list of the settings that she should check to make sure that her computer not only supports Windows Aero, but also that Windows Aero and its features are fully enabled on her computer.
9. Submit your document to your instructor, either in printed or electronic form, as requested.

Apply | Case Problem 3

Use the skills you learned in the tutorial to develop a plan for customizing a computer's power settings.

There are no Data Files needed for this Case Problem.

Innovative Entrepreneurs Selene Ochoa works as a technical support manager at Innovative Entrepreneurs, a firm that provides venture capital for entrepreneurs of new Internet companies. As one of the company's reps, you rely on the use of your company laptop when you visit new clients. You want to adjust the power management settings on your laptop so that you can conserve power while at the same time guaranteeing that your laptop is immediately available when you need to use it. Before you meet with Selene to discuss how best to adjust power settings on your computer, you decide to examine and document your laptop's current power management settings.

Use a word processing application, such as Microsoft Word or WordPad, to prepare your answers to these questions. Complete the following:

1. What type of computer do you use? Desktop computer, laptop, notebook, or handheld? Do you use an Uninterruptable Power Supply (or UPS unit) with your computer?
2. Open the Power Options window from the Control Panel. What type of power plan does your computer currently use? Does it meet your current needs with respect to providing power and optimizing performance?
3. Choose the option for viewing settings for your computer's Power button. What are your current Power button settings? Examine the list of Power button options for Plugged in or On battery. What other options might you want to use, and what benefit would you derive from them?
4. Return to the Power Options window, and then choose the option to edit your current plan settings. What settings does your computer currently use for turning off the display? What changes, if any, might you want to make to these settings, and why?
5. What settings does your computer currently use for switching to a Sleep state? What changes might you want to make to these settings, and why?
6. Choose the option for changing advanced power settings. What settings does your computer use for turning off the hard disk? What changes might you want to make to these settings?
7. Examine your computer's settings for Hybrid Sleep and Hibernation. Does your computer support Hybrid Sleep and, if so, what are its current settings? Is Hibernation enabled on your computer and, if so, what are its current settings?

EXPLORE

8. Examine your computer's settings for Power buttons and lids. What action does your computer take when you press the Power button on your system unit? What action does your computer take when you use the Start menu's Power button?

EXPLORE

9. If available, examine the Battery power management settings. What action does Windows Vista take when the battery reaches a Critical level? What percentage of battery capacity remaining is used for Low Battery level and Critical Battery level? Is Low Battery notification enabled? What action does Windows Vista take when the battery capacity reaches the low level?
10. Close the Power Options dialog box and Edit Plan Settings window without making any changes.
11. Submit your document to your instructor, either in printed or electronic form, as requested.

Challenge | Case Problem 4

Explore how to create custom toolbars for a fixed-rate mortgage company.

There are no Data Files needed for this Case Problem.

Reliable Financiers, Inc. Reliable Financiers, Inc. is a Hawaiian firm that provides fixed-rate mortgages for new homeowners and for homeowners who want to refinance adjustable rate mortgages. Kilani Ka-hale-wai, a loan officer at Reliable Financiers, wants to create custom toolbars that will allow him to quickly access drives, folders, and files on his computer so that he can respond quickly to customer requests on the telephone. Since you've recently customized your computer, you offer to show him how to create toolbars.

As you customize Windows Vista, keep a record of your original computer settings so that you can restore your computer after you finish. Also, use a word processing application, such as Microsoft Word or WordPad, to prepare your answers to these questions. Complete the following:

1. If necessary, unlock the taskbar.

EXPLORE

2. Use the taskbar shortcut menu to add the Address toolbar to the taskbar. Where does Windows Vista place the Address toolbar on the taskbar? Describe the appearance of the Address toolbar.
3. Make sure that your Internet connection is active, and then type **microsoft.com** in the Address toolbar, press the Enter key, and then describe what happens.
4. Type **google.com**, press the Enter key, and then describe what happens.
5. Click the Address box list arrow. What options does Windows Vista display? How do these options resemble and differ from the Address Bar in your Web browser? Would this type of toolbar have any value to you in your everyday use of your computer? Explain. Close the Address toolbar and close your Web browser.

EXPLORE

6. Use the taskbar shortcut menu to display a Desktop toolbar on the taskbar. Where does Windows Vista place the new Desktop toolbar on the taskbar? How do you view the options available from this toolbar? What system folders can you access from this toolbar, and what happens when you point to one of these folders? Try each of these options and note the types of content that you can access from this toolbar. What other options does Windows Vista display on this toolbar? Close this toolbar.

EXPLORE

7. Use the taskbar shortcut menu to create a new toolbar, and then select the Documents folder. What does Windows Vista display on the Documents toolbar menu? What happens if you point to a folder on the Documents toolbar menu? Can you open a file from the Documents toolbar menu and, if so, how do you perform this operation? Close the Documents toolbar.

8. Describe at least one feature on each toolbar that might prove beneficial to you now or in the future.
9. Submit your document to your instructor, either in printed or electronic form, as requested.

Review | Quick Check Answers

Session 2.1

1. theme, color scheme
2. Windows Aero, Windows Vista Basic, Windows Standard, Windows Classic
3. font-smoothing
4. ClearType
5. desktop composition
6. True

Session 2.2

1. True
2. links, menus
3. taskbar grouping
4. True
5. False
6. desktop toolbar

Session 2.3

1. resolution
2. True
3. 32
4. refresh rate
5. True
6. Hybrid Sleep

Ending Data Files

There are no ending Data Files needed for this tutorial.

Tutorial 3

Objectives

Session 3.1
- Examine how Windows Vista organizes folders and files
- Consider a file-management strategy
- View the contents of a folder
- Examine paths, long filenames, and aliases
- Organize files in groups and stacks

Session 3.2
- Use Instant Search
- Search for folders and files from a folder window
- Perform an advanced search with Search Explorer
- Examine search and indexing settings

Managing Folders and Files

Organizing Client Files

Case | Cabral Advertising, Inc.

Maya Cabral operates a fast-growing advertising firm called Cabral Advertising, which provides a wide range of design and advertising services for her clients in the New Orleans area. She designs company logos, brochures, newsletters, annual reports, catalogs, ads, business cards, and wine bottle labels. She scans and restores photos, creates illustrations and cartoons, designs eye-catching Web advertising, and offers contract training on the use of graphic software and advertising design principles. Maya stores the files for her client projects, contracts, proposals, and designs on a computer connected to a network. She also stores her business and personal records on that same computer. Because her business is growing and turnaround times on projects are always tight, she asks you to help her develop a more effective strategy for organizing and locating files stored on her computer.

Starting Data Files

Tutorial.03 →

Tutorial
- Business Records
- Client Projects
- Company Performance
- Company Projections
- Contract Training
- Personal Records
- Sales Analyses

Review
- Business Records
- Client Projects
- Company Performance
- Company Projections
- Contract Training
- Personal Records
- Sales Analyses

Case1

(none)

Case2
- Business Records
- Client Projects
- Company Performance
- Company Projections
- Contract Training
- Personal Records
- Sales Analyses

Case3
- Business Records
- Client Projects
- Company Performance
- Company Projections
- Contract Training
- Personal Records
- Sales Analyses

Case4
- Business Records
- Client Projects
- Company Performance
- Company Projections
- Contract Training
- Personal Records
- Sales Analyses

Session 3.1

Organizing Folders and Files

One of the most important tasks you face is managing disks, drives, folders, and files. As storage capacities of hard disks double each year, and as you work with even newer types of software products and create and download from the Internet a wide array of files, you need to organize your folders and files so that you can quickly locate what you need.

Windows Vista provides you with a variety of tools for organizing, managing, customizing, backing up, and locating programs, folders, files, and specific information contained within files. Some of these tools were available in earlier versions of Windows, some are improved over earlier versions of these same tools, and some are new. No matter how you set up your original folder structure, you should periodically analyze your current needs and re-evaluate how you organize folders and files so that you can simplify access to your software and personal files, improve your productivity, and optimize your computer's performance. Fortunately, organizing folders and files is easier than ever thanks to new features in Windows Vista.

When the Windows Vista setup program installs Windows Vista on a computer, it creates a folder structure on the hard disk for the Windows operating system, other installed software, and for each user account. This setup program installs most of the files that constitute the operating system in a newly created Windows folder. The setup program also creates a Program Files folder for all other installed software. As you install new applications, utilities, and games on your computer, the setup program for each of those products usually installs the files for the software in a separate folder in the Program Files folder. However, if you are installing a new software product, and if the setup program proposes to install the software in a folder other than the Program Files folder, you can change the location of the installed software so that it's stored in the Program Files folder. Doing so guarantees that all your installed software is located in one folder on your hard disk. Although most of the files for the Windows Vista operating system are installed in the Windows folder, some components are installed in subfolders under the Program Files folder.

Windows Vista also creates a Users folder on the hard disk, and within that Users folder, Windows Vista creates a user account folder for the first designated user of that computer. If more than one person has a user account on the same computer, each user will have their own user account folder. Within each user account folder, Windows Vista creates a set of subfolders for storing specific types of files, as illustrated in Figure 3-1.

Figure 3-1 How Windows Vista organizes folders for a user account

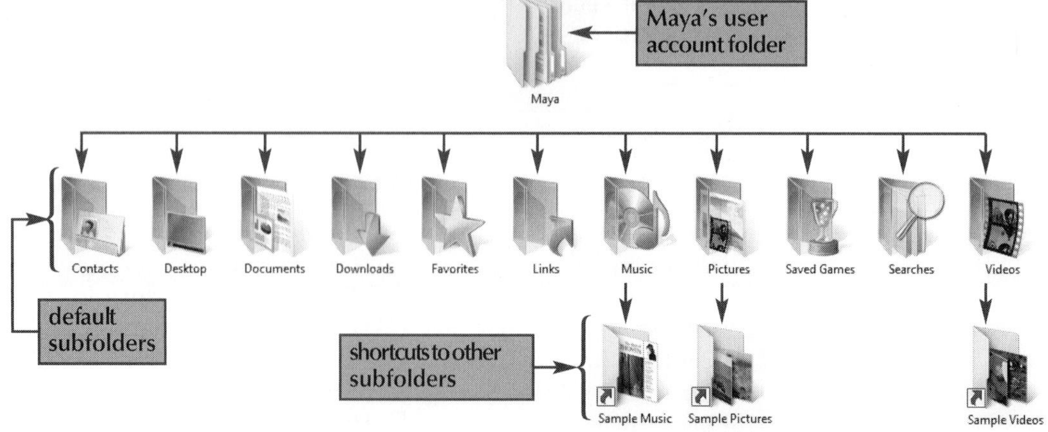

These custom folders are as follows:

- **Contacts** The Contacts folder stores information on all your contacts, whether they are friends, family, coworkers, colleagues, business associates, companies, or organizations. Within this folder, you can create a contact where you store the name, e-mail address(es), street address, phone numbers, Web site address, family information, and notes for a person or business. The information for each contact is stored in a **contact file** with the "contact" file extension. When creating a new user account, Windows Vista automatically creates a contact file for that user. For example, when Maya first created her user account, Windows Vista created a contact named "Maya.contact". You can also customize contacts by adding a picture for each contact. Then you select a contact by quickly examining pictures. If you use Windows Mail as your e-mail program, you can select a personal or business e-mail address from the contacts in the Contacts folder. You can also create **contact groups**, or mailing lists, that combine several contacts into one group, so that you can send the same e-mail message to each contact in the group at the same time. As noted in Tutorial 1, you can also add the Contacts gadget to the Windows Sidebar so that you have easy access to your contacts.
- **Desktop** Windows Vista stores any folders, files, shortcuts, or favorites that you place on your desktop in this folder.
- **Documents** The Documents folder is the central location for storing most of your personal files. By default, most applications save a document to a file in this folder. Likewise, most applications also assume that files you want to open are stored in the Documents folder. Since most people prefer to store all their personal files in the Documents folder, these default assumptions that applications and other types of programs make save you one important step by selecting the right drive and folder for your document file. All you need to do next is to select (or create) the subfolder within the Documents folder where you want to save the file. You can also override these default assumptions if you want to store a file in a folder other than the Documents folder or if you want to store a file on another disk drive. No matter where you store your personal files, you can create subfolders so that you can organize your files into logical groups of related files. For example, you might store different versions of your résumé in a folder called Résumés.
- **Downloads** The Downloads folder contains software and files that you download from the Internet. By keeping downloaded software in one folder, you can quickly find software that you need to reinstall.
- **Favorites** The Favorites folder contains any Internet shortcuts (or bookmarks) that you create with Microsoft Internet Explorer.
- **Links** The Links folder contains shortcuts to the Documents, Music, Pictures, Public, Recently Changed, and Searches folders.
- **Music** You can use the Music folder to store all your music files in one central location. This folder also contains a shortcut to the Sample Music folder (in the Public Music folder) with sample music files, along with their cover art and other information about the music files, such as genre (i.e., jazz, Latin, or classical). You can also play and listen to any music contained in this folder.
- **Pictures** You can use the Pictures folder to store all your pictures in one central location, and you can organize your pictures into subfolders, such as Family, Friends, and Vacations. This folder also contains a shortcut to the Sample Pictures folder (in the Public Pictures folder) with sample picture files that you can also use as desktop backgrounds. You can also view the pictures in this folder as one continuous slide show.

- **Saved Games** If you start a game but stop before you finish it, or if you want to save the settings for a game so that you can resume playing at that point, you can save your game settings when you close the game. Windows Vista creates a file in the Saved Games folder with your game settings. You can open the saved game settings directly from the Saved Games folder. You can also open a saved game from the Games folder or Start menu; in that case, you are asked whether you want to continue with your saved game.
- **Searches** The Searches folder contains virtual folders with shortcuts to various types of files. A **virtual folder** is a folder created as the result of an operation that Windows Vista or you perform, such as displaying a list of recent documents that Windows Vista created or that you opened. Windows Vista automatically creates Search folders with the names Recent Documents, Recent E-mail, Recent Music, Recent Pictures and Videos, Recently Changed, and Shared By Me. If you search for information or files on your computer, you can save your search in the Searches folder.
- **Videos** You can use the Videos folder to store all your video files in one central location. This folder also contains a shortcut to the Sample Videos folder (in the Public Videos folder) with sample video files that you can view and use as desktop backgrounds. You can also view the videos in this folder as one continuous slide show.

In addition to the first user, Windows Vista creates a Public user so that two or more people using the same computer with different user accounts can share files. You can also share files with other users who are part of the same network. The Public folder contains the following subfolders (similar to those you just examined): Public Documents, Public Downloads, Public Music, Public Pictures, and Public Videos.

Organizing Your Personal Folders

If you operate a business, you will want to develop a plan for organizing your business folders so that you can quickly find information for your clients or customers and your business. For example, suppose you operate a small business and perform contract work for various clients. Under the Documents folder, you can create a subfolder named Clients to track all client information, as shown in Figure 3-2. Within that folder, you might create a subfolder for each client. Since you perform the same type of work for each client, you will probably have the same types of subfolders for each client so that you can track similar information. For example, in each client folder, you might have folders for contracts, invoices, and projects. For certain clients, you might have additional folders where you store records specific to that client. You probably will also have a folder for your business records where you can maintain business information, such as annual reports, assets, business plans, cash flow, and taxes. If you work on multiple projects for only a single client or employer, you might prefer to organize folders and files by project rather than by client.

Designing a folder structure for work and personal files — Figure 3-2

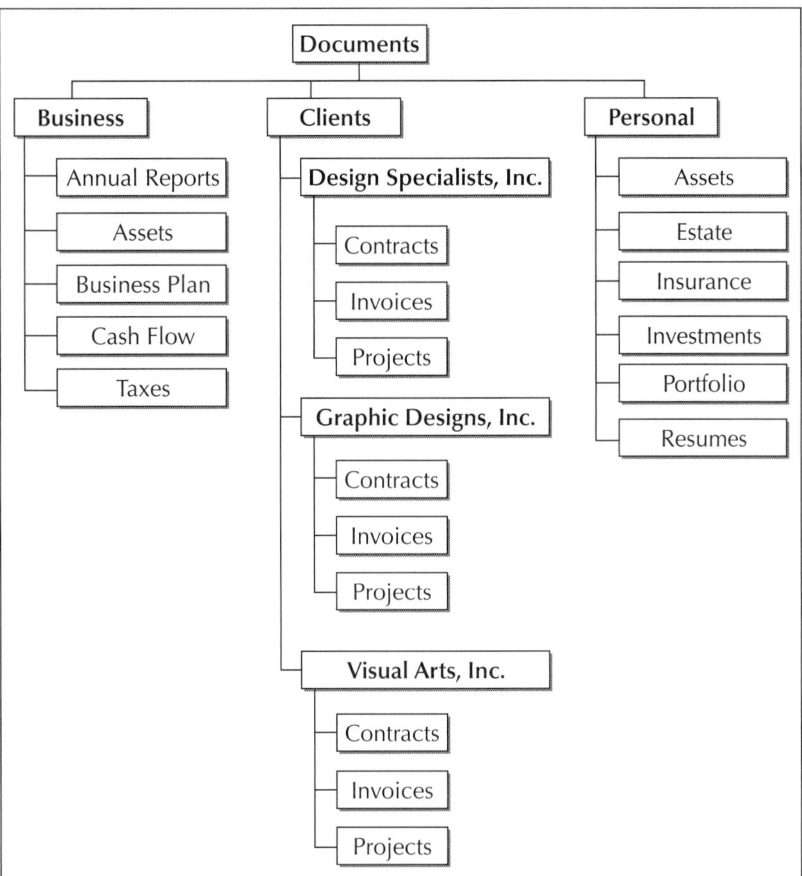

You might also have a personal folder for tracking important personal information, such as your personal portfolio, personal assets (useful for bank loans and insurance), investments, estate information (such as a will), insurance information, and résumés (for use with project proposals where you or your client are seeking venture capital).

If you efficiently organize your folder structure, you can quickly locate what you need and store new files with other files that contain similar types of information. For example, if you need to locate a contract for a specific client, you know exactly where to find that document (i.e., in the Contracts folder for that client). If you need to print a monthly cash flow report for your business or update your database of personal assets, you know which folders contain those files. Another advantage of efficiently organizing your folders and files is that you can quickly back up important folders and files and be assured that you have a copy of all your important documents. When searching for files, an organized folder structure gives you a head start on locating the exact document you need.

InSight | Organizing Your Class Files

You can use these same strategies and approaches to organize files for the different college courses you take. For example, if you were taking a Windows class, a Robotics class, and a Computer Forensics class, you could create a Windows folder, a Robotics folder, and a Computer Forensics folder on the flash drive you use for your classes. Within each of these folders, you could create a Class Notes folder where you store notes that you take for each class; a Lab Assignments folder for all your completed lab assignments; an Online Resources folder where you store saved copies of Web pages that contain course information, the syllabus, class outlines, class handouts, and other course information materials; a Data Files folder where you store downloaded and extracted copies of the electronic files for a course; and perhaps even a Shortcuts folder where you store shortcuts to Web sites that you frequently visit to obtain information for a course. For example, you might have a shortcut to Microsoft's Knowledge Base Web site for your Windows class. If you use your flash drive to store other information not related to the courses you take, you can create a Classes folder and store all the subfolders for all your classes within the Classes folder and keep all that information separate from the other contents of your flash drive.

Getting Started

To complete this tutorial, you need to display the Computer icon on the desktop, switch your computer to single-click activation, and activate the option for displaying file extensions. In the following steps, you will check, and if necessary, change those settings.

To set up your computer:

1. If Windows Vista does not display a Computer icon on the desktop, click the **Start** button, right-click **Computer**, and then click **Show on Desktop**.
2. If you need to enable single-click activation, double-click the **Computer** icon on the desktop, click the **Organize** button on the command bar, click **Folder and Search Options**, and on the General property sheet in the Folder Options dialog box, click the **Single-click to open an item (point to select)** option button, and then click the **Underline icon titles only when I point at them** option button if it is not already selected.
3. Click the **View** tab, click the **Hide extensions for known file types** check box and remove the check mark to display file extensions, click the **OK** button to close the Folder Options dialog box and apply these changes, and then close the Computer window.

Now, as you work with files, you will see their file extensions so that you can associate file extensions with specific programs on your computer.

Some tutorials, like this one, require that you use Data Files to complete the steps in this tutorial. You can obtain these Data Files in one of two ways:

- Download a self-extracting executable file containing the Tutorial.03 Data Files from CENGAGE Learning's Web site to your Documents folder or the Public Documents folder or to a flash drive, and then extract the contents of the self-extracting executable file to a subfolder within the Documents folder or the Public Documents folder on your hard disk or to a flash drive. An **executable file** is a file that contains program code that Windows Vista can load into memory and run. A **self-extracting executable file** is an executable file that contains a set of folders and files stored in a compressed format to reduce the size of the file. It also contains a program for extracting the contents of the executable file (i.e., the folders and files contained with the self-extracting executable file).

- Copy the Tutorial.03 Data Files from a network folder in your computer lab to a flash drive.

If you prefer to download the Data Files from CENGAGE Learning's Web site, follow the instructions on the inside back cover of this book. When you download the Data Files to your computer's hard disk, store the downloaded Data Files in a subfolder with a name such as Windows Vista Data Files, within your Documents folder or on a flash drive. Then you can make duplicate working copies of the Data Files that you need for different tutorials. Each tutorial that uses Data Files specifies the name of the folder where you should store the extracted Data Files.

If you are working on a computer that's connected to a network in a computer lab, your instructor or technical support staff may have already placed a copy of the Data Files in a folder on your computer lab's network so that you can copy the files from a network location to a flash drive or to another location where you will be working with the files.

The files you need for this tutorial are stored in the Tutorial folder of the Tutorial.03 folder provided with your Data Files. You are going to place a copy of the Tutorial folder in the Public Documents folder on the computer that you are using so that you can take advantage of Windows Vista's new Instant Search feature later in the tutorial. You can perform this operation in one of three ways:

- If you download the Tutorial.03 Data Files from CENGAGE Learning's Web site to your own computer, you can store the downloaded file in your Documents or Public Documents folder, and then extract the Tutorial.03 Data Files to a subfolder in the Documents or Public Documents folder. The tutorial instructions assume you will be using the Public Documents folder. If you choose to use your Documents folder instead, you will need to adapt the instructions in the tutorial steps to take this difference into account.
- If you are working on a computer in a computer lab, you can copy the extracted Tutorial.03 Data Files from your computer lab's network to the Public Documents folder on the computer you are using or to another folder on that computer. Your instructor or technical support staff will provide you with any additional information you need to know to perform these operations and to work with the Tutorial.03 Data Files. If you copy the files to a folder other than the Public Documents folder, adapt the instructions in the tutorial steps to take this difference into account.
- If you download and extract Tutorial.03 Data Files to your flash drive, you can attach your flash drive to the computer you are using and copy Tutorial.03 Data Files to your own computer or to a computer in your college's computer lab. Your instructor or technical support staff will provide you with any additional information you need to know to perform these operations and to work with the Tutorial.03 Data Files.

The next three sections step you through the process for performing these three different ways of copying the Tutorial folder in the Tutorial.03 folder provided with your Data Files to the Public folder on the computer you are using. Determine which approach you want to use for working with these Data Files, and then complete the steps in that section only. After you copy the Tutorial folder to the Public folder, continue with the "Renaming a Folder" section.

Copying Files to Your Computer's Public Documents Folder

If you downloaded the Tutorial folder in the Tutorial.03 folder provided with your Data Files to your own computer and want to copy it from the Documents folder (or any other folder) to your computer's Public Documents folder, complete the following steps.

To copy the Tutorial folder to your computer's Public Documents folder:

1. Make sure you have downloaded and extracted your copy of the Windows Vista for Power User Tutorial.03 Data Files.

   Trouble? If you don't have the Data Files for this tutorial, you need to get them before you can proceed. Your instructor will ask you to obtain them from a specified location (such as a network drive). If you have any questions about obtaining Data Files, ask your instructor or technical support person for assistance.

2. Close all open windows.
3. On the Start menu, open **Documents**, and in the Navigation pane on the left side of the Documents window, click **Public**. Windows Vista opens the Public folder.
4. In the Public folder window, click **Public Documents**.
5. On the Start menu, open **Documents** again, and in the Documents window, locate and open the **Tutorial.03** folder.
6. Right-click the **taskbar,** and then click **Show Windows Side by Side**. Windows Vista adjusts the two open folder windows so that they are placed side by side on the desktop and are equal in size. Windows Vista places the last folder window that you open on the left side of the desktop.
7. Hold down the **Ctrl** key while you drag the **Tutorial** folder to the Public Documents folder window, release the Ctrl key, and then release your left mouse button. Windows Vista copies the Tutorial folder to the Public Documents folder.
8. Close the Documents subfolder window that contains the Tutorial.03 Data Files but keep the Public Documents folder window open.
9. After reading the next three paragraphs in this section of the tutorial, continue with the section entitled "Renaming a Folder."

If you drag folders or files from one folder window to another folder window on the same drive, Windows Vista moves the folders or files. If you hold down the Ctrl key while you drag, Windows Vista copies the files instead.

When you drag folders or files from one drive to another, Windows Vista makes a duplicate copy of the folders or files. If you hold down the Shift key while you drag, Windows Vista moves the files instead.

If you hold down the right mouse button as you drag folders or files from one window to another or from one drive to another, Windows Vista displays a shortcut menu that includes the options for moving or copying the folders or files. This latter approach guarantees that Windows Vista performs the type of operation that you want (i.e., a move or a copy).

Copying Files from a Network Folder to the Public Folder

If you are working in a computer lab and want to copy the Tutorial folder in the Tutorial.03 folder provided with your Data Files from your computer lab's network to the Public Documents folder or another folder on your computer, complete the following steps.

To copy the Tutorial folder from the network to the Public Documents folder:

1. Make sure you have your copy of the Tutorial.03 Data Files.

   Trouble? If you don't have the Data Files for this tutorial, you need to get them before you can proceed. Your instructor will ask you to obtain them from a specified location (such as a network drive). If you have any questions about obtaining Data Files, ask your instructor or technical support person for assistance.

2. Close all open windows.
3. On the Start menu, open **Documents**, and in the Navigation pane on the left side of the Documents window, click **Public,** or if your instructor or technical support staff want you to use another folder, locate and open that folder. Windows Vista opens the Public folder (or the folder your instructor or technical support staff recommended).
4. If you are using the Public folder, click **Public Documents**.
5. Follow the instructions provided by your instructor or technical support staff for opening the network folder that contains the Windows Vista for Power Users **Tutorial.03** folder.
6. Right-click the **taskbar,** and then click **Show Windows Side by Side**. Windows Vista adjusts the two open folder windows so that they are placed side by side on the desktop and are equal in size. Windows Vista places the last folder window that you open on the left side of the desktop.
7. Drag the **Tutorial** folder from the network folder window to the Public Documents folder window (or to the folder recommended by your instructor or technical support staff), and then release your left mouse button. Windows Vista copies the Tutorial folder to the Public Documents folder (or to the window for the folder recommended by your instructor or technical support staff).
8. Close the network folder window, but keep the Public Documents folder window open (or the window for the folder recommended by your instructor or technical support staff).
9. Read the next paragraph, and then continue with the section entitled "Renaming a Folder."

If you drag folders or files from a network folder window to a folder window on the computer you are using, Windows Vista copies the folders or files.

Copying the Data Files from a Flash Drive

If you downloaded and extracted the Tutorial folder in the Tutorial.03 folder provided with your Data Files to a flash drive, complete the following steps to copy the Tutorial folder to the Public Documents folder on your own computer or to the Public Documents folder (or another folder recommended by your instructor or technical staff) on a computer in your college's computer lab.

To attach your flash drive:

1. Make sure you have downloaded and extracted your copy of the Windows Vista for Power User Tutorial.03 Data Files.

   Trouble? If you don't have the Data Files for this tutorial, you need to get them before you can proceed. Your instructor will ask you to obtain them from a specified location (such as a network drive). If you have any questions about obtaining Data Files, ask your instructor or technical support person for assistance.

2. Attach your flash drive to a USB port or to a USB cable on the computer you are using. Windows Vista might display a Microsoft Windows dialog box warning about potential problems with the flash drive, an AutoPlay dialog box so that you can select what type of operation you want to perform on the disk, or a window displaying the contents of the flash drive, or Windows Vista might not display any dialog boxes or windows.
3. Complete the appropriate section or sections that follow and complete the section entitled "To copy the Tutorial folder from your flash drive to the Public Documents folder (or another folder)."

If Windows Vista displays a dialog box asking if you want to scan and fix your removable disk, complete the following steps.

If Windows Vista displays a Microsoft Windows dialog box:

1. If Windows Vista displays a Microsoft Windows dialog box asking you if you want to scan and fix your removable disk, click **Scan and fix (recommended)**. See Figure 3-3. As Windows Vista notes, this operation will prevent future problems when copying files to the flash drive.

Figure 3-3 Option for scanning and fixing flash drive

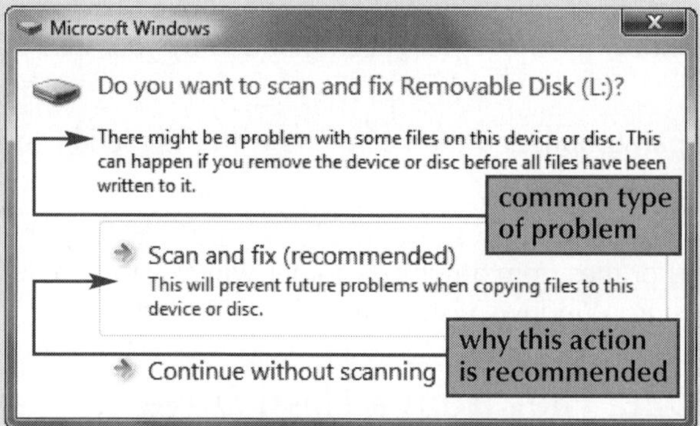

Windows Vista then displays a "Check Disk Removable Disk" dialog box where you can select two disk options. See Figure 3-4. Windows Vista has already enabled the first option for automatically fixing file system errors. This option takes the least time and repairs any problems with the file system on the flash drive. The second option scans for and attempts to recover defective sectors on the flash drive and takes longer than the first option. For a flash drive, you can check the file system because the flash drive stores data differently than a hard disk drive does.

Figure 3-4 Viewing Check Disk options

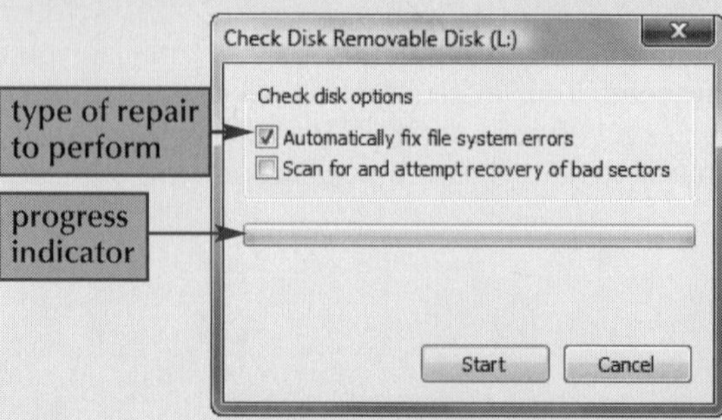

2. Click the **Start** button. Windows Vista might display a "Checking Disk Removable Disk" dialog box in which it informs you that your device or disc was successfully scanned. See Figure 3-5. In this case, Windows Vista notes that it did not find any problems with the flash drive, and the flash drive is ready to use. Windows Vista also explains that if you removed the device or disc before all the files were completely written to the disk, you might be missing parts of some of your files. In that case, you should return to the original set of files (the source) and copy the files again.

Figure 3-5 Results of disk scan

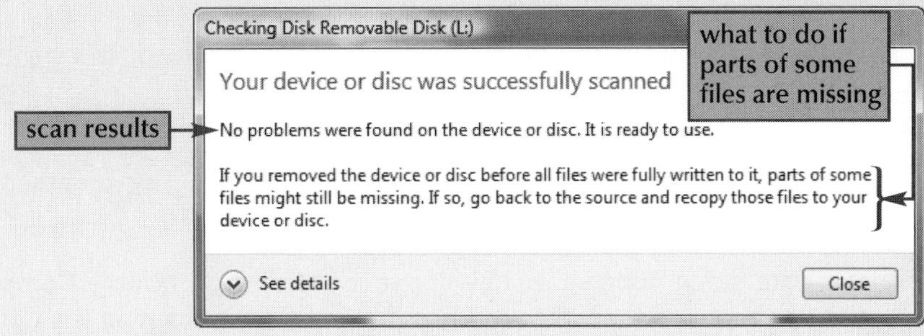

3. Windows Vista might next display an AutoPlay dialog box, as shown in Figure 3-6, or open a window displaying the contents of the flash drive, or it might not display the AutoPlay dialog box or a flash drive window.

Figure 3-6 AutoPlay dialog box options

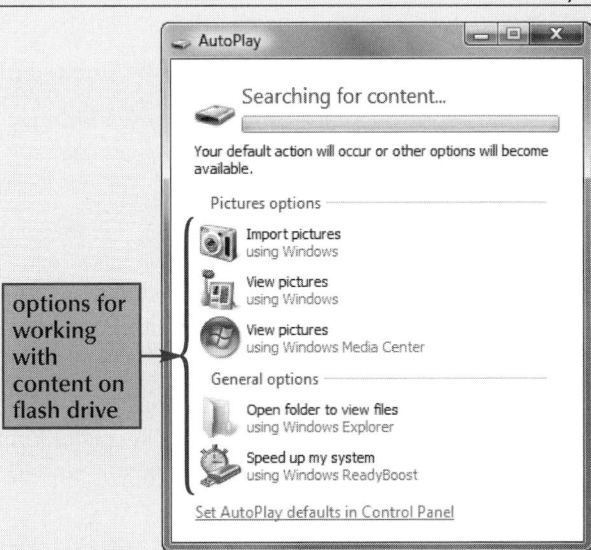

4. If Windows Vista displays an AutoPlay dialog box, complete the next section; otherwise, continue with the steps entitled "To copy the Tutorial folder from your flash drive to the Public Documents folder (or another folder)."

If Windows Vista displays an AutoPlay dialog box when you insert a flash drive into a USB port, complete the following steps.

If Windows Vista displays an AutoPlay dialog box:

1. In the AutoPlay dialog box under General options, click **Open folder to view files**. Windows Vista opens a window displaying the contents of the flash drive.
2. Keep the window open for the next section.

After opening a folder to view files on your flash drive, you are ready to copy the Tutorial to a folder on your hard disk.

To copy the Tutorial folder from your flash drive to the Public Documents folder (or another folder):

1. If Windows Vista did not open a window for your flash drive, click the **Computer** icon on the desktop, and then click the **icon for your flash drive** in the Computer window.
2. Locate and open the **Tutorial.03** folder on your flash drive.
3. On the Start menu, open **Documents**, and in the Navigation pane on the left side of the Documents window, click **Public**. If your instructor or technical support staff want you to use another folder, locate and open that folder. Windows Vista opens the Public folder (or the folder your instructor or technical support staff recommended).
4. If you are using the Public folder window, click **Public Documents**.
5. Right-click the **taskbar,** and then click **Show Windows Side by Side**. Windows Vista adjusts the two folder windows so that they are placed side by side on the desktop and are equal in size. Windows Vista places the last folder window that you open on the left side of the desktop.
6. Drag the **Tutorial** folder from the Tutorial.03 flash drive folder window to the Public Documents folder window (or to the folder recommended by your instructor or technical support staff), and then release your left mouse button. Windows Vista copies the Tutorial folder to the Public Documents folder window (or to the window for the folder recommended by your instructor or technical support staff).
7. Close the Tutorial.03 flash drive folder window, but keep the Public Documents folder window open (or the window for the folder recommended by your instructor or technical support staff).
8. Read the next three paragraphs, and then continue with the section entitled "Renaming a Folder."

When you drag folders or files from one drive to another, Windows Vista automatically makes a duplicate copy of the folders or files. If you hold down the Shift key while you drag, Windows Vista moves the files instead.

If you drag folders or files from one folder window to another folder window on the same drive, Windows Vista moves the folders or files. If you hold down the Ctrl key while you drag, Windows Vista copies the files instead.

If you hold down the right mouse button as you drag folders or files from one window to another or from one drive to another, Windows Vista displays a shortcut menu that includes the options for either moving or copying the folders or files. This latter approach guarantees that Windows Vista performs the type of operation that you want (i.e., a move or a copy).

Renaming a Folder

Next, you want to rename the Tutorial folder you just copied to the Public Documents folder. First, you want to make sure that the Public Documents folder does not contain a folder with the same name that you intend to use.

To rename the copied folder:

1. Examine the names of folders in the Public Documents folder on the computer you are using (or in the window for the folder recommended by your instructor or technical support staff).
2. If you find a folder named Cabral Advertising, right-click the **Cabral Advertising** folder name, click **Rename** on the shortcut menu, press the **Right Arrow** key to go to the end of the folder name, press the **Spacebar**, type **(Previous)**, and then press the **Enter** key. Windows Vista adds "(Previous)" to the end of the existing folder name.
3. Right-click the **Tutorial** folder you just copied to the Public Documents folder (or to the folder recommended by your instructor or technical support staff), and then click **Rename** on the shortcut menu. Windows Vista highlights the folder name.
4. Type **Cabral Advertising** and then press the **Enter** key. Windows Vista renames the folder.

Now you're ready to examine the Data Files for this tutorial.

Viewing the Contents of a Folder

Before she leaves for her client training session, Maya asks you to examine the folder structure and the files in the Cabral Advertising folder. She notes that you will be adding more files to the folder, so you need to be familiar with the folder structure and the location of files.

To view the contents of the Cabral Advertising folder:

1. Open the **Cabral Advertising** folder and if necessary, maximize the window.
2. Click the **Views button arrow** on the command bar, and while viewing the contents of the Cabral Advertising folder window, drag the **slider tab** along the Views menu slider bar and position it between Extra Large Icons and Large Icons so that you can see all the folder icons within the window. Windows Vista displays a partial view of the actual contents of documents within files on the folder icons except for the Contract Training folder icon. See Figure 3-7. The Contract Training folder icon shows that this folder contains subfolders. Your view of this window may differ.

Figure 3-7 Viewing the Cabral Advertising folder

This new Windows Vista feature for scaling icons in a folder and the new feature for displaying the content within files as part of folder icons make it easier to work and find what you need.

To continue your exploration of this folder:

1. Open the **Contract Training** folder and then open the **Presentations** folder.
2. If you do not see a Preview Pane on the right side of the window, click the **Organize** button on the command bar, point to **Layout**, and then click **Preview Pane**. You can use the Layout menu to display or hide the Navigation, Details, and Preview Panes as well as display a classic menu bar similar to what is found in previous Windows versions. You can also adjust the width or height of these three panes by dragging a border.
3. Point to the border between the Preview Pane and the file list pane. When you see a double-headed arrow that points to the left and right ⇔, hold down the left mouse button and drag the border of the Preview Pane to the left until it occupies half of the space that the file icons previously occupied.
4. Use the **Views button arrow** on the command bar to adjust your view to a setting between Extra Large Icons and Large Icons that permits you to see all three file icons in the Presentations folder. Windows Vista displays thumbnail previews of each file, and in the lower-right corner of the thumbnail, also displays a file icon that denotes the type of file (in this case, a Microsoft Office PowerPoint presentation). See Figure 3-8. The thumbnail preview helps you quickly spot content in a file that you want to use.

Figure 3-8 Custom view of folder contents

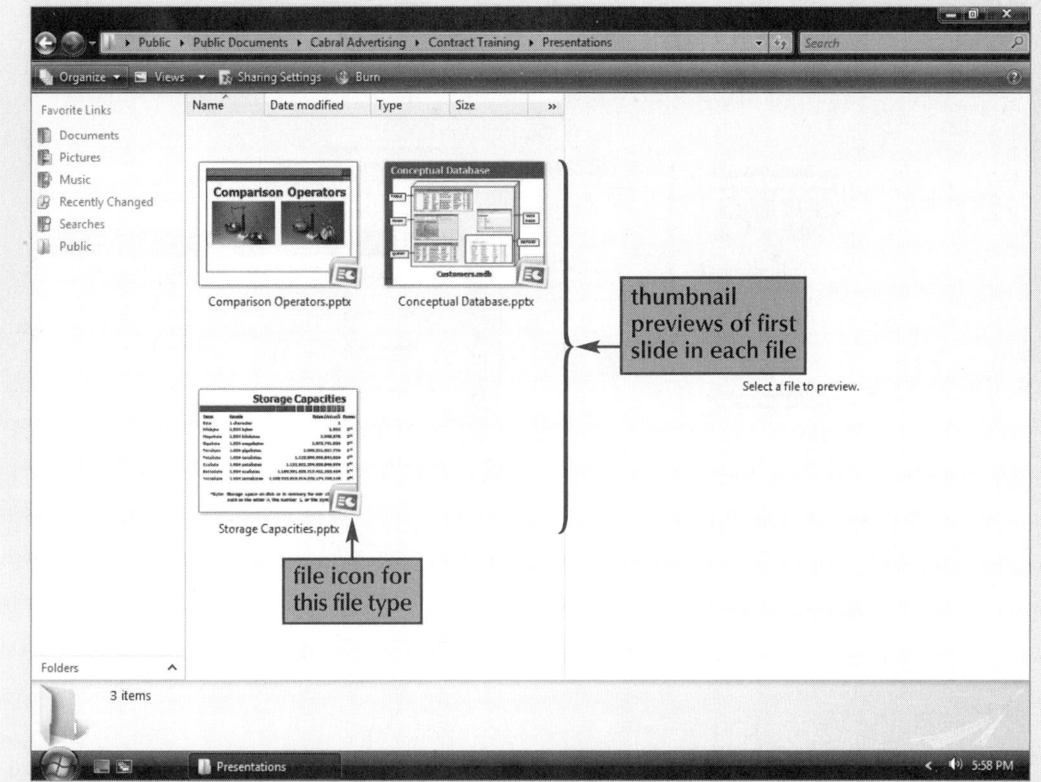

5. Point to **Comparison Operators.pptx** and watch the Preview Pane. Windows Vista displays the first slide in this presentation and plays the animation on this slide.

6. At the bottom of the vertical scroll bar in the Preview Pane, click the **Next Slide** button ▼. Windows Vista displays the next slide in this presentation. See Figure 3-9.

Tip

You can also right-click the Preview Pane and then click Next to advance one slide.

Figure 3-9 **Previewing a presentation**

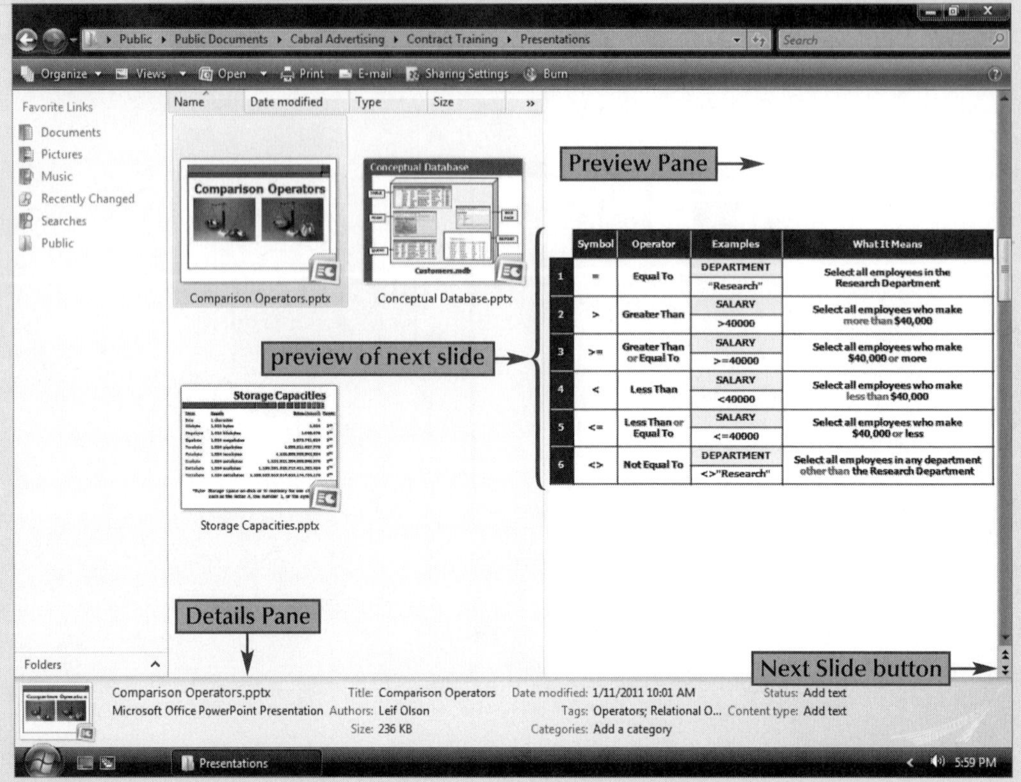

7. Use the **Next Slide** button to view the remainder of the slides in this presentation.

8. Point to **Conceptual Database.pptx**. Windows Vista displays the one slide in this presentation in the Preview Pane.

Tip

Use the Previous Slide button to back up a slide.

Windows Vista provides support for previewing the contents of some types of Office files (such as Microsoft Word, Microsoft Excel, and Microsoft PowerPoint files, but not Microsoft Access database files), Web pages saved with different Web browsers, text files (including Rich Text Format files), e-mail messages, e-mail attachments, audio files, video files, games, contacts, and font files. Software that you purchase and install on your computer might extend this preview capability of Windows Vista for specific types of files that you create with that software. For example, you might be able to preview Adobe Portable Document Format (PDF) files.

If you need to examine the content of different files, you do not need to open each file, examine its contents, close the file, and then open the next file. Furthermore, you don't have to open different types of programs for each type of file you examine. Instead, you can use the Preview Pane to examine the contents of each file by pointing to the file icon, and then scrolling through the content of the file in the Preview Pane. Furthermore, you can use the Preview Pane to step through the mouse-controlled animation in a PowerPoint presentation.

You can also copy the contents of what you view in the Preview Pane, and then place that copy in a new document. For example, if you want to copy one of the slides you examined and use it in a new presentation, you right-click the slide shown in the Preview Pane, click Copy Slide, open or switch to a new or existing presentation in Microsoft Office PowerPoint, and then choose the option for pasting the slide into the presentation. Instead of opening and closing two or more presentations, you can work directly from the Preview Pane.

While you cannot do in the Preview Pane everything that you can do in an application window (at least not yet), the Preview Pane can streamline the way you work, make you more productive, and make your work environment more interesting.

Checking Folder View and Behavior Settings

Maya points out that you can customize your view by changing the way Windows Vista displays the content of folder windows as you browse and view folders and files. She recommends you check these settings to make sure Windows Vista displays your view of folders and files in the way you prefer.

To examine folder settings:

1. Click **Organize** on the command bar, click **Folder and Search Options**, and then click the **View** tab in the Folder Options dialog box. In the Advanced settings list box on the View property sheet, Windows Vista displays a variety of settings for controlling the view and behavior of folders and files. See Figure 3-10.

Figure 3-10 **Examining advanced folder view and behavior settings**

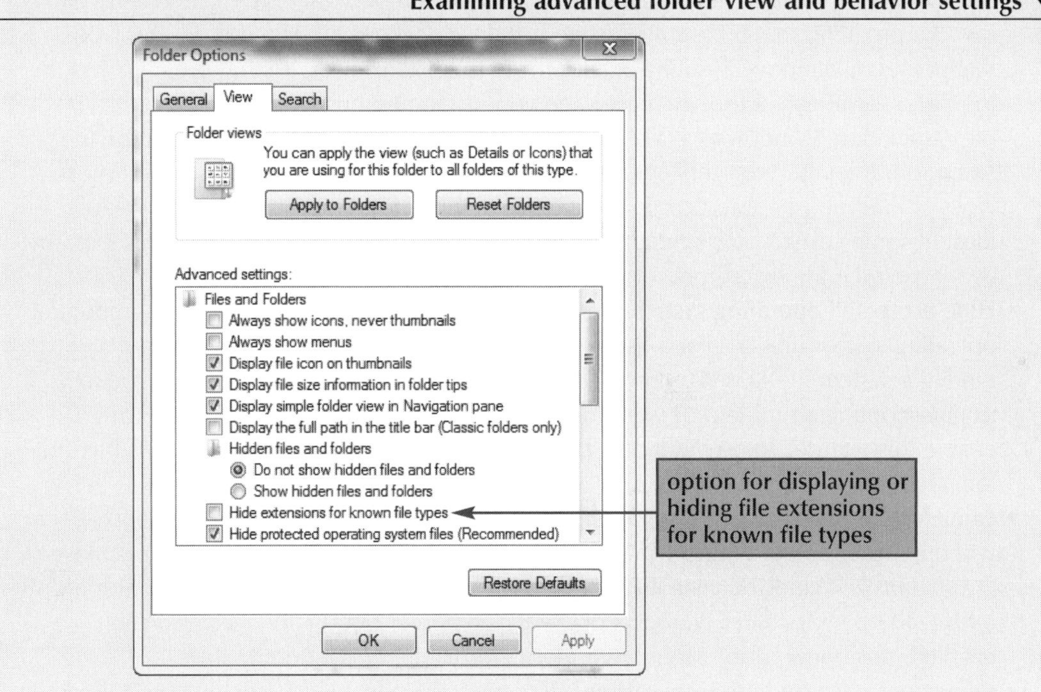

The following Advanced settings options improve the way you work with folders and files, or let you choose an alternate way to work that you prefer:

- **Always show icons, never thumbnails** By default, Windows Vista displays thumbnails, or what are called thumbnail previews, of files in a folder, where possible, rather than simple or static (that is, unchanging) file icons so that you can quickly view and identify the content within a file. However, you can enable this feature if you prefer the classic file icon view or if you notice that it takes too long to display thumbnail previews of every folder and file in a window.
- **Always show menus** By default, Windows Vista does not display the classic menu bar above the command bar. If you want to always have access to the classic menu bar and its submenus, you can enable this feature. The command bar will still be visible, so you can use both the command bar and menu bar.

- **Display file icon on thumbnails** Windows Vista includes a small file icon on the thumbnails of files so that you can identify the types of files contained in a folder and so that you can identify the application associated with each file type.
- **Display file size information in folder tips** By default, when you point to a file, Windows Vista displays a ToolTip that contains information about a file, including the file type (such as Microsoft Office PowerPoint Presentation), the Author, the document's Title, the file Size, and the Date (and time) the file was modified. You can use this feature to quickly view information about a file. If you turn off this feature, Windows Vista does not show the file size in the ToolTip.
- **Hidden folders and files** By default, Windows Vista does not display user or system folders and files that are marked as hidden folders and files. If you want to view hidden folders and files, whether to troubleshoot a problem or just to learn more about the subtle details of the Windows Vista system folder and file structure, you can choose the option "Show hidden files and folders." These hidden file and folder icons then become visible, but the folder and file icon icons appear faint.
- **Hide extensions for known file types** By default this option is enabled, and Windows Vista does not show file extensions for known file types, or registered files. A **registered file** is a file associated with an application or program on your computer. When you install a program, that program registers certain file types with Windows Vista. From that point on, Windows Vista associates those file extensions with that program (assuming the associations do not change when you install another program). As part of the file association, Windows Vista uses the same file icon for all files with the same file extension. If you turn off this option, Windows Vista displays file extensions for most types of files, and as noted earlier, you can use this information to help you identify files. In some cases, you might also be able to more quickly identify malicious software by viewing the file extension.
- **Hide protected operating system files (Recommended)** Windows Vista hides important operating system files so that a user cannot accidentally delete, move, rename, or modify a system file that Windows Vista needs to operate properly. Again, if you're troubleshooting a problem or want to view these operating system files, you can enable this feature. These hidden system folder and file icons then become visible, but the folder and file icons appear faint.
- **Launch folder windows in a separate process** If you enable this option, Windows Vista will open each folder window in a different part of memory. This option can increase the stability of Windows Vista and is obviously useful if you frequently encounter problems with opening folder windows or if your computer frequently crashes. When enabled, this option also slows down the performance of your computer.
- **Remember each folder's view settings** By default, Windows Vista remembers any view settings you have applied to a folder.
- **Restore previous folder windows at logon** If you enable this setting, Windows Vista will restore any windows that were open when you last shut down your computer. This feature allows you to quickly return to those folders where you were last working.
- **Show drive letters** When you open the Computer window, Windows Vista displays the friendly name of a drive, such as Local Disk for a hard disk drive, and the drive name in parentheses (such as C:). If you turn off this setting, you see only the friendly name, not the drive name.
- **Show pop-up description for folder and desktop items** By default, Windows Vista displays a ToolTip when you rest your mouse pointer on a desktop or folder icon. If you turn off this option, Windows Vista does not display ToolTips.

- **Show preview handlers in preview pane** A **preview handler** is a component of the Windows Vista operating system that displays the contents of certain types of files in the Preview Pane. If you turn off this feature, you can no longer preview the content of files with the Preview Pane.
- **Use check boxes to select items** When you enable this new Windows Vista feature, Windows Vista displays a small check box next to each file icon when you point to the file icon. You can click this check box to select the file, as shown in Figure 3-11. This option can be useful if you want to select a group of files, whether they are located side by side or scattered around the folder window, for an operation such as copying, moving, or deleting. Another approach to selecting folders and files in a window is to hold down the Ctrl key as you point to each folder or file (assuming you are using single-click activation). However, if you enable the use of check boxes, you cannot use the Ctrl key to select multiple files. As you select a file's check box, you may also see a ToolTip that identifies the file type, authors, title, size, and date modified.

Selecting files using their check boxes

Figure 3-11

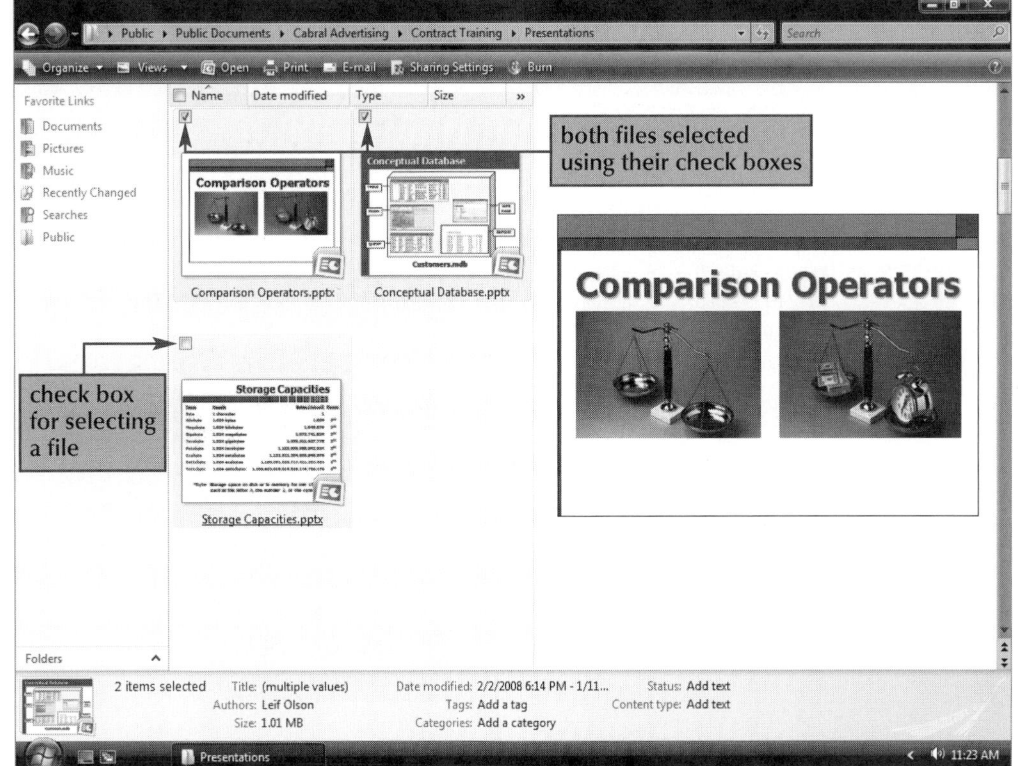

- **When typing into list view** By default, Windows Vista uses the "Select the typed item in the view" option under this category. When enabled, Windows Vista can perform a character search of the contents of a folder. If you want to quickly locate a folder or file in a folder window, you can type the first character of that folder and file and Windows Vista highlights the first folder or file that starts with that character. You don't need to use the scroll bars. This feature saves time and effort because you do not have to scroll through a long list of folders or files to locate the folder or file you want to use. If you switch this setting to "Automatically type into the Search box," any character you type appears in the folder's Search box at the top of the window. The option is useful if you frequently use the new Windows Vista Instant Search feature (which you can examine in more detail later in this tutorial) to locate folders and files in the current folder and its subfolders.

You can use the Restore Defaults button to restore all the options in the Advanced settings list box to their original settings. Under Folder Views, you can use the Apply to Folders button to apply the view you've selected for the current folder to every other folder. For example, if you prefer a specific view, such as Extra Large Icons view, you can switch to that view and then use this option in the Folder Options dialog box to apply that setting to other folders. You can use the Reset Folders to restore the default view settings for all folders.

To continue your examination of this folder's contents:

1. Click the **Cancel** button to close the Folder Options dialog box without making any changes to your computer.
2. Point to **Comparison Operators.pptx**. Windows Vista selects the file and displays information about the file in the Details Pane. See Figure 3-12. The Details Pane provides the same information that you see in a ToolTip when you rest the mouse pointer on a file. Depending on the file type, the Details Pane might also display additional information not found in a ToolTip, such as the category or status of the file.

Figure 3-12 Using the Details Pane to view file information

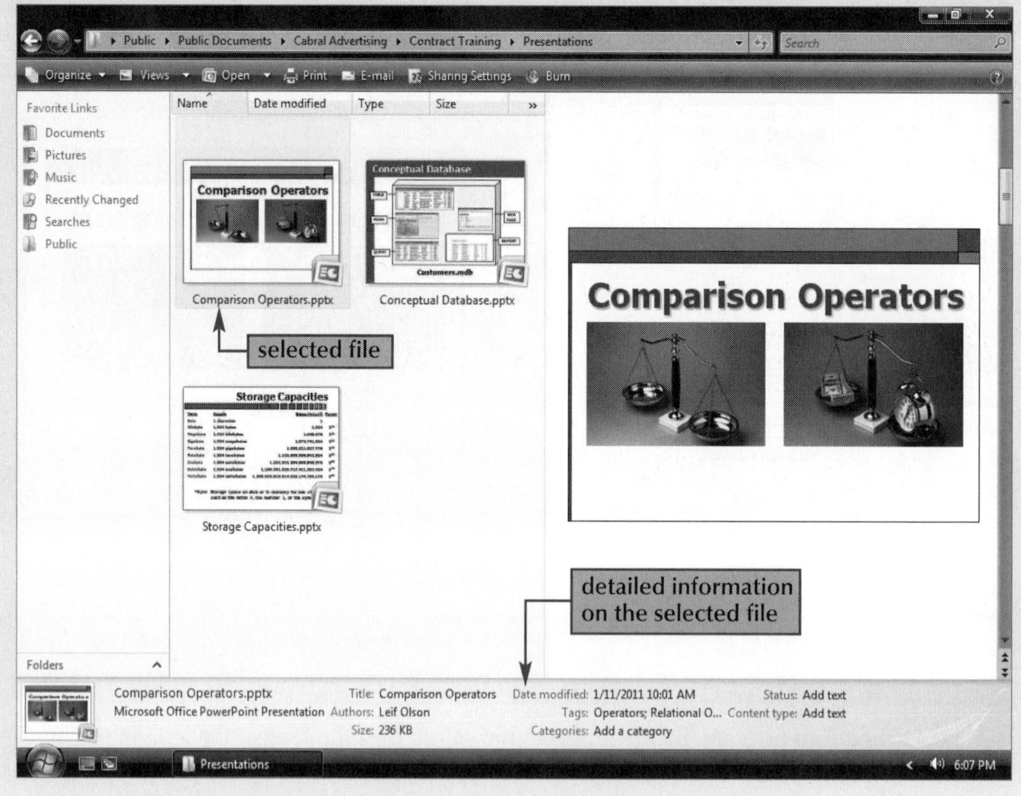

After you select a file, you can make changes to the information about the file in the Details Pane or specify new information. You will examine this use of the Details Pane later in the tutorial.

Viewing Properties of Files

Earlier, Maya noted that another way to view information about a file is to view its properties. You do so by opening a file's Properties dialog box. You decide to compare this method with the use of ToolTips and the Details Pane.

A file's Properties dialog box displays file properties, such as its name and size. It also provides other information, such as a file's attributes. An **attribute** is a setting applied to a folder or file by the operating system; however, you can also change these settings on the General property sheet or in a command-line environment. Using a file's Properties dialog box, you can also calculate the amount of **slack**, or wasted space, allocated to the file but not actually used by the file. You will examine slack and its impact on a computer in more detail in Tutorial 5.

To view properties of a file:

1. Right-click **Comparison Operators.pptx** and then click **Properties** on the shortcut menu. On the General property sheet of the Comparison Operators.pptx Properties dialog box, Windows Vista shows the file icon, the filename, the type of file, the name of the program that opens this file, the location of the file, the size of the file, the storage space that this file uses on disk, and the date the file was created, modified, and accessed as well as the amount of time that has elapsed. See Figure 3-13. On the computer used for this figure, the location of the file is: C:\Users\Public\Documents\Cabral Advertising\Contract Training\Presentations (although you can't see the full location listed on the General property sheet). The file size is reported in KB (or kilobytes) and that information is then translated into bytes. If you divide 242,031 bytes by 1,024 (the number of bytes in a kilobyte), you obtain approximately 236 KB (rounded off). The difference between the number of bytes for "Size on disk" and "Size," namely, 3729 bytes, is the amount of slack. Note that the property sheet also contains check boxes labeled Read-only and Hidden next to Attributes. If you enable the Read-only attribute by adding a check mark to the Read-only check box, and then apply this setting, the program you use to open the file will open it in read-only mode. That means you cannot save any changes you make to the file under the original filename; however, you can save the changes to a file with a new filename. Read-only therefore protects a file from changes. If you enable the Hidden attribute, Windows Vista does not display the file icon in the folder unless you choose the option to "Show hidden files and folders." You can use the Change button to associate this file type with another application.

Tip

To view the full location, click the location and use the arrow keys, End key, or Home key to adjust your view.

Figure 3-13 Viewing properties of a file

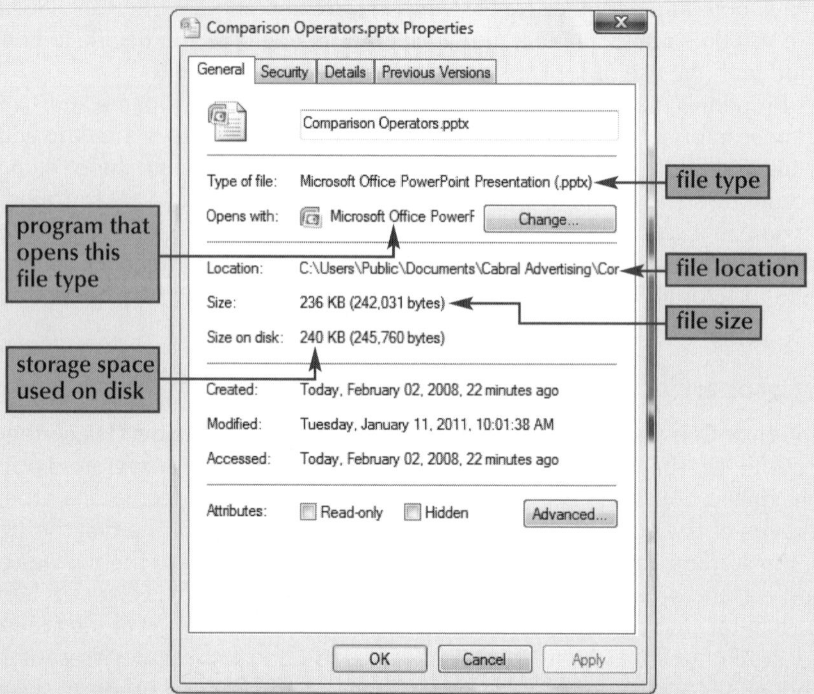

2. Click the **Details** tab. Windows Vista provides more details about the properties of this file under the Description and Origin sections, including the Authors (in this case, Leif Olson, an employee at Cabral Advertising). See Figure 3-14. If you scroll further down this property sheet and locate the Content section, Windows Vista displays information about the content of the file (in this case, information such as the word count and number of slides). Windows Vista displays more information about the file in the File section at the bottom of the Details property sheet (including the name of the computer on which this file is stored).

Figure 3-14
Viewing details on file properties

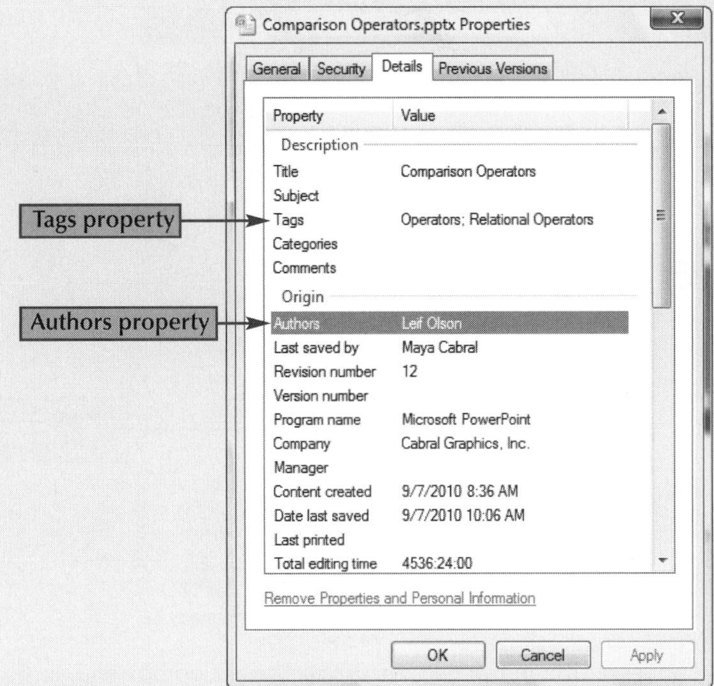

3. Click the **Remove Properties and Personal Information** link at the bottom of the Details property sheet. Windows Vista opens a Remove Properties dialog box. See Figure 3-15. At the top of this dialog box, Windows Vista notes that some of the file properties may contain personal information. Then, it displays two options. You can create a copy of this file with all possible properties removed, or you can pick which properties you want to remove from the file. If you click the "Remove the following properties from this file" option button, you can select and remove all the properties listed under Description and some of the properties listed under Origin and Content, but you cannot select and remove properties listed under File. Also, for files produced for previous versions of applications (such as previous versions of Microsoft Office), you may not be able to remove any properties. Each file property sheet identifies what properties you can remove for that file type.

Figure 3-15 Viewing options for removing file properties

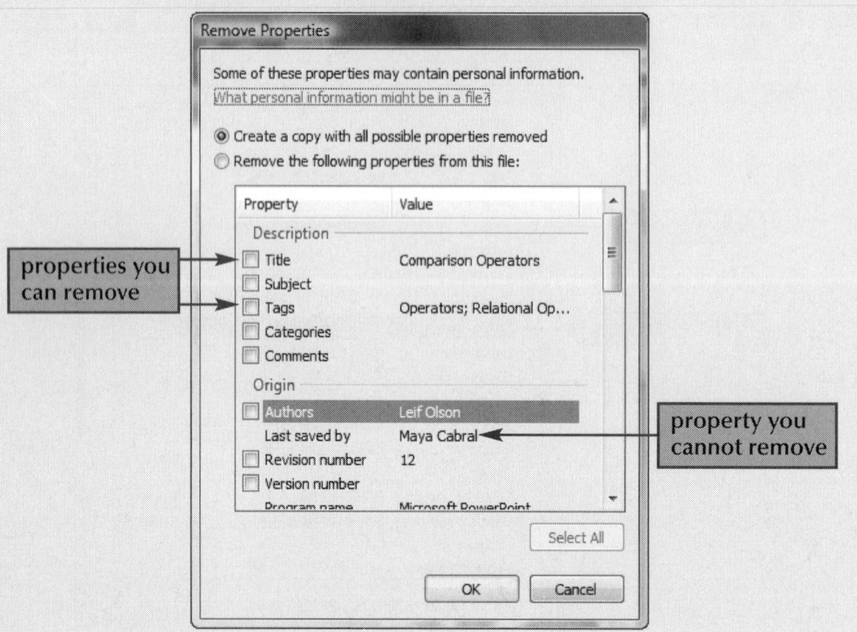

4. Click the **Cancel** button in the Remove Properties dialog box and in the Comparison Operators.pptx Properties dialog box, but keep the Presentations folder window open.

You can also view properties of a group of files.

To view properties of a group of files:

Tip

You can also use the Ctrl+A keyboard shortcut to select all the contents of a folder.

1. Click the **Organize** button on the command bar and then click **Select All**. Windows Vista selects all the files in this folder. In the Details Pane, Windows Vista lists information that applies to all the selected files. See Figure 3-16. For example, Leif Olson is listed because he is the author of all the files. Where file properties vary, such as the Title of the file (its filename), Windows Vista displays "(multiple values)."

Figure 3-16 Viewing details on group properties

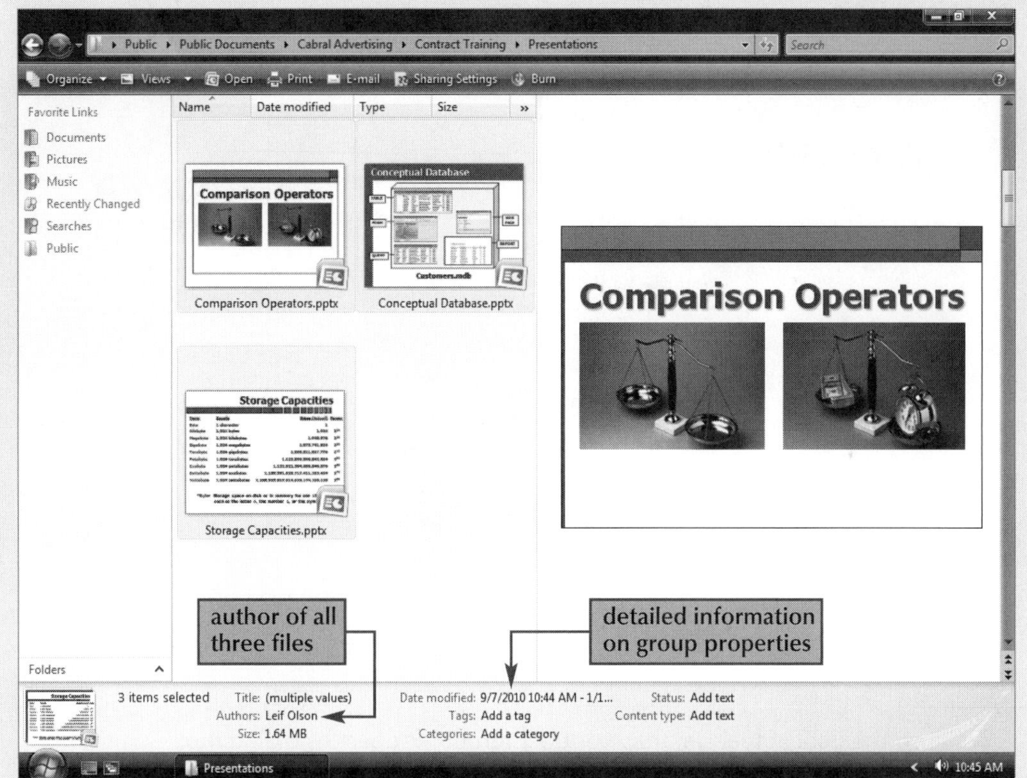

2. Carefully right-click **Conceptual Database.pptx** without losing the selection of the three files, and then click **Properties** on the shortcut menu. On the General property sheet in the Conceptual Database.pptx, ... Properties dialog box, Windows Vista displays group properties for all three files. See Figure 3-17. The ellipsis (...) after the beginning of the Properties dialog box name indicates that you are viewing a collection of files; however, you only see the name of the first file in that group. Windows Vista identifies the total number of files and folders for which you are viewing properties. For File, Windows Vista displays "All of type Microsoft Office PowerPoint Presentation," and for Location, Windows Vista displays "All in C:\Users\Public\Documents\Cabral Advertising\Contract Training\Presentations" (although the entire path is not visible). Windows Vista also reports on the total file size and total size on disk required for all three files. From the Details property sheet, you can remove properties from multiple files.

Trouble? If your Properties dialog box does not match the one shown in Figure 3-17, click the Cancel button, click the Organize button on the command bar, click Select All, click the Organize button again, and then click Properties.

Figure 3-17 Viewing group properties of three files

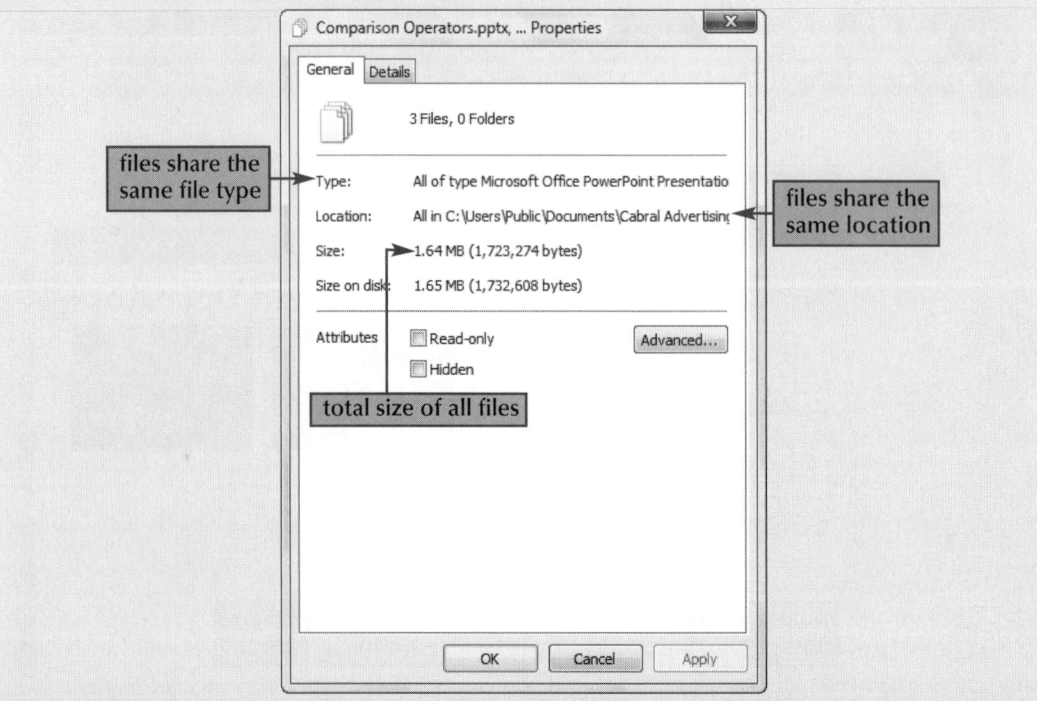

3. Close the Conceptual Database.pptx, ...(group) Properties dialog box.

You have multiple ways in which you can view information about files, and each approach provides some of the same information and some new information (or perhaps a new way of looking at the same information), plus new options (for example, the option for removing properties and personal information).

Viewing Properties of Files | Reference Window

- If you want to view the property of a single file, select the file, and then examine the Details Pane. For more information, right-click the file, click Properties on the shortcut menu, and then examine the General property sheet. If you want to view more information about a file's properties, click the Details tab. If you want to remove properties or personal information from a file, click the "Remove Properties and Personal Information" link at the bottom of the Details property sheet.
- If you want to view properties of two or more files, select each of the files, and then view the information in the Details Pane. For more information, right-click one of the selected files, click Properties on the shortcut menu, and then examine the General property sheet. If you want to view more information about the files' properties, click the Details tab. If you want to remove properties or personal information from the files, click the "Remove Properties and Personal Information" link at the bottom of the Details property sheet.
- If you want to view properties of all the files in a folder, click Organize on the command bar, click Select All, right-click one of the files, click Properties on the shortcut menu, and then examine the General and Details property sheets.

If you want to copy a large file to a flash drive, you can examine the size of the file and the available space on the flash drive to determine if there's room for a copy of the file. Removing properties of a file can enhance your privacy, especially if you decide to e-mail a copy of a file to someone else.

Viewing Properties of Folders

In addition to viewing the properties of files, you can view properties of one or more folders.

To view properties of a folder:

1. Click the **Back** button to return to the Contract Training folder, right-click the **Presentations** folder icon, and then click **Properties** on the shortcut menu. On the General property sheet of the Presentations Properties dialog box, Windows Vista displays the icon used for this folder, the folder name (which you can change), the type of folder (a File Folder), the location of the folder, the size of the folder and its contents, the size on disk of the folder and its contents, the number of files and folders within this folder (three files, but no other folders), the date and time the folder was created, and any attributes assigned to the folder. See Figure 3-18. Again, note that the size on disk is greater than the total size of the folder and its contents. The location of the file is: C:\Users\Public\Documents\Cabral Advertising\Contract Training (although you can't see the full location listed on the General property sheet).

Tip

If you open a folder, you can right-click the folder background and then click Properties to view folder properties.

Figure 3-18 Viewing properties of a folder

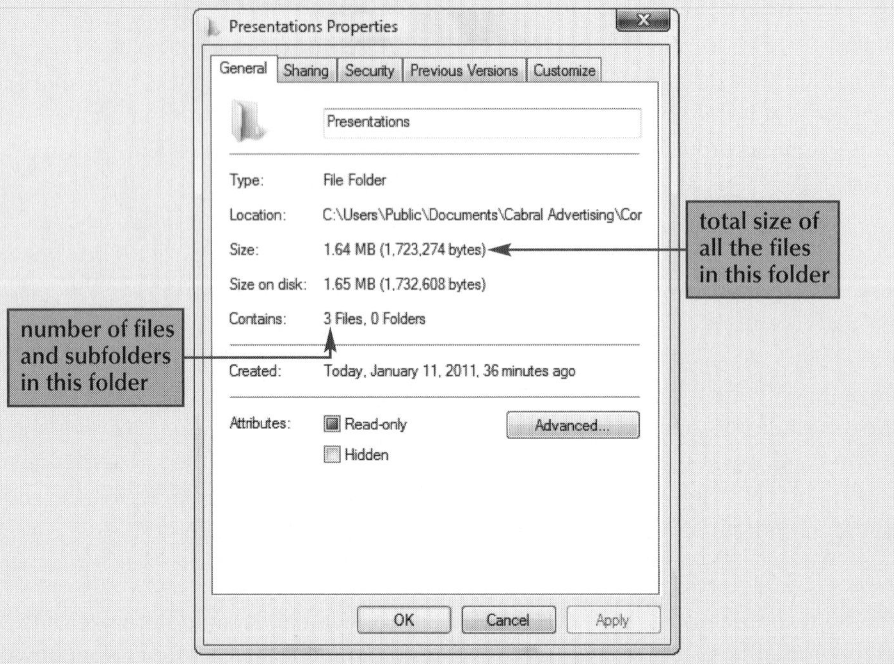

2. Close the Presentations Properties dialog box, but keep the Contract Training folder window open.

Reference Window | Viewing Properties of Folders

- If you want to view the property of a single folder, right-click the folder, click Properties on the shortcut menu, and then examine the General property sheet.
- If you want to view properties of two or more folders, select the folders, right-click one of the folders, click Properties on the shortcut menu, and then examine the General property sheet.
- If you want to view properties of all the subfolders within a folder, click the Organize button on the command bar, click Select All, right-click one of the folders, click Properties on the shortcut menu, and then examine the General property sheet.

By viewing properties of one or more folders, you can determine the total storage capacity required of all those folders before you copy the folders to another disk, such as a flash drive. This is especially important if you need to make a backup, or duplicate copy, of important folders and their files, or to use the folders and files on another computer.

Understanding Paths

When you examined the properties of files and folders, Windows Vista displays the location of the file, files, or folder on the General property sheet. For example, the location of the Presentations folder was listed as:

C:\Users\Public\Documents\Cabral Advertising\Contract Training

This notation is called a **path** because it identifies the exact location of a folder. The C:\ identifies the disk drive where the folder is located (namely, drive C, the hard disk drive), and the backslash (\ ) symbol is a special notation for the top-level folder on a disk drive. The **top-level folder** is the first folder created on a disk when the disk is prepared to store data, and once the top-level folder is created, you can create and store folders and files on the disk. After the notation for the top-level folder, Windows Vista displays the sequence of folders that you follow to get to a specific folder or file. All of the backslashes other than the one that follows the drive name are called **delimiters**, because these backslashes serve to separate folder names. Only the backslash after the drive name refers to the top-level folder or what used to be called the **root directory**. Basically, the full path describes the route (or path) that you (or Windows Vista) use to locate a specific folder or file.

One way to navigate to this folder would be to open Computer, open drive C, open the Users folder, open the Public folder, open the Cabral Advertising folder, and then open the Contract Training folder. If you used this approach, you would be stepping through the path, one drive and folder at a time. As you've seen, there are other and faster ways to access a folder.

As noted earlier, if you open the Contract Training folder to view the Presentations folder, the sequence of folders shown in the Address Bar path closely matches the path shown on the property sheet for the location of the current folder, as illustrated here:

▶ Public ▶ Public Documents ▶ Cabral Advertising ▶ Contract Training

The only piece of information not shown in the Address Bar is the name of the Users folder, which contains all user accounts, including the Public account.

The full path to the Comparison Operators file in the Presentations folder is:

C:\Users\Public\Public Documents\Cabral Advertising\Contract Training\
Presentations\ Comparison Operators.pptx

The path of a file includes the full filename at the end of the path (with the file extension), and the filename is separated from the folder name where it is located by a backslash.

When you open a recently used file, Windows Vista uses the path to locate the file, and it also uses the path for the program associated with that file type to open the program that works with that file type. For example, if you open the Presentations folder and click the Comparison Operators file icon (or thumbnail), Windows Vista opens the file in Microsoft Office PowerPoint and displays the presentation. The path to the Microsoft Office PowerPoint program (assuming you are using Microsoft Office 2007) is:

C:\Program Files\Microsoft Office\Office12\POWERPNT.EXE

POWERPNT.EXE is the name of the file that contains the Microsoft Office PowerPoint application. As noted earlier, files with the file extension "exe" are executable files that contain program code that Windows Vista can load into memory and run. Windows Vista displays POWERPNT.EXE in uppercase because it follows the conventions for naming folders and files under the DOS operating system that preceded the Windows operating environments and Windows operating systems. Likewise, Office12, the name of the folder that contains the Microsoft Office PowerPoint program, follows DOS conventions for naming folders and files. The next section describes conventions for naming files under Windows and under DOS.

The path is critical to the proper performance of Windows Vista. It uses the path to locate and open programs, folders, and files.

Using Long Filenames and Aliases

As noted in Tutorial 1, under any of the Windows operating systems, you can use long filenames to more clearly identify the contents and purpose of a file. You can also include special symbols or characters, such as the ampersand (&), pound sign (#), dollar sign ($), percentage symbol (%), and apostrophes, as well as opening and closing parentheses and spaces. You can also assign long folder names to folders so that you can clearly identify the types of files stored within those folders.

Under the DOS operating system that preceded the Windows operating systems, filenames could be 1 to 8 characters in length. You could also use an optional file extension of up to 3 characters; however, the file extension was not needed for document files. Therefore, these filenames were called short filenames or **8.3 filenames** (that is, names that allow eight characters, a period to separate the main part of the filename from the file extension, a three character file extension, and no spaces in the filename or file extension). Like Windows filenames, the file extension was separated from the main part of the filename by a period (or what computer-savvy people call a "dot"). A filename could not include spaces or more than one period, and like the Windows operating system, you could not use certain symbols in a filename because those symbols were reserved for special operations performed by the operating system. Also, the DOS operating system used only uppercase characters for filenames.

Under Windows Vista and previous versions of the Windows operating system, if you assign a long filename to a file or a long folder name to a folder, Windows Vista creates an alias to provide backward compatibility with DOS and Windows 3.x applications (for example, applications designed for Windows 3.1 and 3.11) that do not recognize long filenames. An **alias** is a filename that follows the rules and conventions for 8.3 filenames. Under the Windows operating system, an alias consists of the first six characters of the long filename, followed by a tilde (~), a number, a period, and the first three characters after the last period in the long filename. Any spaces or symbols in a long filename are not used in the alias.

Take the Cabral Advertising folder name as an example. Windows Vista assigns it the alias CABRAL~1 (assuming no other file has that same alias). If another file in the same folder had already been assigned the alias CABRAL~1, Windows Vista then uses an **algorithm**, or a formula or procedure, to increment the number until it creates a unique filename. To continue with the example, Windows Vista would then check to see if another folder (or file if the file has no file extension) used the alias CABRAL~2. If not, it would use this alias for the Cabral Advertising folder. Note that lowercase (which Windows Vista recognizes) is converted to uppercase (the default for the DOS operating system).

If a folder contains five or more files whose long filename starts with the same set of characters (for example, Five Year Sales Projection.xls, Five Year Sales Analysis.xls, Five Year Growth Plan.xlsx, Five Year Growth Plan Template.xls, and Five Year Budget Summary.xls), and assuming no other files have the same six characters at the beginning of the filename (omitting spaces and symbols), Windows Vista (like Windows XP) follows the approach just described to create short filenames for the first four files (namely, FIVEYE~1.XLS, FIVEYE~2.XLS, FIVEYE~3.XLS, and FIVEYE~4.XLS). But for each file after the fourth file, Windows Vista uses a different approach to creating the short filename. It uses the first two characters of the long filename, followed by four characters that are mathematically generated from the remainder of the characters in the long filename, and then a tilde followed by a unique number (for example, the fifth file would have the short filename FIB7A5~1.XLS). If the file extensions for these five files were "xlsx" instead of "xls", the short filenames would be exactly the same.

You and the applications that you use cannot specify the alias that Windows Vista assigns for long filenames. Also, operating system and applications files follow the DOS naming conventions so that they work properly when a Windows Vista computer is connected to a network with other computers that use operating systems that do not recognize Windows long filenames or that handle long filenames differently.

Under Windows Vista, you might see a folder, shortcut, and file with the same name; however, the file extension (if present) differs, and each has a different alias. Folders usually do not have a file extension (though temporary folders for installed software might have the "tmp" extension). Shortcuts have the file extension "lnk" (for Link) or, in the case of shortcuts to DOS applications, "PIF" (for Program Information File). (*Note*: The first character in the "lnk" file extension is the lowercase character "l", not the number "1.") Filenames have a file extension assigned by the program that created the file. That file extension depends on the file type the program uses or the file type that you choose during the save operation.

The alias is important for DOS and Windows 3.x applications that you might use under Windows Vista or an earlier version of the Windows operating system because those applications do not recognize long folder names and long filenames. Instead, these applications can "see" only the alias (or short filename) for folders and files.

If you use a DOS application or a Windows 3.x application (such as an earlier version of Microsoft Word), you will see only the short filenames in Open and Save As dialog boxes. This can make it difficult to know which folder or file to open or which file to replace because files like the ones described will have very similar short filenames. For example, how would you know whether FIVEYE~1.XLS, FIVEYE~2.XLS, FIVEYE~3.XLS, or FIVEYE~4.XLS contained the Five Year Growth Plan.xlsx that you need?

The DOS operating system truncated file extensions with more than three characters. In other words, if a file extension extended three characters, any extra characters were removed. Today, many programs, including Microsoft Office, work with files that have more than three characters in the file extension. When Windows Vista creates an alias or short filename for a file with a file extension that exceeds three characters, it removes any extra characters in the file extension so that the alias or short filename has only three characters in the file extension.

Understanding Aliases and Filenames | InSight

You should understand how Windows Vista and other versions of the Windows operating system work with long and short filenames if you work with DOS, Windows 3.x, and applications designed for other versions of Windows on the same or different computer systems. You should also understand long and short filenames if you provide support to clients who might have a variety of software configurations on their computers, if you troubleshoot problems, and if you set up, configure, and customize computers for other users. In these instances, if you need to create a set of files with similar names, think carefully about how you name those files. You might want to use names that begin with different characters. For example, instead of using the filenames "Five Year Growth Plan.xlsx" and "Five Year Plan Template.xlsx," you could use the filenames "Five Year Growth Plan.xlsx" and "Template for a Five Year Growth Plan.xlsx." Then you could easily tell these files apart using their short filenames (FIVEYE~1.XLS and TEMPLA~1.XLS).

Organizing Files in Groups and Stacks

Windows Vista provides new ways for organizing files in a folder window so that you can find and focus on the files you need. As in Windows XP, you can organize files by various criteria, such as file type or file size. With Windows Vista, you can group files by various criteria and you can now organize files into stacks by various criteria. A **stack** is a virtual folder that contains a group of related files. You specify the relationship when you create the stack.

To organize files by type:

1. In the Address Bar, click the **New Location arrow button** ▶ to the right of Cabral Advertising, and then click **Client Projects**. Windows Vista switches to the Client Projects subfolder within the Cabral Advertising folder.
2. Click the **Visual Arts, Inc** folder icon, and if you see a Preview Pane after Windows Vista opens the Visual Arts folder, click **Organize** on the command bar, point to **Layout**, and then click **Preview Pane**. Windows Vista closes the Preview Pane.

3. Click the **Views button arrow** on the command bar and then click **Large Icons**. Above the icons are headings that allow you to organize files in a folder.
4. If Windows Vista does not display the Type heading, right-click the **empty area to the right of the headings** (or right-click any heading), and then locate and click **Type**. Windows then displays the Type heading.
5. Point to the **Type** heading, and when Windows Vista displays the Type button arrow, click the **Type button arrow**, and then click **Group**. Windows Vista arranges the files in groups by file type. See Figure 3-19. The three types of file types are JPEG Image, Microsoft Office Excel Worksheet, and Microsoft Office Word Document. If you are looking for a specific type of file, this is an easy and fast way to find all files that fall within a specific file type group.

Figure 3-19 Files grouped by file type

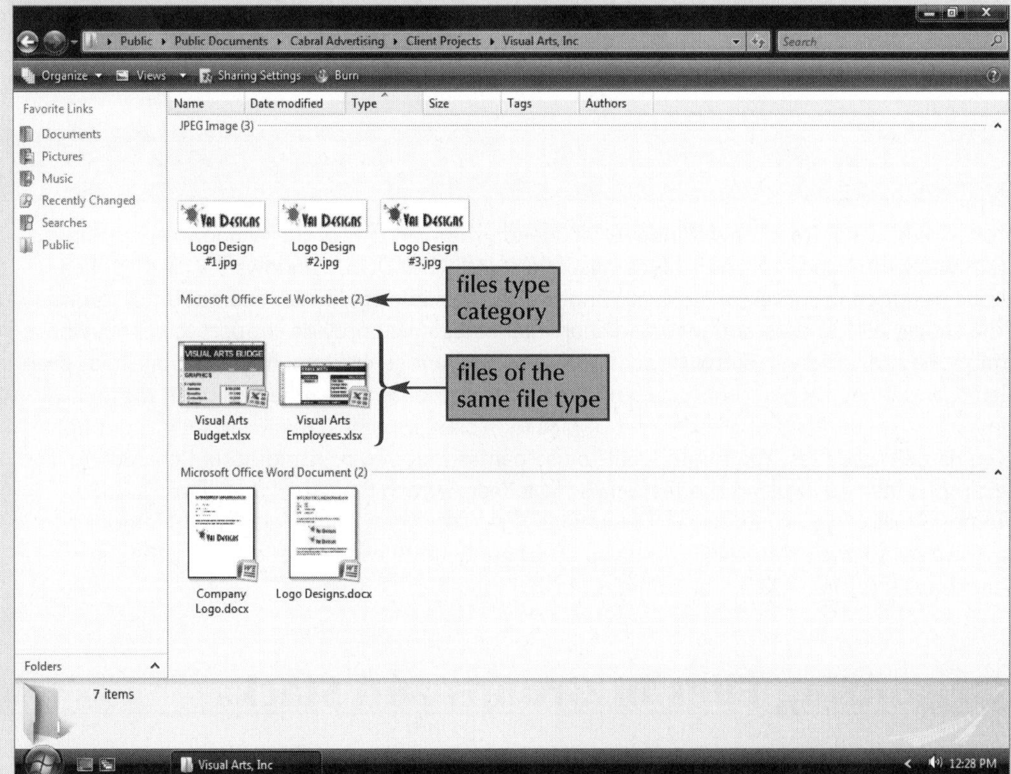

6. If Windows Vista does not display the Authors heading, right-click the **empty area to the right of the headings** (or right-click any heading), and then click **Authors**. Windows displays the Authors heading.
7. Point to the **Authors** heading, click the **Authors button arrow**, and then click **Group**. Windows Vista arranges the files in groups by author. See Figure 3-20. If you are looking for files that you created or that someone else created, this is an easy and fast way to find those files.

Figure 3-20 Files grouped by author

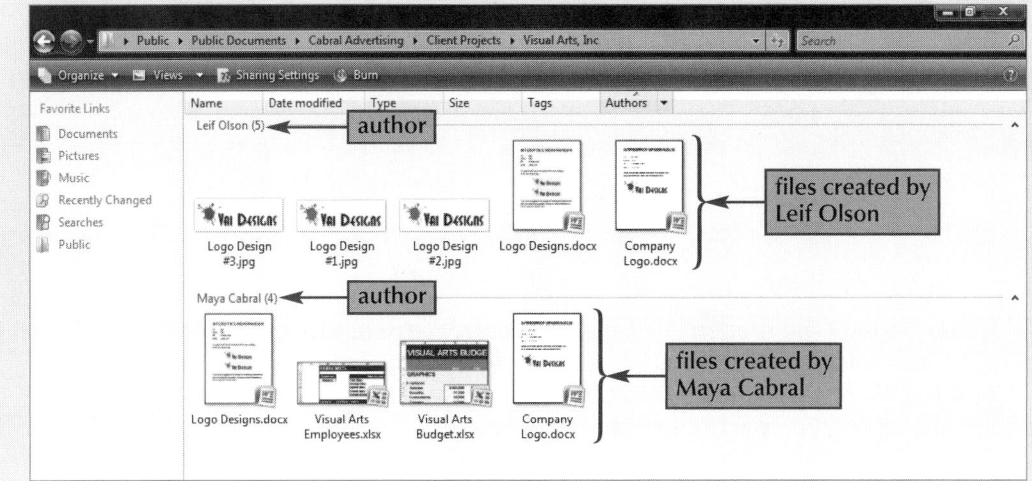

You can also sort the contents of a folder. If you click a heading, Windows Vista sorts the contents of the folder by that file property in ascending order (alphabetical order). If you click the heading a second time, Windows Vista sorts the contents of the folder by that file property in descending order (reverse alphabetical order). You can use this feature to quickly rearrange folders in a file so that you can find what you want.

Besides organizing files by groups, you can exclude all other files and focus on a specific group.

To focus on a specific group of files:

1. Point to the **Authors** heading, click the **Authors button arrow**, and then click **Sort**. Windows Vista removes the grouping by Authors and displays all the files.
2. Point to the **Type** heading, click the **Type button arrow**, and then click the **Microsoft Office Excel Worksheet** check box. Windows Vista selects and displays only Microsoft Office Excel Worksheets in the Visual Arts, Inc folder. See Figure 3-21. If you want to view more than one file type, you can choose each file type by clicking its check box.

Figure 3-21 Viewing files of only one file type

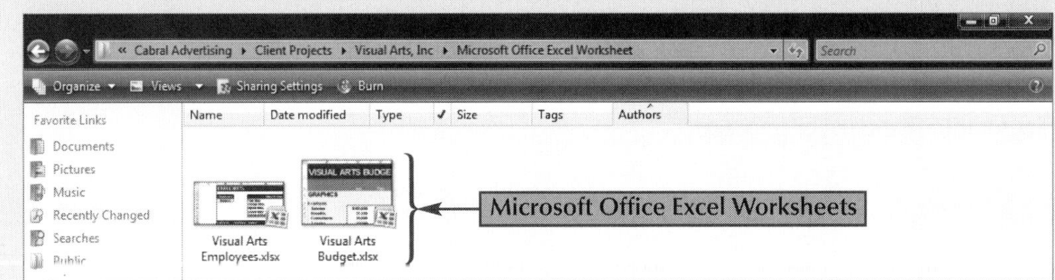

3. Point to the **Type** heading, click the **Type button arrow** with a check mark, and then click the **Microsoft Office Excel Worksheet** check box. Windows Vista removes the selection for Microsoft Excel Worksheets only, and then displays all the files.
4. Point to the **Authors** heading, click the **Authors button arrow**, and then click the **Leif Olson** check box. Windows Vista selects and displays all files created by Leif Olson. See Figure 3-22.

Figure 3-22 Viewing files created by one author

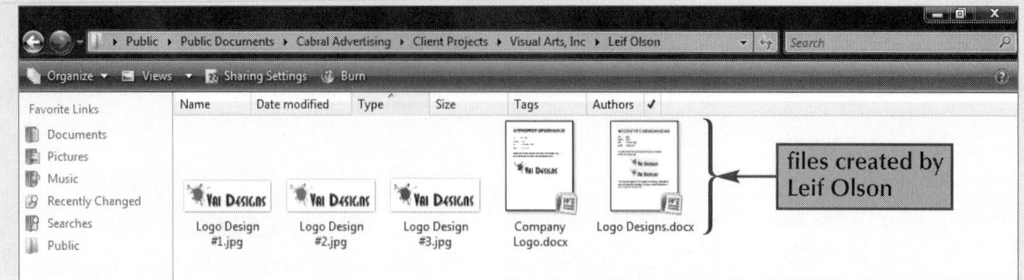

5. Point to the **Type** heading, click the **Type button arrow**, and then click the **Microsoft Office Word Document** check box. Windows Vista selects and displays only Microsoft Office Word files created by Leif Olson. See Figure 3-23. Since you did not clear the previous Authors selection for files created by Leif Olson, Windows Vista now applies two criteria. This feature is particularly handy if you have a folder with many files, and if you want to focus on a group of files that share two or more properties.

Figure 3-23 Files selected using two file properties

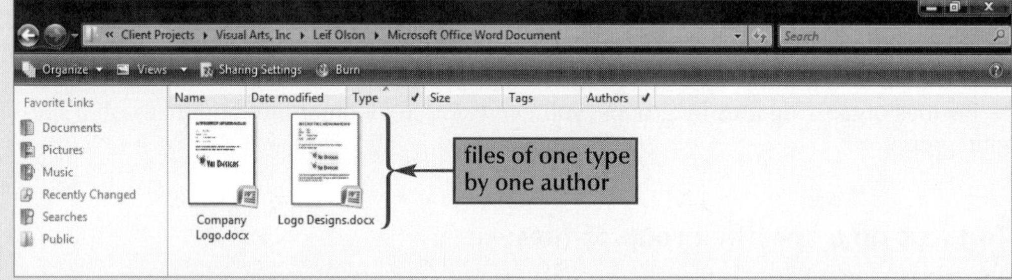

6. Point to the **Type** heading, click the **Type button arrow**, and then click the **Microsoft Office Word Document** check box. Windows Vista clears the selection and shows all file types created by Leif Olson.
7. Point to the **Authors** heading, click the **Authors button arrow**, and then click the **Leif Olson** check box. Windows Vista clears the selection and shows all file types created by all authors.

You can also create stacks that group files into virtual folders.

To stack files into groups:

1. Point to the **Type** heading, click the **Type button arrow**, and then click **Stack by Type**. Windows Vista creates three stacks for each of the three file types in this folder—JPEG Image, Microsoft Office Excel Worksheet, and Microsoft Office Word Document. See Figure 3-24. If you had many more types of files in this folder, you would see many more stacks. Notice that the Address Bar now displays the name of the virtual folder, namely, "Search Results in Visual Arts, Inc."

Figure 3-24 Stacks of files by file type

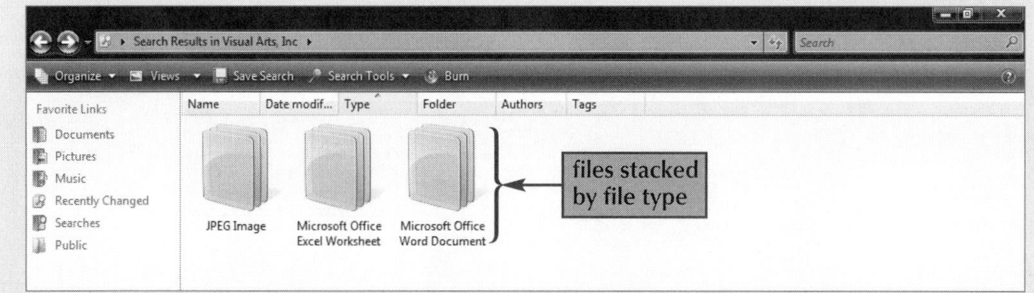

2. Click the **JPEG Image** stack. Windows Vista opens this folder and displays only JPEG Image files. See Figure 3-25. Notice that the Address Bar now shows "Search Results in Visual Arts, Inc ▶ JPEG Image". You are now viewing files within a stack.

Figure 3-25 Viewing files within a stack

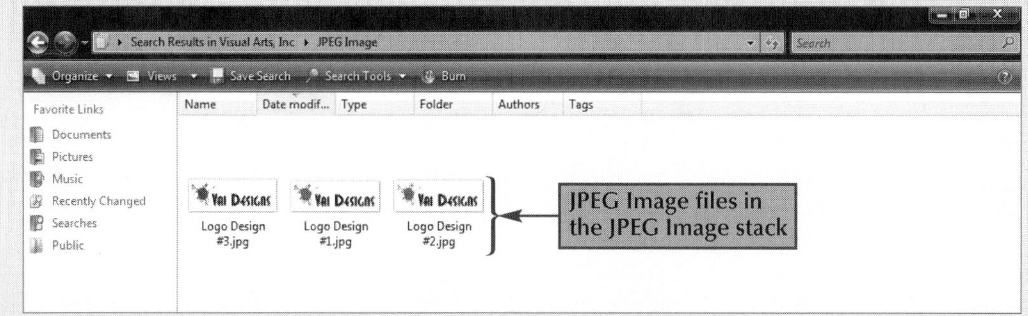

3. Click the **Back** button *twice*. Windows Vista returns to the Visual Arts, Inc window, removes the stacks, and displays all the files.

4. Point to the **Authors** heading, click the **Authors button arrow**, click **Stack by Authors**, and if necessary, switch to Large Icons view. Windows Vista creates two stacks—one with files created by Leif Olson and the other with files created by Maya Cabral. See Figure 3-26.

Figure 3-26 Stacking files by author

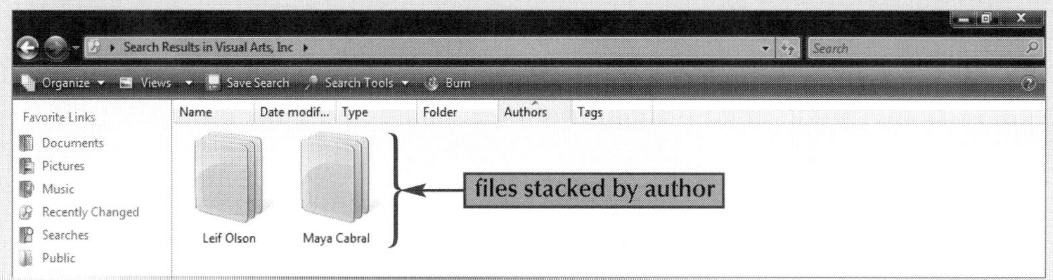

5. Click the **Maya Cabral** stack. Windows Vista displays files created by Maya Cabral. See Figure 3-27. Notice that the Address Bar now shows "Search Results in Visual Arts, Inc ▶ Maya Cabral."

Figure 3-27

Viewing files with an author stack

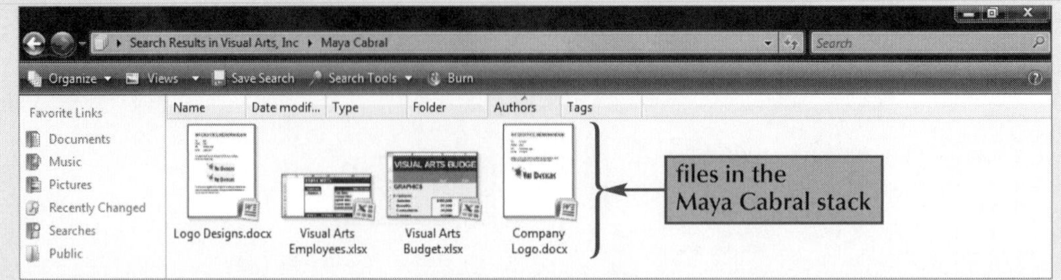

6. Point to the **Type** heading, click the **Type button arrow** with the check mark, and then click **Stack by Type**. Windows Vista creates two stacks for the two types of Maya Cabral files in this folder—Microsoft Office Excel Worksheet and Microsoft Office Word Document. See Figure 3-28. You just created stacks within stacks.

Figure 3-28

Viewing stacks within stacks

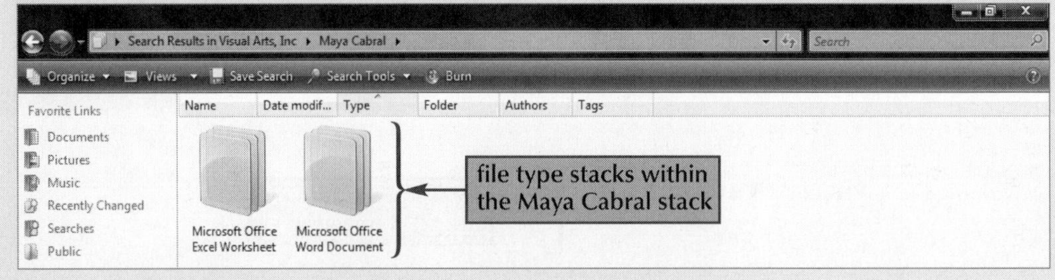

7. Close the Search Results in Visual Arts, Inc window.

You can also combine these features. For example, you can stack files by Authors, open a stack for a specific author, and then group files by file type or view files of one specific file type.

Organizing Files by Groups and Stacks | Reference Window

- If you want to organize files by a column heading that is not shown in the folder window, right-click the empty area to the right of the headings (or right-click any heading), and then click the heading you want. If you don't see the heading you want, click More, and in the Choose Details dialog box, locate and click the check boxes for headings in the Choose Details list box that you want to use, and then click the OK button.
- To arrange all the files into groups, point to a column heading, click the heading's button arrow, and then click Group.
- To remove the grouping, point to a column heading, click the heading's button arrow, and then click Sort.
- To group selected files, point to a column heading, click the heading's button arrow, and then click the check box for one of the group options.
- To remove the grouping of selected files, point to a column heading, click the heading's button arrow, and then remove the check mark from the check box (or check boxes) that you previously selected.
- To stack files, point to a column heading, click the heading's button arrow, and then click Stack by (the heading).
- To remove stacks, click the Back button one or more times to return to the original folder view.

If you work with a long list of files, you can quickly reorganize them by sorting, grouping, or stacking, or use some combination of sorting, grouping, and stacking, to focus on the files you want and to view them in a specific way.

Session 3.1 Quick Check | Review

1. The majority of the Windows operating system files are installed in the ________________ folder, and application software, utilities, and games are typically installed in the ________________ folder.
2. True or False. A virtual folder is a folder created as the result of an operation that Windows Vista or you perform, such as displaying a list of recent documents that Windows Vista created or that you opened.
3. What folder can users with different user accounts, or network users, use to share files?
4. True or False. The Details Pane displays a preview of the contents of a file you select.
5. A(n) ________________ is a file that is associated with an application or program on your computer.
6. The ________________ is a notation that identifies the exact location of a folder or file.
7. What symbol does Windows Vista use to denote the top-level folder on a disk?
8. A(n) ________________ is a virtual folder that contains a group of related files.

Session 3.2

Using Instant Search

One of the major new enhancements in Windows Vista is the Search feature, now called Instant Search. When you start to enter the name of a program, folder, or file you want to locate in the Search box, either from the Start menu or a folder window, Instant Search immediately displays search results. As you continue to type search criteria, Windows Vista narrows your search results.

To provide Search results quickly, the Windows Vista Indexing service constantly indexes folder and filenames as well as the content and properties (or metadata) of files on your computer. A **service** is a Windows Vista program that runs in the background and provides support to other programs. An **index** is a file that contains a collection of information about the folders and files on your computer. By cataloging and compiling data from programs, folders, and files, Instant Search can more quickly locate what you need by using the index rather than repeatedly searching folders and file content each time you search. **Metadata** is data about other data. The title, author, and company are examples of metadata associated with, and stored within, a file. The Indexing service converts documents with different file formats into plain text so that the Search service can index, or catalog, the content. In some cases, the Indexing service also extracts metadata, or file properties, for use in a search.

The Indexing service indexes the Start Menu folder because it contains shortcuts to all the installed software on your computer and provides access to Windows tools. It also indexes the content of the Users folder except for the Default User folder. The Users folder contains a user account folder for all users on a computer. Windows Vista uses the content of the Default User folder as the foundation for creating new user accounts. The Indexing service also indexes the Offline Files cache, a local folder on your computer that acts as a temporary storage location for copies of network files. The Offline Files folder provides you with faster access to the files as well as access to the files when a computer is not connected to the network. When the connection is re-established, Windows Vista updates the network copies of the files (or vice versa). You can also search the content of removable drives, such as flash drives.

The Indexing service does not index everything on your computer. Windows Vista excludes the ProgramData folder, which holds the Search index, so that the Indexing service does not index its own index. Also, protected operating system files are not indexed. The Indexing service indexes folders and files when your computer is inactive (during idle periods) and does not interfere with your use of the computer.

You can initiate a search in one of several ways:

- **Search text box on the Start menu** This option is useful if you want to quickly locate programs on your computer. You start typing the program name and immediately view Search results.
- **Search option on the Start menu** If you choose this option, Windows Vista opens Search Explorer, a specialized search tool, in a window where you can specify what types of files you want to see in your Search results—All (files), E-mail, Document, Picture, Music, and Other. You can also enable the option for an Advanced Search where you can specify the location that you want to use for the search as well as the folder or filename, tags, author, file date, and file size. A **tag** is a word or phrase that you assign as a property to a folder or file to help you organize and locate folders and files. You can assign multiple tags to folders and files and cross-reference them. Search Explorer allows you to specify multiple Search criteria so that you can limit the Search results.
- **Search box in a folder window** The Search box in a folder window is designed to search the contents of that folder and all of its subfolders and therefore provides a more focused search.

- **Using Search folders** Windows Vista creates a set of preconfigured Search folders for each user so that a user can quickly find recently changed files. If you open the Documents window and click Searches in the Navigation pane, Windows Vista displays a list of these preconfigured Search folders—Recent Documents, Recent E-mail, Recent Music, Recent Pictures and Videos, Recently Changed, and Shared by Me (for files you choose to share with other users). You might also see other Search folders, such as Everywhere and Indexed Locations. After you perform a Search, you can save the Search results as a separate virtual folder in the Searches folder. When you open a Saved search, Windows Vista updates the contents of the Search folder using the search criteria you previously provided.
- **Control Panel Search box** If you need to quickly locate a Control Panel applet (or program), you can use the Search box in the Control Panel.

If you use Windows Mail or Microsoft Office Outlook, Instant Search locates e-mail messages and communications.

Searching from the Start Menu

If you need to find a program quickly, you can search for that program from the Start menu. You can also search for folders and files, e-mail contacts and e-mail messages, and Internet favorites (or bookmarks) from the Search box at the bottom of the Start menu.

Maya and you have scheduled an appointment for reviewing the progress of a new client project, so you want to open Windows Calendar and add that appointment to your calendar, plus check your upcoming appointments.

To locate a program using the Start menu Search box:

1. Press the **Windows** key. Windows Vista opens the Start menu and places the insertion point in the Search box, so you are ready to enter your search criterion.
2. Type **w** and then examine the Search results on the Start menu. Windows Vista organizes Search results into categories—Programs, Favorites and History (with links to Web sites that you've bookmarked or visited), Files (which also includes folders), and Communications (contacts and e-mail messages). See Figure 3-29. Under Programs on the computer used for Figure 3-29, Windows Vista lists programs and tools that contain the character "w" somewhere in the program name (including, for example, Microsoft Office Word 2007 on the computer used for this figure). Included in this list is Windows Calendar. Note that you also have an option at the bottom of the Search results for searching the Internet.

Figure 3-29 Searching from the Start menu

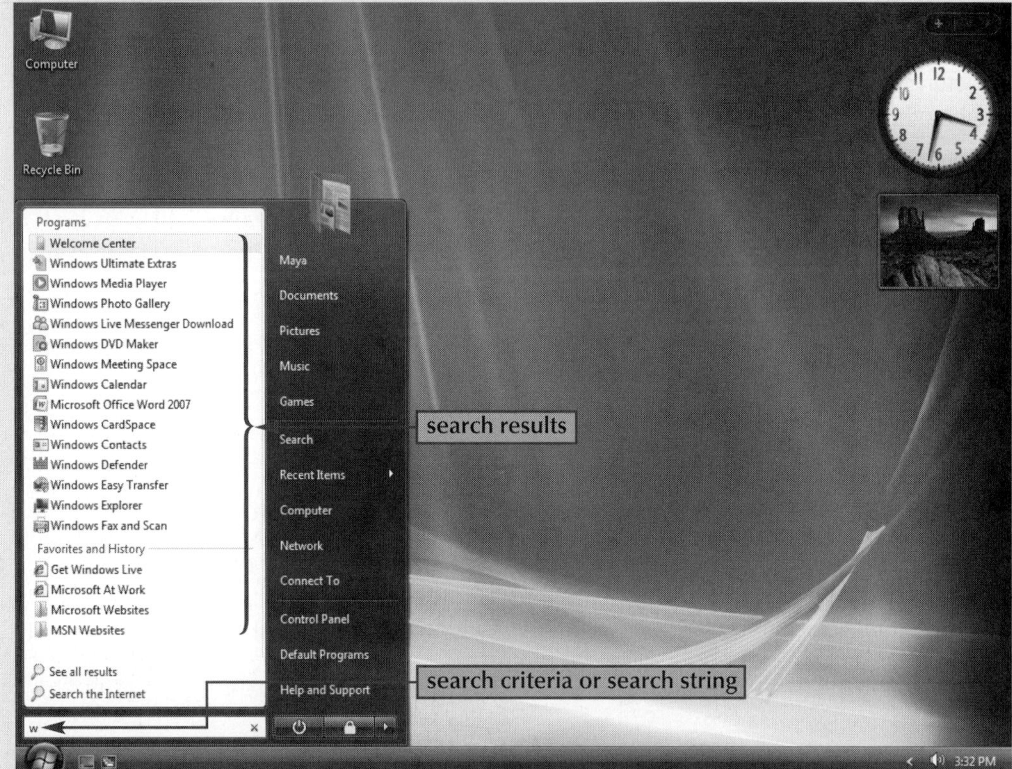

3. Click **Windows Calendar** in the Search results. Windows Vista opens Windows Calendar so that you can view your appointments for the day and enter new appointments.
4. Close Windows Calendar.

This approach is also useful for locating programs that you do not use frequently, such as the Calculator accessory.

The search criterion that you type is called a **search string**. A **string** is a set of characters (or perhaps even a single character) that is not modified by Windows Vista (or any other program).

Searching a Folder

You can also use the Search box on the Start menu to open frequently used folders, such as the Contacts and Videos folders. After you open a folder, you can use the Search box in the folder window to locate a file in the folder or one of its subfolders.

To help her quickly meet an important deadline during a busy day, Maya asks you to locate the Break-Even Analysis file for a new client.

To search using the Search box in a folder window:

1. Press the **Windows** key, type **pu**, and under Files in the Search results, click **Public Documents**. Windows Vista opens the Public Documents folder. Maximize this window, if necessary.

Trouble? If Windows Vista does not display Public Documents in the Search results, but does display Public, click Public in the Search results, and after the Public window opens, click Public Documents, and maximize the Public Documents window.

2. Click the **Cabral Advertising** folder icon, click the **Views button arrow** on the command bar, and then click **Details**. Windows Vista switches to Details view. Note that the Cabral Advertising folder contains seven subfolders.

Tip

You can also right-click the folder background, point to View, and then click Details to switch to Details view.

3. In the Search box located in the upper-right corner of the window, type **b** and then examine the Search results. Instant Search lists every folder and file (in this example, 28 items) that contains the character "b" somewhere in the folder or filename or in the file itself. Searches are case insensitive; in other words, Instant Search looks for "b" and "B".

4. Point to the **thin border** after the Name column, and when the mouse pointer changes to a resizing shape ↔, double-click the **border** after the Name column. Windows Vista adjusts the Name column width to a best fit that accommodates the longest folder or filename in the Name column.

5. Click in the Search box after the letter "b", type **re** and examine the Search results. Instant Search narrows the selection to Break-Even Analysis.xlsx, the one file that has the characters "bre" in the filename or in the file itself. See Figure 3-30. After you locate a file, you can click the file icon to open the file directly from the Search results window.

Figure 3-30 Searching from a folder window

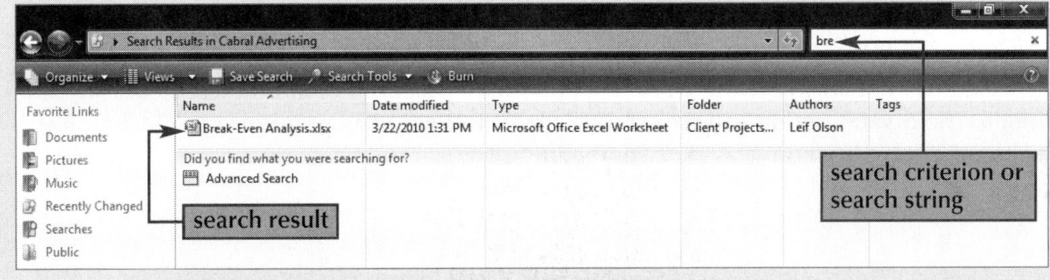

6. Right-click **Break-Even Analysis.xlsx** in the Search results and examine the shortcut menu. You can use Open, the first option on the shortcut menu, to open the file. See Figure 3-31. You can use Print to print the document without opening it. Actually, Windows Vista opens the document and the application, prints the document, and then closes the application and document. In some cases, you can use the "Open with" option to open the document in another program that supports the same file format. You can use the Send To menu option to send a copy of the file to another disk, such as a flash drive.

Figure 3-31 **Viewing actions on a file's shortcut menu**

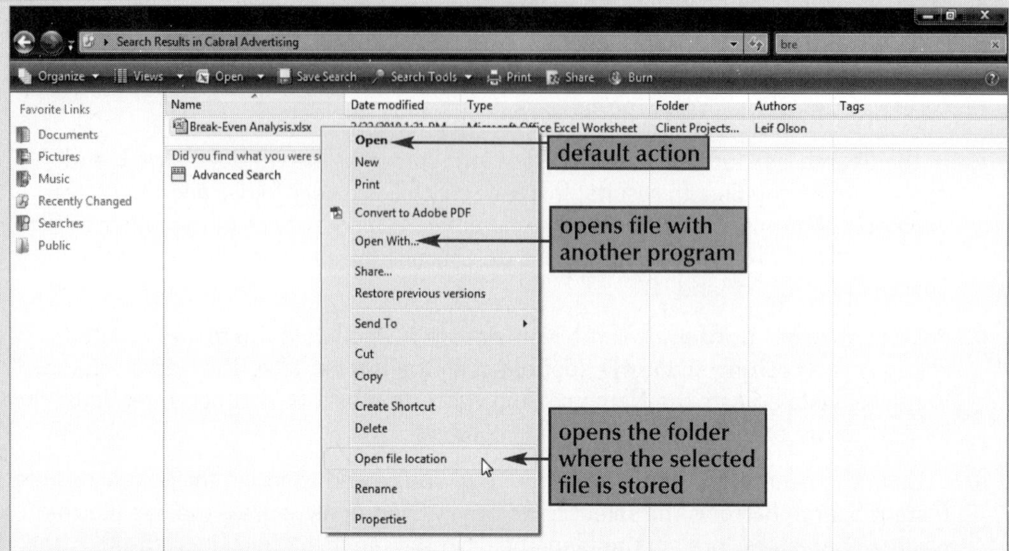

7. Click **Open file location**. Windows Vista opens the Client Projects folder that contains this file in a new folder window. You can then create or work with any other files in the window (presumably ones related to the one that you searched for).
8. Close the Client Projects folder window.

Windows Vista displays the default action for an object in bold on the object's shortcut menu. The **default action** is the operation that Windows Vista performs on a file if you click (or double-click in Classic style) the file icon.

InSight | **Searching for Files by Name**

When searching for filenames, you usually need to enter only a few characters of the filename to find the file. The characters can be the characters at the beginning of the filename or anywhere in the filename. You can also find what you want by entering a unique combination of characters found in the filename of the file you are looking for, but not in other filenames.

Searching Using a File Property or File Type

If you want to search using a file property, such as Authors, you can type all or part of the name, or you can precede the author's name with the name of the property. For example, if you want to find all files for Maya Cabral, you can enter "Maya" (or "Maya Cabral" or "Cabral") in the Search box. The advantage of using "Cabral" is that you locate only those authors with this last name. If you use "Maya", you locate all authors with the first name Maya. You can also be more specific and enter "authors:Maya" or "authors:Maya Cabral" or "authors:Cabral". You can use the latter approach to locate files using approximately 270 different file properties.

Next, you want to display a list of Maya's files so that you can make sure you have everything you need for the next project.

To search using the author property:

1. Click after "bre" in the Search box, use the **Backspace** key to delete "bre," and then type **authors:Maya** and examine the Search results. Instant Search lists every folder and file (in this example, 15 items) that contains "Maya" in the Authors property.
2. Right-click the **Authors** heading, and then click **Size Column to Fit** on the shortcut menu. Note that Maya Cabral is the sole author for all the files except two. On those two other files, she is a coauthor with Leif Olson. See Figure 3-32. The second command on the shortcut menu—Size All Columns to Fit—adjusts the widths of all columns, though some might not be visible if the window is not wide enough to display them. Then you have to scroll to the right.

Figure 3-32 Searching by the Authors property

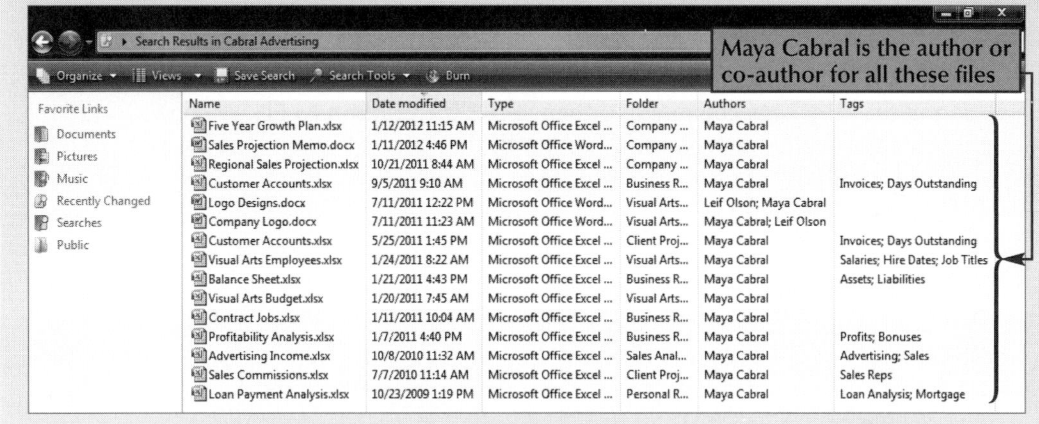

You can also search by specifying a file type—such as "folder" or "document."

Next, you need to prepare a list of all the folders and the files that contain pictures for Maya.

To locate only folders:

1. In the Search box, delete the previous search string, and then type **folder**. Windows Vista displays a list of all the folders in alphabetical order. Note that there are 12 folders. When you opened the Cabral Advertising folder earlier, there were only seven folders. The additional folders (Loan Analysis Models, Presentations, Spreadsheet Design, Tips, and Visual Arts, Inc) are subfolders of two of the folders under the Cabral Advertising folder.
2. In the Search box, delete the current search string, and then type **picture**. Windows Vista lists all the files that contain images or pictures—namely, Logo Design #3.jpg, Logo Design #1.jpg, and Logo Design #2.jpg.
3. In the Search box, delete the current search string, and then type **xlsx**. Windows Vista finds all the Microsoft Office Excel Worksheet files (in this case, 21 files) with the "xlsx" file extension.

> **Tip**
> To also include pre Office 2007 files, use the same Search string but do not include the "x" at the end of the file extension.

You can also search for Music, Videos, and Document to locate these three different classes of files. With the Document search criteria, Windows Vista will find all your text, spreadsheet, and presentation files. However, when you perform these broad types of searches, your Search results might include other types of files that contain the word "picture," "music," "videos," and "document" within the files or in the file properties.

Searching for Tags

To make it easier to organize your folders and files or perform a search, you can specify tags for folders and files. For example, you can use tags to group files in a window, similar to the way you grouped files earlier in the tutorial by type and author. Tags also speed up searches. By assigning multiple tags to the same file, you can locate the file by using whatever word or phrase comes to mind (and that matches one of the tags you've specified).

Maya asks you to find the file that contains a list of the company's assets and liabilities.

To locate the file with the company's assets and liabilities:

1. If you do not see the Tags heading and column in the folder window, right-click **one of the column headings**, and then locate and click **Tags**.
2. In the Search box, delete the current search string, and then type **tags:a**. Windows Vista displays a list of files that meet the Search criteria.
3. Right-click the **Tags** column, and then click **Size Column to Fit**. Windows Vista adjusts the Tags column width to a best fit that accommodates the longest tag or set of tags. Windows Vista located all the files with the character "a" in one of the tags. See Figure 3-33.

Tip

To locate the one Cabral Advertising file that contains "assets" in its tags, you enter "tags:assets" in the Search box.

Figure 3-33 Searching for a file using a tag

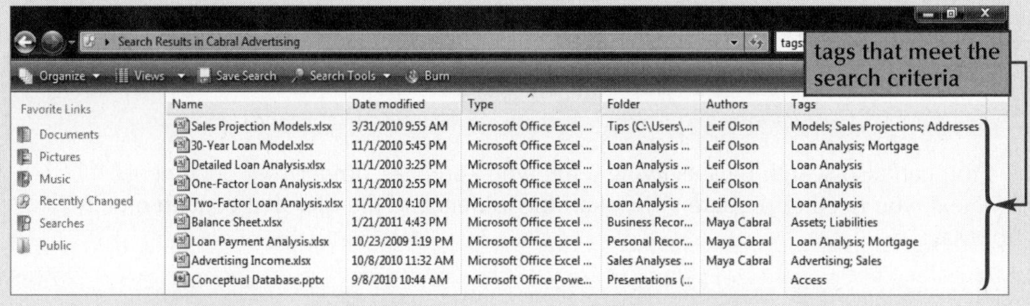

4. Click the **Back** button to return to the Cabral Advertising folder.

Reference Window | Searching Using a File Property, File Type, or Tags

- To search a folder using a file property, click inside the Search box and type the name of a property (or a heading name), followed immediately by a colon (such as name:, date modified:, type:, size:, or tags:), followed immediately by the search string.
- To search for just folders, click inside the Search box and type folder.
- To search for a tag, click inside the Search box, type tags: (with the colon), followed immediately by all or part of the text found in a tag.

Maya wants to create a Best Case Scenario and a Worst Case Scenario of her Five Year Growth Plan. To distinguish this file from the new versions she intends to create, she asks you to add the tag "Most Likely Case" to the current Five Year Growth Plan file.

To assign a tag to a file:

1. In the Search box, type **five**. The Five Year Growth Plan file is listed as one of the two files found by Windows Vista. The "Sales Projection Memo" file was included in the Search results because it contains the phrase "five years" in the text of the file.
2. Point to the **Five Year Growth Plan.xlsx** file icon. In the Details Pane, Windows Vista displays information about this file. See Figure 3-34. Next to the file property Tags is "Add a tag."

Figure 3-34 Using the Details Pane to add a tag to a file

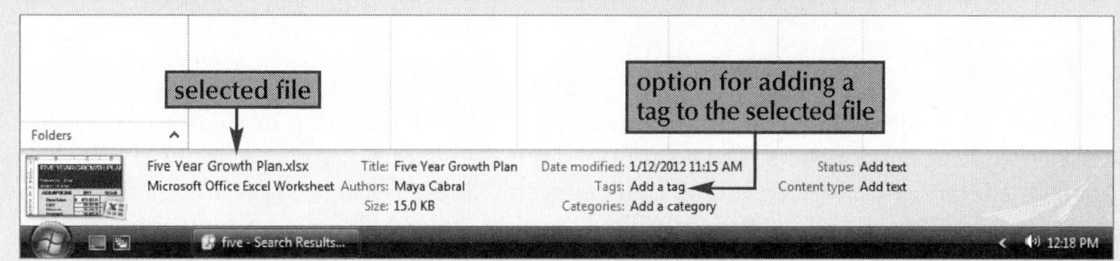

3. Click **Add a tag** in the Details Pane (next to the word Tags), type **Most Likely Case** in the Tags box, and then click the **Save** button in the Details Pane. Windows Vista adds a tag to this file.
4. Use the **Back** button to return to the Cabral Advertising folder.
5. To test your new tag, type **tags:case** in the Search box. Windows Vista finds one file, Five Year Growth Plan.xlsx, which contains the word "case" in the file's tag. See Figure 3-35.

Figure 3-35 Searching for a file with a specific tag

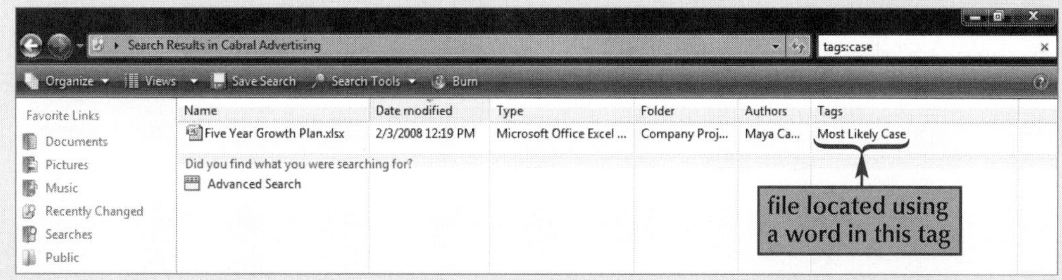

6. Use the **Back** button to return to the Cabral Advertising folder window.

Assigning a Tag or Tags to a File | Reference Window

- Locate or search for the file that you want to assign tags to, and then select the file.
- In the Details Pane, click "Add a tag," and then type the first tag; if you want to assign more than one tag to a file, type each tag followed by a semicolon.
- Click the Save button in the Details Pane.

In the Details Pane, you can enter, update, or change the Author, Title, Category, Tags, Status, and Content Type properties. Also, you can add more than one tag to the Tags box. After you type a tag, you type a semicolon (;) to separate the first tag from the next one. The semicolon acts as a delimiter between tags.

InSight | Specifying File Properties and Tags

For some applications, you can enter properties and tags for the file before you save it. However, the approach that you use may vary with the application and perhaps even with the version of that application. For example, you specify file properties in different ways in Microsoft Office 2003 and Microsoft Office 2007. For files created with applications developed before the introduction of Windows Vista, the options for specifying file properties may be limited. Where available, tags are a great way to cross-reference files and efficiently find what you need.

Using Boolean Filters

You can use Boolean filters to perform more precise searches and quickly narrow a long list of possible search results. The term Boolean is derived from George Boole, a British mathematician who invented a type of algebra in which every equation always results in a value of TRUE or FALSE. A **Boolean filter** consists of a word (called a **logical operator**) or a symbol (called a **comparison operator** or **relational operator**) that allows you to specify more than one search condition or compare two items (whether values or text). When Instant Search evaluates the Boolean filters, it determines whether the Boolean filter is TRUE or FALSE. If TRUE, Instant Search displays the folder or filename in the list of search results. If FALSE, the folder or filename does not appear in the search results. In essence, it allows you to use simple logic to maximize the effectiveness of searches. Whenever you use a search engine, such as Google, to search for information, you are performing a similar type of operation. The search engine compares the search criteria that you specify with the content of Web pages it examines. The search engine then locates and displays a list of search results that meet the criteria you specified. (Rather than searching the Web each time you do a search, search engines rely on previously indexed information of Web sites to quickly locate and display the information you want.) Figure 3-36 lists the Boolean filters, illustrates each Boolean operator with an example, and describes what types of results Windows Vista displays using the example.

Boolean filters | Figure 3-36

Boolean Filter	Example	Finds
AND	project AND proposal	• All files that contain "project" and "proposal" in the filename, file contents, or file properties • All folders that contain "project" and "proposal" in the folder name
OR	project OR proposal	• All files that contain "project" or "proposal" somewhere in the filename, file contents, or file properties • All folders that contain "project" or "proposal" in the folder name
NOT	project NOT proposal	• All files that contain "project" but not "proposal" somewhere in the filename, file contents, or file properties • All folders that contain "project" but not "proposal" in the folder name
" "	"project proposal"	• All files that contain the exact phrase "project proposal" somewhere in the filename, file contents, or file properties • All folders that contain the exact phrase "project proposal" in the folder name
( )	(Specialty Travel)	• All files that contain "Specialty Travel" or "Travel Specialty" in the filename, file contents, or file properties • All folders that contain "Specialty Travel" or "Travel Specialty" in the folder name
>	date modified:>1/1/2011	All folders and files with a modified file date after 1/1/2011
<	size:<1 MB	All folders and files with a file size of less than 1 MB (megabyte)

Here's how the different Boolean filters work:

- **AND** This Boolean filter combines two criteria and requires that any folders or files listed in the search results meet both conditions. For example, if you enter the Boolean filter "project AND proposal" without the quotation marks, the search results include all folders and files with both words, "project" and "proposal," somewhere in the folder or filename, the contents of a file, or the file properties.
- **OR** This Boolean filter combines two criteria and requires that any folders or files listed in the search results meet one of the two conditions. For example, if you enter the Boolean filter "project OR proposal" without the quotation marks, the search results include all folders and files with one of the two words, "project" or "proposal," somewhere in the folder or filename, the contents of the file, or the file properties. If a folder or file contains both words in the folder or filename, the contents of a file, or the file properties, the folder or file is included in the search results.
- **NOT** This Boolean filter combines two criteria and requires that any folders or files listed in the search results meet the first condition and not include the second condition. For example, if you enter the Boolean filter "project NOT proposal" without the quotation marks, the search results includes all folders and files with the word "project" but not the word "proposal" in the folder or filename, the contents of a file, or the file properties.

- **" " (quotation marks)** If you enclose words or a phrase in quotation marks, the search results include exactly what you type. For example, if you enter the search condition "project proposal" with quotation marks around the two words, the search results include any folder or file with the phrase "project proposal" somewhere in the folder or filename, the contents of a file, or the file properties.
- **( ) (parentheses)** If you enclose a phrase in parentheses, the search results include all the words in the phrase; however, the words can be arranged in any order. For example, if you enter (Specialty Travel) with the parentheses, the search results include all folders and files with "Specialty Travel" or "Travel Specialty" in the folder or filename, the contents of the file, or the file properties.
- **> (greater than)** You can also use the **greater than comparison operator (>)** to determine if the setting or value for a property, such as the file date or file size, exceeds a certain date or value. As noted earlier, a comparison operator or relational operator compares two items in a specific way. For example, if you specify the search condition "date modified: >1/1/2010" without the quotation marks, the search results include only folders and files modified after 1/1/2010. "Date Modified" is a file property.
- **< (less than)** Similarly, you can use the **less than comparison operator (<)** to determine if the setting or value for a property, such as the file date or file size, is less than a certain date or value. For example, if you specify the search condition "date modified: <1/1/2010", the search results include only folders and files modified before 1/1/2010. When checking for dates, remember that Windows Vista keeps track of different types of file dates (such as date created, date modified, and date accessed) for each file, and you want to make sure you are using the correct date property.

When you use the AND, OR, and NOT Boolean filters, you must type them in all uppercase for them to work properly.

Maya asks you to locate and print several files that she needs for a new client and for an upcoming workshop. Maya recommends that you use Boolean filters to quickly locate those files. She also notes that you can combine Boolean filters and file properties.

To locate a file with a Boolean filter:

1. In the Cabral Advertising window, type **loan analysis AND mortgage** in the Search box. Instant Search locates two files that contain these two criteria in the files' tags. See Figure 3-37. Both files also have the phrase "loan analysis" in the file itself, but not the word "mortgage." You could have also specified the Tags property for both criteria, as follows: tags:loan analysis AND tags:mortgage.

Figure 3-37 Using the AND Boolean filter to find files

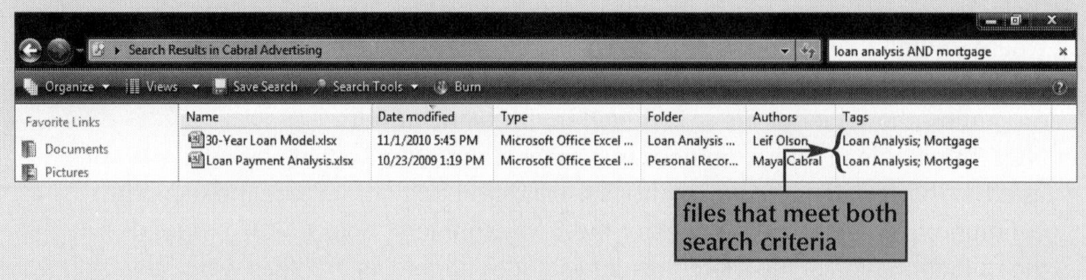

2. In the Search box, delete the current search criteria, and then type **projections OR analysis** in the Search box. Instant Search locates 14 items—two folders and 12 files, nine of which contain one of these words in the folder or filename, in the contents of the file, or in one of the file's properties. The Sales Projection Memo, Regional Sales Projection, and Five Year Growth Plan files do not contain either word in the filename, file's contents, or file properties, but these three files are contained in the only folder, i.e., Company Projections, whose name contains one of the two criteria (namely, "projections"). See Figure 3-38. You have located all of the files Maya needs for projecting and analyzing sales. Because you more than likely will perform this same search again, you decide to save the search.

Figure 3-38 Using the OR Boolean filter to find files

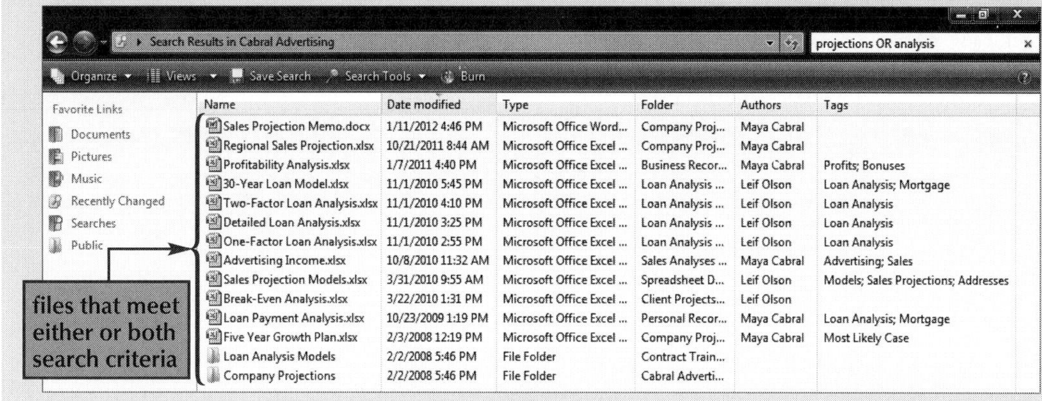

3. Click the **Save Search** button on the command bar. Windows Vista displays a Save As dialog box and prompts you for a filename. It proposes to use your search criteria as the filename and will add the "search-ms" file extension to the filename. Also, Windows Vista will save your search in the Searches folder. See Figure 3-39.

Figure 3-39 Saving a search

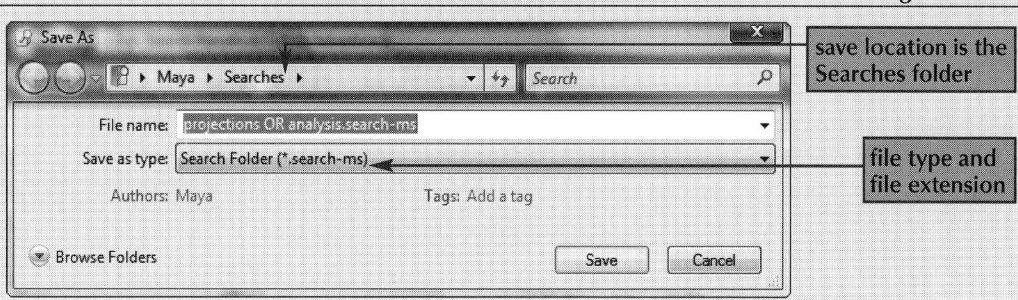

4. Click the **Save** button and then click **Searches** in the Navigation pane. After saving your Search, Windows Vista switches to your Searches folder. See Figure 3-40. You now have a virtual folder named "projections OR analysis".

Figure 3-40 Viewing a saved search in the Searches folder

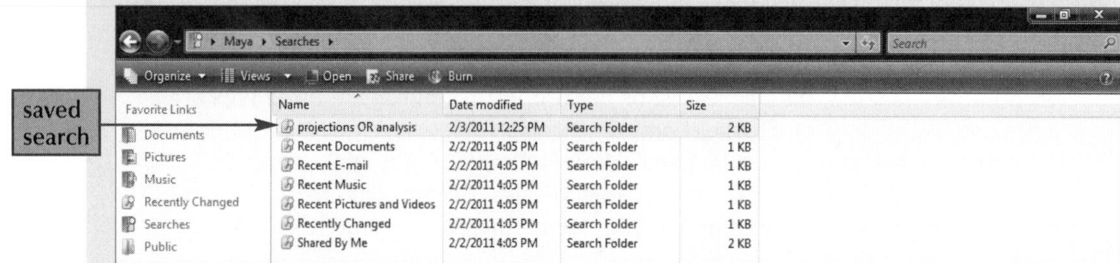

5. Click the **projections OR analysis** folder. Windows Vista opens the folder and displays a copy of the files that it located with your search criteria. See Figure 3-41.

Figure 3-41 Viewing files in a saved search

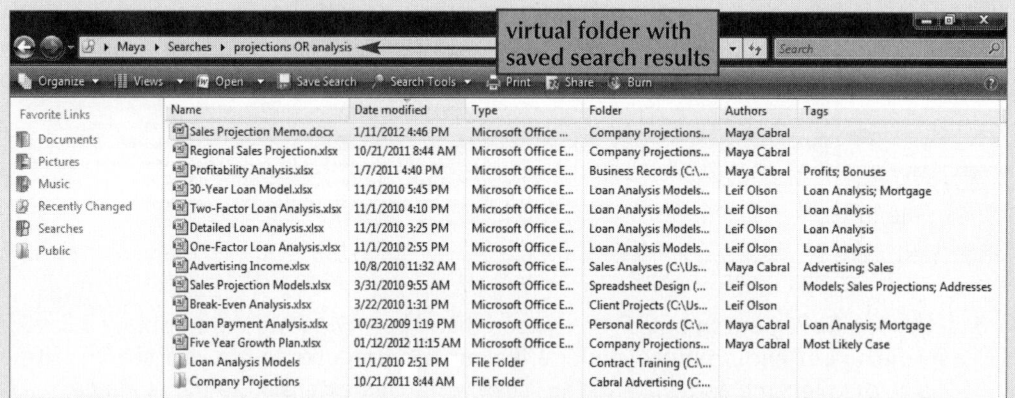

6. In the Navigation pane, click **Public**, click **Public Documents** in the Public folder window, and then click **Cabral Advertising** in the Public Documents folder.
7. In the Search box, type **"excel tips"** (with the quotation marks). Windows Vista locates the only file by this name. If you had entered Excel without the quotation marks, your search results would include all Microsoft Office Excel Worksheets. If you had entered Tips as your search criteria, your search results would include the Tips folder and the Excel Tips file in that folder.
8. Delete the search condition in the Search box, and then type **tags:models OR tips** in the Search box. Windows Vista locates the Sales Projection Models.xlsx file, the Tips folder, and Excel Tips.xlsx file. Here you used a file property as one of the criteria for the Boolean filter. The two files are the ones Maya needs to prepare for an upcoming training session. See Figure 3-42.

Figure 3-42 Combining a tag with a Boolean filter in a search

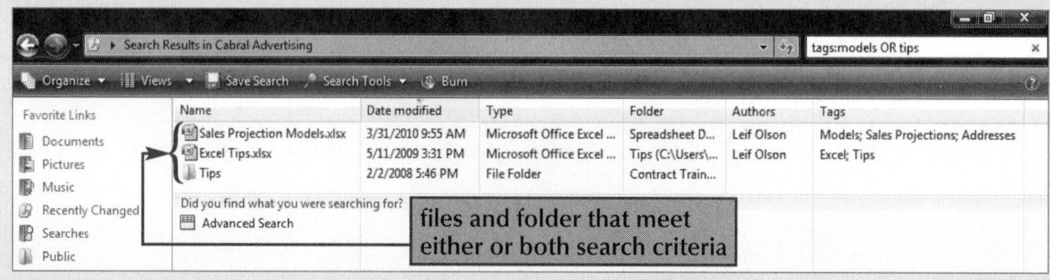

9. Drag the **Sales Projection Models.xlsx file** and drop it on the Tips folder icon, and then click the **Tips** folder icon. Windows Vista moves the Sales Projection Model.xlsx file into the Tips folder. Now Maya has the two files she needs for her contract training workshop.
10. Close the Cabral Advertising folder window.

By combining Boolean filters and file properties, you can quickly locate whatever combination of folders and files you need for a project. In some cases, you may discover valuable files that you have not used in a while.

Using the Search Explorer

If you open Search from the Start menu, you can perform a simple or a more advanced custom search using a specialized search tool called Search Explorer. From Search Explorer, you can search your entire computer system.

Maya asks you to update the list of contract jobs for the last week. To save time, she recommends that you use Search Explorer and specify the Clients tag.

To use Search Explorer:

1. Right-click the **Start** button, click **Properties** on the shortcut menu, click the **Customize** button next to the Start menu option button next to the Start menu option button, add check marks to the **Search**, **Search communications**, **Search favorites and history**, **Search this user's files**, and **Search programs** check boxes (if necessary), and then click the **OK** button. Click the **OK** button to close the Taskbar and Start Menu Properties dialog box.
2. On the Start menu, click **Search** (not the Search box). Windows Vista opens Search Explorer. See Figure 3-43. If you want to perform a simple search and locate a specific type of document, such as E-Mail, Document, Picture, or Music, you can select that option before you enter your search string in the Search box. The All option is the default option for searching all types of files. The Other option locates files other than E-Mail, Document, Picture, and Music files.

Tip

You also use the Windows+F keyboard shortcut to open Search Explorer.

Figure 3-43 Search Explorer window

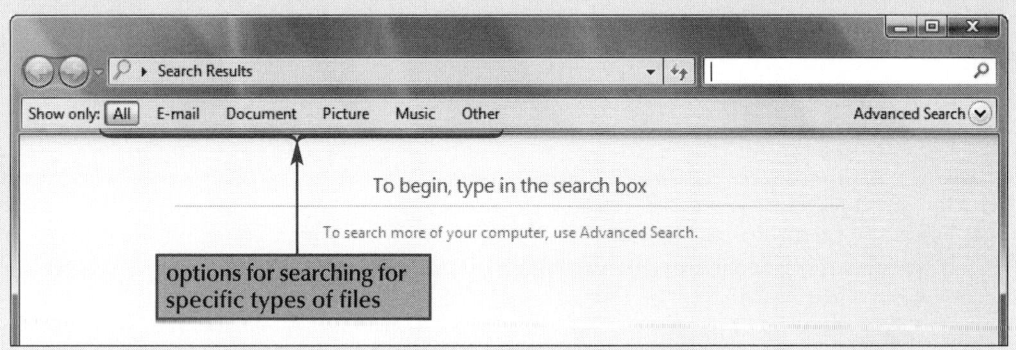

3. To the right of "Advanced Search," click the **Show advanced filters** button. Windows Vista displays options for customizing your search. See Figure 3-44. By default, Windows Vista searches indexed locations, but you can use the Location button to select a location on your computer, including Computer itself or a specific drive, for starting the search. You can use the Date button to locate a file by date, including the modified date or created date, and then you can specify "any" for any date, "is" for an exact date, "is before" for a date preceding the one you specify, or "is after" for a date following the one you specify. If you want to search for files based on size (in KB or kilobytes), you can specify "any" for all file sizes, "equals" for a match to the file size you specify, "is less than" for a file size smaller than the one you specify, or "is greater than" for a file size larger than the one you specify. You can specify a filename, tags, and authors in the Name, Tags, and Authors text boxes, and you can choose the option for searching nonindexed, hidden, and system files. The latter option is slower but is valuable when troubleshooting a problem on a computer.

Figure 3-44 Viewing advanced search options

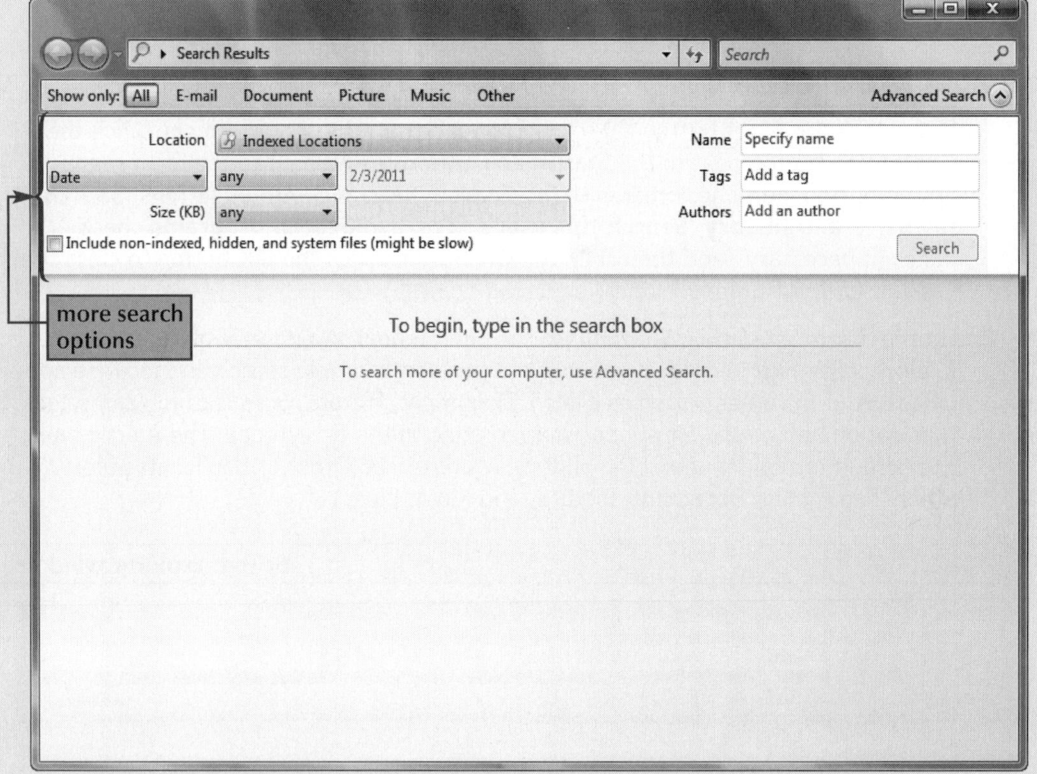

4. Click the **Location** button, note the list of drives from which you can select, click **Choose search locations** at the bottom of the Location list, and in the Choose Search Locations dialog box, click the small **Expand arrow** to the left of Public, click the small **Expand arrow** to the left of Public Documents, and then click the **Cabral Advertising** check box. Windows Vista lists this location in the "Summary of selected locations" list box. See Figure 3-45. You can add more than one location for the search.

Figure 3-45 Viewing and choosing search locations

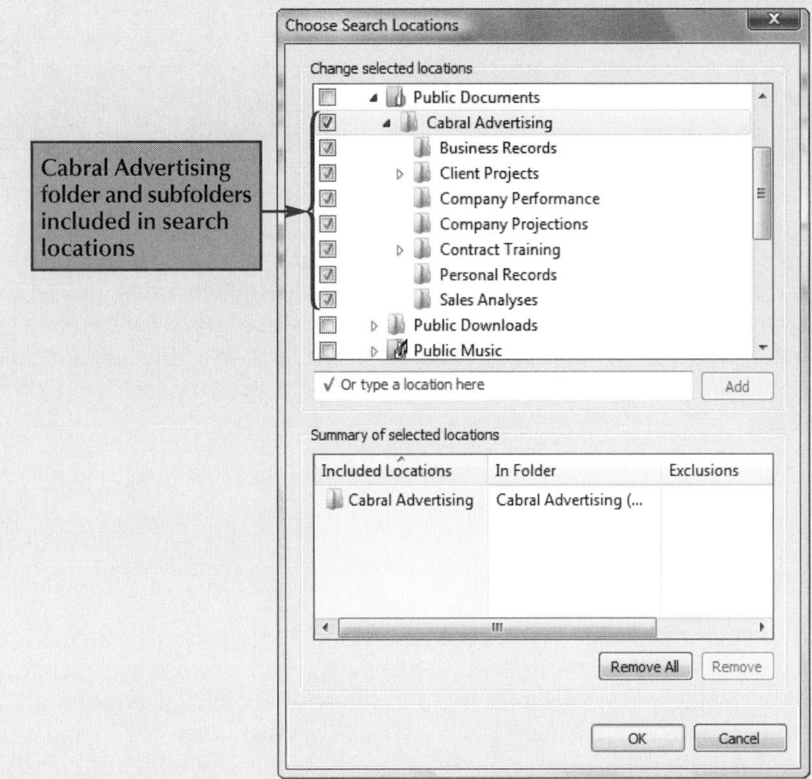

5. Click the **OK** button in the Choose Search Locations dialog box. Search Explorer displays "Cabral Advertising" on the Location button.

6. In the Tags box, type **clients** and in the Search box, type **Solar** (for Maya's Solar-Winds client), and then maximize the Search Results window. Search Explorer locates the one file that matches the search criteria that you specified—namely Contract Jobs.xlsx. See Figure 3-46. Note that this file has one tag, Clients. Within this file is a listing for the "SolarWinds, Inc." contract job. If you wanted to open the folder that contains this file, you would right-click the file and choose "Open file location."

Figure 3-46 Using advanced search options to locate a file

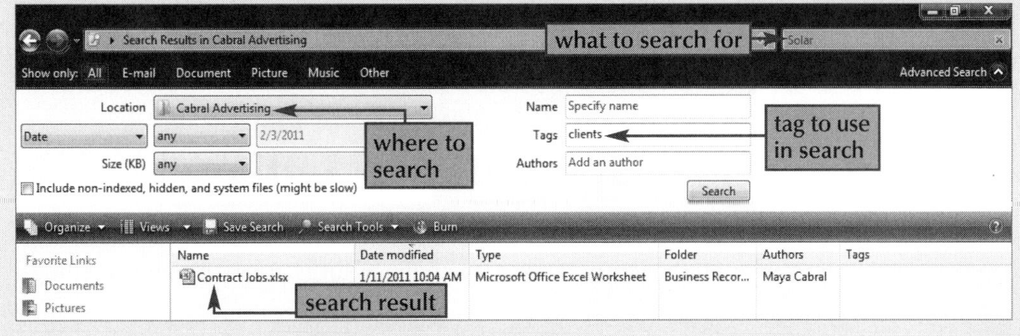

7. Close the Search Results in the Cabral Advertising window.

Reference Window | **Using the Search Explorer**

- On the Start menu, click Search (not the Search box).
- For "Show only," click E-Mail, Document, Picture, or Music to search for a specific type of file, or click Other to search for other types of files, or click All to search for all files, and then type a search string in the Search box.
- To perform an advanced search, click the Show advanced filters button. Use the Location button to choose the location for the search, or use "Choose search locations" to specify another location (such as a folder) for the search. To search by date, choose Date, Date modified, or Date created, choose any, is, is before, or is after, and then choose a specific date from a drop-down calendar. To search using file size, choose any, equals, is less than, or is greater than, and then type a file size. To search by name, type all or part of a filename in the Name box. To search by Tags, type one or more tags separated by semicolons in the Tags box. To search by an author's name, type all or part of the author name in the Authors box. Finally, click the Search button or enter a search string in the Search box.

Search Explorer can help you locate a file or group of files that meet specific criteria from the thousands of files on your computer.

Using Wildcards in Searches

In previous versions of Windows, you could use wildcards to perform searches and locate files with specific patterns in their filenames. You can also use these wildcards in Windows Vista. **Wildcards** are symbols that substitute for one character or for all characters in the folder name or filename. The two wildcards are an asterisk (*) and a question mark (?). The **asterisk wildcard** substitutes for all characters in a folder or filename. For example, to search for all Microsoft Office Word Document files, you could enter the criteria *.doc (pronounced "star dot doc") to locate all Word document files created by any version of Word. In this case, the asterisk substitutes for all characters in the filename before the period that separates the filename from the file extension. The **question mark wildcard** substitutes for one character in a folder name or filename. For example, if you have different files with sales summaries for several years in a row and if all the filenames start with the year (for example, 2009 Sales Summary, 2010 Sales Summary, and 2011 Sales Summary), you can enter the search criteria "20?? Sales Summary" to locate all these files. In this instance, the two question marks instruct Windows Vista to look for any character in the third and fourth positions of the filename. You could also use 20*Sales Summary to locate these same files. In this case, the asterisk substitutes for the last two digits of the year and the space between the year and "Sales Summary." The wildcard *.* selects all files. The first asterisk substitutes for any filename, and the second asterisk substitutes for any file extensions. Open dialog boxes typically have an "All Files (*.*)" option so that you can view all files in a folder rather than files with a specific file extension.

Examining Search and Indexing Settings

Maya recommends that you examine your current indexing and search settings to determine whether you can optimize your searches by changing or customizing those settings.

To examine Indexing options:

1. On the Start menu, open **Control Panel**, click **System and Maintenance**, and then click **Indexing Options**. Windows Vista opens the Indexing Options dialog box. See Figure 3-47. Windows Vista identifies the number of items that are indexed (yours will differ) and informs you that indexing is complete, that indexing speed is reduced because of user activity, or that indexing is in progress. In the "Index these locations" list box, Windows Vista identifies what locations are included and excluded in indexing. By default, Windows Vista indexes the Start Menu folder, the Offline Files folder, and the Users folder (except for Default User). Your settings may differ. If you add a location for indexing, Windows Vista displays the path to that location in this list box.

Tip

You can also press the Windows key, type ind (or type index) in the Search box, and then click Indexing Options in the Search results.

Figure 3-47 Indexing Options dialog box

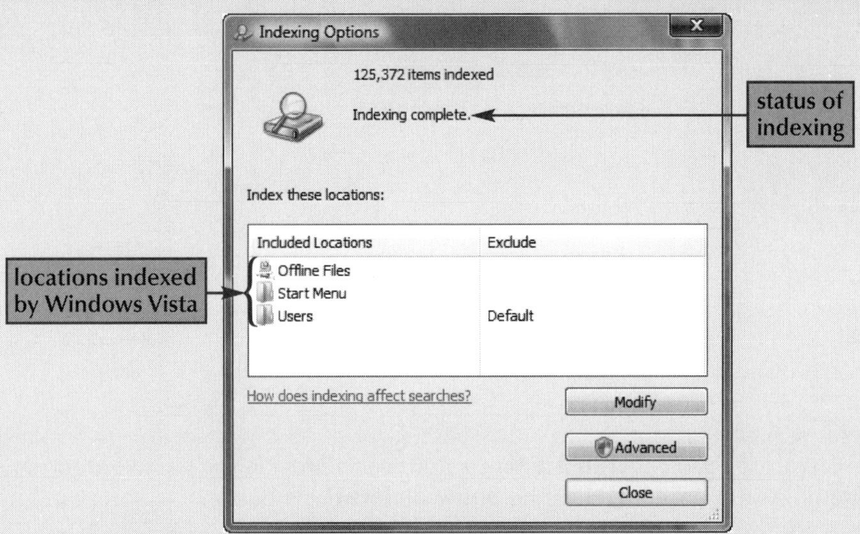

2. Click the **Modify** button in the Indexing Options dialog box. Windows Vista opens an Indexed Locations dialog box and provides two boxes where you can change selected locations and view a summary of selected locations. See Figure 3-48. Your settings may differ. To view all indexed locations, you must use the "Show all locations" button and either choose the option to continue if your account is an Administrator account or provide the password for an Administrator account.

Figure 3-48 Indexed Locations dialog box

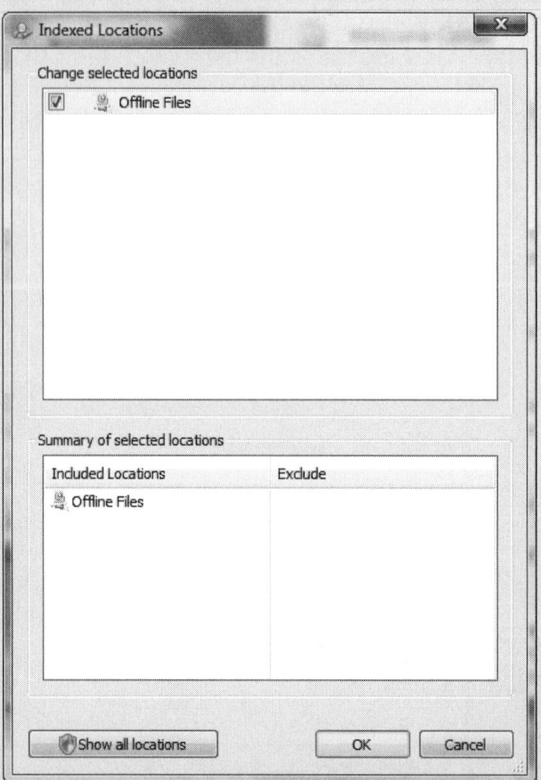

3. If you are logged on as an Administrator or can provide the password for an Administrator account, click the **Show all locations** button.

   Trouble? If you are not logged on as an Administrator or cannot provide a password for an Administrator account, read but do not perform the next two steps.

4. In the User Account Control dialog box, click the **Continue** button or select an **Administrator account** and enter the **password** for that Administrator account, and then click the **Continue** button. Windows Vista updates the contents of the Indexed Locations dialog box and provides more details on indexed locations. Your settings may differ.

5. In the "Change selected locations" list box, click the small **Expand arrow** ▷ to the left of Local Disk (C:) to expand the list for this drive, and then click the small **Expand arrow** ▷ to the left of Users. Note that Windows Vista does not index the Program Files or Windows folders, but does index all user account folders except for Default User. See Figure 3-49. Your settings will differ. In this dialog box, you can change which user accounts are indexed and which folders within a user account or system folder are indexed.

Figure 3-49 Viewing details on indexed locations

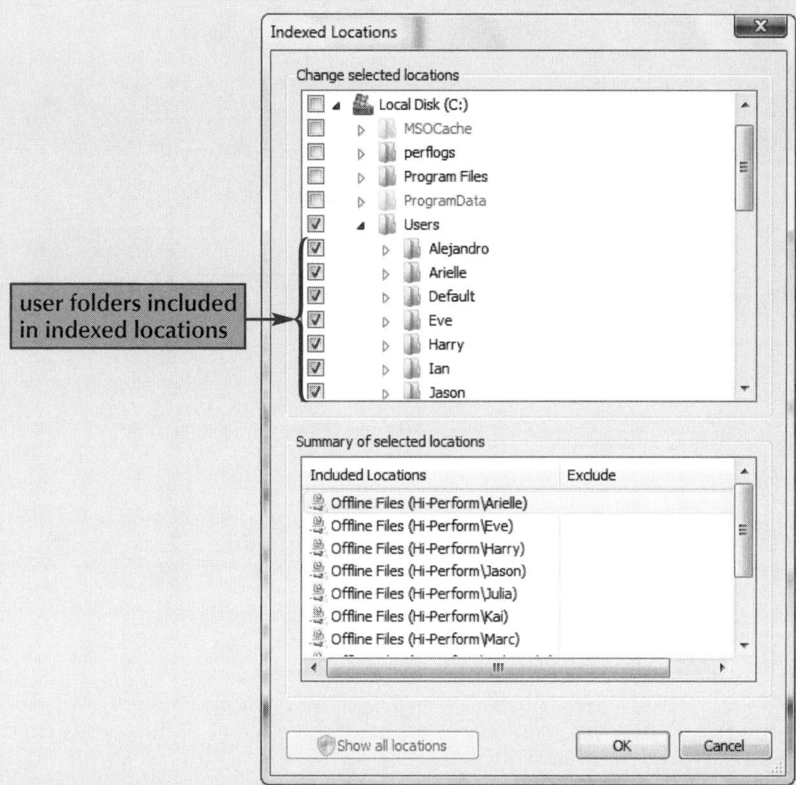

6. Click the **Cancel** button to close the Indexed Locations dialog box without making any changes.
7. If you are logged on as an Administrator or can provide a password for an Administrator account, click the **Advanced** button in the Indexing Options dialog box.

   Trouble? If you are not logged on as an Administrator or cannot provide a password for an Administrator account, read but do not perform the next two steps.
8. In the User Account Control dialog box, click the **Continue** button or select an **Administrator account** and enter the **password** for that Administrator account, and then click the **Continue** button. Windows Vista opens the Advanced Options dialog. See Figure 3-50. Under File Settings, indexing of encrypted files is disabled on the computer used for this figure; however, you can enable this option. Your setting may differ. Encryption is a technique for securing data in a file so that only the authorized user has access to the file. Also by default, words with and without diacritics (or accents), such as jalapeño and jalapeno, are considered the same words for indexing purposes, but you can change this setting if you want to treat words with and without diacritics differently. Under Troubleshooting, you can rebuild your index if you discover that it is not finding files and folders that you know you have. However, you should first check to make sure that those locations are included for indexing, because rebuilding an index can take hours. You can also restore your index to its default settings. If you choose this option, Windows Vista deletes the index the next time you start your computer and then re-indexes all locations marked for indexing. Again, this process takes a lot of time. Under Index location, Windows Vista shows the path to the folder where it stores the index. You have the option of specifying another location.

Figure 3-50 **Advanced Options dialog box**

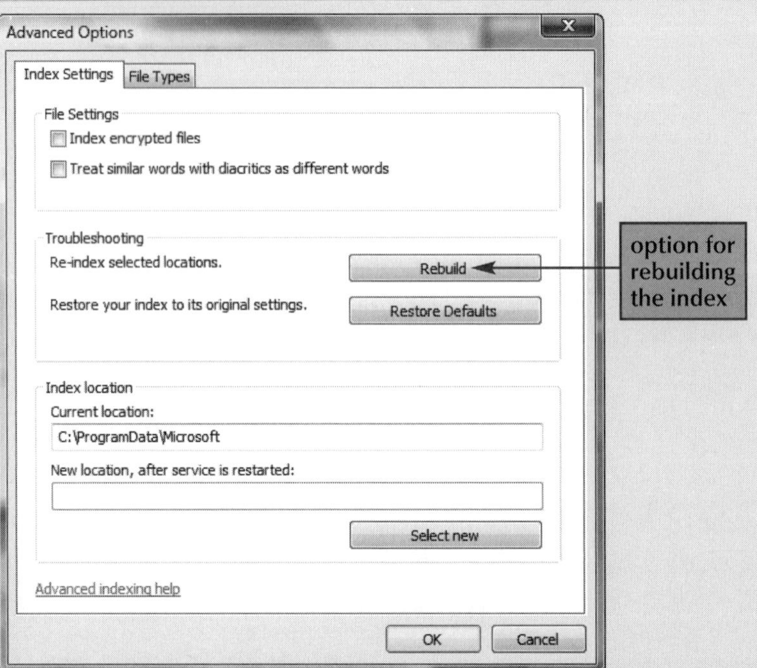

9. Click the **File Types** tab. Windows Vista displays a list of all file types that are included in the index. See Figure 3-51. Here you can examine, and if necessary, change whether Windows Vista indexes a specific file type (identifiable by file extension), and if so, whether it should index only the file properties or both the file properties and file content. You can also add new file extensions in the Add new extension box at the bottom of the dialog box, and then customize the settings for that new file extension.

Figure 3-51 **Viewing file types included in indexing**

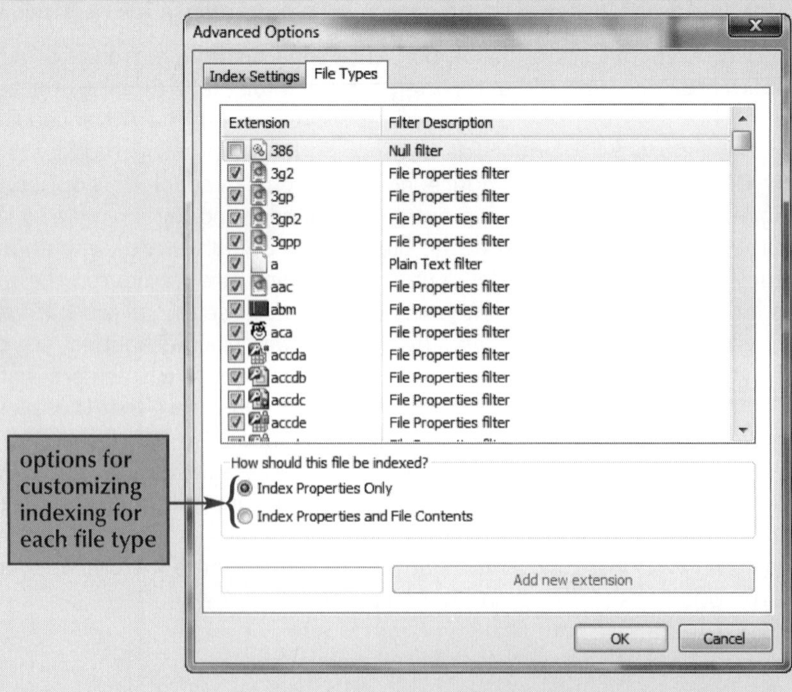

10. Click the **Cancel** button in the Advanced Options dialog box to exit without making any change to the settings on your computer, close the Indexing Options dialog box, and then close the System and Maintenance window.

Examining Search and Index Settings | Reference Window

- On the Start menu, click Control Panel, click System and Maintenance, and then click Indexing Options.
- In the Indexing Options dialog box, click the Modify button, click the "Show all locations" button in the Indexed Locations dialog box, provide Administrator credentials, review, and if necessary, choose locations to index in the "Change selection locations" box, and then click the OK button.
- In the Indexing Options dialog box, click the Advanced button, provide Administrator credentials, review, and if necessary, change File Settings on the Index Settings property sheet, use the Rebuild button to re-index selection locations, or use the Restore Defaults to restore your index to its original settings. Click the File Types tab, select a file type in the Extension column, review, and if necessary, change the option for indexing this file type, and then click the OK button.
- Close the Indexing Options dialog box and then the System and Maintenance window.

You can also customize Search options by using the Folder Options dialog box. In the "How to search" section of the Search property sheet, Instant Search is set to search subfolders and find partial matches, such as when you enter the first few characters of a folder or filename. If you specify that it use natural language search, Instant Search interprets your search string as natural language. For example, if you search for "e-mail from Maya Cabral," Instant Search searches for and displays all e-mail messages from Maya Cabral. If you enable the option for not using the index when searching the file system, Instant Search uses only filenames for the search and does not search the content of files.

If you enable the options for including system **directories** (a command-line term for "folders") and including compressed files under "When searching non-indexed locations," Instant Search searches system folders by examining only filenames, though it also searches filenames and file contents of files stored in compressed files. A **compressed file** is a single file that contains files, or folders and files, stored in a way that reduces the amount of storage space required on disk. You can also use the Restore Defaults button to restore the default Search settings listed in this dialog box.

To examine Search options:

1. On the Start menu, open **Documents**, click the **Organize** button on the command bar, click **Folder and Search Options**, and then click the **Search** tab in the Folder Options dialog box. Under "What to search" on the Search property sheet of the Folder Options dialog box, Instant Search is set to search both filenames and contents for indexed locations. In non-indexed locations, it searches only filenames. See Figure 3-52. You can specify that it always search filenames and contents (which might be slow) or only search filenames (which is faster, but might not produce what you need). The Restore Defaults button restores default search settings.

Figure 3-52 Viewing search settings

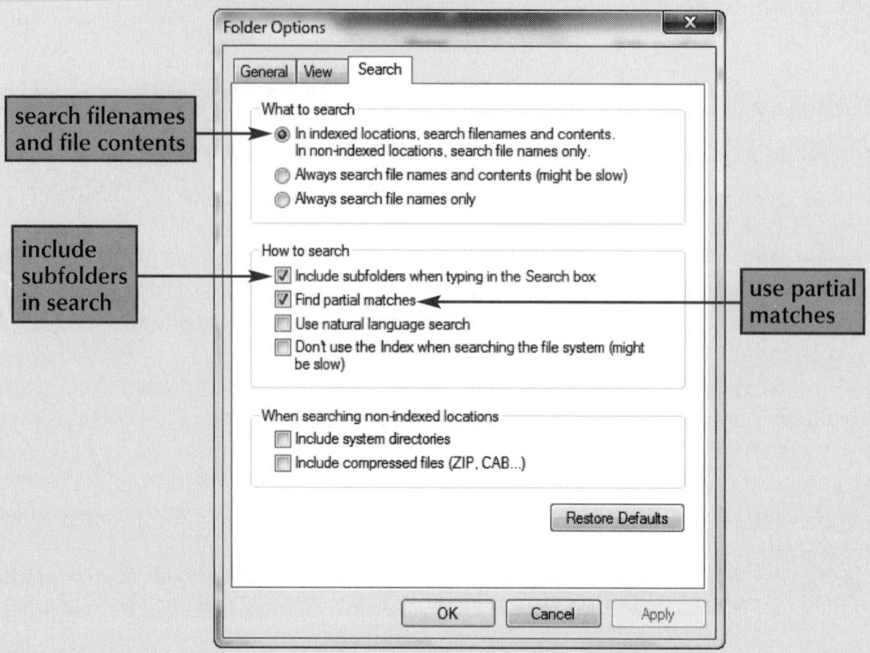

2. Click the **Cancel** button to close the Folder Options dialog box without making changes to your computer, and then close the Documents window.

Reference Window | **Customizing Search Options**

- Open the Documents window (or another folder window), click the Organize button on the command bar, click Folder and Search Options, and then click the Search tab in the Folder Options dialog box.
- Review, and if necessary, change Search settings under "What to search," "How to search," and "When searching non-indexed locations."
- Use the Restore Defaults button to restore default Search settings.
- Click the OK button to close the Folder Options dialog box, and then close the folder window.

You have now examined all the options in the Folder Options dialog box for specifying default Windows settings, and you now know how to restore these default settings.

Restoring Your Computer's Settings

If you are using your own computer and want to restore the original settings, complete the following steps. If you are working in a computer lab or on a company network and the computers are not configured to restore their original settings with a simple reboot, complete the following steps to restore the original display settings on your computer. If the computers in your computer lab are set up so that a reboot restores the computer to its previous states (and undoes all changes you've made to Windows Vista), choose the option to restart your computer so that the next person who uses the computer is not affected by changes you have made.

To restore your computer's display settings:

1. To restore double-click activation, click the **Computer** icon on the desktop, click the **Organize** button on the command bar, click **Folder and Search Options**, and on the General property sheet in the Folder Options dialog box, click the **Double-click to open an item (single-click to select)** option button.
2. To hide extensions for known file types, click the **View** tab in the Folder Options dialog box, click the **Hide extensions for known file types** check box if it does not contain a check mark, click the **OK** button to close the Folder Options dialog box and apply these changes, and then close the Computer window.
3. Open the **Documents** folder from the Start menu, double-click **Public** in the Navigation pane, and then click **Public Documents** in the Public folder window.
4. If you want to copy the Cabral Advertising folder to your flash drive before you remove it from the Public Documents folder, right-click the **Cabral Advertising** folder icon, point to **Send To** on the shortcut menu, and then click the **drive name for your flash drive**.
5. If you want to delete the Cabral Advertising folder from your computer, or if you are working in a computer lab where other people might complete the same assignment on the same computer, click the **Cabral Advertising** folder icon, press the **Delete** key, and in the Delete Folder dialog box, click the **Yes** button.
6. Open the Searches folder, select **projections OR analysis**, press the **Delete** key, and in the Delete Folder dialog box, click the **Yes** button.
7. To remove the Computer icon on the desktop, open the Start menu, right-click **Computer**, and then click **Show on Desktop**.

Maya is impressed with the progress that you have made in using the Windows Vista Instant Search feature. Not only will it save time and effort, but it will help both of you meet critical deadlines.

Session 3.2 Quick Check | Review

1. A(n) ________________ is a word or phrase that you assign as a property to a folder or file so you can organize and locate folders and files.
2. The search criterion that you type in a Search box is called a(n) ________________ .
3. How can you identify the default option on a shortcut menu?
4. True or False. A Boolean filter consists of a word called a logical operator that allows you to specify more than one search condition.
5. A(n) ________________ operator is a symbol that compares two items during a search.
6. What Boolean filter can you use to specify that one of two conditions must be true to select a folder or file during a search? What Boolean filter can you use to specify that two conditions must be true to select a folder or file during a search?
7. What operator can you use to locate all files with a file size greater than 1 MB during a search?
8. True or False. You cannot combine file properties with Boolean filters in a search string.

Review | Tutorial Summary

In this tutorial, you examined the types of system folders that Windows Vista creates for each user and the organization of those folders. You also explored how best to organize your own personal folders and files. After you copied files to the Public folder, you used the Preview Pane to work with those files. Then you worked with view and behavior settings for folder windows. You viewed properties of a file, a set of files, and a folder. You also learned about the importance of the path and the use of long filenames and aliases. You organized files into groups and stacks so you could more easily locate and work with a set of files. You used the enhanced Instant Search feature in Windows Vista to search in a variety of ways. You searched for a program from the Start menu. You searched files in a folder window using filenames, file content, and file properties, including tags. You used Boolean filters and file properties to specify more complex criteria for locating files, and you opened Search Explorer and used its advanced search features. Finally, you viewed Windows Vista search and index settings so that you can understand better how Instant Search works and so that you can customize searches and indexing to meet your daily needs.

Key Terms

“ ”
( )
>
<
8.3 filename
algorithm
alias
AND
attribute
asterisk wildcard
Boolean filter
comparison operator
compressed file
contact file
contact group
default action
delimiter
directory
executable file
greater than comparison operator
index
less than comparison operator
logical operator
metadata
NOT
OR
path
preview handler
question mark wildcard
registered file
relational operator
root directory
search string
self-extracting executable file
service
slack
stack
string
tag
top-level folder
virtual folder
wildcard

Practice | Review Assignments

Practice the skills you learned in the tutorial.

For a list of Data Files in the Review folder, see page 137.

Maya recently hired Charlene Gosney to help her with client projects. On Charlene's first day of work, Maya describes the types of client support that the two of them must provide to successfully complete their projects. Maya asks you to show Charlene the folder structure and file system used on her computer so that Charlene can adapt a similar structure on the computer she will use.

As you complete each step, record your answers to questions so that you can submit them to your instructor. Use a word processing application, such as Microsoft Office Word or WordPad, to prepare your answers to the questions in the Review Assignments. Also, if you change any settings on the computer you are using, note the original settings so that you can restore them later. You will need a copy of the Data Files for this tutorial to complete this assignment. Complete the following steps:

1. On the Start menu, open your user account folder (the one with your user account name). What folders did Windows Vista create for your user account? List their names.
2. Open the Searches folder. What search folders did Windows Vista create for your user account? List their names.
3. Open your Documents folder, your flash drive, or a network folder that contains an original copy of the Tutorial.03 folder. Open the Tutorial.03 folder. Open a second Documents window, switch to the Public folder, and then switch to the Public Documents folder. Tile the windows so Windows Vista places the two windows side by side. Copy the extracted Review folder from your Documents folder, flash drive, or a network folder to the Public Documents folder. Rename the Review folder in the Public Documents folder to Cabral Advertising.
4. Open the Cabral Advertising folder, and if necessary, display the Preview Pane and adjust the Preview Pane so that it is approximately half of the window's width.
5. Use the Views button to adjust your view of the folder's contents to a setting between Extra Large Icons and Large Icons view so that all the folder icons fit within the window.
6. Open the Client Projects folder, and if necessary, use the Views button to adjust your view of the folder's contents to a setting between Extra Large Icons and Large Icons view so that all the folder icons fit within the window.
7. On the Organize menu, choose Folder and Search Options, and then select the View tab. On the View property sheet, turn off the "Display file icon on thumbnails" setting, and then apply this change and close the Folder Options dialog box. Examine the thumbnails of the files in this folder. Open the View property sheet again and enable the "Display file icon on thumbnails" option, and then close the Folder Options dialog box and apply this change. Examine the thumbnails of the files in this folder. Describe how this setting affects your view of these files.
8. Point to the Break-Even Analysis thumbnail, and in the Preview Pane, view the contents of the first sheet in this file. At the bottom of the Preview Pane, click the tab to the right of the one labeled "Break-Even Analysis," and then scroll right to view the contents of this sheet. What does Windows Vista display on the second worksheet?
9. Examine the Details Pane. Who is listed as the author of this file? What is the file size? When was the file last modified? Next to the Tags property, click "Add a tag," and then type three tags: **Income from Sales; Total Cost; Units Sold**. Use the Save button to save and apply your changes.

10. Right-click Break-Even Analysis.xlsx and choose the option for viewing its properties. What is this file's file type? What program opens this file? What is the location for this file? What is this file's size? What is this file's size on disk? How much storage space is wasted on disk for this file? (*Hint*: To make it easier to record this information, you can drag to select any of these file properties, right-click the selected text, select Copy, switch to Microsoft Office Word or WordPad, and then click the Paste button.)
11. Click the Details tab, click "Remove Properties and Personal Information," and then click "Remove the following properties from this file" option button. Under Origin, can you remove the Authors and Program name properties? Use the Cancel button to close the Remove Properties dialog box and the Break-Even Analysis.xlsx Properties dialog box without making changes to the file's properties.
12. In the Client Projects window, use the Select All option on the Organize menu to select the contents of this folder, right-click one of the files or the folders, and then choose the option to view properties. In the group properties dialog box, how many files and folders are stored in this folder? What is the total size of the contents of this folder? How much storage space on disk do the contents of this folder require? How much storage space is wasted? Close the group properties dialog box.
13. Click the background of the Client Projects folder window to remove the selection, and then right-click the Visual Arts, Inc folder and view its properties. What type of object is this folder? What is its size? How much storage space does it use on disk? What does it contain? Close the Visual Arts, Inc Properties dialog box.
14. Right-click the background of the Client Projects folder window, and then choose the option to view its properties. What is the path to the location of the Client Projects folder? Close the Client Projects Properties dialog box.
15. Open the Visual Arts, Inc folder. Turn off the display of the Preview Pane and switch to Details view. If necessary, display the Date Modified, Type, Size, Tags, and Authors headings. Click the Size heading. What happens, and how does this change affect your view of the files in this folder? Click the Size heading again. What happens, and how does this change affect your view of the files in this folder? Click the Name heading. What happens, and how does this change affect your view of the files in this folder? How might you benefit from these features?
16. Click the Name heading button arrow, and then choose the option to group filenames. What happens, and how does this change affect your view of the files in this folder? Click the Name heading button arrow, and then click I-P. What happens, and how does this change affect your view of the files in this folder? How might you benefit from this feature? Remove the option for grouping files by the I-P group, and then sort filenames in alphabetical order.
17. Click the Tags heading button arrow, and then choose the option for stacking files by tags. What happens, and how does this change affect your view of the files in this folder? Click the Hire Dates stack. What file does Windows Vista list in this stack? Click the Back button, and then open the Job Titles stack. What file does Windows Vista list in this stack? Go back to the previous folder, and then open the Salaries stack. What file does Windows Vista list in this stack? How might you benefit from assigning tags to files and organizing files into stacks by tags? Return to the previous folder, and then use the Tags heading list to sort by Tags. Close the Search Results in Visual Arts Inc window.

18. Open the Start menu, and then use the Search box to locate and open the AutoPlay component of the Control Panel. What search string did you enter to locate AutoPlay? How can you use the options in the AutoPlay window? Click the Software and games button arrow. What options are available if you insert a disk that contains software or games? Close the AutoPlay window.
19. Open the Cabral Advertising folder, and if necessary, maximize the window, switch to Details view, and display the Date Modified, Type, Size, Tags, and Authors headings. Use the folder's Search box to locate the file with the filename Balance Sheet. What search string did you enter to locate this file and narrow the search results?
20. Use the folder's Search box to locate all files with "Cabral" as part of the Authors property. If necessary, adjust the width of the Authors column to view the details of this file property. How did you specify the search criteria? How many files did Windows Vista locate, and what feature did they have in common?
21. In the folder's Search box, type **JPEG**. How many files does Windows Vista find, and what features do they have in common?
22. In the folder's Search box, use the tags property to locate all tags with the letter "l" as the first character in the tag. What search criteria did you enter? How many files did Windows Vista find? If necessary, adjust the width of the Tags column. What tags meet the search criteria you specified? Modify the search criteria to locate only files with the "Loan Analysis" tag. What search criteria did you use, and how many files did Windows Vista find? Delete the search criteria in the Search box.
23. In the Search box, enter * (an asterisk) as search criteria to locate all folders and files in the Cabral Advertising folder. How many folders and files does Windows Vista find?
24. Locate and select the file named **Conceptual Database.pptx**. In the Details Pane, add **Database Concepts** as a tag to this file's Tags property. Use the folder's Search box to locate this file using each of the two tags separately.
25. Use Boolean filters to locate all Excel files with Leif Olson as the author. What search string did you specify, and how many files did Windows Vista find?
26. Modify the Boolean filter to locate all Excel files or all files created by Leif Olson. What search string did you specify? How many files did Windows Vista find? Sort the Name heading, and if necessary, adjust the Type and Authors columns so that you can see the full file type and full author's (or authors') name(s). What types of files did Windows Vista find, and why? What authors did Windows Vista find, and why?
27. Save the search and choose Searches in the Navigation pane. What is the name of the Search folder you just created? Select and delete the saved search you just created, but do not delete the other Search folders. Use the Back button to return to the Cabral Advertising folder.
28. In the Search box, enter **"Customer Accounts"** (with the quotation marks) as the search criteria. How can Windows Vista find two files with the same filename? Close the Search Results window.
29. Open Search Explorer from the Start menu, and in the Search Results window, choose the option for showing advanced search filters. Use the Location button to locate and select the Cabral Advertising folder as the location to use for the search, enter **salaries** in the Tags box, and enter **dubois** in the Search box. What two files does Search Explorer find? What does this tell you about the contents of these two files? List five criteria that Search Explorer used to find these two files. Close the Search Results window.

30. Use the Start Search box to open Indexing Options. How many files did Windows Vista index on your computer? What is the status of the indexing operation? What two locations does Windows Vista include in the index? Close the Indexing Options dialog box.
31. If you are finished with the Review Assignments, open the Public Documents folder and delete the Cabral Advertising folder. If necessary, restore any settings that you changed on the computer you are using.
32. Submit your answers to the questions in these Review Assignments to your instructor, either in printed or electronic form, as requested.

Apply | Case Problem 1

Use the skills you learned in the tutorial to set up a new folder structure on a computer.

There are no Data Files needed for this Case Problem.

Coberley Child Care Parents who are preparing themselves to re-enter the job market rely on the childcare services provided by Coberley Child Care, a nonprofit agency. Federal, state, and county agencies, as well as corporations, fund the agency's programs with special grants and donations of computer equipment for its administrative staff. Recently, Jan Hostetler, the office manager, acquired a computer for a new employee and asks you to set up its folder structure using the following guidelines:

- All the employee's folders and files should be stored in one central location and easily accessible by Microsoft Office, other software applications, and the new employee.
- The new employee will need folders to keep track of the following types of information:
    - Services provided by Coberley Child Care, including childcare, job referrals, and job training workshops
    - Agency progress reports, including required federal, state, county, and city status reports as well as agency annual reports
    - Grant proposals and funding sources, such as federal, state, county, city, local, and corporate grants, plus small donor contributions
    - Budget documents, income and expense projections, and tax documents
    - Equipment donations, including computers, printers, and office furniture
    - Volunteer information, including volunteer schedules and performance appraisals
    - Documents that employees and volunteers need to share on the agency's network
    - E-mail contact information for clients, donors, corporate sponsors, and volunteers as well as federal, state, city, and local officials
    - Software downloads and file uploads
- Certain files must be accessible by other users who also have an account on the same computer.

Use a word processing application, such as Microsoft Office Word or WordPad, to prepare a list of recommendations on how you might implement these guidelines. In preparing your report, consider what folders Windows Vista provides for each user account and how they might be used to implement these guidelines. Describe how you would organize the final folder structure for different types of documents listed above. Include a diagram of your proposed folder structure. Submit your document to your instructor, either in printed or electronic form, as requested.

Apply | Case Problem 2

Use the skills you learned in the tutorial to sort, group, and create stacks for computer files

For a list of Data Files in the Case2 folder, see page 137.

Mobile Technology Plus, Inc. Javier Estevez works as a writer for Mobile Technology Plus, a magazine that focuses on rapidly changing technologies for handheld and other mobile devices. To meet tight publication deadlines, he asks you to help him sort, group, and create stacks so that he can more quickly locate and assemble information from files for articles.

Use a word processing application, such as Microsoft Office Word or WordPad, to prepare your answers to the questions in the following steps.

To complete this Case Problem, you must have an extracted copy of the Data Files for this tutorial. You also need to allow Windows Vista time to index this new folder. Complete the following steps:

1. Copy the extracted Tutorial.03\Case2 folder to the Public Documents folder, change the name of the Case2 folder to Mobile Technology Plus, and then open this folder.
2. **EXPLORE** In the Mobile Technology Plus window, turn off the display of the Navigation pane so that you can view more columns of data in the window. (*Hint*: Use the Layout option on the Organize menu.)
3. Display the column headings for Date Modified, Type, Authors, Size, and Tags (if necessary), remove the Folder column heading (if necessary), and then choose the option for sizing all columns to fit.
4. **EXPLORE** In the Search box, type **size:>1 KB** to display all files. Verify that Windows Vista found 30 items in the search results. What types of objects are not included in the search results?
5. Click the Name heading. How does Windows Vista display the search results? Click the Name heading again. How does Windows Vista display the search results? Does Windows Vista group the search results, and if so, how? How might you benefit from the use of this feature in your work?
6. Click the Type heading. How does Windows Vista display the search results? Click the Type heading again. How does Windows Vista display the search results? How might you benefit from the use of this feature in your work?
7. Click the Authors heading. How does Windows Vista display the search results? Click the Authors heading again. How does Windows Vista display the search results? How might you benefit from the use of this feature in your work?
8. Click the Size heading. How does Windows Vista display the search results? Click the Size heading again. How does Windows Vista display the search results? How might you benefit from the use of this feature in your work?
9. Use the Type heading button arrow to group the files by type. How does Windows Vista display the files? List the names of the groups and the number of files in each group. How might you benefit from the use of this feature in your work?
10. Use the Type heading button arrow to stack the files by type. How does Windows Vista display the search results? List the names of the stacks and the total file size of each stack. How might you benefit from the use of this feature in your work?
11. Use the Type heading button arrow to sort the files. What happens, and how does Windows Vista display the search results?
12. Use the Authors heading button arrow to display files where Maya Cabral is the author. How many files does Windows Vista display, and how does Windows Vista display the search results?

13. Use the Type heading button arrow to stack these files by type. How does Windows Vista display the search results? List the names of the stacks and the total file size of each stack.
14. Open the Microsoft Office Excel Worksheet stack. Use the Tags heading button arrow to stack the files by tags. How does Windows Vista display the search results?
15. Restore the display of the Navigation pane, and then close the Search Results window.
16. Submit your document to your instructor, either in printed or electronic form, as requested.

Challenge | Case Problem 3

Go beyond what you've learned to test different search criteria for a contract training company.

For a list of Data Files in the Case3 folder, see page 137.

Yoshiko Learning Center, Inc. Yoshiko Tanaka and her staff at Yoshiko Learning Center provide customized training for employees of companies in Tokyo. Recently, a new client contracted with Yoshiko Tanaka for a three-day training session on how to perform searches. To prepare for this training session, Yoshiko asks you to test different search criteria and use the information you gather to help her prepare a list of examples that she can use to demonstrate different search features. She intends to also use the information you compile as a handout for the training session.

Use a word processing application, such as Microsoft Office Word or WordPad, to prepare your answers to the questions in the following steps.

To complete this Case Problem, you must have an extracted copy of the Data Files for this tutorial. You also need to allow Windows Vista time to index this new folder. Complete the following steps:

1. Copy the extracted Tutorial.03\Case3 folder to the Public Documents folder, change the name of the Case3 folder to Yoshiko Learning Center, and then open this folder.
2. **EXPLORE** Turn off the display of the Navigation pane so that you can view more columns of data in the window. (*Hint*: Use the Layout option on the Organize menu.)
3. Display the column headings for Date Modified, Type, Authors, Size, and Tags (if necessary), remove the Folder column heading (if necessary), and then choose the option for sizing all columns to fit.
4. What search criteria can you enter in the Search box to locate files with "sales" in their filenames?
5. What search criteria can you use to locate files with "sales" and "projections" in their filenames?
6. What search criteria can you use to locate files with "sales" or "projections" in their filenames?
7. **EXPLORE** What search criteria can you use to locate all files with the exact filename "Five Year Growth Plan.xlsx"?
8. What search criteria can you use to locate all Microsoft Office Word files?
9. What search criteria can you use to locate all files with "sales" in their Tags property?
10. **EXPLORE** What search criteria can you use to locate all files with today's date in the Date Modified property?
11. **EXPLORE** What search criteria can you use to locate all files created before today in the Date Modified property?

EXPLORE

12. What search criteria can you use to locate all folders and files with sizes less than 50 KB?
13. What search criteria can you use to locate all files created by Leif with "models" in the Tags property?
14. What search criteria can you use to locate all files with the tags "invoices" and "days outstanding"?
15. Restore the Navigation pane, and then close the Search Results window.
16. What Start menu search criteria can you use to display a list of Microsoft Office programs?
17. Submit your document to your instructor, either in printed or electronic form, as requested.

Challenge | Case Problem 4

Go beyond what you've learned to search for files for a financial investment company.

For a list of Data Files in the Case4 folder, see page 137.

Hamer Investment Group You work for the Help Desk for Hamer Investment Group, a multinational corporation with its headquarters in Berlin, Germany. To help staff locate important documents quickly, you rely on the use of Boolean filters, comparison operators, and file properties. To maximize the use of these features, you decide to test some new search criteria to determine their usefulness in your job.

Use a word processing application, such as Microsoft Office Word or WordPad, to prepare your answers to the questions in the following steps.

To complete this Case Problem, you must have an extracted copy of the Data Files for this tutorial. You also need to allow Windows Vista time to index this new folder. Use this folder to test the following criteria:

1. Copy the extracted Tutorial.03\Case4 folder to the Public Documents folder, change the name of the Case4 folder to Hamer Investment Group, and then open this folder.
2. Right-click the background of the Hamer Investment Group folder and choose the option to view properties. How many folders and files are contained in the Hamer Investment Group folder? Add these values together. How many total objects are contained in this folder? Close the Hamer Investment Group Properties dialog box.

EXPLORE

3. Use a simple criterion in the Search box in the folder window to answer the following questions:
   a. Enter this search string in the Search box: *
      Examine the Details Pane. How many items does Windows Vista find? What does this information and the search results tell you about the use of this search string (called a wildcard)?
   b. Use the Back button to return to the Hamer Investment Group folder.
   c. Enter this search string in the Search box: **file**
      Examine the Details Pane. How many items does Windows Vista find? What does this information and the search results tell you about the use of this search string?
   d. Enter this search string in the Search box: **folder**
      Examine the Details Pane. How many items does Windows Vista find? What do the search results tell you about the use of this search string?

EXPLORE

4. Combine criteria in the Search box in the folder window to answer the following questions:
   a. Enter this search string in the Search box: **NOT folder**
      How many items does Windows Vista find? What do the search results tell you about the use of this search string?
   b. Enter this search string in the Search box: **NOT excel**
      What do the search results tell you about the use of this search string?
   c. Enter this search string in the Search box: **xlsx**
      What do the search results tell you about the use of this search string?
   d. Enter this search string in the Search box: **project**
      How many items does Windows Vista find? Click the Type column. What types of file types are listed in these search results?
   e. Modify your search string to the following: **project NOT folder**
      How does this search string change the search results you found in the previous step?

EXPLORE

5. Enter this search string in the Search box: **20??**
   What files does Windows Vista find? What do the search results tell you about the use of ? (another wildcard)?

EXPLORE

6. Specify file properties as criteria in the Search box in the folder window to answer the following questions:
   a. Enter this search string in the Search box: **name:20**
      What files does Windows Vista find? How does this search string affect the search results?
   b. Enter this search string in the Search box: **authors:(Maya AND Leif)**
      How does this search string affect the search results?
   c. Enter this search string in the Search box: **name:sales OR name:project**
      How does this search string affect the search results?
   d. Enter this search string in the Search box: **name:sales OR name:project NOT folder**
      How does this search string affect the search results?
7. Restore the Navigation pane, and then close the Search Results window.
8. Submit your document to your instructor, either in printed or electronic form, as requested.

Review | Quick Check Answers

Session 3.1

1. Windows, Program Files
2. True
3. Public
4. False
5. registered file
6. path
7. \ (a backslash)
8. stack

Session 3.2

1. tag
2. search string (or string)
3. The default action is displayed in bold.
4. True
5. comparison
6. OR, AND
7. > (greater than)
8. False

Ending Data Files

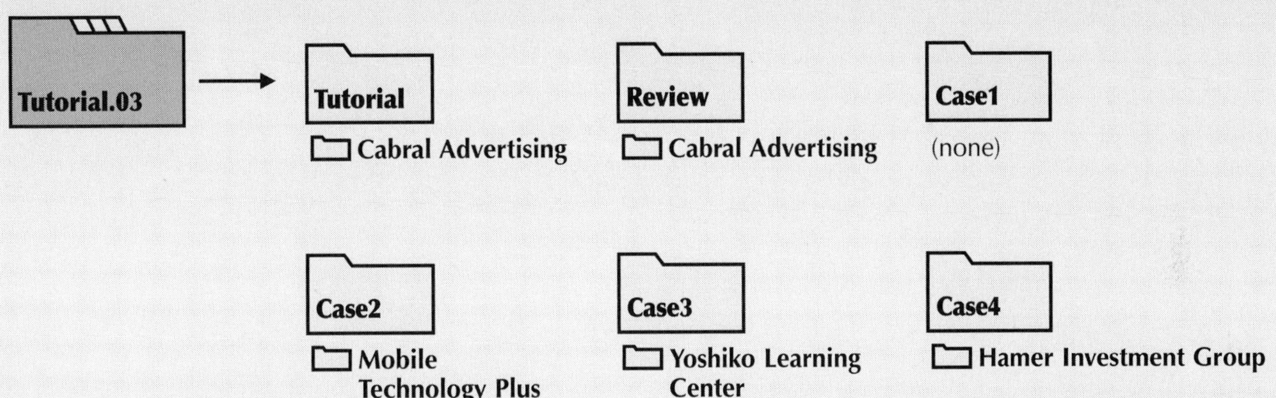

Objectives

Session 4.1
- Create shortcuts to drives, folders, and files
- View shortcut properties
- Customize shortcuts
- Create shortcuts to applications and programs
- Create a new shortcut from an existing shortcut
- Update shortcut paths automatically

Session 4.2
- Add shortcuts to the Start Menu
- Create a Control Panel shortcut
- Customize the Navigation Pane
- Customize a drive icon
- Create Internet shortcuts
- Create e-mail shortcuts

Creating and Customizing Shortcuts

Working Smart with Shortcuts

Case | Upsilon Air

Upsilon Air in San Diego, California, offers airline service to major vacation spots along the Pacific Rim and throughout Oceania. Lance Quattrone, an employee in the advertising group at Upsilon Air, develops custom advertising to showcase their travel packages. To increase his productivity, Lance relies on shortcuts to quickly locate documents, folders, files, and Web sites as well as Windows Vista resources on his desktop and laptop computers. Lance also develops advertising for a new division that will offer suborbital flights so that customers can view the earth just like astronauts.

In this tutorial you will create shortcuts to drives, folders, and files and then view shortcut properties and customize shortcuts. You will create shortcuts to applications and programs, create new shortcuts from existing shortcuts, and update shortcut paths. You will add new shortcuts to the Start menu, create Control Panel shortcuts, and customize the Navigation Pane using shortcuts that act as direct links to folders. You will customize drive icons and create Internet and e-mail shortcuts.

Starting Data Files

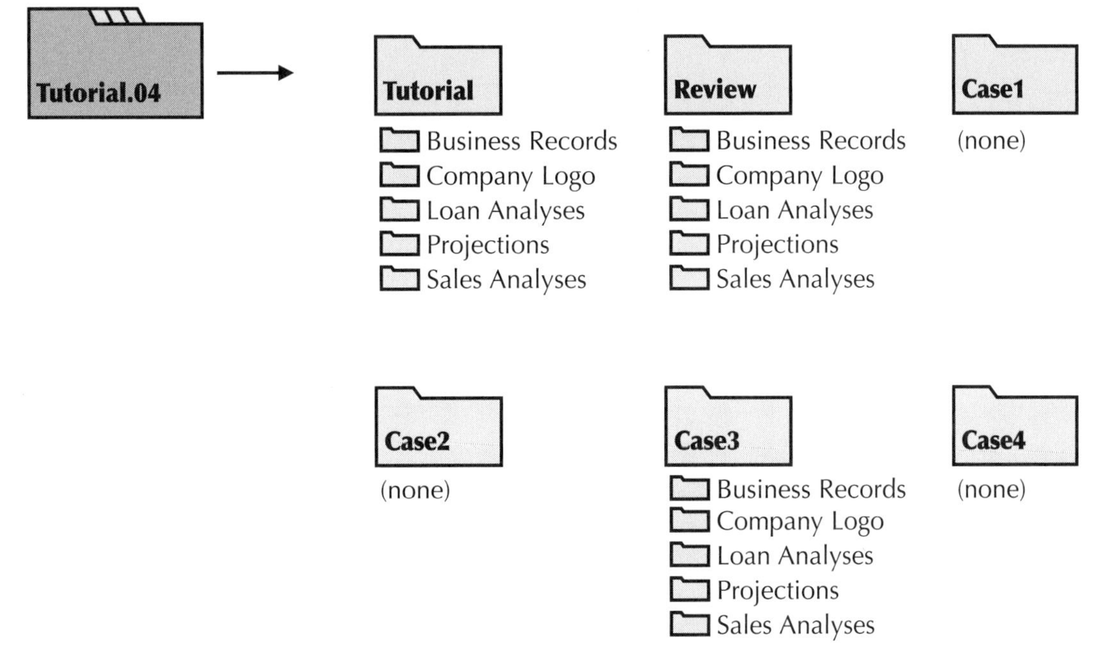

Session 4.1

Using Shortcuts

A **shortcut** is a special type of file that contains the path to an object and as a result, is a direct link to that object. When you click (or double-click) a shortcut, Windows Vista locates and opens the object referenced by the shortcut. The object of a shortcut might be a program, drive, folder, or file. An Internet shortcut is a special type of shortcut that contains the URL (Uniform Resource Locator) for a specific Web site and therefore serves as a direct link to a Web site. Network shortcut paths include two backslash characters at the beginning of the path. For example, \\HI-TECH identifies a computer on a network. This type of path is called the **UNC path** (for Universal Naming Convention) and is a standard approach used to reference servers, printers, and other resources on a network. Figure 4-1 and Figure 4-2 contain examples of different types of shortcuts that you can create on your computer. As you can tell from these figures, the shortcut icon contains a small box with an arrow in its lower-left corner .

Figure 4-1 Examples of hardware, software, and folder shortcuts

Type of Shortcut	Shortcut	Path or Object Name
Hardware Shortcuts		
Drive C	 Local Disk (C)	C:\
Flash Drive	 Flash Drive	F:\
CD Drive	 CD Drive	D:\
DVD Drive	 DVD Drive	E:\
Software Shortcuts		
Microsoft Office Word 2007	 Microsoft Office Word 2007	Microsoft Office Word 2007 ("C:\Program Files\Microsoft Office\Office12\WINWORD.EXE")
Microsoft Office Outlook 2007	 Microsoft Office Outlook 2007	Microsoft Office Outlook 2007 ("C:\Program Files\Microsoft Office\Office12\OUTLOOK.EXE")
Internet Explorer	 Internet Explorer	"C:\Program Files\Internet Explorer\iexplore.exe"
Windows Calendar	 Windows Calendar	"%ProgramFiles%\Windows Calendar\WinCal.exe"
Command Prompt (Command Line)	 Command Prompt	%SystemRoot%\system32\cmd.exe
Folder Shortcuts		
Documents	 Documents	C:\Users\Lance\Documents
Client Projects	 Client Projects	"C:\Users\Public\Documents\Client Projects"
Folder Options	 Folder Options	Control Panel\Folder Options

Figure 4-2 Examples of document, network, Internet, and e-mail shortcuts

Type of Shortcut	Shortcut	Path or Object Name
Document Shortcuts		
Sales Projection Memo (Word Document)	 Sales Projection Memo	"C:\Users\Public\Documents\Company Projections\Sales Projection Memo.docx"
Five Year Growth Plan (Excel Document)	 Five Year Growth Plan	"C:\Users\Public\Documents\Company Projections\Five Year Growth Plan.xlsx"
Company Logo (Icon File)	 Company Logo	"C:\Users\Public\Documents\Company Logo\Delta.ico"
OAM's Blues	 OAM's Blues	"C:\Users\Public\Music\Sample Music\OAM's Blues.wma"
Network Shortcuts		
Network Computer	 HI-TECH	\\HI-TECH
Mapped Network Drive Z:		\\HI-TECH\Templates
Network Printer	 Photosmart	\\HI-TECH\Photosmart
Network Documents Folder	 Documents	\\HI-TECH\Documents
Internet & Web Shortcuts		
Course Technology Web Site	 Course Technology	http://course.com
E-Mail Shortcuts		
New E-Mail Message	 Quick Reminder	mailto:
Quick Reminder	 Weekly Project Meeting	mailto:LanceQuattrone@upsilonair.com?subject=Quick%20Reminder

Shortcut icons to system objects, such as drives, are identical to the icon that Windows Vista uses for the object itself. The same is true for application shortcuts and document shortcuts. If you create a shortcut to a folder, Windows Vista uses a similar type of folder icon, but customizes it. Likewise, if the shortcut references a system folder, such as Pictures, it also has a custom icon. Shortcuts to network drives and folders have a custom shortcut icon. Internet shortcuts use an icon that identifies the default Web browser used to open the Internet shortcut.

You can place shortcuts on the desktop or in folders where you frequently work. For example, you might place a shortcut to your word processing application, or even to a document that you work on daily, on the desktop or on the Quick Launch toolbar. You might store copies of the same shortcut in different places so that you can quickly access the object from those locations. Shortcuts are also useful in networked environments because you do not have to browse the network looking for a network resource, such as a printer or a network folder; instead, you can use a shortcut to go directly to that resource from the desktop or Quick Launch toolbar.

Getting Started

To complete this tutorial, you need to display the Computer icon on the desktop, switch your computer to single-click activation, activate the option for displaying file extensions, and copy the Tutorial folder provided with your Data Files to the Public Documents folder.

To set up your computer:

1. If Windows Vista does not display a Computer icon on the desktop, open the **Start** menu, right-click **Computer**, click **Show on Desktop**, and if necessary, close the Start menu.
2. If you need to enable single-click activation and display file extensions for known file types, double-click the **Computer** icon on the desktop, click the **Organize** button on the command bar, click **Folder and Search Options**, and on the General property sheet in the Folder Options dialog box, click the **Single-click to open an item (point to select)** option button if it is not already selected, and then click the **Underline icon titles only when I point at them** option button if it is not already selected.
3. Click the **View** tab, click the **Hide extensions for known file types** check box if it contains a check mark (and remove that check mark), click the **OK** button to close the Folder Options dialog box and apply these changes, and then close the Computer window.

Now you can copy your Data Files to the Public Documents folder.

Copying Data Files to the Public Documents Folder

Next, you are going to copy the Tutorial folder provided with your Data Files from the Documents folder, your flash drive, or a network folder to the Public Documents folder.

To copy the Data Files to your Public Documents folder:

1. Make sure you have created your copy of the Windows Vista for Power User Data Files and that your computer can access them.

   Trouble? If you don't have the extracted Data Files for this tutorial, you need to get them before you can proceed. Your instructor will ask you to obtain them from a specified location (such as a network folder) or download them from Course Technology's Web site. In either case, make a backup copy of the Tutorial.04 folder before you start so that you will have the original files available in case you need to start over. If you have any questions about obtaining or extracting the Data Files, see your instructor or technical support person for assistance.

2. Close any open windows, and then open a window onto the Documents folder, your flash drive folder, or the network folder that contains a copy of the Tutorial.04 folder, and then open the **Tutorial.04** folder.
3. On the Start menu, open **Documents**, click **Public** in the Navigation Pane, and then click the **Public Documents** folder icon.
4. Right-click the **taskbar**, and then click **Show Windows Side by Side**. Windows Vista adjusts the two open windows so that they are placed side by side on the desktop and so that they are equal in size. Windows Vista places the last window that you open on the left side of the desktop.
5. Hold down the **Ctrl** key while you drag the **Tutorial** folder to the Public Documents folder window, and then release your left mouse button. Windows Vista copies the Tutorial folder to the Public Documents folder window. If you hold down the Ctrl key while you drag a folder, file, or set of files, Windows Vista always copies the selected folder, file, or set of files. That guarantees that you have your original set of files.

Tip

You can also right-drag the folder, file, or set of files and choose either Copy Here or Move Here from the shortcut menu.

6. Point to the **Tutorial** folder icon in the Public Documents folder, press the **F2** key (the Rename key), type **Upsilon Air** and then press the **Enter** key.
7. Close the Public Documents folder window and the folder window that contains the original copy of the Tutorial folder with the Data Files.

Now you're ready to create shortcuts.

Creating Shortcuts

If you want to create a desktop shortcut to a drive, folder, file, or program, you can use any of the following techniques:

- **Dragging** To create a shortcut to a drive, you can open the Computer window and drag a drive icon to the desktop. You can also select more than one drive and drag all the drive icons to the desktop to create several shortcuts at once. However, you should not use this approach to create a shortcut to a folder that contains installed software or to a folder or file in your Documents folder because Windows Vista will move the program, folder, or file instead of creating a shortcut. To be on the safe side, do not drag the file icon for an application or any other type of program from a folder where it's installed to the desktop.
- **Right-dragging** If you right-drag the icon for a drive, folder, file, or program to the desktop, Windows Vista displays a shortcut menu, which includes an option for creating a shortcut.

- **Right-clicking** If you right-click the icon for a drive, folder, file, or program, you can choose the option for creating a shortcut to that object from its shortcut menu. If you perform this operation on a drive in the Computer window, Windows Vista places the shortcut on the desktop. If you perform this operation on the Windows folder or one of its subfolders or files, or if you perform this operation on one of the folders or files in the Program Files folder, Windows Vista informs you that it cannot create a shortcut in this location and asks you if you want to place the shortcut on the desktop instead. If you perform this operation on a folder or file in the Documents folder, Windows Vista creates the shortcut in that folder. You can then move the shortcut to the desktop.
- **Using the Send To menu** If you right-click a folder, file, or program, and then point to Send To on the shortcut menu, you can choose Desktop (create shortcut) to place a shortcut to that object on the desktop. This approach is the easiest, fastest, and the safest one to use.

As you step through the tutorial, you will use these techniques and other techniques to create shortcuts. Then, as you work on your computer, you can use the technique that best suits your needs and your way of working.

Creating Shortcuts to Drives

To meet the increase in customer interest in its Pacific Rim flights and its forthcoming new division that will offer suborbital flights, Upsilon Air hired you to assist Lance in the advertising department. After setting up your new computer, Lance suggests that you customize your computer and create the shortcuts you will need for your new job. Lance recommends that you start by creating a desktop shortcut to your flash drive.

To create a desktop shortcut to your flash drive:

1. If necessary, attach your flash drive to the computer you are using. If Windows Vista displays an AutoPlay dialog box for your flash drive or opens a window or dialog box onto the flash drive, close the window or dialog box. If Windows Vista displays a Microsoft Windows dialog box and asks if you want to scan your flash drive, click **Scan and fix (Recommended)**, click the **Start** button in the Check Disk Removable Disk dialog box, and after Windows Vista checks the disk, click the **Close** button in the Checking Disk Removable Disk dialog box.

   Trouble? If you do not have a flash drive, you can create a shortcut to another disk drive, such as your hard disk drive, usually identified as Local Disk (C:) in the Computer window. If you decide to create a shortcut to another drive, such as a DVD or CD drive, insert a DVD or CD disk into your DVD or CD drive first. The information you examine for another drive may differ from that described in the subsequent steps and that shown in the figures.
2. Click the **Computer** icon on the desktop, and if Windows Vista maximizes the Computer windows, click the **Restore Down** button, and then, if necessary, resize and drag the window to the right so that you can see the left side of the desktop.
3. Drag your **flash drive** icon from the Computer window to the desktop. As you do, Windows Vista displays an icon for your flash drive and a ToolTip with a shortcut arrow icon and the text "Create link in Desktop." See Figure 4-3.

Figure 4-3 Creating a drive shortcut using drag and drop

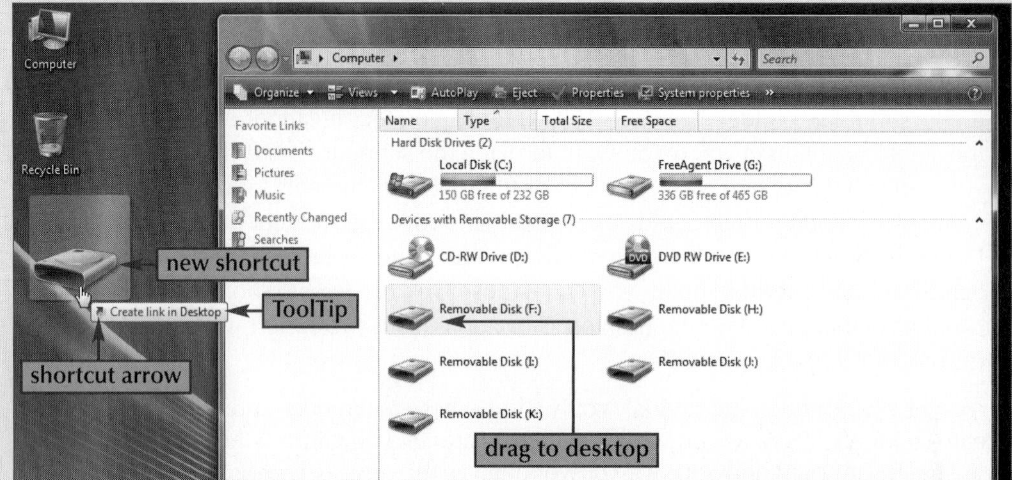

4. Release the left mouse button. Windows Vista creates a desktop shortcut to your flash drive. See Figure 4-4. If you have not assigned your flash drive a different name, Windows Vista names the flash drive shortcut "Removable Disk" followed by the actual drive name letter, a space, a dash, another space, and then the word Shortcut, such as Removable Disk (F) - Shortcut. Your drive name may differ from that shown in Figure 4-4. Your flash drive icon might be identical to the default drive icon used for removable disk drives, as shown in Figure 4-4, or it might have a custom icon.

Figure 4-4 New Removable Disk drive desktop shortcut

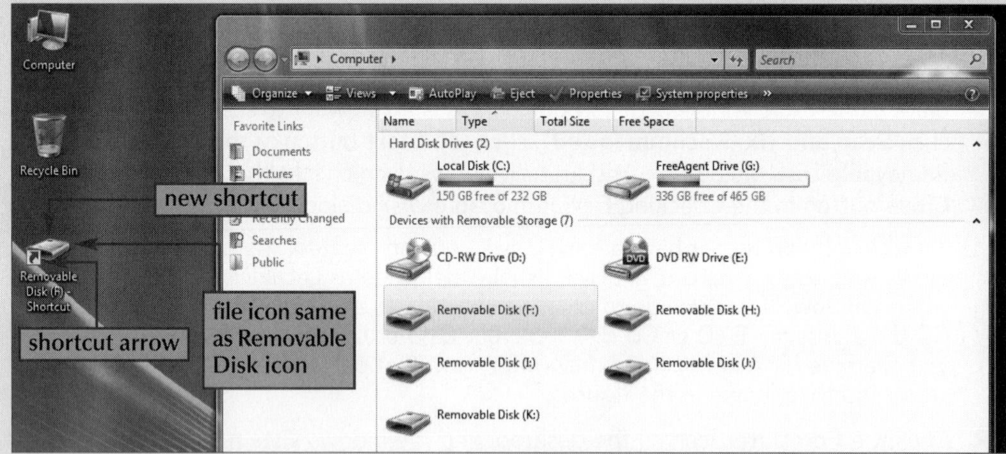

5. Close the Computer window.
6. Right-click the **flash drive shortcut**, click **Rename** on the shortcut menu, type **Flash Drive**, and then press the **Enter** key to change the shortcut's name.
7. Click the **Flash Drive** shortcut icon. Windows Vista opens a window for your flash drive.
8. Close the window for your flash drive.

Lance notes that although Windows Vista displays an AutoPlay dialog box with an option for opening a folder for the flash drive when you first attach it to your computer, the flash drive shortcut on the desktop is still useful. For example, you might close the flash drive window and then later need to open it again, so the shortcut will speed up access to the flash drive. Lance also mentions that if your flash drive window is not open, and if you do not have this shortcut, you will need to click the Computer icon on the desktop, and then click the flash drive icon in the Computer window to view the contents of your flash drive. That operation would require two steps each time you opened a window onto your flash drive. If you do not have a Computer icon on the desktop, you have to open the Computer window from the Start menu, requiring a total of three steps. This shortcut requires only one step each time you use it, saving you one or two steps each time you use it, and providing faster access to the contents of your flash drive. If you move the flash drive shortcut to your Quick Launch toolbar, you can quickly access your flash drive's contents while working in a maximized window that covers the desktop.

Creating a Shortcut to a Flash Drive | Reference Window

- If necessary, attach your flash drive to the computer you are using. If Windows Vista displays an AutoPlay dialog box for your flash drive or opens a window or dialog box onto the flash drive, close the window or dialog box. If Windows Vista displays a Microsoft Windows dialog and asks if you want to scan your flash drive, click Scan and fix (Recommended), click the Start button in the Check Disk Removable Disk dialog box, and after Windows Vista checks the disk, click the Close button in the Checking Disk Removable Disk dialog box.
- Click the Computer icon on the desktop or open the Computer window from the Start menu.
- If the Computer window is maximized, click the Restore Down button, and resize and move the Computer window so that you can also see the desktop.
- Drag the icon for your flash drive (or any other drive) from the Computer window to the desktop, release the left mouse button, and if necessary, rename the shortcut.
- Close the Computer window.

Instead of creating drive shortcuts one at a time, you can select all of the drives for which you want to create shortcuts, drag them to the desktop or right-click one of the selected drives, and then click Create Shortcut. You can use any of the following approaches to select multiple objects in a window:

- **Using Ctrl+point** If you are working in Web style with single-click activation, you select the first object by pointing to it until Windows Vista highlights it, hold down the Ctrl key, point to each of the next objects, and then release the Ctrl key. The selected objects constitute a **collection**; in other words, a group of objects that may or may not be located adjacent to each other. If you need to remove an object from a collection, you point to it again while you press and hold the Ctrl key.
- **Using Ctrl+click** If you are using double-click activation instead, you click the first object, hold down the Ctrl key while you click each of the next objects, and then you release the Ctrl key. If you click too quickly, Windows Vista might make duplicate copies of all the objects you've selected.
- **Using Shift+point** If you are using single-click activation and want to select objects adjacent to each other, point to the first object to select it, hold down the Shift key, point to the last object, and then release the Shift key. Windows Vista selects all the objects between the first and the last objects that you selected.

- **Using Shift+click** If you are using double-click activation and want to select objects adjacent to each other, click the first object to select it, hold down the Shift key, click the last object, and then release the Shift key. Windows Vista selects all the objects between the first and the last objects that you selected.
- **Using check boxes** If you enable the option for using check boxes to select objects within a window, you can click the check box for each object. You can also use this feature to select desktop objects.
- **Using a selection rectangle** If the objects you want to select are located next to each other, you can drag a selection rectangle around the objects with the mouse pointer. You can also use this feature when you are selecting objects on the desktop.

After trying various selection techniques, you can decide which one you prefer. You should also be familiar with different approaches for performing the same type of task in case you work on computers set up in different ways.

Viewing Properties of a Shortcut

Like any other type of object, you can right-click a shortcut and choose the option to view its properties. Lance encourages you to use this technique so you can learn more about how shortcuts work and how to customize shortcuts.

To view shortcut properties:

1. Right-click the **Flash Drive** shortcut icon, and then click **Properties**. Windows Vista opens the Flash Drive Properties dialog box and displays information about the shortcut on the Shortcut property sheet. See Figure 4-5. Windows Vista displays the shortcut's icon, the shortcut's name, the Target type (Removable Disk), the Target location (for example, F:\), and the Target's path (for example, F:\). Your Target location and Target path may differ. As you can tell from the backslash in the Target box path, the shortcut points to the top-level folder of your flash drive. In the Run list box, Windows Vista displays "Normal window," indicating that Windows Vista displays the window at the same size and in the same position as the last time you opened or resized the window. From the Run list, you can also choose to open the object in a maximized window (full screen) or a minimized window (as a button on the taskbar). If you always work in a maximized window, adjusting this setting saves you an additional step. You can also define a keyboard shortcut for use with the shortcut, create a ToolTip by entering text in the Comment box, open the file location, or change the shortcut's icon.

Viewing properties of a flash drive shortcut **Figure 4-5**

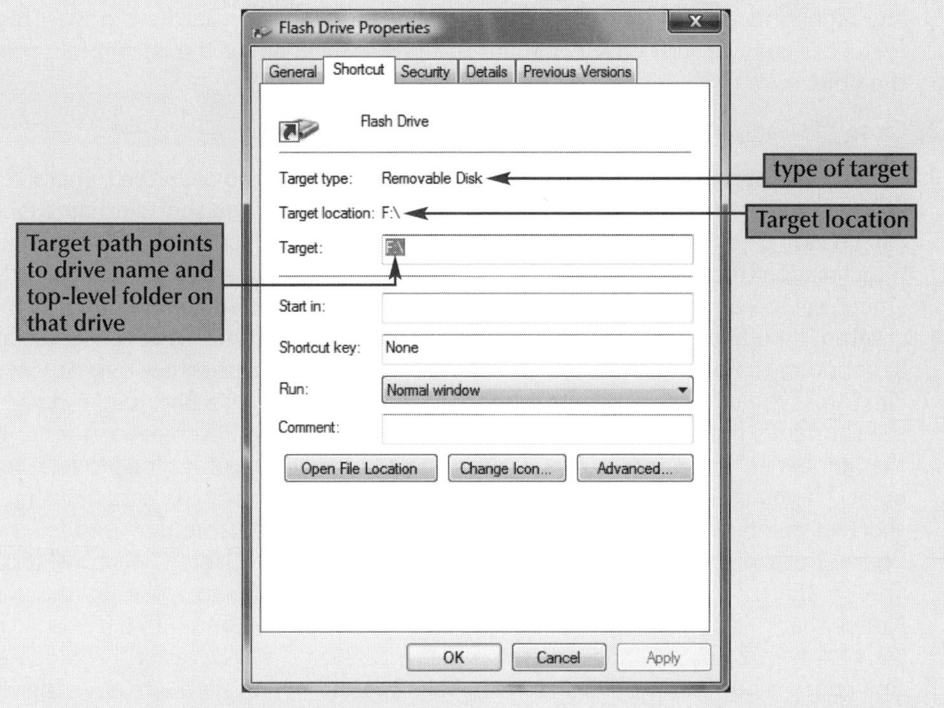

2. Click the **Run arrow button**, click **Maximized**, and then click the **Apply** button. The next time you use this desktop shortcut, Windows Vista will maximize the flash drive window.
3. Keep the Flash Drive Properties dialog box open for the next set of steps.

Creating Keyboard Shortcuts for Desktop Shortcuts | InSight

If much of your computer work involves creating and modifying files, such as word processing documents and spreadsheets, you can save time by creating keyboard shortcuts for your desktop shortcuts. For example, you can use a keyboard shortcut to access the files on your flash drive without leaving your document. To assign a keyboard shortcut, you open the Properties dialog box for the shortcut, click inside the Shortcut key text box and type a character that you want to use for the keyboard shortcut (such as "F" for "Flash Drive"). Windows Vista inserts "Ctrl + Alt + F" (for example) in the Shortcut text box. To use this keyboard shortcut, you press and hold the Ctrl and Alt keys while you press the F key, and then release all the keys. Keyboard shortcut keys for shortcuts take precedence over the same key combination used in a Windows application. If you assign a keyboard shortcut and want to remove it later, click in the Shortcut key text box on this property sheet, and then press the Backspace or Delete key. Windows Vista then displays "None" in the Shortcut key.

Besides viewing and changing general shortcut properties, you can examine advanced attributes or settings assigned to the shortcut file. After you first create a shortcut, Windows Vista notes in the Advanced Attributes dialog box that your file is ready for archiving. That means your backup software will include the file in your next backup (covered in more detail in Tutorial 10). **Backup software** is software that copies folders and files from your hard disk drive to a disk or another hard disk drive; the resulting copy is called a **backup**. Windows Vista also indexes this file for faster searching.

To locate the target and view other shortcut properties:

1. Click the **Open File Location** button. Windows Vista opens the Computer window and highlights the target for the desktop shortcut, namely, your flash drive. This feature is one way for quickly opening the Target location (or the parent folder for the object).
2. Close the Computer window.
3. Click the **General** tab in the Flash Drive Properties dialog box. On the General property sheet, Windows Vista displays information about the shortcut name (you can change it to another name here), the type of file (Shortcut (.lnk)), the shortcut file's location (the path to the folder with the shortcut), the shortcut's file size, the amount of storage space it uses on disk, and the dates and times the shortcut was created, modified, and accessed. Windows Vista also identifies what attributes are assigned to the object. See Figure 4-6. The details for your shortcut may differ. Next to "Type of file," Windows Vista identifies the object as a Shortcut and notes the shortcut's file extension in parentheses. "lnk" (with the lowercase letter "l", not the number "1") stands for "Link," indicating that the shortcut is a link to another object. If you create a shortcut on the desktop, the path for the Location of the shortcut points to the folder for your user account. On the computer used for this figure, the shortcut is stored in Lance's desktop folder—C:\Users\Lance\Desktop. The Location of your Desktop folder will differ from that shown in the figure. Notice that this shortcut, which is 179 bytes in size, is allocated 4,096 bytes (4.00 KB, or 4 × 1,024 bytes/kilobyte) on the disk; however, 3,917 bytes of the allocated disk space is not used by the shortcut and is therefore unavailable to any other file. You will examine this issue in more detail in Tutorial 5.

Figure 4-6 Viewing general flash drive shortcut properties

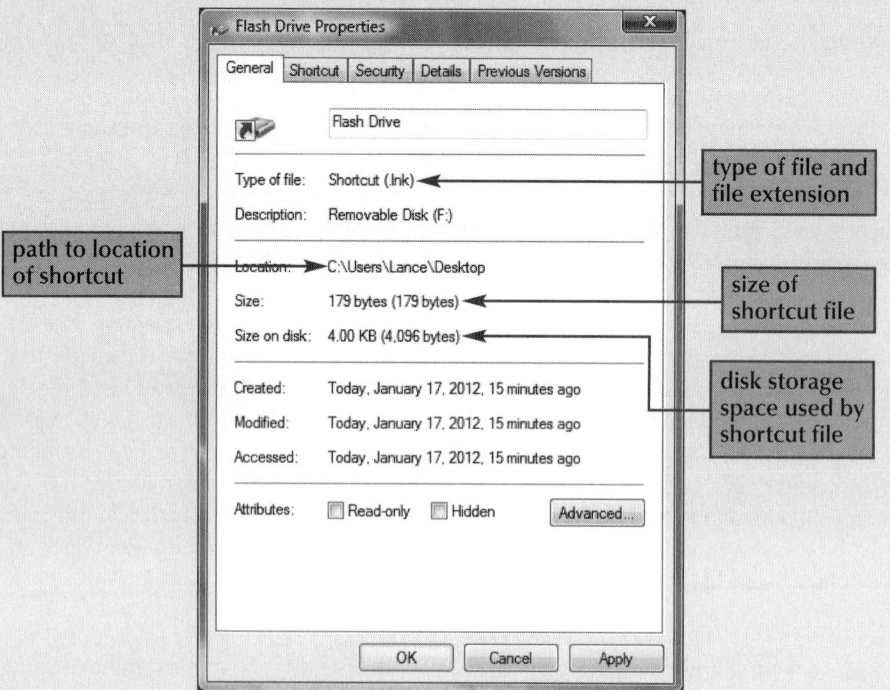

4. Click the **Advanced** button. Windows Vista opens the Advanced Attributes dialog box. See Figure 4-7. Since you just created this shortcut, Windows Vista notes that your file is ready for archiving and that it is indexed for faster searching.

Viewing advanced attributes

Figure 4-7

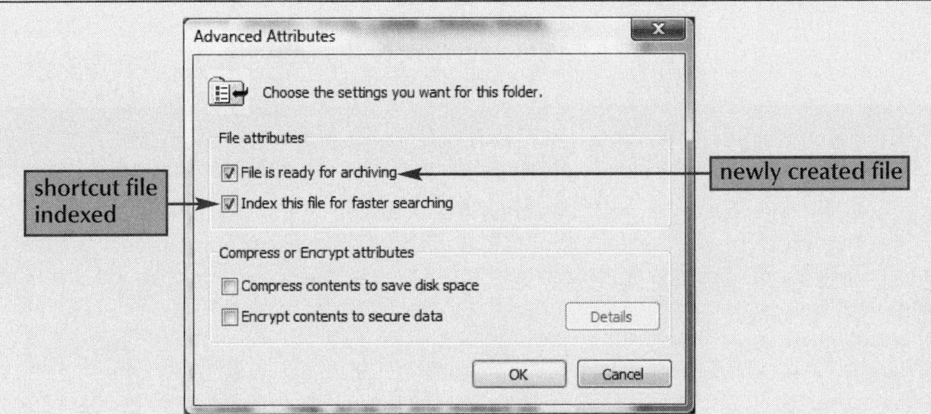

5. Click the **Cancel** button to close the Advanced Attributes dialog box (without inadvertently making changes).
6. Click the **Details** tab. On the Details property sheet, Windows Vista displays file properties for this shortcut. See Figure 4-8. Note that Windows Vista identifies the Owner of this file and the name of the Computer that contains this shortcut. Your file properties will differ. Next to name, Windows Vista shows the full filename of this shortcut.

Viewing details of flash drive shortcut properties

Figure 4-8

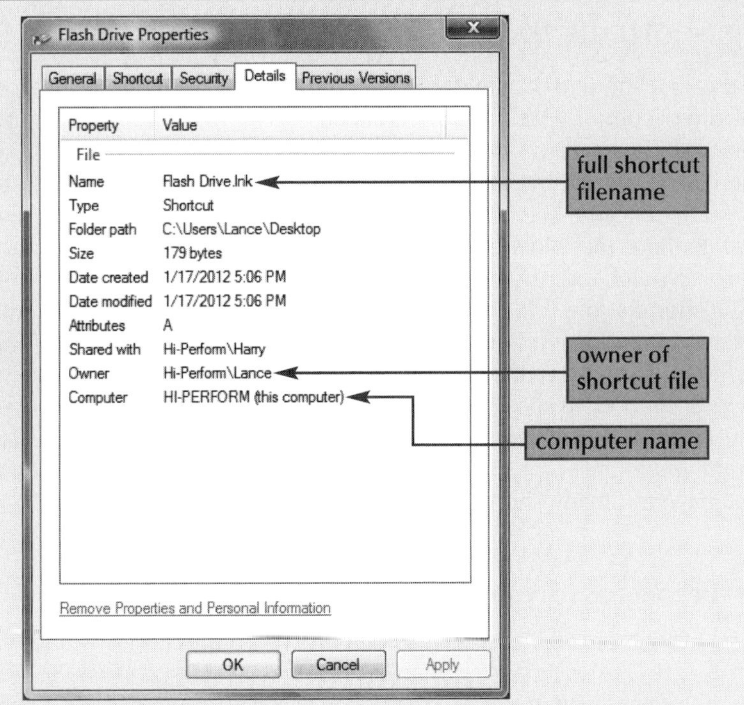

7. Click the **Cancel** button to close the Flash Drive Properties dialog box.

The full filename for the Flash Drive shortcut is "Flash Drive.lnk". The alias, or short filename, for this shortcut is (most likely) FLASHD~1.LNK.

Lance points out that by comparing the amount of storage space used on disk with the size of the shortcut, you can tell that shortcuts waste a disproportionate amount of space compared to their size; however, the tradeoff is that they are very useful. One way to gain additional storage space on your hard disk is to remove shortcuts that you no longer use.

Reference Window | **Viewing Properties of a Shortcut**

- Right-click a shortcut's icon and then click Properties.
- In the Properties dialog box for the shortcut, use the Shortcut property sheet to view a shortcut's target, specify a shortcut key, choose how to open the target window, include a comment for use as a ToolTip, and open the location where Windows Vista stores the shortcut file.
- Click the General tab to view information about the path, actual size, allocated space, and attributes of a shortcut or to change the shortcut name and change attribute settings.
- Click the Advanced button to view information about advanced attributes, such as whether a file is ready for archiving and whether Windows Vista indexes the file for faster searching.
- Use the Details tab to view file properties that you can use when searching for this shortcut.
- Close the Properties dialog box for the shortcut.

Shortcuts simplify many routine tasks that you perform daily and allow you to work smart. If you frequently work with other drives, including the hard disk drive itself, a DVD drive, a CD drive, or drives for memory cards, you can create shortcuts for these drives, and thereby save yourself time and effort when you need to access their contents.

Creating Shortcuts to Folders

When you create a shortcut to a folder, you *cannot* drag that folder to the desktop as you dragged the drive icon for your flash drive because Windows Vista will *move* the folder if the folder is on the same drive as the Desktop folder for your user account (i.e., drive C). Instead, you can right-click the folder, drag it to the desktop, and then choose the option to create a shortcut from the shortcut menu. You can also create the folder shortcut in the window that contains the folder and then drag the shortcut to the desktop; however, you must make sure you choose the correct object to drag (the shortcut, not the folder). If you are creating a shortcut to a folder that contains software (or even a document folder), it is *safer* to use the option for sending an object to the desktop as a shortcut. Then you will not drag the original folder to the desktop by mistake.

Because your flash drive shortcut has proved useful, Lance suggests you create shortcuts to folders that you use every day, starting with your Documents folder. Lance also points out that you might want to move some shortcuts to the Quick Launch toolbar if you find you have too many shortcuts on your desktop.

Tip

You can also right-click Documents, point to Send To, click "Desktop (create shortcut)," and then click the Start button.

To create a shortcut to your Documents folder:

1. Click the **Start** button and drag **Documents** from the Start menu to the desktop. Windows Vista creates a desktop shortcut to your Documents folder. See Figure 4-9. As you drag Documents from the Start menu, Windows Vista displays a shortcut arrow icon under the image of the Documents icon to provide a visual clue about the type of operation it will perform. Note that the shortcut has a custom icon.

Figure 4-9 Viewing the new Documents folder shortcut

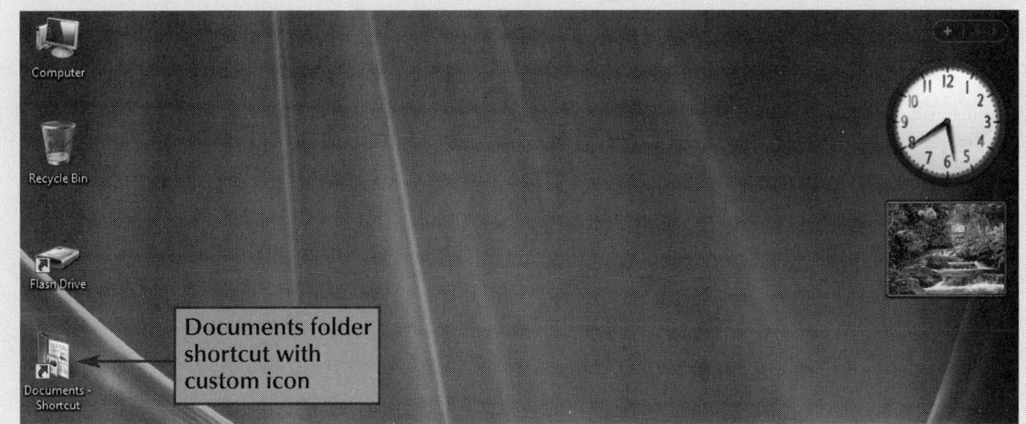

2. Point to the **Documents - Shortcut** icon, press the **F2** key, double-click **Shortcut** in the shortcut's name, press the **Backspace** key four times, and then press the **Enter** key. Windows Vista changes the shortcut name to "Documents."
3. Right-click the **Documents** shortcut, and then click **Properties**. Windows Vista opens the Documents Properties dialog box. See Figure 4-10. Windows Vista notes the Target location (in this figure, "Lance") and the path to the target (in this figure, C:\Users\Lance\Documents). The Target location indicates that the shortcut points to the Documents folder located in the Lance folder (Lance's user account folder). Your user account name will differ; however, the target is still the Documents folder for your current user account.

Figure 4-10 Viewing properties of the Documents folder shortcut

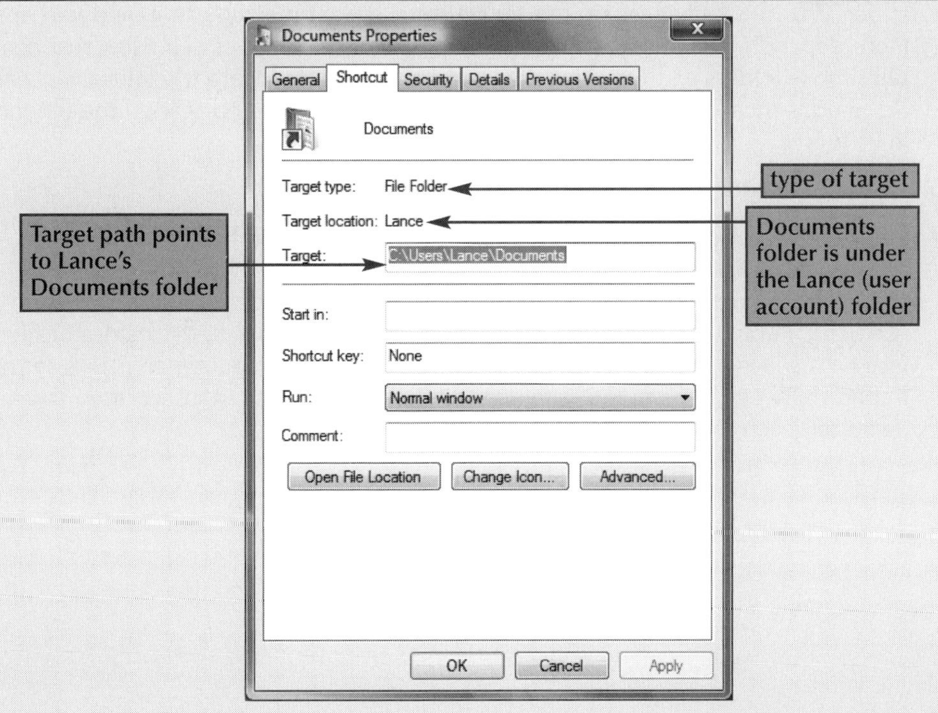

4. Click the **General** tab. Note that the Documents shortcut is larger than the Flash Drive shortcut but takes up the same amount of storage space on disk.
5. Close the Documents Properties dialog box.

Since everyone needs quick access to their Documents folder and its subfolders and files, this desktop shortcut provides fast access to that folder and its contents. Furthermore, Windows Vista does not include an option for displaying the Documents icon on the desktop, so you can use this shortcut instead. (However, if you right-click your user account name on the Start menu, you can display an icon for your user account on the desktop, and then access the Documents folder by first opening your user account folder from its desktop icon.)

To further benefit from the use of folder shortcuts, Lance points out that you can also create desktop shortcuts to specific folders within the Documents folder or the Public Documents folder.

To create a shortcut to the Upsilon Air folder:

1. Click the **Documents** shortcut, click **Public** in the Navigation Pane, and then click the **Public Documents** folder icon to open the Public Documents folder.
2. Right-click the **Upsilon Air** folder icon, point to **Send To** on the shortcut menu, and then click **Desktop (create shortcut)**. Windows Vista creates a shortcut to the Upsilon Air folder on the desktop. The shortcut icon indicates that the Upsilon Air folder contains subfolders.
3. Close the Public Documents folder window.
4. Change the name of the Upsilon Air - Shortcut to **Upsilon Air**.
5. Click the **Upsilon Air** desktop shortcut. Windows Vista opens the Upsilon Air folder. This shortcut saves you up to five steps every time you use it (and perhaps more depending on how you access this folder). In the case of a window that contains many folders and files, you do not have to scroll to locate the folder you want. Scrolling is time-consuming and causes unnecessary wear and tear on the tendons in your arm.
6. Close the Upsilon Air folder window.
7. Right-click the **Upsilon Air** shortcut, and then click **Properties**. Windows Vista opens the Upsilon Air Properties dialog box. See Figure 4-11. The Target box on the Shortcut property sheet shows the path for the target: "C:\Users\Public\Documents\Upsilon Air". If a path includes folder names or filenames with spaces, Windows encloses the entire path within quotation marks so that a space between two parts of a folder name or filename is not interpreted as a delimiter (such as the backslash).

Figure 4-11

Viewing properties of the Upsilon Air folder shortcut

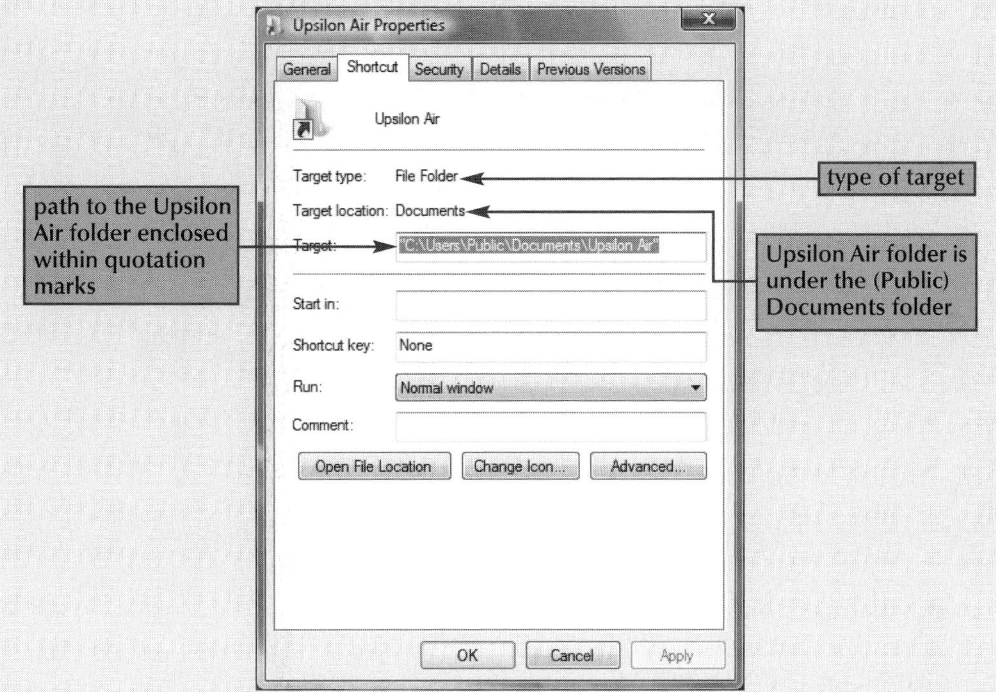

8. Click the **General** tab. Notice that this shortcut is even larger than the Documents shortcut, but again, it takes up the same amount of space on disk as the other two shortcuts you created. Shortcut sizes vary slightly because they point to objects stored in different locations on your computer, and thereby their path is different. Also, settings stored as file properties, such as the path to the file with the shortcut icon or a comment, affect shortcut file sizes.
9. Keep the Upsilon Air Properties dialog box open for the next set of steps.

As you look over the shortcuts you've created on the desktop, you note that the Upsilon Air folder shortcut icon looks similar to other folder icons. Also, you noticed earlier that Lance uses custom icons for folder shortcuts on his desktop. Lance says that you can change the icon for a shortcut if you prefer to use an icon for a shortcut that more clearly distinguishes it from other similar desktop shortcuts.

To change the icon for a shortcut:

1. Click the **Shortcut** tab in the Upsilon Air Properties dialog box, click the **Change Icon** button. In the Change Icon dialog box, Windows Vista displays the path to a file named imageres.dll. See Figure 4-12. This file is located in the System32 folder under the Windows folder, and the icons contained within this file are ones that Windows Vista uses for system components. The current icon has a blue background around the icon (see the third icon in the first column). Windows Vista customizes this basic folder icon to reflect the type of content in the Upsilon Air folder (i.e., multiple subfolders). You can select another icon contained within this file or you can browse for another file with icons.

Figure 4-12 Choosing a custom icon for the Upsilon Air shortcut

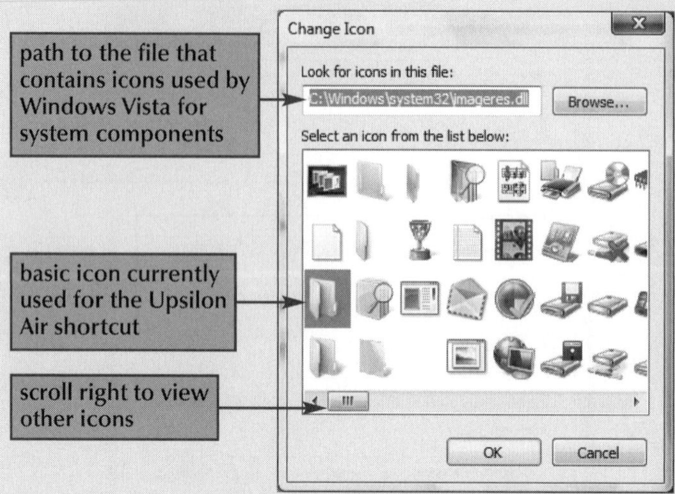

2. Use the horizontal scroll bar to scroll to the right and view all the icons.
3. Locate and click the blue **Pie Chart** icon in the next to last column (on the third row), and then click the **OK** button. Windows Vista closes the Change Icon dialog box. On the Shortcut property sheet, Windows Vista now displays the new shortcut icon. See Figure 4-13.

Figure 4-13 Viewing the custom icon on the Shortcut property sheet

4. Click the **OK** button to close the Upsilon Air Properties dialog box, right-click the **desktop**, and if necessary, click **Refresh** to update your view of the desktop. Windows Vista now displays the new custom icon for the Upsilon Air shortcut. See Figure 4-14.

Figure 4-14 Viewing the custom Upsilon Air shortcut icon

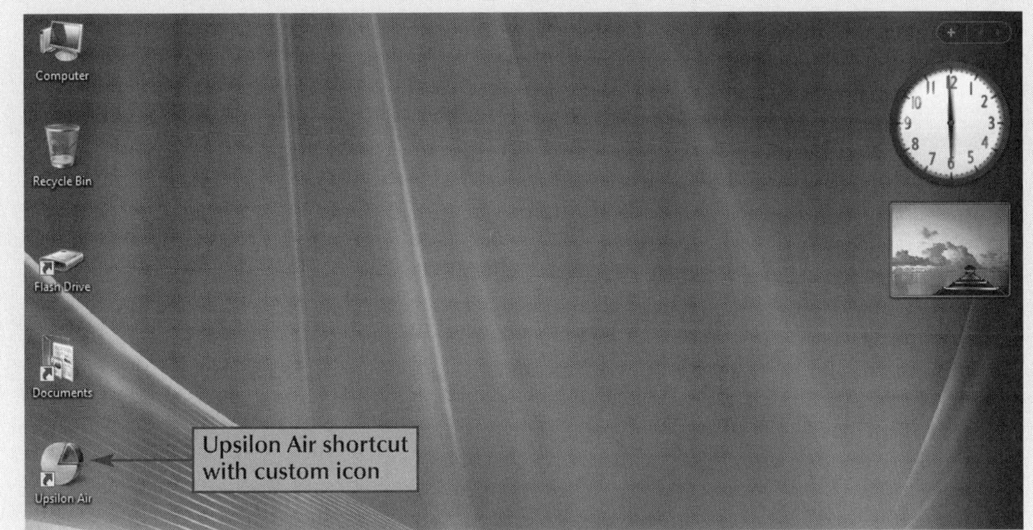

You can find custom icons in files with the "exe" (for executable), "dll" (for dynamic link library), "ico" (for Icon), "icl" (for Icon Library), or "pif" (for Program Information File) file extension; however, not all "exe" and "dll" files contain icons. A **dynamic library file** is a file that contains program code that one or more programs can use.

Creating a Shortcut to a Folder and Customizing the Shortcut Icon | Reference Window

- Locate the folder for which you want to create a shortcut.
- Right-click the folder icon, point to Send To on the shortcut menu, and then click Desktop (create shortcut).
- Close the folder window.
- If you want to change the shortcut's icon, right-click the shortcut, click Properties, click the Change Icon button on the Shortcut property sheet, and locate and select a new icon or browse for an icon file.
- Once you've selected an icon, click the OK button to close the Change Icon dialog box, and then click the OK button to close the Properties dialog box for the shortcut.

It's not uncommon for people to move a subfolder that contains their documents to the desktop for ease of access. However, if you create a shortcut to that folder, you can leave the folder in its original location.

Creating a Shortcut to a File

If you work with the same file every day, or work with a specific file for the duration of a project, you can create a desktop shortcut to that file so that you can immediately open it after your computer boots to the desktop. You can use the same approach to create a shortcut to a file as you used to create a shortcut to a folder.

Because you are experimenting with different designs for a new company logo, Lance recommends that you create a desktop shortcut to one of the files that contains a design for the new company logo.

To create a shortcut to a file:

1. Click the **Upsilon Air** shortcut, maximize the window (if necessary), and then click the **Company Logo** folder.
2. Right-click **Logo #1.jpg**, point to **Send To**, click **Desktop (create shortcut)**, and then close the Company Logo folder window. Windows Vista creates a shortcut to this JPEG image file on the desktop. See Figure 4-15. Notice that the name of the shortcut includes the file extension, which can be misleading, because you might think this object was the actual file unless you noticed the shortcut arrow icon . You can remove the file extension from the shortcut name without affecting the shortcut or the file that it references. Note also that the shortcut icon shows a thumbnail view of the file's contents.

Figure 4-15 Viewing the Logo #1 file shortcut

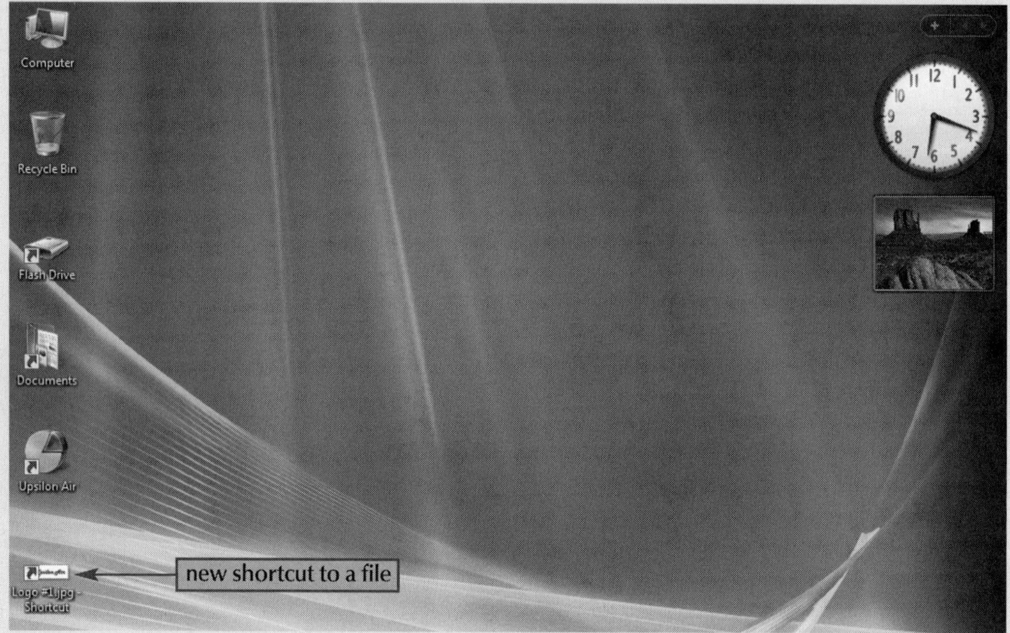

3. Change the **Logo #1.jpg - Shortcut** name to **Logo** (without the file extension).
4. Click the **Logo** shortcut. Windows Vista displays the image in the file using Windows Photo Gallery. See Figure 4-16.

   Trouble? If Windows opens the file in another application, the "jpg" file extension is associated with that application on your computer. Continue with step 5. The important point is that the shortcut worked.

Figure 4-16

Logo #1 file opened with shortcut

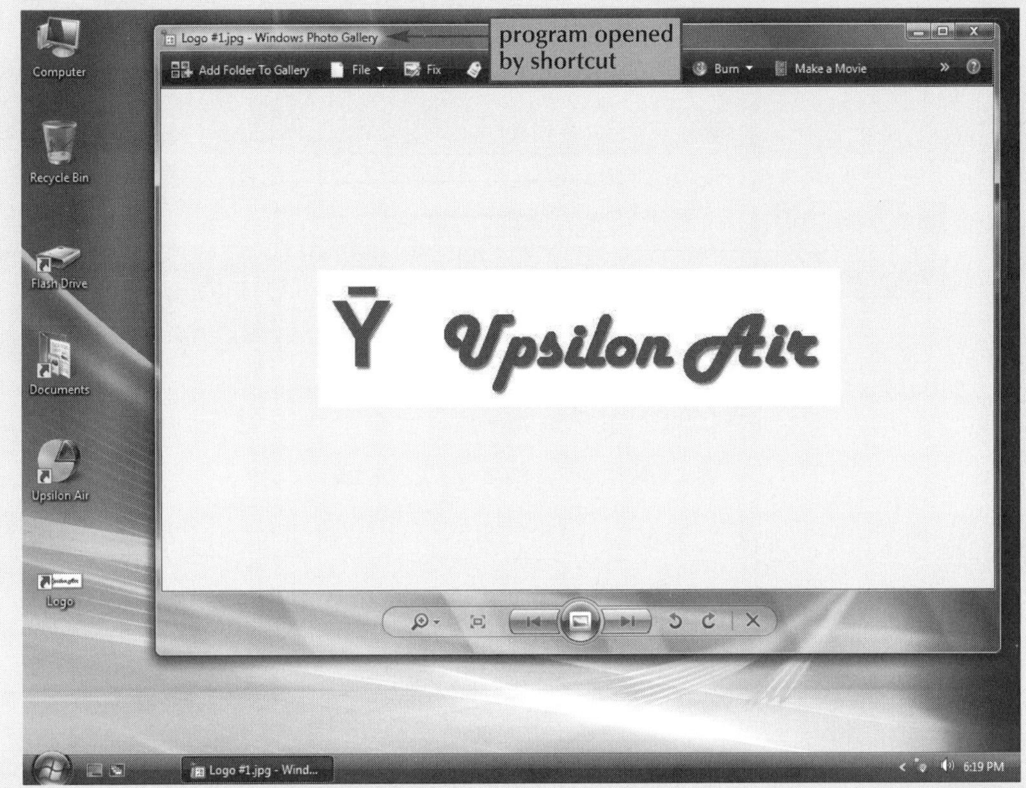

5. Close the Windows Photo Gallery window (or the application window) displaying the contents of the Logo #1 file.
6. Right-click the **Logo** shortcut and then click **Properties**. Windows Vista opens the Logo Properties dialog box. Note that this Target type is a JPEG Image.
7. Click the **path** in the Target box, and then press the **Home** key. Windows Vista moves the insertion point to the beginning of the path so you can see the first part of the path.
8. Press the **End** key. Windows Vista moves to the end of the path so you see the rest of the path. See Figure 4-17. The path to the file referenced by this shortcut is "C:\Users\Public\Documents\Upsilon Air\Company Logo\Logo #1.jpg". The path in the "Start in" box is "C:\ Users\Public\Documents\Upsilon Air\Company Logo". The "Start in" box identifies the folder that contains the object or related files that a program might need.

Figure 4-17 Viewing properties of a file shortcut

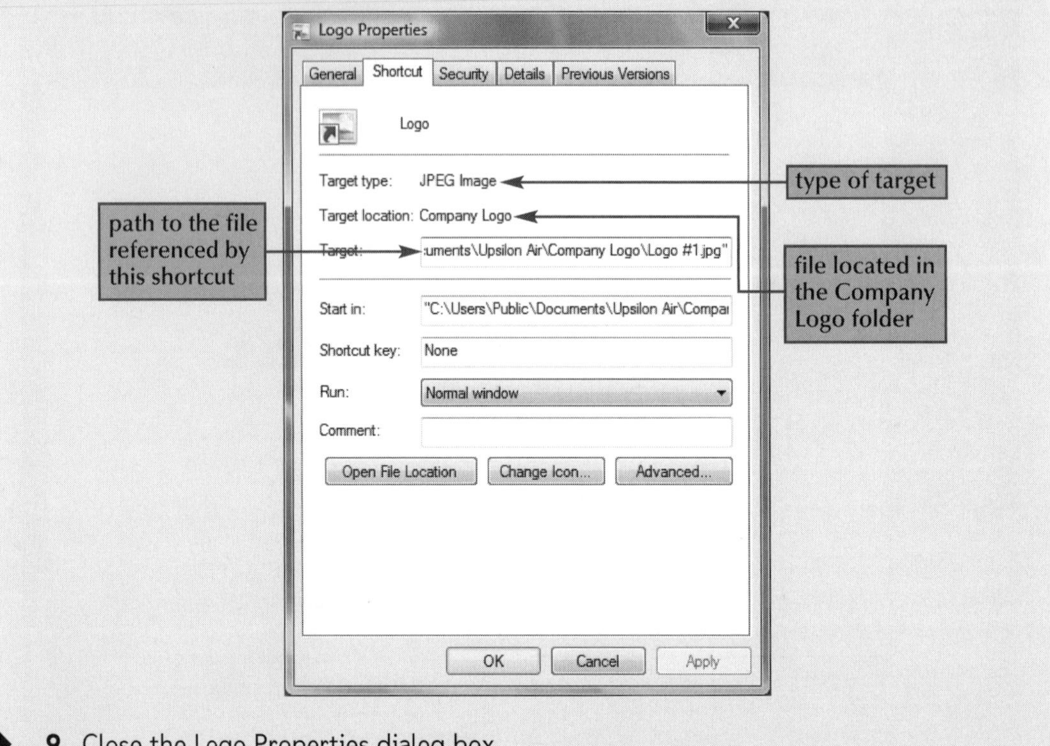

9. Close the Logo Properties dialog box.

The use of shortcuts and the document-oriented nature of Windows Vista simplify the process for locating and opening files.

For each project on which you work, you can create a set of shortcuts to folders and files that you need to open. After your computer boots to the desktop, a single-click means you are ready to work.

Creating a Shortcut to an Application

Even though you can open all the installed software on your computer from the All Programs menu, using this menu often requires many steps to locate and open a program. Instead, you can create shortcuts to applications, utilities, and games on your computer so that you can open them directly from the desktop. As you've seen, once you create the shortcut, it's a one-step process to open the target.

You can use several approaches to create shortcuts for installed software. If you know the location and name of the program file, you can open the folder where the program file is stored, right-click the program file icon, and use the option on the Send To menu for creating a desktop shortcut—just as you did when creating shortcuts to folders and document files.

Another approach is to use the Create Shortcut Wizard to browse for the program file and customize the shortcut at the same time. You right-click the desktop, point to New, and click Shortcut on the desktop shortcut menu. The Create Shortcut Wizard then asks you to enter the location of the item (in other words, its path), or you can browse and locate the program, folder, file, computer, or Web site. Once you've located the object for which you want to create a shortcut, the Create Shortcut Wizard asks you for a name for the shortcut. Click Finish and you're done. When you locate the object by browsing, you are providing Windows Vista with the path to that object. The only problem with this approach is that you have to browse your computer looking for the object, which can be time consuming. You also might not know where to look for the program.

Tip

If you use the Start menu Search box to locate a program, you can right-click the program file, point to Send To, and then click "Desktop (create shortcut)."

Understanding Program Filenames | InSight

With a little understanding of how Microsoft and software developers name their program files, you can usually figure out the filename of a program file while browsing for that program manually or with the Create Shortcut Wizard or Search Explorer. Program files for applications, utilities, and games have the file extension "exe" (for Executable program file). Since the main part of the filename for a program file is limited to eight characters, you might have to guess the main part of the filename or search for a name that is similar to your guess. For example, in the Microsoft Office suite, the program file for Microsoft Excel is Excel.exe, the Microsoft Outlook program file is Outlook.exe, the Microsoft PowerPoint program file is Powerpnt.exe, the Microsoft Access program file is Msaccess.exe, and the Microsoft Word program file is Winword.exe.

A faster and easier way is to send a copy of the shortcut for a program from the All Programs menu to the desktop. The All Programs menu is the obvious first place to check for a shortcut for an application, utility, or game.

So that you can stay on top of your appointments, Lance recommends that you create a desktop shortcut to Windows Calendar.

To create a shortcut to a program:

1. Open the **Start** menu, point to **All Programs**, right-click **Windows Calendar**, point to **Send To**, click **Desktop (create shortcut)**, and then click the **Start** button again to close the Start menu. Windows Vista places a copy of the Windows Calendar shortcut on the desktop. See Figure 4-18.

Figure 4-18 Viewing the Windows Calendar desktop shortcut

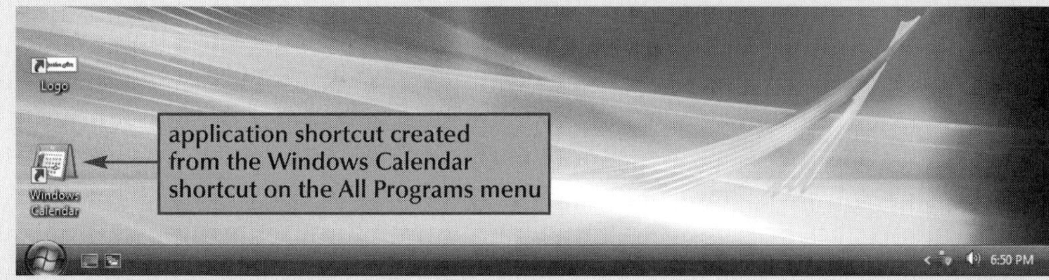

2. Right-click the **Windows Calendar** desktop shortcut and then click **Properties**. Windows Vista opens the Windows Calendar Properties dialog box. The Target box on the Shortcut property sheet shows that the path for the Windows Calendar shortcut is: "%ProgramFiles%\Windows Calendar\wincal.exe". See Figure 4-19. Note that the Target type is "Application." Windows Vista displays the text in the Comment text box as a ToolTip when you point to and rest the mouse pointer over the shortcut.

Figure 4-19 Viewing properties of a Windows application shortcut

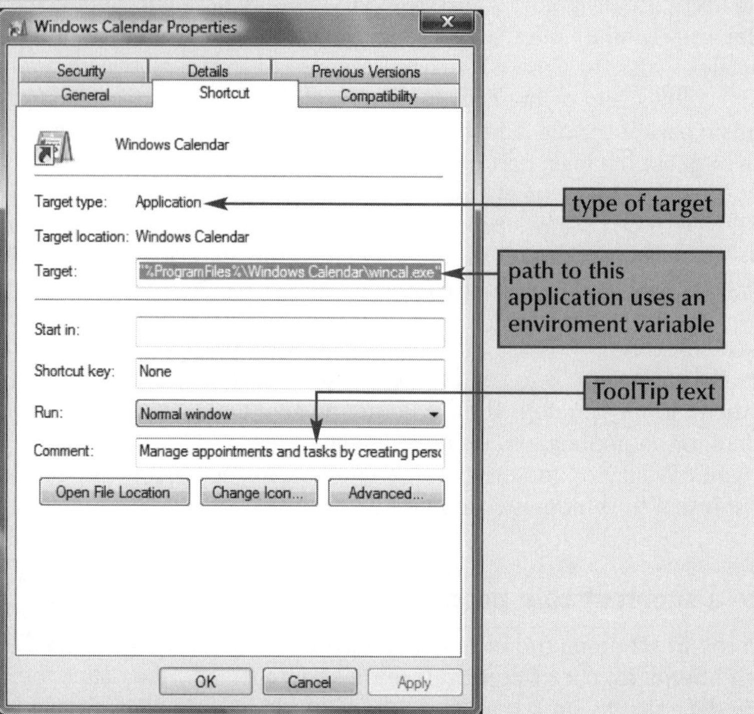

3. Keep the Windows Calendar Properties dialog box open for the following explanation of environment variables.

ProgramFiles is an example of an environment variable. An **environment variable** is a name assigned to a Windows Vista system setting. The name of the environment variable (in this case, ProgramFiles) and its associated setting are stored in an area of memory called the **Windows environment**. Windows Vista and other programs check the Windows environment for settings. The percentage symbols before and after an environment variable identify it as an environment variable, and indicate that it is a placeholder for a setting that can vary.

When a path includes %ProgramFiles%, Windows Vista substitutes the actual setting for the environment variable. If the Program Files folder is on drive C (as is typically the case), the setting for the ProgramFiles variable is "C:\Program Files". In this example, Windows Vista substitutes "C:\Program Files" for %ProgramFiles%" in the path to derive the actual path, namely: "C:\Program Files\Windows Calendar\wincal.exe"

On another computer, Windows Vista might be installed on drive D, and the path to the Program Files folder on that drive would be "D:\Program Files" rather than "C:\Program Files". When that computer boots, Windows Vista can locate files for programs like Windows Calendar because "D:\Program Files" is assigned to the ProgramFiles environment variable and the path to the Windows Calendar program is then "D:\Program Files\Windows Calendar\wincal.exe". The use of environment variables therefore provides flexibility for different types of installations and configurations of Windows Vista and guarantees that the operating system works properly.

To test your Windows Calendar shortcut:

1. Close the Windows Calendar Properties dialog box.
2. Click the **Windows Calendar** desktop shortcut. Windows Vista opens Windows Calendar, and you can now check your appointments and add appointments.
3. Close the Windows Calendar window.

Another important environment variable is SystemRoot. This environment variable specifies the path where Windows Vista is installed. That path includes the drive name and folder name for the Windows folder, which is typically "C:\Windows". You will examine environment variables in more detail in Tutorial 8.

Creating a Shortcut to an Application | Reference Window

- From the Start menu, point to All Programs, and then locate the application or program for which you want to create a shortcut.
- Right-click the application or program name, point to Send To, and then click Desktop (create shortcut).
- Click the Start button to close the Start menu.

The All Programs menu is the easiest way to locate shortcuts for applications, utilities, games, and other programs.

Creating a New Shortcut from an Existing Shortcut

You can make a copy of an existing shortcut and change its path to create a new shortcut. If you change the path so that it points to a different type of object, Windows Vista changes the new shortcut's icon.

Because you also need to work with other files in the Company Logo folder, Lance recommends you create a shortcut to that folder from the Logo shortcut because the target of the Logo shortcut contains the path to the Company Logo folder.

To create a Company Logo folder shortcut from the Logo file shortcut:

1. Right-click the **Logo** shortcut, and then click **Copy** on the shortcut menu.
2. Right-click the **desktop**, and then click **Paste** on the shortcut menu. Windows Vista creates a copy of the Logo shortcut and names it "Logo - Copy."
3. With the shortcut still selected, press the **F2** key, type **Company Logo**, and then press the **Enter** key. Windows Vista changes the name of the new desktop shortcut to "Company Logo" but as evidenced from the shortcut icon, the shortcut still points to the Logo file.
4. Right-click the **Company Logo** shortcut, and then click **Properties**. Windows Vista opens the Company Logo Properties dialog box, displays the Shortcut property sheet, and highlights the target of the shortcut. The path is currently set at "C:\Users\Public\Documents\Upsilon Air\Company Logo\Logo #1.jpg". Note that the Target type is JPEG Image.
5. Press the **End** key, press the **left arrow** key once to position the insertion point to the left of the closing quotation mark, and then use the **Backspace** key to delete "\Logo #1.jpg" from the target's path.

Tip

You can use the Home and End key to navigate to the beginning or end of any entry in a text box.

6. Verify that the new path is "C:\Users\Public\Documents\Upsilon Air\Company Logo".
7. Click the **OK** button. Windows Vista displays a new icon for the Company Logo shortcut. See Figure 4-20. Windows Vista now uses a folder icon instead of a file icon for the shortcut.

Figure 4-20 Viewing a folder shortcut created from a file shortcut

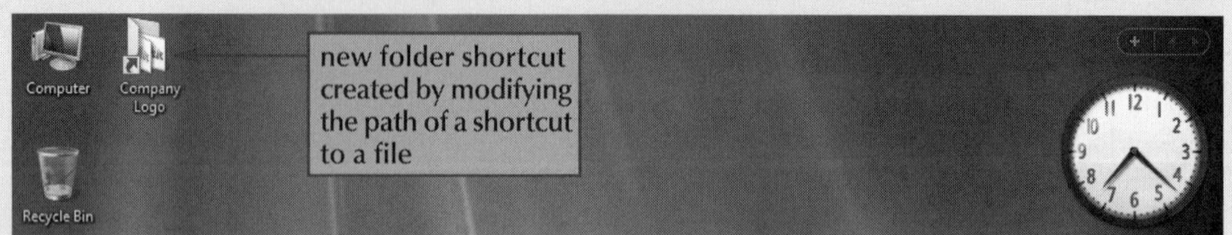

8. Right-click the **Company Logo** shortcut and then click **Properties**. The Company Logo Properties dialog box now identifies the Target type as "File Folder." See Figure 4-21.

Figure 4-21 Viewing the Company Logo folder shortcut properties

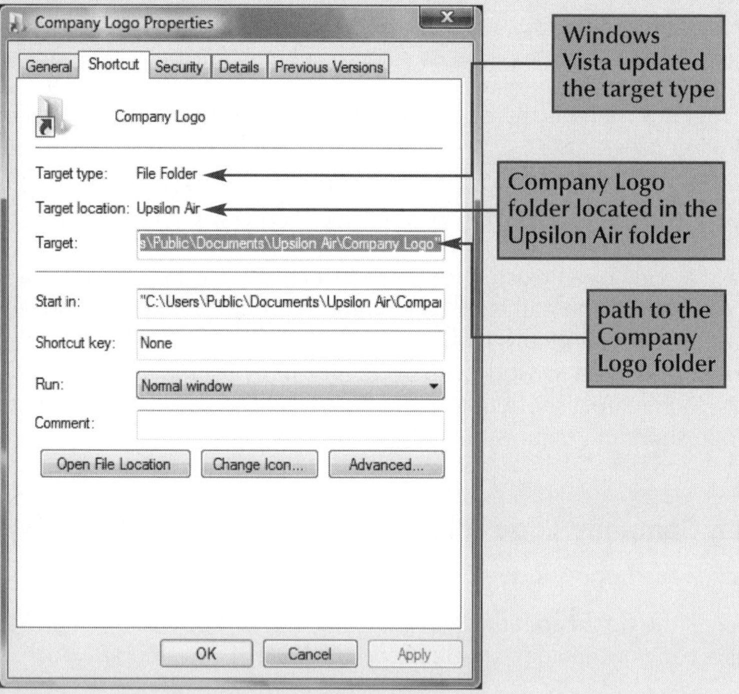

9. Close the Company Logo Properties dialog box.

Lance reminds you that, like the Upsilon Air shortcut, you can change the shortcut icon if you prefer.

Creating a New Shortcut from an Existing Shortcut

| Reference Window

- Right-click a desktop shortcut and then click Copy.
- Right-click the desktop and click Paste.
- Press the F2 key, type a new name for (or edit the name of) the new desktop shortcut, and press the Enter key.
- Right-click the new desktop shortcut, click Properties, and in the Target box on the Shortcut property sheet, modify the path, and then click the OK button.

If you are familiar with the use of the Windows path, you can easily create new shortcuts from existing shortcuts.

Automatic Updating of Shortcut Paths

When you create a shortcut to an object, Windows Vista stores the path to that object as part of the shortcut. If you change the name of the object to which the shortcut points or if you move the object, the shortcut still works. In each case, Windows Vista updates the path so that the shortcut still points to the same object.

Lance informs you that senior management wants to redesign Logo #1.jpg and use it to create a new company logo. He asks you to change the name of the Logo #1 file to Company Logo.

To change the name of the Logo #1 file:

1. Click the **Company Logo** shortcut. Windows Vista opens the Company Logo folder.
2. In the Files list, right-click **Logo #1.jpg**, click **Rename** on the shortcut menu, change the name from "Logo #1" to **Company Logo** and then press the **Enter** key.
3. Close the Company Logo folder window.
4. Click the **Logo** shortcut. Windows Vista opens the Company Logo file for previewing in Windows Photo Gallery. The full filename is shown on the title bar. The shortcut works; in other words, it finds its target.

   Trouble? If Windows Vista opens the file in another program, that's okay. The point is that the shortcut still works.
5. Close the Windows Photo Gallery window.

Next, view the path for the Logo desktop shortcut.

To view the path for the Logo shortcut:

1. Right-click the **Logo** shortcut, and then click **Properties**. Note that Windows Vista updated the path so that it includes the new name of the file—namely, Company Logo.jpg. See Figure 4-22. Notice that the Target Location is Company Logo (the name of the folder that contains the file).

Figure 4-22 Target path updated after renaming the target file

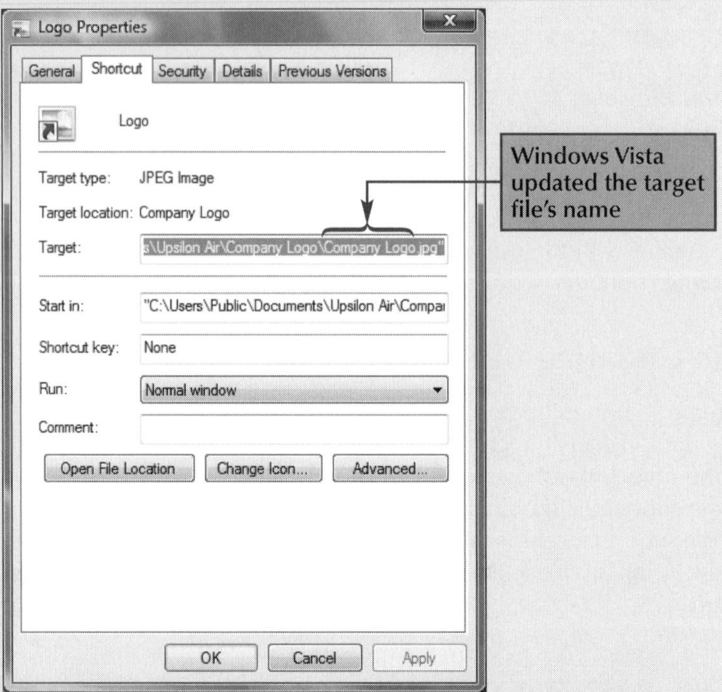

2. Close the Logo Properties dialog box.

Next, you decide to move the Company Logo file to a new folder where you will be preparing an Annual Report.

To move the Company Logo file to a new folder:

1. Click the **Company Logo** shortcut, right-click the **Company Logo.jpg** file, and then click **Cut**.
2. Click **Upsilon Air** in the Address Bar, click the **Organize** button on the command bar, click **New Folder**, type **Annual Report** for the new folder's name, and then press the **Enter** key. Windows Vista assigns a name to this new folder.
3. Click **Annual Report** to open the Annual Report folder, right-click the **folder background**, and then click **Paste**. Windows Vista moves the Company Logo.jpg file to this folder.
4. Close the Annual Report folder window.
5. Click the **Logo** shortcut. Windows Vista opens the Company Logo file for previewing in Windows Photo Gallery (or whatever program is associated with JPEG Image files on your computer). The shortcut still works; in other words, it finds its target.
6. Close the Windows Photo Gallery window.
7. Right-click the **Logo** shortcut, and then click **Properties**. Note that Windows Vista again updated the path to include the name of the Annual Report folder where this file now resides. See Figure 4-23. The Target Location is now Annual Report.

Tip

If you move a file to another folder, Windows Vista updates the path in all shortcuts that reference the file.

Figure 4-23 Updated path includes new folder name for the target file

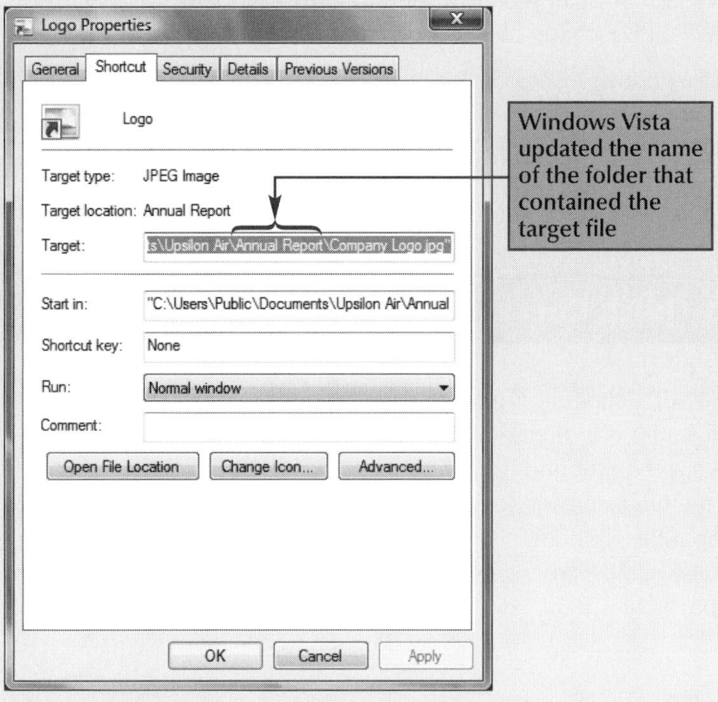

8. Close the Logo Properties dialog box.

Later, you accidentally delete the Company Logo file and then discover the problem when you attempt to use the Company Logo desktop shortcut later.

To delete the Company Logo file:

1. Click the **Upsilon Air** shortcut, open the **Annual Report** folder, right-click **Company Logo.jpg**, click **Delete**, and in the Delete File dialog box, click the **Yes** button to move the file to the Recycle Bin.
2. Close the Annual Report folder window.
3. Click the **Logo** shortcut. Windows Vista displays a Problem with Shortcut dialog box, informs you that the file that the shortcut refers to has been deleted, and asks if you want to restore the file from the Recycle Bin or delete the shortcut. See Figure 4-24.

Figure 4-24 Problem locating a file with its shortcut

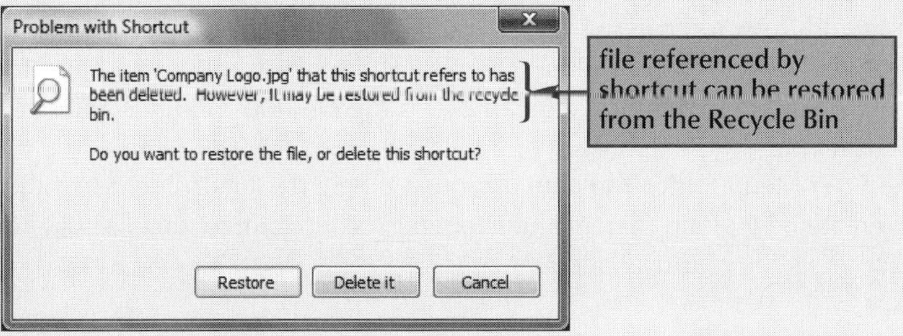

4. Click the **Restore** button. Windows Vista restores the deleted file to the folder where it was previously located, and then opens the Company Logo file that the desktop shortcut points to in Windows Photo Gallery (or whatever program is associated with JPEG Image files on your computer).
5. Close the Windows Photo Gallery window.

As you rename, copy, and move files and folders around on your computer, Windows Vista updates the path that shortcuts use to reference these objects so that your shortcuts continue to work.

Review | Session 4.1 Quick Check

1. True or False. A shortcut is a special type of file that contains the path to an object and, as a result, is a direct link to that object.
2. How does a shortcut find its target?
3. What is the file extension for a desktop shortcut, and what does that file extension imply about the shortcut?
4. True or False. Unlike other types of files, shortcuts do not waste storage space on disk.
5. What types of files use "exe", "dll", and "ico" file extensions?
6. A(n) ________________ is a name assigned to a Windows Vista system setting.

Session 4.2

Adding Shortcuts to the Start Menu

If you are working in a maximized application window such as Microsoft Word or viewing a Web page with Windows Internet Explorer, you might not want to minimize the window just to locate and click a desktop shortcut, and then later have to maximize the window. However, the Start button and taskbar are always accessible. If you place a shortcut on the Start menu or on a taskbar toolbar, such as the Quick Launch toolbar (as you saw in Tutorial 2), you can leave your application window maximized and then still locate and use the shortcut.

If you want to customize the Start menu, you can add new group folders and shortcuts to the Start menu, All Programs menu, and other menus in the following ways:

- **Using the Taskbar and Start Menu Properties dialog box** In Tutorial 2, you opened the Taskbar and Start Menu Properties dialog box and customized the Start menu to include those options that you need for your work.
- **Using drag-and-drop** You can use drag-and-drop to rearrange, move, or copy group folders and program shortcuts on the Start and All Programs menus and also to drag them from one menu to another. You can even drag desktop shortcuts and drop them on the Start menu.
- **Using the Start Menu folder** You can also open the Start Menu folder for your user account, create new group folders and shortcuts, or reorganize the existing group folders and shortcuts for your user account.

The approach you use will depend on how you prefer to work, the types of changes you want to make, and the degree to which you want to customize the Start and All Programs menus.

Pinning a Program to the Start Menu

Because you use the Windows Photo Gallery daily to work with images and videos from various projects, Lance suggests that you pin the Windows Photo Gallery to the Start menu.

To pin Windows Photo Gallery to the Start menu:

1. Before you change the Start menu, click the **Start** button and examine the pinned items list in the upper-left corner of the Start menu. On Lance's computer, only two items appear in this area—an option for opening Internet Explorer and an option for opening Microsoft Office Outlook to compose, send, and receive e-mail messages.
2. Point to **All Programs**, right-click **Windows Photo Gallery**, and then click **Pin to Start Menu**.
3. Click (or point to) the **Back** button. Windows Vista displays the previous view of the Start menu. The pinned items list now contains a shortcut to the Windows Photo Gallery. See Figure 4-25.

Figure 4-25 Pinning an application to the Start menu

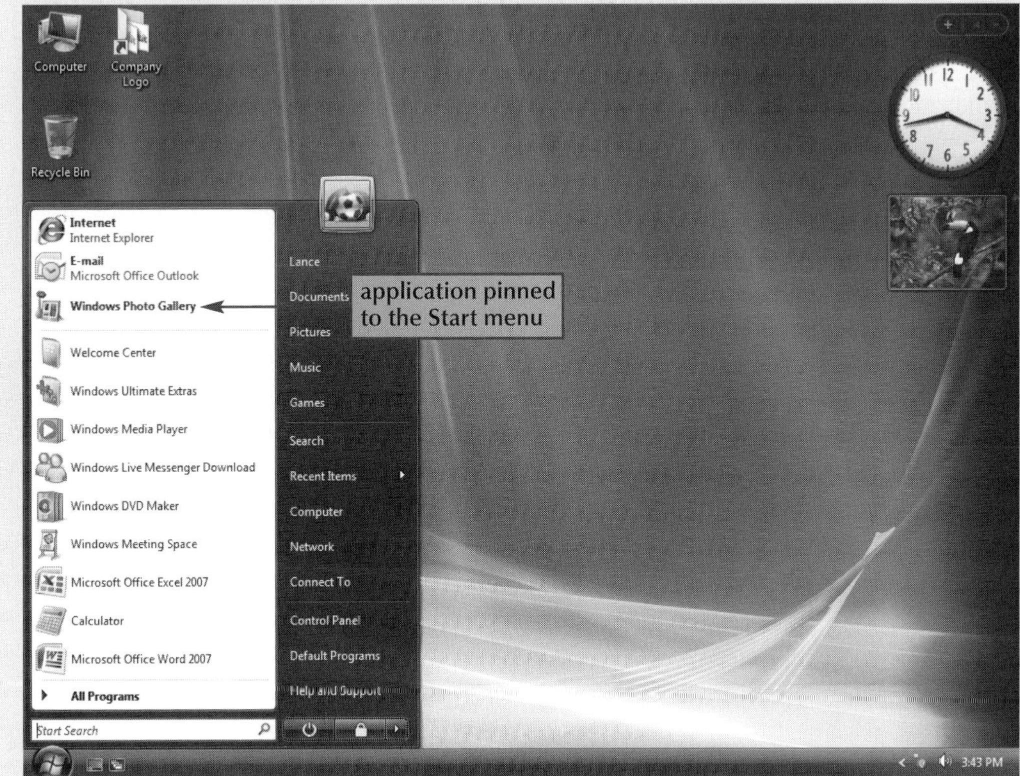

4. Click **Windows Photo Gallery**. Windows Vista opens the Windows Photo Gallery and displays thumbnails of pictures and videos.
5. Close the Windows Photo Gallery window.

If you prefer to move a pinned item to another location on the Start menu's pinned item list, just drag it to the new location. If you later decide to remove a pinned program from the pinned items list, you just point to it, right-click, and then choose the option "Unpin from Start Menu."

Reference Window | Pinning and Unpinning Programs on the Start Menu

- To pin an item to the Start menu's pinned items list, open the Start menu, locate, and then right-click the program that you want to pin to the Start menu, and then click "Pin to Start Menu."
- To move a program in the Start menu's pinned items list, drag the program to a new location on the pinned items list.
- To remove an item from the Start menu's pinned items list, open the Start menu, right-click the program that you want to remove from the pinned items list, and then click "Unpin from Start Menu."

The pinned items list is a logical place to store shortcuts to programs that you rely on every day.

Adding Shortcuts to the Start Menu

To add a desktop shortcut to your Start menu, you drag it from the desktop and drop it on the Start button. Windows Vista then copies the shortcut to the Start menu and places it in the pinned items list. The original shortcut remains on the desktop.

Lance invariably finds that he needs to switch to his Upsilon Air folder while he is working in an application window or examining a Web site with Windows Internet Explorer. Rather than switch to the desktop to access the Upsilon Air shortcut and later reopen the window where he was working, he decides it would be faster to add the Upsilon Air shortcut directly to the Start menu so that all he has to do is click the Start button, and then click the Upsilon Air shortcut. He can then keep his application window open while he selects the Upsilon Air shortcut on the Start menu. He asks you to also add the Upsilon Air desktop shortcut to your Start menu.

Tip

To control the placement of the shortcut on the Start menu, point to the Start button, wait for the Start menu to open, and then drag the shortcut to where you want to place it in the pinned items list.

To add a desktop shortcut to the Start menu:

1. Drag the **Upsilon Air** shortcut from the desktop to the Start button, release the mouse button, and then click the **Start** button if Windows Vista does not display the Start menu. Notice that Windows Vista added a copy of the Upsilon Air shortcut to the pinned items list. See Figure 4-26.

Figure 4-26 Pinning a folder shortcut to the Start menu

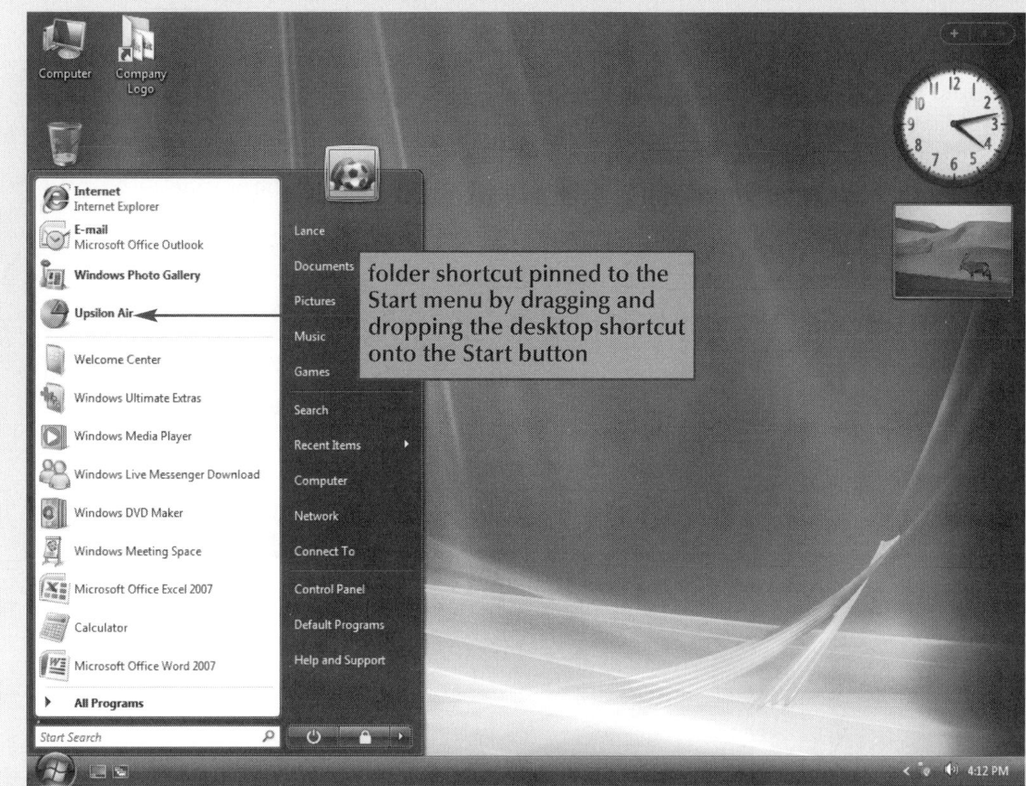

2. Click **Upsilon Air** on the Start menu. The Upsilon Air shortcut on the Start menu works just like the desktop shortcut and opens the Upsilon Air folder.
3. Close the Upsilon Air folder window.

To remove a program from the Start menu's pinned items list, right-click the program and choose "Unpin from Start Menu." To remove other types of shortcuts, like a folder shortcut, from the Start menu's pinned items list, right-click the shortcut and choose "Remove from this list."

Adding a Desktop Shortcut to the Start Menu

| Reference Window

- To add a desktop shortcut to the Start menu's pinned items list, drag the desktop shortcut to the Start button and then release the left mouse button.
- To remove a shortcut from the Start menu's pinned items list, open the Start menu, right-click the shortcut that you want to remove from the pinned items list, and then click "Unpin from Start Menu" or click "Remove from this list."

As Lance has discovered from working on his computer, you might find it useful to have the same shortcut in two or more places for quick access from wherever you are working.

Creating a Control Panel Shortcut

If you find that you use a Control Panel tool, or applet (a small application), frequently, you can create a desktop shortcut to that Control Panel applet so that you don't have to navigate to that applet in the Control Panel. The shortcut will save you many steps.

While working with you, Lance notices that you frequently open the Folder Options dialog box to make changes to folder and file settings. He suggests that you can save time and effort if you create a shortcut to that dialog box in the Control Panel.

To create a Control Panel shortcut:

1. From the Start menu, open the **Control Panel**.
2. In the Control Panel Search box, type **f** and wait for the Search results. Windows Vista displays Control Panel features that meet your search criteria. See Figure 4-27.

Figure 4-27 Searching for Folder Options in the Control Panel

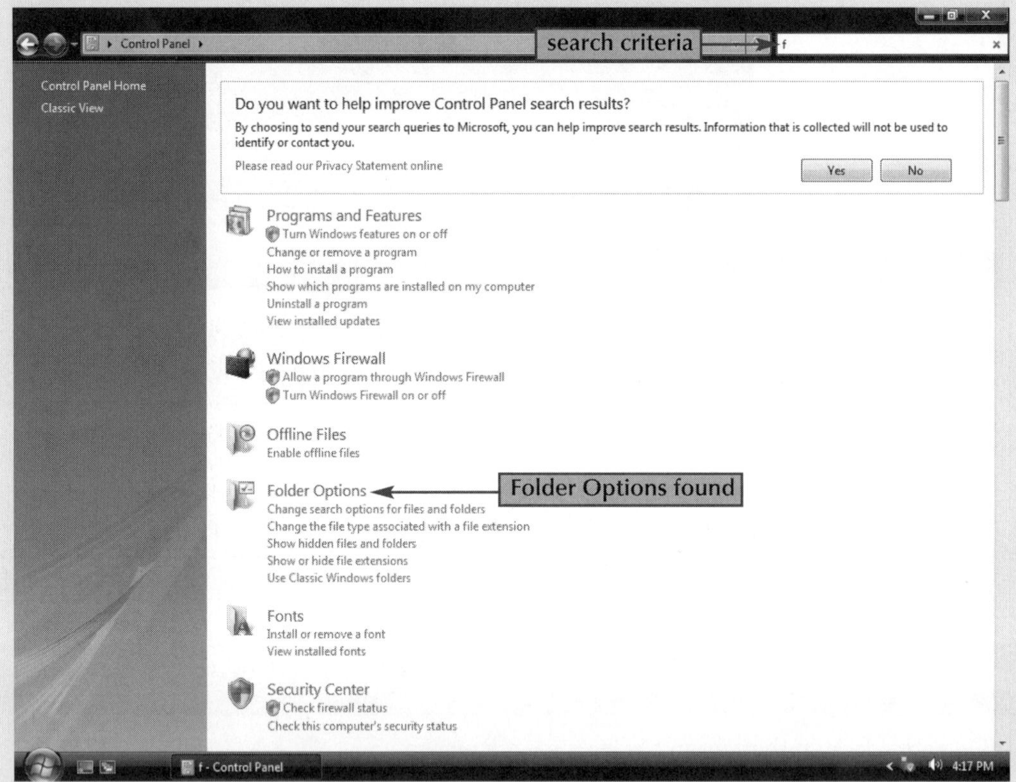

3. Right-click **Folder Options**, click **Create Shortcut**, and then close the Control Panel window. Windows Vista places a desktop shortcut to Folder Options in the Control Panel.
4. Select **Folder Options - Shortcut** and change its name to **Folder Options**.
5. Click the **Folder Options** shortcut. Windows Vista opens the Folder Options dialog box. See Figure 4-28. This shortcut saves multiple steps because you don't have to open a folder window and use the Organize menu to open the Folder Options dialog box.

Figure 4-28 Folder Options dialog box opened from desktop shortcut

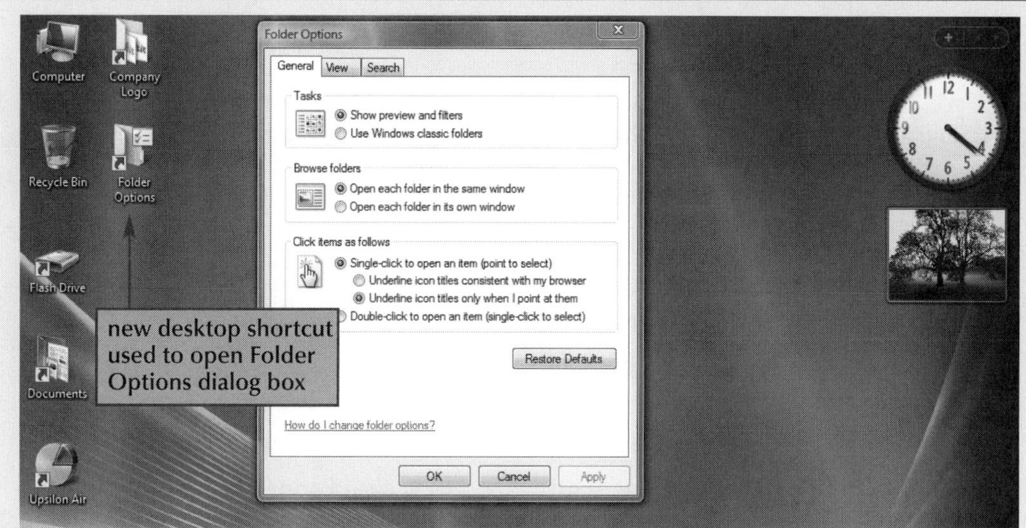

6. Close the Folder Options dialog box.
7. Right-click the **Folder Options** shortcut, and then click **Properties**. Windows Vista opens the Folder Options Properties dialog box. See Figure 4-29. In the Target box on the Shortcut property sheet, Windows Vista displays the target used by this shortcut: Control Panel\Folder Options. The target is dimmed, which means you cannot change the target.

Figure 4-29 Viewing properties of the Folder Options shortcut

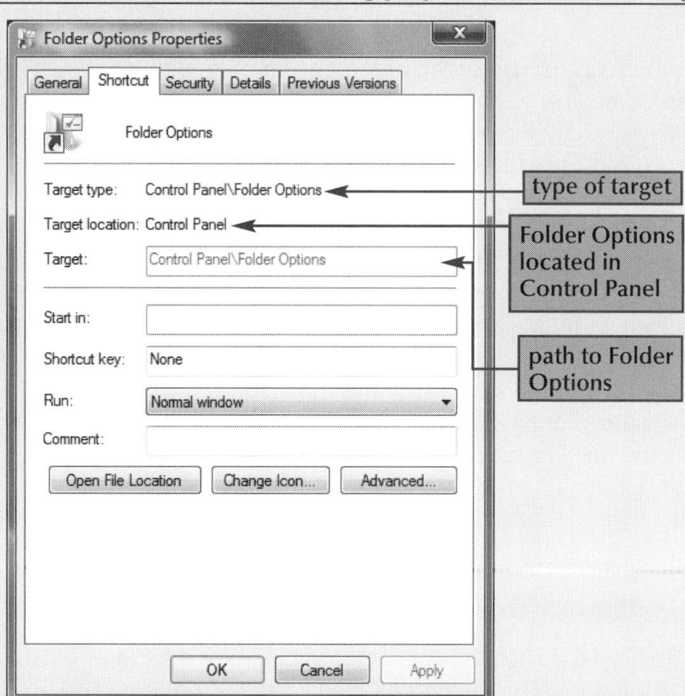

8. Click the **Details** tab. On the Details property sheet, Windows Vista shows the filename of this shortcut: Folder Options.lnk
9. Close the Folder Options Properties dialog box.

If you manage user accounts on your computer, you can create a shortcut to User Accounts in the Control Panel so that you have a direct link to the tools you need to create, modify, and manage user accounts.

You decide that it might also be a good idea to create a custom ToolTip for this shortcut to remind other staff members who use your computer the purpose of this shortcut.

To customize the ToolTip for a shortcut:

1. Point to the **Folder Options** shortcut and rest the mouse pointer on this shortcut. Windows Vista displays a ToolTip with the following text: Location: Control Panel

   Trouble? If you do not see a ToolTip, click the Desktop background and try again.
2. Right-click the **Folder Options** shortcut and then click **Properties**.
3. In the Comment box on the Shortcut property sheet, type the following text: **Use to customize folder views and search settings**
4. Click the **OK** button to close the Folder Options Properties dialog box and apply the new setting.
5. Point to the **Folder Options** shortcut and rest the mouse pointer on this shortcut. Windows Vista displays a ToolTip with the custom text that you specified for the Comment.

   Trouble? If Windows Vista does not display the comment you specified, right-click the desktop, click Refresh, and then try this step again.

If you create shortcuts for users who are not as familiar with Windows Vista as you are, you can add comments to each shortcut so that these users know the function of each shortcut. As you show them how to use a shortcut, you can also show them how to display a shortcut's ToolTip with the custom comment.

Customizing the Navigation Pane

The **Navigation Pane** in folder windows contains links to commonly used folders, including the Documents, Pictures, Music, Recently Changed, Searches, and Public folders. If you frequently use other folders, you can add those folders to the Navigation Pane and Windows Vista creates shortcuts to those folders in your user account Links folder.

As you work, you need to quickly switch between the Documents folder and the Upsilon Air folder, so with Lance's assistance you add an Upsilon Air folder link to the Navigation Pane.

To add the Upsilon Air folder to the Navigation Pane:

1. Click the **Upsilon Air** shortcut. Windows Vista opens a window onto the Upsilon Air folder.
2. Click **Public Documents** in the Address Bar. Windows Vista switches to the Public Documents folder.

3. Drag the **Upsilon Air** folder in the Public Documents folder and place it under the last link listed under Favorite Links, as shown in Figure 4-30. As you drag, Windows Vista displays a horizontal black bar that indicates where the new link will be positioned when you release the left mouse button. Windows Vista also displays a ToolTip with a shortcut arrow and the text "Create link in Links."

Figure 4-30 Creating a Favorite Link using drag and drop

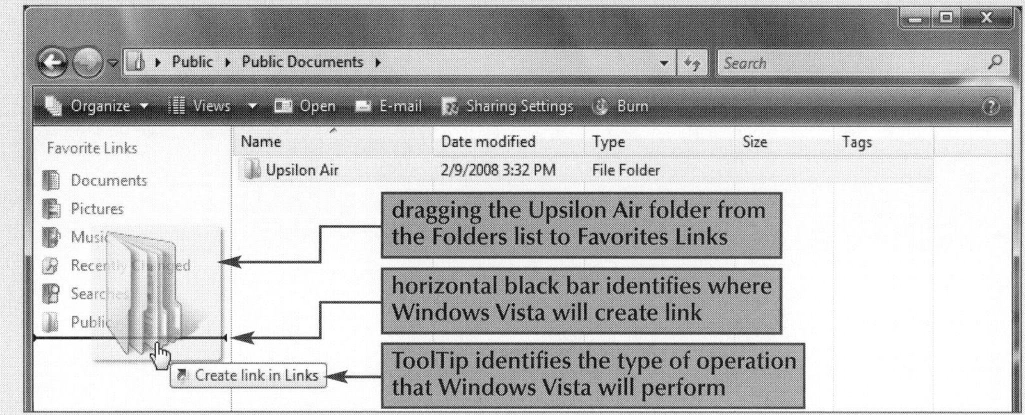

4. Release the mouse button. Windows Vista creates an Upsilon Air link under Favorite Links. See Figure 4-31. If you are working with files in another folder, you can now use the Upsilon Air link to switch quickly to the Upsilon Air folder.

Figure 4-31 Newly created Favorite Link

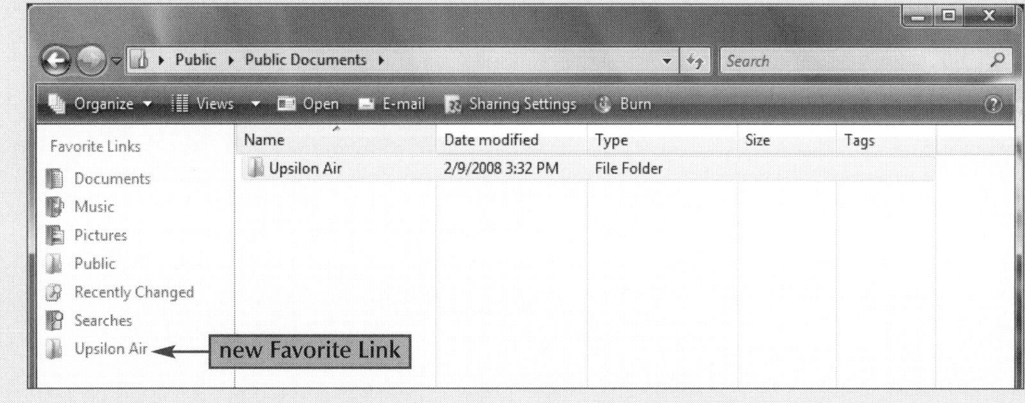

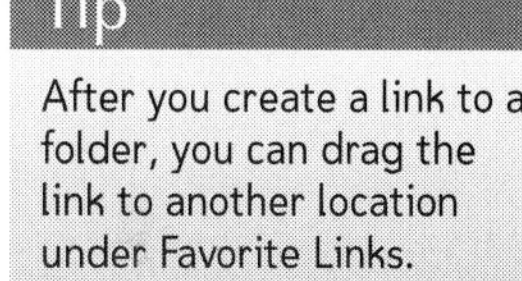

Tip

After you create a link to a folder, you can drag the link to another location under Favorite Links.

5. Right-click one of the links under Favorite Links and then click **Sort by Name**. Windows Vista arranges the Favorite Links in alphabetical order.
6. In the Navigation Pane, click **Documents** to open your Documents folder.
7. In the Navigation Pane, click **Upsilon Air**. Windows Vista opens the Upsilon Air folder and displays its contents in the Files list.

Next, you decide to view the shortcut for your new Upsilon Air link.

To view the shortcut for the Upsilon Air link:

1. In the Address Bar, click the **New Location button arrow** ▸ to the left of Public and then click your user account name. Windows Vista switches to your user account folder.
2. Click the **Links** folder icon, click the **Views button arrow** on the command bar, and then click **Large Icons**. Windows Vista opens the Links folder and switches to Large Icons view. The link to the Upsilon Air folder under Favorite Links in the Navigation Pane is actually a shortcut in the Links folder. See Figure 4-32.

Figure 4-32 Viewing shortcuts in the Links folder

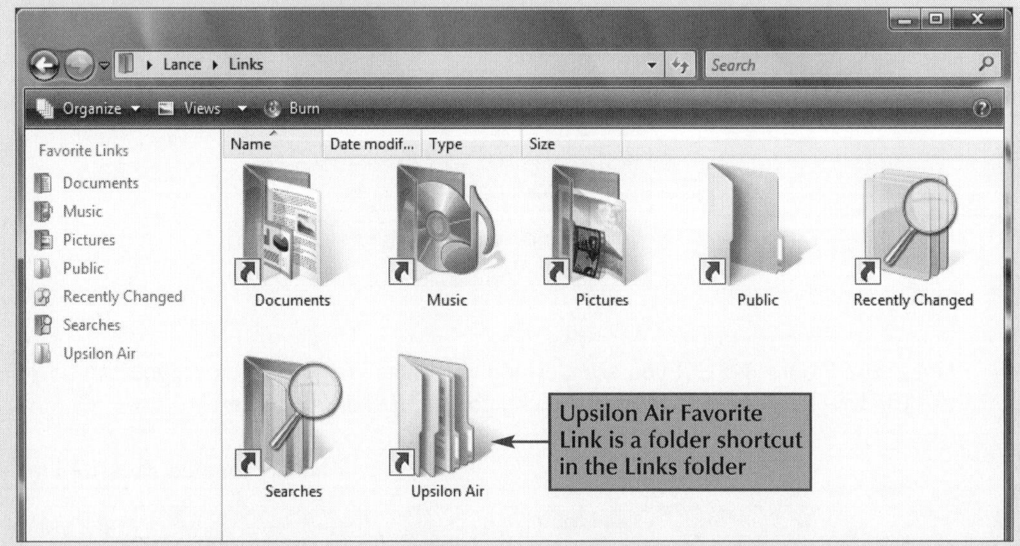

3. Click the **Upsilon Air** shortcut in the Files list of the Links folder window. Windows Vista opens the Upsilon Air folder.

Lance points out that if you no longer need a link under Favorite Links, you can delete it and Windows Vista will remove it from the Links folder. He suggests that you delete the Upsilon Air link so that you know how to remove links under Favorite Links, and then you can add it back to your Favorite Links right afterwards.

To remove the new Upsilon Air link:

1. Click the **Back** button. Windows Vista returns to the Links folder.
2. Right-click the **Upsilon Air** link under Favorite Links in the Navigation Pane, and then click **Remove Link**.
3. In the Delete File dialog box, click the **Yes** button to confirm that you want to move this file to the Recycle Bin. Windows Vista deletes the Upsilon Air link under Favorite Links, and the Links folder no longer contains an Upsilon Air shortcut.
4. Right-click the **Links folder background**, and then click **Undo Delete**. Windows Vista restores the Upsilon Air link under Favorite Links and displays the Upsilon Air shortcut in the Links folder.
5. Close the Links folder window.

If you perform a task, such as deleting a shortcut, file, or folder, and then switch to another drive, folder, or the desktop, you can right-click the background of the current folder and undo the last task you performed (or use the Ctrl+Z Undo keyboard shortcut), as long as you performed that operation on the hard disk drive. You cannot undo, for example, a file you deleted from your flash drive. In fact, when you delete the file from your flash drive, Windows Vista will ask you if you are sure that you want to *permanently* delete this file.

Adding and Removing Links in the Navigation Pane | Reference Window

- To add a link to a folder under Favorite Links in a folder window, drag the folder and drop it in the Navigation Pane.
- To move a link under Favorite Links, drag the link to another location in the Favorite Links list.
- To remove a Favorite Links, right-click the link, and then click Remove Link.

As you work in different folders on your computer, you can add links to other folders in the Navigation Pane to streamline access to important folders.

Customizing a Drive Icon

If you have several removable disk drives in your computer, Windows Vista uses the default Removable Disk icon and name (i.e., Removable Disk) for each of those drives. For example, you might have one or more memory card drives and one or more flash drives, all of which are identified with the same icon in the Computer window. Although you can distinguish one drive from another by each drive's name (i.e., F: and G:), you can also specify a custom icon for each drive to more easily distinguish them. Windows Vista will also use that same icon for your flash drive desktop shortcut.

To specify a custom icon for a flash drive, you must first locate or create a small icon file with the "ico" or "bmp" file extension. Then you create a folder named **autorun** in the top-level folder of your flash drive and put the icon file in the autorun folder. Finally, you use Notepad to create an autorun.inf file where you designate the location of the file icon. Assuming your icon file is named Upsilon Air.ico, you first put that file in the autorun folder, and then you set up the autorun.inf file as follows:

```
[autorun]
icon=autorun\Upsilon Air.ico
```

[autorun] is a section name, and icon= specifies the path for the location of the icon file (in this example, in the autorun folder). If you create this autorun.inf file on a flash drive, Windows Vista uses the icon in the autorun folder as the default icon for the flash drive when you attach it to your computer and for any shortcuts to the flash drive.

If you do not have a flash drive, then read the tutorial steps and examine the figures but do not keystroke the steps.

Lance steps you through the process for creating your first autorun.inf file.

To copy an icon file to your flash drive:

1. If necessary, attach your flash drive to the computer you are using, and then close any dialog boxes or window that opens.
2. Click the **Flash Drive** shortcut, and if necessary, adjust the size of the Flash Drive window so that you can see the Upsilon Air shortcut on the desktop. Windows Vista opens the top-level folder of your flash drive.

3. Click the **Upsilon Air** desktop shortcut, and then click the **Company Logo** folder icon. The symbol displayed in the Upsilon Air.ico file is the Greek symbol for upsilon.
4. Right-click the **taskbar**, and then click **Show Windows Side by Side**. Windows Vista places the windows side by side.
5. Drag the **Upsilon Air.ico** file from the Company Logo folder window to the Removable Disk drive window, and if necessary, use the **Views** arrow button to switch to Large Icons view. Windows Vista copies the Upsilon Air.ico file to the top-level folder of your flash drive.
6. Close the Company Logo window and then maximize your flash drive window.

Now you're ready to create the autorun folder and an autorun.inf file.

To specify a custom icon for your flash drive:

1. Click the **Organize** button on the command bar, click **New Folder**, type **autorun** and then press the **Enter** key.
2. Drag the **Upsilon Air.ico** file and drop it onto the **autorun** folder. Windows Vista moves the Upsilon Air.ico file into the autorun folder.
3. Right-click the **Removable Disk folder background**, point to **New** on the shortcut menu, click **Text Document** and after Windows Vista creates a new file named "New Text Document.txt," type **autorun.inf** and then use the **Delete** key to delete the **.txt** file extension.
4. Press the **Enter** key. In the Rename dialog box, Windows Vista warns you that changing a file's extension may make the file unusable.
5. Click the **Yes** button. Windows Vista displays a custom icon for the autorun.inf file. See Figure 4-33. In the Details Pane (not shown in the figure), Windows Vista identifies this "inf" file as a Setup Information file.

Figure 4-33 Viewing the autorun Setup Information file icon

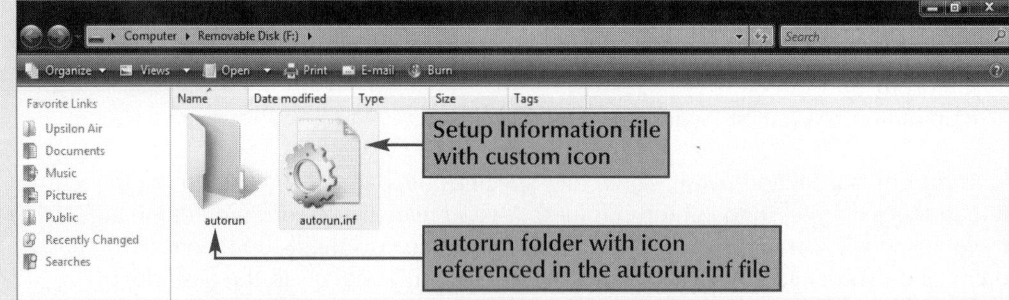

6. Click the **autorun.inf** file icon. Windows Vista opens the file in Notepad.
7. Type **[autorun]** (with the square brackets) on the first line, press the **Enter** key, type **icon=autorun\Upsilon Air.ico** on the second line, and then press the **Enter** key.
8. Compare what you've entered with Figure 4-34, and if necessary, make any corrections.

Figure 4-34 Referencing a custom icon in the autorun.inf file

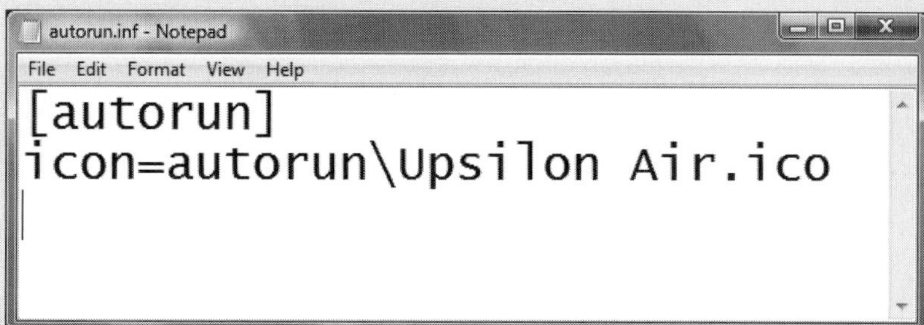

9. Click **File** on the Notepad menu bar, click **Save**, close the Notepad window, and then close the Removable Disk window.

To test your autorun.inf file, you have to remove your flash drive and then reattach it.

To view your flash drive's custom icon:

1. Click the **Safely Remove Hardware icon** in the notification area, click the **drive name for your flash drive**, and after Windows Vista displays a Safe To Remove Hardware dialog box and informs you that this device can be safely removed, remove your flash drive, and then click the **OK** button in the Safe To Remove dialog box.

   Trouble? If Windows Vista informs you that it can't stop your 'Generic volume' device because it is in use, close any programs or windows that might be using the drive, or close any file you might have opened from the flash drive, and then try this step again.

2. Examine the current icon used for your Flash Drive desktop shortcut.
3. Click the **Computer** icon on the desktop.
4. Attach your flash drive, and if necessary, close the AutoPlay dialog box or any other dialog box or window that opens. Windows Vista displays the new custom icon used for your flash drive in the Computer window. See Figure 4-35. However, your Flash Drive desktop shortcut still uses the previous Removable Disk icon.

Figure 4-35 Viewing a flash drive's custom icon

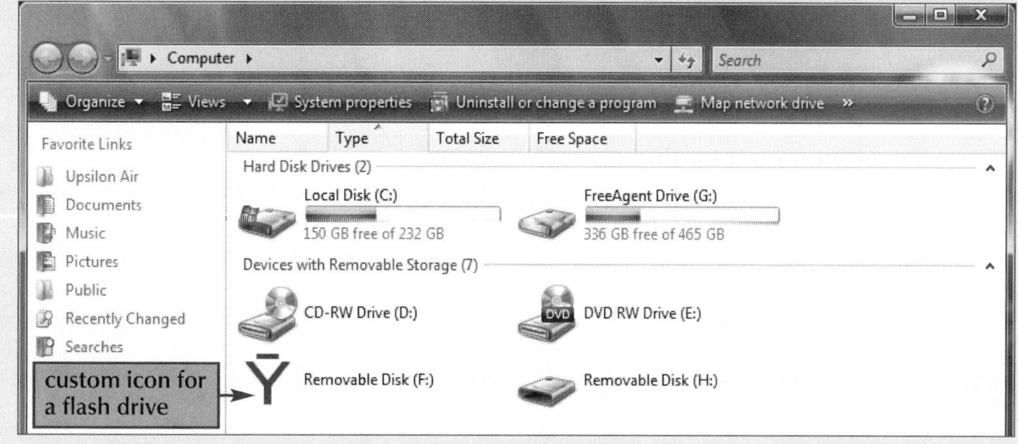

Tip

If you attach your flash drive to another computer, you will see the same custom icon.

5. Close the Computer window.

6. Click the **Flash Drive** shortcut on your desktop. In the Removable Disk window, Windows Vista displays the custom icon for this drive on the left side of the Address Bar, similar to the way Internet Explorer displays custom icons for Web sites.
7. Close the Removable Disk window.

Finally, you want to change the icon for your Flash Drive shortcut so that it matches the icon used for the flash drive icon in the Computer window. If Windows Vista does not automatically update the icon used for your flash drive shortcut, complete the next set of steps.

To change your Flash Drive shortcut's icon:

1. Right-click the **Flash Drive** shortcut icon and then click **Properties**. Windows Vista opens the Flash Drive Properties dialog box.
2. On the Shortcut property sheet, click the **Change Icon** button. Windows Vista opens the Change Icon dialog box and displays the path to the icon in the Upsilon Air.ico file on your flash drive: F:\autorun\Upsilon Air.ico (Your drive name may differ.)
3. Click the **OK** button in the Change Icon dialog box, and then click the **OK** button in the Flash Drive Properties dialog box. Windows Vista updates the icon for the Flash Drive desktop shortcut. See Figure 4-36.

Figure 4-36 Custom flash drive shortcut icon

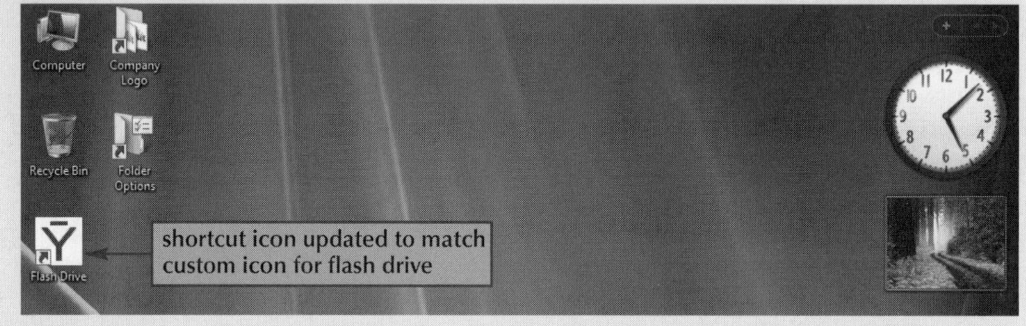

Customizing a Flash Drive Icon | Reference Window

- Locate or create an icon file (with the "ico" file extension) and copy or move the file to the top-level folder of your flash drive.
- Click the Organize button on the command bar, click New Folder, type autorun and then press the Enter key.
- Drag the icon file and drop it onto the autorun folder.
- Right-click the Removable Disk folder background, point to New, click Text Document, and after Windows Vista creates a new file named "New Text Document.txt", type autorun.inf and then use the Delete key to delete the ".txt" file extension. Press the Enter key, and when prompted about changing a file's extension, click the Yes button in the Rename dialog box.
- Click the autorun.inf file icon to open the file for editing.
- Type [autorun] (with the square brackets) on the first line, press the Enter key, type icon=autorun\ followed immediately by the filename of the icon file (for example, icon=autorun\Upsilon Air.ico) on the second line, and then press the Enter key.
- Click File on the Notepad menu bar, click Save, close the Notepad window, and then close the Removable Disk window.
- Click the Safely Remove Hardware icon in the notification area, click the drive name for your flash drive, and after Windows Vista displays a Safe To Remove Hardware dialog box and informs you that this device can be safely removed, remove your flash drive, and then click the OK button in the Safe To Remove dialog box.
- Click the Computer icon on the desktop.
- Attach your flash drive, and if necessary, close the AutoPlay dialog box or any other dialog box or window that opens.
- Close the Computer window.
- If you want to change the icon for a Flash Drive desktop shortcut so that it matches the icon used for the flash drive icon in the Computer window, right-click the Flash Drive shortcut icon, click Properties, click the Change Icon button on the Shortcut property sheet, and after Windows Vista opens the Change Icon dialog box and displays the path to the icon in the Icon File on your flash drive, click the OK button in the Change Icon dialog box, and then click the OK button in the Flash Drive Properties dialog box.

Setup Information files with the "inf" file extension are commonly used by Windows Vista to install device drivers for hardware on your computer, but as you can see, you can also use them to customize drive icons.

Creating Internet Shortcuts

An Internet shortcut is similar to a desktop shortcut, except that the target is the address (or URL) of a Web site. When you visit a Web site with Windows Internet Explorer, you can use the Add to Favorites button to create an Internet shortcut to the current Web site. That Internet shortcut, called a **favorite** (or **bookmark**) is stored in your Favorites folder. When you open Windows Internet Explorer, you can select an Internet shortcut for the Web site you want to visit by using the Favorites button, or if you are already in the Favorites folder or have added the Favorites menu to your Start menu, you can click an Internet shortcut in the Favorites folder or on the Favorites menu to open Windows Internet Explorer and connect your computer to the Web site referenced by the Internet shortcut. You can also copy an Internet shortcut from the Favorites menu or Favorites folder and paste it onto the desktop so that you have a direct link to a Web site you visit regularly. For example, you might have shortcuts on your desktop and flash drive for quickly opening Web pages for your online classes or for opening Web pages posted by your instructor for your in-person class.

If you right-click the background of a Web page (in Internet Explorer), you can create a desktop shortcut to that Web page, or you can drag the icon to the left of the URL in the Address Bar to the desktop or Quick Launch toolbar to create an Internet shortcut.

Even if you regularly use another Web browser, the next set of tutorial steps calls for you to use Windows Internet Explorer. You can adapt what you learn using Internet Explorer to other Web browsers.

Since you frequently check Microsoft's Web site for the latest news on product upgrades and features, as well as for technical troubleshooting information, you decide to create an Internet shortcut to Microsoft's Web site.

Tip

The first time you open Windows Internet Explorer, Windows Vista adds a Launch Internet Explorer Browser shortcut to your Quick Launch toolbar.

To create an Internet shortcut to Microsoft's Web site:

1. Open **Internet Explorer** from the Start menu's pinned items list, the All Programs menu, or the Quick Launch toolbar, and if necessary, maximize the Windows Internet Explorer window.
2. After Windows Internet Explorer displays your home page, maximize the Windows Internet Explorer window, click the **Address Bar icon** to the left of the URL for your home page (this icon may vary depending on your home page), type **microsoft.com**, and press the **Enter** key.
3. After Windows Internet Explorer displays Microsoft's home page, right-click the **background** of the Web page shown in the Windows Internet Explorer browser window. Windows Vista displays a shortcut menu and includes an option for creating a desktop shortcut to this Web site. See Figure 4-37.

   Trouble? If your shortcut menu does not contain a Create Shortcut menu option, you might have right-clicked an object on the background of the Web page. Right-click another part of the background of the Web page and verify that the shortcut menu has a Create Shortcut menu option.

   Trouble? The Mozilla Firefox shortcut menu does not contain an option for creating a desktop shortcut. To create this desktop shortcut, restore down and resize the Mozilla Firefox window so that you can see a portion of the desktop and then drag the icon to the left of the URL in the Address Bar to the desktop. Then continue with Step 5.

Figure 4-37 Viewing the shortcut menu for a Web page

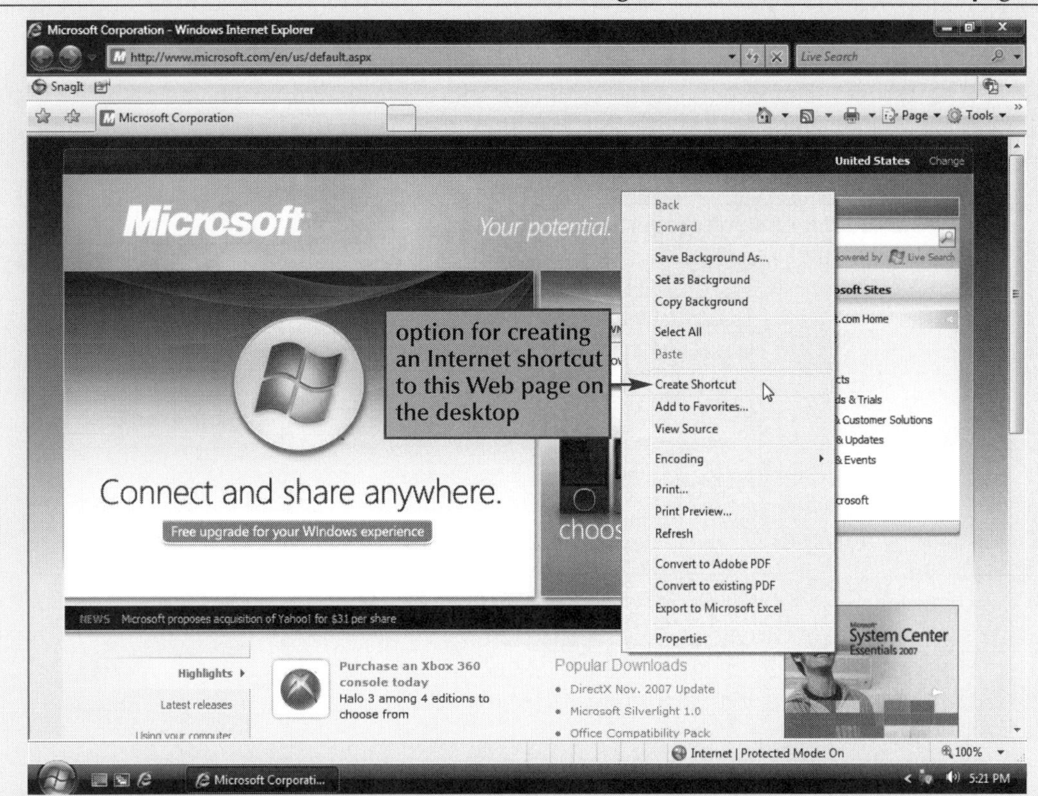

4. Click **Create Shortcut**, and in the Internet Explorer dialog box that gives you the choice of placing the shortcut on the desktop, click the **Yes** button.
5. Close the Windows Internet Explorer window. On your desktop, you now have an Internet shortcut labeled "Microsoft Corporation." See Figure 4-38. Your Internet shortcut name may differ.

Figure 4-38 Microsoft Corporation Internet shortcut

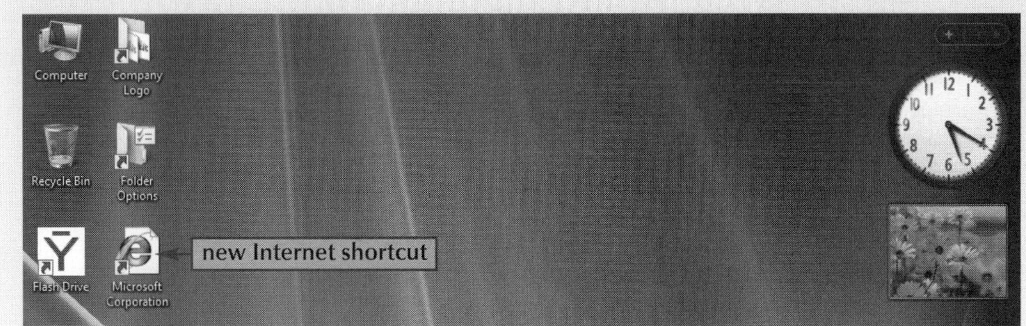

Tip

You can drag the icon to the left of the URL in the Address Bar to the desktop to create an Internet shortcut.

6. Click the **Microsoft Corporation** Internet shortcut. Windows Internet Explorer (or your default Web browser) displays Microsoft's home page.
7. Close the Windows Internet Explorer window.

Next, view properties of the Microsoft Corporation Internet shortcut so that you can compare it to other desktop shortcuts.

To view properties of an Internet shortcut:

1. Right-click the **Microsoft Corporation** Internet shortcut and then click **Properties**. Windows Vista opens the Microsoft Corporation Properties dialog box. See Figure 4-39. Your dialog box name may differ. On the Web Document property sheet, the URL box contains the complete address for Microsoft's home page. Notice that you have the option of changing the icon for the Internet shortcut, and you can specify a keyboard shortcut.

Figure 4-39 Viewing the Web document properties of an Internet shortcut

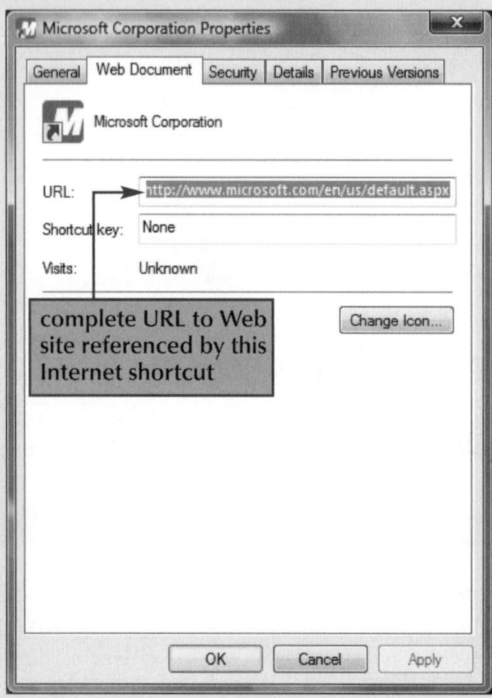

2. Click the **General** tab. On the General property sheet, Windows Vista shows the type of file (Internet Shortcut), the location of the shortcut (the Desktop folder for your logon account under the Users folder), and other details about the shortcut. See Figure 4-40. As shown on this property sheet, the file extension for an Internet shortcut is "url". Notice that Internet shortcuts, like regular desktop shortcuts, are relatively small in size and use a disproportionate amount of storage space on disk relative to their size.

Figure 4-40 Viewing General properties of an Internet shortcut

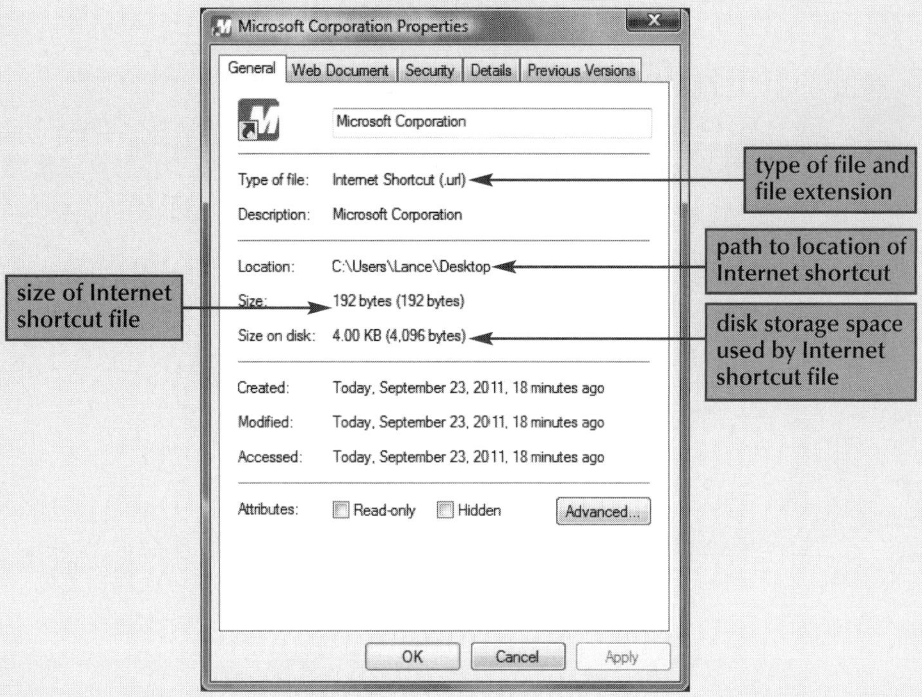

3. Click the **Details** tab. Under the General section, you see the full URL to this Web site.
4. Close the Microsoft Corporation Properties dialog box.

The filename of the Microsoft Corporation Internet shortcut is "Microsoft Corporation.url" and its short filename is most likely MICROS~1.URL

If you browse to a Web site and notice a link to another Web page or Web site, you can drag that link to your desktop to create an Internet shortcut to that Web page or Web site. This feature is useful if you don't have time to visit that Web page or Web site and add it to your Favorites list.

You notice a link of interest to you on Microsoft's Web page and want to create a shortcut to the Web page referenced by that link.

To create a shortcut to a link on a Web page:

1. Click the **Microsoft Corporation** Internet shortcut.
2. Use the **Restore Down** button to restore your Windows Internet Explorer window so that it does not cover the desktop, and if necessary, resize or move the Windows Internet Explorer window so that you can see enough of the left side of the desktop to create a shortcut.
3. Locate a link of interest to you on Microsoft's home page, drag that link to the desktop, and when Windows Internet Explorer displays an Internet Explorer dialog box that asks you if you want to move or copy files from this zone, click the **Yes** button. Windows Vista creates an Internet shortcut to the Web site referenced by the Web page link. See Figure 4-41. On the computer used for this figure, Windows Vista created an Internet shortcut to the Microsoft's Support Web page—a useful Web site when you need to locate information on troubleshooting a problem with Windows Vista.

Figure 4-41 Creating an Internet shortcut using a Web page link

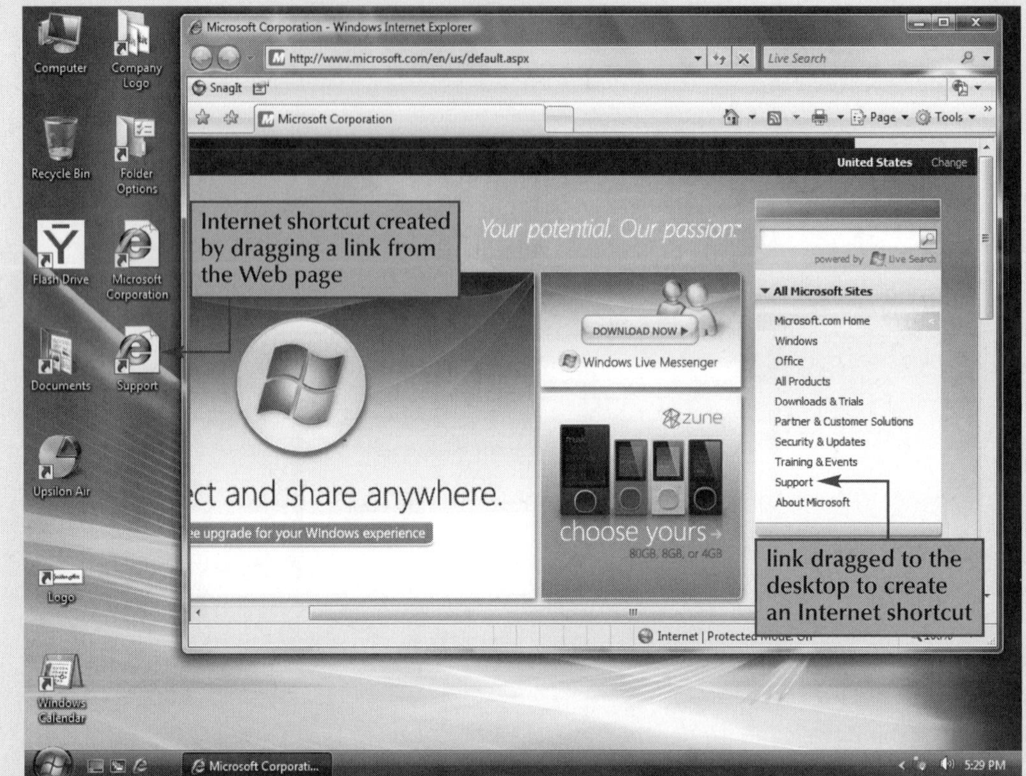

4. Close the Windows Internet Explorer window.
5. Click the new Internet shortcut that references a link to another Web page. Windows Vista opens Windows Internet Explorer and then displays the Web page referenced by the Internet shortcut.
6. If necessary, move the Windows Internet Explorer window so that you can view your Microsoft Corporation Internet shortcut on the desktop.
7. Drag the Microsoft Corporation Internet shortcut and drop it in the Windows Internet Explorer window. Windows Internet Explorer navigates to the Web page referenced by the URL in the Microsoft Corporation Internet shortcut and takes you to Microsoft Corporation's home page.
8. Close the Windows Internet Explorer window.

Dragging Web page links to the desktop is a quick and easy way to create Internet shortcuts to other Web sites that you might want to visit in the future without having to navigate to those Web sites.

Using Internet Shortcuts in Different Web Browsers | InSight

If you work with more than one Web browser on your computer or different computers at various locations, you can use the same Internet shortcuts in different Web browsers. For example, if you open the Mozilla Firefox Web browser and drag a Windows Internet Explorer shortcut and drop it in the Mozilla Firefox window, the Mozilla Firefox Web browser navigates to the site referenced by the URL in the Windows Internet Explorer shortcut. Likewise, you can drag a Mozilla Firefox Internet shortcut and drop it in a Windows Internet Explorer window, and Internet Explorer navigates to the site referenced by the URL in the Mozilla Firefox Internet shortcut.

Creating an Internet Shortcut on the Desktop | Reference Window

- Open Windows Internet Explorer and locate the Web site for which you want to create an Internet shortcut.
- Right-click the background of the Web page, click Create Shortcut on the shortcut menu, and then click the Yes button in the Internet Explorer dialog box to indicate that you want to put the shortcut on your desktop.
- To create an Internet shortcut from a link on a Web page, drag the link to the desktop.
- Close your Web browser.

You can copy your Internet shortcuts to a flash drive and carry them with you wherever you go so that you can quickly access Web sites that you frequently visit using whatever computer and Web browser is available. You might also want to post your bookmarks or access already posted bookmarks from online sites that offer this service.

Creating E-mail Shortcuts

If you use Microsoft Office Outlook or the new Windows Mail in Windows Vista, you can create desktop shortcuts for composing new e-mail messages and automatically include one or more of the following items:

- One or more e-mail addresses in the TO box
- One or more e-mail addresses in the Cc (or carbon copy) box
- One or more e-mail addresses in the Bcc (or blind carbon copy) box
- A Subject line
- One or more lines of text in the body of the e-mail message

Also, instead of specifying individual e-mail addresses, you can specify a group list that contains the e-mail addresses of a group of individuals or businesses with a common interest.

You can use the Create Shortcut Wizard to create any type of shortcut, including an e-mail shortcut. When you create an e-mail shortcut, you use the following format for specifying the contents of the e-mail message:

mailto:E-mail Address**?Cc=**E-mail Address(es)***&Bcc=***E-mail Address(es)***&subject=***Text***&body=***Text

The e-mail shortcut must start with *mailto:* or with *mailto:*E-mail Address. If you want to specify any additional options, such as a Cc, Bcc, Subject, or text in the body of the message, you follow mailto: E-mail Address with a question mark (?), and then specify one or more additional options. You separate each additional option by an ampersand (**&**). To specify a Cc and/or a Bcc, you type *Cc*= or *Bcc*= followed by one or more e-mail addresses separated by commas. To specify a Subject or text in the body of the message, you type *subject*= or *body*= followed by a subject line and/or the text of the message. These additional options can be in any order that you want, but each option must be separated from the next option by an ampersand (&), as noted earlier. For the body of a message, you more than likely will use a standard opening or standard text that you typically include in an e-mail message. Whatever you specify for an e-mail shortcut cannot exceed 255 characters.

You decide to start by creating a simple generic e-mail shortcut.

The remaining steps in this section of the tutorial require that you have Microsoft Office Outlook or Windows Mail installed on your computer and that you already have set up an e-mail account in one of these e-mail software products. If you do not have any of these e-mail software products installed on your computer, read, but do not keystroke, the following steps so that you are familiar with the process for creating e-mail shortcuts. Although you might not have access to Microsoft Office Outlook or Windows Mail on the computers in your computer lab or on your home computer, your current employer or a future employer might rely on Microsoft Office, so you should be familiar with the process for creating e-mail shortcuts. The figures for this section of the tutorial assume that Microsoft Office Outlook is the default e-mail program.

Also, you will be creating e-mail shortcuts addressed to one or more fictional persons with fictional e-mail addresses working at a fictional company. You do not want to attempt to send these e-mail messages, but rather view and benefit from the techniques for creating e-mail shortcuts.

To create a simple e-mail shortcut:

1. Right-click the **desktop background**, point to **New** on the shortcut menu, and then click **Shortcut**. Windows Vista opens the Create Shortcut Wizard. See Figure 4-42. The wizard notes that you can create shortcuts to local or network programs, files, folders, computers, or Internet addresses.

Figure 4-42 Using the Create Shortcut Wizard

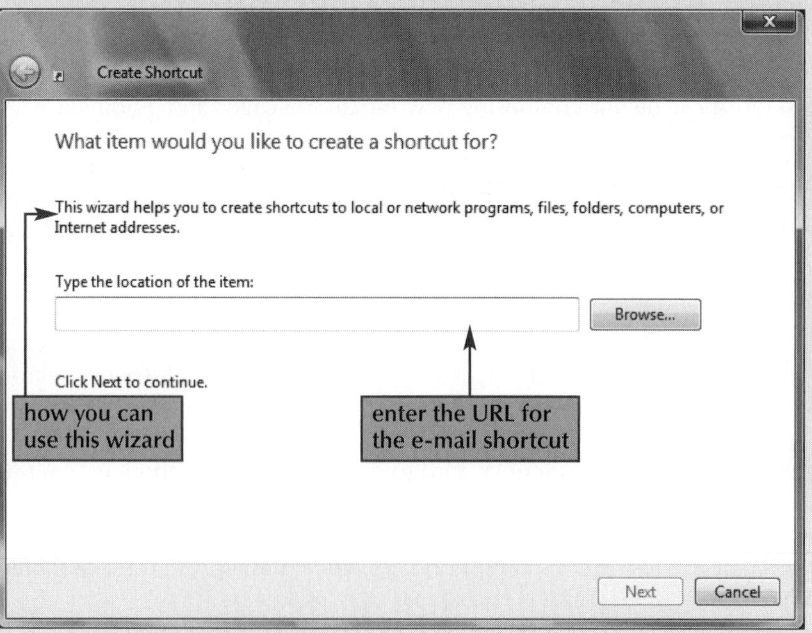

2. In the "Type the location of the item" box, type **mailto:** (you must type mailto without any spaces and the colon after "mailto"), and then click the **Next** button. The Create Shortcut Wizard now prompts you for a name for this shortcut.

3. Type **New E-mail Message** and then click the **Finish** button. Windows Vista creates an e-mail message shortcut. See Figure 4-43. The e-mail message shortcut icon in this figure is a Microsoft Outlook icon because Microsoft Outlook is installed as the default e-mail program on the computer used for this figure. If you are using Windows Mail instead, your e-mail shortcut uses the Windows Mail icon shown in Figure 4-44.

Figure 4-43 Newly created Microsoft Outlook e-mail shortcut

Figure 4-44 Newly created Windows Mail e-mail shortcut

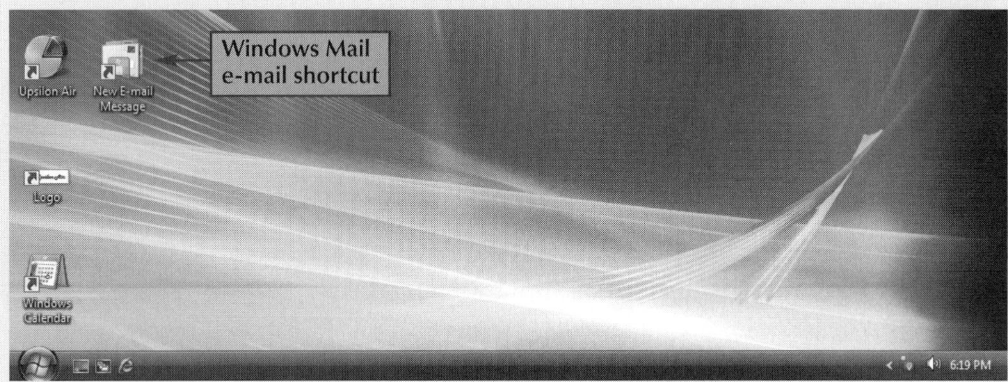

4. Click the **New E-mail Message** shortcut. On the computer used for the figure, Windows Vista opens a Microsoft Outlook window entitled "Untitled – Message (HTML)" and you are ready to compose a new e-mail message. See Figure 4-45.

Figure 4-45 New e-mail message opened from an e-mail shortcut

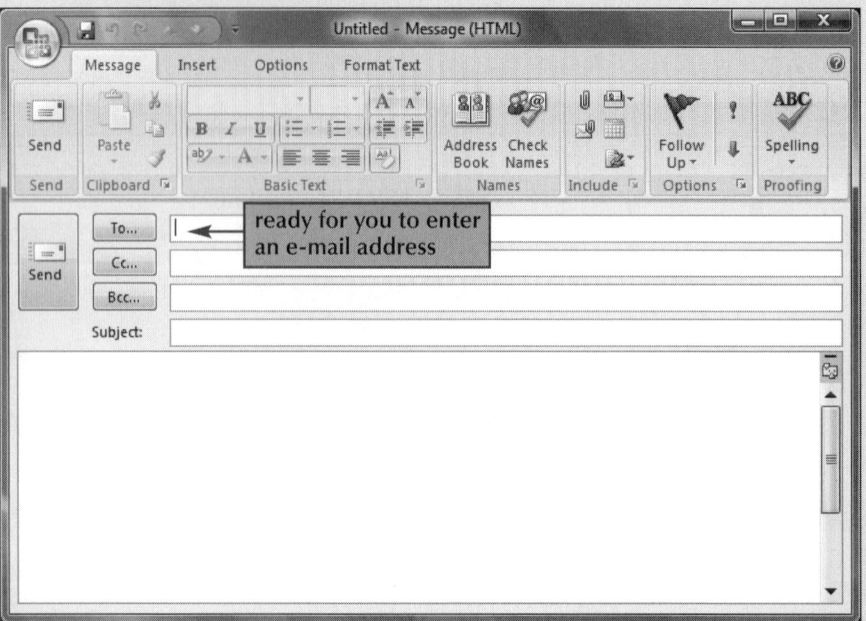

5. Close the e-mail message window, and when prompted to save changes, click the **No** button.

This type of e-mail shortcut saves you multiple steps when you want to open your e-mail software and compose a new e-mail message.

Now, you want to examine the properties of the e-mail shortcut.

To view properties of an e-mail shortcut:

1. Right-click the **New E-mail Message** shortcut and then click **Properties**. Windows Vista opens the New E-mail Message Properties dialog box. In the URL box on the Web Document property sheet, Windows Vista displays the e-mail URL that you typed when you created the e-mail shortcut. See Figure 4-46.

Figure 4-46 Viewing the URL for an e-mail shortcut

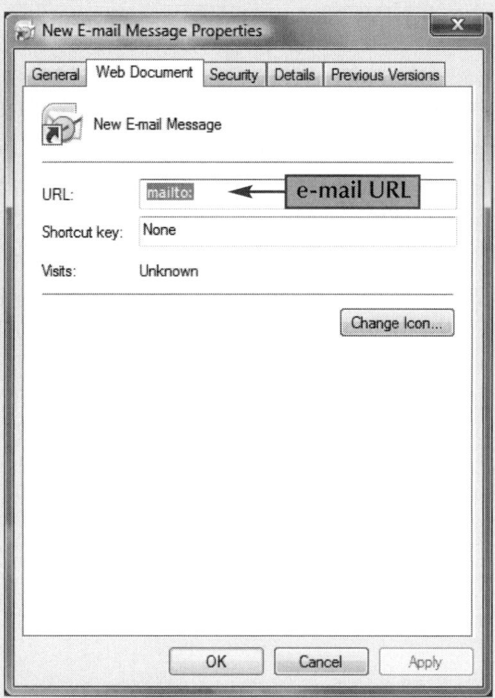

2. Click the **General** tab. Windows Vista identifies this object as an Internet shortcut with the "url" file extension. See Figure 4-47.

Figure 4-47 Viewing General properties of an e-mail shortcut

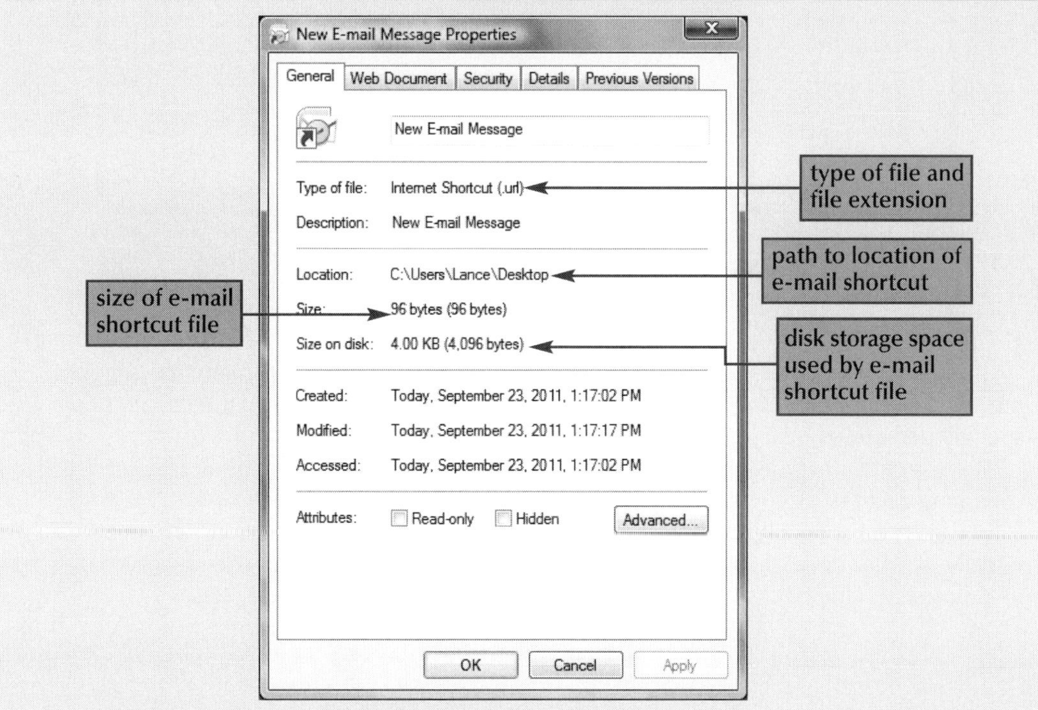

3. Close the New E-mail Message Properties dialog box.

You can open the Properties dialog box for an e-mail shortcut if you need to check or correct the URL for an e-mail shortcut.

Next, create a new e-mail shortcut and designate a recipient's e-mail address.

To create an e-mail shortcut with a recipient's e-mail address:

1. Right-click the **desktop background**, point to **New** on the shortcut menu, click **Shortcut**, type **mailto:LanceQuattrone@upsilonair.com** (with no spaces), click the **Next** button, type **Lance**, and then click the **Finish** button. Windows Vista creates another e-mail message shortcut.
2. Click the **Lance** e-mail shortcut. On the computer used for the figure, Windows Vista opens a new e-mail message in Microsoft Outlook and inserts Lance Quattrone's e-mail address in the To box. See Figure 4-48.

Figure 4-48 Preaddressed new e-mail message

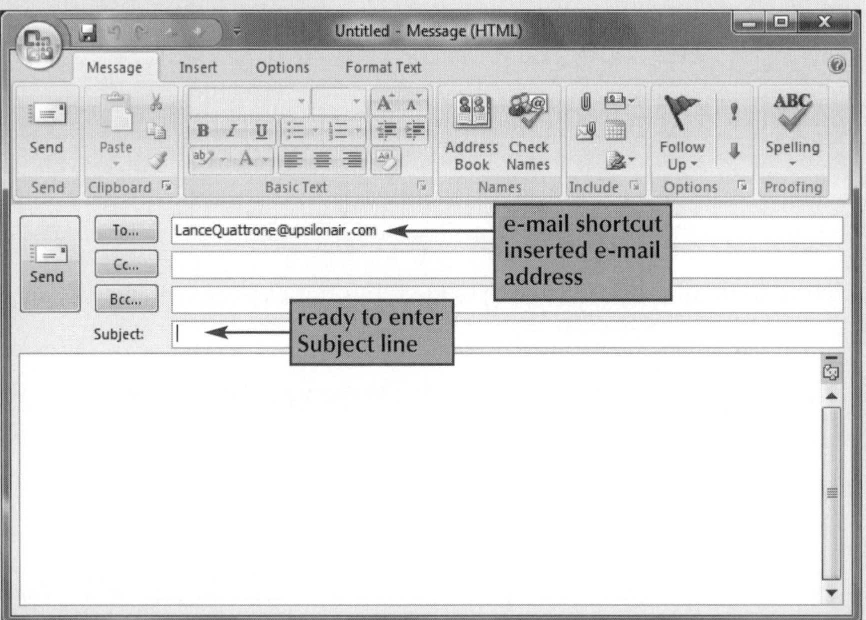

3. Close the e-mail message window, and when prompted to save changes, click the **No** button.

This type of preaddressed e-mail shortcut is useful when you send many messages to the same person (or to the same group). Instead of addressing the e-mail message to a specific person, you can specify a mailing list or mailing group.

Next, create a new e-mail shortcut and designate a recipient's e-mail address and a Cc e-mail address.

Because you are going to address an e-mail message to a fictional person with a fictional e-mail address working at a fictional company and specify a carbon copy for another fictional person in the next set of steps, you do not want to send the e-mail message.

To create an e-mail shortcut with an e-mail address for a recipient and a carbon copy to another person:

1. Right-click the **desktop background**, point to **New** on the shortcut menu, click **Shortcut**, type **mailto:LanceQuattrone@upsilonair.com?Cc=annmarieparker@upsilonair.com** (with no spaces), click the **Next** button, type **Lance & Ann Marie**, and then click the **Finish** button. Windows Vista creates another customized e-mail message shortcut.
2. Click the **Lance & Ann Marie** e-mail shortcut. On the computer used for the figure, Windows Vista opens a new e-mail message in Microsoft Outlook, inserts Lance Quattrone's e-mail address in the To box, and inserts Ann Marie Parker's e-mail address in the Cc box. See Figure 4-49.

   Trouble? If your e-mail shortcut does not work properly, close the e-mail message window without saving, right-click the e-mail shortcut, click Properties, correct the URL for the e-mail message so that it matches what is shown in the previous step, click the OK button to close the Properties dialog box for this e-mail message, and then try this step again.

Figure 4-49 Preaddressed e-mail message with To and CC addresses

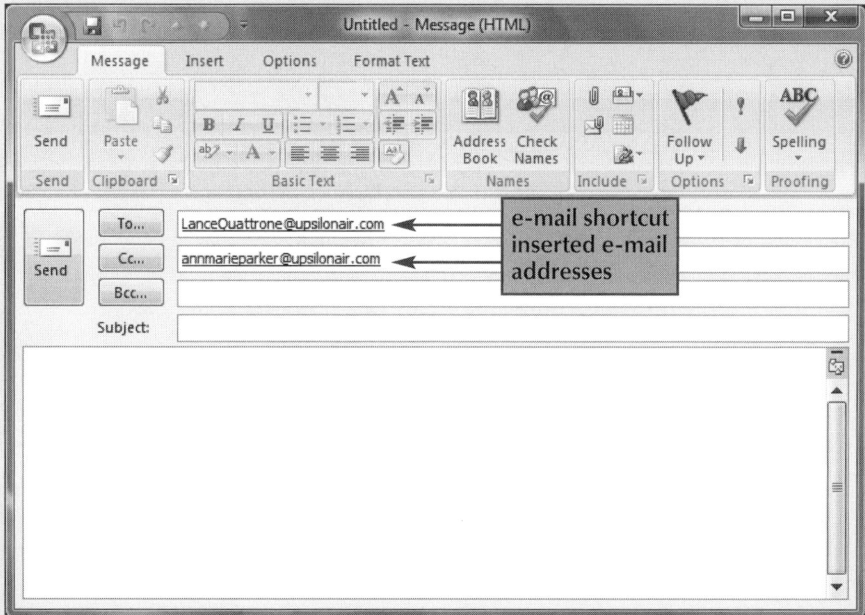

3. Close the e-mail message window, and when prompted to save changes, click the **No** button.

Next, create a new e-mail shortcut and designate a recipient's e-mail address and a subject. For the subject line, you will use "Quick Reminder." Since this subject contains a space, you must replace the space with the URL-encoded hexadecimal code %20 for the space character so that your subject line reads "Quick%20Reminder." **URL encoding** includes a % symbol before the hexadecimal code for the character and allows you to specify a character, such as a space, that is not allowed in a URL. Also, after entering a URL in the Address Bar of a Web browser, you may have noticed that the URL sometimes changes to include %20 for a space.

To create an e-mail shortcut with an e-mail address for a recipient and a subject line:

1. Right-click the **desktop background**, point to **New** on the shortcut menu, click **Shortcut**, type **mailto:LanceQuattrone@upsilonair.com?subject=Quick%20 Reminder** (with no spaces), click the **Next** button, type **Quick Reminder**, and then click the **Finish** button. Windows Vista creates another customized e-mail message shortcut.
2. Click the **Quick Reminder** e-mail shortcut. On the computer used for the figure, Windows Vista opens a new e-mail message in Microsoft Outlook, inserts Lance Quattrone's e-mail address in the To box, and inserts Quick Reminder in the Subject box. See Figure 4-50.

   Trouble? If your e-mail shortcut does not work properly, close the e-mail message window, right-click the e-mail shortcut, click Properties, correct the URL for the e-mail message so that it matches what is shown in the previous step, click OK to close the Properties dialog box for this e-mail message, and then try this step again.

Figure 4-50 New e-mail message with To e-mail address and subject

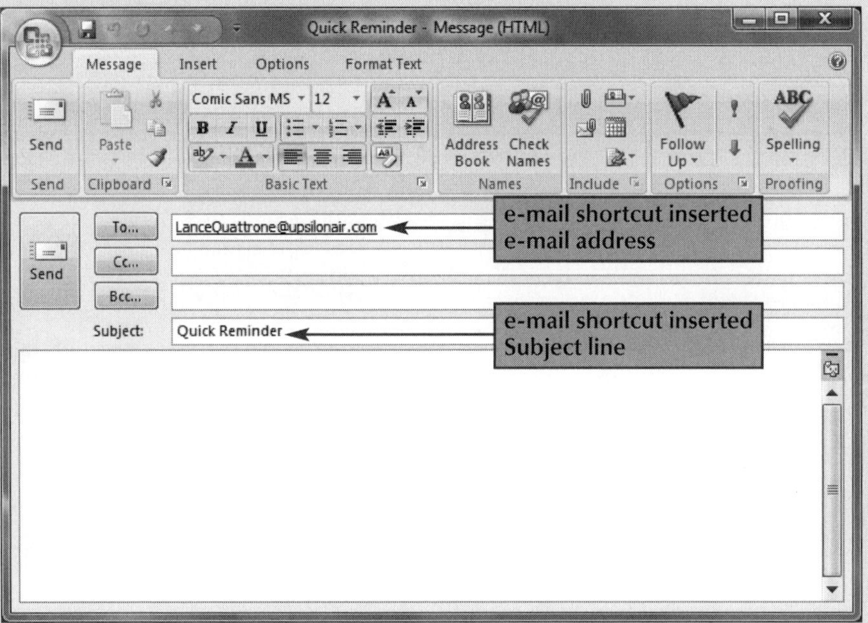

3. Close the e-mail message window, and when prompted to save changes, click the **No** button.

By including a subject line in the e-mail shortcut, you guarantee that the e-mail message uses the specific subject you want, plus it saves you one more step in preparing e-mail messages that require the same subject line.

Next, create a new e-mail shortcut and designate a recipient's e-mail address, subject, and text in the body of the message. If you want to include text on multiple lines in the body of the message, you must use the URL-encoded hexadecimal codes %0D%0A (where 0D is the hexadecimal code for a carriage return and 0A is the hexadecimal code for a line feed) to separate lines of text. You will also have to use the URL-encoded hexadecimal code %20 wherever a space occurs in the subject and the body of the text.

To create an e-mail shortcut with a recipient's e-mail address, a subject line, and text in the body of the e-mail message:

1. Right-click the **desktop background**, point to **New** on the shortcut menu, click **Shortcut**, type **mailto:LanceQuattrone@upsilonair.com?subject=Quick%20 Reminder&body= Weekly%20Meeting%0D%0A%0D%0AFriday,%203%20PM** (all on one line with no spaces), click the **Next** button, type **Weekly Meeting**, and then click the **Finish** button. Windows Vista creates another customized e-mail message shortcut.
2. Click the **Weekly Meeting** e-mail shortcut. On the computer used for the figure, Windows Vista opens a new e-mail message in Microsoft Outlook, inserts Lance Quattrone's e-mail address in the To box, inserts "Quick Reminder" as the subject of the e-mail message in the Subject box, and inserts one line with "Weekly Meeting" followed by a blank line and then a line with "Friday, 3 PM" in the body of the message. See Figure 4-51.

   Trouble? If your e-mail shortcut does not work properly, close the e-mail message window, right-click the e-mail shortcut, click Properties, correct the URL for the e-mail message so that it matches what is shown in the previous step, click OK to close the Properties dialog box for this e-mail message, and then try this step again.

Figure 4-51 Preaddressed e-mail message with subject and text

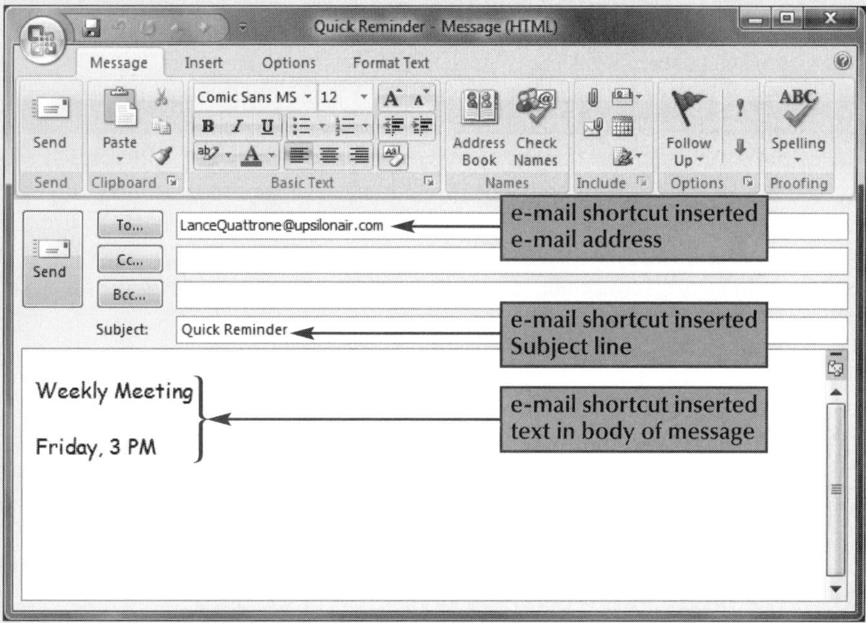

3. Close the e-mail message window, and when prompted to save changes, click the **No** button.

This type of e-mail shortcut is useful when you have to send e-mail messages on the same topic, such as a regularly scheduled meeting or a project. While setting up an e-mail message with text in the body of the message involves more attention to detail and the use of hexadecimal codes for spaces and blank lines, once you create, test, and correct any problems with this type of shortcut, you can save yourself time and effort later in composing new e-mail messages.

Reference Window | Creating E-mail Shortcuts

- To create a generic e-mail shortcut for composing a new e-mail message, right-click the desktop, point to New, click Shortcut, and in the Create Shortcut dialog box, type mailto: (including the colon), click the Next button, type a name for your e-mail shortcut, and then click the Finish button.
- To create an e-mail shortcut for composing a new e-mail message with a recipient's e-mail address, right-click the desktop, point to New, click Shortcut, and in the Create Shortcut dialog box, type mailto: (including the colon) followed immediately by the e-mail address of a person, click the Next button, type a name for your e-mail shortcut, and then click the Finish button.
- To create an e-mail shortcut for composing a new e-mail message with a recipient's e-mail address and a Cc e-mail address, right-click the desktop, point to New, click Shortcut, and in the Create Shortcut dialog box, type mailto: (including the colon) followed immediately by the recipient's e-mail address, followed by ?Cc= and then the Cc e-mail address. Click the Next button, type a name for your e-mail shortcut, and then click the Finish button.
- To create an e-mail shortcut for composing a new e-mail message with a recipient's e-mail address and subject line, right-click the desktop, point to New, click Shortcut, and in the Create Shortcut dialog box, type mailto: (including the colon) followed immediately by the recipient's e-mail address, followed immediately by ?subject= and then the text of the Subject line (you must replace any spaces with %20). Click the Next button, type a name for your e-mail shortcut, and then click the Finish button.
- To create an e-mail shortcut for composing a new e-mail message with a recipient's e-mail address, subject line, and text in the body of the e-mail message, right-click the desktop, point to New, click Shortcut, and in the Create Shortcut dialog box, type mailto: (including the colon) followed immediately by the recipient's e-mail address, followed immediately by ?subject= and the text of the Subject line (you must replace any spaces with %20), followed immediately by &body= and the text for the body of the e-mail message (you must replace any spaces with %20, and you must use %0D%0A for each new line you want to insert between lines of text). Click the Next button, type a name for your e-mail shortcut, and then click the Finish button.

E-mail shortcuts are yet another way to customize the use of Windows Vista and your computer system. If a course calls for you to periodically contact your instructor or to submit assignments via e-mail, you can create e-mail shortcuts with your instructor's address and a subject line formatted in accordance with class submission guidelines.

Customizing Startup with Shortcuts

If you place desktop shortcuts, Internet shortcuts, or e-mail shortcuts in the Startup folder for your user account, Windows Vista will automatically open the drives, folders, files, dialog boxes, Web sites, and preaddressed e-mail messages referenced by those shortcuts. The use of the Startup folder therefore represents one more way in which you can customize the use of your computer.

Effectively Using the Startup Folder | InSight

If you use the same program or programs, the same folders, or the same files every workday, you can place shortcuts to those programs, folders, and files in the Startup folder, and Windows Vista will open them immediately upon displaying the desktop. Likewise, if you check e-mail the first thing every day, or visit a specific Web site every day (such as a news Web site), you can place Internet shortcuts in the Startup folder and Windows Vista opens those Web sites immediately after displaying your desktop. In some cases, software you install on your computer places program shortcuts in the Startup folder so that specific programs automatically open after you power on your computer and perform a full boot, but not after you wake your computer from Sleep or Hibernation. You can check the Startup folder for these types of programs and decide whether you want them to automatically start them each time you start up your computer.

When you place shortcuts in your personal Startup folder, you can copy or move existing shortcuts you have on your desktop, Quick Launch toolbar, Start Menu, and Favorites folder, or you can use the Create Shortcut Wizard to create the shortcuts from scratch.

Lance suggests that you place a copy of the Windows Calendar shortcut in your Startup folder.

To copy the Windows Calendar shortcut to your Startup folder:

1. Right-click the **Windows Calendar** shortcut, and then click **Copy**.
2. Right-click the **Start** button and then click **Open**. Windows Vista opens the Start Menu folder and displays the Programs folder. Your view might differ.
3. Open the **Programs** folder. Windows Vista displays group folders found on the All Programs menu, such as Accessories, Maintenance, and Startup, as well as program shortcuts, such as Internet Explorer, Windows Mail, and Windows Media Player.
4. Open the **Startup** folder, right-click the **folder background**, and then click **Paste**. Windows Vista places a copy of your Windows Calendar shortcut in this folder. See Figure 4-52.

Figure 4-52 Windows Calendar shortcut in Startup folder

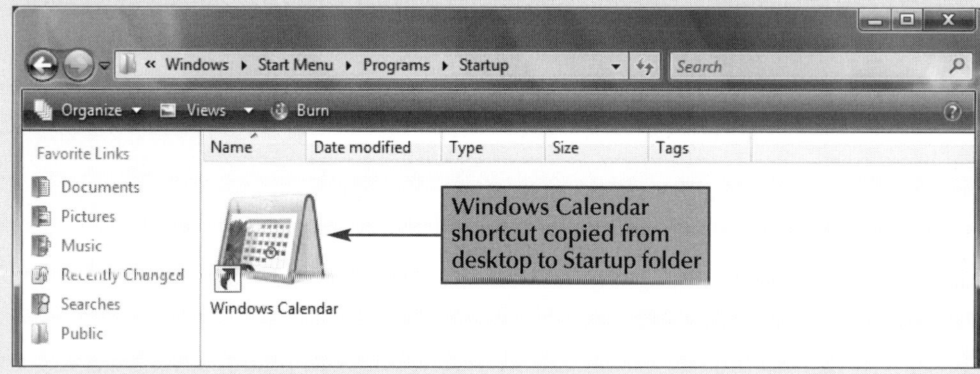

5. If you are working on your own computer and want to reboot your computer so that you can see how Windows Vista opens Windows Calendar after your computer starts up, close the Startup folder window, and then choose the Start Menu option to restart your computer. If you are working on your own computer and want to remove the Windows Calendar from your Startup folder, right-click the **Windows Calendar** shortcut, click **Delete** on the shortcut menu, and in the Delete Shortcut dialog box, click the **Yes** button, and then close the Startup folder window. If you are working on a computer in your college's computer lab and have permission not only to place shortcuts in this folder but also to reboot your computer, close the Startup folder window and choose the Start Menu option to restart your computer.
6. If you are working on a computer in a college computer lab whose lab policy does not permit you to reboot your computer, or if your college's computers restore their original settings after a reboot, right-click the **Windows Calendar** shortcut, click **Delete** on the shortcut menu, and in the Delete Shortcut dialog box, click the **Yes** button, and then close the Startup folder window.

By placing important shortcuts in your Startup folder, you can maximize the performance of your computer, have what you need at your fingertips when your computer starts, and be ready to work at a moment's notice.

Reference Window | Adding Shortcuts to Your Startup Folder

- Locate and right-click the shortcut that you want to add to your Startup folder, and then click Copy.
- Right-click the Start button and then click Open.
- In the Start Menu folder, open the Programs folder.
- In the Programs folder, open the Startup folder, right-click the folder background, and then click Paste.
- To remove a shortcut from the Startup folder, right-click the Start button, click Open, click Programs, click Startup, right-click the shortcut, click Delete, and in the Delete Shortcut dialog box, click the Yes button.

Shortcuts unlock the power of Windows Vista by bypassing many of the intermediate steps that you would otherwise perform as you work on your computer, and by taking you directly to what you need to use, whether it's on your computer, another computer, or the World Wide Web.

Restoring Your Computer's Settings

If you are working in a computer lab, or if you want to restore your desktop computer to the settings that existed prior to working on this tutorial, complete the following steps.

To restore your computer:

1. Click the **Start** button, right-click **Windows Photo Gallery** in the pinned items list, and then click **Unpin from Start Menu**.
2. Click the **Start** button, right-click **Upsilon Air** in the pinned items list, and then click **Remove from this list**.
3. Click the **Upsilon Air** desktop shortcut, right-click **Upsilon Air** under Favorite Links, click **Remove Link**, and then click the **Yes** button.

4. Click **Public Documents** in the Address Bar, right-click the **Upsilon Air** folder, click **Delete**, click the **Yes** button in the Delete Folder dialog box, and then close the Public Documents folder window.
5. If you want to remove the custom icon for your flash drive, click the **Flash Drive** shortcut, hold down the **Ctrl** key, point to the **autorun** folder and then to the **autorun.inf** file, press the **Delete** key, click the **Yes** button in the Delete Multiple Items dialog box, and then close your flash drive window.
6. Hold down the **Ctrl** key while you point to each of the desktop shortcuts that you want to delete, press the **Delete** key, and click the **Yes** button in the Delete Multiple Items dialog box.
7. To restore double-click activation, click the **Computer** icon on the desktop, click the **Organize** button on the command bar, click **Folder and Search Options**, and on the General property sheet in the Folder Options dialog box, click the **Double-click to open an item (single-click to select)** option button.
8. To hide extensions for known file types, click the **View** tab in the Folder Options dialog box, click the **Hide extensions for known file types** check box if it does not contain a check mark, click the **OK** button to close the Folder Options dialog box and apply these changes, and then close the Computer window.

Session 4.2 Quick Check | Review

1. An Internet shortcut is similar to a desktop shortcut, except that its target is ________________ .
2. Windows Internet Explorer stores Internet shortcuts as ________________ in your ________________ folder.
3. True or False. You can create an Internet shortcut by dragging a link on a Web page to the desktop.
4. What Windows folder contains shortcuts for the Favorite Links in the Navigation Pane?
5. True or False. If you delete a folder, file, or shortcut on your flash drive, the Windows Undo feature can restore the folder, file, or shortcut from the Recycle Bin.
6. What file extension does Windows use for a Setup Information file?

Review | Tutorial Summary

In this tutorial, you created desktop shortcuts to drives, folders, and files, and then you viewed properties of, and in some cases, customized these shortcuts. You also created shortcuts to applications and programs, created a shortcut from an existing shortcut by modifying its path, and examined how Windows Vista updates the path of a shortcut when you rename the file and when you move the file to another location. You added shortcuts to the Start menu's pinned items list, you created a Control Panel shortcut, and you created a link to a folder in the Navigation Pane. You visited a Web site, created a desktop Internet shortcut to that Web site, and dragged a link on a Web page to create an Internet shortcut to yet another Web page. You then dragged a shortcut into the Windows Internet Explorer window to navigate to that Web site. You customized the icon for a flash drive, and you used the Create Shortcut Wizard to create a variety of e-mail shortcuts for automating the process of sending e-mail messages.

Key Terms

&
autorun
backup
backup software
bookmark
collection
dynamic library file (dll)
environment variable
favorite
Navigation Pane
shortcut
UNC path
URL encoding
Windows environment

Practice | Review Assignments

Practice the skills you learned in the tutorial.

For a list of Data Files in the Review folder, see page 209.

Lance recently hired another advertising associate, Elsa Vandenberg, to help him with client projects. On her first day of work, Lance explains to Elsa how he works with Windows Vista and describes the types of support that they must provide for other employees. Since time seems to always be at a premium, Lance asks you to create shortcuts to the drives, applications, folders, and files that Elsa will be using on a daily basis.

Use a word processing application, such as Word or WordPad, to prepare your answers to questions in the following steps. Also, if you change any settings on the computer you are using, note the original settings so that you can restore them later. If you are using another browser, adapt the instructions to that browser.

1. Copy the Review folder under the Tutorial.04 folder to the Public Documents folder, and then change the name of the Review folder to Upsilon Air.
2. Open the Computer window and then adjust the size and placement of the window so that you can also see part of the desktop.
3. Create a desktop shortcut to your DVD or CD drive. Which drive did you use to create a shortcut? What type of icon does Windows Vista use for the shortcut? Change the shortcut name to DVD Drive or CD Drive. Open the Properties dialog box for the DVD Drive or CD Drive. What is the target's type? What is the shortcut's target? What file extension does this shortcut have? What is the full filename of the shortcut (including the file extension)? What is the size of the shortcut? How much disk storage space does the shortcut use? How much storage space does the shortcut waste on disk? Who is the owner of this shortcut? What is the name of the computer where this shortcut is located? Close the DVD Drive or CD Drive Properties dialog box. Close the Computer window.
4. If you created a DVD Drive shortcut, insert a DVD disc with data in the DVD drive and close the AutoPlay dialog box and any other window or dialog that opens. If you created a CD Drive shortcut, insert a CD disc with data in the CD drive and close the AutoPlay dialog box and any other window or dialog box that opens. What happens when you click the DVD Drive or CD Drive shortcut? Close the window opened by the DVD Drive or CD Drive shortcut.
5. For what other types of drives on your computer might you want to create desktop shortcuts? Explain.
6. Create a shortcut to the Control Panel on the desktop. Change the name of the new shortcut to **Control Panel** and remove the "- Shortcut" label. What type of icon does Windows Vista use for the Control Panel shortcut? What happens when you click the shortcut? Close the window opened by the Control Panel shortcut.
7. Open the Properties dialog box for the Control Panel shortcut. What is the target's type? What is the shortcut's target? What file extension does this shortcut have? What is the full filename of the shortcut (including the file extension)? What is the size of the shortcut? How much disk storage space does the shortcut use? How much storage space does the shortcut waste on disk? Close the Control Panel Properties dialog box.
8. Open the Public Documents folder, open the Upsilon Air folder, and then create a shortcut to the Sales Analyses folder within the Upsilon Air folder. What is the name of the new shortcut? Describe the appearance of the Sales Analyses shortcut icon. Change the name of the shortcut to **Sales Analyses**. Because Windows Vista does not permit two objects in a folder window to have the same name, how can you have a Sales Analyses folder and a Sales Analyses shortcut in the Upsilon Air folder?

9. Drag the Sales Analyses shortcut to the desktop and then close the Upsilon Air folder window. Did Windows Vista move or copy the Sales Analyses shortcut? Explain.
10. Open the Properties dialog box for the Sales Analyses shortcut. What is the target's type? What is the shortcut's target? What file extension does this shortcut have? What is the full filename of the shortcut (including the file extension)? What is the size of the shortcut? How much disk storage space does the shortcut use? How much storage space does the shortcut waste on disk?
11. From the Shortcut property sheet, choose the option for changing the icon used for the shortcut, browse to and open the Pifmgr.dll file, choose one of the icons contained in this icon library file, apply the changes to your computer, and then close the Sales Analyses Properties dialog box. Refresh the desktop to update the icon for the shortcut. What happens when you click the Sales Analyses shortcut? Close the window opened by the Sales Analyses shortcut.
12. Right-click the Sales Analyses shortcut and then choose "Open folder location." What window does Windows Vista open? Close the window.
13. Create a desktop shortcut to the Logo #3.jpg file in the Company Logo folder and then close the Company Logo folder window. Change the name of the shortcut to **Logo #3**. What type of icon does Windows Vista use for the shortcut? What happens when you click the Logo #3 shortcut? Close the window opened by the Logo #3 shortcut.
14. Open the Properties dialog box for the Logo #3 shortcut. What is the target's type? What is the shortcut's target? What is the target's location? What file extension does this shortcut have? What is the full filename of the shortcut (including the file extension)? What is the size of the shortcut? How much disk storage space does the shortcut use? How much storage space does the shortcut waste on disk? Close the Logo #3 Properties dialog box.
15. From the Start menu, open the All Programs menu, click Accessories, right-click Snipping Tool, click Copy, and then close the Start menu. Right-click the desktop and then click Paste. What happens? What is the name of this shortcut, and what type of icon does Windows Vista use for this new shortcut? What happens when you click this new shortcut? (*Optional*: Use the Snipping Tool to select part of the desktop view, and then close the Snipping Tool window without saving the image.)
16. Open the Properties dialog box for the Snipping Tool shortcut. What is the target's type? What is the target's location? What is the shortcut's target? What file extension does this shortcut have? What is the full filename of the shortcut (including the file extension)? What is the size of the shortcut? How much disk storage space does the shortcut use? How much storage space does the shortcut waste on disk? Close the Snipping Tool Properties dialog box.
17. On the desktop, create a copy of the DVD Drive or CD Drive shortcut. What happens? What type of icon does Windows Vista use for this new shortcut? Open the Properties dialog box for this new shortcut. Replace the target in the Target box with the following path: **C:\Users\Public\Documents** What happens as you type this new path? Change the icon for the DVD Drive (or CD Drive) shortcut to one of the icons in the imageres.dll file in the System32 folder, and then close the DVD Drive (or CD Drive) Properties dialog box and apply the changes.
18. Change the name of the DVD Drive (or CD Drive) shortcut to **Public Documents**, and then view its properties. What is the target's type now? What is the new Target location? Close the Public Documents Properties dialog box. Click the Public Documents shortcut. What happens? Close the window opened by the shortcut.

19. Open the location of the file associated with the Logo #3 desktop shortcut, change the name of the file to **Logo.jpg** and then close the folder window. Click the Logo #3 shortcut. What program opened this file? What filename does Windows Vista display at the top of the window? Originally the Logo #3 shortcut opened Logo #3.jpg, but you changed the name of this file to Logo.jpg. Explain how Windows Vista located and opened this file. Close the window.
20. Open the location of the file associated with the Logo #3 desktop shortcut, create a new folder named **Logo Design** in this location, drag the **Logo.jpg** file into the Logo Design folder, and then close the folder window.
21. Click the Logo #3 shortcut. What happens? What program opened this file and what filename does Windows Vista display at the top of the window? Close the window opened by this shortcut.
22. Open the Logo #3 Properties dialog box for the Logo #3 desktop shortcut. What is the path for this shortcut? Did the path of this shortcut change, and if so, how? Close the Logo #3 Properties dialog box.
23. Open the Start menu, locate and then right-click Snipping Tool, and then choose the option for pinning this program to the Start menu. Describe what happens and then close the Start menu.
24. Drag the Public Documents shortcut to the Start button, drop it onto the Start button, and then examine the Start menu. Where did Windows Vista place the Public Documents shortcut? Move the Public Documents shortcut so that it appears before the Snipping Tool (in alphabetical order). Click the Public Documents shortcut on the Start menu. Does this shortcut work in the same way as the desktop shortcut? Close the window opened by this shortcut.
25. Open the Control Panel using your Control Panel desktop shortcut. Open Hardware and Sound. Drag Power Options to the Start button and drop it onto the Start button. Close the Hardware and Sound window and then examine the Start menu. What happened when you dragged Power Options from the Control Panel and dropped it on the Start button? Drag Power Options from the Start menu to the desktop. Describe what happens.
26. Right-click the Sales Analyses desktop shortcut and choose the option for opening the target folder's location. Drag the Company Logo and Sales Analyses folders to Favorite Links in the Navigation Pane. Describe what happens. Right-click Company Logo in the Navigation Pane and choose "Sort by Name." Describe what happens. Remove the Company Logo and Sales Analyses links under Favorite Links.
27. Open the Company Logo folder. If necessary, attach your flash drive to the computer, open a window onto the flash drive from the AutoPlay dialog box, or if your flash drive is already attached to your computer, open a window onto the flash drive from the Computer window, and then stack the windows side by side.
28. Create an autorun folder, and then drag the **Upsilon Air.ico** file from the Company Logo folder to the autorun folder. Create a new Text Document file, name it **autorun.inf**, open autorun.inf in Notepad, specify Upsilon Air.ico as the file containing the icon to use for the flash drive icon, and then save and close the autorun.inf file. Close the Company Logo and flash drive windows, safely remove and reattach your flash drive, and if necessary, close the AutoPlay dialog box or any other dialog box or window that opens. Open a Computer window, right-click your flash drive icon, and then view properties of your flash drive. What icon does Windows Vista display on the title bar of the Properties dialog box for your flash drive? Close the Properties dialog box for your flash drive, and then close the Computer window.

29. Open Windows Internet Explorer (or another Web browser), navigate to the google.com Web site, adjust the size and placement of the Windows Internet Explorer window so that you can see a portion of the desktop, and then drag the Internet Explorer icon located on the left side of the Address Bar to the desktop. Close Windows Internet Explorer, and then click the Google shortcut. What happens? If necessary, drag the browser window to the right so that you can see the Internet shortcut on the desktop.
30. Drag the Maps link (or one of the other links on Google's home page) to the desktop and choose the option to move or copy files from this zone. Close your Web browser window, click the Maps link (or another Google link you created), and describe what happens. Drag the first Google shortcut and drop it in your Web browser window, and then describe what happens. Close your Web browser window.
31. View properties for the Google shortcut. What is the target URL for this Internet shortcut? What file extension does Windows use for this Internet shortcut? What is the full filename of the shortcut (including the file extension)? What is the size of the shortcut? How much disk storage space does the shortcut use? How much storage space does the shortcut waste on disk? Close the Google Properties dialog box.
32. If Microsoft Outlook or Windows Mail is installed on your computer, and if you have set up an account in one of these e-mail programs, use the Create Shortcut Wizard to create an e-mail shortcut named **Elsa & Lance** that creates a preaddressed e-mail message with Elsa Vandenberg's e-mail address in the To box and Lance Quattrone's e-mail address in the Cc box. Assume Elsa Vandenberg's e-mail address is ElsaVandenberg@upsilonair.com and assume Lance's e-mail address is LanceQuattrone@upsilonair.com. What URL did you specify for this e-mail shortcut? Test your shortcut to make sure it works properly, and if necessary, open the Properties dialog box for the e-mail shortcut, correct the URL, and then test it again. Close this e-mail shortcut without saving your changes.
33. From the Elsa & Lance Properties dialog box, modify the URL so that it contains a Subject line with the text "Project Overview" (do not include the quotation marks in the Subject line). What URL did you specify for this e-mail shortcut? Test your shortcut to make sure it works properly, and if necessary, open the Properties dialog box for the e-mail shortcut, correct the URL, and then test it again. Close this e-mail shortcut without saving your changes.
34. To restore your computer:
    - Open the Public Documents folder with your desktop shortcut and delete the Upsilon Air folder.
    - Open the Start menu and choose the option to unpin, or remove, the Power Options, Public Documents, and Snipping Tool from the pinned items list on the Start menu.
    - Delete the e-mail shortcut, the Internet shortcuts, and the desktop shortcuts that you created in this Review Assignment.
    - If you no longer want the custom icon for your flash drive, open the Computer window, open your flash drive, delete the autorun.inf file, delete the autorun folder, and then close the flash drive window.
35. Submit your document to your instructor, either in printed or electronic form, as requested.

Apply | Case Problem 1

Use the skills you learned to create shortcuts for accessing important resources at a learning center.

There are no Data Files needed for this Case Problem.

Toulumney Learning Center The Toulumney Learning Center provides highly focused courses for people seeking to hone their college entry skills, prepare for certification exams, and develop basic computer skills. Lynsey Bivins, the manager, wants to create shortcuts on the classroom computers that students use so that they can quickly access the programs and resources they need for their coursework. Because the upcoming session is only a week away, she asks you to help her determine which shortcuts students need and then create the shortcuts.

Use a word processing application, such as Word or WordPad, to prepare your answers to the questions in this case problem. Also, if you change any settings on the computer you are using, note what the original settings were so that you can restore them later.

1. Create a desktop shortcut to the Public Documents folder. Describe the method that you used to create this desktop shortcut. Examine its properties. What is the path to the Public Documents folder? Change the icon for the Public Documents folder to another icon in the imageres.dll file in the Windows system32 folder. What icon did you use?
2. Make a copy of the Public Documents shortcut, change its name to **Public Downloads**, view its properties, and then change the path of the shortcut to reference the Public Downloads folder. What path did you specify for this shortcut? Test the shortcut and verify that it works, and then close the Public Downloads folder window. Change the icon for the Public Downloads folder to another icon in the shell32.dll file in the Windows system32 folder. What icon did you use?
3. Open the Control Panel, search for Printers, and then create a desktop shortcut to Printers in the Control Panel. Describe the method that you used to create this shortcut. Describe the icon used for this shortcut. Change the name of this shortcut to Printers.
4. View properties of the Printers shortcut. What is the target for this shortcut? What is the target's location? What is the target type? What file extension does this shortcut have? What is the full filename of the shortcut (including the file extension)? What is the path for the location of this shortcut? What is the size of the target? How much disk storage space does the shortcut use? How much storage space does the shortcut waste on disk? Where does Windows Vista get the icon for this shortcut? Close the Printers Properties dialog box.
5. What does Windows Vista open when you click the Printers shortcut? What is contained in this window? List the names of each of the items in this window. Close the window.
6. Create a desktop shortcut to the Ease of Access Center (not the Ease of Access link) in the Control Panel. What method did you use to create a shortcut to the Ease of Access Center? What type of icon does Windows Vista use for this shortcut? Change the name of this shortcut to **Ease of Access Center**.
7. View properties of the Ease of Access Center shortcut. Where does Windows Vista obtain the icon for this shortcut? What is the target for this shortcut? What is the target's location? What is the target type? What file extension does this shortcut have? What is the full filename of the shortcut (including the file extension)? What is the path for the location of this shortcut? What is the size of the target? How much disk storage space does the shortcut use? How much storage space does the shortcut waste on disk? Close the Ease of Access Center Properties dialog box.

8. What does Windows Vista open when you test the Ease of Access Center shortcut? Is there anything unique about the Ease of Access Center? What is contained in this window?

EXPLORE

9. In the Ease of Access Center, click "Start On-Screen Keyboard" and describe what happens. Close the On-Screen Keyboard window and then close the Ease of Access Center window.
10. Create a folder with the name **Resources** within the Documents folder. Create a desktop shortcut to the Resources folder. Describe the method that you used to create this shortcut.
11. View properties of the Resources desktop shortcut. What is the target type? What is the target for this shortcut? What is the target's location? Close the Resources Properties dialog box.
12. Drag the Public Documents, Public Downloads, Printers, and Ease of Access Center shortcuts and drop them on the Resources shortcut. Use the Resources shortcut to open the Resources folder. What is stored in the Resources folder? How did this happen? Can you think of why it would be useful to have a Resources folder for storing desktop shortcuts? Can you think of a way in which you might adapt this feature to your work or play? Explain.
13. Click the Public Downloads shortcut in the Resources folder. Describe what happens. Close the Resources folder.
14. What new features of shortcuts did you discover from this Case Problem?
15. To restore your computer, delete the Resources folder within the Documents folder and the Resources shortcut on the desktop.
16. Submit your answers to this case problem's questions to your instructor, either in printed or electronic form, as requested.

Apply | Case Problem 2

Use the skills you learned in the tutorial to create a toolkit with useful shortcuts.

There are no Data Files needed for this Case Problem.

On the Edge Troubleshooting On the Edge Troubleshooting is a Milwaukee firm that uses cutting edge computer troubleshooting techniques for its clients. Brice McCray, a networking systems specialist, provides his clients with fast, reliable, and effective network, computer, and laptop support and troubleshooting. Furthermore, he offers top-notch services for optimizing and tweaking the performance of networks and computers. Brice carries on his flash drive shortcuts to common operating system folders and troubleshooting utilities as well as Internet shortcuts to resources at Microsoft's Web site. Since you are working this summer as one of his interns, he recommends that you put together a toolkit of shortcuts that you use to assist clients seeking information on new trends in operating system software.

Use a word processing application, such as Word or WordPad, to prepare your answers to these questions. Also, if you change any settings on the computer you are using, note what the original settings were so that you can restore them later.

1. Open your Web browser, navigate to the Microsoft Web site, and then locate and drag the Support link from Microsoft Corporation's home page to the desktop.
2. Drag the Support Internet shortcut into the Windows Internet Explorer window, and at Microsoft's Support Web page, drag the Knowledge Base link to the desktop.

3. From Microsoft Corporation's home page, search for **Windows Vista** using the Search box. Locate and drag the link for the Windows Vista Home Page to the desktop, and then change the name of the Windows Vista Internet shortcut to Windows Vista. View the properties of this Internet shortcut. What is the URL to this Web site? (*Hint*: You can right-click the URL, select Copy from the shortcut menu, and then paste the URL into your Word or WordPad document.)
4. Search for the Microsoft TechNet Web site using **technet** as your search string, drag the link for the TechNet Web site (with the URL technet.microsoft.com) to the desktop, and then change the name of the Internet shortcut to TechNet.
5. Search for Microsoft's MSDN (Microsoft Developer Network) Web site using **msdn** as your search string, drag the link for the MSDN Home Page site to the desktop, and then change the name of the Internet shortcut to MSDN. View the properties of this Internet shortcut. What is the URL to this Web site?
6. Drag the Knowledge Base, Windows Vista, TechNet, and MSDN Internet shortcuts into the Windows Internet Explorer window, one at a time. Describe what happens in each case. Close the Windows Internet Explorer window.

EXPLORE

7. Use the Create Shortcut Wizard to create a shortcut to the Google Web site (google.com). What icon does Windows Vista use for this shortcut? Did Windows Vista obtain a new icon? If so, from where? Test this shortcut and then close your Web browser window.

EXPLORE

8. Drag the Windows Vista Internet shortcut, and then the Google Internet shortcut, to the Start button. Open the Start menu. Where does Windows Vista place these shortcuts?
9. From the All Programs menu, open the Maintenance group folder, pin "Problem Reports and Solutions" to the Start menu, open the Accessories, and then the System Tools group folders, and pin Task Scheduler to the Start Menu.
10. From the Control Panel, drag "System and Maintenance" from the Control Panel window to the desktop. Use this same approach to add Security, Hardware and Sound, and Network and Internet shortcuts to the desktop. Then close the Control Panel and remove the "- Shortcut" label from the four Control Panel desktop shortcuts. Have you used the System and Maintenance shortcut icon previously? If so, explain. Test each of these shortcuts, identify what each shortcut opens, and close each window.
11. Drag Problem Reports and Solutions and Task Scheduler from the pinned items list to the desktop. View properties of each of these two desktop shortcuts and list the path for each of these desktop shortcuts. What is SystemRoot? Explain the purpose and advantage of using %SystemRoot% in each path.
12. If you want access to these shortcuts no matter where you go, where could you store them?
13. To restore your computer, choose the option to either unpin or remove the shortcuts that you added to the Start menu's pinned items list, and then select and delete the desktop shortcuts that you created in this Case Problem.
14. Submit your answers to this case problem's questions to your instructor, either in printed or electronic form, as requested.

Challenge | Case Problem 3

Explore what you've learned to customize the Start menu on a laptop for a toy company sales rep.

For a list of Data Files in the Case3 folder, see page 209.

Next Generation Toys Julio Vargas, a sales rep for Next Generation Toys, depends on his company laptop to keep in touch with his company's headquarters as he travels and meets with prospective clients. Since he depends on his laptop for his business, he makes every effort to safeguard and improve his computer's performance. He asks you for ideas on how to customize the Start menu on his laptop so that he can quickly access important Windows options for maintaining, troubleshooting, and improving the performance of his computer. He asks you to help him create these shortcuts and add them to a folder on his All Programs menu.

Use a word processing application, such as Word or WordPad, to prepare your answers to these questions. Also, if you change any settings on the computer you are using, note what the original settings were so that you can restore them later.

1. Copy the Data Files from the Case3 folder under the Tutorial.04 folder to the Public Documents folder, and then change the name of the Case3 folder to **Next Generation Toys**. Close the Public Documents folder window.
2. Use the techniques you learned in this tutorial to create new desktop shortcuts for the following Windows components and tools:
   - Disk Cleanup and System Information on the System Tools menu
   - Windows Update and Windows Defender on the All Programs menu
   - Power Options, Folder Options, Indexing Options, and Offline Files in the Control Panel (*Hint*: Use the Search box to locate Offline Files.)
   - Your user account Downloads and Searches folders

   What are the Target paths for the Disk Cleanup, System Information, Windows Update, and Windows Defender shortcuts? Why does Windows Vista enclose the path for the Windows Defender shortcut's Target path within quotation marks?
3. If necessary, remove the "- Shortcut" label from any shortcut names.
4. **EXPLORE** Create a desktop folder named Quick Tools and drag the new desktop shortcuts onto the Quick Tools folder. Describe what happens.
5. **EXPLORE** Right-click the Start button, choose Open, and in the Start Menu folder window, open the Programs folder.
6. **EXPLORE** If necessary, adjust the position of the Programs window so that you can see the Quick Tools desktop folder, and then drag the Quick Tools desktop folder into the Programs window. Describe what happens. Close the Programs window.
7. **EXPLORE** Open the All Programs menu, locate and open Quick Tools. What does the Quick Tools group folder contain?
8. Test the Downloads, Power Options, and System Information menu options in the Quick Tools group folder.
9. Open the Next Generation Toys folder.
10. Create new desktop shortcuts for the following files:
    - **Payments.xlsx** in the Loan Analyses folder
    - **Growth.xlsx** and **Profits.xlsx** in the Projections folder
    - **AdSales.xlsx** in the Sales Analyses folder
11. Close the Sales Analyses folder window. Create a desktop folder named "My Important Files" (without the quotation marks), move the new file desktop shortcuts into the My Important Files folder, open the My Important Files folder, and remove the file extension and the "- Shortcut" label from each shortcut name.

EXPLORE 12. Close the My Important Files folder, open the Start Menu folder, open the Programs folder, drag the My Important Files folder into the Programs window, and then close the Programs folder window.

EXPLORE 13. Open the All Programs menu, locate and open the My Important Files group folder. What does the My Important Files group folder contain? If Microsoft Office Excel 2007 is installed on your computer, open **Profits.xlsx**, examine the file, and then close the workbook.

14. What new features of shortcuts did you discover from this case? How can you use these new features to customize your computer's Start menu?
15. To restore your computer:
    a. Open the All Programs menu, right-click the My Important Files group folder, and then choose the option to delete this group folder. After removing the My Important Files group folder, remove the Quick Tools group folder from your computer.
    b. Open the Public Documents folder, delete the Next Generation Toys folder, and then close the Public Documents folder window.
16. Submit your answers to this case problem's questions to your instructor, either in printed or electronic form, as requested.

Challenge | Case Problem 4

Explore what you've learned to create e-mail shortcuts for a contract job assignment.

There are no Data Files needed for this Case Problem.

Fluent Interpreters, Inc. Nadia Mikhaylov works as a Russian-English translator for Fluent Interpreters. Nadia has just landed a contract job assignment with a small Seattle business that is currently helping Pravdin Associates, a Russian firm, develop spreadsheet templates, projections, and financial analyses. In order to keep in daily contact with employees at this Russian firm, Nadia wants to create e-mail shortcuts on her desktop so that she can quickly prepare e-mail messages.

Use a word processing application, such as Word or WordPad, to prepare your answers to these questions. Also, if you change any settings on the computer you are using, note what the original settings were so that you can restore them later.

To complete this case problem, you must have Microsoft Outlook or Windows Mail installed on your computer, and you must also have set up an e-mail account in one of these e-mail software products. Also, since you will be creating e-mail shortcuts addressed to a fictional person with a fictional e-mail address working at a fictional company, you should not attempt to send these e-mail messages.

1. Use the Create Shortcut Wizard to create an e-mail shortcut for brand new e-mail addresses and name the e-mail shortcut **New Message**. Set up this e-mail shortcut so that it opens an e-mail message for you to compose, but does not enter the recipient's e-mail address or any other information. Test the e-mail shortcut and verify that it is working properly, and then close the e-mail message without saving it. What URL did you specify for this e-mail shortcut? If necessary, open the Properties dialog box for this shortcut, correct the URL, and then test the e-mail shortcut again.

EXPLORE

2. Use the Create Shortcut Wizard to create an e-mail shortcut for Alexei Pravdin at Pravdin Associates. Set up this e-mail message so that it inserts his e-mail address. Assume that alexeipravdin@pravdinassociates.com is his e-mail address. Name the shortcut **Alexei Pravdin**. Test the e-mail shortcut and verify that it is working properly, and then close the e-mail message without saving it. What URL did you specify for this e-mail shortcut? If necessary, open the Properties dialog box for this shortcut, correct the URL, and then test the e-mail shortcut again.

EXPLORE

3. Copy the Alexei Pravdin e-mail shortcut, paste the new e-mail shortcut on your desktop, and change the name of the shortcut to **Pravdin Associates**. Open the Pravdin Associates Properties dialog box and modify the URL so that it includes a Subject line that reads "Pravdin Associates Web Site" (without the quotation marks). Test the e-mail shortcut and verify that it is working properly, and then close the e-mail message without saving it. What URL did you specify for this e-mail shortcut? If necessary, open the Properties dialog box for this shortcut, correct the URL, and then test the e-mail shortcut again.

EXPLORE

4. Make a copy of the Pravdin Associates e-mail shortcut and change the name of the new shortcut to **Pilot Project**. Open the Pilot Project Properties dialog box and modify the URL so that the Subject line reads "Pravdin Associates Pilot Project" (without the quotation marks) and modify the URL so that the e-mail shortcut includes "Project Status" (without the quotation marks) in the body of the message. Test the e-mail shortcut and verify that it is working properly, and then close the e-mail message without saving it. What URL did you specify for this e-mail shortcut? If necessary, open the Properties dialog box for this shortcut, correct the URL, and then test the e-mail shortcut again.

EXPLORE

5. Make a copy of the Alexei Pravdin shortcut, change the name of the shortcut to **Alexei & Tatyana**. Open the Alexei & Tatyana Properties dialog box and modify the URL so that Tatyana's e-mail address appears in the To box. Assume that her e-mail address is tatyanaivanov@pravdinassociates.com. Test the e-mail shortcut and verify that it is working properly, and then close the e-mail message without saving it. What URL did you specify for this e-mail shortcut? If necessary, open the Properties dialog box for this shortcut, correct the URL, and then test the e-mail shortcut again.
6. To restore your computer, delete the five e-mail desktop shortcuts that you created in this Case Problem.
7. Submit your answers to this case problem's questions to your instructor, either in printed or electronic form, as requested.

Review | Quick Check Answers

Session 4.1

1. True
2. by using the path to the target
3. "lnk" is the file extension used for desktop shortcuts, and it implies that a shortcut is a link to another object.
4. False
5. The "exe" file extension is found on executable program files. The "dll" file extension stands for "dynamic link library," and files with this file extension contain program code used by one or more programs. The "ico" file extension stands for "Icon File," and it implies that the file contains an image.
6. environment variable

Session 4.2

1. the URL of the Web site
2. Favorites (or bookmarks), Favorites folder
3. True
4. Links
5. False
6. inf

Ending Data Files

There are no ending Data Files needed for this tutorial.

Objectives

Session 5.1
- Describe the concept and use of a file system
- Examine how to format a hard disk
- Understand the role of the Master Boot Record (MBR)
- Compare the NTFS and FAT file systems
- Check the file system used by different drives
- Use the Disk Management snap-in

Session 5.2
- Compress and uncompress folders and files
- Create and extract from Compressed (zipped) Folders
- Encrypt and decrypt folders and files
- Examine BitLocker Drive Encryption

Examining Windows Vista File Systems

Managing Data in the NTFS File System

Case | Cooper & Bauman

Cooper & Bauman, a corporation with its headquarters in Melbourne, Australia, produces a variety of consumer products, including household and personal care products as well as small household appliances. As Cooper & Bauman's information systems expert, Cadence Soubeiran is responsible for managing the handling, storage, and protection of vital company information. Cadence determines which employees have access to information and what type of access to provide. She also develops guidelines for securing, protecting, and releasing company information. Cadence and her staff are constantly evaluating and learning how to implement new Windows Vista features to increase the security of the company's computers and their data. Her current focus is on the Windows Vista NTFS file system and its support for high-performance, high-capacity drives and for accessing and managing data.

Starting Data Files

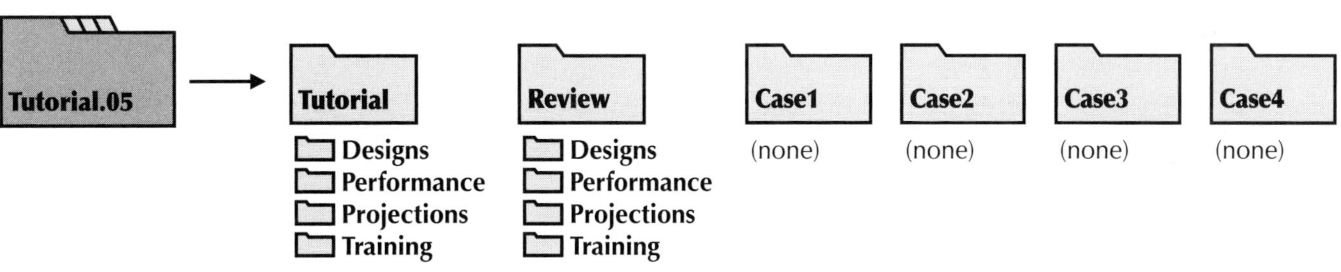

Session 5.1

Exploring the Windows Vista File Systems

The term **file system** refers to the data structures that an operating system uses to track information about folders and files stored on a disk as well as information about the disk and file system itself. Just as an address book keeps track of the street addresses and phone numbers for an individual (for example), the file system keeps track of the physical location of a file on disk and details of the file, such as its filename and file size.

Because you will be working with the terms "disk," "drive," and "volume" as you examine different file systems and the drives on your computer, you should understand what these terms mean and how they differ. A **disk** is a physical device, such as a hard disk, DVD, or CD. A **volume**, a logical concept, consists of all or part of a disk, uses a specific file system, and is assigned a drive name (such as C: for drive C). On a hard disk, you might have a single volume or you might have two or more volumes. A single hard disk can have multiple volumes on that one disk, or a volume can span, or stretch across, multiple hard disks. A **drive,** another logical concept, consists of all or part of a single disk, uses a specific file system, and is assigned a drive name. It is not uncommon for these terms to be used interchangeably.

InSight | Distinguishing the Boot and System Volumes

The boot volume is the volume that contains the Windows Vista operating system files located in the Windows folder. The system volume is the volume that contains the files and data structures for loading Windows Vista. The files and data structures required to boot your computer are stored on the system volume rather than the boot volume (logically backwards). Likewise, the operating system files are stored in the Windows folder on the boot volume, not the system volume (also logically backwards). Fortunately, the boot volume and system volume are usually the same, but they can be different. If you have one hard disk and if there is only one volume on that disk (for drive C), the boot volume and system volume are the same.

A file system determines how an operating system allocates storage space to folders and files, how effectively it uses the storage space on a disk, what type of access it provides to specific folders and files, what options are available for maintaining and restoring the integrity of the file system, and any additional features unique to that file system. Different types of file systems can be used for different types of disks, and different versions of the Windows operating systems differ in their support for specific file systems. Even the same file system can differ in terms of the support provided in different versions of Windows. Windows Vista supports the following common types of file systems for different types of storage media:

- **NTFS**, the New Technology File System, for internal and external hard disk drives
- **FATFS**, the File Allocation Table File System, for smaller hard disks, USB flash drives, and floppy disks
- **Extended FAT File System (exFAT)**, a new file system designed for mobile devices
- **UDF**, the Universal Disk Format file system, for DVDs
- **CDFS**, the Compact Disc File System, for CDs
- **Live File System**, a new Windows Vista DVD and CD file system

Before you can use a disk, the operating system or another application or utility must prepare the disk so that Windows can record data to and retrieve data from the disk. That includes hard disks, DVDs, CDs, and flash drives, to name a few. When you purchase a computer, the computer manufacturer or dealer has already formatted or prepared the hard disk so that it can store data, and the computer manufacturer or dealer has already installed a version of the Windows operating system on the disk. However, it is possible to purchase an unformatted hard disk and then use a Windows Vista DVD to format the hard disk first before installing the operating system. Also, if you encounter a serious problem with your computer, you might need to make copies of any important files on the hard disk (if possible) and then reformat the hard disk, reinstall the operating system, reinstall all your applications, and restore your personal data from a backup.

If you install an upgrade to your existing operating system, the installation program may give you the option of also upgrading to a newer file system. In some cases, you might decide to convert a file system for a specific disk to a different file system so you can take advantage of its features.

You can only use one file system on your hard disk drive. However, you can partition or subdivide the hard disk into multiple volumes and format each volume to use a different file system. Windows Vista, however, can only be installed on an NTFS volume.

Formatting a Hard Disk

When Windows Vista formats a hard disk, it creates concentric recording bands known as **tracks** on each side of each platter of a hard disk, as illustrated in Figure 5-1. A hard disk may contain one or more **platters**, or metallic disks, for storing data. Also, both sides of each platter store data. Each track is subdivided into small storage compartments referred to as **sectors**, and each sector is usually 512 bytes in size. Tracks located at the same position on different platters are known as cylinders. A **cylinder** is therefore a three-dimensional way of viewing multiple tracks on different platters while a track is a two-dimensional way of viewing single concentric recording bands on a platter.

Figure 5-1 Cylinders, tracks, and sectors on a hard disk

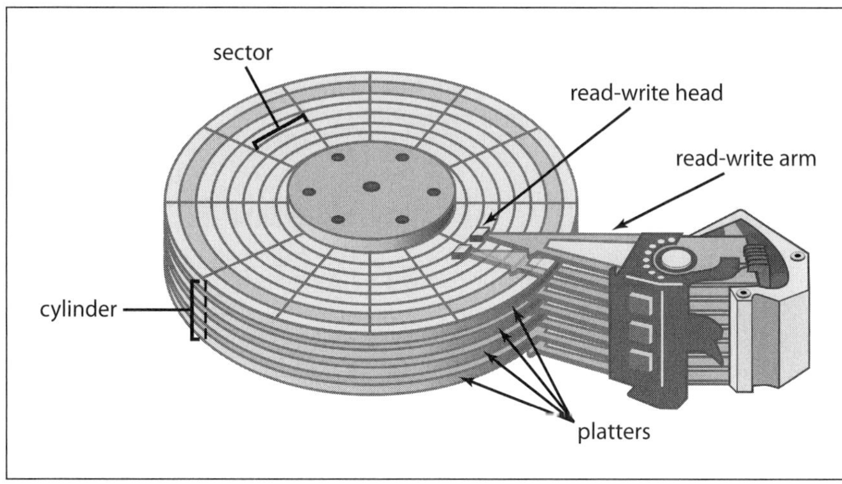

Although a sector is the basic storage compartment on a disk, the Windows Vista operating system does not allocate storage space sector by sector. Instead, Windows Vista allocates storage space cluster by cluster. A **cluster** (or **allocation unit**) consists of one or more sectors of storage space that Windows Vista allocates as a single unit or block to all or part of a file (depending on the file size). The number of sectors per cluster depends on several factors, including the file system used on the disk, the size of the volume, and the operating system itself. For example, on a 1 GB USB flash drive, a cluster may consist of 32 sectors while on a 750 GB hard disk a cluster may consist of 8 sectors. If you create a one-page document that requires 7 sectors of storage space on a disk, and if you save that document to a file on the 1 GB USB flash just described, Windows Vista allocates 1 cluster of storage space for that file. If each cluster on that USB flash drive consists of 32 sectors, that file uses 32 sectors of storage space even though it requires only 7 sectors. That means that the extra 25 sectors of storage space are wasted storage space that no other file can use. Storage space allocated to a file, but not used by that file, is called **slack**. If you save that same file to the 750 GB hard disk with 8 sectors per cluster, Windows Vista still allocates 1 cluster of storage space for that file. However, since each cluster on that hard disk consists of 8 sectors, that same file would use only 7 sectors of storage space. Unlike the USB flash drive, only 1 sector of storage space is wasted.

On the now-obsolete 3½ HD (High-Density) floppy disk, each cluster contained 1 sector, making this type of disk more efficient for storing data with the least amount of wasted storage space, or slack. If you saved a one-page document that required 7 sectors of storage space to a file on a floppy disk, Windows Vista would allocate 7 clusters for the file. If the file did not fill the last sector of storage space in the last cluster, that would be the only wasted storage space. However, not only was the total amount of storage space on floppy disks limited, but floppy disks had a short useful life.

During the formatting process, Windows Vista verifies that it can write to and read from each sector on the disk. If it discovers any sectors that it cannot write to or read from, it marks the clusters that contain those defective sectors as unusable and does not store data in those clusters. Clusters that contain one or more defective sectors are called **bad clusters**. At the end of the formatting process, Windows creates a file system on the disk and a top-level folder. The **top-level folder** (or **root directory**) is the first folder (or **directory**) created on a disk after Windows Vista formats the disk. When you open a Computer window and click (or double-click) an icon for a disk drive, the window that opens is a window onto the top-level folder of that disk. After the disk has a file system and top-level folder, you can install software onto the disk and add your own personal folders and files. The process for creating tracks and sectors on a disk is called **low-level formatting** while the process for creating a file system on the disk is called **high-level formatting**.

Identifying the Role of the Master Boot Record

When Windows Vista prepares a disk for use with a specific file system, it creates a Master Boot Record (MBR) at the beginning of the hard disk drive. The **Master Boot Record** (**MBR**) is a critical data structure that plays an important role in the booting process. The MBR also contains information about the hard disk's partitions. A **partition** is a subdivision of a physical hard disk that functions as if it were a separate physical disk. The **primary partition** is the bootable (or active) partition that contains the operating system (usually drive C). An **extended partition** does not contain operating system files, but rather can be subdivided into additional logical drives, such as drive D, etc. You can have as many as 23 logical drives (drive D through drive Z). Network drives, another type of logical drive, are assigned to network folders, and network drive names are assigned in reverse alphabetical order, starting with the drive name Z:.

Within the Master Boot Record is a table called the **Hard Disk Partition Table**, which contains information about the partitions on the hard disk. The Hard Disk Partition Table identifies where each partition starts and ends and which partition boots the computer. That partition (usually drive C) contains the Windows Vista operating system files for loading the operating system. The Master Boot Record also contains a boot program called the **Master Boot Code**, which locates the bootable partition then transfers control to the boot sector of the volume that contains the installed operating system. The **boot sector**, or **boot record**, is the sector at the beginning of a partition. It contains information about the layout of the volume, the file system structures, and in the case of a bootable volume, code for locating and loading the operating system files that start loading a specific operating system.

When your computer finds the hard disk during booting, it reads the MBR, finds the location of the boot drive (drive C), and then reads the boot record on drive C. The bootstrap loader then locates and loads the operating system from the hard disk.

Exploring the NTFS File System

NTFS (the **NT File System** or "New Technology File System") is the native file system for Windows Vista and its predecessors in the Windows NT product line, including Windows XP and Windows 2000 Professional. NTFS relies on the use of a **Master File Table (MFT)** to keep track of folders and files as well as information about the volume and the Master File Table itself. The MFT contains at least one record (or listing) for each file on disk. Each **record** in this table consists of a row of file information organized into columns. If you are familiar with the use of Microsoft Access database tables, Microsoft Excel tables, or Microsoft Word tables, and how they organize data in a table format, you can visualize the organization of the MFT.

When Windows Vista prepares a hard disk to use NTFS, it creates the MBR on the hard disk and then creates an NTFS boot sector for the volume where you install Windows Vista as well as the MFT and other NTFS data structures. Windows Vista keeps a second copy of the first four records or entries (or the first cluster, whichever is larger) in the MFT as a backup in case a problem prevents access to critical information stored in these records of the MFT. This backup copy is referred to as the **Master File Table Mirror** (**MFTMirr**). These first four records contain information about the MFT, the MFTMirr, a transaction log file used for recovery (covered later), and the volume. If the first four records in the MFT are damaged, Windows Vista may be able to recover from the damage and replace the first four records of the MFT with the first four records from the MFTMirr.

The first 16 records in the MFT consist of **metadata**, or data about data, and include not only information about the first four records described in the previous paragraph, but also information about which clusters are available and which clusters are in use, which clusters are bad clusters, and other key information needed by NTFS.

The NTFS boot sector contains information about the volume formatted for NTFS, including:

- Number of bytes per sector
- Number of sectors per cluster
- **Media descriptor**, or a setting that identifies the type of disk
- Total number of sectors
- Location of the MFT
- Location of the MFTMirr
- Number of clusters used for each record in the MFT
- Volume serial number

The NTFS **transaction log file** contains a record of operations performed on a volume, such as renaming or deleting a file. Each operation is called a **transaction**. If a problem occurs, Windows Vista uses the information in the transaction log file to roll back operations that were not completed and thereby restore the integrity of the file system. Any operations listed as complete in the transaction log file are repeated to ensure that the corresponding changes were actually made on disk.

The MFT also includes **attributes**, or settings assigned to files by the operating system to indicate a specific state, such as:

- **Archive Attribute** Windows Vista assigns the **Archive attribute** to newly created or newly modified files so that a backup utility can identify which files should be backed up. (This attribute is covered in more detail in Tutorial 10.) If you display the Attributes column in a folder window, files with this attribute are identified by the code "A".
- **Read-Only Attribute** If a file is assigned the **Read-Only attribute**, you can open and view (or read) the contents of the file, but you cannot save changes to the file under the same filename. This attribute therefore guarantees that important system folders and files are not modified. For example, the Program Files and the Documents folders are assigned the Read-Only attribute. If you display the Attributes column in a folder window, files with this attribute are identified by the code "R".
- **Hidden Attribute** If a folder or file is assigned the **Hidden attribute**, Windows Vista does not display the folder or file in folder windows (unless you choose the option to display all hidden folders and files). Even then, the icons for hidden folders and files are fainter in appearance to remind you that they are assigned this attribute. The Hibernation file is an example of a file assigned the Hidden attribute. If you display the Attributes column in a folder window, files with this attribute are identified by the code "H".
- **System Attribute** Folders and files with the **System attribute** are important operating system files. Typically, system files are also assigned the Hidden attribute, and in some cases, the Read-Only attribute to protect them. That means a file can be assigned more than one attribute. The Fonts folder is assigned the System and Read-Only attributes. If you display the Attributes column in a folder window, files with the System attribute are identified by the code "S".
- **Compress Attribute** Any folders and files that you explicitly choose to compress (to save disk storage space) are assigned the **Compress attribute**. If you display the Attributes column in a folder window, files with this attribute are identified by the code "C".
- **Encrypt Attribute** Any folders and files that you explicitly choose to encrypt (or encode for security) are assigned the **Encrypt attribute**. If you display the Attributes column in a folder window, files with this attribute are identified by the code "E".
- **Not Content Indexed Attribute** Folders and files with the **Not Content Indexed** attribute are excluded from indexing. The Hibernation file is an example of a file which is not indexed for faster searching. If you display the Attributes column in a folder window, files with this attribute are identified by the code "N".

Figure 5-2 shows cluster sizes for NTFS volumes with different storage capacities. As the size of a volume increases, the number of sectors per cluster increases. Smaller volumes have smaller cluster sizes (with fewer sectors per cluster), and larger volumes have larger cluster sizes (with more sectors per cluster). Smaller volumes therefore use storage space more efficiently. The limit of 2 TB for a volume size is not a shortcoming of NTFS, but rather a limitation imposed by the Hard Disk Partition Table in the MBR. This table can only store information on volumes up to 2 TB. To work with NTFS volumes over 2 TB, you must use Windows Vista to convert **simple volumes**, which rely on the MBR, to **dynamic volumes**, which use a relational database to keep track of information about volumes.

Cluster sizes for NTFS volumes **Figure 5-2**

Volume Size			Cluster Size	
From	To	Sectors/Cluster	Bytes	Kilobytes (KB)
7 MB	512 MB	1	512	0.5
513 MB	1 GB	2	1,024	1
1 GB+	2 GB	4	2,048	2
2 GB+	2 TB	8	4,096	4
1 sector = 512 bytes				

Theoretically, NTFS supports volume sizes of 2^{64} clusters (less one cluster), for a total of 18,446,744,073,709,551,615 clusters. As currently implemented, NTFS supports volume sizes of 2^{32} clusters (less one cluster) using 64 KB clusters (or 128 sectors per cluster), for a total volume capacity of 256 TB (terabytes) (or 281,474,976,710,656 bytes less one cluster). At the default cluster size of 8 sectors per cluster, the maximum size for an NTFS volume is 16 TB (terabytes) less one cluster of 4 KB (kilobytes). 16 TB is equal to approximately 16,384 gigabytes.

As a quick review, recall that a byte is equivalent to the storage space on disk for one character. 1,024 bytes constitute a kilobyte (approximately one thousand bytes). 1,024 kilobytes constitute a megabyte (approximately one million bytes). 1,024 megabytes constitute a gigabyte (approximately one billion bytes), and 1,024 gigabytes constitute a terabyte (approximately one trillion bytes).

Calculating the Number of Sectors in a Cluster | InSight

Cluster sizes are commonly expressed as kilobytes (KB) rather than the actual number of sectors per cluster; however, occasionally, cluster sizes are expressed as the number of sectors per cluster. If you need to convert cluster sizes expressed as KB to the number of sectors per cluster, you use the following approach:

To convert a 64 KB cluster size into the number of sectors per cluster:

64 KB × 1,024 bytes per KB = 65,536 bytes

65,536 bytes / (512 bytes per sector) = 128 sectors

Likewise, if you know the number of sectors per cluster and want to express the cluster size in KB (kilobytes), you use the following approach:

To convert 8 sectors per cluster into kilobytes per cluster:

8 sectors per cluster × 512 bytes per sector = 4,096 bytes

4,096 bytes / (1,024 bytes per KB) = 4 KB

NTFS has additional features not available in the FAT file systems (which you will examine next), including the following:

- **Folder and File Permissions** A **permission** is a rule that determines who has access to a resource, such as a folder or file, and how they can use the resource. For example, an Administrator might deny you access to a specific folder, assign you read-only access, or permit you to create, modify, and delete files in a folder. This feature helps maintain the security of data on networked and non-networked computers.

- **Distributed Link Tracing** If you create a shortcut to a file on an NTFS volume, Distributed Link Tracing stores a unique object ID in the shortcut file and in the file to which the shortcut points. Windows Vista can then update the shortcut to the file if you rename the file, move it to another folder on the same volume or to a different volume on the same computer, move the file from a shared network folder to another shared network folder, or move the volume to another computer within the same domain. A **domain** consists of a group of networked computers administered as a unit using the same rules and procedures and sharing the same database and security policy.

  Windows and applications create unique GUIDs for objects, as needed. A **GUID** (**Globally Unique Identifier**), also referred to as an **UUID** (**Universally Unique Identifier**), is a unique randomly generated 128 bit (or 16 byte) number. If you raise 2 to the 128th power (2^{128}), you discover that there are a total of 340,282,366,920,938,000,000,000,000,000,000,000,000 (or 340 billion, billion, billion, billion) possible numbers. The chances that another object might be assigned the same GUID is improbable.

- **Multiple Data Streams** NTFS supports files that contain multiple data streams. A **data stream** consists of a set of data stored within a file. All files have a data stream that consists of the actual data stored in the file by the file's creator, and that data stream is visible to all file systems, but additional data streams, such as file properties or a thumbnail of the file's contents, can be attached to a file. Each data stream has its own name so that the application that created the data stream can access what's stored in the data stream. If you copy a file with additional data streams from an NTFS volume to a FAT volume, Windows informs you that the extra information attached to the file will be lost during the copy operation and asks you whether you want to proceed.
- **Disk Quotas** An Administrator can specify how much storage each user can have on a disk. You will examine this feature in Tutorial 6.
- **Mounted Drives** Using the Disk Management Snap-in tool (which you will examine later in this tutorial), you can attach a drive, such as a USB flash drive, to an empty folder that you have already created on an NTFS volume (for example, to an empty folder under the Documents folder). You can then access the contents of the drive (such as a flash drive) by opening the folder on your NTFS volume. The mounted drive appears as part of a group of related folders and provides a way for extending storage of files outside the current volume. You might use this feature if you do not have enough storage space on your hard disk for the contents of the other disk. Mounted drives, also called volume mount points or drive paths, are assigned a label or name instead of a drive letter.
- **Hard Links** A **hard link** is a link to a file on an NTFS volume. When you create the hard link, you assign a filename to the hard link. You now have two ways to open the same file: You can open the original file, or you can use the hard link to open the file. In fact, for all practical purposes, the hard link looks like and acts like the actual file. For example, if you have a file named Project Status.xlsx in a folder on your hard disk, you can create a hard link named Project Status.xlsx in another folder to the actual file named Project Status.xlsx. You can then open the same file from either folder. Any changes you make apply to the actual file. One advantage of using a hard link is that you do not need to keep two copies of the same file in different folders and run the risk of updating one copy of the file without updating the other copy of the file.

As noted, a hard link can have the same name as the file that it points to if it is stored in another folder. The hard link can also have a different name from the file that it points to, whether it's stored in a different folder or the same folder as the original file. As you've seen, you can also use a shortcut to quickly access a file. However, if you permanently delete the original file that a shortcut points to, you've lost the entire file. The shortcut still exists, but it cannot find the file it references. In contrast, if you permanently delete the original file that you've created a hard link to, you can still access the file's contents via the hard link.

- **Sparse Files** Certain files, such as catalog files used for indexing files, contain specific data and long runs of zeroes. Rather than allocate disk storage space to those portions of the file that contain the long runs of zeroes, Windows can mark the file as a sparse file and allocate disk storage space only to the meaningful data, not to the long runs of zeroes. That means Windows can store potentially very large files more efficiently on disk and take up less disk storage space. When accessing the file, Windows can restore the sparse file to its original state.
- **Encryption** As you will discover in the second session of this tutorial, you can encrypt (or encode) folders and files so that only you have access to your files.
- **Compression** As you will discover in the second session of this tutorial, you can compress folders and files so that they use less storage space on disk.

As you can see, NTFS is a complex, yet full-featured, file system that supports current and future disk storage capacities.

Understanding the FAT File System

The FAT file system was introduced with the first version of the DOS operating system and was incorporated in Windows 95, the first Windows operating system. The FAT file system relies on the use of a File Allocation Table (FAT) to keep track of cluster usage on disk. When Windows formats a disk with the FAT file system, it creates the following four tables in the system area of the disk:

- Boot record
- File Allocation Table #1 (or FAT1)
- File Allocation Table #2 (or FAT2)
- Directory table

The **system area** is the outer track of the disk (called Track 0), and it is used exclusively for these data structures. Right after the system area is the **files area** where you store your document files. The following sections describe each of these four tables.

The Boot Record

The boot record (sometimes called the boot sector) is a table that contains the name and the version number of the operating system used to format the disk, as well as information on the physical characteristics of the disk, including the following:

- Number of bytes per sector
- Number of sectors per cluster
- Number of File Allocation Tables
- Maximum number of files allowed in the top-level folder or root directory
- Total number of sectors
- Media descriptor, which identifies the type of disk
- Number of sectors for the FAT

- Number of sectors per track
- Number of sides formatted
- Drive number
- Volume serial number (calculated from the date and time on the computer)
- Volume label (an electronic label)
- Type of file system
- Number of hidden, reserved, and unused sectors

The boot sector also contains a **bootstrap loader** program for loading the operating system from a FAT volume.

When Windows Vista accesses a drive, it reads the boot record so that it knows how to work with and allocate storage space on that disk drive. The boot sector is therefore important because different types of disks (including hard disks) have different storage capacities and allocate storage space differently.

The File Allocation Tables

After the boot sector, the operating system creates two copies of a table called the **File Allocation Table** to keep track of which clusters (or allocation units) are available or unused, which ones store the contents of files and are therefore used, which are defective and unusable, and which are reserved for use by the operating system. Figure 5-3 shows a diagrammatic representation of a File Allocation Table. In this figure, you are looking at information on two files that use clusters 1500–1505 and 1506–1508. Each cluster contains the number of the next cluster (called a **pointer**) for that same file (shown in the column labeled "FAT"). The last cluster of a file contains an **end-of-file** (**EOF**) code or marker. Because the operating system can determine the cluster number by counting the entries in the table, the File Allocation Table only contains the information shown in the last column.

Figure 5-3 Cluster usage in the File Allocation Table

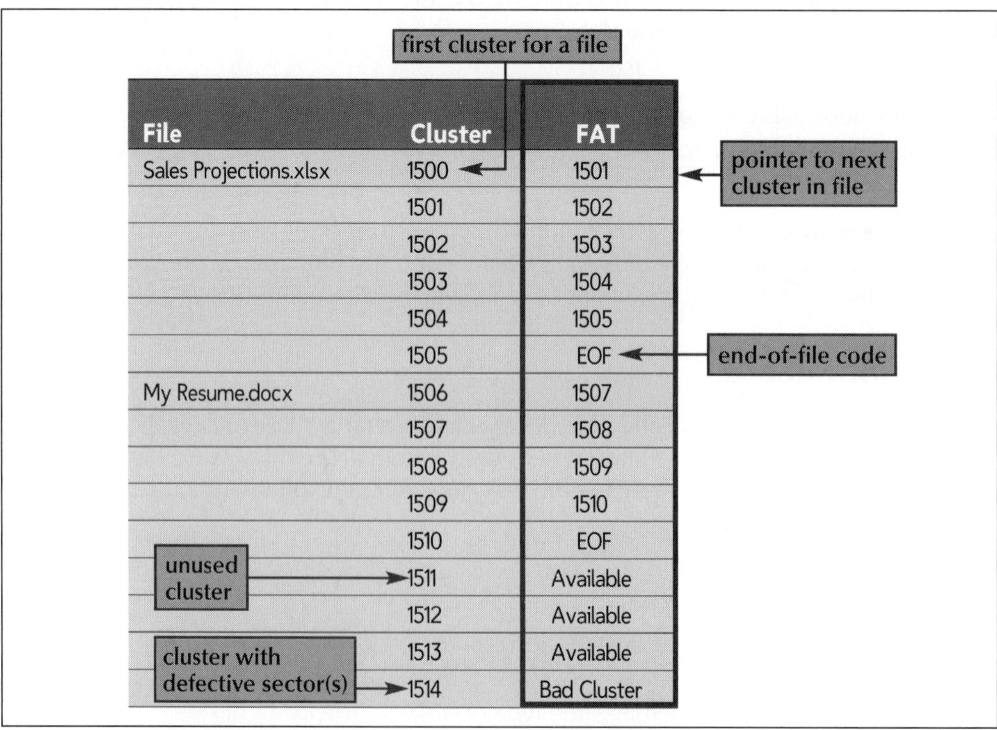

The operating system places two copies of the File Allocation Table on a disk. One copy is called **FAT1**, the other, **FAT2**. Each time the operating system saves a new or modified file to a disk, it updates both tables. FAT2 is therefore a backup of FAT1. If FAT1 is damaged, Windows can use FAT2 to access information about the use of clusters on disk.

The Directory Table

The **directory table** keeps track of information on the folders and files stored in the top-level folder or root directory. This table contains the names of folders and files, as well as information on their sizes, dates and times of creation, last accessed date, dates and times of modification, and any special attributes assigned to the folder or file by the operating system. Figure 5-4 contains a partial view of the contents of a directory table.

Figure 5-4 **Directory table for top-level folder**

folder (or directory)

Filename	Extension	Attributes	File Time	File Date	Starting Cluster	Size (Bytes)
Portfolio		D	08:30:02	10/14/2010	156	
Brochure	docx	A	10:31:58	10/27/2010	157	75,968
Company Logo	psd		16:32:19	03/21/2011	298	1,312,335
Display Ad	psd	A	09:27:43	02/07/2011	835	693,712
Newsletter	docx		14:01:32	11/15/2010	1890	521,690

document files

The directory table only keeps track of the folders and files located in the top-level folder. This table does not keep track of the folders and files contained within subfolders below the top-level folder. Each subfolder below the top-level folder is actually a directory table, like the one for the top-level folder, and each directory table tracks the folders and files contained within that subfolder. In essence, the operating system divides the labor of tracking folders and files on a hard disk among different directory tables.

When you save a file, you specify the drive and folder where you want to store the file. Because you consider the folder as a container for a file, you visualize the file as being stored within the folder. However, that is not the case. A folder is a file that keeps track of other files, and it's stored at a certain location on disk, just like any other file. When you save a file in a folder, you are really designating the directory table or folder file that will keep track of the file. So, a folder is a logical concept, not a physical concept.

In the FAT file system, the directory table keeps track of the Archive, Read-Only, Hidden, and System attributes.

The directory table also contains the number of the starting cluster for each folder and file on a disk. By using the directory table and the File Allocation Table, Windows Vista can locate all the clusters used by a folder or file on a FAT volume and reassemble the file so that you can work with the document in that file.

The FAT12, FAT16, and FAT32 File Systems

FAT12 is the file system used on small media, namely, floppy disks and volumes less than 32 MB. FAT12 supports a maximum of 4,096 clusters (or 2^{12} clusters) on a floppy disk. All versions of the Windows operating system support FAT12. If you have a floppy disk drive and examine the properties of a floppy disk, Windows Vista identifies the file system used on the disk as FAT (for FAT12).

The original version of Windows 95 and Windows 95a used the FAT16 file system. **FAT16** supports a maximum of 65,536 clusters (or 2^{16} clusters) on a disk. Since some clusters are reserved, the actual limit is 65,524 clusters. Another feature of the FAT16 file system is that the boot record, File Allocation Table #1, File Allocation Table #2, and directory table are fixed in size. The size of the File Allocation Tables cannot exceed 128 KB, which affects the usage of storage space on hard disks because the File Allocation Table can only track a specific number of clusters, no matter how large the disk. As hard disk storage capacities increase, the number of sectors per cluster must therefore increase because the number of clusters cannot increase. Figure 5-5 shows cluster sizes on different-sized volumes that use FAT16. Notice that for hard disks that range in capacity from 1 GB up to 2 GB, each cluster is 64 sectors in size. FAT16 volumes can actually support up to 4 GB of storage (at 128 sectors per cluster, or 64 KB clusters); however, applications might not work properly on volumes of that size. The theoretical and practical storage limits of file systems vary because they depend on the support Microsoft builds into each version of the Windows operating system for each file system and take into accounts other issues, such as support by applications.

Figure 5-5 Cluster sizes for FAT16 volumes

Volume Size			Cluster Size	
From	To	Sectors/Cluster	Bytes	Kilobytes (KB)
7 MB	16 MB	4	2,048	2
17 MB	32 MB	1	512	0.5
33 MB	64 MB	2	1,024	1
65 MB	128 MB	4	2,048	2
129 MB	256 MB	8	4,096	4
257 MB	512 MB	16	8,192	8
513 MB	1 GB	32	16,384	16
1 GB	2 GB	64	32,768	32
1 sector = 512 bytes				

Because the directory table for the top-level folder of a hard disk that uses FAT16 is fixed in size, it can only track a total of 512 folders and files. You must also limit the use of long filenames for folders and files in the top-level folder because long folder names and filenames take more than one directory entry in the Directory table and therefore use up the available **directory space**. That's why you should organize files into folders on disks that use FAT16 so that the top-level folder or root directory does not become full.

FAT32, a variation on the FAT file system, was introduced in Windows 95B and was supported in all later versions of Windows except for Windows NT Workstation 4.0. FAT32 supported even larger volumes than FAT16 and used disk storage space more efficiently than FAT16.

The boot record on FAT32 drives is larger and contains a backup of critical data structures. Furthermore, a backup of the boot sector is stored elsewhere on the volume. Unlike FAT16, the File Allocation Tables and directory table in the FAT32 file system are not fixed in size, and these system files can "spill over" from the system area to the files area of the disk where you store document folders and files. Also, FAT32 supports up to 65,536 folders and files in the top-level folder.

FAT32 supports a maximum of 268,435,456 clusters (or 2^{28} clusters) on a hard disk, so cluster sizes can be smaller. Although FAT32 uses 32 bits for each entry in the File Allocation Table, and therefore would theoretically support a maximum of 4,294,967,296 clusters (or 2^{32} clusters), the first 4 bits of each entry are reserved.

Figure 5-6 shows cluster sizes on different-sized volumes that use FAT32. On a 2 GB hard disk that uses FAT32, a cluster consists of only 8 sectors (as compared to 64 sectors for the same-sized volume under FAT16). FAT32 can support much larger hard disks, theoretically up to 8 TB (terabytes); however, FAT32 volumes are limited to 32 GB in size because Windows can only create FAT32 volumes up to 32 GB. For volumes larger in size than 32 GB, you must use NTFS.

Figure 5-6 **Cluster sizes for FAT32 volumes**

Volume Size			Cluster Size	
From	To	Sectors/Cluster	Bytes	Kilobytes (KB)
33 MB	64 MB	1 sector	512	0.5
65 MB	128 MB	2 sectors	1,024	1
129 MB	256 MB	4 sectors	2,048	2
257 MB	8 GB	8 sectors	4,096	4
8 GB	16 GB	16 sectors	8,192	8
16 GB	32 GB	32 sectors	16,384	16
1 sector = 512 bytes				

Comparing Slack in FAT16, FAT32, and NTFS

Although large files take a lot of storage space on a volume, small files waste a lot of storage space relative to their size. For example, on a 2 GB hard disk that uses FAT16, a 256-byte shortcut requires only a half-sector of storage space, but actually uses 64 sectors of storage space because the operating system allocates one cluster (or 64 sectors) to the shortcut. That shortcut wastes 63½ sectors (which becomes slack), as illustrated in Figure 5-7. On a 2 GB hard disk that uses the FAT32 file system, the operating system still allocates one cluster to that shortcut, but since a cluster contains 8 sectors, only 7½ sectors of storage space are wasted (and end up as slack). On a 2 GB volume that uses NTFS, the operating system allocates one cluster of storage space; however, since a cluster contains 4 sectors for a 2 GB volume, only 3½ sectors of storage space are wasted (and become slack). From Figure 5-7, it's clear that FAT32 is far more efficient than FAT16 on small volumes and that NTFS uses storage space even more efficiently and thereby reduces slack.

Figure 5-7 How file systems affect slack

Volume Size	File System	Shortcut Size	Allocated	Cluster Size	Slack
2 GB	FAT16	1/2 sector	1 cluster	64 sectors	63½ sectors
2 GB	FAT32	1/2 sector	1 cluster	8 sectors	7½ sectors
2 GB	NTFS	1/2 sector	1 cluster	4 sectors	3½ sectors

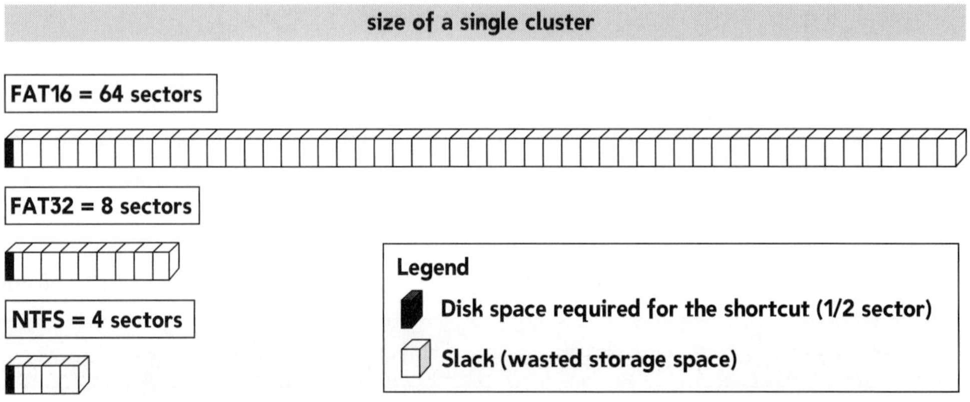

If you compare the largest-size volume supported by FAT32, namely 32 GB, with a similar 32 GB volume that uses NTFS, it's even more obvious that as volume sizes increase, NTFS is more efficient at using disk storage space. Continuing with the previous example of a shortcut that requires only a half-sector of storage space, Windows Vista allocates one cluster of storage space to the shortcut, but on a 32 GB volume, the cluster size for FAT32 consists of 32 sectors, so 31½ sectors of storage space are wasted. In contrast, on a 32 GB volume that uses NTFS, the cluster size is smaller and consists of only 8 sectors so that same shortcut wastes only 7½ sectors of storage space on disk. See Figure 5-8.

How FAT32 and NTFS affect slack

Figure 5-8

Volume Size	File System	Shortcut Size	Allocated	Cluster Size	Slack
32 GB	FAT32	1/2 sector	1 cluster	32 sectors	31½ sectors
32 GB	NTFS	1/2 sector	1 cluster	8 sectors	7½ sectors

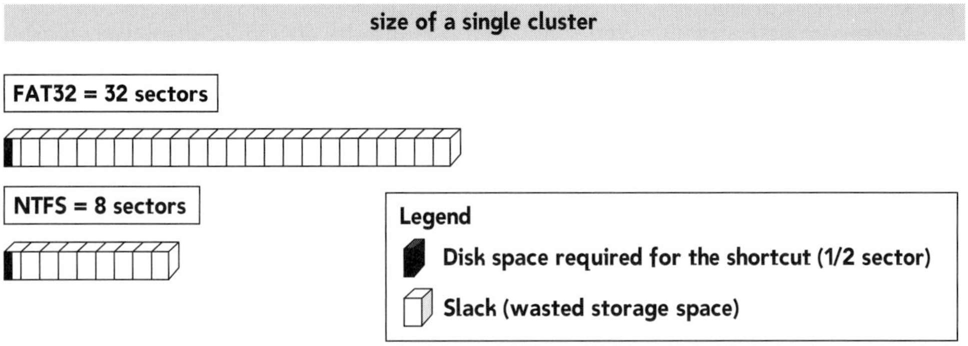

size of a single cluster

FAT32 = 32 sectors

NTFS = 8 sectors

Legend

Disk space required for the shortcut (1/2 sector)

Slack (wasted storage space)

Today, storage capacities of hard disks far exceed those used in the preceding examples, and hard disk storage capacities double almost every year. NTFS is the only Windows Vista file system that supports these larger capacity hard disk drives. Furthermore, even as hard disk storage capacities increase, NTFS still uses storage space efficiently.

Tip

You can store more files on FAT16 and FAT32 flash drives if you use 8.3 filenames instead of long filenames.

The Extended FAT File System

Microsoft introduced the **Extended FAT** (known by its popular name **exFAT**) file system in the Windows Vista Service Pack 1 upgrade to provide support for larger storage capacities on flash memory storage devices. The Extended FAT file system is also an important file system for mobile devices. Devices that use the exFAT file system can store data in excess of 4 GB, support up to 1,000 files per folder (or directory), and support larger file sizes for storing multimedia files.

Checking the File System of a Drive

To find out what file system your computer uses for a specific drive or volume, you can view properties of that drive or volume. The General property sheet for a drive or volume identifies the file system and provides other information, such as the amount of used space, the amount of free space, and the total capacity of the drive or volume. Windows Vista or any operating system works more slowly with a disk that is full or nearly full than one that has plenty of free space, so this information can help you manage your computer resources and improve performance.

On the General property sheet, you can assign a name to a disk by entering a **volume label** (an electronic label). You can select a volume label that identifies the contents or purpose of the drive, or you can enter all or part of your last name to identify that you own the disk in case you misplace it and need to claim it later. For NTFS volumes, you can use up to 32 characters for the volume label. You can also use any symbols you want as part of the volume label, and you can mix different cases (uppercase and lowercase characters). FAT volume names are limited to 11 characters.

In response to a request by an employee in the Advertising department, Cadence asks you to evaluate the file systems and storage capacities on that employee's computer to make sure it meets that employee's needs and ensures the privacy and security of the data on the hard disk drive.

To check the file systems used on your computer:

1. If necessary, display the Computer icon on the desktop, switch your computer to single-click activation (or Web style), and activate the option for displaying file extensions.
2. Open a Computer window, right-click the **icon for the hard disk drive** (usually drive C), and then click **Properties** on the shortcut menu. Windows Vista opens the Local Disk (C:) Properties dialog box and displays information on the General property sheet. On the computer used for Figure 5-9, Windows Vista reports that the file system used on Local Disk (C:) is NTFS, and the text box to the right of the drive icon is blank. Your drive C friendly name may differ if you or your computer manufacturer changed it. If you have changed the default name for drive C from Local Disk, the name you specified appears on the title bar of the dialog box and in the text box to the left of the drive icon. The pie chart represents the amount of used space and free space for the total storage capacity of the volume. As you can tell from this property sheet, Windows Vista automatically indexes this drive for faster searching. NTFS volumes also contain a check box for compressing the drive to conserve storage space.

Tip

If you point to a hard disk drive, Windows Vista displays the drive's file system and its total, free, and unused space in the Details Pane.

Figure 5-9 Viewing hard disk drive properties

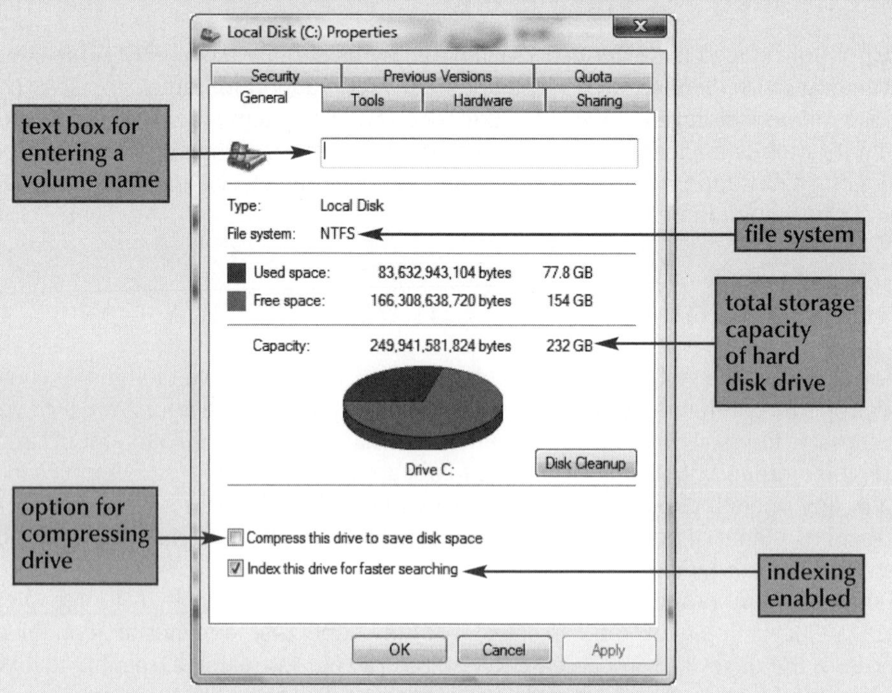

3. Click the **Hardware** tab, and in the "All disk drives" box, double-click the **border** after the Type and then the Name columns (in that order) for a best fit of the contents in each column. On the Hardware property sheet, Windows Vista lists all the disk drives in your computer. See Figure 5-10. Your drives will differ and may include references to USB devices. Although Windows Vista identifies drives in the Computer window, this property sheet has the added advantage of identifying the manufacturer and model of each drive, where that information is known. If you select a drive in the "All disk drives" box, the Device Properties section identifies the manufacturer, the physical location, and the device status (whether the device is working properly). If you select a hardware device and then click the Properties button, Windows Vista opens a Properties dialog box that provides more information for that device. You will examine hardware properties in more detail in Tutorial 12.

Viewing a list of disk drives on a computer **Figure 5-10**

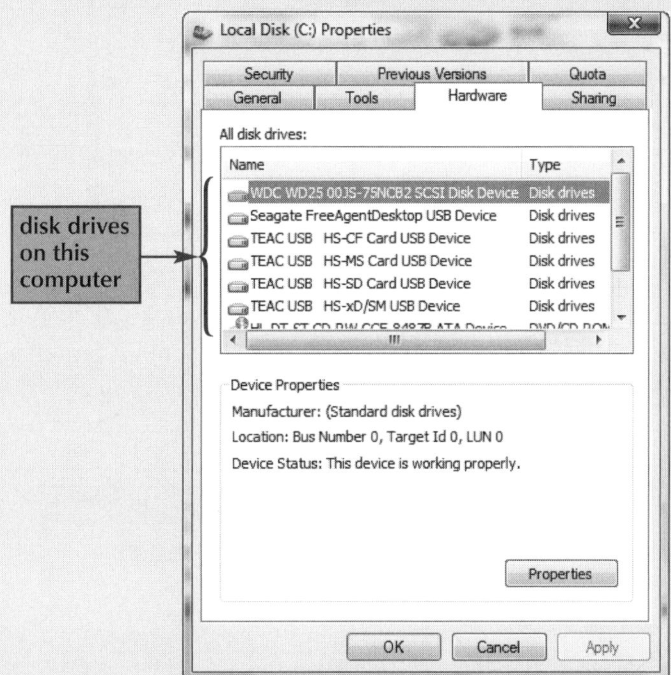

4. Close the Local Disk (C:) Properties dialog box.

5. Examine the drives in the Computer window, attach your flash drive, and if necessary, close any window or dialog box that opens. After you attach a flash drive, Windows Vista displays a drive icon for the flash drive in the Computer window.

6. Right-click your **flash drive** icon and then click **Properties**. Windows Vista opens a Removable Disk Properties dialog box for that drive. See Figure 5-11. If you or the manufacturer has assigned a volume label to this drive (as is the case for the flash drive in the figure), the volume label replaces the default name "Removable Disk" in the title bar and in the Computer window. For the flash drive used in Figure 5-11, Windows Vista reports the file system as FAT32. If a flash drive uses the FAT16 file system, Windows Vista reports the file system as FAT, so you can easily distinguish between FAT16 and FAT32 volumes.

Figure 5-11 Viewing properties of a USB flash drive

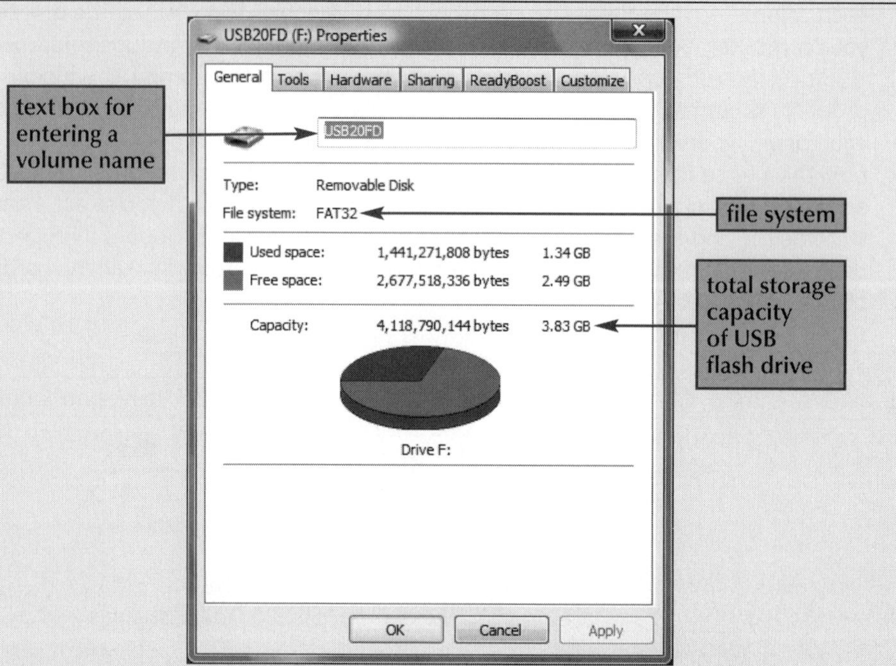

7. Click the **Hardware** tab. The flash drive is now included in "All disk drives" list box. See Figure 5-12. Windows Vista identifies this flash drive as a "PNY USB 2.0 FD USB Device." Your flash drive might be reported as another brand or as a "Generic USB Flash Disk USB Device."

Figure 5-12 Flash drive included in list of disk drives

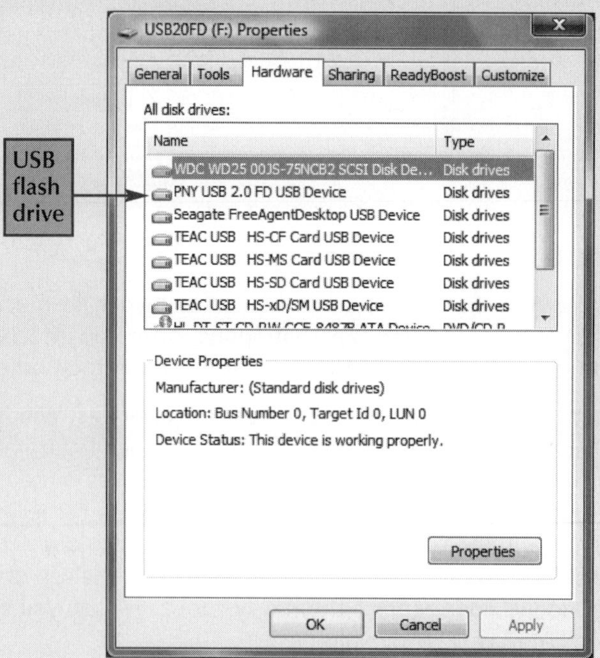

8. Close the Properties dialog box for your flash drive.

You can also view the file system used for other types of drives, including DVD and CD drives. If you only have a DVD drive or a CD drive, then complete the steps for the type of drive that you have.

To examine the file systems used on other types of drives:

1. Insert a DVD with data into a DVD drive on your computer, if possible, wait a moment, and if Windows Vista displays an AutoPlay dialog box, close the AutoPlay dialog box.
2. Right-click the **DVD drive** icon in the Computer window, and then click **Properties**. On the General property sheet for the DVD drive, Windows Vista identifies the drive type as a CD Drive and the file system as UDF. See Figure 5-13. The Universal Disk Format (UDF) file system is a successor to the Compact Disc File System (CDFS) originally designed for CDs. UDF provides support for long filenames (greater than 64 characters) and a multitier folder structure. For the DVD-RW drive used on this computer, the total storage capacity of the Windows Vista Ultimate DVD is 2.49 GB. Your DVD properties will differ.

Figure 5-13 Viewing properties of a DVD disk drive

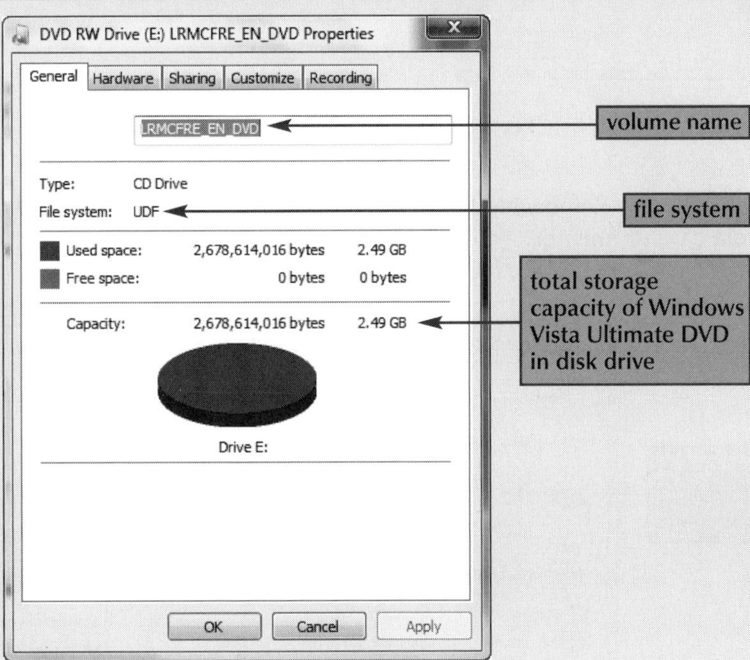

3. Close the DVD Drive Properties dialog box.
4. Insert a CD with data into a CD drive, if possible, wait a moment, and if Windows Vista displays an AutoPlay dialog box, close the AutoPlay dialog box.
5. Right-click the **CD drive** icon in the Computer window, and then click **Properties**. On the General property sheet for the CD drive on the computer used for Figure 5-14, Windows Vista identifies the file system as CDFS (for Compact Disc File System). For the CD-RW drive used on this computer, the total storage capacity of the Microsoft Office Professional 2007 CD is 410 MB.

Figure 5-14 Viewing properties of a CD disk drive

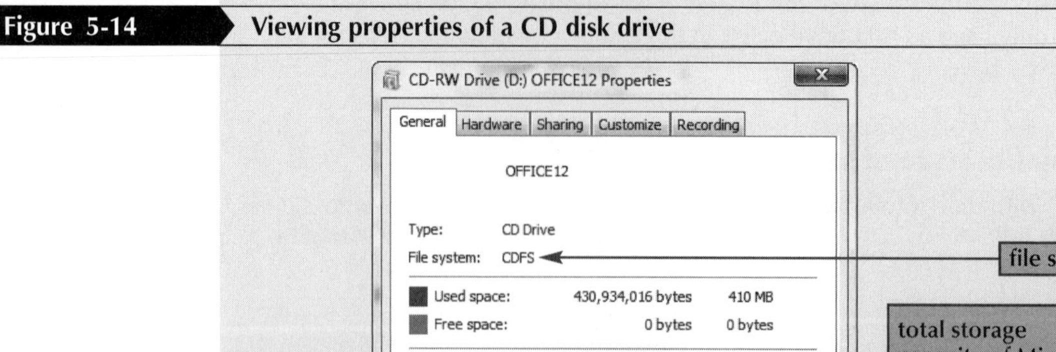

6. Close the CD drive's Properties dialog box and then close the Computer window.

Figure 5-15 shows a Removable Disk Properties dialog box for a 2 GB SD (Secure Digital) media card (or memory card) used to store photos in a digital camera. Notice that Windows Vista identifies the file system as FAT (for FAT16).

Figure 5-15 Viewing properties of a memory card

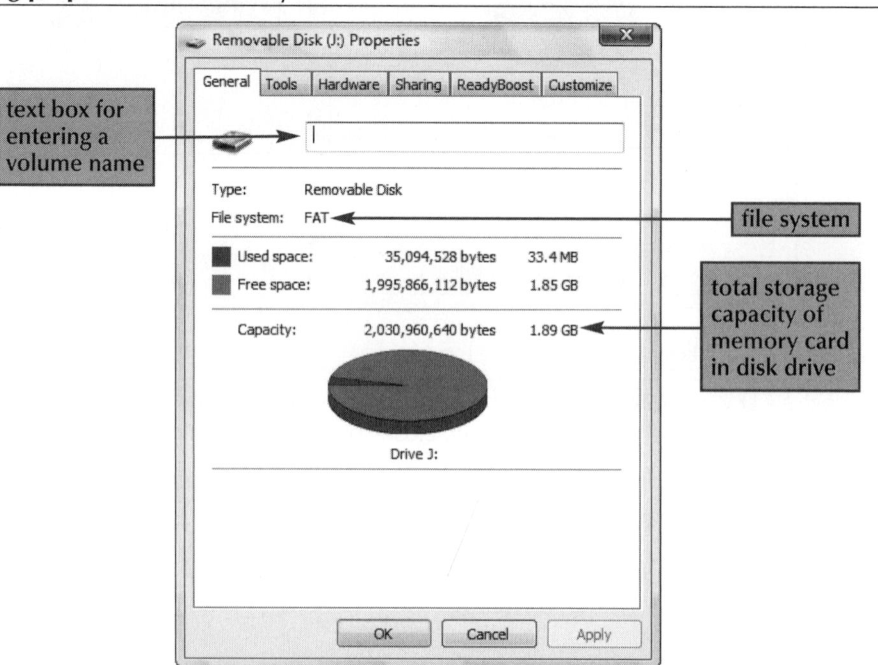

Identifying a Drive's File System | Reference Window

- From the Start menu or a Computer desktop icon, open a Computer window.
- Right-click a drive icon and then click Properties on the shortcut menu.
- Check the General property sheet for the file system used on the disk and check the drive's file system.
- Close the Properties dialog box for the drive, and then close the Computer window.

The new Windows Vista **Live File System** allows you to work with DVDs and CDs as if they were flash drives. That means that you can copy files to a DVD or CD as you work. You no longer have to select a group of files, indicate that you want to copy them to a DVD or CD, and then wait for Windows to burn the files on the DVD or CD. The Live File System is compatible with Windows Vista, but not earlier Windows versions.

Using the Disk Management Snap-In Tool

If your user account is an Administrator account, you can open a system administrative tool known as Computer Management and then use the Disk Management snap-in to display more detailed information about disks and drives on your computer. By default, the Business, Ultimate, and Enterprise Editions of Windows Vista contain the Disk Management snap-in.

Computer Management is a console (or administrative tool) within the Microsoft Management Console (MMC). The **Microsoft Management Console** is a Windows component that provides access to administrative tools created by Microsoft and other software manufacturers so that you can manage hardware, software, and networks. A **snap-in** is a program for managing Windows, and it operates within the Microsoft Management Console. You access snap-ins from the Administrative Tools folder in the Control Panel.

The Disk Management snap-in tool identifies the type of file system each volume uses and whether a volume is a primary partition or a logical drive on an extended partition. As noted earlier, a primary partition is a partition on a **basic disk**, a physical disk that uses a Master Boot Record and a Hard Disk Partition Table to identify the **active partition**—the partition that contains the files for booting a computer. A basic disk can contain up to four primary partitions, or three primary partitions and one extended partition. An **extended partition** is a partition that contains one or more logical drives.

In Windows Vista Ultimate, you can convert a basic disk into a dynamic disk using the Disk Management snap-in. A **dynamic disk** is a physical hard disk containing dynamic volumes that support features not available on basic disks. Dynamic disks use an operating system-specific database to keep track of disks and volumes and provide features that are not available on basic disks (though basic disks are simpler to manage). A dynamic volume is a volume that you create on a dynamic disk. The Business, Home Premium, Home Basic, and Starter Editions of Windows Vista do not support dynamic disks. You can create one of the following types of dynamic volumes with Windows Vista Ultimate or Windows Vista Enterprise:

- **Simple volume** A **simple volume** consists of a single region of storage space on one physical disk or multiple regions of storage space on one physical volume.
- **Spanned volume** A **spanned volume** combines unused storage space from more than one physical hard disk into one logical volume. That means the volume extends across more than one physical hard disk, so you must have at least two physical hard disks to create this type of volume.
- **Striped volume** A **striped volume** (also known as RAID-0) records data across multiple physical hard disks in a pattern known as stripes, thereby improving performance.

RAID stands for **Redundant Array of Independent Disks**, and it provides a way of storing data on more than one disk to improve performance or reliability. There are two other types of dynamic volumes:

- **Mirrored volume** A **mirrored volume** (also known as RAID-1 and supported by Windows Server 2008) consists of two physical hard disks, one of which contains an identical copy of the contents of the other hard disk. By duplicating data on another volume (called **data redundancy**), this type of dynamic disk is **fault-tolerant**. If one physical hard disk fails, the operating system uses the second physical hard disk that has a duplicate copy of the contents of the physical hard disk that failed. Your computer continues to operate without problems.
- **RAID-5 volume** A **RAID-5 volume** is fault-tolerant and stores data and parity information in stripes across three or more physical hard disks. **Parity** is a calculated value derived from data (or an error-checking) feature that enables the operating system to reconstruct lost data if one physical hard disk fails. After restoring the lost data on the failed physical hard disk, your computer continues to operate without problems.

Simple, spanned, and striped volumes are not fault-tolerant. Obviously, if the disk that contains a simple volume fails, you cannot access data on the simple volume. If one disk in a spanned or a striped volume fails, you cannot access data on the spanned or striped volume.

At a weekly meeting with her staff, Cadence and her staff examine and discuss new features of the Windows Vista Disk Management snap-in. She asks you to set up a demonstration of this important tool for the upcoming meeting.

To complete the next section of the tutorial, your user account must be an Administrator account, or you must provide the password for an Administrator account. If your user account is not an Administrator account, and if you do not know the user name and password for an Administrator account, read the following steps and examine the figures so that you are familiar with this important tool, but do not keystroke the steps. Also, if Administrative Tools is not displayed as an option on the Start or All Programs menus, you will need to add this option to the Start menu and All Programs menu to simplify access to the Disk Management snap-in tool.

If you are working in a college computer lab, you can ask your instructor and technical support staff whether you have permission to use the Disk Management snap-in tool to view information about volumes on the computers in your college computer lab. If your edition of Windows Vista does not contain the Disk Management snap-in, read the steps in this section of the tutorial and examine the figures but do not keystroke the steps.

To add Administrative Tools to the Start and All Programs menus:

1. Right-click the **Start** button, click **Properties** on the shortcut menu, and on the Start Menu property sheet, click the Start menu option's **Customize** button. Windows Vista opens the Customize Start Menu dialog box.
2. Scroll to the bottom of the list box that provides options for customizing how links, icons, and menus look and behave on the Start menu; locate System Administrative Tools; click the **Display on the All Programs menu and the Start menu** option button; click the **OK** button in the Customize Start Menu dialog box; and then click the **OK** button in the Taskbar and Start Menu Properties dialog box.

Now you're ready to open Computer Management and view information about the drives in your computer.

To open Computer Management:

1. On the Start menu, point to **Administrative Tools** and then click **Computer Management**. Windows Vista switches to Secure Desktop Mode and displays a User Account Control dialog box.
2. If you are logged on under an Administrator account, click the **Continue** button, or if you are logged on under a Standard user account, enter the **password** for an Administrator account, and then click the **OK** button. Windows Vista opens the Computer Management window. From the Computer Management window, you can open specific snap-ins such as Disk Management.
3. Maximize the Computer Management window and then, under Storage in the console tree pane on the left, click **Disk Management** and wait for Windows Vista to connect to the Virtual Disk Service and load disk configuration information. The Details pane in the middle of the window provides information about the volumes and disks on your computer. See Figure 5-16. At the top of the Details pane is the Volume List area, and at the bottom is the Graphical View area. The view in your Details pane will differ from that shown in the figure.

Tip

You can also right-click the desktop Computer icon, click Manage, and then click Disk Management under Storage in the console pane in the Computer Management window.

Figure 5-16 Using Disk Management to view information on volumes

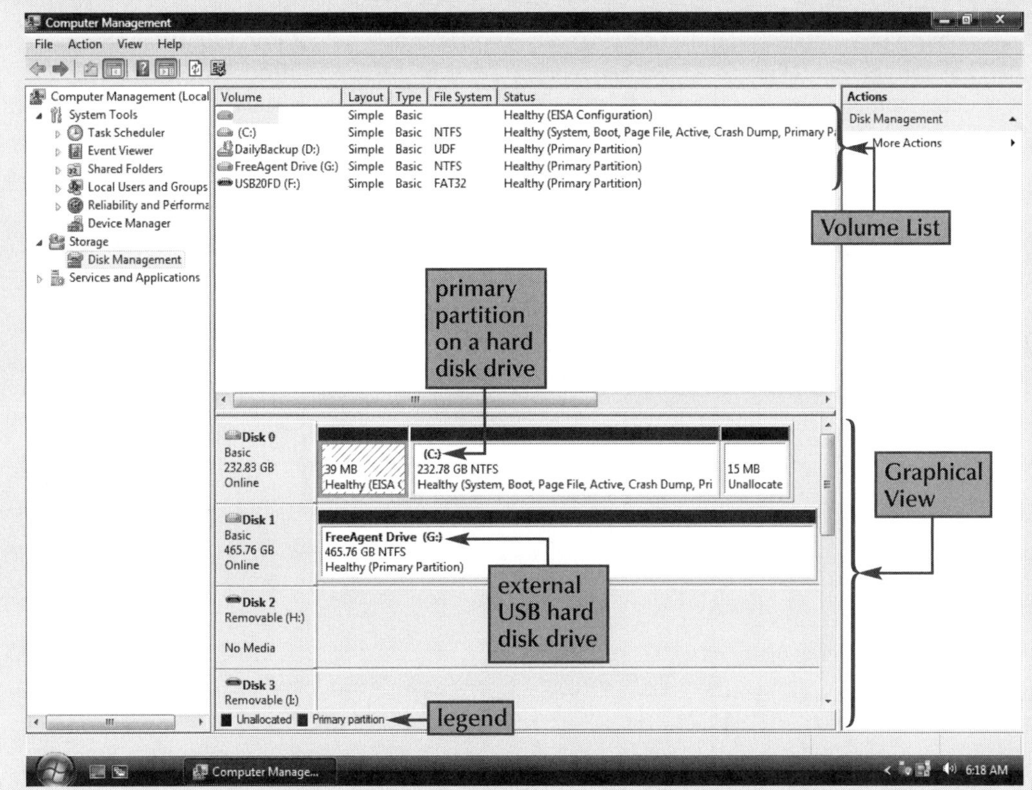

4. To more clearly identify these two areas in the Details Pane, click **View** on the menu bar, and then click **Customize**. The Customize View dialog box opens.

Tip

Right-click a disk or partition to display a shortcut menu of actions that you can perform on the disk or partition.

5. Click the **Description bar** check box to enable this feature, and then click the **OK** button. The bar at the top of the Details pane identifies the two views in the Details pane (i.e., Volume List + Graphical View). On the computer used for the figures in this section, the Graphical View area shows one hard disk (identified as Disk 0) with a storage capacity of 232.83 GB. Disk 0 is divided into two primary partitions: a hidden partition set up by the computer manufacturer, and a partition identified with the drive C letter (C:). This hard disk also has a small, unallocated region. The legend at the bottom of the Details pane identifies the disk regions shown in the Graphical View area. Drive C is a primary partition that uses NTFS. Disk 1 is an external USB hard disk drive that also uses NTFS. If you do not see a specific disk in the Graphical View area, you can adjust your view by scrolling, or you can examine the Volume List at the top of the Details pane. In the Volume List, the Disk Management snap-in identifies Disk 0 (Drive C) as a basic volume that uses NTFS. In the Status column for this disk, "Healthy" indicates that the volume is accessible and does not have any known problems. In parenthesis, Disk Management notes that this volume is both the system volume and the boot volume (as is typically the case). Drive F, a flash drive, is identified as Healthy and has a primary partition that uses FAT32.
6. Click **View** on the menu bar, point to **Top**, and then click **Disk List**. The view at the top of the Details pane changes to show a listing of Disks by disk number or CD-ROM number. See Figure 5-17. The Status column identifies whether a disk is online or whether it contains no media. The Device Type column identifies the type of connection (USB for a USB hardware device and IDE for Integrated Drive Electronics). The Partition Style column identifies all these disks as MBR disks, or disks that use a Master Book Record. Your details will differ.

Figure 5-17 Using Disk Management to view information on disks

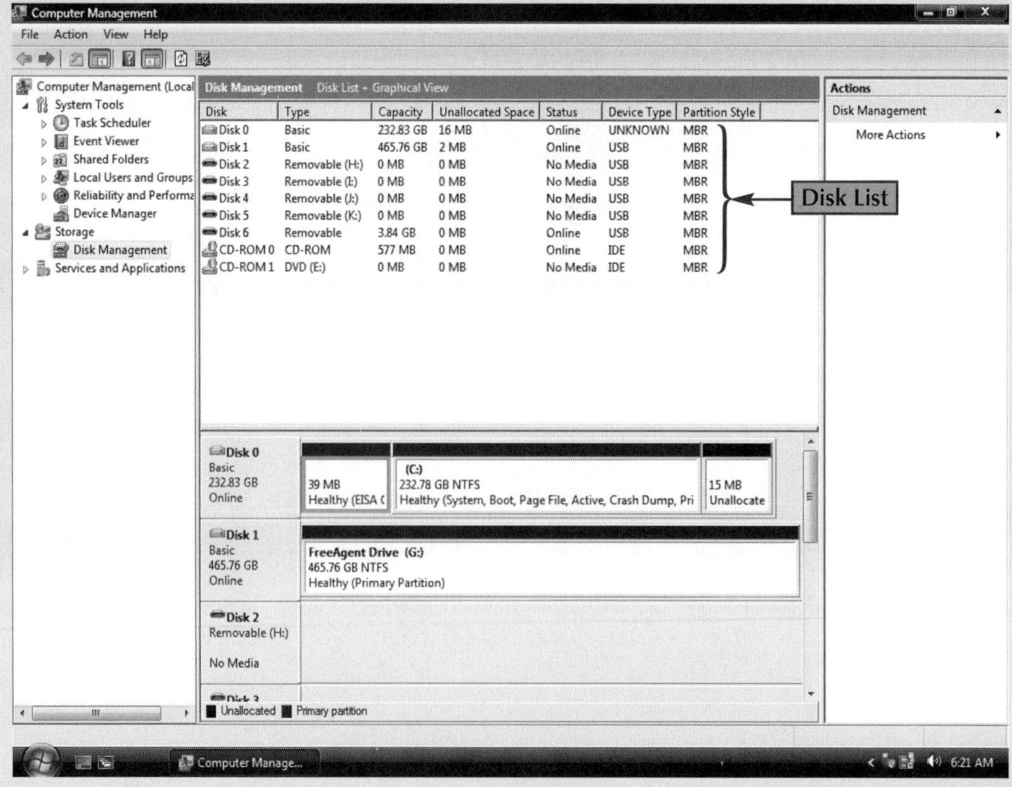

7. To restore your default settings before closing the Computer Management window, click **View** on the menu bar, point to **Top**, and then click **Volume List**.

8. Next, click **View** on the menu bar, click **Customize**, and in the Customize View dialog box, click the **Description bar** check box to enable this feature, click the **OK** button, and then close the Computer Management window.

You can use the Disk Management snap-in to perform a variety of tasks on disks, partitions, volumes, and logical drives, including identifying and troubleshooting problems. Under Windows Vista, you can now extend a primary partition or logical drive to use additional unallocated disk storage space or to shrink the size of a partition or a logical drive so that you can create unallocated disk storage space for use as a new partition. If you shrink a partition or logical drive, files are moved, if necessary, so that you do not lose any data.

Using the Disk Management Snap-In Tool | Reference Window

- If Administrative Tools is not displayed on the All Programs menu, right-click the Start button, click Properties on the shortcut menu, and on the Start Menu property sheet, click the Start Menu option's Customize button. Scroll to the bottom of the list box that provides options for customizing how links, icons, and menus look and behave on the Start menu, locate System Administrative Tools, click the "Display on the All Programs menu and the Start menu option button," click the OK button in the Customize Start Menu dialog box, and then click the OK button in the Taskbar and Start Menu Properties dialog box.
- On the Start menu, point to Administrative Tools, click Computer Management, and in the User Account Control dialog box, click the Continue button, or enter the password for an Administrator account, and then click the OK button.
- Under Storage in the console tree pane on the left, click Disk Management and wait for Windows Vista to load disk configuration information.
- To more clearly identify the two areas in the Details pane, click View on the menu bar, click Customize, and in the Customize View dialog box, click the Description bar check box to enable this feature, and then click the OK button.
- To view disk information by disk number and CD number, click View on the menu bar, point to Top, and then click Disk List.

Session 5.1 Quick Check | Review

1. A(n) ________________ is a physical device, such as a hard disk, whereas a(n) ________________ is a logical concept and consists of all or part of a disk, uses a specific file system, has a drive name, and may span multiple hard disks.
2. A(n) ________________ is a subdivision of a track and stores 512 bytes, whereas a(n) ________________ is the smallest amount of storage space that Windows Vista allocates to a file or part of a file.
3. Storage space allocated to a file, but not used by that file, is called ________________.
4. What table does NTFS use to keep track of folders and files on a hard disk?
5. What new Windows Vista file system permits copying to a DVD or CD on an as-needed basis?
6. What is the difference between the boot volume and the system volume?

Session 5.2

Setting Up a Folder for Data Files

To complete the steps in this session of the tutorial, you will need to copy the extracted Tutorial folder provided with your Data Files from the Documents folder, your flash drive, or a network folder to the Public Documents folder, and then rename the new folder.

To copy the Data Files to your Public Documents folder:

1. Make sure you have your copy of the Windows Vista for Power Users Tutorial.05 Data Files.

   Trouble? If you don't have the Data Files for this tutorial, you need to get them before you can proceed. Your instructor might ask you to obtain them from a specified location (such as a network drive) or download them from Course Technology's Web site. If you have any questions about the Data Files, see your instructor or technical support person for assistance. If you download the Data Files, you must extract them before you can use them.

2. Close all open windows, open a window onto the Documents subfolder, your flash drive folder, or the network folder that contains a copy of the Tutorial folder in the Tutorial.05 folder provided with your Data Files.
3. From the Start menu, open **Documents**, click **Public** in the Navigation Pane, and then click **Public Documents**. Windows Vista opens the Public Documents folder window.
4. Right-click the **taskbar** and then click **Show Windows Side by Side**. Windows Vista places the two open windows side by side on the desktop and makes them equal in size. Windows Vista places the last window that you open on the left side of the desktop.
5. Hold down the **Ctrl** key while you drag the **Tutorial** folder to the Public Documents folder window, and then release your left mouse button. Windows Vista copies the Tutorial folder to the Public Documents folder window.
6. Change the name of the Tutorial folder to **Cooper & Bauman**.
7. If necessary, change to Large Icons view.
8. Open the **Cooper & Bauman** folder, right-click the **Performance folder icon**, click **Cut**, click the **Back** button, click the **Organize** button on the command bar, and then click **Paste**. Windows Vista moves the Performance folder to the Public Documents folder.
9. Close the Tutorial.05 folder window that contains the original copy of the Tutorial folder, and then maximize the Public Documents folder.
10. Keep the Public Documents folder window open for the next section of the tutorial.

Now, you're ready to examine NTFS folder and file compression.

Compressing and Uncompressing Folders and Files

On an NTFS volume, you can compress files, folders, or even an entire drive, but not on a FAT volume. Once a file is compressed, NTFS handles the decompression and recompression of files as you work on them in applications. Window Vista follows certain rules when you copy or move uncompressed or compressed folders and files from one location to another within an NTFS volume:

- When you *move* a folder or file to another folder, the file keeps its compression state after the move. Therefore, if you move an uncompressed folder or file to a compressed folder, the file remains uncompressed. Likewise, if you move a compressed folder or file to an uncompressed folder, the folder or file remains compressed.
- When you *copy* a folder or file to another folder, the file takes on the compression state of the folder. Therefore, if you copy a compressed file to an uncompressed folder, the file is uncompressed. Likewise, if you copy an uncompressed file to a compressed folder, the file is compressed.
- If you copy a file to a folder and that folder contains a file by the same name, the copied file takes on the compression state of the file already stored in that folder.

Copying Files Between FAT and NTFS Volumes | InSight

If you copy a file from a folder on a FAT volume to a folder on an NTFS volume, the file takes on the compression state of the folder on the NTFS volume. If you copy a compressed folder or file from an NTFS volume to a FAT volume, the folder or file is uncompressed. Likewise, if you e-mail a compressed file, the person who receives that message receives an uncompressed file attached to the message.

In the following steps, you are going to compress and uncompress a folder on an NTFS volume. If you are working in a college computer lab, ask your instructor or technical support staff for permission to compress and uncompress a folder. If you do not have permission to use the NTFS compression feature on a volume, read the steps and examine the figures so that you are familiar with this feature, but do not keystroke the following steps.

Cadence asks you to show a new employee how to compress folders and files on his computer so that he can archive important files and free up valuable storage space.

To compress a folder and its contents:

1. Right-click the **Cooper & Bauman** folder and then click **Properties** on the shortcut menu. On the General property sheet in the Cooper & Bauman Properties dialog box, Windows Vista reports that this folder and its subfolder and files are 5.83 MB (6,118,056 bytes) in size, use 5.87 MB (6,160,384 bytes) of storage space on the disk, and currently contain 24 files in 3 folders. See Figure 5-18. That means this folder and its subfolders and files waste 42,328 bytes of storage space on the disk because of slack.

Tip

If a folder or file is already selected, you can press the Alt+Enter keys to open the folder or file's Properties dialog box.

Figure 5-18 Viewing properties of the Cooper & Bauman folder

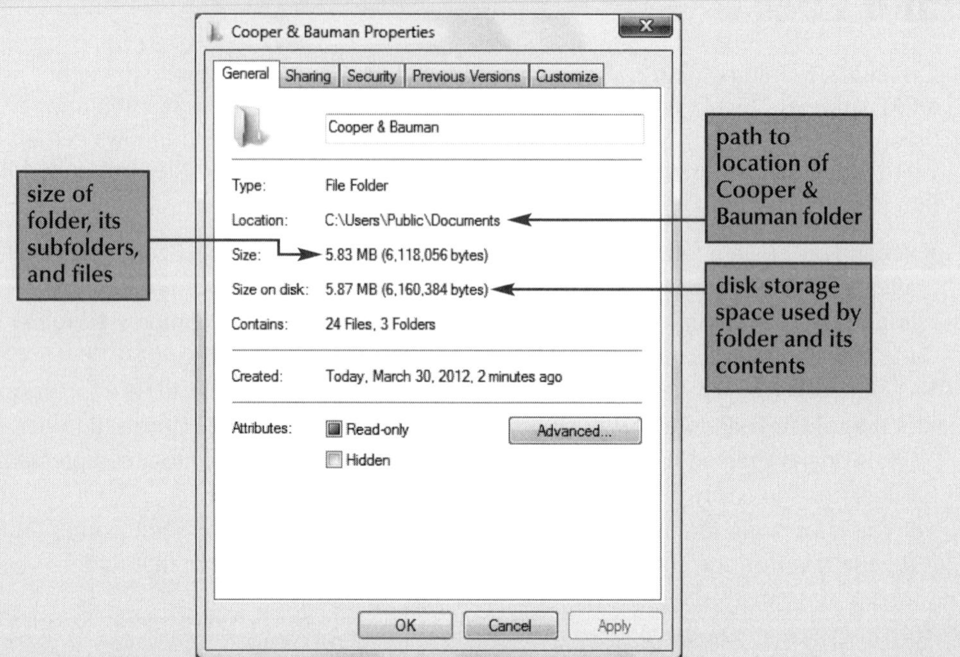

2. Click the **Advanced** button. Windows Vista opens the Advanced Attributes dialog box. See Figure 5-19. Under the Compress or Encrypt attributes section is an option for compressing the contents of the folder to save disk space.

Figure 5-19 Advanced Attributes dialog box

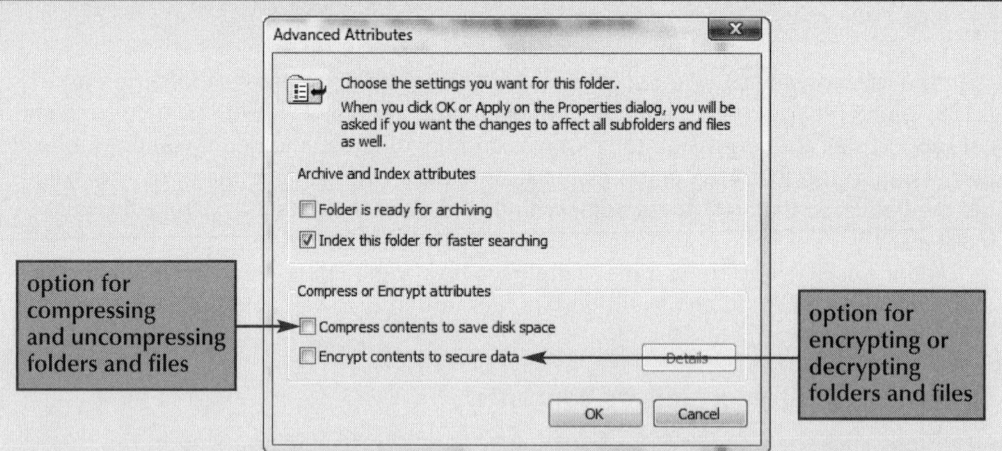

3. Click the **Compress contents to save disk space** check box, click the **OK** button in the Advanced Attributes dialog box, and then click the **Apply** button in the Cooper & Bauman Properties dialog box. The Confirm Attribute Changes dialog box informs you that you have chosen to apply the Compress attribute. See Figure 5-20. You have the option of applying this change to only the Cooper & Bauman folder, or you can apply the change to the Cooper & Bauman folder and all its subfolders and files. Windows Vista automatically selects the latter option.

Figure 5-20 Confirm Attribute Changes dialog box

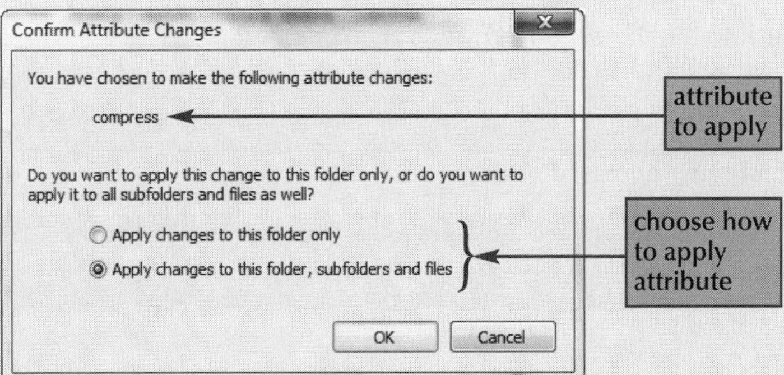

4. If it is not already selected, click the **Apply changes to this folder, subfolders and files** option button, and then click the **OK** button. On the General property sheet in the Cooper & Bauman Properties dialog box, Windows Vista reports that this folder and its subfolder and files are still 5.83 MB (6,118,056 bytes) in size, but it now uses only 2.35 MB (2,468,184 bytes) of storage space on the disk. See Figure 5-21. Windows Vista has reduced the amount of disk space used by this folder by 3,688,271 bytes (or approximately 3.5 MB). Windows Vista compressed the folder by almost 60% so that the folder is about 40% of its original size. That's a substantial reduction in the amount of storage space that the folder now uses on disk.

Figure 5-21 Viewing properties of a compressed folder

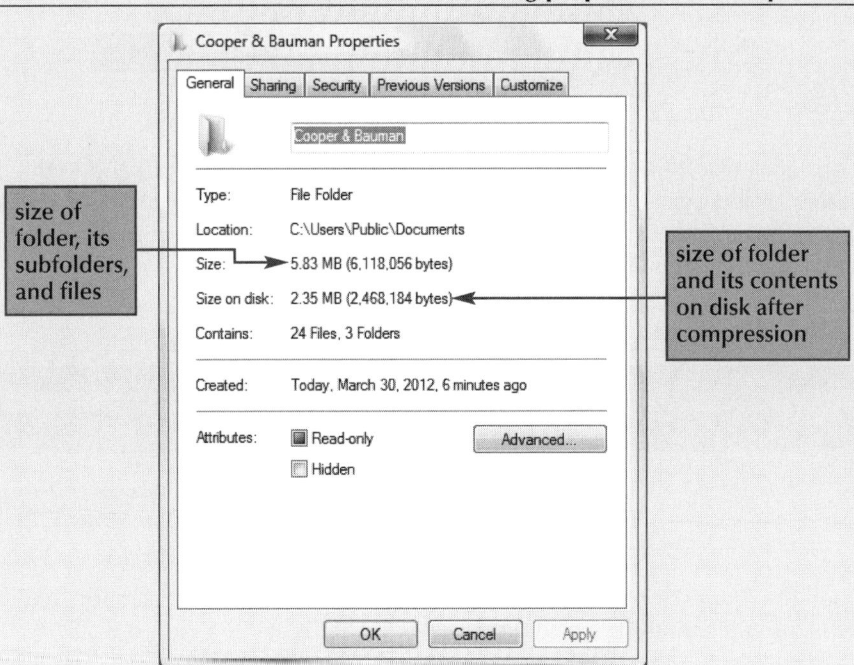

5. Click the **OK** button to close the Cooper & Bauman Properties dialog box, click the **folder window background**, and notice that the Cooper & Bauman folder name is displayed in bright blue to indicate that the folders contents are compressed. See Figure 5-22. In contrast, the Performance folder is uncompressed, as evidenced by the folder name appearing in black.

Trouble? If Windows Vista does not display compressed folders and files in bright blue, click the Organize button on the command bar, click Folder and Search Options, click the View tab, and in the Advanced settings list box, locate and add a check mark to the "Show encrypted or compressed NTFS files in color" check box, and then click OK to close the Folder Options dialog box and apply the new setting.

Figure 5-22 Compressed and uncompressed folders

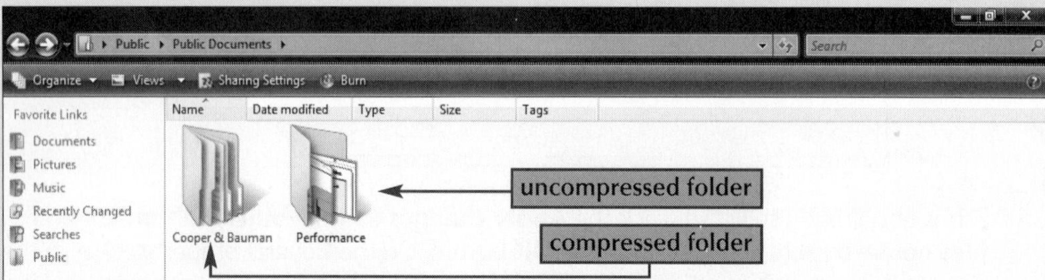

Tip

If a folder or file is already selected, you can press the Enter key to quickly open the folder or file.

6. Open the **Cooper & Bauman** folder, change to Details view (if necessary), and notice that the subfolder names are also shown in bright blue. See Figure 5-23.

Figure 5-23 Viewing compressed subfolders

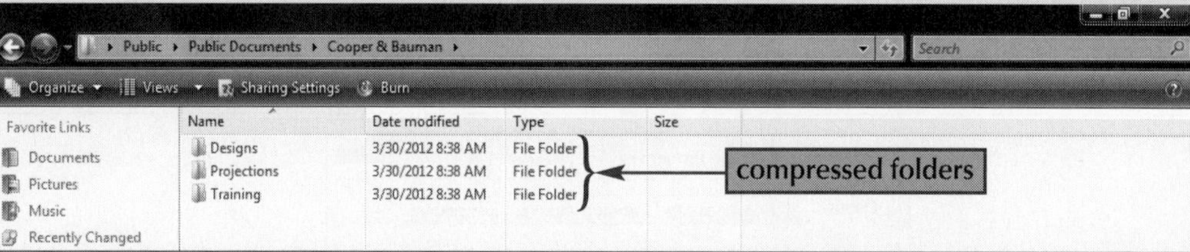

7. Right-click a **column heading**, click **More** on the shortcut menu, and in the Choose Details dialog box, locate and click the **Attributes** check box, and then click the **OK** button. Windows Vista displays an Attributes column. "C" in the Attribute column stands for the Compress attribute. See Figure 5-24.

Figure 5-24 Viewing the Compress attribute

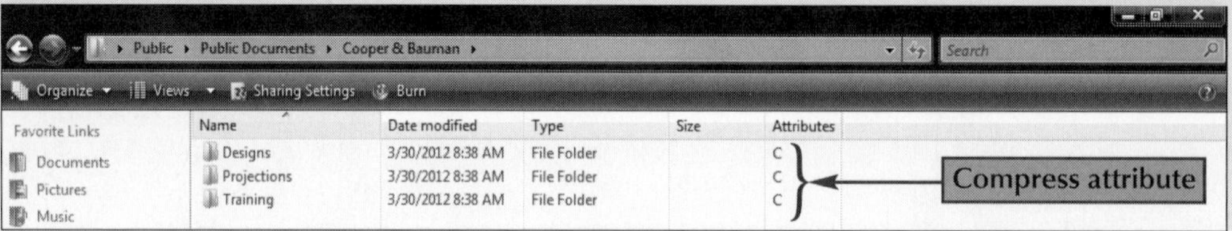

8. Open the **Projections** folder, change to Large Icons view (if necessary), and notice that all the filenames are also displayed in bright blue. See Figure 5-25.

Figure 5-25 Viewing compressed files in a compressed folder

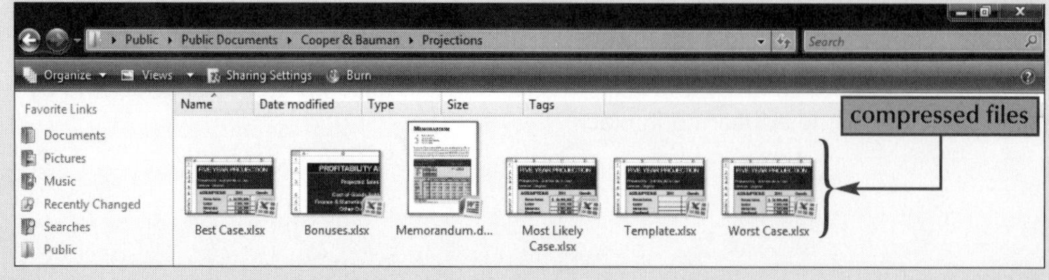

9. Click **Public Documents** in the Address Bar to return to the Public Documents folder.

Next, you want to move the Performance folder to the Cooper & Bauman folder and then copy the Projections folder from the Cooper & Bauman folder to the Public Documents folder and examine changes in compression states.

To move the Performance folder to the Cooper & Bauman folder:

1. Drag the **Performance** folder and drop it onto the **Cooper & Bauman** folder icon. Windows Vista moves the Performance folder into the Cooper & Bauman folder.
2. Open the **Cooper & Bauman** folder, and if necessary, change to Details view. Notice that Windows Vista did not compress the Performance folder after the move (the folder name is shown in black rather than blue). See Figure 5-26. Also, the Attributes column does not contain "C" for Compressed. That means the folder is not compressed.

Figure 5-26 Viewing an uncompressed folder after a move

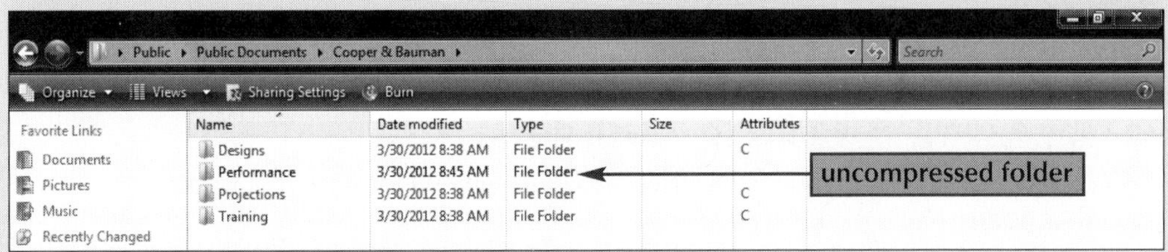

3. Open the **Performance** folder. The files in this folder are not compressed (the filenames are shown in black rather than blue).
4. Click the **Back** button, right-click the **Projections** folder, click **Cut**, click **Public Documents** in the Address Bar, right-click the **background** of the Public Documents window, and then click **Paste**. Notice that the Projections folder retains its compression state when moved from the Cooper & Bauman folder (the folder's name is shown in bright blue).
5. Open the **Projections** folder. Notice that the files within this folder are still compressed.
6. Click **Public Documents** in the Address Bar, and then drag the **Projections** folder to the **Cooper & Bauman** folder. Windows Vista moves the Projections folder back into the Cooper & Bauman folder. If you open the Cooper & Bauman folder, you will find that the Projections folder retains its original compressed state (as you would expect).

Tip

You can press the Backspace key to back up to the previous window.

Next, you are going to copy a folder from the Cooper & Bauman folder and then copy an uncompressed file into the Cooper & Bauman folder.

To copy a compressed folder and its files from a compressed folder:

1. In the Cooper & Bauman folder, right-click the **Training** folder, click **Copy**, click the **Back** button, right-click the **background** of the folder window, and then click **Paste**. Notice that the copy of the previously compressed Training folder is now uncompressed (it takes on the compression state of the current folder, and the folder name is now shown in black).

2. Open the **Training** folder. Notice that the files within this folder are now uncompressed.
3. Right-click the **Spreadsheets.pptx** file, click **Copy**, click the **Back** button, open the Cooper & Bauman folder, right-click the **background** of the folder window, and then click **Paste**. Notice that the Spreadsheets.pptx file now takes on the compression state of the current folder (it's now compressed). See Figure 5-27.

Figure 5-27 Viewing a newly-compressed file after a copy

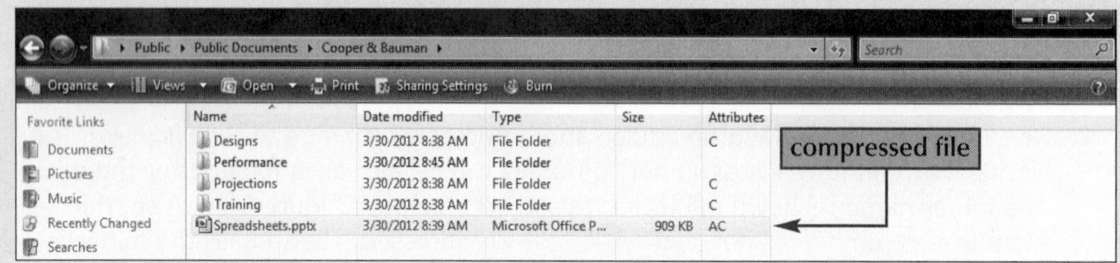

4. Keep this folder open for the next set of steps.

You need to copy a file from the Cooper & Bauman folder to your flash drive.

To copy a compressed file to a flash drive:

1. If necessary, attach your flash drive and close any window or dialog box that opens.
2. Right-click **Spreadsheets.pptx**, point to **Send To**, and then click the **option for your flash drive** on the Send To menu. Windows Vista copies this compressed file to your flash drive.
3. Click the **New Location** arrow to the left of Public in the Address Bar, click **Computer**, and then click **your flash drive icon**. Windows Vista opens a window onto your flash drive. Notice that the Spreadsheets.pptx file is now uncompressed because you copied it to a FAT32 volume. After moving this file, you change your mind and want to remove it from your flash drive.
4. Right-click the **background** of your flash drive window, click **Undo Copy**, and in the Delete File dialog box where Windows Vista asks if you want to permanently delete this file, click the **Yes** button.
5. Click the **Recent Pages** button and then click **Public Documents**.
6. Right-click the Training folder icon, click **Delete**, and in the Delete Folder dialog box, click the **Yes** button. Windows Vista deletes this duplicate copy of the Training folder.
7. Open the **Cooper & Bauman** folder, right-click **Spreadsheets.pptx**, click **Delete**, and in the Delete File dialog box, click the **Yes** button. Windows Vista deletes this duplicate copy of the Spreadsheets.pptx file.
8. Click the **Back** button to return to the Public Documents folder.
9. Keep the Public Documents folder window open for the next set of steps.

Tip

You can undo your last action by pressing the Ctrl+Z keys.

Now, you are going to reverse the compression process and uncompress the Cooper & Bauman folder and its contents.

To uncompress a folder and its contents:

1. Right-click the **Cooper & Bauman** folder, click **Properties** on the shortcut menu, and on the General property sheet of the Cooper & Bauman Properties dialog box, click the **Advanced** button.
2. In the Advanced Attributes dialog box, click the **Compress contents to save disk space** check box to remove the check mark, click the **OK** button, and then click the **Apply** button in the Cooper & Bauman Properties dialog box. Windows Vista displays the Confirm Attribute Changes dialog box and asks how you want to apply this change.
3. Click the **Apply changes to this folder, subfolders and files** option button (if necessary), and then click the **OK** button. On the General property sheet in the Cooper & Bauman Properties dialog box, Windows Vista reports that this folder and its subfolder and files are 5.93 MB (6,220,759 bytes) in size, and the 29 files and 4 folders now use 5.98 MB (6,270,976 bytes) of disk storage space.
4. Click the **OK** button to close the Cooper & Bauman Properties dialog box.
5. Keep the Public Documents folder open for the next section of the tutorial.

In summary, if you *copy* a file (compressed or uncompressed) to a folder on an NTFS volume, the file takes on the compression state of the folder (compressed or uncompressed). If you *move* a compressed or uncompressed file from one folder to another on an NTFS volume, the file remains as it originally was (compressed or uncompressed), no matter whether the folder is compressed or uncompressed. Also, the ability to compress and uncompress folders and files is a feature of NTFS volumes and is not available on FAT volumes.

Compressing and Uncompressing a Folder | Reference Window

- Locate the folder you want to compress, right-click that folder, click Properties, and then click the Advanced button on the General property sheet in the Properties dialog box for that folder.
- In the Compress or Encrypt attributes section of the Advanced Attributes dialog box, add a check mark to the "Compress contents to save disk space" check box to compress the folder or remove the check mark from the "Compress contents to save disk space" to uncompress the folder, click the OK button in the Advanced Attributes dialog box, and then click the OK button in the Properties dialog box for the folder.
- In the Confirm Attribute Changes dialog box, click the "Apply changes to this folder, subfolders and files" option button, and then click the OK button.

You just successfully compressed and then uncompressed a folder and its contents. If you need to archive important files that you no longer use on a daily basis, but want to keep in case you need them in the future, you can compress them so that they use less storage space on your hard disk. Then you can copy or move the compressed files to another disk, such as a DVD, for long-term storage.

Using Compressed (Zipped) Folders

Windows Vista supports Compressed (zipped) Folders on both NTFS and FAT volumes. A **Compressed (zipped) Folder** is a file that contains a group of files, or one or more folders and files, in a single file. Any folders or files you place within a Compressed (zipped) Folder are compressed, so they require less storage space on disk. If you need to send someone a set of files, you do not have to attach each file separately to the e-mail message. Instead, you store the files in a single Compressed (zipped) Folder and attach that one file to your e-mail message. The person who receives your e-mail message saves the Compressed (zipped) Folder on the hard disk, and then extracts the files within the Compressed (zipped) Folder. Likewise, instead of posting many files at a Web site or FTP site where someone might have to download each file individually, you can package them in a single Compressed (zipped) Folder. Someone can then download only one file and extract the contents from the Compressed (zipped) Folder. An **FTP site** is an Internet site for uploading and downloading files between computers. The **File Transfer Protocol (FTP)** is a standard set of formats and procedures for transferring files between computers over the Internet.

When you create a Compressed (zipped) Folder, Windows Vista uses a custom icon with a zipper for the Compressed (zipped) Folder. The Compressed (zipped) Folder behaves exactly like a zip file created with a file compression utility, such as WinZip. When you copy a Compressed (zipped) Folder to another computer with a version of Windows that does not support Compressed (zipped) Folders, the Compressed (zipped) Folder appears as a zip file with the "zip" file extension. If you open this compressed zip file on another computer with a file compression utility, such as WinZip, you can view the files contained with the original folder, and you can extract the files from the compressed zip file.

Cadence asks you to convert the Cooper & Bauman folder into a Compressed (zipped) Folder so that she can send the entire folder to another coworker via e-mail. She also asks you to extract the files afterwards on your computer so that you know how to extract folders and files from e-mail attachments with a Compressed (zipped) Folder.

If you have a file compression utility (such as WinZip) installed on your computer, that utility might be associated with the file extension used for Compressed (zipped) Folders, and Windows Vista will use that utility to compress and uncompress files. In this case, read the following steps and examine the figures, but do not keystroke the following steps.

To create a Compressed (zipped) Folder:

1. Right-click the **Cooper & Bauman** folder, point to **Send To**, click **Compressed (zipped) Folder**, and then press the **Enter** key to accept the filename that Windows Vista proposes. Windows Vista creates a Compressed (zipped) Folder named "Cooper & Bauman.zip." See Figure 5-28. Notice that you still have your original Cooper & Bauman folder.

Figure 5-28 Compressed (zipped) Folder with a custom folder icon

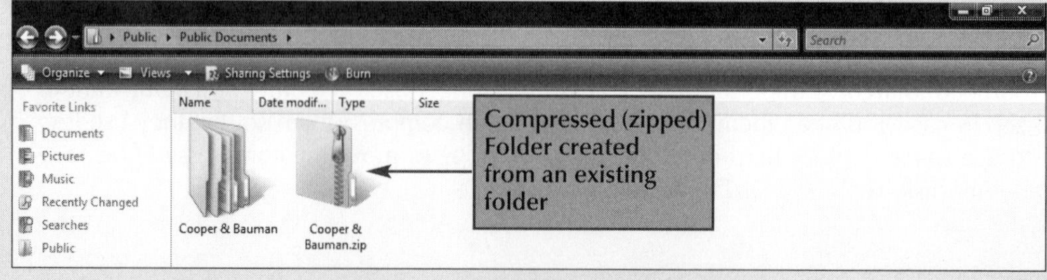

2. Right-click the original **Cooper & Bauman** folder, click **Delete**, and then click the **Yes** button in the Delete Folder dialog box.

3. Right-click **Cooper & Bauman.zip** and then click **Properties**. In the Cooper & Bauman.zip Properties dialog box, Windows Vista reports that the size of this folder and its contents is now 1.73 MB (1,817.902 bytes) and that its size on disk is now 1.73 MB (1,818,624 bytes). See Figure 5-29. The size of the folder and its contents has decreased 4,402,857 bytes (or approximately 4.2 MB), and its size on disk has decreased 4,452,352 bytes (or approximately 4.25 MB). Windows Vista compressed this folder and its subfolders and files by 71% so that the Compressed (zipped) Folder is only 29% of the size of the original Cooper & Bauman folder. That's a substantial reduction in size.

Figure 5-29 Viewing properties of a Compressed (zipped) Folder

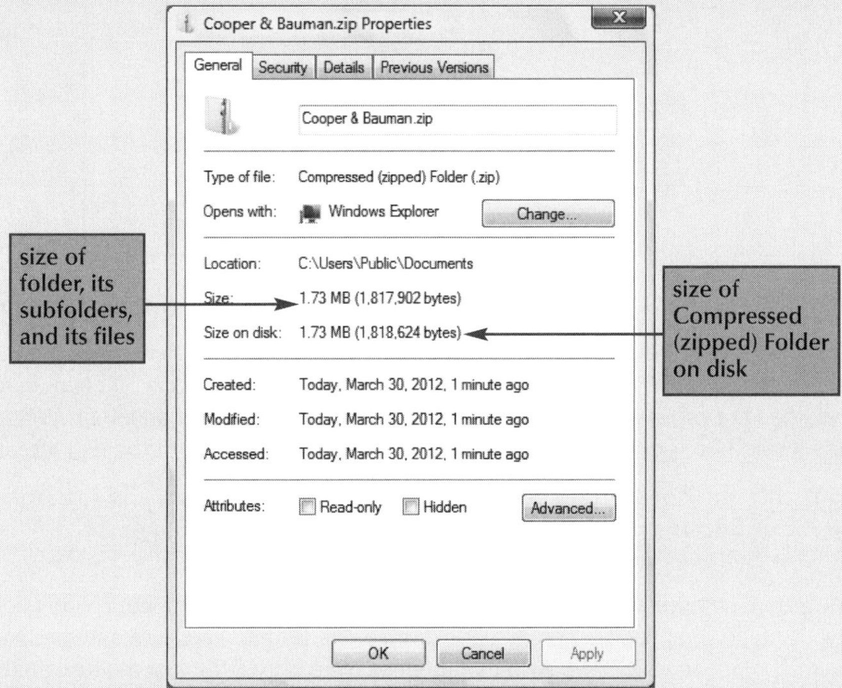

4. Close the Cooper & Bauman.zip Properties dialog box, and then click the **Cooper & Bauman.zip** Compressed (zipped) Folder. Within this Compressed (zipped) Folder is the original Cooper & Bauman folder.

5. Click the **Cooper & Bauman** folder. Within this folder are all the Cooper & Bauman subfolders.

6. Click the **Extract all files** button on the command bar. In the Extract Compressed (Zipped) Folders dialog box, Windows Vista prompts you for the destination folder for the extracted files. See Figure 5-30. Windows Vista proposes to use the path: "C:\Users\Public\Documents\Cooper & Bauman". If you do not change this path, Windows Vista creates a Cooper & Bauman folder within another Cooper & Bauman folder when it extracts the files.

Figure 5-30 **Extract Compressed (Zipped) Folders dialog box**

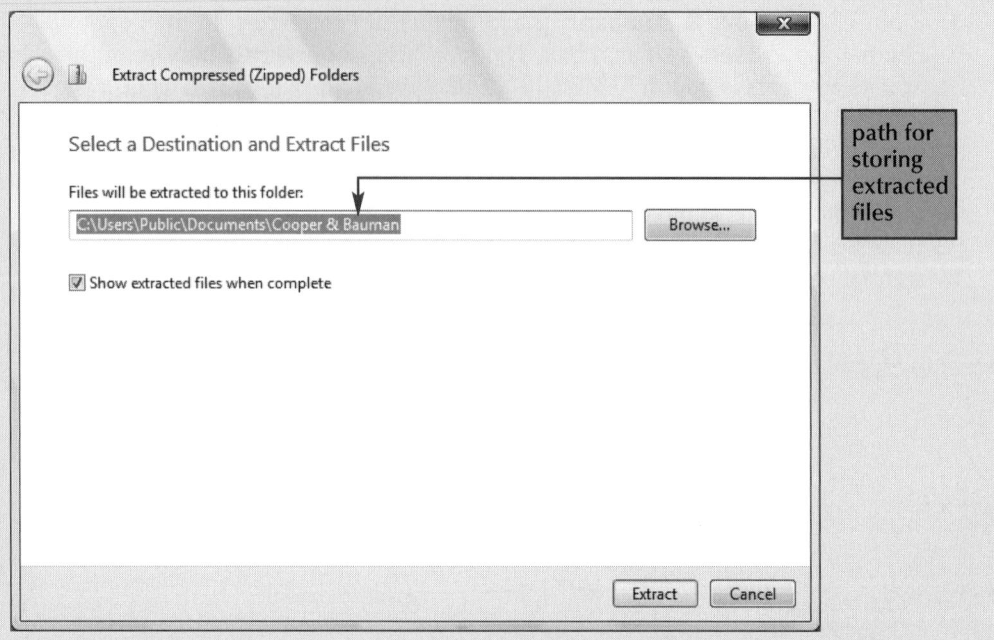

7. Change the path to **C:\Users\Public\Documents** by deleting "\Cooper & Bauman".
8. Click the **Extract** button. Windows Vista extracts the files and then opens the Public Documents window. You now have an extracted copy of the Cooper & Bauman folder. If you had not removed the previous copy of the Cooper & Bauman folder, Windows Vista would have prompted you to replace the previous copy with the extracted copy.
9. Right-click the **Cooper & Bauman** taskbar button, click **Close**, and then maximize the Public Documents window, keeping it open for the next set of steps.

Tip

You can also extract folders and files by copying them from a Compressed (zipped) Folder.

The degree of compression that you achieve using Compressed (zipped) Folders depends on the types of files that you compress. For example, the Bitmap Image files in the Designs folder were compressed by 77-95% so that the files were only 5-23% of their original size. Most of the Microsoft Excel 2007 spreadsheet files in the Performance, Projections, and Training folders were compressed by 11-24% (though one compressed by 74%).

You might ask, "How does NTFS compression compare with compression in a Compressed (zipped) Folder?" If you take the original Cooper & Bauman folder and compress it using NTFS compression, the folder, its subfolders, and files use 2.44 MB of storage space rather than 5.92 MB. That means Windows Vista compressed the folder and its contents by 59% so that the amount of storage space used by the folder and its contents is only 41% of the uncompressed folder. In contrast, if you create a Compressed (zipped) Folder from this same Cooper & Bauman folder, the compressed size is 2.58 MB. That means Windows Vista compressed the folder and its contents by 56% so that the amount of storage space used by the Compressed (zipped) Folder is only 44% of the size of the original folder. While NTFS compression achieves a slightly greater degree of compression with this mix of folders and files, the two approaches essentially yielded comparable results. However, if you compress the Designs folder (which contains Bitmap Images) using both approaches, you achieve a substantially greater compression by using a Compressed (zipped) Folder (in fact, 50% more compression). You can create and work with Compressed (zipped) Folders on *both* NTFS and FAT volumes.

Cadence recommends that you copy the Compressed (zipped) Folder to your flash drive so that you have a backup copy of these important files.

To copy a Compressed (zipped) Folder to a flash drive:

1. Right-click the **Cooper & Bauman.zip** folder, point to **Send To**, and then click the **option for your flash drive**. Windows Vista copies the Compressed (zipped) Folder to your flash drive.
2. Click the **New Location** arrow ▸ to the left of Public in the Address Bar, click **Computer**, and then click **your flash drive icon**. Windows Vista opens a window onto your flash drive. Notice that you have a copy of Cooper & Bauman.zip on your flash drive.
3. To restore your flash drive to its original state, right-click **Cooper & Bauman.zip**, click **Delete**, and in the Delete Folder dialog box, click the **Yes** button.
4. Click **Public** in the Navigation Pane and then click **Public Documents**. Now that you extracted the Cooper & Bauman folder, you no longer need the Compressed (zipped) Folder.
5. Right-click **Cooper & Bauman.zip**, click **Delete**, and in the Delete Folder dialog box, click the **Yes** button.

Once you create a Compressed (zipped) Folder, you can copy or move files to or from the Compressed (zipped) Folder, and you can delete folders and files within a Compressed (zipped) Folder. You can open a file from a Compressed (zipped) Folder; however, the file is Read-Only. If you make changes to the file, you cannot save the changes to the file in the Compressed (zipped) Folder. Instead, you have to save the changes in a file with a new filename in another location.

Creating and Extracting a Compressed (Zipped) Folder | Reference Window

- To compress a folder, locate the folder you want to compress, right-click that folder, point to Send To, click Compressed (zipped) Folder, and then press the Enter key to accept the filename proposed by Windows Vista or type a new filename and press the Enter key.
- To extract a Compressed (zipped) Folder, open the Compressed (zipped) Folder, click the "Extract all files" button on the command bar, adjust the path in the Extract Compressed (Zipped) Folders dialog box (if necessary), and then click the Extract button.

Compressed (zipped) Folders are also useful if you need to transport a set of folders and files, or just files, from one location to another with your flash drive.

Encrypting and Decrypting Folders and Files

With the Windows Vista **Encrypting File Service** (**EFS**), you can encrypt and decrypt folders and files on hard disks to protect your important documents. **Encryption** encodes data so that only the original user can access that data. This protection can be important if you share your computer with other users, use a portable computer, or connect your computer to a larger network, including the Internet.

The Encrypting File Service works with NTFS and therefore is only available on NTFS volumes. The Business, Ultimate, and Enterprise editions of Windows Vista support this feature; however, encryption is not fully supported in the Home Basic, Home Premium, and Starter editions of Windows Vista.

If you open an encrypted file, NTFS uses the Encrypting File Service to automatically decrypt the file. When you save a file to disk, NTFS uses the Encrypting File Service to re-encrypt it. In other words, the process is transparent to you, and you can work with the contents of your files just as you would if they were not encrypted. Although you can encrypt files one by one, a more effective approach is to encrypt the folder that contains your files, and then all files stored in that folder are automatically encrypted. You cannot, however, encrypt system files.

If you *copy* or *move* an unencrypted file to an encrypted folder on an NTFS volume, the unencrypted file is automatically encrypted. If you *copy* or *move* an encrypted file to an unencrypted folder on an NTFS volume, the file remains encrypted.

InSight | Copying and Moving Files Between FAT and NTFS Volumes

If you copy an unencrypted folder or file from a FAT volume to an encrypted folder on an NTFS volume, Windows Vista automatically encrypts the folder (and its contents) or the file. If you move or copy an encrypted folder or file to a FAT volume, Windows Vista removes the encryption because FAT volumes do not support encryption. If you attach an encrypted file to an e-mail message, Windows Vista removes the encryption.

If you are working in a college computer lab, ask your instructor or technical support staff whether you have permission to encrypt and decrypt a folder and its files. If you do not have permission to use encryption on an NTFS volume, read the steps and examine the figures so that you are familiar with this feature, but do not keystroke the following steps. Because this feature is only available on NTFS volumes, you cannot use a flash drive with the FAT file system. Instead, you must use an NTFS volume.

With the increasing attention paid to security, Cadence discusses with her staff the potential value of the Windows Vista Encrypting File Service. She asks you to encrypt and decrypt the Cooper & Bauman folder so that you are familiar with this process.

If you are using the Home Basic, Home Premium, or Starter edition of Windows Vista, read the tutorial steps in this section of the tutorial and examine the figures but do not keystroke the steps.

To encrypt a folder and its contents:

1. Right-click the **Cooper & Bauman** folder, click **Properties**, and after Windows Vista opens the Cooper & Bauman Properties dialog box, click the **Advanced** button on the General property sheet. The Advanced Attributes dialog box includes an option for encrypting the contents of this folder under "Compress or Encrypt attributes."
2. Click the **Encrypt contents to secure data** check box, click the **OK** button in the Advanced Attributes dialog box, and then click the **OK** button in the Cooper & Bauman Properties dialog box. The Confirm Attribute Changes dialog box asks you how you want to apply the Encrypt attribute.
3. Click the **Apply changes to this folder, subfolders and files** option button (if necessary), and then click the **OK** button. Windows Vista now displays an Applying Attributes dialog box and encrypts this folder and all the files within this folder.

   Trouble? Windows Vista may display a balloon and suggest that you back up your file encryption key. Click the "Back up your file encryption key" balloon, and in the Encrypting File System dialog box, click "Back up later", and then Windows will remind you the next time you log on. Windows Vista may also display an "Encrypting File System - Back up your file encryption key" icon in the notification area.
4. Click the **folder window background** and notice that the Cooper & Bauman folder name is displayed in green to indicate it is encrypted.

Trouble? If Windows Vista does not display encrypted folders and files in green, click the Organize button on the command bar, click Folder and Search Options, click the View tab, and in the Advanced settings list box, locate and add a check mark to the "Show encrypted or compressed NTFS files in color" check box, and then click the OK button to close the Folder Options dialog box and apply the new setting.

5. Open the **Cooper & Bauman** folder, right-click a **Heading** column button, click **More**, locate and click the **Attributes** check box, and then click the **OK** button. Notice that Windows Vista displays all the subfolder names in green to indicate that they are encrypted. In the Attributes column, "E" indicates "Encrypted." See Figure 5-31.

Figure 5-31 Viewing encrypted folders

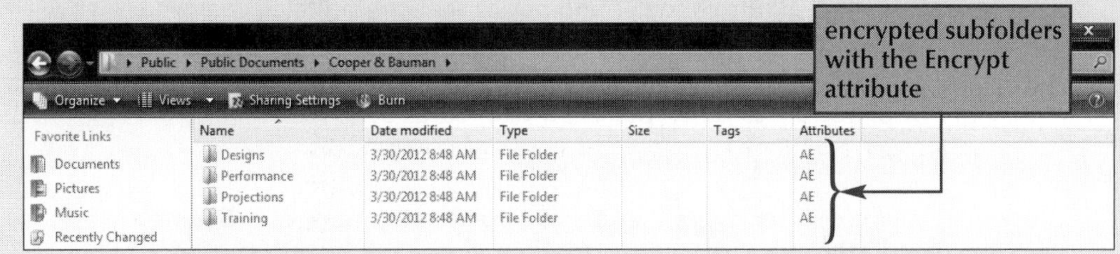

6. Open the **Performance** folder and notice that Windows Vista displays the filenames in green to indicate that they are encrypted.

7. Right-click **Best Return.xlsx**, click **Copy**, click **Public Documents** in the Address Bar, right-click the **background** of the folder window, and then click **Paste**. Windows Vista copies the encrypted file to the Tutorial folder. Notice that the file remains encrypted.

8. Right-click **Best Return.xlsx**, click **Properties**, click the **Advanced** button on the General property sheet, click the **Encrypt contents to secure data** check box, click the **OK** button in the Advanced Attributes dialog box, and then click the **OK** button in the Best Return.xlsx Properties dialog box. Windows Vista removes the encryption from the file.

9. Right-click **Best Return.xlsx**, click **Copy**, click the **encrypted Cooper & Bauman** folder, right-click the **background** of the Cooper & Bauman folder window, and then click **Paste**. Windows Vista encrypts the unencrypted file as it is copied into the encrypted folder.

10. Click **Public Documents** in the Address Bar, and then keep the Public Documents window open for the next set of steps.

You work with encrypted folders and files just as you work with unencrypted folders and files; however, Windows Vista does not index encrypted files (though, as covered in Tutorial 3, you can enable this option). However, if you copy an encrypted folder or encrypted files to a flash drive that uses FAT, Windows Vista will decrypt the folder and files. NTFS encryption is not supported on FAT volumes.

Now, you're going to reverse this process and decrypt the Cooper & Bauman folder and its contents.

To decrypt a folder and its subfolders and files:

1. Right-click the **Cooper & Bauman** folder, click **Properties**, click the **Advanced** button on the General property sheet in the Cooper & Bauman Properties dialog box, click the **Encrypt contents to secure data** check box and remove the check mark, click the **OK** button in the Advanced Attributes dialog box, click the **OK** button in the Cooper & Bauman Properties dialog box, click the **Apply changes to this folder, subfolders and files** option button, and then click the **OK** button. Windows Vista removes the encryption from this folder and its subfolders and files.
2. Click the **folder window background** and notice that the Cooper & Bauman folder name is now shown in black to indicate that it is no longer encrypted.
3. Open the **Cooper & Bauman** folder and notice that the subfolder names are now shown in black. Windows Vista removed the encryption that you applied earlier to the Cooper & Bauman folder. Also, in the Cooper & Bauman folder, Windows Vista no longer displays "E" for "Encrypt" in the Attributes column.
4. Click **Public Documents** in the Address Bar.
5. To restore your computer, press the **Ctrl** key, point to the **Cooper & Bauman** folder, point to **Best Return.xlsx**, release the **Ctrl** key, right-click **Best Return.xlsx**, click **Delete**, and in the Delete Multiple Items dialog box, click the **Yes** button.
6. Close the Public Documents folder window.

The process for encrypting a folder or file is similar to that for compressing a folder or file. However, you cannot apply both compression and encryption to the same folder or file.

Reference Window | Encrypting and Decrypting a Folder

- Locate the folder you want to encrypt or decrypt, right-click the folder, click Properties, and then click the Advanced button on the General property sheet in the Properties dialog box for that folder.
- In the Compress or Encrypt attributes section of the Advanced Attributes dialog box, click the "Encrypt contents to secure data" check box, click the OK button in the Advanced Attributes dialog box, and then click the OK button in the Properties dialog box for the folder.
- In the Confirm Attributes dialog box, click the "Apply changes to this folder, subfolders and files" option button (if necessary), and then click the OK button.

If you encrypt folders or files on your computer, Windows Vista will remind you of the importance of backing up your file encryption certificate and encryption key in the event the original certificate and key are lost or corrupted; otherwise, you will not be able to access your files if a problem occurs. If you choose to back up your file encryption certificate and encryption key, Windows Vista will store this information in a file on a disk you specify (such as a USB flash drive). Like the house key you use to lock and unlock the door to your home, an **encryption key** is a code that Windows Vista uses to encrypt and decrypt files. During this process of backing up the encryption certificate and key, Windows Vista explains that a **certificate**, issued by a certification authority (such as Microsoft), confirms your identity and contains information used to protect data or to establish secure network connections. It also explains that a **certificate store** is the system location where certificates are kept. In the next step, the Certificate Export Wizard asks you to select from one of a variety of file formats for exporting certificates. You can click a link in this dialog box to learn more about certificate file formats so that you can pick the one you prefer. The Certificate Export Wizard then prompts you for a password, the name of the file you want to export, and the name of the file where you want to back up this information. After you encrypt a file, you can start the Certificate Export Wizard from the Details property sheet for the encrypted file.

If you rely on NTFS encryption, you should make sure that you back up this critical information and make sure that you have unencrypted backups stored in a secure location.

BitLocker Drive Encryption

BitLocker Drive Encryption, only available in Windows Vista Enterprise and Windows Vista Ultimate, is a new feature for increasing the security of a computer by encrypting the boot volume. With BitLocker Driver Encryption, your system remains encrypted even if someone who has authorized or unauthorized access to your computer removes your hard disk drive and inserts it into the system unit of another computer with the intent of accessing your data on that computer. Your system is also protected if someone who has authorized or unauthorized access to your computer attempts to access the contents of your hard disk drive by installing or loading another operating system. If malicious software alters important Windows startup files, BitLocker Drive Encryption can detect those changes and prevent access to your computer.

BitLocker Drive Encryption uses a **Trusted Platform Module (TPM) microchip** on the motherboard to store and protect the information needed to encrypt and decrypt the boot volume. At each boot, the Trusted Platform Module microchip verifies that the hard disk is in the correct computer system and that important system files have not been altered in any way before it unlocks access to the hard disk drive, the operating system, and your data. It is also possible to use the Trusted Platform Module microchip with a USB flash drive to store a Startup Key that validates your identity; however, as many people easily discover, it's easy to forget or misplace a flash drive, and it's also easy for someone else to pick up a flash drive in a split second. You do have the option of storing a second copy of the Startup Key on another USB flash drive. You can also validate your identity using a PIN (or Personal Identification Number).

If BitLocker Drive Encryption detects a problem or a change to the hard disk or system files, it boots in recovery mode, and you must enter a 48-digit recovery password using the function keys on the keyboard to gain access to your computer. When setting up BitLocker Drive Encryption, you have the option of saving this password to a USB flash drive or a local or remote folder, and you can print the password.

For maximum security, BitLocker Drive Encryption requires that your computer have an enabled Trusted Platform Module v 1.2 or later microchip. You must also have a BIOS that supports this feature, and you must enable the Trusted Platform Module via the BIOS. Also, your computer must have a separate NTFS boot volume (which is encrypted) with the Windows operating system files and your personal files as well as a separate NTFS system volume (which is unencrypted) with the hardware-specific files needed to boot your computer. The system volume can be relatively small in size (i.e., 1.5 GB). Data on the boot volume is protected, but data on the system volume is not protected. If you are seriously considering the use of BitLocker Drive Encryption, you should examine the information that Microsoft makes available at its Web site prior to purchasing a computer and prior to installing Windows Vista. Then, you can verify that the computer contains the hardware needed to support this feature, and that you have the ability to create the partitions needed to implement BitLocker Drive Encryption. These requirements depend on how you intend to implement BitLocker Drive Encryption and the degree of security that you want to use. Also, while you can use BitLocker Drive Encryption on a computer that does not have a Trusted Platform Module microchip, BitLocker Drive Encryption cannot verify the integrity of boot files, and it cannot detect a hard disk moved to another computer.

If you need to upgrade or replace your motherboard or BIOS, repartition the hard disk, install a new operating system, or install updates to hardware firmware, you can disable BitLocker Drive Encryption and then re-enable it afterwards. You can also remove BitLocker Drive Encryption and then re-encrypt your hard disk afterwards. If a computer is at the end of its useful life, you can delete the BitLocker encryption keys from the volume so that no one can ever access the hard disk.

BitLocker Drive Encryption also prevents hackers from accessing information on your computer, such as passwords, and it is useful on laptops that contain sensitive data and that might be easily misplaced or stolen. However, its use is more applicable to an enterprise environment where it can be implemented properly and where reliable security and backup measures are already in place.

You can combine the use of BitLocker Drive Encryption and NTFS encryption of folders and files to further protect a computer. BitLocker Drive Encryption can encrypt system files. NTFS can encrypt your personal files, but not system files.

Restoring Your Computer's Settings

If you are working in a computer lab, or if you want to restore your desktop computer to the settings that existed prior to working on this tutorial, complete the following steps.

To restore your computer:

1. To restore double-click activation, click the **Computer** icon on the desktop, click the **Organize** button on the command bar, click **Folder and Search Options**, and on the General property sheet in the Folder Options dialog box, click the **Double-click to open an item (single-click to select)** option button.
2. To hide extensions for known file types, click the **View** tab in the Folder Options dialog box, click the **Hide extensions for known file types** check box if it does not contain a check mark, click the **OK** button to close the Folder Options dialog box and apply these changes, and then close the Computer window.
3. To remove the Computer from the desktop, right-click **Computer** on the Start menu, and then click **Show on Desktop**.

Review | Session 5.2 Quick Check

1. Which file system(s) supports (support) compression and encryption?
2. True or False. When you move a file to another folder, the file takes on the compression state of the new folder.
3. True or False. When you copy a file to another folder, the compression state of the file does not change.
4. What happens if you copy a compressed file from an NTFS volume to a FAT volume?
5. If you want to send a folder with a set of files as a single e-mail attachment, you can create a ________________ from the folder.
6. True or False. If you *copy* or *move* an unencrypted file to an encrypted folder on an NTFS volume, the unencrypted file is automatically encrypted.
7. True or False. If you *copy* or *move* an encrypted file to an unencrypted folder on an NTFS volume, the file remains encrypted.

Tutorial Summary | Review

In this tutorial, you learned how to format a hard disk and place a file system on the hard disk. Then, you examined the data structures and features of the NTFS and FAT file systems and compared how these file systems use storage space on disk. You opened a Computer window and viewed properties of different types of drives, including their file system. You used the Disk Management Snap-in tool to look at more detailed information about partitions and disks. You compressed and uncompressed folders and files and then encrypted and decrypted folders and files. You also created a Compressed (zipped) Folder and compared that compression method to NTFS compression. Finally, you examined the new Windows Vista BitLocker Drive Encryption feature found in Windows Vista Enterprise and Windows Vista Ultimate.

Key Terms

active partition
allocation unit
Archive attribute
attribute
bad cluster
basic disk
BitLocker Drive Encryption
boot partition
boot record
boot sector
bootstrap loader
certificate
certificate store
cluster
Compress attribute
Compressed (zipped) Folder
compression
cylinder
data redundancy
data stream
directory
directory space
directory table
disk
domain
drive
dynamic disk
dynamic volume
Encrypt attribute
Encrypting File Service (EFS)
encryption
encryption key
end-of-file (EOF)
Extended FAT (exFAT)
extended partition
FAT1
FAT12
FAT16
FAT2
FAT32
fault-tolerant
File Allocation Table (FAT)
file system
File Transfer Protocol (FTP)
files area
FTP site
GUID (Globally Unique Identifier)
Hard Disk Partition Table
hard link
Hidden attribute
high-level formatting
Live File System
low-level formatting
Master Boot Code
Master Boot Record (MBR)
Master File Table (MFT)
Master File Table Mirror (MFTMirr)
media descriptor
metadata
Microsoft Management Console (MMC)
mirrored volume
Not Content Indexed attribute
NTFS
parity
partition
platter
pointer
primary partition
RAID-5 volume
Read-Only attribute
record
Redundant Array of Independent Disks (RAID)
root directory
sector
simple volume
slack
snap-in
spanned volume
striped volume
system area
System attribute
top-level folder
track
transaction
transaction log file
Trusted Platform Module (TPM) microchip
UUID (Universally Unique Identifier)
volume
volume label

Practice | Review Assignments

Practice the skills you learned in the tutorial.

For a list of Data Files in the Review folder, see page 281.

Cadence just acquired several laptop computers for use by Cooper & Bauman staff members when they are traveling on company business. She asks you to examine the file systems used on those laptops and verify that employees can compress, uncompress, encrypt, and decrypt folders and files without any problems. She also asks you to create a Compressed (zipped) Folder with your most recent folders and files for an upcoming conference.

If you are using the Home Basic, Home Premium, or Starter edition of Windows Vista, which do not fully support encryption, you cannot complete those steps that call for encrypting and decrypting folders and files.

Use a word processing application, such as Word or WordPad, to prepare your answers to questions in the following steps. Complete the following:

1. If necessary, display the Computer icon on the desktop, switch to single-click activation, choose the option for displaying file extensions, copy the Review folder from the Tutorial.05 folder provided with your Data Files to the Public Documents folder, change its name to **Cooper & Bauman**, attach your USB flash drive, and close any open dialog boxes or Windows.
2. Open a Computer window and view properties of your hard disk drive. Which drive name is assigned to your hard disk drive? What is the friendly name of your hard disk drive? What file system does Windows Vista use on your hard disk drive? How much used space, free space, and disk storage capacity in GB does your hard disk drive have? Does Windows Vista index this drive for faster searching? Is the drive compressed or uncompressed?
3. Select the Hardware property sheet. What type of hard disk drive is installed in the computer you are using? Close the Properties dialog box for your hard disk drive.
4. Open the Cooper & Bauman folder in your Public Documents folder, open the Designs folder, and if necessary, switch to Details view, remove the Preview Pane, and adjust column widths to the widest entry in each column.
5. View the properties of the Design #8.bmp file. What is its size in KB and bytes? How much storage space does it use on disk in KB and bytes? How much slack does this file have? Close the Properties dialog box for this file.
6. Add the Attributes column to this folder window. Identify the attributes currently assigned to this file.
7. Create a Compressed (zipped) Folder from the Design #8.bmp file, and then view properties of this file. What is the file's size in KB and bytes? How much storage space does it use on disk in KB and bytes? How does this slack compare to that used by the original file? How much less disk storage space does the Compressed (zipped) Folder use than the original file? Close the Properties dialog box for this file.
8. Compress Design #8.bmp (using NTFS compression). What is the compressed file's size in KB and bytes? How much storage space does it use on disk in KB and bytes? How much less disk storage space does the compressed file use than the original file? What attributes does this file have after compression? Remove the compression from Design #8.bmp. Close the Properties dialog box for this file.

9. Prepare a table that lists the size and size on disk in KB of the original uncompressed file, the Compressed (zipped) Folder, and the compressed file, using the following format:

Filename	Size (KB)	Size on Disk (KB)
Original Design #8.bmp		
Design #8.zip		
Compressed Design #8.bmp		

10. Using the data in this table, which file has the smallest file size? Which file uses the least storage space on disk?
11. If you are using Windows Vista Business, Ultimate, or the Enterprise Edition, encrypt Design #8.zip, and when asked whether you want to encrypt the parent folder and the file or just the file, choose the "Encrypt the file only" option. What is the file's size in KB and bytes? How much storage space does it use on disk in KB and bytes? How do these values compare to the original zip file? What attributes does this file have after encryption? Close the Properties dialog box for this file, and then delete the encrypted Design #8.zip file.
12. Return to the Public Documents folder, switch to Details View, and display the Attributes column. What attributes, if any, are assigned to the Cooper & Bauman folder?
13. View properties of the Cooper & Bauman folder. What is the size of this folder and its contents in KB and bytes? How much storage space does this folder and its contents use on disk in KB and bytes? How many files and folders does the Cooper & Bauman folder contain? Close the folder's Properties dialog box.
14. Create a Compressed (zipped) Folder from the Cooper & Bauman folder and accept the filename proposed by Windows Vista. Did Windows Vista assign any new attributes to the Compressed (zipped) Folder? If so, what are they?
15. View properties of the Cooper & Bauman Compressed (zipped) Folder. What is the size of this Compressed (zipped) Folder in KB and bytes? How much storage space does this Compressed (zipped) Folder use on disk in KB and bytes? Close the Compressed (zipped) Folder's Properties dialog box.
16. Compress the original Cooper & Bauman folder and its subfolders and files using NTFS compression. View properties of the compressed Cooper & Bauman folder. What is the size of this folder and its contents in KB and bytes? How much storage space does this folder and its contents use on disk in KB and bytes? How many files and folders does the Cooper & Bauman folder contain? What attributes does this file have after compression? Close the compressed Cooper & Bauman Properties dialog box.
17. Prepare a table that lists the size and size on disk in MB of the original uncompressed Cooper & Bauman folder, the Cooper & Bauman Compressed (zipped) Folder, and the compressed Cooper & Bauman folder, using the following format:

Folder Name or Filename	Size (MB)	Size on Disk (MB)
Original Cooper & Bauman folder		
Cooper & Bauman.zip		
Compressed Cooper & Bauman folder		

18. Using the data in this table, which folder or file has the smallest file size? Which folder or file uses the least storage space on disk?

19. If you are using the Windows Vista Business, Ultimate, or Enterprise Edition, encrypt the compressed Cooper & Bauman folder, its subfolders, and files. Did the attributes of the Cooper & Bauman folder change after encryption? Explain. Is the folder and its contents still compressed? Explain. Decrypt the Cooper & Bauman folder.
20. To restore your computer, delete the Cooper & Bauman folder and its contents, and then delete the Cooper & Bauman Compressed (zipped) Folder.
21. Submit the results of the preceding steps to your instructor, either in printed or electronic form, as requested.

Apply | Case Problem 1

Use the skills you learned in the tutorial to inform a PC users group.

There are no Data Files needed for this Case Problem.

Middletown PC Users Group Each month, your local PC users group meets to discuss and share information on a specific topic. The next meeting will focus on disks, partitions, and drives, and you have been asked to lead the discussion. You decide that now is a good time to compile information about your computer system that you can use to illustrate various concepts at the users group. You can also demonstrate how to use the Disk Management snap-in.

To complete this Case Problem, your edition of windows Vista must contain the Disk Management snap-in and you must provide Administrator credentials to use this tool.

Use a word processing application, such as Word or WordPad, to prepare your answers to questions in the following steps. Complete the following:

1. Attach your USB flash drive to your computer, and if you have a media card reader, insert a memory card into the media card reader.
2. Insert a DVD with data in your DVD drive (if available) and a CD with data in your CD drive (if available).
3. Open the Disk Management snap-in and change the top of the Details Pane to Disk List view.
4. Use the Computer window and the Disk Management snap-in to prepare a table of information on the hard disk drive, DVD or CD drive (or both), flash drive, and memory card (if available) in your computer. Include the following information:
   - Type of drive
   - Drive name
   - Volume type
   - File system
   - Volume status
   - Storage capacity
5. Identify by drive type which volume or volumes are system volumes, boot volumes, primary partitions, extended partitions, and logical drives.
6. Identify whether a volume contains unallocated space.
7. Include any other information that helps you understand disks, partitions, and drives on your computer.
8. Submit your answers to your instructor, either in printed or electronic form, as requested.

Research | Case Problem 2

Use the skills you learned to research information on DVD file systems.

There are no Data Files needed for this Case Problem.

Nguyen Mai Consulting Nguyen Mai is a young professional computer consultant adept at finding the right solutions for her clients while working for an advanced degree in expert systems. One of Mai's steady clients heard of the new Windows Live File System for burning DVDs and wants to know whether this file system will meet her specific needs. Mai has to meet two upcoming deadlines for other clients, so she enlists your help. She asks you to research the Windows Live File System using the Internet and the Windows Vista Help and Support system, including its Online Help.

Use a word processing application, such as Word or WordPad, to prepare your answers to questions in the following steps. Complete the following:

1. Use Windows Help and Support, Windows Online Help, and a search engine of your choice to locate information on the features, advantages, disadvantages, and compatibility of the following:
   - Windows Vista Live File System
   - Mastered disc format
   - Various DVD and CD formats
2. As you conduct your research, keep track of the sources you find, including the article topic or Web site name and the URLs of those Web sites.
3. Prepare a two- to three-page report that summarizes the information that you located. At the end of your report, list the sources that you used for the report. Include the article topic or Web site name as well as the URLs of those Web sites.
4. Submit your document to your instructor, either in printed or electronic form, as requested.

Apply | Case Problem 3

Use the skills you learned in this tutorial to analyze file systems.

There are no Data Files needed for this Case Problem.

Carpelan & Thakur Jatan Thakur is a partner in a Computer-Aided Design/Computer-Aided Manufacturing business that manufactures machine parts for companies that want to replace worn-out components no longer made by the original manufacturer. As one of his close friends, he asks you to help him determine the best file system to use on his 2 GB USB flash drive. Using the information covered in this tutorial, evaluate the use of the FAT16, FAT32, and NTFS file systems on this USB flash drive.

Use a word processing application, such as Word or WordPad, to prepare your answers to questions in the following steps. Complete the following:

1. Prepare a one- to two-page report in which you evaluate the FAT16, FAT32, and NTFS file systems.
2. Include the following information in your evaluation:
   - Identify the cluster sizes on this 2 GB volume for each file system.
   - Recommend the file system that you think would best use storage space on this disk.
   - Note the file system that the manufacturer would most likely use.
   - When you identify cluster sizes for each file system, list the cluster sizes as the number of sectors per cluster and the number of kilobytes per cluster.
3. Evaluate and describe other features of each of the three file systems that enhance, and any problems that limit, the use of a particular file system on this USB flash drive.

4. If Jatan purchased a 4 GB flash drive, what file systems could he use on that drive, and how would each file use storage space on the flash drive?
5. Submit your document to your instructor, either in printed or electronic form, as requested.

Apply | Case Problem 4

Use the skills you learned in the tutorial to optimize file storage.

There are no Data Files needed for this Case Problem.

Video OnStream Landon Evans works as a technical support person for Video OnStream, a video production firm in Los Angeles, California. Some employees work exclusively at home, and others complete projects on their home computers. Employees ask Landon for his advice on how to optimize the storage of files on their computer's storage devices and how to protect their data. Evaluate each of the following scenarios encountered by employees and explain what you think Landon should recommend.

Use a word processing application, such as Word or WordPad, to prepare your answers to questions in the following steps. Complete the following:

1. Erica has just purchased a 16 GB USB flash drive and wants to know which file system it uses. What file systems are supported on a flash drive with that storage capacity, and what do you think would be the most likely file system used on that flash drive? How can Erica determine the file system used on that flash drive?
2. Alec's flash drive has a storage capacity of 1 GB and uses the FAT16 file system. Would Alec benefit from reformatting the flash drive for FAT32? Explain.
3. Janine wants to compress a large folder and its contents on her flash drive, but the General property sheet does not have an Advanced button for accessing the option for compressing folders and files. What is the cause of this problem? Is there any other option that Janine can use to compress this folder and its contents?
4. Ivan wants to e-mail several digital images that he's captured with his digital camera to friends, but his digital images exceed the allowable size for file attachments. How can Ivan resolve this problem?
5. Selene just received an e-mail message with an attachment that has the "zip" file extension. She does not know the person that sent the e-mail message, and she wants to know whether it is safe to open the attachment. What type of file is this attachment, and what is the most likely content of this file? Also, what would you recommend that Selene do?

EXPLORE

6. Trevor's computer has a 750 GB hard disk that's partitioned into one volume. He wants to know which file system the disk uses and whether Windows Vista would use disk storage space more efficiently if he partitioned, or subdivided, the hard disk into two volumes. What file system does this hard disk drive use? Would he benefit from partitioning the hard disk into two volumes? If so, how? If not, are there any other ways in which he might be able to improve the usage of disk storage space on this hard disk?
7. Submit your document to your instructor, either in printed or electronic form, as requested.

Review | Quick Check Answers

Session 5.1

1. disk, volume
2. sector, cluster
3. slack
4. Master File Table
5. Live File System
6. The boot volume contains the Windows Vista operating system files located in the Windows folder while the system volume contains the hardware-specific files for loading Windows Vista.

Session 5.2

1. NTFS
2. False
3. False
4. Windows Vista uncompresses the file.
5. Compressed (zipped) Folder
6. True
7. True

Ending Data Files

There are no ending Data Files needed for this tutorial.

Optimizing Your Hard Disk

Optimizing the Storage of Files on Disks

Objectives

Session 6.1

- Remove unneeded files with the Disk Cleanup Wizard
- Use the Error-Checking Tool and Check Disk utility
- Examine the problems posed by lost clusters and cross-linked files

Session 6.2

- Identify file fragmentation on a volume
- Examine how Windows Vista uses Disk Defragmenter
- Produce a defragmentation analysis of a hard disk drive
- Set disk quotas for users
- Schedule tasks with Task Scheduler

Case | Celedon Global Marketing, Inc.

Celedon Global Marketing, Inc., a technology marketing business in Princeton, New Jersey, provides its client companies with the expertise to achieve success in global markets. Aaron Larsen, a business technology IT specialist, assists clients in understanding and maximizing the use of new technologies important to their businesses. As new employees join the firm, Aaron assists them with their first client projects so he can explain and demonstrate techniques for optimizing and maintaining their computers.

In this tutorial, you use the Disk Cleanup Wizard to check hard disks for files that can safely be deleted. You also learn how to use the Error-Checking Tool and the Check Disk utility to examine disks for errors and how to use Disk Defragmenter to defragment a hard disk. You also examine how to set disk quotas and learn how to schedule computer maintenance tasks.

Starting Data Files

There are no starting Data Files needed for this tutorial.

Session 6.1

The Importance of Optimizing Your Computer

To achieve the best performance from your computer, you can use powerful Windows Vista utilities to periodically optimize the hard disk. For example, you can:

- Search for and remove unneeded files from your hard disk and thereby reclaim valuable disk storage space.
- Identify and correct file system and hard disk errors that prevent access to files on the hard disk and affect the stability and performance of the operating system itself.
- Optimize the storage of programs, folders, and files on disk.
- Apportion disk storage space when multiple users share the same computer.
- Schedule preventive maintenance tasks.

Besides optimizing and improving the performance of your computer, these utilities protect your investment in your computer and extend the useful lifetime of your hard disk.

Using the Disk Cleanup Wizard

The Disk Cleanup Wizard searches for and removes the following types of files and components:

- **Downloaded Program Files** Downloaded program files consist of ActiveX controls and Java applets that Windows Internet Explorer automatically downloads and stores in the Downloaded Program Files folder under the Windows folder. An **ActiveX control** is a small program, such as an animated counter, that is automatically downloaded from a Web page so that it can run locally on your computer. A **Java applet** is similar to an ActiveX control; however, the program is written in the Java programming language. You can safely remove program files that Windows Internet Explorer automatically downloads to the Downloaded Program Files folder from Web sites. Note that the Downloaded Program Files folder does not contain programs that you download and then install for use on your computer. Nor does it include Web browser plug-ins, device drivers, or program updates (such as Acrobat or QuickTime updates) that you download and install on your computer. Furthermore, it does not store other types of files, such as clip art, images, video, or music that you download to your computer for your personal or professional use. When you download and install software or programs on your computer, you can store each downloaded file in a subfolder under your user account's Downloads folder in case you need to reinstall a program later.
- **Temporary Internet Files** Temporary Internet files are files that Windows Internet Explorer downloads and stores in the Temporary Internet Files folder for your user account. Whenever you access a Web page, all of the components on the Web page—graphics, animation, audio, video, and the HTML code for the Web page itself, and other types of files—are downloaded to the Temporary Internet Files folder. These files constitute what is commonly known as your **Internet cache**. A **cache** (pronounced "cash") is a folder or area of memory where Windows Vista or a program temporarily stores data. The Disk Cleanup Wizard can locate and remove all of these files, but it does not change your personalized settings for Web pages. Because the Disk Cleanup Wizard does not identify files cached by other browsers, such as Mozilla Firefox, you must use those other Web browsers to remove temporary Internet files that they download and store locally on your computer.

- **Offline Web Pages** Offline Web pages are Web pages that are stored on your computer so that you can view them without being connected to the Internet.
- **Hibernation File Cleaner** The hibernation file stores information about the state of your computer when it enters hibernation. If you enable or use hibernation, you want to keep this file. If you do not rely on hibernation, you can remove this file to free up disk space. If you remove this file, Windows Vista disables hibernation; however, as noted in Tutorial 2, you can always re-enable it by using Power Options.
- **Debug Dump Files** Windows Vista creates these files when a problem occurs on your computer. Microsoft tech support can then use these files to help you resolve a problem with your computer.
- **Recycle Bin** You can also remove deleted folders and files in the Recycle Bin, but then they are no longer available if you need to restore folders or files on your hard disk drive.
- **Setup Log Files** Setup log files are files that contain information about the installation of Windows Vista or other software.
- **System error memory dump files** and **System error minidump files** Windows creates these files when an error occurs so that a Microsoft tech can analyze these files for the source of a problem. Dump files contain information about the state of the operating system at the time a problem occurs.
- **Temporary files** Temporary files are files that the operating system and applications create when you are performing some type of operation or working with a document in an application. The operating system and applications use these temporary files for processing data. When you complete an operation or close a program or a file, any temporary files created by the operating system or application are deleted from disk. However, if a power failure or some other type of problem occurs, any open temporary files remain on disk. You can use the Disk Cleanup Wizard to identify and remove these files.

You can even view the process of creating a temporary file. For example, Figure 6-1 shows a tiled view of a Microsoft Office Word 2007 window and a folder window that contains a Microsoft Office Word 2007 file named Financial Performance.docx. After opening the file in Microsoft Word, Windows Vista updates the view of the folder window to show a temporary file called ~$nancial Performance.docx. See Figure 6-2. (To view temporary files, you must enable the options for showing hidden folders and files and for displaying protected operating system files.) After closing Microsoft Word, Windows Vista again updates the folder window to show that the temporary file no longer exists. See Figure 6-3. If the power fails while you are working on this file, the temporary file will remain on disk. According to Microsoft, you can safely remove any temporary files that have not been modified in over a week.

Figure 6-1 Viewing a Microsoft Word file in a folder window

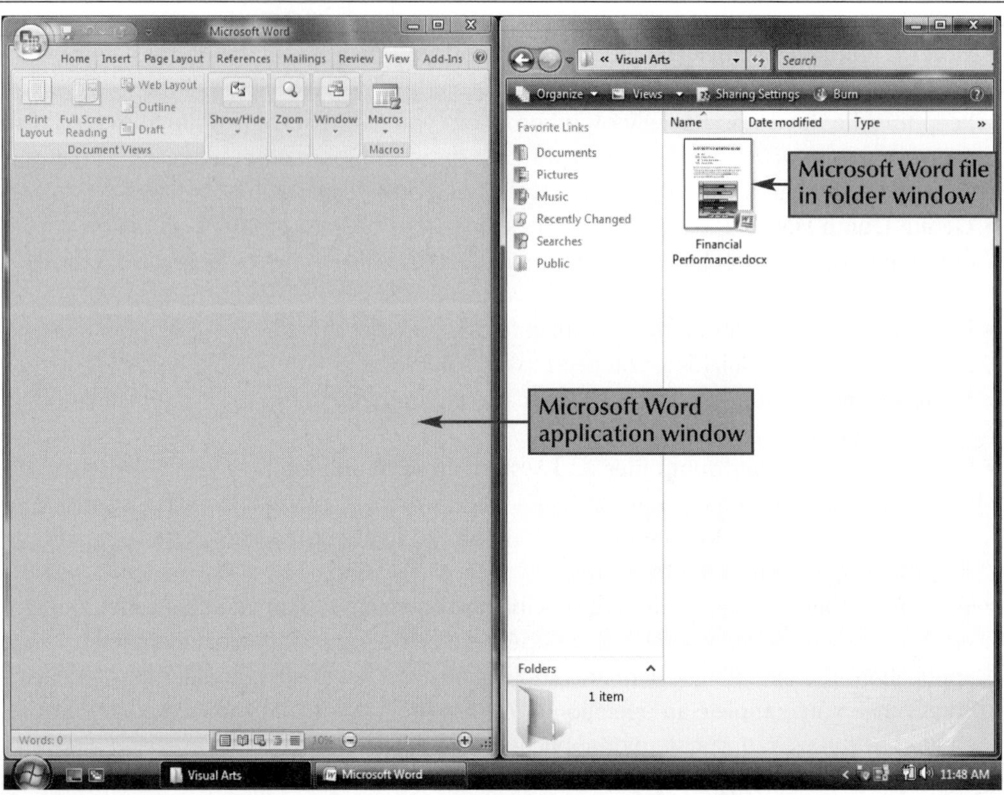

Figure 6-2 Temporary file created after opening a Microsoft Word file

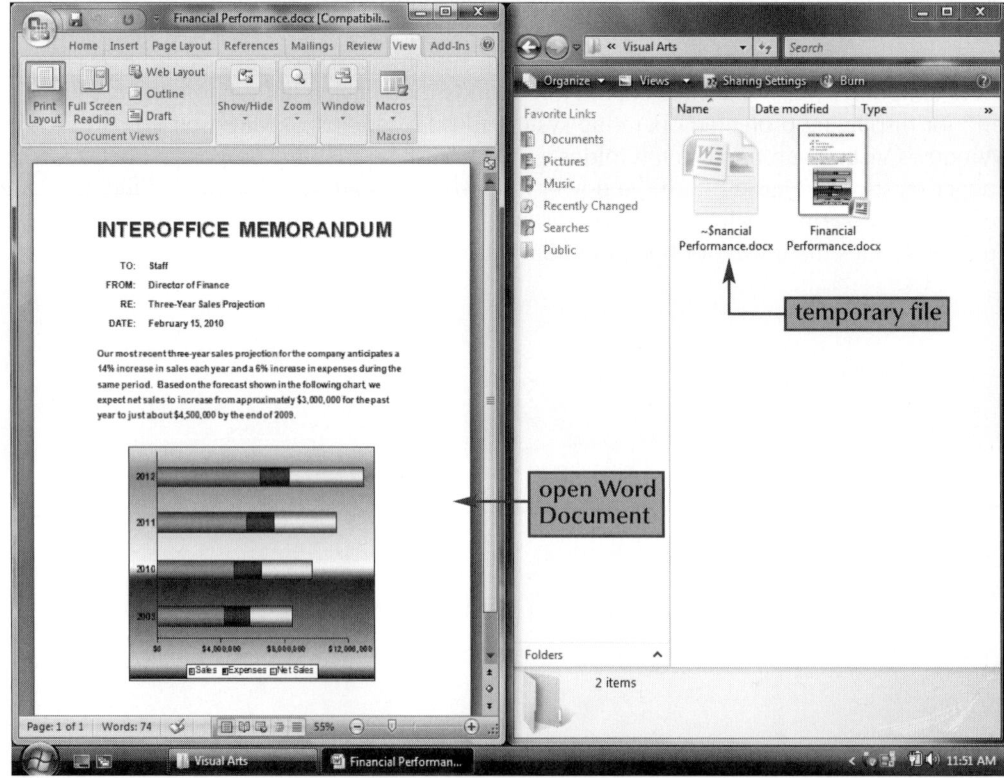

Figure 6-3 Viewing a folder's contents after closing a Microsoft Word file

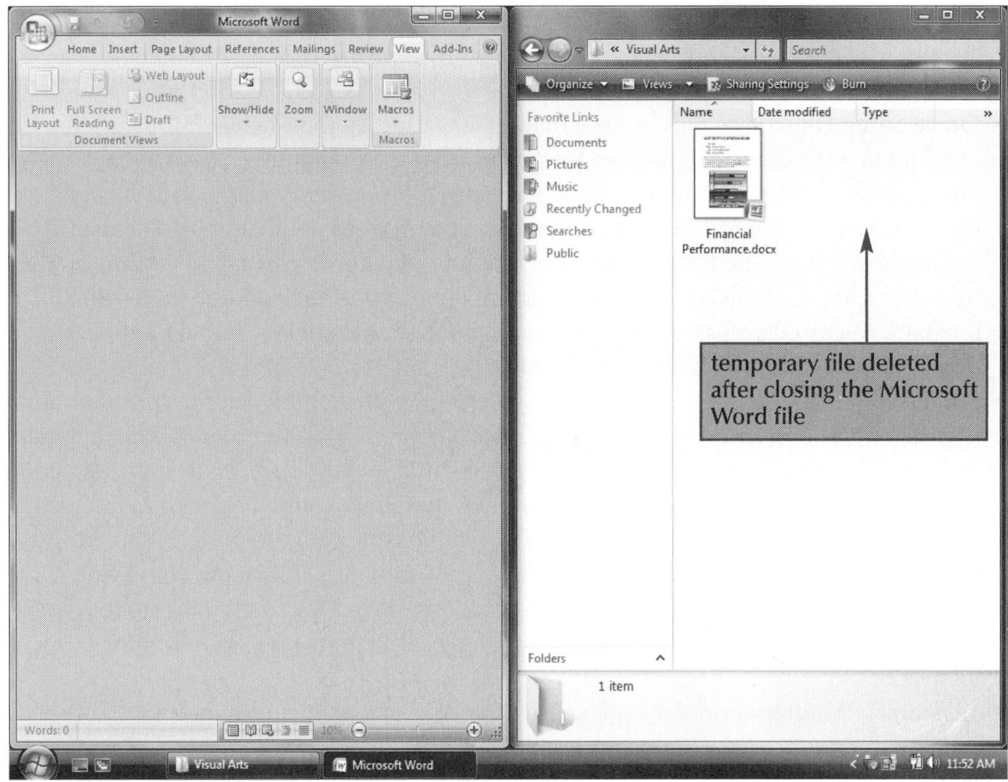

- **Thumbnails** Windows Vista creates and keeps a copy of thumbnails for your picture, video, and document files so that it can quickly redisplay the thumbnails when you open a folder. If you remove these thumbnails, Windows Vista will re-create them when you open a folder.
- **Per user archived Windows Error Reporting Files**, **Per user queued Windows Error Reporting Files**, **System archived Windows Error Reporting Files**, and **System queued Windows Error Reporting Files** Windows Vista creates and uses these files for error reporting and solution checking.

Balancing Speed and Storage Space | InSight

If you visit the same Web sites repeatedly, Windows Internet Explorer can display Web pages more quickly because it doesn't have to download them; instead, it accesses the files for those Web pages in the Temporary Internet Files folder and, if necessary, updates them if the content of the Web page you visit has changed. To benefit from this performance boost while on the Web, you will more than likely want to retain the contents of the Temporary Internet Files folder. If you do not visit the same Web sites, the number of files in the Temporary Internet Files folder will increase and consume more storage space on your hard disk, which can impair the performance of your computer. Under these conditions, you can use the Disk Cleanup Wizard to periodically empty the Temporary Internet Files folder, reclaim valuable storage space, and improve the performance of your computer. Another important reason for emptying the Temporary Internet Files is that it may contain malicious software that was downloaded to your computer when you viewed a Web page at a Web site. You can also specify that Internet Explorer empty the Temporary Internet Files folder when you close your Web browser. You can apply the same concepts to other Web browsers, such as Firefox.

The Disk Cleanup Wizard might identify other categories of files that can be safely deleted, such as the following:

- **Temporary Setup Files** These files were created by a previous setup installation program and are no longer needed.
- **Office Setup Files** These files are installation files used by the Microsoft Office setup installation program. If you remove these files from your computer, you may be prompted to insert your original Office installation disc when you reinstall Microsoft Office, when you choose the option to repair your current installation of Microsoft Office, or when you perform a patch operation to update your installed version of Microsoft Office. A **patch** consists of program code that is inserted into an executable program. Microsoft recommends that you retain these files unless you always have access to your Microsoft Office installation disc.
- **Old Chkdsk files** The Check Disk utility, which you will examine later in this tutorial, checks a disk drive for errors, and where possible, repairs those errors. During a repair operation, it might save recovered file fragments that are no longer part of any file and that are no longer needed. This option removes these recovered files from a disk drive and frees up valuable storage space.
- **Previous Windows installation(s)** This category consists of files from a previous Windows installation that may conflict with a new installation of Windows. These files are moved to a folder named Windows.old so that you can access data from a previous Windows installation.
- **Temporary Windows installation files** This category of files includes installation files used by a Setup program during an installation of Windows. These files can be safely deleted.
- **Files discarded by Windows upgrade** This category includes files from a previous Windows installation. Windows upgrade keeps a copy of any files that were not moved to the new version of Windows and that were not identified as Windows system files. If you are sure that no user's personal files are missing after an upgrade, you can delete these files.

The Disk Cleanup Wizard is only available for use on internal and external hard disk drives.

Aaron asks you to show Kimberly, the company's graphic design specialist, how to use the Disk Cleanup Wizard as part of her regular disk maintenance program.

In the following steps, you will determine how much storage space you can free on your hard disk. If you are working in a computer lab, the technical support staff might already use the Disk Cleanup Wizard on a regular basis and might prefer that you not make any changes to the computer without their permission. Ask your instructor or technical support staff whether you can use the Disk Cleanup Wizard in your computer lab.

To run the Disk Cleanup Wizard:

1. If necessary, display the Computer icon on the desktop, switch your computer to single-click activation (or Web style), and activate the option for displaying file extensions.
2. Open a Computer window, right-click the **Local Disk (C:)** hard disk drive icon, click **Properties** on the shortcut menu, and then click the **Disk Cleanup** button on the General property sheet. Windows Vista opens the Disk Cleanup Options dialog box and asks you to choose which files to clean up. See Figure 6-4. You can clean up only your own files or you can clean up files for all users on the computer. The Security icon indicates that you need to use an Administrator account or must provide the password for an Administrator account if you clean up files for all users.

Tip

You can also press the Windows Logo key, type cleanmgr or Disk Cleanup in the Search box, and then press the Enter key.

Figure 6-4

Choosing which files to clean up

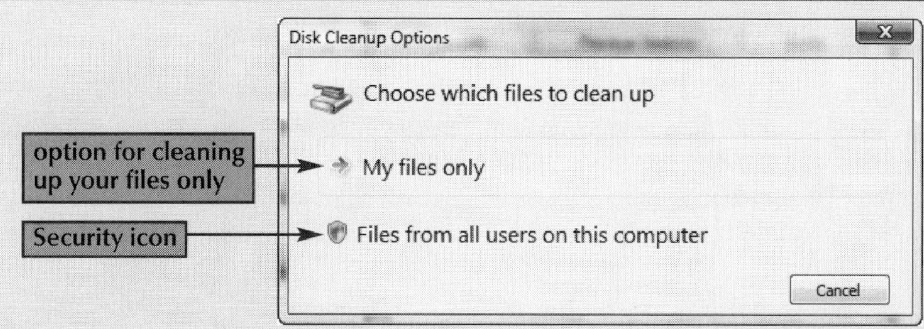

3. Click **My files only**. Disk Cleanup Wizard examines the hard disk drive, as shown in Figure 6-5, and then reports on its findings, as shown in Figure 6-6. The options shown in the "Files to delete" list box vary and depend on how your computer is set up, which file system Windows Vista uses for a drive, and what the Disk Cleanup Wizard finds. On the computer used for this figure, the Disk Cleanup Wizard reports that it can free up to 3.66 MB of disk storage space on drive C by deleting all of the files identified in the "Files to delete" list box. Or it can delete 5 GB if you select all of the options in the "File to delete" list box. On the computer used for the figure, the Disk Cleanup Wizard, however, marks only three options—Downloaded Program Files, Temporary Internet Files, and Thumbnails—for deletion. *To be on the safe side, only delete files that the Disk Cleanup Wizard specifically marks as safe to remove (i.e., those categories with a check mark in the check box next to the category).* For some of the options listed in the Files to delete box (such as Downloaded Program Files), you can view the files in the folder where Windows Vista or an application stores the files. To do so, you first select an option, and then click the View Files button.

Figure 6-5

Scanning for unneeded files

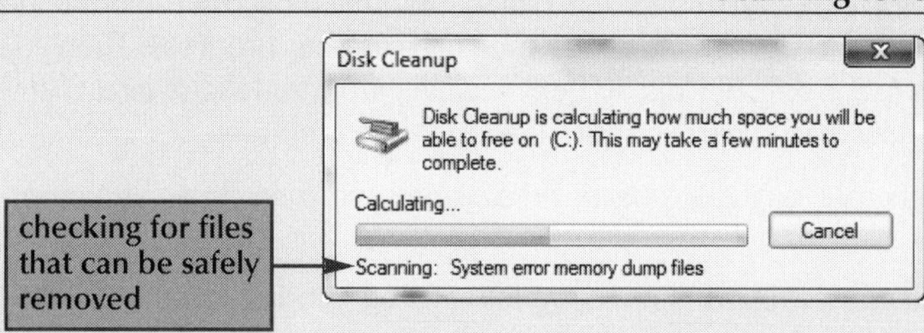

Figure 6-6 Evaluating files to remove from a hard disk

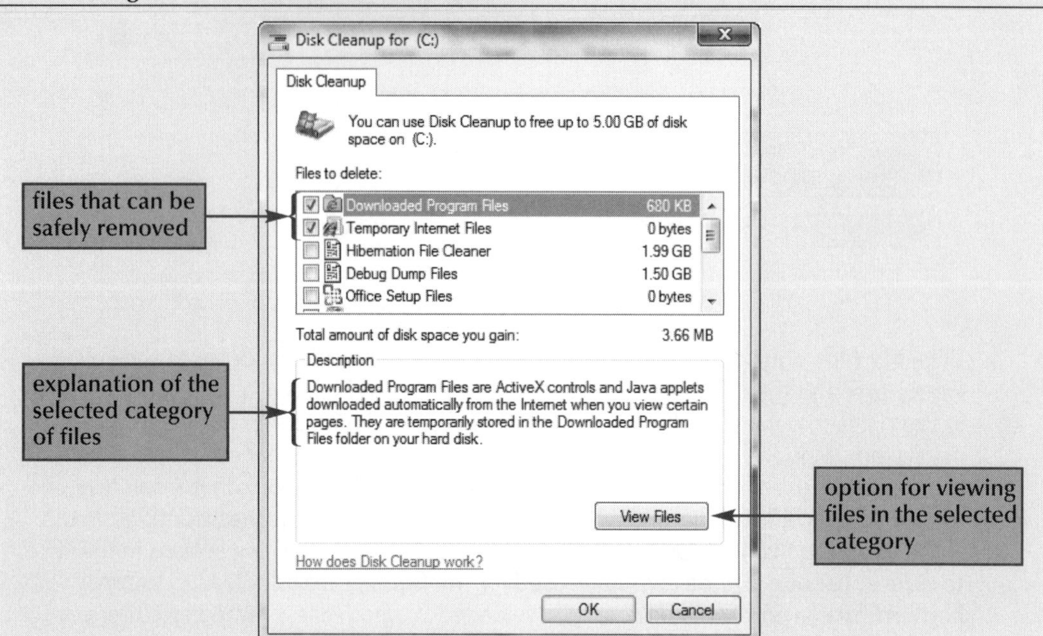

4. If you are working on your own computer and want to free storage space by removing the categories of files identified by the Disk Cleanup Wizard as safe to remove, click the **OK** button, and in the Disk Cleanup dialog box, verify that you want to permanently delete these files by clicking the **Delete Files** button. If you are working on your own computer and do not want to delete any of these files, or if you are working in a computer lab where you do not have permission to remove these files, click the **Cancel** button in the Disk Cleanup for (C:) dialog box. If you choose the option for removing specific files, the Disk Cleanup dialog box charts your progress. Then you return to the Local Disk (C:) Properties dialog box. The cleanup may take several moments, depending upon how many files the Disk Cleanup Wizard removes.
5. Close the Local Disk (C:) Properties dialog box and then close the Computer window.

The Disk Cleanup Wizard is one simple way you can improve the performance of your computer.

Using the Disk Cleanup Wizard | Reference Window

- Open Computer, right-click the icon for a hard disk drive, and then click Properties.
- On the General property sheet, click the Disk Cleanup button.
- In the Disk Cleanup Options dialog box, click "My files only" to clean up only your files, or click "Files from all users on this computer" if you want to clean up files for all users. In the latter case, click the Continue button if you are logged on under an Administrator account, or enter the password for an Administrator account, and then click the OK button.
- After the Disk Cleanup Wizard reports on its findings, check each type of file category listed under "Files to delete," and decide whether you want to remove that category of files. *To be on the safe side, only delete files that the Disk Cleanup Wizard specifically marks as safe to remove (i.e., those categories with a check mark in the check box next to the category).* For some categories, you can use the View Files button to examine the folder with those files and make sure you do not remove files you want to keep.
- Click the OK button to remove the files you selected.
- Close the Properties dialog box for the drive, and then close the Computer window.

You can also use Windows Internet Explorer to delete your browsing history, Temporary Internet files (or your Internet cache), cookies, form data, and Web site passwords. A **cookie** is a simple text file that contains information about your visit to a Web site. Not all Web sites place cookies on your computer. In addition, you can delete files and settings created by **add-ons** (or programs used with your Web browser). Aaron recommends you also show Kimberly this option.

To use Windows Internet Explorer to empty the Internet cache:

1. Open Windows Internet Explorer, click the **Tools** button on the Windows Internet Explorer command bar, and then click **Delete Browsing History**. In the Delete Browsing History dialog box, you can delete Temporary Internet Files, Cookies, History, Form data, and Passwords. See Figure 6-7. Windows Internet Explorer notes that cookies are files placed on your computer by Web sites you visit to store your personal user preferences. It also notes that History contains a list of Web sites that you visited, that Form data consists of data you've typed into forms, and that Passwords include passwords that are automatically entered when you revisit the same Web site. You can pick and choose which of these categories of information you want to delete, or you can use the Delete all button to delete all these files and data that Windows Internet Explorer saves on your hard disk.

Tip

Emptying the Internet cache might prove useful if you experience a problem while using Internet Explorer.

Figure 6-7 Options for deleting your browsing history

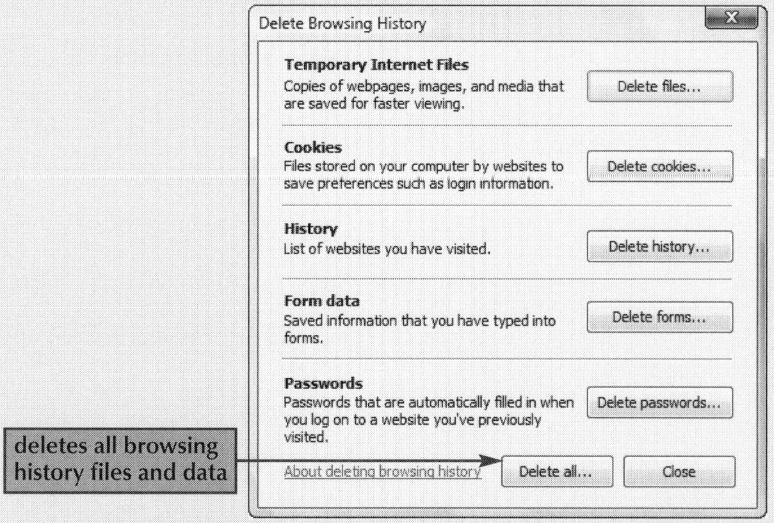

2. If you want to delete one or more of these categories of information, click the button for deleting that category of information and verify the operation. If you want to delete the information for all of these categories, click the **Delete all** button, verify the operation, and then click the **Close** button. If you do not want to delete information from any of these categories, click the **Close** button.

3. Close Windows Internet Explorer.

Add-ons include ActiveX controls, Browser Helper Objects (BHOs), and toolbars that work with your Web browser. A **Browser Helper Object** is a small program that works with your Web browser so that you can view specific types of Web content or that provides additional features in your Web browser. An example of a BHO is Adobe PDF Reader Link Helper from Adobe Systems. This BHO enables you to view PDF files within Windows Internet Explorer. A **PDF (Portable Document Format)** file is a file that contains an image of the contents of another file so that you can view and print that file. PDF files are considered a safe file format for distributing the contents of other files, and they are commonly used by different Web sites to post articles, documents, white papers (technical documents), and tax forms (to name a few examples).

If you choose to delete your browsing history, Windows Internet Explorer does not delete your favorite bookmarked Web sites, and it does not delete feeds to which you have subscribed. A **feed** (also known as an **RSS feed**) consists of Web site content (such as news headlines or digital content, such as video) automatically delivered to your Web browser; other programs, such as e-mail software; or your desktop.

Using the Check Disk Utility

Problems with the file system on a disk might arise from insufficient power, a power failure, a brownout (a diminished supply of power), a power surge, an improper shutdown, or after a system lockup that requires a reboot. File system problems can also arise from an infection by malicious software, faulty or failing hardware, software problems, and even limited disk storage space (because the disk is almost full). Although the Disk Cleanup Wizard can help you free up valuable storage space on a disk, you might also need to move folders and files from the hard disk to some type of permanent storage medium for long-term storage. You should also consider the use of an uninterruptible power supply, or backup power unit, that provides a steady supply of enough power to support your computer and all of its hardware.

To check for errors to the file system or the hard disk, you can use the Windows Vista command-line Check Disk utility or the Error-Checking Tool (the GUI version of the command-line Check Disk utility). Both tools fall into a category of software called disk analysis and repair utilities, and both help you protect your investment in your hard disk and other types of disks, including flash drives.

The Check Disk utility and Error-Checking Tool examine a disk for file system errors and repair those errors where possible. They can also check the physical structure of a disk and evaluate the integrity of sectors on a disk's surface. Checking the file system is relatively fast; however, checking the integrity of a disk's surface is time-consuming. Fortunately, you only need to check the physical integrity of a disk's surface if you suspect or encounter a major problem with the hard disk. If that happens, you should immediately back up important files on your computer before you run either utility. Also, if you attempt to use these utilities on the system volume (the volume from which Windows Vista boots), Windows Vista informs you that you must perform the disk check during the next boot.

You can use the Check Disk utility and Error-Checking Tool in one of three ways:

- **Perform a diagnostic check** If you run one of these utilities in **Diagnostic Mode** or **Read-Only Mode**, it examines a disk for errors and reports on any errors that it finds, but it does not correct the errors. Instead, it reports what it would do if you decide to correct the file system errors. After using this approach, you can decide whether to make a backup of the contents of your computer's hard disk before you correct file system errors. Another advantage of this option is that you can check the system volume without rebooting.
- **Check and repair file system errors** This option checks for and attempts to fix file system errors, but it does not check for bad sectors. If you are checking the system volume, Windows Vista must reboot the computer before checking the file system on the volume.
- **Check and repair file system errors and bad sectors** Although this option is the most thorough, it is the most time-consuming. If you are checking the system volume, you must reboot the computer. If you check the integrity of the hard disk, and either utility finds a bad cluster that contains data, it attempts to recover the data from the bad cluster by moving the data to another cluster on the disk.

The Check Disk utility was originally introduced with the first version of the DOS operating system on the first IBM PCs in 1981 and was included in every subsequent version of the DOS operating system and every version of the Windows operating system in both the Windows 9.x and Windows NT product lines. This utility is still available in Windows Vista. The Windows 9.x product line also contained a ScanDisk utility, which was also introduced originally in the DOS operating system. Both utilities are disk analysis and repair utilities that work in a similar way; however, ScanDisk is typically used in the Windows GUI in the Windows 9.x product line, whereas Check Disk is used in a command-line window in both product lines. The Windows 9.x product line also had a command-line version of ScanDisk. Windows Vista, Windows XP, and Windows 2000 have a GUI version of Check Disk called the Error-Checking Tool.

Microsoft has included (and updated) the Check Disk utility in every version of the DOS and Windows operating systems, which emphasizes the importance of this command-line utility in checking and repairing disk problems.

Using the Error-Checking Tool on an NTFS Volume

Because the file systems for NTFS and FAT volumes differ, the Error-Checking Tool and Check Disk utility examine different data structures important to tracking folders and files on each type of volume.

When you use the Error-Checking Tool or command-line Check Disk utility on an NTFS volume, the utility makes three passes of the volume and examines all the data used to keep track of all the folders and files on a volume. As it does, it performs three types of checks:

- **File verification** During the first pass or phase, the Error-Checking Tool and command-line Check Disk utility verify files. They examine each file record segment in the volume's Master File Table (MFT) for internal consistency and identify which file record segments and clusters are in use. A **file record segment (FRS)** is a 1,024-byte entry in the Master File Table for a file or folder. At the completion of this phase, the Error-Checking Tool and command-line Check Disk utility compare the information that they compile to information that NTFS maintains on disk to find discrepancies or problems, such as corrupted file record segments.

- **Index verification** During the second pass or phase, the Error-Checking Tool and command-line Check Disk utility verify **indexes**, or **NTFS directories** (folders), on the volume. They examine each directory on the volume for internal consistency by making sure that every directory and file is referenced by at least one directory and that the file record segment reference for each file and subdirectory (subfolder) in the Master File Table is valid. During this pass, the Error-Checking Tool and command-line Check Disk utility also verify time stamps (file dates and times) and file sizes. From the information garnered during this phase, the Error-Checking Tool and command-line Check Disk utility can determine whether the volume contains any orphaned files. An **orphaned file** has a valid file record segment in the Master File Table, but is not listed in any directory. An orphaned file might occur if the parent folder is overwritten or modified in some way, but the file record segment in the MFT for the orphaned file still refers to that parent folder. The Error-Checking Tool and command-line Check Disk utility can restore an orphaned file to its original directory if that directory still exists. If that directory does not exist, the Error-Checking Tool and command-line Check Disk utility create a directory in the top-level folder or root directory for that file. If these utilities find a file record segment that is no longer in use or that does not correspond to the file in the directory, they remove the directory entry. This phase takes the most time.
- **Security descriptor verification** In the third pass or phase, the Error-Checking Tool and command-line Check Disk utility verify the integrity of security descriptors for each folder and file. A **security descriptor** contains information about the owner of the folder or file, permissions granted to users and groups for that directory or file, and information on security events to be audited for that directory or file. These utilities only verify that the security descriptors are properly formed, not whether they are appropriate.

If you specify the "Scan for and attempt recovery of bad sectors" option with the Error-Checking tool or specify the **Repair switch (/R)** with the command-line Check Disk utility, these utilities step through two additional phases that determine whether they can read from, and write to, sectors in each cluster on disk. During the fourth phase, these utilities verify all used clusters (that contain data), and in the fifth phase, they verify all unused clusters (that do not contain data). These two phases are time-consuming.

Before you run the Error-Checking Tool and command-line Check Disk utility, you should close all other programs and windows to make sure that no open program accesses folders or files on the disk that you intend to check; otherwise, that open program might interfere with the Error-Checking Tool and command-line Check Disk utility. In the case of the command-line Check Disk utility, it might report nonexistent errors.

If the Error-Checking Tool and command-line Check Disk utility cannot lock (or prevent access to) the drive, they offer to check the hard disk drive the next time you start the computer. If the drive you're checking is not the system volume, the Error-Checking Tool and command-line Check Disk utility might be able to dismount the volume so that it has exclusive access to the volume. When Windows dismounts a volume, that volume is no longer available for use. Windows Vista must mount the volume later to make it available for use. If you do not want to dismount a volume, you can instead schedule the Error-Checking Tool and command-line Check Disk utility to check the disk at the next boot.

If you want to use the Error-Checking Tool and command-line Check Disk utility to examine your hard disk, but have never used them before, you should first back up the hard disk or at least your important files. If the Error-Checking Tool and command-line Check Disk utility detect and then repair errors in the file system or move data from bad clusters to good clusters, you might lose important information.

Aaron emphasizes the importance of using the Error-Checking Tool regularly to check and maintain the integrity of hard disks that contain important company documents. He points out that it is easier to repair problems while they are relatively minor, rather than wait until the problems become more serious and perhaps impossible to repair. To become familiar with the Error-Checking Tool, Aaron suggests you use it to check your hard disk drive.

In the next set of steps, you are going to use the Error-Checking Tool to check your hard disk drive. As noted earlier, the Error-Checking Tool is the version of the command-line Check Disk utility that operates in the graphical user interface. Later in the tutorial, you will use the command-line Check Disk utility. If Windows Vista cannot boot to the desktop, but rather boots to a command-line environment, you must use the command-line Check Disk utility to troubleshoot file system problems on your computer.

To check your hard disk drive, you must log on under an Administrator account or provide Windows Vista the password for an Administrator account. If you have an external hard disk drive, you can check that hard disk drive instead of the system volume (most likely drive C:). If you do check an external hard disk drive, Windows Vista can check the volume directly without requiring a reboot. If you do not have a backup of your hard disk (or don't want to make any changes to your hard disk), you can either perform a Diagnostic or Read-Only check of your hard disk, or you can read the following steps and examine the figures so that you are familiar with this utility.

If you are using a computer in a college computer lab, make sure that you have permission to use the Error-Checking Tool. In some cases, computers in a college lab may be set up so that you cannot check the hard disk drive during the next boot. If you don't have permission to use the Error-Checking Tool or do not have the option of rebooting and then checking a computer's hard disk drive, just read the steps and examine the figures.

To use the Error-Checking Tool to check a hard disk drive:

1. Open a Computer window, right-click the **Local Disk (C:)** drive icon, click **Properties**, and then click the **Tools** tab in the Local Disk (C:) Properties dialog box. On the Tools tab, you have the option of performing three important operations, all of which you will examine in this and another tutorial. See Figure 6-8.

Figure 6-8 Local Disk (C:) Tools property sheet

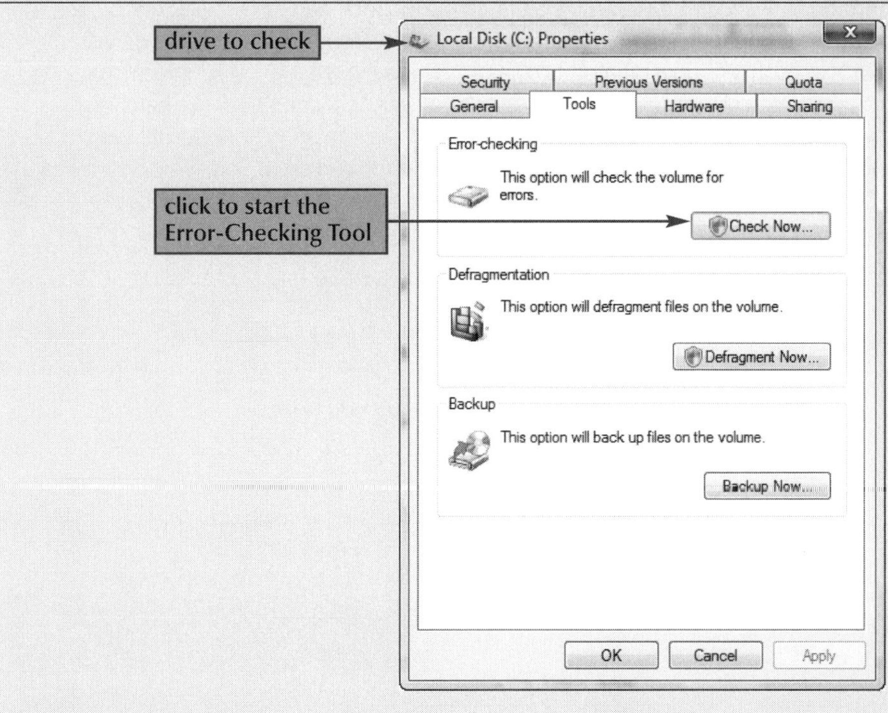

2. Under Error-checking, click the **Check Now** button. Windows Vista displays a User Account Control dialog box and prompts for Administrator credentials.

3. In the User Account Control dialog box, click the **Continue** button if you are already logged on under an Administrator account, or when prompted by Windows Vista, enter the **password** for an Administrator account and then click the **OK** button. Windows Vista displays a Check Disk Local Disk (C:) dialog box with two options for checking a disk. See Figure 6-9. The first option, "Automatically fix file system errors," is already enabled. This option checks the file system and repairs file system errors. The second option, "Scan for and attempt recovery of bad sectors," checks each sector on the disk, and if any defective sectors are found, the Error-Checking Tool attempts to recover the data from the bad sectors and moves the data to good sectors. You can use either option, or both options.

Figure 6-9 Verifying options for checking a hard disk drive

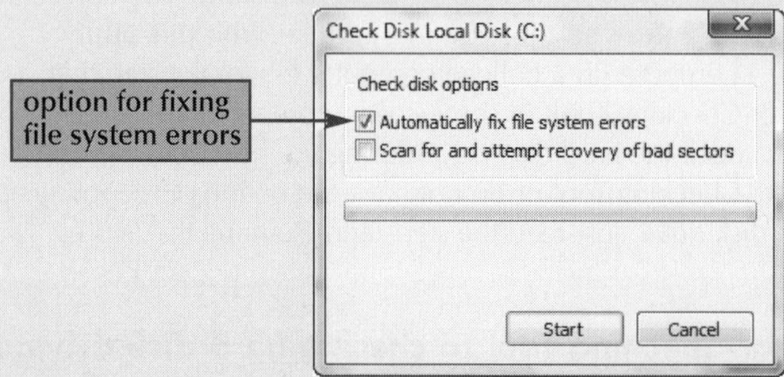

4. If you want to perform a Diagnostic or Read-Only check of your hard disk drive (or an external hard disk drive), click the **Automatically fix file system errors** check box to remove the check mark, and make sure there is no check mark in the "Scan for and attempt recovery of bad sectors" check box. If you want to check your hard disk (or an external hard disk) for errors and repair those errors, make sure the "Automatically fix file system errors" check box contains a check mark, and then click the **Start** button. If you indicate that you want to check and repair your system volume, Windows Vista displays a Microsoft Windows dialog box, as shown in Figure 6-10, and informs you that it cannot check the disk while it's in use; however, you can check for hard disk errors the next time you start the computer. If you are checking an external hard disk, Windows Vista immediately checks the file system on that disk. If you are performing a Diagnostic or Read-Only check, Windows Vista immediately performs the check.

Figure 6-10 Option for checking the system volume at next boot

5. If you want to check and repair your system volume, click the **Schedule disk check** button, click the **Lock menu** button on the Start menu, and then click **Restart**. (If you decide not to check the hard disk during the next reboot, click the **Cancel** button.) During the reboot, Windows Vista checks the file system on your system volume. After the check of the hard disk or an external hard disk is complete, Windows Vista reports on whether it found and corrected any problems with the file system, and then Windows Vista boots the computer. Figure 6-11 shows the results produced by checking a 250 GB hard disk drive that is both the system and boot volume. If you checked an external hard disk drive, Windows Vista displays a Checking Disk dialog box and (hopefully) reports that your device or disk was successfully scanned, that no problems were found, and that the disk is ready for use, as shown in Figure 6-12.

   Trouble? If you are checking an internal hard disk, you do not need to perform any additional steps. Examine the results that the Check Disk utility reports.

Figure 6-11 Check Disk results for NTFS volume

```
Checking file system on C:
The type of the file system is NTFS.

A disk check has been scheduled.
Windows will now check the disk.
CHKDSK is verifying files (stage 1 of 3)...          <- stage 1
  196864 file records processed.
File verification completed.
  172 large file records processed.
  0 bad file records processed.
  2 EA records processed.
  140 reparse records processed.
CHKDSK is verifying indexes (stage 2 of 3)...        <- stage 2
  736360 index entries processed.
Index verification completed.
  5 unindexed files processed.
CHKDSK is verifying security descriptors (stage 3 of 3)...   <- stage 3
  196864 security descriptors processed.
Security descriptor verification completed.
  24447 data files processed.
CHKDSK is verifying Usn Journal...
  37428664 USN bytes processed.
Usn Journal verification completed.
Windows has checked the file system and found no problems.

 244083577 KB total disk space.
  78853284 KB in 171862 files.
     77360 KB in 24448 indexes.
         0 KB in bad sectors.
    308061 KB in use by the system.
     65536 KB occupied by the log file.
 164844872 KB available on disk.

      4096 bytes in each allocation unit.            <- cluster size
  61020894 total allocation units on disk.
  41211218 allocation units available on disk.
```

Figure 6-12 Results of using Error-Checking Tool on an external hard disk drive

Checking Disk FreeAgent Drive (F:)

Your device or disc was successfully scanned

No problems were found on the device or disc. It is ready to use.

If you removed the device or disc before all files were fully written to it, parts of some files might still be missing. If so, go back to the source and recopy those files to your device or disc.

See details Close

no problems on external hard disk drive

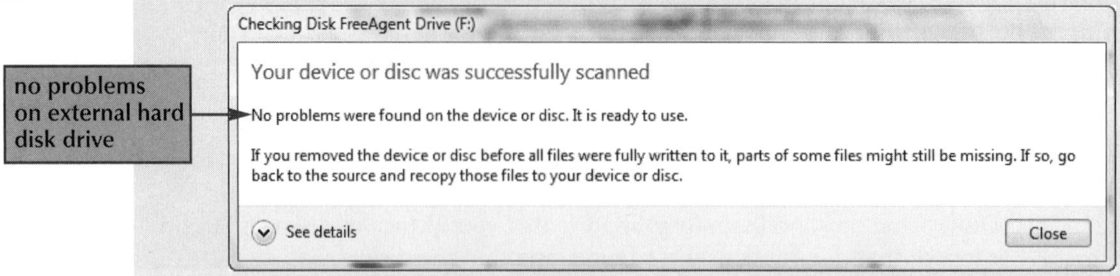

6. If you checked an external hard disk drive or performed a Diagnostic check of your hard drive, click the **See details** button in the Checking Disk dialog box. Windows Vista summarizes the results of checking the external hard disk drive. On the computer used for Figure 6-13, a check was performed on a 500 GB external hard disk drive. Your results will differ.

Figure 6-13 Results from checking an external hard drive for errors

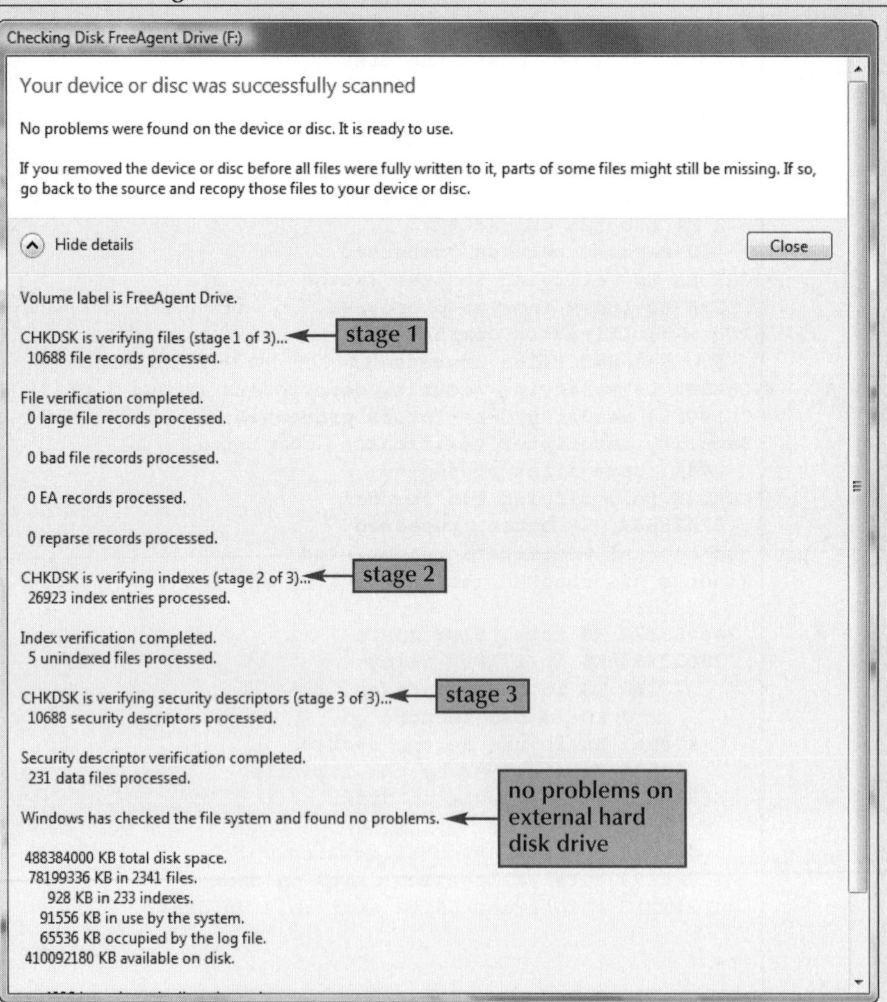

7. Close the Checking Disk dialog box, and then close the Properties dialog box for that disk drive.
8. Close the Computer window.

At the beginning of the system volume check, the Check Disk utility identifies the file system on the disk, and then starts verifying files. During this phase (and other phases), it displays the percent complete for the number of file records processed, and then it notes that file verification is completed. Next, indexes, or NTFS directories (folders), are verified. This phase takes more time, but once complete, Windows Vista notes the number of index entries processed and that the Index verification is completed. In the third stage, security descriptors are verified. At the end of this phase, Windows Vista reports the number of security descriptors processed, notes that the security descriptor verification is completed, and reports on the number of data files processed.

Next, the **Usn Journal** (also called the Change Journal), which keeps track of changes made to folders and files on an NTFS volume, is verified. Windows Vista reports on the number of USN bytes processed, and then notes that Usn Journal verification is completed. After this last check, Windows Vista either reports that it checked the file system and found no problems, or it reports on specific problems. The **USN** (**Update Serial Number**) is a unique number assigned to each change to a folder or file listed in the Usn Journal. The USN is also recorded in the Master File Table record for a folder or file so that the file system has a record of the last change made to a folder or file.

Finally, Windows Vista summarizes information on the usage of disk storage space and allocation units (or clusters). First, it reports on the total disk storage space, the number of kilobytes used by files, the total number of files, the number of kilobytes used by indexes, the total number of indexes, the number of kilobytes in bad sectors, the number of kilobytes used by the system, the total number of kilobytes used by the log file (the Usn Journal), and the total available kilobytes on disk. The storage space used by the system includes the Master File Table and other NTFS metafiles (files that contain data about other files). Then, it reports on the number of bytes in each allocation unit (or cluster), the total allocation units on disk, and the total available allocation units on disk. If you divide the total number of bytes in each allocation unit by 512 bytes, you know how many sectors are contained in each cluster. For the computer used for Figure 6-11, there are 8 sectors per cluster.

If the Error-Checking Tool and command-line Check Disk utility detect a problem with the file system or identify bad or failing clusters, they try to fix the problem, but this feature is no substitute for backups.

Reference Window | **Using the Error-Checking Tool to Check the File System on a Hard Disk Drive**

- Open a Computer window, right-click the Local Disk (C:) drive icon or the drive icon for an external hard disk drive, click Properties, and then click the Tools tab in the Properties dialog box for the specific drive you chose.
- Under Error-checking on the Tools tab, click the Check Now button.
- After Windows Vista displays a User Account Control dialog box, click the Continue button if you are already logged on under an Administrator account, or when prompted by Windows Vista, enter the password for an Administrator account, and then click the OK button.
- After Windows Vista displays a Check Disk dialog box (with the name of the disk drive), click the "Automatically fix file system errors" check box, click the Start button, and if Windows Vista displays a Microsoft Windows dialog box and informs you that it cannot check the disk while it's in use, click the Schedule disk check button.
- If you are checking your system volume, click the Lock menu button on the Start menu, click Restart, and as Check Disk examines your system volume, view the results of the disk check.
- If you checked an external hard disk drive, review the results reported in the Checking Disk dialog box, close the Checking Disk dialog box, close the Properties dialog box for that disk drive, and then close the Computer window.

Using new self-healing features of NTFS, Windows Vista can detect and repair file system errors while your computer is up and running. This new Windows Vista feature not only reduces the number of file system problems on NTFS volumes, but also reduces the likelihood that you (or an Administrator) might need to manually resolve those problems. This self-healing feature is especially useful in a business environment because a hard disk check is time-consuming and can result in loss of productivity when an employee's computer is not available. If the self-healing capabilities of NTFS do not resolve file system problems, Windows Vista schedules a check of the disk during the next boot.

In previous versions of Windows, it was common practice to recommend a periodic check of the hard disk, preferably once a week or no longer than once a month, to check for and remove problems before they became more serious. Even though the NTFS self-healing features help protect the hard disk, Microsoft still recommends periodic preventive maintenance. Microsoft notes that because problems with the file system and disks commonly result in problems that are difficult to troubleshoot, they recommend the Check Disk utility as one of the first tools you use to diagnose and repair problems, especially if you have not made a change to your system's settings or configuration.

Using the Error-Checking Tool on FAT Volumes

The self-repairing and self-healing features of NTFS are not found in the FAT file system, so the use of the Error-Checking Tool or the command-line Check Disk utility on FAT volumes is more important. Flash drives typically use the FAT file system, and you might need to check the file system if you experience problems with accessing data on the flash drive.

When checking the file system on a FAT volume, the Error-Checking Tool and command-line Check Disk utilities check the File Allocation Tables (FAT1 and FAT2), the directory table for the top-level folder (or root directory), the folder (or directory) structure, the integrity of files, and the validity of long filenames. As you may recall from Tutorial 3, the File Allocation Table contains information on cluster usage. Also, the operating system keeps and updates two copies of the File Allocation Table (FAT1 and FAT2). When these utilities examine the File Allocation Tables, they trace the chain for each file and account for all clusters in use by each file.

As you will recall from Tutorial 3, the directory table for the top-level folder (or root directory) in the FAT file system tracks information on the folders and files that are stored in the top-level folder of a disk, including the starting cluster for each file and its size. When checking the directory table, the Error-Checking Tool or command-line Check Disk utility verifies that the size of each file matches the total amount of storage space assigned to clusters for each file in the File Allocation Table.

Checking the folder or directory structure is also important because Windows Vista must be able to navigate it to locate and store files on a disk. The Error-Checking Tool and command-line Check Disk utility therefore navigate the entire directory structure of a disk to ensure that it is functional and intact.

Checking for Lost Clusters

When the Error-Checking Tool and the command-line Check Disk utility verifies the integrity of files, they look for lost clusters and cross-linked files. A **lost cluster** is a cluster on a FAT volume that contains data that once belonged to a program, document, or another type of file, such as a temporary file. In the File Allocation Table, there is no pointer to the lost cluster; therefore, the lost cluster is not associated with any file, and you cannot view the data in the lost cluster. The cluster is still allocated to the lost cluster, so the lost cluster wastes disk storage space. A **pointer** is the cluster number of the next available cluster for a folder or file.

Like other types of file system problems, lost clusters might develop when a power failure occurs, when you reboot a computer system after it locks up, when a brownout or a power surge occurs, or when you do not properly shut down Windows Vista. In these cases, lost clusters develop because the operating system might not be able to record any remaining information it has on the location of the clusters for a file in the File Allocation Table or the information it has on the starting cluster of the file in the folder or directory file.

Figure 6-14 illustrates this common problem on FAT volumes. Assume you are looking at the part of the FAT where Windows Vista tracks the usage of cluster numbers 1500 through 1512. In this example, assume that Windows Vista has assigned clusters 1500 through 1505 to a file named Financial Analysis.xlsx, and that it assigned clusters 1506 through 1512 to a file named Project Overview.docx. As a result of a power failure, assume the pointer for cluster 1509 for the Project Overview file changes to an end-of-file code (EOF). If you open the Project Overview file in the application that produced it, Windows Vista reads clusters 1506 through 1509 and then stops because it finds an end-of-file code for cluster 1509. If you examine the end of this file (assuming you can open it at all), you discover that part of the file is missing and that the file contains uninterpretable characters. Clusters 1510 through 1512, which once belonged to the Project Overview file, are now lost clusters. In fact, they constitute one **chain** of lost clusters because they are derived from a single file. A chain of lost clusters is also called a **file fragment**. The FAT shows those clusters as being in use (i.e., they contain data). However, those clusters are not associated with any file on disk because the FAT does not contain a pointer to cluster 1510. The operating system cannot use or access the storage space occupied by these lost clusters, so they waste valuable storage space on disk. Because lost clusters arise so easily, they are the most common type of problem encountered on FAT volumes.

Figure 6-14 How lost clusters might occur on a FAT volume

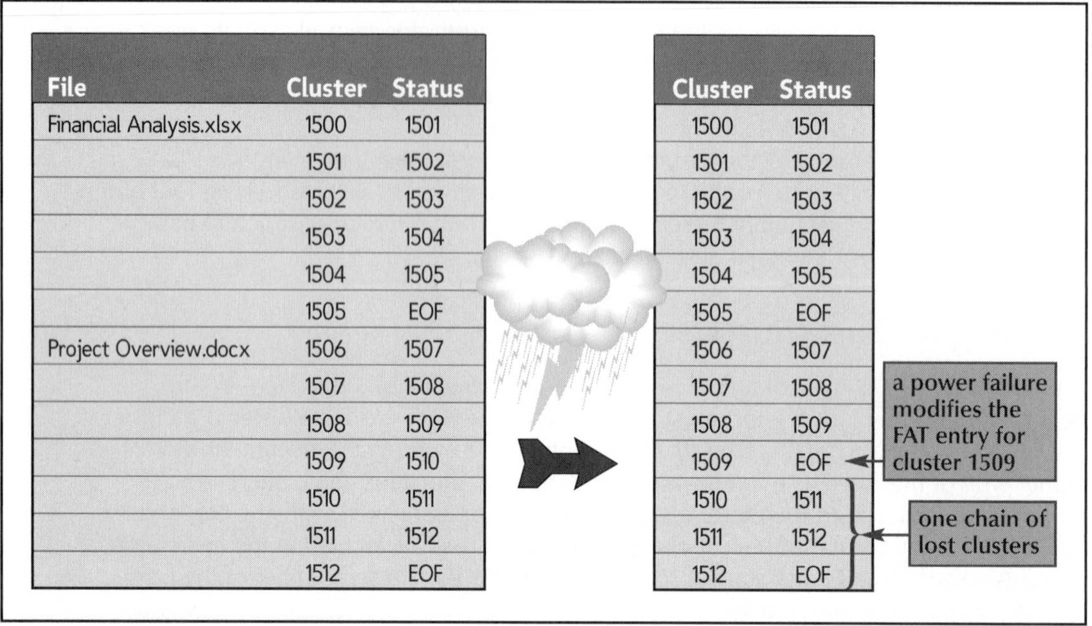

Likewise, if a power problem occurs near the end of a file save operation, you might end up with lost clusters on a disk, or the entire file that you had open may end up as lost clusters. In this case, Windows might report the file size as 0 (zero). That means all of the clusters originally assigned to the file are now lost clusters. If a FAT volume has lost clusters, it might appear that all of the disk storage space is available because you cannot see the lost clusters in a folder window. However, the disk could have lost clusters that are not visible when viewing the contents of the disk. You can use the Error-Checking Tool or the command-line Check Disk utility to recover those lost clusters and free up valuable storage space on the disk. If a disk contains lost clusters, the command-line Check Disk utility will report that it found errors on the disk and then ask if you want to convert the lost chains to files. A **lost chain** is a sequence of lost clusters that once belonged to a single file. The Error-Checking Tool converts the lost chains to files without asking you.

As it recovers lost clusters, the Error-Checking Tool or command-line Check Disk utility creates a hidden system folder named FOUND.nnn in the top-level folder of the disk that it checks (where nnn is a sequential number, starting with 000) for each chain of lost clusters, and then stores the recovered clusters in a file named FILE0000.CHK within that folder. If these utilities find more than one chain of lost clusters, they name the second chain FILE0001.CHK, the third chain FILE0002.CHK, and so on. The file extension "chk" stands for Check Disk. To view the FOUND.000 folder in a folder window, you have to open the Folder Options dialog box and choose the options for showing hidden files and folders and for displaying hidden, protected operating system files.

After recovering lost clusters, you can delete the FOUND.000 folder and recover the disk storage space used by lost clusters. Or, you can open the FOUND.000 folder, open each file with recovered lost clusters, and then attempt to determine if these files contain anything of value to you. You can open each file in Notepad and try to determine what type of content is contained in the file, close the file, and then open the program that you think created the file to determine if the file can be opened by that program and, if so, whether the file has any useful information you need. If you open a file in Notepad, you might not be able to distinguish what type of content is stored in the file; however, if you examine the beginning of the file, you will see a code, such as JPEG or GIF, which identifies the file type. Close Notepad, change the file extension to the appropriate file type, and open the file with the program associated with that file type. If the file contains useful information, and if you do not have a copy of that information elsewhere, you can save it using an appropriate filename related to its contents. If the file does not contain anything of value to you, or if you still cannot tell which application produced the file or what type of information was contained in the file (typically the case), delete the file to recover the disk space used by the file. Later, if you discover that you are missing part of a file, you can restore the file from a backup.

Over time, lost clusters can increase in number on FAT volumes, waste more valuable disk space, and lead to further disk errors. In most cases, you delete the files that contain lost clusters and reclaim valuable storage space on your hard disk.

Checking for Cross-Linked Files

Another important but less common problem on FAT volumes is cross-linked files. A **cross-linked file** is a file that contains at least one cluster that belongs to or is shared by two (or perhaps more) files. For example, as shown in Figure 6-15, one file might be cross-linked with only one other file through one cluster. In this example, the problem that caused the file system error might modify the end-of-file code for one file so that it points to a cluster that's part of another file.

How a cross-link might occur on a FAT volume | **Figure 6-15**

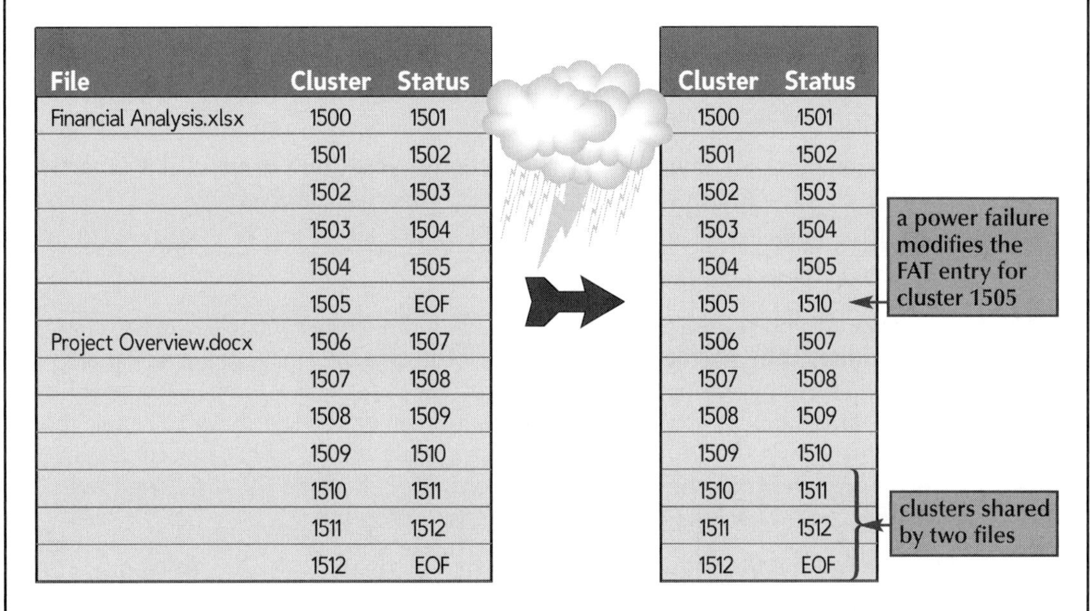

File	Cluster	Status
Financial Analysis.xlsx	1500	1501
	1501	1502
	1502	1503
	1503	1504
	1504	1505
	1505	EOF
Project Overview.docx	1506	1507
	1507	1508
	1508	1509
	1509	1510
	1510	1511
	1511	1512
	1512	EOF

Cluster	Status
1500	1501
1501	1502
1502	1503
1503	1504
1504	1505
1505	1510
1506	1507
1507	1508
1508	1509
1509	1510
1510	1511
1511	1512
1512	EOF

Again, assume you are looking at cluster usage in the File Allocation Table for the same two files you examined earlier. Also, assume that as a result of a power problem, the end-of-file (EOF) code for the last cluster of the file Financial Analysis.xlsx changes so that it points to a cluster assigned to the file Project Overview.docx. In this example, the end-of-file code for cluster 1505 now points to cluster 1510. Cluster 1509 for the Project Overview file also points to cluster 1510. If you open the Financial Analysis file, Windows reads clusters 1500 through 1505, and then, because it finds a pointer to another cluster (and not an EOF code), Windows reads clusters 1510 through 1512 (which were originally part of the Project Overview file). Windows then stops when it encounters the EOF code for cluster 1512. If you examine the Financial Analysis file (assuming you can open it at all), you will discover lost data and uninterpretable characters in the file where the cross-link occurs and perhaps in other parts of the file as well. If you open the Project Overview file, Windows reads clusters 1506 through 1512, the clusters originally assigned to this file before the cross-link occurred. Again, if you examine this file, you will discover uninterpretable characters and perhaps lost data where the cross-link occurs.

How do you repair cross-linked files? You can copy each file to a new location and remove the original files so that the files are no longer cross-linked. You then open both files (if possible), examine them, and edit the files to remove the uninterpretable characters and add any data that might have been lost. Or, you can use the Error-Checking Tool or command-line Check Disk utility to eliminate the cross-links between files by providing each file with a copy of the same cross-linked cluster(s). However, you will have to open and examine each file (if possible) and then edit the contents of the file where the cross-link occurred.

Checking a Flash Drive with the Error-Checking Tool

Aaron recommends that you check your flash drive with the Error-Checking Tool so that you become familiar with how to check other types of drives and disks.

Before you check your flash drive for errors (and repair any errors that are found), make sure you have backup copies (or duplicate copies) of any important files on your flash drive. To be on the safe side, you could copy everything on your flash drive to a folder named Flash Drive in the Public Documents folder (similar to how you copy Data Files to the same folder). In the following steps, you can also choose the option for performing a Diagnostic or Read-Only check of your flash drive.

To use the Error-Checking Tool to check a flash drive:

1. If necessary, attach a flash drive to your computer and close any dialog boxes or windows that Windows Vista opens.
2. Open a Computer window, right-click the **icon for your flash drive**, click **Properties**, and then click the **Tools** tab in the flash drive's Properties dialog box.
3. Under Error-checking, click the **Check Now** button. Windows Vista opens the Check Disk Removable Disk dialog box.
4. If you want to perform a Diagnostic or Read-Only check of your flash drive, click the **Automatically fix file system errors** check box to remove the check mark and make sure there is no check mark in the "Scan for and attempt recovery of bad sectors" check box. If you want to check your flash drive for errors and repair those errors, make sure the "Automatically fix file system errors" check box contains a check mark, and then click the **Start** button. After checking the disk, Windows Vista displays a Checking Disk Removable Disk dialog box.
5. Click the **See details** button. The Checking Disk Removable Disk dialog box expands to display information about the Check Disk operation. See Figure 6-16. On the computer used for this figure, Windows Vista checked a 1 GB USB flash drive and found no problems with the disk drive's file system. Windows Vista reports on the total disk space; the amount of storage space used by hidden files, folders, and files; and the amount of available disk storage space remaining on the disk. Windows Vista also reports that each allocation unit (or cluster) contains 4,096 bytes. If you divide that value by 512 bytes per sector, you find that this USB flash drive has 8 sectors per cluster. That means this 1 GB USB flash drive uses the FAT32 file system. A FAT16 volume of this size would have cluster sizes of 16,384 bytes with 32 sectors per cluster. Finally, Windows Vista reports the total and available number of allocation units (or clusters) on the USB flash drive.

Check Disk results for a FAT volume **Figure 6-16**

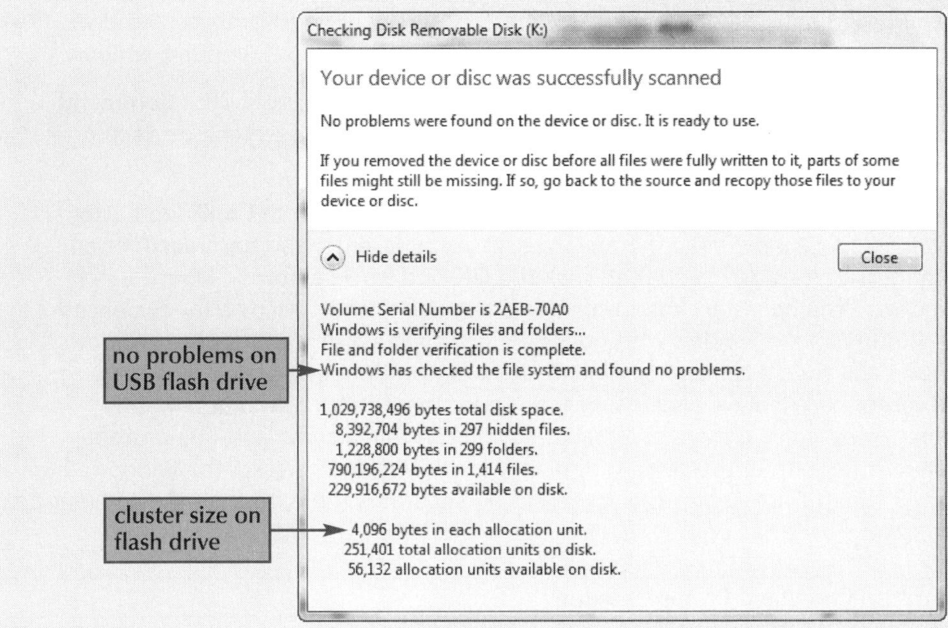

6. Click the **Close** button to close the Checking Disk Removable Disk window, close the Removable Disk Properties dialog box, and then close the Computer window.

You do not need to perform a surface scan of a flash drive because data is written to a flash drive in a different way than for a hard disk drive.

Using the Command-Line Check Disk Utility

You use the command-line Check Disk utility in a command-line environment either under the Windows Vista graphical user interface or in a command-line user interface. You can open a command-line window by using Command Prompt on the Accessories menu. In the command-line window, you enter one command at a time at the command-line prompt (or operating system prompt). Windows Vista locates and opens the program, the program performs its intended task and reports its results, and then Windows Vista displays another command-line prompt so that you can enter another command. You will work with the command-line environment in more detail in Tutorial 14, but this next section will introduce you to its use and an important command-line utility.

Also, to use the command-line Check Disk utility, you must open a Command Prompt window in **Admin Approval Mode**. In other words, you must open Command Prompt in a way that Windows Vista prompts you for Administrator permission or provides you with the option of entering a password for an Administrator account.

Aaron recommends that you check your flash drive with the command-line Check Disk utility and compare its use with the Error-Reporting Tool.

In the following steps, you are going to open the command-line Check Disk utility in Admin Approval Mode and then use Diagnostic or Read-Only Mode to check your flash drive. You therefore must log on under an Administrator account or provide Windows Vista the password of an Administrator account. If you are using a computer in a college computer lab, make sure that you have permission to open and use the command-line Check Disk utility. If you don't have permission to open and use the command-line Check Disk utility, read the following steps and examine the figures, but do not keystroke the steps.

To complete this next section, you need to know the drive name for your flash drive.

To open a command-line window and check a flash drive with the Check Disk utility:

Tip

You can also click the Safely Remove Hardware icon in the notification area to determine the drive name assigned to your flash drive.

1. If you don't know the drive name for your flash drive, open a Computer window, locate the drive name for your flash drive, and then close the Computer window.
2. On the Start menu, point to **All Programs**, click **Accessories**, right-click **Command Prompt**, and then click **Run as administrator**. Windows Vista switches to Secure Desktop Mode and displays a User Account Control dialog box.
3. If you are logged on under an Administrator account, click the **Continue** button, or if you are logged on under a Standard user account, enter the **password** for an Administrator account, and then click the **OK** button. As shown in Figure 6-17, Windows Vista opens an Administrator: Command Prompt window (as evidenced by the title on the window's title bar). Windows Vista also identifies the Windows version and then displays a command-line prompt. Windows 6.0.6000 is the original version of Windows Vista. "C:\Windows\System32>" is the command-line prompt where you enter a command. As you can tell, a command-line prompt includes the path to the current directory (or folder); in this case, the Windows System32 folder. The greater-than symbol (>) separates the path from the command you enter.

Figure 6-17 Administrator: Command Prompt window

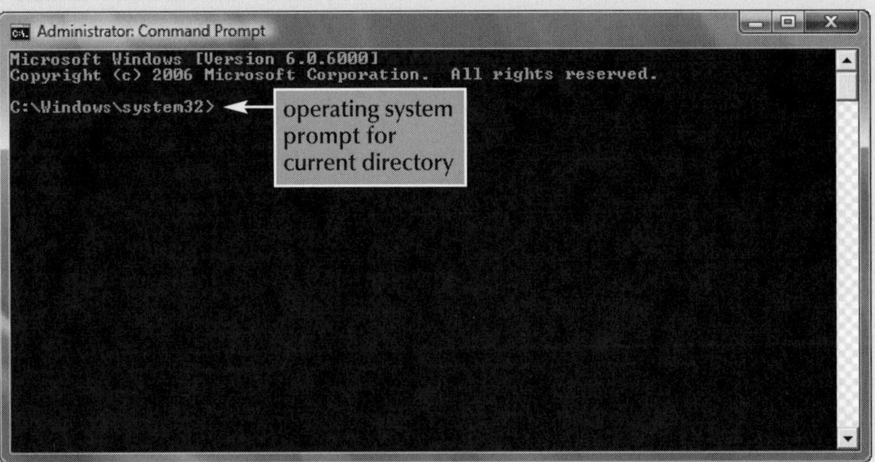

Tip

You can use lowercase or uppercase for a command and any options that you specify with the command.

4. Type **CHKDSK** (in uppercase or lowercase), press the **Spacebar**, type the **drive name for your flash drive**, and then press the **Enter** key. For example, if your flash drive is identified as drive F in the Computer window, you type CHKDSK F: and press the Enter key. The Check Disk utility checks the disk and then reports on its findings. See Figure 6-18. Your results will differ. On the 1 GB flash drive attached to the computer used for this figure, Windows Vista found no problems with the file system. In the status report, it displays the same information that you saw in the previous section when you used the Error-Checking Tool (assuming you used the same flash drive and assuming you did not make any further changes to that flash drive before this step). If you do not specify a drive to check, the Check Disk utility assumes you want to check the current drive.

   Trouble? If Windows Vista informs you that the command you entered is not recognized as an internal or external command, operable program, or batch file, you mistyped the command or did not include a space between the command and the drive name. Repeat this step and enter the command properly.

Trouble? If Windows Vista informs you that it cannot open the volume for direct access, you typed the wrong drive name. If necessary, open a Computer window, verify the flash drive's drive name, close the Computer window, and then repeat this step with the correct drive name.

Trouble? If Windows Vista informs you that the drive, the path, or the file name is not valid, you did not type a colon after the drive name. Repeat the step and enter the drive letter followed by a colon.

Checking a flash drive with the Check Disk utility **Figure 6-18**

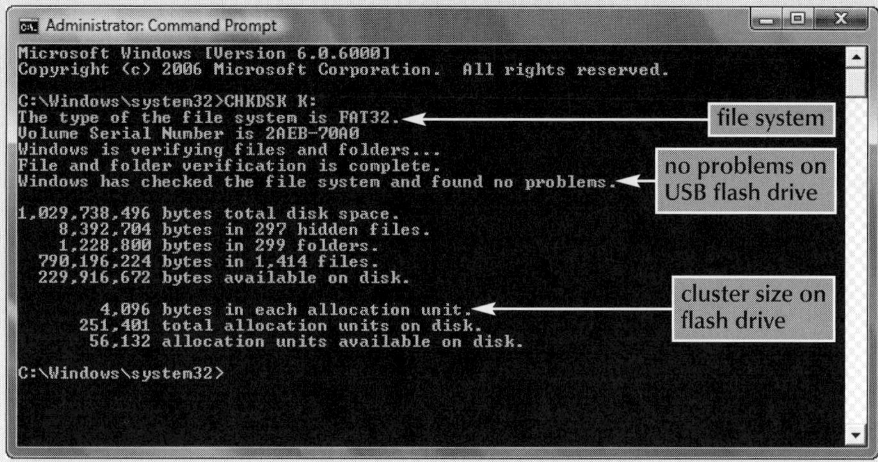

5. To close the Command Prompt window, type **EXIT** and press the **Enter** key.

Tip

Like any other window, you can also use the Command Prompt window Close button to close the window.

After the Check Disk utility reports problems with a disk, you back up your important files, and then use the Check Disk **Fix switch** (**/F**) to repair the problems with the file system (if at all possible). A **switch** is an optional parameter that you use with a command to change the way the command works. Check Disk can also check the physical integrity of sectors on a disk if you use the Repair switch (/R). When you use this switch, Check Disk attempts to recover data stored in bad sectors before marking the clusters with those sectors as unusable. Any recovered data is recorded in other unused, but good, sectors on the disk. If you are using the Repair switch to check sectors on a disk, Check Disk can take a long time, making the disk volume unavailable until the Check Disk utility completes its check and repair of the disk. Microsoft notes that if you interrupt the Check Disk utility when it is running with this switch, it cannot guarantee the integrity of your disk.

If Windows reports that an NTFS directory is corrupt and unreadable (which means you cannot open the folder), run the Error-Checking Tool or command-line Check Disk utility to recover the directory (or folder) and all the subfolders and files. After you open the FOUND.000 folder, you will find a folder named dir0000.chk that contains your recovered folder, its subfolders, and files. You can select this folder and copy its contents to a new location on your hard disk. Windows Vista might be able to recover all or some of your original folders and files.

If Windows Vista detects a problem with a disk during booting, it automatically runs Autochk.exe, a version of Check Disk that runs only at the next boot before Windows Vista boots the computer to the desktop. If you schedule a Check Disk for the next boot, Windows Vista runs Autochk.exe at the next boot.

As you've discovered, the Error-Checking Tool and the Check Disk utility perform comparable operations. Figure 6-19 summarizes how you perform the three basic types of checks discussed at the beginning of this section of the tutorial, using these tools.

Figure 6-19 **Comparison of Error-Checking Tool and Check Disk utility**

Operation	Error-Checking Tool	Check Disk Utility
Diagnostic or Read-Only Mode	Check Disk options: Remove check mark from the following check boxes: • Automatically fix file system errors • Scan for and attempt recovery of bad sectors	CHKDSK [*drivename*] Example: CHKDSK C
Fix file system errors	Check Disk options: • Add a check mark to the Automatically fix file system errors check box • Remove the check mark from the Scan for and attempt recovery of bad sectors check box	CHKDSK [*drivename*] /F Example: CHKDSK C: /F
Fix file system errors and recover bad clusters	Check Disk options: Add a check mark to the following check boxes: • Automatically fix file system errors • Scan for and attempt recovery of bad sectors	CHKDSK [*drivename*] /F /R Example: CHKDSK C: /F /R

You cannot use the Error-Checking Tool or the command-line Check Disk utility to check DVDs or CDs; rather, you use a third-party utility to scan and repair these types of discs.

Reference Window | Using the Check Disk Utility in a Command Prompt Window

- If necessary, open a Computer window, locate the drive name for the drive you want to check, and then close the Computer window.
- From the Start menu, point to All Programs, click Accessories on the All Programs menu, right-click Command Prompt, and then click Run as administrator.
- In the User Account Control dialog box, click the Continue button if you are logged on under an Administrator account, or if you are not logged on under an Administrator account, enter the password for an Administrator account, and then click the OK button.
- To perform a Diagnostic or Read-Only check, type CHKDSK (in uppercase or lowercase) in the Command Prompt window, press the Spacebar, type the drive name for the drive (including the colon) you want to check, and then press the Enter key.
- To check and repair file system errors, type CHKDSK, press the Spacebar, type the drive name, press the Spacebar, type /F and then press the Enter key.
- To check and repair file system errors and bad sectors, type CHKDSK, press the Spacebar, type the drive name, press the Spacebar, type /F /R and then press the Enter key.
- After examining the status report and repairing file system errors and bad clusters, type EXIT and press the Enter key (or click the Command Prompt window's Close button) to close the Command Prompt.

The Check Disk utility is a powerful tool for maintaining the integrity of the file system on a computer.

Troubleshooting with Check Disk | InSight

You can use the command-line Check Disk utility to check for and resolve many types of problems that arise on a computer. If you experience a problem with hardware, software, folders, or files on your computer, first try the Error-Checking Tool or command-line Check Disk utility because the source of the problem may actually result from an error in the file system. These utilities take only a few minutes to check your computer, and if the problem you are experiencing results from a problem in the file system, these utilities can correct the problem in most instances and save you valuable time and money.

Session 6.1 Quick Check | Review

1. True or False. Temporary files are files that applications create when you are working with a document or that Windows creates while performing an operation.
2. What utility or utilities can you use to check a hard disk for errors, and where possible, repair those errors?
3. A(n) ________________ is an NTFS directory (or folder).
4. What NTFS file system component contains information about the owner of the folder or file, permissions granted to users and groups for that directory or file, and information on security events to be audited for that directory or file?
5. A(n) ________________ is a cluster on a FAT volume that contains data that once belonged to a program, document, or another type of file, such as a temporary file, but which is no longer associated with any file.
6. A(n) ________________ is an optional parameter that you use with a command in a command-line environment to change the way in which the command typically works.

Session 6.2

Understanding File Fragmentation

As you create, modify, and save files to a hard disk, Windows attempts to store the different parts of each file in **contiguous**, or adjacent, clusters; in other words, one right after the other. However, as you add, delete, and modify files, Windows might then store different parts of the same file in **noncontiguous** or nonadjacent clusters that are scattered across the surface of a disk because the disk does not have enough space to store the file in contiguous clusters. The file is then called a **fragmented file**. Over time, file fragmentation can build up, affect the performance of a hard disk, and as noted by Microsoft, place undue stress on the hard disk.

A hard disk's read/write heads retrieve data from and record data on the surface of the hard disk. Each time you instruct a program to retrieve a file from a hard disk, the hard disk must move the read/write heads to different positions on the hard disk to locate each cluster for a file and reassemble its contents so that you can work with the file. When retrieving a file that is stored in contiguous clusters, the read/write heads can quickly reassemble the entire file from one location on the hard disk. However, when retrieving a fragmented file, the read/write heads must keep moving to different positions on the hard disk to locate and then reassemble the entire file. Therefore, the overall process takes longer, and you spend more time waiting for a file to open.

Likewise, when you issue a command to save a new or modified file to a disk, Windows Vista must locate available clusters for that file on disk. If a file is stored in noncontiguous clusters, it takes the read/write heads longer to write the file to the disk because the read/write heads must move to different positions on the hard disk to record data. Obviously, the problem is compounded if all or most of the files on a disk are fragmented. Furthermore, as fragmentation builds up on a disk, it not only means that you spend more time waiting for files to open and save, it also results in more disk access, and that in turn causes increased wear and tear on the hard disk.

To understand how file fragmentation occurs, consider a simple example. Assume that over the last six months you added files to a hard disk, and you deleted and modified files on the hard disk. Also assume that you created and saved a project overview report, a bid proposal, and a financial projection and that these three files are each stored in contiguous clusters, one file after another. As shown in Figure 6-20, the Project Overview report is stored in seven contiguous clusters (clusters 1100 through 1106), the Bid Proposal in 10 contiguous clusters (clusters 1107 thru 1116), and the Financial Projection in 21 contiguous clusters (clusters 1117 through 1137). Clusters 1138 through 1160 are currently unused clusters, and the remainder of the hard disk stores many other files that you have added to the hard disk over time.

Figure 6-20 **Files arranged in contiguous clusters**

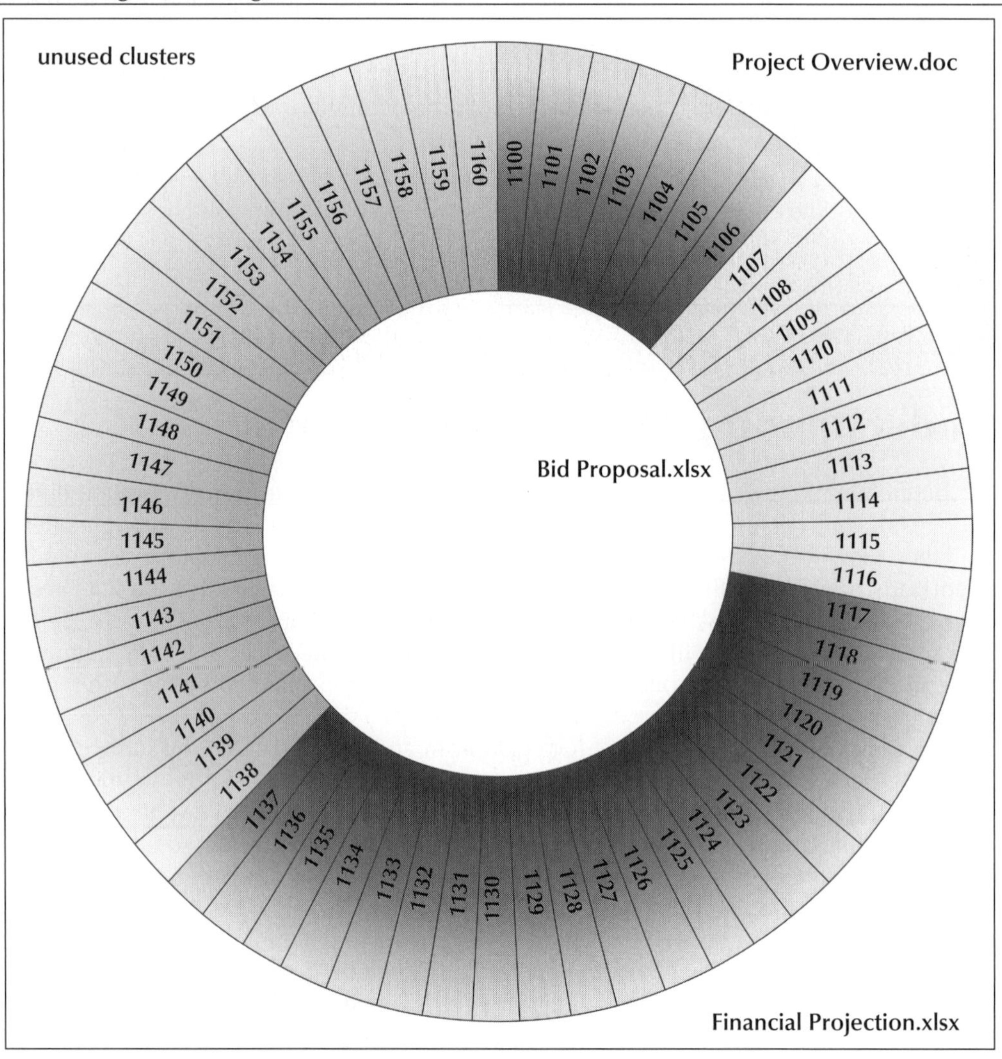

You decide you no longer need the Bid Proposal, so you delete this file. By removing this file, you free up ten clusters, as shown in Figure 6-21.

Clusters freed after deleting a file **Figure 6-21**

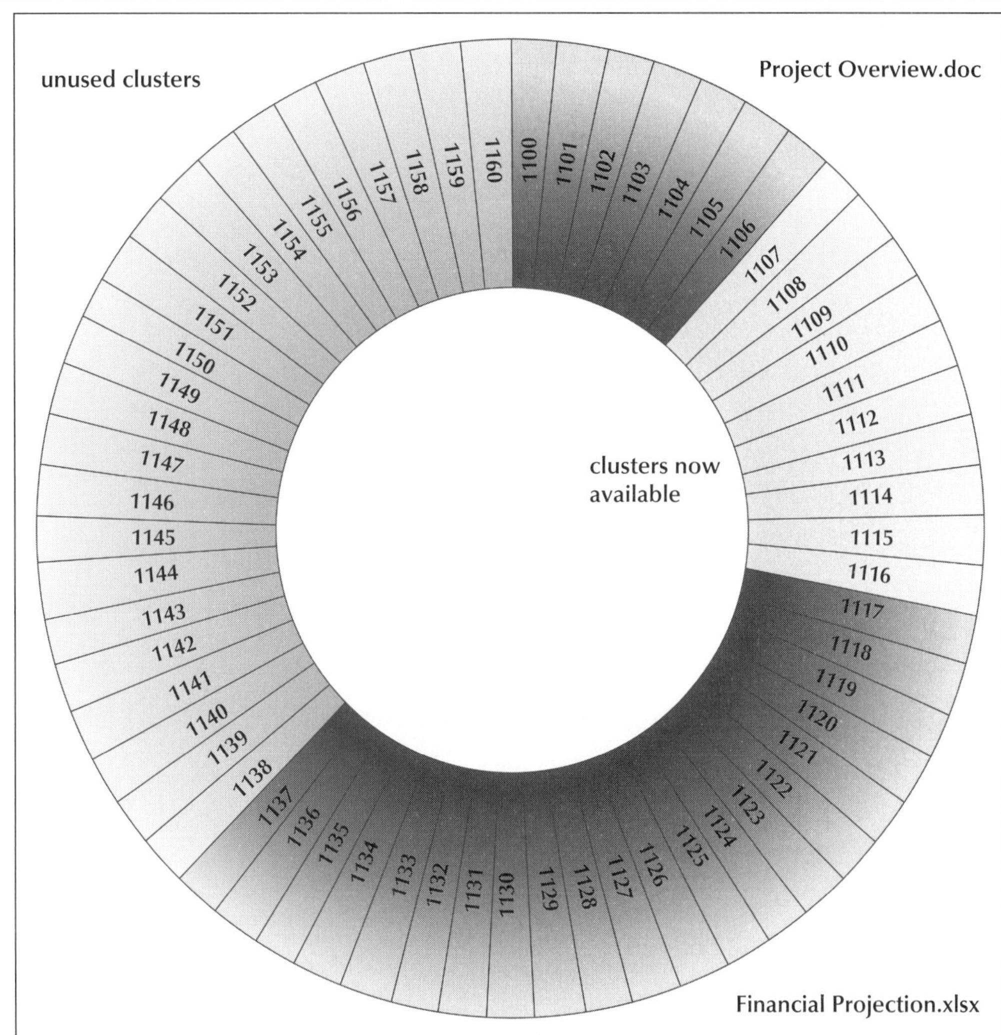

Next, you prepare and save a Portfolio for an upcoming project. Let's assume that this file initially requires 10 clusters and that Windows uses the clusters that were previously occupied by the Bid Proposal. A short while later, you open the file again and add a new section to the portfolio so that the final file size requires 28 clusters of storage space on disk. When Windows allocates storage space for the file with the Portfolio, it might use the next available set of contiguous clusters for the additional 18 clusters required for this file, right after the clusters for the file with the Financial Projection, as shown in Figure 6-22.

Figure 6-22 Fragmented file stored in two noncontiguous blocks

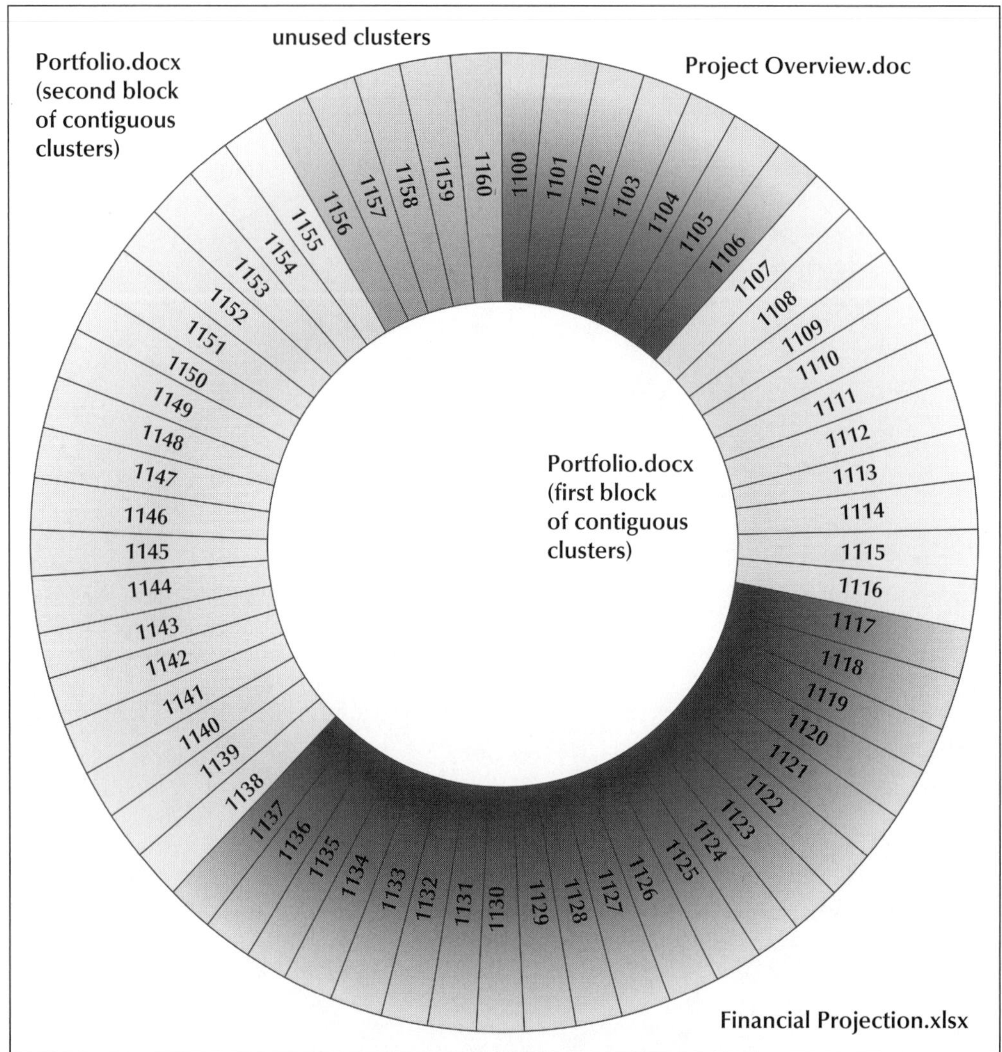

The Portfolio file is a fragmented file because it is stored in two blocks of noncontiguous clusters. The first part of the file is stored in clusters 1107 through 1116, and the second part of the file is stored in clusters 1138 through 1155. Clusters 1156 through 1160 remain unused. From this example, you can see that if you reduce the size of files or delete files from a disk, you free clusters that Windows might use later for part of another file. If you increase the size of files or add new files to a disk, and the disk does not contain enough consecutive clusters to hold the entire file, Windows stores the files in noncontiguous clusters. Over time, the number of fragmented files increases and the performance of your computer decreases.

To reduce file fragmentation, you can use the Windows Vista Disk Defragmenter utility. Disk Defragmenter reorganizes the clusters assigned to each file so that they are located in contiguous clusters, and it also rearranges files so that they are stored one right after another. This latter operation reduces free space fragmentation by removing free space (or unused space) between files that would result in even more fragmentation later. **Free space fragmentation** occurs when the available free space is scattered around the disk rather than consolidated in adjacent clusters in one area of the disk. If all of the clusters for a file are stored in adjacent clusters, the read/write heads can quickly retrieve the contents of that file, improving the response time and performance of your computer and reducing stress on your hard disk.

Microsoft has modified Disk Defragmenter in Windows Vista so that it defragments a hard disk in a slightly different way than Disk Defragmenter found in previous versions of Windows. The Windows Vista Disk Defragmenter does not attempt to defragment a noncontiguous block in a file if the noncontiguous block is larger than 64 MB because the performance gain is minimal. Also, unlike previous versions of Disk Defragmenter, it does not graphically display the progress of analyzing and then defragmenting a disk.

In previous versions of Windows, you opened Disk Defragmenter and then analyzed and defragmented a disk. However, in Windows Vista, Disk Defragmenter is scheduled to run every Wednesday at 1 a.m. to keep your hard disk(s) optimized. If your computer is turned off at this time, Disk Defragmenter runs when you start your computer. This feature guarantees a weekly defragmentation of your hard disk. You can change this schedule, and you can also manually perform a defragmentation of your hard disk(s).

Opening Disk Defragmenter

The time it takes to defragment a hard disk depends on the size of the hard disk, the number of folders and files on the disk, the amount of storage space already in use on the hard disk, the amount of fragmentation that already exists on the volume, the available system resources (such as memory), and how often you run the defragmenting utility. The first time you optimize your hard disk with a defragmenting utility like Disk Defragmenter, it may take a long time to defragment the hard disk, but it is well worth the time and effort. If you run a defragmenting utility frequently, it takes less time to defragment the disk because most of the disk is already optimized. If disk fragmentation builds up quickly, the amount of time required to defragment the disk increases. Frequent use of the Windows Disk Defragmenter or another defragmenting utility was important in previous versions of Windows, but as just noted, the Windows Vista Disk Defragmenter automatically defragments hard disks every week, starting from your initial purchase of a computer, so your hard disks are constantly being optimized.

Aaron recommends that you show Kimberly how to adjust the schedule for Disk Defragmenter on her computer so that she can pick a date and time that works best for her.

In the following steps, you are going to open Disk Defragmenter and view the current schedule for defragmenting your computer's hard disk. You will not defragment your hard disk in these steps because it could take anywhere from a few minutes to a few hours, and you have no way of knowing how long it will take. To change the schedule for defragmenting your hard disk or to manually defragment the hard disk, you must log on under an Administrator account or provide Windows Vista the password of an Administrator account. If you are using a computer in a college computer lab, make sure that you have permission to open Disk Defragmenter. If you don't have permission to open Disk Defragmenter, read the following steps and examine the figures, but do not keystroke the steps.

To open Disk Defragmenter:

1. On the Start menu, click **Control Panel**, click **System and Maintenance** in the Control Panel window, click **Performance Information and Tools**, click **Advanced tools**, and then click **Open Disk Defragmenter**. Windows Vista switches to Secure Desktop Mode and displays a User Account Control dialog box.

Tip

You can also open a Computer window, right-click your hard disk drive icon, click Properties, click the Tools tab, and then click the Defragment Now button.

2. If you are logged on under an Administrator account, click the **Continue** button, or if you are logged on under a Standard user account, enter the **password** for an Administrator account, and then click the **OK** button. Windows Vista opens the Disk Defragmenter dialog box. See Figure 6-23. Windows Vista explains how Disk Defragmenter improves the performance of your computer and displays the current schedule for running Disk Defragmenter. On the computer used for Figure 6-23, the schedule is the default schedule built into Windows Vista. Windows Vista also reports on when Disk Defragmenter last defragmented your hard disk(s) and the next scheduled run. It also notes that scheduled defragmentation is enabled and that your disks will be defragmented at the scheduled time. You can use the Defragment now button to manually start a defragmentation of your hard disks. Your defragmentation schedule may differ if you or the tech support staff in your college's computer lab changed the default schedule built into Windows Vista.

Figure 6-23 Viewing Disk Defragmenter settings

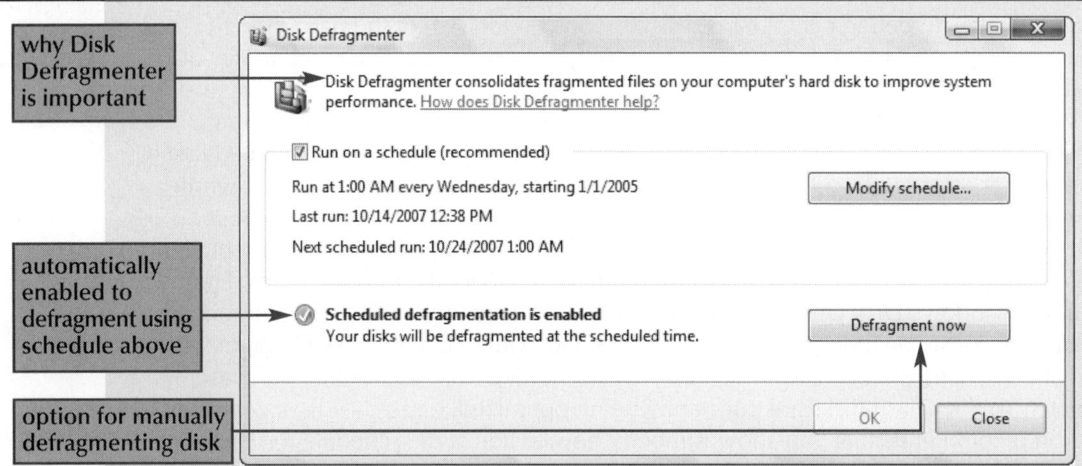

3. If the scheduled defragmentation is enabled, click the **Modify Schedule** button. In the Disk Defragmenter: Modify Schedule dialog box, you can specify a new schedule. See Figure 6-24.

Figure 6-24 Dialog box for modifying disk defragmenter's schedule

4. Click the **How often** button, and then examine the options. Notice that you can schedule Disk Defragmenter to run Daily, Weekly, or Monthly. You can also pick a specific day of the week by using the "What day" button and a specific hour during the day by using the "What time" button.

5. Click the **How often** button again to close the list, and then click the **Cancel** button to close the Disk Defragmenter: Modify Schedule dialog box without making any changes to your defragmentation schedule.
6. Click the **Close** button to close the Disk Defragmenter dialog box without making any changes to your scheduled defragmentation.
7. Close the Advanced Tools window.

If you click the Defragment now button, you can close the Disk Defragmenter dialog box and continue to work on your computer as Disk Defragmenter defragments the hard disk(s). Windows Vista will note that the defragmentation may take minutes or hours depending on the amount of fragmentation on your hard disk(s). If you click the Defragment now button and then change your mind, click the Cancel defragmentation button, and then close the disk Defragmenter dialog box.

Opening Disk Defragmenter | Reference Window

- On the Start menu, click Control Panel, click System and Maintenance in the Control Panel window, click Performance Information and Tools in the System and Maintenance window, click Advanced Tools under Tasks in the Performance Information and Tools window, and then click Open Disk Defragmenter.
- In the User Account Control dialog box, click the Continue button if you are logged on under an Administrator account, or if you are not logged on under an Administrator account, enter the password for an Administrator account, and then click the OK button.
- If you want to modify the Disk Defragmenter's schedule on your computer, make sure the scheduled defragmentation is enabled, and then click the Modify Schedule button. Use the "How often," "What day," and "What time" buttons to set a new schedule, and then click the OK button.
- If you want to perform a manual defragmentation as you work, click the Defragment now button, and then click the Close button to close the Disk Defragmenter dialog box.

Defragmenting your hard disk(s) is an important process that extends the longevity of your hard disk and improves the performance of your computer and, fortunately, in Windows Vista, it is now automated so that you do not overlook this important type of preventive maintenance.

Using the Command-Line Defrag Utility

Windows Vista also includes a command-line utility called Defrag for defragmenting a disk. Unlike the graphical user interface version, you have more control over defragmentation. Using this command-line utility, you can:

- **Perform a fragmentation analysis of a specific volume** The Defrag utility displays a short report with information about the volume size, the amount of free space, the largest contiguous free space, and the percent file fragmentation. It also advises you whether you need to defragment the volume. You can also choose which volume you want to examine. For example, you can analyze fragmentation on your hard disk or on an external hard disk drive.
- **Perform a full defragmentation** With this option, the Defrag utility attempts to consolidate all file fragments regardless of their size. As noted earlier, by default, Disk Defragmenter only consolidates file fragments smaller than 64 MB.

- **Force defragmentation of a volume when the free space is low** To effectively defragment a hard disk, Disk Defragmenter must have access to enough unused disk space for defragmenting files. If the free space is low, defragmentation is not as effective. With this option, the Defrag utility can force defragmentation of a volume with a limited amount of free space. For effective defragmentation of a disk, Microsoft has noted that 15% of the hard disk should be free for use by Disk Defragmenter, and if possible, you should keep 30% of the hard disk free for sorting file fragments.

If you perform a fragmentation analysis of a volume, you can also specify a Verbose switch (/V) so that the Defrag utility provides more information about fragmentation on a disk. The report includes the following information:

- Volume size, cluster size, used space, free space, and percent free space
- Percent file fragmentation, total movable files, average file size, total fragmented files, total excess fragments, average number of fragments per file, and total unmovable files
- Amount of free space, total contiguous free space, average free space per contiguous region, and largest free space per contiguous region
- Total number of folders, number of fragmented folders, and excess folder fragments
- Total Master File Table size, total number of MFT records, percent MFT in use, and total MFT fragments

To produce a detailed fragmentation analysis report, you enter the DEFRAG command at the command prompt and then specify two switches: -A or /A (for Analysis) and -V or /V (for Verbose). The Analysis switch instructs the Defrag utility to analyze the volume rather than defragment it. The Verbose switch instructs the Defrag utility to provide more detailed information about the analysis and defragmentation than it would otherwise provide.

To use the command-line Defrag utility, you must open a Command Prompt window in Admin Approval Mode and provide Administrator credentials.

So that you can more effectively analyze defragmentation on employee computers, Aaron offers to demonstrate how to use the Defrag utility to produce a detailed fragmentation analysis report for your computer's hard disk.

In the following steps, you are going to open the command-line Defrag utility in Admin Approval Mode and produce a fragmentation analysis report for your computer's hard disk. You therefore must log on under an Administrator account or provide Windows Vista the password of an Administrator account. If you are using a computer in a college computer lab, make sure that you have permission to open and use the command-line Defrag utility. If you don't have permission to open and use the command-line Defrag utility, read the following steps and examine the figures, but do not keystroke the steps.

To produce a fragmentation analysis report for a hard disk:

1. On the Start menu, point to **All Programs**, click **Accessories**, right-click **Command Prompt**, and then click **Run as administrator**. Windows Vista switches to Secure Desktop Mode and displays a User Account Control dialog box.
2. If you are logged on under an Administrator account, click the **Continue** button, or if you are logged on under a Standard user account, enter the **password** for an Administrator account, and then click the **OK** button. Windows Vista opens an Administrator: Command Prompt window (as evidenced by the title on the window's title bar).
3. Maximize the Administrator: Command Prompt window. Note that the Command Prompt window does not maximize in the same way that other windows maximize.

4. In the Administrator: Command Prompt window, type **DEFRAG C: -A -V** (in uppercase or lowercase) at the command-line prompt, press the **Enter** key, and wait for the fragmentation analysis report. Figure 6-25 shows a fragmentation analysis report for a 250 GB volume although Windows Vista reports the volume size as 233 GB in the fragmentation analysis report. Your fragmentation analysis results will differ. The Insight after the following explanation of the fragmentation analysis report explains why this volume size discrepancy occurs.

Tip

You can also enter the command DEFRAG C: /A /V to produce the same fragmentation analysis report.

Figure 6-25 Fragmentation analysis of a hard disk

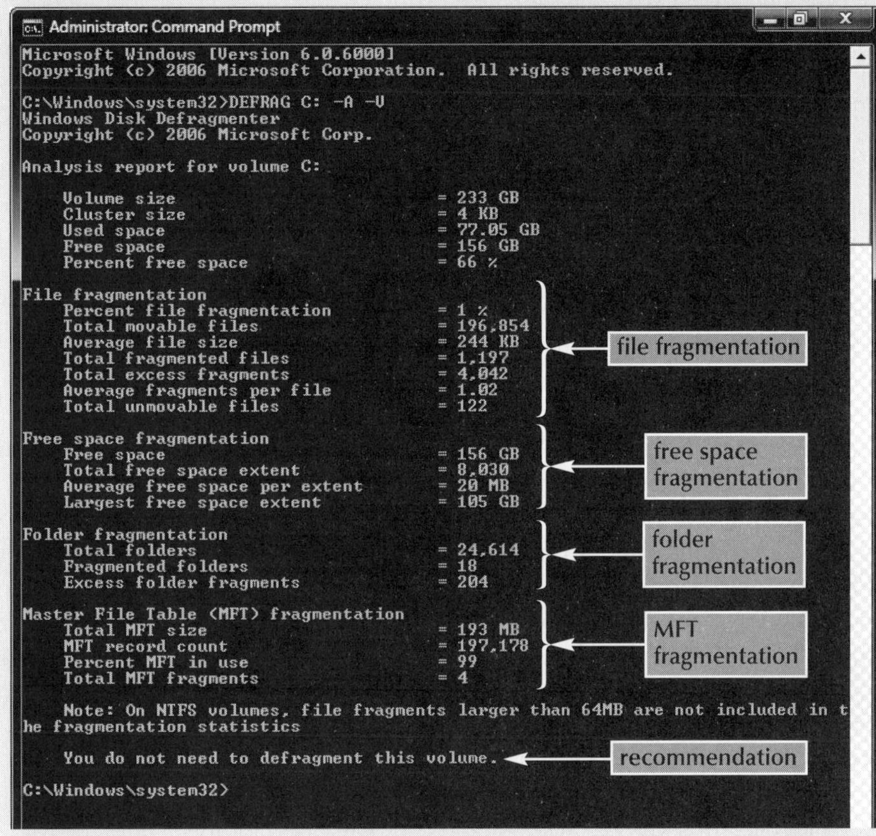

The defragmentation analysis report is divided into these sections:

- **Volume information** The first part of the report provides information on the volume size, the cluster size, the amount of used space, the free space, and the percent free space. On the 250 GB hard disk drive with a volume size of 233 GB used for this fragmentation analysis, cluster sizes are 4 KB, meaning that there are 8 sectors per cluster. (4 KB × 1,024 bytes/KB = 4096 bytes, and 4,096 bytes ÷ 512 bytes/sector = 8 sectors per cluster.) The volume size and free space is rounded off to the nearest gigabyte. The 66% free space means that this volume has more than enough available storage space for defragmenting the hard disk.

- **File fragmentation** The second part of the report provides information on file fragmentation. On the hard disk used for this figure, there is only 1% file fragmentation, a very low value. In the past Microsoft has recommended defragmenting a hard disk if fragmentation exceeded 10%. "Total movable files" identifies the number of files that Disk Defragmenter can move to defragment the disk. On the hard disk used for this figure, there are 1,197 fragmented files. While it might be ideal to have no fragmented files, the files that are fragmented represent only a very small fraction (1%) of the total number of files and are more than likely to be files that have file fragments greater than 64 MB in size. The "Total excess fragments" refers to the number of file fragments in excess of two file fragments per file and therefore indicate more highly-fragmented files. The "Average fragments per file" is another measure of file fragmentation. A value of 1.00 for the average number of fragments per file indicates that all the files (or nearly all) are not fragmented. If the value is 1.10, 10% of the files, on average, are stored as two file fragments. If the value is 1.20, 20% of the files, on average, are stored as two file fragments. This hard disk's value of 1.02 means that 2% of the files, on average, are stored as two file fragments (almost perfect defragmentation for a volume this size). The "Total unmovable files" are operating system files that cannot be moved when defragmenting a disk.
- **Free space fragmentation** The third part of the report focuses on free space fragmentation. For the hard disk used in this figure, there are 8,030 regions of free space with an average of 20 MB per region of contiguous free space. The largest region of free contiguous space is 105 GB. The more consolidated free space you have on a disk, the less fragmentation builds up.
- **Folder fragmentation** The fourth part of the report deals with folder fragmentation. Here, the Defrag utility reports on the total number of fragmented folders out of the total number of folders on the disk. In this example, 18 fragmented folders is 7 ten-thousandths of a percent of the total number of folders, a very low degree of folder fragmentation. "Excess folder fragments" refers to the number of folder fragments in excess of two fragments per folder and therefore indicates more highly-fragmented folders.
- **Master File Table fragmentation** Finally, Defrag reports on the size of the MFT and the number of records within the MFT. In this example, it's 193 MB in size and contains 197,178 records (or 197,178 files). On the computer used for this figure, the MFT contains four file fragments.

If you decide that you want to defragment your hard disk after examining a defragmentation analysis, you would enter the same command without the switches. The command for defragmenting the disk is:

DEFRAG C:

Also remember that the defragmentation could take hours.

To end your command-line session:

1. To close the Administrator: Command Prompt window, type **EXIT** and press the **Enter** key (or click the Administrator: Command Prompt window Close button).

Interpreting Reported Sizes for Hard Disks | InSight

Assume you purchase a 500 GB hard disk and then you discover that Windows Vista reports the hard disk size as approximately 466 GB. The rated size of 500 GB for the hard disk means that the hard disk has a storage capacity of 500,000,000,000 bytes. That value is calculated as follows: 500 GB × 1,000 megabytes per gigabyte × 1,000 kilobytes per megabyte × 1,000 bytes per kilobyte. However, when measuring disk storage capacities, Windows Vista uses 1,024 megabytes per gigabyte; 1,024 kilobytes per megabyte; and 1,024 bytes per kilobyte. To find the hard disk storage capacity reported by Windows Vista, you perform this calculation: 500,000,000,000 bytes ÷ 1,024 bytes per kilobyte ÷ 1,024 kilobytes per megabyte ÷ 1,024 megabytes per gigabyte = 466 GB. This approach used by manufacturers in measuring hard disk storage capacities means that a hard disk's storage capacity is actually less than the rated storage capacity.

Producing a Fragmentation Analysis Report Using the Command-Line Defrag Utility | Reference Window

- On the Start menu, point to All Programs, click Accessories, right-click Command Prompt, and then click Run as administrator.
- In the User Account Control dialog box, click the Continue button if you are logged on under an Administrator account. If you are not logged on under an Administrator account, enter the password for an Administrator account, and then click the OK button.
- In the Administrator: Command Prompt window, type DEFRAG C: -A -V or type DEFRAG C: /A /V (in uppercase or lowercase) at the command-line prompt, press the Enter key, and wait for the fragmentation analysis report.
- After examining the fragmentation analysis report, type EXIT and press the Enter key to close the Administrator: Command Prompt window.

Command-line tools can be quite powerful and can provide more options for examining, evaluating, and fine-tuning the performance of a computer. Tutorial 13 focuses on command-line tools and techniques.

Setting Disk Quotas on NTFS Volumes

Windows Vista supports the use of disk quotas for controlling and tracking the usage of storage space on an NTFS volume. **Disk quotas** are settings designed to limit the amount of hard disk storage space that is available to individual users who share the same computer so that one user's files do not take up a disproportionate amount of storage space on the hard disk or fill the hard disk and prevent other users from using and creating files. For example, in a business that runs three shifts with 10 computers and 30 employees (each of whom must use a computer), three employees working different shifts might share the same computer and therefore an Administrator would need to set disk quotas for each user on each computer.

In addition to assigning a disk quota for each user, Administrators can prevent users from further access to a disk if they exceed their disk quota, or the Administrator can opt to permit users to exceed their disk quota. In either case, the Administrator can keep track of disk space usage with a log. Not only can the Administrator set a disk quota for a user, but the Administrator can specify that a warning be issued when the user nears his or her quota limit. For example, an Administrator might set a user's disk quota to 100 GB, and then set the disk quota warning level to 95 GB. Disk quotas apply only to NTFS volumes, not to FAT volumes.

Aaron asks you to set up disk quotas on a new computer shared by Marc and Julia, two employees working two different shifts.

In the following steps, you are going to examine the use of disk quotas on a computer. You must log on under an Administrator account or provide Windows Vista the password of an Administrator account. Also, as noted, disk quotas are supported only on NTFS volumes, not on FAT volumes. If you are using a computer in a college computer lab, make sure that you have permission to work with disk quotas on an NTFS volume. If you don't have permission to work with disk quotas, or if the hard disk that you're examining is a FAT volume, read the following steps and examine the figures, but do not keystroke the steps.

To enable, set, and examine disk quotas:

1. Open a Computer window, right-click the **Local Disk (C:)** drive icon (for an NTFS volume), click **Properties** on the shortcut menu, and in the Properties dialog box for the drive, click the **Quota** tab. Windows Vista displays the Quota property sheet shown in Figure 6-26 and explains that your hard disk supports space limits for each user so that a single user cannot fill the entire volume.

Figure 6-26 Quota property sheet for a hard disk

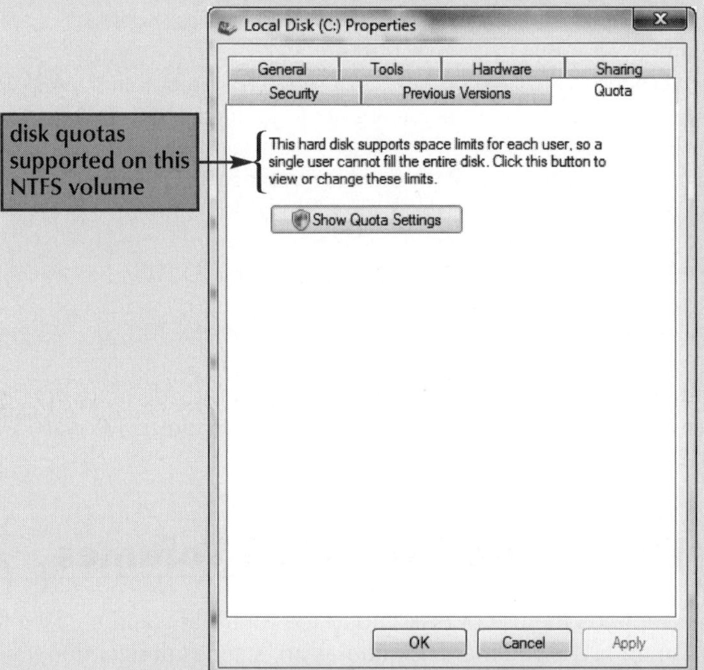

2. Click the **Show Quota Settings** button. Windows Vista switches to Secure Desktop Mode and displays a User Account Control dialog box.
3. If you are logged on under an Administrator account, click the **Continue** button, or if you are not logged on under an Administrator account, enter the **password** for an Administrator account, and then click the **OK** button. Windows Vista opens the Quota Settings for C: dialog box. See Figure 6-27. On the computer used for this figure, quota settings have not yet been enabled.

   Trouble? If disk quotas are already enabled on the computer you are using, read, but do not keystroke, the remaining steps in this section.

Figure 6-27 Quota settings for a hard disk

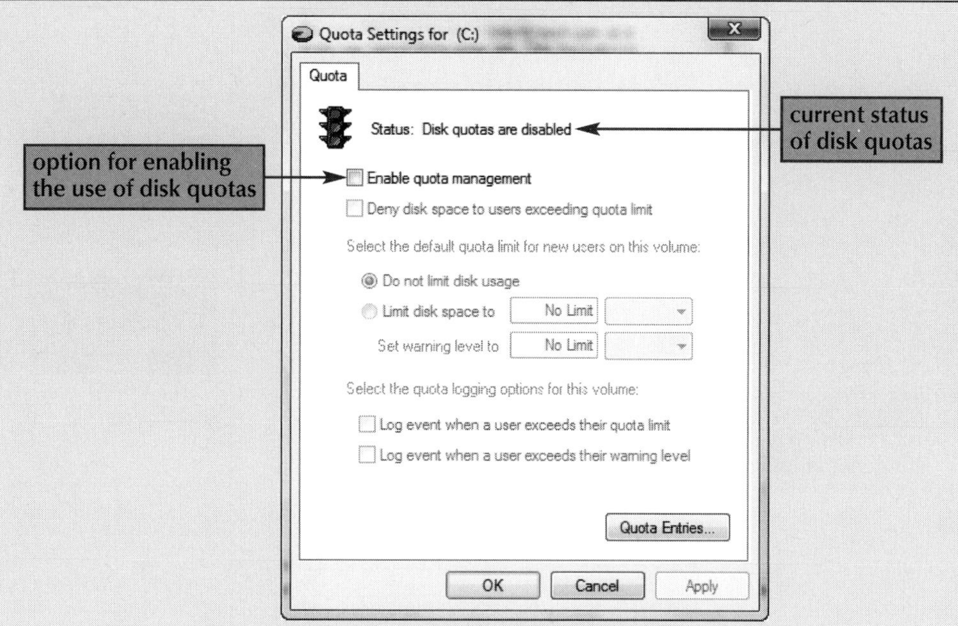

4. If you want to enable disk quotas, click the **Enable quota management** check box. All the other options on the Quota property sheet now become available.

5. Click the **Apply** button. The Disk Quota dialog box warns you that you should enable the quota system only if you intend to use disk quotas on the volume. See Figure 6-28. It also notes that it takes several minutes to update disk usage statistics before enabling the quota system.

Figure 6-28 What to expect after enabling disk quotas

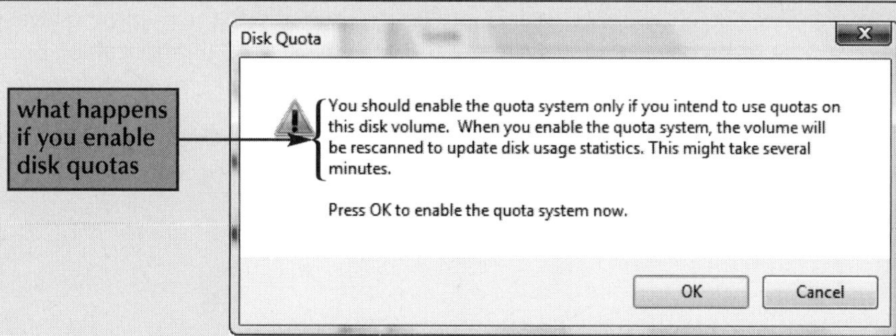

6. If you want to proceed, click the **OK** button; otherwise, click the **Cancel** button to cancel the operation, and then just read the following steps and examine the figures. Once you click the OK button, the stoplight icon changes to a yellow light while the volume is rescanned to update the disk usage statistics. After that process is complete, the stoplight icon changes to green, and the disk quota system is active. The Quota property sheet has an option for denying disk space to users who exceed their quota limit. You can choose to not limit disk usage or specify a limit on disk space and a warning level. You can also enable quota logging when a user exceeds their quota limit and their warning level. Figure 6-29 shows a quota limit of 25 GB and a warning level of 24 GB for each new user, and the quota logging options are enabled.

Figure 6-29 Quota settings for a hard disk

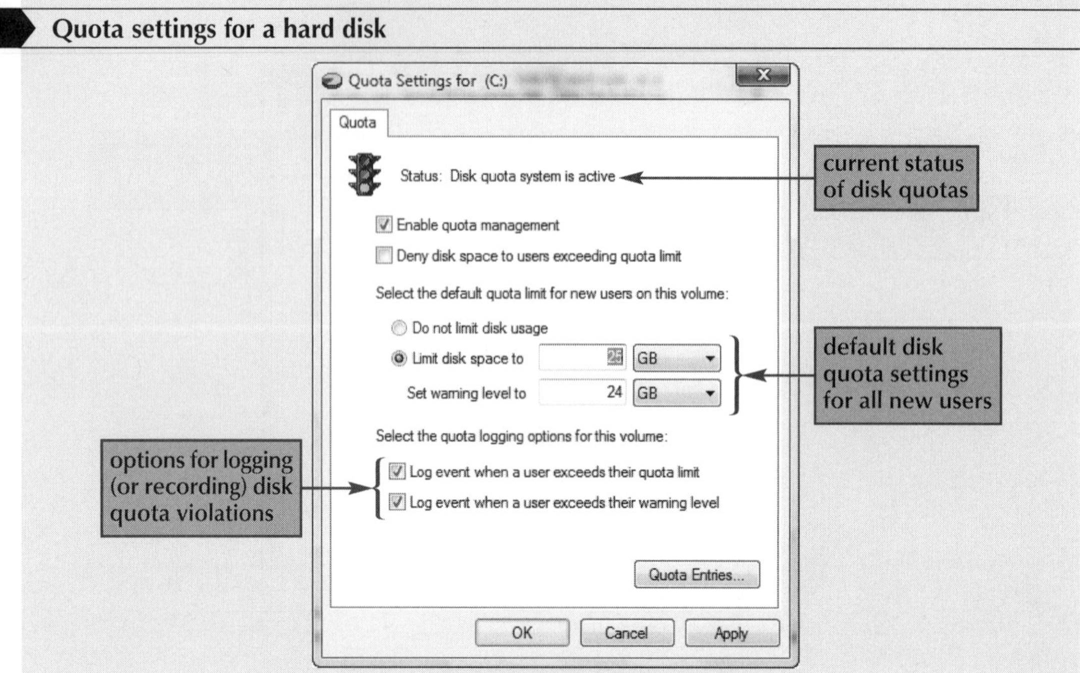

Before you apply these changes, you can specify or examine quota entries for all users and, if necessary, change a specific user's quota limit or warning level.

To examine quota entries for all users:

1. Click the **Quota Entries** button. Windows Vista displays the status for each user. (You may want to maximize this window to view the information more easily.) See Figure 6-30. Windows Vista shows the account name for each user, the amount of storage space they are currently using, their quota limit (if specified), their warning level (if specified), and the percent of their quota that they have used (if applicable). Because quotas were just enabled on the computer used for this figure, the quota limit and warning level for existing users is set as "No Limit."

Quota entries

Figure 6-30

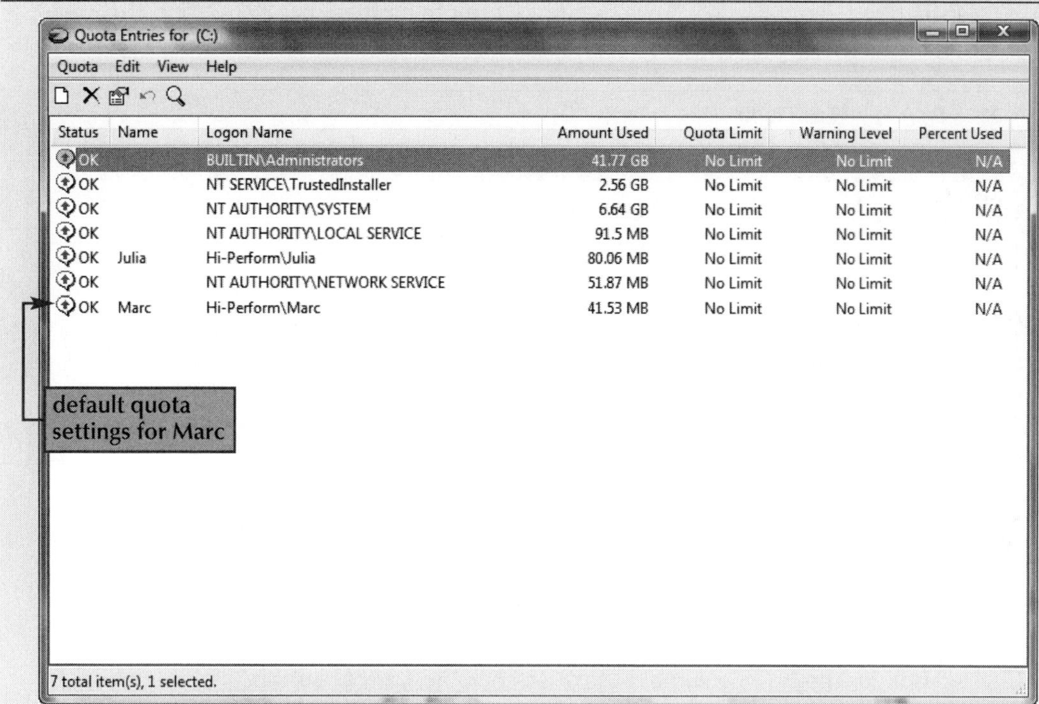

2. If you want to examine or specify a quota for a user, click the entry for that user account, click **Quota** on the menu bar, and then click **Properties**. Windows Vista displays the Quota Settings for the selected user (in this example, Marc, one of the new employees). See Figure 6-31. You can now set the limits you want for the user you selected. If the quota settings for the user are set to "No Limit," you can click the "Limit disk space to" option button, and then customize those settings for this one user.

Marc's default quota settings

Figure 6-31

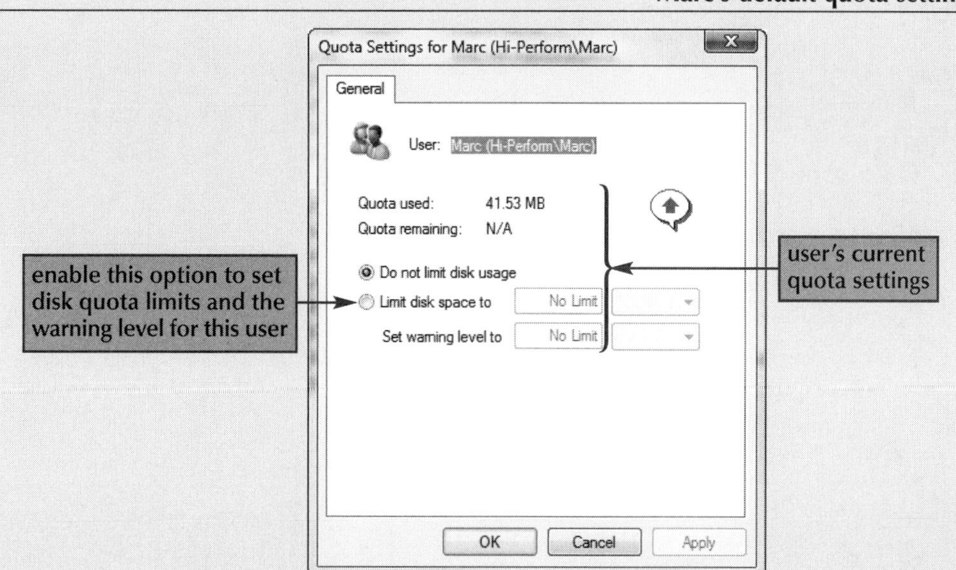

Tip

You can also view a user's quota settings by double-clicking a user's quota entry or by right-clicking a user's quota entry, and then selecting Properties.

3. If you changed a user's quota limit and warning and want to apply those settings, click the **OK** button; otherwise, click the **Cancel** button to leave the settings unchanged. Figure 6-32 shows that Marc's quota limit is now 25 GB, and the warning level is now 24 GB.

Figure 6-32 **Marc's new quota settings**

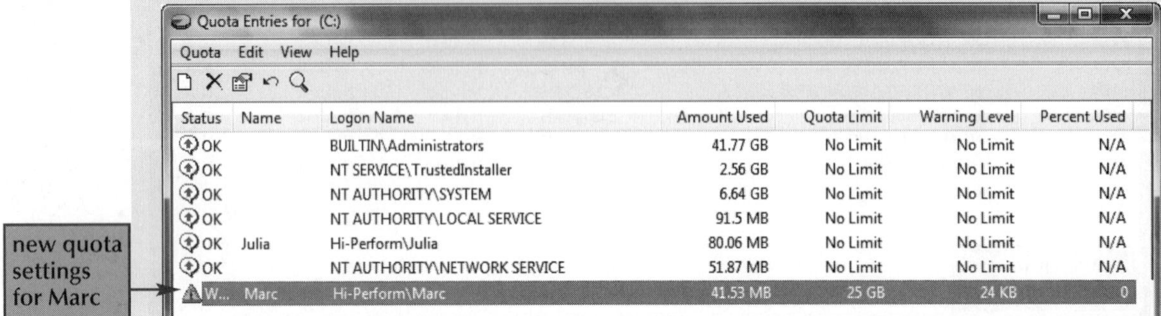

4. Close the Quota Entries window, and then click the **OK** button to close the Quota Settings dialog box for the NTFS volume, or click the **Cancel** button to close the Quota Settings dialog box without making any changes.

5. If you made changes you want to keep, click the **OK** button in the Properties dialog box for the NTFS volume; otherwise click the **Cancel** button.

6. Close the Computer window.

If you enable quotas and then later decide to dispense with disk quotas, you can disable the quota system in the Quota Settings dialog box.

Setting Disk Quotas | Reference Window

- Open the Computer window, right-click the drive icon for an NTFS volume, click Properties, and in the Properties dialog box for the drive, click the Quota tab.
- Click the Show Quota Settings button, and in the User Account Control dialog box, click the Continue button if you are logged on under an Administrator account. If you are not logged on under an Administrator account, enter the password for an Administrator account, and then click the OK button.
- If you want to enable disk quotas, click the "Enable quota management" check box in the Quota Settings dialog box, and then click the Apply button.
- In the Disk Quota dialog box, click the OK button to continue; otherwise, click the Cancel button to cancel the operation.
- In the next Quota Settings dialog box, choose the disk quota options you want to apply to new users.
- Click the Quota Entries button, and in the Quota Entries window, click the entry for the user you want to examine or change, click Quota on the menu bar, and then click Properties. (You also can double-click a user's quota entry or right-click a user's quota entry, and then click Properties.)
- In the Quota Settings dialog box for the user you chose, make whatever changes you want to make for that user, and then click the OK button, or click the Cancel button to close the Quota Settings dialog box.
- Close the Quota Entries window, and then click the OK button to close the Quota Settings dialog box for the NTFS volume, or click the Cancel button to close the Quota Settings dialog box without making any changes.
- If you made changes you want to keep, click the OK button in the Properties dialog box for the NTFS volume; otherwise, click the Cancel button.
- Close the Computer window.

After you set disk quotas for this new computer, you have a mechanism for tracking disk usage by the two new employees and ensuring that these users have a reasonable and equal share of the resources of the computer on which they work.

Creating a Scheduled Task

You can use the Windows Vista Task Scheduler to automate tasks on a computer. For example, you can schedule the Disk Cleanup Wizard to run at a specific time each week to guarantee that you do not forget to clean your disk of unneeded files. Like many other programs, the Disk Cleanup Wizard does not include a built-in scheduling feature, so you can use Task Scheduler to set up a schedule for the Disk Cleanup Wizard.

Aaron asks you to set up a scheduled task that runs the Disk Cleanup Wizard weekly for Marc to remind him of the need to remove unnecessary files from his computer. Because you need to know the location and name of the program file for the Disk Cleanup Wizard to create the scheduled task, Aaron shows you how you can use the All Programs menu to locate this information.

To determine the location and program filename for the Disk Cleanup Wizard:

1. On the All Programs menu, click **Accessories**, click **System Tools**, right-click **Disk Cleanup**, and then click **Properties**. Windows Vista opens the Disk Cleanup Properties dialog box. See Figure 6-33. The Target location identifies the System32 folder as the location of the Disk Cleanup program. The Target box shows the full path to the Disk Cleanup program and the name of the program file: %SystemRoot%\System32\cleanmgr.exe. The program filename is "cleanmgr.exe" and it is located in the System32 folder, which is located under %SystemRoot%. As you learned in Tutorial 4, SystemRoot is an environment variable that contains the setting for the path to the folder where Windows Vista is installed. On most computers that setting is C:\Windows. Also, as you may recall, the percent symbols identify SystemRoot as a replaceable parameter. In other words, Windows Vista replaces %SystemRoot% with the setting for the actual path to the Windows folder to determine the path for the Disk Cleanup program on any given computer.

Figure 6-33 Viewing the path to the Disk Cleanup program

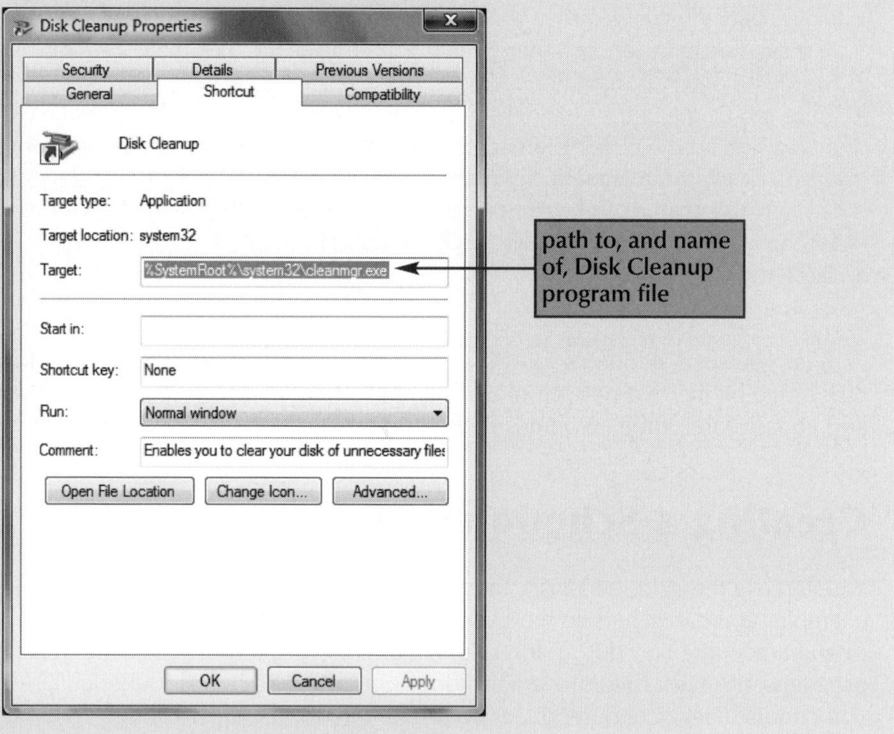

2. Close the Disk Cleanup Properties dialog box.

Aaron notes that you can use this power user technique to locate the names and paths for other programs installed on your computer, including Windows Vista utilities, for which you might want to create scheduled tasks.

Now that you know the location and name of the program for the Disk Cleanup Wizard, you are ready to create your scheduled task. So that you can easily locate and, if necessary, modify the scheduled task later, Aaron recommends that you set up a folder for the scheduled task after you open Task Scheduler.

In the following steps, you are going to create a scheduled task. If you are working in a computer lab, ask your instructor or technical support staff for permission to create a scheduled task. The lab staff might have already set up a regular maintenance schedule for each computer (including a scheduled task for Disk Cleanup). If that is the case, read the steps and examine the figures so that you are familiar with how to create and remove scheduled tasks, but do not keystroke the following steps.

To open Task Scheduler and set up a folder for a scheduled task:

1. On the Start menu, point to **Administrative Tools**, click **Task Scheduler**, and if prompted for Administrator credentials for an Administrator account in a User Account Control dialog box, click the Continue button if you are logged on under an Administrator account, and then click the OK button.

2. Maximize the Task Scheduler window. The Task Scheduler window is organized into three areas: a Scope Pane on the left, an Actions Pane on the right, and a Results Pane in the center. See Figure 6-34. When you first start Task Scheduler, it displays a Task Scheduler Summary in the Results Pane. Under Overview of Task Scheduler, it informs you that you can use Task Scheduler to create and manage common tasks that your computer will carry out automatically at the times you specify. It also informs you that tasks are stored in the Task Scheduler Library (in the Scope Pane on the left) and that you can select a task from the Task Scheduler Library to view information about the task or to make changes to the task. Under Task Status, Task Scheduler lists tasks that have started in the last 24 hours and summarizes how many are running, how many succeeded, how many stopped, and how many failed. Then, you see a list of tasks by name. Under Active Tasks in the Results Pane, it notes that active tasks are ones that are currently enabled and have not expired. If you scroll further down the Results Pane, you will find a preview pane that shows more details of the tasks listed under Task Status. Your list of tasks may differ.

Tip

You can also open the All Programs menu, click Accessories, click System Tools, and then click Task Scheduler.

Figure 6-34 Task Scheduler window

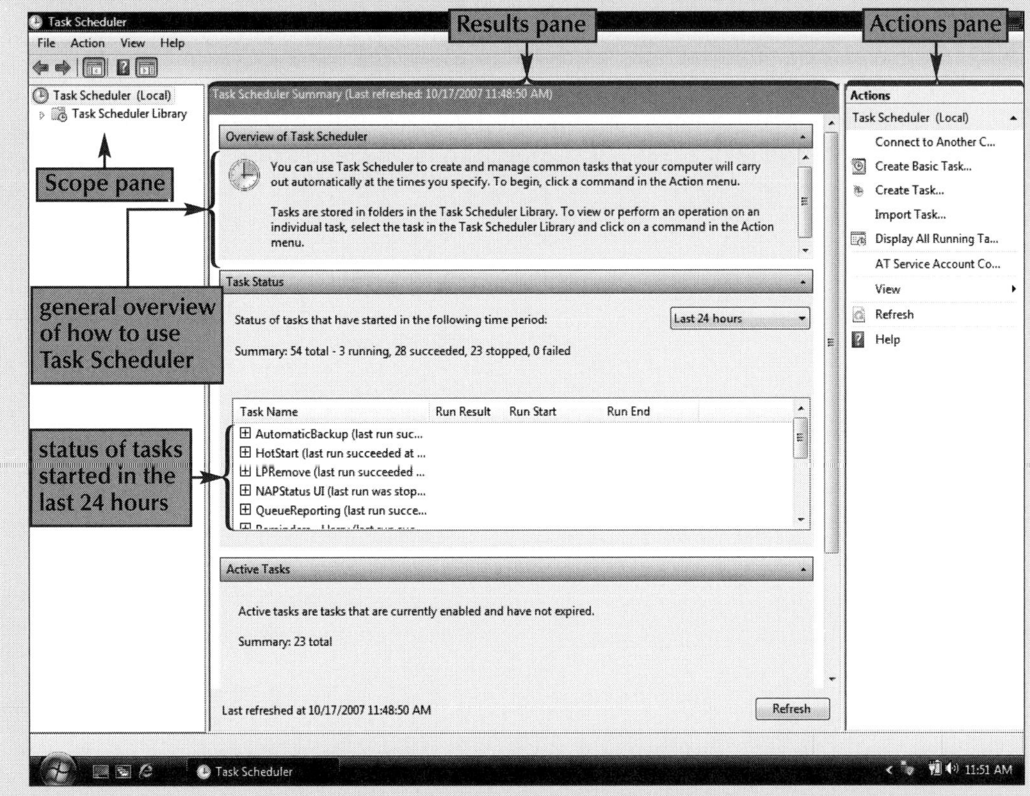

3. Double-click **Task Scheduler Library** in the Scope Pane on the left and verify whether your computer already has a folder named Disk Cleanup under the Task Scheduler Library folder. Note the Microsoft folder under the Task Scheduler Library folder. This folder contains scheduled tasks for various components of the Windows Vista operating system. For example, the Defrag folder contains a predefined scheduled task for the built-in automatic defragmentation of your hard disk.
4. Click **New Folder** in the Actions Pane on the right side of the window, and in the "Enter name of the new folder" dialog box, type **Disk Cleanup** in the Name text box, and then click the **OK** button. Task Scheduler displays a Disk Cleanup folder.

   Trouble? If the Task Scheduler Library already contains a Disk Cleanup folder, you can create a second Disk Cleanup task by specifying another name for the new folder (such as Clean Disk or Disk Clean).
5. Click the **folder** that you just created for the Disk Cleanup task.

Now, you're ready to set up the task. You can set a task to start and run daily, weekly, or monthly (common options), or you can specify that a task run only once, when the computer starts, when you log on, or when a specific event is logged. An **event** is a significant incident or occurrence in the system or in an application that is recorded in an Event Log, which you can view using Windows Vista's Event Viewer. After you select the trigger for a task, you specify the name of the program or script that should run. In addition, you can include optional arguments for the program or script and specify where the task starts. A **trigger** is a set of criteria that specify when a task begins. A trigger can be a time-based trigger or an event-based trigger. A **script** is a file that contains a list of executable commands processed without user intervention. You are going to examine these options as you set up a task.

Tip

To bypass the Create Basic Task Wizard and manually define a task, click Create Task in the Actions Pane.

To specify the details for a task:

1. Click **Create Basic Task** in the Actions Pane. Task Scheduler opens the Create Basic Task Wizard dialog box, as shown in Figure 6-35, and notes that you can use this wizard to quickly schedule a common task. It also notes that if you want to create a task that has multiple actions or triggers, you use the Create Task command instead. In this first dialog box, you can type a name for the task and provide any additional optional information about the task in the Description box. On the left is a list of operations that you will perform to define this task.

Figure 6-35 Specifying a name for a basic task

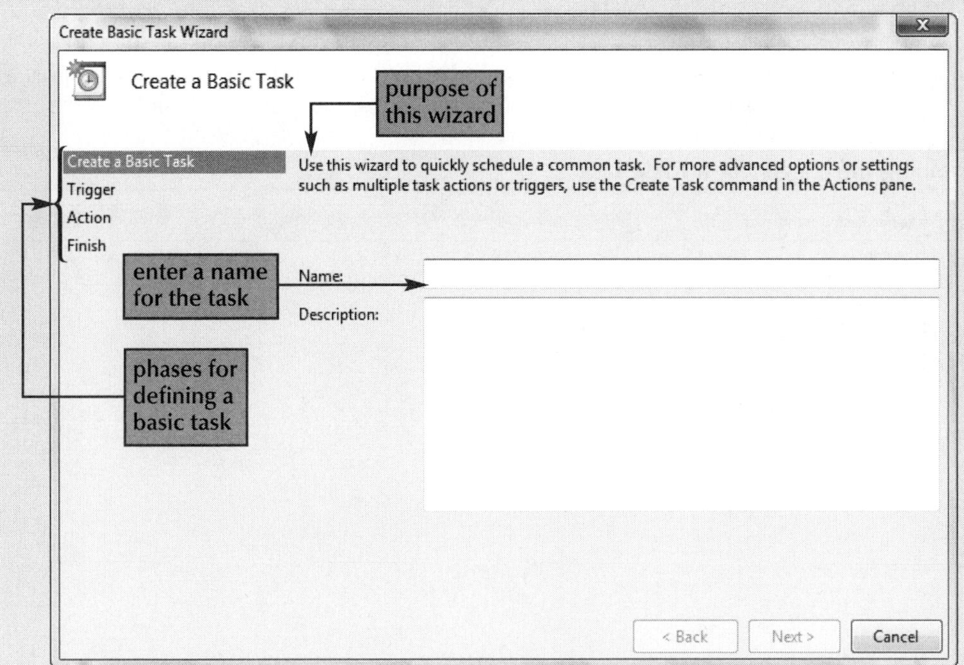

2. Type **Disk Cleanup** in the Name box, type **Run the Disk Cleanup Wizard once a week** in the Description box, and then click the **Next** button. In the next step, you specify the Task Trigger. In other words, you specify the criteria under which you want the task to start. See Figure 6-36.

Figure 6-36 Choosing a trigger for a basic task

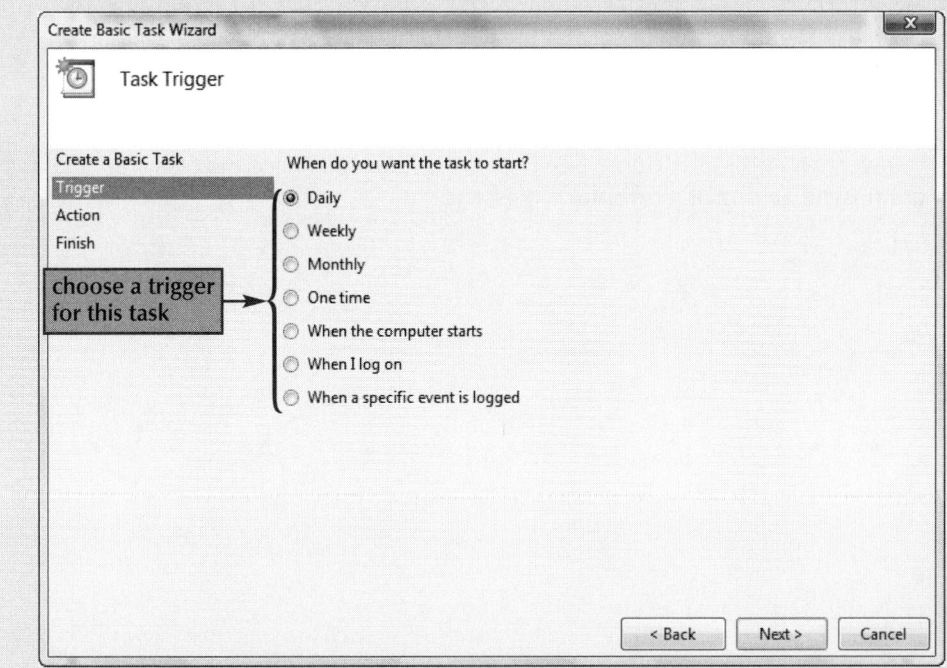

3. Click the **Weekly** option button, and then click the **Next** button. In the next step, you specify the date and time for starting the task the first time, and you can specify how frequently the task repeats (once a week, for example) and the day of the week for repeating the task. See Figure 6-37. In the Start box is the current date. You can use the Start list button to the right of the current date to display a navigable calendar so that you can select the date you want the task to start.

Figure 6-37 **Refining the trigger for a basic task**

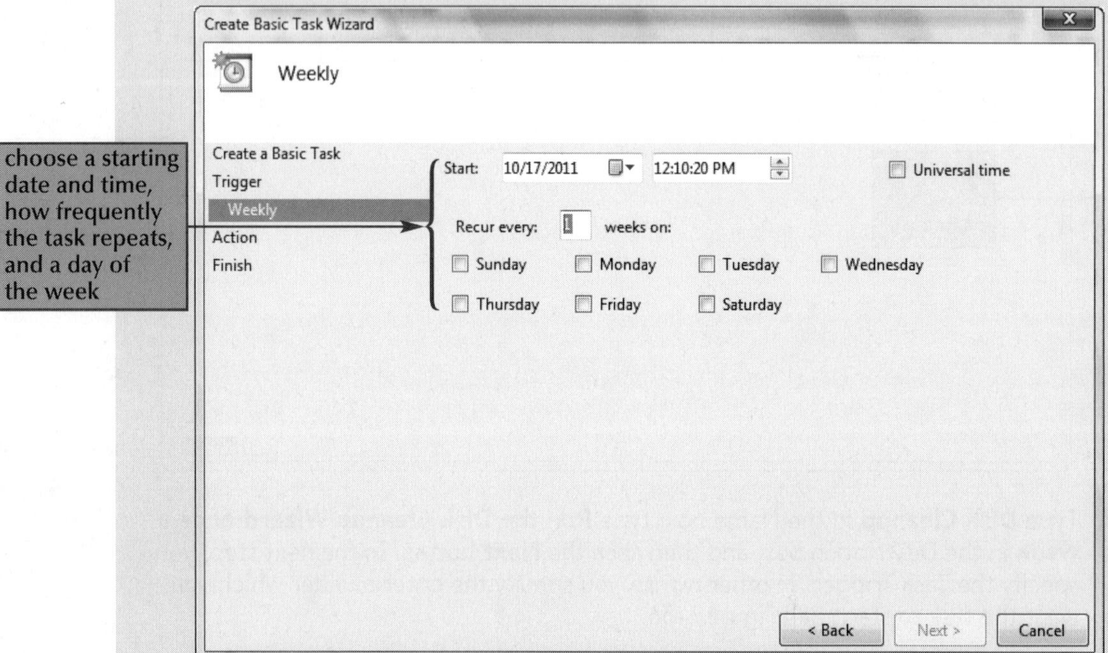

4. Make sure the task is set to start on the current date, click the **minutes** in the time, use the **up** button to set the time so that it is 5 to 10 minutes (or more) ahead of the current time (so that you can complete the remaining steps before the task is scheduled to start), click the **check box for the current day of the week**, and then click the **Next** button. In the next step, you specify what action you want the task to perform. See Figure 6-38. You can have the task start a program, send an e-mail, or display a message.

Figure 6-38

Choosing an action

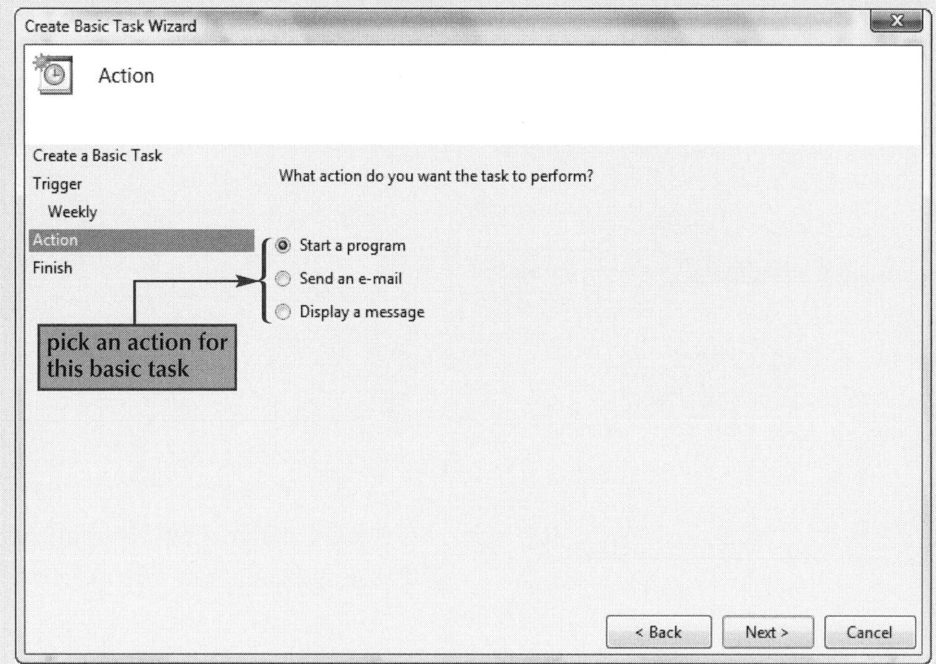

5. Make sure the "Start a program" option button is already selected, and then click the **Next** button. In the next step, you specify the name of a program or script, and you can also add optional arguments for the program or script and specify where the task starts. See Figure 6-39. Options on this page depend on what you selected on the previous Action page. You now have to locate the program for starting the Disk Cleanup Wizard. The program name is "cleanmgr.exe" and it is stored in the Windows System32 folder. The System32 folder and its subfolders contain many of the programs and utilities provided with Windows Vista, as well as important components of the operating system, such as dynamic link libraries, files with configuration settings, Control Panel components, device drivers, event logs, system files, and the Windows Vista Registry files (to name a few).

Figure 6-39 **Providing details on the program to start**

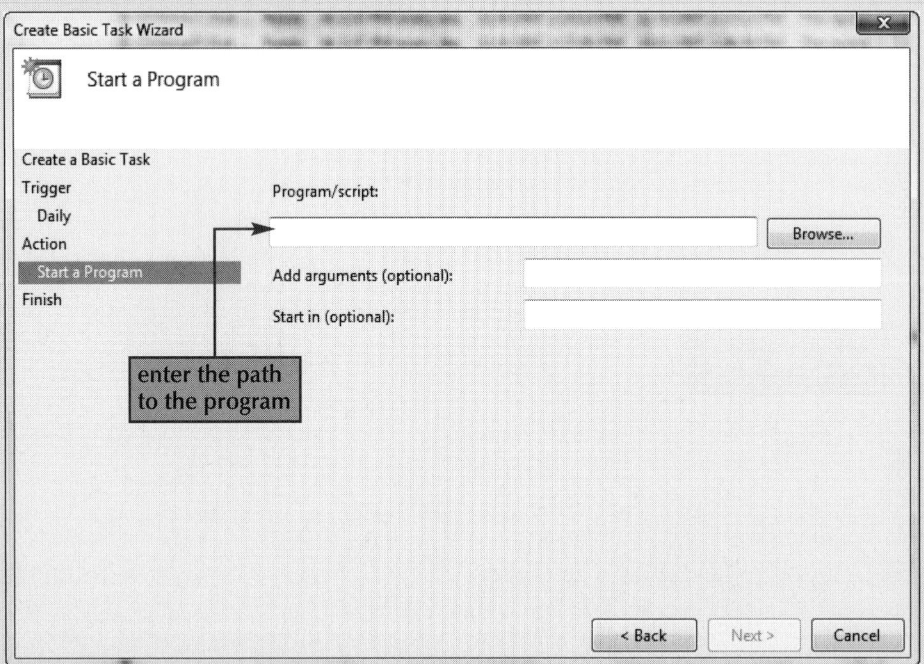

6. Click the **Browse** button. Windows Vista displays an Open dialog box and then displays the contents of the System32 folder (under the Windows folder). See Figure 6-40.

Figure 6-40 **Browsing for a program for a scheduled task**

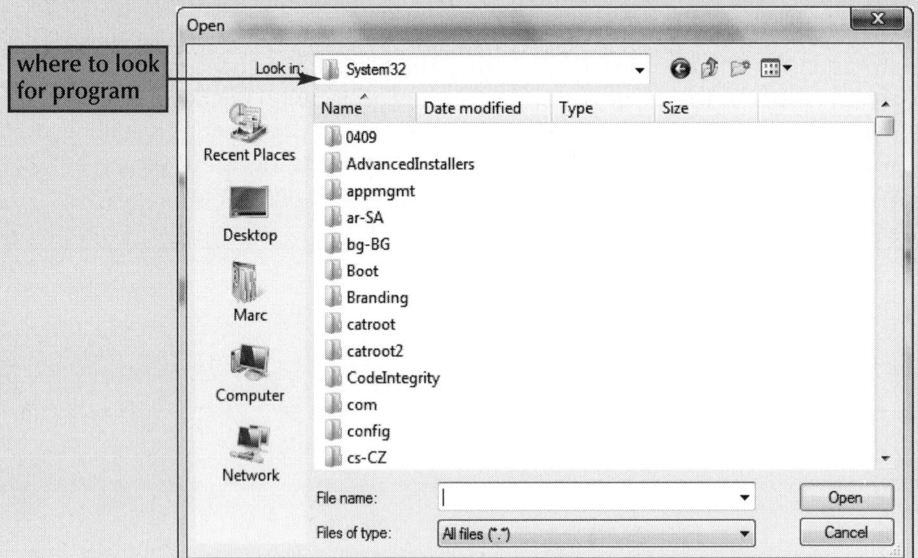

7. In the File name box, type **cle** (for cleanmgr.exe), and after Windows Vista displays the program name in the Filename list box, click **cleanmgr.exe**, and then click the **Open** button. Windows Vista displays the full path to the program for running the Disk Cleanup Wizard. See Figure 6-41. In the Add arguments (optional) text box, you can specify additional parameters, such as a switch, to change the way that a command works. For example, if you want a scheduled task to check an external hard disk drive in drive F, you would enter the following Drive switch (/D) in the Add arguments (optional) text box and specify the drive you want to check: /D F:

Figure 6-41 Program settings for a scheduled task

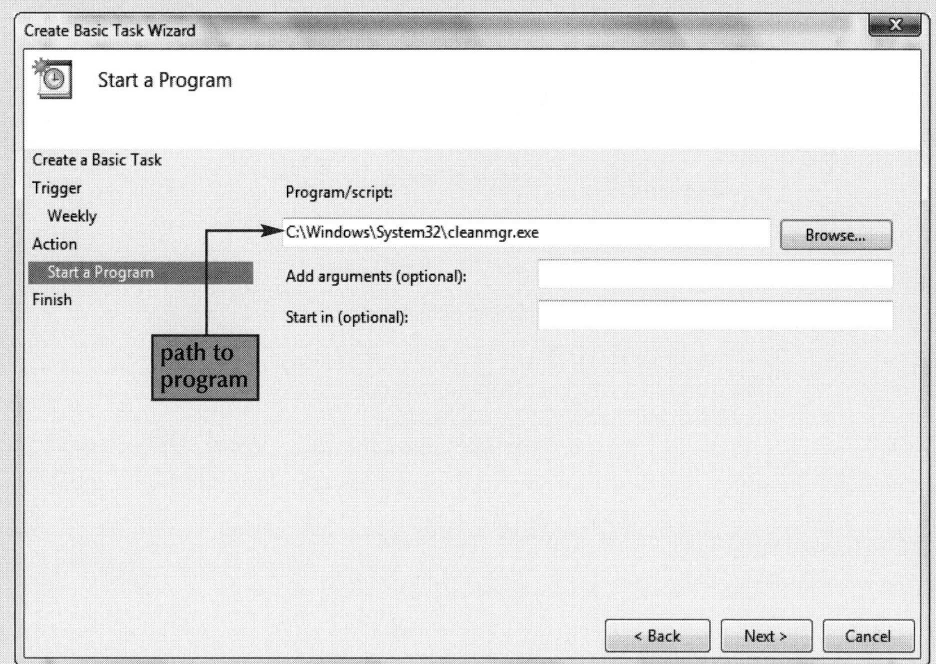

8. Click the **Next** button. Windows Vista displays a summary of the options you specified for the task. See Figure 6-42. You can review these options, and if you want to make any last-minute changes, you can use the Back button to return to an earlier step, make the change, and then use the Next button to return to this summary.

Figure 6-42 Summary of settings for a scheduled task

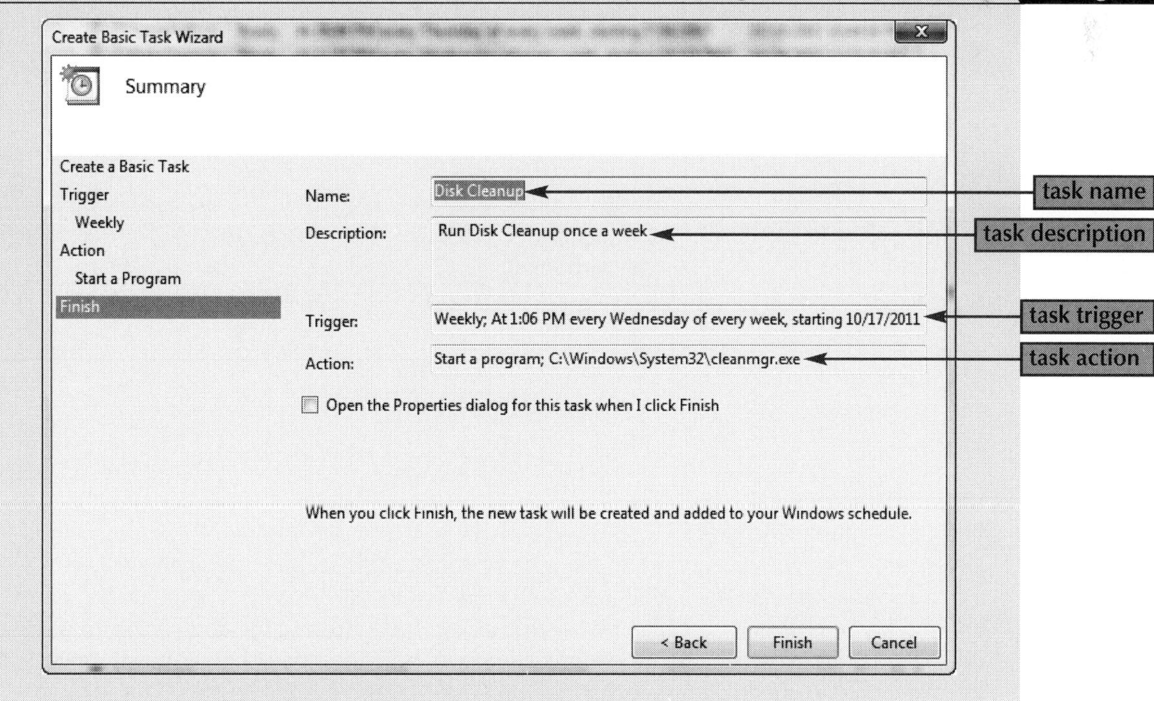

9. Click the **Finish** button, minimize the Task Scheduler window, and then wait for the task to start. At the time you specified, Windows Vista opens the Disk Cleanup Options dialog box. See Figure 6-43.

Figure 6-43 **Program started using a scheduled task**

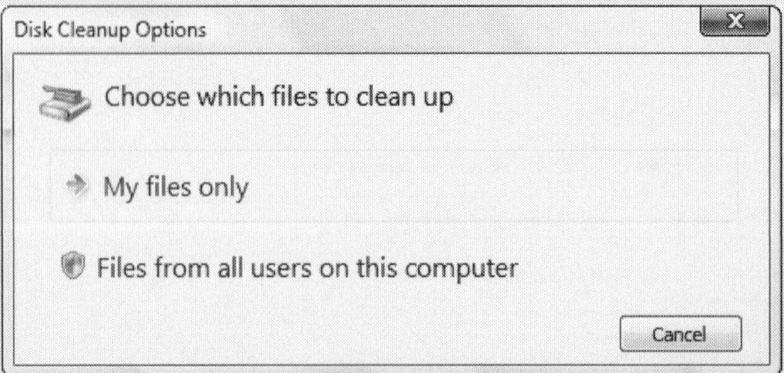

10. Now that you've tested the scheduled task, close the Disk Cleanup Options dialog box.

InSight | Working with Coordinated Universal Time (UTC)

The Universal time check box in the Create Basic Task Wizard (Figure 6-37) specifies that the task start based on Coordinated Universal Time (UTC) or what was once referred to as Greenwich Mean Time (GMT) rather than using local time (i.e., the current time zone). Coordinated Universal Time (UTC), also referred to as Universal Coordinated Time, is based on a 24-hour clock adjusted for time zone differences and Daylight Savings Time, as necessary. If you work in a field such as meteorology and aviation, you probably need to specify times and dates using UTC. The following examples illustrates how you would convert times to a 24-hour clock and adjust for the time zone differences:

Location	Time	Time Zone	24-Hour Clock*	Time Zone Difference	UTC**
Los Angeles	10:30 AM	PST (Pacific Standard Time)	1030	+8 Hours	1830
Los Angeles	3:45 PM	PST (Pacific Standard Time)	1545	+8 Hours	2345
New York City	10:30 AM	EST (Eastern Standard Time)	1030	+5 Hours	1530
New York City	3:45 PM	EST (Eastern Standard Time)	1545	+5 Hours	2045

*To convert a PM time to a 24-hour clock, add 12 to the hour.

**If UTC exceeds 2359, the date changes to the next day.

You can schedule tasks for other important types of operations, such as opening the Backup and Restore Center so that you can back up your entire computer, opening Windows Defender so that you can perform a full scan of your computer, and opening Windows Update so that you can manually check for Windows updates for your computer. You can also modify predefined scheduled tasks, such as the one for defragmenting your hard disk drive. If you discover that you are periodically performing the same operation, you might want to create a scheduled task to start the program you use for this operation at some specific interval of time, such as once a month.

Creating a Scheduled Task

| Reference Window

- From the Start menu, point to Administrative Tools and click Task Scheduler.
- Double-click the Task Scheduler Library folder in the Scope Pane on the left.
- Click New Folder in the Actions Pane on the right, and in the "Enter name of the new folder" dialog box, type a folder name for the new task in the Name text box, and then click the OK button.
- Under the Task Scheduler Library folder, click the folder where you want to store the new task.
- In the Actions pane on the right, click Create Basic Task.
- In the Create Basic Task Wizard dialog box, type a name for the task in the Name box, type a brief description about the task in the Description box (optional), and then click the Next button.
- In the next step, specify when you want the task to start by clicking the proper option button, and then click the Next button.
- In the next step, specify the trigger for starting the task, and then click the Next button.
- In the next step, specify what action you want the task to perform (such as start a program, send an e-mail, or display a message), and then click the Next button.
- In the next step, specify the details for the action you selected in the previous step.
- In the next step, review the task summary, and if necessary, use the Back button to back up to a previous step to make a change, use the Next button to advance to this last step, and finally, click the Finish button.
- Close the Task Scheduler window.

Now, you want to view the settings for your scheduled task.

To view the settings for your scheduled task:

1. Restore the Task Scheduler window, and in the Actions Pane on the right, click **Refresh,** click **Disk Cleanup** in the list of tasks at the top of the Results Pane, and then press the **Ctrl** and **+** keys (that is, hold down the Ctrl key and then press the plus key) to adjust column widths for a best fit. Task Scheduler shows the status of the task (Ready), its triggers, the next run time, the last run time, the last run result, the author, and the date and time the task was created. (To view all these options, you must scroll to the right.) See Figure 6-44. Under the task list are the property sheets with all the information for this scheduled task. On the General property sheet, it identifies the task name, the author (i.e., Marc), the description, and any security options associated with the task. This scheduled task is set to run only when the user is logged on the computer.

Figure 6-44 Viewing properties of a scheduled task

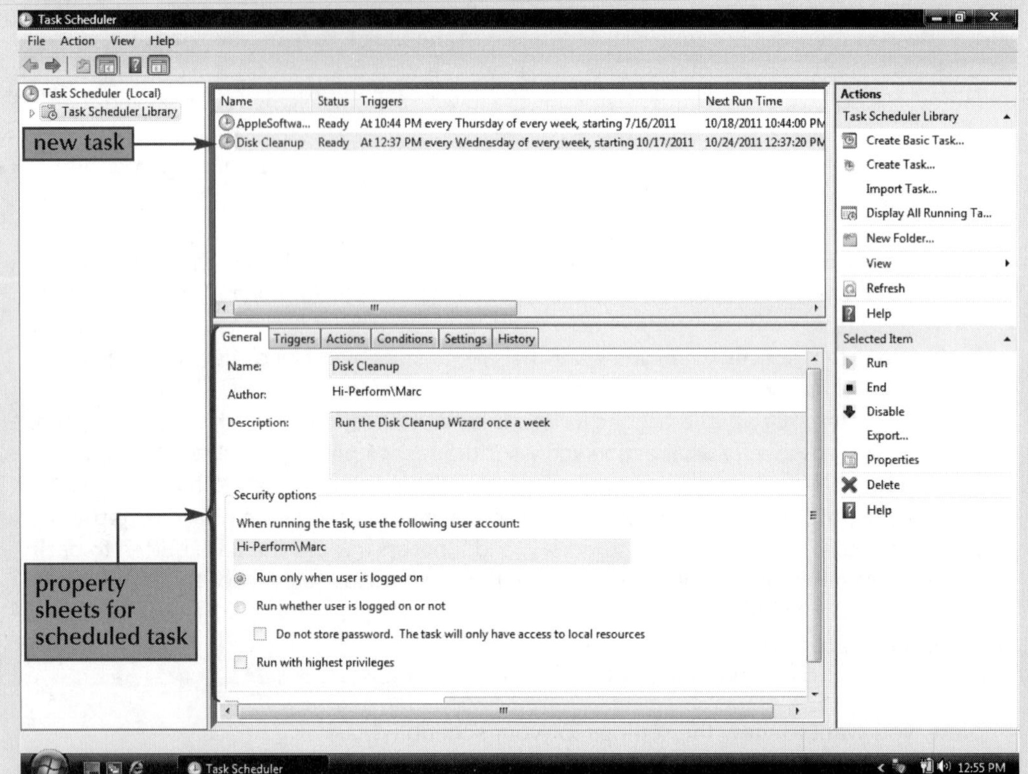

2. Click the **Triggers** tab. Task Scheduler shows how frequently the task is triggered, details on the task (including the time and day of the week that the task is designated to start, the starting task date, and whether the task is enabled (and active).
3. Click the **Actions** tab. Task Scheduler identifies the type of action performed by this task (i.e., start a program) and the path to the program opened by this task.
4. Click the **Conditions** tab. Task Scheduler identifies any other conditions associated with starting the task, such as how the task operates when the computer is idle and how the power state affects the task. This scheduled task starts only if the computer is on AC power, and it stops if the computer switches to battery power.
5. Click the **Settings** tab. Task Scheduler lists any additional settings that affect the behavior of the task. This scheduled task can be run on demand; the task will stop if it runs longer than 3 days, and if the task does not end when requested, Windows Vista will force it to stop.
6. Click the **History** tab. Task Scheduler identifies a list of events associated with this task, such as when the task was initially registered (defined) and when the task completed. See Figure 6-45.

Figure 6-45 History property sheet for scheduled task

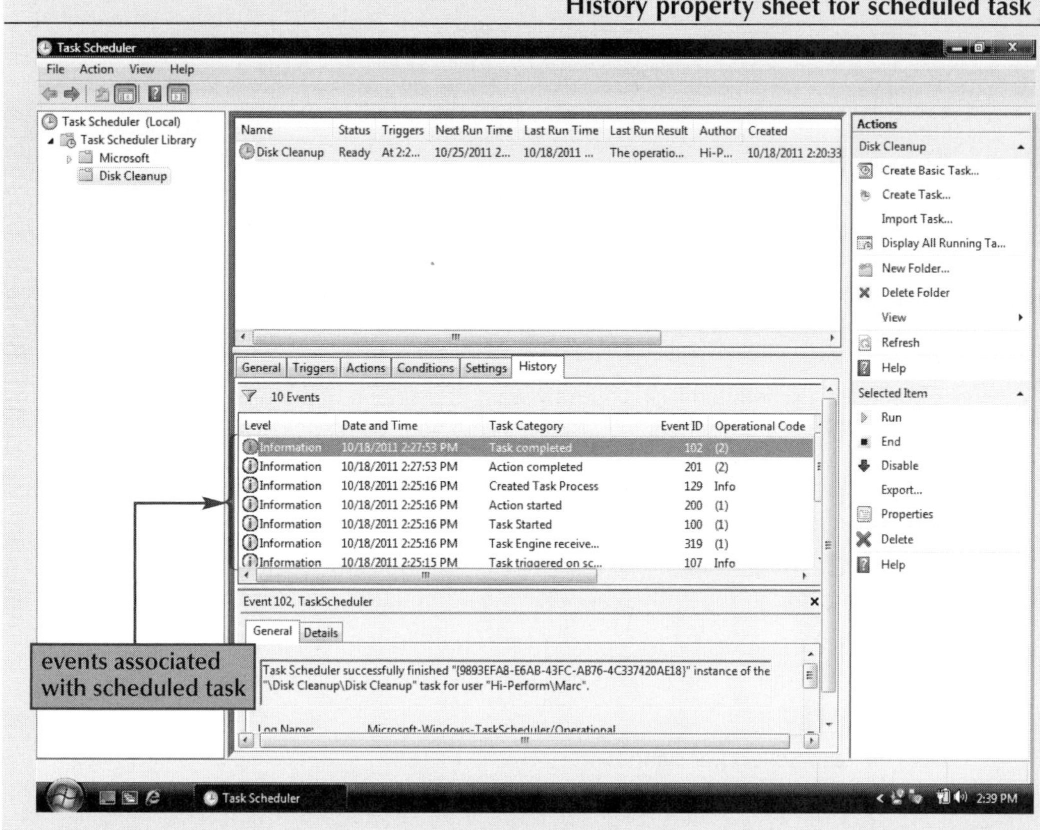

If you select a task and then click Properties in the Actions pane, Task Scheduler will display the same information in a Disk Cleanup Properties dialog box, as shown in Figure 6-46. You can examine and make changes to the task from this task's Properties dialog box. Options that were not available when you created the task with the Task Scheduler Wizard are available here, so you can fine-tune settings for a task.

Figure 6-46 Viewing properties of a scheduled task

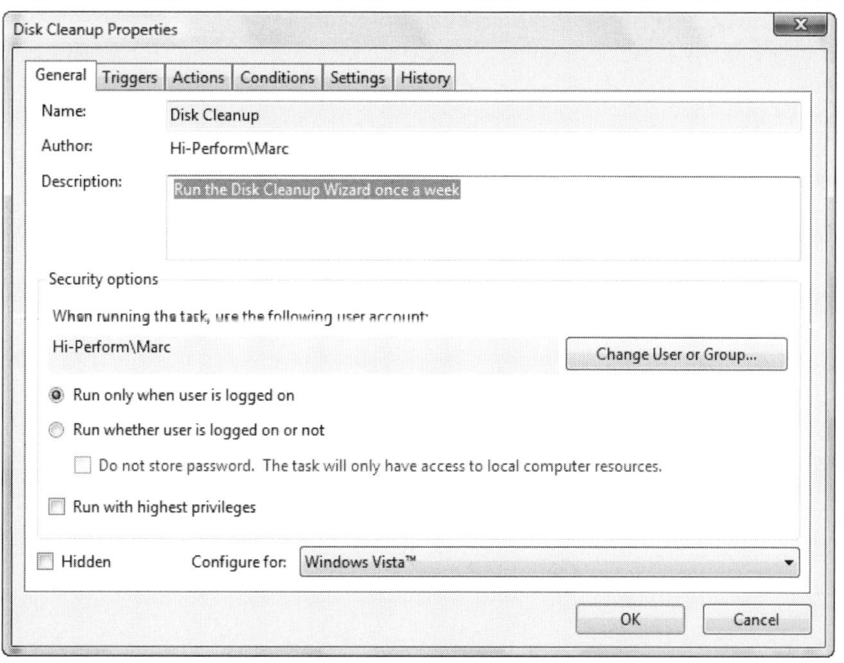

Reference Window | Checking Settings for a Scheduled Task

- On the Start menu, point to Administrative Tools, and click Task Scheduler.
- Click the Expand indicator to the left of Task Scheduler Library in the Scope Pane on the left side of the window.
- Click the folder name where you stored the task, and if necessary, select the task in the Results Pane.
- Click the General, Triggers, Actions, Conditions, Settings, and History tabs to view detailed information about the task.
- To view properties of the task and modify task settings, click Properties in the Actions pane, and then review details about the task.
- Close the Task Scheduler window.

After you create a scheduled task, you may want to delete it. In the next set of steps, you will delete the Disk Cleanup scheduled task to restore your computer to its original state.

To delete your scheduled task:

1. Click **Disk Cleanup** in the list of tasks in the Results Pane, click **Delete** in the Actions Pane, and in the Task Scheduler dialog box, click the **Yes** button.
2. Click the **Disk Cleanup** folder under Task Scheduler Library in the Scope Pane, click **Delete Folder** in the Actions Pane, and in the Task Scheduler dialog box, click the **Yes** button.
3. Close the Task Scheduler window.

You might have more than one task in the same folder, so you should always select the folder, and then select and delete the task first. If the folder has only one task (and you've deleted that task), you can then delete the folder if you do not want to keep it.

Reference Window | Deleting a Scheduled Task

- On the Start menu, point to Administrative Tools, and click Task Scheduler.
- In the Task Scheduler window, click the Expand indicator to the left of Task Scheduler Library in the Scope Pane on the left side of the window.
- In the list of Ready tasks, locate and click the name of the folder that contains the task you want to delete.
- Click the task name in the list of tasks in the Results Pane, click Delete in the Actions Pane, and in the Task Scheduler dialog box, click the Yes button.
- If there is only one task in the folder, and if you want to delete the folder as well, click the folder name in the Scope Pane that contained the scheduled task, click Delete Folder in the Actions Pane, and in the Task Scheduler dialog box, click the Yes button.
- Close the Task Scheduler window.

You can use Task Scheduler Wizard to schedule common types of tasks that you perform on your computer every day. Scheduled tasks not only streamline the use of your computer, but they also free up your time so that you don't have to remember what tasks you need to perform and when you need to perform them.

Restoring Your Computer's Settings

If you are working in a computer lab, or if you want to restore your desktop computer to the settings that existed prior to working on this tutorial, complete the following steps.

To restore your computer:

1. To restore double-click activation, click the **Computer** icon on the desktop, click the **Organize** button on the command bar, click **Folder and Search Options**, and on the General property sheet in the Folder Options dialog box, click the **Double-click to open an item (single-click to select)** option button.
2. To hide extensions for known file types, click the **View** tab in the Folder Options dialog box, click the **Hide extensions for known file types** check box if it does not contain a check mark, click the **OK** button to close the Folder Options dialog box and apply these changes, and then close the Computer window.
3. If you want to remove the Computer icon from the desktop, open the Start menu, right-click **Computer**, and then click **Show on Desktop**.

Session 6.2 Quick Check | Review

1. If a file is stored in noncontiguous clusters, the file is a(n) ________________ .
2. What two types of fragmentation can arise on a hard disk?
3. What can you use to produce a defragmentation analysis of a drive?
4. To limit the amount of storage space used by a user on a hard disk, you enforce ________________ .
5. If you need to perform the same operation at regular intervals on your computer, what can you do to automate that operation?

Review

Tutorial Summary

In this tutorial, you used the Disk Cleanup Wizard to identify and remove unneeded files on a computer. You examined the features and importance of the Error-Checking Tool and command-line Check Disk utility. You used the Error-Checking Tool to check an NTFS volume for errors. You examined the problems posed by lost clusters and cross-linked files on a FAT volume, and you then used the command-line Check Disk utility to check a FAT volume for errors. You examined how file fragmentation and free space fragmentation arise on a volume, and you examined the current settings for the Windows Vista Disk Defragmenter. You used the command-line Defrag utility to produce a defragmentation analysis of a hard disk drive. You learned how to set disk quotas on an NTFS volume for multiple users. Finally, you used Task Scheduler to create and run the Disk Cleanup Wizard.

Key Terms

ActiveX control
add-on
Admin Approval Mode
Browser Helper Object (BHO)
cache
chain
contiguous
cookie
cross-linked file
Diagnostic Mode
disk quota
event
feed
file fragment
file record segment (FRS)
Fix switch (/F)
fragmented file
free space fragmentation
index
Internet cache
Java applet
lost chain
lost cluster
noncontiguous
NTFS directory
orphaned file
patch
PDF (Portable Document Format)
pointer
Read-Only Mode
Repair switch (/R)
RSS feed
script
security descriptor
switch
trigger
USN (Update Sequence Number)
Usn Journal

Practice | Review Assignments

Practice the skills you learned in the tutorial.

There are no Data Files needed for the Review Assignments.

Aaron just hired Michael Everett to assist him with his duties. After showing Mike his desk and his computer system, he asks you to show Mike how to perform a thorough check of his computer and customize it for his new job.

Try to use a computer that is different from the one that you used for the tutorial so that you can compare your results with those from the tutorial. Also, to perform some of these operations, you must log on as Administrator or under a user account with Administrators privileges.

As you complete each step in the Review Assignments, record your answers to questions so that you can submit them to your instructor. Use a word processing application, such as Word or WordPad, to prepare your answers to these questions. Also, if you change any settings on the computer you are using, note the original settings so that you can restore them later. Complete the following:

1. Open a Computer window, and if necessary, switch to Tiles view. If Windows Vista does not organize drives by type, right-click the folder window background, point to Group, and then click Type. How many hard disk drives does your computer have, and what are their names? Are these drives internal or external hard disk drives? Point to and select each hard disk drive icon, and then examine the information in the Details Pane. What file system does each hard disk drive use? What is the total storage capacity of each hard disk drive?
2. If you have one drive; select it; if you have two or more drives, select a drive that you did not use in the tutorial, start the Disk Cleanup Wizard, and choose the option to remove only your files. What hard disk drive did you check? How much storage space can the Disk Cleanup Wizard free on your hard disk drive? What types of files does it propose to remove? After you finish using the Disk Cleanup Wizard, close it, and then close the Properties dialog box for the drive. Also close the Computer window.
3. Suppose you opened a Word document stored in a file named Sales Projection Memo.docx and then noticed another file named ~$les Projection Memo.docx in the folder window with the Sales Projection Memo.docx file. What type of file is ~$les Projection Memo.docx? If you close Sales Projection Memo.docx, what would happen to ~$les Projection Memo.docx? Would the Disk Cleanup Wizard locate and propose to remove this file if it remained on disk? Explain.
4. Run the Error-Checking Tool on your flash drive in Diagnostic or Read-Only mode by turning off the options for automatically fixing file system errors and scanning for and attempting recovery of bad sectors. Did the Error-Checking Tool find any problems? If so, what were the problems? How many bytes of storage space are allocated in each cluster (or allocation unit)? How many sectors are in each cluster (or allocation unit) on the flash drive? After you finish using the Error-Checking Tool, close all open windows.

5. Open and then maximize the Command Prompt window. Use the command-line Check Disk utility without any switches to check the same flash drive for errors in read-only, or diagnostic, mode (without making any changes to the flash drive). Also, make sure you specify the flash drive name as it may be different from the default drive used by Windows Vista in the Command Prompt window. What file system is used on your flash drive? Does Check Disk report any errors or problems? If so, what are they? What is the total disk space on the flash drive? Close the Command Prompt window.

To complete Steps 6-8, you need to log on under an Administrator account or know the user name and password for an Administrator account. Also, in Step 9, you must provide Administrator credentials if you are logged on under an Administrator account.

6. Open the Disk Defragmenter. Is Disk Defragmenter automatically enabled on your computer, and if so, what is its schedule? Close the Disk Defragmenter dialog box.
7. Open and then maximize an Administrator: Command Prompt window. Enter the command for producing a full fragmentation analysis report for your flash drive (using Verbose mode). What command did you enter to perform this operation? List your answers to the following questions:
   - What is the volume size?
   - What is the cluster size?
   - What is the percent free space?
   - What is the percent file fragmentation?
   - What is the total number of fragmented files?
   - What is the largest free space extent?
   - What is the total number of fragmented folders?
   - Does Disk Defragmenter recommend that you defragment this volume?
   - To defragment the flash drive, what command would you enter?

   Close the Administrator: Command Prompt window.
8. Before examining disk quotas on an NTFS volume, ask your instructor and technical support staff for permission to check disk quotas on an NTFS volume if you are working in a computer lab. Are disk quotas enabled on the computer you are using? If so, what is the default disk quota for new users, and what is your disk quota? If disk quotas are not enabled on your computer, is there any condition under which you might use disk quotas? Explain. Close all open windows without making any changes to the quota settings.
9. Before using Task Scheduler, obtain permission from your instructor or technical support staff to use the Task Scheduler to schedule a task if you are working in a computer lab. Open Task Scheduler, select the Task Scheduler Library in the Scope Pane, and then create a new folder named Clean Disk. (If there is another folder by this name, use another folder name.) Expand the Task Scheduler Library folder and select the folder you just created. Use the Create Basic Task Wizard to schedule the following task:
   - Create a basic task named **Disk Cleanup** with a daily trigger.
   - Set the start time so that it is five or 10 minutes later than the current time.
   - The Disk Cleanup task should start the cleanmgr.exe program. What is the path for this program?

After the task starts, click the Disk Cleanup Options taskbar button, and then close the Disk Cleanup Options dialog box. Maximize the Task Scheduler window, select the newly scheduled Disk Cleanup task in the Results Pane, and then answer the following questions:

- Who is identified as the Author on the General property sheet?
- What user account does this task use when it runs?
- Under Security Options, what condition must be met for this task to run?
- Select the Conditions property sheet. What condition determines whether this task runs when the computer is idle?
- Under what power conditions will the task start or stop?

Delete the Disk Cleanup task in the Results Pane, delete the folder that you created for this task, and then close the Task Scheduler window.

10. Which of the techniques covered in this tutorial have you used in the last three months to optimize the storage of files on your hard disk and optimize the performance of your computer? Are there any techniques or tasks that you want to implement in the future? Explain.
11. Submit the results of the preceding steps to your instructor, either in printed or electronic form, as requested.

Apply | Case Problem 1

Use the skills you learned in this tutorial to analyze disk fragmentation.

There are no Data Files needed for this Case Problem.

McCuen Refinancing Specialists Jarod McCuen assists homeowners in refinancing the mortgages on their homes so that they can switch from an adjustable rate mortgage to a fixed rate mortgage. Since Jarod must respond quickly to meet tight deadlines and provide the best possible service for his clients, he asks you to check the performance of his computer by analyzing fragmentation on his hard disk.

To complete this step, you need to log on under an Administrator account or know the user name and password for an Administrator account. If you are working in a computer lab, make sure you have permission to use the command-line Defrag utility to analyze a computer's hard disk. You will also have to allow time for a defragmentation analysis of your computer's hard disk drive.

As you complete each step in this case, record your answers to questions so that you can submit them to your instructor. Use a word processing application, such as Word or WordPad, to prepare your answers to these questions. Also, if you change any settings on the computer you are using, note the original settings so that you can restore them later. Complete the following:

1. View the General property sheet for your hard disk drive. What is the total storage capacity of this drive? How much storage space on the drive is already used? How much is available? Close the Local Disk (C:) Properties dialog box and the Computer window.
2. Open an Administrator: Command Prompt from the Accessories menu, and then maximize the window. Note your starting time. Enter the following command (on one line): **DEFRAG C: -A -V** When the fragmentation analysis is complete, note the ending time.

3. Using the fragmentation analysis report, list your results for the following items in the Analysis report:
   - Cluster size
   - Percent free space
   - Percent file fragmentation
   - Total fragmented files
   - Total excess (file) fragments
   - Average fragments per file
   - Average free space per extent
   - Largest free space extent
   - Fragmented folders
   - Excess folder fragments
   - Total MFT size
   - MFT record count
   - Percent MFT in use
   - Total MFT fragments
4. How long did it take for the fragmentation analysis? Based on this information, how frequently might you perform a fragmentation analysis?
5. Using the information in the Analysis report, what would you conclude about file fragmentation on your computer? In your conclusion, note which information in the Analysis report led you to your conclusion.
6. Using the information in the Analysis report, what would you conclude about folder fragmentation on your computer? In your conclusion, note which information in the Analysis report led you to your conclusion.
7. Using the information in the Analysis report, what would you conclude about MFT fragmentation on your computer? In your conclusion, note which information in the Analysis report led you to your conclusion.
8. Using the information in the Analysis report, what would you conclude about free space fragmentation on your computer? In your conclusion, note which information in the Analysis report led you to your conclusion.
9. Do you need to defragment this volume?
10. Close the Administrator: Command Prompt window.
11. Submit your document to your instructor, either in printed or electronic form, as requested.

Apply | Case Problem 2

Use the skills you learned in the tutorial to analyze and repair errors on a hard disk.

There are no Data Files needed for this Case Problem.

Dubuisson International Foods, Inc. Jacquelyn Dubuisson is owner and manager of Dubuisson International Foods, Inc. Like many small businesses experiencing rapid growth, she and her staff depend on their computers to track and fulfill orders as well as manage all financial transactions. Recently, she's experienced some problems accessing files on her computer, so she asks you to check the hard disk on her computer to make sure it is functioning properly.

To complete this step, you need to log on under an Administrator account or know the user name and password for an Administrator account. If you are working in a computer lab, make sure you have permission to use the Check Disk utility to perform a diagnostic or read-only check of the hard disk drive.

As you complete each step in this case, record your answers to questions so that you can submit them to your instructor. Use a word processing application, such as Word or WordPad, to prepare your answers to these questions. Also, if you change any settings on the computer you are using, note the original settings so that you can restore them later. Complete the following:

1. View the General property sheet for Local Disk (C:). What is the total storage capacity of this drive? How much storage space on the drive is already used? How much is available?
2. Note your starting time. Select the Tools property sheet for your hard disk, choose the option for running the Error-Checking Tool, and then turn off the option for automatically fixing file system errors so that you can perform a diagnostic, or read-only, check. Once the Error-Checking Tool has checked the hard disk, note the ending time.
3. Choose the option to view details of the Check Disk operation. Did it find any problems? If so, list the problems that Check Disk found.
4. From the detailed check disk results, answer the following questions:
   - How many file records did it process?
   - How many bad file records did it process?
   - How many index entries did it process?
   - How many bytes for the Usn Journal did it process?
   - What is the size of each allocation unit (or cluster) in bytes and in sectors?

   Close the Checking Disk dialog box, then close the Properties dialog box for Local Disk (C:) and the Computer window.
5. How long did it take for the disk check? Based on this information, how frequently might you check this disk?
6. **EXPLORE** Open, and then maximize an Administrator: Command Prompt window. Note your starting time. Enter the CHKDSK command followed by a space, and then the drive name of the NTFS volume. What command did you enter? When the Check Disk is complete, note the ending time.
7. How do you know that Check Disk performed a diagnostic, or read-only, check of your hard disk drive?
8. How long did it take for the disk check?
9. Do the Check Disk results match what you found by using the Error-Checking Tool?
10. Close the Administrator: Command Prompt window.
11. Submit your document to your instructor, either in printed or electronic form, as requested.

Challenge | Case Problem 3

Extend the skills you learned in this tutorial to schedule a task for a pharmaceutical company.

There are no Data Files needed for this Case Problem.

Vasquez Pharmaceuticals Vasquez Pharmaceuticals is a major distributor of low-cost pharmaceuticals and medical supplies for hospitals, clinics, and healthcare services throughout Latin America. Danielle Diaz, a healthcare services manager, wants to optimize the availability of disk storage space on her computer by removing unneeded files daily from not only her internal hard disk drive, but also her external hard disk drive. She decides to create scheduled tasks that automatically start the Disk Cleanup Wizard each Friday afternoon and check a specific hard disk drive.

As you complete each step in this case, record your answers to questions so that you can submit them to your instructor. Use a word processing application, such as Word or WordPad, to prepare your answers to these questions. Also, if you change any settings on the computer you are using, note the original settings so that you can restore them later. Complete the following:

1. Open Task Scheduler, and in the Task Scheduler Library, create a new folder named Clean Drive for these scheduled tasks, and then open the Clean Drive folder. *Note*: If the computer you are using already has a Clean Drive folder with one or more scheduled tasks that you do not want to change, use a different name, such as Drive C Disk Cleanup, for the new scheduled task you create.
2. EXPLORE In the Actions Pane, choose the Create Task option, and on the General property sheet, enter the following name and description:
   Name: **Drive C Disk Cleanup**
   Description: **Check drive C for unneeded files**
3. EXPLORE Select the Triggers property sheet and use the New button to specify the following conditions:
   Begin the task: On a schedule
   Settings: Daily, starting 10 minutes from the current time on the current date (*Hint*: If you think you need more time to set up the scheduled task, increase the number of minutes.)
   Close the New Trigger dialog box and save the settings you've specified.
4. EXPLORE Select the Actions property sheet and use the New button to specify the following action:
   Action: Start a program
   Program/script: Browse for and select the program cleanmgr.exe in the Windows System 32 folder
   In the Add arguments (optional) text box, enter: **/D C:** (*Hint* Make sure you leave a space between /D and C:)
   Save the New Action you specified.
5. EXPLORE Select the Settings property sheet and specify the following settings:
   Enable: Run task as soon as possible after a scheduled start is missed
   Enable: If the task fails, restart every 1 minute
   Turn off: Stop the task if it runs longer than 1 hour
   Save the settings you specified.
6. Wait for the scheduled task to begin, and if necessary, open the Disk Cleanup Options dialog box from the Disk Cleanup Options taskbar button. Then, choose the option for checking your files only.
7. What types of files does the Disk Cleanup propose to remove from your computer, and how much storage space will you gain overall and for each category?

8. If you decide to remove all the files identified by the Disk Cleanup Wizard, how much total disk space would you free up?
9. Remove the files that the Disk Cleanup Wizard automatically marks for removal.

EXPLORE

10. If you have an external hard disk drive and want to create a second scheduled task for the Disk Cleanup Wizard, what optional argument would you specify for the Action? Assume the external hard disk drive is assigned the drive name D: *Note*: If you have an external hard disk drive, you can create a second scheduled task in the Disk Cleanup folder, and then test it. You can also change the trigger for the scheduled task that checks drive C so that it starts just before the scheduled task for your external hard disk drive. After the first task opens, complete this task so that the next one can start.
11. Delete the scheduled task(s) that you just created in the Clean Drive folder, delete the Clean Drive folder, and then close Task Scheduler.
12. Submit your document to your instructor, either in printed or electronic form, as requested.

Challenge | Case Problem 4

Extend your skills to create shortcuts for optimizing a client's hard disk.

There are no Data Files needed for this Case Problem.

Troy Hansen Computer Consulting As a self-employed computer consultant, Troy Hansen helps his clients customize and streamline their computer systems. His next client asks Troy to show him how he can optimize the performance of his computer and protect the integrity of his hard disk drive. Troy asks you to create shortcuts for performing a Disk Cleanup operation, a diagnostic check of the hard disk for file system errors, and a fragmentation analysis report of this new client's hard disk. Complete the following:

EXPLORE

1. Right-click the desktop, point to New, and then click Shortcut. In the Create Shortcut dialog box, type the path for the Disk Cleanup Wizard and specify that it check drive C, as follows:

   c:\windows\System32\cleanmgr.exe /d c:

   Note: This path includes a switch for specifying the drive to check.

   In the next step, enter a name for your shortcut (such as Drive C Disk Cleanup), and then choose the option to finish the process of creating a shortcut. Test your new desktop shortcut and explain what happens. List the files the Disk Cleanup Wizard proposes to delete and the total amount of storage space you will gain. Remove any files you no longer need.

EXPLORE

2. Use the Create Shortcut Wizard again to create a shortcut to the command-line Check Disk utility. However, this time you have to specify the path to the program for opening a command-line window and keeping the window open as well as the path to the Check Disk program and the drive you want to check. Enter the following command-line path and name your shortcut Drive C Check:

   c:\windows\System32\cmd.exe /k c:\windows\System32\chkdsk.exe c:

   Note: The program cmd.exe opens a command-line window, and the /k switch keeps the window open.

EXPLORE

3. Open the Properties dialog box for this new shortcut and use the Advanced button to open the Advanced Properties dialog box. Enable the option for running this program as an Administrator, and then save the changes you have made and close the dialog box.

4. Test your Drive C Check shortcut and explain what happens.

EXPLORE

5. Right-click your Drive C Check shortcut, choose the option to copy the shortcut, right-click the desktop, and choose the option to paste the copy on the desktop. Then, change the name of the new desktop shortcut to Drive C Fragmentation Analysis. Display the Properties dialog box for this shortcut and modify the target to use the Defrag program instead of the Check Disk program, as follows: **c:\windows\System32\cmd.exe /k c:\windows\System32\defrag.exe c: -a –v** *Hint:* Change "chkdsk.exe" to "defrag.exe" and add the -a and -v switches after the path for the Defrag program.
6. Test your Drive C Fragmentation Analysis shortcut and explain what happens. Close the command-line window.
7. Describe the icons used by the three shortcuts.
8. If you no longer need the three desktop shortcuts you created, select and delete them.
9. Submit your document to your instructor, either in printed or electronic form, as requested.

Review | Quick Check Answers

Session 6.1

1. True
2. Error-Checking Tool and the command-line Check Disk utility
3. index
4. security descriptor
5. lost cluster
6. switch

Session 6.2

1. fragmented file
2. file fragmentation and free space fragmentation
3. command-line Defrag utility
4. disk quotas
5. create a scheduled task

Ending Data Files

There are no ending Data Files needed for this tutorial.

Tutorial 7

Objectives

Session 7.1
- Protect your computer's security and privacy
- Use Windows Defender to scan for malicious software
- Use Software Explorer to view program information
- Explore user accounts and User Account Control
- Use Windows Firewall

Session 7.2
- Use Windows Update to check for updates
- Check security settings with Windows Vista Security Center
- Check Windows Internet Explorer security and privacy settings
- Examine Internet Explorer's Security Status Bar

Enhancing Your Computer's Security

Protecting a Computer and Its Data

Case | Joyner Security Consulting Services, Inc.

Joyner Security Consulting Services specializes in computer security and privacy services for global companies, small businesses, and nonprofit organizations. Arielle Joyner, the founder and president, relies on a small staff of dedicated professionals and skilled contractors to handle the security needs of different types of businesses. To enhance your major in computer security with real-world experience, you have enrolled in a college work experience program that recently placed you as a college intern with Joyner Security Consulting Services, Inc. Arielle Joyner asks you to work directly with her to evaluate the computer security and privacy settings on the computer systems for a new client.

In this tutorial you examine important security and privacy issues and features available in Windows Vista and Windows Internet Explorer for protecting the security and privacy of your computer system.

Starting Data Files

There are no starting Data Files needed for this tutorial.

Session 7.1

Setting Up Your Computer

Set up your computer so that the operations that you perform match the steps in the tutorial.

To set up your computer:

1. If the Windows Sidebar is not visible on the desktop, open the **All Programs** menu, click **Accessories**, and then click **Windows Sidebar**.
2. If necessary, display the Computer icon on the desktop, open a Computer window, enable single-click activation, and then close the Computer window.

Now, you're ready to examine various techniques for protecting your computer's security and privacy.

Protecting the Security and Privacy of Your Computer

To effectively protect the security of your computer and the privacy of information stored on it while using the Internet, you should be familiar with the types of threats that you might encounter and understand how best to handle them. Many of these threats result from **malware**, a catch-all term for different types of malicious software. The following list describes various types of malware that might infect your computer when you are browsing the World Wide Web and while you are using e-mail:

- **Computer Virus** A **computer virus** is a program that can damage or adversely affect the performance of a computer or compromise its security. A computer virus typically requires a host (such as a program or file) to which it is attached, or it might be contained within an e-mail attachment. When you open the program, file, or attachment that contains the computer virus, it becomes active, makes copies of itself, and spreads to other computers.
- **Internet Worm** An **Internet worm** is an independently functioning program that adversely affects the performance of a computer and may compromise its security. Like a computer virus, it makes copies of itself and spreads from computer to computer via a network (such as the Internet). In the process, it ties up system and network resources and creates congestion on a network. Like a computer virus, it can gain access to a computer via an e-mail attachment.
- **Trojan Horse** A **Trojan Horse** is a program that masquerades as a legitimate program, but once you open the program, the Trojan Horse performs some type of malicious action on the computer or compromises its security by placing a program called a **backdoor** on the computer so that an intruder or hacker can gain access to the computer without detection. Unlike computer viruses or Internet worms, Trojan Horses do not replicate or make copies of themselves. Instead, they are spread via computer viruses, worms, or downloaded software.

- **Browser Hijacker** A **browser hijacker** is malicious software that changes your Web browser's home page to the Web site of the maker of the hijacker software or to another Web site, hijacks your computer and takes it to that Web site without your permission, and prevents you from navigating to other Web sites and from changing your Web browser settings back to what you originally specified. A well-known example of this type of malicious software is CoolWebSearch, which hijacks your Web browser and takes it to the Web site for CoolWebSearch or to another associated Web site.
- **Keylogger** A **keylogger** is malicious software that can monitor your computer, record keys that you press, and send the information it compiles via e-mail to a third party. That information may include passwords, PINs, a social security number, and credit card numbers. It can also track and report your Web browsing habits, and it can become active when you connect to a secure Web site, such as your online banking Web site.
- **Rootkits** A **Rootkit** is malicious (or perhaps even legitimate) software that, when installed on your computer, uses stealth techniques to hide itself from the operating system, other software, and you. Once installed, a Rootkit can modify or integrate itself into the operating system and intercept and filter operations so that it can hide itself and information about itself, such as references to itself in the Windows Registry. A Rootkit can also hide the activity of other malicious software, such as computer viruses, Internet worms, Trojan Horses, and backdoors, which permit an intruder or hacker to remotely control a computer. To remove a Rootkit, you use a Rootkit detector program to find the name of the Rootkit or you can search the Internet for software designed to specifically remove the Rootkit or for any other known way to remove it. After you remove a Rootkit, you may also need to remove other malicious software hidden by the Rootkit. If you cannot find a way to remove a Rootkit, you back up your document files, reformat your hard disk, and reinstall Windows Vista and your software. That approach may, in fact, prove to be the most reliable and least time-consuming way to resolve the problem.

The following list describes other types of threats and problems that might affect your computer when you are browsing the Internet:

- **Cookies** A **cookie** is a text file placed on your computer by a Web site that you visit. The cookie contains the Web site's address as well as information about the date and time of a visit, which Web pages you examined, the expiration date and time of the cookie, and other information, such as your preferred language or country setting. A cookie might also contain personal information you provide a Web site, such as your user name and user preferences. You can block or remove cookies using your Web browser.
- **Web Bug** A **Web bug** uses links on a Web page, in a document, or in an e-mail message to reference another Web site that in turn monitors your Web browsing habits to develop a profile of your interests, track copyrighted documents, or track the flow of e-mail from one person to another.
- **URL Poisoning** A Web site can use **URL poisoning** to track your Web browsing habits by adding an ID number to the URL displayed in the Web browser's Address Bar. The Web site can then determine which Web pages you examine at that site.
- **Remote Surveillance Tools** This category of software called **remote surveillance tools** can perform a wide variety of operations on a computer, such as view the contents of your monitor, capture user passwords, listen to sounds in a room, steal programs and data from a computer, and control the hardware and software on your computer.

- **Packet Sniffer** A **packet sniffer** is software that enables a third party to eavesdrop on computer transmissions, collect user names and passwords, convert Internet transmissions into readable data, and identify weaknesses in a computer's security. You can also use a packet sniffer to identify an intruder or to identify unauthorized transmissions from your computer.
- **Spyware** This type of software monitors your activities on the Internet and reports information about your browsing habits to a third party, such as an advertising company, without your knowledge or consent. **Spyware** may be installed on your computer with or without your consent, or it might be packaged with other software that you download and install on a computer. It is not uncommon for spyware to adversely affect the performance of a computer and even prevent you from connecting to the Internet. To complicate matters, some antispyware products that claim to remove spyware from your computer might actually be spyware.
- **Adware** Originally designed to display advertising in pop-up windows, **adware** can also be spyware that displays unsolicited advertising (usually in pop-up windows), monitors your activity on the Internet, and reports that information to a third party without your authorization or knowledge.
- **Phishing** In a technique called **phishing** (pronounced "fishing"), you receive an e-mail message that appears to be sent from a reputable company with which you do business (such as an ISP or bank) in an attempt to trick you into disclosing personal and financial information, such as bank account numbers, PINs, SSN, and your mother's maiden name, to steal your assets or identity (or both). The e-mail message typically informs you that you need to immediately update account information, or your account will be closed or suspended. The e-mail message also includes a bogus URL that you can click to go to the presumed company's Web site and update an account. The URL and the Web site may look similar or identical to that of the online company with which you have an account; however, if you point to the URL with the mouse pointer and then examine the status bar at the bottom of the Web browser window, you will see a completely different URL—the actual one that's used when you click the URL in the e-mail message. You can use this technique to quickly identify a phishing threat. If you receive this type of e-mail message, do not respond to the e-mail message. Instead, contact the company in question by telephone or in person to verify whether it wants you to update your account information and to let the company in question know about a potential problem that its customers face.
- **Pharming** Like phishing, **pharming** (pronounced "farming") relies on e-mail messages that inform you to immediately update account information. However, pharming may use malicious software or tamper electronically with a URL to redirect your Web browser to a Web site that appears identical or very similar to that of a company with which you do business to obtain personal and financial information without your knowledge or permission. Again, if you receive this type of e-mail, you should contact the company via phone or in person to verify whether the request is legitimate.
- **Denial of Service (DoS) and Distributed Denial of Service (DDoS) Denial of Service** refers to the use of techniques to shut down a Web site by sending it repeated requests to allocate resources for a connection. Because the Web server is forced to keep allocating resources, it eventually exhausts its available resources or cannot handle any additional requests and therefore cannot accept any more connections. **Distributed Denial of Service** relies on the use of hundreds or thousands of interconnected home computers (called **zombies**) infected with malware and controlled remotely by a single user to overwhelm a Web site with traffic and thereby shut down the Web site. These home user networks are referred to as **bots** or **botnets**. The home user does not even know that their computer is a zombie.

- **Bot software** This type of software is used to remotely control a set of computers, usually computers of home users, to attack a Web site or send spam. The Bot software may place different types of malicious programs on a set of home computers or exploit weaknesses in the security of the computer or the operating system and remotely control the computers. These home users do not realize that their computer is part of a botnet.
- **Hoaxes** A **hoax** is an e-mail message sent from a family member, friend, or co-worker warning you of a problem that poses a risk to your computer. The problem sounds plausible, and the e-mail message usually includes technical information to make you believe it's true. Furthermore, the e-mail message quotes an expert or company to make you believe the threat is real. The e-mail message recommends that you send an e-mail message to everyone you know and warn them of the threat, and have them in turn send an e-mail message to everyone they know, warning of a problem that does not actually exist. The end result is that the e-mail traffic overloads and might even shut down e-mail servers. If you receive this type of message, first check its validity by visiting a Web site that contains information about e-mail hoaxes (such as Symantec's Web site) before you forward that e-mail message to everyone you know and contribute to the problem.

Malicious software can gain access to your computer via one or more of the following ways:

- E-mail attachments
- Internet downloads
- Downloaded toolbars
- Infected Web pages, programs, documents, or disks
- Web browser plug-ins or add-ons
- Pop-up windows

To protect yourself from these types of threats, you can take the following precautions:

- **Use Internet Security or antivirus software** Purchase, install, and use Internet Security or antivirus software to detect and remove malicious software that gains access to your computer. These products typically include an option for checking for updates daily so that they can detect and remove new types of malicious software that appear. If you turn off the automatic update feature, remember to manually check for updates on a frequent basis. Some companies allow you to download and use a personal edition of their antivirus software for free as long as you use your computer for personal use and are not using it for business purposes.
- **Use antispyware software** Although antivirus software might remove certain types of spyware, you also need an antispyware software product to provide additional protection against spyware and other malicious software not detected by antivirus software. Windows Vista includes an antispyware program called Windows Defender that you will examine in the next section of the tutorial. Also, some companies allow you to download and use a personal edition of their antispyware software for free as long as you use your computer for personal use and are not using it for commercial purposes.
- **Use firewall software on your computer** Although Windows Vista includes a firewall, you can purchase, install, and use third-party firewall software or the firewall. **Firewall** software protects your computer from hackers and from malicious software that has already gained access to your computer. Later in the tutorial, you will examine firewall software in more detail and examine the firewall included with Windows Vista.

- **Windows Automatic Updates** Windows Vista can automatically download and install new security updates and updates to the operating system that add further protection to your computer. Furthermore, it can also identify and download important security updates for your version of Microsoft Office. Make sure that this feature is enabled on your computer. You will examine this feature in more detail later in this tutorial.
- **Use caution in opening e-mail attachments** Many types of malicious software are spread via e-mail attachments. If you receive an e-mail message from someone you cannot identify or that does not contain a subject line, do not open the e-mail message—delete it. If someone asks you why you did not respond to an e-mail message, ask that person if he or she clearly identified themselves and included a subject line in their e-mail message. Ask that person to note in their message that they included an attachment and to briefly identify its contents. If you open a message that contains an e-mail attachment, check the name of the e-mail attachment to verify that it is the type of document you expect from the sender. Also, check the file extension of the e-mail attachment to determine the type of file. Certain file types, such as program files with the "exe" file extension, might contain malicious software. An e-mail attachment with the "vbs" file extension might contain an Internet worm.

Figure 7-1 contains three tables that identify commonly used file extensions for different file formats that may be safe or unsafe. The file extensions listed in Table I are generally considered unsafe. If an e-mail attachment contains one of these file extensions, do not open the file extension unless you know that the person who sent you the e-mail message attached a file that you specifically requested. If you are not sure whether it's safe to open the file, don't open it. Instead, contact the person who sent you the e-mail message and ask them about the e-mail attachment. HTML (for Hyper Text Markup Language) identifies the document as a Web page, and the HTML file format is now considered insecure because it can harbor malicious software. The file extensions listed in Table II are file extensions for common types of document formats, and they may be safe or unsafe. Use the same approach as you would when dealing with file extensions shown in Table I. The file extensions listed in Table III are generally considered safe; however, make sure that the e-mail attachment is one that you specifically requested or know about before opening it. Because the criteria for safe and unsafe file extensions changes over time, you can best use this information to heighten your awareness and pay more attention to file extensions and potential problems.

Be cautious of e-mail attachments that appear to have two file extensions, such as "txt.vbs". When you notice what appears to you as the file extension (namely, "txt"), you might not pay attention to the actual file extension (namely, "vbs") and inadvertently open an e-mail message with an Internet worm.

As previously noted, ask friends and co-workers and anyone else with whom you correspond via e-mail to specifically identify and note that they have included an e-mail attachment. Because some people use handles instead of their real name for the user ID portion of their e-mail address, also recommend that they include their name in the e-mail message. Also, someone might send you an e-mail message without knowing that their computer is infected with malicious software, and that malicious software might attach a copy of itself to a message as your e-mail software sends the message.

Unsafe and safe file extensions | Figure 7-1

Table I: Unsafe File Extensions

Extension	File Type
bat	Windows Batch File
cmd	Command Script
com	Command (MS-DOS Application)
docm	Microsoft Word Document (Macro-Enabled Open XML Format)
exe	Executable (Application, Utility, or Game)
htm or html	Hypertext Markup Language File (Web Page)
inf	Setup Information File
js	JavaScript Source Code
jse	JavaScript Encoded Script File
pif	Windows Program Information File
ppsm	Microsoft PowerPoint Slide Show (Macro-Enabled Open XML Format)
pptm	Microsoft PowerPoint Presentation (Macro-Enabled Open XML Format)
scr	Screen Saver (Program File)
shb	Windows Shortcut into a Document
shs	Windows Shell Scrap Object File
vb or vbs	VBScript File
vbe	VBScript Encoded Script File
wsc	Windows Script Component File
wsf	Windows Script File
wsh	Windows Script Host Settings File
xlsm	Microsoft Excel Workbook (Macro-Enabled Open XML Format)

Table II: Safe or Unsafe File Extensions

Extension	File Type
doc	Microsoft Word Document; WordPad Document
mdb	Microsoft Access Database
pps	Microsoft PowerPoint Slide Show
ppt	Microsoft PowerPoint Presentation
rtf	Rich Text Format
xls	Microsoft Excel Workbook
zip	Zip File (Compressed File); Compressed (zipped) Folder

Figure 7-1 Unsafe and safe file extensions (continued)

Table III: Safe File Extensions

Extension	File Type
bmp	Windows Bitmap Graphics
csv	Comma Separated Values (Text File)
docx	Microsoft Word Document (Open XML Format)
gif	Graphics Interchange Format (Graphics Image)
jpg, jpeg, or jpe	Joint Photograph Experts Group (Graphics Image)
pdf	Adobe Portable Document Format
ppsx	Microsoft PowerPoint Slide Show (Open XML Format)
pptx	Microsoft PowerPoint Presentation (Open XML Format)
psd	Adobe Photoshop Document
pub	Microsoft Publisher Document
snp	Microsoft Access Report Snapshot
tif or tiff	Tagged Image File Format
txt	Text Document
xlsx	Microsoft Excel Workbook (Open XML Format)
xps	XML Paper Specification

- **Change the message format used for e-mail messages** Your e-mail software may use HTML as its default message format. If that's the case, you can change your e-mail message format to the more secure Plain Text file format. For example, the default message format in Microsoft Outlook is HTML; however, you can change it to Rich Text Format (RTF) or Plain Text format, both of which are more secure than HTML. **Rich Text Format (RTF)** is a file format for storing formatted text. Since many different software programs can create and open files saved in Rich Text Format, this file format is commonly used to exchange files with individuals who use software products different from the ones you use.
- **Beware of phishing and pharming e-mail messages** As noted earlier, do not respond to e-mail messages that attempt to scare you into updating personal, financial, and account information; instead, directly contact the company in question via phone or in person to verify the authenticity of the message and any request to update account information. If you are sure that your computer is secure and is not infected with malicious software, you can visit the actual company's Web site and review your account information or contact the actual company from its Web site about the need for updating account information. Later in the tutorial, you will examine the new Phishing Filter in Windows Internet Explorer which helps detect phishing Web sites.
- **Be cautious of spam** Do not open or respond to **spam** or unsolicited e-mail messages; instead, delete or block the unsolicited e-mail messages. E-mail software includes an option for blocking messages from specific e-mail addresses as well as from specific domains (Web sites). Furthermore, you can add specific e-mail addresses and domains to a safe list to guarantee that messages from specific individuals or businesses are not inadvertently treated as spam and placed in a Junk Mail or Bulk Mail folder. Also, if an unsolicited e-mail message recommends that you respond to the message to have your name removed from their list, do not respond to the message because it will only verify that your e-mail address is legitimate and you may very well continue to receive spam. Use your e-mail software to automatically block or delete unsolicited e-mail.

- **Use secure Web sites to conduct online transactions** If you are entering sensitive information at a Web site, purchasing a product online, or conducting a bank transaction online, verify that you are at a secure Web site by making sure that the URL of the Web site includes "https" ("s" for "secure") rather than "http" in the URL for the Web site. Also, look for a padlock icon on your Web browser's Address Bar or status bar to indicate that any transactions you perform are encrypted and therefore secure. Later in the tutorial, you will examine Windows Internet Explorer's Security Status Bar, which helps you identify secure and insecure Web sites.
- **Check your Web browser's security settings and enable options for enhancing the security of your computer** You can use your Web browser to control the use of cookies and pop-up windows. You will examine these options in Internet Explorer later in the tutorial.
- **Use caution in downloading programs, files, and toolbars** Downloaded programs and files may contain malicious software, and some toolbars may include a spyware component. If a Web site prompts you to accept an agreement for using their product, carefully read that agreement because it might note that you are agreeing to download not only the product you're interested in, but one or more additional components that you might not otherwise be aware of and may prefer not to have on your computer.
- **Acquire special-purpose software** For certain types of threats or issues, you might need to acquire special software to further protect your computer. As noted earlier, you might find that some companies provide their software free of charge if you use it only for personal use.

Today, and in the foreseeable future, an Internet Security Suite or antivirus software, antispyware software, and firewall are indispensable to the security of your computer. Safe computing practices also enhance your computer's security and your personal privacy.

Using Windows Defender

Windows Defender, an antispyware program included with Windows Vista, detects and removes spyware on computers used by small office and home users. Windows Defender automatically scans a computer every day for malicious software. By default, it performs a quick scan at 2 a.m. every day; however, you can specify a different schedule if you prefer. A **quick scan** is a fast scan that examines specific components, such as memory and the Windows Registry, which might be infected with malicious software.

Malicious software must be loaded into memory before it can become active. Once malicious software gains access to a computer, it can insert a setting in the Windows Registry to guarantee that it is automatically loaded with each boot. Windows Defender therefore examines the Registry when a computer boots to check programs that are automatically loaded into memory.

After your computer boots, Windows Defender continually monitors your computer for software that attempts to make changes to your system or to install itself. If Windows Defender finds harmful, or what it refers to as potentially unwanted software, it displays a warning, identifies how many harmful or potentially unwanted items it found, permits you to review the items, and provides an option for taking one of four possible actions. You can ignore the item, in which case it allows you to install the software or allows that software to run, but if the software attempts to change security settings, it alerts you again. You can allow software to run without any further alerts, and you can also choose to quarantine or remove harmful or potentially unwanted software. If you **quarantine** the program, Windows Defender moves the program to another location and prevents it from becoming active again (usually by changing the file extension). Later, you can remove or restore the quarantined item.

You can also specify that Windows Defender perform a full scan and examine every file on a computer; however, a full scan can take hours. You would more than likely perform a full scan if you wanted to verify that you have completely removed malicious software from your computer. You can still work on your computer during a full scan, but your computer will operate more slowly.

When Windows Defender identifies suspicious or potentially unwanted software, it assigns one of the following alert levels to the software:

- **Severe** This alert level includes malicious software that is well-known or dangerous. Since this software can affect your computer's security and your privacy, Windows Defender will recommend that you immediately remove this software.
- **High** This alert level includes software that changes system settings or collects personal information without your knowledge or consent and that can therefore affect your computer's security and your privacy. Windows Defender will also recommend that you immediately remove this software.
- **Medium** This alert level is similar to the High alert level; however, Windows Defender will recommend that you review the software before you install or run the software. The software might be legitimate, or it might affect your computer's security and your privacy or possibly display advertising.
- **Low** This alert level includes software that operates according to its licensing terms; however, the software might make changes to system settings or collect information about your use of your computer. Therefore, Windows Defender recommends that you review the software to be sure you want to use it.
- **Not yet classified** This last alert level includes software that is more than likely not dangerous, but has not been analyzed by Microsoft. You can choose to use it, send it to Microsoft for analysis, or check Microsoft's SpyNet community and find out how other users handle this software.

Arielle recommends that you use Windows Defender to perform a quick scan of your new laptop computer, and then scan your flash drive before installing software you've downloaded to your flash drive.

If Windows Defender is not installed on your computer, read the steps and examine the figures so that you are familiar with how Windows Defender works, but do not keystroke the steps.

To perform a quick scan of your computer and then scan your flash drive:

1. On the Start menu, point to **All Programs**, and then click **Windows Defender**. In the Windows Defender window, you are reminded that this program offers protection against malicious and unwanted software. See Figure 7-2. On the computer used for this figure, Windows Defender notes that it has not found any harmful or unwanted software and that the computer is running normally. In the Status area, it notes when it performed the last scan, the type of scan, the scan schedule, whether real-time protection is on or off, and the definition version. Real-time protection means that the option for constantly monitoring a computer for potentially unwanted software is enabled. Definition version refers to the most recent update that contains files Windows Defender uses to detect harmful or potentially unwanted software and prevent the installation or use of that software.

Figure 7-2 Viewing the status of a computer

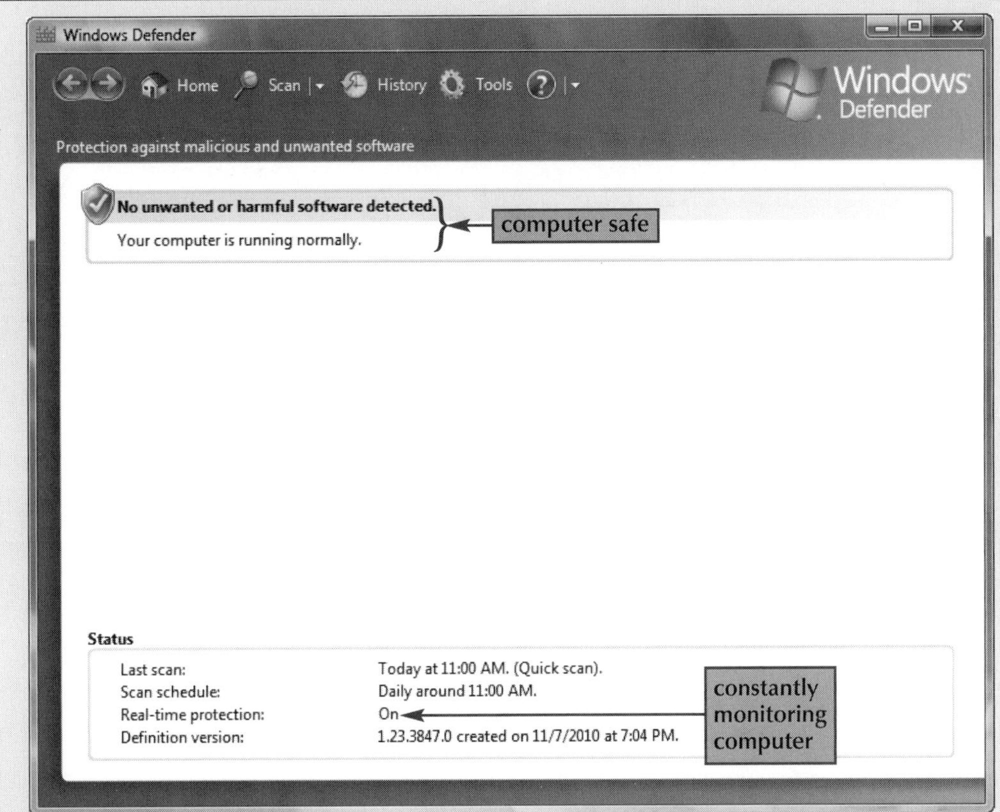

Trouble? If you see a Windows Defender dialog box that informs you that Windows Defender is turned off, check with your instructor or tech support staff to determine whether you can turn it on. If so, click the "Turn on and open Windows Defender" link in the Windows Defender dialog box, and then provide Administrator credentials.

2. Click the **Scan** link on the command bar. Windows Defender performs a quick scan of your computer. See Figure 7-3. During the scan, it checks Registry settings as well as files in the Windows and Program Files folders. After the scan is complete, it informs you of its findings. On the computer used for Figure 7-4, it reports it did not detect any unwanted or harmful software and notes that the computer is running normally.

Figure 7-3 Performing a quick scan

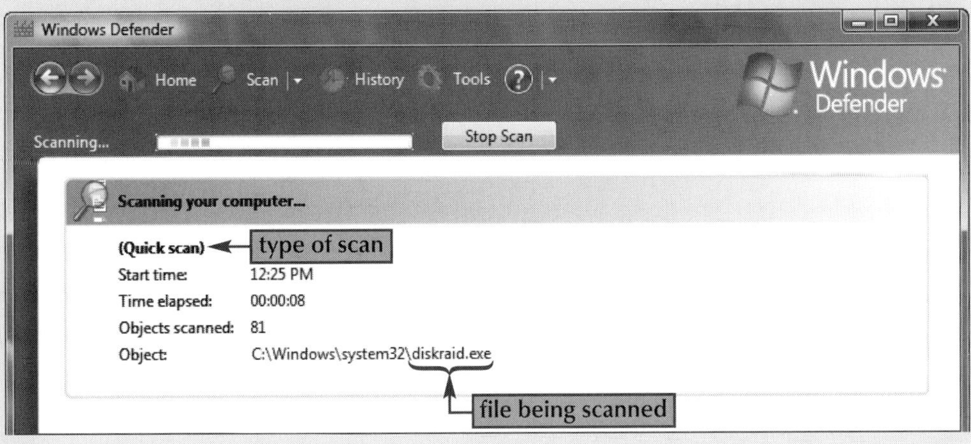

Figure 7-4 **Quick scan results**

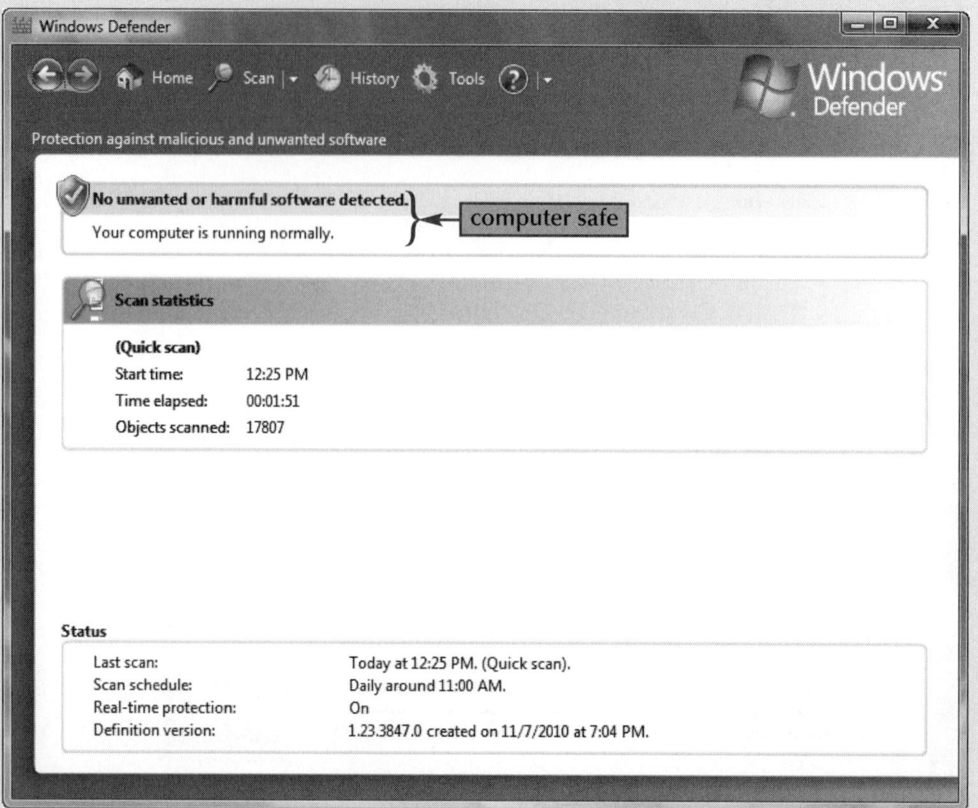

3. Attach your flash drive, and if necessary, close any dialog boxes or windows that open.
4. Click the **Scan list button** (not the Scan link), and then click **Custom Scan**. Under Select scan options, you can select a quick scan, a full system scan, or drives and folders you want to scan. See Figure 7-5. If you point to the Scan list button, you see a ToolTip with the text "Scan options."

Figure 7-5 **Scanning options**

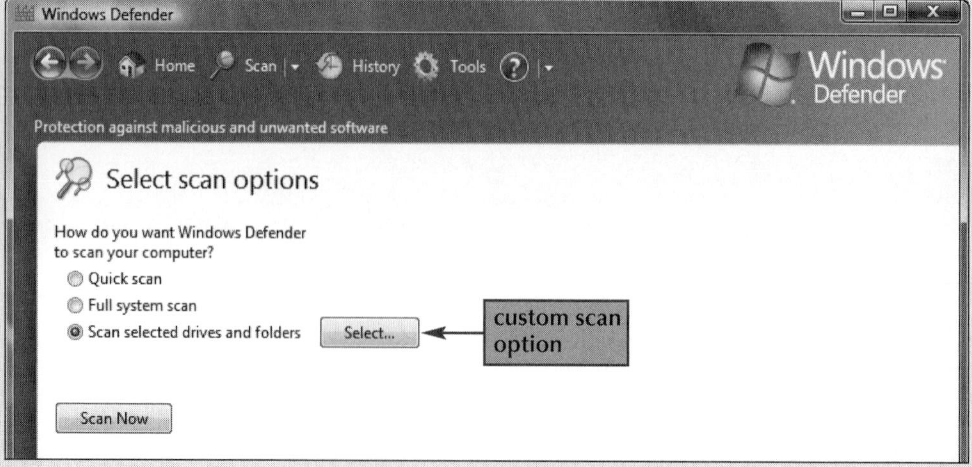

5. Click the **Select** button. In the Windows Defender dialog box, you can select a drive or expand and view the folder structure for a drive if you want to scan only a folder. See Figure 7-6.

Figure 7-6 Selecting a drive to scan

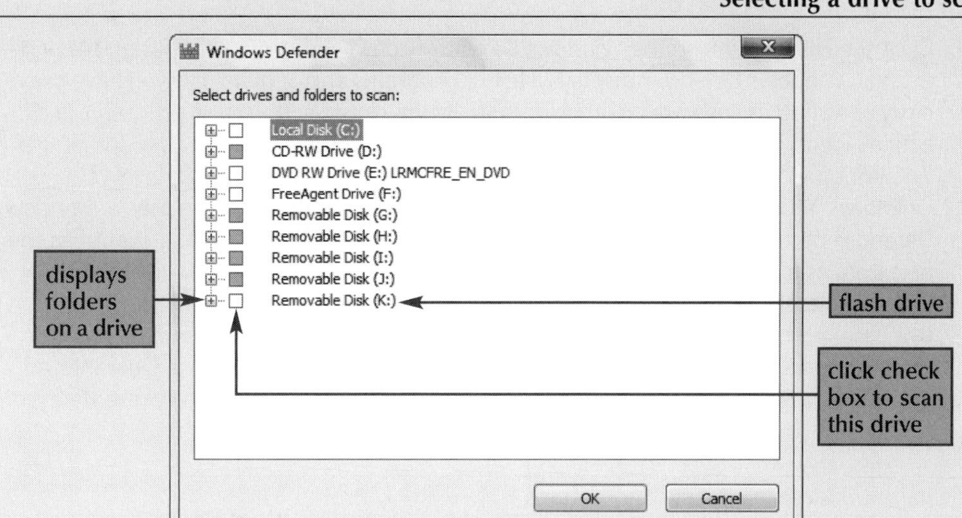

Tip

Gray check boxes indicate that the drive does not contain removable media.

6. Click the **check box for your flash drive**, and then click the **Expand** button ⊞ to display the folders on your flash drive. Windows Defender will scan all folders (and subfolders and files) on the flash drive, and then report on its findings.
7. Click the **OK** button, and then click the **Scan Now** button. Windows Defenders scans your flash drive. Depending on the capacity of your flash drive and the amount of files it contains, the full scan may take several minutes.
8. After the scan is complete, examine the results and the amount of time required for the scan (for future reference).
9. Keep the Windows Defender window open for the next section of the tutorial.

Tip

To scan a folder, click the Expand button for a drive, and then click the check box for the folder you want to scan.

Tip

If a scan takes longer than you expect, click the Stop Scan button.

If you store all software and file downloads in a specific folder, such as the Downloads folder for your user logon or the Public Downloads folder, you can scan only that folder before you install any downloaded software or open any downloaded files.

Using Windows Defender to Scan a Drive | Reference Window

- On the Start menu, point to All Programs, click Windows Defender, and in the Windows Defender window, review information about the previous scan of your computer.
- To perform a quick scan of your computer, click the Scan button on the command bar.
- To scan a specific drive, click the Scan button arrow (not the Scan link), click Custom Scan, click the Select button, click the check box for the drive that you want to scan, or click the expand indicator for the drive you want to scan and select the folder or folders you want to scan, and then click the OK button.
- Click the Scan Now button.
- After reviewing the scan results, close the Windows Defender window.

Arielle recommends that you examine your laptop's scan history and find out if Windows Defender identified any unknown software and what action Windows Defender took.

To view your scan history:

1. Click the **History** link on the Windows Defender command bar. Under Programs and actions, Windows Defender displays a list of programs and actions that you have previously specified as spyware or other potentially unwanted software or programs and actions identified and taken by Windows Defender. On the computer used for Figure 7-7, Windows Defender identifies two items as Unknown, with an Alert level of Unknown. Your results may differ. The Action Taken indicates that the user or Windows Defender permitted these actions. Under Resources, Windows Defender identifies the first item as a Registry setting for the start page of Internet Explorer. Under Category (not completely visible in the figure), it reports that this item is not yet classified. In this case, both actions are the same. You can use the Allowed items link to review or monitor items permitted to run on your computer, and you can use the Quarantined items link to remove or restore items that Windows Defender currently prevents from running on your computer.

Figure 7-7 Viewing monitored programs and actions

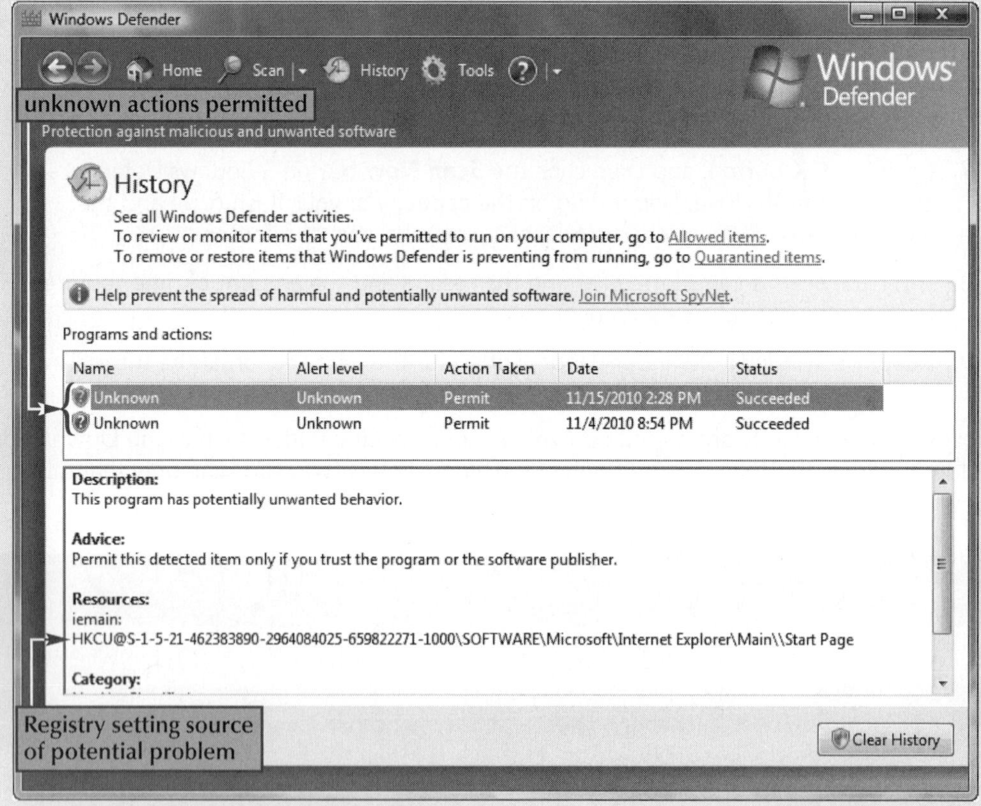

2. Click the **Tools** link on the command bar. Windows Defender displays two categories (Tools and Settings) where you can change settings and use specific Windows Defender Tools. See Figure 7-8.

Windows Defender tools and options **Figure 7-8**

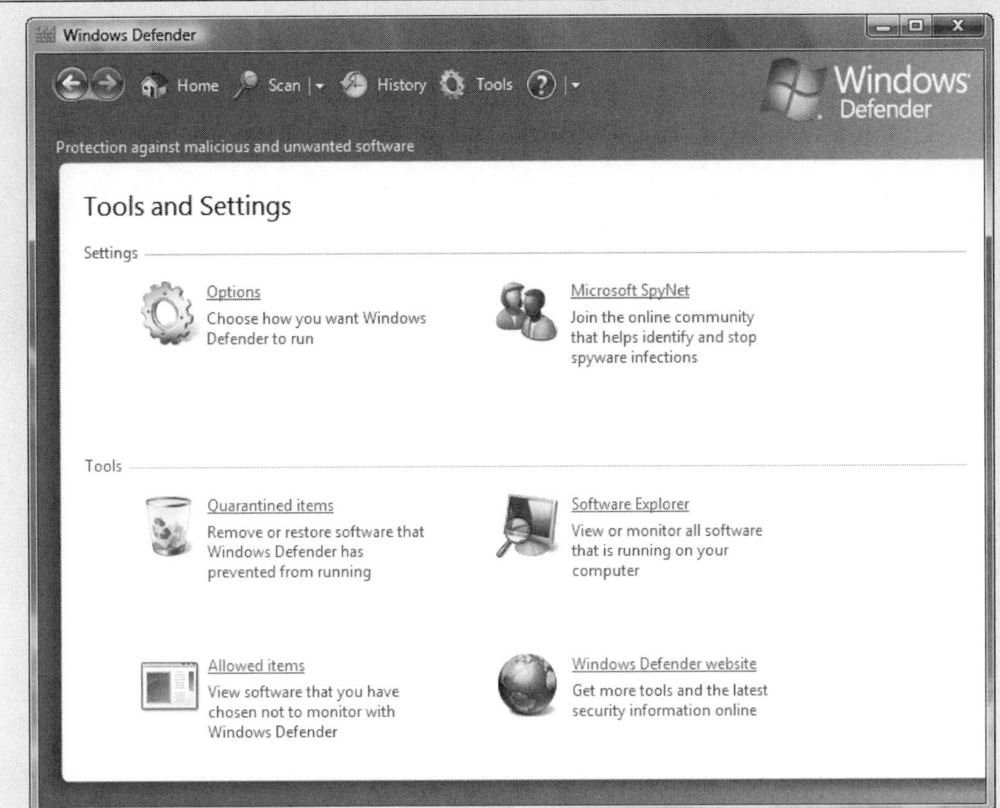

3. Under Tools, click the **Allowed items** link. Windows Defender displays a list of items allowed to run on your computer (if any) and notes that it does not inform you of any risks these items pose to your privacy or your computer. It further notes that if you remove an item from this list, Windows Defender will continue to monitor the item. You do not want to restore items with a Severe or High Alert Level because they are likely to pose a risk to your computer and your privacy.
4. Click the **Back** button, and then click **Quarantined items**. Windows Defender displays a list of items that are quarantined (if any) and therefore not allowed to run on your computer. You can select an item and remove or restore it. As for Allowed items, you do not want to restore items with a Severe or High Alert Level because they are likely to pose a risk to your computer and your privacy.
5. Keep Windows Defender open for the next section of the tutorial.

Viewing your scan history is important because you may not be aware of actions already taken by Windows Defender.

Reference Window | Viewing Your Scan History

- On the Start menu, point to All Programs, click Windows Defender, and in the Windows Defender window, click the History link on the Windows Defender command bar and examine the information on programs and actions taken by Windows Defender under Programs and actions.
- To view information on Allowed items, click the Tools link on the command bar, click the Allowed items link, and review the information on any allowed programs and their alert levels.
- To view information on Quarantined items, click the Tools link on the command bar, click Quarantined items, and then review the information on quarantined items and their alert levels.
- After reviewing History and information on Allowed and Quarantined items, close the Windows Defender window.

Next, you can use Software Explorer to view information about the software on your computer.

Using Software Explorer

You can use a Windows Defender tool called **Software Explorer** to view information about all software running on your computer. You can also use Software Explorer to remove or disable programs that you do not want to run on your computer. In Software Explorer, you can view information about the following types of programs:

- **Startup programs** that Windows automatically loads during booting. Although you may know that certain programs, such as antivirus software, load when your computer starts, you might not know about all of the other programs that load and that can affect the performance and security of your computer as well as your privacy.
- **Currently running programs**
- **Network connected programs,** or programs you use to connect to the Internet or to your home or office computer.
- **Winsock service providers**, or programs or processes that provide networking and communication services for Windows Vista and other programs. These programs often have access to important components of the operating system. A **service** is a program, routine, or process that runs in the background and provides support to other programs. A **process** refers to the memory allocated to a program and the information needed for the execution of the program.

Arielle asks you to examine Software Explorer so that you are familiar with the types of programs that load and run on your laptop.

To use Software Explorer to view information about programs:

1. Click the **Back** button, and on the Tools and Settings page, click the **Software Explorer** link. On the computer used for Figure 7-9, Software Explorer displays a list of Startup programs organized by category. In the Category list on the left, the first category displays programs developed by Microsoft Corporation. In the pane on the right, Software Explorer displays detailed information about the first program in the first category of the Category list. Because different types of programs are installed on different computers, your list of programs will differ.

Figure 7-9 Viewing a list of startup programs

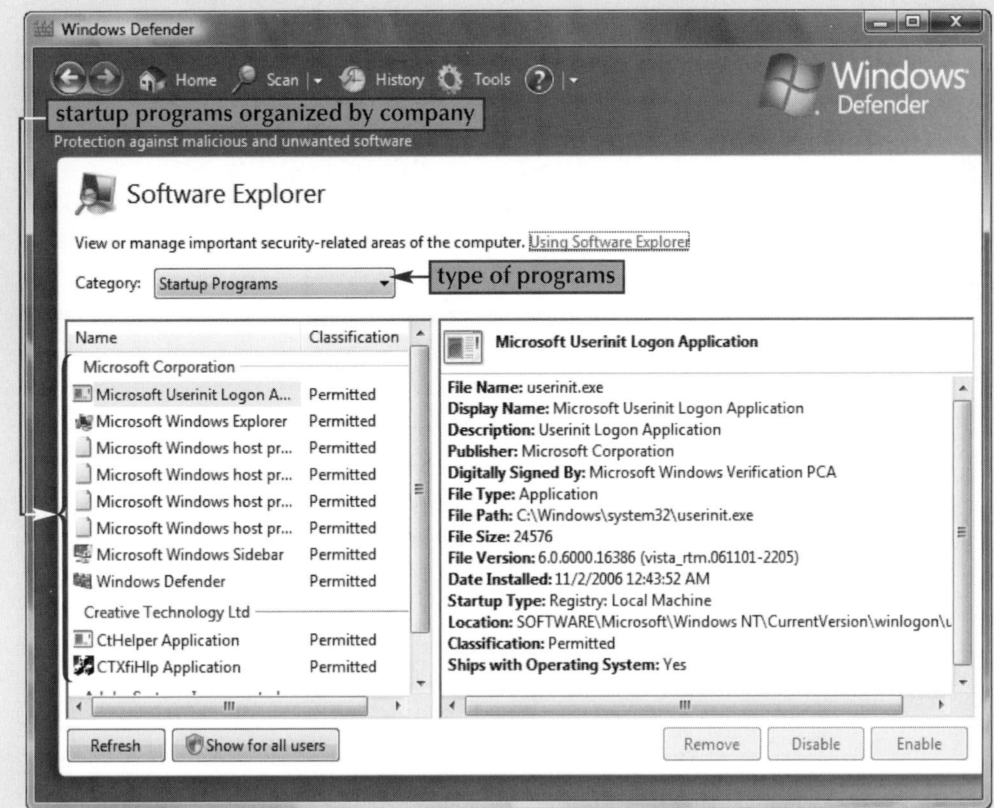

2. In the Category list on the left, locate and click **Windows Defender** under the Microsoft Corporation category. In the pane on the right, note that the Startup Type is identified as Registry: Local Machine. See Figure 7-10. That means that Windows Defender itself loads from a setting in a portion of the Windows Registry called Local Machine. The exact path to that part of the Registry is shown for Location. The File Path shows the full path to the Windows Defender program, and the Startup Value listed just before the File Path also shows the full path.

Figure 7-10 Viewing information on the Windows Defender startup program

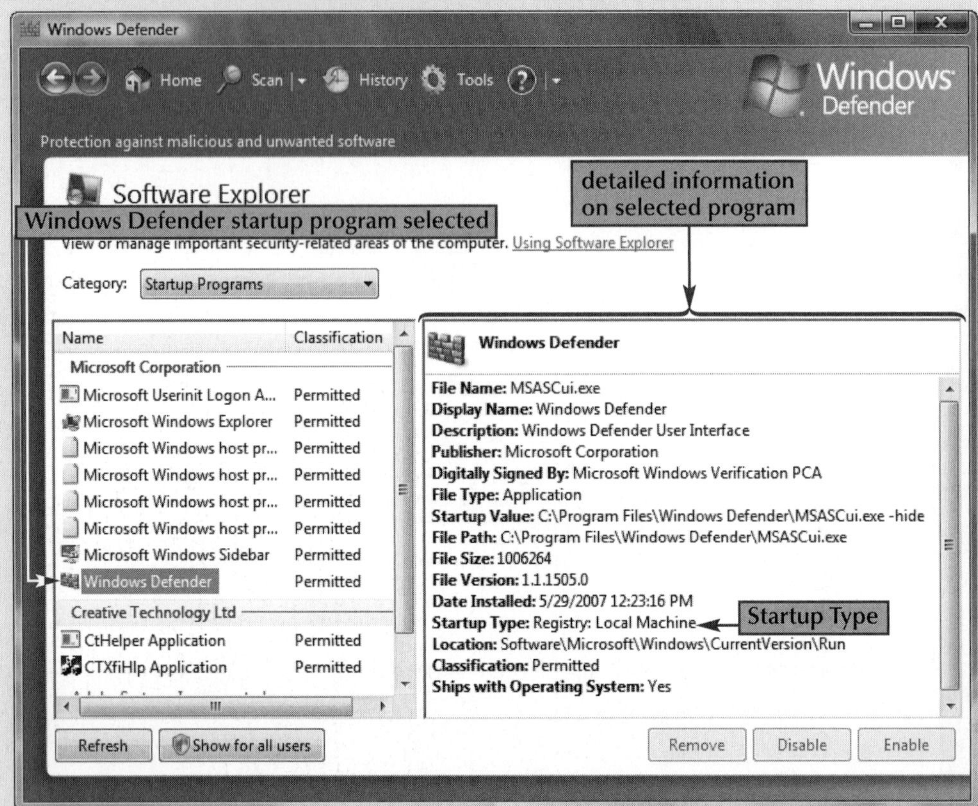

3. Click the **Category** list button above the Category list, and then click **Currently Running Programs**. Software Explorer displays a list of all currently running programs and shows their classification.

4. Under the Microsoft Corporation in the Category list, locate and click **Microsoft Windows Sidebar**. Software Explorer displays information about this Windows Vista component. See Figure 7-11. If Windows Sidebar is set to start when Windows starts on your computer, the detailed information about Microsoft Windows Sidebar will show the Auto Start value set to "Yes." The Classification for Windows Sidebar is set to "In Progress," which indicates that Windows Defender has already analyzed the program and determined that it poses no risk to your computer and your privacy. Also, you may see Microsoft Windows Desktop Manager in the Category list under Microsoft Corporation. As noted in Tutorial 1, this is the Windows Vista component that manages the use of Windows Aero for those versions of Windows Vista that support Windows Aero.

Figure 7-11 Viewing information on Windows Sidebar startup program

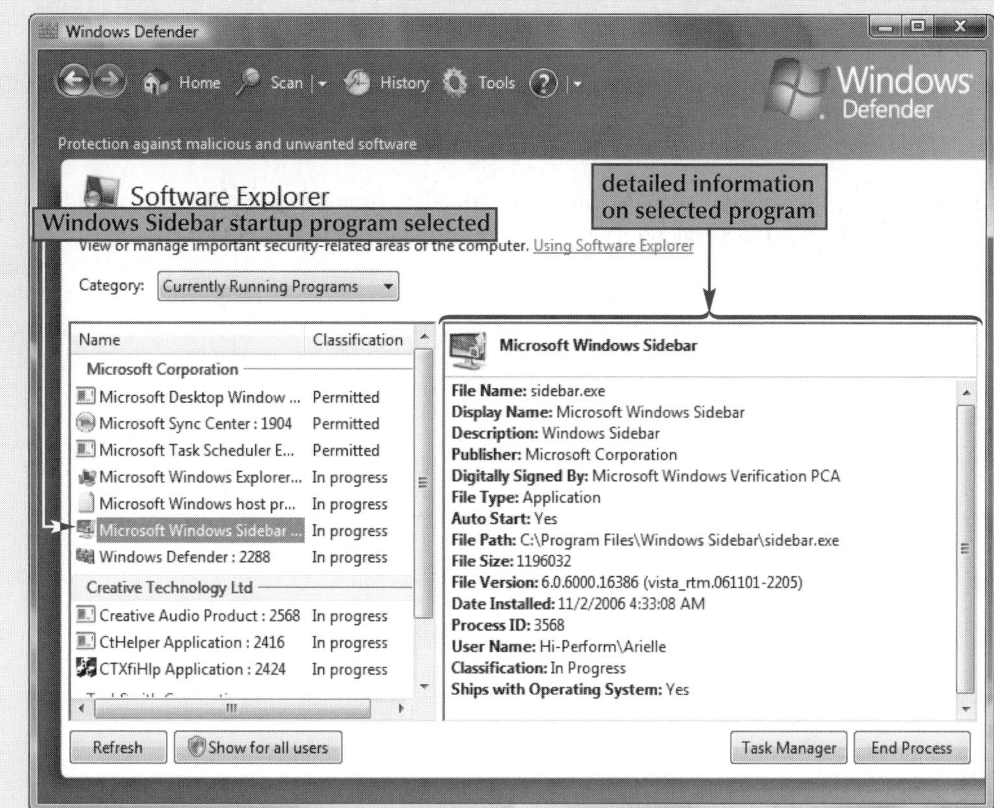

5. Keep the Windows Defender window open for the next section of the tutorial.

As noted earlier, some programs, including malicious software, load during the early stages of booting from settings stored in the Windows Registry. Other programs might load from the All Users Startup folder or your personal user account Startup folder during booting. And yet, other programs might load as services during booting. Since Windows loads programs in different ways on your computer, Software Explorer is an important tool because it provides a list of all running programs no matter how they load.

Using Software Explorer | Reference Window

- On the Start menu, point to All Programs, click Windows Defender, click the Tools link on the command bar, click Software Explorer, select a program in the Category list, and then view information about that Startup program.
- Use the Category list button to select another category (Currently Running Programs, Network Connected Programs, or Winsock Service Providers), select a program in the Category list, and then examine information about that program.
- After viewing information on programs, close the Windows Defender window.

Arielle asked you earlier to check Windows Defender settings to make sure they meet your needs.

To examine Windows Defender settings:

1. Click the **Tools** link on the command bar. Under Tools, a link to the Microsoft Windows Defender Web site lets you obtain more tools and the latest information on Windows Defender. Under Settings, you can join the SpyNet online community to help identify and stop spyware infections.
2. Under Settings, click the **Options** link. Under Automatic scanning, you can change the frequency, approximate time, and type of scan you prefer. See Figure 7-12. The option for checking for definition updates before performing a scan is automatically enabled so that Windows Defender can perform scans of your computer with the latest information on potentially dangerous software. Under Default actions, you can choose the action that Windows Defender takes for programs that it identifies as High, Medium, and Low level alerts. Your Default actions for each alert level include the Default action (definition-based) option, Ignore, and Remove.

Figure 7-12 Viewing Windows Defender options and settings

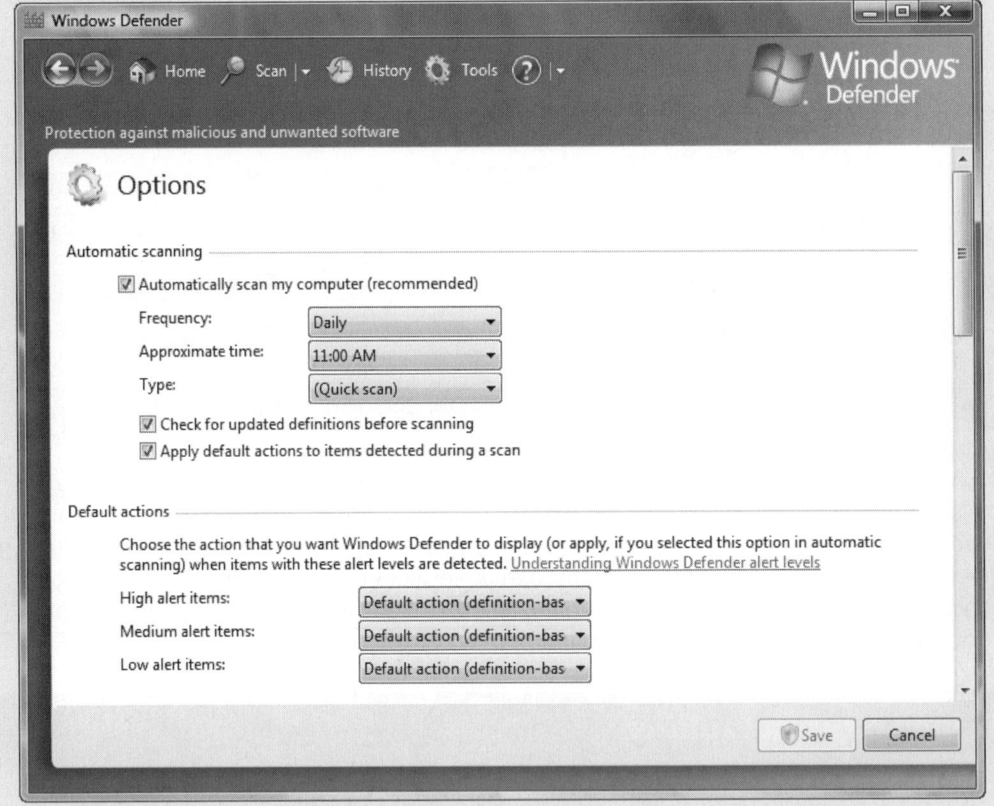

3. Click the **Help options button arrow** on the command bar (not the Help icon). You can use this menu to check for updates to Windows Defender at any time (after you provide Administrator credentials).
4. Close the Windows Defender window.

Examining Windows Defender Settings | Reference Window

- On the Start menu, point to All Programs, click Windows Defender, click the Tools link on the command bar, and then click the Options link under Settings.
- Under Automatic scanning, review, and if necessary, change the options for automatically scanning your computer.
- Under Default actions, review, and if necessary, change the settings for the action Windows Defender takes for programs that it identifies as High, Medium, and Low level alerts.
- Close the Windows Defender window.

Windows Defender helps to protect your computer and your privacy. You can also use Windows Defender to view information about all running programs, allowed items, and quarantined items to identify malicious or potentially dangerous software, verify that a program you installed is working, and discover why a particular program that you've installed might not be working.

Although Windows Defender is an important tool, you should also acquire and install antivirus software on your computer to protect against other types of malicious software.

The Importance of User Accounts and User Account Control

A **user account** is a collection of settings that identifies you to Windows Vista and determines what you can do on your computer. For example, a user account:

- Identifies which folders and files you can access
- Provides access to your personal settings (such as desktop and folder settings)
- Determines what types of changes you can make to the computer (such as installing software and hardware, updating software, and managing user accounts)
- Determines what types of system settings you can access, view, and change

When you install Windows Vista on a computer, you must create an Administrator account for setting up the computer. Not only do you provide a user account name, but you also provide a secure password for added protection of your computer. When you create additional user accounts for new users, you specify the type of user account for each new user and provide a user account name and (optional) password. Each user can then specify or change their password.

Windows Vista supports three types of user accounts:

- **Administrator** An **Administrator account** provides you with complete access to your computer. You can change system settings (including security settings); manage user accounts (your account and other user's accounts); install, configure, update, troubleshoot, and uninstall software and hardware; and access all folders and files on a computer (including folders and files of other users).
- **Standard User** A **Standard User account** provides you with access to the full capabilities of a computer but prevents or restricts you from making changes to system settings; managing your user account and other user accounts; installing, configuring, updating, troubleshooting, and uninstalling software and hardware; and accessing other user's folders and files. A Standard User can use installed software and hardware, make certain changes to their own user account, specify personal desktop and folder settings, and create folders and files.

- **Guest** A **Guest account** is an account designed for a user (such as a visitor or friend) who needs temporary access to the features on your computer, such as the ability to use software, connect to the Internet, and browse the Web. A user of a Guest account faces the same restrictions as those for a Standard User account. However, a Guest account does not have a password, and a temporary user cannot specify a password. A user with Administrator privileges must enable the Guest account on a computer before a guest can use it.

Windows Vista also includes a built-in Administrator account that is automatically disabled. However, under certain conditions (which you examine in the next tutorial), you have access to that Administrator account.

InSight | Effectively Implementing User Accounts on a Computer

If you are the only person that uses your computer, you can have both an Administrator account and a Standard User account. You use your Administrator account only when you need to make changes to your computer. The rest of the time, you use your Standard User account so that you do not inadvertently make changes to your computer that you do not want and so that you can safely browse the Internet and World Wide Web under more secure conditions. That way a hacker or a malicious Web site that accesses your computer does not have Administrator rights on your computer.

If several people use your computer, you set up each user with a Standard User account so that they can use the computer but not make any changes to its configuration. You do not want to have only an Administrator account that you share with all other users because those others users (including children) will then have full access to the computer and can make whatever changes they want.

To enhance the security of Windows Vista over previous versions of Windows, Microsoft has included in Windows Vista an important feature known as User Account Control. **User Account Control (UAC)** prompts you (and any other users of the same computer) for permission or for the user name and password of an Administrator account before performing an operation that affects the operation of your computer or that affects other users. By prompting for permission or Administrator credentials, User Account Control also prevents the installation of malicious software or spyware on your computer without your knowledge.

Also, when you log on under an Administrator account under Windows Vista, you work as a Standard User in what's called **Admin Approval Mode**, without Administrator privileges. If you start to perform an operation that requires Administrator credentials, Windows Vista switches to Secure Desktop Mode and displays a **Consent Prompt** in a User Account Control dialog box. In **Secure Desktop Mode**, you can perform only one operation, namely, the specific operation that you initiated. Secure Desktop Mode, a new Windows Vista feature, prevents another operation that you might not even be aware of (such as installing malicious software) from being performed on your computer once you provide Administrator credentials. Also, Secure Desktop Mode prevents other software from interacting with the user interface while you are performing an operation that requires Administrator credentials. Only Windows processes can access Secure Desktop Mode, preventing what are called silent installs of malicious software. **Silent installs** are ones performed without your knowledge or consent. This feature also applies when you are on the Internet or World Wide Web. Hackers or Web sites cannot silently install malicious software on your computer.

If you provide Administrator credentials, perform the task you initiated, and then decide to repeat that same task, Windows Vista switches to Secure Desktop Mode again and prompts you to provide Administrator credentials again.

If you log on under a Standard User account and start an operation that requires Administrator credentials, Windows Vista switches to Secure Desktop Mode and displays a **Credentials Prompt** in a User Account dialog box. You must select an Administrator account and provide the password for that account before you can perform the operation.

In certain dialog boxes, Windows Vista displays a security shield icon next to an option to let the user know that the option requires Administrator credentials. For example, as shown in Figure 7-13, the option for changing the date and time in the Date and Time dialog box requires Administrator credentials.

Figure 7-13 Date and Time dialog box options

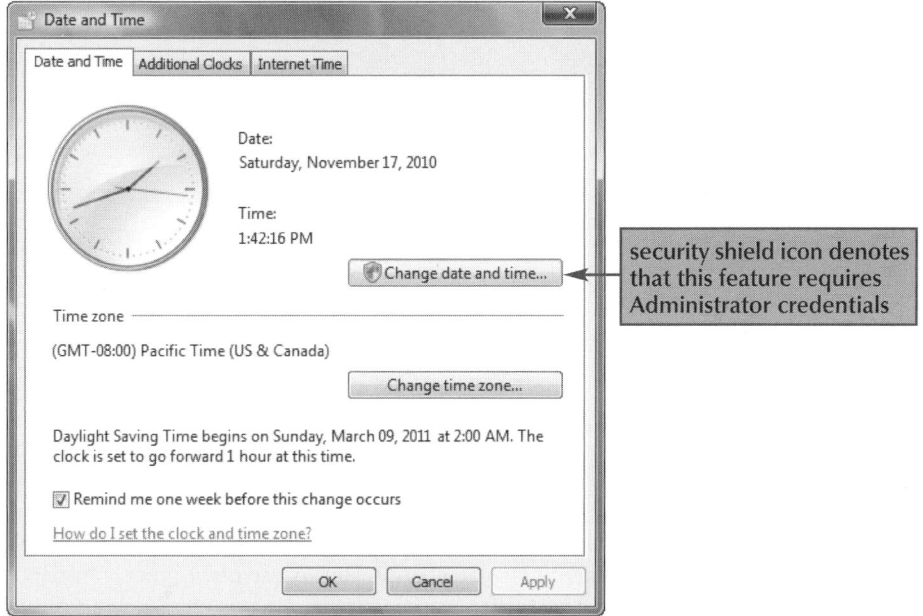

You might discover that certain applications do not run properly on your computer because they were originally designed to run with Administrator privileges. To correct this problem, you upgrade to a newer version designed for Windows Vista that does not require Administrator privileges.

By default, User Account Control is enabled on a computer.

To view information about user accounts or change settings for a user account, you open User Accounts from the Control Panel. You can also create a **Password Reset Disk** in case you forget the password to your user account. To create a Password Reset Disk, you can use a flash drive or a memory card.

After discussing the value of having a Password Reset Disk with other members of Arielle's staff, you decide to make one for your user account.

To open User Accounts and create a Password Reset Disk:

1. If necessary, attach your flash drive to your computer, and then close any dialog boxes or windows that open.

2. On the Start menu, click **Control Panel**, click the **User Accounts and Family Safety** link in the Control Panel window, and then click the **User Accounts** link. Windows Vista opens the User Accounts window and displays information about your user account. See Figure 7-14. You can change or remove your password or change your account picture without Administrator credentials. If you want to change your account name, account type, manage another account, or turn User Account Control on or off, you must provide Administrator credentials, as evidenced by the security icon to the left of those options.

   Trouble? If you are using the Business Edition of Windows Vista, you do not have a Family Safety link. Instead, click the first, and then the second, User Accounts link to access the window for managing user accounts.

Figure 7-14 Options for managing a user account

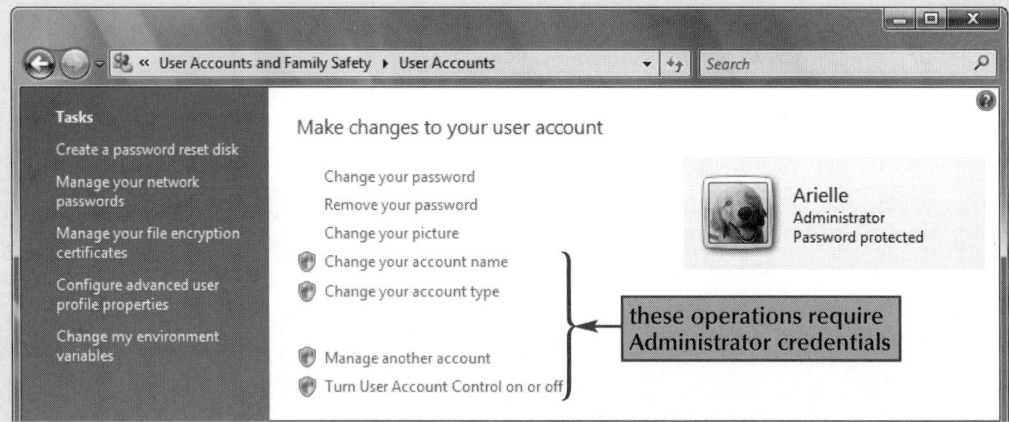

3. Under Tasks in the left pane, click the **Create a password reset disk** link. Windows Vista opens the Forgotten Password Wizard dialog box. See Figure 7-15. Windows Vista notes that no matter how many times you change your password, you only need to create this disk once. Windows Vista also warns you that anyone can use your password reset disk to reset the password and gain access to your user account. However, the trade-off is that you have a way to access your computer if you forget your password.

Figure 7-15 Forgotten Password Wizard

4. Click the **Next** button. The Forgotten Password Wizard prompts for the location of the disk where it will store your password information. See Figure 7-16. You can use a removable disk or an external hard disk drive, but not your internal hard disk drive.

Figure 7-16 Choose a drive for the password key

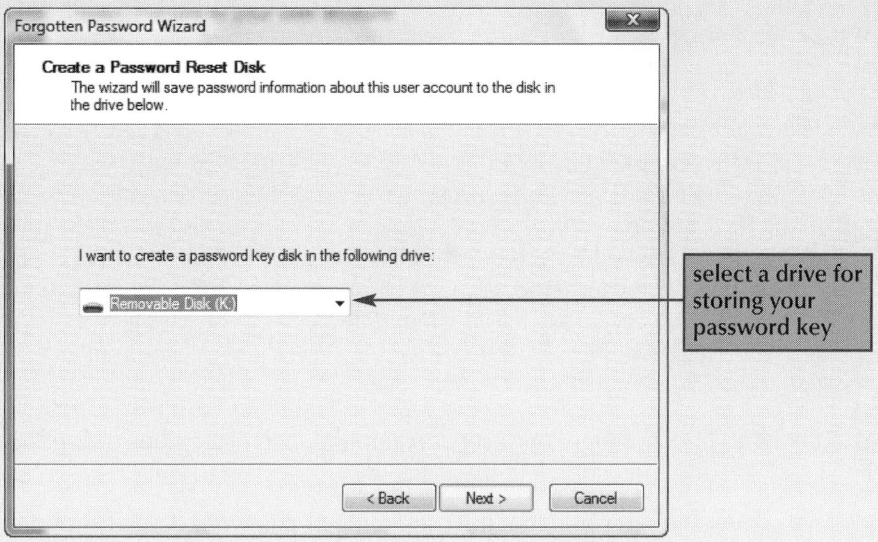

Forgotten Password Wizard

Create a Password Reset Disk

The wizard will save password information about this user account to the disk in the drive below.

I want to create a password key disk in the following drive:

Removable Disk (K:)

< Back | Next > | Cancel

select a drive for storing your password key

5. Click the **I want to create a password key disk in the following drive** list arrow, select the disk drive that contains your flash drive, and then click the **Next** button. At the next step, the Forgotten Password Wizard prompts for the password to your user account.
6. In the Current user password box, type your **current password**, and then click the **Next** button. The Forgotten Password Wizard then shows you the progress of creating the Password Reset Disk.
7. After the Forgotten Password Wizard notes that the operation is complete, click the **Next** button. In the last step, the Forgotten Password Wizard recommends that you keep this disk in a safe place.
8. Click the **Finish** button to close the Forgotten Password Wizard dialog box, and then close the User Accounts window.

Tip

After you create a Password Reset Disk, you want to test it so that you can be sure it works when you need it.

If you examine your flash drive, you will discover a new file with the name "userkey.psw" that contains information for resetting your user account password if you forget your password.

Reference Window | Creating a Password Reset Disk

- If necessary, insert a flash drive, DVD, or CD, and then close any windows that open.
- On the Start menu, click Control Panel, click the User Accounts and Family Safety link in the Control Panel window, and then click the User Accounts link. (If you are using the Business Edition of Windows Vista, click the first and second User Accounts link after you open the Control Panel.)
- Under Tasks, click the Create a password reset disk link and read the information about creating a Password Reset Disk in the Forgotten Password Wizard dialog box.
- Click the Next button, and then click the "I want to create a password key disk in the following drive" list arrow, select a disk drive, and then click the Next button.
- At the next step, type your current password in the "Current user password box," and then click the Next button.
- After the Forgotten Password Wizard creates a Password Reset Disk in the next step, click the Next button, and at the last step, click the Finish button to close the Forgotten Password Wizard dialog box.
- Close the User Accounts window.

If you attempt to log on under your user account and can't remember your password, enter any password and then complete these steps:

- After Windows Vista informs you that the user name or password that you entered is incorrect, click the OK button, and when prompted to log into the same account again, click Reset password.
- After Windows Vista opens the Password Reset Wizard dialog box, it explains the purpose of this wizard. When ready, advance to the next step where the Password Reset Wizard prompts you to insert your Password Reset Disk.
- Insert your Password Reset Disk, and then advance to the next step where the Password Reset Wizard prompts you to select the disk drive with your Password Reset Disk.
- Select the disk drive, and then advance to the next step where you reset your user account password and provide a new password hint. The Password Reset Wizard also notes that your new password will replace your old password, but everything else about your user account remains the same.
- Enter a new password in the "Type a new password" box, enter the same password again in the "Type the password again to confirm" box, enter a new hint in the "Type a new password hint" box, and then advance to the next step.
- The Password Reset Wizard informs you that you've successfully reset the password and notes that you can now log on with the new password. Click the Finish button to complete this process and return to the Welcome screen so that you can now log into your user account.

Many users occasionally forget account passwords, especially when they have so many different types of accounts with different passwords and PINs. To guarantee access to your user account, you can make sure that you have a way back in if you forget your user account password.

Creating Strong Passwords

No matter what type of account you have, you should have a strong password that reduces the chances that someone might guess your password or that someone might use a program to crack your password. The latter also applies to hackers and malicious Web sites.

Microsoft's Help and Support recommends the following approach to creating strong passwords:

- Create a password that contains eight or more characters (the more the better). In certain networked environments, you might need to limit the number of characters in a password. You can ask your network administrator if there are any restrictions or limitations for passwords.
- Do not use all or part of your name or your company's name as a password. Likewise, do not use your child's name, your pet's name, or the name of someone close to you as a password.
- Do not use a complete word as your password; instead, modify it in some way that's easy for you to remember. For example, you might remove or replace certain characters or scramble the characters in some way.
- In your password, mix uppercase and lowercase characters, include one or more numbers and symbols, and include spaces so as to further reduce the chance of someone cracking the password. You can also use numbers or other characters that resemble actual characters in a password. By randomly combining different characters, numbers, symbols, and spaces, you can create an even stronger password; however, the password also becomes more difficult to recall.
- Use misspellings in your password. In other words, substitute other characters for correctly used characters in a password.

If feasible, change your password on a regular basis. Make sure your next password is not similar to your previous password. Since people today rely on many different passwords for many different types of accounts and access systems, you may need to record your passwords on paper or in an encrypted or password-protected file in case you forget a password. If you record a password on paper, make sure you do not identify it as a password or as a password for a specific account, but instead identify it using some personal association unique to the way you think.

Using Windows Firewall

A firewall is software (or perhaps hardware) that performs two basic types of operations:

- **Monitors incoming traffic from the Internet or a network** A firewall protects your computer from hackers that attempt to gain access to your computer while you are on the Internet and from Web sites that attempt to install malicious software on your computer. A firewall can also prevent Internet worms from gaining access to your computer while you are connected to the Internet or another type of network.
- **Monitors outgoing traffic from your computer to the Internet or a network** A firewall also prevents malicious software (and other programs) already installed on your computer from connecting to the Internet, a Web site, or another computer network without your knowledge or permission.

In both instances, the firewall can permit or block incoming or outgoing traffic. For example, if you open your Web browser and initiate a request to visit a specific Web site, your firewall knows that this request originated from your computer. When the Web server at the Web site responds, the firewall permits traffic from that Web site so that you can view its Web page. If a hacker or Internet worm attempts to access your computer, the firewall knows that you did not originate that request from your computer, so it blocks access and prevents the hacker or Internet worm from gaining access to your computer. If an unknown program on your computer attempts to connect to the Internet or to a Web site, your firewall will either prevent that outgoing communication or warn you of the problem and ask you what you want to do. You also can specify which Web sites you will accept communications from and which ones you want to block. To allow communications to or from a program, you can create an **exception**, which is a rule for a program or service that permits the program or service to communicate through a firewall.

Arielle asks you to examine Windows Firewall so that you can later compare it with other firewall products that you might recommend to her new client.

To open Windows Firewall and examine your firewall settings:

1. On the Start menu, click **Control Panel**, click the **Security** link, and then click the **Windows Firewall** link. In the Windows Firewall window, Windows Vista provides you with information about the current state of Windows Firewall. See Figure 7-17. On the computer used for this figure, Windows Firewall is on (the recommended option), it is blocking inbound (unsolicited) communications that do not have an exception, it is set to display a message when it blocks a program, and the network location is a public network. On the left side of the window, you can turn Windows Firewall on or off, and you can allow a program through Windows Firewall.

Figure 7-17 Viewing Windows Firewall settings

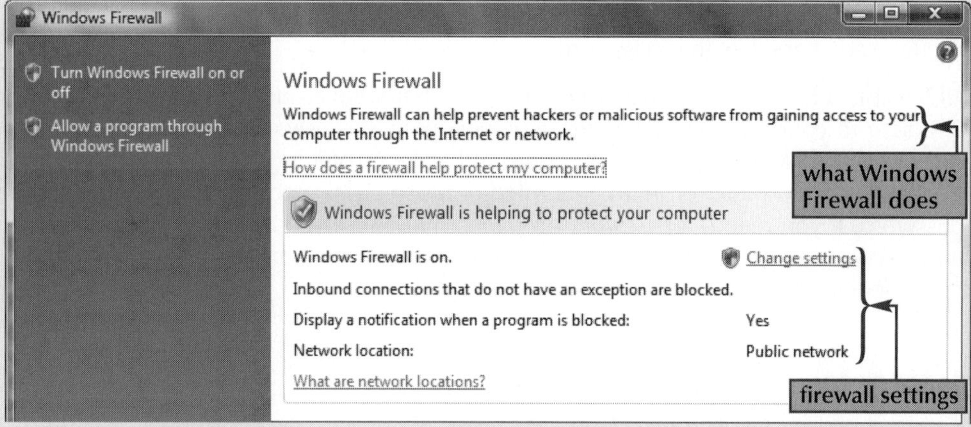

2. Click the **Change settings** link. Windows Vista displays a User Account Control dialog box.
3. In the User Account Control dialog box, click the **Continue** button if you are logged on under an Administrator account, or enter a **password** for an **Administrator account,** and then click the **OK** button if you are logged on under a Standard User account. Windows Vista opens a Windows Firewall Settings dialog box. See Figure 7-18.

Figure 7-18 Viewing general Windows Firewall settings

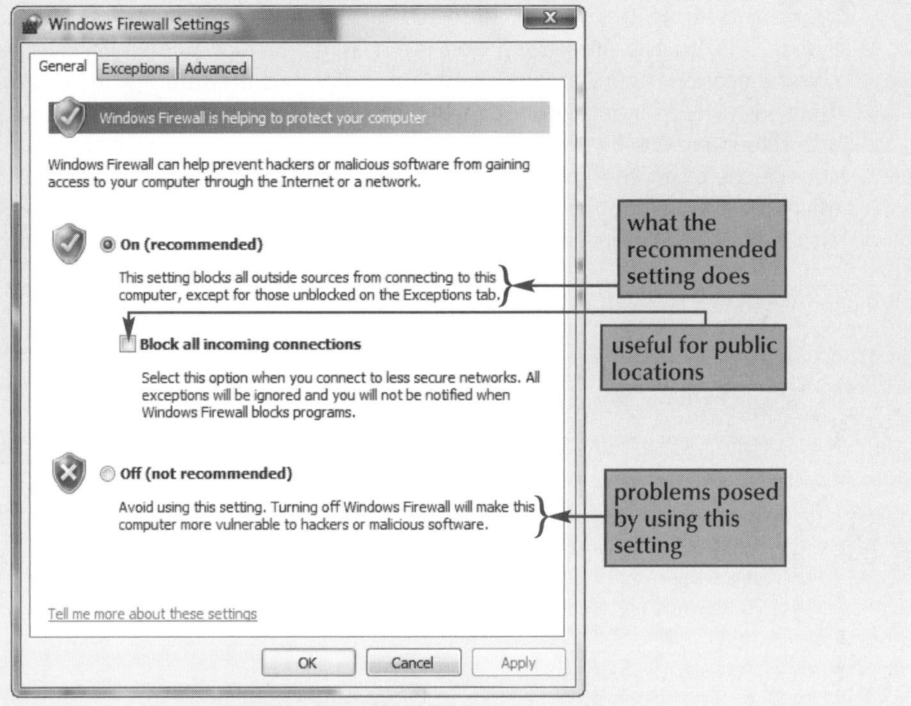

On the General property sheet, Windows Vista notes that Windows Firewall can help prevent hackers or malicious software from gaining access to your computer through the Internet or a network. The General property sheet also shows whether Windows Firewall is enabled. The default On (recommended) option blocks all outside sources from gaining access to your computer unless you specifically authorize access on the Exceptions property sheet. You only use the Off (not recommended) option if you rely on another firewall software product.

Choosing the Right Network Location | InSight

When you first connect to a network, you choose one of three network locations: Home, Work, or Public place. The Home or Work network locations are appropriate choices for small home and office networks where you trust the people and devices on the network. The Public place network location is useful when you connect to a network in a public place, such as an airport. This option makes your computer invisible to other computers on the same network and therefore offers additional protection for your computer.

If you use Windows Firewall, and if you need to connect to a less secure network or the Internet, such as a network in a public place, you can enable the option for blocking all incoming connections, and Windows Firewall will ignore all exceptions. However, you will still be able to originate a request from your computer and view most Web pages as well as send and receive e-mail messages and instant messages.

To continue your examination of firewall settings:

1. Click the **Exceptions** tab. From this property sheet, you can enable specific programs and services as well as add and edit exceptions for programs and ports. See Figure 7-19. In this situation, a port is a specific location in memory over which a communication occurs between your computer and the Internet (or vice-versa). That port acts as a gateway into and out of your computer. (You can think of a port as a telephone line for transmissions from another phone to your phone or from your phone to another phone.) On this computer, an exception is enabled for Microsoft Office Outlook so that it can communicate through the firewall. Notice also that Windows Firewall automatically informs you if it blocks a program.

Figure 7-19 Viewing Windows Firewall exceptions

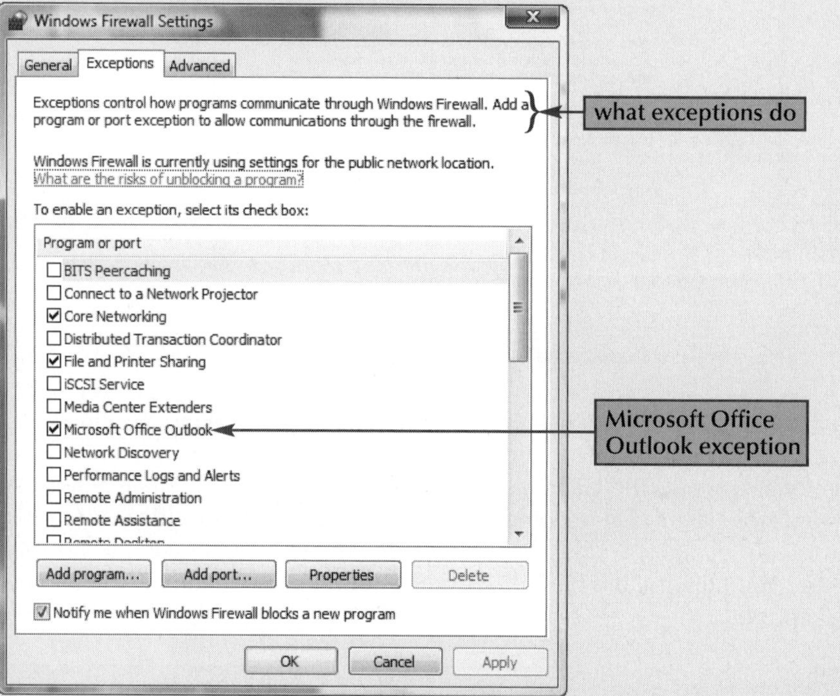

You can use the Add program button to select a program installed on your computer, such as Adobe Acrobat Reader, so that it can communicate through the firewall. When you specify a program exception, Windows Firewall allows the program to communicate through the firewall only when you use the program to access the Internet or a network.

2. Click the **Advanced** tab. Under Network connection settings, Windows Firewall identifies which connections it protects. See Figure 7-20. You can use the Restore Defaults button under Default settings to restore Windows Firewall's original settings.

Viewing firewall-protected network connections — Figure 7-20

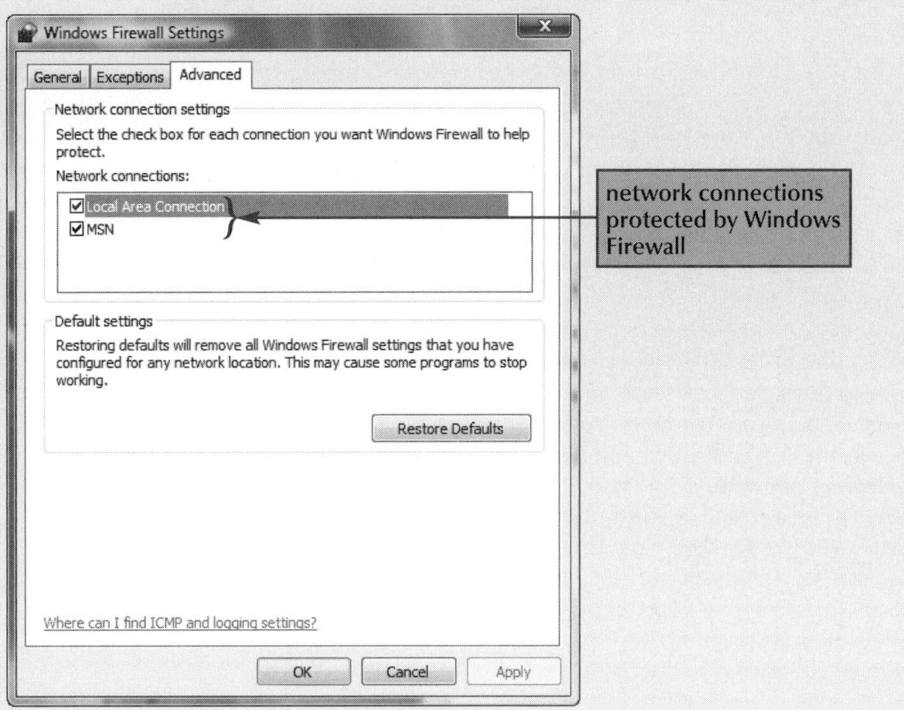

3. If you have made changes to Windows Firewall settings on your computer that you want to keep, click the **OK** button; otherwise, click the **Cancel** button to close the Windows Firewall Settings dialog box.
4. Close the Windows Firewall window and the Security window.

Microsoft recommends that you use only one firewall software product on your computer because two firewalls might conflict with each other.

Reference Window | Viewing and Changing Windows Firewall Settings

- On the Start menu, click Control Panel, click the Security link, and then click the Windows Firewall link.
- Verify that Windows Firewall is enabled on your computer if you do not use any other firewall, or if you do use another firewall, verify that Windows Firewall is turned off.
- Click the Change Settings link, and after Windows Vista displays a User Account Control dialog box, click the Continue button if you are logged on under an Administrator account, or enter a password for an Administrator account, and then click the OK button if you are logged on under a Standard User account.
- On the General property sheet of the Windows Firewall Settings dialog box, verify that Windows Firewall is on if you do not use any other firewall, or turn Windows Firewall off if you use another firewall.
- Click the Exceptions tab, review the list of programs and exceptions, enable or disable exceptions, and if necessary, use the Add program button to select and enable a program installed on your computer so that it can communicate through the firewall.
- Click the Advanced tab, and under Network connection settings, verify that Windows Firewall protects the network connections on your computer, or use the Restore Defaults button under Default settings to restore Windows Firewall's original settings.
- Click the OK button to close the Windows Firewall Settings dialog box and apply changes to Windows Firewall settings, or click the Cancel button to exit without making any changes to your current Windows Firewall settings.
- Close the Windows Firewall window and the Security window.

With the combined efforts of Windows Defender, User Account Control, and Windows Firewall, Windows Vista provides far more protection for your computer than previous versions of Windows.

Review | Session 7.1 Quick Check

1. A(n) ________________ is a program that masquerades as a legitimate program, but once a user opens the program, it performs some type of malicious action on the computer or compromises its security.
2. What type(s) of software monitors a user's activities on the Internet and reports information about a user's browsing habits to a third party, such as an advertising company, without that user's knowledge or consent?
3. What two types of techniques rely on the use of e-mail messages that appear to be sent from a reputable company with which a user does business to trick a user into disclosing personal and financial information in order to steal a user's assets or identity?
4. If you receive an e-mail message with an attachment that has the "vbs" file extension from someone you do not know or recognize, would it be safe to open the file extension? Explain.
5. In Windows Defender, ________________ is an important tool that you can use to view information about software running on your computer.
6. ________________ prompts you (and any other users of the same computer) for permission or for the user name and password of an Administrator account before performing an operation that affects the operation of your computer or that affects other users.
7. True or False. In Secure Desktop Mode, you can multitask and perform more than one operation.
8. What type of software monitors incoming traffic from, and outgoing traffic to, the Internet or a network?

Session 7.2

Using Windows Update

Another important tool for protecting your computer is Windows Update. This tool identifies your computer's make and model, the Windows version on your computer, and any other Microsoft software on your computer. Then, it locates and installs software updates that enhance the security and privacy of your computer, improve its performance, and provide new features. Some updates are critical updates, such as security updates, and others are optional, such as driver updates.

Windows Vista enables automatic updating on your computer to automatically identify, download, and install security updates and other important updates. Optional updates are not automatically downloaded and installed; however, you might find some of the optional updates useful. You can also review and choose which updates you want to download. These updates are identified, downloaded, and installed on your computer when you are connected to the Internet. Microsoft notes that the automatic updating of software does not interfere with other operations that you are performing on your computer or with Web browsing. If you disconnect your computer from the Web during a download, that same download picks up where it left off the next time you have an Internet connection.

If you turn off automatic updating, you must remember to periodically check for recommended and optional updates and download and install them on your computer to maintain its security and your privacy.

Since Windows updates are critical to protecting your laptop computer, you and Arielle decide to check for updates.

In the next set of steps, you are going to check for updates for the computer you are using. If you are working in a computer lab where the lab staff is responsible for updating the lab computers, you may not be able to download and install updates. If that is the case, read the following steps and examine the figures, but do not keystroke the following steps.

To open Windows Update and manually check for updates:

1. On the Start menu, point to **All Programs**, and then click **Windows Update**. Windows Vista opens the Windows Update window and displays information about your most recent check for updates, when it last installed updates, your current Automatic Updates setting, and what types of updates it installs on your computer. See Figure 7-21. On the computer used for this figure, Windows Update automatically started checking for Windows updates. You can use the Check for updates link to check for new updates at any time.

Figure 7-21 Checking for Windows updates

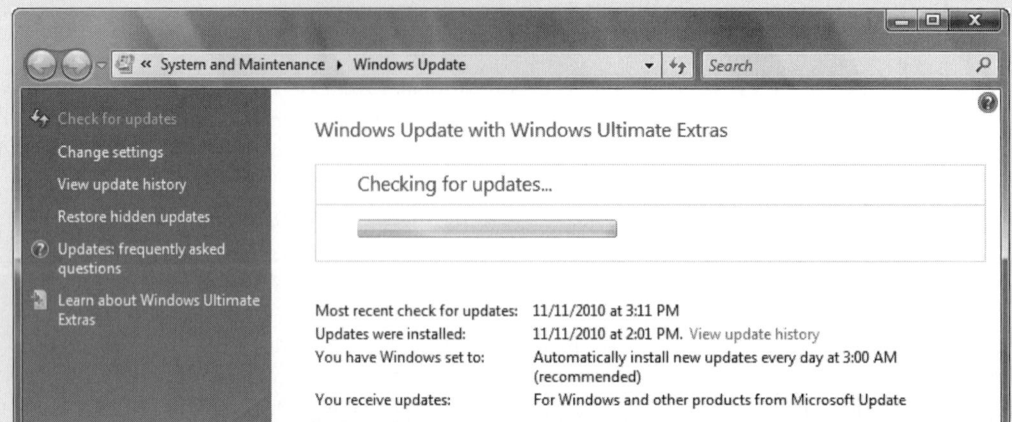

2. Click the **Check for updates** link (if necessary). After checking for updates, Windows Update identifies the number of important updates, the number of optional updates, and any extra updates that are available for your version of Windows. See Figure 7-22. On the computer used for this figure, Windows Update identified 8 important updates, 37 optional updates, and 2 Windows Ultimate Extras updates. Your results will differ. If there are any important updates, you can use the Install updates button to install those updates now, or you can click the View available updates link to examine the proposed updates.

Figure 7-22 Results of scanning a computer for Windows updates

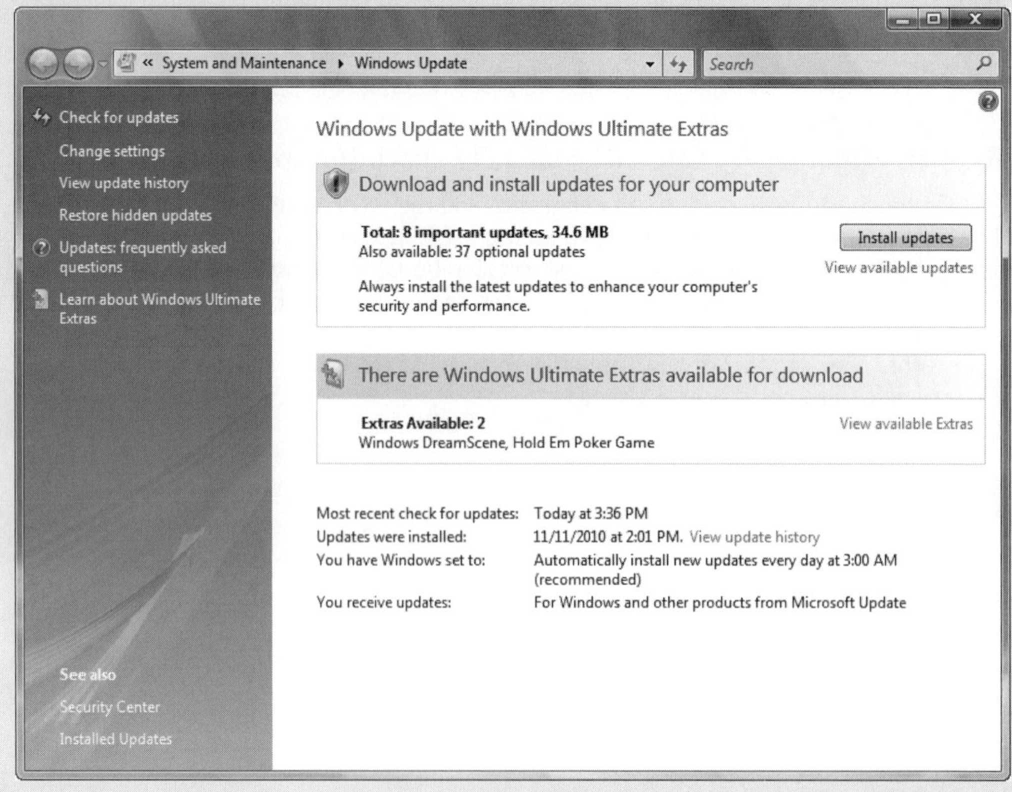

3. If Windows Update identified important updates for your computer, click the **View available updates** link. In the View available updates window, Windows Update lists all the updates currently available for your computer, groups those updates into categories, and identifies whether the updates are important, recommended, or optional. See Figure 7-23. On the computer used for this figure, Windows Update recommends an update to the Windows Malicious Software Removal Tool and a definition update for Windows Defender. The Windows Malicious Software Removal Tool checks for infections by well-known malicious software and helps you remove any infection it finds. Your list of updates will vary since it depends on what updates are available at the time you use Windows Update and on what updates you've previously downloaded and installed. You can pick the updates you want to download and remove those you do not want to download. If automatic updating is enabled on your computer, Windows Update downloads and installs the updates.

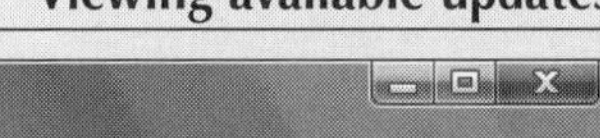
Figure 7-23 Viewing available updates

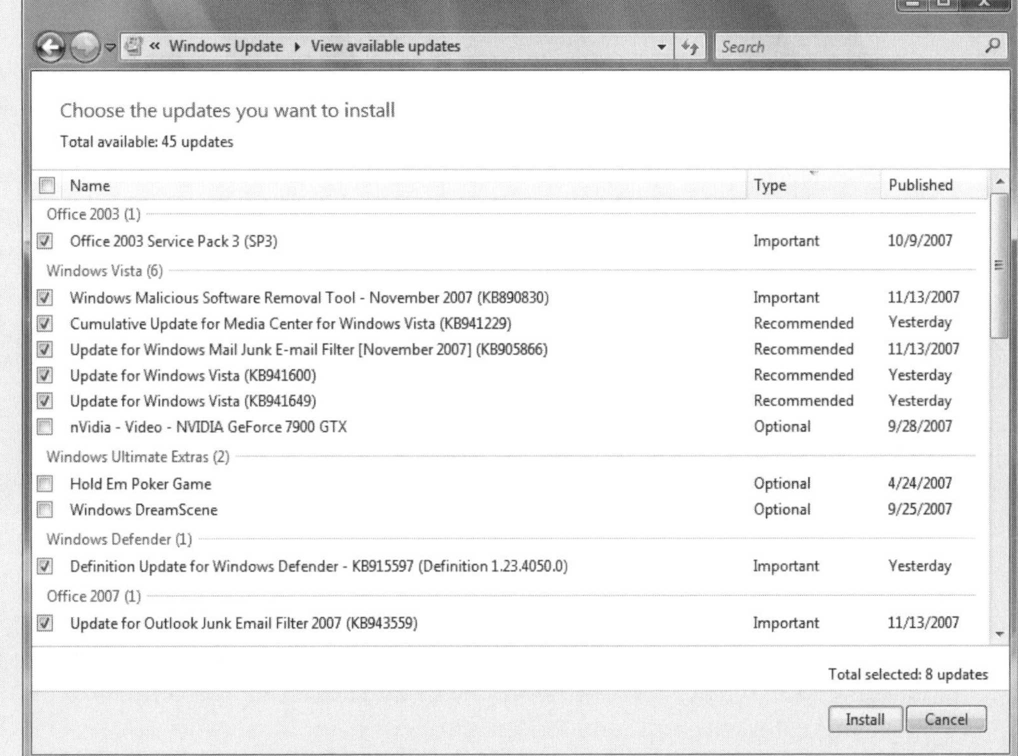

4. If automatic updating is not enabled on your computer, or if you do not want to install any updates, click the **Cancel** button and read the remainder of this step and the next step. If automatic updating is not enabled on your computer, and if you want to download and install updates identified for your computer, select those updates, and then click the **Install** button. Windows Vista displays a User Account Control dialog box.

5. Click the **Continue** button if you are logged on under an Administrator account, or enter the **password** for an Administrator account if you are not logged on under an Administrator account. If you chose the option for downloading one or more updates, Windows Vista shows the progress of downloading the update or updates you selected in the Windows Update window. See Figure 7-24. After downloading and installing updates, Windows Update either informs you that you have to restart your computer to install the updates, or it identifies whether the updates were successfully installed and if more updates are available. See Figure 7-25.

Figure 7-24 Progress of downloading updates

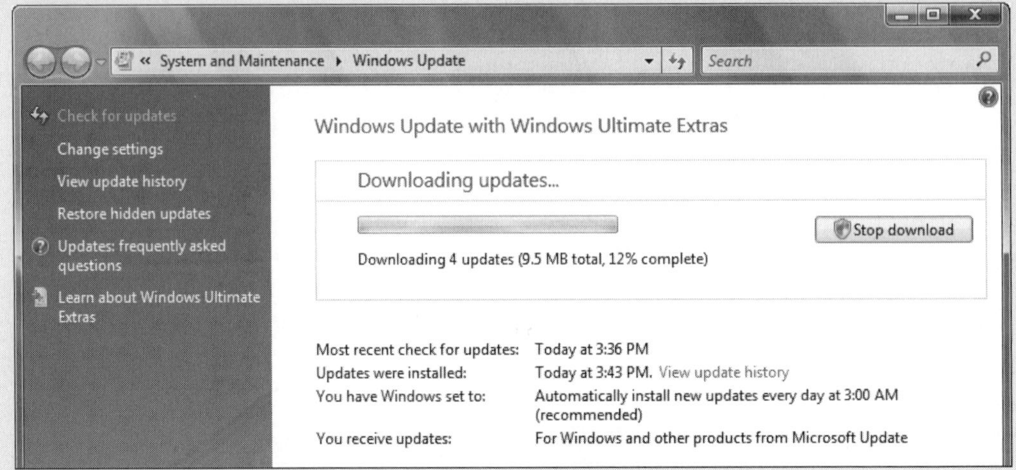

Figure 7-25 Updates successfully installed

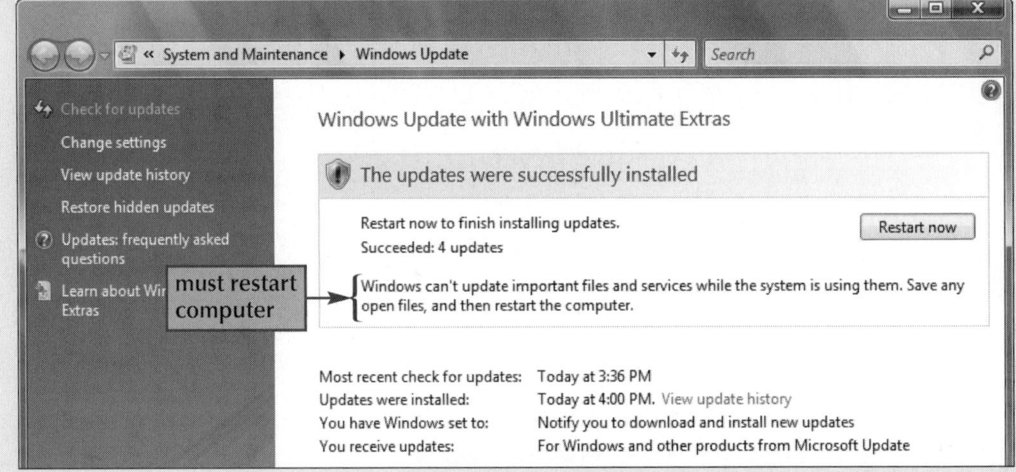

6. If Windows Update informs you that you must restart your computer now to finish installing updates, do not click the Restart now button. You can finish installing those updates later.

7. Keep the Windows Update window open for the next section of the tutorial.

In some cases, you might need to restart your computer to complete the installation of one or more updates. Also, in some cases, Windows Update might need to install an update on your computer before it can install other updates.

Software that you acquire from other software manufacturers may include an option for automatically checking for and downloading updates. If not, it's a good idea to periodically visit the software manufacturer's Web site and manually check for updates. Windows Update might also identify device driver updates for hardware on your computer, or you might need to visit the Web site of a hardware manufacturer to check for and download updated device drivers, and perhaps, also download and install other software for those hardware devices. However, if your hardware is working properly, you should be wary of downloading and installing hardware updates that may affect your use of your hardware.

Using Windows Update | Reference Window

- On the Start menu, point to All Programs, click Windows Update, and in the Windows Update window, examine the information on your most recent check for updates, when Windows Update last installed updates, your current setting for automatically updating Windows Vista, and what types of updates Windows Update installs on your computer.
- To check for updates, click the Check for Updates button, and after Windows Update completes the check for updates, examine the information on the number of important updates, the number of optional updates, and any extra updates that are available for your version of Windows.
- If Windows Update identified important updates for your computer, click the View available updates link and examine the list of updates currently available for your computer.
- If you want to download and install updates identified for your computer, select those updates, click the Install button, and in the User Account Control dialog box, click the Continue button if you are logged on under an Administrator account, or enter the password for an Administrator account if you are not logged on under an Administrator account.
- After downloading and installing updates, close the Windows Update window.

Because software technology changes rapidly, and new updates are constantly available to protect and secure your computer and enhance its features, you should make sure that your computer's software is up to date.

Checking Your Update History and Windows Update Settings

You might need to check your update history and verify that all important updates are installed, or you might want to remove updates if you encounter an unexpected problem after downloading and installing an update. You should also check and verify that the settings that Windows Update uses for automating your computer meet your specific needs.

After downloading updates for your computer, you decide to take a moment to review a history of updates made to your laptop computer.

To view your update history and Windows Update settings:

1. In the Windows Update window, click the **View update history** link in the left pane. In the View update history window, Windows Vista lists the names of all successfully installed, pending, failed, and canceled updates. It also notes whether each update was an important, recommended, or optional update. On the computer used for Figure 7-26, Windows Vista shows important and recommended updates that are pending or were successful or canceled. If you want to remove an update, you can click the Installed Updates link to select and uninstall that update.

Figure 7-26 **Viewing your Windows Update history**

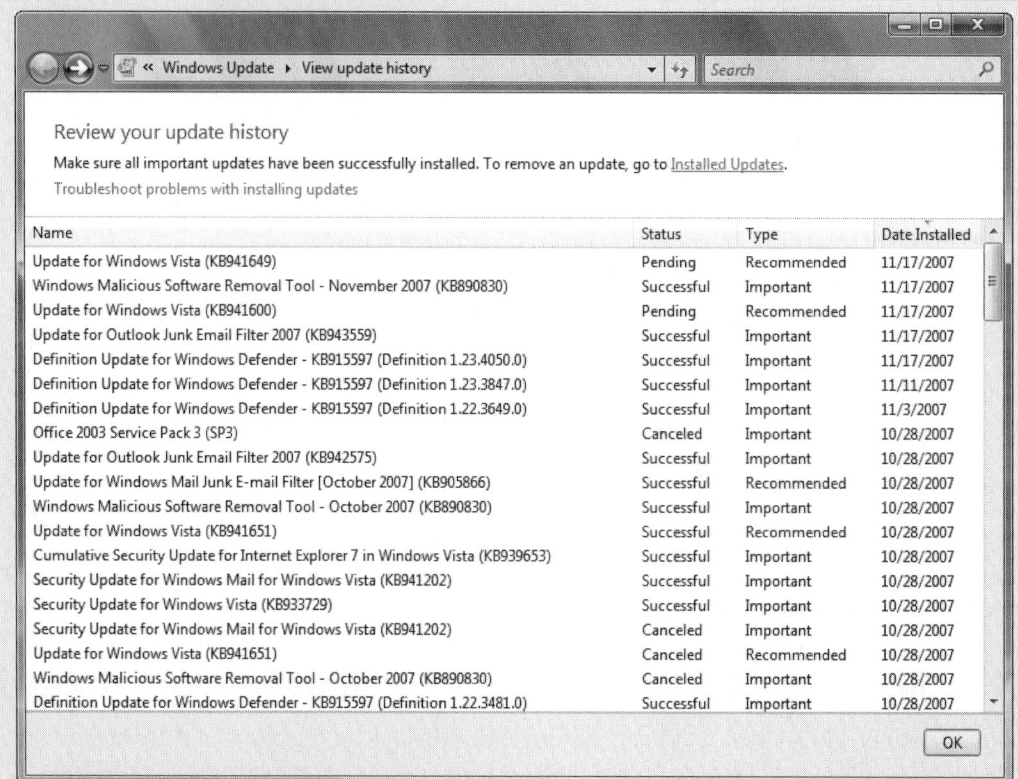

2. Click the **Installed Updates** link. In the Installed Updates window, Windows Vista organizes updates into groups, identifies the update by name, which program the update applies to, and the publisher of each update, and lists when the update was installed. See Figure 7-27. If you want to uninstall or change an update, you first select the update, and then click the Uninstall or Change button on the command bar. Microsoft Windows and Microsoft Office updates include a Knowledge Base article number after the update name in parentheses (with KB at the beginning of the Knowledge Base article number). If you want more information about an update, you can visit the Microsoft Web site and search for the Knowledge Base article by using its article number.

Figure 7-27 Viewing installed updates

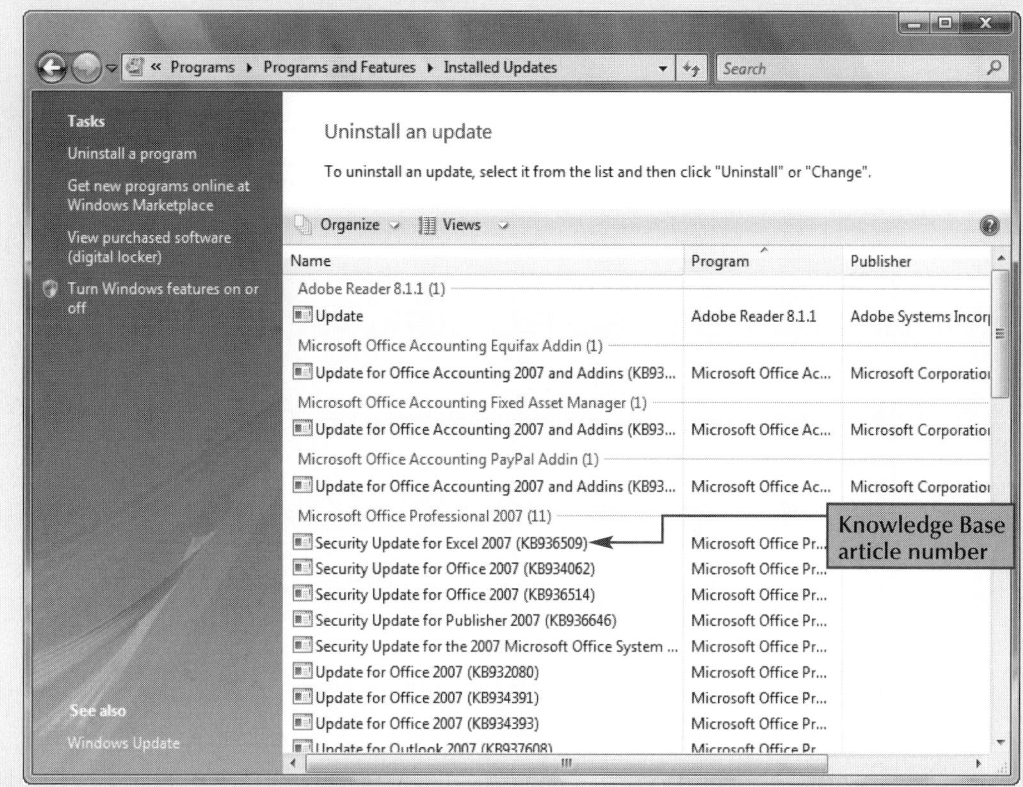

3. Click the **Windows Update** link at the bottom of the left pane to return to the Windows Update window. The "Restore hidden updates" link in the left side of the window displays a list of updates that you had previously instructed Windows Vista not to automatically install or to notify you about. Once you display hidden updates, you can choose to install them if you have changed your mind.

4. Click the **Change settings** link on the left side of the window. In the Change settings window, you can choose how Windows Vista installs updates. See Figure 7-28. The first option, "Install updates automatically (recommended)," is the default option used by Windows Vista because it guarantees that your computer always has the most recent updates. Windows Vista automatically checks for updates each day at 3:00 a.m.; however, you can change this schedule. The second option, "Download updates but let me choose whether to install them," makes updates available by downloading them to your computer, and then you can choose when to install them. The third option, "Check for updates but let me choose whether to download and install them," informs you of when updates are available, but lets you review those updates and decide what you want to download and when you want to download them. This option is useful if you have a slow dial-up connection or a slower connection with your ISP. The last option, "Never check for updates (not recommended)," turns off automatic updating but requires that you remember to check for and download and install updates. Under Recommended updates, you can decide whether Windows Update downloads, installs, and notifies you of recommended updates. If the "Use Microsoft Update" option under Update Service is enabled, you will receive updates for Windows and other products from Microsoft Update.

Figure 7-28 Viewing Windows Update settings

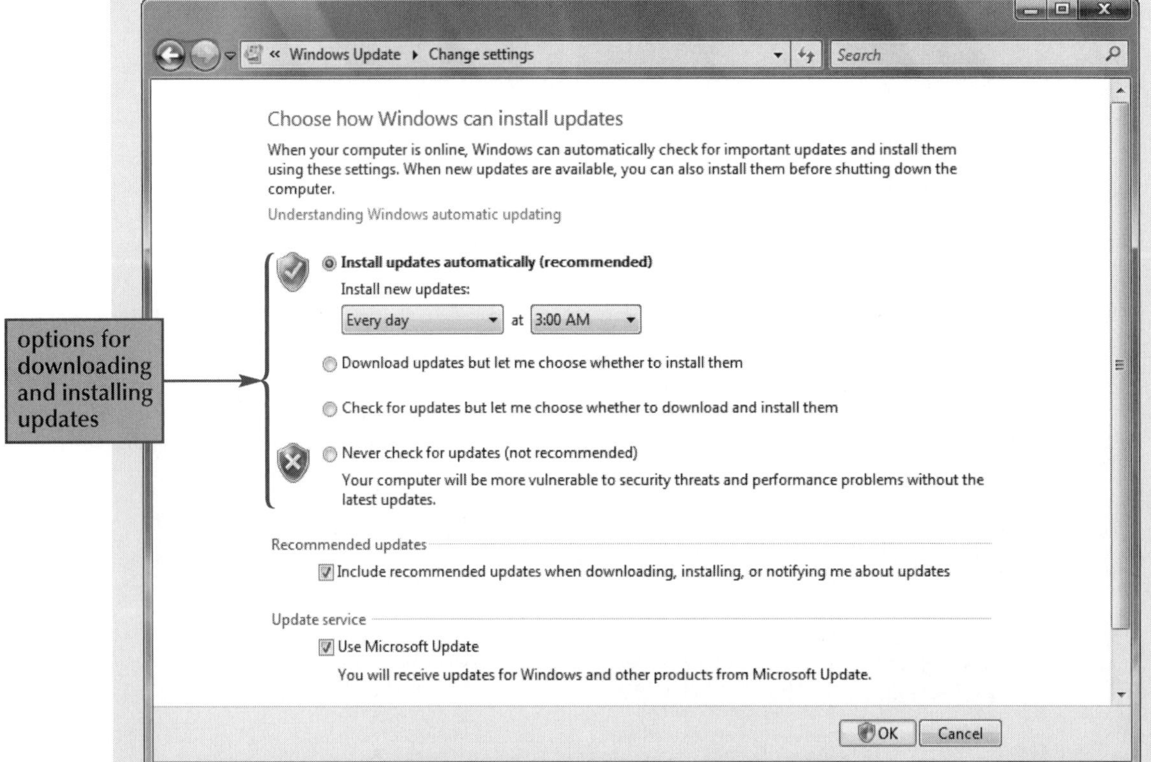

5. If you want to exit the Change settings window without making any changes to Windows Update settings, click the **Cancel** button. If you made any changes to Windows Update settings that you want to apply to your computer, click the **OK** button, and then click the **Continue** button in the User Account Control dialog box if you are logged on under an Administrator account, or enter the **password** for an Administrator account, and then click the **OK** button.
6. Close the Windows Update window.

Because of the frequency with which Microsoft releases new security and critical Windows updates, you should choose one of the options for downloading and installing updates or of informing you of the availability of updates.

Checking Your Windows Update History and Settings | Reference Window

- On the Start menu, point to All Programs, click Windows Update, and view the information on the current status of Windows updates.
- Click the View update history link in the left pane, and then examine the information on successfully installed, pending, failed, and canceled updates.
- To view more detailed information about installed updates or to remove an update, click the Installed Updates link, and then examine information on installed updates.
- If you want to uninstall or change an update, select the update, and then click the Uninstall button or the Change button on the command bar.
- Click Windows Update at the bottom of the left pane.
- To view a list of updates that you had previously instructed Windows Vista not to automatically install or to notify you about, click the "Restore hidden updates" link on the left side of the window. If you want to install a hidden update, select the update and choose the option to install it.
- To view or change Windows Update settings, click the Change settings link on the left side of the window; select the option you want to use for installing updates; choose whether you want Windows Update to download, install, and notify you of recommended updates; and decide whether you want to receive updates for Windows and other products from Microsoft Update.
- If you want to exit the Change settings window without making any changes to Windows Update settings, click the Cancel button. If you made any changes to Windows Update settings that you want to apply to your computer, click the OK button, and then click the Continue button in the User Account Control dialog box if you are logged on under an Administrator account, or enter the password for an Administrator account, and then click the OK button.
- Close the Windows Update window.

The Automatic Updates feature is a convenient way to protect your computer and to improve the capabilities of Windows Vista and your other Microsoft software.

Using the Windows Vista Security Center

The Windows Vista Security Center provides information about the following settings on your computer:

- **Firewall** The Security Center identifies the name of the firewall used to protect your computer and its status, namely, whether it is enabled or not. If you are not using a firewall, or if Windows Firewall is not enabled, it informs you of this security issue. Since Windows Vista may not detect all firewalls, you might need to specify that you have a firewall that you will take responsibility for monitoring.
- **Automatic updating** If you have chosen an option other than the default setting of installing updates automatically, Windows Vista will report that automatic updating is off and recommend that you turn on automatic updating to enhance the security and performance of your computer.
- **Malware protection** The Security Center identifies the antivirus software and the antispyware software used to protect your computer against spyware and other malicious software. Since Windows Vista may not detect all antivirus and antispyware, you might need to specify that you have antivirus and antispyware that you will take responsibility for monitoring.

- **Other security settings** The Security Center also identifies whether your Internet security settings are set to their recommended levels and whether User Account Control is enabled.

If Windows Vista detects a problem with one of these security settings, it flags that security setting in the Security Center and displays a Security Center icon in the notification area of the taskbar to alert you of the security problem found by the Security Center. You can then double-click the Security Center icon in the notification area to open the Windows Security Center and check, adjust, or troubleshoot security settings.

Because these settings affect the security of your computer, it is a good idea to check them and to pay attention to Windows Security Alerts displayed in the notification area.

As a follow-up to examining the security settings already recommended by Arielle, you decide to open the Security Center and examine the status of all your security settings.

To open the Security Center and check security settings:

1. On the Start menu, click **Control Panel**, click the **Security** link, and then click the **Security Center** link. Windows Vista opens the Security Center and provides information on your Firewall, Automatic updating, Malware protection, and Other security settings. On the computer used for Figure 7-29, the Windows Security Center notes that the Firewall, Automatic updating, and Malware protection are On and that Other security settings are OK. This is the ideal state and affords your computer the maximum amount of protection. Your settings may differ. The Security Center might report that a specific setting is off, not monitored, or that you need to check your settings. Also, if the Security Center detects a problem with one of the security settings, it expands the category automatically after you open the Windows Security Center so that you can immediately view information about the problem.

Figure 7-29 Viewing Windows Security Center settings

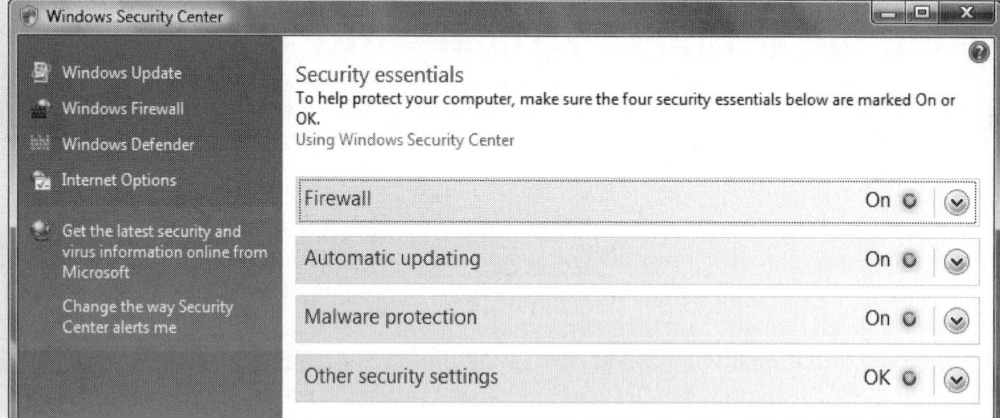

2. Click the **Details** button on the right side of the Firewall section to expand this section and view your current firewall settings. As shown for the computer in Figure 7-30, the Security Center reports that Windows Firewall is actively protecting the computer. If you use another firewall, the Security Center will either report the name of the firewall or note if it cannot detect it. As pointed out earlier, it also notes that you should not use two or more firewalls at the same time because they might conflict with each other. Your firewall setting may differ.

Viewing the status of a computer's firewall — Figure 7-30

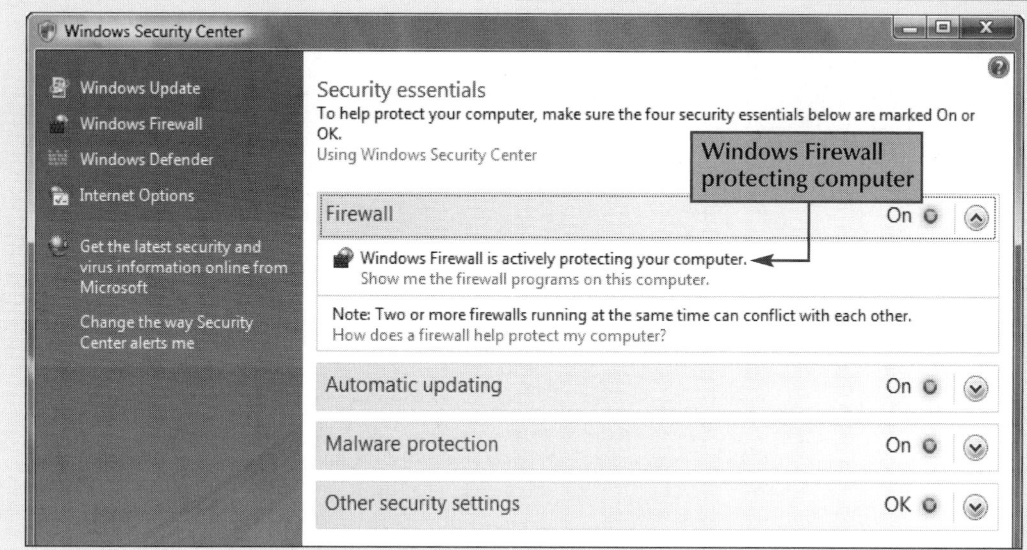

3. Click the **Details** button on the right side of the Firewall section to hide the details of your firewall settings.

4. Click the **Details** button on the right side of the Automatic updating section to view your current settings for updating Windows and other Microsoft software. If Automatic updating is enabled, the Security Center informs you that Windows Vista installs updates as they become available. If Automatic updating is set to notify you after updates are downloaded and ready to install, or if Automatic updating is set to notify you when updates are available and ready to download and install, the Security Center will inform you that Automatic updating is "Not automatic." If you have specified that you do not want Windows Vista to automatically check for updates, the Security Center will inform you that Automatic updating is off.

5. Click the **Details** button on the right side of the Automatic updating section to hide the details of your Windows Update settings.

6. Click the **Details** button on the right side of the Malware protection section. The Security Center shows the status of Virus protection as well as Spyware and other malware protection. As shown in Figure 7-31, the Windows Security Center identifies the antivirus software used on this computer (in this case, PC Tools AntiVirus), and it reports that the antivirus software is up to date and that virus scanning is on. The Windows Security Center also reports that Windows Defender is actively protecting this computer against spyware and malware. Your antivirus and malware protection programs might differ, and your Windows Security Center settings for your antivirus and malware protection might differ.

Figure 7-31 **Viewing Windows Security Center settings**

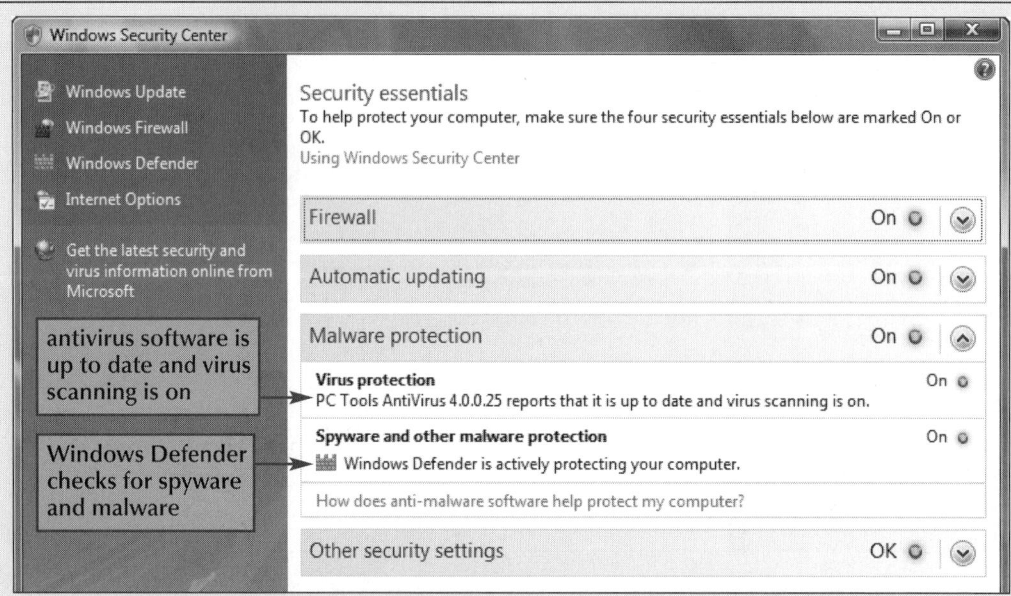

If you are not using antivirus software on your computer, or if the Security Center does not detect any antivirus software on your computer, it will report that it did not find any antivirus software on your computer. You can click the "Show me my available options" link to specify that you will monitor your antivirus software or specify that the Security Center should not monitor your virus protection. In either case, the Security Center will not monitor the status of your antivirus software, will not alert you if your antivirus software is out-of-date and needs updating, and will not alert you if your virus protection is turned off. If you click "Find a program," then Windows Vista connects you to the Windows Vista Security Software Providers Web page where Microsoft lists security software that is compatible with Windows Vista, as shown in Figure 7-32. Your view may differ.

Figure 7-32 Security software providers

7. Click the **Details** button on the right side of the Malware protection section to hide the details on your Malware protection settings.

8. Click the **Details** button on the right side of the Other security settings section to expand and view this section. The Security Center shows you the status of your Internet security settings (which you will examine in more detail in the next section of the tutorial) and your User Account Control setting. As shown in Figure 7-33, the Security Center also notes that the Internet security settings on the computer used for this figure are OK. These Internet security settings, however, only apply to Windows Internet Explorer. If you use another Web browser, you need to check the security and privacy settings for that Web browser. Your User Account Control setting should be on, especially if you decide not to use antivirus or antispyware software on your computer. Your settings may differ.

Figure 7-33 **Viewing Internet security and User Account Control settings**

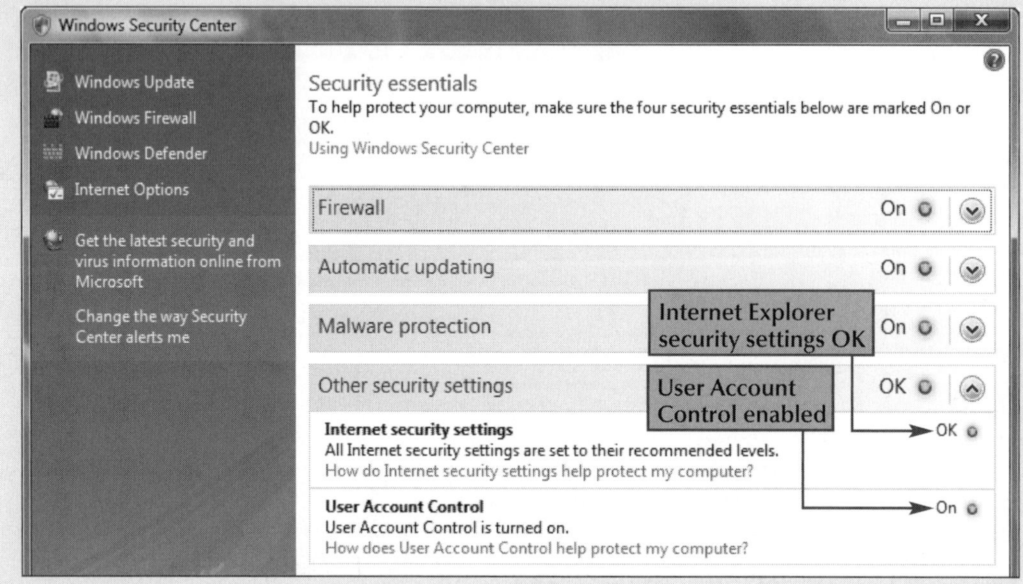

9. Close the Windows Security Center window and the Security window.

These types of checks by the Windows Security Center alert you to problems and are critical to maintaining a secure computer system.

Checking Windows Internet Explorer Security and Privacy Settings

If you use the Windows Internet Explorer Web browser (or any other Web browser), you should examine its security and privacy settings and verify that your Web browser is properly configured for your needs. If you use more than one Web browser, you should check each Web browser's security and privacy settings.

You can check Windows Internet Explorer settings in several ways:

- **Using Windows Internet Explorer** You can open Windows Internet Explorer and use the Tools menu to examine Internet Options (Internet security and privacy settings) and to examine other security features of Windows Internet Explorer.
- **Using Windows Security Center** You can use the Internet Options link in the Windows Security Center to open the Internet Properties dialog box, where you can examine security and privacy settings.
- **Using the Start menu** If Windows Internet Explorer is set as your default Web browser, you can open the Start menu, right-click Internet in the pinned items list, and then chose Internet Properties to examine security and privacy settings.

For other Web browsers, such as Firefox, you must open the Web browser and locate, examine, and adjust its security and privacy settings.

Checking Windows Internet Explorer Security Settings

Windows Internet Explorer organizes Web sites into four security zones, each of which determines the security settings for a Web site.

- **Local intranet** Local intranet sites are Web sites that are part of your company's or organization's intranet. An **intranet** is a private network that relies on the use of Internet technologies and **protocols** (the rules and conventions for transmitting data over a network) and that is limited to a specific group of people, such as employees within a company. By default, these Web sites are secure Web sites that use the **HTTPS protocol** to encrypt and decrypt Web pages that you request and information that you transmit to the Web site. HTTPS stands for "Hypertext Transfer Protocol over Secure Socket Layer" or "HTTP over SSL."
- **Trusted sites** Trusted sites are Web sites that you add to this security zone because you trust that they will not damage your computer or its data.
- **Restricted sites** Restricted sites are Web sites that you designate as ones that could potentially damage your computer or its data.
- **Internet** This security zone includes Web sites not included in the previous three security zones.

You can assign specific Web sites to the Local intranet sites, Trusted sites, and Restricted sites security zones and that, in turn, affects the security setting for those Web sites. Also, each security zone has its own default security level; however, you can also change the security level for each security zone. The security level for the four security zones are as follows:

- **Medium-high for the Internet zone** Windows Internet Explorer prompts you before downloading potentially unsafe content, and it does not download unsigned ActiveX controls without a trusted digital signature. **ActiveX controls** are programs downloaded from a Web site you visit, and they run on your local computer to provide you with access to features at that Web site, such as interactive content. A **digital signature** is an electronic security mark added to a program to verify the publisher of the program (such as Microsoft) and to verify that the program has not been changed. Even if a program has a valid digital signature, that does not mean that it is harmless. You have to use your best judgment as to whether to trust the content in the program by deciding whether you trust the publisher and whether you trust the Web site that downloads the content. **Unsigned ActiveX controls** are ones that have not been verified as safe. You can change the setting for the Internet zone to Medium, Medium-high, or High. A Medium setting is the same as Medium-high. Microsoft notes that a High setting provides the maximum safeguards from potentially harmful content and disables less secure features. Microsoft also notes that Medium-high is appropriate for most Web sites and that High is appropriate for Web sites that might have harmful content. The Medium, Medium-high, and High security levels determine the specific setting used for 46 different types of security settings, all of which you can manually adjust.
- **Medium-low for Local intranet** In most case, Windows Internet Explorer does not prompt you before running content, but like the Internet zone, it does not download unsigned ActiveX controls. You can adjust this level to Low, Medium-low, Medium, Medium-high, and High, or specify custom settings.
- **Medium for Trusted sites** Windows Internet Explorer prompts you before downloading potentially unsafe content and does not download unsigned ActiveX controls. You can adjust this level to Low, Medium-low, Medium, Medium-high, or High, or specify custom settings.

- **High for Restricted sites** This setting provides the maximum protection for your computer from Web sites that you suspect might contain harmful content. You can also specify custom settings for this security zone.

Protected Mode is enabled for three of the four security zones. In **Protected Mode**, Windows Internet Explorer operates with limited privileges and therefore cannot make changes to Windows Registry settings and to files in system and user folders. That, in turn, protects your computer from Web sites that attempt to install malicious software on your computer and from hackers or intruders who attempt to make changes to your computer system. However, Windows Internet Explorer can make changes to specific locations, such as the Temporary Internet Files, History, Cookies, Favorites, and other temporary file folders so that it can provide access to content from Web sites that you visit. If a Web site or Web browser Add-on requires more privileges than otherwise allowed by Protected Mode, a User Account Control dialog box will prompt for Administrator credentials. Also, Protected Mode does not apply to Trusted sites, for obvious reasons.

To protect the security and privacy of client's computers, Arielle and her staff configure Windows Internet Explorer on each computer and work with client's employees on an ongoing basis to make sure their security and privacy settings meet their needs and the company's needs. Arielle asks you to examine and configure Internet Explorer settings on your computer so that they are appropriate for your use.

To examine Windows Internet Explorer Security settings:

Tip

On the right side of the status bar, Windows Internet Explorer indicates whether Protected Mode is On or Off.

1. Open Windows Internet Explorer, click the **Tools** button on the command bar, click **Internet Options**, and then click the **Security** tab in the Internet Options dialog box. Windows Vista displays four security zones—Internet, Local intranet, Trusted sites, and Restricted sites. See Figure 7-34. You can select a security zone to view (by clicking the zone's icon) and, if necessary, change security settings for that security zone. Once you select a security zone, information about that security zone appears under the area that identifies the four security zones. Under "Security level for this zone," Windows Internet Explorer shows the default (or custom) security level for the security zone selected at the top of the property sheet and summarizes features of the security level setting. The default setting for the Internet security zone is Medium-high, but you can change that setting to Medium or High, or you can specify custom settings by using the Custom level button. Also, notice that the Enable Protected Mode check box indicates that Windows Internet Explorer uses Protected Mode for the Internet security zone.

Internet Explorer security settings **Figure 7-34**

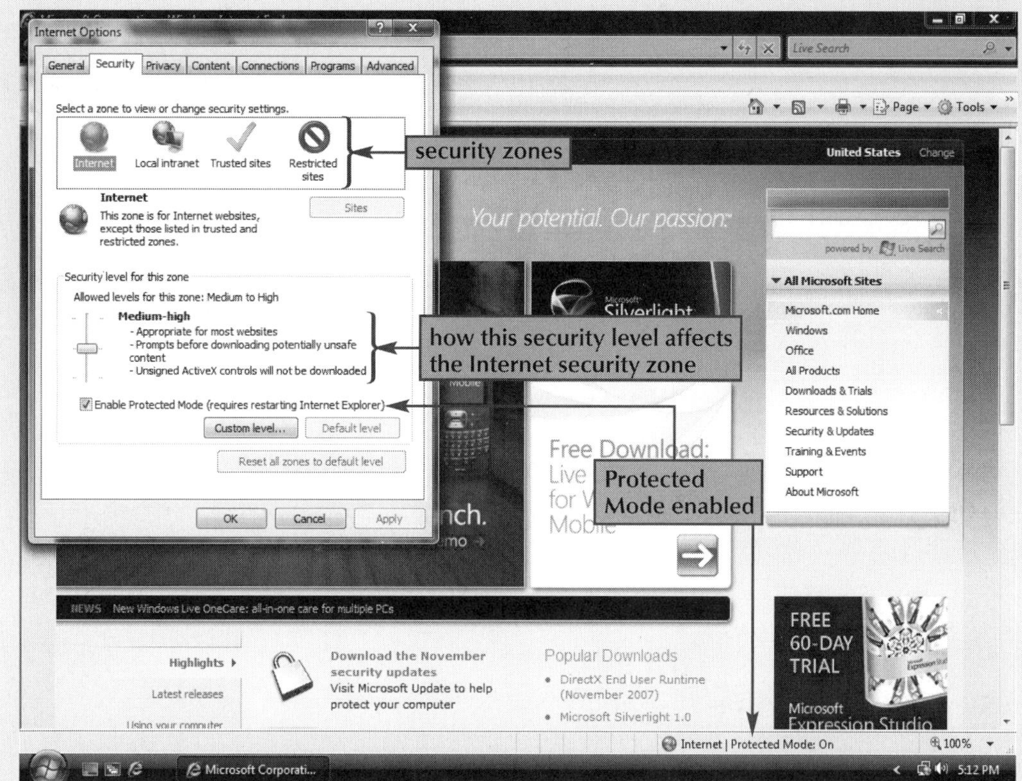

2. Click the **Trusted sites** icon. Notice that the Enable Protected Mode check box indicates that this feature is not enabled for the Trusted sites security zone because you trust Web sites you place in this zone not to harm your computer.

3. Click the **Sites** button. In the Trusted sites dialog box, you can enter the URL for a specific Web site and add it to your Trusted sites security zone if it is a secure site that uses the HTTPS protocol. Windows Internet Explorer notes that all Web sites in this zone will use this zone's security settings. Windows Internet Explorer automatically inserts the URL of the current Web site in the "Add this website to the zone" text box. You might, for example, want to add your online banking Web site to the Trusted sites security zone. See Figure 7-35. If you add a Web site to this security zone and then change your mind, you can open this dialog box, select the Web site, and remove it from this security zone. You can also add Web sites to the Local intranet and Restricted sites security zones in the same way.

Figure 7-35 Option for adding Web sites to the Trusted sites security zone

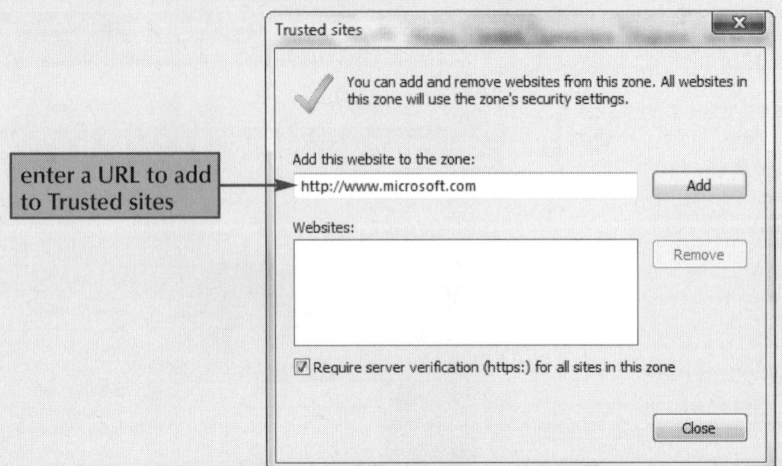

4. Click the **Close** button to close the Trusted sites dialog box.

Using these security zones, you can apply the right security zone settings to the Web sites that you visit.

Controlling Cookie Usage

As noted earlier, a cookie is a text file placed on your computer by a Web site you visit, and it contains information about your visit to that Web site. Although not all Web sites use cookies, their use by many Web sites has raised the issues of **online profiling** and **online privacy** and how information stored in a cookie might be used by the Web site that created the cookie, and perhaps by other Web sites. Advertising agencies are obviously interested in the use of cookies because they can develop a profile of your interests from the Web sites that you visit, and then use this information to develop more effective marketing strategies that promote products you are likely to find interesting and that display that information in customized banner advertising. If you decide that you do not want a Web site unknown to you tracking information about you and developing an online profile of your interests, you can use your Web browser to remove and block future cookies from that Web site.

Cookies can also be useful to you, so you do not want to arbitrarily block all cookies. For example, if you frequently visit the same Web site, and if that Web site requires you to identify yourself, a cookie stored on your computer the first time you visit the site will expedite your access to that same site later. If you visit an interactive gaming site, and advance to different skill levels, that Web site can use a cookie on your computer to identify the skill level you last attained so that you can pick up where you left off when you return. Cookies are also used to track information in online transactions, such as purchasing products or online banking. If you visit a Web site that sells products in different countries, that site might place a cookie on your computer that identifies your country (and therefore your language system). Also, you need to use cookies to access your online e-mail software.

The next group of settings that you want to examine on your laptop is its privacy settings.

To examine Privacy settings:

1. In the Internet Options dialog box, click the **Privacy** tab. Under Settings, Windows Internet Explorer displays the current setting for handling cookies in the Internet security zone. See Figure 7-36. You can use the Settings slider bar to choose an alternate privacy setting, such as Block All Cookies, High, Medium High, Low, or Accept All Cookies.

Figure 7-36 Viewing Internet Explorer privacy settings

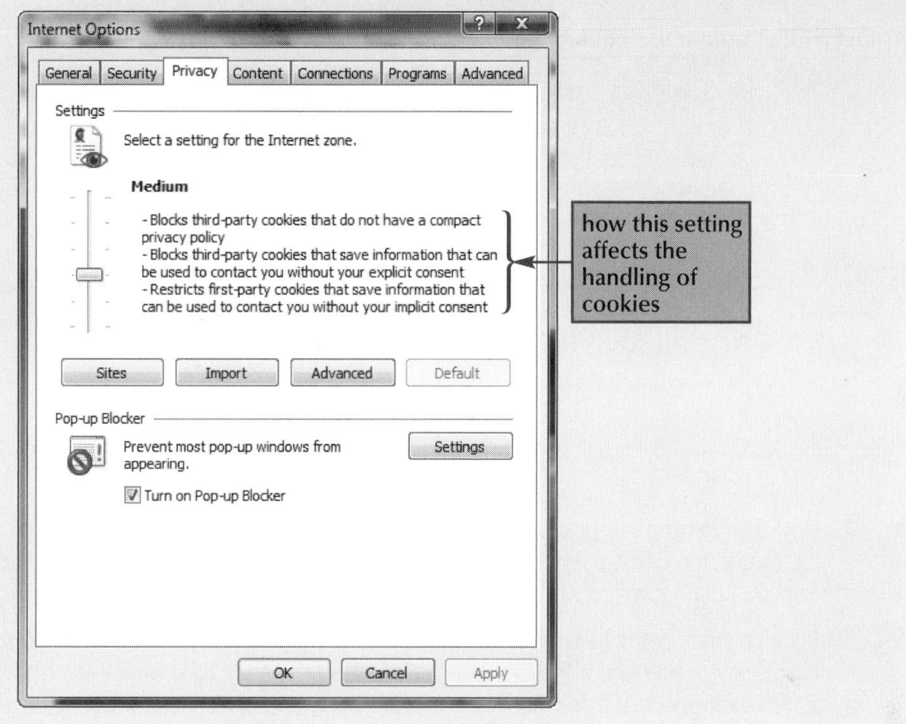

If the security level is set at Medium (the default setting), Windows Internet Explorer blocks cookies from third-party Web sites that do not have a **compact privacy policy** (a condensed privacy statement that you can read), blocks cookies from third-party Web sites that save information that can be used to contact you without your explicit consent, and restricts cookies from first-party Web sites that save information that can be used to contact you without your implicit consent. A **first-party Web site** is a Web site whose Web page you are currently viewing, whereas a **third-party Web site** is another Web site that provides content (such as banner advertising and images) to the Web site you're visiting. **Explicit consent** means that you specifically agreed (in some way) that a Web site can use information it collects about you to contact you. **Implicit consent** means that you have not informed a Web site that you do not want it to use information it collects about you to contact you. In other words, you have not opted out. As you might imagine, what constitutes implicit consent is hard to define.

Windows Internet Explorer lets you override automatic cookie handling and choose to accept or reject a cookie when prompted. You can also specify whether you want to always allow **session cookies**—temporary cookies that expire and are deleted when you close Windows Internet Explorer. In contrast, a **persistent cookie** is one that remains on your computer and that can be read by the Web site that created it when you next visit that Web site.

To further protect your laptop, you want to examine the options for overriding automatic cookie handling.

To override automatic cookie handling:

1. Click the **Advanced** button on the Privacy property sheet, and then click the **Override automatic cookie handling** check box. In the Advanced Privacy Settings dialog box, you can override automatic cookie handling by Windows Internet Explorer and specify whether you want to accept or block first-party and third-party cookies, or whether you want Windows Internet Explorer to always prompt you before accepting a cookie. See Figure 7-37. In the latter case, you can choose to accept or reject a cookie. You can also specify whether you want to always allow session cookies.

Figure 7-37 Overriding automatic cookie handling

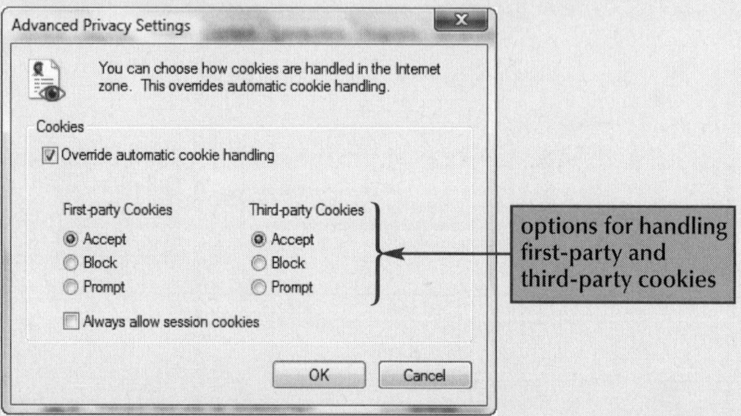

2. Click the **Prompt** option button under First-party Cookies, click the **Prompt** option button under Third-party Cookies, click the **OK** button to close the Advanced Privacy Settings dialog box, and then click the **OK** button in the Internet Options dialog box.
3. Browse to a Web site that you frequently visit (such as microsoft.com or google.com), and if you see a Privacy Alert dialog box similar to the one shown in Figure 7-38, examine the information in the dialog box and verify the URL of the Web site attempting to place a cookie on your computer, click the **Apply my decision to all cookies from this website** check box, click the **Block Cookie** button to block all first-party cookies, and then determine whether blocking cookies affects your access to that Web site. If you see another Privacy Alert dialog box while accessing that same site, examine the information to determine if the cookie comes from another Web site (a third-party Web site with a different URL), click the **Apply my decision to all cookies from this website** check box, and then click the **Block Cookie** button to block all third-party cookies. Since more than one third-party Web site might place cookies on your computer when you visit a Web site, you might see more Privacy Alert dialog boxes for those other third-parties. You will use the information you glean from these Web sites in this step and the following step to allow or block Web sites in the next section.

Figure 7-38 Privacy alert for first-party cookie

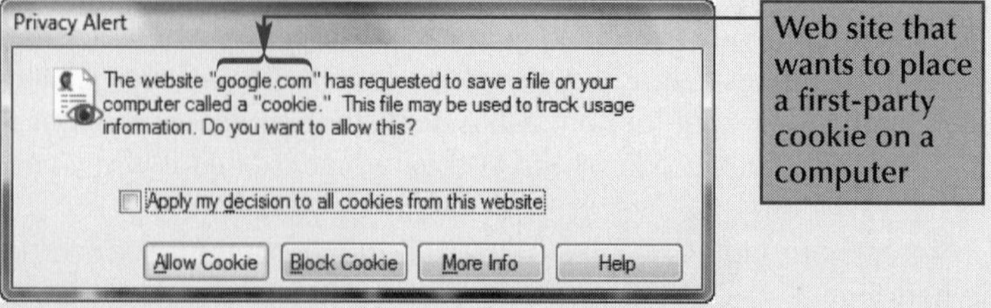

4. Use this same approach to visit several other Web sites that you frequently visit and to block cookies from both first-party and third-party Web sites while at the same time noting which Web sites are placing cookies on your computer. Now, you know which of these Web sites place cookies on your computer and whether other third-party Web sites (typically advertising Web sites) are placing cookies on your computer. You can also use these URLs to visit third-party Web sites to determine the company name and its business purpose, and then decide whether you want them to place cookies on your computer.
5. Click **Tools** on the Windows Internet Explorer command bar, click **Internet Options** on the Tools menu, click the **Privacy** tab in the Internet Options dialog box, click the **Advanced** button on the Privacy property sheet, click **the Override automatic cookie handling** check box (to turn this feature off), click the **OK** button in the Advanced Privacy Settings dialog box, and then click the **Apply** button in the Internet Options dialog box. If you now visit the same Web sites you just visited, they will place cookies on your computer, and Windows Internet Explorer will not display Privacy Alerts.

Now that you know some of the Web sites that place cookies on your computer, you can allow or block cookies from those specific Web sites.

To allow or block cookies from specific Web sites:

1. Click the **Sites** button on the Privacy property sheet. In the Per Site Privacy Actions dialog box, you can specify the URLs of Web sites that are always permitted to use cookies, and you can specify the URLs of Web sites that cannot ever use cookies, regardless of their privacy policies. See Figure 7-39. If you blocked first-party and third-party cookies from an earlier Web site, those Web sites are displayed in the Managed websites list box, and cookies from those Web sites are always blocked, as shown on the computer used for this figure.

Specifying cookie usage by Web site — Figure 7-39

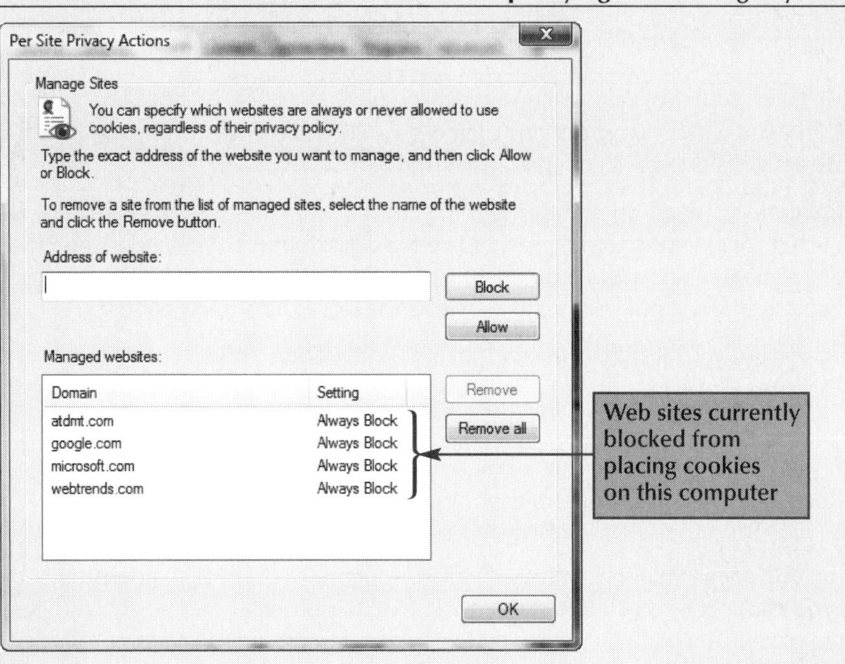

2. In the Managed websites list box, click the **URL** of a Web site that you just visited, and then click the **Remove** button. Windows Internet Explorer removes that Web site from the Managed websites list box, and if you visit that Web site again, Windows Internet Explorer will accept first-party cookies from that Web site. If you also blocked cookies from a third-party Web site earlier, Windows Internet Explorer will continue to block third-party cookies from that Web site.

3. In the Address of website text box, type the **URL** of the Web site that you just removed from the Managed websites list box, and then click the **Allow** button. The URL for that Web site is added to the Managed websites list box, and Windows Internet Explorer will now always accept first-party cookies from that Web site. For example, on the computer used for Figure 7-40, Windows Internet Explorer now accepts all cookies from Microsoft's Web site.

Figure 7-40 **Web site allowed to place cookies on a computer**

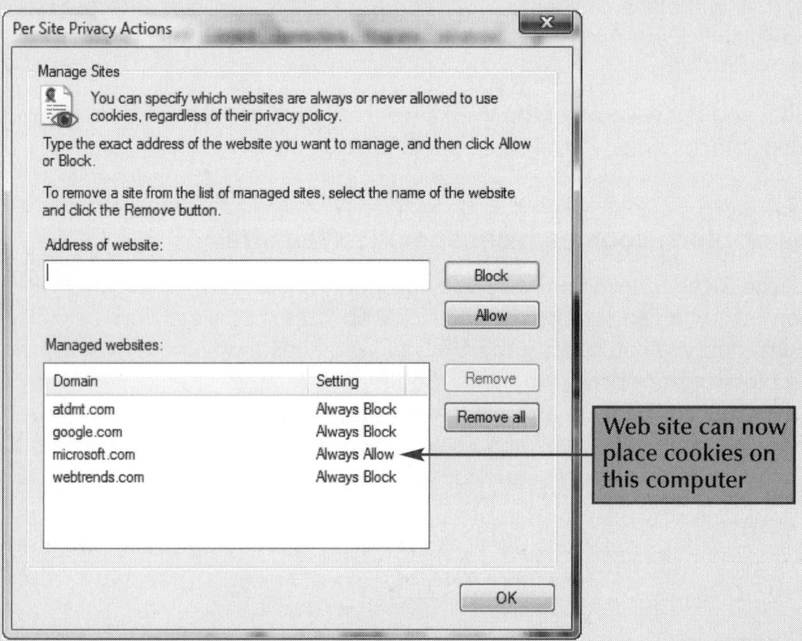

4. In the Per Site Privacy Actions dialog box, click the **OK** button, and in the Internet Options dialog box, click the **OK** button.

5. Navigate to yet another Web site that you frequently visit, and then use the **Back** button to return to the previously visited Web site. You no longer see Privacy Alert dialog boxes for first-party and third-party cookies; however, Windows Internet Explorer now allows first-party cookies and blocks third-party cookies.

6. To restore your original privacy settings, click **Tools** on the command bar, click **Internet Options**, click the **Privacy** tab, click the **Sites** button, click the **Remove all** button, click the **OK** button in the Per Site Privacy Actions dialog box, and then click the **OK** button in the Internet Options dialog box.

7. Keep Windows Internet Explorer open for the next section of the tutorial.

If you enable the Windows Internet Explorer option for overriding automatic cookie handling, you can specify that Windows Internet Explorer prompt you for each Web site that wants to place a first-party and third-party cookie on your computer. As you visit Web sites, you can identify which ones place cookies on your computer. Then, you can specify in the Per Site Privacy Actions dialog box which Web sites you will accept cookies from and which

Web sites are not allowed to put cookies on your computer. By using this approach, you guarantee that you can access and use Web sites for your e-mail software, online banking, and other types of online transactions, such as purchases of products or services, while preventing other Web sites, such as marketing and advertising Web sites, from developing an online profile of your browsing activities and interests by placing cookies on your computer.

Using Windows Internet Explorer's Pop-Up Blocker

Pop-up windows are commonly used to display advertising from Web sites that you visit. The pop-up window may appear above your Web browser window, blocking part of your view onto a Web page, or in the background behind the Web browser window. In the latter case, you do not see the pop-up window until you close or minimize your Web browser window. While many people find pop-up windows annoying when they are trying to browse the Web and view Web pages, Web sites can also use pop-up windows to place malicious software on your computer, so you need to control the use of pop-up windows like you control cookie usage.

Windows Internet Explorer has a Pop-up Blocker that can prevent many different types of pop-up windows from automatically opening. However, if you deliberately click a link or button for a pop-up window, that pop-up window will open unless you adjust Pop-up Blocker settings. The Pop-up Blocker feature will also prevent pop-up windows that are larger than the viewable screen or outside the viewable screen area from opening.

Next, you want to examine your Pop-up Blocker settings as you continue your thorough check of your new company laptop.

To view Pop-up Blocker settings:

1. In the Windows Internet Explorer window, click **Tools** on the command bar and point to **Pop-up Blocker**. You can use the Pop-up Blocker menu to turn off Pop-up Blocker or view Pop-up Blocker settings. If you or someone else turns off Pop-up Blocker, you can use this same menu to turn on Pop-up Blocker.
2. Click **Pop-up Blocker Settings**. Under Exceptions, Windows Internet Explorer notes that pop-ups are currently blocked because Pop-up Blocker is automatically enabled in Windows Internet Explorer. See Figure 7-41. It also notes that you can allow pop-up windows from a specific Web site by adding the site to the Allowed sites list box. You just type the URL of the Web site in the "Address of website to allow" text box, and then click the Add button to allow that Web site to display pop-up windows. Later, if you no longer want to allow pop-ups from an allowed site, you select that site in the Allowed sites box and click the Remove button.

Tip

You can also check Pop-up Blocker settings on the Privacy property sheet in the Internet Options dialog box.

Figure 7-41 **Pop-up Blocker settings**

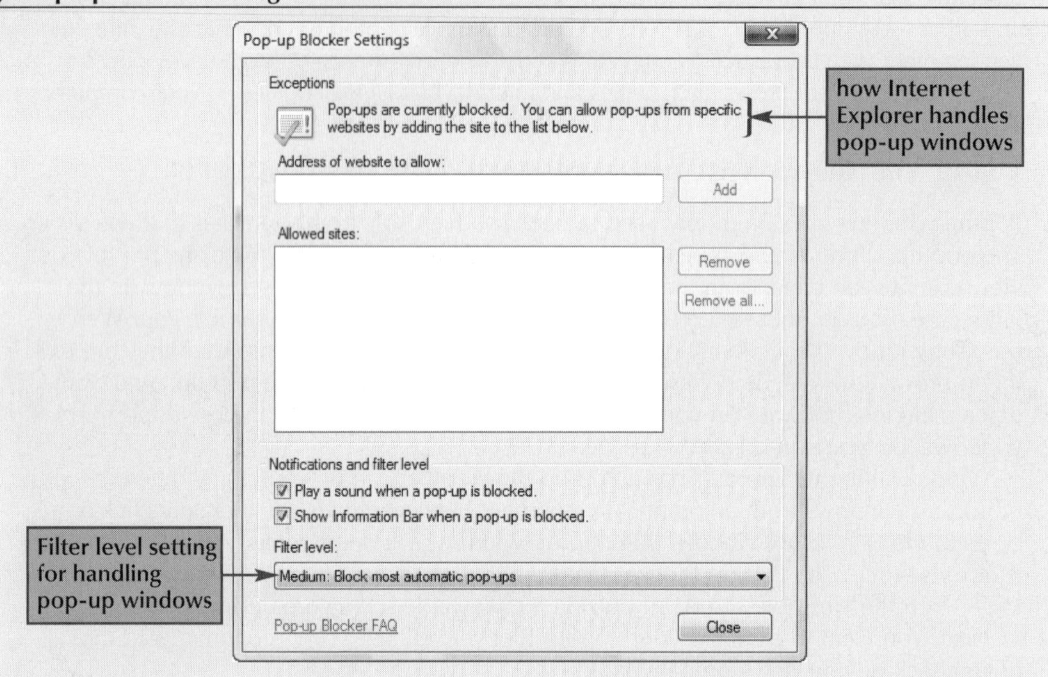

Under Notifications and filter level, you can specify whether you want a sound to play and whether to show an Information Bar when a pop-up window is blocked. In the Filter level list box, you can specify one of three settings for pop-up windows. The High setting blocks all pop-up windows, the Medium setting is the default and blocks most automatic pop-up windows, and the Low setting allows pop-up windows from secure sites. If you select the High setting, Internet Explorer will block all pop-up windows, even those that appear after you click a link or button.

When Pop-up Blocker blocks a pop-up window from opening, Windows Internet Explorer displays an Information Bar dialog box, shown in Figure 7-42, asks if you noticed the Information Bar, explains the purpose of the Information Bar, and points to where you can find the Information Bar so that you can specify how to handle the pop-up window. (The Information Bar is a light yellow bar extending across the top of the Web page you're examining.) Windows Internet Explorer displays the following message on the left side of the Information Bar: "Pop-up blocked. To see this pop-up or additional options click here..."

Figure 7-42 **Viewing the purpose of the Information Bar**

If you click the Information Bar, it displays a menu with the following options:

- Temporarily Allow Pop-ups
- Always Allow Pop-ups from This Site...
- Settings
- More information

"More information" opens Windows Help and Support and displays Help information on the Internet Explorer Information Bar.

If you point to Settings, you see a cascading menu with these options:

- Turn Off Pop-up Blocker
- Show Information Bar for Pop-ups
- More Settings...

"Show Information Bar for Pop-ups" is enabled, and "More Settings" opens the Pop-up Blocker Settings dialog box.

Windows Internet Explorer also uses the Information Bar to display information about security risks (such as installing an unsafe ActiveX control or security settings below recommended levels), downloads, and other activities (all of which are described in detail in Windows Help and Support).

Even if Pop-up Blocker is enabled, you might still see pop-up windows if spyware is installed on your computer. In this case, you have to use antispyware software to remove the spyware from your computer.

Troubleshooting Problems with Pop-up Windows | InSight

Many Web sites display pop-up windows, so your first inclination might be to block all pop-up windows. However, you might need to display certain types of pop-up windows from specific Web sites. For example, your Web-based e-mail software may display your Address Book with e-mail addresses for your important contacts in a pop-up window, or your online banking Web site might display a pop-up window for conducting an online transaction. In these instances, you want to make sure that these Web sites can display pop-up windows by adding them to your Allowed sites list. Also, if you experience problems accessing a feature at a Web site, Windows Internet Explorer might be blocking a pop-up window that you need to access. Add that site to your Allowed sites list and determine whether that resolves the problem. If not, you can always remove the site from your Allowed sites list.

To close the Pop-up Blocker Settings dialog box:

1. Click the **Close** button to close the Pop-Up Blocker Settings dialog box.
2. Keep Windows Internet Explorer open for the next section of the tutorial.

The Pop-up Blocker is a useful tool because some Web sites overwhelm the user by displaying one pop-up window after another and block your view of a Web page or leave pop-up windows all over your desktop after you close your Web browser.

Managing Windows Internet Explorer Add-ons

You can now view information about Windows Internet Explorer **Add-ons**, or programs that work with Windows Internet Explorer. You can enable or disable an Add-on program, and you can examine information on how frequently Windows Internet Explorer uses an Add-on. This feature is yet one more tool for protecting the security of your computer and privacy because an Add-on might contain harmful program code and affect your use of your Web browser and your computer.

After discussing potential problems caused by Internet Explorer Add-ons at your weekly meeting with Arielle, you decide to examine information about the Add-ons on your laptop.

Tip

To start Internet Explorer without loading Add-ons, open the All Programs menu, click Accessories, click System Tools, and then click Internet Explorer (No Add-ons).

To view Add-on settings:

1. In Windows Internet Explorer, click **Tools** on the command bar, click **Manage Add-ons**, and then click **Enable or Disable Add-ons**. The Manage Add-ons dialog box points out that disabling or removing Add-ons might prevent your Web browser from properly displaying some Web pages. See Figure 7-43. Your Add-ons will differ.

Figure 7-43 Viewing Internet Explorer Add-ons

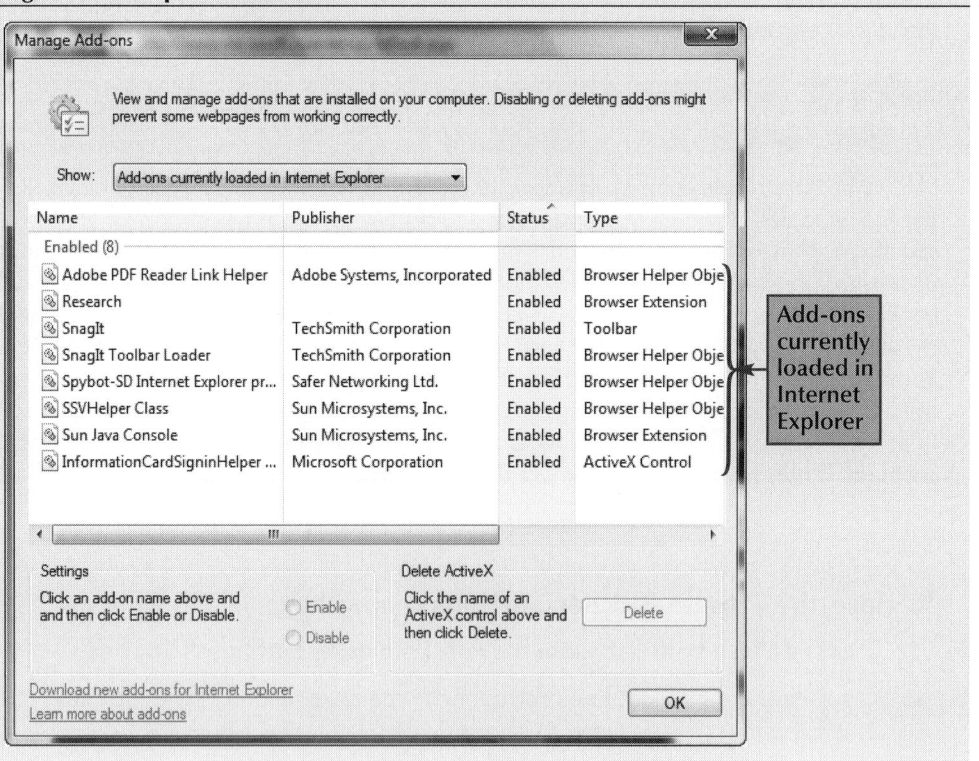

The Manage Add-ons dialog box displays a list of Add-ons that are currently loaded in Internet Explorer. The Manage Add-ons dialog box shows the name of each Add-on, the publisher, the status (enabled or disabled), the type of object, and the associated file. The object type might be identified as a Browser Helper Object (BHO), Browser Extension, Toolbar, or ActiveX Control. If you want to enable or disable an Add-on, just select that Add-on in the Name column, and then the Enable and Disable buttons become visible in the Settings area. You can also use the Show button to view the following types of Add-ons:

- Add-ons that have been used by Internet Explorer
- Add-ons that run without requiring permission
- Downloaded ActiveX controls (32 bits)

To make proper use of this dialog box, you can research the various types of Add-ons listed in the four types of categories described in the previous paragraph. You can search the documentation for software installed on your computer, or you can use a search engine to try to find information on specific Add-ons. For example, in Figure 7-43, Research is listed as a currently loaded Browser Extension. You might search Google using the following criteria:

Research "Browser Extension"

If you try this option, you will discover that this Add-on is installed as part of Microsoft Office, but the publisher is not identified in the Manage Add-ons dialog box. Although people in several online forums had different ideas on how it was installed and what Office product is associated with it, one Windows expert noted that this Browser Extension displays a Research pane on the left side of a Windows Internet Explorer so that you can search a variety of online reference tools and Web sites. This Windows expert also noted that you can display the Research Pane from the Tools menu by pointing to Toolbars, and then Explorer Bar, and then selecting Research.

As another example, Help information included with the SnagIt screen capture program explained that the SnagIt Toolbar Loader (identified as a Browser Helper Object) displays a toolbar in the Windows Internet Explorer window for quickly capturing screens. The SnagIt toolbar itself is listed as SnagIt (with object type identified as Toolbar) and is visible under the Address Bar. The SnagIt Add-Ins Help information also explains how to use the SnagIt Setup installation program to uninstall Microsoft Internet Explorer SnagIt Add-Ins.

InSight | Researching Browser Helper Objects and Other Add-ons

More than likely, you will discover an extensive number of Add-ons in Windows Internet Explorer, and therefore, researching all the Add-ons quickly becomes time-consuming. To save time, you can initially focus on those with no identified publisher or those that seem suspicious to you. Then, you can decide whether you want to search for information on Add-ons from companies that you trust. You can use a search engine to locate Web sites, such as sysinfo.org, with extensive lists of Browser Helper Objects that also include information about other types of Add-ons. These Web sites provide whatever information is available about an Add-on and typically identify an Add-on as legitimate, spyware or malware, "open to debate," or of unknown status. To err on the side of caution, you should examine several Web sites and compare and verify the consistency of information provided about Add-ons and Browser Helper Objects (BHOs). Another option for protecting the security of your computer and your privacy is to load Windows Internet Explorer with all Add-ons disabled (as explained in the Tip for Step 1).

To complete your examination of Add-ons:

1. Click the **Close** button to close the Manage Add-ons dialog box. If you disabled (or enabled) any Add-ons, Windows Internet Explorer warns you that you might need to restart your computer to apply the changes.
2. Keep Windows Internet Explorer open for the next two sections of the tutorial.

Add-ons, especially Browser Helper Objects and toolbars, are an easy medium for introducing malicious software to your computer, so individuals who diagnose and resolve computer problems must take into account these types of objects when troubleshooting a problem on a computer.

Using the Security Status Bar

When you visit a Web site, such as an online banking Web site, where you disclose confidential and personal information, the URL for that Web site changes to indicate that it is a secure Web site. The "http" changes to "https" to indicate a secure connection that uses encryption to protect information transmitted to the Web site. Also, in earlier versions of Internet Explorer or in other Web browsers, you typically saw a gold padlock on the status bar of the Web browser window.

Unlike earlier versions of Internet Explorer, Windows Internet Explorer displays a more prominent Security Status Bar with a gold padlock on the right side of the Address Bar. If you click the Security Status Bar, Windows Internet Explorer displays a Website Identification dialog box with information about the Web site. If the Web site is legitimate, the Website Identification dialog box identifies the name of the authority that certifies the authenticity of Web sites (such as VeriSign), identifies the Web site, and notes that the connection to the Web server at this Web site is encrypted. Figure 7-44 shows a Website Identification dialog box for Microsoft's Windows Live Hotmail Web site. If you click the View Certificates link, Windows Internet Explorer opens a Certificate dialog and provides more information on the certifying authority. The Address Bar and Security Status Bar also have a green background to denote that the Web site is safe.

Using the Security Status Bar **Figure 7-44**

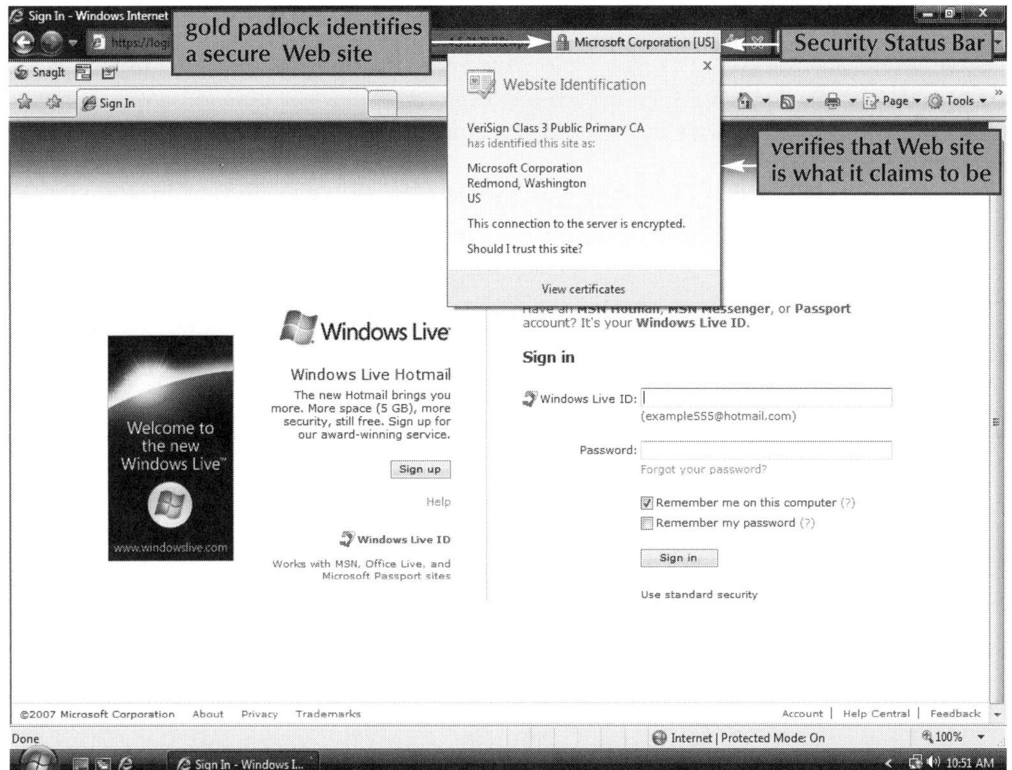

If a Web site has an invalid security certificate, Windows Internet Explorer notes that there is a problem with the Web site's security certificate. This warning Web page also notes that this problem might indicate that the Web site is attempting to fool you or is attempting to intercept data that you send to that Web site. This warning Web page will recommend that you close this Web page and do not visit the Web site. Also, the Address Bar and Security Status Bar have a red background to denote that the Web site is not safe.

Using Windows Internet Explorer's Phishing Filter

As noted at the beginning of the tutorial, phishing refers to attempts to try to trick a user into disclosing personal and financial information, such as bank account numbers, credit card numbers, PINs, and a user's SSN, to steal a user's assets or identity (or both). A user receives an e-mail message from what appears to be a reputable company with which the user does business (such as an ISP or bank). The e-mail message informs the user that they need to immediately update their account information or risk suspension or closure of the account. The e-mail message contains a link for updating that account information, but if the user clicks the link, they are directed or redirected to a Web site that appears similar or identical to the Web site of the company with which they do business. Then they are prompted to update their account information.

To counteract this threat to users, Microsoft has included a phishing filter in Windows Internet Explorer. This phishing filter uses three approaches to checking Web sites for phishing activities. First, it compares URLs of Web sites that a user enters against a list of legitimate Web sites stored on the user's computer. Second, it sends URLs to an online service dedicated to detecting phishing and compares those URLs against URLs on a constantly updated list of reported phishing Web sites. Finally, the phishing filter analyzes Web sites visited by users to determine if the Web sites exhibit characteristics of phishing Web sites.

If Windows Internet Explorer identifies a Web site as a known phishing Web site, it displays a warning Web page that notes the Web site is a reported phishing Web site and recommends that you close the Web page and not visit the Web site. If a Web site is not a known legitimate Web site and is not a known reporting phishing Web site, but instead is a suspected phishing Web site, Windows Internet Explorer displays a Suspicious Website button in the Address Bar. You can then click that button to obtain more information about the Web site.

An online service with a constantly updated list of reported phishing Web sites is essential because these Web sites appear for a short time and then move to a new location to evade detection.

Because of the widespread use of phishing and pharming, Arielle recommends that you set up all client computers with the Phishing Filter enabled and explain the use of this feature to clients.

To check the status of Internet Explorer's Phishing Filter:

1. Click **Tools** on the Windows Internet Explorer command bar, and then point to **Phishing Filter**. Windows Internet Explorer displays the Phishing Filter menu. If your Phishing Filter menu contains the option "Turn On Automatic Website Checking," then your phishing filter is turned off, and Windows Internet Explorer analyzes Web sites for characteristics of phishing Web sites but does not forward the information to Microsoft. If your Phishing Filter menu contains the option "Turn Off Automatic Website Checking," then your phishing filter is turned on, and Windows Internet Explorer is checking Web sites that you visit. If a Web site is not on the legitimate list, the Phishing Filter automatically sends the Web site's URL to Microsoft so that it can analyze the Web site.
2. If your phishing filter is turned off, and if you want to enable the phishing filter, click **Turn On Automatic Website Checking**. Windows Internet Explorer opens the Microsoft Phishing Filter dialog box and enables the option for using the phishing filter. See Figure 7-45.

Figure 7-45 Internet Explorer's Phishing Filter enabled

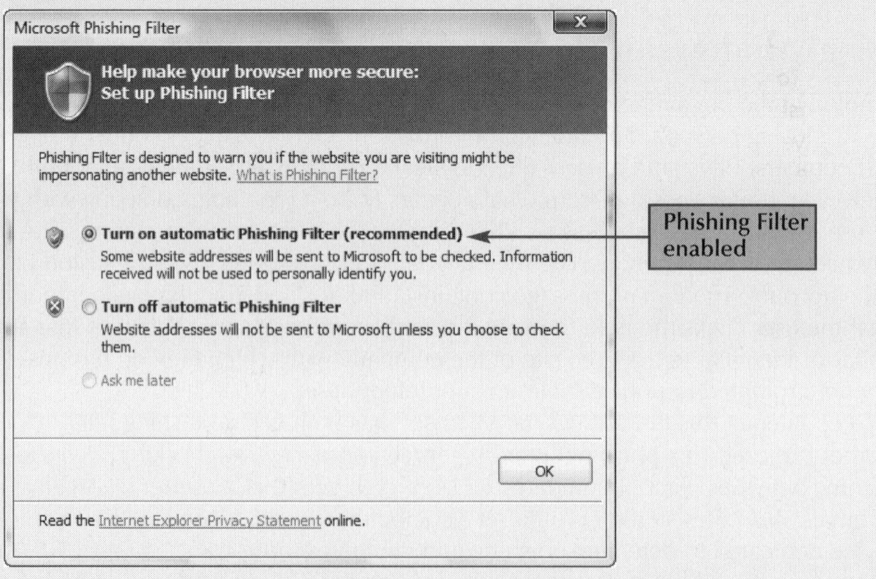

3. If you opened the Microsoft Phishing Filter dialog box, click the **OK** button to close it and apply the setting you selected.
4. Keep Windows Internet Explorer open for the next section of the tutorial.

If you visit a Web site and want to check to determine whether it is a phishing Web site, you can use the "Check This Website" option on the Phishing Filter menu. This option is useful if you turned off the Phishing Filter, but then decide you want to check a Web site you visit. You can use the "Report This Website" option on the Phishing Filter menu to report the Web site you're visiting to Microsoft so that it can check to determine whether it is a phishing Web site.

Deleting Your Browsing History

Another way to protect your computer and your privacy is to periodically delete your browsing history. That browsing history includes Temporary Internet Files, cookies, History (Web sites you've visited), form data (or information that you've entered into forms at Web sites), and passwords that are automatically filled in when you visit the same Web site again. If you decide to delete all of these items, Windows Internet Explorer then asks if you want to delete files and settings stored by Add-ons.

Although retaining the various components of your browsing history can improve your browsing experience on the Web, malicious software in the form of Web pages can be downloaded by your Web browser and stored in the Temporary Internet Files folder (or your Internet cache). To reduce the risk to your computer, you can empty the Temporary Internet files folder and remove that malicious software from your computer. Also, if you use a public computer, such as a library computer or college computer, you should delete your personal browsing history when you finish using that computer. You should also make sure you remember to sign out of your e-mail software account; otherwise, the next person who uses the same Web browser on that computer right after you might have access to your e-mail.

As part of raising the awareness of security and privacy issues for new clients, Arielle asks that you show the employees of new clients how to delete their browsing history.

To delete your browsing history:

1. Click **Tools** on the Windows Internet Explorer command bar, and then click **Delete Browsing History**. In the Delete Browsing History dialog box, you can delete each of the five components of your browsing history separately, or you can delete all of them in one step. See Figure 7-46. If you are working on your own computer, you can choose which items you want to remove from a computer and which items you want to keep.

Tip

You can access these same options by choosing Internet Options from the Tools menu and clicking the Delete button under Browsing history on the General property sheet.

Figure 7-46 Options for deleting browsing history

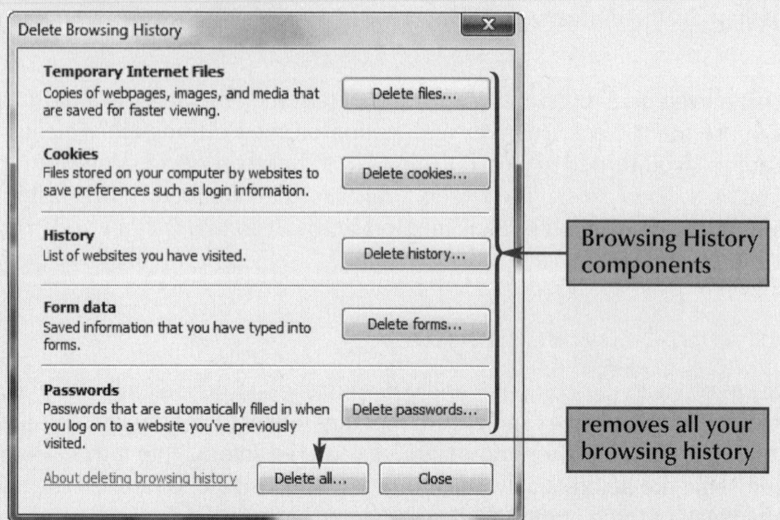

2. If you do not want to delete your browsing history or any of the items in the Delete Browsing History dialog box, click the **Close** button. If you want to delete all of these options, click the **Delete all** button, and in the Delete Browsing History dialog box, click the **Also delete files and settings stored by add-ons** check box if you also want to include this option, and then click the **Yes** button. If you want to delete specific items, click the **Delete** button for those items, and then click the **Yes** button; after you delete all of the items you want to delete, click the **Close** button.

3. Close the Windows Internet Explorer window.

Tip

If you are working on a public computer, close Windows Internet Explorer and restart the computer to remove cookies still stored in RAM.

Disk Cleanup also removes Temporary Internet Files and Downloaded Program Files, but it does not remove cookies, your browsing history, form data, and passwords.

If you delete your browsing history, Windows Internet Explorer does not delete your Favorite bookmarks, and it does not delete RSS feeds that you subscribe to. Also, if you use another Web browser (or if you use both Windows Internet Explorer and another Web browser), you must use that other Web browser's options for removing these same options from your computer.

Checking Internet Explorer Security and Privacy Settings | Reference Window

- Open Windows Internet Explorer, click Tools on the command bar, and then click Internet Options.
- Click the Security tab to view and specify security settings for Internet sites, Local intranet sites, Trusted sites, and Restricted sites. Select each security zone, verify the security level for each zone, and verify that the option for enabling Protected Mode is turned on for Internet, Local intranet, and Restricted sites. Use the Sites button to add or remove Web sites to the Local intranet, Trusted sites, and Restricted sites security zone. Use the Custom Level button on the Security property sheet to change individual security settings.
- Click the Privacy tab to select a privacy setting for the Internet zone. Use the Advanced button to display the Advanced Privacy Settings dialog box and override automatic cookie handling by Internet Explorer, specify whether you want to accept or block first-party and third-party cookies, or whether you want to be prompted as to how to handle cookies. Use the Sites button to block or allow cookies from specific Web sites.
- Click the General tab, and then click the Delete button under Browsing history to delete temporary Internet files, cookies, history, form data, and passwords; verify the operation and decide whether to delete files and settings for Add-ons; click the Yes button; and then click the OK button to close the Internet Options dialog box.
- Click Tools on the command bar, point to Pop-up Blocker, and if necessary, click Turn On Pop-up Blocker. Click Tools, point to Pop-up Blocker, click Pop-up Blocker Settings, specify the Filter level for pop-up windows, enable the option for showing an Information Bar when Windows Internet Explorer blocks a pop-up window (if necessary), add or remove the URLs of Web sites that can display pop-up windows, and then click the Close button.
- Click Tools on the command bar, click Manage Add-ons, and then click Enable or Disable Add-ons. Use the Show button to display "Add-ons currently loaded in Internet Explorer," "Add-ons that have been used by Internet Explorer," "Add-ons that run without requiring permission," and "Downloaded ActiveX Controls (32 bit)," and then review the Add-ons displayed in each category. If you want to disable (or enable) an Add-on, select the Add-on, and then click the Disable (or Enable) button. Click the OK button to close the Manage Add-ons dialog box.
- Click Tools on the command bar, point to Phishing Filter, and then click Turn On Automatic Website Checking (if the Phishing Filter is off). To check a specific Web site that you've visited, click Tools, point to Phishing Filter, and then click Check This Website. To report a Web site that you suspect to be a phishing Web site, click Tools, point to Phishing Filter, and then click Report This Website.

As noted earlier, it is a good idea to examine the settings on the different property sheets for Windows Internet Explorer, or whatever Web browser you use, and make sure your Web browser is set up the way you prefer rather than rely on the default settings built into the Web browser.

Session 7.2 Quick Check | Review

1. ________________ is a Windows Vista component or tool for identifying important updates for the Windows operating system, device driver updates, and updates for other Microsoft software.
2. What Windows Vista component can you use to check the status of your computer's firewall, Windows' automatic updating feature, your computer's malware protection, Internet settings, and User Account Control settings?
3. True or False. You cannot override automatic cookie handling by Windows Internet Explorer.
4. What is the name of the Windows Internet Explorer feature for blocking pop-up windows?

5. True or False. The Windows Internet Explorer Security Status Bar provides information about whether a Web site provides a secure, encrypted connection.
6. What is the name of the Windows Internet Explorer feature for determining whether a Web site is a known or suspected phishing Web site?
7. What components does Windows Internet Explorer remove from your computer when it deletes your browsing history?

Review | Tutorial Summary

In this tutorial, you examined various types of malware and other threats that might affect your computer's security and your privacy while browsing the Web. You explored the different ways in which malicious software might gain access to your computer and how you can protect your computer's security and your privacy. You learned how Windows Defender alerts you to suspicious software on your computer, used Windows Defender to perform a quick scan of your computer and flash drive, viewed your scan history, and examined Windows Defender settings. You also used Software Explorer to view information about software running on your computer. You learned about the importance of user accounts and the new Windows Vista User Account Control feature. You created a Password Reset Disk for your user account. You explored Windows Firewall settings and Automatic updating settings on your computer. You checked your computer for important Windows updates, and you verified your installed update history and Windows Update settings. You opened the Windows Vista Security Center to see the status of your firewall, Automatic updating, and malware protection as well as other security settings. You examined Windows Internet Explorer's security zone settings, privacy settings, Pop-up Blocker, option for managing Add-ons, Security Status Bar, and Phishing Filter as well as the use of protected mode. You also deleted your browsing history.

Key Terms

ActiveX controls
Add-on
Admin Approval Mode
Administrator account
adware
backdoor
bot or botnet
browser hijacker
compact privacy policy
computer virus
Consent Prompt
cookie
Credentials Prompt
Denial of Service (DoS)
digital signature
Distributed Denial of Service (DDos)
exception
explicit consent
firewall
first-party Web site
Guest account
hoax
HTTPS protocol
implicit consent
Internet worm
intranet
keylogger
malware
online privacy
online profiling
packet sniffer
password reset disk
persistent cookie
pharming
phishing
pop-up window
process
Protected Mode
protocol
quarantine
quick scan
remote surveillance tool
Rich Text Format (RTF)
Rootkit
Secure Desktop Mode
service
session cookie
silent install
Software Explorer
spam
spyware
Standard User account
third-party Web site
Trojan Horse
unsigned ActiveX control
URL poisoning
user account
User Account Control (UAC)
Web bug
Winsock Service Provider
zombie

Practice | Review Assignments

Practice the skills you learned in the tutorial.

There are no Data Files needed for the Review Assignments.

In preparation for an upcoming training session on ways to protect a computer's security and the privacy of a new client, you decide to review what you will cover during that training session. To complete Step 2, Windows Defender must be installed on your computer. As you complete each step in the Review Assignments, record your answers to questions so that you can submit them to your instructor. Use a word processing application, such as Word or WordPad, to prepare your answers to these questions. Complete the following:

1. In the first section of the tutorial, review the information on types of malicious software, other types of threats, the ways in which malicious software gains access to a computer, and precautions you can take to protect your computer's security and your privacy. Then, prepare a list of steps and precautions that you use to protect your computer and your privacy.
2. Open Windows Defender, and then complete the following steps:
   a. What information does Windows Defender report about the status of your computer? What was the last type of scan performed by Windows Defender? Is Real-time protection on or off?
   b. Use the Scan options list arrow to select a Custom Scan. Then use the Select button to open the Windows Defender folder where you select the drives and folders you want to scan. Expand the folder structure for Local Disk (C:), expand the folder structure for the Users folder, expand the folder structure for the Public folder, and then select the Public Downloads folder as the folder to scan. Apply that setting, and then perform a scan of the Public Downloads folder. What are the results of scanning this folder for malicious software? Why would you want to especially check this specific folder? What other user folder might you also want to include in a custom scan?
   c. Use the History link on the command bar to view a history of all Windows Defender activities. What are the names, alert levels, and action taken by Windows Defender on the programs and actions listed in your History?
   d. Use the Tools link to display Windows Defender tools and settings, and then open Software Explorer. List the first three categories of company names shown for Startup Programs. Select the entry for Microsoft Windows Explorer. What is the program name for this file? What is the file path for this program? What is its startup type? Does this program ship with the Windows operating system? Close Windows Defender.
3. Open the Control Panel, open User Accounts and Family Safety, and then open User Accounts. (If you are using the Business edition of Windows Vista, open the first and second links for User Accounts.) What type of account do you have? Does your account type permit you to install and remove software and hardware, change system settings, and manage other user accounts? Explain. Is your account password protected? How can you tell which options in User Accounts require Administrator credentials? Close User Accounts.
4. Open the Control Panel, open Security, and then open the Security Center.
   a. What is the status of your firewall? What is the name of the firewall you use on your computer?

b. If you use Windows Firewall on your computer, use the Windows Firewall link in the left pane to open Windows Firewall. How does Windows Firewall handle inbound connections? What does Windows Firewall do when it blocks a program? What type of network location does Windows Firewall protect? Close the Windows Firewall window.
c. What is the setting for Automatic updating in the Windows Security Center? Use the Windows Update link in the left pane to open Windows Update, and then use the Change settings link in the Windows Update window to view your Automatic updating settings. What setting does your computer use for updating Windows? Would you benefit from using another setting for Automatic updating? Explain. Does Windows Update also download recommended updates? Close the Change settings window.
d. Under Malware protection in the Windows Security Center, what type of virus protection and malware protection does your computer use?
e. What is the status of your Other security settings?
f. Close the Windows Security Center window and the Control Panel window.

5. From the All Programs menu, open Windows Update, and if necessary, choose the option for checking for updates. What, if any, updates are available for your computer? If necessary, use the View available updates link to view those updates, and then identify what updates are available.
6. If necessary, use the Back button to return to the Windows Update window. Choose the option to view your update history. Which of the following types of updates has Windows Update downloaded and installed on your computer: Windows Defender, the Windows Malicious Software Removal Tool, Windows Mail, and Microsoft Office? Close the View update history window.
7. Open Windows Internet Explorer, open the Internet Options dialog box, and select the Security tab. What security level setting does Windows Internet Explorer use for the Internet security zone? What advantage, if any, would the High or Medium security level settings have? Which security zones use Protected Mode?
8. Select the Privacy tab. What setting does Windows Internet Explorer use for your Internet zone? If you chose the option for blocking all cookies, can Web sites read cookies already stored on your computer? What advantage would the Medium High setting have over the Medium setting? Use the Advanced button to view Advanced Privacy Settings. Would overriding automatic cookie handling be beneficial to you on your computer? Explain. How would you implement the handling of first-party and third-party cookies if you used this option? Close the Advanced Privacy Settings dialog box. How can you allow first-party cookies and block third-party cookies from specific Web sites?
9. Choose the option to view Pop-up Blocker settings from the Privacy property sheet. What filter level does Pop-up Blocker use? What can you do to allow specific Web sites to display pop-up windows that might otherwise be blocked? Have you implemented this option, and if so, how? Close the Pop-up Blocker Settings dialog box.
10. Select the Programs tab, and then choose the option for managing Add-ons. What types of Add-ons are currently loaded in Internet Explorer? How can you disable an Add-on shown in the Enabled list? Are there any Add-ons that do not have a publisher listed, and if so, what are the names of the Add-ons? How might you find information for these Add-ons? Close the Manage Add-ons dialog box, and then close the Internet Options dialog box.

11. If you access your e-mail via an online Web site, visit that Web site's home page or logon page. What options (if any) does your online e-mail Web site have for remembering you on the computer you are using and remembering your password? How might you benefit from these options? Does your online e-mail software have an option for a secure logon? Explain. If so, enable that option, and then use the Security Status Bar to view a security report. What information does the Security Status Bar provide about the Web site's identification when you point to the Security Status Bar?
12. Use the Phishing Filter to check this Web site. What does the Phishing Filter report about this Web site? Close the Phishing Filter dialog box.
13. From the Tools menu, choose the option for deleting your browsing history. Which of the five types of files do you delete from your computer, and which types of files do you keep? Explain. Close the Delete Browsing History dialog box.
14. Close Windows Internet Explorer.
15. Submit the results of the preceding steps to your instructor, either in printed or electronic form, as requested.

Apply | Case Problem 1

Use the skills you learned in the tutorial to prepare a security report on Rootkits.

There are no Data Files needed for this Case Problem.

Talcott Security Systems Unlimited As a computer security specialist working for Talcott Security Systems Unlimited in Saint Louis, Missouri, Zhi Lin is frequently called upon to present papers, prepare background information, and moderate conferences on various types of security threats and risks. For an upcoming forum on Rootkits, he needs to prepare background information on Rootkits and Rootkit detection software for participants and thereby set the stage for a more focused and in-depth discussion. He asks you to assist him in preparing background information on Rootkits and Rootkit detection software. As you complete each step in the Review Assignments, record your answers to questions so that you can submit them to your instructor. Use a word processing application, such as Word or WordPad, to prepare your answers to these questions. Complete the following:

1. From the Microsoft Web site (*www.microsoft.com*), search for information on Rootkits.
2. In the first page of search results, locate and read information on RootkitRevealer or any other type of Microsoft Rootkit detection product.
3. Answer the following questions or provide the following information:
   a. What is a Rootkit?
   b. What are the four types of Rootkits?
   c. What is a persistent Rootkit?
   d. How does RootkitRevealer (or any other type of Microsoft Rootkit detection product) detect a Rootkit?
   e. How might a Rootkit evade detection by RootkitRevealer (or another Rootkit detection program)?
   f. How does RootkitRevealer evade detection from a Rootkit when you open it?
   g. The names of at least three Rootkits.
4. From Microsoft's Web site, search for information on the Strider GhostBuster Project. How does Strider GhostBuster detect Rootkits, and what fundamental weakness of Rootkits does it use to detect Rootkits?
5. Search for information on the Strider HoneyMonkey Project. What is a HoneyMonkey, and what is its purpose?

6. Include a list of references that you used to prepare this paper, including the URLs of Web sites that contained information on Rootkits.
7. Submit the results of the preceding steps to your instructor, either in printed or electronic form, as requested.

Apply | Case Problem 2

Use the skills you learned in the tutorial to document startup programs and other software.

There are no Data Files needed for this Case Problem.

California Marine Protection Foundation In addition to handling the funding for specific marine protection projects along the California coast, Julianne Lauchland provides tech support for other employees who work at the California Marine Protection Foundation. When she sets up a computer for a staff member, she documents the startup programs and other software running on the computer so that she can troubleshoot problems that might arise later. Since she is currently faced with a tight deadline for submitting a fund proposal, she asks you to help her document software on a new computer. To complete this Case Problem, Windows Defender must be installed on your computer. As you complete each step in the Review Assignments, record your answers to questions so that you can submit them to your instructor. Use a word processing application, such as Word or WordPad, to prepare your answers to these questions. Complete the following:

1. Open Windows Defender, open Software Explorer, and then display a list of currently running programs.
2. List the Display Name, Description, File Name, File Path, Auto Start setting, and Classification of the following Microsoft Corporation products (if present):
   a. Microsoft Desktop Window Manager
   b. Microsoft Internet Explorer
   c. Microsoft Task Scheduler Engine
   d. Microsoft Windows Sidebar
   e. Windows Defender

   Note: If any of these startup programs are not available on your computer, note that fact for those startup programs.
3. Display a list of startup programs and list the name of the companies for each category of startup programs.
4. If Adobe Acrobat is listed as one of your startup programs, list the information for the Display Name, Description, Publisher, Digitally Signed By, Startup Type, Classification, and Ships with Operating System.
5. What is the purpose of Microsoft Desktop Window Manager?
6. Use the "Using Software Explorer" link to display Help information on Software Explorer in Windows Help and Support. Under "Understanding Software Explorer details," explain the value of the information listed for Auto Start, Startup Type, Classification, and Digitally Signed By. Close Help and Support and close Windows Defender.
7. Submit your answers to the preceding steps to your instructor, either in printed or electronic form, as requested.

Apply | Case Problem 3

Use the skills you learned in the tutorial to evaluate Web browser Add-ons.

There are no Data Files needed for this Case Problem.

Arenales Books Agustín Martínez manages the acquisition of books for Arenales Books, an online supplier of computer books that focus on computer security. Agustín also provides technical support for updating Arenales Books' Web site. To guarantee that this computer remains free of malicious software, he periodically checks Add-ons that load with his Web browser. As his assistant, he asks you to help him document and research new Add-ons. As you complete each step in the Review Assignments, record your responses so that you can submit them to your instructor. Use a word processing application, such as Word or WordPad, to prepare your responses. Complete the following:

1. Open Windows Internet Explorer, and then choose the option for opening the Manage Add-ons dialog box.
2. Prepare a list of the Add-ons currently loaded in Internet Explorer on the computer you are using. Include in your list the name of the Add-on, its Publisher, its Status, its Type, and its filename.
3. Compare the list you prepared in the previous step with a list of Add-ons that have been used by Internet Explorer. If you find any additional Add-ons not listed with Add-ons currently loaded in Internet Explorer, add them to your list of Add-ons from the previous step.
4. **EXPLORE** Use a search engine such as Google to locate information about specific Add-ons or to locate Web sites that contain lists of information about Browser Helper Objects. Locate information on at least five Add-ons in your list (including at least one Browser Helper Object, one Toolbar, and one Browser Extension). Use the information provided for each Add-on (such as its name, publisher, type, and filename) in the Manage Add-ons dialog box to verify that you have located the right information for an Add-on. (*Hint*: For example, when searching lists of Browser Helper Objects, you might want to use only part of an Add-on name, such as "Adobe," to locate a list of related Adobe Add-ons.) List the following types of information on each Add-on you research (where available):
   a. The status of the Add-on (i.e., whether the Add-on is a legitimate program or malicious software, if known)
   b. The nature of the Add-on (i.e., BHO or TB, or both)
   c. The description of the Add-on (how it's identified, e.g., hijacker, spyware, adware, etc., or by its malicious software name)
   d. Any other useful information
5. Include a list of references that you used to prepare this paper, including the URLs of Web sites that contained information on Add-ons.
6. Submit the results of the preceding steps to your instructor, either in printed or electronic form, as requested.

Research | Case Problem 4

Work with the skills you've learned and use the Internet to evaluate the latest security threats and risks.

There are no Data Files needed for this Case Problem.

Eberhardt Strategic Assessments Corina Puzon, a specialist in computer security and privacy issues, works as a computer analyst for Eberhardt Strategic Assessments. As part of her job, she evaluates new threats and risks to identify new patterns in the development and distribution of these threats and risks. Recently, she's noticed a steep rise in new threats, and she asks you to help her evaluate these threats. As you complete the following steps, use Microsoft Word or WordPad to prepare a summary in your own words on a new security threat or risk. Complete the following:

1. Visit the Symantec Web site (*www.symantec.com*), and then locate (or search for) Threat Explorer to view a list of the latest threats and risks.
2. Choose one of the latest threats or risks and view information about that threat or risk.
3. Prepare a summary that contains the following information:
   a. Threat or risk name
   b. Type of threat (e.g., computer virus, Internet worm, Trojan Horse, etc.)
   c. Risk impact, or threat or risk level (i.e., how serious is the threat)
   d. Systems affected (i.e., Windows versions)
   e. Its specific target or targets (Registry, system files, Web browser, etc.)
   f. Publisher (if known)
   g. How it spreads (e.g., via e-mail attachment, etc.)
   h. Technical details, such as a more detailed description of its effect or effects
   i. An overview of the basic approach (but not a detailed step-by-step list) for removing the threat or risk
   j. Your personal perspective or conclusions about this threat or risk
4. Include a list of references that you used to prepare this paper, including URLs of Symantec Web sites (or other Web sites).
5. Submit the results of the preceding steps to your instructor, either in printed or electronic form, as requested.

Review | Quick Check Answers

Session 7.1

1. Trojan Horse
2. Spyware (*Note*: Adware can also be spyware)
3. phishing and pharming
4. No. An e-mail attachment with a vbs extension might contain an Internet worm.
5. Software Explorer
6. User Account Control
7. False
8. Firewall

Session 7.2

1. Windows Update
2. Security Center
3. False
4. Pop-up Blocker
5. True

6. Phishing Filter
7. Temporary Internet files, cookies, history, form data, and passwords (*Note*: You also have the option for removing files and settings stored by Add-ons.

Ending Data Files

There are no ending Data Files needed for this tutorial.

Objectives

Session 8.1
- Develop a strategy for troubleshooting problems
- Analyze your computer's performance
- Use Event Viewer to view event logs
- Create a restore point with System Protection
- Use System Restore to view restore points

Session 8.2
- Use the BIOS Setup utility
- Boot in Safe Mode
- Use Task Manager to view running processes and services
- Analyze startup programs and environment variables
- Examine System Recovery Tools

Troubleshooting Windows

Using Windows Vista Troubleshooting Tools and Resources

Case | Carbon Sink, Unlimited

Carbon Sink, Unlimited is a Swiss consortium of international companies that work cooperatively to research and develop new strategies and technologies for removing carbon dioxide from the atmosphere and thereby tackling the immediate and long-term effects of global warming. Julien Cottier, a network specialist with a strong background in climate science, assists the scientists and research technicians with configuring, customizing, optimizing, and troubleshooting their computer systems.

In this tutorial, you examine a strategy for troubleshooting problems, use Reliability Monitor to evaluate the current performance level of your computer, use Event Viewer to examine detailed information on events that occur on your computer, check System Protection settings, use System Protection to create a restore point, and use System Restore to view existing restore points. You open the BIOS Setup utility during booting and view your computer's boot sequence, and then you examine the Windows Vista boot process. You view running processes and services in Task Manager and learn how to shut down nonresponding programs. You use System Configuration and System Information to view information on startup programs, and you learn how to use System Configuration to control the loading of those programs during booting. Finally, you examine System Recovery Tools provided with Windows Vista.

Starting Data Files

There are no starting Data Files needed for this tutorial.

Session 8.1

Developing a Troubleshooting Strategy

Since the recent formation of Carbon Sink, Unlimited, research groups have been interviewing, hiring, and assembling staff with multidisciplinary backgrounds in climate science. Julien Cotter not only trains his staff in the latest troubleshooting tools and techniques, but he also determines how each new staff person can assist the specialized needs of the different research groups important to the company's mission. With each new employee, Julien discusses the importance of developing a troubleshooting strategy to quickly identify and resolve problems.

When faced with a problem on your computer system, you can adapt and apply the following approach for troubleshooting problems.

- **Define the problem**. First, make sure you know the exact nature of the problem. For example, if you observe a change in the performance of Windows Vista, ask yourself questions that provide you with the information you need to clearly identify the nature and possible cause of the problem. For example, exactly how does this problem affect your computer system? Does Windows Vista report any error messages? If so, do the messages provide clues for troubleshooting the problem? Is this the first time you've encountered this type of problem? If you encountered the problem before, how did you resolve the problem? Did you or someone else recently make a change in any important Windows Vista settings or its configuration? Did you recently download and install a new software product or device driver? Did you recently install any new hardware? Did you change a Windows setting? Did you modify the Windows Registry?
- **Analyze the problem**. Next, analyze the problem by evaluating your responses to the questions you ask yourself. For example, if you recently changed the configuration of your computer, such as downloading and installing a new video display driver, and then notice problems with components of the graphical user interface, including Windows Aero, could the problem result from the installation of the new video display driver? Or might some other type of error be causing the problem, such as a problem with the file system? Could the monitor be failing, or could important system files be damaged?
- **Devise ways to test the possible cause of the problem**. To obtain more information about the nature of a problem, devise other tests that help you identify the cause of the problem. For example, if you experienced a problem with the video display after installing an update for a video display adapter and then discover a change in one of your video display settings, adjust that setting and determine whether it resolves the problem. If the problem persists, restore the previously used device driver and determine whether that resolved the problem. (In Tutorial 15, you will examine the use of Roll Back Driver, which permits you to restore the previously used device driver for a hardware device.) If not, try other possible sources for the problem, such as file system errors.
- **Draw on all the resources you have to resolve the problem**. What tools are available in Windows Vista for obtaining more information about the problem or for identifying and analyzing the problem? How can you best use those tools to help you identify or solve a problem? For example, did Windows Vista send a problem report to Microsoft, and if so, what information does it provide in Problem Reports and Solutions in the Control Panel on the nature of the problem and the availability of a solution?

Check hardware and software settings and examine information about recent events that occurred on your computer. Check any reference manuals provided with your hardware or software. If the manufacturer of the product you purchased has a technical support line, call and talk to a technical support person about the problem. That person might know the answer immediately or might be able to replicate the problem and then determine how toresolve it. Many companies provide assistance via their Web sites, publish answers to frequently asked questions (FAQs), and post updates, such as device drivers, that users can download. Microsoft's Help and Support and its online Knowledge Base (*http://support.microsoft.com*) is another valuable source for information on Windows Vista, Internet Explorer, Office applications, and other software products.

- **Decide how best to proceed in resolving the problem**. For example, if you recently installed an update to your video display driver, and if that is the only change made to your computer, evaluate what options are available for resolving the problem. Can you uninstall the driver update? Can you restore the previously used video display driver that worked? If you encounter a more serious problem, can you restore your entire computer to an earlier working state? Make one change at a time, determine whether the change resolved the problem, and if not, decide whether you want to (for example) use Windows Update to reinstall the updated device driver, and then try the next logical troubleshooting option. If you decide to make a major change to your computer system, stop and make a backup first of important files and, if necessary, your computer system itself. Tutorial 10 covers ways to back up your computer system and your important files.
- **Consider other alternatives**. If you attempt to troubleshoot a problem and cannot resolve it, consider other possible causes, such as the possibility that your computer is infected with malicious software or that a hacker or intruder might have gained access to your computer and modified it in some way.

If your field of specialty is technical support and troubleshooting, you might want to develop a system for reporting problems that includes the following:

- **A database of problems and solutions to those problems**. You can create a database of problems that users have already encountered or are likely to encounter, identify the operating systems and applications for each problem and solution, include specific steps for resolving each problem, and include warnings. You can design the database for yourself and other technical support staff who need to quickly consult this resource, and you can prepare an online version of this database for users so that they can search for and resolve common problems that do not require major changes to the configuration of a computer, such as modifying the Registry. Cross-reference the information so that users can more easily locate solutions to problems. You can also include links to Microsoft's Knowledge Base or other Web sites that provide troubleshooting information or assistance.
- **Online form for reporting problems**. Rather than relying on recording information via the telephone or after a conversation, you can create an online form for reporting problems that gathers all of the necessary information, provides the detail you need, and standardizes the reporting process. Show staff members how to use the Windows Vista Snipping Tool accessory or the Alt+Print Screen keys to capture an image of a message box that identifies an error, or in the case of Alt+Print Screen, how to paste the image into a new document.
- **Remote control of user's screen**. You might also want to use a software tool, such as Windows Remote Assistance, to assist a user with a problem from your computer, or use Remote Desktop Connection or Remote Desktop Web Connection to troubleshoot the user's problem from another computer.

Because of the complexity of troubleshooting problems with an operating system, as well as all the other software and all the hardware on a computer, you should become familiar with all the tools and features provided with the operating system for identifying, analyzing, and troubleshooting problems.

Getting Started

To complete this tutorial, you must display the Computer icon on the desktop, switch your computer to single-click activation, and display Administrative Tools on the Start menu. In the following steps, you check and, if necessary, change these settings.

To set up your computer:

1. If necessary, display a Computer icon on the desktop.
2. If you need to enable single-click activation, double-click the **Computer** icon on the desktop, click the **Organize** button on the command bar, click **Folder and Search Options**, and under "Click items as follows" on the General property sheet in the Folder Options dialog box, click the **Single-click to open an item (point to select)** option button, click the **Underline icon titles only when I point at them** option button, click the **OK** button to close the Folder and Options dialog box, and then close the Computer window.
3. If Administrative Tools is not displayed on the Start menu, right-click the **Start** button, click **Properties**, and on the Start Menu property sheet, click the **Customize** button to the right of the Start menu style option, scroll to the bottom of the list of options for customizing the Start menu, and under System administrative tools, click the **Display on the All Programs menu and the Start menu** option button, click the **OK** button to close the Customize Start Menu dialog box, and then click the **OK** button to close the Taskbar and Start Menu Properties dialog box.

Next, Julien suggests you investigate a tool new to Windows Vista called the Reliability Monitor.

Using Reliability Monitor

Reliability Monitor is a new Windows Vista tool that monitors the reliability and stability of your computer. If a problem arises, Reliability Monitor identifies the cause of the problem, such as a Windows, application, or hardware failure, and you can view information on a specific problem that occurred on a specific day. You can also get a sense of the overall performance of your computer and determine whether its performance is improving or decreasing. Reliability Monitor also assigns a reliability rating on a scale of 1 to 10 to reflect the current reliability of your computer. (See the "How Windows Vista Assigns Reliability Ratings" Insight for more information on how Windows Vista assigns this rating.) That reliability rating is called the **System Stability Index**.

Reliability Monitor provides information on five types of events that affect system stability:

- **Software (Un)Installs** Reliability Monitor uses this category to report information about the installation, configuration, updating, and removal of software, including Windows Vista.
- **Application Failures** Reliability Monitor uses this category to report information about problems with applications, such as a nonresponding application.

- **Hardware Failures** Reliability Monitor uses this category to report information about hardware failures that involve the hard disk and memory.
- **Windows Failures** Reliability Monitor uses this category to report information about operating system failures, such as system crashes, boot failures, and sleep failures (power management problems).
- **Miscellaneous Failures** Reliability Monitor uses this category to report information on shutdown problems.

If a significant date and time change occurred, Reliability Monitor also displays a System Clock Changes category if you select the day on which the date and time occurred.

How Windows Vista Assigns Reliability Ratings | InSight

On the day you install Windows Vista, it assigns your computer a reliability rating of 10.0 (the highest possible score). Whenever a problem occurs, Windows Vista lowers your computer's reliability rating. If your computer does not experience any problems on a given day, Windows Vista increases your computer's reliability rating. The **reliability rating** is therefore a setting that reflects the overall performance of your computer. Reliability ratings range from 1.0 (for least stable) to 10.0 (for the highest degree of stability). When calculating reliability ratings, Reliability Monitor does not include days when your computer is off or in a sleep state. You can use your computer's reliability rating to monitor changes to the health of your computer.

So that you can monitor the health of your new computer, Julien recommends that you use Reliability Monitor to produce a System Stability Report and use that as a baseline for tracking changes to the performance of your computer.

To access the full functionality of Reliability Monitor, you must provide Administrator credentials. If you are not logged on under an Administrator account or cannot provide the password for an Administrator account, read the following steps and examine the figures so that you are familiar with the use of Reliability Monitor, but do not keystroke the steps.

To open Reliability Monitor and examine a System Stability Report for your computer:

1. On the Start menu, point to **Administrative Tools**, and then click **Reliability and Performance Monitor**. If your account is an Administrator account, Windows Vista switches to Secure Desktop Mode and displays a User Account Control dialog box. If your account is a Standard User account, Windows Vista opens Reliability and Performance Monitor but warns you that you must be a member of either the Administrators group or the Performance Log Users group to enable the full functionality of these tools.

   Trouble? If you want to open Reliability and Performance Monitor with Administrator credentials, close the current Reliability and Performance Monitor window, point to Administrative Tools on the Start menu, right-click Reliability and Performance Monitor, click Run as administrator, and then provide Administrator credentials.

2. When prompted for Administrator credentials for your Administrator account, click the **Continue** button in the User Account Control dialog box.

   Trouble? If warned that an Administrator might need to enable a scheduled task to update or display data in Reliability Monitor under a Standard user account, click the OK button in the Reliability Monitor dialog box, and then Windows Vista opens the Reliability and Performance Monitor window.

Tip

You can also right-click the Computer icon, select Manage, provide Administrator credentials, and then select Reliability and Performance in the Computer Management window's console pane.

3. In the console tree pane on the left side of the window, double-click **Monitoring Tools** to expand this category (if necessary), click **Reliability Monitor**, and then maximize the window. Reliability Monitor displays a System Stability Chart. See Figure 8-1. The line chart plots your computer's System Stability Index (or reliability rating) over time. The System Stability Index value also shows your computer's current reliability rating. On the computer used for this figure, the System Stability Index increased from a low of 5.68 to a high of 9.78 over a 30-day period, indicating that the reliability of the system improved substantially. The System Stability Chart contains information for the last 30 days; however, you can scroll to the left to view earlier dates or use the Calendar control to the right of the chart to select a specific date. Below the plot of data on the line chart, Reliability Monitor displays red error icons for Application, Hardware, Windows, and Miscellaneous failures; yellow warning error icons for software install or uninstall failures; and informational icons for successful software installs and uninstalls. Your System Stability Chart details will differ.

Figure 8-1 **Viewing a System Stability Chart in Reliability Monitor**

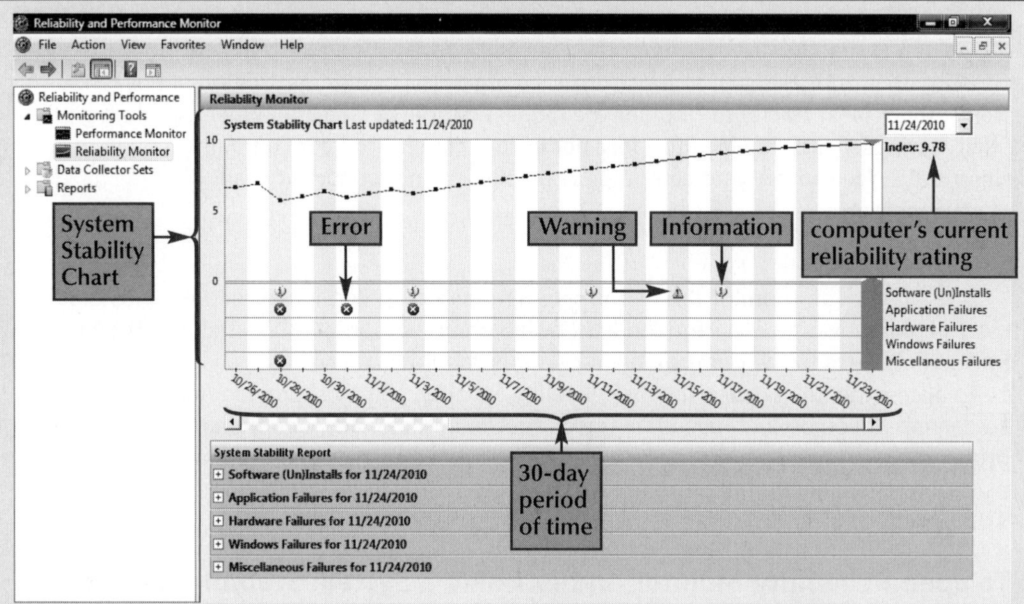

4. If Reliability Monitor displays one or more red error icons for an Application, Hardware, Windows, or Miscellaneous failure, click a **red error** icon on the day where it appears. Reliability Monitor expands the category for Application, Hardware, Windows, or Miscellaneous Failures in the System Stability Report under the chart and displays details about the errors that occurred on that day. On the computer used for Figure 8-2, Reliability Monitor displays information about an Application Failure and reports that OUTLOOK.EXE (the program filename for Microsoft Outlook) stopped responding on Halloween. The Version number indicates that the program in question is Microsoft Outlook 2007. The System Stability Index dipped to a low of 5.88 that day. On this computer, all three application failures involved Outlook. If the same application failure appears repeatedly, you need to follow up and research the cause of the problem.

Figure 8-2 Viewing information about an application failure

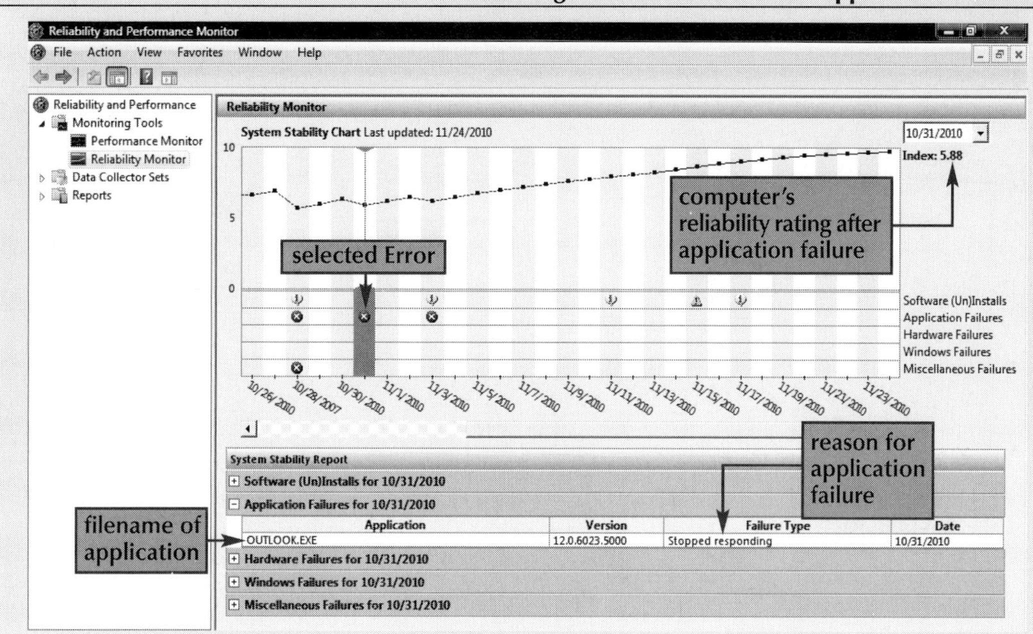

On the computer used for Figure 8-3, Reliability Monitor reported that an application configuration change for SnagIt (a screen capture program) failed.

Figure 8-3 Viewing information about another application failure

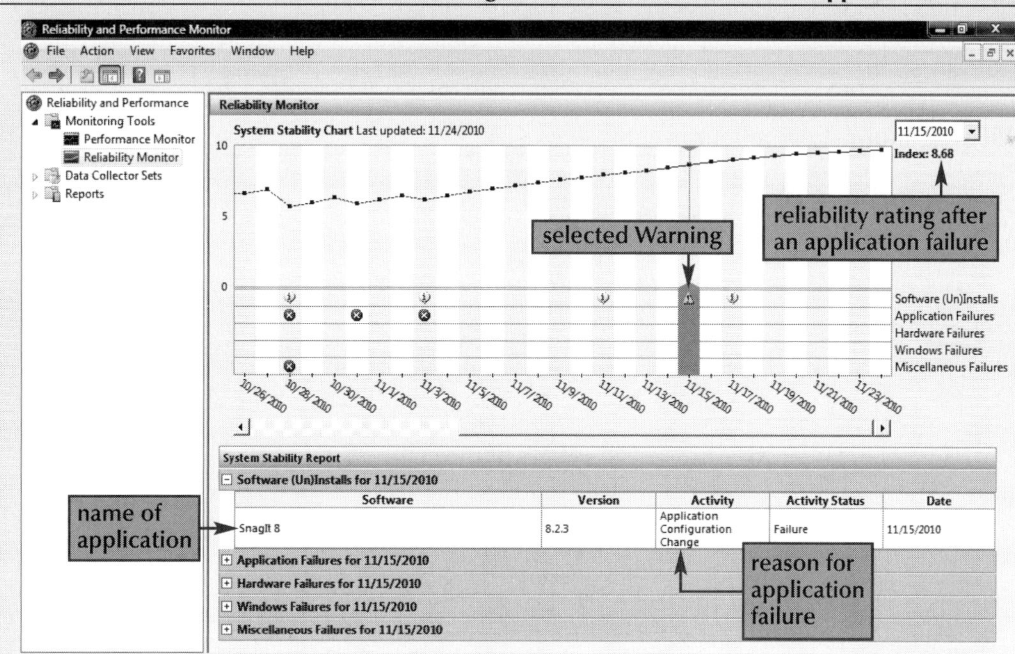

On the computer used for Figure 8-4, Reliability Monitor reported a successful installation of a definition update for Windows Defender.

Figure 8-4

Viewing information on a successful software update

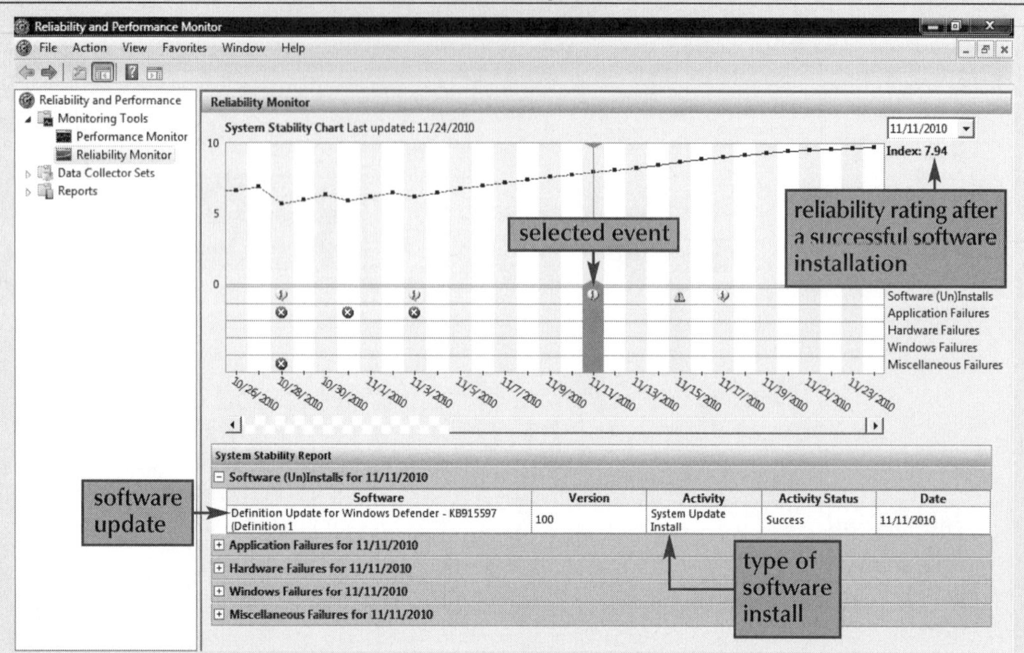

If you select a date that contains more than one icon for the five categories in the System Stability Chart, Reliability Monitor displays information for each category where a problem occurred or where a successful install or uninstall of an application occurred. Figure 8-5 shows a date that includes another Outlook application failure, a successful application install and configuration change for Adobe Reader, and a successful install of a system definition update for Windows Defender.

Figure 8-5

Viewing information on four events

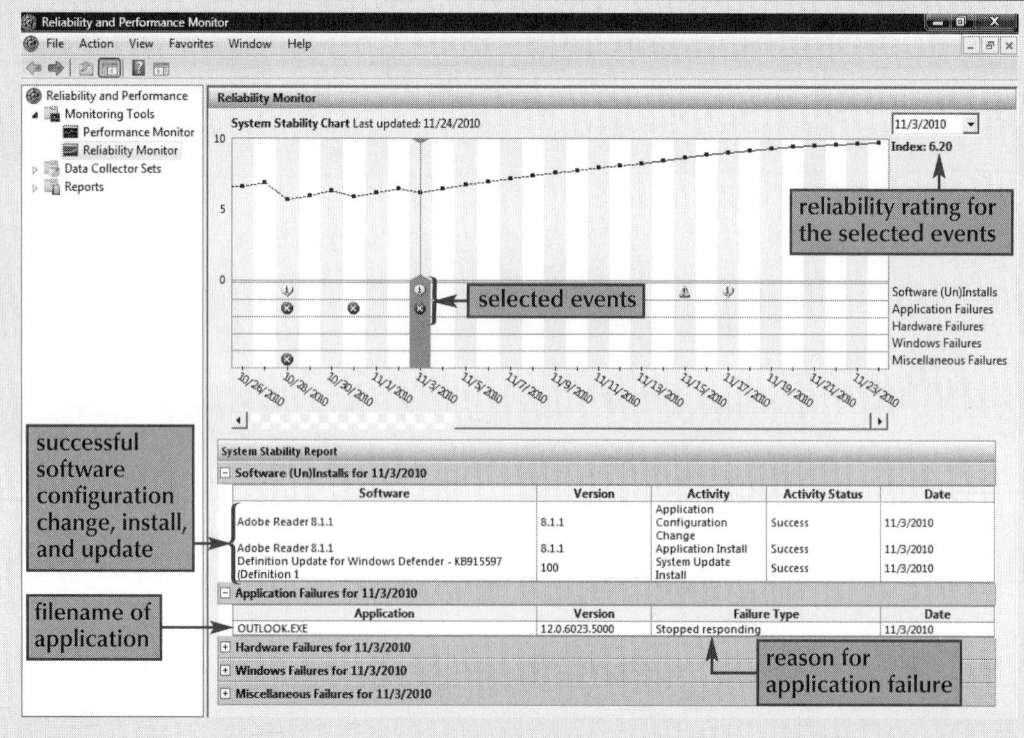

During the period examined for this computer, there were no hardware failures. The one Miscellaneous failure was identified as a Disruptive Shutdown when the computer was not shut down properly. The other informational icons indicated successful system updates for the Windows Malicious Software Removal Tool, Windows Mail Junk E-mail Filter, and Outlook Junk E-mail Filter, as well as Windows Vista general and security updates, definition updates for Windows Defender, a cumulative security update for Windows Vista Internet Explorer 7, Microsoft Office Professional 2007 application installs and configuration changes, SnagIt configuration change, and driver installs for USB hardware, Microsoft Composite Battery, Microsoft ACPI-Compliant System, and HID UPS Battery (though not all of these updates are visible in the figures).

Figure 8-6 shows a later date when a Windows failure occurred. On that date, there was a successful installation of an update for Windows Defender; however, the OS also stopped working that day. A Stop Error (or Blue Screen of Death) occurred when Windows Vista awoke from a Sleep state; however, Windows Vista immediately recovered from the Stop Error and restored the computer and itself. Notice also that the System Stability Index dropped from 10.0 (the highest possible score) to 6.79 as the result of a series of Application failures that primarily resulted from merging multiple Microsoft Word documents with comments into one document.

Viewing information on a Windows failure

Figure 8-6

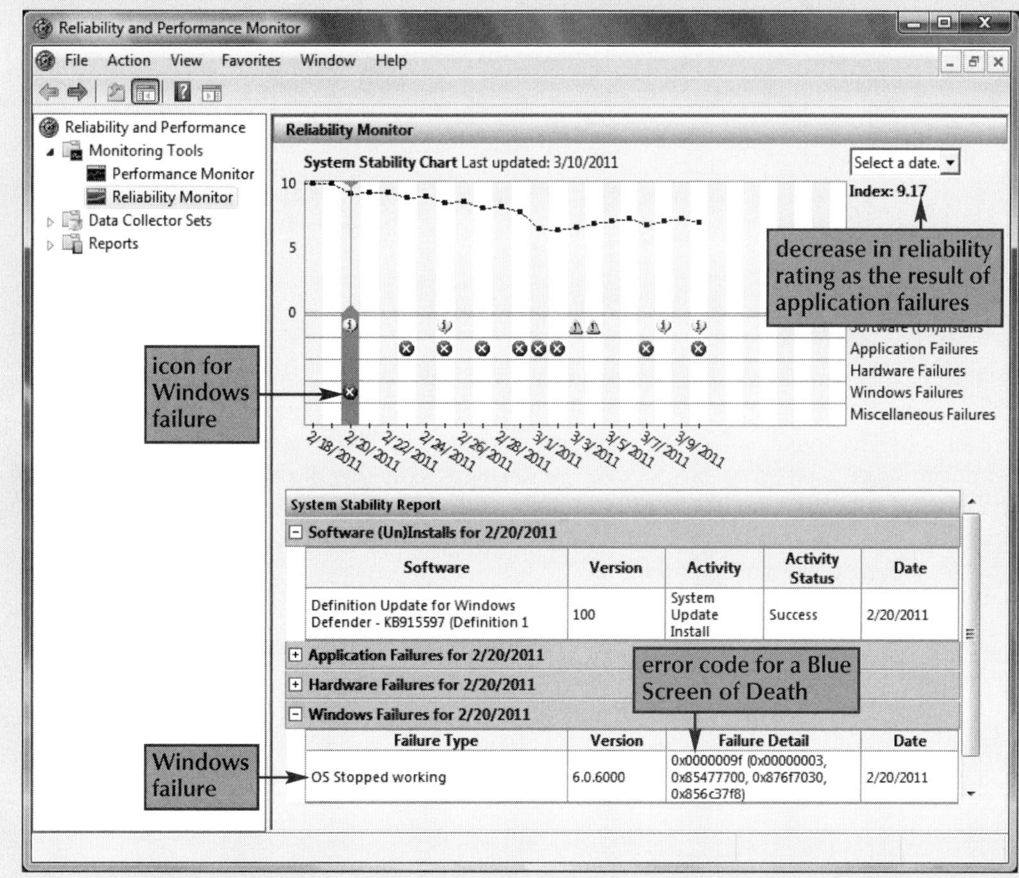

Tip

You can click the Collapse or Expand box to the left of a category to hide or display the detail within a category.

5. Click the **Calendar control** list arrow in the upper-right corner, and then click **Select all**. Under System Stability Report, Reliability Monitor reports information for all Software (Un)Installs. See Figure 8-7. If you scroll further down the System Stability Report, Reliability Monitor displays detailed information on events for all five categories. Your details will differ.

Figure 8-7 **Viewing information on all events**

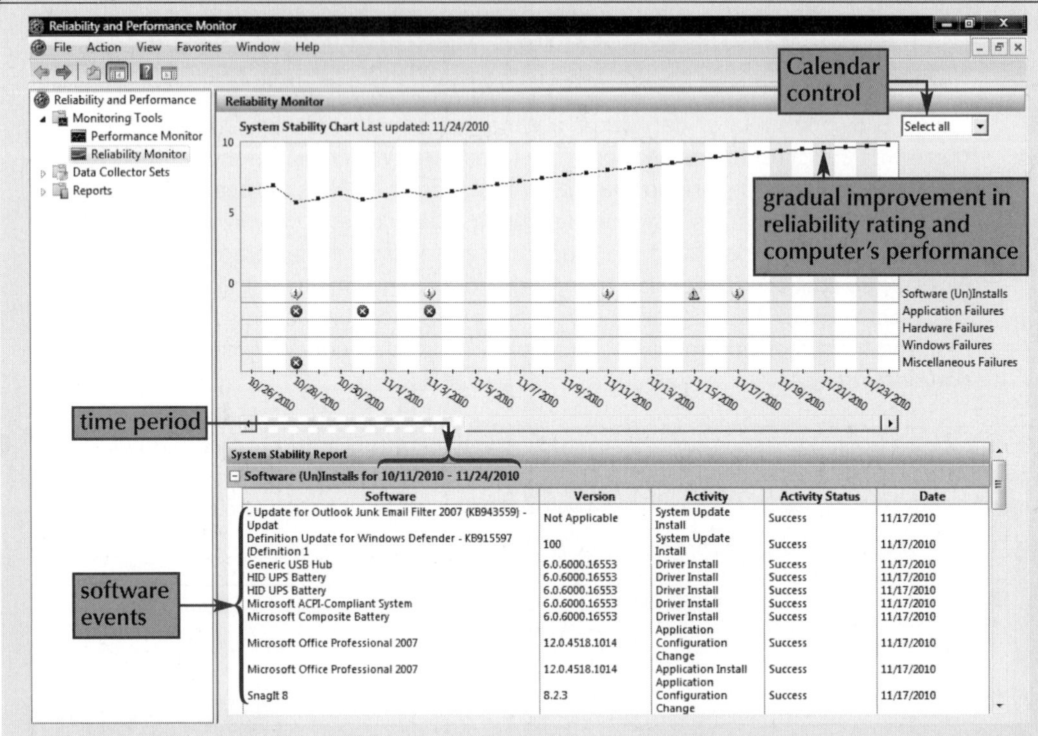

6. Close the Reliability and Performance Monitor window.

If you expand the Application Failures category after choosing Select all in the Calendar control list box, Reliability Monitor lists all programs that stopped responding or that stopped working. By viewing all failures for a specific category, you can more easily identify problems with specific programs or spot trends or changes in the performance of your computer that require your attention. The problems might relate to the specific software or to limited resources on your computer. You can also use Reliability Monitor Help for assistance in troubleshooting performance problems.

Using Reliability Monitor

| Reference Window

- On the Start menu, point to Administrative Tools, and then click Reliability and Performance Monitor.
- If your account is an Administrator account, click the Continue button in the User Account Control dialog box after Windows Vista switches to Secure Desktop Mode. If your account is a Standard User account, Windows Vista opens Reliability and Performance Monitor but warns you that you must be a member of either the Administrators group or the Performance Log Users group to enable the full functionality of these tools.
- In the console tree pane on the left side of the Reliability and Performance Monitor window, click Reliability Monitor, and then maximize the window.
- Examine the System Stability Chart for changes in your computer's Reliability Stability Index and for information about Software (Un)Installs, Application Failures, Hardware Failures, Windows Failures, and Miscellaneous Failures.
- If Reliability Monitor displays one or more red error or yellow warning icons for Software (Un)Installs and Application, Hardware, Windows, or Miscellaneous Failures, click one of the error or warning icons to view information about all errors and events that occurred on that date.
- To view information about all Software (Un)Installs or all Application, Hardware, Windows, and Miscellaneous Failures, click the Calendar control list arrow, click Select all, and then examine the events listed in the System Stability Report.
- Close the Reliability and Performance Monitor window.

Reliability Monitor's System Stability Chart and System Stability Report are useful tools for identifying problems, trends, and changes that affect the stability and performance of your computer.

Using Event Viewer

Event Viewer is a more advanced and more comprehensive Windows Vista troubleshooting tool that provides detailed information about every event that occurs on a computer. An **event** is a significant change in your computer system or to a program that either requires notifying the user or users of that computer or recording the event in a log. Information about events is stored in files called **event logs**.

Event Viewer displays information on the following types of events that occur on a computer:

- **Application Events** Event Viewer identifies an application or program event as an Error, Warning, or Information.
- **Security Events** Event Viewer identifies a security-related event as an Audit Success or Audit Failure. Examples of an Audit Success include a successful user account logon or logoff, a successful start of Windows Firewall, and a change in the system time. An example of an Audit Failure is an inability of Windows Firewall to inform a user that it successfully blocked an application from receiving an incoming connection.
- **Setup Events** This category contains information about events on a domain controller. A **domain controller** is a computer that functions as a server on an Active Directory network. An **Active Directory network** is one that manages user logons and provides access to network and shared resources.

- **System Events** Event Viewer displays information about events triggered by components of the Windows operating system. Examples of system events include the start or stop of system services (such as the Security Center, Windows Update, Windows Search, Windows Error Reporting, and Windows Backup), the system uptime, and the start and completion of a Windows Defender scan. Examples of system errors include a driver problem, the failure to assign a specific resource to a hardware device, recovery of a corrupted Registry entry for a specific user logon, an unexpected shutdown of the system, and a nonfunctioning device attached to the computer.
- **Forwarded Events** These events are ones forwarded from another computer.

When you open Event Viewer, it displays a Summary of Administrative Events and groups specific types of events into one of six categories: Critical, Error, Warning, Information, Audit Success, and Audit Failure. You can expand one of these categories to view a list of events that fall in that category. Then, you can double-click an event to view more detail about that event.

After recently encountering a couple of problems on your computer, Julien and you decide to use Event Viewer to identify the source of those problems.

To examine a Summary of Administrative Events:

Tip

You can also press the Windows Logo key, type event, and then click Event Viewer in the Search results.

1. On the Start menu, point to **Administrative Tools**, click **Event Viewer**, and if prompted for Administrator credentials for an Administrator account, click the **Continue** button in the User Account Control dialog box. (If your account is a Standard User account, Windows Vista opens Event Viewer.) Event Viewer compiles a Summary of Administrative Events in the Details pane in the center of the window. See Figure 8-8. Obviously, Critical, Error, and Warning are three groups of events that you want to examine, and if possible, troubleshoot and resolve.

Figure 8-8 Viewing a Summary of Administrative Events

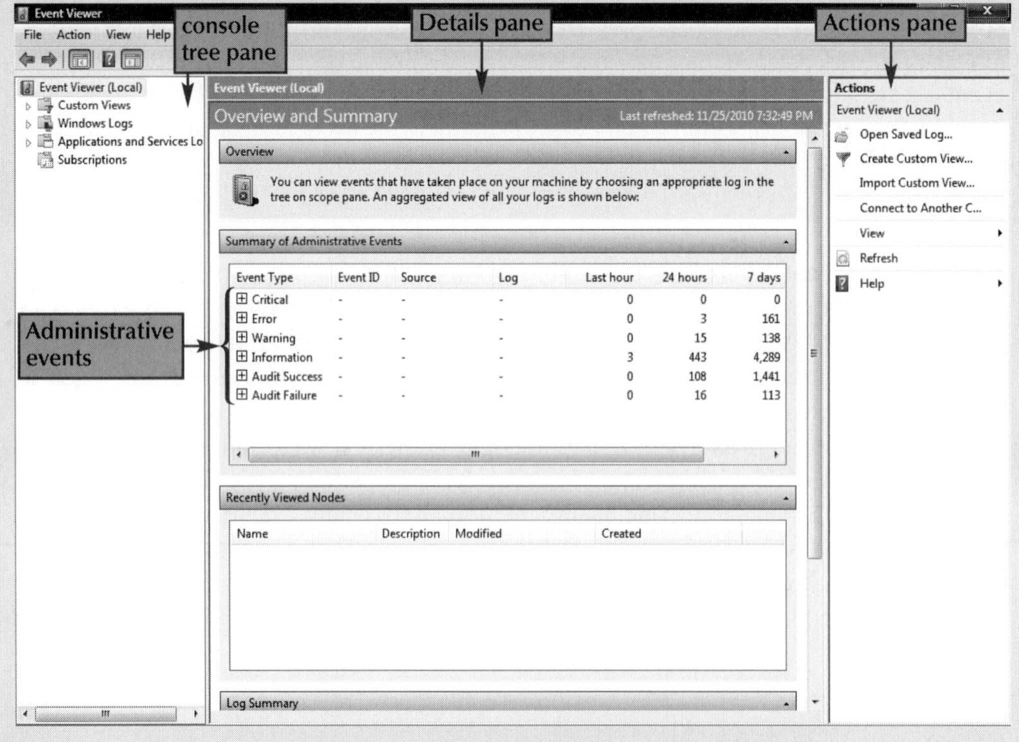

2. Click the **Expand** box ⊞ to the left of Critical in the Summary of Administrative Events pane. On the computer used for Figure 8-9, Event Viewer lists three Critical events. Your events will differ. The Kernel-Power Critical event is a power management problem that occurred when the computer switched to a sleep state, and the DriverFrameworks-UserMode Critical events relate to a problem with a USB flash drive device driver.

   Trouble? If Event Reviewer does not display an Expand box to the left of the Critical Event Type category, click the Expand box for one of the other categories, preferably Error, Warning, and then Information (in that order).

Figure 8-9 Viewing a list of Critical events

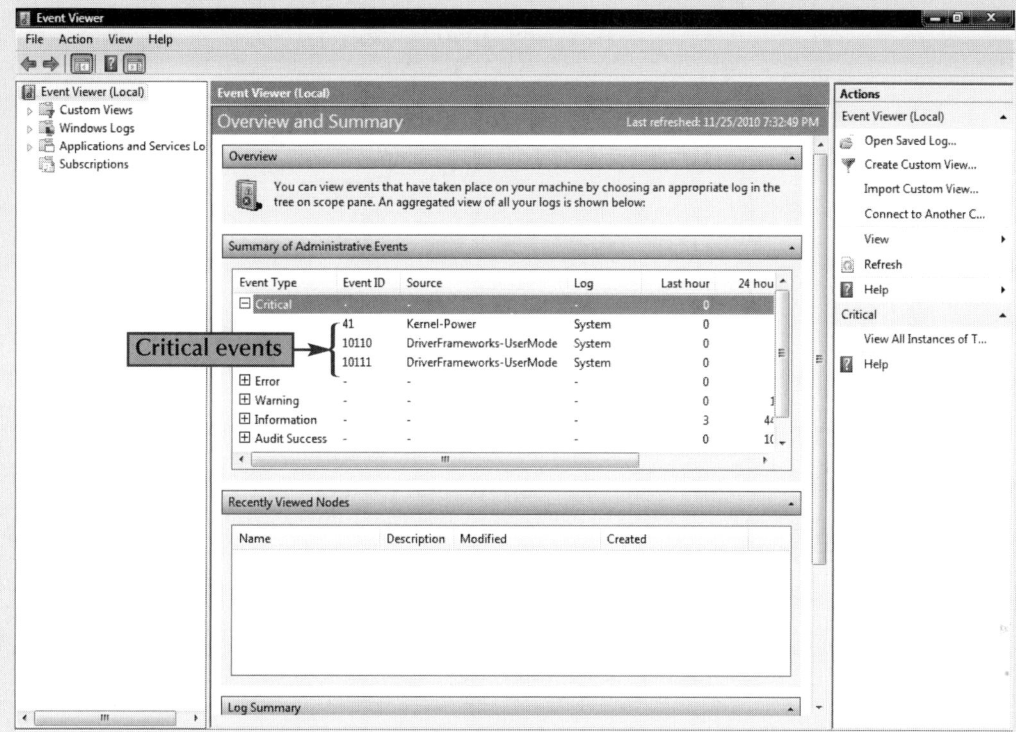

3. Double-click an **event** under one of the Event Type categories. On the computer used for Figure 8-10, Event Viewer displays information about a Kernel-Power Critical event and noted that the last sleep transition was unsuccessful. Event Viewer notes that this problem might have resulted if the system stopped responding, failed, or lost power in the last sleep transition. Your event and event information may differ.

Tip

For online assistance, click the Help link in the Actions pane, and then click Event Log Online Help.

Figure 8-10 **Viewing details of a Critical event**

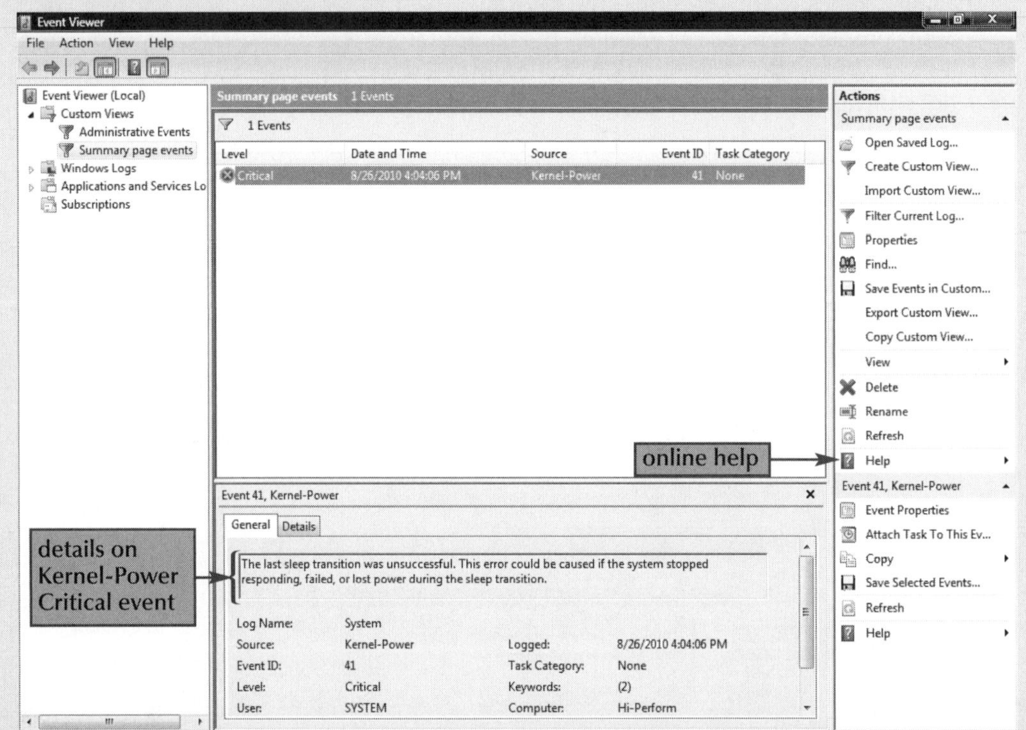

4. Use the **Back** button on the Standard toolbar to return to the Summary of Administrative Events. Event Viewer recompiles the Summary of Administrative Events from event logs.

5. View an event in one of the other event categories that you have not already examined so that you are familiar with other types of events, and then return to the Summary of Administrative Events.

6. Keep Event Viewer open for the next section of the tutorial.

You can also choose to view a category of events, such as Application Events, Security Events, and System Events. Furthermore, you can **filter**, or select, events by applying one or more criteria so that you can focus on one specific type of event, such as all Application Event Errors.

To examine Application events:

1. In the console tree pane on the left, double-click **Windows Logs** (or click the Expand box to the left of Windows Logs) to expand this category. In the Details pane in the center of the window, Event Viewer lists the total number of events that appear in each of the five Windows logs.

2. In the console tree pane, click **Application** under Windows Log. Event Viewer displays a list of events that fall in this category and lists them from the most recent event to the oldest event.

3. Click an **Application event** in the Details pane and review the information reported on that event on the General sheet. On the computer used for Figure 8-11, Event Viewer reports that the Windows Backup application successfully completed a file backup. Your event and event details will differ.

Viewing details on an Information event **Figure 8-11**

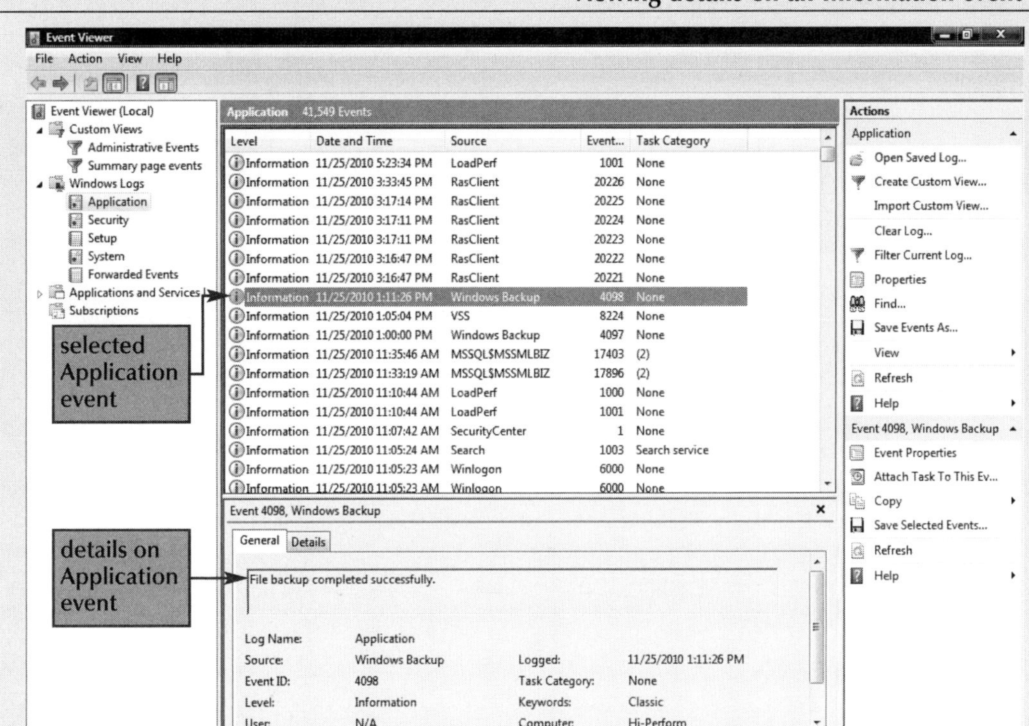

4. In the Actions pane on the right, click the **Filter Current Log** link. Event Viewer displays a Filter Current Log dialog box. See Figure 8-12. You can now specify criteria for filtering events and thereby display only those that meet the criteria you specify. For Application events, you can choose the Error, Warning, or Information check boxes under Event level.

Figure 8-12 Filter Current Log dialog box for specifying filter criteria

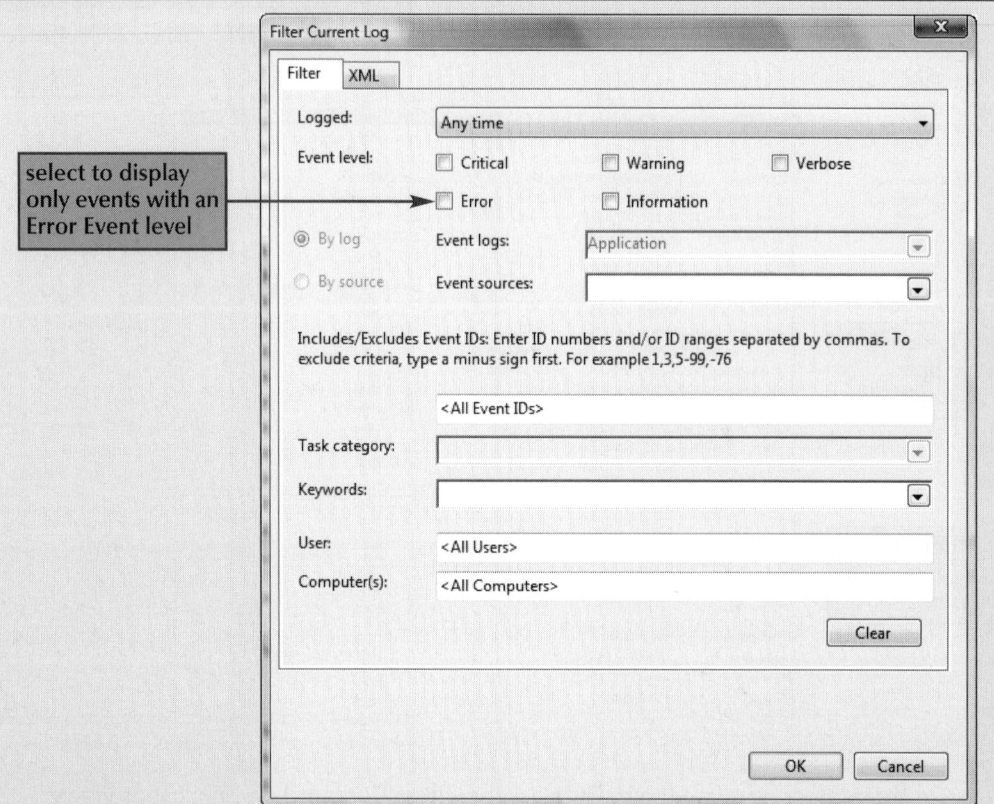

5. Under Event level, click the **Error** check box, and then click the **OK** button. Event Viewer filters events and displays all events assigned the Error level.
6. Double-click **one event** in the list of filtered Application events. On the computer used for Figure 8-13, Event Viewer opens an Event Properties dialog box and displays details about an Application Hang event on the General sheet. Event Viewer notes that OUTLOOK.EXE stopped interacting with Windows and therefore was closed. Event Viewer then suggests that the user view Windows Vista's problem history by opening Problem Reports and Solutions in the Control Panel.

Figure 8-13 Viewing information on an Application Hang

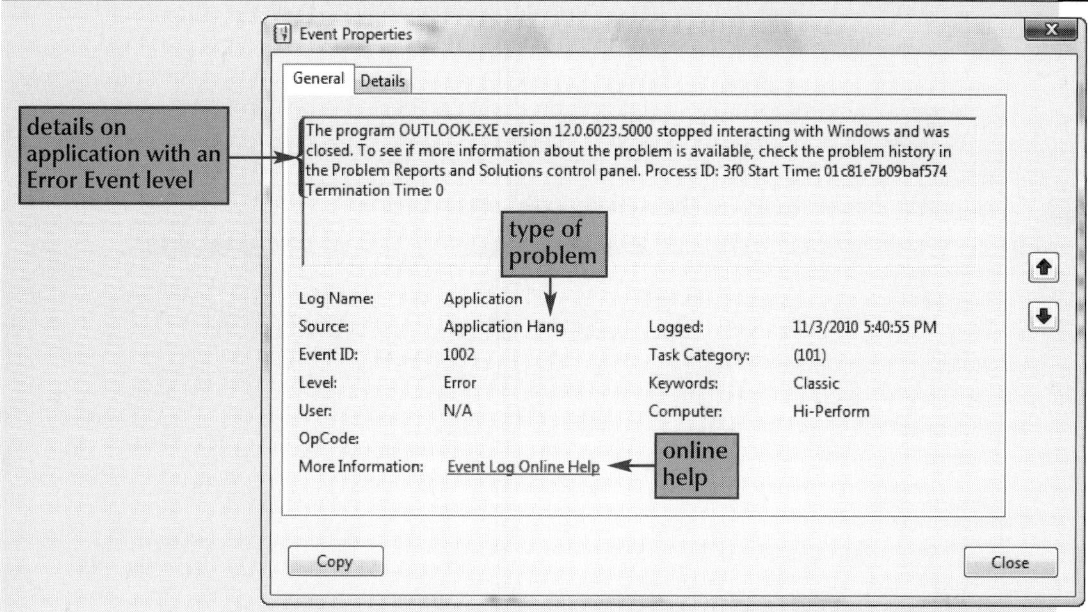

7. Click the **Close** button in the Event Properties dialog box.
8. In the Actions pane, click **Clear Filter**. Event Viewer removes the filter you applied to the list of Application events.
9. Keep the Event Viewer window open for the next section of the tutorial.

You can use the same approach to examine System events with an Error level so that you can focus on problems with Windows and Windows services.

If you want to examine security problems, select Security under Windows logs. Event Viewer then displays a list of Security events in the Details pane. The first column, labeled Keywords, identifies the event as an Audit Success or Audit Failure. If you want to see just Audit Failures, you choose the Filter Current Log option, click the Keywords list arrow, click the Audit Failure check box, and then apply the filter. Now, you can focus on security-related problems.

You can also view events related to a specific service, such as Reliability Monitor, Windows Update, and User Account Control as well as Microsoft Office sessions (i.e., Word, Excel, PowerPoint, and Access sessions).

To examine events for a specific service:

1. In the console tree pane on the left, double-click **Applications and Services Logs** (or click the Expand View box to the left of Applications and Services Logs) to expand this category.
2. Under Applications and Services Log in the console tree pane, double-click **Microsoft**, and then double-click **Windows**. Event Viewer expands each category.

3. Under Windows, locate and double-click **Reliability-Analysis-Engine**, and then click **Operational** under Reliability-Analysis-Engine in the console tree pane. In the Details pane, Event Viewer lists events for the Reliability Analysis component that updates your computer's System Stability Index every day. See Figure 8-14. All of the 1,630 events recorded for the Reliability-Analysis-Engine on this computer are events at the Information Level. In other words, there are no Error Level events. Your events and event details will differ.

Figure 8-14 Viewing Windows events for the Reliability-Analysis-Engine

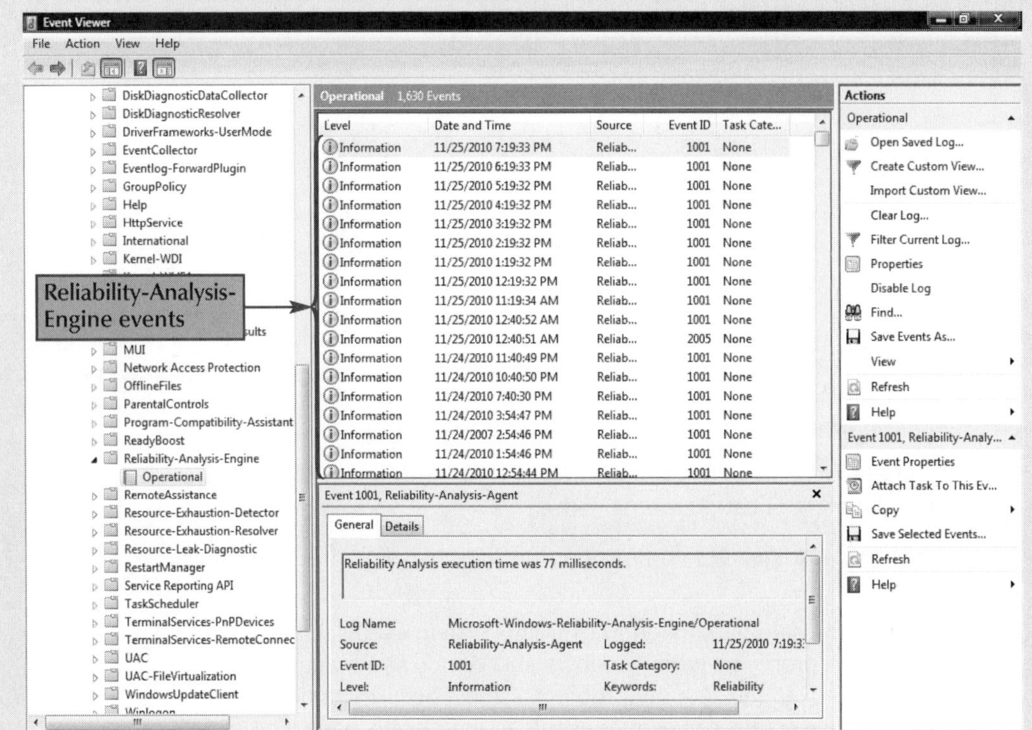

4. If Microsoft Office is installed on your computer, locate and click **Microsoft Office Sessions** in the console tree pane; otherwise, read this step. Event Viewer displays event information for each application session you open in Microsoft Office. You can use the same approach you used earlier to filter events and display only those events with an Error level so that you can examine and then troubleshoot Office problems. Of the 2,135 events recorded on Microsoft Office applications, there were only two Error Level events where the application crashed.

5. Close the Event Viewer window.

Event Viewer records information on every single event that occurs on your computer. On the computer used for these figures, there were a total of 126,919 events. By using filters, you can narrow down events so that you can focus on the most serious events and attempt to troubleshoot the problems that occurred. Also, after an error condition occurs on your computer, you can use Event Viewer to view information about the event and decide how best to troubleshoot the problem. You can use Event Viewer Help or Event Log Online Help to assist you with troubleshooting problems using Event Viewer.

Using Event Viewer | Reference Window

- On the Start menu, point to Administrative Tools, click Event Viewer, and if prompted for Administrator credentials for an Administrator account, click the Continue button in the User Account Control dialog box. (If your account is a Standard User account, Windows Vista opens Event Viewer.)
- In the Summary of Administrative Events, click the Expand box to the left of each Event Type category you want to examine, examine the list of events, and if you want to view information about a specific event, double-click that event, examine information about that event, and then use the Back button on the Standard toolbar to return to the Summary of Administrative Events.
- To view Application Events, Security Events, and System Events, double-click Windows Logs in the console tree pane to expand this category, click Application, Security, or System under Windows Logs, select an event in the Details pane, and review the information reported on that event on the General sheet.
- To filter events, click the Filter Current Log link in the Actions pane on the right, and in the Filter current Log dialog box, select or specify one or more criteria for filtering events, click the OK button, and then select and examine an event in the list of filtered events.
- To remove a filter, click Clear Filter in the Actions pane.
- To examine events for a specific Windows component or service, double-click the Applications and Services Logs in the console tree pane to expand this category, double-click Microsoft, double-click Windows, locate and double-click the Windows component you want to examine, click Operational in the console tree pane under the Windows component you selected, and in the Details pane, review the information on events or select and examine specific events.
- If Microsoft Office is installed on your computer, locate and click Microsoft Office Sessions, and then examine the information on Microsoft Office application events.
- Close the Event Viewer window.

As you may have discovered from working with Event Viewer, it provides an alternate approach to viewing some of the same information that you can examine with the Reliability Monitor. However, it provides more information about all the events that occur on your computer. Also, you can use different approaches to locate and filter events so that you can examine and troubleshoot problems or assure yourself that your system is working properly.

Using System Protection to Create a Restore Point

If you encounter a problem after installing an operating system upgrade, a software product, or a device driver for a hardware device, you can use System Restore to roll back your computer to the point before you installed or updated that software on your computer. Likewise, if you make a change to a system setting, or if your computer sustains damage from malicious software, you might be able to use System Restore to roll back your computer to an earlier working state. If you roll back your computer to an earlier point in time to resolve a problem, any other changes you've made to your computer during that same period of time, such as updates to installed software, are also restored to their previous state.

System Protection is the Windows component that creates and saves restore points so that you can roll back your computer with System Restore and restore it to an earlier working state. Each **restore point** contains information about the state of system files and system settings on a computer at a specific point in time. System Protection creates restore points at specific intervals of time and when it detects an operation that will change the state of the computer. Although System Protection keeps track of changes to system files and system settings, *it does not save copies of your personal files, such as documents, photos, e-mail messages, or favorites (bookmarks for Web sites)*. Also, System Protection creates restore points on NTFS volumes, but not on FAT32 volumes.

System Protection creates restore points under the following conditions:

- **New installation of or upgrade to Windows Vista** System Protection creates an initial system checkpoint when you first start a new computer with Windows Vista or after you upgrade a computer to Windows Vista. A **system checkpoint** is a scheduled restore point.
- **Before installing Windows updates** System Protection creates a restore point before Windows Update installs any new Windows updates.
- **Before installing and uninstalling certain types of software** System Protection creates a restore point before you install a program using Windows Installer or InstallShield. Windows Installer is the Windows component that manages the installation and removal of programs on your computer. InstallShield is a software tool developed by Macrovision Corporation for packaging and reliably installing and uninstalling software. When you use System Restore to roll back your computer to a restore point created before installing a program, System Restore removes the installed software and Registry settings for the installed software and restores programs and system files that were altered during the installation of the new program. If you later decide you want to use this software product, you must reinstall it. Also, System Protection does not create restore points for software installed without Windows Installer or an InstallShield Wizard, so you must create those restore points manually.
- **Before installing unsigned device drivers** If you install a device driver that has not been digitally signed or certified by Microsoft's Windows Hardware Quality Labs (WHQL), System Protection creates a restore point before installing the device driver. If a problem arises after installing an updated device driver, you can use the restore point to roll back your computer and restore your previous device driver. In Tutorial 12, you will examine a feature called Roll Back Driver that is designed for problems caused by installing a new device driver or a device driver update.
- **Daily** System Protection is scheduled to create a system checkpoint every day at 12 a.m. If your computer is in a sleep state, Windows Vista does not wake up the computer to perform the scheduled task. However, if your computer is off or in a sleep state, System Protection creates the scheduled system checkpoint as soon as possible when your computer is up and running.
- **At system startup** System Protection is scheduled to create a restore point when your computer system starts up. The scheduled task that System Protection uses to create this restore point does not wake up the computer to create a restore point. System Protection creates the restore point only if the computer is idle for one minute, and it waits only five minutes for an idle state. You will examine scheduled tasks in more detail later in the tutorial.
- **Before restoring files from a backup** System Protection creates a restore point before you back up or restore backed-up files if either operation alters the state of the operating system.
- **Before restoring your computer using a restore point** If you roll back your computer using a restore point, System Protection creates a new restore point first so that if a problem develops after the restore operation, you can roll your computer forward to its original state before the restore operation. However, if you roll back your computer while in Safe Mode (described later in the tutorial), System Protection does not create a restore point that would allow you to undo the restore operation.

- **When you create manual restore points** You can use System Protection to manually create restore points before you make changes to your computer. For example, before you make changes to Registry settings or other system settings, or before you install a downloaded program that does not use Windows Installer, you can create a restore point in the event a problem develops.

If you have Windows Vista Ultimate, Windows Vista Business, or Windows Vista Enterprise on your computer, and if you make Windows Backups using Windows Vista's Backup and Restore Center, System Restore can use those backups as restore points.

Windows Vista enables System Protection on all hard disk drives and uses up to 15% of the storage space on those hard disk drives for restore points. System Protection requires a minimum of 300 MB of hard disk storage space, and it does not work on hard disk drives with less than 1 GB of total disk capacity.

Examining System Protection Settings

As a precautionary measure, Julien asks all of his support staff to make a manual restore point before modifying the Windows Registry on their own computers and on the computers used by the company's research staff.

Before you create a restore point in the following steps, you will examine the System Protection settings on the computer you are using. To complete the following steps, you need to provide Administrator credentials. If you are not logged on under an Administrator account or cannot provide the password for an Administrator account, read the following steps and examine the figures so that you are familiar with the use of System Restore, but do not keystroke the steps.

To open System Restore and view System Protection settings:

1. Right-click the **Computer** desktop icon, click **Properties**, and under Tasks in the System window, click the **System protection** link. Windows Vista switches to Secure Desktop Mode and displays a User Account Control dialog box.
2. In the User Account Control dialog box, click the **Continue** button if you are logged on under an Administrator account, or if you are logged on under a Standard User account, enter the **password** for an Administrator account, and then click the **OK** button. Then, wait for System Protection to update information on Automatic restore points. Windows Vista displays the System Protection property sheet in the System Properties dialog box. See Figure 8-15. Under Automatic restore points, System Protection identifies the hard disks for which it creates restore points, and it identifies the most recent restore point for each hard disk it protects. On the computer used for this figure, System Protection creates restore points only for Local Disk (C:), the System volume, and it notes the date and time of the most recent restore point (a system checkpoint). It does not create restore points for an external hard disk drive that stores automated daily backups. You can use the check box next to each drive to enable or turn off System Protection. Your System Protection settings will differ.

Tip

Press the Windows Logo and Break keys to open the System window.

Figure 8-15 Viewing System Protection settings

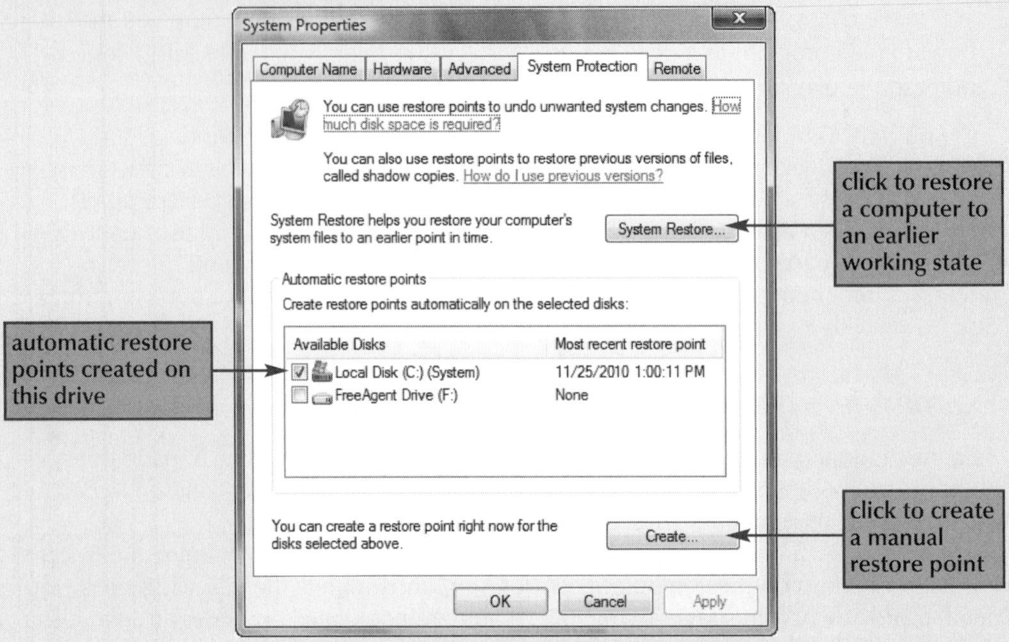

3. Keep the System Properties dialog box open for the next section of the tutorial.

If you turn off System Protection, System Restore deletes all existing restore points and does not create any new restore points.

Reference Window | Checking System Protection Settings

- To view System Protection settings, right-click the Computer icon, click Properties, and under Tasks in the System window, click the System Protection link.
- After Windows Vista switches to Secure Desktop Mode and displays a User Account Control dialog box, click the Continue button if you are logged on under an Administrator account, or if you are logged on under a Standard User account, enter the password for an Administrator account, and then click the OK button.
- On the System Protection tab in the System Properties dialog box, check the settings for creating restore points under Automatic restore points, enable or disable System Protection for each hard disk drive, and then click the OK button to close the System Properties dialog box and apply the changes you made. *Warning*: If you turn off the option for automatically creating restore points, System Protection warns you that all existing restore points are deleted and no new restore points are made. If you do not want to lose your existing restore points, do not turn off System Protection.

Although Windows Vista automatically enables System Protection, you should check the System Protection settings to make sure it creates restore points.

Creating a Restore Point

Although System Protection creates restore points automatically under certain conditions, you can also manually create a restore point before you make an important change to your computer that might cause a problem that you don't anticipate, such as changing a Registry setting.

Since many employees also carry work home and use their own computer systems, Julien asks his assistants to show employees how to create manual restore points as a precautionary measure before they make a significant change to their computer.

To create a restore point:

1. In the System Properties dialog box, click the **Create** button on the System Protection property sheet. System Protection prompts you to enter a description that identifies the purpose of the restore point. See Figure 8-16. It also notes that it will add the date and time to the description.

Figure 8-16 Specifying a description for a manual restore point

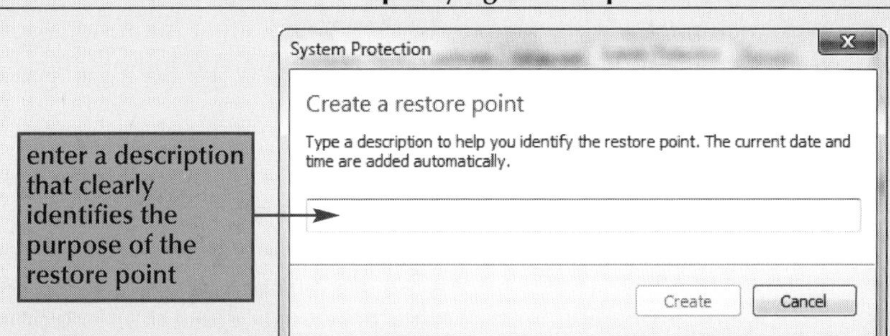

2. Type **Manual Restore Point** and then click the **Create** button. System Protection then displays a dialog box to let you know that it is creating a restore point. When it finishes creating the restore point, it displays a dialog box to let you know that it successfully created the restore point.
3. Click the **OK** button in the System Protection dialog box.
4. Keep the System Properties dialog box open for the next section of the tutorial.

You've created a manual restore point as a safeguard against critical system problems.

Naming Manual Restore Points | InSight

When you create a manual restore point, enter a description that clearly identifies the type of restore point. For example, if you are going to install a new game that you've downloaded from the Internet, you could enter the description "Installation of" or "Before installing" followed by the actual name of the game. By being as specific as possible, you can locate the exact restore point you need later and easily distinguish it from the automatic restore points made by System Protection.

Reference Window | Creating a Manual Restore Point

- To create a manual restore point, right-click the Computer icon, click Properties, and then click the System protection link in the System window.
- After Windows Vista switches to Secure Desktop Mode and displays a User Account Control dialog box, click the Continue button if you are logged on under an Administrator account, or if you are logged on under a Standard User account, enter the password for an Administrator account, and then click the OK button.
- In the System Properties dialog box, click the Create button on the System Protection property sheet, enter a description for the restore point in the System Protection dialog box, and click the Create button.
- After System Protection informs you that it successfully created a restore point, click the OK button in the System Protection dialog box, and then click the OK button to close the System Properties dialog box.

Along with system restore points automatically made by System Protection, manual restore points improve the chances that you can restore your computer to an earlier functioning state and resolve a problem. Because rolling back your computer is a major change to its configuration, you also have to weigh the effect that the restore point has on other changes you made to your computer during the same period of time.

Viewing Restore Points

If you run into a problem on your computer and decide to roll back your computer, you must first choose a restore point from a list of available restore points.

Julien also reminds his assistants to step employees through the process of restoring their computer to an earlier operating state with a previously created restore point and show them how to view their list of restore points.

To view restore points:

1. In the System Properties dialog box, click the **System Restore** button. In the System Restore dialog box shown in Figure 8-17, System Restore points out that it can help you fix problems that cause your computer to run slowly or stop responding. It also points out that choosing a restore point does not affect any of your personal documents, pictures, or data and that the process is completely reversible. If the most recent restore point occurred as a result of a new Windows update, driver, or software installation, you see a Recommended restore option in the System Restore dialog box for undoing that installation, as shown in Figure 8-17.

Figure 8-17 Viewing System Restore options for restoring system files and settings

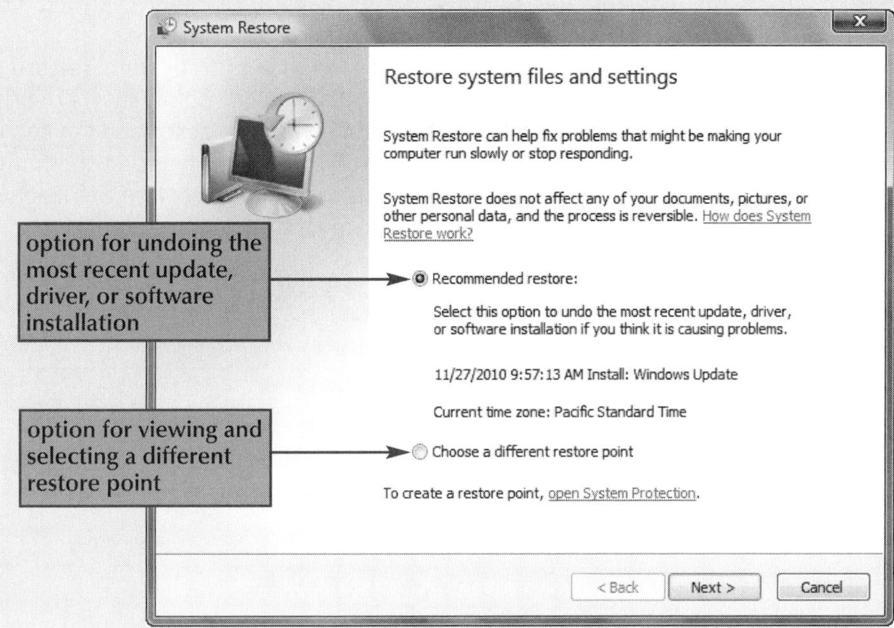

If you have already used a restore point to roll back your computer to an earlier point in time, System Restore includes an option for undoing that task, as shown in Figure 8-18. If you recently rolled back your computer, you also have the option for choosing a different restore point.

Figure 8-18 System Restore option for undoing a restore

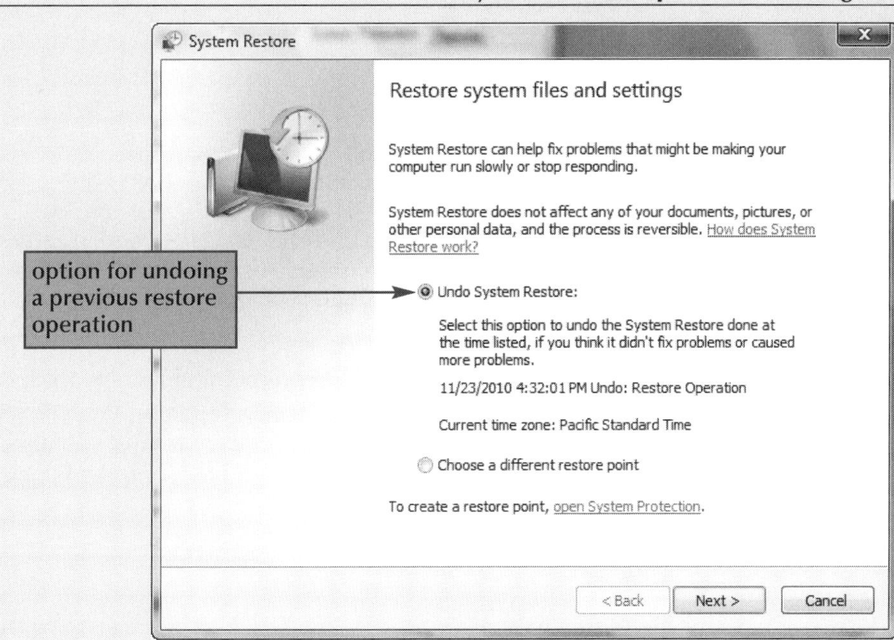

2. If System Restore displays an option for choosing a different restore point, click the **Choose a different restore point** option button, and then click the **Next** button; otherwise, if System Restore does not display an option for choosing a different restore point, click the **Next** button. System Restore displays a list of restore points made during the last five days. See Figure 8-19. System Restore lists restore points in reverse order from the most recent restore point, shows the date and time when it created each restore point, and includes a description of each restore point. Since you just made a manual restore point, it's listed at the top of the list. To see earlier restore points, you can click the "Show restore points older than 5 days" check box. On the computer used for this figure, System Restore listed "System: Scheduled Checkpoints" restore points, "System: Windows Backup" restore points, "Install: Windows Update" restore points, and "Undo: Restore Operation" restore points (though not all are visible in the figure).

Figure 8-19 Types of restore points available for restoring a computer

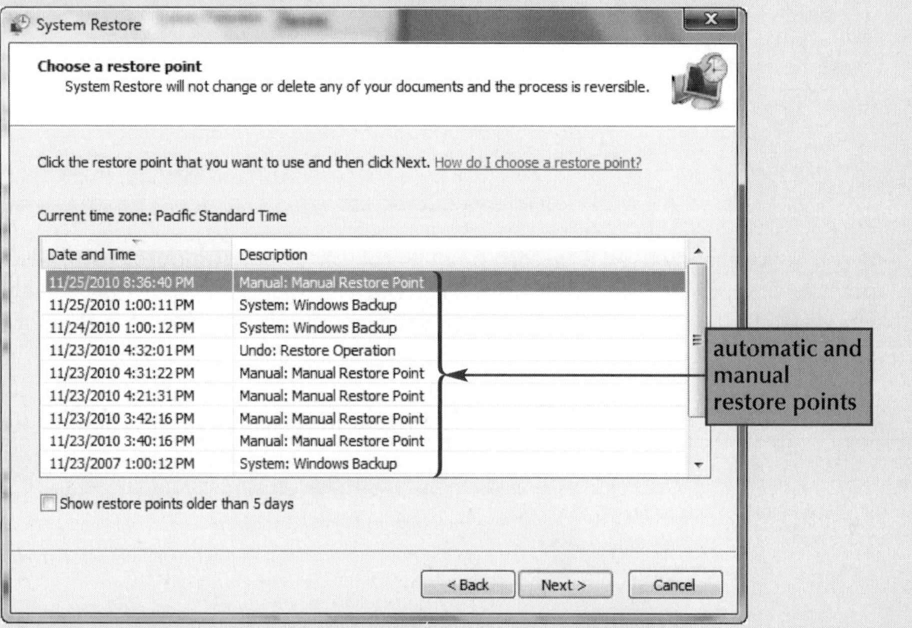

3. So that you do not inadvertently roll back your computer to an earlier working state with a restore point, click the **Cancel** button to cancel this operation and close the System Restore dialog box, and then close the System Properties dialog box.

If you want to roll back your computer, you select a restore point, and then advance to the next dialog box, where System Restore prompts you to confirm your choice. See Figure 8-20. If the selected restore point is not the one that you want to use, you click the Back button, select the correct restore point, click the Next button, and then confirm the restore point you've chosen before you click the Finish button.

Confirm the restore point you selected **Figure 8-20**

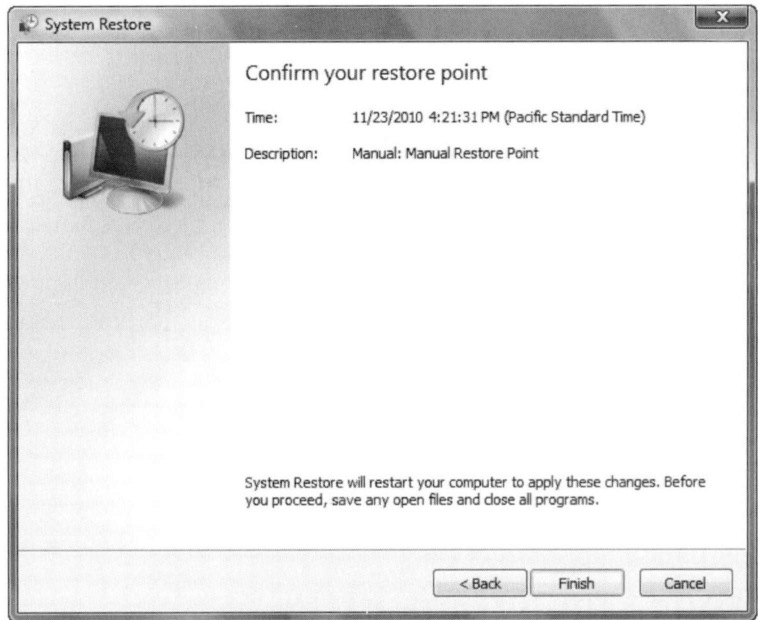

After you click the Finish button, a System Restore dialog box warns you that once started, you cannot interrupt System Restore, and you cannot undo the changes System Restore makes until it restores your computer to the restore point you chose. Finally, it asks if you are sure you want to continue.

Next, you see a System Restore dialog box with the message "Preparing to restore your system" and a progress indicator. As your computer system shuts down, System Restore displays the message "Please wait while your Windows files and settings are being restored." After your computer reboots, you log on under your user account and wait while System Restore finishes restoring your computer. System Restore then displays a System Restore dialog box verifying that System Restore completed successfully. It also notes that your system has been restored to a specific date and time and that your documents have not been affected. See Figure 8-21.

System Restore successfully completed **Figure 8-21**

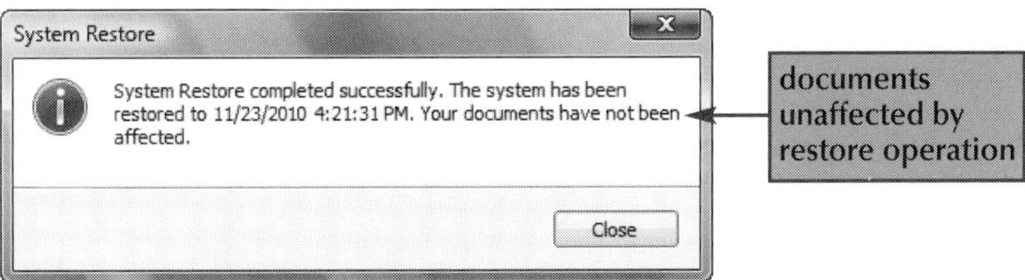

System Restore provides you with a powerful tool for reversing changes that affect the performance of your computer system; however, don't assume that it can resolve every problem you encounter. Although System Protection is designed to create restore points prior to operations that affect the use of your computer, such as installing new software, you can use System Protection to manually create restore points before you make changes to your computer. Furthermore, while System Restore is invaluable, it does not substitute for backups, so you still must back up your important documents on a regular basis.

Review | Session 8.1 Quick Check

1. What tool can you use to produce a System Stability Chart and System Stability Report?
2. A(n) ________________ is a significant change in your computer system or a program that either requires notifying users or recording information in a log.
3. You can specify criteria to ________________ events in an event log and thereby display only those that meet the criteria you specify.
4. ________________ creates and saves restore points so that you can roll back your computer with ________________ and restore it to an earlier working state.
5. What two tools can you use to locate information on specific problems that occur on your computer?
6. A(n) ________________ is a scheduled restore point.

Session 8.2

Using Your Computer's BIOS

As you discovered in Tutorial 1, the BIOS (Basic Input/Output System) plays an important role during the initial stages of booting, including locating and loading the operating system on a computer. The BIOS also contains important system settings that are retained after you power off your computer and that are used during the next boot to help configure your computer. The term **firmware** refers to a hardware device, such as the BIOS, which contains embedded software that controls how the device interacts with the operating system.

To view and change BIOS settings, you open a computer's built-in BIOS Setup utility during booting by pressing a specific key (or combination of keys), such as F2 or F1. During the very early stages of booting, most computers (but not all) display a message on the initial startup screen to identify the key or keys to press to open the BIOS Setup utility, as shown in Figure 8-22. On some computers, the option for displaying these keys (also called **hotkeys**) is turned off to prevent someone from inadvertently opening the BIOS Setup utility and making changes that might adversely affect a computer.

Initial startup screen **Figure 8-22**

The BIOS might also display a message that identifies which hotkey to press to open a Boot Device Menu. Figure 8-23 shows a Boot Device Menu from a Dell computer. From the Boot Device Menu, you can choose which device to use to boot your computer. On this computer, you use the Onboard or USB CD-ROM to boot from a DVD (i.e., your Windows Vista DVD). Your Boot Device Menu might also display other options, including the option for entering System Setup (opening the BIOS Setup utility). You can customize this menu using the BIOS Setup utility.

Boot Device menu **Figure 8-23**

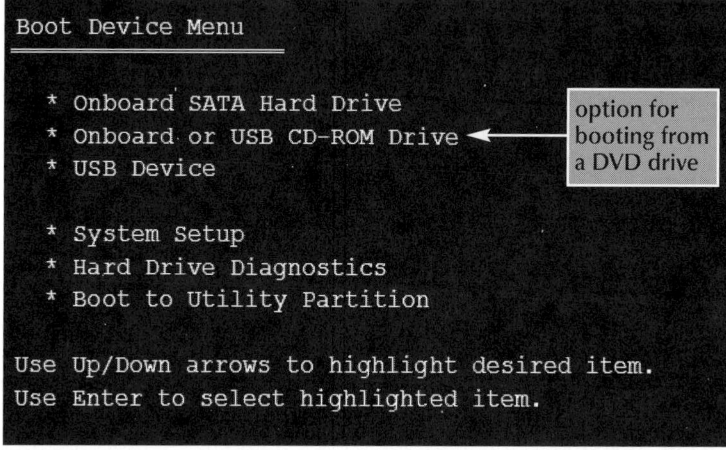

After you open the BIOS Setup utility, you can view and change certain BIOS settings. However, you also want to make sure that you do not accidentally change a setting that might affect the performance of your computer system or prevent your computer from booting. Before you make a change, make a note of the original BIOS setting, the new setting, and the date of the change. That way, you can restore a setting that proves problematic later.

You can use the BIOS Setup utility to perform the following tasks:

- **Check and change the boot sequence** The **boot sequence** (or boot order) consists of a list of devices that the BIOS examines during booting in order to locate the operating system. Typically, the hard disk drive is listed first, followed by other devices, such as a CD drive or USB device. If you want to boot from a device other than the default (or first) device, you might need to change the boot sequence. If you want to install Windows Vista from the Windows Vista DVD, you might need to adjust BIOS settings so that your computer can boot from your DVD drive (as is the case for the computer used for figures in this section of the tutorial).
- **Locate important information about your computer** The BIOS contains detailed information about the computer system itself. For example, you can view information about the memory slots available in your computer, determine how much RAM is located in each memory slot, and determine which memory slots are used and which are empty.
- **Specify security settings** If you want to prohibit an unauthorized user from changing BIOS configuration settings, you can specify an Admin password. If you want to prevent an unauthorized user from booting your computer, you can also specify a System password.
- **View and change power management settings** For example, you can specify an Auto Power On setting to turn your computer on every day, or only weekdays, at a specific time. You can also specify what happens after a power loss, namely, whether the system stays off, powers itself on, or returns to its previous state (on or off) after power is restored.
- **Adjust POST behavior settings** As you may recall from Tutorial 1, POST (for Power-On Self-Test) refers to initial tests performed to verify the presence and working state of boot devices. You can specify whether your computer displays messages that identify which keys to press at startup to open the BIOS Setup utility or Boot Menu. You can also specify whether to display either the Setup or Boot Menu message, or specify that the BIOS display no messages so that an unauthorized user does not know which keys to press to open the Setup utility or Boot Menu. You can also specify whether the Num Lock key is on or off after your computer boots.

To open the Setup utility, you must reboot your computer, or if your computer is already off, you must power on your system and identify the key or keys needed to open the Setup utility. As your computer starts up, pay close attention to the information displayed on the monitor so that you know what you need to press to open the Setup utility. You must press the key or keys for opening the BIOS Setup utility at that point, before booting continues. Otherwise, you must let Windows Vista boot to the desktop, restart Windows Vista, and then try again.

If you are working in a computer lab, your technical support staff might have already password-protected the Setup utility so that only the technical support staff can access and change these settings. In some cases, you might be able to open the Setup utility, but not make any changes to BIOS settings. If you are working in a computer lab, and if the Setup utility is not password-protected, do not perform the following steps without the permission of your instructor or technical support staff. If you cannot or prefer not to open the Setup utility until you are more familiar with how it is organized and the BIOS settings it contains, read the following steps and examine the figures, but do not keystroke the following steps.

Julien asks you to check and adjust BIOS settings on a new computer purchased for a new research scientist.

Read the following steps before you perform them because you may not have enough time to read them and check the information displayed on the monitor at the same time.

To open the BIOS Setup utility:

1. If your computer is turned off, power on your computer. If you already logged on your computer, close all open applications, windows, and dialog boxes, and then restart your computer.
2. During booting or rebooting, watch the monitor for a message that identifies which key or keys to press to open the Setup utility, and then very quickly press that key or combination of keys. At that point, you may see the message "Entering Setup" displayed on the monitor, and then the BIOS Setup utility opens. Figure 8-24 shows BIOS settings for a Dell System DXG051 computer. Your view of BIOS settings may differ because different companies manufacture different types of BIOSes, and they change and improve their BIOSes over time.

   Trouble? If you see the Windows Vista logo, you've passed the point when you can open the BIOS Setup utility. Wait for Windows Vista to boot to the desktop, restart your computer, and then try again. In some cases, a computer might boot so quickly that you do not see any messages displayed on the monitor. However, if you press the Pause key, you can temporarily halt booting so that you can see what's displayed on the screen. To resume booting, press the Enter key. If you do not see a message on how to open Setup, check your computer documentation, the manufacturer's Web site, or use a search engine to locate this information, or try pressing F2 or F1 in the first few seconds of the boot process. In the latter case, if the key you press is not the key for opening the Setup utility, you must wait until Windows boots to the Welcome Screen or desktop, and then restart your computer and try another key.

BIOS settings **Figure 8-24**

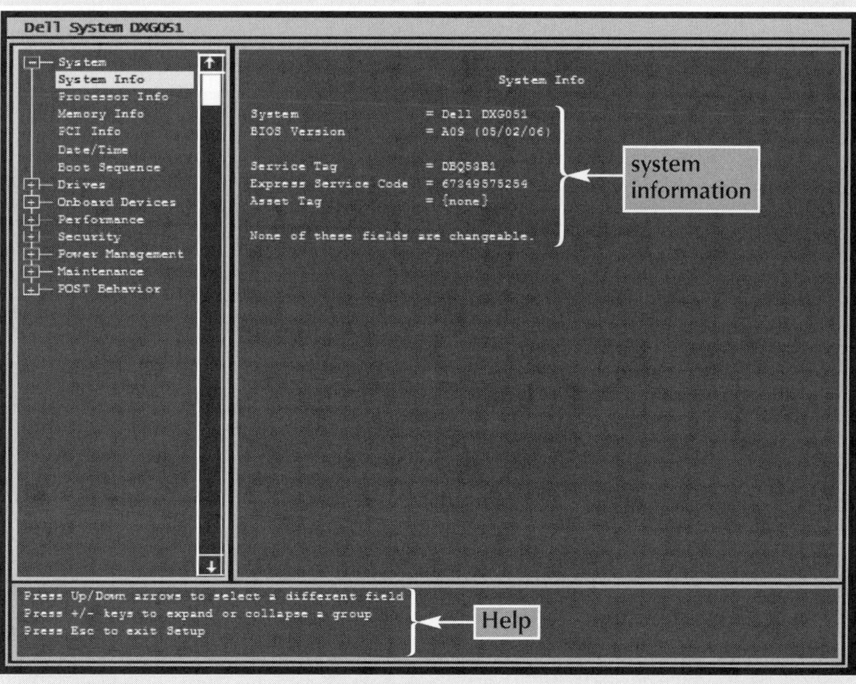

On the computer used for Figure 8-24, the pane on the left side of the screen displays different categories from which you can access specific BIOS settings. On this computer, the BIOS Setup utility selects the first category, System, expands this category, highlights System Info, and in the right pane, displays System Info settings. The System group contains basic system information as well as options for changing the date, time, and boot sequence. The System field identifies the computer system as a Dell DXG051. A **field** refers to the name of a specific type of setting and the setting itself. At the bottom of the screen, the BIOS setup utility displays information on how to select another field, expand or collapse a group, and exit the BIOS Setup utility. For example, on this computer, you press the Up and Down arrow keys to select a different group or a different field, press the plus and minus keys to expand or collapse a group of settings, and press the Esc key to exit the BIOS Setup utility. It also notes that you cannot change the fields in this category. While the BIOS on your computer might differ from the one shown in Figure 8-24, it provides information on how to use the BIOS Setup utility, and it should also contain similar options, though they might be organized and labeled in a different way. The logic for working with different types of BIOSes is the same.

Next, you want to examine your computer's boot sequence.

To examine your computer's boot sequence:

1. Examine each category of options available on your computer and locate and select the field that contains information on the boot sequence or boot order of your computer. After selecting Boot Sequence under the System group or category in the left pane on the computer used for Figure 8-25, the BIOS Setup utility lists five bootable devices, some of which are not present; however, the settings shown are the manufacturer's settings. The Setup utility notes that only devices preceded by a number are bootable. In this case, it also informs you that you can use the Space key (i.e., the Spacebar) to control whether a specific device is bootable. Your BIOS settings will differ.

Figure 8-25 BIOS Boot Sequence settings

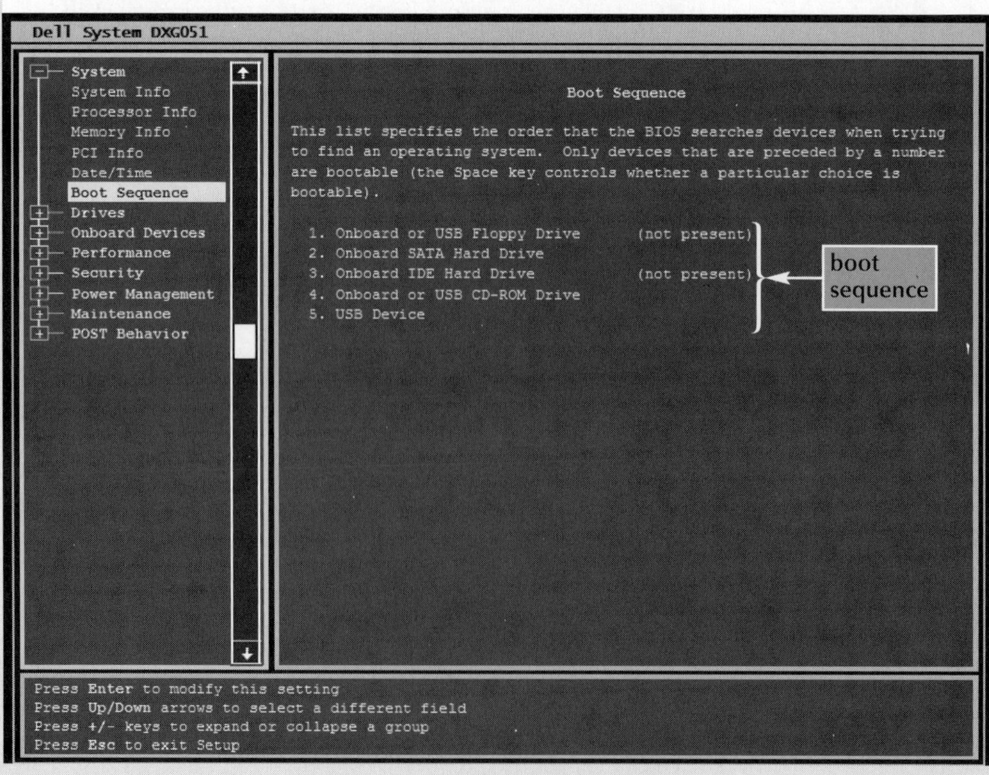

On the computer used for this figure, the first bootable device is the Onboard SATA Hard Drive, followed by an Onboard or USB CD-ROM Drive, and then a USB Device. **SATA** (for Serial ATA or Serial Advanced Technology Attachment) is a newer technology for connecting a hard disk drive to a computer to achieve far faster data transfers than was possible with the previous **PATA** (for Parallel ATA or Parallel Advanced Technology Attachment) hard disk drives.

When this computer boots, the BIOS routine responsible for locating and loading the operating system checks the SATA hard disk drive first, and since Windows Vista is installed on this hard disk drive, it boots the computer from that drive. However, if there is a problem with that drive that prevents the BIOS routine from accessing it, the BIOS routine then examines the next drive listed in the boot sequence for the operating system. If it locates the operating system on that next drive, it boots the computer; otherwise, it examines the next drive listed in the boot sequence. If you want to boot from another drive or from another type of bootable device, such as a DVD or CD drive, you can change the boot sequence so that the DVD or CD drive is listed before the option for booting from the hard disk drive. Even if the DVD or CD drive is not listed first in the boot sequence, a computer might detect it during booting if it contains a DVD or CD, and then prompt you to press a key to boot from that disk drive.

As shown in the Help pane at the bottom of the window, you can use the Enter key to change the boot sequence. Select the first boot device (in this example, the SATA hard drive), press the Enter key, use the Down and Up arrow keys to select another drive in the menu, and then press the Enter key.

After you save changes to one or more BIOS settings, you use the Esc key to exit the BIOS Setup utility. As shown in Figure 8-26, the BIOS Setup utility used on this computer provides two options after pressing the Esc key: Remain in Setup and Exit. It prompts you to choose one of these options, and it explains what each option does. When you exit the BIOS Setup utility, your computer reboots with the new settings you specified.

BIOS Exit options **Figure 8-26**

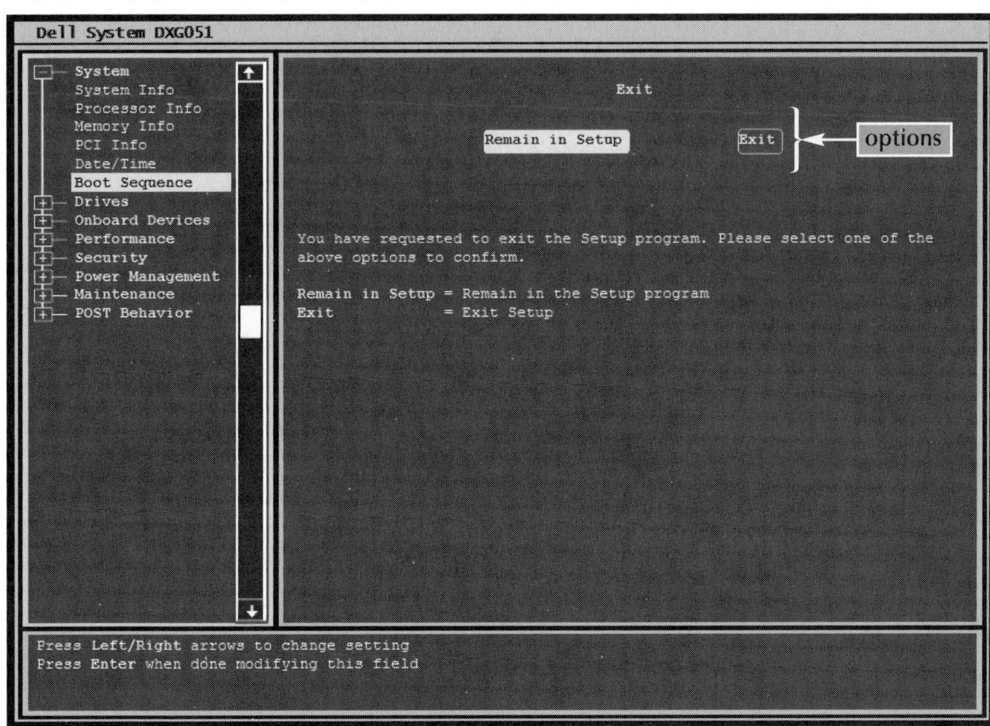

To close the BIOS Setup utility and reboot your computer:

1. If you changed your computer's BIOS settings, note the changes in case you need to reverse them later, and then choose the option to save your changes and exit (if available) or the option to exit. If you did not make any changes to BIOS settings, or want to exit without saving changes, choose the option to exit without saving changes (if available) or the option to exit.
2. After your computer reboots, log onto your user account.

You can also use the BIOS Setup utility to document important system settings, troubleshoot problems, or reconfigure your computer for new hardware.

Reference Window | **Changing the Boot Sequence**

- If your computer is turned off, power on your computer. If you have already started Windows Vista and booted to the desktop, close all open applications, windows, and dialog boxes, and then restart Windows Vista.
- During the initial stages of booting, watch the monitor for a message that identifies which key or keys to press to enter the BIOS Setup utility, and then press the key or keys shown on the monitor.
- Locate the category that contains the settings for changing your computer's boot sequence, examine and make a record of the current boot sequence order, and then change the boot sequence so that it lists devices in the order in which you want the BIOS to boot your computer.
- Choose the option that allows you to save your changes and exit Setup.

Because BIOS settings affect the performance of your computer, you should check the materials that came with your computer to see if they contain any information on its BIOS settings. If not, visit the manufacturer's Web site and download manuals for your specific computer. You can also use a search engine to locate other Web sites that contain information about BIOS settings and about troubleshooting problems using the BIOS Setup utility.

Your BIOS documentation should also explain how to reset BIOS passwords (and therefore bypass existing password protection), how to clear and reset BIOS settings, and how to replace the battery that stores computer configuration and date and time information.

Reviewing the Windows Vista Boot Process

Windows Vista relies on the following system components to boot your computer:

- **Boot Configuration Data** On BIOS-based systems, the **Boot Configuration Data (BCD)** is a database file that contains boot configuration settings and information about the location of boot files that, in turn, determine how the Windows operating system loads from disk. The data in this file is stored in a format similar to that of the Windows Registry, so it is referred to as a Registry file (and called a data store). The file that contains boot configuration data is named BCD, and it is stored in the Boot folder (\Boot) under the top-level folder on the system volume (the volume from which Windows Vista boots).

- **Windows Boot Manager** The **Windows Boot Manager** starts the process of loading the Windows Vista operating system by examining the BCD to determine whether another operating system is installed on the computer. If so, it displays a menu so that you can choose which operating system you want to use. If you choose an operating system other than Windows Vista, the Windows Boot Manager passes control to the operating system loader for that operating system. If no other operating system is installed on the computer, it passes control to either the Windows Boot Loader or Windows Resume Loader. If the BCD does not contain information about a hibernation file, it passes control to the Windows Boot Loader; otherwise, it passes control to the Windows Resume loader. The Windows Boot Manager is stored in a file named bootmgr in the top-level folder of the system volume.
- **Windows Boot Loader** The Windows Boot Loader, stored in a file named WinLoad.exe in the Windows System32 folder (C:\Windows\System32\WinLoad.exe), loads the Windows Vista operating system and basic hardware device drivers.
- **Windows Resume Loader** The Windows Resume Loader, stored in a file named WinResume.exe in the Windows System 32 folder (C:\Windows\System32\WinResume.exe), reads the hibernation file and restores Windows Vista to its previous state before Windows Vista switched to hibernation.

These Windows components are hidden system folders and files. To view them, you must enable the options for displaying hidden files and folders and for displaying protected operating system files.

During booting, the BIOS uses the boot sequence settings to locate the hard disk drive. Then, it reads the MBR, loads the boot code and Hard Disk Partition Table contained in the MBR into memory, and passes control to the MBR boot code. The Hard Disk Partition Table identifies which partition is the boot partition. The MBR code locates and reads the boot sector on the boot partition to determine the location of the Windows boot manager. Next, it loads the Windows Boot Manager. Windows Boot Manager starts the Windows Boot Loader or the Windows Resume Loader, which in turn loads Windows Vista. Figure 8-27 provides a general overview of this booting process on a basic volume.

Figure 8-27 Overview of the booting process on a basic volume

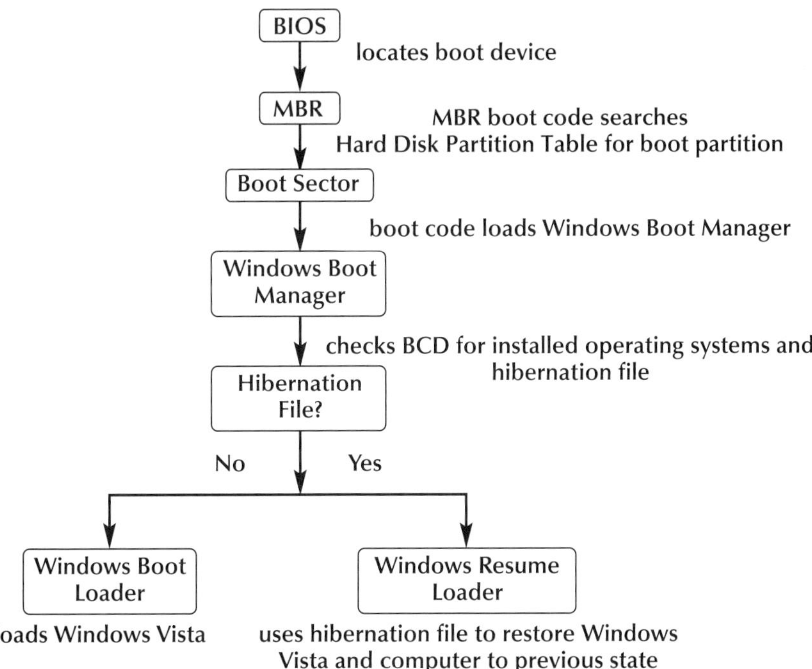

Using the Windows Advanced Boot Options Menu

At a weekly meeting with his assistants, Julien notes that staff members might occasionally encounter a problem booting Windows Vista. When that situation occurs, they may have to troubleshoot the problem using the Advanced Boot Options menu. In the ensuing discussion, Julien and his assistants review the different options on the Advanced Boot Options menu.

This menu, shown in Figure 8-28, contains a list of options that provide alternate approaches to booting Windows Vista. To display the Advanced Boot Options menu, you press the F8 function key after the initial startup screen before you see the Windows logo.

Figure 8-28 **Advanced Boot Options menu**

```
                        Advanced Boot Options

Choose Advanced Options for: Microsoft Windows Vista
(Use the arrow keys to highlight your choice.)

    Safe Mode
    Safe Mode with Networking
    Safe Mode with Command Prompt

    Enable Boot Logging
    Enable low-resolution video (640x480)
    Last Known Good Configuration (advanced)
    Directory Services Restore Mode
    Debugging Mode
    Disable automatic restart on system failure
    Disable Driver Signature Enforcement

    Start Windows Normally

Description: Start Windows with its regular settings.

ENTER=Choose                                              ESC=Cancel
```

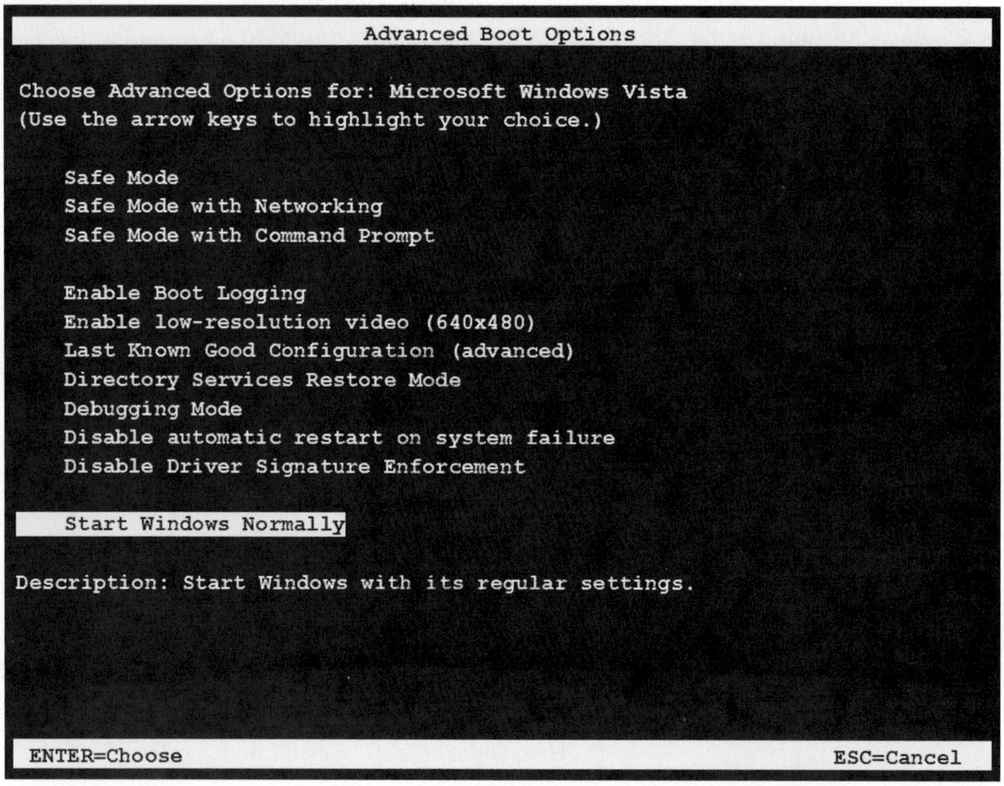

You can use the Up and Down arrow keys to highlight a boot option, and a brief description of that boot option appears at the bottom of the Advanced Boot Options menu.

The Advanced Boot Options menu provides you with access to these boot options:

- **Start Windows Normally** The Start Windows Normally option is the default boot option that Windows Vista uses when you don't display the Advanced Boot Options menu. If you choose this option from the Advanced Boot Options menu, Windows Vista performs a full boot.
- **Enable Boot Logging** This boot option is identical to the Start Windows Normally option, except Windows Vista creates a special startup log file named ntbtlog.txt (for NT Boot Log) in the Windows folder during booting and logs all the drivers that it loads (or fails to load). By examining the drivers that failed to load, you might be able to identify the exact cause of a problem and eliminate its possible cause. Figure 8-29 shows part of the NT Boot Log in the file ntbtlog.txt.

Viewing an NT boot log **Figure 8-29**

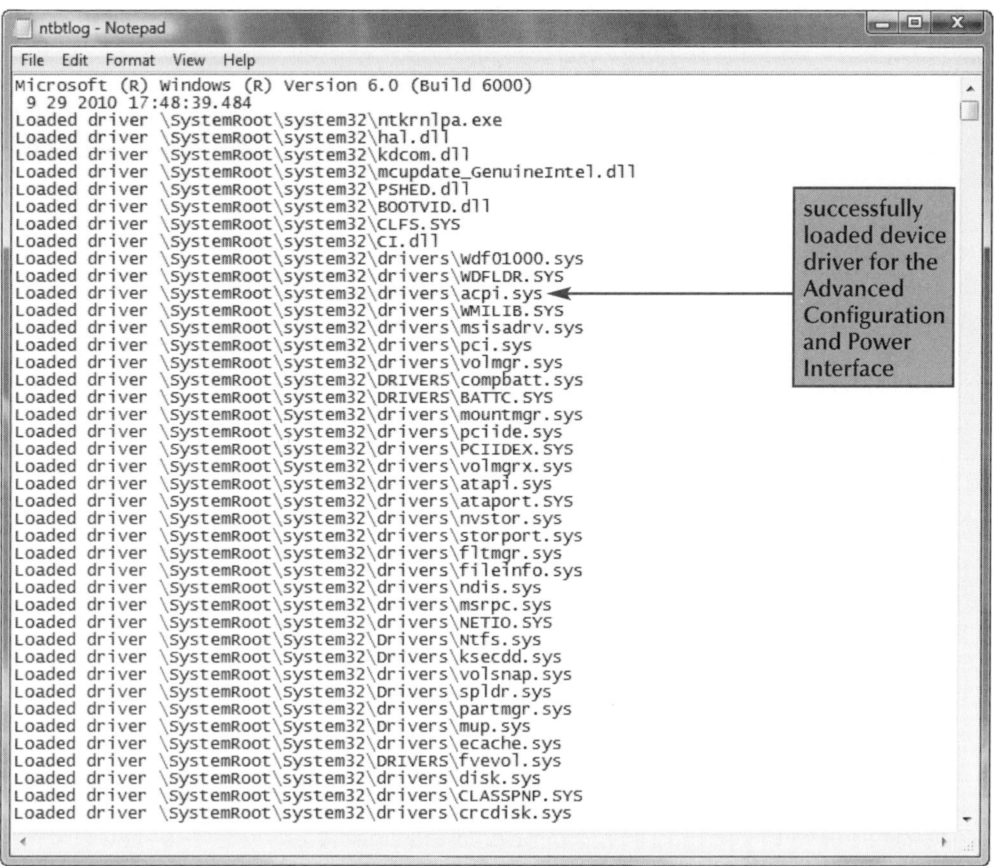

- **Last Known Good Configuration (advanced)** This boot option starts Windows Vista with the boot configuration saved in the Windows Registry by the operating system from the last successful boot. If you encounter startup problems, or if your system is unstable, a recent change to system settings and device drivers might be the source of the problem, and you can use the Last Known Good Configuration to start your computer with settings that worked during your last successful boot. Because this boot option restores previously used device drivers and the previous set of Registry settings from the last successful boot, you could lose any changes to the configuration of your computer that you recently made. However, that may make all the difference if you are otherwise unable to boot your computer. Microsoft recommends that you use the Last Known Good Configuration boot option before you try other boot options because the other startup and troubleshooting options are more complex, and the Last Known Good Configuration may immediately resolve the problem.
- **Enable low-resolution video (640×480)** This boot option is similar to a normal boot but with one difference. Although it uses your current video display adapter device driver, it switches your video display to a low resolution (640×480) and a lower refresh rate so that you can troubleshoot a problem with your video display settings or your video display driver. If you install a new device driver for your video display adapter, or if a problem develops with your current video display adapter device driver, you can start your computer with this boot option and troubleshoot the problem. This boot option is therefore useful if you experience a problem that does not permit you to see an image on the monitor. Also, you still have access to your network and to the Internet after choosing this boot option.

- **Safe Mode** The **Safe Mode** boot option is a troubleshooting option that has been available in all versions of the Windows operating system. It starts Windows Vista but loads only basic device drivers and essential Windows services. After your computer is up and running, you can troubleshoot the source of the problem or problems you were experiencing. This boot option switches the video display to a lower resolution of 800 × 600. You might use Safe Mode to troubleshoot problems caused by newly installed device drivers, newly installed software, software upgrades, startup background programs, or changes to system settings. Startup background programs (which you will examine in the next section of the tutorial) are programs that are loaded at each boot and operate in the background. However, in Safe Mode, Windows Vista does not load startup background programs because they might be the cause of the problem that you encountered when you booted your computer in normal mode. If the problem that caused you to choose the Safe Mode boot option does not appear in Safe Mode, basic device drivers and settings loaded by Windows Vista during Safe Mode are not the source of the problem. Rather, the problem more likely involves a new device that you've added to your computer or a change in device drivers for a hardware component. When you boot in Safe Mode, you can also use the Error-Checking Tool to repair a problem with the file system.
- **Safe Mode with Networking** This boot option is similar to Safe Mode; however, Windows Vista establishes network connections so that you can troubleshoot a problem that requires network access.
- **Safe Mode with Command Prompt** This boot option is similar to Safe Mode, but Windows Vista boots to a command prompt instead of the desktop. That means you must have command-line skills so that you can use the command-line operating environment to troubleshoot system problems. After selecting this boot option, you are prompted for the operating system to load, and then you log on as Administrator. Figure 8-30 shows the command-line environment after choosing the Safe Mode with Command Prompt boot option. You do not have access to your network. Even though you are working in a command-line environment, you can still load components of the graphical user interface, such as the Display Settings dialog box.

Figure 8-30 Safe Mode with Command Prompt user interface

- **Disable automatic restart on system failure** When Windows Vista encounters an error that prevents it from booting, it restarts, only to encounter the same problem again. This boot option turns off that feature so that you can boot your computer and view any error codes or information needed to troubleshoot the problem. For example, if you see a **Blue Screen of Death (BSOD)**, you've encountered a **Stop Error**, a fatal error from which it cannot recover and therefore requires a reboot. The reboot may resolve the problem, or you might see the same BSOD again. If you disable the automatic restart on system failure, you can view the BSOD, record the Stop Error codes, and then search Microsoft Support for information on the problem (or problems) that might have caused the Stop Error.

- **Disable Driver Signature Enforcement** This boot option allows you to install device drivers that do not contain the proper driver signatures because those device drivers might be the only ones available for you to use. As noted previously, signed drivers have a digital signature (or electronic security mark) that identifies and verifies the integrity of the publisher and indicates whether the original content of the driver software package has been changed. The use of signed drivers protects the stability and security of your computer, so you should make every effort to use signed drivers.
- **Directory Services Restore Mode** This boot option applies only to Windows domain controllers on a server operating system. An Administrator can use this option to restore the SYSVOL (system volume) directory and the Active Directory service on a domain controller. SYSVOL is a shared directory that stores the server copy of the domain's public files. A **domain** is a group of computers that are part of a network and that share a common directory database and security policy. A domain controller is a server that uses Active Directory to manage user logon and user access to a network and shared resources. Active Directory is a Windows service that tracks information about resources on a network, such as computers, printers, groups, and users.
- **Debugging Mode** This boot option is a more advanced troubleshooting option that enables an Administrator to send debugging (or troubleshooting) information through a cable to another computer as Windows Vista starts so that an Administrator (or perhaps Microsoft tech support) can examine the information.
- **Repair your computer** This boot option is displayed on the Advanced Boot Options menu only if a set of Windows Vista system recovery tools are installed on your computer. You can also access these tools by booting from your Windows Vista DVD. The system recovery tools include the following features for troubleshooting your computer:
    - Startup Repair (for repairing startup problems)
    - System Restore
    - Windows Complete PC Restore
    - Windows Memory Diagnostic Tool
    - Command Prompt

You've already examined System Restore, and you will examine Startup Repair later in this tutorial. You will examine Windows Complete PC Restore in Tutorial 10 and the Command Prompt in Tutorial 13.

Booting Your Computer in Safe Mode

So that you are familiar with Safe Mode in case you need to troubleshoot a problem, Julien recommends that you use the Advanced Boot Options menu to boot in this mode.

In the next set of steps, you are going to boot your computer in Safe Mode. If you are using a computer in your college computer lab, verify with your instructor or technical support staff that you have permission to boot in Safe Mode. Also, to complete the following steps, you must log on under an Administrator account. If you do not have permission to boot your computer in Safe Mode, or if you cannot log on under an Administrator account or provide the password for an Administrator account, read the following steps and examine the figures, but do not keystroke the steps.

When you reboot your computer, you need to press the F8 key after the initial startup screen and before you see the Starting Windows screen with the progress indicator. If you pass this point, Windows Vista boots to the desktop. Also, when you switch from one boot mode to another, Windows Vista boots your computer more slowly, so you must be patient. If you are unsure when to press the F8 key, you can press and release it several times during the initial stages of booting, but make sure you include a slight pause between each press of the F8 key so that the BIOS does not display a keyboard error condition. Also,if you use the

Up or Down Arrow key on the numeric keypad to choose an option from the Advanced Boot Options menu, you might need to first press the Num Lock key to turn Num Lock off.

To boot in Safe Mode:

1. On the Start menu, choose the option to restart your computer on the Lock menu.
2. After the initial startup screen with configuration information, and before you see the Windows logo, press and release the **F8** key (several times, if necessary). Windows Vista displays the Advanced Boot Options menu, as shown in Figure 8-31.

Figure 8-31 **Choosing Safe Mode from the Advanced Boot Options menu**

```
                      Advanced Boot Options

Choose Advanced Options for: Microsoft Windows Vista
(Use the arrow keys to highlight your choice.)

    Safe Mode
    Safe Mode with Networking
    Safe Mode with Command Prompt

    Enable Boot Logging
    Enable low-resolution video (640x480)
    Last Known Good Configuration (advanced)
    Directory Services Restore Mode
    Debugging Mode
    Disable automatic restart on system failure
    Disable Driver Signature Enforcement

    Start Windows Normally

Description: Start Windows with only the core drivers and services. Use
             when you cannot boot after installing a new device or driver.

 ENTER=Choose                                                ESC=Cancel
```

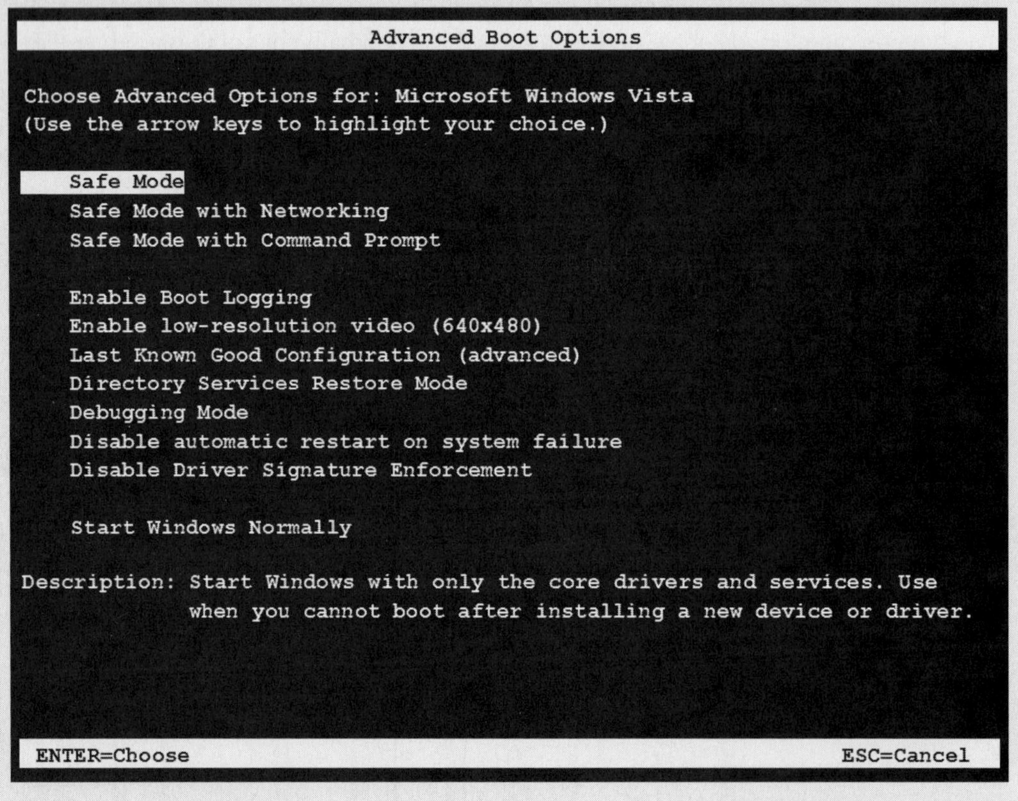

3. Use the **Up** or **Down** arrow key to point to and highlight the **Safe Mode** menu option, and then press the **Enter** key. Windows Vista system files are loaded and listed on the monitor on a line-by-line basis. At the Welcome screen, you are prompted to select your user name and enter your password.

4. Log onto your computer under your user account if it is an Administrator account, or log on under another Administrator account. After Windows Vista displays the desktop, it opens Windows Help and Support and explains that Safe Mode is a troubleshooting option that starts your computer in a limited state. See Figure 8-32. Windows Vista notes that if an existing problem does not appear in Safe Mode, you can eliminate default settings and basic device drivers as possible causes of the problem. It further notes that if you don't know the cause of the problem, you can use the process of elimination to ascertain the problem. In this respect, it recommends that you open the programs that you typically use, including the programs in the Startup folder, one at a time, to determine whether one of these programs caused the problem. If Windows Vista starts in Safe Mode, a recently installed program or device might prevent Windows Vista from starting normally. In this case, it suggests you use System Restore to resolve the problem.

Figure 8-32 **Help and Support window opened after booting into Safe Mode**

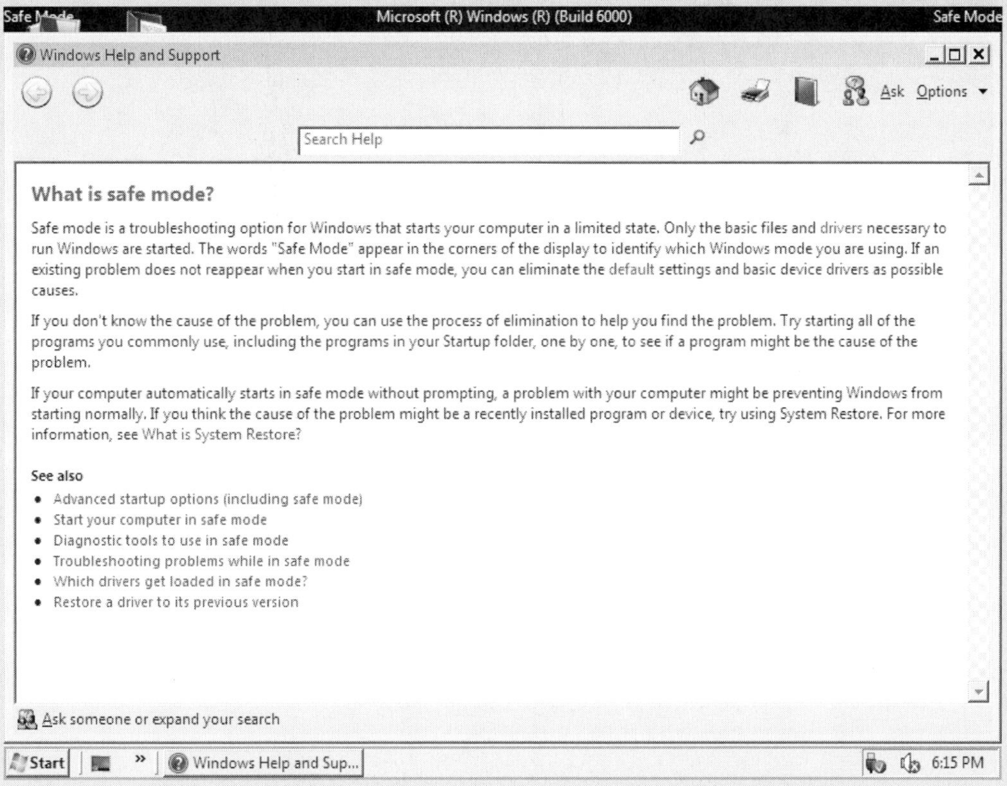

Safe Mode | Microsoft (R) Windows (R) (Build 6000) | Safe Mode

Windows Help and Support

Ask Options

Search Help

What is safe mode?

Safe mode is a troubleshooting option for Windows that starts your computer in a limited state. Only the basic files and drivers necessary to run Windows are started. The words "Safe Mode" appear in the corners of the display to identify which Windows mode you are using. If an existing problem does not reappear when you start in safe mode, you can eliminate the default settings and basic device drivers as possible causes.

If you don't know the cause of the problem, you can use the process of elimination to help you find the problem. Try starting all of the programs you commonly use, including the programs in your Startup folder, one by one, to see if a program might be the cause of the problem.

If your computer automatically starts in safe mode without prompting, a problem with your computer might be preventing Windows from starting normally. If you think the cause of the problem might be a recently installed program or device, try using System Restore. For more information, see What is System Restore?

See also

- Advanced startup options (including safe mode)
- Start your computer in safe mode
- Diagnostic tools to use in safe mode
- Troubleshooting problems while in safe mode
- Which drivers get loaded in safe mode?
- Restore a driver to its previous version

Ask someone or expand your search

Start | Windows Help and Sup... | 6:15 PM

5. Close the Windows Help and Support window. In the four corners of the screen, Windows Vista displays the message "Safe Mode." See Figure 8-33. Windows Vista no longer displays your wallpaper, and your view of windows, dialog boxes, and menus is more like the view found in Classic View in earlier versions of Windows. At this point, you can implement the suggestions recommended in the Windows Help and Support window to determine the cause of the problem. You can also open the Control Panel to check and change system settings as necessary, and then restart Windows Vista.

Figure 8-33 Safe Mode desktop

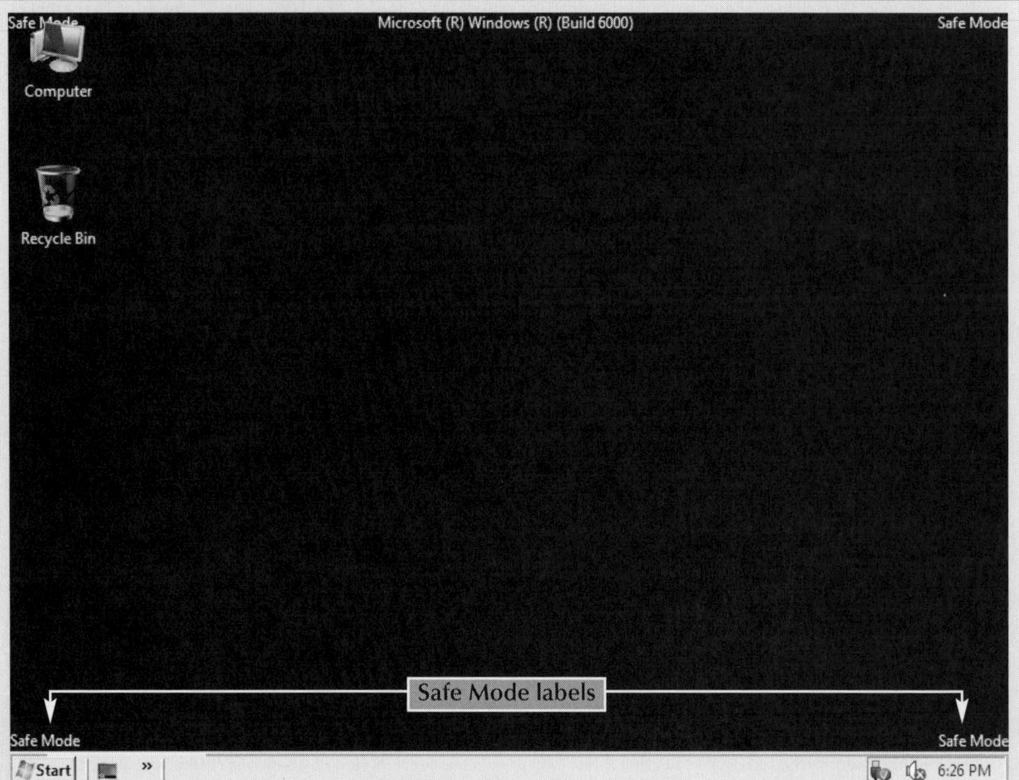

6. Right-click the **desktop**, click **Personalize** on the shortcut menu, and in the Personalization window, click the **Display Settings** link. As shown in the Display Settings dialog box on the computer used for Figure 8-34, Windows Vista is configured for a (Default Monitor), a Screen resolution of 800 by 600 pixels, and the Highest (32-bit) color setting. If you use the Advanced Settings button to open the (Default Monitor) and Properties dialog box, Windows Vista displays "<unavailable>" or "n/a" for Adapter Information. Furthermore, the screen refresh rate is set at "Use hardware default setting." These display settings enable Windows Vista to boot the computer so that you can see an image on the monitor.

Figure 8-34 Safe Mode display settings

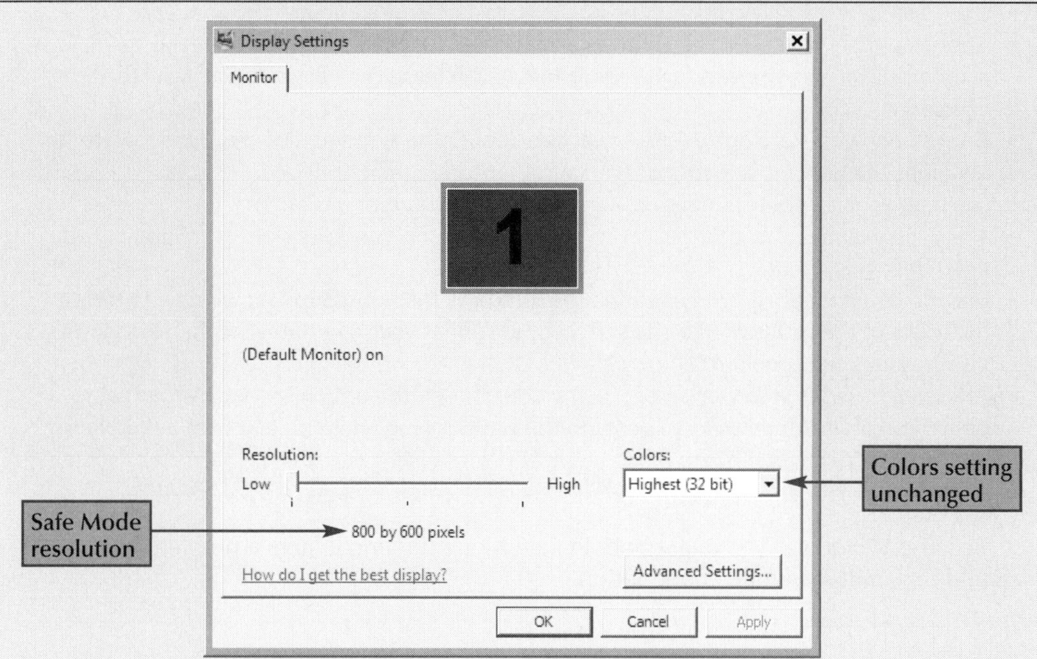

7. Click the **Cancel** button to close this dialog box without changing any video display settings, and then close the Personalization window.
8. On the Start menu, choose the option to restart your computer from the Lock menu, and after Windows Vista boots to the desktop, log on your computer under your user account.

The first thing you might want to try after rebooting in Safe Mode is to restart Windows Vista to determine if it can rebuild damaged files and reconfigure itself. If you cannot repair a problem in Safe Mode, you can still use the Last Known Good Configuration boot option.

Reference Window | Booting in Safe Mode

- Open the Start menu and choose the option to restart your computer from the Lock menu.
- After the initial startup screen with information about the configuration of your computer, and before you see the Windows logo, press and release the F8 key (several times, if necessary).
- After Windows Vista displays the Advanced Boot Options menu, use the Up arrow key to highlight the Safe Mode menu option, and then press the Enter key.
- Log onto your computer under an Administrator account.
- After you examine the information on Safe mode in the Windows Help and Support window, close this window.
- Use the approaches recommended in the Windows Help and Support window to locate the cause of the problem you encountered, or reboot your computer to see if Windows Vista resolves the problem.
- After you have finished working in Safe Mode, choose the option to restart your computer, and after Windows Vista boots to the desktop, log on your computer under your user account.

Because Windows Vista might boot in Safe Mode if it encounters a problem, you should be familiar with this boot option.

Using Windows Task Manager

Where possible, you should always shut down your computer properly. However, if you are using an application that stops responding or responds too slowly, first try to close the application before you shut down your entire computer system and run the risk of losing changes to other documents or damaging system files. If that approach does not work, you can use **Windows Task Manager** to shut down a nonresponding application or any other type of program. Windows Task Manager provides information about applications, processes, services, and processor and memory usage. As noted earlier, a process is an executable program, such as Explorer, Microsoft Word, or Task Manager; a service, such as the Print Spooler service that handles the printing of files in the background; or a subsystem, such as the one for Windows Vista applications. A service is a program, routine, or process that provides support to other programs.

After you open Task Manager, you can view a list of running applications and determine whether a program is not responding. If so, you can instruct Windows Vista to shut it down so that you can continue to use your computer.

You mention to Julien that an application on your computer occasionally stops responding when you are multitasking, and you want to know how you should handle this problem so that you do not lose any of your other work. Julien recommends that you first try Task Manager to shut down the application.

To open Task Manager and view information about processes:

1. On the Start menu, point to **All Programs**, click **Accessories**, click **Paint**, and then minimize the Paint window.

2. Right-click the **taskbar**, click **Task Manager** on the shortcut menu, and then click the **Applications** tab (if necessary) in the Windows Task Manager window. On the Applications sheet of the Windows Task Manager window, Windows Vista displays a list of running applications, including "Untitled - Paint," in the Task column. See Figure 8-35. "Untitled" is the temporary name for the new Paint document. If you have other open applications, windows, or documents, they are also listed as tasks. In the Status column, Task Manager shows whether a process is running or is not responding. If it is not responding, you can select that process in the Task box, click the End Task button, and have Windows Vista close it so that you can continue to use your computer. If you end a task, you lose any unsaved changes you made to a document with that program. You can also use the Switch To button to switch to an application or document that you first select in the Task column. If you click the New Task button, Task Manager opens a Create New Task dialog box where you can enter the name of a program, folder, document, or Internet resource (or browse to locate what you want to open).

Tip

You can also press the Ctrl+Alt+Del keys, and then click Start Task Manager to open Task Manager.

Figure 8-35 Viewing running applications with Task Manager

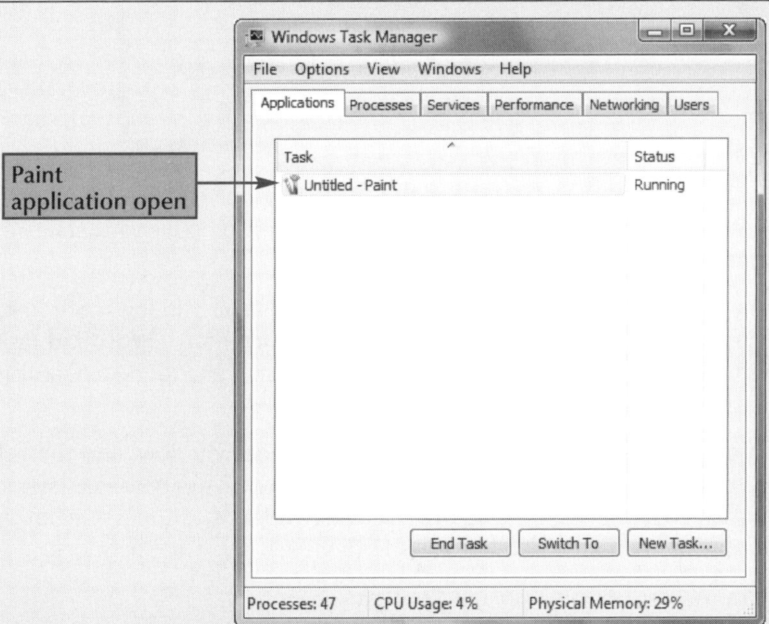

At the bottom of the dialog box, Windows Vista lists information about the number of processes currently running on your computer, the percent of CPU usage, and the amount of physical memory in use. You will examine this information in more detail in Tutorial 9.

3. On the Start menu, point to **All Programs**, click **Accessories**, click **WordPad**, and then minimize the WordPad window. Task Manager now lists "Document - WordPad" as a task. "Document" is the temporary name for the new WordPad document.

4. Click the **Processes** tab in the Windows Task Manager window. Task Manager displays a list of running processes in alphabetical order by Image Name. See Figure 8-36. In the Image Name column, Task Manager lists mspaint.exe, the name of the file that contains the Paint program. If you scroll to the bottom of this list of processes, Task Manager lists wordpad.exe, the name of the file that contains the WordPad program. Your list of other processes will differ.

Figure 8-36 Viewing running processes with Task Manager

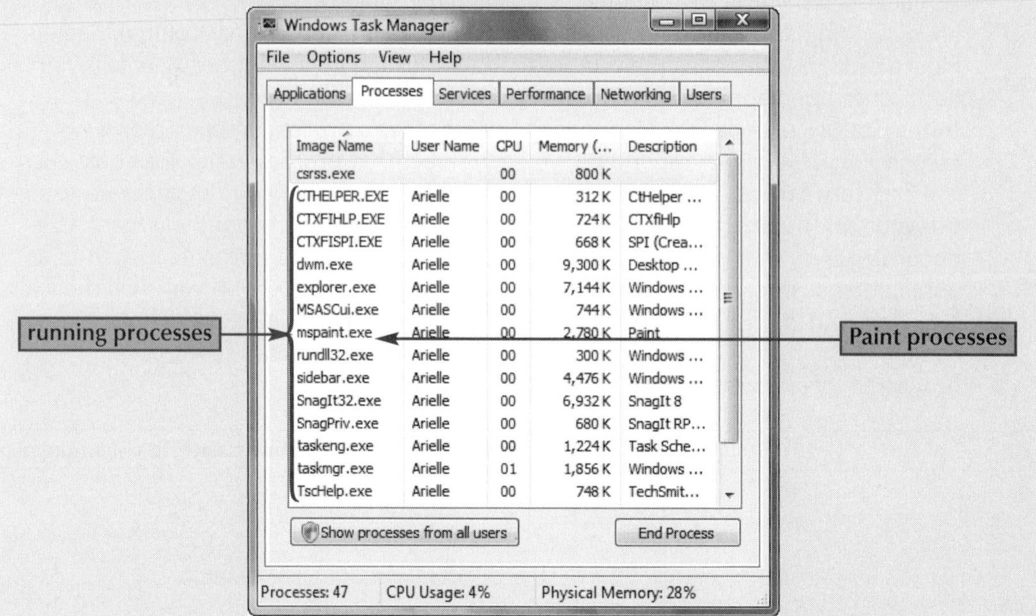

5. Right-click the **Untitled - Paint** taskbar button, and then click **Close**. After Paint closes, Task Manager updates its list of processes and no longer lists mspaint.exe as a running process.
6. Click the **Applications** tab in the Windows Task Manager window, note that Untitled - Paint is not listed as an open task, right-click the **Document** - **WordPad** taskbar button, and then click **Close**. After WordPad closes, Task Manager no longer lists it as an open task.
7. Click the **Services** tab in the Windows Task Manager window, and then click the **Name** column button to display an alphabetical list of the names of services. In the Description column, Task Manager more clearly identifies the nature of the service (although you need to widen the column to view the full descriptions).
8. Close the Windows Task Manager windows.

Although you might use Task Manager only occasionally to shut down a nonresponding program, remember that it is available. It lets you shut down a program that is tying up your computer system without affecting any other open programs and without losing valuable documents or data in other windows. A complete shutdown clears all memory, so it's better to try Windows Task Manager first. Task Manager is also useful if you want to see what applications are loaded when you notice that your computer is not performing optimally. You can also identify programs such as Microsoft Word that remain open after you have closed them and that prevent you from preforming certain operations on the file you just worked on or the folder that contains that file.

Using Task Manager to Shut Down a Nonresponding Program | Reference Window

- Right-click the taskbar, and then click Task Manager.
- After Windows Vista opens the Windows Task Manager window, select the nonresponding program in the Task column of the Applications sheet, click the End Task button, and then verify that you want to close the nonresponding program.
- Close the Windows Task Manager window.

Using System Configuration

Microsoft considers System Configuration one of the most important troubleshooting tools because it claims that startup programs are a leading cause of problems for Windows users. As noted earlier, a **startup program** is one that loads during booting and then operates in the background as you use your computer. For example, a startup program might provide you with quick access to a media player; however, if you do not use that program, it wastes valuable resources and memory as it runs in the background. Likewise, you might open the media player only occasionally, but a startup program loads at every boot and uses system resources. Instead, you can open the program directly from the Start menu when you need it. Startup programs can also include malicious software that loads at every boot, and therefore you can use System Configuration to confirm that malicious software loaded during booting.

You can also use System Configuration to control the startup process by specifying which startup programs and services load during booting. You can use its list of startup items to research your startup programs to determine whether they are useful, necessary, or malicious. If you suspect that a particular program is the source of a problem, you can temporarily turn off that program in System Configuration so that Windows Vista does not load it during the next boot. If the problem you experienced does not recur after you reboot your computer, you've identified the source of the problem. If the problem remains, the startup item that you turned off is not the source of the problem. You can turn on the option to load that startup item again, and then repeat the process with another startup item or service. Using this strategy, you can identify and isolate the source of a problem.

Because staff members periodically run into problems with background programs, Julien sets aside some time to show you and his other assistants how to use System Configuration to troubleshoot startup programs that cause problems.

To open System Configuration, you must be logged on under an Administrator account or provide the password for an Administrator account. If your account is a Standard User account, and if you do not know the password for an Administrator account, read the following steps and examine the figures, but do not keystroke the steps.

To examine your computer system's startup programs:

1. On the Start menu, point to **Administrative Tools**, and then click **System Configuration**. Windows Vista switches to Secure Desktop Mode and then displays a User Account Control dialog box.

Tip

You can also press the Windows Logo key, type system, and then click System Information in the Search results.

2. In the User Account Control dialog box, click the **Continue** button if you are logged on under an Administrator account, or if you are logged on under a Standard User account, enter the **password** for an Administrator account, and then click the **OK** button. Windows Vista opens the System Configuration dialog box. See Figure 8-37. Under Startup selection on the General property sheet, Normal startup is selected as the default option for starting your computer unless you have already used the System Configuration Utility to modify the startup process on your computer (as is already the case on the computer used for this figure). As noted, Normal startup loads all device drivers and services. If you choose Diagnostic startup (a troubleshooting option), Windows Vista loads only basic devices and services during the next boot. This option also turns off the loading of all startup programs during the next boot. Selective startup allows you to pick which system services and startup items (also called startup programs) are loaded during booting.

Figure 8-37 System Configuration startup options

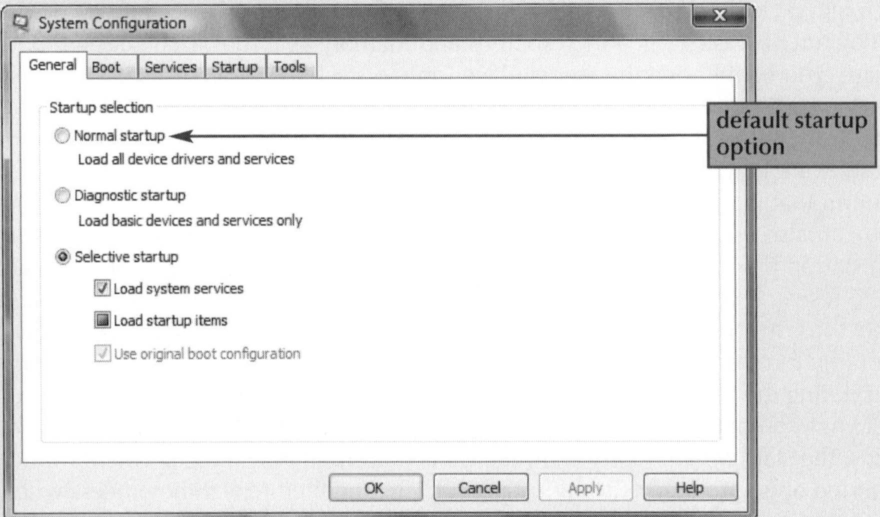

3. Click the **Services** tab in the System Configuration dialog box. This property sheet lists the names of all services that load during booting, the manufacturer (if known), whether the service is currently running or stopped, and the date that you disabled a service. See Figure 8-38. You can turn off or turn on specific services when troubleshooting problems. However, under the list of services, a note indicates that some secure Microsoft services may not be disabled. There might easily be 125 or more different services on your computer, and to effectively troubleshoot problems on your computer, you need to know not only what each service does, but also what happens if you turn off the service and whether one service is dependent on the availability of another service. To learn more about services, you can open Services from the Administrative Tools menu and view the names and descriptions of services as well as each service's status and startup type, such as Automatic (Delayed Start), Automatic, Manual, or Disabled. If you double-click a service, you can modify settings for services and determine whether they depend on another service or services.

Figure 8-38

Viewing Microsoft and non-Microsoft services

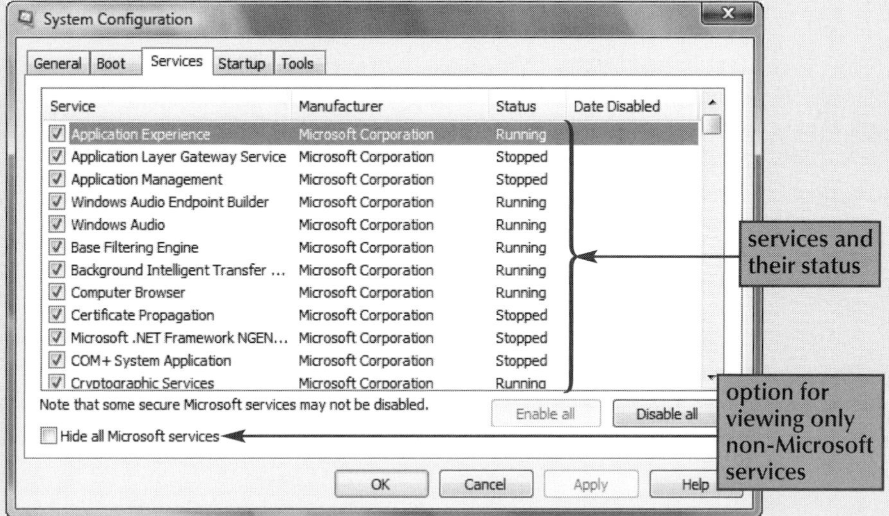

4. Click the **Hide all Microsoft services** check box on the Services property sheet. Now, you only see a list of non-Microsoft services (if any). When you troubleshoot system startup problems, seriously consider the possibility that a non-Microsoft or third-party service might be the cause of the problem after you have already eliminated startup programs as the cause of the problem. Microsoft recommends that you not turn off the loading of a service unless you know that it is not an essential service. An example of an important (and therefore essential) service is Windows Security Center.

5. Click the **Hide all Microsoft services** check box on the Services property sheet to redisplay all services.

6. Click the **Startup** tab in the System Configuration dialog box, and if the list of Startup items is not displayed in alphabetical order, click the **Startup Item** column button above the list of startup items. The Startup property sheet lists startup items, or startup programs, that load during booting, along with the name of the manufacturer (if known). The Manufacturer column shows the name of the software developer (if known). The Command column displays the path for the startup program or the name of the program file itself. The Location column shows how the startup item loads. Startup items whose locations start with HK are programs that load from the Registry at each boot. If you have already disabled a startup program or item, the date and time of that change is noted in the Date Disabled column (the last column not visible in this figure). See Figure 8-39. The first Microsoft® Windows® Operating System startup item on this computer loads the Windows Sidebar at each boot. If you do not want Windows Vista to display the Windows Sidebar, you can open the Windows Sidebar Properties dialog box and turn off the option for starting Sidebar when Windows starts. Five of the startup items load programs or dynamic link libraries that provide full support (or almost full support) for the video display adapter and sound system on this computer, and therefore, they are necessary startup items. The LUMIX Simple Viewer startup item is a program for transferring pictures from a digital camera's memory card, viewing and printing pictures, sending pictures via e-mail, and exporting pictures to a memory card. By disabling this item, this program does not automatically open when a memory card is inserted, but rather can be manually opened from the Start menu when needed. At the bottom of this property sheet is a button for disabling all startup items (so that they do not load during the next boot) and a button for enabling all startup items (so that they all do load during the next boot). Some startup programs display icons in the notification area, but this list provides a more complete accounting of startup programs.

Figure 8-39 Viewing Startup programs

Tip

This method for adjusting column widths works elsewhere in Windows Vista and in applications, such as Microsoft Excel and Microsoft Access.

Tip

To widen all columns, click the window or dialog box background (if necessary), and then press the Ctrl and + keys.

7. Point to the border between the Startup Item and Manufacturer columns, and when the mouse pointer changes to ↔, double-click the **border** to adjust the width of the column for a best fit. Now you can see the full name of all the startup items (helpful for viewing the names of startup programs so that you can research the use and need for startup programs).
8. Use the same approach to adjust the widths of the remaining columns (including the Date Disabled column) so that you can see all the information in each column. Scroll right to view other columns and adjust their widths. When troubleshooting the use of startup programs, you may need to rely on all this information (see the following Insight).
9. Click the **Tools** tab in the System Configuration dialog box. From this property sheet, you have quick access to various tools for troubleshooting your computer—including System Restore, Event Viewer, the Security Center, Task Manager, the Internet Options dialog box, and System Information (which you will examine in the next section of the tutorial).
10. Click the **Cancel** button to close the System Configuration dialog box without making any changes.

Trouble? If you make a change in the System Configuration dialog box and then click the OK button, another System Configuration dialog box informs you that you may need to restart your computer to apply the changes. It also recommends that you close any open programs or files before doing so. Click the Exit without restart button to close the System Configuration dialog box without restarting your computer.

Although System Configuration provides an option for disabling the loading of startup items, you might achieve the same effect by trying one of these options first:

- If a startup program displays an icon in the notification area, you can right-click the icon to look for a shortcut menu option for disabling or closing the startup program. In some cases, you can click the icon to display a menu of options for that startup program. You may also be able to view an object's properties and permanently turn off the option for loading when Windows starts (such as described earlier for the Windows Sidebar). The primary limitation with this approach is that most startup programs do not display an icon in the notification area.

- You can open the program that displays an icon in the notification area or that loads a startup item and determine whether it contains an option for turning off the loading of the startup item when Windows starts or an option for displaying an icon in the notification area.
- For certain startup items, you might have to start the Setup program for a software product and uninstall a specific component that loads a startup item. This approach is especially useful for removing startup items that reload after you disable them with System Configuration.

You might also find yourself wondering how all these startup programs are installed on a computer. Some startup programs are installed when you install other programs, such as an application or office suite. They are designed to provide quick access to program components or extra features or to verify that you are a licensed user of software installed on your computer. When you download software from a Web site, read the license agreement before you agree to it so that you know whether you are also agreeing to the installation of other programs (including malicious software) that you may not want or need. After you start the installation program for a software product, you can view the license agreement and choose which options you want to install.

InSight | Analyzing Startup Items

You can use several strategies to locate the source of a problem that might be caused by a startup item:

- **Approach #1** Identify questionable startup items and use an Internet search engine such as Google (and perhaps Microsoft Support) to locate information about those startup items. If you know the software manufacturer, try searching their Web site for information about a startup item. You can then disable a startup item that you've identified as unnecessary, malicious, or unknown; reboot your computer; and determine whether your change corrected the problem. If not, restore that startup item and then test another questionable startup item until you've determined which (if any) caused the problem. If you determine that none of those startup items caused the problem, look at other startup items and non-Microsoft services. Among the many sites that contain information about startup programs (and Browser Helper Objects), *Sysinfo.org* is a recognized and valuable resource for PC Tech Support and users who want to troubleshoot computer performance problems. As of mid-2007, this Web site had a comprehensive list of over 14,000 startup programs. Also, *Symantec.com* maintains a comprehensive list of threats posed by malicious software. As you research startup items and services, check more than one site so that you do not rely on information provided by one Web site. When analyzing startup items, use information that System Configuration provides for the startup name, manufacturer, command, and location to verify that your startup item matches information you find about a legitimate startup program. Doing so distinguishes it from a malicious startup program that might have a similar (disguised) startup item or program name, but loads from another location on a computer.
- **Approach #2** If you do not know which startup item might be the source of a problem on your computer, and if you do not want to test each startup item separately (each of which requires a reboot), you can reduce the amount of time that it would take to locate the startup item causing the problem by disabling the loading of half of the startup items and then restarting your computer. If the problem remains, you've eliminated the startup items you just disabled prior to rebooting as the cause of the problem because those startup items did not load during the reboot. You can open System Configuration and then continue to test half of the remaining startup items using the same approach until you locate the one that is the source of the problem. If the problem no longer appears after you disable half of the startup items, you know that the problem was caused by a startup item that you disabled and that did not load. Then you can use the same strategy by enabling half of the startup items you disabled until you find the startup item that caused the problem. This approach, referred to as "divide and conquer," is useful for reducing the number of reboots required to identify the problem. For example, if you have 16 startup items, you might only need to reboot a maximum of four times instead of 16 times. If you eliminate all the startup items as the source of the problem, examine non-Microsoft services using the same approach.
- **Approach #3** You can disable all the startup items, and then reboot your computer. If the problem remains, you know that none of the startup items are the likely cause of the problem you experienced. You can then examine non-Microsoft services using the same approach. If you disable all the startup items, and the problem disappears, you know that the likely cause of the problem is one of the startup items. You can then use a similar approach to the previous one in which you enable and load half of the startup items to determine the source of the problem. You keep repeating this approach until you locate the startup item that causes the problem.

The only problem posed by these approaches is that you may turn off essential startup items or services and therefore lose some functionality of your computer. However, by researching the startup items as described in the first approach, you might be able to minimize or eliminate this problem. As noted earlier, avoid disabling services that are essential to the proper functioning of your computer. By researching information about these services at the Microsoft Web site or other Web sites, you can make an informed decision. As you make changes with System Configuration, make sure you document each change you make so that you can reverse it later.

If you discover that a startup program is the source of a problem on your computer, and if you want the features available in that startup program, check for an upgrade or new version of the program that might function on your computer without causing any problems. Another software product might also offer the same features without creating problems.

Using System Configuration | Reference Window

- On the Start menu, point to Administrative Tools, and then click System Configuration.
- In the User Account Control dialog box, click the Continue button if you are logged on under an Administrator account, or if you are logged on under a Standard User account, enter the password for an Administrator account, and then click the OK button.
- On the General property sheet in the System Configuration dialog box, choose the type of Startup selection you want to use. Use Normal startup to load all device drivers and services (as well as all startup items). Use Diagnostic startup to load only basic devices and services at the next boot when troubleshooting problems caused by startup items and services. Use Selective startup to pick those startup items and services you want to load at the next boot.
- Use the Services property sheet to specify which services load at the next boot as part of your troubleshooting strategy. Click the "Hide all Microsoft services" check box to view a list of non-Microsoft services that might cause a problem on your computer.
- Use the Startup property sheet to specify which startup items load at the next boot so that you can identify and isolate the program that is the source of the problem.
- Use the Tools property sheet to open troubleshooting and diagnostic tools.
- Close the System Configuration dialog box, and if necessary, restart your computer to apply the changes you made for loading startup items and services.

If you need to restore the loading of all startup configuration files, services, and programs, choose Normal startup on the General property sheet and reboot your computer.

Using System Information

Another useful tool for locating information about your computer is System Information. In addition to a System Summary, it provides information on the use of hardware resources, hardware components, and your software environment. You can use the System Summary to verify the Windows edition on a computer (important for troubleshooting).

Julien shows you an alternate approach for locating information on startup programs using System Information. In the process, he reviews how Windows Vista uses environment variables.

To open the System Information utility:

1. On the Start menu, point to **All Programs**, click **Accessories**, click **System Tools**, click **System Information**, and then maximize the System Information window. In the Category pane on the left, System Information organizes more detailed information into three categories—Hardware Resources, Components, and Software Environment. In the Details pane on the right, System Information displays a System Summary that contains basic information about your computer, such as your Windows Edition (e.g., Microsoft® Windows Vista™ Ultimate), your Windows version and build (e.g., Version 6.0.6000 Build 6000 for the first version of Windows Vista), the computer manufacturer and model, the processor, the BIOS version and date (which is also available via the BIOS Setup utility), the path for the Windows directory and the System directory, the boot device, time zone, and memory usage (which you will examine in Tutorial 9). See Figure 8-40. Your System Summary details will differ.

Tip

You can also press the Windows Logo key, type info, and then click System Information in the Search results.

Figure 8-40 System Summary in System Information

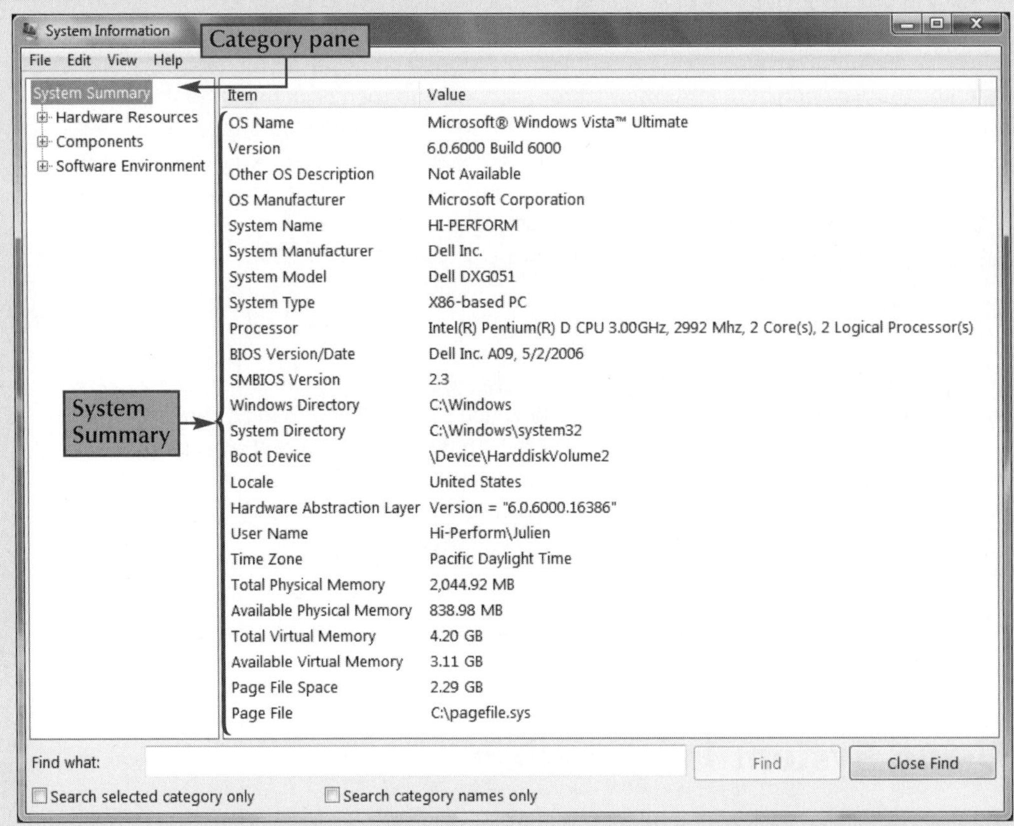

2. Click the **Expand View** box ⊞ to the left of the Software Environment category. The Software Environment category provides detailed information on the software currently loaded in the computer's memory, such as drivers, running tasks, startup programs, and loaded modules, as well as other related information.

3. Under Software Environment, click **Startup Programs**. System Information displays information about startup programs in the Details pane. See Figure 8-41. You can compare this information to that found on the Startup property sheet in the System Configuration dialog box. For example, System Configuration lists the first startup item shown on the computer in this figure as "AcroTray - Adobe Acrobat Distiller helper application;" however, System Information identifies the startup item as "Acrobat Assistant 7.0." You can verify that these two listings are the same because they have the same command (path). In contrast, the three startup programs for the video display adapter are more clearly identified in System Configuration. For example, the program NvSvc listed in System Information is the same as "NVIDIA Driver Helper Service, Version 163.71" in System Configuration. Again, you can verify that these two listings are for the same startup program by comparing their command (paths). Note that the Command for Windows Defender is "%programfiles%\windows defender\msascui.exe -hide". %programfiles% is yet another example of an environment variable (covered in the next step).

Figure 8-41 Viewing startup programs in System Information

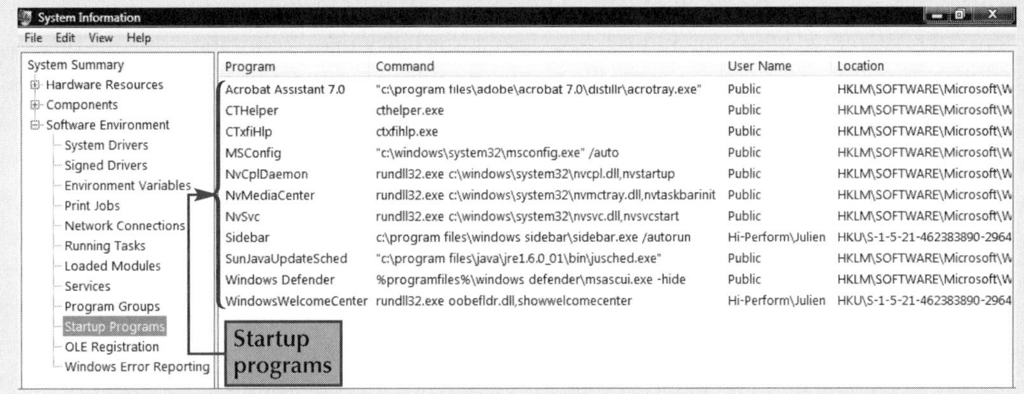

4. Under Software Environment, click **Environment Variables**, and in the Details pane, double-click the borders between each column for a best fit (or click the Details pane background and then press the Ctrl and + keys). The Details pane lists environment variables and their corresponding values. See Figure 8-42. Your environment variable names and settings might differ from those shown in the figure (and described after the figure).

Figure 8-42 Environment variables and their settings

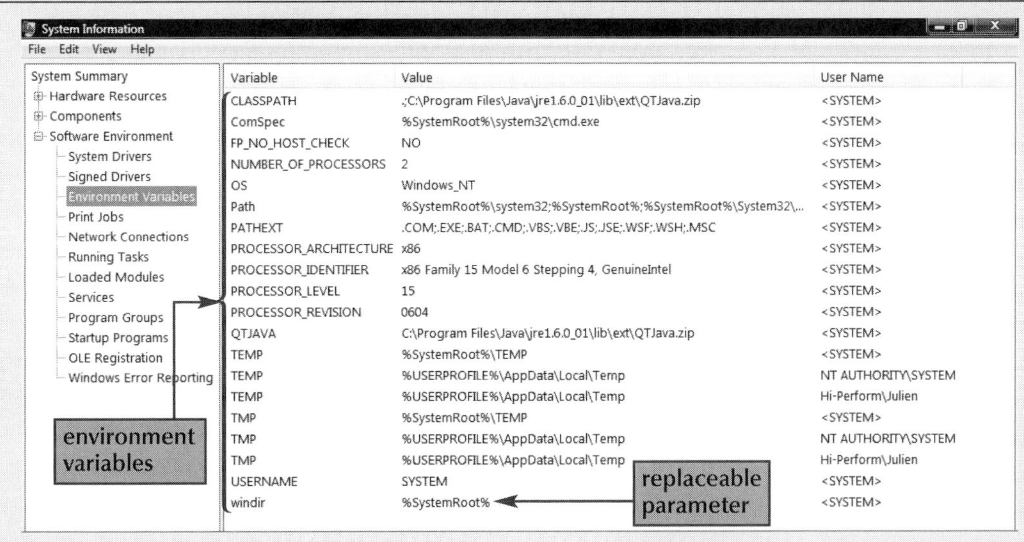

As you learned earlier, an **environment variable** is a symbolic name (such as OS) associated with a specific setting (such as Windows_NT for the OS environment variable). The environment variable therefore acts as a pointer to a setting, such as a system setting or an application setting. Environment variables and their settings are stored in an area of memory known as the **Windows environment** (previously known as the DOS environment under the DOS operating system) and identified as Software Environment by System Information. Windows Vista, applications, and other programs check the Windows environment for settings.

Understanding these environment variables gives you a better sense of how Windows Vista works. For example, the windir environment identifies the location of the Windows folder (or directory). This environment variable is assigned the value %SystemRoot%. (*Please note that in any sentence that contains a period or comma after an environment variable name, setting, or path, the period or comma is not part of the setting or path.*) SystemRoot is the environment variable name that refers to the folder that contains the Windows Vista operating system files. Though not shown here, the SystemRoot environment variable is assigned the path to the Windows folder. If the Windows folder is located on drive C, the value for the SystemRoot environment variable is C:\Windows. If the Windows folder is located on drive D, the value for this variable is D:\Windows. Since the Windows folder might be located on a hard disk drive other than drive C on another computer, Windows assigns the setting for this environment variable during booting. Therefore, since the path for the Windows folder can vary, it's stored in an environment variable. When the environment variable is used in a path, it is enclosed within percent symbols to indicate that it is a **replaceable parameter**. In other words, it's a variable value (meaning it can change or be different on different computers) that is replaced by the actual path on a specific computer.

Other important environment variables are:

- **ComSpec** This environment variable (a holdover from the DOS operating system) identifies the path of the **command interpreter**, the program that interprets commands you enter in a command-line environment. The setting for this environment variable is %SystemRoot%\system32\cmd.exe. As already noted, if the Windows folder is located on drive C, the SystemRoot environment variable is assigned the setting C:\Windows. When interpreting a path that contains %SystemRoot%, Windows Vista replaces %SystemRoot% with C:\Windows so that the final and actual path for ComSpec is C:\Windows\System32\cmd.exe (the exact path to this program on this computer). If you boot in Safe Mode with Command Prompt, Windows Vista starts this program so that you can work in a command-line environment.
- **Path** This environment variable (a holdover from the DOS operating system) identifies a sequence of directories (or folders) that contain program files Windows Vista searches to locate and load a program from disk. This path differs on different computers because they have different software products installed on them. On the computer used for this figure, the path is as follows (all on one line without any spaces after the semicolons):

  %SystemRoot%\system32;%SystemRoot%;%SystemRoot%\System32\Wbem;
  c:\Program Files\Microsoft SQL Server\90\Tools\binn\;
  C:\Program Files\QuickTime\QTSystem\

  When Windows Vista substitutes C:\Windows for %SystemRoot% in each part of the path that uses this replaceable parameter, the final path used by Windows Vista to locate programs is (again all on one line and without spaces after the semicolons):

  C:\Windows\system32;C:\Windows;C:\Windows\System32\Wbem;c:\Program Files\Microsoft SQL Server\90\Tools\binn\;C:\Program Files\QuickTime\QTSystem\

  The path for each folder must be separated from the previous one by a semicolon.

If you issue a command to use a specific program, Windows Vista searches the current folder first to see if the program file is contained in that folder. If it finds the program file, it loads the program into memory. If it does not find the program file, it checks the path defined by the Path variable, starting with the first folder listed in the path and proceeding from folder to folder until it locates the program. For example, when checking the path shown previously for a program file, Windows Vista first checks the System32 folder (C:\Windows\System32) because it is listed first in the path. If the program is not found in the System32 folder, it checks the Windows folder next (in this case, C:\Windows). If the program is not found in the Windows folder, it checks the Wbem folder (C:\Windows\System32\Wbem). If the program is not found in the Wbem folder, it checks the binn folder (C:\Program Files\Microsoft SQL Server\90\Tools\binn). If the program is not found in the binn folder, it checks the QTSystem folder (C:\Program Files\QuickTime\QTSystem\).

- **PATHEXT** This environment variable identifies a set of file extensions that are used to locate a program file, and therefore, it is used in combination with the Path variable. For example, if the Run command is displayed on the Start menu, you can click Run, type a command, program filename, folder name, path, or URL in the Open text box in the Run dialog box, and then press the Enter key (or click the OK button), Windows opens the program, folder, file, or Web site. If you enter the command CMD in the Run dialog box's Open text box, and then press the Enter key, Windows Vista opens a command-line window.

The command CMD that you type is actually the main part of the filename for the program file (e.g., the program file for the CMD command is named CMD.EXE). Windows Vista then checks the current folder and each of the other folders listed in the path, in the order in which they are listed, for the program file. However, since program files can have different file extensions, Windows Vista looks for that program file using the command you type and different possible file extensions in each directory. In each folder Windows Vista checks, it looks for a program using the first file extension in the PATHEXT environment variable (in this case, COM) and searches for a file named CMD.COM. If it finds a program by that name, it loads the program into memory so that you can use it. If it does not find a program by this name, it looks for a program using the next file extension in the PATHEXT variable (in this case, EXE), and then searches for a file named CMD.EXE in the same directory. As it turns out, CMD.EXE is the name of the program for opening a command-line window, so it finds and loads this program from the System32 folder, the first folder it checks in the path. If this folder does not contain a program by this name, it repeats the same process using the next file extension listed in the PATHEXT environment variable, on a folder-by-folder basis, until it locates the program.

Some computer viruses use the same filename as a legitimate program with an EXE file extension, but the computer virus' filename uses the COM file extension. Since the COM file extension is the first one listed in the PATHEXT environment variable, this approach guarantees that Windows locates and loads this program file with the computer virus. Then the computer virus can pass control to the file with the EXE file extension so that it also loads, and you are not even aware that a computer virus has been loaded into memory, but it now has access to your entire system. However, if you are more specific and type CMD.EXE in the Run Open text box, Windows Vista searches for a file by that filename and that file extension using the folders listed in the Path variable. That's why it pays to enter the full filename of a program file.

The DOS operating system used the same technique for locating program files; however, it looked only for files with the COM, EXE, and BAT file extensions (in that order). Those program file extensions were carried over to the Windows operating system, and additional file extensions are now included in the PATHEXT environment variable. Recall from the previous tutorial that these file extensions are currently considered unsafe and therefore potentially dangerous if they are the file extensions of an e-mail attachment.

Other categories under Software Environment provide the following types of information:

- **System Drivers** This category includes a list of the names of all system drivers, a description for each driver (such as Windows Firewall Authorization Driver), the path to the file that contains each driver, the type of driver (kernel driver or file system driver), whether the driver started (i.e., loaded), the Start Mode of each driver (Auto, Boot, Disabled, Manual, or System), and the State of each driver (Running or Stopped).
- **Signed Drivers** This category includes a list of the names—such as Dell 2007WFP (Digital), a monitor driver—or filenames of all drivers; whether the driver is signed (Yes, No, or Not Available); the device class (such as DISKDRIVE or MONITOR); driver version number and date; and INF name (the name of the Setup Information File for installing driver support).
- **Running Tasks** This category includes detailed information about all running tasks (most of which have the exe file extension), including their filenames and their path (if known).
- **Loaded Modules** This category includes detailed information on all loaded modules of program code with the dll, drv, exe, and cpl file extensions, including the names and paths to each module. "dll" is the file extension for dynamic link libraries, "drv" for drivers, "exe" for executable files, and "cpl" is the file extension for Control Panel applets.
- **Services** This category includes detailed information on all services, including the name (such as WinDefend), the display name (such as Windows Defender), the State (Running or Stopped), the Start Mode (Auto, Disabled, or Manual), and the path.
- **Program Groups** This category contains the group name (such as Start Menu, Start Menu\Programs, and Start Menu\Programs\Accessories) of all the group folders on the Start Menu for Default Users, Public User, and the currently logged-on user.
- **Windows Error Reporting** This category contains a list of errors that have occurred on the computer you are using and shows the date and time of each error, the type of error (such as Application Error, Application Hang, and Windows Error Reporting), and details on each error. This information is similar to what you saw earlier using Event Viewer. If you are trying to troubleshoot a problem with an application, you might want to examine this information.

System Information is an invaluable tool for locating information that can help you identify and perhaps resolve problems you encounter on your computer. You can also use System Information to learn more about your own computer system.

Using System Information | Reference Window

- On the Start menu, point to All Programs, click Accessories, click System Tools, click System Information, and then maximize the System Information window.
- In the Category pane on the left, click the Expand box to the left of the Software Environment category, and then click Startup Programs and examine the information on Startup Programs in the Details pane on the right.
- In the Category pane on the left, click Environment Variables under Software Environment, and in the Details pane, examine the information on environment variables and their settings.
- Close the System Information window.

Using the Windows Recovery Environment

The **Windows Recovery Environment (WinRE)** is a special environment for troubleshooting computer startup problems, such as a Windows Vista boot failure. Within the Windows Recovery Environment, you have access to the following set of five tools, called System Recovery Tools, for manually troubleshooting a computer:

- **Startup Repair** This recovery tool checks for and fixes problems with system files, boot configuration settings, the Master Boot Record, Hard Disk Partition Table, boot sector, Registry settings, device drivers, Windows updates, and file system problems that prevent your computer from starting properly (or at all). Startup Repair cannot repair problems with BIOS settings, improperly functioning hardware, incorrect hardware configuration, incorrect device driver settings, or hardware failures. It cannot repair problems caused by malicious software, and it cannot help you recover your personal documents. It can detect, but not repair, problems caused by bad RAM or the hard disk hardware. A computer manufacturer might also choose to customize or replace this tool. In the latter case, Startup Repair would not be available.
- **System Restore** You can use this recovery tool to roll back your computer to an earlier working state. Startup Repair might also begin restoring your computer using System Restore to repair a problem with starting Windows. You can also use this option if you change the password for an Administrator account and then forget that password or if Windows Vista does not recognize the password for some reason. You can also use System Restore if you make a change to an Administrator account that subsequently prevents you from logging on under that account (such as changing the Administrator account to a Standard User account).
- **Windows Complete PC Restore** You can use this recovery tool to restore your entire computer from your last full system backup. If you choose this option, you lose any files that you created or modified since that last backup.
- **Windows Memory Diagnostic Tool** You can use this recovery tool to perform a thorough check of the RAM in your computer. This tool is stored in the \Boot folder; however, you can only run it in the Windows Recovery Environment.
- **Command Prompt** With this recovery tool, you can use certain command-line tools, such as the Check Disk utility, to troubleshoot problems with a computer. Some types of command-line tools, including network command-line tools, are not available because Windows Vista is not running on the computer. Instead, you work in the Windows Recovery Environment (WinRE).

To access these System Recovery Tools, you:

1. Insert your Windows DVD into a DVD drive.
2. Restart your computer.

3. Choose the option for booting from your DVD drive.
4. In the first Install Windows dialog box, verify the "Language to install," "Time and currency format," and "Keyboard or input method" settings.
5. In the next Windows dialog box, choose the "Repair your computer" option.
6. In the System Recovery Options dialog box, choose the operating system you want to repair, or if Microsoft Windows Vista is not listed, use the Load Drivers button to load drivers for your hard disk first.
7. In the next System Recovery Options dialog box, shown in Figure 8-43, choose one of the five recovery tools described previously.

Figure 8-43 System Recovery Options dialog box

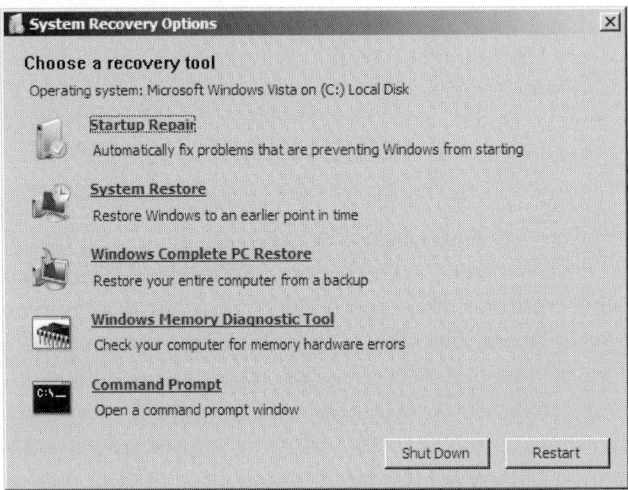

If Windows Vista could not start during your last boot, the Startup Repair tool starts, checks your computer for the possible source of the problem, and then fixes the problem if possible. Or the Startup Repair tool might prompt you to restore your computer with System Restore. If the Startup Repair tool successfully diagnoses and repairs the problem, it displays information about the nature of the problem, including the source of the problem and how the problem was resolved.

If your computer manufacturer preinstalled the Windows Recovery Environment (WinRE) with the System Recovery Tools on your computer, you can display the Advanced Boot Options menu by pressing F8 during booting and choose the "Repair your computer" option. After you select a keyboard layout, you enter your user name and password, and then choose Startup Repair from the System Recovery Options menu. If the Windows Recovery Environment is not preinstalled on your computer, make sure you can locate your Windows Vista DVD.

Although it is possible to install the Windows Recovery Environment on a computer, it's an involved process that requires creating a new hidden partition with a specific partition style defined by Microsoft so that you can boot your computer from this partition if Windows Vista fails to boot from the partition where it is installed. Also, this partition must be located before the Windows partition on the hard disk. After setting up this partition, you copy the files needed for the Windows Recovery Environment and then configure the Windows Recovery Environment. You must also take into account whether you're using BitLocker Drive Encryption in those Windows Vista Editions that support this feature.

Restoring Your Computer

If you are working in a computer lab, or if you want to restore your desktop computer to the settings that existed prior to working on this tutorial, complete the following steps.

To restore your computer:

1. To remove Administrative Tools from the Start and All Programs menu, right-click the **Start** button, click **Properties**, and on the Start Menu property sheet, click the **Customize** button to the right of Start menu, scroll to the bottom of the list of options for customizing the Start menu, and under System administrative tools, click the **Don't display this item** option button, click the **OK** button to close the Customize Start Menu dialog box, and then click the **OK** button to close the Taskbar and Start Menu Properties dialog box.
2. To restore double-click activation, click the **Computer** icon on the desktop, click the **Organize** button on the command bar, click **Folder and Search Options**, and on the General property sheet in the Folder Options dialog box, click the **Double-click to open an item** (**single click to select**) option button, click the **OK** button to close the Folder Options dialog box, and then close the Computer window.
3. To remove the Computer icon from the desktop, open the **Start menu**, right-click **Computer**, and then click **Show on Desktop**.

Julien is confident you can now help him configure, customize, optimize, and troubleshoot the computer systems at Carbon Sink, Unlimited.

Session 8.2 Quick Check | Review

1. ________________ is a term commonly used to refer to a hardware device, such as the BIOS, which contains embedded software that interacts with the operating system.
2. What term is used to refer to the name of a BIOS setting and the setting itself?
3. ________________ contains boot configuration settings and information about the location of boot files, which in turn determine how the Windows operating system loads from disk.
4. What happens if you select Last Known Good Configuration on the Advanced Boot Options menu?
5. What program can you use to shut down a nonresponding program?
6. What are startup programs, and how can you control the loading of those programs?
7. What is an environment variable?

Review | Tutorial Summary

In this tutorial, you examined common strategies for troubleshooting problems on a computer. You used Reliability Monitor to produce a System Stability Chart, and then you used that chart to identify the nature of specific problems on a computer. You also used Event Viewer to analyze event logs and locate information on various types of events, including critical events and other events that produced errors on a computer. You examined System Protection settings and used System Protection to create a restore point. Then, you used System Restore to view your new restore point. You opened the BIOS Setup utility and examined BIOS boot sequence settings. You examined the Windows Vista boot process and data structures used for booting. You used the Advanced Boot Options menu to examine different Windows boot options, and you started Windows Vista in Safe Mode. You used Task Manager to view running processes and services, and you examined how to use it to shut down nonresponding programs. You opened System Configuration and evaluated the loading of startup programs and services. You used System Information to examine information about startup programs and environment variables. Finally, you examined the use of Windows Vista System Recovery Tools.

Key Terms

Active Directory network
BIOS
Blue Screen of Death (BSOD)
Boot Configuration Data (BCD)
boot sequence
command interpreter
domain
domain controller
environment variable
event
event logs
Event Viewer
field
filter
firmware
hotkeys
Parallel Advanced Technology Attachment (PATA)
Reliability Monitor
reliability rating
replaceable parameter
restore point
Safe Mode
Serial Advanced Technology Attachment (SATA)
startup program
Stop Error
system checkpoint
System Stability Index
Windows Boot Loader
Windows Boot Manager
Windows environment
Windows Recovery Environment (WinRE)
Windows Resume Loader
Windows Task Manager

Practice | Review Assignments

Practice the skills you learned in the tutorial.

There are no Data Files needed for the Review Assignments.

Sencia Bacay, one of Julien's coworkers, recently downloaded and installed plug-ins, or add-ons, for her Web browser. Now she notices a problem with the performance of her computer, and she is experiencing problems establishing an Internet connection. You offer to help her troubleshoot this problem.

To complete some of these steps in the Review Assignments, you must log on under an Administrator account or provide the password for an Administrator account. As you complete each step in the Review Assignments, record your answers to questions so that you can submit them to your instructor. Use a word processing application, such as Word or WordPad, to prepare your answers to these questions. Also, if you change any settings on the computer you are using, note the original settings so that you can restore them later. Complete the following:

1. If necessary, display the Computer icon on the desktop, switch to single-click activation, and display Administrative Tools on the Start menu and All Programs menu.
2. What is the likely cause or source of the problems that Sencia is currently experiencing on her computer?
3. What troubleshooting strategy or approach can Sencia use to solve her computer problems? Briefly outline the steps she should use prior to actually troubleshooting the problem.
4. Open Reliability and Performance Monitor, select Reliability Monitor, and if necessary, provide Administrator credentials for an Administrator account, or close the Reliability Monitor dialog box if your account is a Standard User account.
5. What is the current reliability rating (or System Stability Index) of your computer? Describe how the reliability rating has changed over the time period represented on the System Stability Chart. Select the icon for the most recent Application, Hardware, Windows, or Miscellaneous failure, or if there have been no failures, select the last icon for the most recent Software (Un)Installs warning or informational event. What type of event did you select? Using the information in the System Stability Report, describe the cause of the failure or the information about the warning or informational event you selected. What, if anything, would you do next? Close the Reliability and Performance Monitor window.
6. Open Event Viewer, and if necessary, provide Administrator credentials. Expand the Critical category in the Summary of Administrative Events. Double-click one of the events with a Critical level, or if there are no Critical events, expand the Error, Warning, or Informational category, and double-click one of the events. What Event Type did you choose? What is the Source of this event? In your own words, describe the information that Event Viewer provides on the nature of this event.
7. In the console tree pane, expand Windows Logs, and then select Application. Use the Filter Current Log action to specify all events with a Critical Event level and an Error Event level. Also, use the Event sources drop-down list button to select Application, Application Error, Application Hang, and Application Management event sources. Apply the filter, and then select one of the recent Application events with a Critical or Error Event level. What is the event Level and Source? In your own words, describe what caused this problem? What recommendations does Event Viewer suggest for troubleshooting the problem (if any)? Clear the filter.

8. In the Event Viewer console tree pane, open Applications and Services Logs, and then select Internet Explorer. Does Event Viewer report any Critical, Error, or Warning events for Internet Explorer? If so, explain. Why might Sencia examine this category of event logs? Then close Event Viewer.
9. Right-click the desktop Computer icon and choose the option to view its properties. In the System window, select System protection under Tasks, provide Administrator credentials, and wait for System Protection to update information on Automatic restore points. List the disks on your computer for which System Protection automatically creates restore points. How much time has elapsed since the last restore point?
10. Use the Create button on the System Protection property sheet to create a manual restore point. Enter a description for the restore point (such as Manual Restore Point) and create the restore point. After System Protection creates the restore point, close the System Protection dialog box, and then close the System Properties dialog box and System window.
11. On the All Programs menu, select Accessories, select System Tools, and then open System Restore. After providing Administrator credentials, advance to the next step, or choose the option for choosing a different restore point, and then advance to the next step. Choose the option for showing restore points older than 5 days. Identify the different types of restore points created by System Protection. Then, close the System Restore dialog box without making any changes to your computer.
12. Read this step before you restart your computer so that you know what types of information to collect during booting to answer the questions in this step. Close all open programs and windows, choose the option to restart your computer, and then open the BIOS Setup utility. (If you are not permitted to open the BIOS Setup utility in your college's computer lab, note that fact as your answer to this step.) What key or keys did you use to open the BIOS Setup utility? Is there a key for opening a Boot Menu, and if so, what key can you use? After opening the BIOS Setup utility, locate the boot sequence, and then list the current boot sequence for your computer. Exit the BIOS Setup utility without making any changes to your computer, and then display the Advanced Boot Options menu as your computer reboots. If your computer boots to the desktop, restart your computer and try again.
13. Choose the "Enable low-resolution video (640×480)" option on the Advanced Boot Options menu and log on under your user account. View the Display settings for your computer's screen resolution and color setting. What is the current setting for Resolution and Colors? What type of monitor and video display adapter does Windows Vista report? Close the Display Settings dialog box. Could you connect to the Internet if you needed to search for information on troubleshooting a problem? Restart your computer, let Windows Vista boot normally, and then log on your user account.
14. Open Windows Internet Explorer, and then open Task Manager. What applications are running on your computer? View processes. Locate the Image Name iexplore.exe for the Windows Internet Explorer task. How much memory does the Windows Internet Explorer task use for its Private Working Set?
15. Select the Services property sheet, and then click the Description column header to alphabetize services by Description. Check the Status column for the Security Center, Windows Defender, Windows Firewall, and Windows Event Log. Are these services running on your computer? If Windows Defender is not installed on your computer, or if you use a firewall other than Windows Firewall, note this information in your response to the question. Close Windows Task Manager and Windows Internet Explorer.

16. Open System Configuration and provide Administrator credentials. What type of Startup selection does your computer use? Select the Startup property sheet, adjust the width of all the columns so you can view all the information displayed in each column, and list the names of the Startup Items that load during booting on your computer. Which Startup Items, if any, are not loaded? Choose one of the Startup Items, and then list the Startup Item's name, the Manufacturer's name (if known), the Command for loading the startup item, and the Location from which Windows Vista loads the startup item. How does this Startup Item load? Close the System Configuration dialog box.
17. From the All Programs menu, open System Information. In the System Summary, list the information provided by System Information on the OS Name, Version, Processor, Windows Directory, System Directory, Boot Device, and Total Physical Memory for your computer. (*Hint*: If all the information for an entry is not visible, rest the mouse pointer on the entry, and then view the information in the ToolTip.)
18. In the Category pane, expand the Software Environment category, and then select Startup programs. Widen the columns in the Details pane so you can view all the information in each column. List the names of the startup programs, and then examine the Location column. What location (or locations) does Windows Vista use to load these startup programs?
19. Select the Environment Variables category. What are the settings for OS and windir environment variables? What value does Windows Vista substitute for the replaceable parameter in the windir environment variable? Explain the purpose and use of the PATHEXT environment variable. Close System Information.
20. Submit the results of the preceding steps to your instructor, either in printed or electronic form, as requested.

Apply | Case Problem 1

Use the skills you learned in the tutorial to troubleshoot problems with Reliability Monitor.

There are no Data Files needed for this Case Problem.

Laskowski Analytics, Inc. Over the years, Hanna Laskowski's software testing and analysis firm has evaluated the performance of applications and utilities under different Windows operating systems. The computers used by her employees must therefore meet the highest performance standards in order to return reliable data about the performance of programs that they test every day. Prior to purchasing newer and higher performance computers to test new Windows operating systems and applications, she asks you to evaluate a new state-of-the-art computer.

To complete this Case Problem, you must provide Administrator credentials if you are logged on under an Administrator account. As you complete each step in this case, record your answers to questions so that you can submit them to your instructor. Use a word processing application, such as Word or WordPad, to prepare your answers to these questions. Also, if you change any settings on the computer you are using, note the original settings so that you can restore them later. Complete the following:

1. Open Reliability Monitor, and then use the System Stability Chart to evaluate the performance of your computer by locating information to answer the following questions:
   - What is the most recent date for which Reliability Monitor has information, and what is the current reliability rating (or System Stability Index) of the computer you are using?
   - Adjust your view in the System Stability Chart and select the earliest date for which Reliability Monitor has information. What date did you select, and what is the reliability rating (or System Stability Index)?

- Locate and select the date for the lowest reliability rating shown in the System Stability Chart over the time period for which information is available. What date did you select, and what is the lowest reliability rating? Which failures or problems account for this low reliability rating?

2. Use the Calendar control to select all dates for which performance data is available. Use the System Stability Report to evaluate problems on your computer, as follows:
   - Examine the activity status for Software (Un)Installs. If Reliability Monitor lists any Software (Un)Installs failures, identify the Software and the Activity for the last failure (if any).
   - Examine Application failures. Identify the Application name and Failure Type for the last application failure (if any).
   - Examine Hardware failures. Identify the Component Type, Device, and Failure Type for the last hardware device failure (if any).
   - Examine Windows failures. Identify the Failure Type for the last Windows failure (if any).
   - Examine Miscellaneous failures. Identify the Failure Type for the last Miscellaneous failure (if any).
3. After analyzing the information you examined, summarize your impression of the performance of your computer over the period of time for which Reliability Monitor contains information on Software (Un)Installs and Application, Hardware, Windows, and Miscellaneous failures. Indicate in your analysis whether the performance of your computer is improving or becoming worse, and if the latter is the case, identify what you must troubleshoot to improve your computer's performance and what options you might explore.
4. Submit the results of the preceding steps to your instructor, either in printed or electronic form, as requested.

Apply | Case Problem 2

Use the skills you learned in the tutorial to analyze events for a cutting-edge troubleshooting firm.

There are no Data Files needed for this Case Problem.

Avant Garde Troubleshooters, Inc. Toru Miyazaki and Isao Nagano cofounded and now manage a cutting-edge troubleshooting firm to help their customers resolve problems caused by different operating systems. Their employees rely on Event Monitor for up-to-date information about problems that arise on the computers they use to remotely troubleshoot problems. Toru asks you to use Event Viewer to evaluate System events on a computer used by one of his new employees.

To complete this Case Problem, you must provide Administrator credentials if you are logged on under an Administrator account. As you complete each step in this case, record your answers to questions so that you can submit them to your instructor. Use a word processing application, such as Word or WordPad, to prepare your answers to these questions. Also, if you change any settings on the computer you are using, note the original settings so that you can restore them later. Complete the following:

1. Open Event Viewer from the Administrative Tools menu, open Windows Logs, and then select System.
2. Create a filter that displays System events with a Critical Event level, and then click the Source column header to list events in alphabetical order. How many events does Event Viewer report for the Critical Event level?

3. If there are any events with the Critical Event level, list the different types of Sources for these events.
4. If there are any events with the Critical Event level, select one event in each different type of Source, and summarize the following information about the events:
   - Source
   - Task Category
   - Nature of the problem
   - Recommended resolution (if any)
5. Change the existing filter so that it displays events with an Error Event level. If there are any events with the Error Event level, select the most recent Error level event and summarize the following information about that event:
   - Source
   - Nature of problem
   - Recommended resolution (if any)
6. Change the existing filter so that it displays events with a Warning Event level, and if necessary, alphabetize that list by Source. (*Hint*: Click the Source heading.) If available, select a Warning event for Windows Defender (if installed) or select the most recent Warning level event and summarize the following information about that event:
   - Source
   - Nature of problem
   - Recommended resolution (if any)

EXPLORE

7. Change the filter so that it displays events for the System Restore Event source. What information does Event Viewer report about the most recent System Restore event? What prompted the creation of a restore point?
8. Open Applications and Services Logs in the console tree pane, open Microsoft, open Windows, open WindowsUpdateClient, and then select Operational. Create a filter that displays events for the Critical, Error, and Warning levels. Click the Level column header to sort events by Level, and then select the most recent Critical, Error, or Warning event. What does Event Viewer report about the Event Level and the nature of this event? Clear the current filter and close Event Viewer.
9. How might you benefit from, or use, Event Viewer on your computer?
10. Submit the results of the preceding steps to your instructor, either in printed or electronic form, as requested.

Challenge | Case Problem 3

Extend what you've learned to examine BIOS settings for a foundation computer.

There are no Data Files needed for this Case Problem.

Euro-Russian Seed Vault Foundation Olga Sergeyev is the director of the Euro-Russian Seed Vault Foundation, a joint Russian and European Community venture designed to store and protect seeds of all known crop and wildflower species in the world to guarantee future crop and wildlife diversity and to recover from ecological disasters and pathogens. As Olga's in-house computer specialist, she has asked you to examine and, if necessary, optimize the BIOS settings on the computers used by foundation staff.

As you complete each step in this Case Problem, record your answers to questions so that you can submit them to your instructor. Use a word processing application, such as Word or WordPad, to prepare your answers to these questions. Also, if you change any settings on the computer you are using, note the original settings so that you can restore them later. Complete the following:

1. Restart your computer and open the BIOS Setup utility.
2. Locate information about the processor, and if available, provide the following information:
   - Processor Type, Clock Speed, Bus Speed, L2 Cache (size), and L3 Cache (size)
   - Multiple Core Capable
   - Hyperthreading Capable
   - 64-bit Technology
3. Locate information about the memory on your computer, and if available, provide the following information:
   - (Amount of) Installed Memory
   - Memory Speed
   - Memory Technology
   - (Type of) Memory Slot and amount of memory used in each memory slot
4. Locate the boot sequence on your computer, and then list the order in which the BIOS searches your computer to locate the drive with the operating system.

EXPLORE

5. Locate information about power management, and if available, indicate the purpose of each of the following settings and provide the following information:
   - Auto Power On setting and options for this field
   - AC Recovery setting and options for this field
   - Suspend Mode setting and any other option(s) for this field

EXPLORE

6. Locate information about Execute Disable, if available. What does this setting do, what is the current setting for this field, and what is the factory default? (*Hint*: Check the Security category for this field.)

EXPLORE

7. Locate information about POST behavior, and if available, indicate the purpose of each of the following settings and provide the following information:
   - Fast Boot setting
   - Numlock Key setting
   - POST Hotkeys
8. Exit the BIOS Setup utility without making any changes to BIOS settings.
9. After your computer restarts, log onto your computer, view properties of your computer, provide the following information, and then close the System window.
   - Processor
   - Memory (RAM)
   - System type
10. Open System Information from the All Programs menu and provide the following information from the System Summary:
    - Processor
    - Total Physical Memory
11. Select the Environment Variables category, provide the following information from environment variables, and then close the System Information window.
    - Number of processors
    - Processor architecture
    - Processor Identifier

12. Submit the results of the preceding steps to your instructor, either in printed or electronic form, as requested.

Research | Case Problem 4

Work with the skills you've learned and use the Internet to evaluate startup programs.

There are no Data Files needed for this Case Problem.

Mostyn Excursions, Inc. Mostyn Excursions, a business located in Wales, provides unique travel tours and packages to exotic, unusual, and quaint locales throughout Wales, Scotland, Ireland, and Britain as well as the Hebrides, Orkney Islands, Shetland Islands, Rockall, and Isle of Man. Cedric Mostyn, the owner of Mostyn Excursions, asks you to evaluate the startup programs used on the computers at Mostyn Excursions to determine how best to optimize those computers.

To complete this Case Problem, you must log on under an Administrator account or know the password for an Administrator account. As you complete each step, record your answers to questions so that you can submit them to your instructor. Use a word processing application, such as Word or WordPad, to prepare your answers to these questions. Also, if you change any settings on the computer you are using, note the original settings so that you can restore them later. Complete the following:

1. Open System Configuration from the Administrative Tools menu, select the Startup property sheet, widen all the columns, and then click the Startup Item column header to sort startup items in alphabetical order.
2. Prepare a list that includes the name of each Startup Item, the program filename, and the name of the folder where the program file is located (where available).
3. Use a search engine to locate one or more Web sites that contain information about startup programs. (*Hint*: Since this company is located in Wales, you might want to use the Sysinfo.org United Kingdom Web site, which contains information on tens of thousands of startup programs.)
4. For each Startup Item on your computer, use the Startup Name, program filename, and program file location to locate and record the following information (where available):
    - The purpose of the Startup Item
    - Whether the Startup item is legitimate or malicious software
    - The recommended option for loading the Startup Item, such as:
    - Safe to load during booting
    - Required
    - Not required or not recommended
    - User's choice
    - Unknown
5. If necessary, check one or two other Web sites to determine whether they provide any more useful information about your startup programs.
6. For each Startup Item, explain whether you would enable or disable the loading of the program and explain how you arrived at that decision.
7. List the names and URLs of any Web sites you used to compile information for this case problem.
8. Close the System Configuration dialog box.
9. Submit the results of the preceding steps to your instructor, either in printed or electronic form, as requested.

Review | Quick Check Answers

Session 8.1

1. Reliability Monitor
2. event
3. filter
4. System Protection, System Restore
5. Reliability Monitor, Event Viewer
6. system checkpoint

Session 8.2

1. firmware
2. field
3. Boot Configuration Data (BCD)
4. Last Known Good Configuration is a boot option that starts Windows Vista with the configuration saved in the Windows Registry by the operating system from the last successful boot.
5. Task Manager
6. A startup program is a program that loads during booting and that operates in the background as you use your computer. You can use System Configuration to specify which startup programs load during booting and which ones do not load.
7. An environment variable is a symbolic name (such as OS) associated with a specific setting.

Ending Data Files

There are no ending Data Files needed for this tutorial.

Objectives

Session 9.1
- Describe RAM, virtual memory, and the paging file
- View the paging file on your computer
- Monitor changes in system performance with Task Manager
- Use Resource Overview to evaluate system performance
- Create a system health report

Session 9.2
- Use Performance Monitor
- Save, print, and analyze performance measurements
- Use Reliability and Performance Monitor
- View virtual memory settings
- Examine Windows ReadyBoost, Superfetch, and ReadyDrive

Evaluating System Performance

Monitoring Memory Usage

Case | Allele Vigor, Inc.

Allele Vigor, Inc. is a Boston-based biotech company that develops new species of plants by using interspecific, intraspecific, interfamilial, intergeneric, and cross-species, gene-splicing techniques. These innovative efforts over the years have resulted in new food crops and new ways of producing fibers for use in a wide array of products. Allele Vigor's employees rely on high-performance and resource-intensive gene modeling and analysis software to develop these new plant species. Cai Shuang, a tech specialist at Allele Vigor, Inc., checks and optimizes the performance of computer systems used by the research staff.

In this tutorial, you will examine the importance of RAM, virtual memory, and the paging file. You will use Windows Task Manager to examine information on processor and memory usage. You will use Resource Overview to evaluate system performance, and you will use Reliability and Performance Monitor to create a system health report and identify potential problems. Then, you will use Performance Monitor to track memory and processor usage as you work on your computer. Next, you examine virtual memory settings on your computer, and you examine how you can use Windows ReadyBoost to optimize memory usage.

Starting Data Files

There are no starting Data Files needed for this tutorial.

Session 9.1

The Importance of RAM

RAM (random access memory) is the hardware component that most affects the performance of a computer. Computers typically come with high-performance processors and high-capacity hard disks with gigabytes of storage space; however, manufacturers provide, and users typically purchase, computers that have less than an optimal amount of RAM for the myriad of ways in which they use their computers. To increase the amount of memory available in a computer, Windows Vista creates a special system file on your hard disk called a **paging file** for use as supplemental RAM. The installed physical RAM and the paging file constitute what is called **virtual memory**. For example, assume you open Microsoft PowerPoint to create a presentation, and then decide that you want to insert a graph from an Excel spreadsheet into your PowerPoint presentation. After you open Microsoft Excel, Windows Vista can temporarily swap most of the Microsoft PowerPoint application and your presentation to the paging file on the hard disk to optimize the amount of physical RAM available to you while you are working in Microsoft Excel. After you open the spreadsheet that contains the graph you want to copy, you select that graph, copy it to the Office Clipboard, and then you switch back to Microsoft PowerPoint and your presentation and paste a copy of that graph into your presentation. When you switched back to Microsoft PowerPoint, Windows Vista swapped Microsoft Excel and the spreadsheet to the paging file on disk, and then swapped Microsoft PowerPoint and your presentation from the paging file to RAM to optimize the amount of physical RAM available to you while you are working in Microsoft PowerPoint.

The segments of memory that Windows Vista swaps to disk are called **pages**, and the process of swapping pages to and from disk is called **paging**, hence, the name of the paging file. Each page is 4 KB (or 4,096 bytes) in size and contains either program code or data. Windows Vista keeps track of how frequently each page is used, and less frequently used pages are the first to be swapped to the paging file on disk. However, programs contain a small set of pages that must remain in memory at all times.

By default, Windows Vista manages the size of the paging file. Windows Vista sets the minimum size of the paging file so that it equals the amount of installed RAM plus 300 MB. If your computer contains 4 GB of RAM, the minimum size of the paging file is approximately 4.3 GB. The 4 GB of RAM plus the 4.3 GB for the paging file provide Windows Vista with a total of 8.3 GB of memory. The absolute minimum size for the paging file is 16 MB.

Windows Vista sets the maximum size of the paging file to three times the amount of installed RAM. If your computer contains 4 GB of RAM, the maximum size of the paging file is 12 GB. The 4 GB of RAM plus the 12 GB for the paging file provide Windows Vista with a total of 16 GB of memory.

Windows Vista dynamically increases the size of the paging file when more virtual memory is needed and reduces its size when less virtual memory is needed. This process is transparent to the user, and Windows Vista provides you with whatever memory is needed for you to work with your applications and documents. When you start your computer, Windows Vista automatically creates the paging file even if it is not needed.

Although the use of a paging file provides you with the additional memory that you need to work with resource-intensive applications and multitask, it does pose a problem. Virtual memory is slower than physical RAM, and therefore, it slows down the performance of a computer. Swapping programs and data to and from disk is slow compared to the speed with which your computer can access programs and data in RAM. If your computer has a limited amount of RAM or does not have enough RAM for the types of applications that you use and the way in which you multitask, it functions more slowly as the operating system swaps pages to and from RAM to the paging file on disk, and from the paging file back into RAM. The more RAM you have, the less you have to rely on virtual memory. The less your computer has to rely on virtual memory, the faster it runs.

Selecting the Right Amount of RAM | InSight

When you buy a computer, you should have some idea of the amount of memory required by the different types of programs you intend to use so that you can purchase the amount of RAM that you need. These programs include the ones you use on an everyday basis, such as a Web browser, e-mail software, and word processing, spreadsheet, graphics, and database applications. They also include the Windows Vista operating system and other programs that operate in the background, such as antivirus software. Consider whether you intend to watch movies or videos, listen to music, and work with graphics and animation on your computer, because all these activities require more RAM. Furthermore, when you multitask and open and use more than one application at the same time, Windows Vista must allocate memory to each application.

The operating system allocates memory to applications that you use and is supposed to reclaim memory after you close an application. Some software developers, however, design their applications so that they leave program code in memory after you close the application. If you open the same application later, or use another application in the same office suite or same family of products that requires some of the same program code, the application opens faster. However, if you don't open the same application again or don't work with another application in the same office suite or family of products, that memory is tied up and unavailable. Furthermore, some applications remain in memory after you close them and can prevent you from performing certain operations, such as changing the name of the folder that contains a file you opened in that application.

This phenomenon, where allocated memory is not reclaimed by the operating system, but rather is tied up by previously open applications or processes, is referred to as a **memory leak** (or **memory overuse**). A memory leak can also be caused by a poorly designed program that does not relinquish memory when you close it. One simple way to deal with this problem is to reboot. When you reboot, everything in RAM is erased, so the amount of memory available to the operating system and applications returns to the original level that was available when you first booted your computer. A better approach to this type of problem is to install updates for the program that causes memory leaks or switch to software that does not create memory leaks.

The following points describe some basic features of memory usage on a computer:

- Windows Vista allocates memory to itself and to startup programs loaded during booting. Furthermore, Windows Vista must load device drivers and the program code required for each hardware device on your computer. While the amount of memory allocated after booting is complete varies with the configuration of your computer system, you should know what Windows Vista requires just to boot your computer. In fact, the operating system uses most of the memory allocated on a computer after your computer boots. (Later in the tutorial, you will examine how much memory Window Vista uses when you boot your computer and how much memory Microsoft Word, a commonly used application, requires.) If you want to limit the amount of memory allocated to startup programs, you can use the System Configuration utility you examined in Tutorial 8 to control the loading of those startup programs.
- Each time you open an application or another type of program, such as a Web browser, e-mail software, game, or utility, Windows Vista allocates memory to that program. That same principle applies to opening folder windows, such as the Computer and Documents folder windows.

- Some programs require more memory than other programs. If you rely on resource-intensive applications like Adobe Photoshop or Adobe Dreamweaver, and if you multi-task with those applications, you should have enough installed RAM to support those applications.
- Multitasking requires more memory than single-tasking because you have more open programs.
- Each time you close an application or another program, Windows Vista reclaims memory allocated to the application or program that opened that window. That same principle applies to closing folder windows, such as the Computer and Documents folder windows.
- After you close all open applications or programs, memory usage may not return to the original level from which you started after booting your computer because Windows Vista may not be able to reclaim all the originally allocated memory.

It's a good idea to purchase the RAM you need for your computer when you first acquire that computer so that you don't encounter performance problems. Anticipate how long you intend to keep your computer and evaluate how you intend to use a new computer before deciding how much RAM you need.

If you increase the amount of installed RAM on your computer, you will see a marked improvement in the performance and speed of your computer, particularly when you are multitasking and have more than one application open at a time, or when you use resource-intensive applications. Note that other factors, such as the processor speed, also affect the performance of a computer. However, studies have shown that the single best way to boost the performance of a computer is to add more RAM.

InSight | Identifying Low Memory Problems

If you notice any of the following types of problems, your computer does not have a sufficient amount of memory for proper performance:

- Windows Vista notifies you that your computer is low on memory or out of memory
- Poor overall performance, including very slow responses to routine operations, such as opening and selecting options from a menu
- Display problems, such as the appearance of blank areas on the monitor after selecting an option on a menu or closing a dialog box, rather than immediately updating your view
- Windows Vista or programs stop responding

These problems might occur only under certain circumstances, such as when you are multitasking or using a resource-intensive application. When you observe these types of problems, evaluate whether you need to purchase and install more RAM in your computer and whether you need to adjust virtual memory settings on your computer.

Your computer must also have sufficient storage space available on the hard disk for virtual memory to work properly. If disk storage space is limited on your computer, you will experience problems opening and using applications. Figure 9-1 lists the amount of storage space reserved for the Master File Table (MFT) zone, restore points, and the Recycle Bin and the amount of free space recommended by Microsoft for effective sorting of file fragments with Disk Defragmenter.

The maximum size for the Recycle Bin is 10 percent of a drive's storage capacity for drives 40 GB in size or smaller. For drives larger than 40 GB, the maximum size for the Recycle Bin is 4 GB plus 5 percent of the disk storage capacity above 40 GB. For example, if your hard disk's storage capacity is 500 GB, the maximum size of the Recycle Bin is 27 GB (or approximately 5.4 percent of the disk storage capacity), calculated as follows: ((500 GB - 40 GB)*.05) + 4 GB.

The **Master File Table Zone** is disk storage space that Windows Vista reserves for future growth of the Master File Table. The size of the Master File Table varies and increases over time as you create, copy, and move folders and files onto your hard disk. These four components might use or require up to 50–70 percent of the available storage space on the hard disk. Windows Vista also needs additional storage space above that amount for the following components:

- **Paging file** Although Windows Vista manages the size of the paging file, you can manually specify lower and upper limits for the size of the paging file. As noted earlier, the downside of relying on more virtual memory is that it slows down your computer.
- **Windows Vista and Microsoft Office updates**
- **Application updates**
- **Hibernation file**
- **Internet Cache and downloaded program files** for use with your Web browser
- **System files**, such as temporary files, spool files, thumbnails, debug dump files, and error-reporting and solution-checking files

You also need whatever disk storage space remains for your document files, e-mail messages, videos, music, television broadcasts, and other files.

Figure 9-1 Amount of disk storage required by Windows components

Windows Component	% of Disk's Storage Capacity
Master File Table (MFT) zone	Up to 12.5%
Restore points	Up to 15%
Recycle Bin	10% or less
Disk Defragmenter	15-30%
Total required or recommended	52.5-67.5%

Getting Started

To complete this tutorial, you must display the Computer icon on the desktop, switch your computer to single-click activation, display file extensions for known file types, choose the option to display hidden files and folders as well as protected operating system files, and display Administrative Tools on the Start Menu. In the following steps, you will check, and if necessary, change these settings.

To set up your computer:

1. If necessary, display a Computer icon on the desktop.

2. If you need to enable single-click activation, display file extensions, and display hidden folders, files, and protected operating system files, double-click the **Computer** icon on the desktop, click the **Organize** button on the command bar, click **Folder and Search Options**, and under "Click items as follows" on the General property sheet in the Folder Options dialog box, click the **Single-click to open an item (point to select)** option button, click the **Underline icon titles only when I point at them** option button, click the **View** tab, and in the Advanced Settings, click the **Hide extensions for known file types** check box (and remove the check mark), click the **Show hidden files and folders** option button, click the **Hide protected operating system files (Recommended)** check box, click the **Yes** button in the Warning dialog box to display protected operating system files, click the **OK** button to close the Folder and Options dialog box, and then close the Computer window.

3. If Administrative Tools is not displayed on the Start menu, right-click the **Start** button, click **Properties**, and on the Start Menu property sheet, click the **Customize** button to the right of the Start menu style option, scroll to the bottom of the list of options for customizing the Start menu, and under System administrative tools, click the **Display on the All Programs menu and the Start menu** option button, click the **OK** button to close the Customize Start Menu dialog box, and then click the **OK** button to close the Taskbar and Start Menu Properties dialog box.

Now you're ready to view the paging file on your computer.

Viewing the Paging File

By default, the paging file, which is named pagefile.sys, is stored in the top-level folder of the system volume (usually drive C). As you will discover later in the tutorial, you can move the paging file to another drive that has more storage space, is faster, or both to improve your computer's performance. If you have multiple hard disks in your computer, you can create a paging file on each hard disk to improve the performance of your computer. Your computer can then process I/O requests concurrently on multiple disks.

Shuang asks you to help her perform a thorough check of several newly acquired computer systems for staff research scientists. She starts by showing you the paging file on one of the new computers.

To view the paging file:

1. Open the Computer window, open a window onto drive C (or your system volume), locate and point to **pagefile.sys**, and then examine the information on the paging file in the Details Pane. On the computer used for Figure 9-2, Windows Vista reports that the paging file is 2.28 GB in size. Since this computer contains 2 GB of RAM, Windows Vista sets the minimum size of the paging file at 2 GB + 300 MB (0.29 GB), or approximately 2.3 GB. Your paging file size may differ. Windows Vista also identifies this file as a System File. Note also that the paging file and the hibernation file (hiberfil.sys) are by far the largest files in the top-level folder of this computer.

   Trouble? If you do not see pagefile.sys in the top-level folder of drive C, make sure that your computer is set to display hidden files and folders as well as protected operating system files. Also, the paging file might be located on another drive. If necessary, examine your other drive(s) and locate the paging file.

Figure 9-2 Viewing the paging file on the system volume

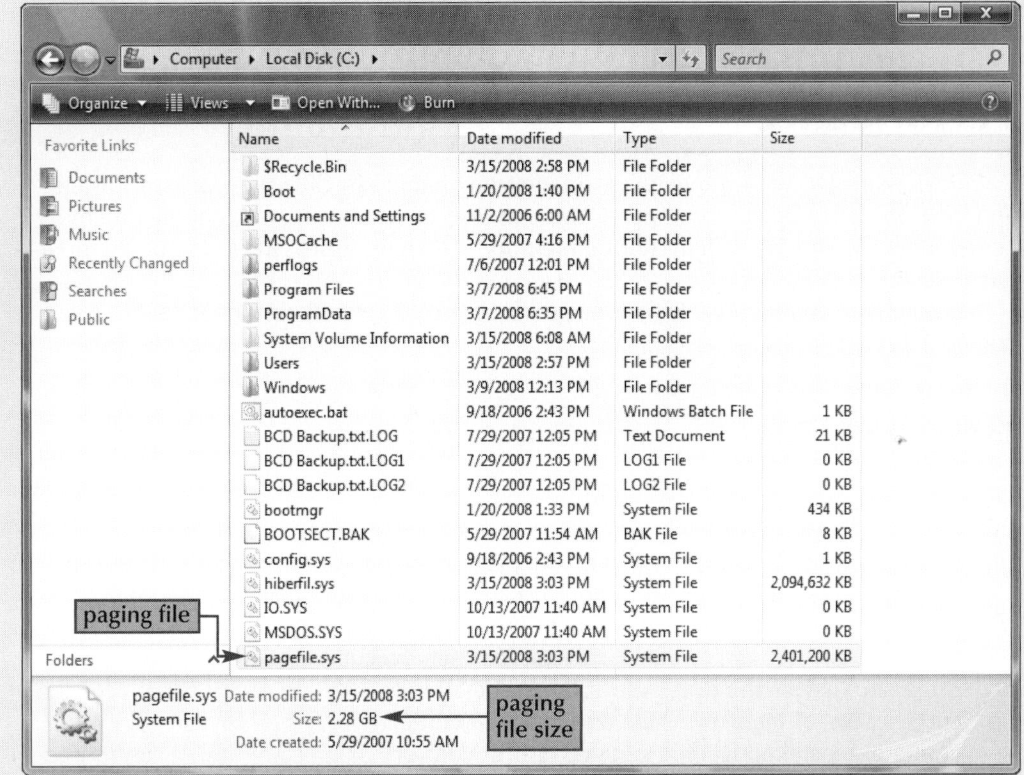

2. Examine other folders and files in this folder. Bootmgr is the Windows Boot Manager. If you use hibernation on your computer, you will see a hibernation file named hiberfil.sys. The Boot folder contains the Boot Configuration Data (BCD). You may also see other startup configuration files that remain after an upgrade to Windows Vista or startup configuration files required for backward compatibility with older programs.

3. Close the Computer window.

It is easier to understand the concept and use of virtual memory if you can associate it with something physical on your computer, such as installed RAM and the paging file.

Locating and Examining the Paging File | Reference Window

- Open a Computer window, and then open a window onto drive C (or your system volume).
- Click the Organize button, click Folder and Search Options, click the View tab, and under Advanced settings, click the "Show hidden files and folders" option button under "Hidden files and folders" (if necessary), and remove the check mark from the "Hide protected operating system files (Recommended)" check box. After Windows Vista displays a Warning dialog box, informing you that you have chosen to display protected operating system files, click the Yes button.
- Click the OK button to close the Folder Options dialog box and apply the changes to your system. The file named pagefile.sys, which is now visible, is the Windows Vista paging file.

Shuang mentions that you can also use the Windows Task Manager to observe changes in the paging file.

Using Windows Task Manager to View System Performance

With Task Manager, you can view information on changes in CPU (or processor) usage and memory usage on your computer. You can also view details about physical memory, kernel memory, and the system. **Kernel memory** is memory reserved for use by the operating system.

Next, Shuang and you use Task Manager to check the overall performance of a new computer.

Tip

You can also press and release the Ctrl+Shift+Esc keys to open Task Manager.

Tip

To display a graph in more detail, double-click it. Double-click a graph again to return to regular view.

To view information on your system's performance:

1. Right-click an empty area of the taskbar, and then click Task Manager.
2. Click the **Performance** tab. At the top of the Performance property sheet, Windows Task Manager displays a bar graph that shows the percent CPU usage. See Figure 9-3. Because the computer used for this figure has a dual-core processor, Task Manager displays two line graphs under CPU Usage History that show the change in (or history of) CPU usage for each execution core in the dual-core processor. Under the graphs for CPU usage, Task Manager displays graphs for the current level of Memory usage and the Physical Memory Usage History. Since the amount of installed RAM in each computer can vary, each computer is configured differently, and the information shown on the Performance property sheet changes as you use your computer, your view and details will differ.

Figure 9-3 Examining performance data in Task Manager

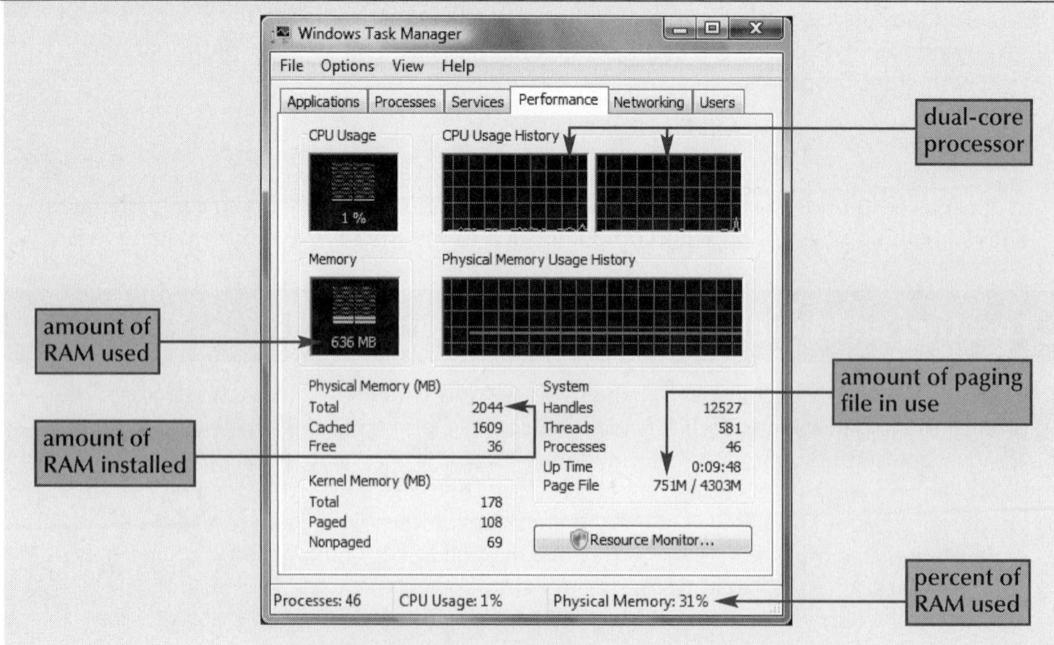

The CPU Usage reflects the activity of the processor at any given point in time. If you use Windows Task Manager on a regular basis, you will find that CPU Usage is low unless you are performing an operation, such as clicking the Start button, opening the Computer window, opening an application, or connecting to the Internet; then, it peaks momentarily before it drops again to an idle level. If the value for CPU Usage remains high, some program might be unduly burdening the CPU with requests for processing, and that affects the performance of your computer. As you discovered in Tutorial 8, you might be able to use the System Configuration utility to identify a program or service adversely affecting the performance of your computer. Once you locate that program (or service), you can prevent it from loading, remove it from your computer, or replace it with another program that does not adversely affect your computer. You can also use Performance Monitor (which you will examine in the second session) to identify rogue programs that affect processor activity.

The Memory bar graph on this computer shows that 636 MB of RAM is currently used on this computer. On the Status Bar at the bottom of the Task Manager window, Task Manager reports for Physical Memory that 31% of the installed RAM is currently in use. Under the Physical Memory (MB) section, Windows Task Manager lists the total amount of installed RAM, the amount of cached RAM, and the amount of free RAM. On the computer used for this figure, the amount of installed RAM is 2044 MB, or almost 2 GB. The Cached value refers to the system cache. The **system cache** is the amount of RAM used to store pages of open files. By maintaining past pages in the system cache, Windows Vista can find information that you need more quickly. In fact, hit rates can be in the high 90 percent range. That means that 90 percent or more of the time Windows Vista finds what you need in the system cache and therefore does not need to retrieve the data from the hard disk. That translates into faster response times and reduces wear and tear on the hard disk drive, thereby extending the useful life of your hard disk. The Free value is the amount of unused RAM.

As noted earlier, kernel memory refers to the memory used by core components of the operating system and by device drivers. On this computer, kernel memory is 178 MB. **Nonpaged kernel memory** is available only to the operating system. Pages in kernel memory cannot be paged to disk. **Paged kernel memory** is memory that can be paged, or swapped, to disk so that other programs can use that memory.

Under the System section, Task Manager reports 46 open processes, 581 threads, and 12,527 handles on the computer shown in the figure. As you may recall, a process is an executable program, a service, or a subsystem. A **thread** is an object within a process that executes instructions (or program code). Windows Vista supports multiple threads for each program so that it can execute instructions from different parts of the same program at the same time. It can also execute multiple instructions from the same part of the same program at the same time. On a computer that has a multiple core processor (such as a dual-core with two execution cores or a quad-core processor with four execution cores) or a computer that has multiple processors, different parts of the same program can run concurrently on different execution cores or different processors. If a program creates threads and does not release those threads when you close the program, you have found the source of a memory leak. A **handle** is an ID that uniquely identifies a resource, such as a file or Registry setting, so that a program can access that resource.

The Up Time shows the amount of time that the computer has been up and running. In this case, the computer has been up and running for slightly under ten minutes, and only one program is open—a screen capture program. The first value shown for Page File (751M) is the amount of storage space in the paging file currently in use. The second value shown for Page File (4303M) is the combined size of the paging file and physical RAM (or total available memory at this point in time).

As you work on your computer, you can use Windows Task Manager to monitor changes in your system so that you have a better idea of what resources your system uses and needs. For example, after you open an application, you can evaluate the change in CPU Usage and memory usage and review the detailed statistics that Task Manager provides.

To monitor changes in your system:

1. Click **Options** on the Windows Task Manager menu bar, and if the Always on Top option does not have a check mark next to it, click **Always On Top**; otherwise, click **Options** a second time to close the menu. The Windows Task Manager window now appears on top of any other open window.
2. Click **Options** on the Windows Task Manager menu bar, and if the Minimize on Use option has a check mark next to it, click **Minimize on Use**; otherwise, click **Options** a second time to close the menu. This option keeps Windows Vista from minimizing Windows Task Manager when you open an application.
3. If Microsoft Word is installed on your computer, open that application; otherwise, open another application that you commonly use. The percent CPU Usage jumps momentarily and then returns to an idle level. See Figure 9-4. Memory usage also increases. On the computer shown in this figure, memory usage increased from 636 MB (as shown in the previous Figure 9-3) to 702 MB (as shown in the current Figure 9-4), an increase of 66 MB when opening Microsoft Office Word 2007. The percent of Physical Memory in use increased by approximately 3 percent, from 31 percent to 34 percent, and the number of processes, threads, and handles increased. The amount of the paging file in use increased from 751 MB to 834 MB (an increase of 83 MB). Again, the details of these changes will differ for your computer.

Figure 9-4 Changes in memory usage after opening Microsoft Word

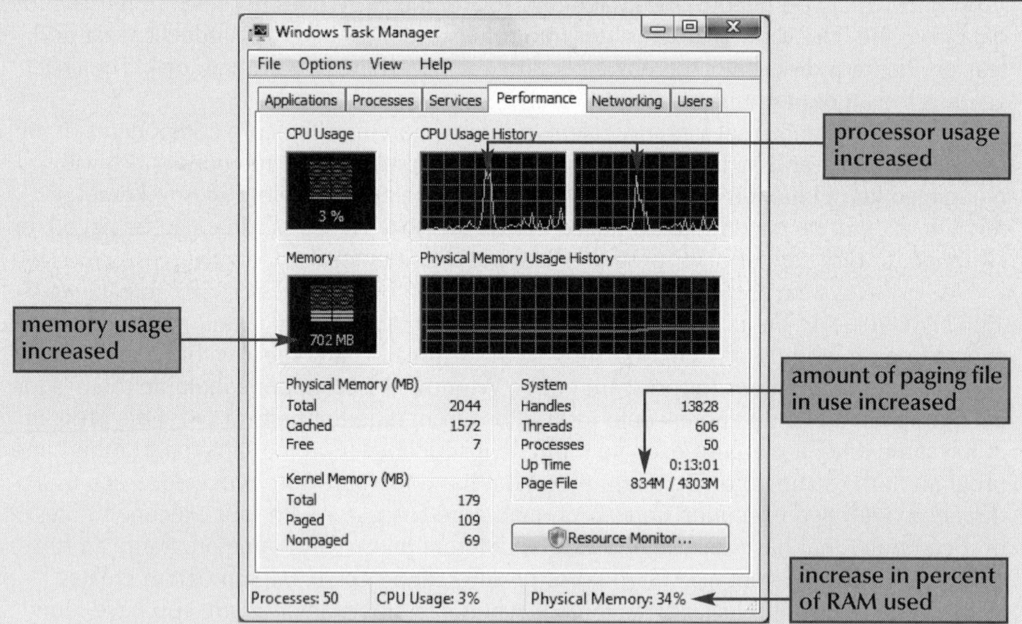

4. If you have Microsoft Excel installed on your computer, open that application; otherwise, open another application installed on your computer. CPU Usage spikes momentarily, and Memory usage again increases. See Figure 9-5. On the computer shown in this figure, memory usage increased from 702 MB (as shown in the previous Figure 9-4) to 720 MB (as shown in the current Figure 9-5), an increase of 18 MB when opening Microsoft Office Excel 2007. The amount of Physical Memory in use increased by 1 percent, from 34 percent to 35 percent. The amount of the paging file in use increased from 834 MB to 861 MB (an increase of 27 MB). As before, the number of processes, threads, and handles increased. Your details will differ.

Changes in memory usage after opening Microsoft Excel

Figure 9-5

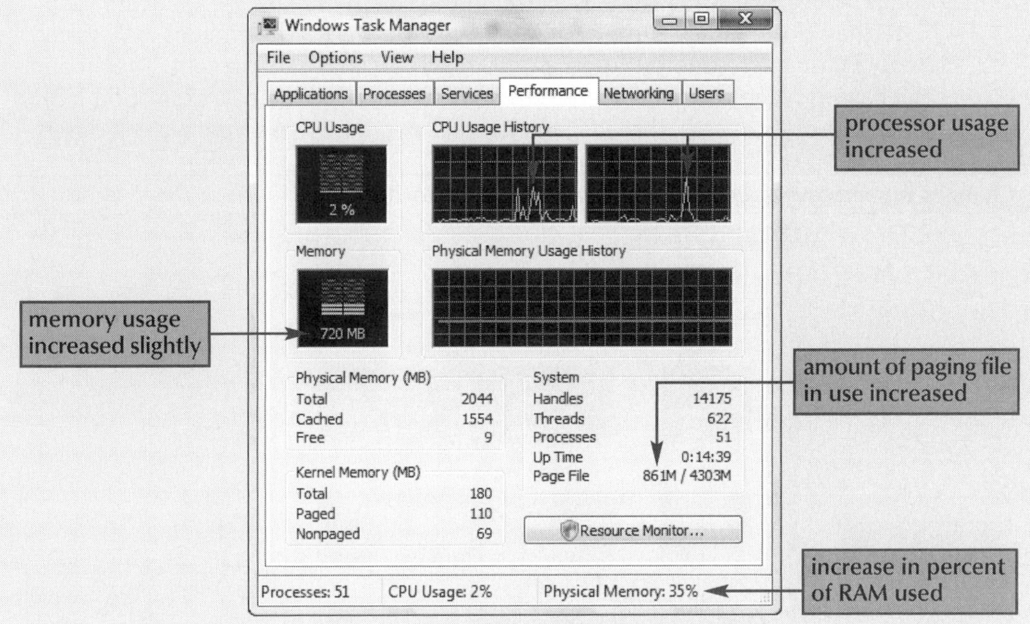

5. Close Microsoft Excel or the application that you opened in the last step. On the computer used for this figure, memory usage dropped from 720 MB (as shown in the previous Figure 9-5) to 713 MB (as shown in the current Figure 9-6), a decrease of 7 MB when closing Microsoft Office Excel 2007. See Figure 9-6. The amount of Physical Memory in use decreased by 1 percent, from 35 percent to 34 percent. The amount of the paging file in use decreased from 861 MB to 845 MB (a decrease of 16 MB). The number of processes, threads, and handles decreased. Your details will differ.

Changes in memory usage after closing Microsoft Excel

Figure 9-6

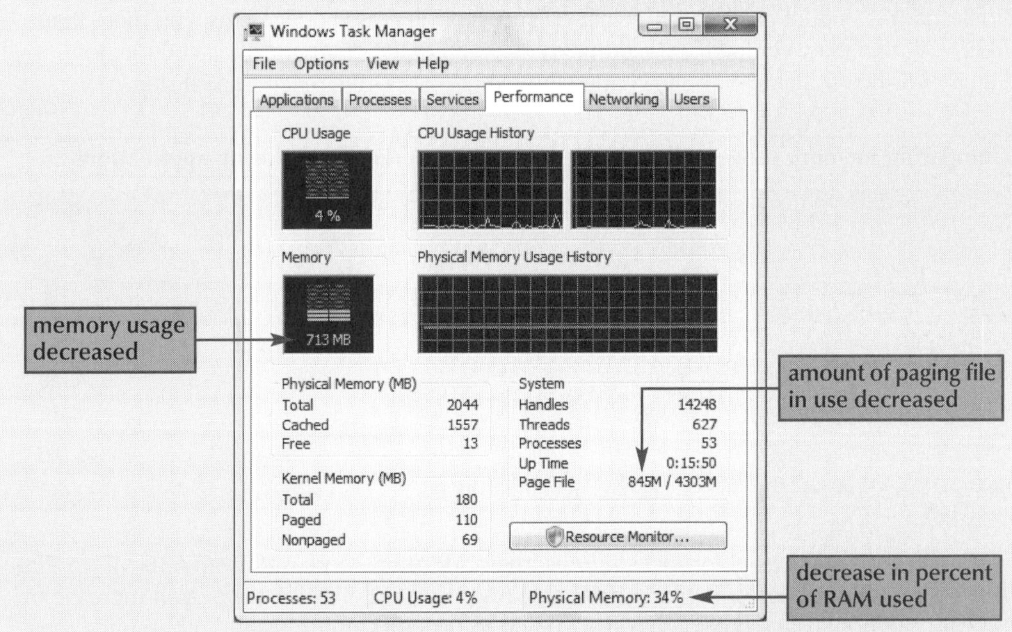

6. Close Microsoft Word or the first application that you first opened. On the computer used for this figure, memory usage dropped from 713 MB (as shown in the previous Figure 9-6) to 665 MB (as shown in the current Figure 9-7), a decrease of 48 MB when closing Microsoft Word 2007. See Figure 9-7. The amount of Physical Memory in use decreased by 2 percent from 34 percent to 32 percent. The amount of the paging file in use decreased from 845 MB to 792 MB (a decrease of 53 MB). The number of processes, threads, and handles decreased. Your details will differ.

Figure 9-7 **Changes in memory usage after closing Microsoft Word**

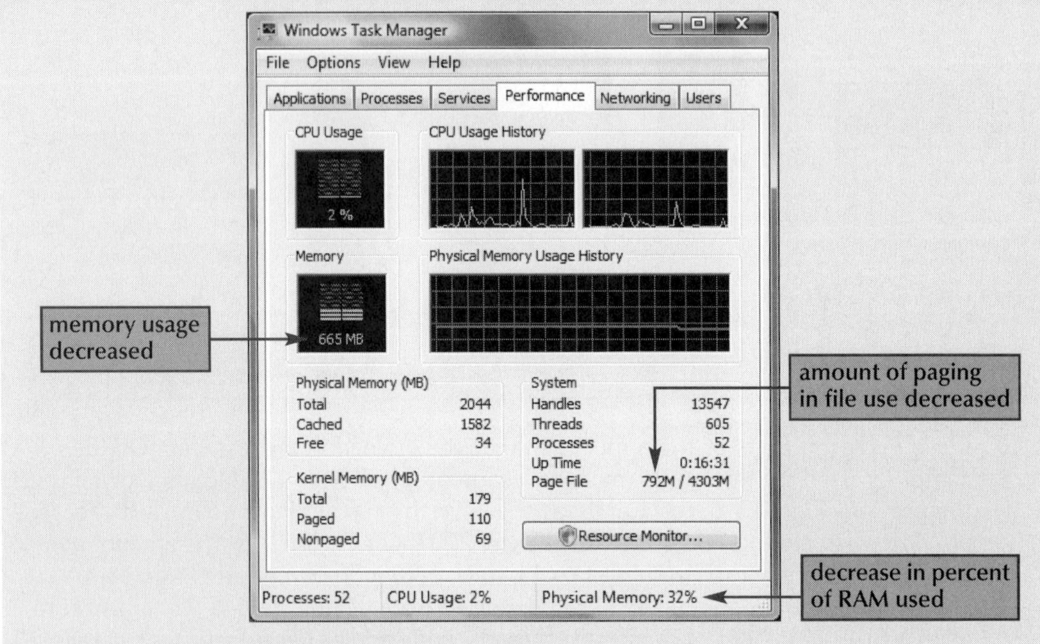

7. Close Windows Task Manager.

If you compare the total amount of memory allocated after opening these two applications and the amount of memory reclaimed after closing these applications, you more than likely will find that Windows Vista did not reclaim all of the originally allocated memory. Figure 9-8 shows a table with the change in memory usage after each tutorial step.

Figure 9-8 **Comparing memory usage and page file size after opening and closing applications**

Operation	Memory Usage	Change in Memory Usage	Physical Memory in Use	Page File Size
Opening Task Manager	636 MB		31%	751 MB
Opening Microsoft Word 2007	702 MB	+66 MB	34%	834 MB
Opening Microsoft Excel 2007	720 MB	+18 MB	35%	861 MB
Closing Microsoft Excel 2007	713 MB	-7 MB	34%	845 MB
Closing Microsoft Word 2007	665 MB	-48 MB	32%	792 MB

On the computer used for these figures, memory usage increased from 636 MB to 720 MB after opening Microsoft Word 2007 and Microsoft Excel 2007, an overall increase of 84 MB. Memory usage dropped from 720 MB to 665 MB after closing both applications, an overall decrease of 55 MB. That means that Windows Vista did not recover 29 MB of the memory it originally allocated. Program code from these applications still remains in memory. This is an example of a memory leak. If this computer is idle for a while, Windows Vista will more than likely reclaim some of that still-used memory. The amount of Physical Memory in use on this computer is 1 percent higher than the original level of 31 percent, and the paging file is 41 MB larger than the original size.

Using Task Manager to Monitor System Performance | Reference Window

- Right-click the taskbar, click Task Manager, and then click the Performance tab in the Windows Task Manager window.
- Click Options on the Windows Task Manager menu bar, and if the Always on Top option does not have a check mark next to it, click Always On Top; otherwise, click Options a second time to close the menu.
- Click Options on the Windows Task Manager menu bar, and if the Minimize on Use option has a check mark next to it, click Minimize on Use; otherwise, click Options a second time to close the menu.
- As you open and close applications or windows, check the CPU Usage, CPU Usage History, Memory, and Physical Memory Usage History on the Performance property sheet for changes in processor activity and memory usage on your computer. Also, examine information on the number of processes, handles, and threads as well as the Page File size and the percent Physical Memory in use.
- When you have finished monitoring your system's performance, close Task Manager.

Task Manager itself uses very little memory, so it is a useful tool for monitoring memory.

Using Resource Overview to Evaluate Memory Usage and System Performance

Resource Overview is a new Windows Vista feature that provides summary information on the use of CPU, disk, network, and memory resources. You can use Resource Overview not only to provide you with an overview of your computer's performance, but you can also use it to identify one or more processes impacting the performance of your computer.

Shuang and you open Resource Overview on a new computer to evaluate how best to make use of this new Windows Vista tool.

To complete the following steps, you must provide Administrator credentials. If you are logged on under a Standard User account and do not provide Administrator credentials, Windows Vista will open Reliability and Performance Monitor, but inform you that you must be a member of either the Administrators group or the Performance Log Users group to enable the full functionality of these tools. Then, you will not be able to examine performance data. If you cannot provide the password for an Administrator account, read the following steps and examine the figures so that you are familiar with the use of Reliability Monitor, but do not keystroke the steps.

Tip

You can also open Resource Overview by clicking the Resource Monitor button on the Task Manager Performance property sheet.

To open Resource Overview:

1. On the Start menu, point to **Administrative Tools**, right-click **Reliability and Performance Monitor**, and then click **Run as administrator**. Windows Vista switches to Secure Desktop Mode and displays a User Account Control dialog box.
2. In the User Account Control dialog box, click the **Continue** button if you are logged on under an Administrator account, or if you are logged on under a Standard User account, enter the **password** for an Administrator account, click the **OK** button, and then maximize the Reliability and Performance Monitor window. Resource Overview displays four line graphs that measure processor, disk, network, and memory usage over a 60-second time frame, followed by a summary for these four resources. See Figure 9-9. On the computer used for this figure, Resource Overview shows that current processor and network usage is relatively low, that disk I/O activity is present and high at times, and that 38 percent of Physical Memory is in use. Your details will differ.

Figure 9-9 Viewing CPU, disk, network, and memory usage

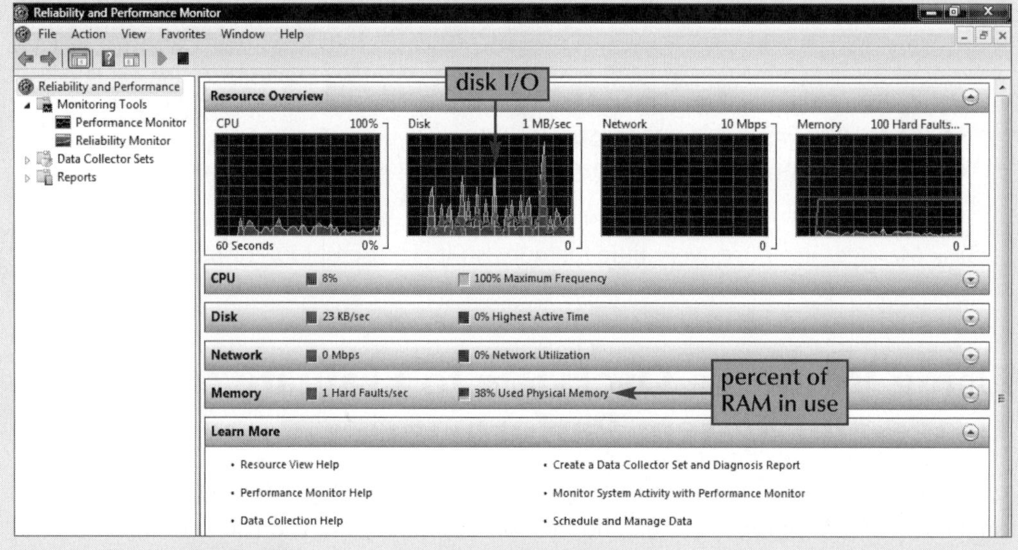

Tip

Clock cycle refers to a regular interval of time during which the processor can execute one (or more) instructions.

3. Click the **Expand Details** button on the right side of the CPU details section under the four minigraphs. The CPU details section expands and lists programs and processes using CPU resources. See Figure 9-10. Resource Overview constantly updates the list of programs and processes using the processor. The Image column lists process names, the PID lists the process ID for each process, Description identifies the process, the Threads column lists the number of open threads for each process, the CPU column lists the number of clock cycles used by the process at any given point in time, and the Average CPU column lists the percent load placed by each process on the CPU. The Desktop Window Manager process updates the desktop window and provides access to Windows Aero features. Note also the increased disk I/O over the previous figure. Your details will differ.

Figure 9-10

Viewing processes that are using the CPU

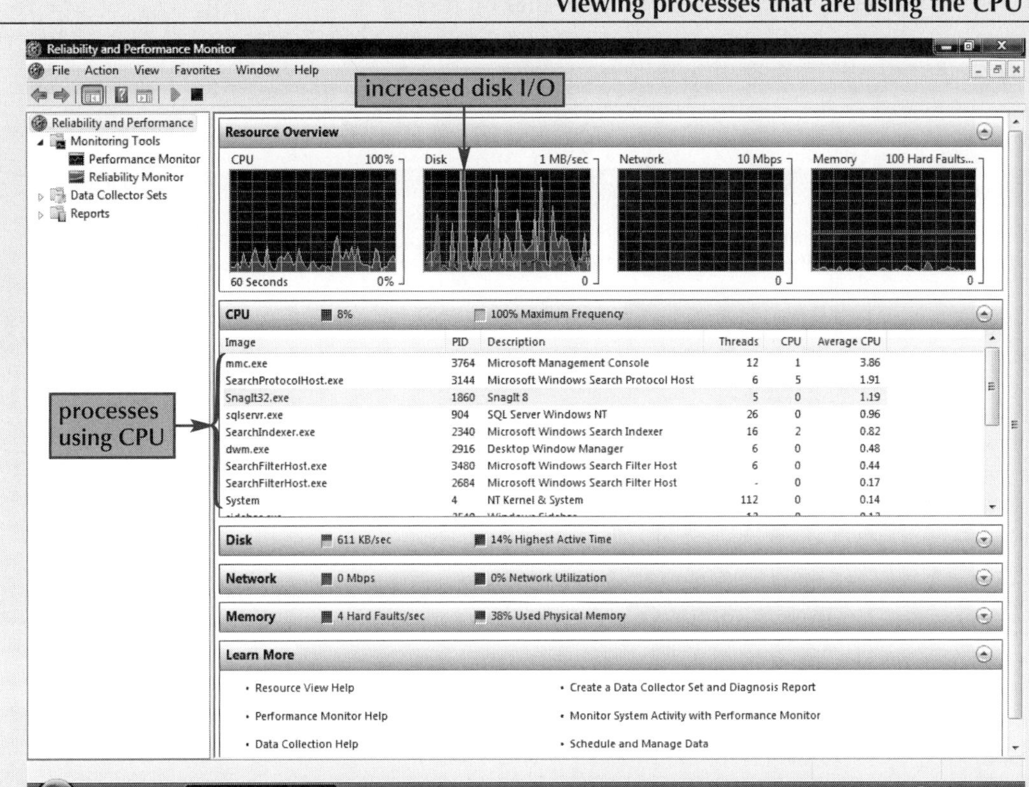

4. Click the **Collapse Details** button for the CPU details section, and then click the **Expand Details** button on the right side of the Disk details section. This section provides details on disk activity. See Figure 9-11. Note that disk I/O has increased over the two previous figures. Your details will differ. The File column lists the path of the file that is currently being read from, or written to, disk. The Read (B/min) and Write (B/min) shows the number of bytes per minute being read from, or written to, the file on disk. The IO Priority column shows the task's priority (such as Normal or Background), and the Response Time (ms) column shows the time in milliseconds for each disk I/O. You might also see System processes for C:\pagefile.sys (Page File), the C:\$Mft (NTFS Master File Table), and the C:\$LogFile (NTFS Volume Log).

Tip

To stop updating the graphs, click the Stop the Resource Monitor button on the Standard toolbar, and then resume updating by clicking the Start the Resource Monitor button.

Figure 9-11 Viewing processes reading and writing to files on disk

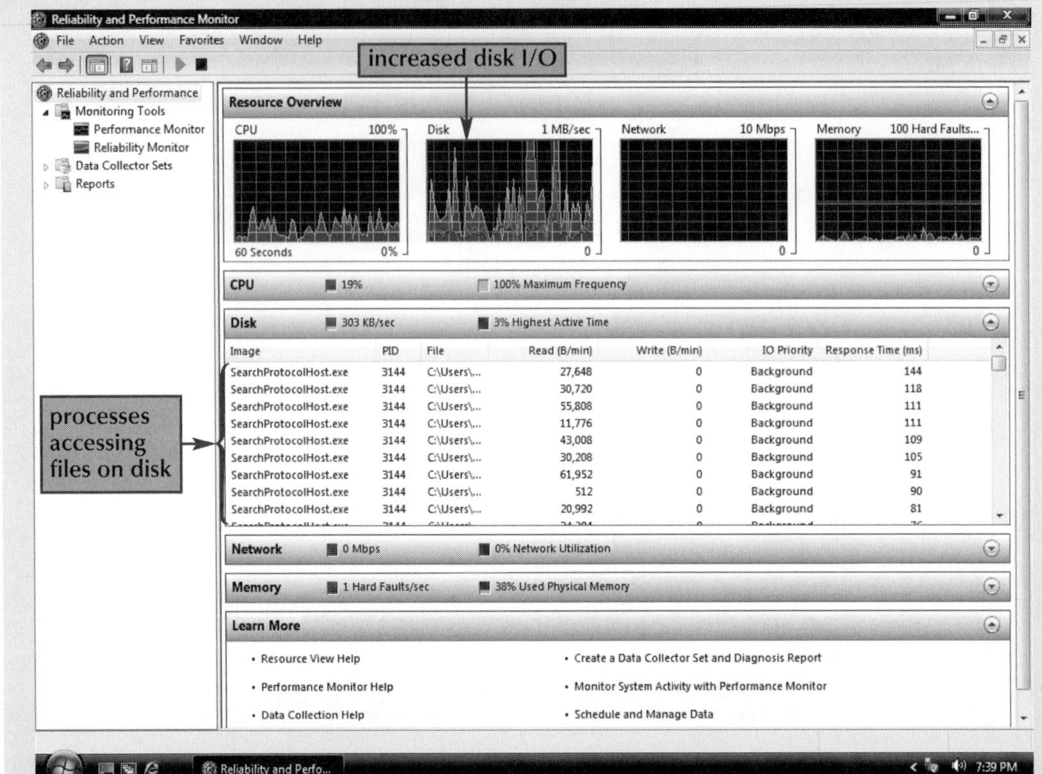

5. Click the **Collapse Details** button for the Disk details section, and then click the **Expand Details** button on the right side of the Memory details section. This section provides details on memory usage by each program or process. See Figure 9-12. Disk I/O has increased yet again on the computer used for this figure. SearchIndexer, the main component of the Windows search engine, is active (because the computer is currently idle), accounting for the increased disk I/O. Your details will differ. The Hard Faults/min column shows the number of hard faults occurring each minute. A hard fault (or hard page fault, or page fault) occurs when a page is no longer available in physical memory, but has instead been paged to disk, and therefore requires a disk read. If disk paging consistently exceeds 70% of total disk activity, you are experiencing a high level of hard faults, and your computer has an insufficient amount of RAM. Commit (KB) lists in kilobytes the amount of memory committed (allocated) for each process. If the Commit (KB) keeps increasing for a process, you've identified a rogue program that's adversely affecting the performance of your computer and may cause it to stop responding or crash. Working Set (KB) lists the amount of physical memory currently used by each process. Shareable (KB) lists the amount of memory allocated to a process that can be shared with other processes. Private (KB) lists the amount of memory in exclusive use by a process (it cannot be shared).

Figure 9-12

Viewing processes and their memory usage

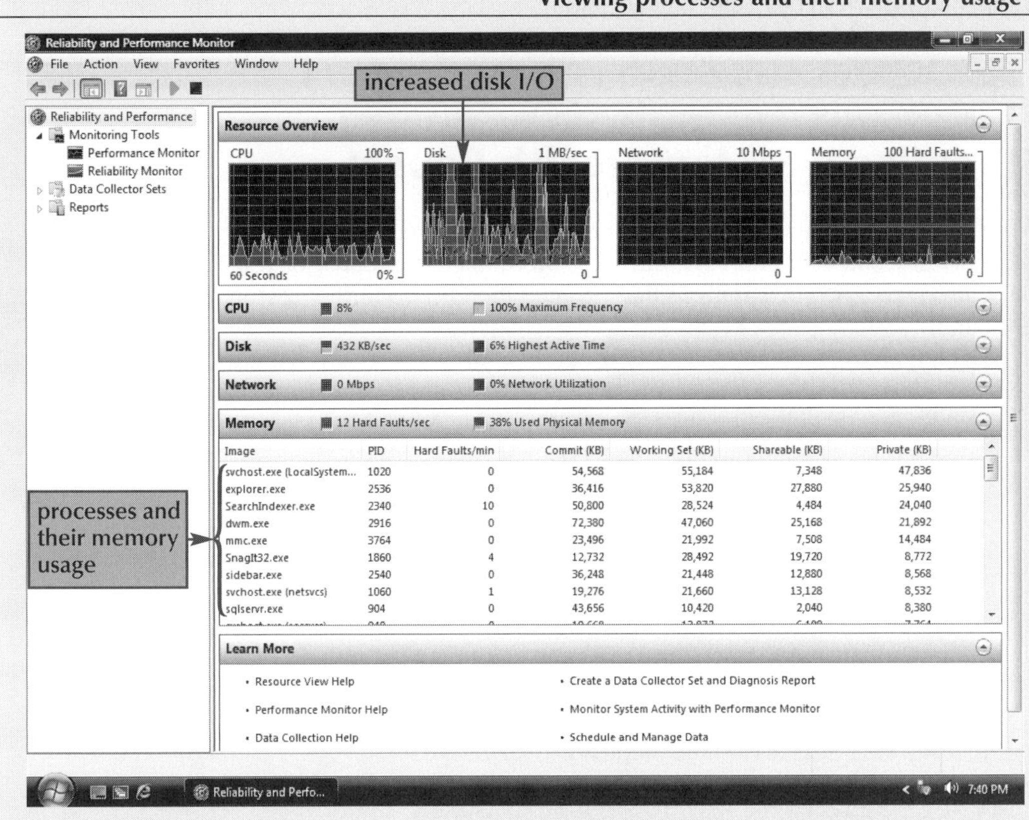

6. Close the Reliability and Performance Monitor window.

The Network graph and Network details section displays information about the current level of network traffic.

Using Resource Overview to Evaluate Memory Usage and System Performance

| Reference Window

- On the Start menu, point to Administrative Tools, right-click Reliability and Performance Monitor, and then click "Run as administrator."
- After Windows Vista displays a User Account Control dialog box, click the Continue button if you are logged on under an Administrator account, or if you are logged on under a Standard User account, enter the password for an Administrator account, and then click the OK button.
- Examine the four Resource Overview minigraphs that show CPU, disk, network, and memory usage activity to spot trends or changes in system performance.
- Expand the CPU, Disk, Network, and Memory sections to examine the effect that individual programs and processes have on the performance of the processor, disk, network, and the use of memory.
- When you have finished evaluating your system's performance, close the Reliability and Performance Monitor window.

Shuang notes that the highest impact on the performance of this computer results from the increased disk I/O caused by the SearchIndexer process updating the search index. However, she says that it is not a problem, but rather a reflection that SearchIndexer is busy updating the search index. She further notes that the computer is currently idle and that Microsoft designed SearchIndexer so that it becomes active when a computer is idle and pauses when the computer is in use or when it detects high I/O. In effect, Windows Vista is optimizing the use of the computer.

Creating a System Health Report

You can use Reliability and Performance Monitor to create a system health report to identify any potential problem with the performance or security of your computer and to also produce a detailed analysis that you can then use to further research potential problems.

Shuang and you decide to follow up on her earlier observation about the impact of SearchIndexer on this computer by producing a system health report.

To complete the following steps, you must provide Administrator credentials. If you are not logged on under an Administrator account or cannot provide the user name and password for an Administrator account, read the following steps and examine the figures so that you are familiar with the use of Reliability Monitor, but do not keystroke the steps.

To create a system health report:

1. On the Start menu, open **Control Panel**, click the **System and Maintenance** link, click the **Performance Information and Tools** link, click the **Advanced tools** link under Tasks, and then click the **Generate a system health report** link. Windows Vista switches to Secure Desktop Mode and displays a User Account Control dialog box.
2. In the User Account Control dialog box, click the **Continue** button if you are logged on under an Administrator account, or if you are logged on under a Standard User account, enter the **password** for an Administrator account, click the **OK** button, and then maximize the Reliability and Performance Monitor window. Reliability and Performance Monitor then starts a System Diagnostics test and notes that this analysis takes 60 seconds. Under System Diagnostics, Reliability and Performance Monitor notes that this report includes suggestions for ways to maximize the performance of your computer and streamline its operation. See Figure 9-13. After that process is complete, you see a System Diagnostics Report. See Figure 9-14. Under Diagnostic Results, Reliability and Performance Monitor display any warnings. Reliability and Performance notes any problems that it found, explains the symptom, cause, steps for resolving the problem, and includes any related links to help you quickly resolve problems. If the Security Center has not recorded an antivirus software product, Reliability and Performance Monitor will note that it is unable to identify an active antivirus application and that either there is no antivirus product installed or it is not recognized. If Windows Update is turned off, Reliability and Performance Monitor reports this information and highly recommends that you run Windows Vista with Windows Update enabled. Under Basic System Checks, Reliability and Performance Monitor identifies the results of OS Checks, Disk Checks, Security Center Checks, System Service Checks, and Hardware Device and Driver Checks and indicates whether the checks passed or failed. You can expand each category and examine the status of each individual test. On the computer used for this figure, Resource Overview shows Normal or Idle for the four different components and reports that 1240 MB of memory is available. Your System Diagnostics Report details will differ.

System Diagnostics analyzing the local computer

Figure 9-13

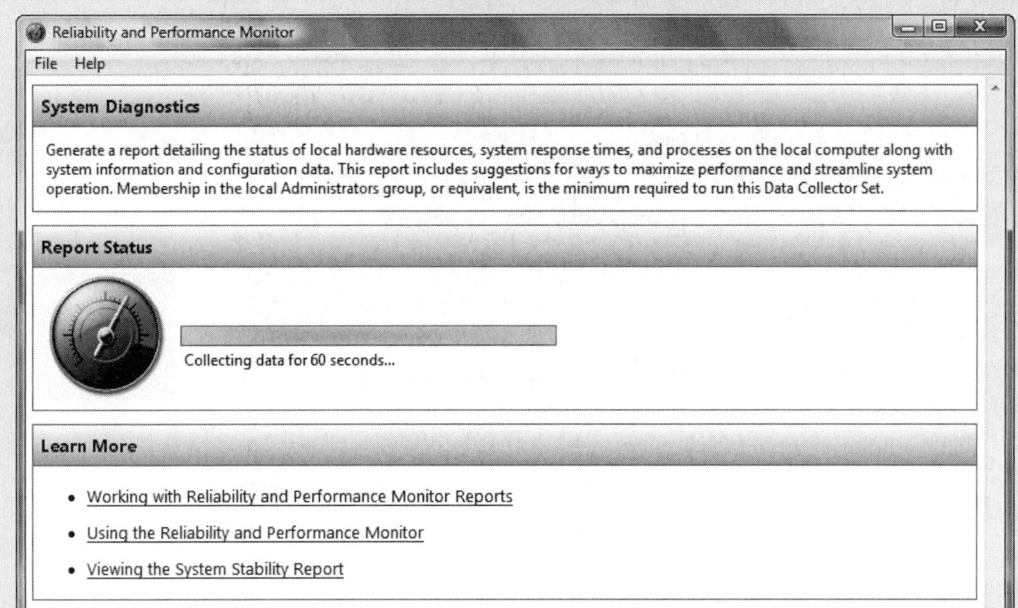

Viewing a System Diagnostics Report

Figure 9-14

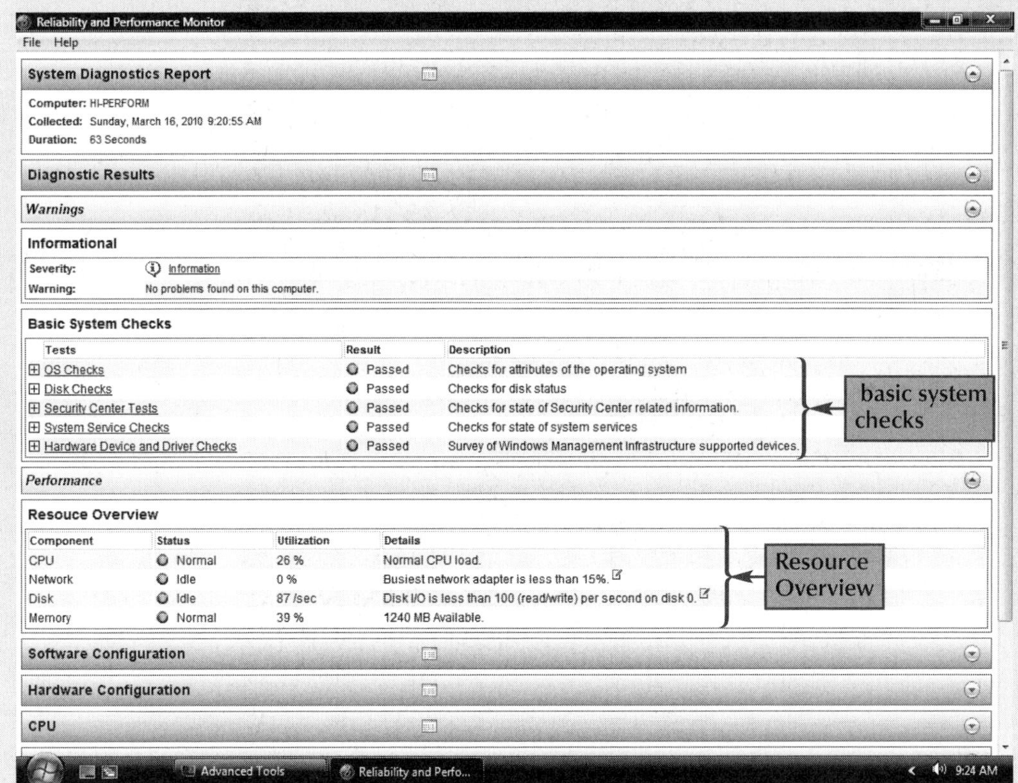

3. If necessary, adjust your view so that you can see the Performance section. The Resource Overview reports on the status, utilization, and details of four components: CPU, Network, Disk, and Memory. If you see a small note icon, you can point to that note icon to display a ToolTip with more detail, as shown in Figure 9-15. As shown in this figure, the Disk note reports on the number of Reads and Writes per second.

Figure 9-15 **Viewing a note on disk details**

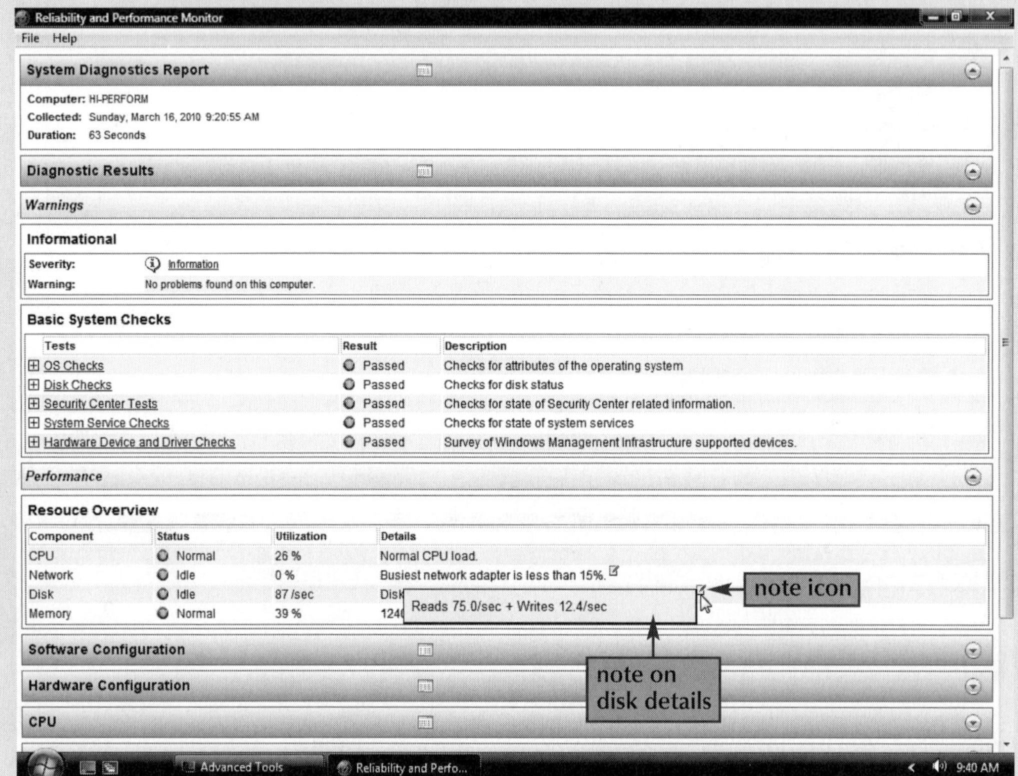

4. Click the **Collapse Details** buttons for the Warnings and Performance sections, click the **Expand Details** button for the Software Configuration details section, click the **Expand Details** button for the Startup Programs section, and then, if necessary, adjust your view so that you can see all your startup programs. Reliability and Performance Monitor displays a list of startup programs and the commands for starting those programs. See Figure 9-16. Your details will differ. The information shown here is similar to that found using System Information (covered in Tutorial 8).

Figure 9-16 Viewing information on startup programs

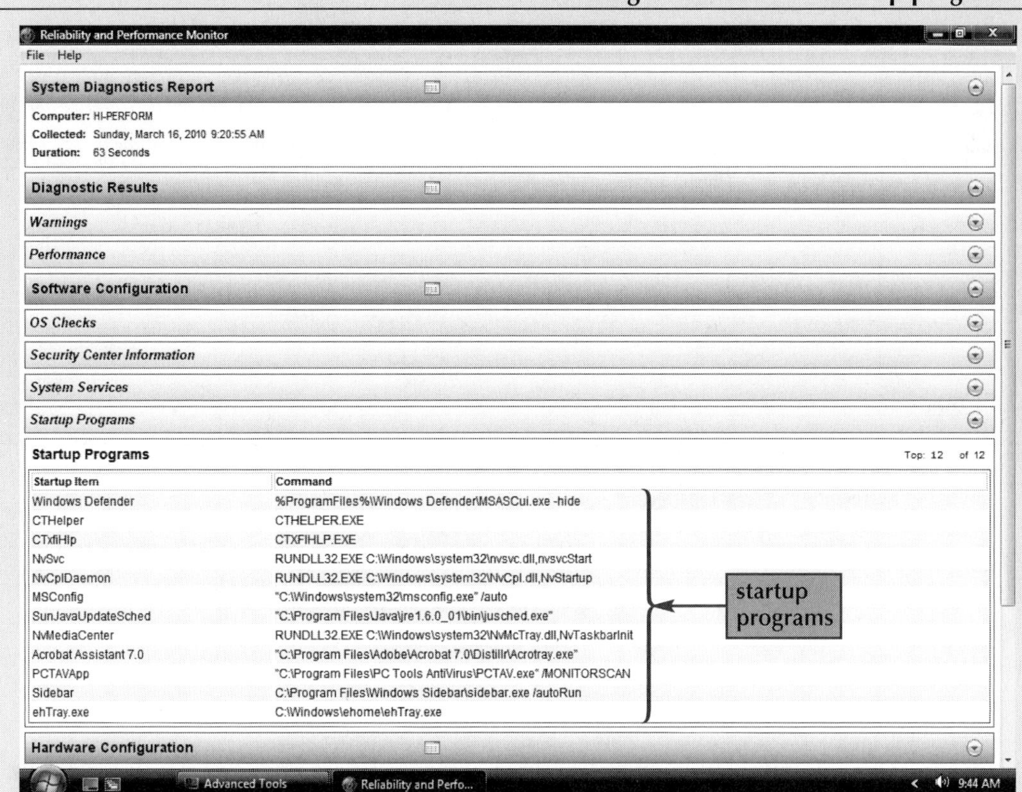

5. Click the **Collapse Details** button for the Software Configuration section, click the **Expand Details** button for the Disk details section, click the **Expand Details** button for Hot Files, and then adjust your view so that you can see all the reported Hot Files. Reliability and Performance Monitor identifies the files that cause the most disk I/Os. If you click the **Expand View** indicator to the left of each file, Reliability and Performance Monitor shows the individual program or programs accessing each file, as shown in Figure 9-17. On this computer, SearchIndexer.exe is one of the programs accessing C:\$Log File (the NTFS Log File).

Figure 9-17 Viewing Hot Files that cause the most disk I/O

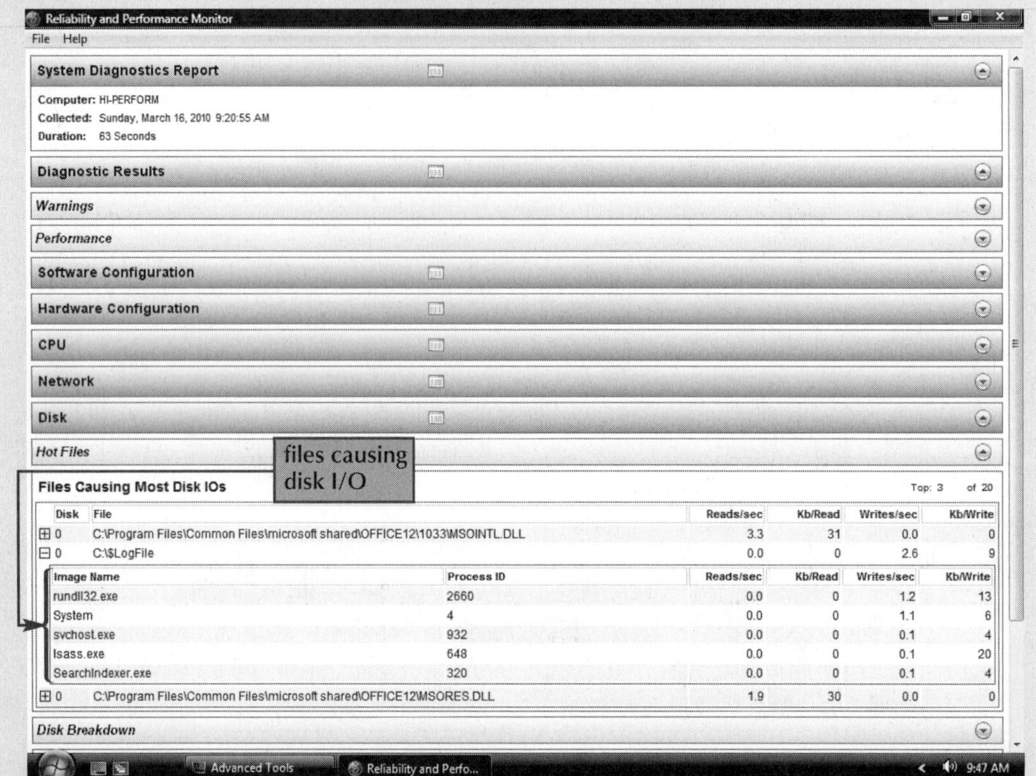

Disk	File	Reads/sec	Kb/Read	Writes/sec	Kb/Write
0	C:\Program Files\Common Files\microsoft shared\OFFICE12\1033\MSOINTL.DLL	3.3	31	0.0	0
0	C:\$LogFile	0.0	0	2.6	9

Image Name	Process ID	Reads/sec	Kb/Read	Writes/sec	Kb/Write
rundll32.exe	2660	0.0	0	1.2	13
System	4	0.0	0	1.1	6
svchost.exe	932	0.0	0	0.1	4
lsass.exe	648	0.0	0	0.1	20
SearchIndexer.exe	320	0.0	0	0.1	4

Disk	File	Reads/sec	Kb/Read	Writes/sec	Kb/Write
0	C:\Program Files\Common Files\microsoft shared\OFFICE12\MSORES.DLL	1.9	30	0.0	0

6. Examine any other diagnostic results of interest to you, close the Reliability and Performance Monitor window, and then close the Advanced Tools window.

Shuang notices that the System Diagnostics report also contains information about memory usage, but she decides to examine that information after she uses Performance Monitor to examine specific performance factors on this computer.

Creating a System Health Report

| Reference Window

- On the Start menu, open Control Panel, click the System and Maintenance link, click the Performance Information and Tools link, click the Advanced tools link under Tasks, and then click the Generate a system health report link.
- After Windows Vista switches to Secure Desktop Mode and displays a User Account Control dialog box, click the Continue button if you are logged on under an Administrator account, or if you are logged on under a Standard User account, enter the password for an Administrator account, click the OK button, and then maximize the Reliability and Performance Monitor window.
- After Reliability and Performance Monitor completes a System Diagnostics test and displays a System Diagnostics Report, examine any warnings displayed under Diagnostic Results and use this information to enhance the performance or security of your computer.
- Under Basic System Checks, examine the results for OS Checks, Disk Checks, Security Center Checks, System Service Checks, and Hardware Device and Drivers.
- Under the Performance section, examine the information in the Resource Overview on the status, utilization, and details of the CPU, Disk, Network, and Memory components. If you see a small note icon to the right of a Resource Overview entry, you can point to that note icon to display a ToolTip with more detail about that component.
- Expand each section and subsection to view more details about the performance of your computer. If you want to examine information on startup programs, expand the Software Configuration details section, and then expand the Startup Programs section. If you want to identify the files that cause the most disk I/O, expand the Disk details section, and then expand Hot Files.
- Close the Reliability and Performance Monitor window and the Advanced Tools window.

You can use the System Diagnostics Report to identify and correct problems and to view information about the status of your computer so that you can decide whether there might be ways to improve the performance of your computer.

Session 9.1 Quick Check

| Review

1. Windows Vista creates a special system file on your hard disk called a(n) ________________ for use as supplemental RAM.
2. True or False. If Windows Vista relies too heavily on the paging file, you may not have enough RAM to support the ways in which you use your computer.
3. The phenomenon where allocated memory is not reclaimed by the operating system, but rather tied up by previously open applications or processes, is called a(n) ________________ .
4. Windows Vista uses the ________________ to store pages of open files to improve the chances that it can locate data that you might need later.
5. A(n) ________________ occurs when a page is no longer available in physical memory, but has instead been paged to disk, and therefore requires a disk read.
6. The installed physical RAM and the paging file constitute what is called ________________ .

Session 9.2

Using Performance Monitor to Evaluate System Performance

Shuang points out that you can use Performance Monitor, another Windows Vista tool, to more closely monitor the performance of your computer, evaluate the use of resources (such as memory), and identify bottlenecks or other problems that interfere with the use of your computer. Unlike other tools, you can pick and choose which performance factors you want to monitor and thereby focus on resolving a specific problem.

When using Performance Monitor, you start by selecting a performance object, such as Memory, Paging File, PhysicalDisk, Process, Processor, or System (to name a few). A **performance object** is a broad category that contains various performance counters for measuring the performance of some aspect of your computer system. A **performance counter** is a specific option for measuring the performance of an object. For example, in the Memory performance object category, you can choose to measure allocated memory and available memory—two different performance counters. The Process performance object contains options for measuring the effects of one or more programs on a resource (such as memory or the processor). For some performance counters, you can also select an instance. An **instance** allows you to sample a performance counter in a specific way. For example, under the Process performance object, you can monitor the % Processor Time (a performance counter) for all programs or for one specific program. If you want to measure % Processor Time for all programs, you would select the _Total instance. If you want to measure % Processor Time for a specific program, such as Microsoft Word, you would select that program's name (for Microsoft Word, you would select WINWORD). By measuring the effect of an individual program on processor usage, you can identify rogue programs that tie up the processor and force it to perform unneeded operations.

Shuang relies on Performance Monitor to track changes in processor and memory resources, two components that significantly affect the performance of computer systems. She asks you to open Performance Monitor and measure the use of processor and memory resources on this new computer. She also suggests you save performance measurements on your flash drive.

To complete the following steps, you must provide Administrator credentials. If you are not logged on under an Administrator account or cannot provide the password for an Administrator account, read the following steps and examine the figures so that you are familiar with the use of Performance Monitor, but do not keystroke the steps. You also need to reboot your computer and log on before you complete the next section. That will clear RAM so that your performance measurements show the effect of opening a program for the first time. Furthermore, you will have a better idea of what Windows Vista needs in order to start your computer.

To open Performance Monitor and specify performance counters:

1. Restart your computer and log on under your user account.
2. Attach your flash drive to the computer you are using, and if necessary, close any windows or dialog boxes that open.
3. On the Start menu, point to **Administrative Tools**, right-click **Reliability and Performance Monitor**, and then click **Run as administrator**. Windows Vista switches to Secure Desktop Mode and displays a User Account Control dialog box.

4. In the User Account Control dialog box, click the **Continue** button if you are logged on under an Administrator account, or if you are logged on under a Standard User account, enter the **password** for an Administrator account, click the **OK** button, and then maximize the Reliability and Performance Monitor window.

5. Under Monitoring Tools in the console tree pane on the left, click **Performance Monitor**. As shown in the Details pane on the right, Performance Monitor is already plotting values for the % Processor Time performance counter on a line graph. See Figure 9-18. Note that % Processor Time ranges from 0 percent to around 15 percent on the computer used for this figure. The last broad peak in processor activity coincides with taking a screen capture of Performance Monitor for this figure. Your details will differ.

Performance Monitor plotting % Processor Time values **Figure 9-18**

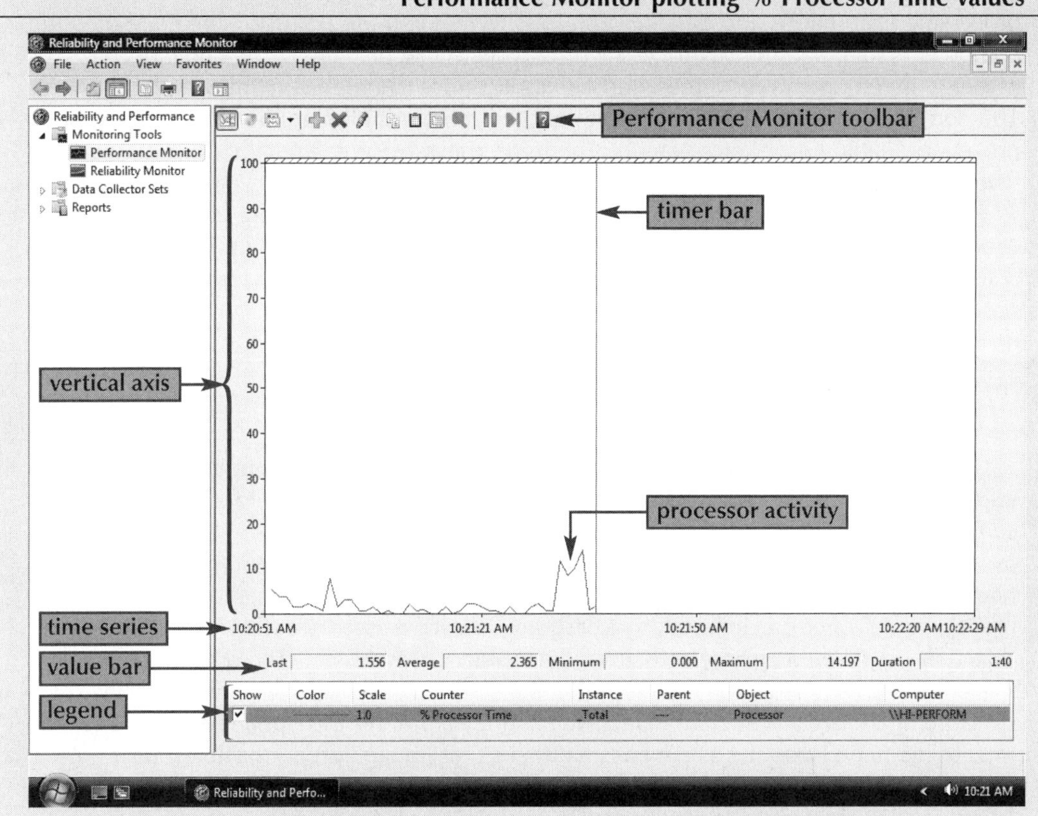

In the **legend** at the bottom of the details pane, Performance Monitor identifies the names of the counters, instances, and objects that it measures. In this case, Performance Monitor is measuring the _Total instance for the % Processor Time performance counter that, in turn, falls within the Processor performance object category. In the legend, Performance Monitor also identifies the name of the computer whose performance it measures, the color code for the corresponding line that represents plotted values in the line graph, and the scale used for this performance counter. In this case, the values shown on the vertical axis (also referred to as the Y axis or value axis) on the left are scaled for the plotted values in the line graph. For example, if the % Processor Time is 100%, the value plotted on the line graph matches the 100 mark on the vertical axis and indicates that the processor is working at its maximum capacity. The horizontal axis is called the time series axis and shows intervals of time. The Show check box in the legend allows you to decide whether or not you want to show the plot of a performance counter on the line graph.

The **value bar** above the legend and below the graph lists the last value, average value, minimum value, maximum value, and duration for the performance counter you select in the legend. Samples are taken every second (by default), and Performance Monitor always plots 100 samples for each counter on the graph (by default). Thus, the duration of 1:40 represents 1 minute 40 seconds, or 100 seconds (one second for each sample). The **timer bar** is the red vertical bar that slowly moves to the right as Performance Monitor samples values each second, plots those values on the graph, and adds the last, average, minimum, and maximum values for that performance counter to the value bar. After sampling 100 values, Performance Monitor displays subsequent samples starting at the left side of the line graph (replacing data already plotted on the line graph), and the timer bar follows the sampling of the next 100 values from left to right across the line graph.

% Processor Time measures the percentage of elapsed time that the processor spends processing instructions and data for a process. When you are not using the computer, the computer is idle, and the % Processor Time is quite low (usually in the range of 0–5 percent). If you open a resource-intensive application, % Processor Time can increase to 100 percent momentarily or for a short period of time until the application finishes the process of loading itself into memory. Then, % Processor Time typically drops to an idle level of 0-5 percent.

The % Processor Time performance counter is therefore the primary indicator of processor activity, though, on computers with fast processors, this value underestimates the actual activity of the processor. However, it can still provide useful information about the state of the processor.

InSight | Troubleshooting High % Processor Times

If % Processor Time peaks but remains high for a short time before dropping down to an idle level, you might be using a resource-intensive application that would work better on a computer with a newer and faster processor. If % Processor Time remains high and does not drop as you are examining the impact of a single program on your computer, you've identified a rogue program that is unduly burdening the processor with repeated requests for processing data. You can uninstall that program, and if necessary, replace it with a program that does not tie up the processor. If you cannot identify a specific program as the cause of this problem, it's time to open the system unit and clean the dust that's built up inside the system unit and around the fan. In fact, you might want to try this option before you spend time trying to find that one single program that's causing high processor times. Dust buildup around the fan can prevent proper circulation of air within the system unit, and dust buildup on the system board acts as insulation to trap heat that can then damage electronic components. Check the manual that came with your computer for the proper approach for opening the system unit and reattaching it later. Also check that manual for the proper techniques for cleaning the system unit and other computer components, such as your monitor. Compressed air is a simple and straightforward way to blow dust out of the inside of a system unit without accidentally damaging a component (such as RAM) on the system board by touching the component. Computer supply stores sell kits that contain what you need to properly clean your computer.

Since Shuang also wants to monitor memory, disk, and page file usage on this computer, she recommends that you add the Available Bytes performance counter to measure available memory, the Committed Bytes performance counter to measure allocated memory, the Pages/sec performance counter to measure disk I/O, and the Page File Bytes performance counter to measure changes in the size of the paging.

Now that you have given your computer time to return to an idle state, you are ready to add performance counters and monitor your computer's performance.

To add performance counters:

1. Click the **Add** button on the Performance Monitor toolbar directly above the line graph. In the Add Counters dialog box, you specify which performance counters you want to track. See Figure 9-19. Under the Available counters section, you can use local computer counters or counters from a specific computer on a network. Under "Select counters from computer," the local computer is identified as the computer to monitor. Performance Monitor also displays a list of performance objects from which you can choose specific performance counters. Since the types of performance objects depend in part on the type of software installed on a computer, your list of performance objects will differ.

   Trouble? If <Local computer> is not displayed under the "Select counters from computer" list box, click the list arrow and select <Local computer>.

Tip

You can also add performance counters by right-clicking the graph and then selecting Add Counters on the shortcut menu.

Figure 9-19 Add Counters dialog box for selecting performance counters

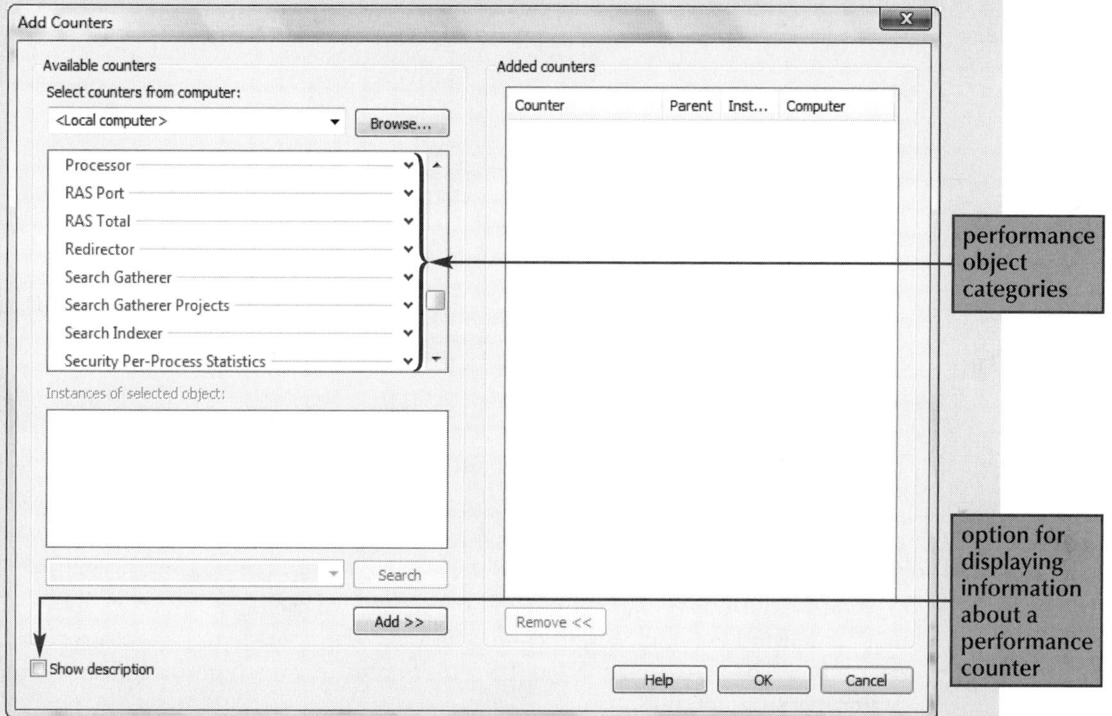

2. In the Available counters section, use the vertical scroll bar to locate Memory, click the **Expand** button to view a list of performance counters under the Memory performance object, click **Available Bytes**, and then click the **Show description** check box (bottom left corner of dialog box). The dialog box expands to show the Description section at the bottom of the Add Counters dialog box. See Figure 9-20. Performance Monitor explains that the Available Bytes performance counter measures the amount of physical memory in bytes that Windows Vista can immediately allocate to a process or for use by the system. Then, Performance Monitor provides more detail on what constitutes Available Bytes. Notice also that there are no instances of this performance counter in the now dimmed "Instances of select object" list box.

Figure 9-20 Viewing information on the Available Bytes performance counter

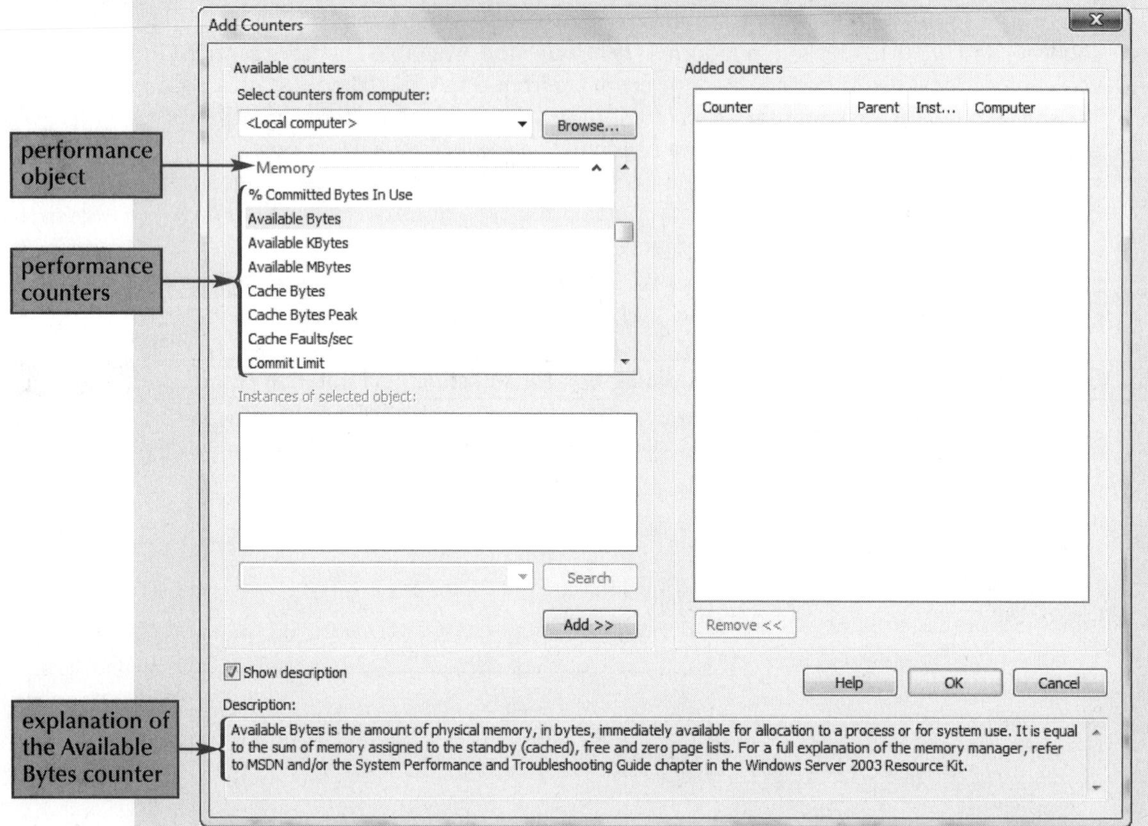

3. Click the **Add** button in the Add Counters dialog box. Performance Monitor lists this performance counter in the Added counters list box on the right.
4. Adjust your view of Memory performance counters, and then locate and click **Committed Bytes**. In the Description section, Performance Monitor explains that Committed Bytes is the amount of committed virtual memory. Then, it explains that committed memory is physical memory for which space has been reserved in the paging file in case it's needed. It further notes that each physical disk can have one or more paging files.
5. Click the **Add** button. Performance Monitor adds this performance counter to the Added counters list box.

6. Adjust your view of Memory performance counters, and then locate and click **Pages/sec**. In the Description section, Performance Monitor explains that Pages/sec measures the number of pages read from or written to disk for hard faults. A hard fault occurs when a process requires program code or data that is not in its working set or elsewhere in physical memory, and therefore must be retrieved from the paging file on disk. A working set is the physical memory allocated to and used by a process. A page fault error (PFE), or invalid page fault, occurs when Windows Vista is unable to find data in the paging file. Performance Monitor also notes that this performance counter is the primary indicator of hard page faults that result in system-wide delays on a computer. That means that this performance counter is useful for monitoring paging activity. Possible causes for this type of problem include an insufficient amount of RAM, an insufficient amount of available disk storage space, a memory conflict between two applications in which one attempts to access data used by the other, a problem in translating virtual memory addresses to physical memory addresses, some other type of corruption or problem in virtual memory, or turning off or reducing the size of the paging file.
7. Click the **Add** button. Performance Monitor adds this performance counter to the Added counters list box.
8. Locate the Process performance object under Available counters, click the **Expand** button [▾] to view a list of performance counters under the Process performance object, locate and click **Page File Bytes**, and make sure the **_Total** instance is selected in the "Instances of selected object" list box. In the Description section, Performance Monitor notes that this performance counter measures the current amount of virtual memory in bytes that all the processes have reserved for use in the paging file. It also notes that the paging file stores pages of memory used by these processes that are not contained in other files, and that since all processes share the paging file, an insufficient amount of storage space in a paging file can interfere with the performance of other processes and their use of memory.
9. Click the **Add** button. Performance Monitor adds this performance counter to the Added counters list box. Note that the performance factors are organized by performance object category. See Figure 9-21.

Figure 9-21 Choosing memory performance counters

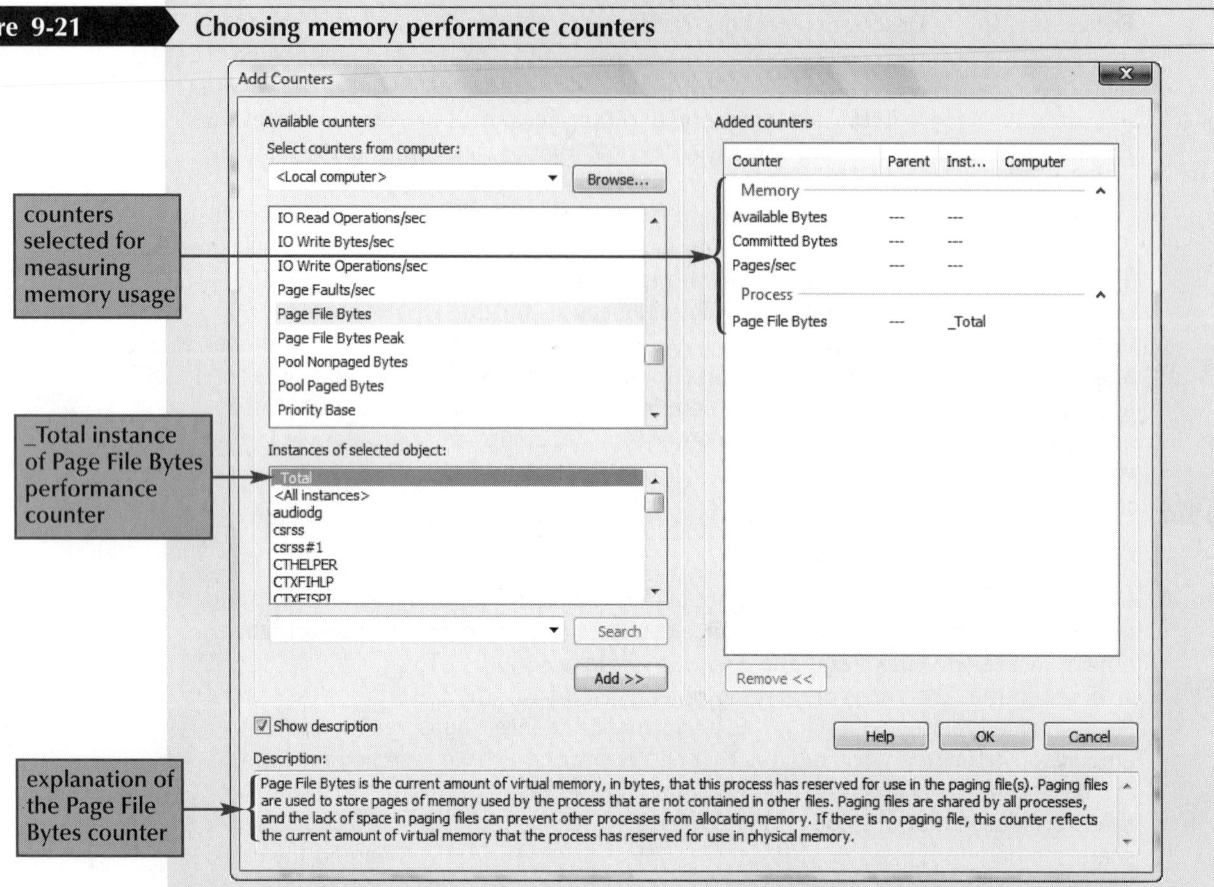

10. In the Add Counters dialog box, click the **OK** button to add these counters to your performance plot.

You have just added the performance counters requested by Shuang, and now you are ready to use these counters to monitor and provide information on the performance of this computer. To simplify that process, you first need to adjust your view of performance counters in the legend and adjust the scale for plotting those values so that all lines plotted on the line graph fall within the range shown on the vertical axis.

To adjust your view of performance counters:

1. Click **one of the performance counters** in the legend, and then press the **Ctrl** key and the **+** key in the numeric keypad for a best fit of the data in all the columns of the legend (or manually adjust each column width so that all the data is visible). Although this approach adjusts the legend so that you can see all the data in each column, you may not see all of the column headings.
2. Click the **Counter column** button. Performance Monitor arranges the performance counters in alphabetical order by counter name—% Processor Time, Available Bytes, Committed Bytes, Page File Bytes, and Pages/sec.

   Trouble? If the performance counters are listed in descending order (reverse alphabetical order), click the Counter column button a second time.

   Trouble? If you are missing one of the five performance counters just described, use the Add button to locate and add that performance counter to the set of performance counters that you are measuring, and then click the Counter column button to sort them in alphabetical order by Counter name.

Trouble? If the same performance counter is listed twice, Performance Monitor might produce spurious results. Select one of the two performance counters, and then click the Delete button on the Performance Monitor toolbar (or press the Delete key).

3. Click the **% Processor Time counter** in the legend (if necessary), and then click the **Highlight** button on the Performance Monitor toolbar. Performance Monitor highlights the line in the graph that contains plotted values for the % Processor counter. The Highlight button separates a single performance measurement from all others and more easily displays plotted values represented by lines with a light color (such as yellow) that are otherwise difficult to see.

4. Click the **Available Bytes** counter in the legend. Performance Monitor highlights the line in the graph that contains plotted values for this counter. Since the plotted values for the Available Bytes counter lie outside the range of values represented on the vertical axis, the line for this counter appears as a dark line at the top of the line graph. Note that the scale value for this counter is 0.000001. That means that the actual values plotted on the line graph for this counter are divided by 0.000001. For example, if you change the vertical axis to show values from 0 to 1500, the value for Available Bytes on this computer is just over 1400. To obtain the actual value, you divide the actual or estimated value of 1400 derived from the vertical axis by 0.000001 to arrive at 1,400,000,000 bytes (or approximately 1.4 GB). The exact value is always shown in the value bar.

5. Right-click the **Available Bytes** counter in the legend and click **Scale Selected Counters** on the shortcut menu. Performance Monitor changes the scale for this plotted counter so that it lies within the range of values on the vertical axis. Note that the scale for this counter is now 0.00000001 (you may have to widen the Scale column). View the vertical axis to estimate 14 or 15 for Available Bytes. To find the actual number of bytes with this new scale, divide 14 or 15 by 0.00000001 to estimate a value of 1,400,000,000 or 1,500,000,000 bytes (approximately 1.4 GB or 1.5 GB). Again, the exact value is shown in the value bar.

6. Click the **Committed Bytes** counter in the legend, notice that the plotted value lies outside the upper limit of the vertical axis, right-click the **Committed Bytes** counter in the legend, and click **Scale Selected Counters** on the shortcut menu. Performance Monitor changes the scale for this plotted counter so that it lies within the range of values on the vertical axis. Note that the scale value for this counter changes from 0.000001 to 0.0000001, and the plotted values are now visible on the graph.

7. Click the **Page File Bytes** counter in the legend, notice that the plotted value lies outside the upper limit of the vertical axis, right-click the **Page File Bytes** counter in the legend, and then click **Scale Selected Counters** on the shortcut menu. The scale value for this counter changes from 0.000001 to 0.0000001, and the plotted values are now visible on the graph.

Tip

You can also press the Ctrl+H keys to enable or turn off the Highlight button.

If you want to scale more than one counter, and if the counters are listed one right after the other in the legend, you click the first counter, hold down the Shift key while you click the last counter, right-click the group, and choose Scale Selected Counters. If the counters are not located one after the other, hold down the Ctrl key while you click each counter you want to scale, right-click the group (now called a collection), and choose Scale Selected Counters.

InSight | Understanding the Scaling of Plotted Values

If the scale for a counter is 1, that means the values plotted on the line graph for the counter are the actual values. You can therefore use the values on the vertical axis to estimate the actual value for a point on the line graph, such as a momentary peak in a value, and your estimated value will be very close to the actual value. For example, if the % Processor Time jumps to 80 on the vertical axis after you open an application, the % Processor Time is actually 80%. If the scale for a counter is 10, the values plotted on the line graph are 10 times larger than the actual values, and you must divide the estimated value you derive from the vertical axis by 10 to determine the actual value for a momentary peak in the line graph. For example, if the vertical axis values range from 0 to 1000, and if you notice that the % Processor Time jumps to 800 after opening an application, the % Processor Time is actually 80 percent. If the scale for a counter is 0.1, the values plotted on the line graph are one-tenth of the actual values, and you must divide the estimated value that you derive from the vertical axis by 0.1 to determine the actual value for a momentary peak in the line graph. For example, if the vertical axis values range from 0 to 10, and if you notice that the % Processor Time jumps to 8 after opening an application, the % Processor Time is actually 80 percent. Simpler yet, you can obtain the actual values from the value bar no matter what scale is used or use the value bar to confirm your estimated value.

Next, you are going to save your line graph so that you have a record of your baseline performance values.

Tip

You can also press the Ctrl+F keys to freeze or unfreeze the display.

To save performance measurements:

1. Click the **% Processor Time** counter in the legend, and then click the **Freeze Display** button on the Performance Monitor toolbar (not the Reliability and Performance Monitor toolbar). Performance Monitor stops plotting counter values. After you click the Freeze Display button it becomes the Unfreeze Display button. The Freeze Display button pauses the plotting of performance data so that you can save the data, analyze the data, select different performance counters in the legend, and examine the details of each measurement in the value bar.
2. Right-click the **line graph**, click **Save Image As** on the shortcut menu, and if necessary, click the **Browse Folders** button in the Save in list box to display a list of locations on your computer. Note that your performance measurements will be saved as an Image file with the "gif" file extension.
3. Click **Computer** under Favorite Links, and then click your **flash drive icon**.
4. Type **Initial Performance Measurements** in the File name box, and then click the **Save** button.
5. Click the **Unfreeze Display** button on the Performance Monitor toolbar. Performance Monitor resumes plotting counter values.

Now, you have a record of baseline values for specific performance counters on your computer. Baseline values are important so that you have a sense of the current state and performance level of the computer you are using. Before you start the next set of steps, wait a minute for your computer to idle down and for performance counters to return closer to the levels they were before you saved performance data.

To examine information on specific counters:

1. Click **% Processor Time** in the legend, and then click the **Freeze Display** button.
2. Point to a **peak for % Processor Time** on the line graph and do not move the pointer. Performance Monitor displays a ToolTip with information about that plotted value in the line graph. See Figure 9-22. The ToolTip identifies the counter, the actual value, and the time and date. On the computer used for this figure, % Processor Time peaked at 4.681 percent after Performance Monitor started plotting a new set of 100 values. The percentage of processor activity is relatively low (or should be low) whenever the computer is idle. On the computer used for this figure, the % Processor Time ranged from 0 to slightly over 13 percent when idle. However, if you perform an operation, you will see a momentary spike in processor activity. Your details will differ.

Tip

You can also select a counter in the legend by clicking its line in the graph.

Viewing information about a plotted value for % Processor Time — **Figure 9-22**

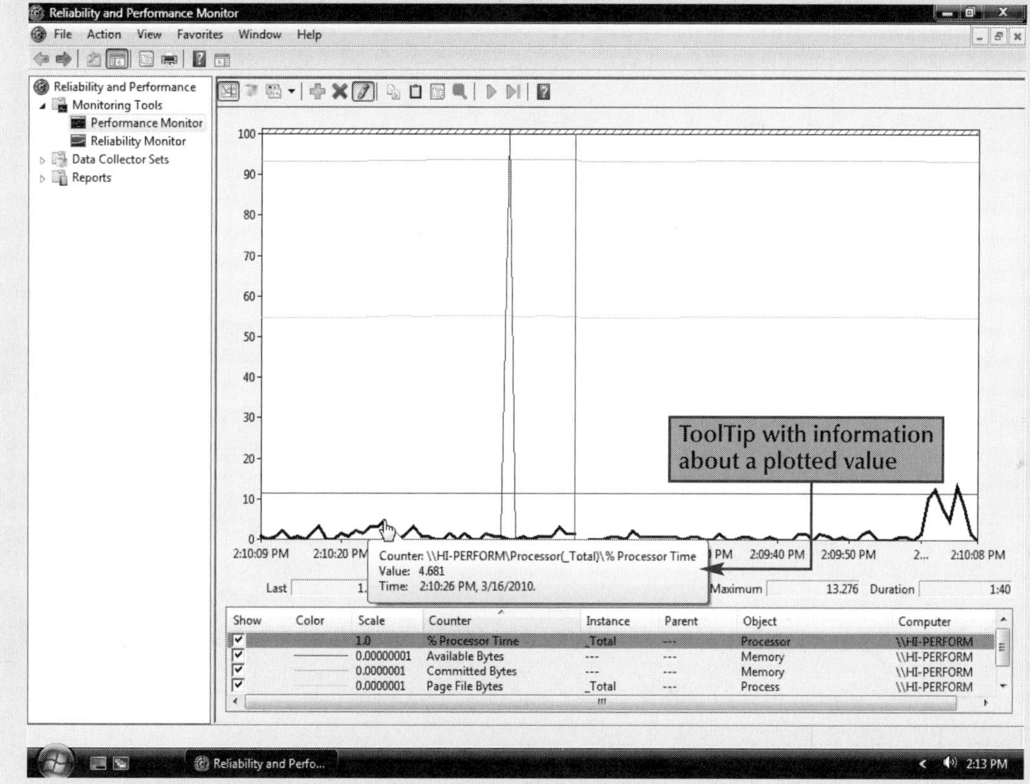

3. Click the **Available Bytes** counter in the legend. On the computer used for Figure 9-23, Available Bytes is steady at a level just above 10 on the vertical axis. Let's assume the value is 12. Since the scale for this counter is 0.00000001, you divide 12 by 0.00000001 to yield 1,200,000,000 bytes (or approximately 1.1 GB of the 2 GB of RAM on this computer). If you examine the value bar, Performance Monitor shows the actual values for this counter. The Last measured value is 1,145,827,328 bytes, or approximately 1.07 GB (1,145,827,328 divided by 1,024 three times). Your details will differ. That means that slightly more than half of this computer's 2G of RAM is available after starting the computer, opening Performance Monitor, and adding performance counters.

Figure 9-23 Viewing initial values for the Available Bytes performance counter

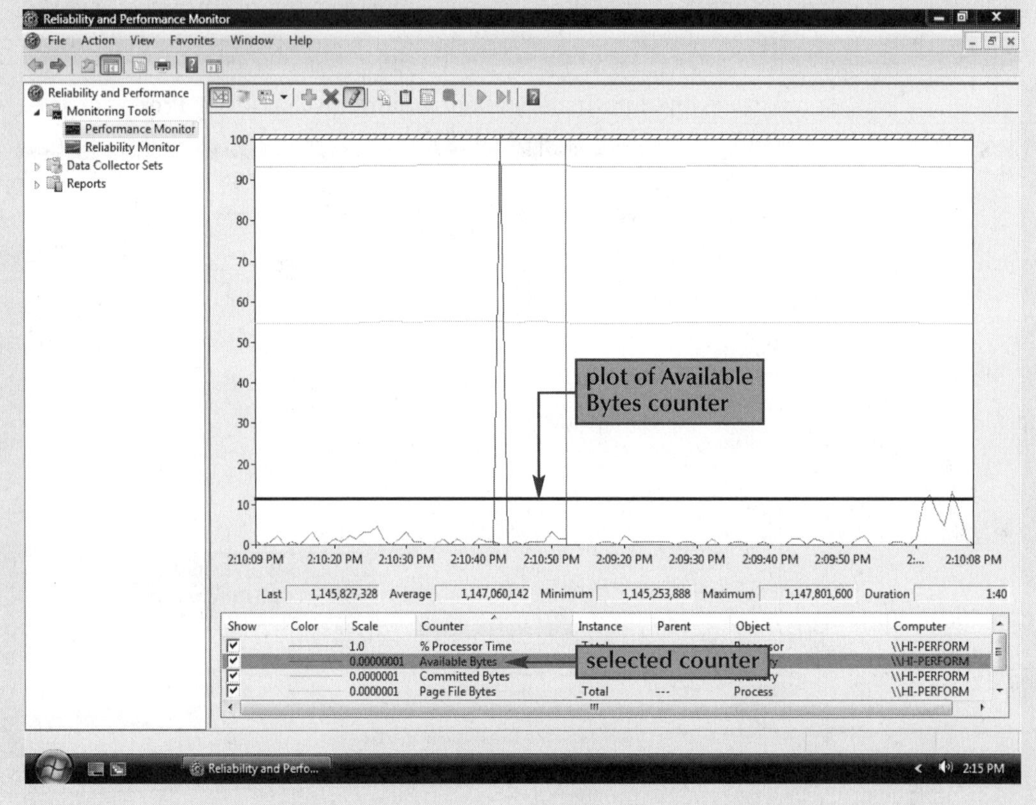

4. Click the **Committed Bytes** counter in the legend. On the computer used for Figure 9-24, Committed Bytes exhibits slight variations; however, it is relatively stable. In the value bar, the Last measured value on the computer used for this figure is 936,833,024 bytes, or approximately 893 MB (936,833,024 divided by 1,024 twice). Your details will differ. That means that less than half of the installed RAM is in use (or committed).

Figure 9-24 Viewing initial values for the Committed Bytes performance counter

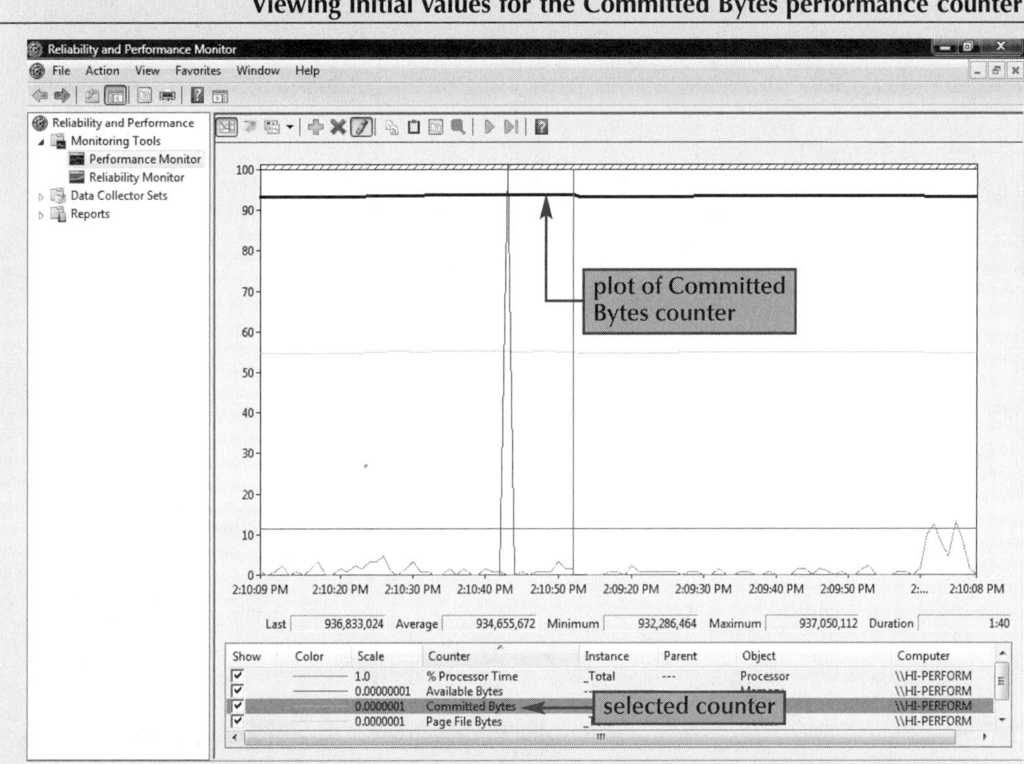

5. Click the **Page File Bytes** counter in the legend. On the computer used for Figure 9-25, Performance Monitor reports the Last measured value as 550,928,384 bytes, or approximately 525 MB, the amount of storage space used in the paging file by all processes. Your details will differ.

Figure 9-25 Viewing initial values for the Page File Bytes performance counter

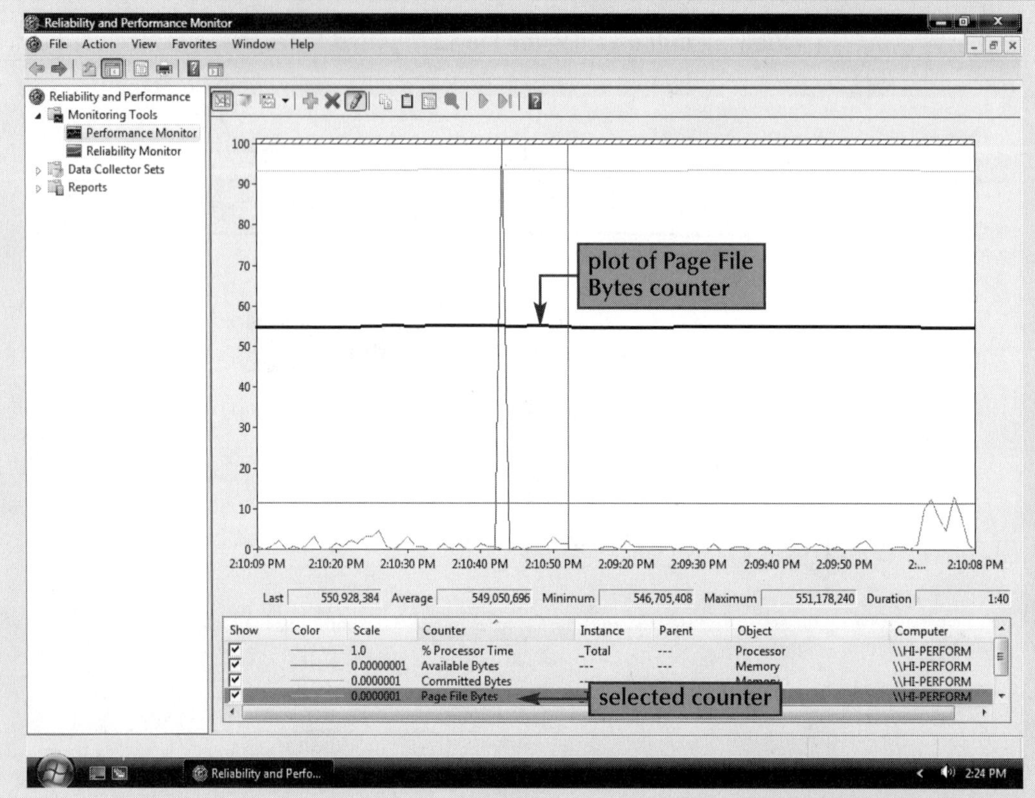

6. Click the **Pages/sec** counter in the legend area (you may need to scroll). From the graph for the computer used in Figure 9-26, values for Pages/sec ranged from 0 to 187 Pages/sec (as shown in the value bar). Even though the values for this performance were relatively low most of the time, there was a momentary peak in the Pages/sec when disk I/O occurred on the computer used for this figure. Your results may differ.

Figure 9-26 Viewing initial values for the Pages/sec performance counter

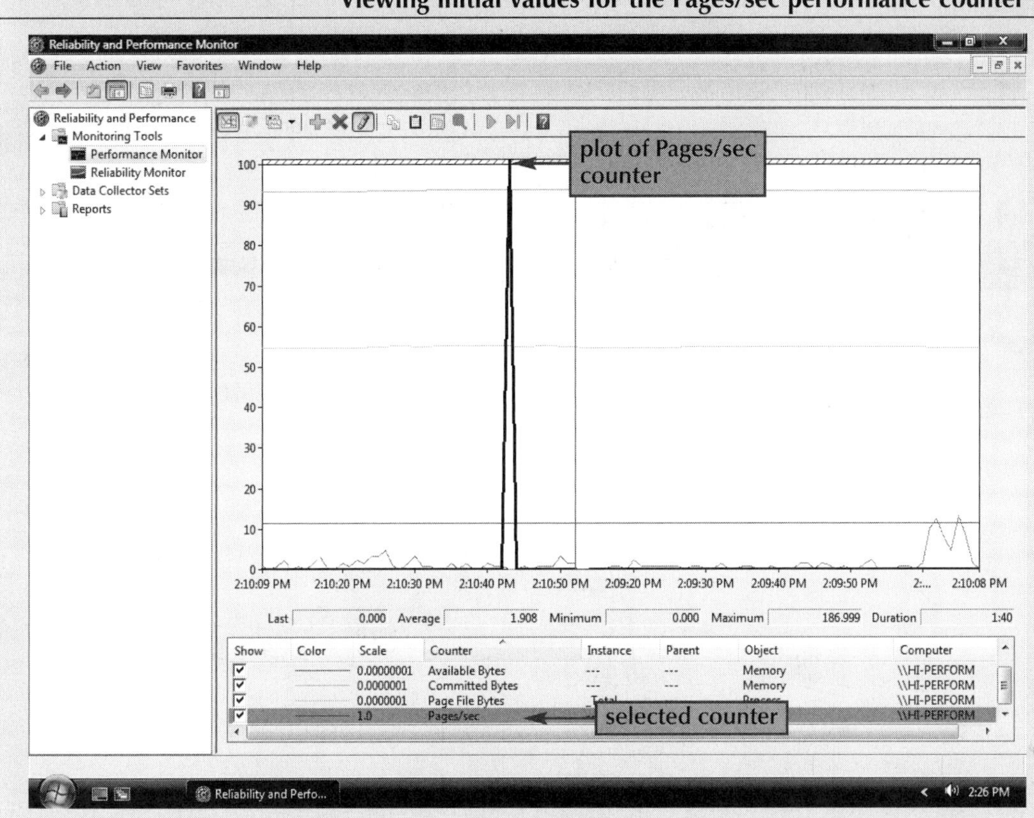

7. Click the **Unfreeze Display** button to resume plotting performance data.

Typically, you check these baseline values after you boot your computer so that you can capture information on changes to performance counters and thereby be able to evaluate the performance of your computer as you continue to work or as you troubleshoot problems.

Now, you're ready to evaluate the performance of this computer after you open a program on your computer. Again, before you start the next set of steps, wait a minute for the performance data on the computer that you are using to "idle down."

To monitor your computer's performance as you open an application:

1. To clear the performance data already plotted, right-click the **graph**, and then click **Clear**. If you clear the graph before performing another operation, the values shown for the performance counters in the value bar relate to that operation.
2. Locate and click the **% Processor Time** counter in the legend.

3. Open **Microsoft Word** or another application on your computer (preferably one you depend on), click the **Reliability and Performance Monitor** taskbar button, wait a few seconds for % Processor Time and Pages/sec to return to levels close to the previous ones, and then click the **Freeze Display** button. On the computer used for this figure, the % Processor Time spiked momentarily at about 51 percent during the time when the processor was busy with the loading of Microsoft Word (also see Maximum value in the value bar). See Figure 9-27. Your details will differ. This spike is higher the first time you open an application and then smaller when you reopen it later, indicating that some of the program was already cached (or stored) in memory. The % Processor Time should drop after a program is loaded into memory and return to a low level. If % Processor Time does not drop after loading a program, you've identified a problem with that particular program impacting the performance of your computer.

Figure 9-27 Viewing an increase in % Processor Time after opening Word

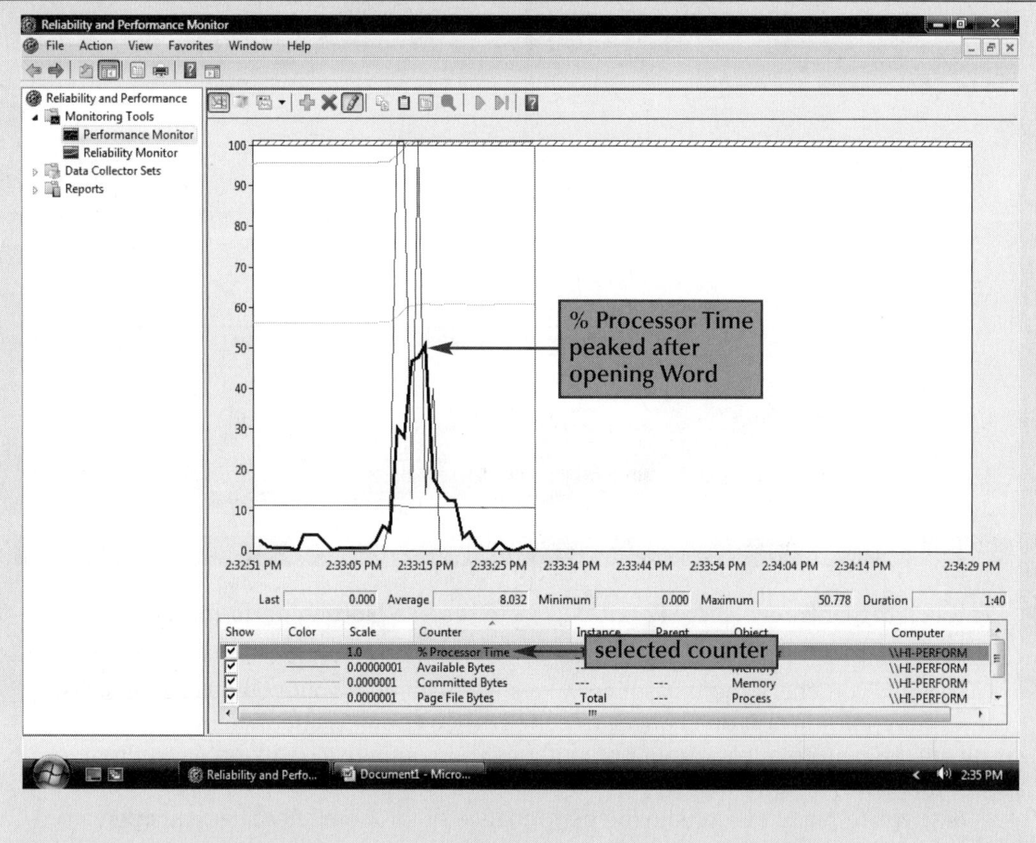

4. Click the **Pages/sec** counter in the legend and examine the line graph. On the computer used for Figure 9-28, there was a lot of disk I/O as Windows Vista loaded Microsoft Word from disk into memory. One major peak reached a maximum value of 341 Pages/sec (as shown on the value bar), and there was another peak near 100 Pages/sec, followed by a smaller peak around 40 Pages/sec. (If you point to a peak, then Performance Monitor displays a ToolTip with the actual value). If you had plotted Page Reads/sec and Page Writes/sec, you would discover that the vast majority of these Pages accessed per second correlated with reading Microsoft Word from disk. Your details will differ.

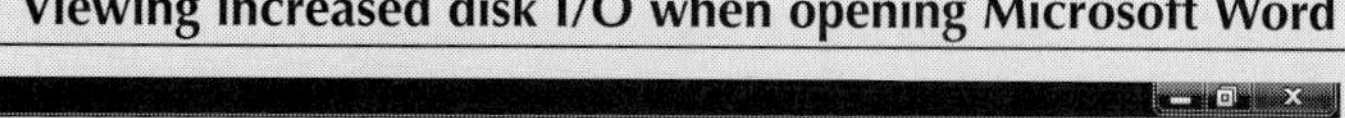

Figure 9-28 Viewing increased disk I/O when opening Microsoft Word

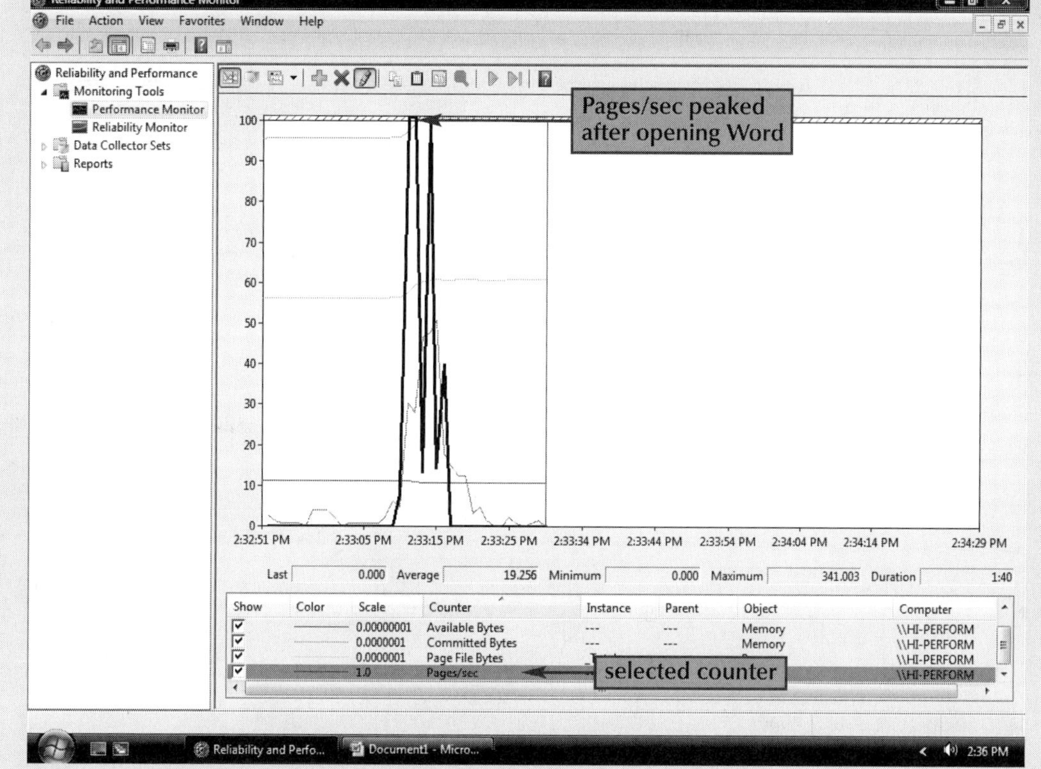

5. Click the **Committed Bytes** counter in the legend and examine the line graph. On the computer used for Figure 9-29, the amount of memory in use after loading Microsoft Word increased from approximately 893 MB to a maximum value of 961 MB (a gain of 68 MB) because Windows Vista allocated memory to Microsoft Word. Note also that the performance values for Committed Bytes now exceed the upper range of the vertical axis. Earlier, when you performed this same operation and examined the change in memory, Task Manager reported a gain of 66 MB (a comparable value) on this computer. Your details will differ.

Figure 9-29 Viewing an increase in memory usage after opening Word

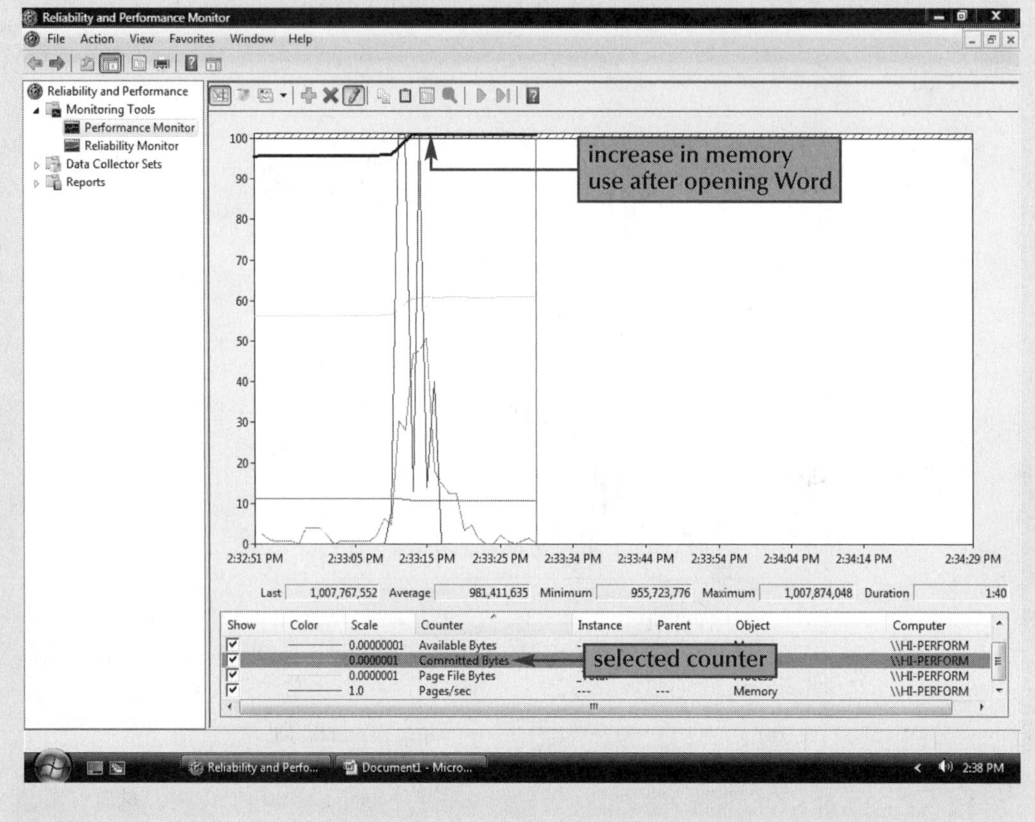

6. Click the **Available Bytes** counter in the legend and examine the line graph. On the computer used for Figure 9-30, the amount of available memory after loading Microsoft Word decreased from 1.07 GB to approximately 1 GB (a decrease of approximately 0.07 GB) because less RAM is available after Windows Vista allocated memory to Microsoft Word. Your details will differ.

Figure 9-30 **Viewing a decrease in available memory after opening Word**

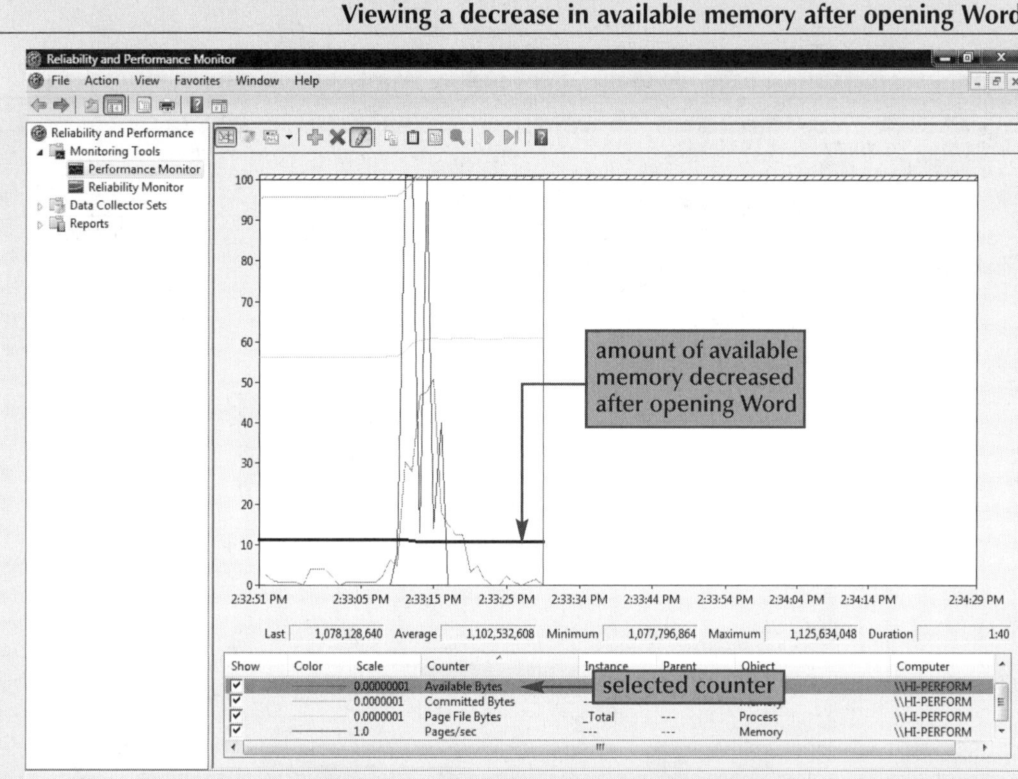

7. Click the **Page File Bytes** counter in the legend and examine the line graph. On the computer used for Figure 9-31, the amount of storage space used in the paging file after loading Microsoft Word increased from 525 MB to approximately 581 MB (a gain of 56 MB). That means data in RAM was swapped to the paging file to optimize the use of memory for Microsoft Word. Your details will differ. The plotted values for Page File Bytes typically follow the same pattern as for Committed Bytes.

Figure 9-31 Viewing an increase in page file usage after opening Word

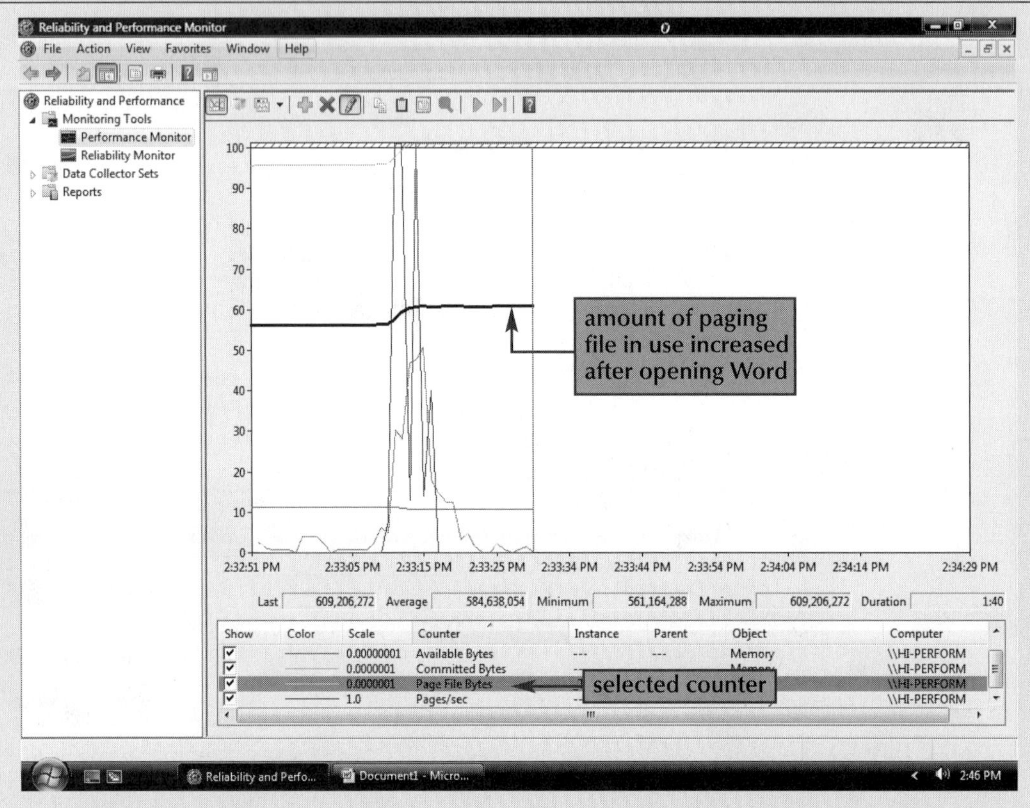

Next, you want to save your line graph with a record of performance values after opening Microsoft Word.

To save performance measurements:

1. Click the **% Processor Time** counter in the legend.
2. Right-click the **line graph**, click **Save Image As** on the shortcut menu, type **After Opening Microsoft Word** (or the name of the application you opened) in the File name box, and then click the **Save** button.

Next, you'll close Microsoft Word, and then examine changes in each of these five performance counters so that you can evaluate how Windows Vista reclaims and handles these valuable resources.

To monitor your computer's performance as you close an application:

1. Click the **Unfreeze Display** button on the Performance Monitor toolbar to resume plotting performance counters.

2. Right-click the **Microsoft Word** taskbar button (or the taskbar button for the application you opened), click **Close**, wait for a few more seconds so that Performance Monitor can plot the changes that just occurred, and then click the **Freeze Display** button. On the computer used for Figure 9-32, % Processor Time showed a spike of much shorter duration than what occurred when opening Microsoft Word. Your details will differ.

Viewing a peak in % processor time after closing Word — **Figure 9-32**

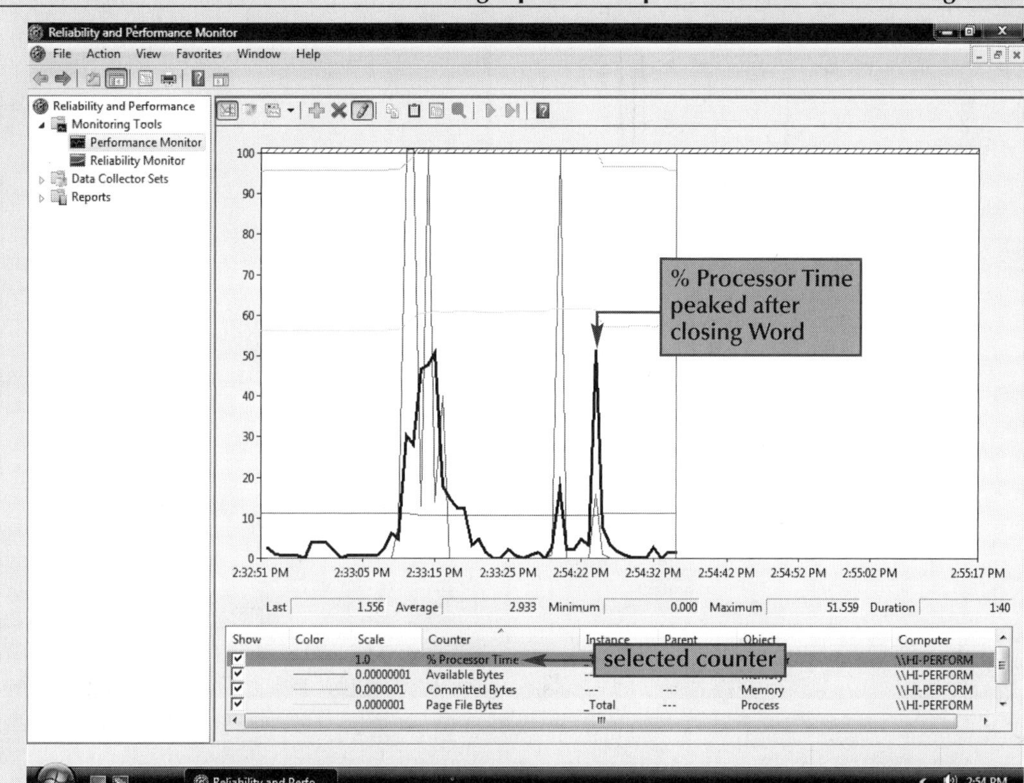

3. Click the **Pages/sec** counter in the legend and examine the line graph and value bar. On the computer used for Figure 9-33, Pages/sec showed a smaller spike as Microsoft Word closed. Your details will differ.

Figure 9-33 **Viewing disk I/O after closing Microsoft Word**

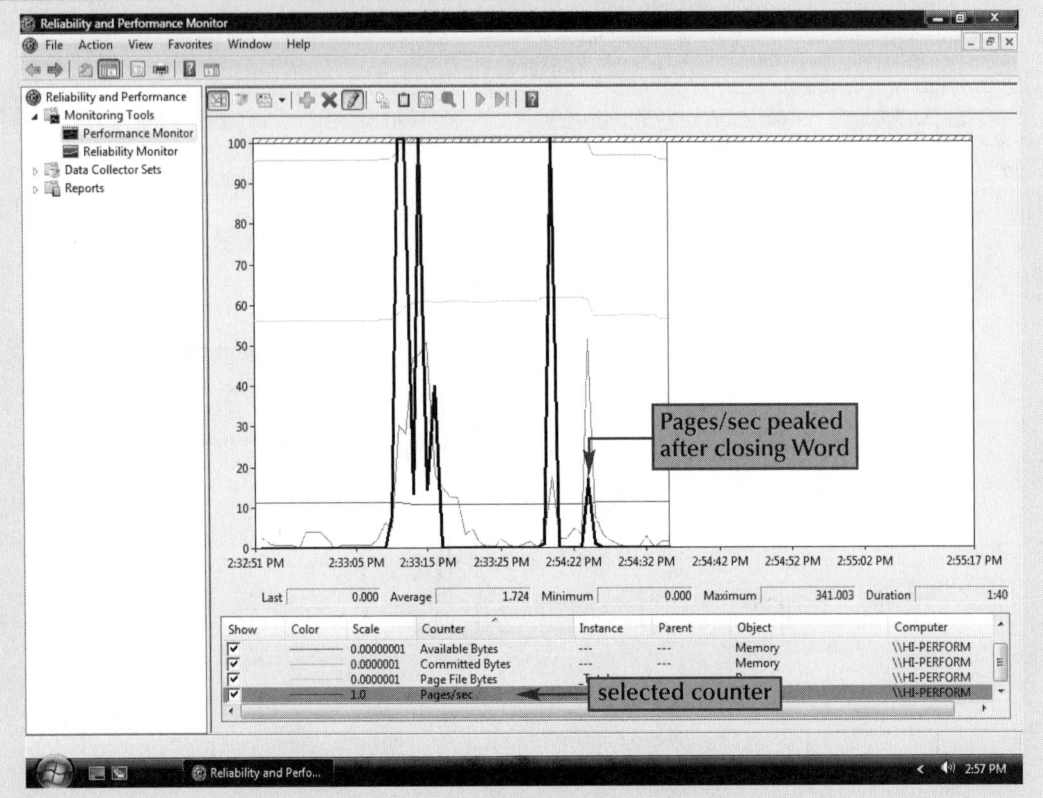

4. Click the **Committed Bytes** counter in the legend and examine the line graph and value bar. On the computer used for Figure 9-34, the amount of memory in use decreased from 961 MB to approximately 914 MB (a decrease of 47 MB) after closing Microsoft Word. The plot of Committed Bytes performance data is now once again visible in the graph. Your details will differ.

Viewing a decrease in memory usage after closing Word **Figure 9-34**

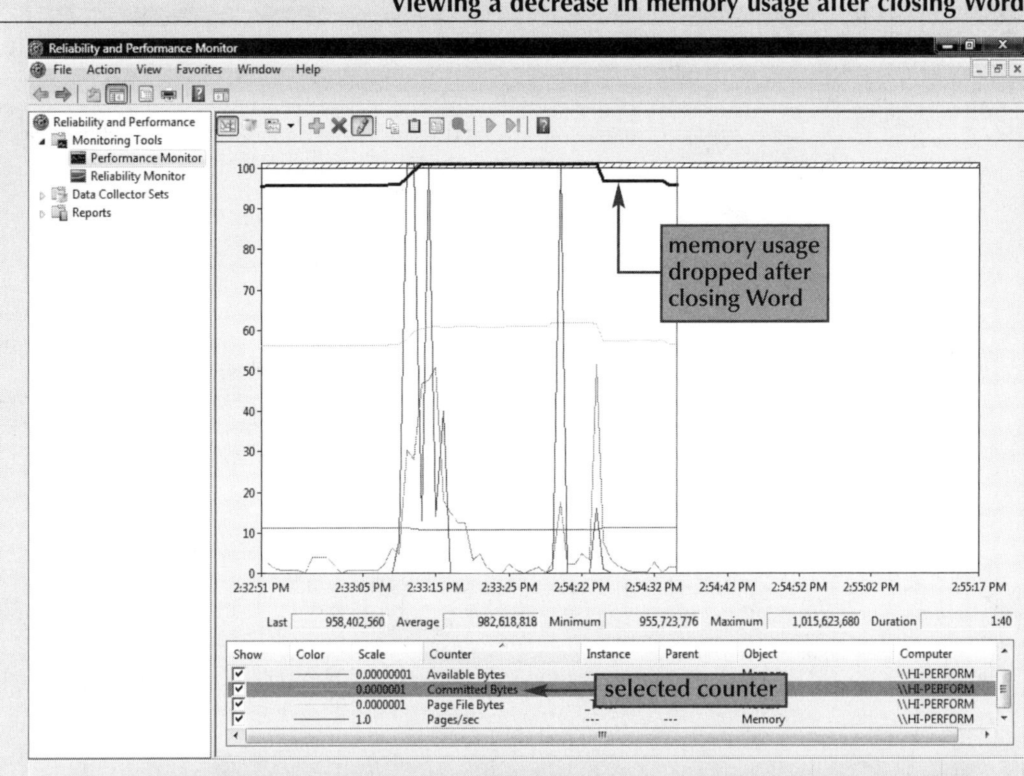

5. Click the **Available Bytes** counter in the legend and examine the line graph and value bar. On the computer used for Figure 9-35, the amount of available memory increased from 1 GB to approximately 1.04 GB (a gain of 0.04 GB) after closing Microsoft Word. Your details will differ.

Figure 9-35 Viewing an increase in available memory after closing Word

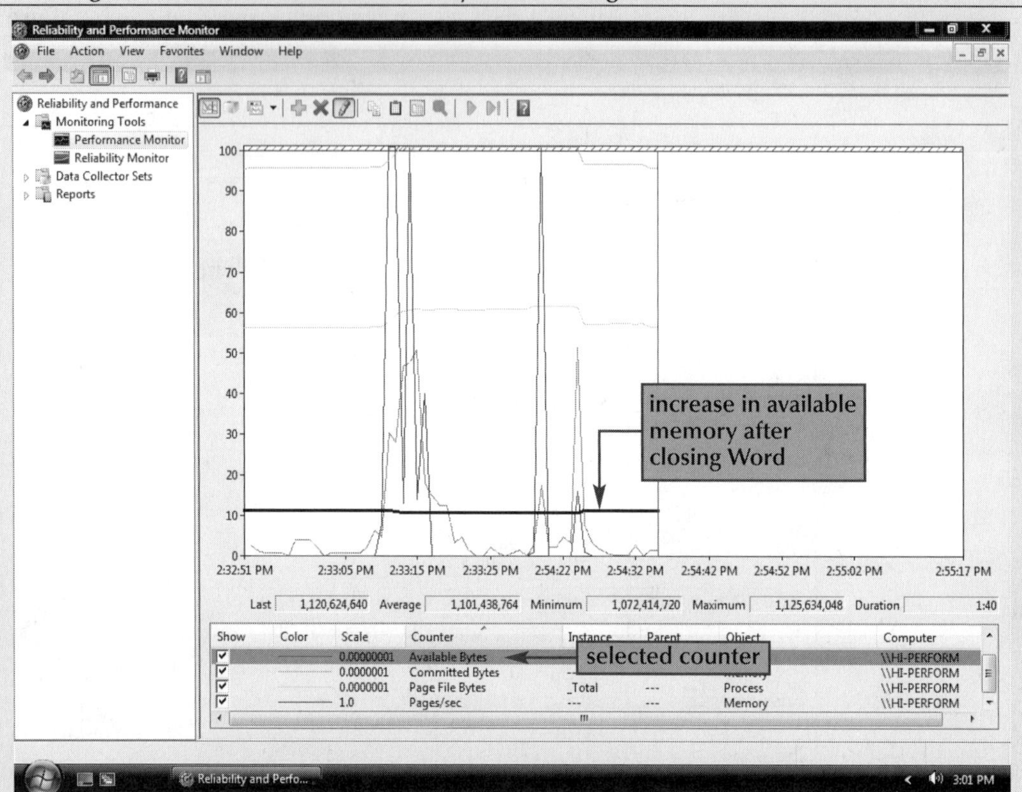

6. Click the **Page File Bytes** counter in the legend and examine the line graph and value bar. On the computer used for Figure 9-36, the amount of used storage space in the paging file decreased from 581 MB to approximately 538 MB (a decrease of 43 MB) after closing Microsoft Word. Your details will differ. The plotted values for Page File Bytes follow the same pattern as for Committed Bytes.

Figure 9-36

Viewing a decrease in page file usage after closing Word

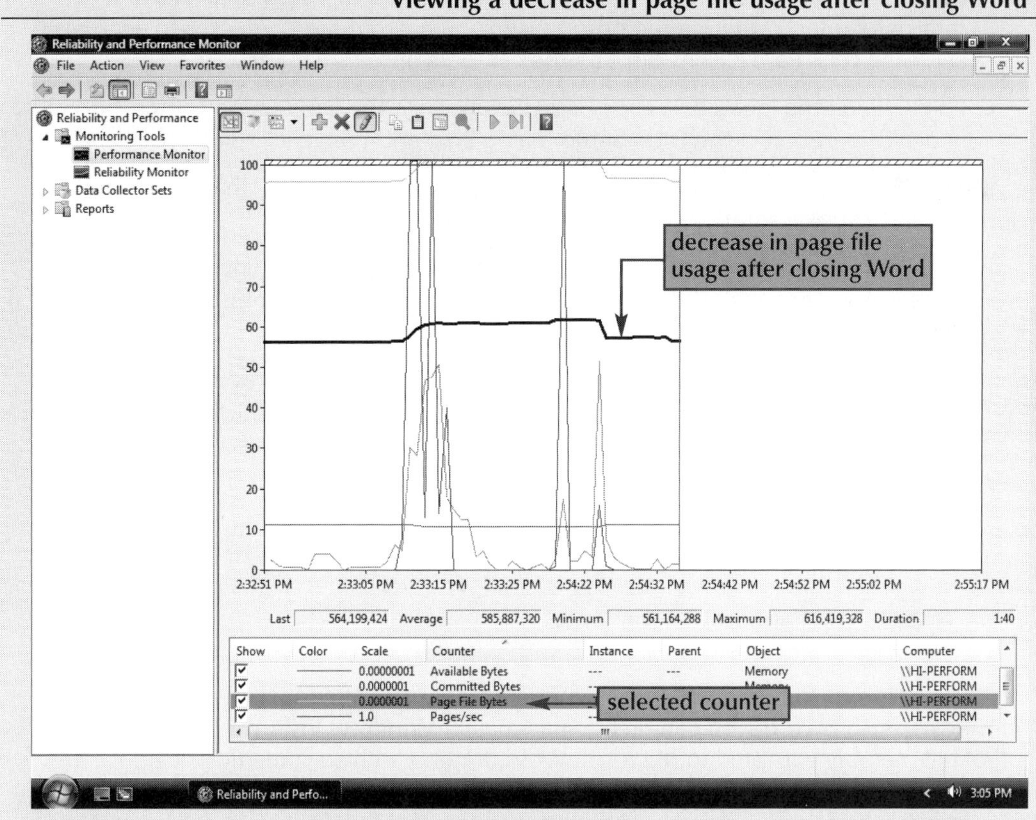

Next, you are going to save your graph so that you have a record of performance values after closing Microsoft Word.

To save performance measurements:

1. Click the **% Processor Time** counter in the legend.
2. Right-click the **line graph**, click **Save Image As** on the shortcut menu, type **After Closing Microsoft Word** (or the name of the application you opened) in the File name box, and then click the **Save** button.
3. Click the **Unfreeze Display** button on the Performance Monitor toolbar.
4. Close the Reliability and Performance Monitor window, and then close the Advanced Tools window.

Next, you want to view and print two of the files that contain information about the performance of your computer after opening and closing Microsoft Word. Although you can open different applications to print the Image files that contain a view of your graphs, you are going to use Paint in the following steps because the Image files have the gif file extension. Plus, Paint is included with the Windows Vista accessories and therefore is available on all computers.

To view and print performance measurements:

1. Open a Computer window, and then open a window onto your flash drive.

2. Locate and right-click **After Opening Microsoft Word.gif**, point to **Open With**, notice that you can open this file type in several different programs (including Internet Explorer, though the programs may vary from one computer to another), and then click **Paint**. Paint displays the contents of the Image file.
3. Click **File** on the menu bar, click **Page Setup**, click the **Landscape option button** under Orientation in the Page Setup dialog box, and then click the **OK** button.
4. Click **File** on the menu bar, and then click **Print Preview**. Now that you switched to Landscape orientation, your graph will print on one page.
5. Click the **Print** button on the Print Preview toolbar, verify that you have chosen the correct printer in the Print dialog box, and then click the **Print** button in the Print dialog box.
6. Click **File** on the menu bar, click **Open**, click Computer under Favorite Links (if necessary), click your flash drive icon (if necessary), and then locate and open **After Closing Microsoft Word.gif** on your flash drive.
7. Click **File** on the menu bar, and then click **Print Preview**.
8. Click the **Print** button on the Print Preview toolbar, and then click the **Print** button in the Print dialog box.
9. Close the Paint application windows.

If you compare the results for the performance counters after opening and then after closing Microsoft Word, you can determine whether Windows Vista was able to reclaim all of the memory allocated to Microsoft Word. If not, you have a memory leak. Figure 9-37 shows the initial performance measurements on memory usage and the performance measurements on memory usage after opening and after closing Microsoft Word. After closing Microsoft Word, the value for Committed Bytes should have returned to its original level prior to opening Microsoft Word; however, that did not occur. The value for Committed Bytes was 21 MB larger after closing Microsoft Word than prior to opening Microsoft Word. That indicates that Windows Vista did not completely reclaim the memory used by this application, resulting in a memory leak of 21 MB. However, the next time you open Microsoft Word or another Office application during that same computer session, that application opens faster, so the program code that remained in memory proves useful. The size of the paging file dropped after closing Microsoft Word but did not return to its original size. The size of the paging file in use (as measured by Page File Bytes) was 13 MB larger after closing Microsoft Word than prior to opening Microsoft Word.

Figure 9-37 **Comparing changes in memory usage**

	Initial Performance Measurements	After Opening Microsoft Word	After Closing Microsoft Word
Available Bytes	1.07 GB	1 GB	1.04 GB
Committed Bytes	893 MB	961 MB	914 MB
Page File Bytes	525 MB	581 MB	538 MB

Other useful options on the Performance Monitor toolbar are the following:

- **Change graph type button** The default graph type is Line, but you can use this toolbar button to switch to Histogram bar or Report. Histogram bar displays the magnitude of values by the height of vertical bars. One nice feature of this view is that you can visually see rapid changes in measurements for performance counters (i.e., vertical bars fluctuating rapidly in size and appearing and disappearing). As shown in Figure 9-38, Report displays the current values for performance counters. If you use the Ctrl+G keys, the keyboard shortcut for the Change graph type button, you can quickly switch between different graph types.

Viewing performance counters in Report view **Figure 9-38**

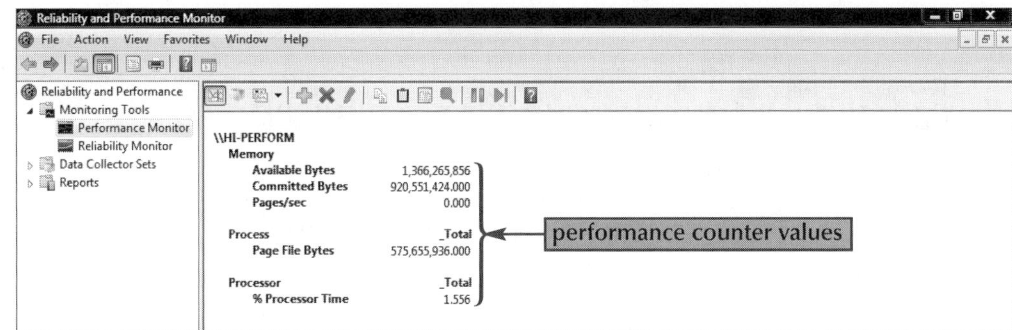

- **Properties button** You can use the Properties button to open the Performance Monitor Properties dialog box and customize your use of Performance Monitor. For example, you can specify which elements (such as the legend, value bar, or toolbar) you want to display, what you want to report for Report and Histogram data (current value, minimum value, maximum value, or average value), how frequently the update occurs (in seconds), the duration of the sampling, whether you want to log (or copy) performance data to a file, specify a minimum and maximum value for the vertical scale axis, specify the use of vertical and horizontal gridlines, specify the use of vertical axis numbers and time axis labels, specify colors for the graph background, choose fonts, and choose borders. You can also specify the line color, scale, line width, and line style for each performance counter. Press the Ctrl+Q keys to quickly open the Performance Monitor Properties dialog box.
- **Update Data button** If you freeze the display, you can use the Update Data button to manually plot one sample at a time. Its keyboard shortcut is Ctrl+U.
- **Delete button** If you select a counter in the legend, you can use this button to remove that counter from your graph.

As noted earlier, Committed Bytes is the amount of memory your computer is using at any given time. By monitoring this value, you can determine how much memory Windows Vista needs after booting, and you can observe the demands on memory by the types of applications that you use and by the way you work (multitasking vs. single-tasking). This information gives you a baseline value (or values) for the amount of memory that Windows Vista needs as you work on your computer. You can use this baseline value to decide whether to add more RAM to your computer, to estimate how much you might need to meet the most demanding applications that you use, and to handle multitasking of resource-intensive applications.

If Performance Monitor continually reports a high value for the Pages/sec performance counter, a memory or disk bottleneck might be degrading the performance of your computer. You can close application and folder windows you no longer use, turn off features that you use in applications (such as optional add-ons), or move the paging file to another disk with more space, less disk activity, and/or a faster speed. Since all processes share the paging file, Windows Vista might not be able to allocate memory to other processes if it cannot expand the size of the paging file when needed. You might need to add more physical memory (more RAM) to your computer to reduce the amount of paging that occurs—paging that also makes excessive demands of your hard disk.

You should monitor the performance of your computer so that you know how resources are allocated from one session to the next and from one way of working to another (such as multitasking vs. single-tasking), so that if problems develop, you can monitor the performance of your computer and compare its current performance to times when those problems did not occur.

Reference Window | Using Performance Monitor to Track Performance

- Open the Start menu, point to Administrative Tools, right-click Reliability and Performance Monitor, click Run as administrator, and then provide Administrator credentials.
- In the console tree pane on the left side of the Reliability and Performance Monitor window, click Performance Monitor.
- If you want to remove any existing performance counters, select each of those performance counters in the legend, and then click the Delete button on the Performance Monitor toolbar.
- If you want to add performance counters, click the Add button on the Performance Monitor toolbar to open the Add Counters dialog box, or right-click the graph, and click Add Counters.
- Select the option to use either local computer counters or counters for a specific computer on your network.
- From the list of Available counters, locate and click the Expand View button for a Performance object.
- Locate and select the counter you want to use, and if necessary, locate and select the instance you want to measure from the "Instances of selected object" box.
- To view information about a performance counter, click the Show Description check box.
- Click the Add button to add the performance counter to the Added Counters list box.
- Repeat this process for each counter you want to use, and then click OK in the Add Counters dialog box.
- To focus on performance measurements for a specific counter, select that counter in the legend area or by clicking on its line in the line graph.
- If you want to highlight a specific performance counter in the graph, click the performance counter in the legend, and then click the Highlight button. Click the Highlight button a second time if you want to turn off the highlight.
- If you want to save the graph, click the Freeze Display button, right-click the graph, click Save Image As on the shortcut menu, select the drive and folder in the Save As dialog box where you want to save the performance information, type a filename in the File name box, and then click Save.
- Click the Unfreeze Display button again to view further updates to the graph.
- When you have finished your performance measurements, close the Reliability and Performance Monitor window.

Performance Monitor is a powerful tool for analyzing nearly every aspect of your computer's performance. Because of the extensive number of performance counters and the ways that you can combine these performance counters to evaluate your computer, you could develop a career devoted exclusively to performance monitoring of computers.

Using Reliability and Performance Monitor to Examine Memory Performance

In the first part of the tutorial, you used Reliability and Performance Monitor to create a system health report to identify any potential problem with the performance or security of your computer and to also produce a detailed analysis so that you can then further research potential problems. As part of the system health report, Reliability and Performance Monitor also provides information on the current memory usage by reporting on the values of key performance counters.

Shuang asks you to create another system health report, and then examine the information on memory usage.

To complete the following steps, you must provide Administrator credentials. If you are not logged on under an Administrator account or cannot provide the password for an Administrator account, read the following steps and examine the figures so that you are familiar with the use of Reliability Monitor, but do not keystroke the steps.

To create a system health report:

1. On the Start menu, open **Control Panel**, click the **System and Maintenance** link, click the **Performance Information and Tools** link, click the **Advanced tools** link under Tasks, and then click the **Generate a system health report** link. Windows Vista switches to Secure Desktop Mode and displays a User Account Control dialog box.
2. In the User Account Control dialog box, click the **Continue** button if you are logged on under an Administrator account, or if you are logged on under a Standard User account, enter the **password** for an Administrator account, click the **OK** button, maximize the Reliability and Performance Monitor window, and wait for Reliability and Performance Monitor to produce the System Diagnostics Report.
3. Locate and click the **Expand Details** button for the Memory section, click the **Expand Details** button for the Counters section, and then adjust your view so that you can see the details on the memory performance counters, as shown in Figure 9-39. The Performance Counter column includes the Available Bytes, Committed Bytes, and Pages/sec performance counters that you used with Performance Monitor as well as many other memory performance counters. The System Diagnostics Report also provides the mean, minimum, and maximum value for each of these memory performance counters. The maximum value for Committed Bytes is 967,217,152 bytes (or 922 MB) of memory currently in use. The minimum value for Available Bytes is 1,291,337,728 (or 1.2 GB) of memory available for use. Pages/sec ranged from 0 to 1,756. Cache Bytes is the amount of memory set aside for storing pages read from disk and kept in the cache in case you need the data in these pages later. That, in turn, obviates the need for reading the pages in from disk again (and again). Page Faults/sec, which ranges from 0 to 16,072, measures the number of requests for pages from either disk or elsewhere in physical memory. Your details will differ.

Tip

You can use Performance Monitor to select and view a description with Help information on each of these counters.

Figure 9-39 Viewing memory performance data

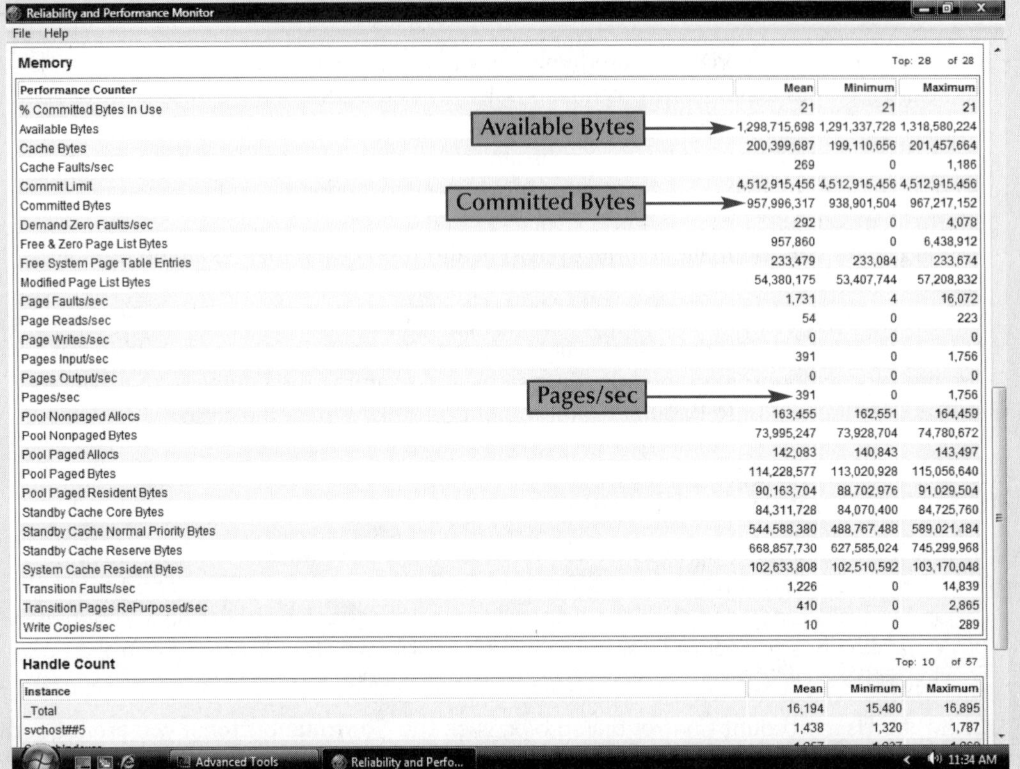

Memory — Top: 28 of 28

Performance Counter	Mean	Minimum	Maximum
% Committed Bytes In Use	21	21	21
Available Bytes	1,298,715,698	1,291,337,728	1,318,580,224
Cache Bytes	200,399,687	199,110,656	201,457,664
Cache Faults/sec	269	0	1,186
Commit Limit	4,512,915,456	4,512,915,456	4,512,915,456
Committed Bytes	957,996,317	938,901,504	967,217,152
Demand Zero Faults/sec	292	0	4,078
Free & Zero Page List Bytes	957,860	0	6,438,912
Free System Page Table Entries	233,479	233,084	233,674
Modified Page List Bytes	54,380,175	53,407,744	57,208,832
Page Faults/sec	1,731	4	16,072
Page Reads/sec	54	0	223
Page Writes/sec	0	0	0
Pages Input/sec	391	0	1,756
Pages Output/sec	0	0	0
Pages/sec	391	0	1,756
Pool Nonpaged Allocs	163,455	162,551	164,459
Pool Nonpaged Bytes	73,995,247	73,928,704	74,780,672
Pool Paged Allocs	142,083	140,843	143,497
Pool Paged Bytes	114,228,577	113,020,928	115,056,640
Pool Paged Resident Bytes	90,163,704	88,702,976	91,029,504
Standby Cache Core Bytes	84,311,728	84,070,400	84,725,760
Standby Cache Normal Priority Bytes	544,588,380	488,767,488	589,021,184
Standby Cache Reserve Bytes	668,857,730	627,585,024	745,299,968
System Cache Resident Bytes	102,633,808	102,510,592	103,170,048
Transition Faults/sec	1,226	0	14,839
Transition Pages RePurposed/sec	410	0	2,865
Write Copies/sec	10	0	289

Handle Count — Top: 10 of 57

Instance	Mean	Minimum	Maximum
_Total	16,194	15,480	16,895
svchost##5	1,438	1,320	1,787

4. Right-click the **background** of the System Diagnostics Report that contains the Memory performance counters, and then click **Print Preview** on the shortcut menu. Print Preview displays the first of two pages for this report. On the computer used for Figure 9-40, note that the first page contains warnings, information on the status of system checks, and a resource overview. Your Print Preview may differ.

Viewing the first page of the System Diagnostics Report

Figure 9-40

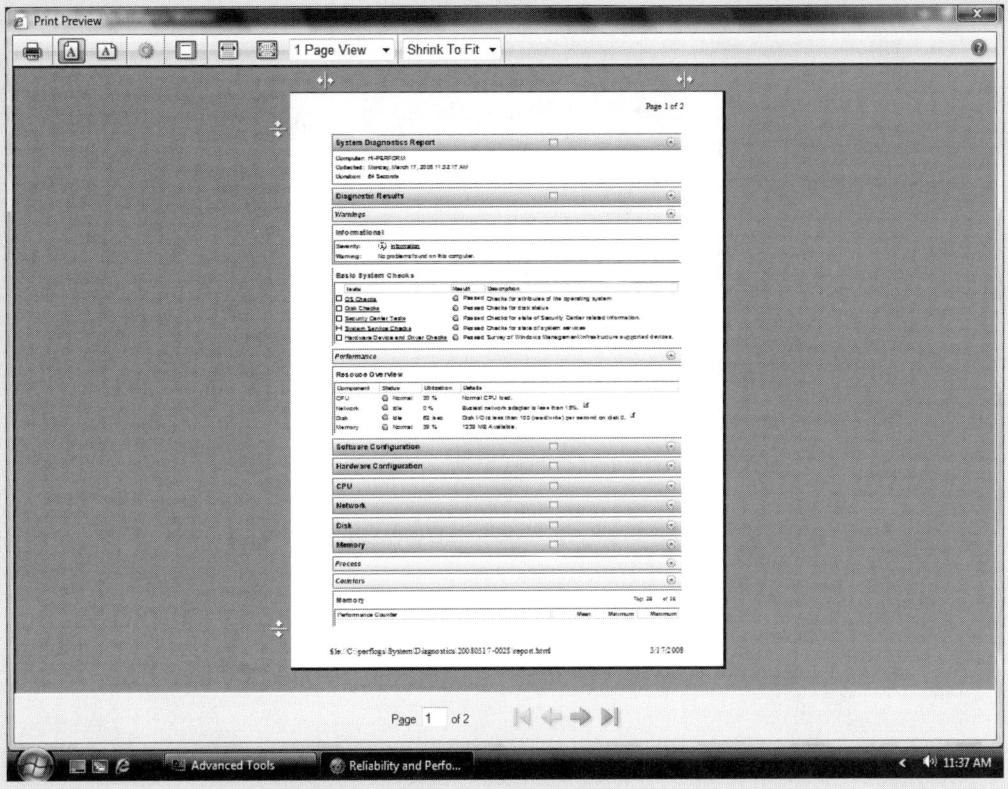

5. Click the **Next Page** button to the right of the Page box on the Status Bar. The next page of this report contains the values for Memory Performance counters at the time you produced the System Diagnostics Report. Your Print Preview may differ. You can print this report, or you can return to the System Diagnostics Report.

6. Close the Print Preview window, close the Reliability and Performance Monitor window, and then close the Advanced Tools window.

When you right-click the Memory performance counter results in Reliability and Performance Monitor, the shortcut menu may also contain an "Export to Microsoft Excel" option which copies the Memory performance counters and their mean, minimum, and maximum values to a new Microsoft Excel spreadsheet so that you can analyze the data further. Figure 9-41 shows an Excel spreadsheet with performance counters exported from the Reliability and Performance Monitor's System Diagnostics Report.

Figure 9-41 Viewing exported performance data in an Excel spreadsheet

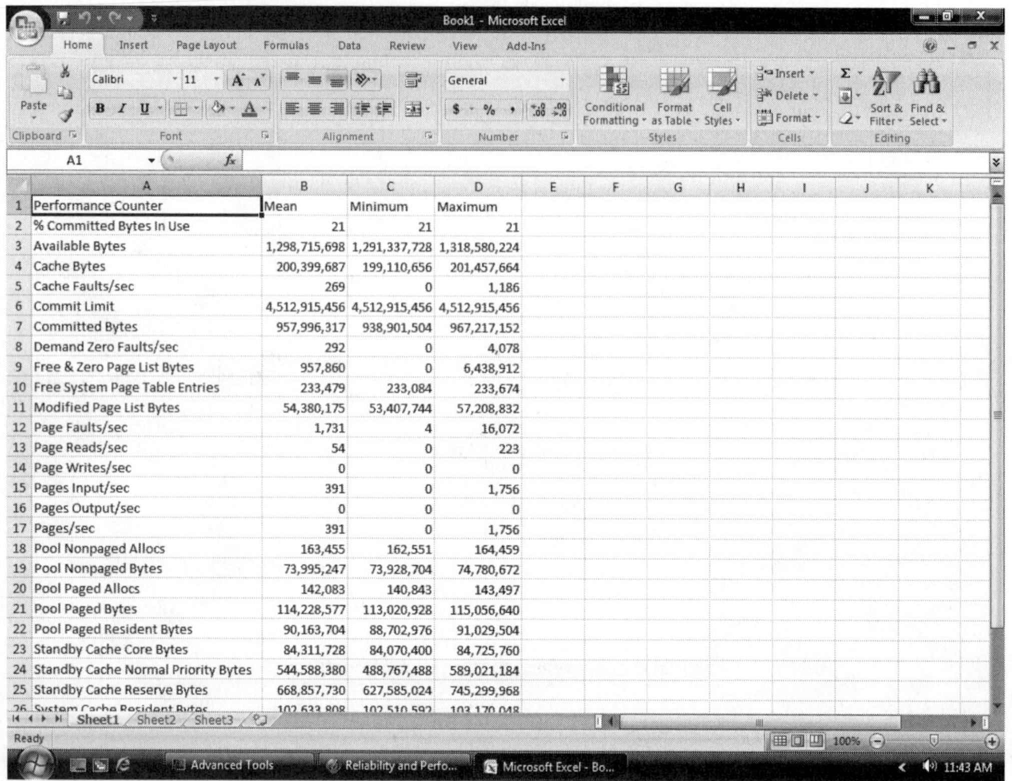

Performance Counter	Mean	Minimum	Maximum
% Committed Bytes In Use	21	21	21
Available Bytes	1,298,715,698	1,291,337,728	1,318,580,224
Cache Bytes	200,399,687	199,110,656	201,457,664
Cache Faults/sec	269	0	1,186
Commit Limit	4,512,915,456	4,512,915,456	4,512,915,456
Committed Bytes	957,996,317	938,901,504	967,217,152
Demand Zero Faults/sec	292	0	4,078
Free & Zero Page List Bytes	957,860	0	6,438,912
Free System Page Table Entries	233,479	233,084	233,674
Modified Page List Bytes	54,380,175	53,407,744	57,208,832
Page Faults/sec	1,731	4	16,072
Page Reads/sec	54	0	223
Page Writes/sec	0	0	0
Pages Input/sec	391	0	1,756
Pages Output/sec	0	0	0
Pages/sec	391	0	1,756
Pool Nonpaged Allocs	163,455	162,551	164,459
Pool Nonpaged Bytes	73,995,247	73,928,704	74,780,672
Pool Paged Allocs	142,083	140,843	143,497
Pool Paged Bytes	114,228,577	113,020,928	115,056,640
Pool Paged Resident Bytes	90,163,704	88,702,976	91,029,504
Standby Cache Core Bytes	84,311,728	84,070,400	84,725,760
Standby Cache Normal Priority Bytes	544,588,380	488,767,488	589,021,184
Standby Cache Reserve Bytes	668,857,730	627,585,024	745,299,968
System Cache Resident Bytes	102,633,808	102,510,592	103,170,048

Using the System Diagnostics Report | Reference Window

- On the Start menu, open Control Panel, click the System and Maintenance link, click the Performance Information and Tools link, click the Advanced tools link under Tasks, and then click the Generate a system health report link.
- After Windows Vista switches to Secure Desktop Mode and displays a User Account Control dialog box, click Continue if you are logged on under an Administrator account, or if you are logged on under a Standard User account, enter the password for an Administrator account, click the OK button, maximize the Reliability and Performance Monitor window, and wait for Reliability and Performance Monitor to produce the System Diagnostics Report.
- Locate and click the Expand Details button for the Memory section, click the Expand Details button for the Counters section, and then adjust your view so that you can see the details on the memory performance counters.
- Examine the information on Memory performance counters, and if necessary, use Performance Monitor to locate Help information on a performance counter.
- If you want to preview and then print the current view of the System Diagnostics Report, right-click the background of the System Diagnostics Report, click Print Preview on the shortcut menu, and examine the preview in the Print Preview window. Click the Print Document button on the Print Preview toolbar to print the report, or close the window to return to the System Diagnostics Report.
- If you want to copy the Memory performance counters and their mean, minimum, and maximum values to a new Microsoft Excel spreadsheet so that you can analyze the data further, right-click the background of the System Diagnostics Report, and then click the "Export to Microsoft Excel" option.
- Close the Reliability and Performance Monitor window, and then close the Advanced Tools window.

The System Diagnostics Report is a snapshot of your computer at a specific point in time. If you are experiencing problems with your computer, such as a slow response time, you can produce a new System Diagnostics Report so that you can examine memory usage and check for any other types of problems that Reliability and Performance Monitor might report.

Examining Virtual Memory Settings

Another way to manage memory is to examine which drives Windows Vista uses for paging files. If your computer has more than one drive, but Windows Vista maintains a paging file on only one drive, such as drive C, you can use the Properties dialog box for your computer to find out whether another drive on your computer has more storage space. If that drive is accessed less frequently than drive C, is a faster drive, and has more storage space, it might make more sense to use that drive for the paging file, and thereby free up valuable storage space on drive C for installed applications and the operating system and reduce disk access. Microsoft recommends that you do not put a paging file on the same drive as the system files, and it also recommends that you do not put multiple paging files on different partitions of the same physical hard disk. Although you can specify no paging file, Microsoft recommends against that option. Unless you have enough physical memory, or RAM, you need at least one paging file on one of the drives. If you specify no paging file, you might not be able to boot your computer. Windows Vista also stores information on serious error conditions in the paging file so that you can send an error report with that information to Microsoft for analysis at the next successful boot of your computer.

As you examine virtual memory settings in the tutorial steps, you will discover that the default setting for managing the paging file is "System managed size." That means that Windows Vista manages the size of the paging file to optimize the performance of your computer, so you may never need to change your virtual memory settings.

For an upcoming professional development day for employees, Shuang asks you to show the staff how to view and analyze additional information about the performance of applications on their computers, environment variable settings, and startup and recovery options.

To complete the following steps, you must provide Administrator credentials. If you are not logged on under an Administrator account or cannot provide the password for an Administrator account, read the following steps and examine the figures, but do not keystroke the steps.

To view virtual memory settings:

1. Right-click the **Computer** icon, click **Properties**, and under Tasks in the System window, click the **Advanced system settings** link. Windows Vista switches to Secure Desktop Mode and displays a User Account Control dialog box.
2. In the User Account Control dialog box, click the **Continue** button if you are logged on under an Administrator account, or if you are logged on under a Standard User account, enter the **password** for an Administrator account, and then click the **OK** button. Windows Vista opens the System Properties dialog box and displays the Advanced property sheet in the foreground. The Advanced property sheet provides access to information about settings for performance, user profiles, startup and recovery, and environment variables. See Figure 9-42.

Figure 9-42 Advanced property sheet in the System Properties dialog box

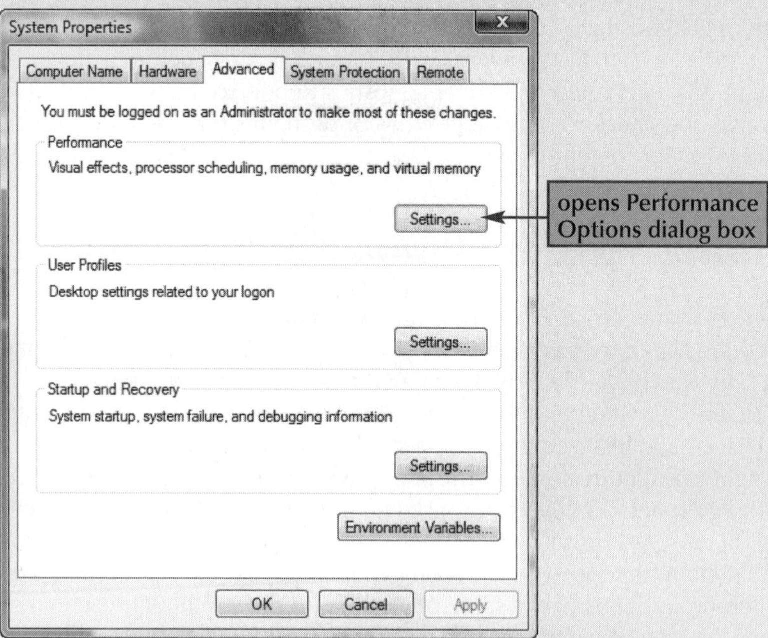

3. Under Performance, click the **Settings** button. On the Visual Effects property sheet, you can let Windows Vista select the best settings for your computer. You can also adjust settings on your computer for either the best appearance or the best performance, or you can choose which settings you want in the Custom box.

4. Click the **Advanced** tab. You can adjust the Processor Scheduling setting and view virtual memory settings. By default, Windows Vista enables the Programs option button under Processor Scheduling, and Windows Vista provides more processor resources to the foreground program than background services. As a result, your foreground program performs more smoothly and faster. If you select the Background services option under Processor Scheduling, all programs receive an equal amount of processor resources.

5. Under Virtual memory, click the **Change** button. Windows Vista by default automatically manages paging files on all drives; however, if you turn off this option, you can select a drive in the "Paging file size for each drive" list box, and then specify a custom size by entering a minimum and maximum size in MB. See Figure 9-43. Once you specify a custom size, you click the Set button to apply that setting. You can also specify no paging file, but that is generally not recommended. At the bottom of the Virtual Memory dialog box, Windows Vista summarizes the total paging file size for all drives. On the computer used for this figure, the recommended size is 3066 MB (or approximately 3 GB), which is 50 percent higher than the amount of installed 2 GB of RAM. The currently allocated size is 2,344 MB (or approximately 2.3 GB). The minimum allowed size is 16 MB. Your settings may differ.

Viewing virtual memory settings

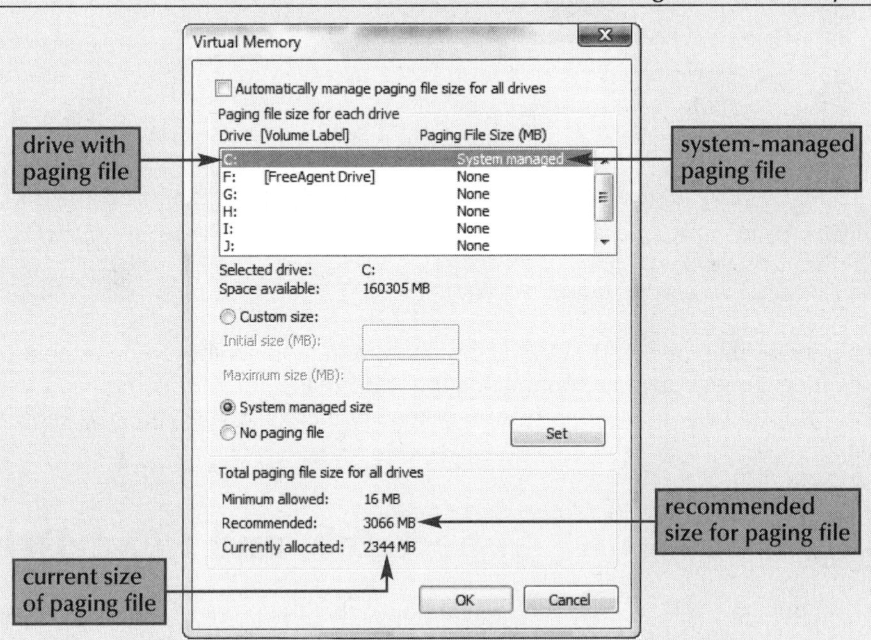

6. Click the **Cancel** button to close the Virtual Memory dialog box without making changes, click the **Cancel** button to close the Performance Options dialog box without making changes, click the **Cancel** button in the System Properties dialog box, and then close the System window.

As you change the way you work with your computer, Shuang mentions that you can adjust these virtual memory settings and optimize the use of paging files on multiple physical hard disk drives. If you routinely use programs that demand a lot of memory, and if you also discover that Windows Vista consistently uses more than 70 percent of the paging file, you can increase the size of the paging file to provide extra memory and thereby optimize performance, or better yet, you can install more RAM. If you want to move the paging file from one drive to another, you select the other drive and specify a paging file. Then, you select the drive from which you want to remove the paging file and choose the "No paging file option" button for that drive.

Reference Window | **Viewing Virtual Memory Settings**

- Right click the Computer icon, click Properties, and click the Advanced system settings link in the System window.
- After Windows Vista switches to Secure Desktop Mode and displays a User Account Control dialog box, click the Continue button if you are logged on under an Administrator account, or if you are logged on under a Standard User account, enter the password for an Administrator account and click the OK button.
- Click the Settings button Under Performance on the Advanced property sheet in the System Properties dialog box, click the Advanced tab in the Performance Options dialog box, and under Virtual memory, click the Change button.
- Examine the virtual memory settings for your computer in the "Total paging file size for all drives" section at the bottom of the Virtual Memory dialog box.
- If you want to specify your own virtual memory settings, remove the check mark from the "Automatically manage paging file size for all drives" check box, select a drive, click the Custom size option button, enter an Initial size and Maximum size for the paging file for the selected drive, click the Set button, click OK to close the Virtual Memory dialog box, click OK to close the Performance Options dialog box, click the OK button to close the System Properties dialog box, and then close the System window. You might need to reboot your computer with the new virtual memory settings.
- To close the Virtual Memory dialog box without making any changes to your virtual memory settings, click the Cancel button to close the Virtual Memory dialog box without making changes, click the Cancel button to close the Performance Options dialog box without making changes, click the Cancel button in the System Properties dialog box, and then close the System window.

Shuang notes that the Windows Vista operating system is rich in resources and tools for evaluating, configuring, and optimizing the performance of your computer. Later, if you need to locate any of this information or modify these settings, you now know where to look.

Using ReadyBoost, Superfetch, and ReadyDrive

When you purchase a flash drive, you might notice that the product label notes that the flash drive is "Enhanced for Windows® ReadyBoost™." **Windows ReadyBoost** is a new Windows Vista feature that uses some of the high-speed storage space on a flash drive to boost the performance of your computer by storing cached data on the flash drive. Accessing and loading small amounts of cached data on a flash drive is far faster than accessing and loading it from the hard disk drive.

When you insert a flash drive or a secure digital (SD) memory card with more than 256 MB of memory in a computer, Windows Vista will check the device to determine if it is fast enough to support Windows ReadyBoost. If so, it displays an AutoPlay dialog box similar to the one shown in Figure 9-44 with the option "Speed up my system using Windows ReadyBoost."

Option for boosting system performance with ReadyBoost **Figure 9-44**

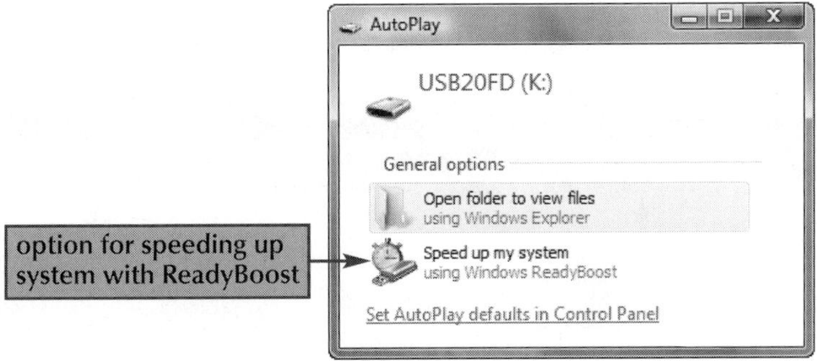

If you select the "Speed up my system" option, Windows Vista opens the Properties dialog box for the flash drive and displays the ReadyBoost property sheet, as shown in Figure 9-45. You can specify whether to use this flash drive to speed up your system by using storage space on the flash drive, and if so, you can specify how much space to reserve for optimizing the speed of your system. On the computer used for Figure 9-45, Windows recommends that 3,830 MB (or 3.74 GB) of the 4 GB of storage space be used for a ReadyBoost cache. That leaves only 98 MB of storage space for other files. If you need more storage space for files on the flash drive, you can adjust the amount of space you want to reserve for the ReadyBoost cache on the ReadyBoost property sheet.

Options for adjusting Windows ReadyBoost settings **Figure 9-45**

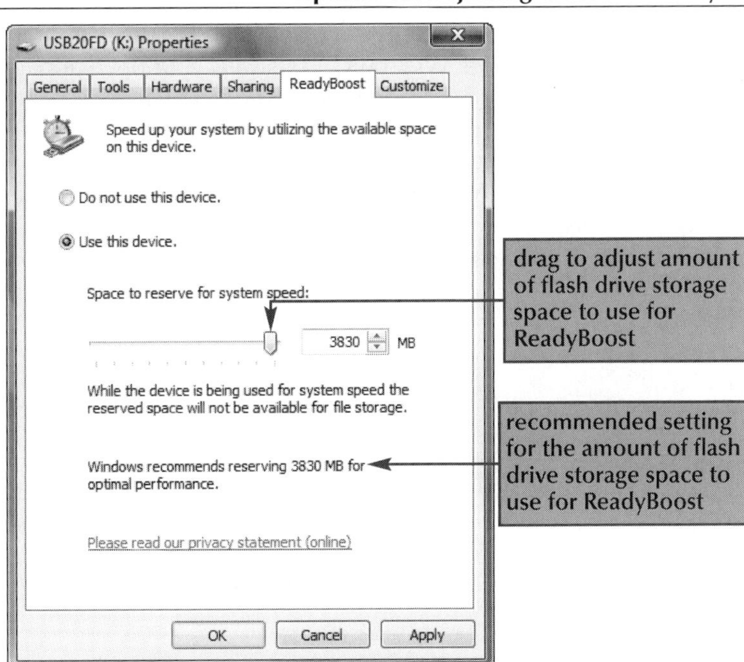

Once you enable ReadyBoost, you will see a ReadyBoost Cache File with the filename ReadyBoost.sfcache on the flash drive when you view its contents. See Figure 9-46.

Figure 9-46 Viewing the ReadyBoost cache file on a flash drive

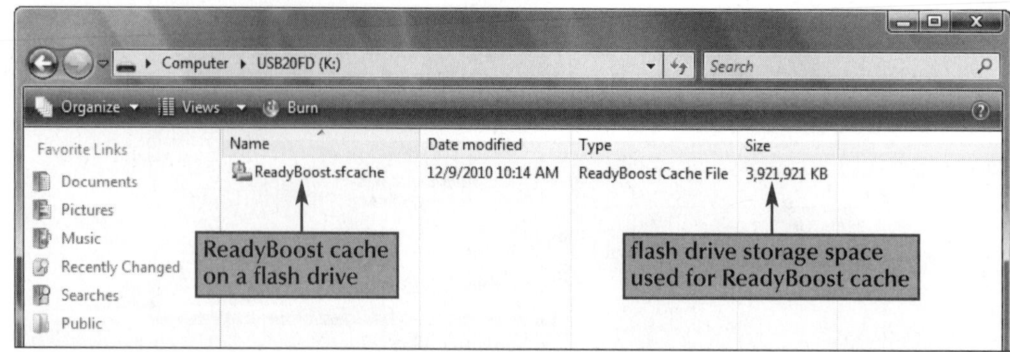

The ReadyBoost cache created on the flash drive is specific to the computer that you used to enable this feature. However, you can remove the flash drive and use it on other computers to store files on that portion of the flash drive not used by Windows ReadyBoost.

Superfetch, another Windows Vista technology, monitors the programs you use, the frequency with which you use those programs, and the dates and times you use those programs over a period of time in order to determine how you use your computer. Then, it preloads those programs so that they are available when you need them. That also means that it can preload different applications on different days of the week and weekend so that the appropriate programs are available to you.

Superfetch performs another important function. If your computer is idle, system background processes (such as SearchIndexer) become active and perform important functions. When they become active, Windows Vista swaps your open applications and programs to the paging file. Once background processes complete their operations, Superfetch quickly restores your applications and programs from the paging file to RAM so that they are ready for you to use.

ReadyDrive is a Windows Vista technology similar to ReadyBoost; however, it works with new types of hard disks called **hybrid hard disks** that contain built-in flash memory where ReadyDrive caches data. ReadyDrive can access this cached data even if the hard disk is turned off or powered down. Therefore, ReadyDrive can start up computers faster from a cold boot or from Sleep or Hibernation. That also means that ReadyDrive can turn off or power down the hard disk sooner, conserve battery power, and reduce wear and tear on the hard disk.

Restoring Your Computer

If you are working in a computer lab, or if you want to restore your desktop computer to the settings that existed prior to working on this tutorial, complete the following steps.

To restore your computer:

1. To remove Administrative Tools from the Start menu, right-click the **Start** button, click **Properties**, and on the Start Menu property sheet, click the Start menu **Customize** button to the right of Start menu, scroll to the bottom of the list of options for customizing the Start menu, and under System administrative tools, click the **Don't display this item** option button, click the **OK** button to close the Customize Start Menu dialog box, and then click the **OK** button to close the Taskbar and Start Menu Properties dialog box.

2. To restore double-click activation, hide file extensions, and not display hidden folders, files, and protected operating system files, click the **Computer** icon on the desktop, click the **Organize** button on the command bar, click **Folder and Search Options**, and on the General property sheet in the Folder Options dialog box, click the **Double-click to open an item (single-click to select)** option button, click the **View** tab, and in the Advanced Settings box, click the **Hide extensions for known file types** check box, click the **Do not show hidden files and folders** option button, click the **Hide protected operating system files (Recommended)** check box, click the **OK** button to close the Folder and Options dialog box, and then close the Computer window.
3. To remove the Computer icon from the desktop, open the **Start** menu, right-click **Computer**, and then click **Show on Desktop**.

Shuang is satisfied that you are prepared to train the staff how to view and analyze the performance information that Windows Vista provides.

Session 9.2 Quick Check | Review

1. A(n) ________________ allows you to sample a performance counter in a specific way.
2. A(n) ________________ is the physical memory allocated to and used by a single process or program.
3. What performance counter is the primary indicator of processor activity?
4. What performance counter is the primary indicator of hard page faults?
5. ________________ is a new Windows Vista feature that uses the high-speed storage space on a flash drive to augment the amount of memory in your computer.
6. Windows Vista's new ________________ feature keeps track of which programs and files you use and preloads them into RAM so that they are available when you need them.

Review | Tutorial Summary

In this tutorial, you examined the importance and use of RAM, virtual memory, and the paging file. You opened a Computer window, and then located and viewed the size of the paging file on your computer. Then, you used Windows Task Manager to examine information about CPU Usage, CPU Usage History, Memory usage, and Physical Memory Usage History on your computer. You opened and closed two applications and monitored changes in CPU and memory usage with Windows Task Manager, and then you analyzed the results to determine if a memory leak occurred. You opened Reliability and Performance Monitor and examined a Resource Overview of CPU, disk, and memory usage for your computer. You also viewed the currently running programs and their impact on CPU, disk, and memory usage. You then used Reliability and Performance Monitor to create a System Diagnostics Report that provided information on the health of your computer system at a specific point in time. In the System Diagnostics Report, you examined warnings, the results of basic system checks, a Resource Overview on the utilization of the CPU, network, disk, and memory. You examined the currently loaded startup programs and a list of hot files that cause the most disk I/Os on your computer. Next, you opened Performance Monitor, selected and customized performance counters, and monitored changes in % Processor Time, Available Bytes, Committed Bytes, Pages/sec, and Page File Bytes after initially starting your computer and after opening and closing an application. You also saved performance results for later analysis and printing. You created another System Diagnostics Report so that you can view a snapshot of memory performance counters. Then, you viewed the virtual memory settings on your computer, and finally, you examined how you can use Windows ReadyBoost to optimize the use of memory and improve your computer's performance.

Key Terms

handle
hybrid hard disks
instance
invalid page fault
kernel memory
legend
Master File Table Zone
memory leak
memory overuse
nonpaged kernel memory
page
paged kernel memory
paging
paging file
performance counter
performance object
RAM
ReadyDrive
Superfetch
system cache
thread
timer bar
value bar
virtual memory
Windows ReadyBoost

Practice | Review Assignments

Practice the skills you learned in the tutorial.

There are no Data Files needed for the Review Assignments.

In preparation for an upcoming staff training session on optimizing memory usage on a laptop, Shuang asks you to evaluate the performance of a laptop she recently acquired and prepare an analysis of its performance that she will use as background information in that training session.

As you complete each step in these Review Assignments, record your answers to questions so that you can submit them to your instructor. Use a word processing application, such as Word or WordPad, to prepare your answers to these questions. Also, if you change any settings on the computer you are using, note the original settings so that you can restore them later. Complete the following:

1. If necessary, display a Computer icon on the desktop, enable single-click activation, display hidden files and folders, display protected operating system files, and display Administrative Tools on the All Programs menu and Start menu.
2. Attach a flash drive to the computer, and if necessary, close any dialog boxes or windows that open.
3. Open a Computer window onto the drive that contains your computer's paging file, and then select and examine information about the paging file using the Details pane. What is the name of the paging file? What type of file is the paging file? How large is the paging file? Close the Computer window.
4. Right-click the taskbar, select the option for opening Task Manager, and then select its Performance sheet. What is the total physical memory on your computer? What percent of that memory is in use? How much of that memory is cached, and how much is free? How much memory is currently used? What is the current size of the paging file, and what is the total possible page file size on your computer?
5. Open a resource-intensive application, such as Internet Explorer, Microsoft Access, Microsoft PowerPoint, Microsoft Outlook, Adobe Dreamweaver, or Adobe PageMaker, but preferably another application, utility, or game that you did not open in the tutorial. What program did you open? What changes occurred in CPU Usage and Memory Usage when you opened that application? What percent of physical memory is in use? What is the current size of the paging file?
6. Close the program you just opened. What changes occurred in CPU Usage and Memory Usage when you closed that program? What percent of physical memory is now used? What is the current size of the paging file? Close Windows Task Manager.
7. Choose the option to open and run Reliability and Performance Monitor as an Administrator. Use the Resource Overview line graphs to describe the changes in CPU, disk, network, and memory usage that are currently occurring on your computer. What percent of physical memory is currently used?
8. Expand the Memory details section of Resource Overview and click the Image column header to sort the programs in alphabetical order. Locate the Image name explorer.exe. What does Resource Overview report on this program's commit bytes, working set, shareable memory, and private memory? Close the Reliability and Performance Monitor window.

9. Create a system health report (Administrator credentials required). Does the System Diagnostics Report display any warnings, and if so, what are they? Did Reliability and Performance Monitor report that any basic system checks failed, and if so, what are they? If necessary, expand the Performance section. In the Resource Overview, how much of memory is currently used, and how much is available? What is the status of the CPU and Disk? How would you rate the performance of your computer? Explain.
10. Expand the Memory section, and then expand the Counters section. What is the mean value for Available Bytes, and how many megabytes or gigabytes does that represent? What is the mean value for Committed Bytes, and how many megabytes or gigabytes does that represent? What is the mean rate of Pages/sec? Close the Reliability and Performance Monitor window and the Advanced Tools window (if necessary).
11. Open Performance Monitor with Administrator credentials. From the Memory performance object category, select and add the Available Bytes, Committed Bytes, and Pages/sec performance counters to the Added counters list box. From the Process performance object category, select and add the Page File Bytes _Total instance performance counter to the Added counters list box. Use the descriptions provided by Performance Monitor in the Add Counters dialog box to explain concisely what each of these performance counters measures. After selecting and adding these two performance counters, close the Add Counters dialog box.
12. Sort the performance counters in the legend in alphabetical order by Counter name. Check the scale for each counter, and if necessary, adjust a counter's scale so that its plotted values appear within the visible area of the graph.
13. Freeze the display and save the current graph view in an Image file named **Initial Performance Measurements** on your flash drive.
14. Choose each counter in the legend and list its last recorded value and its maximum value.
15. Unfreeze the display and open an application, utility, or game that you have not yet opened on your computer. Freeze the display after activity correlated with the opening of this program stabilizes, and then save the current graph view on your flash drive in an Image file named **After Opening** followed by the name of the program. What program did you choose?
16. Choose each counter in the legend, and then list its last recorded value and its maximum value.
17. Select each counter in the legend again and *concisely* describe the changes in the performance counters and how each change affected your computer as Windows Vista opened the program you chose.
18. Unfreeze the display, close the program, and then freeze the display after activity correlated with the closing of this program stabilizes. Save the current graph view on your flash drive in an Image file named **After Closing** followed by the name of the program.
19. Choose each counter in the legend, and then list its last recorded value and its maximum value.
20. Select each counter in the legend again and *concisely* describe the changes in the performance counters and how each change affected your computer as the program closed.

21. Prepare a table that lists the last recorded value for Available Bytes, Committed Bytes, and Page File Bytes prior to opening a program, after opening a program, and then after closing a program. Examine the results. Was Windows able to reclaim all of the allocated memory, or was there a memory leak? If there was a memory leak, what was the size of the memory leak? Are there any other conclusions that you can draw from this data? If so, concisely describe them.
22. Based on your observations of what happened when you opened and then closed a program, what would you expect to happen if you opened and then later closed a different program on your computer (one that you had not opened previously)? Close the Reliability and Performance Monitor window.
23. Choose the option to view properties of the Computer icon, and then open Advanced system settings. After providing Administrator credentials, use the Settings button under Performance to display the Performance Options dialog box, and then choose the Advanced tab and use the Change button under Virtual memory to view virtual memory settings. Does Windows Vista manage the paging file, or have you (or someone else) set a custom initial size and maximum size, and if so, what are these sizes? On what drive is the paging file located? What is the recommended and currently allocated size of the paging file? What other drives, if any, are available on your computer for creating paging files? Use the Cancel button to close the Virtual Memory, Performance Options, and System Properties dialog box without making changes to your computer. Then close the System window.
24. Open a Computer window, right-click your flash drive, and choose the option to view its properties. Select the ReadyBoost property sheet. Does Windows Vista report that this flash drive supports the Windows ReadyBoost feature? If so, how much space is actually allocated for optimizing system speed, or how much space does Windows Vista recommend for optimizing the performance of your computer? How much total storage space does your flash drive have? Close the flash drive Properties dialog box.
25. Submit the results of the preceding steps to your instructor, either in printed or electronic form, as requested.

Apply | Case Problem 1

Use the skills you learned to evaluate the performance of a computer for a self-employed writer.

There are no Data Files needed for this Case Problem.

Trent Danford Trent Danford is a successful, self-employed writer who regularly contributes articles on innovative scientific and technological inventions to national magazines. Since Trent must meet frequent deadlines for contributing articles, he needs a reliable computer that is configured for optimal performance. He enlists your help in evaluating the performance of his computer during a typical workday.

To complete this case problem, you will need to provide Administrator credentials to open Reliability and Performance Monitor and use Performance Monitor. As you complete each step in this case, record your answers to questions so that you can submit them to your instructor. Use a word processing application, such as Word or WordPad, to prepare your answers to these questions. Also, if you change any settings on the computer you are using, note the original settings so that you can restore them later. Complete the following:

1. View your computer's System Properties. What version of Windows Vista are you using? What is your computer's Windows Experience Index rating? What type of processor does your computer use, and what is its clock speed? How much memory (RAM) does your computer have? Is your Windows Vista version a 32-bit or 64-bit operating system? Close the System window.
2. Open Performance Monitor with Administrator credentials, add the following performance counters, sort the legend in alphabetical order by counter name, and then scale the counters to automatically fit within the plotting area of the line graph:
   - Available Bytes for the Memory performance object
   - Committed Bytes for the Memory performance object
   - Pages/sec for the Memory performance object
   - Page File Bytes Peak and _Total instance for the Process performance object
   - Virtual Bytes Peak and _Total instance for the Process performance object
3. Verify that the % Processor Time performance counter is listed in the legend; if not, add this counter.
4. After adding these performance counters, freeze the display, and then record the last measured value for each of the performance counters in a table. Use "Activity" for the first column heading, use % Processor Time for the second column heading, and then use the names of the performance counter names listed in Step 2 as the column headings for each of the next five columns. Save a copy of your graph in an Image file named **Initial Performance Measurements**.
5. For the remainder of your work session, use your computer as you typically would, but where possible, note the basic types of tasks that you perform, such as checking e-mail, browsing the Web, using an application, attaching and unattaching your flash drive, opening a folder, searching the Web, or playing a game, etc. List each activity you perform in the first column, and list the performance measurements for each performance counter in the next six columns. After you open a program, freeze the display, update the table of measurements that you are tracking by briefly describing the operation you performed and recording the Maximum measured value for % Processor Time and Pages/sec and the Last measured value for the other performance counters, and then unfreeze the display to continue plotting performance counters.
6. After you complete your workday, save your graph in an Image file named **End of Session Performance Measurements**.
7. Analyze the information that you've collected on the performance of your computer. What conclusions would you draw about the impact of different types of operations (such as opening or closing applications, utilities, folders, and files, etc.) on the resources available in your computer? Were there any bottlenecks or problems? If so, what are they? Are there any ways in which you might be able to improve the performance of your computer? Was Windows Vista able to reclaim all of the memory it allocated during your work session, or was there a memory leak? Explain.
8. Submit the results of the preceding steps to your instructor, either in printed or electronic form, as requested.

Apply | Case Problem 2

Use the skills you learned to evaluate the performance of a computer for a Project Management company.

There are no Data Files needed for this Case Problem.

Aschbacher Project Managements, Inc. Shannon Longbotham works as a project management specialist for Aschbacher Project Management, Inc., an American corporation in Chicago. She works closely with her company's Fortune 500 clients to develop strategies for organizing, implementing, and evaluating company projects. Shannon needs a high-performance computer that is optimally configured so that she can manage multiple client projects. She asks you to perform a thorough analysis of her computer.

To complete this case problem, you will need to provide Administrator credentials to open Reliability and Performance Monitor and use Performance Monitor. You also must work on a computer with Microsoft Office or one that has four major software applications.

As you complete each step in this case, record your answers to questions so that you can submit them to your instructor. Use a word processing application, such as Word or WordPad, to prepare your answers to these questions. Also, if you change any settings on the computer you are using, note the original settings so that you can restore them later. Complete the following:

1. View your computer's System Properties. What edition of Windows Vista are you using? What is your computer's Windows Experience Index rating? What type of processor does your computer use, and what is its clock speed? How much memory (RAM) does Windows Vista report for your computer? Is your Windows Vista version a 32-bit or 64-bit operating system?
2. View, and then list your Windows Experience Index subscores. Close the System window.
3. Open Performance Monitor with Administrator credentials and add performance counters for tracking allocated memory, available memory, the number of pages per second read from or written to disk, the number of bytes used by all processes in the paging file, and the maximum amount (or peak value) for the amount of bytes used by all processes in the paging file. Verify that you have also included the performance counter for measuring the percent of processor time. List the names of the performance objects and their corresponding performance counters.
4. Sort the legend in alphabetical order by counter name, and then scale the counters to automatically fit within the plotting area of the line graph.
5. **EXPLORE** Use the Change graph type button on the Performance Monitor toolbar to switch to Report view.
6. Read this step before you record performance data. Freeze the display, and then record the values for each of the performance counters in a table. In the first column, note that the measurements are your initial or starting performance measurements, and in the next six columns, list the names of the performance counters, and then record the initial or starting performance values you record for each performance counter on the next line in the table. (*Note*: To accommodate this wide table, use Page Setup on the File menu to change your page orientation to landscape.) Also, for long performance counter names, enter the names on two lines so that you can include all columns in one table. If performance counters contain decimal values with zeroes (such as .000), do not record the zeroes.

7. Unfreeze the display, and then open the following applications on your computer, one right after the other: Microsoft Word, Microsoft Excel, Microsoft PowerPoint, Microsoft Access (if the latter is installed on your computer), and Microsoft Outlook (if you use this e-mail software and if you have already configured it). List the names of the applications you opened.
8. Freeze the display, and then record the values for each of the performance counters in your table. In the first column, note that the next set of measurements are ones taken after you opened Microsoft Office applications.
9. Unfreeze the display, close all of the open applications, freeze the display again, and then record the current settings for your performance counters in your table. In the first column, note that the next set of measurements are ones taken after you closed all Microsoft Office applications.
10. Analyze your performance measurements to determine the impact of Microsoft Office applications on your computer, and then answer the following questions:
    a. What was the impact on memory of opening four major software applications?
    b. After you closed all applications, did Windows Vista reclaim all of the memory it originally allocated before opening the applications, or was there a memory leak? Explain.
    c. What was the impact on the paging file of opening and multitasking with four major software applications?
    d. What was the impact on the processor of opening four major software applications?
    e. Does your computer have enough installed RAM to support multitasking of major applications? Explain.
    f. Do any of these changes in system performance correlate with your Windows Experience Index subscores? Explain.
11. Submit the results of the preceding steps to your instructor, either in printed or electronic form, as requested.

Challenge | Case Problem 3

Use the skills you learned to identify tools for collecting information at a consulting firm.

There are no Data Files needed for this Case Problem.

Prescott Systems, Inc. Xavier Calderon works as a Security Specialist for Prescott Systems, Inc., a New York state consulting firm that provides network security services for local government agencies. One of Xavier's coworkers has noticed an extensive amount of disk I/O and thrashing (excessive paging) on his computer, and Xavier has asked you to help this coworker identify tools that he might use to collect more information about this potential problem.

Use a word processing application, such as Word or WordPad, to prepare your answers to these questions.

EXPLORE

1. Identify how Xavier's coworker might use each of the following Windows Vista tools to locate information about disk I/O and paging.
    a. Windows Task Manager
    b. Resource Overview
    c. System Diagnostics Report
    d. Performance Monitor

   Be as specific as possible when you provide information about the use of these tools.

EXPLORE

2. Are there other tools that you examined in previous tutorials that Xavier's coworker might use to assist him?

EXPLORE

3. Would the following factors affect overall disk I/O, and if so, how?
   a. RAM
   b. Paging File
   c. Windows ReadyBoost
   d. Processor
4. Submit the results of the preceding steps to your instructor, either in printed or electronic form, as requested.

Apply | Case Problem 4

Use the skills you learned in the tutorial to evaluate startup programs on computers at a Welsh travel firm.

There are no Data Files needed for this Case Problem.

Portnoy Designs Celeste Portnoy is a fashion designer who recently launched her own firm after working in the fashion industry for many years with other firms. Recently, she experienced problems with her laptop, and she asks you to ascertain the source of the problem. You decide to start by creating a system health report for her laptop.

As you complete each step in this case, record your answers to questions so that you can submit them to your instructor. Use a word processing application, such as Word or WordPad, to prepare your answers to these questions. Also, if you change any settings on the computer you are using, note the original settings so that you can restore them later.

1. After examining the System Diagnostics Report for Celeste's laptop, you notice the following findings:
   - The System Stability Report includes the following warnings under Diagnostic Results:
     - The Security Center reports that Windows Update is disabled.
     - The Security Center has not recorded an antivirus product.
     - The average disk queue length is 2. The disk may be at its maximum transfer capacity due to throughput and disk seeks.
   - Under Basic System Checks, one of the Disk Checks tests notes that Drive C has 21 percent free disk space.
   - Resource Overview shows a high level of disk I/O during certain periods of time when the computer is presumably idle.
   - Under the Disk details section, the System Diagnostics Report shows that a component of the Windows Vista Search engine and one of the startup programs on the laptop are causing the most disk I/Os.
   - Under Report Statistics, you discover that the laptop has 1024 MB of RAM.
2. After reviewing these findings, what changes would you recommend to Celeste's laptop? Also explain why you would make these recommendations.
3. Based on the information that you found, what other tools might you use to further analyze this problem? Be as specific as possible.
4. Submit the results of the preceding steps to your instructor, either in printed or electronic form, as requested.

Review | Quick Check Answers

Session 9.1

1. paging file
2. True
3. memory leak (or memory overuse)
4. system cache
5. hard fault
6. virtual memory

Session 9.2

1. instance
2. working set
3. % Processor Time
4. Pages/sec
5. Windows ReadyBoost
6. Superfetch

Ending Data Files

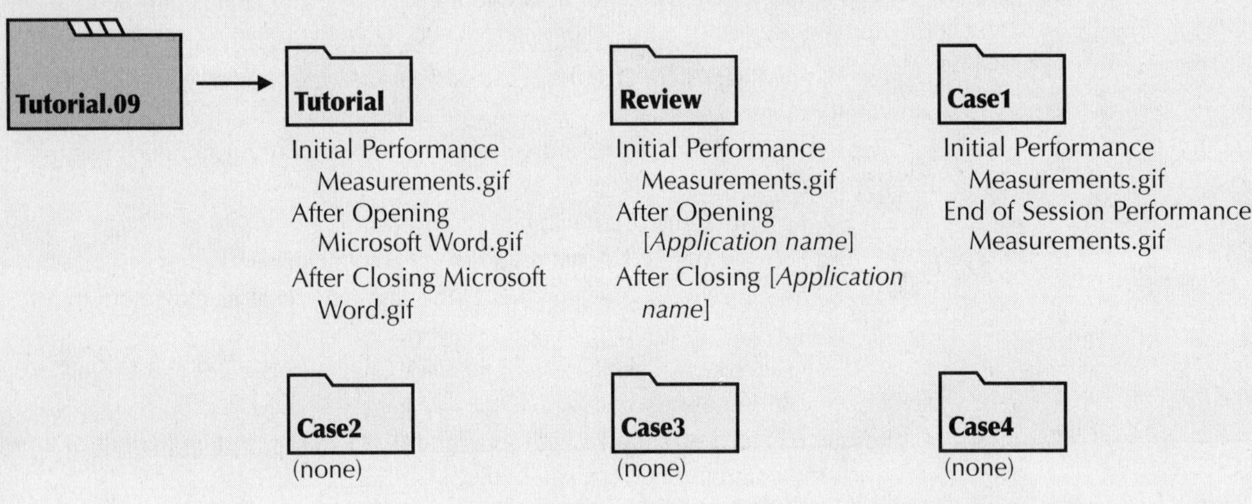

Objectives

Session 10.1
- Learn why backups are important
- Examine backup strategies
- Evaluate how backup software uses the Archive attribute
- Compare two ways to back up and restore files

Session 10.2
- Examine shadow copy technology
- Restore previous versions of files
- Use the Windows Briefcase to synchronize and update files
- Examine the Windows Vista Sync Center

Backing Up and Restoring Files

Protecting Your Important Files

Case | Gaia Cartographics

Gaia Cartographics is a small company in Santa Fe, New Mexico, that specializes in aerial, satellite, and digital mapping. Thiago Ribeiro, a mapping specialist, is currently preparing maps of the Amazon River and the Brazilian rainforest, a biome that contains a greater variety of plant and animal life than any other region of the world. To ensure that he has backup copies of all his maps, Thiago relies on the Backup and Restore Center in his Business Edition of Windows Vista.

In this tutorial, you examine the importance of backing up your computer and explore backup strategies that combine the use of full backups with differential or incremental backups. You evaluate the use of the Archive attribute in identifying files to include in a backup. You open the Backup and Restore Center and compare options for backing up folders and files, restoring folders and files, making a Complete PC backup, and restoring a Complete PC backup. Then, you investigate the use of Previous Versions and shadow copies for restoring folders and files. You also view Previous Versions of files on your computer. You create a Briefcase and use the Briefcase to synchronize changes in files in two locations—your hard disk drive and the Briefcase on a flash drive. You also examine the use of the new Windows Vista Sync Center.

Starting Data Files

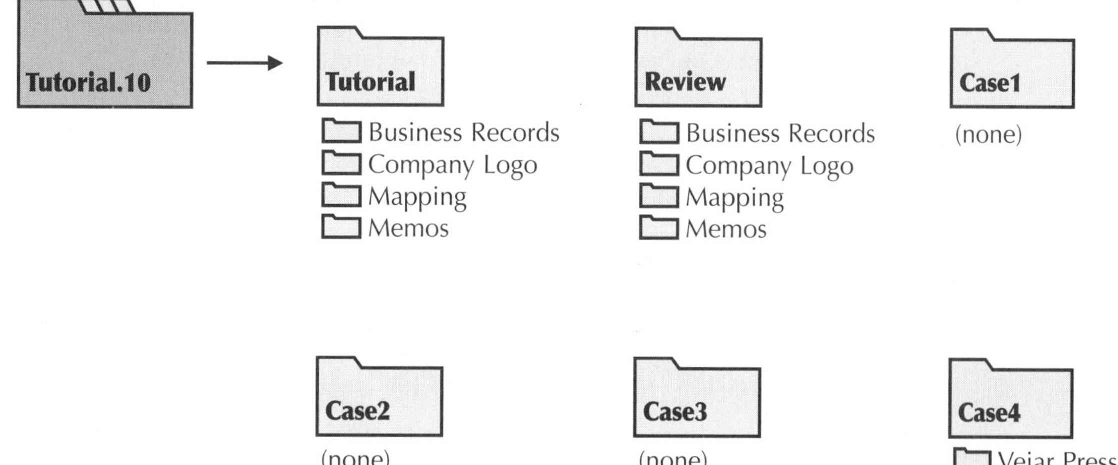

Session 10.1

Setting Up Your Computer

To complete this tutorial, you must display the Computer icon on the desktop and switch your computer to single-click activation. In the following steps, you will check, and if necessary, change these settings, copy the Data Files needed for this tutorial to the Public Documents folder, and then reboot your computer.

To set up your computer:

1. If Windows Vista does not display a Computer icon on the desktop, open the **Start** menu, right-click **Computer**, click **Show on Desktop**, and then close the Start menu.
2. If you need to enable single-click activation, double-click the **Computer** icon on the desktop, click the **Organize** button on the command bar, click **Folder and Search Options**, and under "Click items as follows" on the General property sheet in the Folder Options dialog box, click the **Single-click to open an item (point to select)** option button, click the **Underline icon titles only when I point at them** option button, click the **OK** button to close the Folder and Options dialog box, and then close the Computer window.

Next, you are going to copy the Data Files that you will need later in the tutorial to the Public Documents folder.

To copy the Data Files to your Public Documents folder:

1. Make sure you have a copy of the Windows Vista for Power User Data Files and that your computer can access them.

   Trouble? If you don't have the starting Data Files, you need to get them before you can proceed. Your instructor will either give you the Data Files or ask you to obtain them from a specified location (such as a network drive). In either case, make a backup copy of the Data Files before you start so that you will have the original files available in case you need to start over. If you have any questions about the Data Files, see your instructor or technical support person for assistance.
2. Close all open windows.
3. Open a window onto the Documents subfolder, your flash drive folder, or the network folder that contains a copy of the Tutorial.10 folder containing the Data Files for this tutorial, click **Tutorial.10** to open this folder, point to the **Tutorial** folder icon, click the **Organize** button on the command bar, and then click **Copy**.
4. On the Start menu, open **Documents**, click **Public** under Favorite Links in the Navigation Pane, click **Public Documents**, click the **Organize** button on the command bar, and then click **Paste**. Windows Vista copies the Tutorial folder from the Tutorial.10 folder to the Public Documents folder.
5. Select the **Tutorial** folder icon, press the **F2** key (the Rename key), type **Gaia Cartographics** and then press the **Enter** key.
6. Close the Public Documents folder window and the folder window that contains the original copy of the Tutorial.10 folder.

In the second session of the tutorial, you will work with these Data Files.

To improve the chances that you will have Previous Versions of these files for the second session of the tutorial, you are going to restart your computer. Windows Vista should create a Previous Version of these files after you shut down and then restart your computer. If you are working in a computer lab where the computer restores itself to its previous state after rebooting, you can skip the next set of steps and continue with the steps for creating a restore point.

To continue the process of preparing your computer:

1. Close any open windows and files.
2. On the Start menu, choose the option for restarting your computer.
3. If necessary, log on your computer under your user account.

Next, you are going to create a restore point for use in the second session of the tutorial. To perform this operation, you must provide Administrator credentials.

To create a restore point:

1. Right-click the **Computer** desktop icon, click **Properties**, and in the System window, click the **System protection** link under Tasks. Windows Vista switches to Secure Desktop Mode and displays a User Account Control dialog box.
2. If you are logged on under an Administrator account, click the **Continue** button. If you are not logged on under an Administrator account, enter the **password** for an Administrator account, and then click the **OK** button. Windows Vista displays the System Protection property sheet in the System Properties dialog box, and then locates and displays information about restore points in the Automatic restore points box.
3. Click the **Create** button, type **Manual Restore Point** in the next System Protection dialog box, click the **Create** button in this same dialog box, wait for System Protection to create a restore point, and then click the **OK** button in the next and last System Protection dialog box.
4. Click the **OK** button to close the System Properties dialog box, and then close the System window.

You have successfully created a restore point.

The Importance of Backing Up Files

Like other professionals who depend on their computers, Thiago understands the importance of regular backups. Several years ago, he accidentally deleted some important client contract files while he was rushing to meet a deadline. Fortunately, he had performed regular backups of his computer, so he quickly restored those client contract files from his backups so that he could complete negotiations on a new contract. Without those backups, he would have had to reconstruct the contract documents from scratch.

Common causes of loss of documents and data include the following:

- User errors (such as accidentally deleting folders and files or overwriting files)
- Malicious software, malicious Web sites, and hackers
- Power failures, power surges, or power brownouts
- Hardware malfunction or failure
- Software problems

- Theft or vandalism of a computer
- Natural disasters, including fires, floods, and earthquakes

The potential for accidentally losing important files is far greater today because of the variety of risks posed by malicious software introduced to a computer via e-mail attachments and Internet downloads. If you do not back up your computer, the time required for restoring important personal or business documents can become substantial. If you operate a business and do not routinely back up important business and client records, and if you lose all of your business and client records as a result of a problem, you could easily be out of business.

InSight | **Reducing the Risk of Problems on Your Computer**

As you've discovered in previous tutorials, you can use Windows tools and features, such as the Check Disk utility, to check and repair the hard disk's file system; Disk Defragmenter to optimize the use of storage space on your hard disk; and Disk Cleanup Wizard to fine-tune your computer on a regular basis. In addition, you should use and frequently update your antivirus software, anti-spyware software, and if necessary, your firewall to protect your computer from malicious software, malicious Web sites, and hackers. You should rely on the Windows Automatic Updates feature to automatically download and install critical security updates. Also, if you implement safe practices, such as using caution when opening e-mail attachments, you further reduce the risk of problems on your computer.

Even though the reliability of hard disk drives has improved considerably and the useful lifetime of a hard disk is estimated at seven years, hard disks are still susceptible to damage and failure. As noted, restoring the contents of a hard disk from scratch would be a formidable task (even if it's at all possible) and one that could cost you a lot of time and money. That's why it's important to regularly back up your hard disk. Think of a backup as an insurance policy that helps you protect your personal and business assets.

Approaches for Backing Up Files

The method you use to back up files on your computer depends on how you work, how much data you store on your hard disk, and how important the data in those files is to you. You can use different approaches to back up important files:

- **Copying files from a hard disk to some type of removable storage** You can copy important folders and files to a flash drive or burn them to a DVD or CD. This approach guarantees that you have at least two copies of important folders and files in two different locations. This backup approach is also useful if you need to make a quick backup at the end of a busy day before you leave the office or before you finish work on your home computer or a mobile PC. However, one potential problem with this approach is that if you store the same file on your hard disk and a flash drive, you might find later that you have made different changes to both copies of the same file so that you now have essentially two versions of that same file. Then, you are faced with the task of reconciling the differences between the two files, or you might inadvertently copy the older version of that file over the most recent version of that file, losing important changes. This problem is compounded if you work on multiple files on your home computer, copy them to a flash drive, and then later use another computer, such as your computer at work, to make revisions to those files. Then, you must remember which files you changed on the flash drive so that you can update those same files on your home computer (and vice versa). Also, if you use a DVD or CD to store copies of important files, you might need to use special software first, to format the discs (a time-consuming operation), and then record copies of those files onto the disc. That process can also take longer than a simple copy operation to a flash drive.

- **Copying files from a hard disk to an external hard disk drive or a network folder** External hard disk drives can easily provide enough storage space for backing up all your files or your entire computer, and this approach also guarantees that you have at least two copies in two different locations. If you have a home computer network, you can copy or back up files to a shared folder on another computer on the network. In fact, you might keep an older, but still useful, computer solely for this purpose. You might also purchase and employ newer technologies, such as Microsoft Home Server, to provided automated backups on networked computers that use Windows Vista.
- **Using a backup utility** If you work with a large number of files stored in many different folders on your hard disk, your best bet is to use a **backup utility** to back up those files onto some type of permanent, high-capacity storage medium, such as an external hard disk. Backup utilities use storage space more efficiently than copying files to a disk, and they can compress files to reduce the amount of storage space or media needed for a backup. You can also use a variety of backup media, such as external hard disk drives, DVDs, CDs, or a flash drive. If you experience a problem that results in the loss of folders and files, or even one file, on your hard disk, you can restore those folders or file, or a single file, from a backup that you made with the backup utility. You can use the Backup and Restore Center in Windows Vista, or you can purchase a backup utility that meets your specific needs.
- **Using shadow copies** Certain editions of Windows Vista automatically make copies of all folders and files on your computer at periodic intervals of time, and these copies are known as shadow copies. Later in this tutorial, you will learn more about shadow copy technology and examine how to restore files and folders using shadow copies. While this backup feature is invaluable when you lose an important file, the downside is that the shadow copies are stored on your hard disk along with the original copies of all your folders and files. If your hard disk fails, you have lost not only your original copies of your folders and files, but also your shadow copies of those same folders and files. That's why you need to make sure that you have at least one other copy of important files stored in a different location, such as on removable media, an external hard disk, or a network.

You might discover that a combination of these approaches serves your needs best, conveniently fits backups into your schedule, and guarantees that you can restore important files to your computer.

Organizing Folders and Files for Backups

Another important facet of backing up folders and files is to organize your folders and files logically so that you can quickly select those folders and files that you want to include in a backup. At certain times, you might want to back up all your folders and files. If your folders and files are stored in a single folder, such as the Documents folder, you can specify that you want to back up the Documents folder, and then immediately start your backup. At other times, you might want to back up only certain folders and files. If you have already organized your files into groups and placed those files into groups of logically related folders, you can more easily select the folders and files that you want to back up and be assured that you have a backup copy of all your important files. If you do not organize your files into folders and do not organize folders into logical groups as subfolders under one main folder, you must perform the time-consuming task of locating all the folders and files that you want to back up and hope that you have found everything you need to include in the backup (such as e-mail messages). You should also periodically reevaluate how you organize files by folder because you may discover a more efficient and more logical approach that makes it easier for you to locate the files you need when you must change those files and when you are ready to back up the files.

You may also want to periodically perform a **full system backup** where you make a backup copy of everything stored on your hard disk. Obviously, a full system backup requires an external hard disk or some other type of backup medium that has enough storage space to store the full system backup. If you encounter a problem later with your computer, you might need that full system backup to restore your entire system, your software applications, or all your folders and files. Although it's easy to reinstall software from DVDs or CDs that contain the software you purchased or by downloading and installing another copy of the software from the Internet, you must then obtain all the updates for the software since you originally installed it on your computer. You also have to devote time to specifying and customizing software settings so the software is set up the way you prefer to use it. If you reinstall software from a backup, you obviate the need for downloading all previous updates, and you retain your custom settings.

Developing an Effective Backup Strategy

To reduce the time, effort, and media required for backups; to guarantee that you have recent backups of important files that you work with daily; and to simplify the processing for restoring folders and files, you should develop and implement an effective backup strategy.

One commonly used backup strategy is to make a full backup at regular intervals, such as every week, month, quarter, or perhaps even every day. The interval of time between each full backup is called the **backup cycle**, and it begins by backing up your whole system, or an important or major part of your computer (such as your user folder, which contains the Documents, Contacts, Music, Pictures, Videos, Favorites, and Downloads subfolders, to name a few); continues with backups of important files at shorter intervals of time within each backup cycle; and then ends with the next full backup. The length of your backup cycle depends on how important your files are to you, how frequently you change your files and add new files, and how frequently you make changes to your computer system. For example, if you use your computer every day, and create and modify many files within a day, you might opt for a weekly or daily backup cycle. This first backup in a backup cycle is typically called a **full backup** or **normal backup** because it includes all your folders and files (or perhaps everything on your computer).

Combining Differential Backups with a Normal Backup

If you perform a full or normal backup each month (for example), you might want to perform either a differential or an incremental backup at the end of each week to streamline backups and save time, effort, and media as well as guarantee that you have backups of files that you create or change between normal backups. On the other hand, if you perform a full backup each week, you might perform a differential or incremental backup at the end of every day.

Unlike a full backup which includes all folders and files you select, a **differential backup** includes only new and modified files since your last full or normal backup. After you perform a full or normal backup, you have a copy of all your folders and files stored in your backup. However, you continue to make changes to the folders and files on your hard disk and create new folders and files. That means that you do not have a backup of the changes to the folders and files you've modified or created until the next full or normal backup. If you stop and perform a differential backup between full or normal backups, that first differential backup includes only those folders and files that you've modified or created since your last full backup. After the first differential backup, you have the most recent copy of every folder and file in either the full backup or the differential backup. Then, you continue to make further changes to your folders and files, and you create even newer folders and files that have not yet been backed up. So, you must continue to make additional differential backups during the backup cycle.

Each additional differential backup that you perform within the same backup cycle includes all the files you backed up during previous differential backups. For example, assume you perform a full or normal backup at the beginning of the month, and then perform differential backups at the end of each week. At the end of the first week after the full or normal backup, you perform your first differential backup. This backup includes all files that you created or modified during the first week, since the previous full or normal backup. That differential backup does not include files that you did not change after the full or normal backup because copies of those files are in your full or normal backup.

At the end of the second week, you perform your second differential backup. This backup includes all files that you created or modified during the first *and* second weeks, again since the full or normal backup.

At the end of the third week, you perform your third and last differential backup. This backup includes all files that you created and modified during the first, second, *and* third weeks, again since the full or normal backup at the start of the backup cycle.

At the beginning of the next month, you perform a new full or normal backup that includes all files, and then you start a new backup cycle. Any folders or files you created or modified during the fourth week of the previous backup cycle are also included in this backup. Then, you continue with differential backups during this next backup cycle.

Figure 10-1 illustrates an example of this approach to combining a full or normal backup with differential backups within a backup cycle. Assume you regularly back up two important folders on your hard disk: a Clients folder and a Business Records folder. At the beginning of the backup cycle, you back up all your client and business records, including your business portfolios. During the first week, assume you change two of your business portfolios—Portfolio 1.docx and Portfolio 2.docx. That means that the copies of these two files in your full or normal backup are no longer your most recent copies of the files. However, after you perform your first differential backup, that differential backup will include these two files.

Figure 10-1 Using a backup strategy that combines full and differential backups

Backup Cycle	New or Modified Files	Type of Backup	Files Backed Up
Beginning of backup cycle		Full backup #1	All folders and files in: • Clients folder • Business Records folder
End of week 1	Portfolio 1.docx Portfolio 2.docx	Differential backup #1	Portfolio 1.docx Portfolio 2.docx
End of week 2	Portfolio 3.docx Portfolio 4.docx	Differential backup #2	Portfolio 1.docx Portfolio 2.docx Portfolio 3.docx Portfolio 4.docx
End of week 3	Portfolio 2.docx Portfolio 5.docx Portfolio Cover Letter.docx	Differential backup #3	Portfolio 1.docx Portfolio 2.docx Portfolio 3.docx Portfolio 4.docx Portfolio 5.docx Portfolio Cover Letter.docx
Start of a new backup cycle	Portfolio 1.docx	Full backup #2	All folders and files in: • Clients folder • Business Records folder

During the second week, assume you change Portfolio 3.docx and Portfolio 4.docx. Your second differential backup will include these two files, plus the two you worked on during the first week; in other words, it contains Portfolio 1.docx, Portfolio 2.docx, Portfolio 3.docx, and Portfolio 4.docx.

During the third week, assume you change Portfolio 2.docx again, create a new portfolio called Portfolio 5.docx, and revise your Portfolio Cover Letter.docx. These three files, plus the others you worked on during the previous two weeks, are backed up when you perform your third differential backup. You now have a copy of Portfolio 2.docx in your first, second, and third differential backups. The copy in your third differential backup is the most recent copy of the file, and the ones in your first and second differential backups are previous versions of that file (and in this example, are identical).

During the last week of the backup cycle, assume you revise Portfolio 1.docx again. At the end of that fourth week, you start a new backup cycle with a new full or normal backup that includes all the files in your Client and Business Records folders plus any new or modified files. That full or normal backup also includes the revision you made to Portfolio 1.docx during the last week of the previous backup cycle (the fourth week of the previous month).

To better understand the concept of differential backups, you can think of each new differential backup after the first differential backup as a "cumulative backup" because each one includes all files included in previous differential backups.

One disadvantage of using a differential backup strategy is that differential backups increase the amount of time and media you need for backups. After the first differential backup, subsequent differential backups take longer because you are backing up more files. Once you complete a differential backup, you do not need to keep the backup media with the previous differential backups in that same backup cycle (unless you want to play it safe and err on the side of caution). Since you do not need to keep previous differential backups, a differential backup strategy is primarily used in those instances in which you need to keep only the most recent version of files that you have worked on during the current backup cycle. For example, if you work in a profession that is constantly changing (such as computer sciences), you frequently update your files and do not need previous versions of those files. (However, if you decide to keep each of your differential backup sets, you might be able to find previous versions of some files in an earlier differential backup set.)

One advantage of differential backups is that it is easier to restore folders and files. For example, if you need to restore all the files in your Clients and Business Records folders, you first restore all the files from your last full or normal backup, and then you restore all the files in the last differential backup for that backup cycle because it contains the most recent copy of all the files you changed after your last full or normal backup. The catch is that you spend more time backing up files than you do restoring files.

Combining Incremental Backups with a Normal Backup

Instead of using a differential backup strategy with your full backups, you can combine a full backup with incremental backups. An **incremental backup** includes only those files that you create or change since your previous backup—whether it was a full backup *or* an incremental backup.

Again, assume that you've just started a new backup cycle and that you've performed a full backup. As noted previously, after you perform a full or normal backup, you have a copy of all your folders and files. However, you continue to make changes to the folders and files on your hard disk, but until you perform the next full or normal backup, you do not have a backup of any folders or files that you created or modified. So, at the end of the first week, you perform your first incremental backup. This backup includes all the files that you created or modified during the first week (and is therefore identical to a differential backup at this point).

At the end of the second week, you perform your second incremental backup. This backup includes all files that you created or modified during the second week *only*. This is the point at which an incremental backup strategy differs from a differential backup strategy. Unlike a differential backup, this next incremental backup would not include folders and files that you created or modified and backed up during the first incremental backup.

At the end of the third week, you perform your third and last incremental backup. This backup includes all files you created or modified during the third week *only*. It does not include folders and files you created or modified during the first and second weeks.

At the end of the month, you perform a new full or normal backup that includes all files, and you start a new backup cycle again, followed by periodic incremental backups. This backup also includes any folders or files you created or modified during the last week of your previous backup cycle.

Figure 10-2 illustrates the use of incremental backups with full or normal backups. Again, assume you regularly back up two folders on your hard disk—a Clients folder and a Business Records folder. At the beginning of the backup cycle, you perform a full or normal backup and back up all files in the Clients and Business Records folders.

Using a backup strategy that combines full and incremental backups **Figure 10-2**

Backup Cycle	New or Modified Files	Type of Backup	Files Backed Up
Beginning of backup cycle		Full backup #1	All folders and files in: • Clients folder • Business Records folder
End of week 1	Portfolio 1.docx Portfolio 2.docx	Incremental backup #1	Portfolio 1.docx Portfolio 2.docx
End of week 2	Portfolio 3.docx Portfolio 4.docx	Incremental backup #2	Portfolio 3.docx Portfolio 4.docx
End of week 3	Portfolio 2.docx Portfolio 5.docx Portfolio Cover Letter.docx	Incremental backup #3	Portfolio 2.docx Portfolio 5.docx Portfolio Cover Letter.docx
Start of a new backup cycle	Portfolio 1.docx	Full backup #2	All folders and files in: • Clients folder • Business Records folder

During the first week, you modify the Portfolio 1.docx and Portfolio 2.docx. Your first incremental backup at the end of the first week includes only those two files.

During the second week, you modify Portfolio 3.docx and create Portfolio 4.docx. Your second incremental backup at the end of that week includes *only* Portfolio 3.docx and Portfolio 4.docx. Unlike a differential backup, it does not include Portfolio 1.docx and Portfolio 2.docx, which you worked on during the first week; rather, the backups for these files are contained in your first incremental backup. If you don't work on these files during the remainder of the backup cycle, this backup is the only one that contains the latest versions of those files.

During the third week, you modify the Portfolio Cover Letter.docx and Portfolio 2.docx, and you also create Portfolio 5.docx. Your third incremental backup at the end of that week includes *only* those three files. It does not include Portfolio 1.docx, Portfolio 3.docx, and Portfolio 4.docx from the first two weeks. The copy of Portfolio 2.docx in your third incremental backup is a more recent version of Portfolio 2.docx than the one in your first incremental backup. So, you now have two versions of this file in your incremental backups (allowing you to return to an earlier version of the same file if needed). In contrast, with a differential backup strategy, you typically have only the most recent version of this file because you recycle backup media sooner.

During the last week of this backup cycle, you revise Portfolio 1.docx. At the beginning of the next month, you start a new backup cycle with a new full or normal backup that includes all the files in your Clients and Business Records folders (including any new or modified files that you worked on during the last week of the backup cycle). That backup also includes the revision you made to Portfolio 1.docx during the last week of the previous backup cycle (the fourth week of the previous month).

Incremental backups have some advantages and disadvantages over differential backups (and vice versa). Incremental backups are faster than differential backups because each new incremental backup includes fewer files than a corresponding differential backup. Also, since each incremental backup does not include files backed up during previous incremental backups, you do not need to use as much backup media. However, unlike a differential backup strategy, you need to keep all your incremental backups so that you can restore all of the files you worked on during a backup cycle.

Incremental backups take longer to restore. For example, if you need to restore all the files in your Clients and Business Records folders, you would first restore all the files from your last full or normal backup, and then you would restore all the files in each of your incremental backup sets in the order in which you produced them during the last backup cycle.

Why do you need to restore folders and files from all the incremental backups? You might have created a new file during the second week of the backup cycle and not worked on that file during the remainder of the backup cycle. The only copy of that file is in the second incremental backup. If you just restore files from the full backup and the last incremental backup, you will not have that file in the second incremental backup, because it's not included in either the full or last incremental backups. If you use differential backups, that file is included automatically in the last differential backup, so you only need to restore the normal backup and the last differential backup.

Why not use a differential background strategy rather than an incremental one? If you've worked on a document every day during a backup cycle, each incremental backup will have a different version of the file that contains that document. Unlike a differential backup strategy, in which you do not typically save previous differential backups, you can restore earlier versions of a file if you use an incremental backup strategy. You just choose the incremental backup that contains the version of the file you want to restore. Also, because incremental backups are faster and require fewer backup media, they are the most common types of backups that businesses and individuals make. As noted earlier, no matter what type of backup strategy you use, you spend more time backing up files than you do restoring files.

If you are faced with the daunting task of performing full or normal backups that require a substantial amount of time, such as 24 hours, you can combine full or normal backups on a less frequent basis with both differential and incremental backups. For example, you might do a full or normal backup at the beginning of the month, perform differential backups on a daily basis, except for the end of each week when you perform an incremental backup. The daily differential backups insure that you have a "cumulative" backup of every folder and file that you create or modify during the week. The end-of-week incremental backups back up all the folders and files you created or modified during the week, and in essence, act like a weekly full or normal backup, but require less time. Furthermore, the incremental backups turn off the Archive attribute on all the folders and files that you created or modified during the week so that you can start with a new set of differential backups the following week that only back up data during the next week. If you need to restore all the data on your computer from these backups, you restore the last full backup, the last incremental backup, and then the last differential backup.

Making Copy and Daily Backups

Even if you employ the use of a differential or incremental backup strategy with full backups, you might also want to implement other types of backups, such as a copy backup and a daily backup. A **copy backup** backs up all the files you select without affecting other types of backups that you create during a backup cycle. You might use a copy backup to make an extra backup within a backup cycle so that you can store the copy backup off-site. For example, if you combine a full backup with an incremental backup strategy, you can use a copy backup at any point during the backup cycle to back up all the files that you select. Any new or modified files that are included in the copy backup are also backed up in the next incremental backup.

In contrast, a **daily backup** backs up all files that have been created or modified the day you perform the daily backup. Like the copy backup, a daily backup does not interfere with an incremental or differential backup strategy. Again, you might use a daily backup to make an extra backup within a backup cycle so that you can store the daily backup off-site. Also, if you've had a particularly busy and productive day and modified many files, you could make a daily backup before your next differential or incremental backup. If a problem occurs before your next differential or incremental backup, and you do not have a backup of the files you worked on that day, you have to reconstruct those files from scratch.

Even if you combine a differential or incremental backup strategy with periodic full backups, remember that you have no backups of changes to files made between each differential or each incremental backup, so you might employ the use of a copy backup or a daily backup for added protection against a potential problem that might arise.

Keeping Multiple Backups

If you back up to an external hard disk or a network folder where you have plenty of storage space, you can keep more backups for a longer period of time. However, if you are backing up to media, such as a flash drive, where the amount of storage space might be limiting, or if you are backing up to a DVD, CD, or any other type of media that you might want to reuse, it is a good habit to keep at least the last four of your most recent backup sets.

When you start your next backup cycle, you can use the backup media from your oldest backup cycle. During the next backup cycle, you have backups from three previous backup cycles that are untouched. After you complete the next backup cycle, you now have backups from your four most recent backup cycles. With each new backup cycle, you repeat this same process. This approach guarantees that you have backups from the three most recent backup cycles in case you encounter a problem while performing a backup during the next backup cycle. If you attempt to restore files from your most recent backup cycle and discover that your most recent backup set is defective, you can turn to the backup set from the previous backup cycle.

If you don't use this approach, but rather decide to record over backups from your previous (and only other) backup cycle, you are taking an unnecessary risk. If the backup, drive, or computer fails during the next backup, you might lose an important backup from your previous backup cycle, and you might also lose everything on your hard disk. Then, you might have no backups and have to re-create all your files from scratch if that is even possible.

Using Multiple Types of Backups

You should not rely on just one backup or even one backup strategy. You might, for example, want to back up important files on your computer to one type of removable storage (such as a flash drive, DVD, or CD) and perform the same backup to a shared network folder or an external hard disk drive so that you can restore the same set of files in one of two different ways. As part of your backup process, you should keep a log of what backups you have made—including the date of the backup, the backup utility (and version) you used, what's included in the backups, and where the backups are stored. As noted earlier, it is a good idea to store at least one set of backups off-site. In fact, your insurance company might require you to store backups off-site before they will insure your data. Like insurance policies, backups are invaluable when you need them.

In the public sector, the federal Sarbanes-Oxley Act of 2002 mandates that publicly held companies and accounting firms maintain and properly store financial data for not less than seven years and also maintain documentation on data integrity necessary for inspecting and auditing the financial practices of firms.

Understanding the Importance of the Archive Attribute

When you perform a full or normal backup, you select the drive(s), folder(s), and file(s) that you want to back up, and then you back up everything you selected. When you perform a differential or incremental backup, the backup utility automatically selects only those folders or files that have been modified or created. The question is, "How does the backup utility know which files to select for a differential or incremental backup?" When you create or modify a folder or file, Windows Vista turns on the Archive attribute or setting for that folder or file. The backup utility then uses that attribute to determine what to include in a backup. Only files with the Archive attribute enabled are selected for differential or incremental backups. The **Archive attribute** is actually a bit that can be turned on or off, and not surprisingly, it's also referred to as the **Archive bit**.

If you want to view the status of the Archive attribute of a file, or if you want to turn on or turn off the Archive attribute of a file, you view properties of that file and choose the Advanced button on the General property sheet to open the Advanced Attributes dialog box, as shown in Figure 10-3. If the Archive attribute is turned on, you will see a check mark in the "File is ready for archiving" check box. If there is no check mark in this check box, a Backup utility has backed up the file and turned off the Archive attribute (or you have deliberately turned it off).

Figure 10-3 Viewing the status of a file's Archive attribute

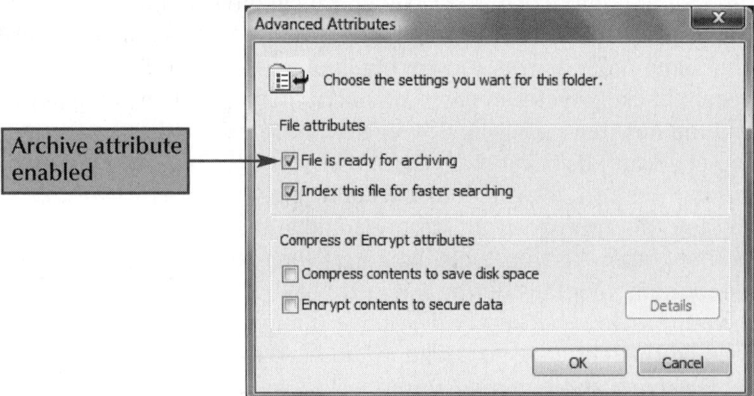

During a full or normal backup, a Backup utility backs up all the folders and files you've selected—whether the Archive attribute is on or off. Once all the folders and files are backed up, the Backup utility turns off the Archive attribute of any file that previously had the Archive attribute enabled, as shown in Figure 10-4. The net result is that all the files that are backed up after a full or normal backup no longer have the Archive attribute enabled.

Archive attribute of a new or modified file before and after a full backup — **Figure 10-4**

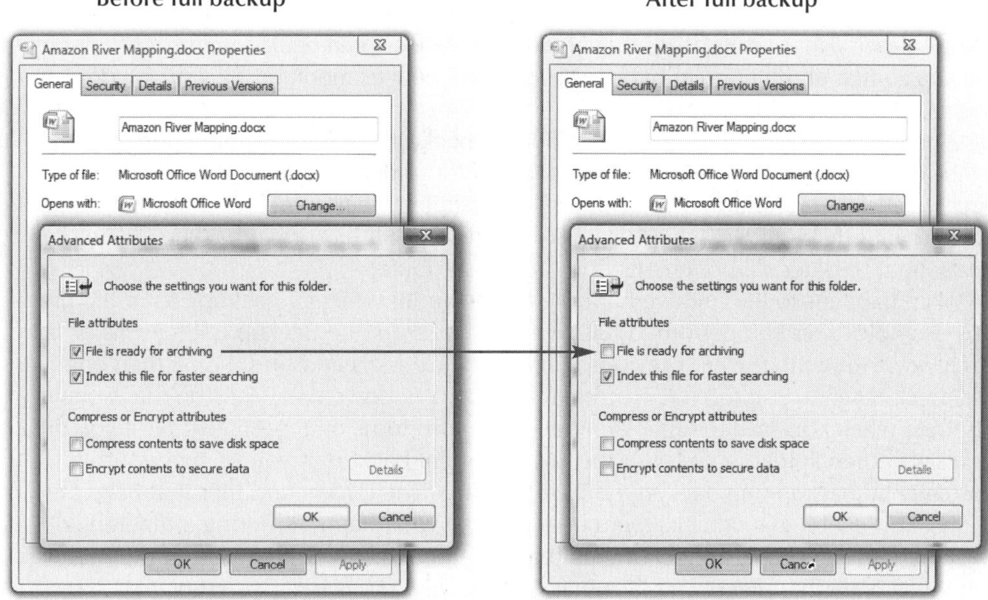

If you open a file and change it after a full or normal backup, Windows Vista turns on the Archive attribute when you save the file. If you create and save a new file, Windows Vista also turns on the Archive attribute. If you then perform a differential backup, the backup utility selects all folders and files that have the Archive attribute turned on (they are either new or modified files) and backs them up. The backup utility does not include folders or files that have the Archive attribute turned off (they have already been backed up). Unlike a full or normal backup, the backup utility does not change the Archive attribute of the files that it backed up during your first differential backup. See Figure 10-5.

Archive attribute of a new or modified file before and after a differential backup — **Figure 10-5**

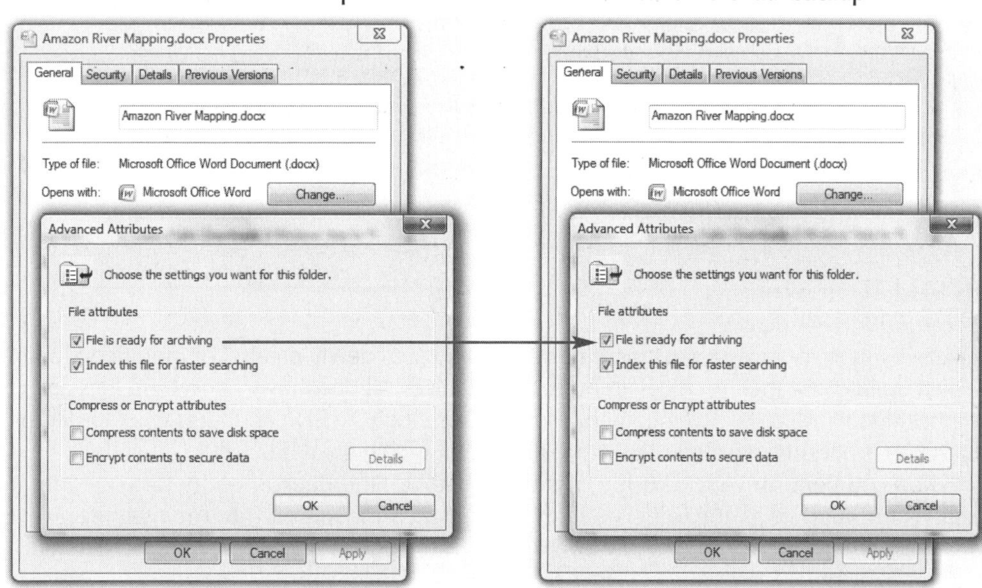

When you perform your next differential backup, any newly created or modified folders and files are backed up because their Archive attribute is enabled on. All files backed up in the previous differential backup are also included in this next differential backup because their Archive bits are still enabled. That process is repeated with each differential backup so that all differential backups contain all new or modified files since your last full or normal backup.

When you perform your next full or normal backup, the backup utility turns off the Archive attributes that were previously enabled for folders and files. The only time Archive attributes are turned off with a backup strategy that combines a full or normal backup with differential backups is when you do the full or normal backup. Therefore, differential backups do not change the Archive attribute.

What happens to the Archive attribute during an incremental backup? As in the previous example, after you perform a full or normal backup, the Backup utility turns off all Archive attributes that were previously enabled for folders and files. If you then open a file and change it after the full or normal backup, Windows Vista turns on the Archive attribute when you save the file. Windows Vista also turns on the Archive bit if you create and save a new folder or file after the full or normal backup. If you then perform an incremental backup, the backup utility selects all those folders and files that have the Archive bit enabled and backs them up—just like what happens during a differential backup. However, after an incremental backup, the Backup utility turns off the Archive attributes of all the folders and files that were backed up. See Figure 10-6.

Figure 10-6 **Archive attribute of a new or modified file before and after an incremental backup**

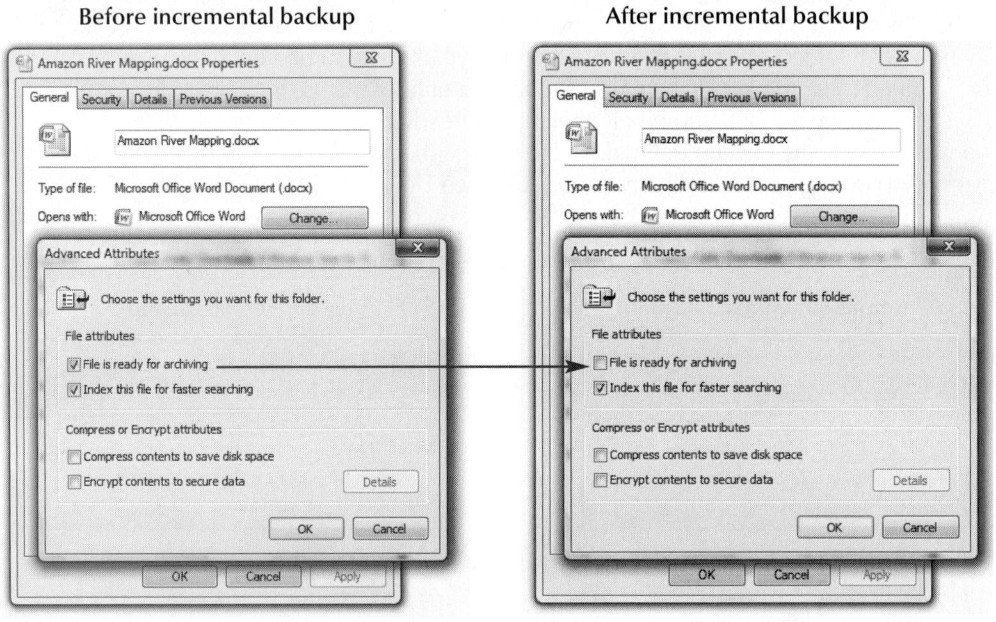

Before incremental backup | **After incremental backup**

When you perform your next incremental backup, any newly created or modified files are backed up because their Archive attributes are enabled. All previously backed up files are not included in the next incremental backup because their Archive attributes were turned off. That same process is repeated with each subsequent incremental backup.

When you perform your next full or normal backup, the Backup utility turns off the Archive attributes of all the folders and files. As shown in Figure 10-6, Archive bits are turned off with this backup strategy after the normal backup and after each incremental backup.

Figure 10-7 summarizes the status of the Archive attribute before and after a full, differential, and incremental backup. Both full and incremental backups turn off the Archive attribute of any new or modified folders and files that are backed up. Differential backups do not change the Archive attribute of any new or modified folders and files that are backed up. Full backups also back up folders and files with the Archive attribute off. Differential and incremental backups do not back up files with the Archive attribute off.

How full, differential, and incremental backups handle Archive attributes **Figure 10-7**

Type of Backup	Archive Attribute	
	Before backup	After backup
Full backup:		
Already backed up files	Off	Off
New files	On	Off
Modified files	On	Off
Differential	On	On
Incremental	On	Off

When you perform a copy or daily backup, the Backup utility does not modify the Archive bit of files selected for the backup. So that means that a copy or daily backup does not interfere with the use of differential or incremental backups.

The Archive bit provides a simple but powerful technique for determining the status of a file for backup operations.

Using the Backup and Restore Center

You can use the Window Vista's new Backup and Restore Center to perform two types of backups; however, the options available also depend on the edition of Windows Vista that you use. These two types of backups are as follows:

- **Complete PC Backup** If you are using Windows Vista Ultimate, Windows Vista Business, or Windows Vista Enterprise, you can perform a Complete PC Backup. During this type of backup, Windows Vista backs up an entire volume to a file with the "vhd" (for Virtual Hard Disk) file extension. This file contains a complete image of your entire hard disk so that you can rebuild your computer if you experience a major problem. During a Complete PC Backup, Windows Vista also compacts this file so that your backup utilizes disk storage space more efficiently. Unlike other types of backups that back up one file at a time, Complete PC also backs up sections of the hard disk in one step, so the backup operation is much faster. You can only store a Complete PC Backup on removable media like an external hard disk or a DVD. The Automated System Recovery (ASR) backup available in Windows XP was used to restore an entire computer, but it is no longer available in Windows Vista.

- **Folders and files** You can use this incremental backup option to back up your user folders and files. This option does not back up system files, programs, encrypted files, and other files like temporary files or deleted files in the Recycle Bin. Instead, you pick and choose the types of user folders and files you want to include in the backup. You can back up your folders and files to a second hard disk, to removable media—such as a writeable DVD, writeable CD, Compact Flash (CF) memory card, or Secure Digital (SD) memory card—or to a shared network folder (except in Windows Vista Home Basic). You can also back up to a flash drive; however, Windows Vista's Help and Support notes otherwise. You cannot back up to the system volume, to the same disk that contains the files that you are backing up, or to a tape drive. Also, you can only back up to disks that use the NTFS, FAT, and UDF (Universal Disk Format) file systems. The first time you perform a backup of your folders and files, the Backup and Restore Center performs a full backup of all your files. After that, you can perform selective backups that include only specific groups of files. The backed-up files are stored in Compressed (zipped) Folders on the backup media. Subsequent backups are incremental backups that back up only changes within files, not the entire files themselves.

The Windows Vista Backup and Restore Center simplifies, and also provides an option for automating, the process for making backups, thus ensuring that you have backups of the valuable data on your computer.

Backing Up Folders and Files

This section of the tutorial describes the process for backing up folders and files. There are no tutorial steps because this backup feature requires that you perform a full backup of your entire computer system the first time you back up your folders and files. That requires time and storage media and also requires that you have more than enough storage space on your backup storage media. If there are multiple users on the same computer, all the users' personal files are backed up, thus increasing the time and amount of storage space on backup media. If you change backup settings (such as changing the location for the backup or changing the schedule), you must perform another full backup of all user data on your computer.

If you have already used the Backup and Restore Center to back up folders and files, the Backup and Restore Center is set to automatically perform an incremental backup of all your folders and files on your computer. If you open a file and make a change to it, during the next scheduled or manual backup, the Backup and Restore Center backs up only the changes within the file—not the entire file. This feature reduces the amount of storage space required for incremental backups. If your computer is operating on battery power, you cannot back up the computer.

You must log on under an Account with Administrator privileges to perform a backup. If you are logged on under a Standard user account and attempt to initiate a backup, Windows Vista displays a Backup and Restore Center dialog box informing you that you need to be an Administrator to run a backup. Then, it suggests that you use Fast User Switching to switch to an account with Administrator privileges or that you log off and then log back on as an Administrator.

The following steps describe the process for backing up folders and files. If you have not yet used the Backup and Restore Center, but want to back up your computer's data and have enough time and enough backup media, you can perform the operations describe in the following steps. For example, on the computer used for these figures, a new, full backup of all User files and folders that resulted in 16.3 GB of compressed backup files took 1.5 hours.

1. **Open the Backup and Restore Center** To open the Backup and Restore Center, you open the Start menu, open the Control Panel, open System and Maintenance, and then open the Backup and Restore Center. Figure 10-8 shows the Backup and Restore Center. The Backup and Restore Center window consists of two basic sections—one for backing up folders and files or your entire computer, and one for restoring folders and files or your entire computer. The information displayed in these sections depends on whether you have already backed up your computer. A full backup of all user folders was already performed on the computer used for this figure, so the Backup and Restore Center is now set up to perform incremental backups of the same files on a weekly basis. After a backup is complete, the Backup and Restore Center window shows the date and time of the last backup, the date and time of the next scheduled backup, and the location to use for saving backups. On the computer used for this figure, a backup is currently in progress. Also, folder and file backups are stored on a 500 GB external hard disk drive that has enough storage space for full backups and ongoing incremental backups. Also on this computer, Complete PC was initially used to create a complete image of the hard disk on the same external hard disk drive so that the computer system could be recovered if a hardware failure occurred. If you have never backed up files and folders, you will not see "Last Backup," "Next backup," and "Where to save files" under "Create backup copies of your files and folders," and there is no Change settings link.

Viewing backup settings in the Backup and Restore Center **Figure 10-8**

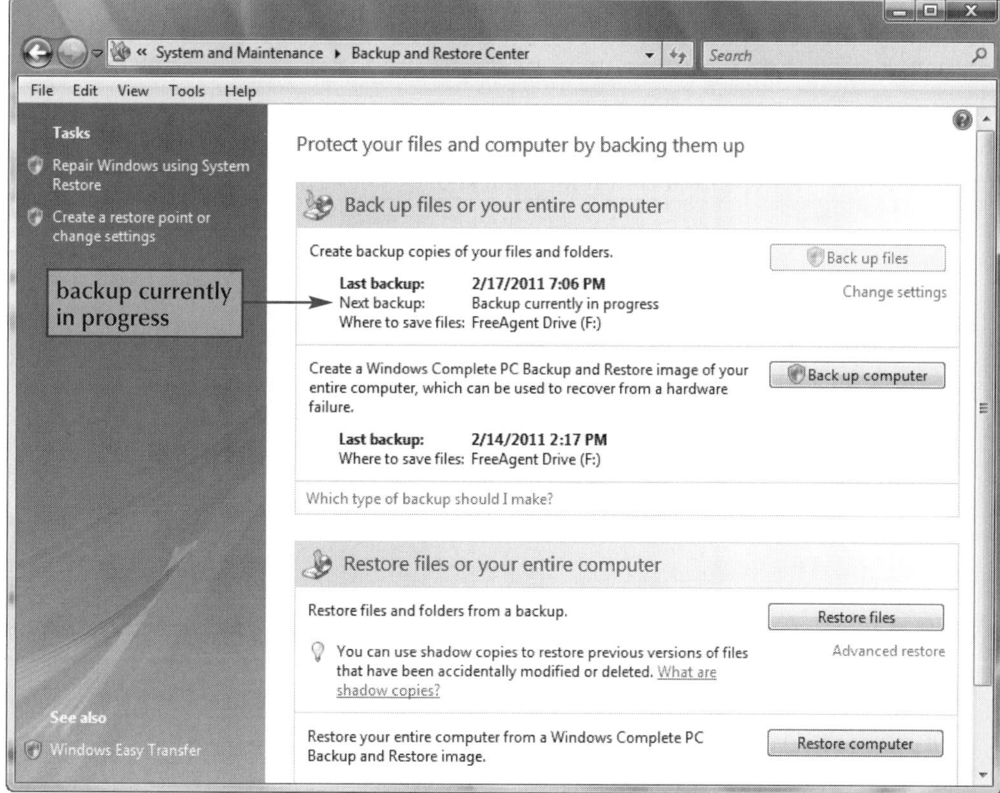

2. **Indicate you want to back up files** To start your first backup or to manually initiate another backup of folders and files, you just click the "Back up files" button. After Windows Vista switches to Secure Desktop mode, you provide Administrator credentials, and then the Backup and Restore Center takes one of three steps:
   - If you've never used the Backup and Restore Center option for backing up folders and files, you must first specify settings for backing up folders and files, as described in Step 3 and subsequent steps.
   - If you've already backed up user folders and files previously, the Back Up Files Wizard immediately performs an incremental backup.
   - If you click the Change settings link, Windows Vista displays a Backup Status and Configuration dialog box with two options:
     Back up now If you choose this option, Windows Vista prompts for Administrator credentials, and then the Backup and Restore Center initiates a backup.
     Change backup settings If you choose this option, Windows Vista prompts you for Administrator credentials, and then the Backup and Restore Center looks for backup devices and prompts for backup settings, as described in Step 3. You also have the option of creating a new, full backup in addition to saving your settings. Then, the Backup and Restore Center initiates the backup at the scheduled time.
3. **Choose a location for the backup** If this is the first time that you have backed up your computer, you click the Back up files button. In the Back Up Files dialog box, the Back Up Files Wizard asks you where you want to save your backup, after checking first for backup devices. See Figure 10-9. If you click the "On a hard disk, CD, or DVD" list button, you will see a list of drives that you can choose from for your backup, as shown in Figure 10-10. This list includes hard disk drives (including internal and external hard disk drives), DVD drives, CD drives, drives for memory cards, and flash drives. You also have the option of backing up to a shared network folder.

Figure 10-9 Selecting a local or network location for a backup

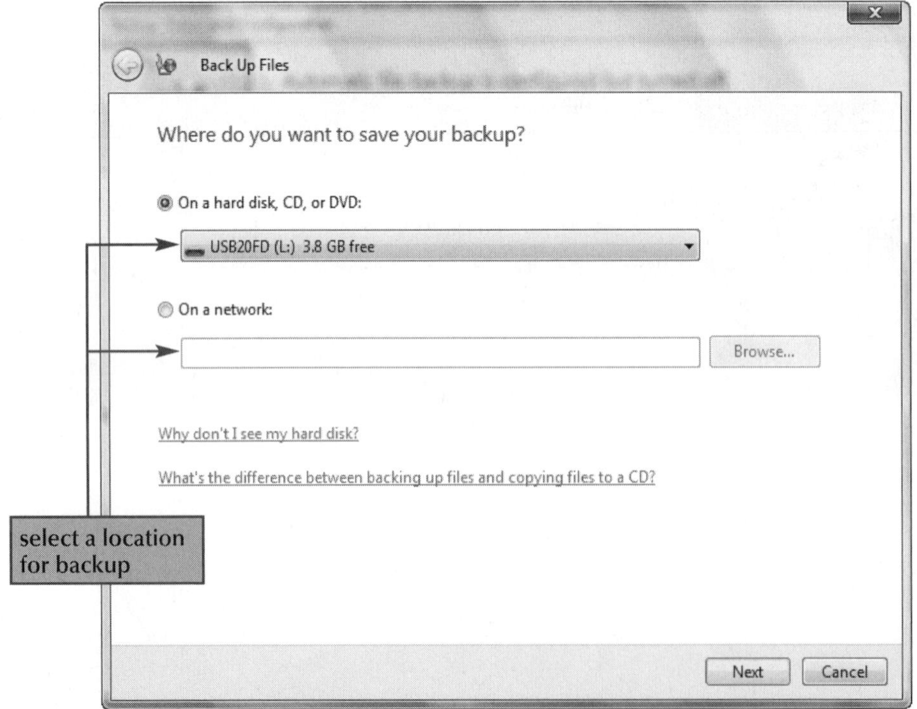

Choosing a location for the backup **Figure 10-10**

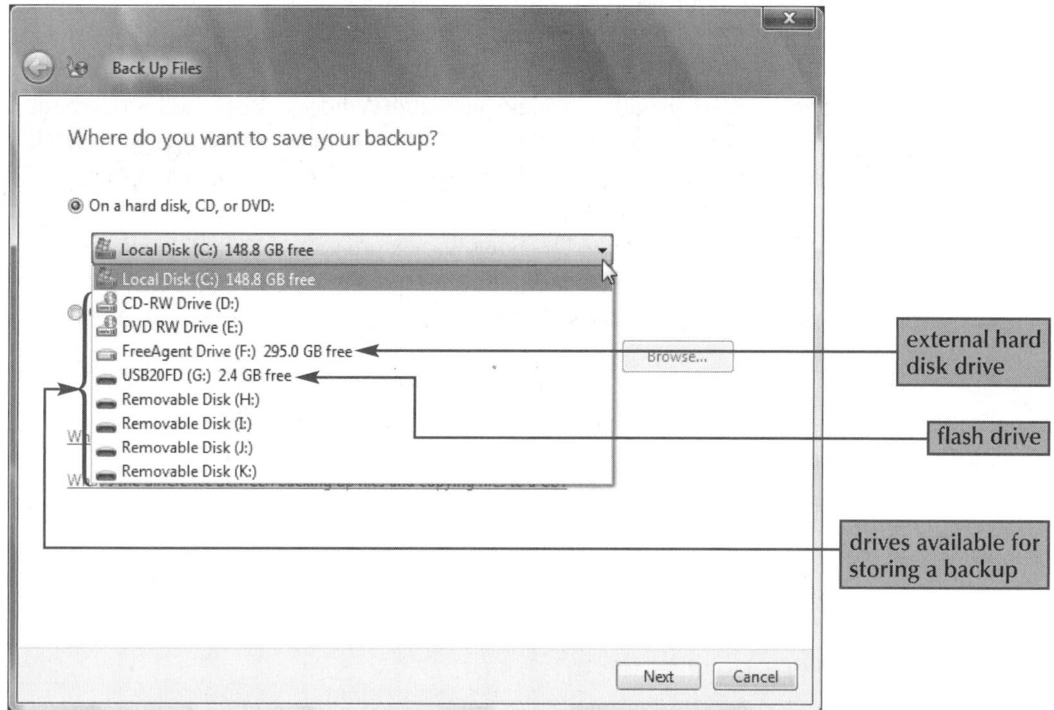

4. **Select the types of files to back up** Next, the Back Up Files Wizard asks you to pick the file types that you want to back up. By default, all the standard types of user files are selected for backup. See Figure 10-11. You can point to one of the file type categories to display details about which files fall in a category. The Back Up Files Wizard notes that all file types that you select will include not only your files but also the same types of files for all other users on the computer, so you must make sure that you have adequate storage space for your backup. Also, note that the Backup and Restore Center only backs up files on NTFS volumes. The following list describes the types of files included in each category of file types shown in the Back Up Files dialog box:
   - **Pictures** This category includes digital photographs, clip art, drawings, scanned pictures, faxes, and other image files, such as JPEG (Joint Photographic Experts Group) and PNG (Portable Network Graphics) files.
   - **Music** This category includes music files, play lists, CD tracks, and other audio files, such as Windows Media Audio and MP3 (MPEG Audio Layer 3) files.
   - **Videos** This category includes video and movie files, such as Windows Media Video, MPEG (Motion Pictures Experts Group), and AVI (Audio Video Interleaved) files.
   - **E-mail** This category includes e-mail messages, contacts, and PST (Microsoft Outlook's Personal Folder File) and EML (Electronic Mail) files on your local computer. (E-mail messages that are stored online are not included in the backup.)

- **Documents** This category includes document files, such as word processing files, spreadsheet files, and presentation files. It also includes PDF (Adobe Portable Document Files) and XPS (XML Paper Specification) files. **XPS (XML Paper Specification)** is a Microsoft specification for creating a high-quality version of a printed document that you can view with the Windows Vista XPS Document Viewer, share with others, and print using printers that support the XPS. **XML (Extensible Markup Language)** is a language for designing Web pages that supports the use of codes to identify and describe data.
- **TV shows** This category includes TV shows you record with Windows Media Center.
- **Compressed files** This category includes compressed, image, and archive format files that contain other files, such as Zip files and Compressed (zipped) Folders with the "zip" file extension, Cabinet files with the "cab" file extension (Windows installation files), ISO files with the "iso" file extension (CD disk image files), Windows Imaging Format files (disk image files) with the "wim" file extension, and Virtual Hard Disk files (disk image files) with the "vhd" file extension.
- **Additional files** This category includes all other files that do not fit in the other categories.

Note that the backup never includes system files, program files, or temporary files.

Figure 10-11 Selecting file types to back up

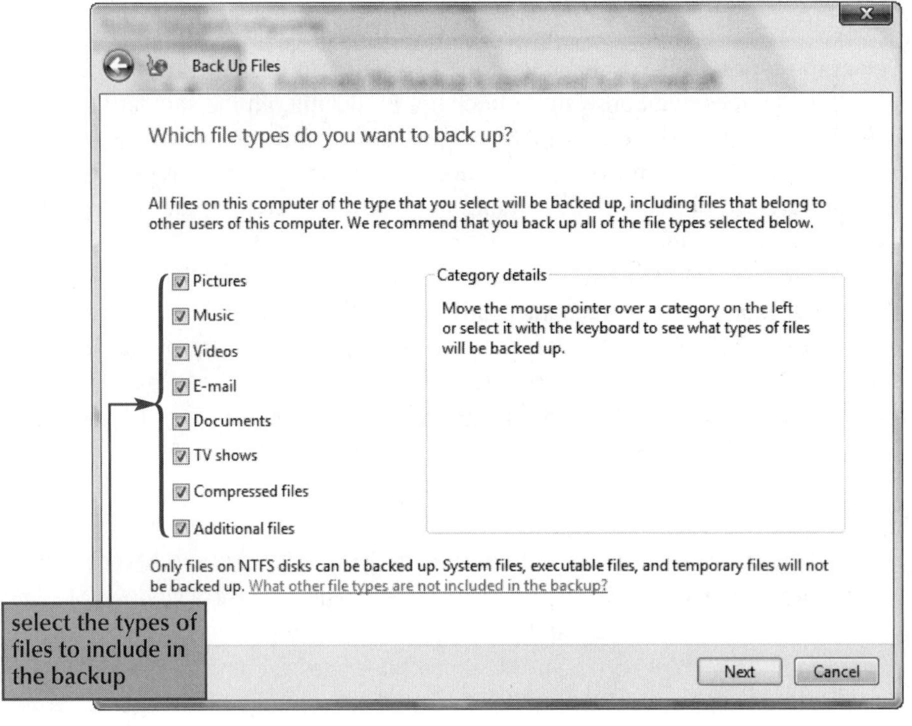

5. **Select a schedule for the backup** After you select the file types you want to back up, the Back Up Files Wizard asks you in the next step how often you want to create a backup. See Figure 10-12. It also notes that new files and files that have changed will be added to your backup according to the schedule that you set. Using the "How often" list button, you choose Daily, Weekly, or Monthly. Using the "What day" list button, you choose any day of the week. Using the "What time" list button, you choose any hour of the day.

Specifying a schedule for the backup **Figure 10-12**

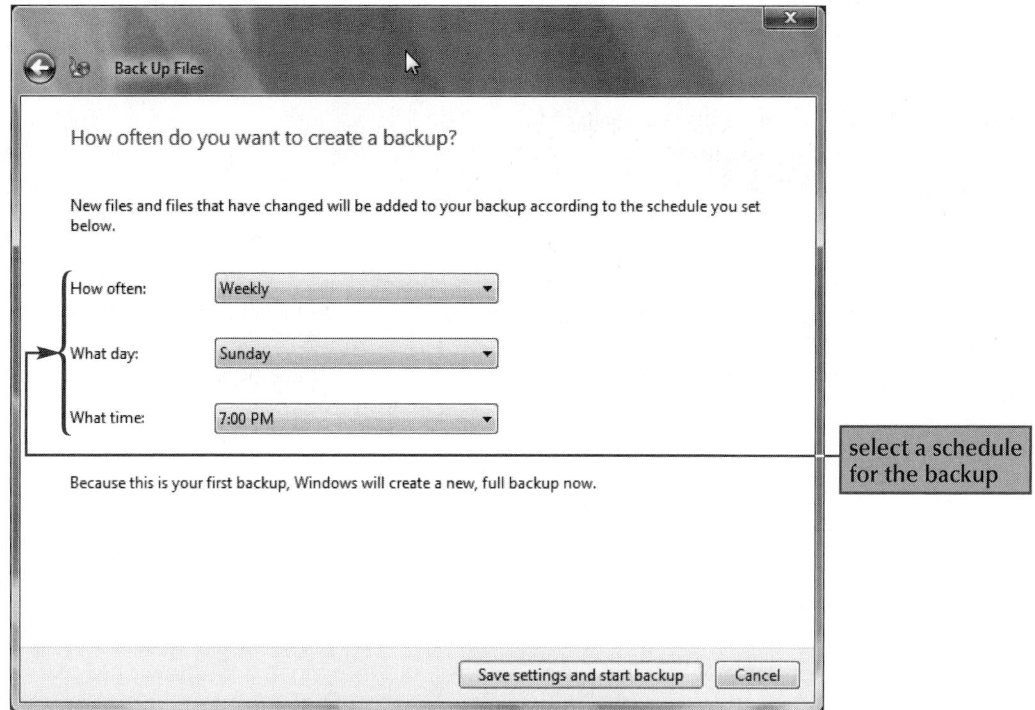

6. **Save your settings and start the backup** When you specify a schedule for the first time, you use the "Save settings and start backup" button to save your backup settings and initiate a full backup of all your files and folders. If you use the Change settings link to change backup settings, you use the "Save settings and exit" button to save your new backup settings. Then, the Backup and Restore Center initiates the backup at the scheduled time. If you are backing up to a DVD or CD, Windows Vista provides you with an estimate of the number of discs that you need. It also informs you when the backup has finished successfully.

When you start your first backup of files and folders on your computer, the Backup and Restore Center displays a Back Up Files dialog box informing you that it is creating a shadow copy, and then it scans for files to include in the backup. The shadow copy takes about a minute, but the process for selecting files to include in the backup can be time-consuming if you have a lot of files and folders to back up. For example, on the computer used for these figures, a new, full backup of all User files and folders that resulted in 16.3 GB of compressed backup files took 45 minutes to select files for the backup and another 45 minutes to perform the backup.

Reference Window | Backing Up Files and Folders

- Log on your computer under an Administrator account, not a Standard User account.
- Open the Start menu, open the Control Panel, open System and Maintenance, and then open the Backup and Restore Center.
- If you want to manually start a backup of folders and files, click the "Back up files" button, and then provide Administrator credentials.
- If you previously performed a backup, and then click the Change settings link, Windows Vista displays a Backup Status and Configuration dialog box with two options. You can click "Back up now" to provide Administrator credentials and initiate a backup using your current backup settings, or you can pick "Change backup settings" to provide Administrator credentials and specify new backup settings (the location for the backup, the types of files to back up, and a backup schedule).
- If you've never used the Backup and Restore Center option for backing up folders and files, you click the "Back up files" button, provide Administrator credentials, and specify settings for backing up folders and files (the location for the backup, the types of files to back up, and a backup schedule).

After you have performed a full backup of your files (and those of any other users) and set a schedule for periodic incremental backups, you can examine your backup storage media. The following bulleted list describes what you will find on the full backup storage media:

- **Backup drive** After you open a Computer window, and then open a window onto the drive that contains the backup media for your backup, you will see a MediaID.bin file and a folder with the name of your computer system. See Figure 10-13. That folder with the name of your computer system contains your current backup and any future backups that you create.

Figure 10-13 **Viewing the contents of the media used for a backup**

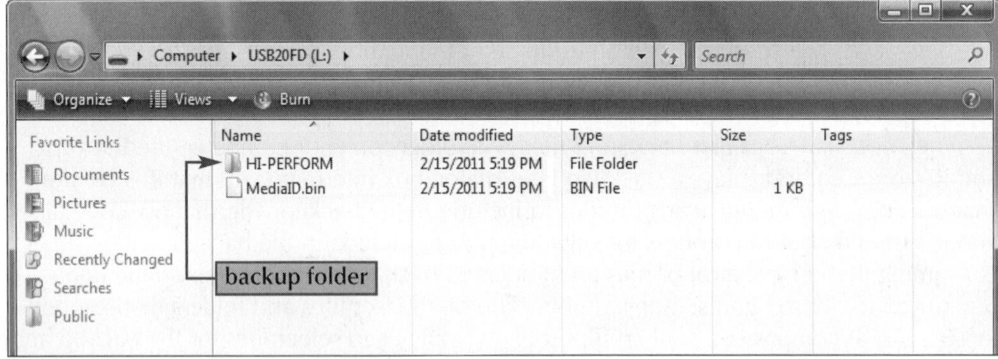

- **Backup sets** After opening the folder with the name of your computer system, you see a folder that contains your backup set or sets (if you have previously backed up your computer). See Figure 10-14. That folder is named "Backup Set" followed by the backup date in the format YYYY-MM-DD followed by the backup time in hours, minutes, and seconds in the format HHMMSS.

Figure 10-14 Backup sets for one computer

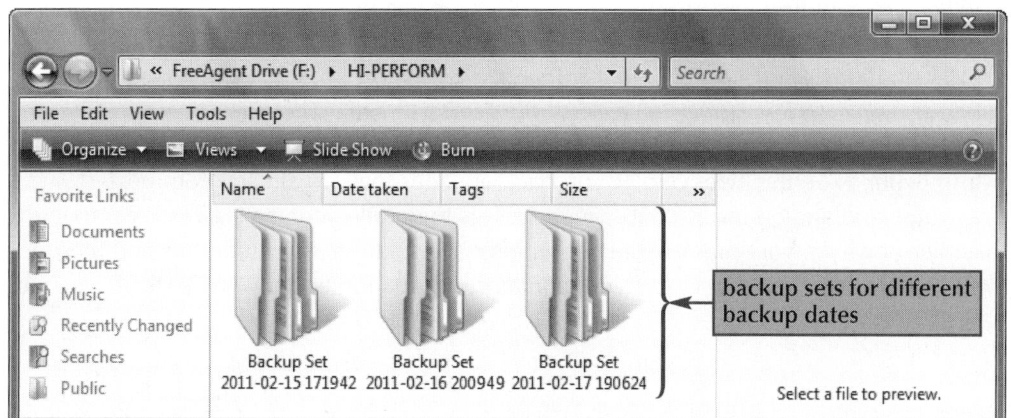

- **Specific backup set** If you open a Backup Set folder, you will find two folders—a Backup Files folder and a Catalogs folder. See Figure 10-15.

Figure 10-15 Identifying the folder with the backed up files

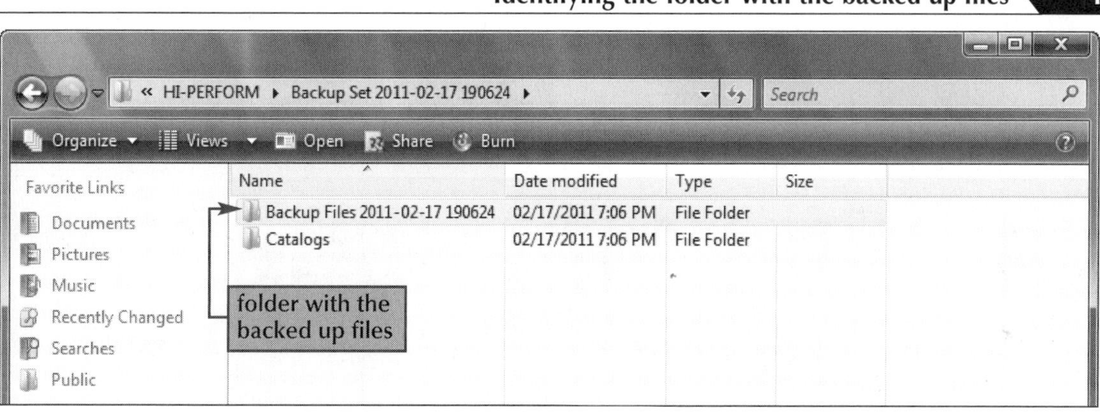

- **Catalogs folder** If you open the Catalogs folder, you will discover that it contains a Windows Backup Catalog File named GlobalCatalog.wbcat, which contains an index (or list) of all the files that are included in this backup, along with the name of the Zip file that contains each file. See Figure 10-16. The Backup and Restore Center uses this catalog to find the location of a file that you want to restore.

Figure 10-16 Viewing the contents of the Catalogs folder

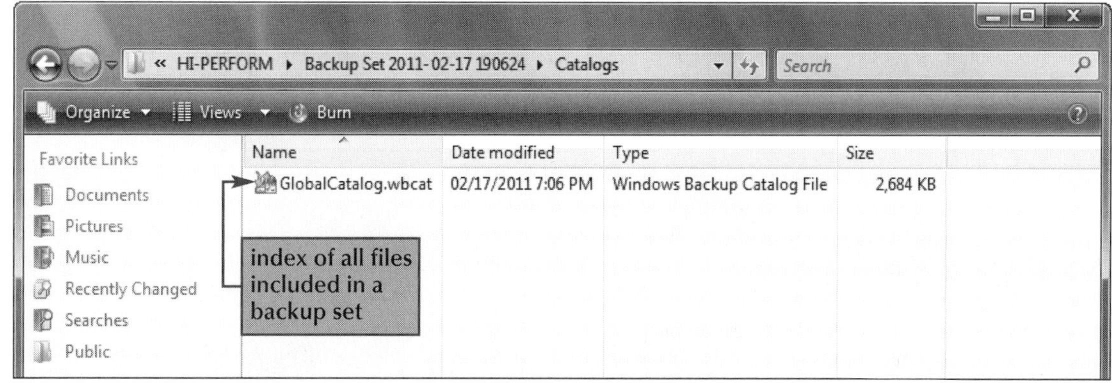

- **Backup Zip files** If you back up one folder level, and then open the Backup Files folder, you will find one or more files with your backups. See Figure 10-17. These files are named "Backup files" followed by a number starting with 1 and the "zip" file extension for Compressed (zipped) Folder. By storing backups as compressed files, your backups take up less storage space on your backup media. The overall compression is typically around 50 percent; however, different types of files compress differently, so it also depends on the types of files you back up. Files that are already compressed, such as video and audio files, do not compress. This folder also contains a hidden Catalogs folder; however, you must enable the option for displaying hidden folders and files to view this folder. That Catalogs folder contains information about what is stored in each backup zip file.

Figure 10-17 **Backup zip files for storing backed up files**

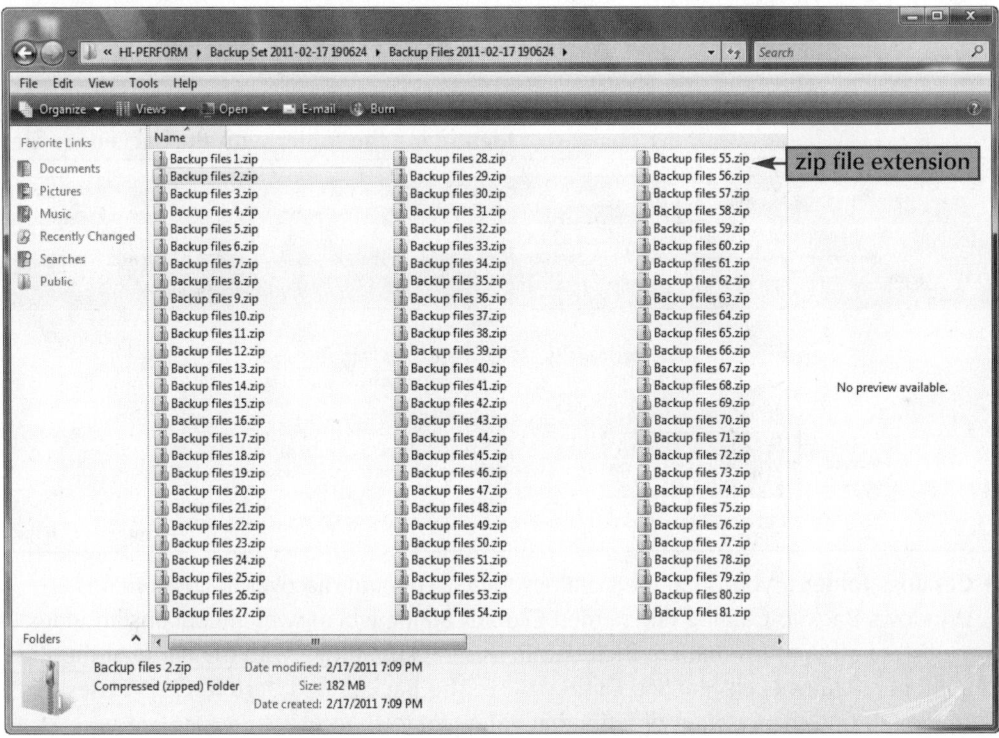

- **Backed up drive folder** You can open the backup zip files because Windows Vista treats them as Compressed (zipped) Folders. Figure 10-18 shows the contents of one of these backup files. This backup zip file contains a folder with the name of the drive that contained the original files that were backed up.

Figure 10-18 **Viewing the contents of a backup zip file**

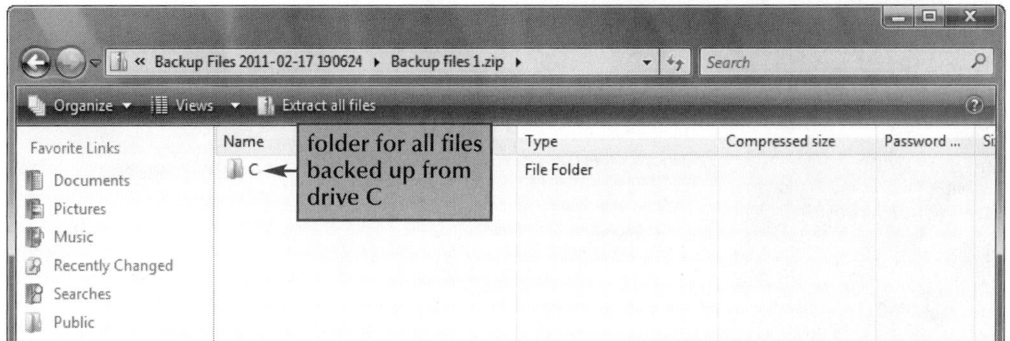

- **Backed up folders and files** If you open the backed up drive folder, you will find folders named after folders on your hard disk drive and perhaps individual files. These folders contain backups of files that match one of the categories of file types that you specified for inclusion in your backup. For example, Figure 10-19 shows a backup zip file with two folders—a Program Files folder and a Users folder. This Program Files folder contains one or more subfolders for software installed on your computer, and those folders also contain files that match one of the file types you specified for your backup. For example, if you chose the option to back up Music files, you might see a folder for Microsoft Office (Clipart, Media, and Office Media folders and files) and another folder for QuickTime. The Users folder contains all user folders (including your user folder, the user folders of any other user of the same computer, and the Public folder) that contain the file types you specified for your backup. Unlike other backup utilities, you can open these folders that contain files with backups and, if necessary, copy them from the Compressed (zipped) Folder to your hard disk.

Tip

You can use the Search feature to search zip files, including backup zip files, to locate files that you want to restore.

Figure 10-19 **Viewing the folders backed up on drive C**

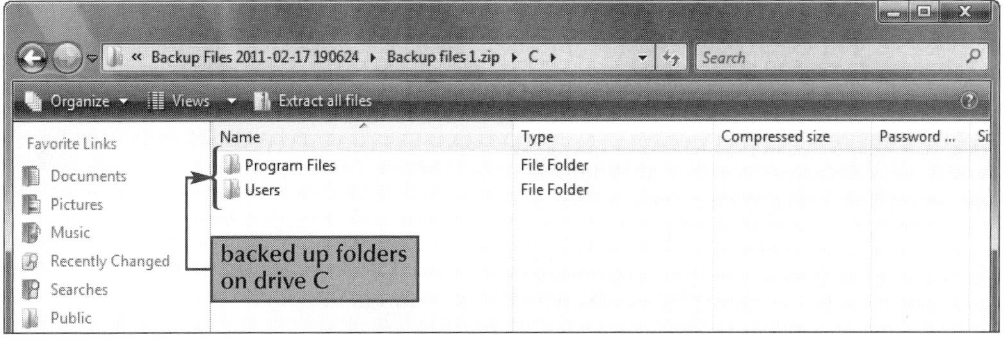

After you complete a backup, the Backup and Restore Center will identify the date and time of the last backup, the date and time of the next backup, and the backup location. See Figure 10-20.

Figure 10-20 Viewing the status of the last backup and next scheduled backup

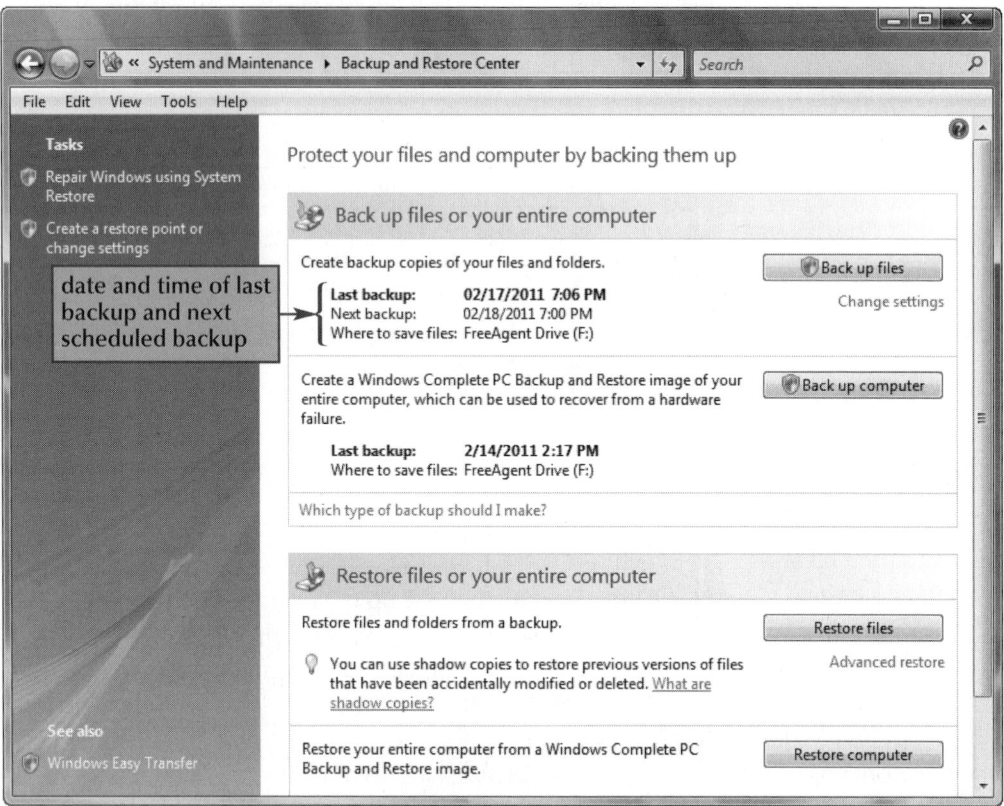

All editions of Windows Vista except Windows Vista Starter Edition contain the option for backing up folders and files, and all editions of Windows Vista except Windows Vista Home Basic permit you to create scheduled backups and to back up to shared network folders. You can, however, use the Back Up Files Wizard in Windows Vista Home Basic to perform a basic backup of your folders and files, and it will remind you to back up your files periodically.

Restoring Folders and Files

Occasionally, a file on your hard disk becomes corrupted or damaged, making it impossible to use the file. A **corrupted file** is a file whose contents have been altered as the result of a hardware or software error, power failure, or a problem with the file system itself. If you find that a file is corrupted, or if you accidentally delete a folder or file, or if your hard disk fails, you can restore folders and files from your backups once you have resolved the problem that occurred with your computer. If your hard disk fails, you have to replace the drive and reinstall Windows Vista. Then, you can restore your personal folders and files on the computer.

The following steps describe the process for restoring folders and files. If you want to perform a "test restore" of a few files right after you backed them up and *before you have made any other changes to those files*, you can perform the operations in these steps.

1. **Select the option for restoring files** Open the Backup and Restore Center, and then click the Restore files button. After you choose this option, the Backup and Restore Center displays a Restore Files dialog box and prompts you whether you want to restore files from the latest backup or from an older backup, as shown in Figure 10-21.

Selecting a backup to restore **Figure 10-21**

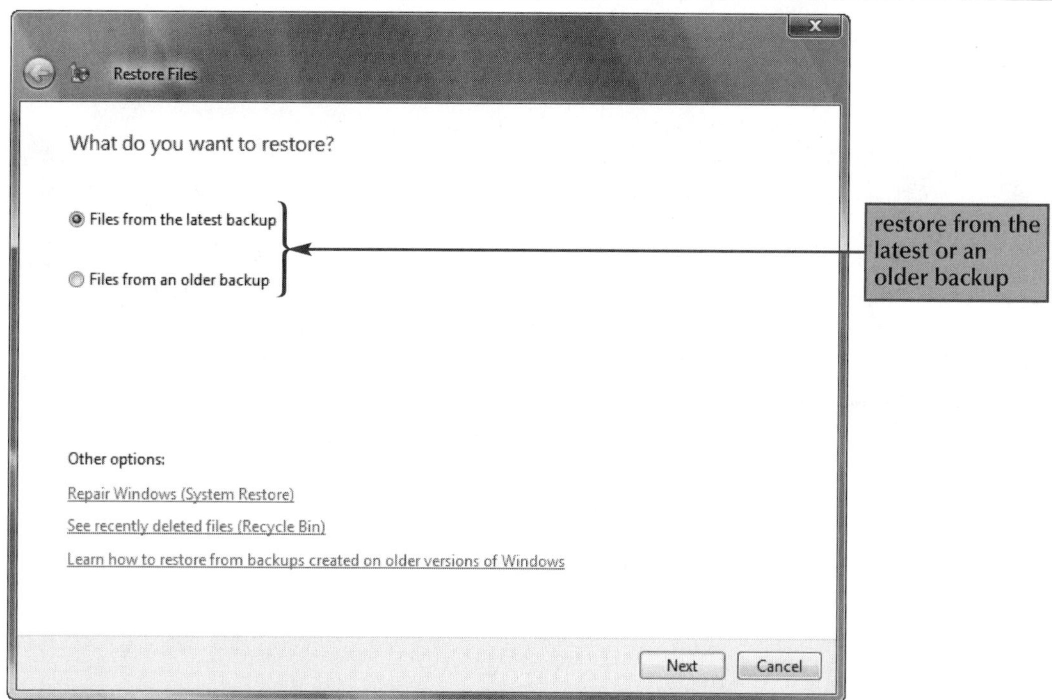

2. **Choose a backup set to restore** If you choose the option for restoring from your most recent backup, the Restore Files Wizard displays another Restore Files dialog box where you can select the folders and files you want to restore. See Figure 10-22. If you choose the option to restore files from an earlier backup, you see a Restore Files dialog box that displays a list of previous backups from which you can choose, as shown in Figure 10-23. After you choose a backup set and advance to the next step, you see the Restore Files dialog box where you pick and choose which folders and files you want to restore.

Figure 10-22 Options for selecting the files and folders to restore

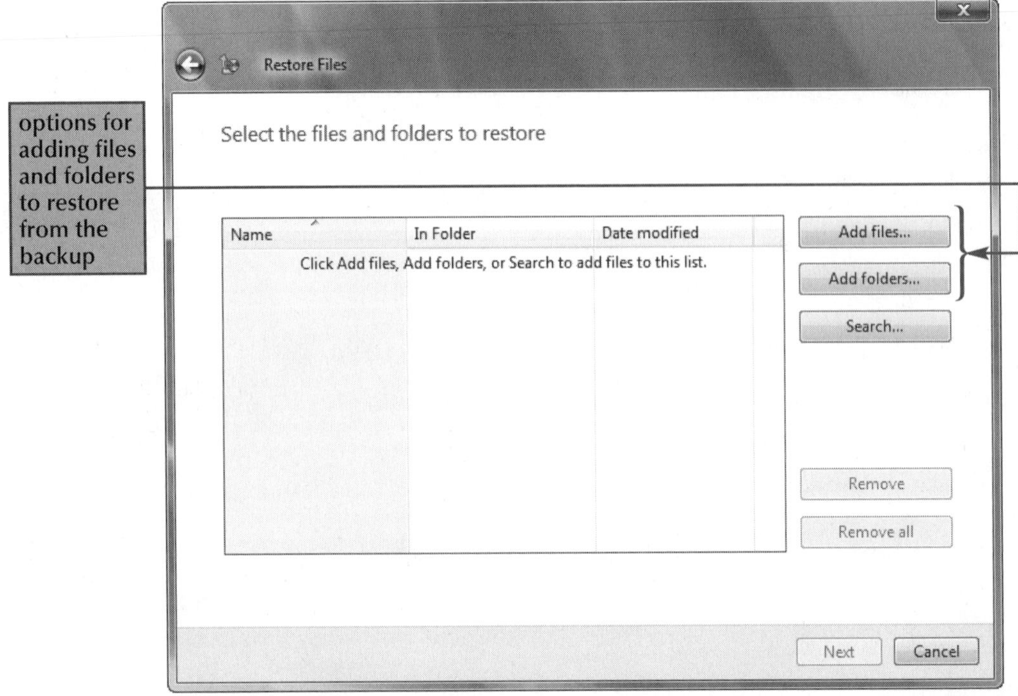

Figure 10-23 Choosing a backup set for a specific date

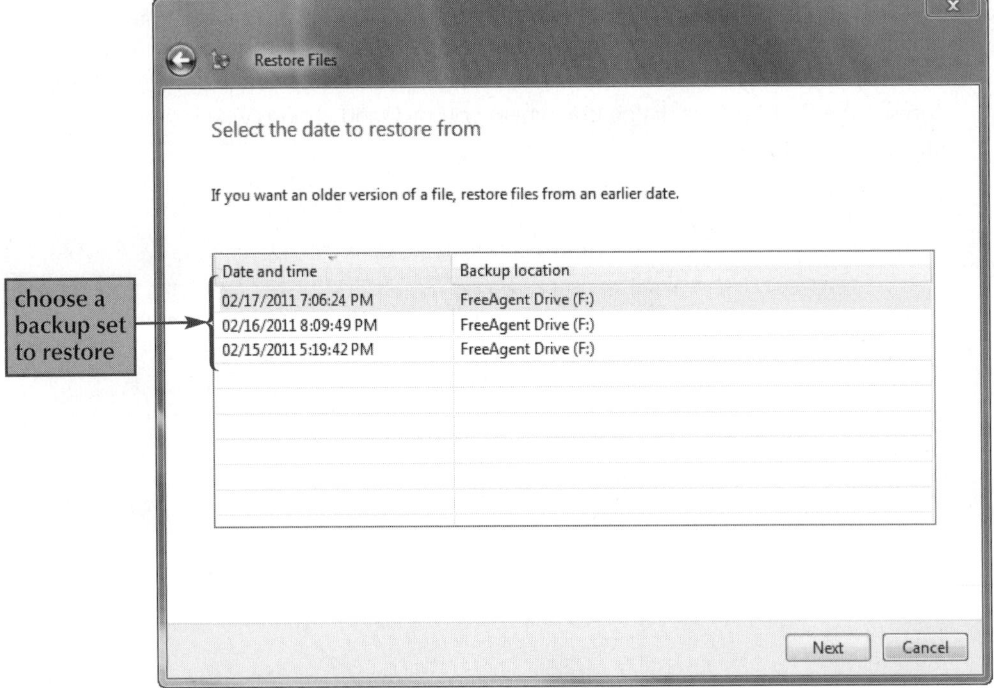

3. **Select the drive to restore** If you choose the Add folders button or Add files button, you browse in the "Add folder to restore" window or the "Add files to restore" window. If you want to restore files to drive C, you select Computer under Favorite Links. As shown in the "Add folder to restore" window in Figure 10-24, you then see the folder for that drive in your backup set.

Selecting the drive that contains the backups to restore **Figure 10-24**

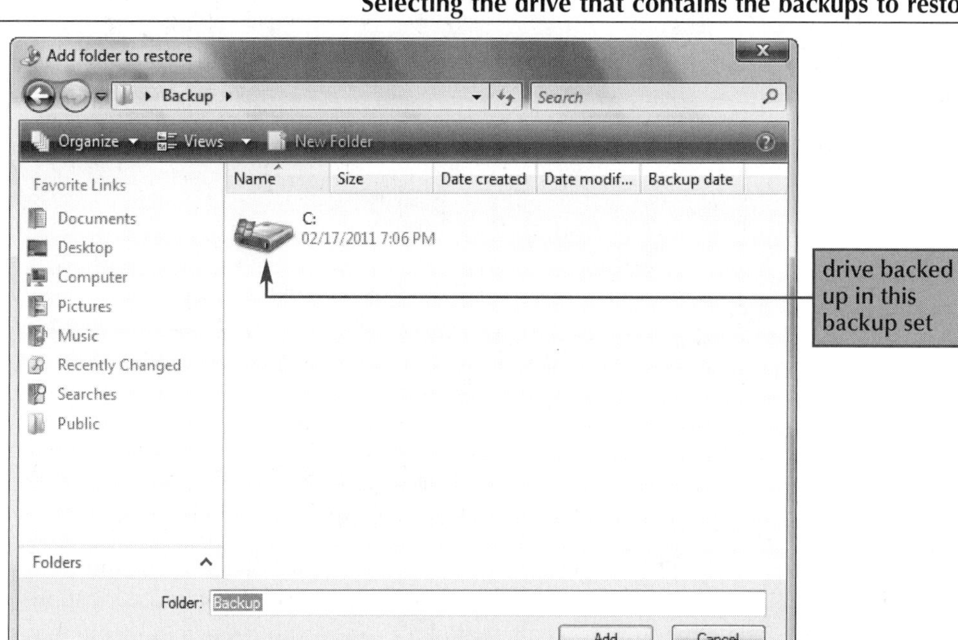

4. **Select the folders and files to restore** Next, you open the drive C folder. If you want to restore your user folder and all its subfolders and files, you select that folder, and then click the Add button. If you want to restore just your Documents folder, you open the Users folder, and then your user account folder. Next, you select the Documents folder, and then click the Add button. If you want to restore a specific folder, you locate that folder, select it, and then click the Add button. After you select a folder (or file), the Restore Files dialog box shows the name of the folder(s) and file(s) you want to restore. You can repeat this process to restore any combination of folders and files. For example, Figure 10-25 shows the Gaia Cartographics folder in the Restore Files dialog box.

Figure 10-25 Gaia Cartographics folder added from backup set

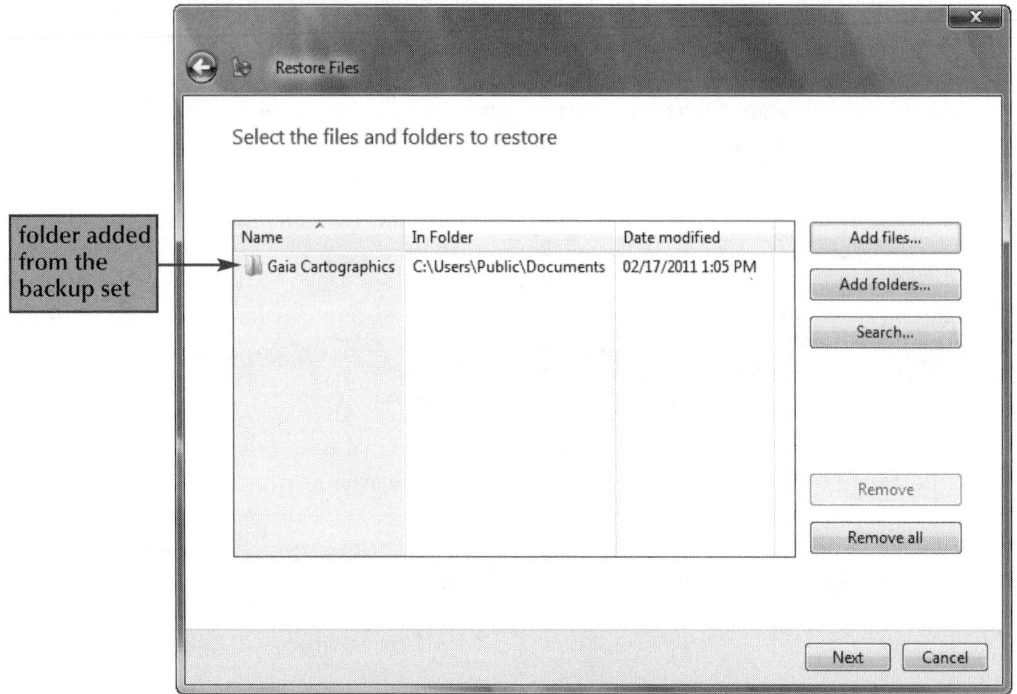

5. **Choose a location for restoring files** After you select the folder(s) and file(s) you want to restore, you advance to the next step where you specify whether you want to restore the folder(s) and file(s) to their original location or to an alternate location. See Figure 10-26. If you choose an alternate location, you browse and locate the folder where you want to restore your folders and files. You can either select an existing folder or create a new folder where you want to restore folders and files.

Figure 10-26 Options for restoring to the original or an alternate location

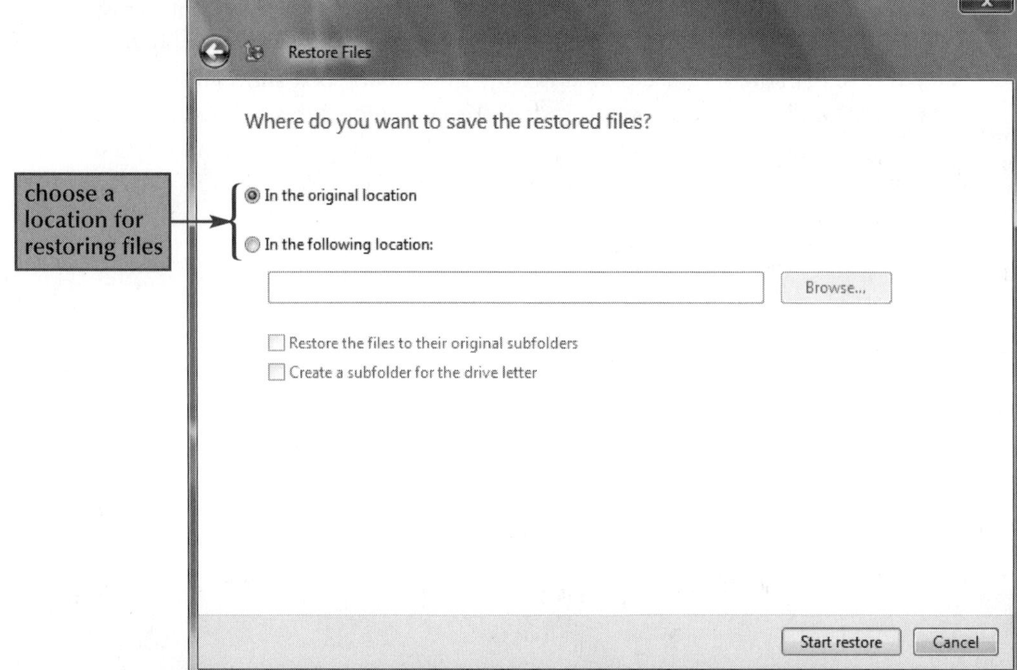

6. **Start restoring the files** Next, you click the Start restore button, and a Restore Files dialog box shows you the progress of the restore operation. If the Restore Files Wizard discovers one or more filenames that match the folders and files you want to restore, it informs you that there is already a file with the same name as a file you want to restore. See Figure 10-27. The Copy File dialog box displays a Copy and Replace, Don't copy, and "Copy, but keep both files" option. If you choose the "Copy, but keep both files" option, the file you restore will have the same name as the existing file in that folder; however, the Restore Files Wizard appends "(2)" to the end of the main part of the filename so that you can distinguish the two different copies. You can use the "Do this for all conflicts" check box to use the same option for every other conflict the Restore Files Wizard encounters rather than let it prompt you for each file that has a filename identical to the one that it is ready to restore.

Deciding how to handle a file conflict during a restore operation **Figure 10-27**

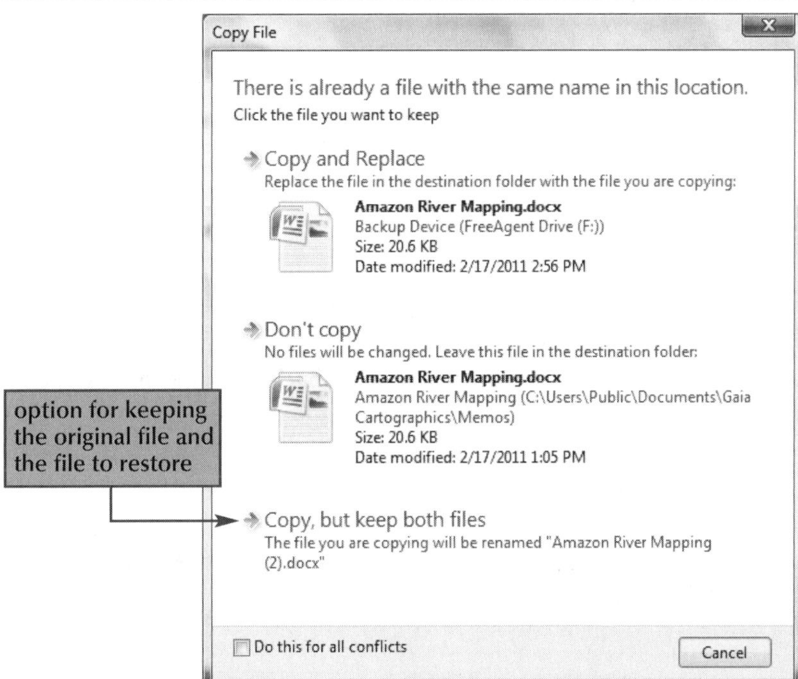

7. **Finish restoring files** After the restore operation is complete, the Restore Files dialog box reports that you successfully restored files.

Reference Window | Restoring Files and Folders

- Log on your computer under an Administrator account.
- Open the Start menu, open the Control Panel, open System and Maintenance, and then open the Backup and Restore Center.
- Click the Restore files button, and then provide Administrator credentials.
- In the Restore Files dialog box, choose whether you want to restore files from the latest backup or from an older backup, and then click the Next button.
- Click the Add files button or the Add folders button to select the files and folders you want to restore, and then click the Next button.
- Choose whether to save the restored files in the original location or an alternate location that you specify, and then click the Start restore button.
- If necessary, select an option in the Copy File dialog box to resolve conflicts where a file being restored has a name identical to an existing file.

InSight | Verifying Backups

A test restore is a good way to check your backup and its media and ensure that you can restore files from that backup and media. You do not want to wait until a serious problem occurs before you attempt to restore files from a backup, and then discover a problem with your backup or your backup media. For example, you can select and rename a folder in your Documents folder, and then restore the original folder from your backup. After you verify that the restore and your backup media worked, you can delete the restored folder and rename your original folder.

Using the Advanced Restore Options

You can also perform an advanced restore from the Backup and Restore Center window, as follows:

Tip

You can open the Backup Status and Configuration dialog box from the System Tools menu.

1. **Choose advanced restore options** If you click the Advanced restore link in the Backup and Restore Center window, you see a Backup Status and Configuration dialog box with an Advanced restore option for restoring files from a backup made on another computer or for restoring files for all users on your computer. See Figure 10-28.

Figure 10-28 Advanced restore options

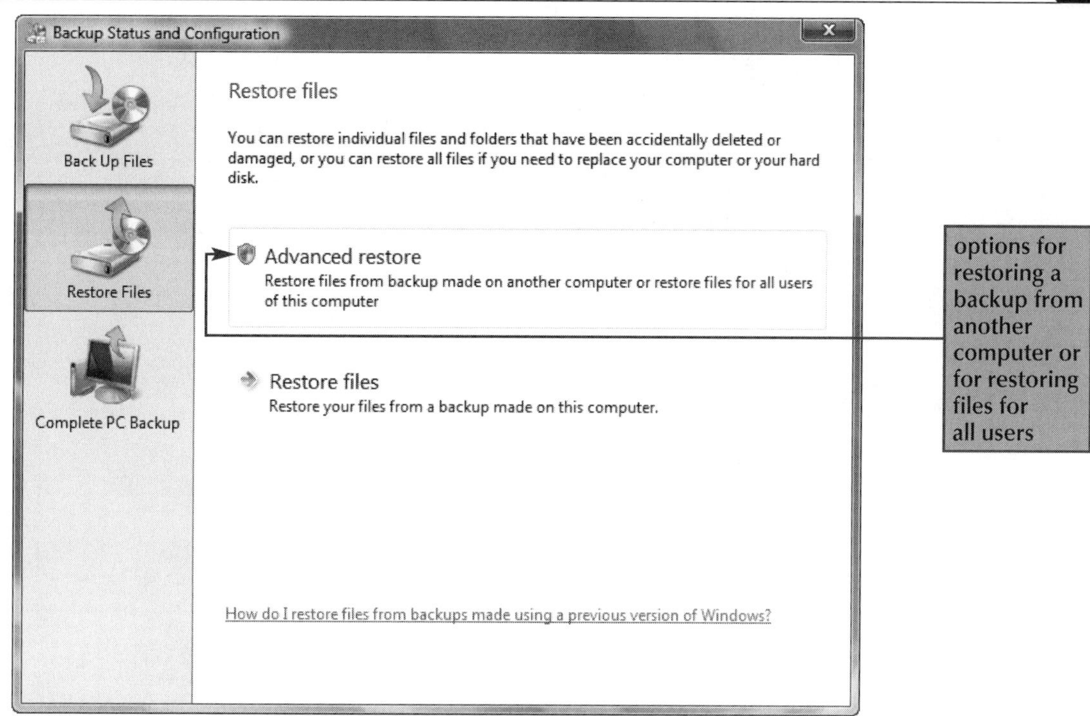

2. **Specify the type of backup set** If you choose the Advanced restore option and provide Administrator credentials, you are prompted to specify the type of backup you want to restore in a Restore Files (Advanced) dialog box. See Figure 10-29. You can:
   - Restore files from the latest backup made on your computer.
   - Restore files from an older backup made on your computer.
   - Restore files from a Windows Vista backup made on another computer.

   If you choose the first option, you can immediately select the folders and files you want to restore. If you choose the second option, the Restore Files Wizard displays a list of all backups made on your computer (including those of other users). After you choose a backup set, you can select the folders and files you want to restore.

Figure 10-29 Choosing an advanced restore option

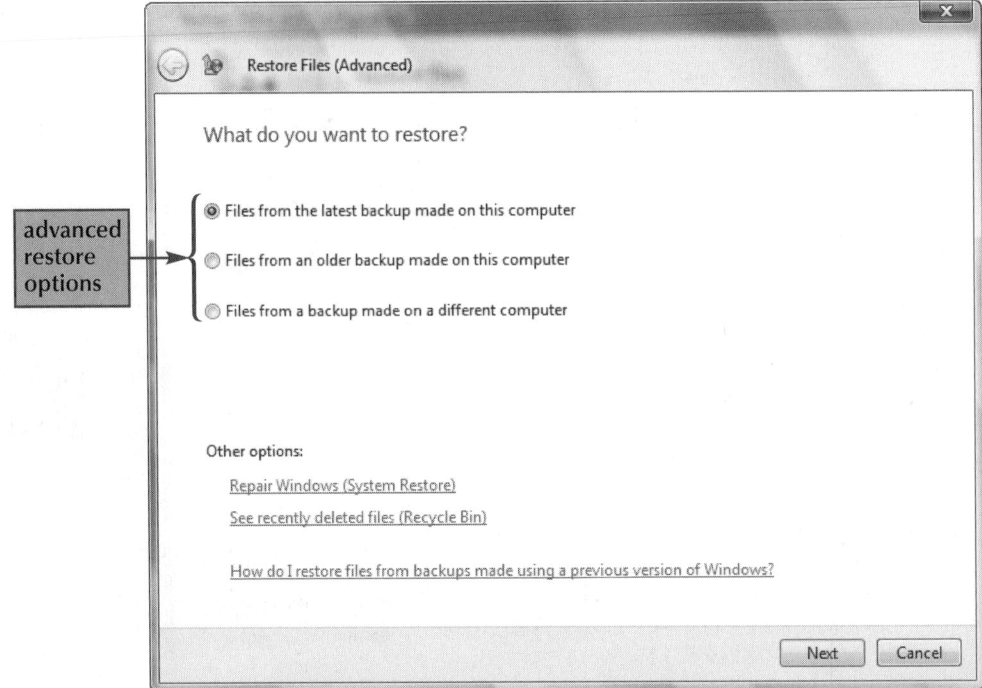

If you choose the third option for restoring from a backup made on a different computer, you are prompted for the location of the backup, as shown in Figure 10-30. The backup you use must be one that you created with the Windows Vista Back Up Files Wizard. This option is also useful if you want to find an even older backup set on your current backup media that is not displayed in the list of available backup sets.

Figure 10-30 Specifying the location of the backup media or network folder

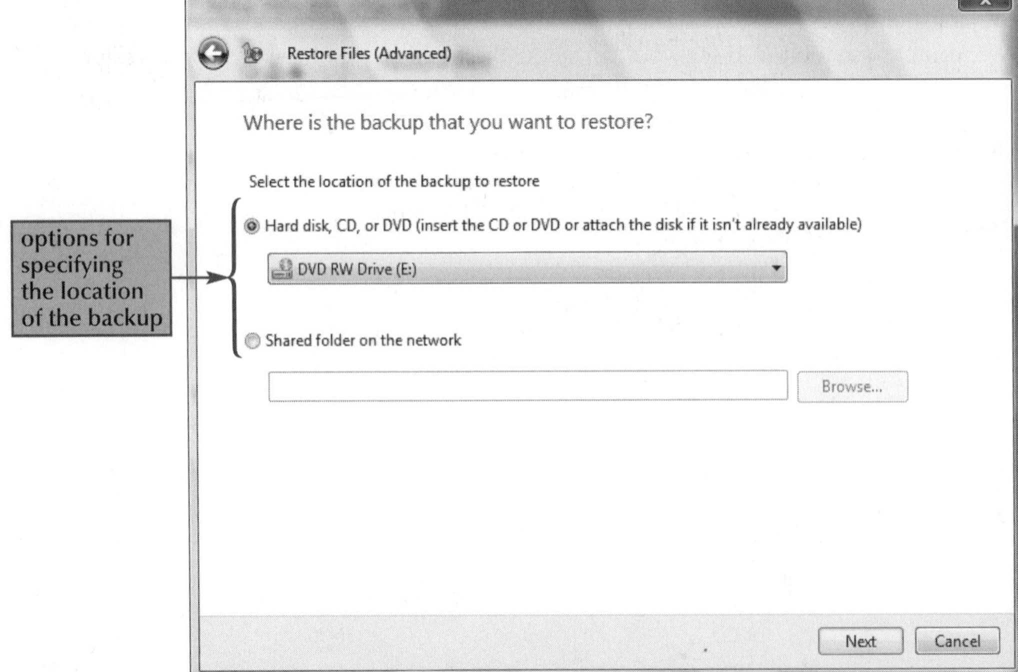

3. **Select backup set and folders and files to restore** After you specify the location of the backup, you can select a backup set, and then step through the process for selecting folders and files to restore, specify the location for the restore operation, and then start the restore.

As a reminder, all editions of Windows Vista except Windows Vista Starter Edition contain the option for backing up folders and files, and all editions of Windows Vista except Windows Vista Home Basic permit you to create scheduled backups and to back up to shared network folders.

Creating a Complete PC Backup and Restore Image

The Complete PC Backup and Restore Image option in Windows Vista Ultimate and Windows Vista Business copies the system volume to a virtual hard disk image file with the "vhd" file extension. That backup must be stored on a volume on your local computer. The first backup is a full backup, but each backup after that is a partial backup that backs up incremental changes *within* files.

The following steps describe the process for performing a Complete PC Backup. If you have not yet performed a Complete PC Backup, but want to back up your system volume and have enough time and enough backup media, you can perform the operations described in the following steps.

Tip

Microsoft recommends that you perform a complete system backup of your computer after you make a significant change to your computer's configuration.

1. **Indicate you want to back up your computer** After you open the Backup and Restore Center, you click the Back up computer button, and then provide Administrator credentials.
2. **Specify the backup location** In the Windows Complete PC Backup dialog box shown in Figure 10-31, you are prompted for the location for saving the backup. Windows Complete PC Backup informs you that it will create a backup of your entire computer, including programs, system settings, and files. It also notes that you can restore your entire computer using the Windows Recovery Environment (WinRE), which you examined in Tutorial 9, and which is reviewed in the next section of the tutorial on restoring files from a Complete PC Backup. You then specify the location of the backup.

Figure 10-31 Specifying a backup location for a Complete PC backup

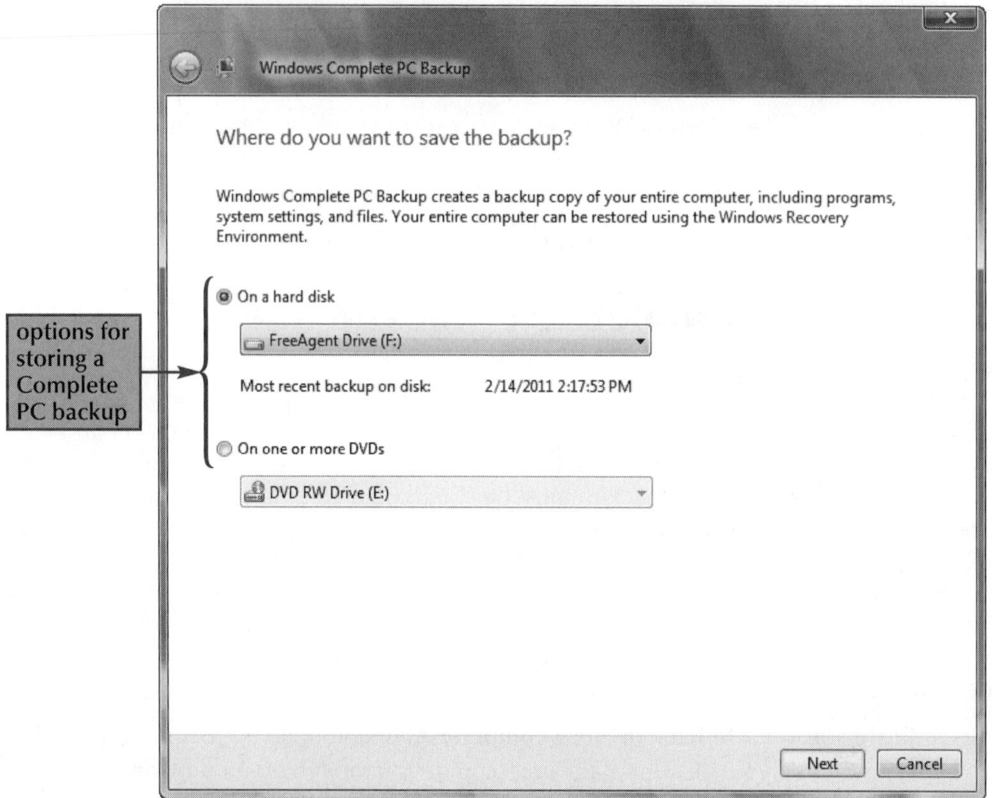

3. **Confirm your backup settings** In the next Windows Complete PC Backup dialog box, you are asked to confirm your backup settings for the backup location and the disks to back up. See Figure 10-32. Windows Complete PC Backup reports on the amount of storage space that might be needed for the backup. On the computer used for this figure, there is already a Complete PC backup stored on the external hard disk, so Windows Complete PC Backup notes that all of the estimated storage space might not be needed and that it will only save differences between the previous Complete PC backup and this next backup. It also notes that if there is not enough storage space on the disk, it will discard one or more of the older backups, starting with the oldest.

Confirming Complete PC backup settings — Figure 10-32

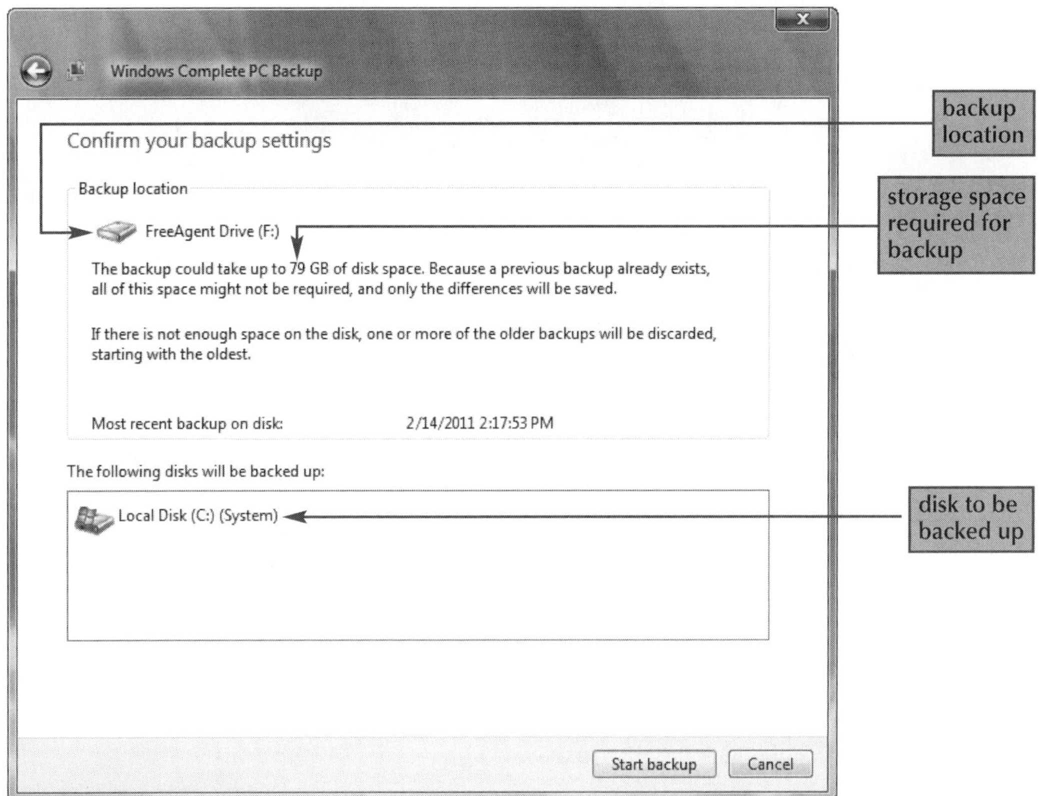

4. **Start the Complete PC Backup** To start the Complete PC Backup, you just click the Start backup button.

Performing a Complete PC Backup | Reference Window

- Open the Start menu, open the Control Panel, open System and Maintenance, and then open the Backup and Restore Center.
- Click the Back up computer button, and then provide Administrator credentials.
- In the Windows Complete PC Backup dialog box, select an external hard disk, memory card drive, CD-RW drive, or DVD-RW drive for the backup.
- In the next Windows Complete PC Backup dialog box, confirm your backup settings, and then click the Start backup button.

After you perform a Complete PC backup, you can examine your backup storage media. You will discover that the folder and file structures for a Complete PC backup are similar to those used for a backup of folders and files described earlier. The following list describes the content of your backup storage media:

- **Image backup folder** After you open a Computer window, and then open a window onto the drive that contains the backup media that you use for your Complete PC backup, you will see a WindowsImageBackup folder. See Figure 10-33.

Figure 10-33 Viewing the folder that contains a Complete PC backup

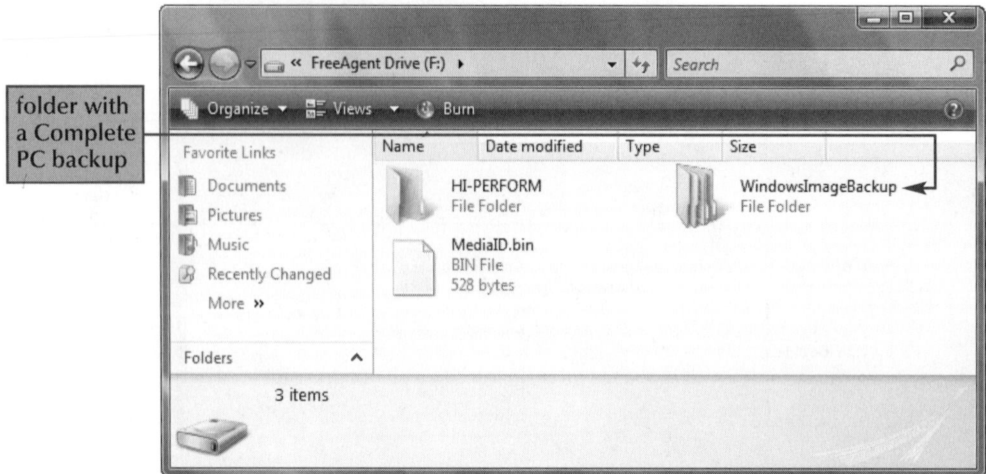

- **Backup set folder** After you open the WindowsImageBackup folder, you will see a folder with your computer's name. Within that folder are two folders—a Catalog folder and a Backup folder with your backup set. See Figure 10-34. The Catalog folder contains two files—GlobalCatalog and BackupGlobalCatalog—that keep track of the Complete PC image versions. The Backup folder name also includes the backup date in the format YYYY-MM-DD followed by the backup time in hours, minutes, and seconds in the format HHMMSS. The folder with your computer's name also contains a MediaID file that identifies the disk image.

Figure 10-34 Viewing the Complete PC backup set folder

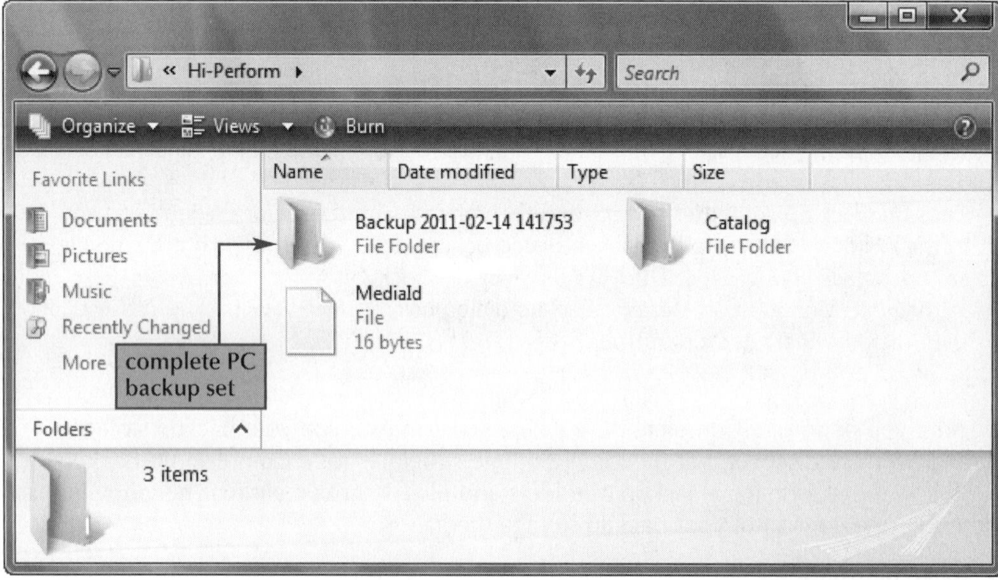

- **Virtual Hard Disk image file and backup configuration files** If you open the Backup folder, you will find a Virtual Hard Disk image file with the "vhd" file extension that contains the complete backup of your computer. See Figure 10-35. On the computer used for this figure, the Virtual Hard Disk image file is approximately 33 GB in size. You will also see XML (Extensible Markup Language) files that store configuration settings for the backup file.

Figure 10-35 Viewing the Complete PC backup files

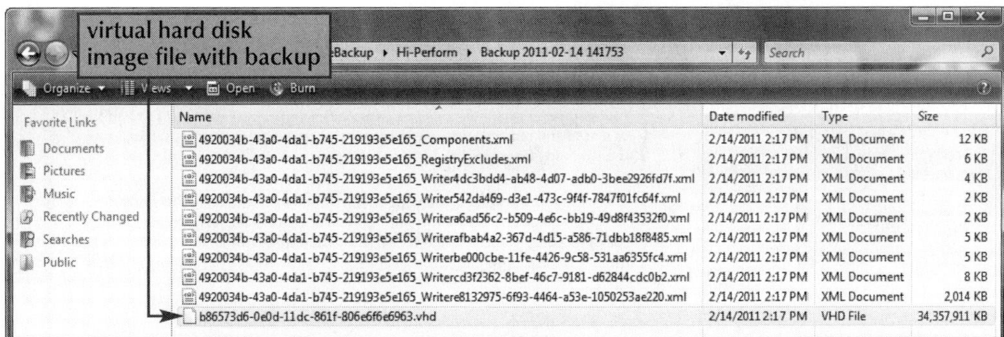

- **Complete PC backup status** After you complete a backup, the Backup and Restore Center will identify the date and time of the last backup, the date and time of the next backup, and the backup location.

If you have Virtual PC (a software environment for running up to four additional operating systems under an existing operating system) installed on your computer, you can mount the virtual hard disk image with the "vhd" file extension as a secondary hard disk drive. You first modify Virtual PC settings in the Virtual PC console for an existing OS (such as Windows XP or Windows 2000 Professional), and then you start that operating system and access the secondary hard disk drive from a Computer window. Next, you access the individual files in your Complete PC Backup as you would folders and files in your Documents folder.

Restoring a Complete PC Backup

If you need to restore your entire system volume from a Complete PC Backup, you must boot from your Windows DVD and open the System Recovery Tools because a complete restore of your computer overwrites everything on the system volume. As noted earlier, a Complete PC Backup is designed for situations in which you have no other choice than to restore the entire system volume, such as after a hard disk failure.

If you need to restore a Complete PC Backup, you can open the Backup and Restore Center, and then click the Restore computer button. Then, a Backup and Restore Center dialog box asks you if you are sure you want to restore your computer. See Figure 10-36. Then, the Backup and Restore Center dialog box points out that this operation reformats your computer's hard disks, erases all programs and user data on the computer, and replaces what you previously had on your computer with the programs and user data from your backups. Then, you are warned to make sure that you have recent backups of your data. It then points out that you must run Windows Complete PC Restore using the System Recovery Options menu from a recovery partition on your hard disk or from a Windows Vista DVD. A **recovery partition** is a hidden hard disk partition that contains software for recovering and restoring your computer. After rebooting your computer from the recovery partition or Windows Vista DVD, you press the F8 key during booting to display the System Recovery Options menu.

Figure 10-36 **Precautionary warning and information for restoring a computer**

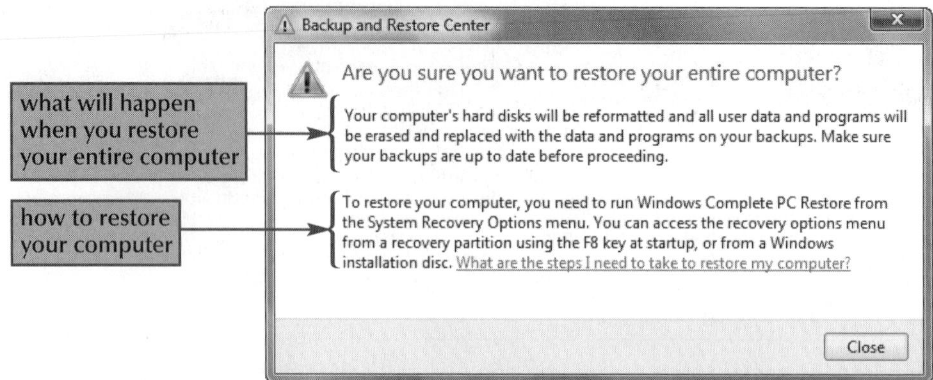

The following steps describe the process for restoring a system volume using a Complete PC Backup. *Do not attempt to perform these steps because doing so overwrites everything on your computer with the contents of a previous Complete PC Backup of your computer.*

1. Insert your Windows Vista DVD and reboot your computer, and if necessary, open the BIOS Setup utility and change the boot sequence so that your computer boots from the drive with your Windows Vista DVD. As your computer reboots, press a key when prompted to boot from your Windows Vista DVD.
2. As your computer boots from the Windows Vista DVD, verify the "Language to install," "Time and currency format," and "Keyboard or input method" settings in the first Install Windows dialog box.
3. In the next Windows dialog box, choose the "Repair your computer" option to work in the Windows Recovery Environment.
4. In the System Recovery Options dialog box, choose the operating system you want to repair, or if no operating system is listed, use the Load Drivers button to load drivers for your hard disk.
5. At this point, the Startup Repair Wizard might automatically start and attempt to recover your computer. If you want to try this option before restoring from a Complete PC Backup, you can let it run. However, if you want to restore your computer from your Complete PC Backup, you choose the option for canceling the Startup Repair Wizard. Likewise, if the Startup Repair Wizard prompts you about running System Restore, you can also cancel this option.
6. In the System Recovery Options dialog box, choose the Windows Complete PC Restore option. Then, a Complete PC Restore Wizard starts.
7. In the first Windows Complete PC Restore dialog box, you specify settings for restoring your entire computer from a backup. At this point, the wizard warns you that everything on your computer will be erased, after which it restores everything from your most recent Complete PC Backup. However, you can choose the "Restore a different backup option" to choose another backup.
8. At the next step, you verify your selections and the disk that you want to restore (for example, C:). If the disk is not formatted, you choose the "Format and repartition disks" option before proceeding.
9. After you verify that you want to perform the operation one more time, the restore operation begins. After it is complete, your computer reboots.

You can restore a Complete PC Backup to another hard disk on the same or another computer even if it's a different size; however, you have to make sure that there is enough storage space on that volume to restore everything from your Complete PC backup.

Session 10.1 Quick Check | Review

1. The interval of time between each full backup is called the ______________ .
2. What type of backup always includes all new and modified files since your last full or normal backup?
3. What type of backup includes only those files that you created or changed since your previous backup—whether it was a full or normal backup or a partial backup?
4. When you create a file or modify and then save an existing file, Windows Vista turns on the ______________ attribute for that file.
5. True or False. When you back up files with the Back Up Files Wizard, it stores backed up files in files with the "zip" file extension.
6. What type of environment must you use to restore a Complete PC Backup?

Session 10.2

Using Previous Versions and Shadow Copies

With Windows Vista Ultimate, Windows Vista Business, and Windows Vista Enterprise, you can use Previous Versions to restore files, folders, or even your entire computer from either a backup or a shadow copy. A **shadow copy** is a copy of a folder or file that Windows creates for a restore point.

System Protection (covered in Tutorial 8) periodically creates restore points that include shadow copies of new files or files that you've modified since the last restore point. If you make a backup with the Backup and Restore Center, Windows Vista uses its Volume Shadow Copy service to take a snapshot of a file that you have open so that the Back Up Files Wizard can back up the file (rather than skipping the open file and excluding it from the backup). You can continue to work on the file, and the Back Up Files Wizard uses the shadow copy of the file for the backup. The shadow copy, which is kept in reserve by the Volume Shadow Copy, then becomes a Previous Version of the file you're backing up.

You can use the VSSADMIN command (the Volume Shadow Copy Service administrative tool), in a command line window to display the storage space reserved on disk for Shadow Copy Storage. On the computer used for Figure 10-37, the amount of storage space used on drive C for the Shadow Copy Storage space is 33.599 GB. By default, Windows Vista reserves 30 percent of a volume's free space or 15 percent of the volume size (whichever is less) for shadow copies. The amount of storage space currently used on the external hard disk drive attached to this computer for Shadow Copy Storage is 1.51 GB, and the maximum storage space reserved on that volume for shadow copies is slightly over 116 GB.

Figure 10-37 Viewing details on Shadow Copy Storage space

Viewing Previous Versions of Folders and Files

Windows Vista can use shadow copies and backup copies of files to restore previous versions of files. However, to view and work with Previous Versions of folders and files, the Windows Vista Volume Shadow Copy must first make shadow copies of the folders and files. The Volume Shadow Copy service does not automatically make a shadow copy (or Previous Version) of each file right after you make a change to a file.

Thiago asks you to check his Amazon Mapping River file in the Memos folder to determine whether there are any Previous Versions of the file, and if so, restore the most recent version of the file so that he can check a change he made in the file.

To complete the following steps, Windows Vista or the Windows Backup and Restore Center must have already created either shadow copies or backups that include the file you examine in this section of the tutorial. If Windows Vista informs you that there are no previous versions for the file, continue to read the following steps so that you are familiar with the use of Previous Versions. Also, you can use the following techniques to examine another file on your computer instead of the file specified in these steps. If you opened that file within the last several days, changed the file, and then saved the changes, you should have a Previous Version of that file.

To check for Previous Versions of a file:

1. Open a **Computer** window, click **Public** under Favorite Links, click the **Public Documents** folder, click the **Gaia Cartographics** folder, and then click the **Memos** folder.
2. Right-click the **Amazon River Mapping.docx** file icon, click **Properties** on the shortcut menu, and then click the **Previous Versions** tab. At the top of this property sheet, Windows Vista informs you that Previous Versions come from shadow copies that are automatically saved to your computer's hard disk or from backup copies. Then, Windows Vista searches for Previous Versions of the file. If it does not find any Previous Versions of the file, it informs you that there are no previous versions. On the computer used for Figure 10-38, Windows Vista found five Previous Versions. Figure 10-39 shows that the Previous Versions of these files are either shadow copies or files stored in a Windows backup. The Previous Versions are grouped by periods of time—such as Today, Yesterday, Earlier This Week, and Last Week. Your Previous Versions will differ.

   Trouble? If no Previous Versions of the Amazon River Mapping.docx file appear in the Properties dialog box for this file, then Windows Vista Volume Shadow Copy may not have made a shadow copy of this file. Open the Properties dialog box for another file that you opened, changed, and saved within the last several days.

Figure 10-38 Viewing Previous Versions of a Microsoft Office Word file

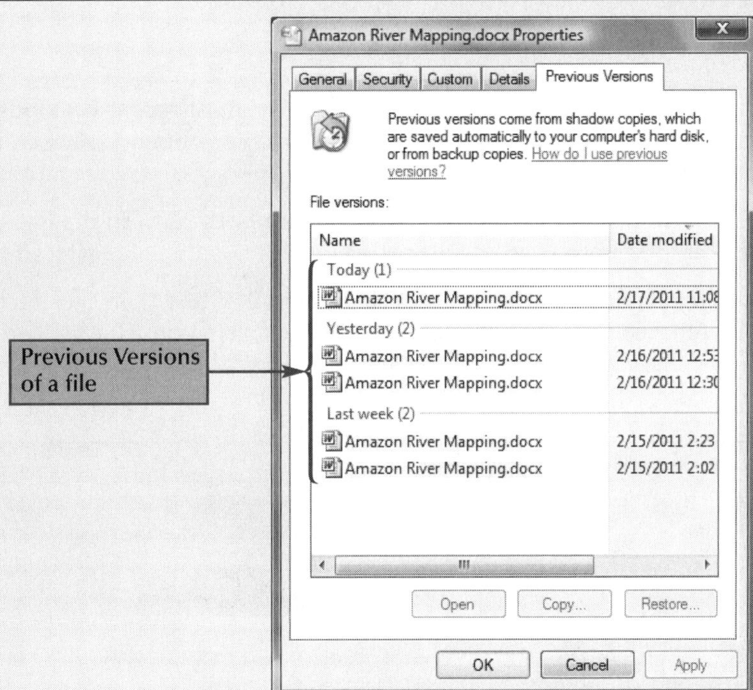

Figure 10-39 Location of Previous Versions of this file

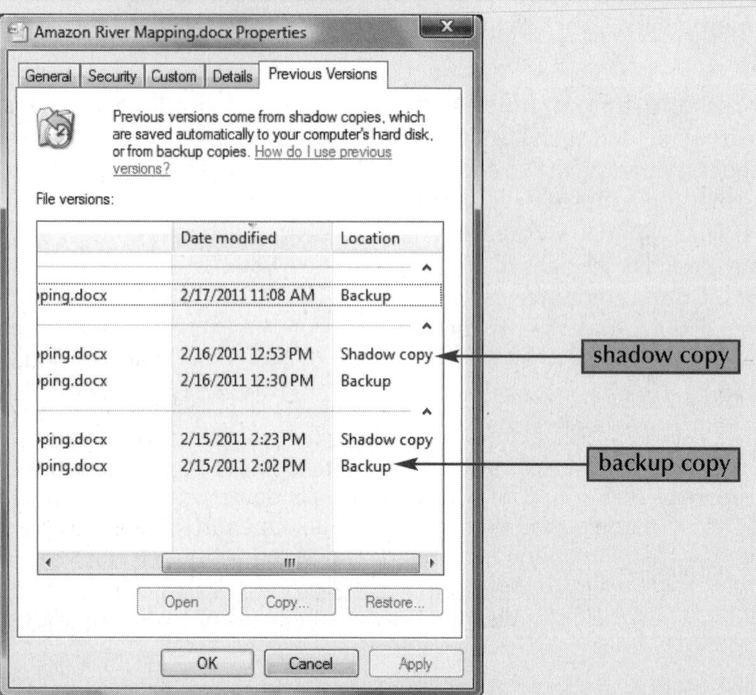

3. If you have a Previous Version of this file, select the most recent **Previous Version** and click the **Restore** button. A Restore Files dialog box opens, followed by a Copy File dialog box.
4. In the Copy File dialog box, click **Copy, but keep both files**. In the Restore Files dialog box, the Restore Files Wizard reports that it successfully restored the file.
5. Click the **Finish** button in the Restore Files dialog box, and then click the **OK** button in the Amazon River Mapping.docx Properties dialog box. In the Memos folder window, you have two versions of this file—the original file and a previous version named "Amazon River Mapping (2).docx." See Figure 10-40.

Figure 10-40 Viewing a restored version of an existing file

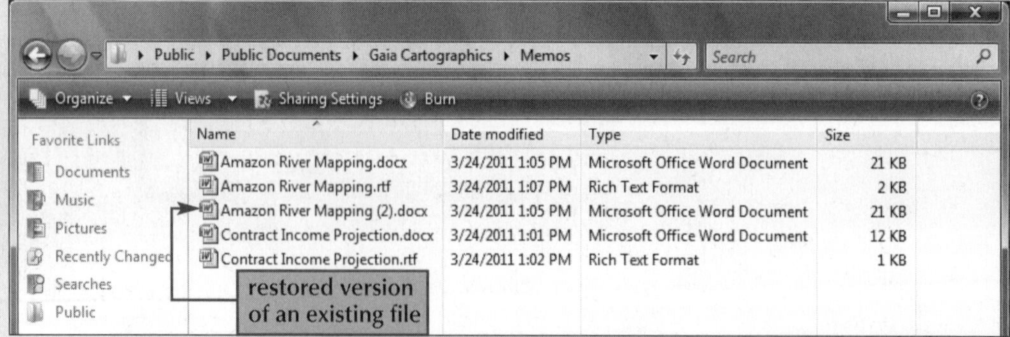

6. Before you start the next section of the tutorial, right-click the **Amazon River Mapping (2).docx** file, click **Delete**, and in the Delete File dialog box, click the **Yes** button.

There are several approaches you can use to retrieve important documents with Previous Versions:

- **Shadow copies and backups of files** If you select a shadow copy of a file from the file's Previous Version property sheet, the Open and Copy buttons become available. You can use the Open button (or just click a Previous Version) to open the Previous Version, and then you can save the file under a new filename. You can use the Copy button to create a copy of the file from a Previous Version, and then you can save it and specify a filename. You can use any of these options (if available) to save previous copies of a file but still retain the current version.
- **Shadow copies and backups of folders** Windows Vista keeps Previous Versions of folders, including the Documents folder, as shown in Figure 10-41. If you choose to open a Previous Version of a folder, you can examine all the files previously contained in that folder and copy or open specific files that you need to another location.

Viewing Previous Versions of the Documents folder | **Figure 10-41**

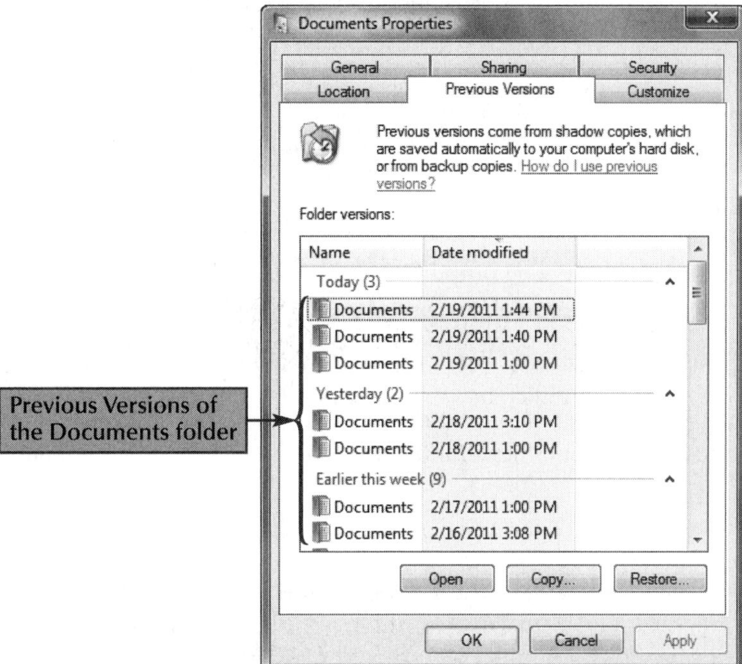

- **Shadow copies and backups of a drive** As shown in Figure 10-42 for drive C, you can also access Previous Versions of your hard disk drive as individual folders, and then retrieve what you need.

Figure 10-42 Viewing shadow copies of a hard disk drive

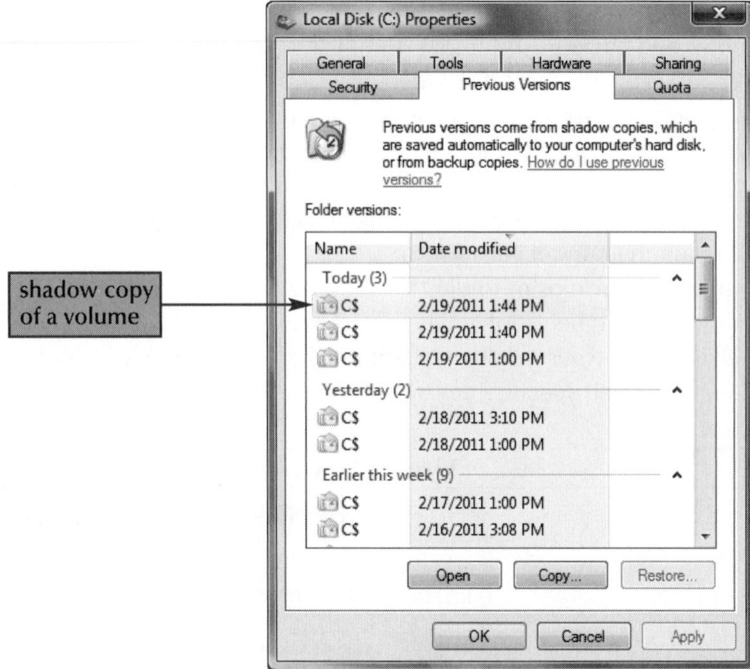

- **Recover deleted files from Previous Versions of a folder's properties** If you delete one or more files in a folder, you can right-click the background of the folder window and choose the options for viewing properties of the folder. Then, from the Previous Versions property sheet, you can recover copies of deleted files.

The use of shadow copies and Previous Versions can be a lifesaver when you accidentally delete or overwrite an important file, or if you need to recover a Previous Version of a file rather than reconstruct the file from scratch or from an existing file. The ability to retrieve previous copies of all files in a folder or the hard disk further enhances this feature.

Using a Briefcase

You can use a **Briefcase** to synchronize copies of files stored in two different locations. To take advantage of this feature, you start by creating a Briefcase folder on a flash drive (for example), and then you copy folders and files on your computer to the Briefcase. The Briefcase keeps track of the full path and name of the original folders and files that you copied. You can then work on the files in the Briefcase using another computer. Later, when you return to the computer that has the original copies of the Briefcase files, you can use the Briefcase to update the original files on that computer's hard disk drive using the changed files in the Briefcase. If you then change the files on that computer's hard disk drive, you can then use the same Briefcase again to update the copies in the Briefcase itself, using the changed files on the hard disk. Likewise, you can use the Briefcase over a network to update copies of the same files stored on two different networked computers.

If you copy a folder to a Briefcase on a flash drive, and then create new files either on your computer or the Briefcase, you can add the new files from your computer to the Briefcase or add new files in the Briefcase to your computer. Likewise, if you delete a file in either location, you can delete the corresponding file in the other location. Essentially, a Briefcase allows you to synchronize files quickly between two different locations.

If you change the original file on your office or home computer, and then later change the same copy of that file in the Briefcase without first updating the original file with the Briefcase, the files are "out of sync," and the Briefcase cannot update the files. Instead, it will recommend that you skip any future updates. Therefore, if you change one of the two copies of a file, you should use the Briefcase to update the other file before you work on it and make further changes.

Tip

The Windows Briefcase feature is available in every version of Windows since Windows 95.

Advantages of Using the Briefcase to Update Files | InSight

Instead of using the Briefcase, why not copy files from your computer to your flash drive, and after you have changed those files on the flash drive, just copy the files back to your computer? One advantage of using the Briefcase over a simple copy-and-paste operation is that it is much faster. It identifies only the files that need to be updated, and then performs the update faster than you could by manually copying the files from one location to another. Furthermore, the Briefcase can update files stored in different locations on your hard disk without your having to locate each location and manually update each file. If you create a Briefcase on a flash drive to store a copy of one or more folders with hundreds of files, the Briefcase can quickly identify only those files that need updating, perform the update, and save you literally hours of time. If you do not use the Briefcase, but try to remember which files you need to update, you run the risk of overlooking some files, and you eventually end up with two or more different versions of those files that you have to manually reconcile. Likewise, if you copy files from different folders into a Briefcase, and then work on them at another location, the Briefcase can update the original files in each of the original folders much faster than you can manually. This is particularly useful if you work on multiple projects and store files for each project in different folders, or if you work for different clients and store your client files in different folders.

Creating a New Briefcase

You can create a new Briefcase on your flash drive, and then copy a set of folders and files to that Briefcase. Then, you can carry that Briefcase with you and work on the folders and files at work, at home, on your laptop, while traveling, or wherever you might have access to a computer. Later, you can update copies of those files on your work or home computer.

Thiago often takes work files home so that he can work on them in the evenings or on weekends. When he travels to a client's office, he takes a copy of his files with him. After he revises a file at home or in a client's office, he needs to copy it to his office computer so that he has the most recent copy of the file in both locations. In the past, he discovered that he had not updated important client files on his office computer, his home computer, or his portable laptop. As a result, he ended up with two or three versions of the same file. To prevent this type of problem from occurring again, he decides to keep a Briefcase on his flash drive for files he might need at home or when visiting a client's office. Since he needs to attend an important meeting with a potential client, he asks you to set up a Briefcase for his files.

To create a Briefcase:

1. Attach your flash drive to the computer, and after Windows Vista displays an AutoPlay dialog box, choose the **Open folder to view files** option in the AutoPlay dialog box, or if necessary, open a Computer window, and then open a window onto your flash drive.

2. On the Start menu, open **Documents**, click **Public** under Favorite Links, click **Public Documents**, click the **Gaia Cartographics** folder icon, and if necessary, use the **Views** button to change the view to Large Icons view.

3. Right-click the **taskbar** and then click **Show Windows Side by Side**. Windows Vista places the windows side by side. Note that the windows are of equal size, and the last window you selected (Gaia Cartographics) is placed on the left side of the desktop.

Tip

If you want to swap the position of the two windows, select the window you want to appear on the left, and then repeat this step.

4. Right-click the **background** of the flash drive window, point to **New**, and then click **Briefcase**. Windows Vista creates a new Briefcase called "New Briefcase."

5. Type **Gaia Cartographics** and press the **Enter** key to rename the Briefcase, and then press the **Enter** key a second time to open the Gaia Cartographics Briefcase. Windows Vista displays a Briefcase dialog box that explains that the primary purpose of a Briefcase is to sync files between a desktop computer and a mobile PC.

6. Click the **Close** button in the Briefcase dialog box.

Now, you're ready to copy files to your new Briefcase.

To copy files to the Briefcase:

Tip

To quickly select all files in a window, press the Ctrl+A keys.

1. Switch to the **Gaia Cartographics** window on the left, click the **Organize** button on the command bar, and then click **Select All**. Windows Vista selects all the folders in the Gaia Cartographics folder window.

2. Drag the **selected folders** from the Gaia Cartographics window to the **Gaia Cartographics Briefcase** window on your flash drive. The Updating Briefcase dialog box shows the progress of copying folders and files to the Gaia Cartographics Briefcase. See Figure 10-43.

Figure 10-43 Copying files from a hard disk to a Briefcase

3. Maximize the **Gaia Cartographics Briefcase** window, use the **Views** button on the command bar to change your view to Details view (if necessary), and then hold down the **Ctrl** key and press the **+** key on the numeric keypad to automatically adjust all column widths for a best fit. The "Sync Copy In" column now displays the entire path for each folder in the Gaia Cartographics folder on your hard disk drive. See Figure 10-44. Since you've just copied these folders to the Gaia Cartographics briefcase, the Status column displays "Up-to-date."

   Trouble? If the Briefcase shows "Needs updating" in the Status column for one or more of your copied folders, click the Back button to return to the previous window, and then click the Forward button to return to the Gaia Cartographics. The Briefcase should now update the window and show "Up-to-date" for all of the copied folders.

Viewing folders copied to a Briefcase from the hard disk

Figure 10-44

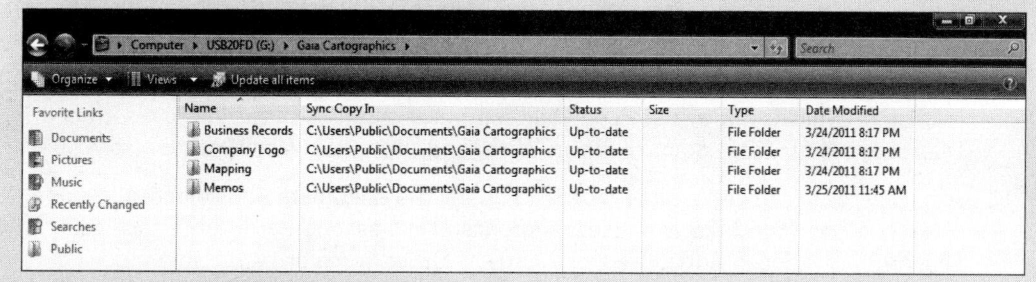

4. Minimize the Gaia Cartographics window on drive C and maximize the Gaia Cartographics Briefcase window.

5. Keep both windows open for the next section of the tutorial.

Like any other briefcase, you can now carry it with you and work on the files wherever you have access to a computer.

Copying Folders and Files to a Briefcase on a Flash Drive

| Reference Window

- Attach a flash drive to your computer, and then choose the "Open folder to view files" option in the AutoPlay dialog box.
- Right-click the background of your flash drive window, point to New, click Briefcase, type a new name for the Briefcase, press the Enter key, and then open your Briefcase.
- Open the folder that contains the files you want to add to a Briefcase.
- Right-click the taskbar, and then click Show Windows Side by Side.
- In the window that contains the files you want to add to your new Briefcase, click the Organize button, and then click Select All.
- Drag the selected folders and files to the Briefcase window on your flash drive.

You can have as many Briefcases as you need—one for each client or each project, for example—so that you have access to the files you need when working at another computer.

Modifying a File in the Briefcase

The Briefcase is similar to other folders you use. If you want to modify a file, you open the Briefcase, open the folder with the file, and then open, modify, and save the file back to its Briefcase folder. Later, you can update the original copy of this same file stored on another computer.

Thiago asks you to update a memo regarding an upcoming staff meeting on an expansion of their current Amazon River mapping project in his Briefcase. Then, he will update the corresponding file on his computer later.

Although you are going to continue to work on the same computer, imagine that you have taken the flash drive with the Briefcase to a client's office and worked on files in the Briefcase.

To modify a Briefcase file:

1. In the Gaia Cartographics Briefcase, click the **Memos** folder icon, and if you cannot see the full name of each file, press the **Ctrl** and **+** keys to adjust columns to a best fit.

Trouble? If you closed the Gaia Cartographics folder under Public Documents on your computer and the Gaia Cartographics Briefcase on your flash drive, open these folders, right-click the taskbar, and then click Show Windows Side by Side.

Tip

You can open an application first, and then open a file directly from a Briefcase.

2. If Microsoft Office 2007 is installed on your computer, click the **Amazon River Mapping.docx** file icon. If you are using an earlier version of Microsoft Office, or if Microsoft Office is not installed on your computer, right-click the **Amazon River Mapping.rtf** file icon, point to **Open With**, and then click **WordPad**.
3. After Microsoft Office Word or WordPad opens the document you selected, change "March 22" to **March 29** in the last sentence of the second paragraph, save your change to this document, close the Microsoft Office Word or WordPad window, and if necessary, adjust the columns in the Memos folder for a best fit. In the Status column, the Briefcase displays "Needs updating" for the Amazon River Mapping file. See Figure 10-45.

Figure 10-45 Recently modified file needs updating

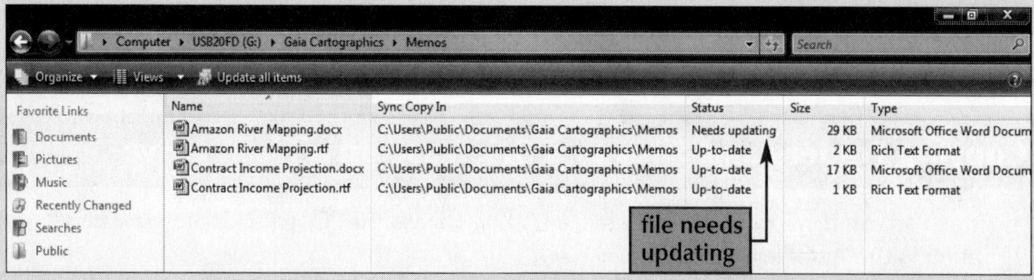

4. Keep the Gaia Cartographics Briefcase and the Gaia Cartographics windows open for the next section of the tutorial.

Reference Window | Modifying a File in a Briefcase

- Open the Briefcase, open the folder that contains the file you want to modify (if necessary), and then click the file icon to open it in the application associated with that file type on your computer, or if necessary, right-click the file icon, point to Open With, and then choose another program that works with the same file type.
- Modify the file, save your changes, and then close the application window.

As you work at home or while traveling, you can modify any file in the Briefcase, and then update your original copies when you return to the computer that contains the original files.

Using a Briefcase to Update Files

If you have updated files on your computer and want to update the copies of those files stored in a Briefcase, or if you have updated files in your Briefcase and want to update the original files on your computer, or if you want to update files in both your Briefcase and your computer at the same time (you might have worked with different files in each location), you open the Briefcase and use the Update all items button. The Briefcase then identifies which files need updating. It also identifies the location of the files to be updated (the original files on your desktop computer or the files in the Briefcase itself). You can perform the update, change the direction of the update (restoring a previous copy of a file), or skip the update.

After Thiago returns to his office, he decides to update the copy of the Amazon River Mapping file stored on his office computer with the new version of that file in his Briefcase on his flash drive.

To update files on your computer using your Briefcase:

1. Click the background of the Memos folder window in your Briefcase to remove the selection from any currently selected file, and then click the **Update all items** button on the command bar. The Update Gaia Cartographics dialog box identifies the file you need to update. See Figure 10-46. Even though you cannot see the full filename or full path, the Briefcase recommends that you replace the unmodified version of the Amazon River Mapping file in the Gaia Cartographics Memos folder on drive C (the one shown on the right) with the more recently modified version in the Briefcase (the one shown on the left). Notice that the times (and perhaps the dates) of the modified and unmodified files on this computer are different and that the modified one on the left is more recent. If you had modified more than one file, the Briefcase would list all of the files you had modified. Your file dates and times will differ.

Tip

If you want to update only one file in your Briefcase, select that file, and then click the Update this item button.

Figure 10-46 Option for updating files between a Briefcase and the hard disk

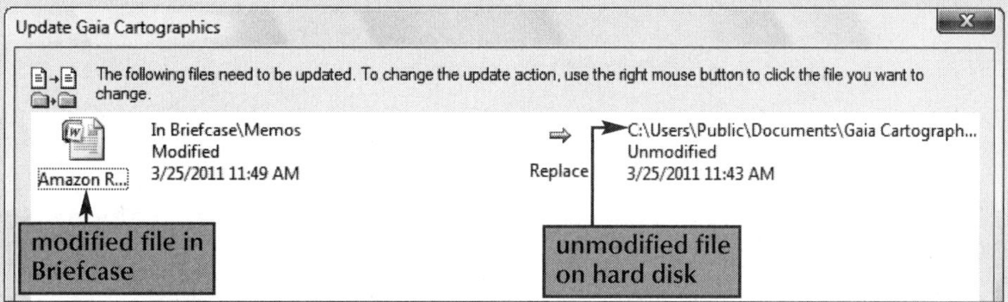

2. Right-click the **Replace** action arrow. As shown in Figure 10-47, the Briefcase displays a shortcut menu that allows you to change the direction of the Replace so that you can restore the modified copy in the Briefcase to its original condition, using the original file stored on drive C. Or, if you do not want to update one of the files listed in this dialog box, you can use the shortcut menu to change the Replace action to a Skip action.

Figure 10-47 Options for updating a file

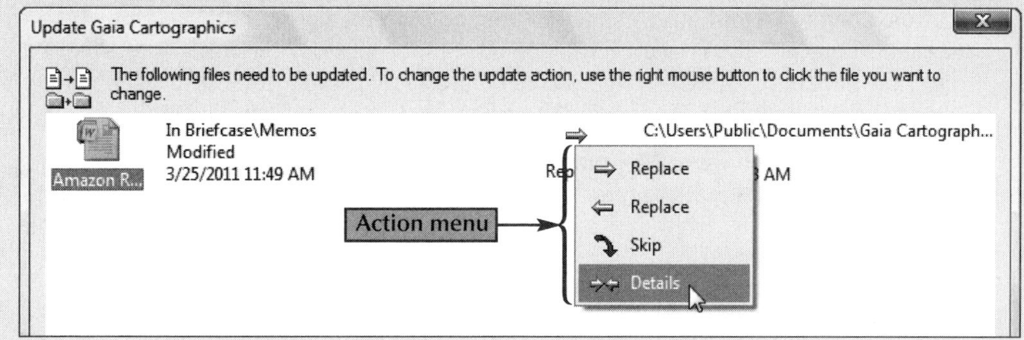

3. Click **Details** on the shortcut menu. In the Resolve Conflict dialog box, you can specify which version to keep (the newer version shown at the top) or the previous version (shown at the bottom). See Figure 10-48. The newer version will have "(newer)" to the right of the information for Date modified. In the Resolve Conflict dialog box, you can see the full name of each file and the full path for each file. Your details will differ if you opened the Rich Text Format (RTF) version of the Amazon River Mapping file.

Figure 10-48 **Options for resolving a file conflict**

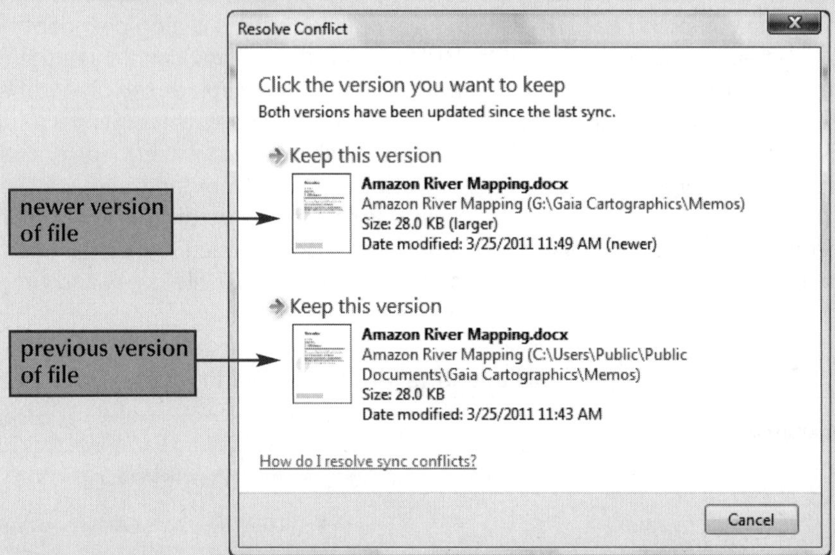

4. Click **Keep this version** to keep the newer version. You return to the Update Gaia Cartographics dialog box.

5. In the Update Gaia Cartographics dialog box, click the **Update** button. The Briefcase updates the previous version of the file on your computer and closes the Update Gaia Cartographics dialog box. In the Status column, the Briefcase shows "Up-to-date" for the Amazon River Mapping file.

6. Click the **Gaia Cartographics** taskbar button to open the Gaia Cartographics window, maximize the Gaia Cartographics window, open the **Memos** folder, and then use the **Views** arrow button on the command bar to change to **Large Icons** view.

7. If you do not see a Preview Pane on the right side of the window, click the **Organize** button, point to **Layout**, click **Preview Pane**, point to the border between the Contents pane and the Preview Pane, and after the mouse pointer changes to ↔, drag the **border** to the left so that you can more easily preview the contents of a file in the Preview Pane without opening the file.

8. Point to the **Amazon River Mapping** file icon for the file you just updated. As shown in Figure 10-49, note that the original file was updated to show the March 29 date for the staff meeting. Your view in the Preview Pane will differ if you opened and modified the Rich Text Format (RTF) version of the Amazon River Mapping Proposal file, but you can still verify that the Briefcase updated the date for the staff meeting in this file.

Figure 10-49 File updated using a newer version from a Briefcase

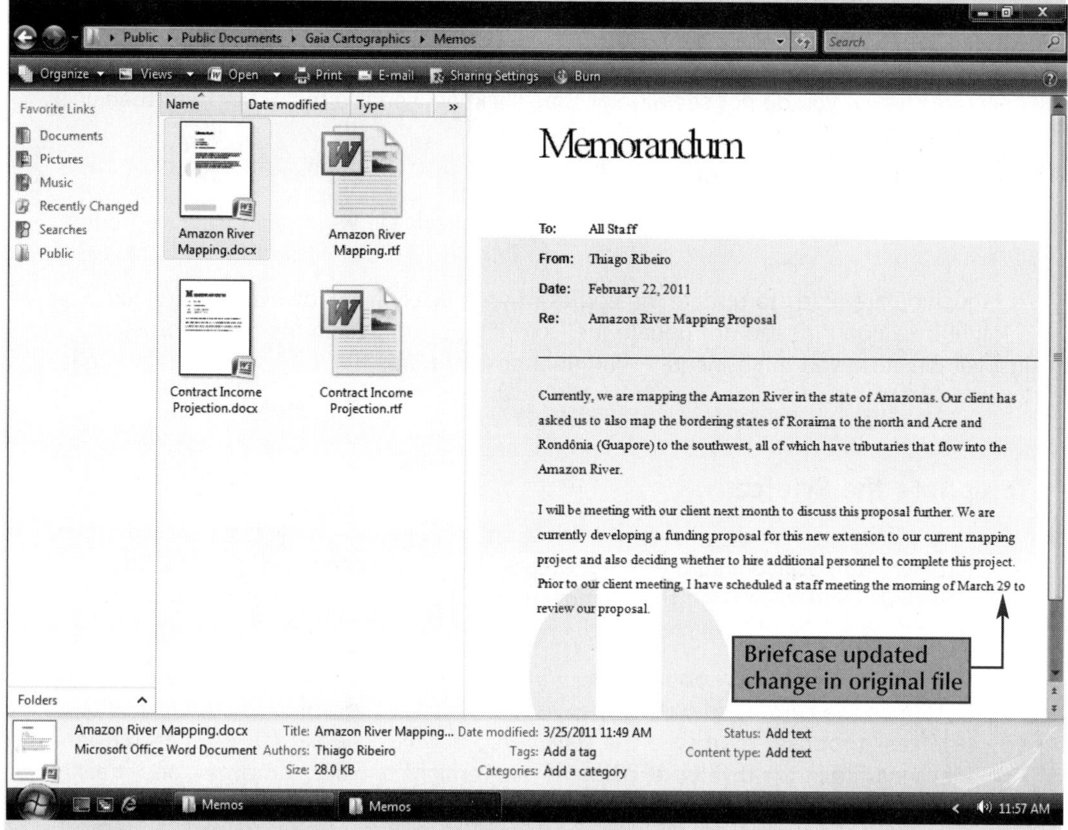

Thiago asks you to make an additional change to the Amazon River Mapping file, delete the Contract Income Projection file, and make a change to the Gaia Cartographics Logo file on his computer. Then, he asks you to update his Briefcase.

To update these files on your computer:

1. If Microsoft Office is installed on your computer, click the **Amazon River Mapping.docx** file icon in the Memos folder. If you are using an earlier version of Microsoft Office, or if Microsoft Office is not installed on your computer, right-click the **Amazon River Mapping.rtf** file icon in the Memos folder, point to **Open With**, and then click **WordPad**.
2. In the first sentence of the first paragraph, change "in the state of Amazonas" to "in the Brazilian state of Amazonas" (without the quotation marks) by inserting the word **Brazilian** before "state," save your changes to this document, and then close Microsoft Word or WordPad.
3. Right-click the **Contract Income Projection.docx** file icon, click **Delete**, and in the Delete File dialog box, click the **Yes** button.
4. In the Address Bar, click **Gaia Cartographics**, click the **Company Logo** folder icon, right-click **Gaia Cartographics Logo.tif**, point to **Open With**, and then click **Paint**.

5. In the Paint window, click the **dark blue** color box on the first row of the Color Box at the top of the window (second color from the end of the first row), and then click the **Fill With Color** button in the Toolbox on the left side of the window, click the **white background** behind the graphic image. Paint fills the background with this color.

   Trouble? If you do not see a Color Box, click View on the menu bar, and then click Color Box.

6. Click **File** on the menu bar, click **Save**, and then close the Paint window.
7. Click the Memos taskbar button to bring the Briefcase window to the foreground.

Now, you are ready to update the copies in your Briefcase. However, you realize that it might be a good idea to not update the Company Logo Design file in your Briefcase just yet, because you might need the original design in this file. Plus, you can update it later.

To update the Briefcase:

1. In the Briefcase window, click the **Back** button to return to the Gaia Cartographics folder. In the Status column, the Briefcase displays "Needs updating" for the Company Logo folder and the Memos folder (the two folders that contained the three files you modified or deleted).
2. Click the **white background** of the window, and then click the **Update all items** button on the command bar. In the Update Gaia Cartographics dialog box, the Briefcase proposes to update the Gaia Cartographics Logo and the Amazon River Mapping file in the Briefcase, using newer versions on your computer, and it also proposes to delete the "Contract Income Projection docx" file in the Briefcase because you deleted this file on your computer. See Figure 10-50. The dates for your modified or deleted files will differ.

Figure 10-50 Updating multiple files in the Briefcase

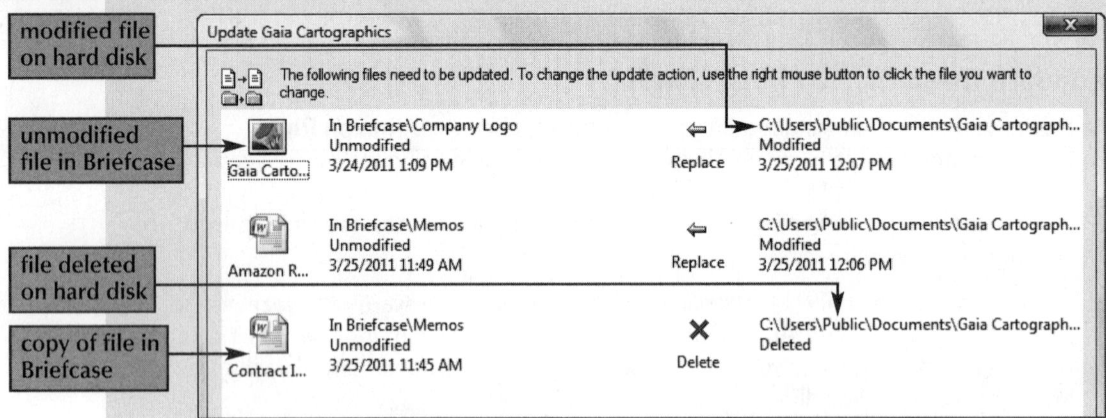

3. Right-click the **Replace** action arrow for the Gaia Cartographics Logo (the first file listed), and then click **Skip**.
4. Right-click the **Delete** action for the last file, the "Contract Income Projection (Initial Draft).docx" file, and then click **Details**. In the Resolve Conflict dialog box, the Briefcase offers you two options. You can keep the version in your Briefcase and copy it back to your computer to replace the file you deleted, or you can delete the version of the file in both locations. See Figure 10-51.

Options for restoring a deleted file or removing both files

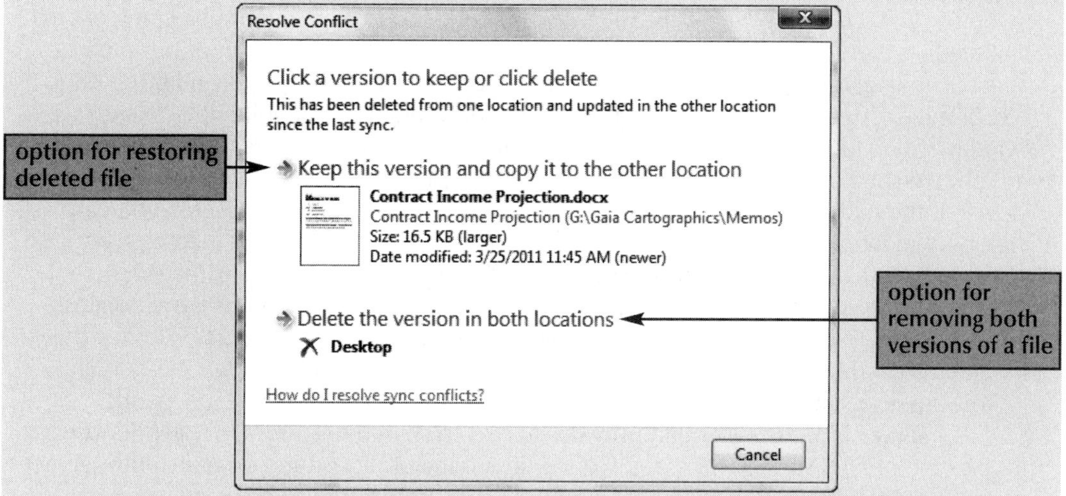

Figure 10-51

5. Click **Delete the version in both locations**, right-click the **Don't Delete** action arrow for the last file and click **Delete**, and then click the **Update** button in the Update Gaia Cartographics dialog box.
6. Open the Briefcase's **Company Logo** folder, use the **Views** button to switch to **Large Icons** view (if necessary), and notice that the original version of the Gaia Cartographics Logo is still in the Briefcase. Your computer still has the revised version of this file.
7. Close the Briefcase Company Logo folder window and your Gaia Cartographics' Company Logo folder window.

A Briefcase simplifies the process of reconciling different versions of the same file on different drives or different computer systems so that you have the most recent version of any file that the Briefcase tracks. You can create a Briefcase for each set of folders and files that you use on more than one computer system. You can use a Briefcase on a network. If you change files on one computer, you can immediately update the corresponding files on other computers in the network.

Updating Files in a Briefcase

| Reference Window

- Open a Computer window, and then open a window for the drive that contains the Briefcase.
- Open the Briefcase, click the Briefcase folder window background, and then click the Update all items button on the command bar.
- Review the files in the Update Briefcase dialog box, and if necessary, right-click the action arrow and change the direction of the replace, choose the option to skip the replace, or choose the option to not delete a file.
- In the Update Briefcase dialog box, click the Update button.
- Close the Briefcase window.

Next, you'll explore the Sync Center, which lets you synchronize files you work on in different locations.

Using the Sync Center

If you store two copies of the same file in two different locations so that you can work on that file in either location, you can use the new Windows Vista **Sync Cente**r to synchronize (or update) one or more files if you make changes to files in one location. You can synchronize files stored on your computer and a flash drive or a mobile device, such as a Windows mobile device, mobile phone, portable music or video player, digital camera, or PDA (Personal Digital Assistant); however, the mobile device must support the Sync Center. If the mobile device does not support the Windows Vista Sync Center, you can check the manufacturer's Web site for the mobile device to determine if there is sync software that enables you to perform the same type of synchronization as the Windows Vista Sync Center. Also, some mobile devices might include an option for synchronizing your contacts. To be able to use your contacts in the Windows Vista Contacts folder, the mobile device must be able to read files with the "contact" file extension.

You can also synchronize files between your computer and folders of a network server. A **server** is a computer that provides access to shared resources for network users. In this type of sync relationship, you work with a copy of files stored on a network server from your Offline Files folder. This latter option, synchronizing files between your computer and folders on a network, is not available in Windows Vista Starter, Windows Vista Home Basic, and Windows Vista Home Premium.

When you use the Sync Center to synchronize files stored in two locations, the Sync Center compares the files in each location to determine whether they are identical or different. If the files differ, the Sync Center copies the more recent version of the files to the other location and overwrites older versions of the files. If you change the same file in both locations, the Sync Center will report a **sync conflict** and asks you which version of the file you want to keep.

If the Sync Center discovers that a file exists in only one location (it's a new file), it copies the file to the other location. Likewise, if you delete a file in one location, the Sync Center deletes the file in the other location.

You can also set up one of two kinds of sync relationships, or what are called **sync partnerships**:

- **One-way sync partnership** In this type of sync relationship, the Sync Center copies files from what you designate as a primary location (such as your hard disk) to a secondary location (such as a flash drive or mobile device). It never copies files from the secondary location to the primary location.
- **Two-way sync partnership** In this type of sync relationship, the Sync Center copies files from a primary location to a secondary location and vice versa.

The Sync Center is a valuable resource for people on the move who need to update files between a desktop computer and a mobile device that supports the features available in the Sync Center.

Restoring Your Computer

Complete the following steps to restore your computer to its original settings.

1. If you want to turn off single-click activation, click the **Computer** icon on the desktop, click the **Organize** button on the command bar, and under "Click items as follows" on the General property sheet in the Folder Options dialog box, click the **Double-click to open an item (single-click to select)** option button.
2. Click the **OK** button to close the Folder and Options dialog box, and then close the Computer window.

3. To remove the Computer icon from the desktop, open the **Start** menu, right-click **Computer**, click **Show on Desktop**, and then close the Start menu.
4. Open a window onto your flash drive, and then select and delete the Gaia Cartographics Briefcase.
5. Delete the Gaia Cartographics folder from the Public Documents folder.

Session 10.2 Quick Check | Review

1. A(n) ________________ is a copy of a folder or file that Windows creates for a restore point.
2. What two types of files can Windows Vista use to restore files to a computer?
3. You can use the ________________ to synchronize copies of files stored in two different locations—such as your hard disk drive and a flash drive.
4. True or False. You can use the Windows Sync Center to synchronize files by using a one-way sync partnership or two-way sync partnership between your computer and a mobile device, such as a mobile phone.
5. True or False. If you rename a file in a Briefcase, the Briefcase deletes the copy of that same file stored on your hard disk, and then creates a new file on the hard disk with the new filename.
6. You can restore Previous Versions of ________________ , ________________ , and ________________ .

Tutorial Summary | Review

In this tutorial, you learned about the importance of making backups and common ways in which people lose important documents and data. You explored different approaches for backing up files and how best to organize your folders and files for backups. You examined options for developing a backup strategy that combined a full backup with either a differential or incremental backup. You also compared specific differences in how differential and incremental backups work, the use of daily and copy backups, and how backup utilities use the Archive attribute to determine which files to back up. You examined the importance of keeping multiple backups, using different types of backup media. You opened the Backup and Restore Center and learned how to back up folders and files or an entire computer and how to restore folders and files or an entire computer. You also viewed the folder structure and types of files used by these different types of backups. You examined the importance and use of shadow copies, as well as backups, for restoring files, using the new Windows Vista Previous Versions feature. You also viewed Previous Versions of a file. You created a Windows Briefcase, copied files from your hard disk to the Briefcase, changed files in both the Briefcase and on your hard disk drive, and then automatically updated files in both locations using the Briefcase. Finally, you explored the Windows Sync Center for synchronizing files between a computer and a mobile device and between a network folder and Offline Files.

Key Terms

Archive attribute
Archive bit
backup cycle
backup utility
Briefcase
copy backup
corrupted file
daily backup
differential backup
full backup
full system backup
incremental backup
normal backup
one-way sync partnership
recovery partition
server
shadow copy
Sync Center
sync conflict
sync partnership
two-way sync partnership
XML (Extensible Markup Language)
XPS (XML Paper Specification)

Practice | Review Assignments

Practice the skills you learned in the tutorial.

For a list of Data Files in the Review folder, see page 611.

Recently, a representative of the local community college contacted Thiago to discuss the possibility of hiring a student intern as part of an independent work-study program. Through a federal program, the college would pay half of the student intern's salary. Thiago interviewed the student and decided to hire him to work on the new expansion of the Amazon River mapping project. Thiago asks you to review and demonstrate options for backing up and restoring files with this intern.

As you complete each step in this Review Assignment, record your answers to questions so that you can submit them to your instructor. Use a word processing application, such as Word or WordPad, to prepare your answers to these questions. If you change any settings on the computer you are using, note what the original settings were so that you can restore them later. Complete the following:

1. Open the Tutorial.10 folder containing an original copy of the Windows Vista for Power Users Data Files and copy the Review folder from the Tutorial.10 folder to the Public Documents folder. Then, change the name of the Review folder to **Mapping Project**.
2. Use System Protection to create a restore point named "Manual Restore Point." Restart your computer and log on under your user account.
3. What edition of Windows Vista is installed on your computer?
4. Describe techniques or strategies you use to ensure that you have backup copies of important files on your hard disk. Include in your discussion how many backups you retain, what type of backup media you use, and how frequently you back up. Do you store any backups off-site?
5. Describe techniques or strategies covered in this tutorial that you might use to ensure that you have backup copies of important files on your hard disk. Also include in your discussion how many backups you would retain, what type of backup media you would use, how frequently you would back up, and whether you would store any backups off-site.
6. Open the Backup and Restore Center. What options are available for backing up and for restoring files on your computer? If the Backup and Restore Center has recently backed up files on your computer, what schedule did you specify for each of your next backups? Where does the Backup and Restore Center store your backups?
7. Does your edition of Windows include Complete PC Backup, and if so, have you performed a Complete PC Backup of your computer? What type of media did you use to store your Complete PC Backup? Close the Backup and Restore Center window.
8. Open the Public folder, open the Public Documents folder, view properties of the Mapping Project folder, and then select the Previous Versions tab. Do you have any Previous Versions of this folder? Explain.
9. Select the most recent Previous Version, and then click Open. What name does Windows Vista show for this folder in the Address Bar? What is the date and time for all the folders in the Mapping Project folder?
10. Open the Memos folder. What does this folder contain? Close this Memos folder with Previous Versions of your files.

11. In the Public Documents folder, open the Mapping Projects folder. What is the date and time for all the folders in the Mapping Projects folder? How much time elapsed between the point when you copied the Review folder from the Tutorial.10 folder to the Public Documents folder and the point at which Windows Vista created Previous Versions?
12. Open the Memos folder. What does this folder contain? How does this Memos folder differ from the one that you opened from the Mapping Project Properties Previous Versions property sheet?
13. Right-click the Amazon River Mapping.docx file, and then select the Previous Versions property sheet. What types of Previous Versions exist for this file (if any)? Close the Amazon River Mapping Properties dialog box.
14. From the Memos folder, return to the Gaia Cartographics folder.
15. On the Start menu, open a Computer window, and then open a window onto your flash drive. Create a new Briefcase on your flash drive, name it Mapping Project, and then open the Mapping Project Briefcase.
16. Display the Mapping Project folder window on your hard disk and the Mapping Project Briefcase windows side by side. Select all the folders in the Mapping Project folder window on your hard disk and drag them to the Mapping Project Briefcase window on your flash drive.
17. Open the Memos folder in the Mapping Project folder window on your hard disk. If you have Microsoft Office 2007 on your computer, open the Contract Income Projection.docx file. If you have an earlier version of Microsoft Office, or if you do not have Microsoft Office 2007 on your computer, open the Contract Income Projection.rtf file in WordPad. Change $22,000,000 to **$25,000,000** and then save and close the file and Microsoft Word.
18. Open the Business Records folder in the Mapping Project Briefcase on your flash drive, and then delete the Break-Even Analysis.xlsx file.
19. Open the Company Logo folder in the Mapping Project window on your hard disk and change the name of the Amazon Mapping Logo.tif file to **Amazon River Mapping Logo.tif**.
20. Switch to the Mapping Project Briefcase window, return to the Mapping Project folder, and then choose the option to update all items. For each proposed update, list the proposed update action, the name of the file, the status of the file in the Briefcase, and the status of the file on the hard disk. (If you examine Details of an action in order to identify the filename, restore the proposed action.) Then, perform the updates.
21. Open the Company Logo folder in the Briefcase. What are the names of the two files in this folder? What did the Briefcase update in this folder?
22. Open the Business Records folder on your hard disk. What change did the Briefcase make to this folder?
23. Delete the Mapping Project Briefcase on your flash drive and the Mapping Project folder on your hard disk.
24. Submit your document to your instructor, either in printed or electronic form, as requested.

Apply | Case Problem 1

Use the skills you learned in the tutorial to develop a backup strategy for a law firm.

There are no Data Files needed for this Case Problem.

Grayson, Sables & O'Toole Morgana Courey, an attorney in the law firm of Grayson, Sables & O'Toole, prepares new bond documents for funding rural water projects. Since most projects require essentially the same type of bond document, she adapts bond documents she prepared for other projects to make it easy to prepare a new bond proposal. Morgana asks you to develop a backup strategy that will guarantee that she can retrieve an earlier version of a bond document and adapt it to a new funding project.

As you complete each step in this case, record your answers to questions so that you can submit them to your instructor. Use a word processing application, such as Word or WordPad, to prepare your answers to these questions. Also, if you change any settings on the computer you are using, note the original settings so that you can restore them later. Complete the following:

1. What would be the best backup strategy for Morgana to use?
2. Assume that her assistant uses backup software that supports full, differential, and incremental backups. Prepare a table that describes how to implement this backup strategy, using a backup cycle of one week. (Assume a five-day work week.) Name the table "Proposed Backup Schedule" and include the following three columns: Stage of Backup Cycle, Type of Backup, and Backup Includes. Identify each stage in the backup cycle, the type of backup, and what types of folders and files are included in the backup. Also identify when the next backup cycle begins.
3. How many copies of each backup set would you recommend that Morgana's assistant keep, and where should he store those backup sets?
4. What other Windows Vista features might Morgana's assistant use to recover earlier versions of previously created bond documents?
5. If Morgana needs to work on copies of bond documents at home, how can she guarantee that she and her assistant have the most recent version of those documents?
6. How might Morgana benefit from a Complete PC Backup?
7. Submit your document to your instructor, either in printed or electronic form, as requested.

Apply | Case Problem 2

Use the skills you learned in the tutorial to devise a backup strategy for a consulting firm.

There are no Data Files needed for this Case Problem.

Thaxton Consulting, Inc. The Middlesworth County's Board of Directors recently contracted with Christopher Thaxton to develop a comprehensive growth management plan for the county. Christopher wants to implement a backup strategy that guarantees access to the most recent version of documents that he prepares. Since each revision of Middlesworth County's comprehensive growth management plan undergoes extensive analysis, review, and public comment, Christopher needs to keep only the most recent versions of documents. Also, since the development of a comprehensive growth management plan takes several years, he works on the same documents each day. Christopher asks you to develop a backup strategy that will meet his needs for this particular project.

As you complete each step in this case, record your answers to questions so that you can submit them to your instructor. Use a word processing application, such as Word or WordPad, to prepare your answers to these questions. Also, if you change any settings on the computer you are using, note the original settings so that you can restore them later. Complete the following:

1. What would be the best backup strategy for Christopher to use?
2. Assume that Christopher's assistant uses backup software that supports full, differential, and incremental backups. Prepare a table that describes how to implement this backup strategy, using a backup cycle of one week. (Assume a five-day work week.) Name the table "Proposed Backup Schedule" and include the following three columns: Stage of Backup Cycle, Type of Backup, and Backup Includes. Identify each stage in the backup cycle, the type of backup, and what types of folders and files are included in the backup. Also identify when the next backup cycle begins.
3. How many copies of each backup set should his assistant keep, and where should he store those backup sets?
4. What can Christopher do in advance to guarantee that he can restore his entire computer and all his files should he encounter a serious problem with his computer?
5. How can Christopher guarantee that the copies of the files he works on in his office and at work are the most recent versions of those files?
6. If Christopher wants to only perform a full backup at the beginning of the month, how might he effectively combine the use of full, differential, and incremental backups?

EXPLORE

7. If you've never performed a full backup of your user files on your own computer, if you have enough time and storage media to perform a full backup of your user files, and if you have access to an Administrator account, open the Backup and Restore Center, create a backup schedule with the Back Up Files Wizard, and then perform a full backup. If you have already specified a backup schedule and performed a previous backup, and if you want to back up changes to folders and files since that previous backup, open the Backup and Restore Center, and then start a backup. Describe the process that Christopher would initially follow if he decided to use Windows Vista's Backup and Restore Center to back up his user files every day. Then, describe how he would perform subsequent backups.

EXPLORE

8. Create a new folder named **Test Restore** in your Documents folder. Then, use the Backup and Restore Center's Restore Files Wizard to restore a folder from the backup to the Test Restore folder.
9. Submit your document to your instructor, either in printed or electronic form, as requested.

Challenge | Case Problem 3

Go beyond what you've learned in the tutorial to examine Previous Versions for an international shipping firm.

There are no Data Files needed for this Case Problem.

CalBay International Shipping, Inc. Iloai Tuilagi works as an accountant for CalBay International Shipping, Inc., which handles shipping for well-known import/export businesses. As part of her job, she occasionally requests copies of financial and supporting documents from company's clients. Iloai asks you to help her with the new Previous Versions feature of Windows Vista so that she can view previous copies of the company's financial documents. You decide to show her how you access Previous Versions of files on your computer.

As you complete each step in this case, record your answers to questions so that you can submit them to your instructor. Use a word processing application, such as Word or WordPad, to prepare your answers to these questions. Also, if you change any settings on the computer you are using, note the original settings so that you can restore them later. Complete the following:

1. What edition of Windows Vista is installed on your computer?
2. **EXPLORE** Open a Computer window, and then select and view Previous Versions of your hard disk drive. What is the most recent Previous Version of your hard disk, and how is it identified (by name)? What options are available for using a Previous Version (i.e., Open, Copy, and/or Restore)? Describe what happens if you open a Previous Version? What does Windows Vista display in the Address Bar? Close the Previous Version's window, and then close the Properties dialog box for your hard disk drive.
3. **EXPLORE** On the Start menu, open your user account folder, right-click the Documents folder, and then select the Previous Versions property sheet. What is the most recent Previous Version of your Documents folder? What options are available for using a Previous Version? Click the most recent Previous Version. Describe what happens and describe the contents of this window. What does Windows Vista display in the Address Bar? Close the Previous Version's window, and then close the Documents Properties dialog box.
4. **EXPLORE** Open the Public folder, view properties of the Public Documents folder, and then select the Previous Versions property sheet. What is the most recent set of Previous Versions of your Public Documents folder? Click the most recent Previous Version and describe what happens. Close the Previous Version's window, and then close the Public Documents Properties dialog box.
5. Open the Public Documents (or Documents) folder, select a file, view its properties, and then select the Previous Versions tab. Describe the types of Previous Versions available and their location(s).
6. If a Shadow copy is available, select that Previous Version and choose the option to make a copy of it. When prompted for the location for the Shadow Copy, open the Public Documents folder, create a new folder named Amazon River Mapping, and then copy the Shadow copy to the Amazon River Mapping folder. If you do not have a Shadow Copy, but you do have a Backup Copy, select that Backup Copy, and then click the Restore button. In the Copy File dialog, choose the option to copy the file, but keep both files (the original and the previous version). Then, close the Restore Files dialog box and the file's Properties dialog box.
7. Comment on your impression of the value of Previous Versions and also note whether you would find this feature useful on your computer.
8. Submit your document to your instructor, either in printed or electronic form, as requested.

Apply | Case Problem 4

Use the skills you learned in the tutorial to create and use a Briefcase for a publishing firm.

For a list of Data Files in the Case4 folder, see page 611.

Vejar Press, Inc. Miguel Vejar's firm publishes books written by Latin American writers. As head of the firm, he frequently reviews manuscripts, contracts, and company documents at home and while traveling. He wants to make sure that the documents he changes on his office computer, his home computer, and his laptop all match. He asks you to create a Briefcase for his files, make changes to files in the Briefcase, and then update his computer with the changes you make.

As you complete each step in this case, record your answers to questions so that you can submit them to your instructor. Use a word processing application, such as Word or WordPad, to prepare your answers to these questions. Also, if you change any settings on the computer you are using, note the original settings so that you can restore them later. To complete certain steps in this exercise, you will need to copy the Case4 folder in the Tutorial.10 folder to the Public Documents folder. Complete the following:

1. Open a window onto the Documents subfolder, your flash drive folder, or the network folder that contains a copy of the Tutorial.10 folder. Open the Tutorial.10 folder, open the Case4 folder, and then select and copy the Vejar Press folder. Open the Public Documents folder, paste the Vejar Press folder into the Public Documents folder, and then open the Vejar Press folder.
2. Open a window onto your flash drive, create a new Briefcase named **Vejar Press**, and then open the Vejar Press folder.
3. Tile the Vejar Press Briefcase window and the Vejar Press Public Documents window so that they are displayed side by side, and then copy all the folders in the Vejar Press window on your hard disk to the Vejar Press Briefcase window.
4. Open the Company Logo folder in your Briefcase, choose the option for opening **Vejar Press Logo.tif** in the Paint accessory, select a light yellow color from the Color Box, select the Fill with Color tool in the Toolbox, change the background color from white to light yellow, use the Save command on the File menu to save your changes, and then close the Paint window.
5. Open the Memos folder in your Briefcase and change the name of Book Titles.docx to **Book Titles Expansion.docx**.
6. Open the Business Records folder in your Briefcase, select the "Balance Sheet.xls" file, select the Copy option on the Organize menu, select the Paste option on the Organize menu to create a second copy of the file, and then change the name of the file to **2011 Vejar Press Balance Sheet.xlsx**.
7. Delete **Balance Sheet.xlsx**.
8. Return to the Vejar Press folder, and then choose the option to update all the files on your hard disk, using the Briefcase. For each proposed update, list the proposed update action, the name of the file, the status of the file in the Briefcase, and the status of the file on the hard disk. (If you examine Details of an action in order to identify the filename, restore the proposed action.)
9. Update all the files.
10. Comment on your impression of the value of the Briefcase and also note whether you would find this feature useful on your computer.
11. To restore your computer, delete the Vejar Press Briefcase on your flash drive, and then delete the Vejar Press folder in the Public Documents folder on your hard disk.
12. Submit your document to your instructor, either in printed or electronic form, as requested.

Review | Quick Check Answers

Session 10.1

1. backup cycle
2. differential
3. incremental
4. Archive
5. True
6. Windows Recovery Environment

Session 10.2

1. shadow copy
2. shadow copies and backups
3. Briefcase, or Sync Center
4. True
5. True
6. files, folders, and drives

Ending Data Files

There are no ending Data Files needed for this tutorial.

Tutorial 11

Objectives

Session 11.1
- Prepare your computer for an operating system upgrade
- Use Windows Vista Upgrade Advisor to evaluate a computer for an upgrade
- Examine the process for installing Windows Vista
- Learn how to use Windows Easy Transfer to transfer files and settings

Session 11.2
- Turn Windows Features on or off
- Examine how to install and upgrade software
- Use the Program Compatibility Wizard
- Uninstall software
- Add or remove Microsoft Office components
- Set program defaults

Installing, Updating, and Troubleshooting Software

Optimizing the Use of Software

Case | NanoAssets, Inc.

NanoAssets, Inc. provides capital to emerging industries and research groups developing new products using nanotechnology, such as fuel-cell research, nanoparticle delivery of medications, nanoparticle textile coatings, and solar panels that use nanotechnology. Kai Acoya evaluates funding proposals submitted by new companies and research groups and tracks the progress of these entrepreneurs. Like other staff members at NanoAssets, Inc., Kai relies on state-of-the-art operating systems and software technologies. She also realizes the importance of updating her Windows Vista operating system, Microsoft Office, project management software, and the other software products she uses every day.

In this tutorial, you examine how to prepare for and perform an upgrade to Windows Vista, use the Windows Vista Upgrade Advisor to evaluate the feasibility of upgrading your computer to another Windows versions or edition, examine the process for installing Windows Vista, and examine how to transfer files and settings from an older computer to a new computer. You also turn Windows features on or off, install and uninstall the Windows Vista Upgrade Advisor, use the Program Compatibility Wizard to correct program compatibility problems, examine how to add or remove Microsoft Office components, and review the options for setting program defaults.

Starting Data Files

There are no starting Data Files needed for this tutorial.

Session 11.1

Getting Started

To complete this tutorial, you must display the Computer icon on the desktop and switch your computer to single-click activation. In the following steps, you will check, and if necessary, change these settings.

To set up your computer:

1. If Windows Vista does not display a Computer icon on the desktop, open the **Start menu**, right-click **Computer**, click **Show on Desktop**, and then close the Start menu.
2. If you need to enable single-click activation, double-click the **Computer** icon on the desktop, click the **Organize** button on the command bar, click **Folder and Search Options**, and under "Click items as follows" on the General property sheet in the Folder Options dialog box, click the **Single-click to open an item (point to select)** option button, click the **Underline icon titles only when I point at them** option button, click the **OK** button to close the Folder and Options dialog box, and then close the Computer window.

Now, you're ready to examine how to prepare for an operating system upgrade.

Preparing for an Operating System Upgrade

Like other software developers, Microsoft continually develops new versions of their Windows operating system and enhances the capabilities of existing Windows editions via updates. These new Windows versions, editions, service pack upgrades, and updates take advantage of the rapid emergence of new hardware and software technologies as well as increasing security and privacy.

Installing or upgrading to a new version of the Windows operating system represents a significant change not only in the way that you use your computer, but also in the configuration of your computer and the support for existing and new software. Before you install or upgrade to Windows Vista or any other operating system, you should take certain steps to protect your work and the integrity of your computer system. These steps also improve the chances that the new Windows operating system installs properly. Once you complete these preparatory steps, you can then install the new Windows operating system.

You should perform the following steps before installing or upgrading to Windows Vista or a future version of the Windows operating system:

- **Compare editions** Windows Vista and its predecessor included a variety of different editions for different types of users. When upgrading to Windows Vista or its successor, you should examine the different editions to find out which one meets your needs. That, in turn, determines the type of computer and computer hardware that you purchase.
- **Check system requirements** Operating systems, as well as software applications, utilities, and games, have specific requirements that you should check before purchasing and attempting to install the software, including specific processor, system memory, hard disk storage capacity, and graphics memory requirements.

- **Consider the upgrade path** With each new operating system, Microsoft posts at its Web site information on the types of upgrade paths. The **upgrade path** identifies whether you can upgrade from your current version or edition of Windows to the next version of Windows or another edition of Windows.
- **Check hardware and software compatibility** If you are buying a new computer, you need to know whether the hardware and software provided with that computer supports a newer version or edition of Windows that you want to purchase and install. Also, if you are buying new hardware for a computer, you need to know whether your existing version and edition of Windows supports that hardware.

If you visit Microsoft's Web site, you can find the information you need to make an informed decision so that you can maximize your investment in a new or existing computer.

The management at NanoAssets has decided to replace the current computer systems with high-performance computers that take advantage of the newer features in Windows Vista Ultimate. At Kai's request, they also agreed to provide higher performance laptops for use by employees who frequently travel on company business. Kai asks you to visit Microsoft's Web site and examine information on how best to upgrade Windows.

Remember that Web sites and software changes over time, so the views shown in the following figures may differ from what you see when you visit Microsoft's Web site.

To compare Windows Vista editions and system requirements:

1. Open Internet Explorer (or the Web browser you use), enter **www.microsoft.com** as the URL, and then press the **Enter** key.
2. Click inside the **Search Input Area** (or search box), type **Windows Vista**, and then press the **Enter** key. On the Search Results page, locate and click the **Windows Vista** link.
3. At the Windows Vista home page, click the **Choose an edition** link. Figure 11-1 shows the Microsoft Windows Vista Web page that provides information on choosing an edition. Here you can examine information about the Windows Vista Ultimate, Home Premium, Home Basic, Business, and Enterprise Editions. You can also download a Windows Vista Product Guide that provides a more comprehensive look at the new features in Windows Vista. A disclaimer at the bottom of the Web page notes that some Windows Vista product features are only available in certain editions of Windows Vista, and those product features may also require new hardware.

   Trouble? If you do not see a "Choose an edition" link, click inside the Search Input Area (or search box), type "Choose an edition," press the Enter key, and examine the Search results for a link to the Windows Vista Web page that showcases Windows Vista editions.

Figure 11-1 Microsoft's Web page on choosing a Windows Vista edition

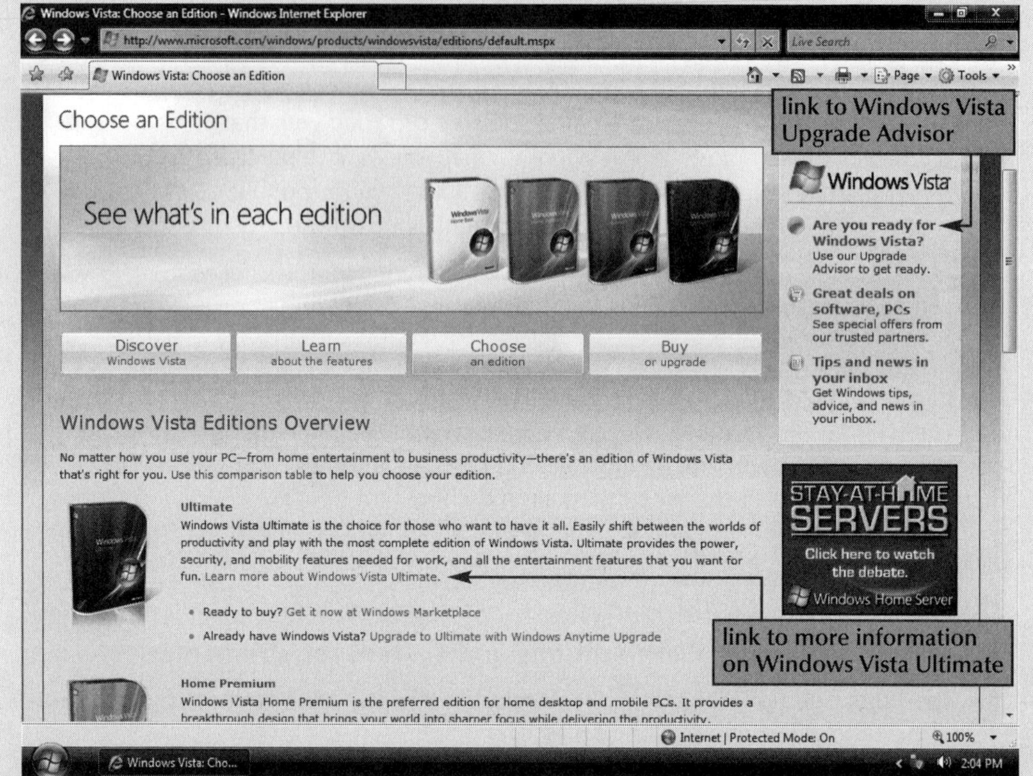

Tip

The check marks in this table are color-coded for the different Windows Vista editions displayed above the table.

4. Scroll to the bottom of this Web page, and then click the **Compare editions** link. The Compare Editions Web page contains a table that compares important features in these editions. See Figure 11-2. From this table, you can quickly identify which versions have which features. For example, Windows Vista Home Basic does not support Windows Aero, but Windows Vista Home Premium, Business, and Ultimate do support Windows Aero. Windows Vista Home Premium and Ultimate support Windows Media Center, but Windows Vista Home Basic and Business do not. Windows Vista Business and Ultimate include Complete PC Backup, but Windows Vista Home Basic and Home Premium do not. Only Windows Vista Ultimate supports BitLocker Drive Encryption. For the more serious computer professional who needs access to all of the features in Windows Vista, as well as more advanced technologies, including networking, the Windows Vista Ultimate or Business Editions are the obvious choices.

   Trouble? If you do not see a "Compare Editions link," click inside the Search Input Area (or search box), type "Compare editions," press the Enter key, and examine the Search results for a link to the Windows Vista Web page that compares Windows Vista editions.

Figure 11-2

Comparing features in different editions of Windows Vista

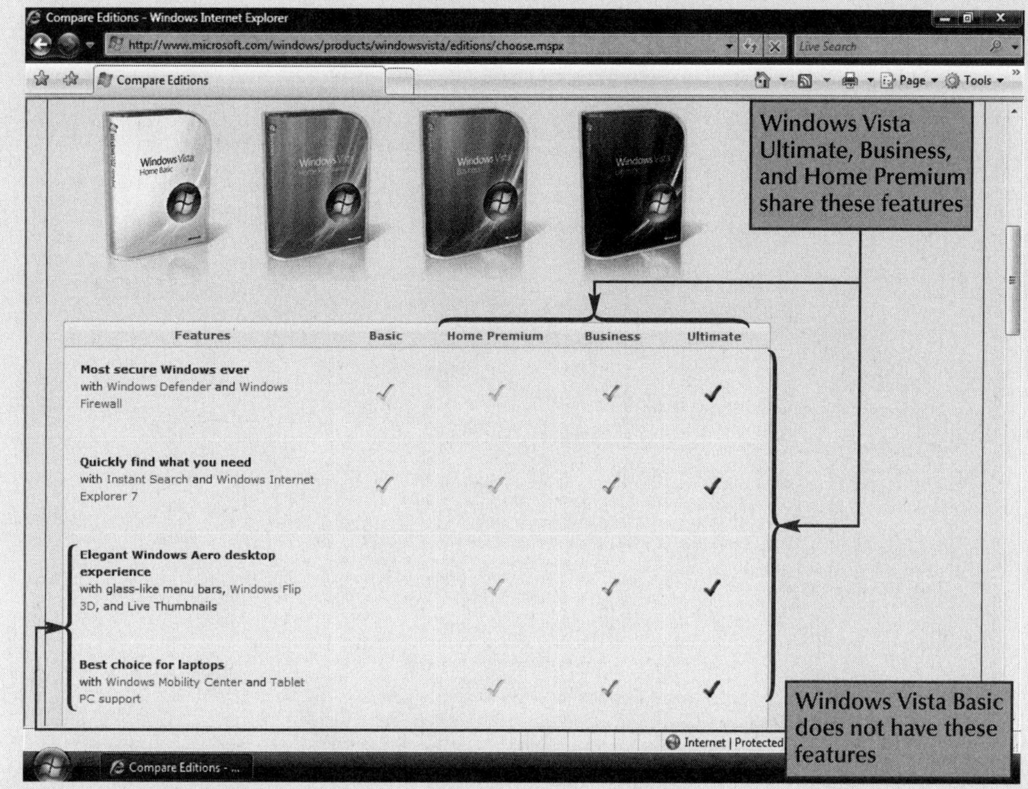

5. Click inside the **Search Input Area** (or search box), type **system requirements** and then press the **Enter** key.

6. In the Search results, locate and click the **Windows Vista: Recommended System Requirements** link. You can now view system requirements for the Windows Vista Home Basic, Home Premium, Business, and Ultimate Editions, as shown in Figure 11-3.

Figure 11-3 System requirements for Windows Vista editions

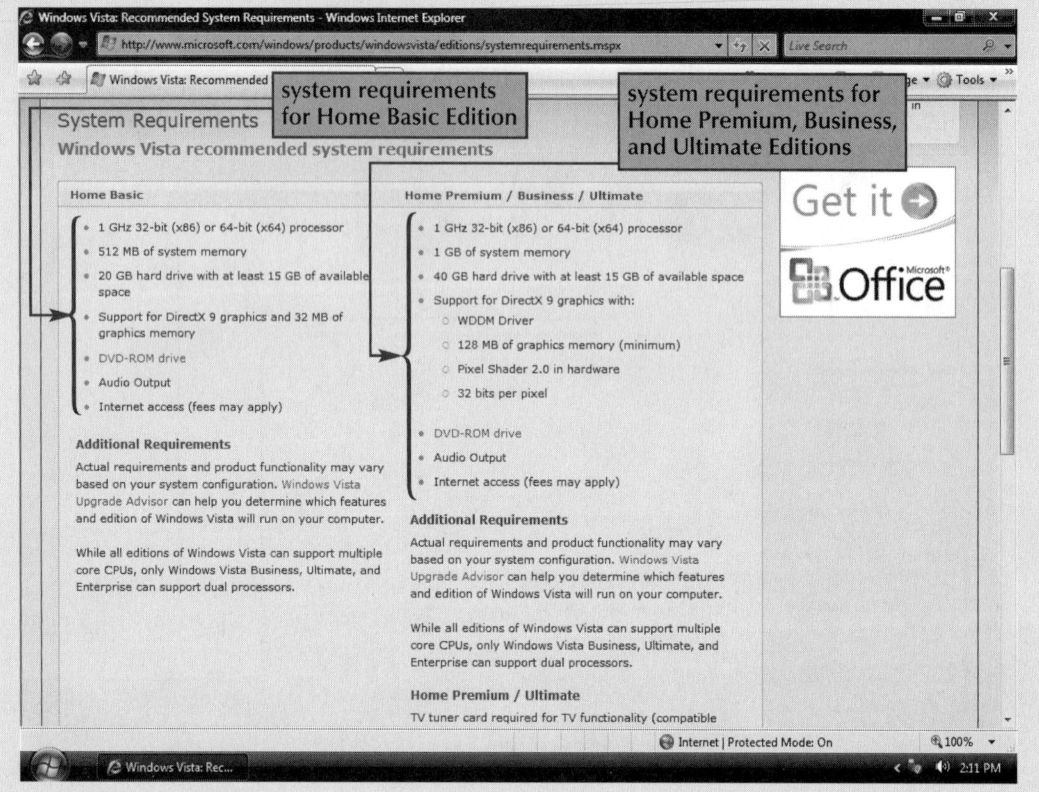

When examining system requirements for Windows Vista or any other operating system upgrade, you want to consider the following factors:

- **Processor** Microsoft recommends a 1 GHz 32-bit (x86) or 64-bit (x64) processor for the Windows Vista Home Basic, Home Premium, Business, and Ultimate Editions. A 32-bit operating system is designed for 32-bit processors that handle 32 bits of data at a time and that support up to 4 GB (2^{32}) of RAM. In contrast, a 64-bit operating system is designed for 64-bit processors that handle 64 bits of data at a time and that, in theory (but not in practice), support up to 2^{64} or 16 EB (16 exabytes or 16 billion gigabytes) of RAM. At the bottom of this Web page (not visible in Figure 11-3), Microsoft notes that an 800 MHz processor is the minimum requirement for all of these Windows Vista editions. Microsoft also notes that all editions of Windows Vista support multiple-core processors (such as dual-core processors), but only the Windows Vista Business, Ultimate, and Enterprise Editions support dual processors (two separate processors). Once you know this information, you have to evaluate whether you can expect reasonable performance with your current processor and its operating speed when you upgrade to Windows Vista or to a new Windows Vista edition. Even if your processor meets the minimum or recommended requirements, an older and slower processor might act as a bottleneck and affect the overall performance of the computer.

- **System memory** Microsoft recommends that you have 512 MB of system memory (or RAM) for the Windows Vista Home Basic Edition and 1 GB of system memory (or RAM) for the Windows Vista Home Premium, Business, and Ultimate Editions. At the bottom of this Web page, it notes that the minimum requirement for system memory (or RAM) for all these Windows Vista editions is 512 MB. Invariably, you need more RAM than the minimum requirement. Likewise, to ensure optimal performance of Windows Vista and the software on your computer, you will need more than even the recommended requirement. If you do not have enough RAM for the Windows Vista operating system and the software that you use, Windows Vista will rely more heavily on the use of virtual memory, which slows down the performance of your computer. You should purchase enough RAM to support everything you need to do over the next several years on your computer.
- **Hard disk storage capacity** To accommodate the demands of users and rapidly emerging hardware and software technologies, the Windows Vista operating systems require a computer with an ever increasing amount of hard disk storage capacity. As shown in Figure 11-3, Microsoft recommends a 20 GB hard disk with at least 15 GB of available space for the Windows Vista Home Basic Edition and a 40 GB hard disk with at least 15 GB of available space for the Windows Vista Home Premium, Business, and Ultimate Editions. The recommended minimum for all these editions is a 20 GB hard disk with at least 15 GB of available space. While a 20 GB or 40 GB hard disk might meet basic needs, generally, you will need a hard disk with a substantially greater storage capacity to support Windows Vista operations and features and so that you can install and use more software and create and store more files on your computer. Certain types of files, such as video and audio files, require an extensive amount of storage space. Also, consider that the Windows operating system and your other software will be downloading and installing updates on a daily basis, thus increasing the need for more storage space on the hard disk. A year after the release of Windows Vista, hard disk storage capacities approached 500 GB to 1 terabyte, so a 20 GB or 40 GB hard disk is very small and limited in comparison.
- **Graphics memory** With the introduction of Windows Aero in the Windows Vista operating system, the amount of graphics memory becomes an increasingly important factor in the performance of your computer. Microsoft recommends 32 MB of graphics memory and support for DirectX 9 graphics in the Windows Vista Home Basic Edition and 128 MB of graphics memory and a graphics processor that supports DirectX9 in the Windows Vista Home Premium, Business, and Ultimate Editions. More specifically, Microsoft notes that Windows Aero requires 64 MB of graphics memory for a single monitor set at a resolution less than 1,310,720 pixels (such as 800 x 600, 1024 x 768, 1280 x 768, and 1280 x 1024), 128 MB of graphics memory for a single monitor at resolutions between 1,310,720 to 2,304,000 pixels (such as 1680 x 1050), and 256 MB of graphics memory for a single monitor set at a resolution greater than 2,304,000 pixels. As you discovered in Tutorial 1, and as noted on this Web page, Microsoft recommends support for Windows Display Driver Model (WDDM) driver, Pixel Shader 2.0 in your video graphics adapter for rendering graphic effects, and 32 bits per pixel (color setting). When you purchase a computer or a video display card for a computer, you should purchase one that has 256 MB or 512 MB (or more) of graphics memory so that Windows Vista and the other software on your computer perform optimally.

- **Other components** For the Windows Vista Home Basic, Home Premium, Business, and Ultimate Editions, Microsoft recommends a DVD-ROM drive so that you can install Windows Vista from a DVD (or CD) as well as audio output and Internet access. If you want TV recording and playback features with Windows Media Center on your computer in the Windows Vista Home Premium and Ultimate Editions, you need a TV tuner card. If you want to use Windows Tablet and Touch Technology in the Windows Vista Home Premium, Business, and Ultimate Editions, you need a Tablet PC or a touch screen. If you want to use Windows Vista Ultimate's BitLocker Drive Encryption, you need a computer with a TPM (Trusted Platform Module) 1.2 chip (covered in Tutorial 5) and a USB flash drive.

Kai also emphasizes the importance of checking upgrade paths before purchasing a Windows Vista edition.

To examine information on upgrade paths:

1. Click the **Buy or Upgrade** button at the top of the Web page that covers Windows Vista system requirements.
2. On the Get Windows Vista Web page, locate and click the **Know your upgrade options** link. This Web page provides information on whether your current version of Windows qualifies for an upgrade to a specific edition of Windows Vista. See Figure 11-4.

Figure 11-4 **Windows Vista upgrade path options**

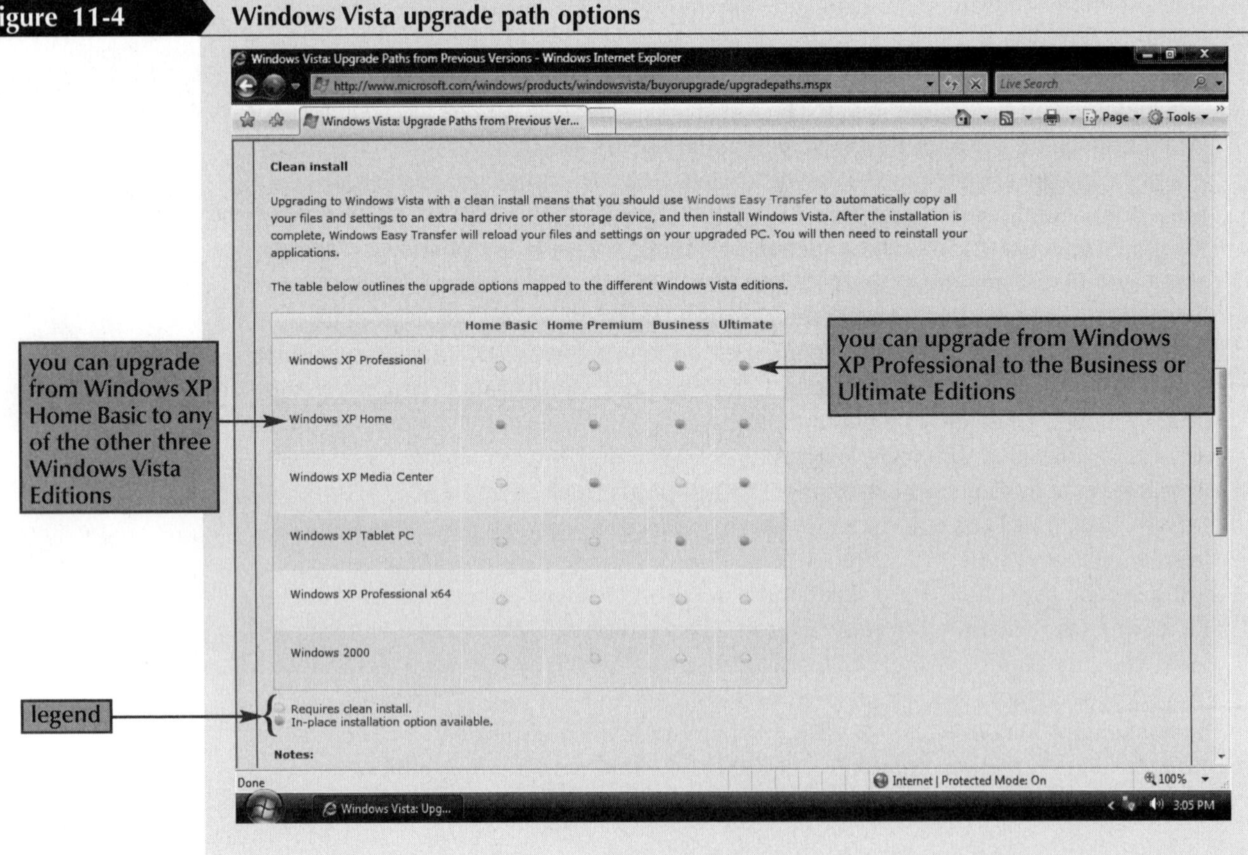

There are two approaches to upgrading. If you want to install a new Windows version over your existing Windows version and keep your installed software, Windows settings, and personal files, you perform an **upgrade-in-place**. In contrast, a **clean install** reformats and erases everything on your hard disk. Then, you install whatever operating system you want on your computer, reinstall all your software, and restore all your personal documents from backups. Before a clean install, it's also a good idea to make sure that you have copies of any device drivers that you might need for your hardware. A clean install is useful if your computer has no operating system, if you want to replace the current operating system with a new operating system, if you want to restore default Windows settings, if you want to repartition your hard disk, if you want to remove malware that cannot be removed in any other way, or if you want to remove everything from your hard disk and rebuild your computer system. As you can imagine, clean installs are time-consuming and require that you anticipate everything that you might need before and after the clean install (no small feat, but it does provide better results). The green circles in the table in the previous Figure 11-4 identify which previous Windows versions and editions support in-place Windows Vista upgrades while the yellow circles identify which Windows versions and editions require clean installs of a Windows Vista edition. For example, you can upgrade in-place from Windows XP Professional to the Windows Vista Business or Ultimate Editions, but you cannot "downgrade" to the Windows Vista Home Basic or Home Premium Editions. However, you could perform a clean install and replace Windows XP Professional with the Windows Vista Home Basic or Home Premium Edition. Figure 11-5 summarizes all the upgrade path options. If you're thinking of an upgrade from Windows Vista Home Basic to any other edition of Windows Vista, you will more than likely have to upgrade the hardware in your computer (especially if you want access to Windows Aero).

Upgrade versus clean install options — **Figure 11-5**

If you have	You can upgrade to	You must do a clean install to upgrade to
Windows XP Home	Windows Vista Home Basic Windows Vista Home Premium Windows Vista Business Windows Vista Ultimate	
Windows XP Media Center	Windows Vista Home Premium Windows Vista Ultimate	Windows Vista Home Basic Windows Vista Business
Windows XP Tablet PC	Windows Vista Business Windows Vista Ultimate	Windows Vista Home Basic Windows Vista Home Premium
Windows XP Professional	Windows Vista Business Windows Vista Ultimate	Windows Vista Home Basic Windows Vista Home Premium
Windows XP Professional x64		Any Windows Vista edition
Windows 2000		Any Windows Vista edition

If you have the Windows XP Professional x64 Edition or Windows 2000 on your computer, you must perform a clean install to upgrade to the Windows Vista Home Basic, Home Premium, Business, or Ultimate Edition. However, these two Windows versions do qualify for an upgrade copy of Windows Vista. An **upgrade copy** is a less-expensive version of a software product that checks for a previous version already installed on a computer before installing itself. The existence of a previous copy is a prerequisite for installing the upgrade.

If you have any other earlier version of the Windows operating system on your computer, you must purchase a full version of Windows Vista, and you must perform a clean install. A **full version** is a more-expensive version of a software product that does not require a previously installed version, but rather just installs itself. If you do not have a previously installed version of a software product on your computer, you must buy a full version.

Microsoft also recommends that you use the Windows Vista Upgrade Advisor, a Web application, to determine whether your computer supports Windows Vista, and if so, what Windows Vista edition best suits your computer and what features your computer supports. Microsoft also notes that you can use the Windows Vista Upgrade Advisor to determine whether you can upgrade to another edition of Windows Vista.

Now, you're ready to locate information on the Windows Vista Upgrade Advisor and then download a copy for use in the second session of the tutorial.

To locate information on the Windows Vista Upgrade Advisor:

1. Scroll to the bottom of the Windows Vista Upgrade Paths Web page, and then click the **Windows Vista Upgrade Advisor** link. As shown in Figure 11-6, you can download the Windows Vista Upgrade Advisor and read the background information before you use the Windows Vista Upgrade Advisor to determine the feasibility of upgrading your computer and its Windows version or edition.

   Trouble? If you cannot find the Windows Vista Upgrade Path Web page or the Windows Vista Upgrade Advisor link, click inside the Search Input Area (or search box), type "Windows Vista Upgrade Advisor," press the Enter key, and examine the Search results for a link to the Windows Vista Web page that provides information about the Windows Vista Upgrade Advisor.

Figure 11-6 Windows Vista Upgrade Advisor Web page

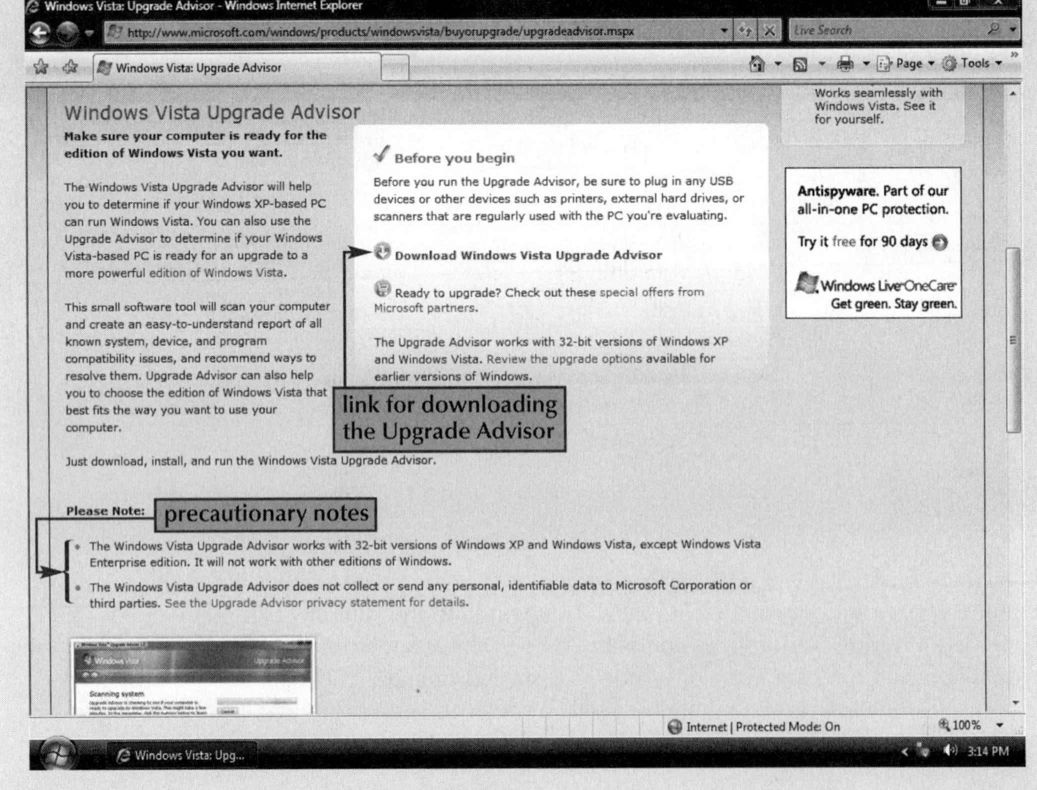

2. Click the **Download Windows Vista Upgrade Advisor** link. At the Download details Web page for the Windows Vista Upgrade Advisor, Microsoft provides a brief overview of the Windows Vista Upgrade Advisor, how you can use the Windows Vista Upgrade Advisor, and the system requirements for running the Windows Vista Upgrade Advisor. See Figure 11-7.

Figure 11-7 Web page for downloading the Windows Vista Upgrade Advisor

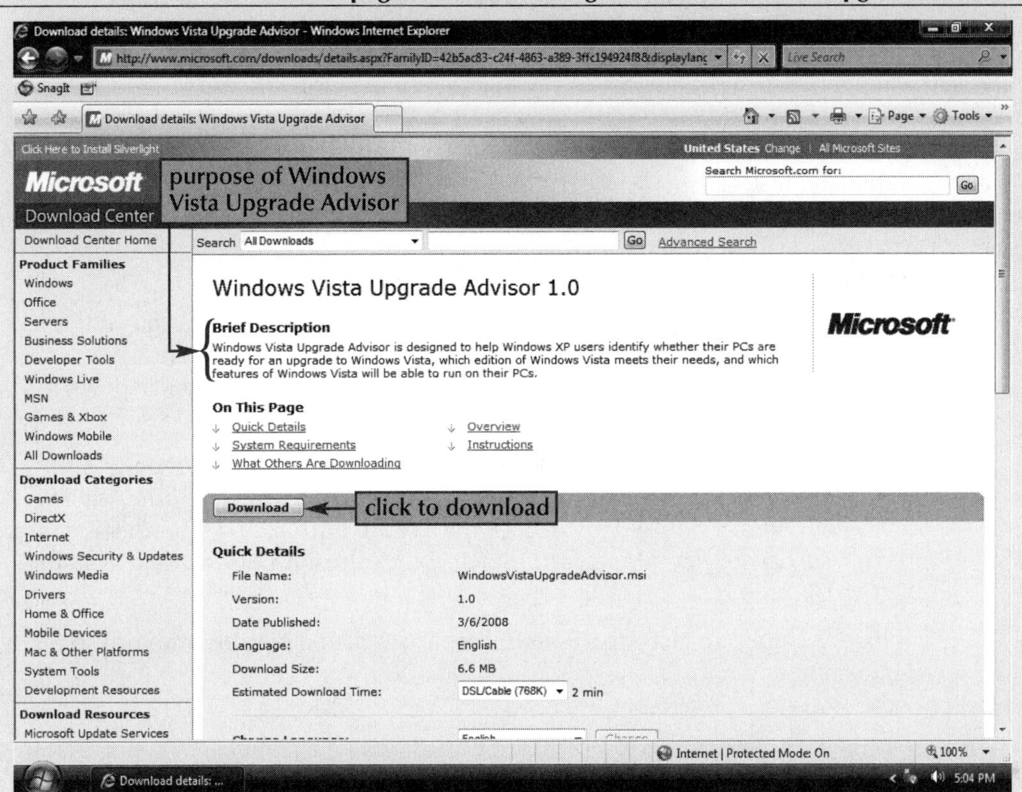

3. Click the **Download** button, and then click the **Close** button in the Information Bar dialog box (if necessary). At the next Web page (entitled "Thank You for Downloading"), click the **Start download** link if the download does not start in 30 seconds, click the **Save** button in the File Download – Security Warning dialog box, click **Documents** under Favorite Links in the Navigation Pane, click the **New Folder** button on the command bar, type **Windows Vista Upgrade Advisor** for the new folder name, press the **Enter** key, and then click the **Save** button in the Save As dialog box. During the download, Windows Vista identifies the downloaded file with the "msi" file extension as a Windows Installer Package. You can use your antivirus and antispyware software to scan this file for malicious software—always a safe practice.

Tip

If you right-click the downloaded file, the shortcut menu may have an option for scanning the file with your antivirus software.

4. After Internet Explorer informs you that the download is complete, close the Download complete dialog box.

5. Close Internet Explorer.

Now, you're ready to install the Windows Vista Upgrade Advisor.

Installing the Windows Vista Upgrade Advisor

Kai wants to upgrade her laptop from Windows Home Premium to Windows Vista Ultimate, so she decides to download and install the Windows Upgrade Advisor so that she can check whether her laptop is compatible with Windows Vista Ultimate. Before she installs the Windows Vista Upgrade Advisor, she decides it's time to create a restore point.

If you want to install the Windows Vista Upgrade Advisor on your computer and check for upgrade options, complete the following steps. If you do not want to install the Windows Vista Upgrade Advisor on your computer and check for upgrade options, read the following steps and examine the figures, but do not keystroke the steps. If you are working in a computer lab and want to download and install the Windows Upgrade Advisor on a computer in your computer lab, ask your instructor or technical support staff for permission first.

To create a restore point:

1. Right-click the **Computer** desktop icon (or right-click the Computer icon on the Start menu), click **Properties**, and after the System window opens, click the **System protection** link, and provide Administrator credentials after Windows Vista switches to Secure Desktop Mode.
2. Click the **Create** button on the System Protection property sheet in the System Properties dialog box, type **Before Installing Windows Vista Upgrade Advisor** in the System Protection dialog box, click the **Create** button, and after System Protection successfully creates a restore point, click the **OK** button in the System Protection dialog box.
3. Click the **OK** button to close the System Properties dialog box, and then close the System window.

If you encounter a problem, you can attempt to uninstall the software first, but if that fails, you can use System Restore to roll back your computer to the manual restore point that you created before you installed that software product.

Now, you're ready to install the Windows Vista Upgrade Advisor.

As noted earlier, the Windows Vista Upgrade Advisor may need to download and install additional software from Microsoft's download Web site before it can install itself properly.

To install the Windows Vista Upgrade Advisor:

1. Open the **Documents** folder, open the **Windows Vista Upgrade Advisor** folder, use the Views arrow button to switch to Details view (if necessary), click the **background** of the folder window, and then press the **Ctrl** and **+** keys to adjust all the columns for a best fit. As shown in Figure 11-8, the name of the file is WindowsVistaUpgradeAdvisor.msi and the Type column identifies the file type as a Windows Installer Package file.

Figure 11-8 Viewing Windows Vista Upgrade Advisor file details

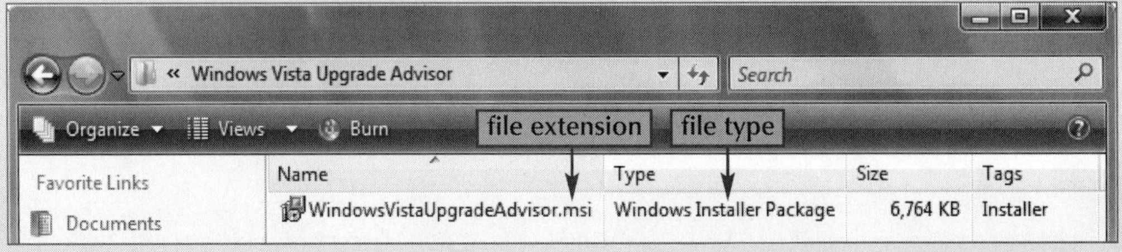

2. Click the **WindowsVistaUpgradeAdvisor.msi** file icon. Windows Vista opens the Windows Installer Package, and the first Windows Vista Upgrade Advisor Setup Wizard dialog box explains that the installer will guide you through the processing for installing this software. See Figure 11-9.

   Trouble? If Windows Vista displays an Open File - Security warning dialog box and asks if you want to run this file, click the Run button.

Figure 11-9 Windows Vista Upgrade Advisor Setup Wizard

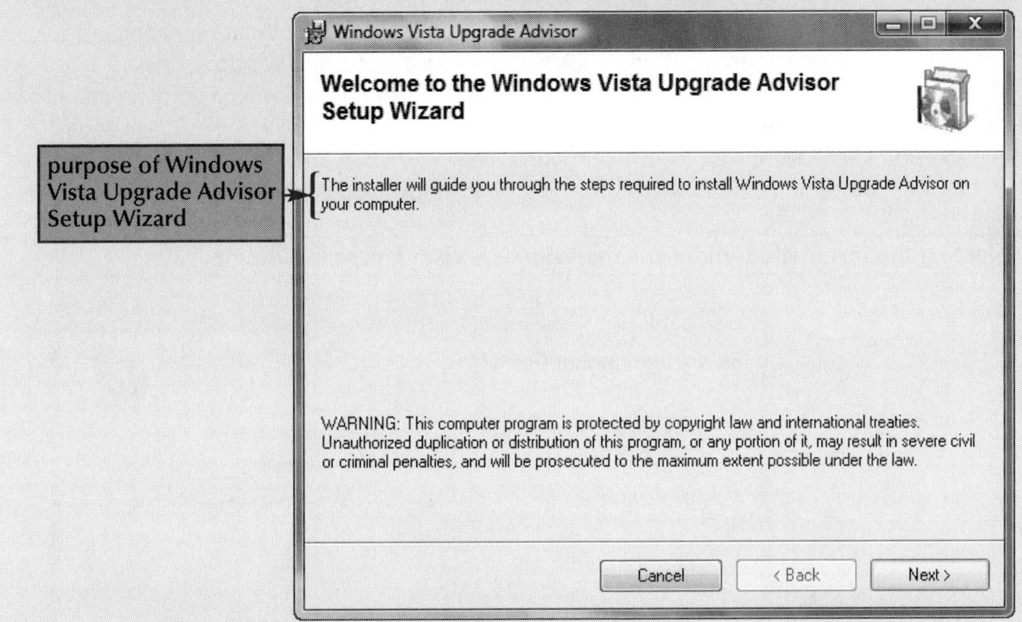

3. Click the **Next** button. In the next step, you are prompted to read the License Agreement. See Figure 11-10. Be sure to read the License Agreement that comes with a software product so that you know what is actually installed with a software product; otherwise, you may assume only one program is installed.

Figure 11-10 Reading the Windows Vista Upgrade Advisor License Agreement

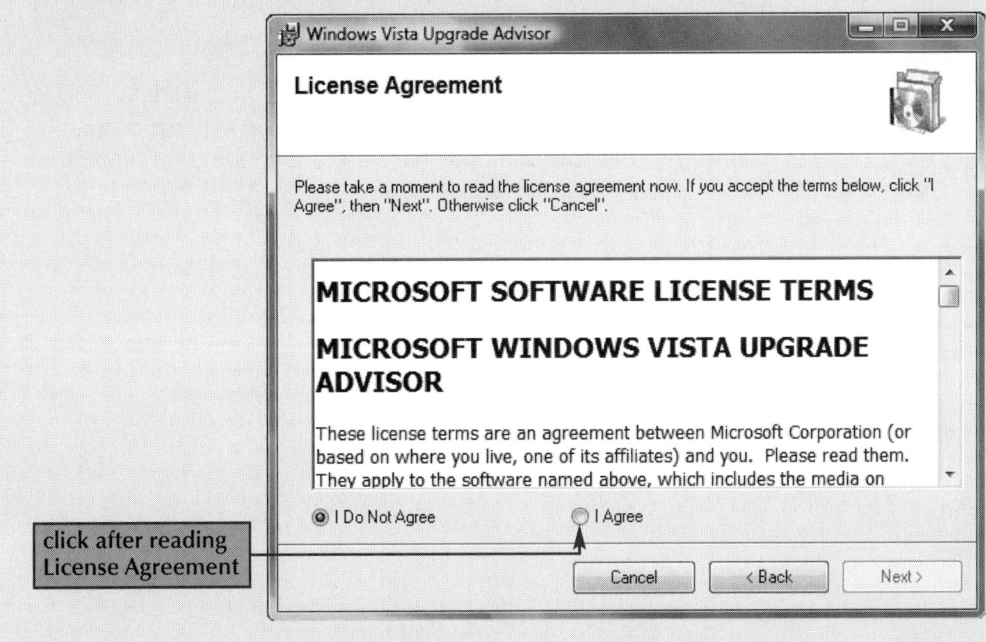

4. After you read the License Agreement, click the **I Agree** option button, and then click the **Next** button. The installer displays the path to the folder where it will install the software. See Figure 11-11. The path to that folder is "C:\Program Files\Microsoft Windows Vista Upgrade Advisor\". That means this software will be installed in a folder named "Microsoft Windows Vista Upgrade Advisor" under the Program Files folder on drive C. As noted earlier, Microsoft encourages software manufacturers to install their software in the Program Files folder rather than in another location. You can use the path proposed by the installation program, you can manually enter a new path, or you can use the Browse button to locate another folder for the software product. Most people use the default location proposed by the installation program. If you click the Disk Cost button, a Windows Vista Upgrade Advisor Disk Space dialog box identifies the drives where you can install the software, as well as each drive's size, available storage space, and the required storage space for installing the software. That way you can verify whether there is enough storage space to install the program before you proceed.

Figure 11-11 Selecting the installation folder for the Windows Vista Upgrade Advisor

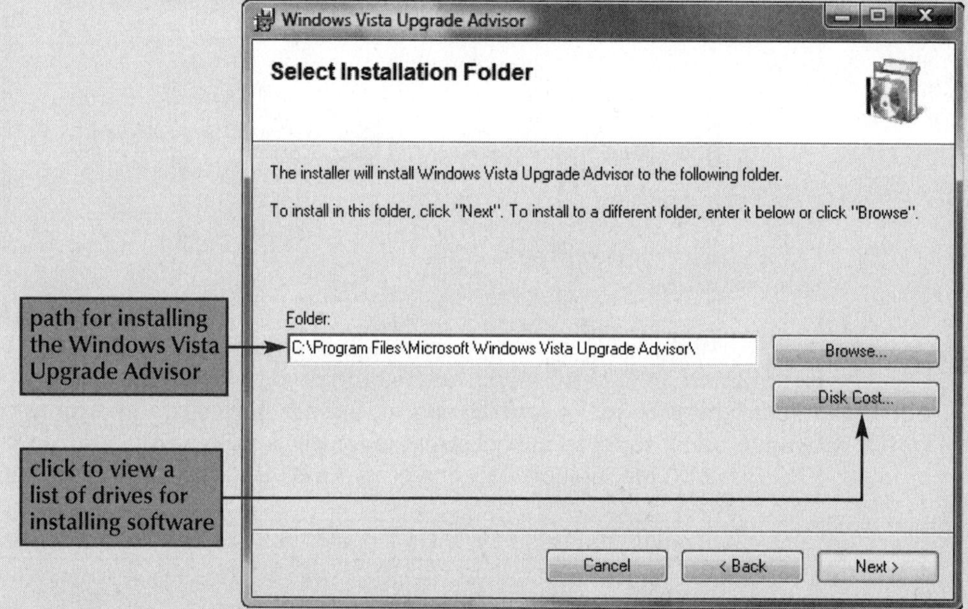

5. Click the **Next** button. In the Confirm Installation dialog box, you are informed that the installer is ready to install the Windows Vista Upgrade Advisor on your computer. See Figure 11-12. At this point you have the option for creating a desktop shortcut to the Windows Vista Upgrade Advisor.

Figure 11-12

Installer is ready to install the Windows Vista Upgrade Advisor

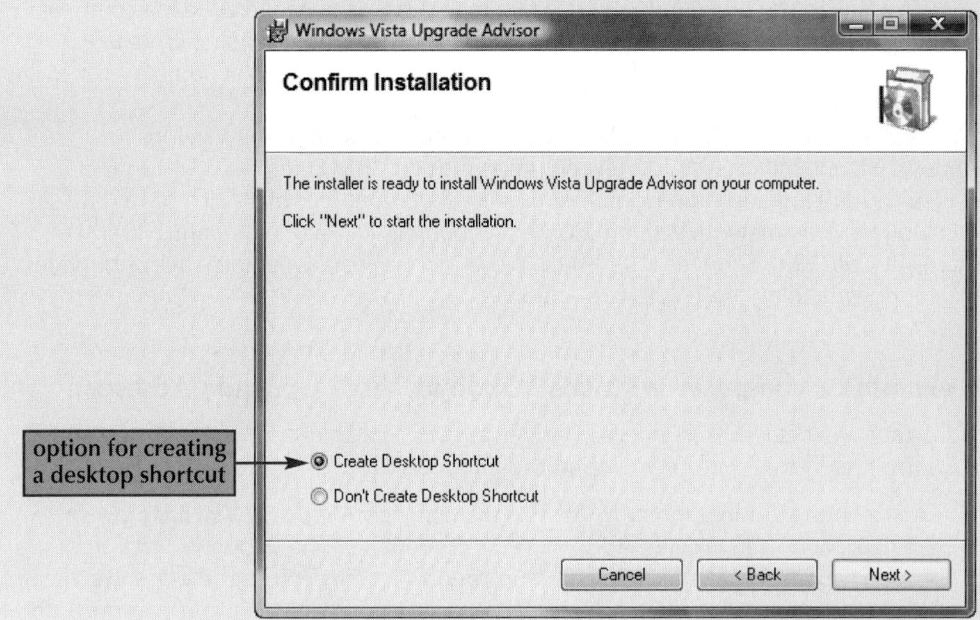

6. Click the **Next** button, and after Windows Vista switches to Secure Desktop Mode, provide Administrator credentials in the User Account Control dialog box. The next and last Windows Vista Upgrade Advisor dialog box informs you that the software was successfully installed.
7. Click the **Close** button.

After you install certain software products, you might need to restart your computer so that Windows Vista can complete the installation. You are notified whether a restart is required.

Installing the Windows Vista Upgrade Advisor

| Reference Window

- To create a manual restore point, right-click the Computer desktop icon, click Properties, click the System protection link under Tasks, provide Administrator credentials, click the Create button on the System Protection property sheet in the System Properties dialog box, enter a name for the restore point, click the Create button, and after System Protection creates a restore point, close the System Protection dialog box, the System Properties dialog box, and the System window.
- Open the folder where you stored the downloaded Windows Vista Upgrade Advisor file, click (or double-click) the WindowsVistaUpgradeAdvisor.msi file icon, click the Next button, read the License Agreement, click the I Agree option button, click the Next button, change the proposed path (if necessary) for the installation, click the Next button, confirm the installation by clicking the Next button, provide Administrator credentials, and then click the Close button after the installation is complete.

Now, you can use the Windows Vista Upgrade Advisor to evaluate a computer.

Evaluating a Computer with the Windows Vista Upgrade Advisor

Kai now wants to use the Windows Vista Upgrade Advisor to analyze the feasibility of upgrading a laptop with Windows XP Professional with a Service Pack 2 Update to Windows Vista. She asks you to follow the process with her so that you know how to use it when you work with other company computers.

You can only use the Windows Vista Upgrade Advisor with 32-bit versions of Windows XP and Windows Vista (except for Windows Vista Enterprise). To run the Windows Vista Upgrade Advisor on a computer, that computer must also have .NET 2.0 (Microsoft .NET Framework Version 2.0 Redistributable Package (x86)) and MSXML6 (Microsoft Core XML Services 6.0); if not, the Windows Vista Upgrade Advisor provides links for downloading these software options.

To examine a computer with the Windows Vista Upgrade Advisor:

1. Attach any devices that you regularly use, such as a printer or scanner, to your computer system before you open the Windows Vista Upgrade Advisor.
2. Open the Start menu, point to **All Programs**, click **Windows Vista Upgrade Advisor**, and then provide Administrator credentials. The Windows Vista Upgrade Advisor opens, checks for updates, and then welcomes you to the Windows Vista Upgrade Advisor. See Figure 11-13. It explains that it will scan your computer to determine which Windows Vista edition will work best on your computer. It also notes that it will also provide you with useful information about which Windows Vista features your computer supports and about the compatibility of your computer's software and hardware. It then recommends that you plug in any devices that you regularly use with your computer, such as a printer, scanner, or external hard disk drive.

Figure 11-13 Windows Vista Upgrade Advisor ready to scan computer

3. Click the **Start Scan** button. During the scan, you can examine the availability of features in different editions of Windows Vista or view information about specific editions. See Figure 11-14. After the scan is complete, it instructs you to click the See Details button to examine the results of the scan.

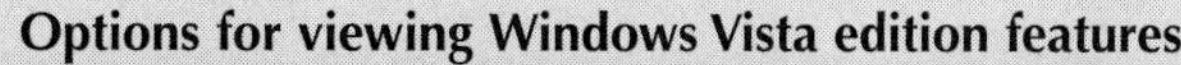
Options for viewing Windows Vista edition features

Figure 11-14

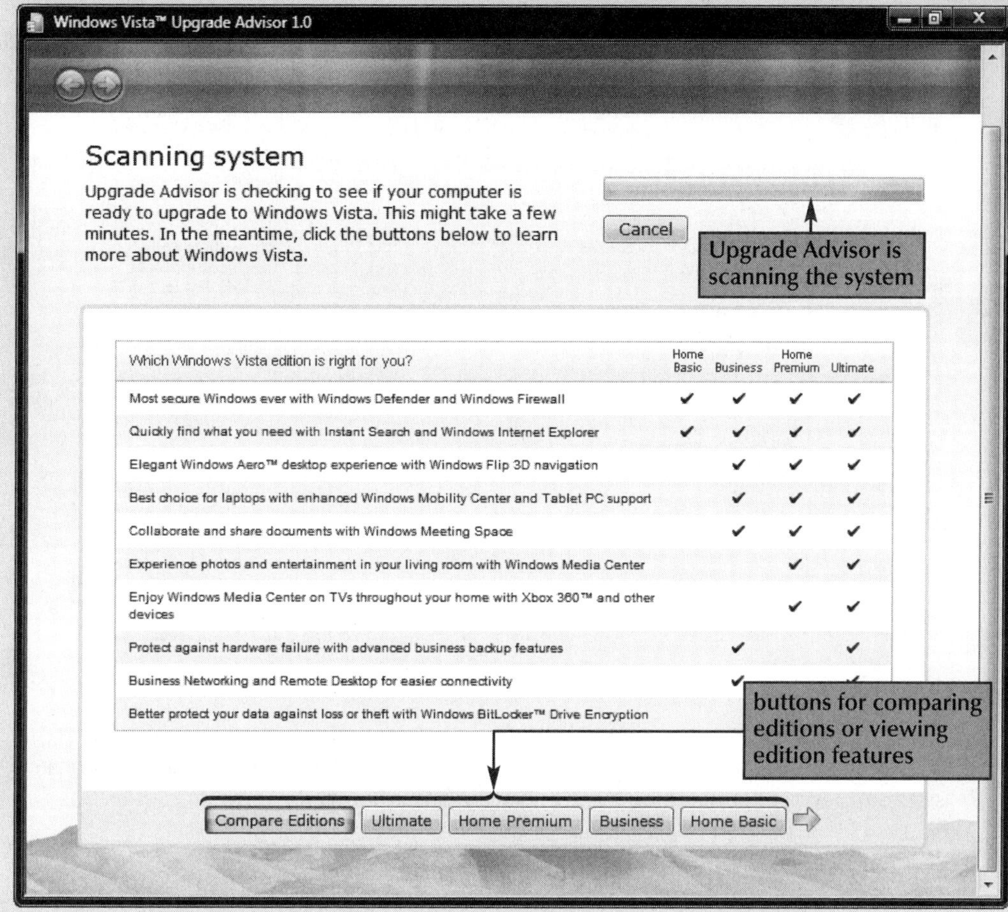

4. Click the **See Details** button. The Upgrade Advisor reports that this Windows XP Professional computer can run Windows Vista, and it recommends the Windows Vista Business Edition on the computer used for this figure. See Figure 11-15. Your Windows version and recommendation may differ.

Figure 11-15 Upgrade Advisor's recommendation

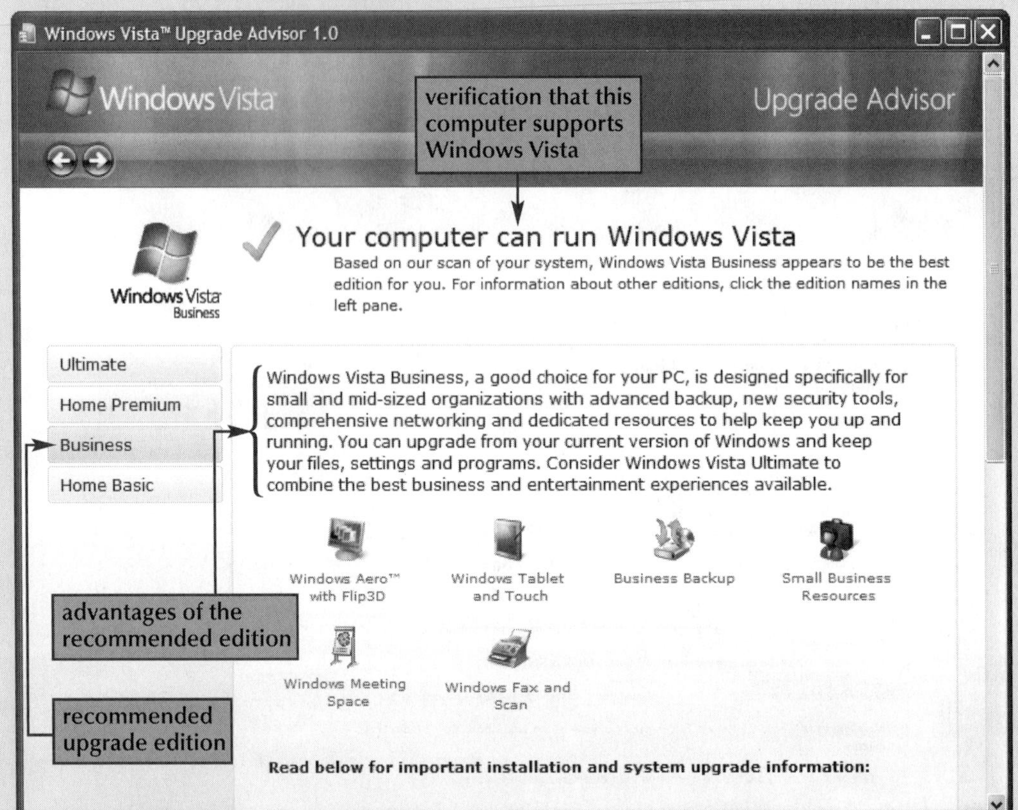

5. Scroll down (if necessary) and view the information under System Requirements. The Upgrade Advisor recommends that you examine system, device, and program issues important to installing Windows Vista and upgrading your computer. See Figure 11-16.

Options for reviewing system, device, and program issues

Figure 11-16

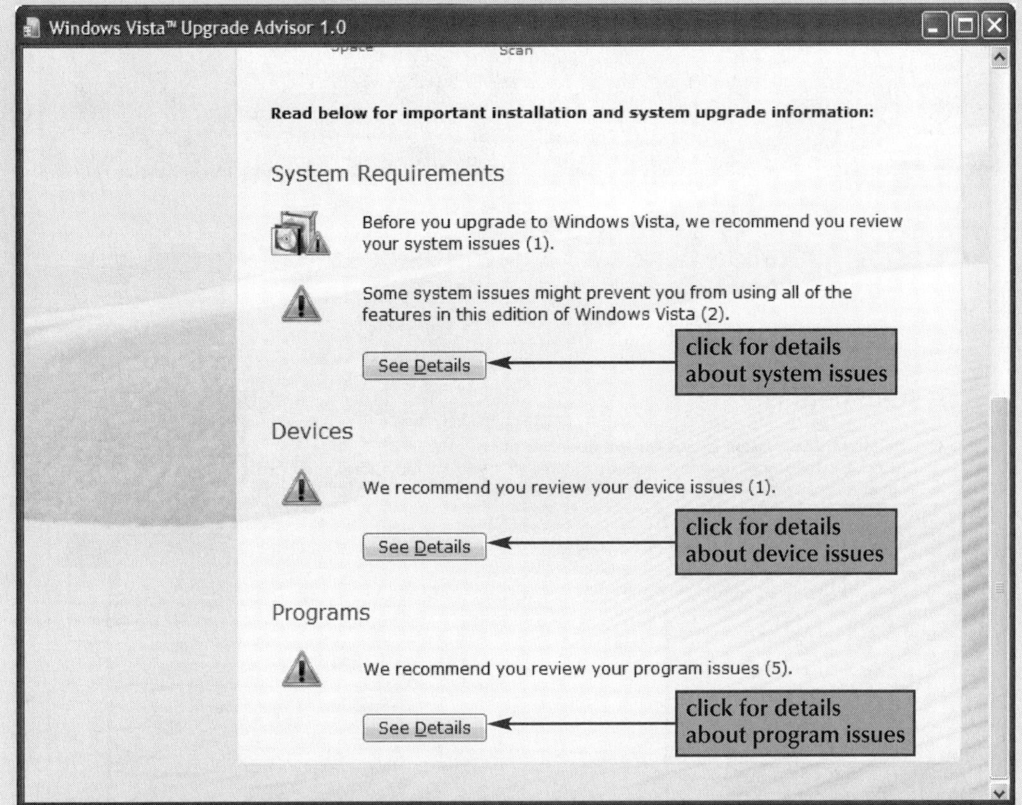

6. Under System Requirements, click the **See Details** button, and then examine the system issues. The first system issue on the computer used for Figure 11-17 is that it doesn't have enough available disk space on drive C to install Windows Vista. In the Explanation column, it notes that Windows Vista requires 15 GB of free hard disk space. It suggests that you remove unwanted files to free up storage space on drive C or that you upgrade the hard disk. In the Action Required column, it recommends you increase the amount of available storage space on this drive (drive C) or install Windows Vista on another drive (in this case, drive D) (which in this case would work). It also notes that your computer's hard disk drive should be at least 40 GB. Your system issues will differ.

Figure 11-17 Reviewing details of a system issue

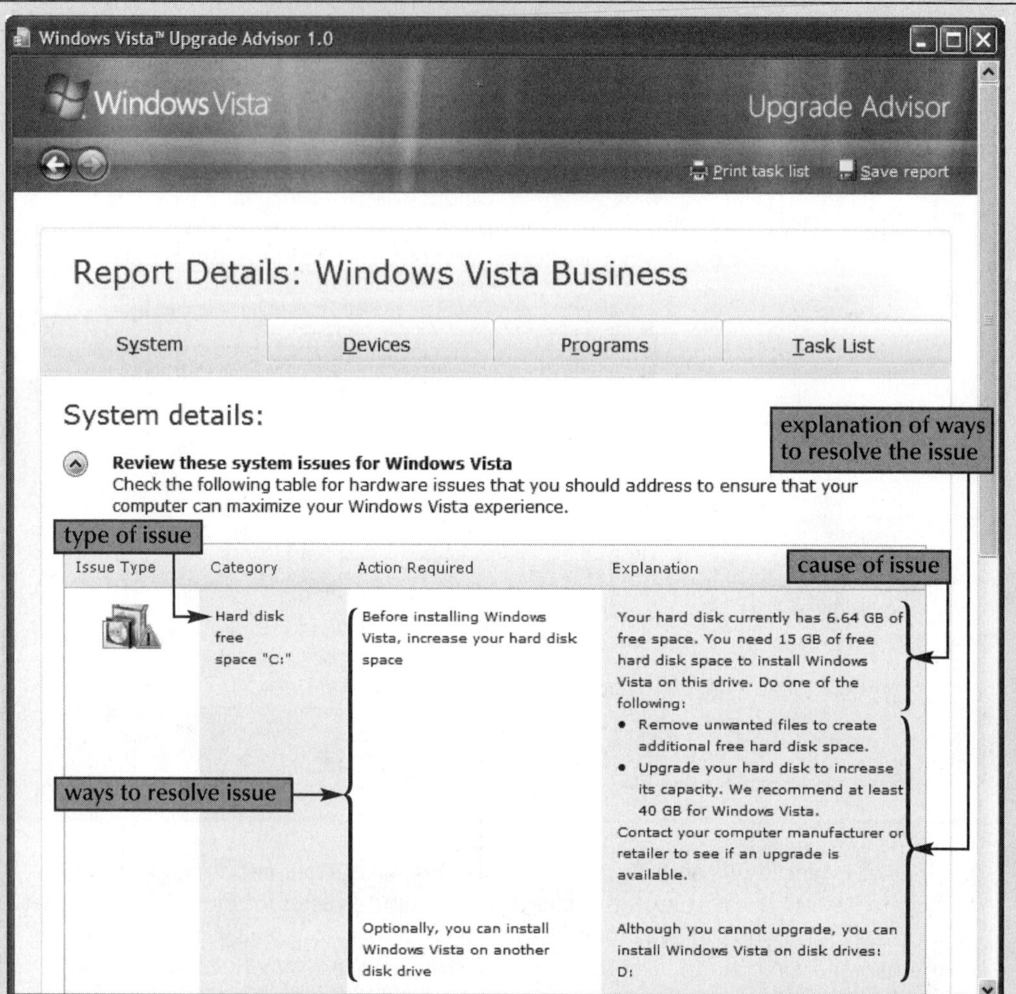

7. Adjust your view (if necessary) so that you can see any additional issues. On the computer used for Figure 11-18, the Upgrade Advisor notes that this video card does not support Windows Aero, and therefore, it recommends an upgrade of the video card. With respect to system memory, the Upgrade Advisor notes that the 512 MB of RAM on this computer supports only Windows Vista core experiences. The Upgrade Advisor recommends a RAM upgrade to a minimum of 1 GB of RAM. It recommends you visit the manufacturer's Web site for the video display adapter card to determine if there is an upgrade. The Upgrade Advisor ends by noting that there are no issues for two other system components—the CPU and the DVD drive. Your system issues may differ.

Figure 11-18

Recommendations for upgrading a video card and RAM

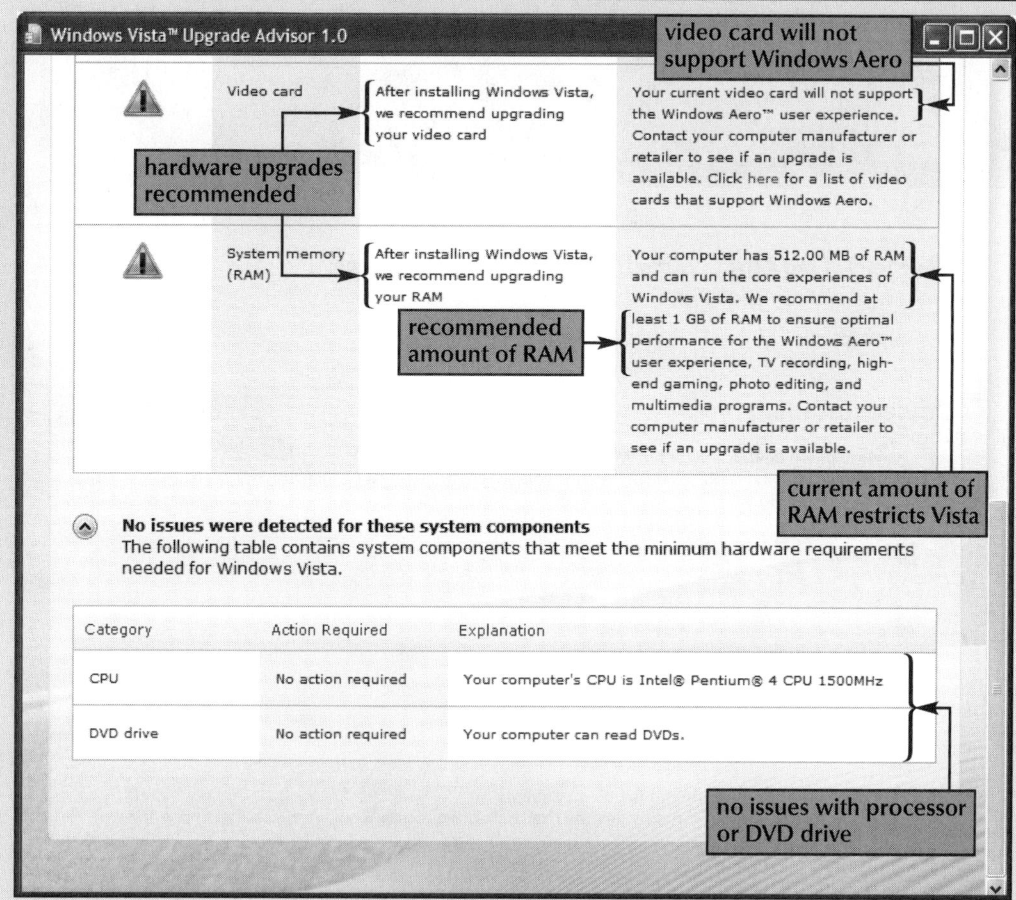

8. Scroll to the top of the Windows Vista Upgrade Advisor window (if necessary), click the **Devices** tab, and examine the information on device issues. As shown for the computer used in Figure 11-19, it notes that the monitor in this computer will not work with Windows Vista, and it recommends that you check the manufacturer's Web site for more information. Your device issues may differ.

Figure 11-19 Viewing information on a device issue

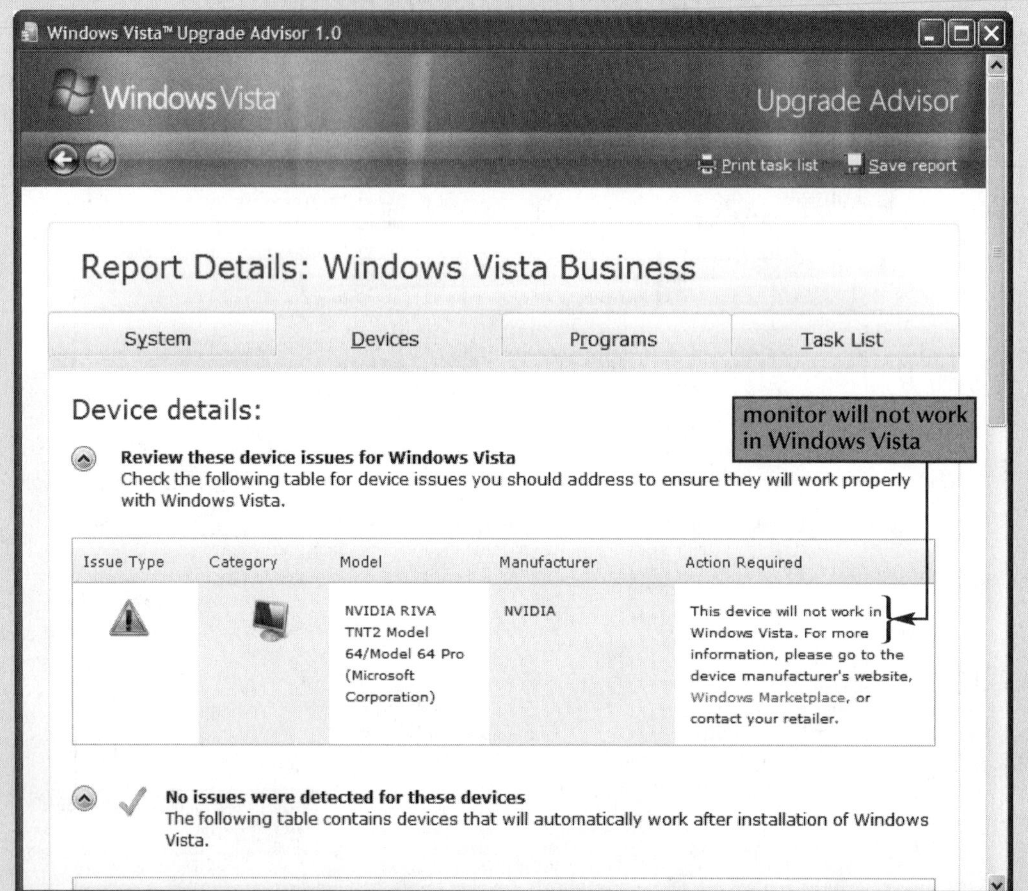

9. Adjust your view (if necessary) so that you can see any additional issues. On the computer used for Figure 11-20, the Upgrade Advisor also notes that there are no compatibility issues with 11 other devices (nine of which are shown in this figure), including a network adapter card, USB UPS (Uninterruptable Power Supply), Hewlett-Packard PhotoSmart 1115 ink-jet printer, and modem. If the Windows Vista Upgrade Advisor does not find any information on specific hardware devices, it groups them in a separate category and notes that there is no compatibility data available for these devices. It then recommends that you check for more information at the manufacturer's Web site. Your device issues will differ.

Figure 11-20

No problems detected for these hardware devices

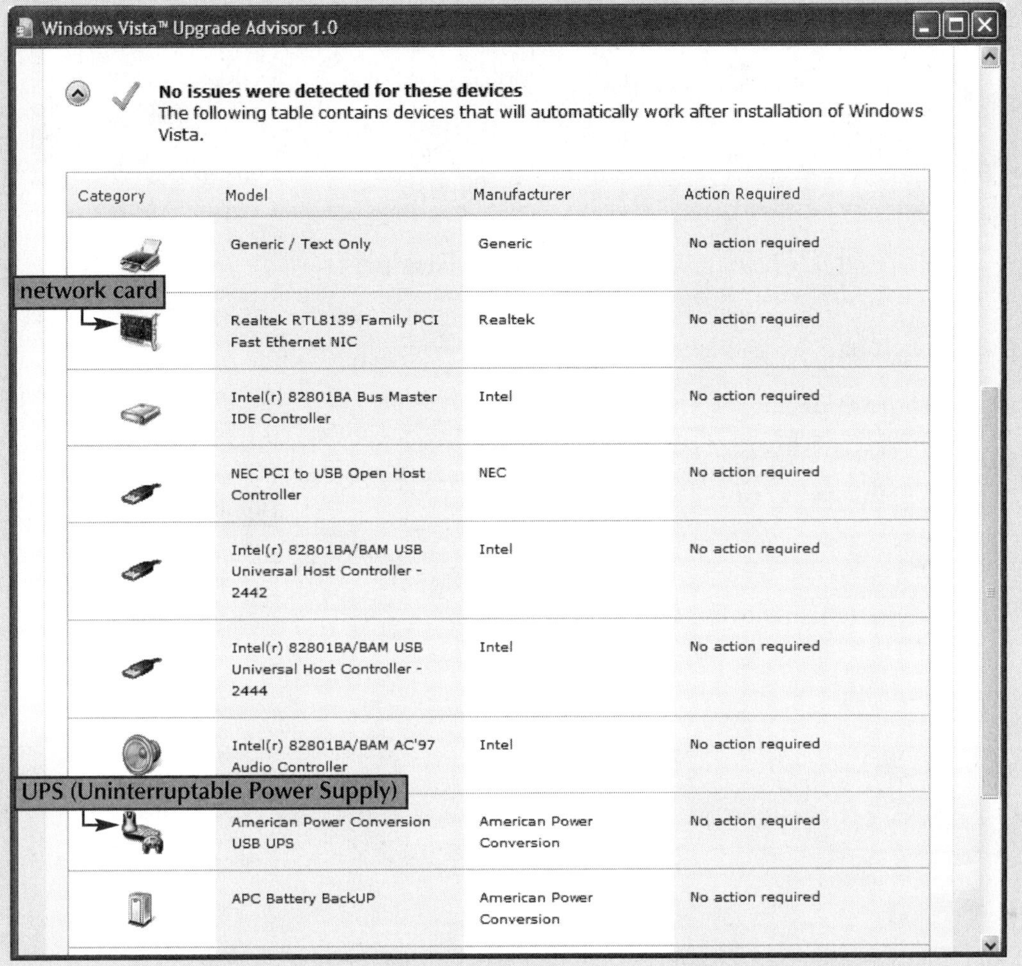

Windows Vista™ Upgrade Advisor 1.0

No issues were detected for these devices
The following table contains devices that will automatically work after installation of Windows Vista.

Category	Model	Manufacturer	Action Required
	Generic / Text Only	Generic	No action required
network card	Realtek RTL8139 Family PCI Fast Ethernet NIC	Realtek	No action required
	Intel(r) 82801BA Bus Master IDE Controller	Intel	No action required
	NEC PCI to USB Open Host Controller	NEC	No action required
	Intel(r) 82801BA/BAM USB Universal Host Controller - 2442	Intel	No action required
	Intel(r) 82801BA/BAM USB Universal Host Controller - 2444	Intel	No action required
	Intel(r) 82801BA/BAM AC'97 Audio Controller	Intel	No action required
UPS (Uninterruptable Power Supply)	American Power Conversion USB UPS	American Power Conversion	No action required
	APC Battery BackUP	American Power Conversion	No action required

Now that you've examined hardware issues, you are ready to examine issues with respect to the software installed on your computer and view a list of tasks that you need to perform to prepare your computer for an operating system upgrade.

To examine software issues:

1. Scroll to the top of the Windows Vista Upgrade Advisor window (if necessary), click the **Programs** tab, and examine the information on program issues. As shown for the computer used in Figure 11-21, the Upgrade Advisor identifies five issues with installed software, namely, Diskeeper Professional Edition, PowerDVD, Microsoft IntelliType Pro 2.2, Messenger, and Microsoft IntelliPoint 5.2 (not all of which are shown in the figure). In each case, the Upgrade Advisor notes that there might be minor compatibility issues after upgrading to Windows Vista, and it again recommends you check the vendor's Web site for more information. The Windows Vista Upgrade Advisor might also note that specific software, such as the Microsoft .NET Framework 2.0, has no known compatibility issues and that the software might have received a "Works with Windows Vista" logo from Microsoft. Your program issues will differ.

Figure 11-21 Minor compatibility problems with existing software

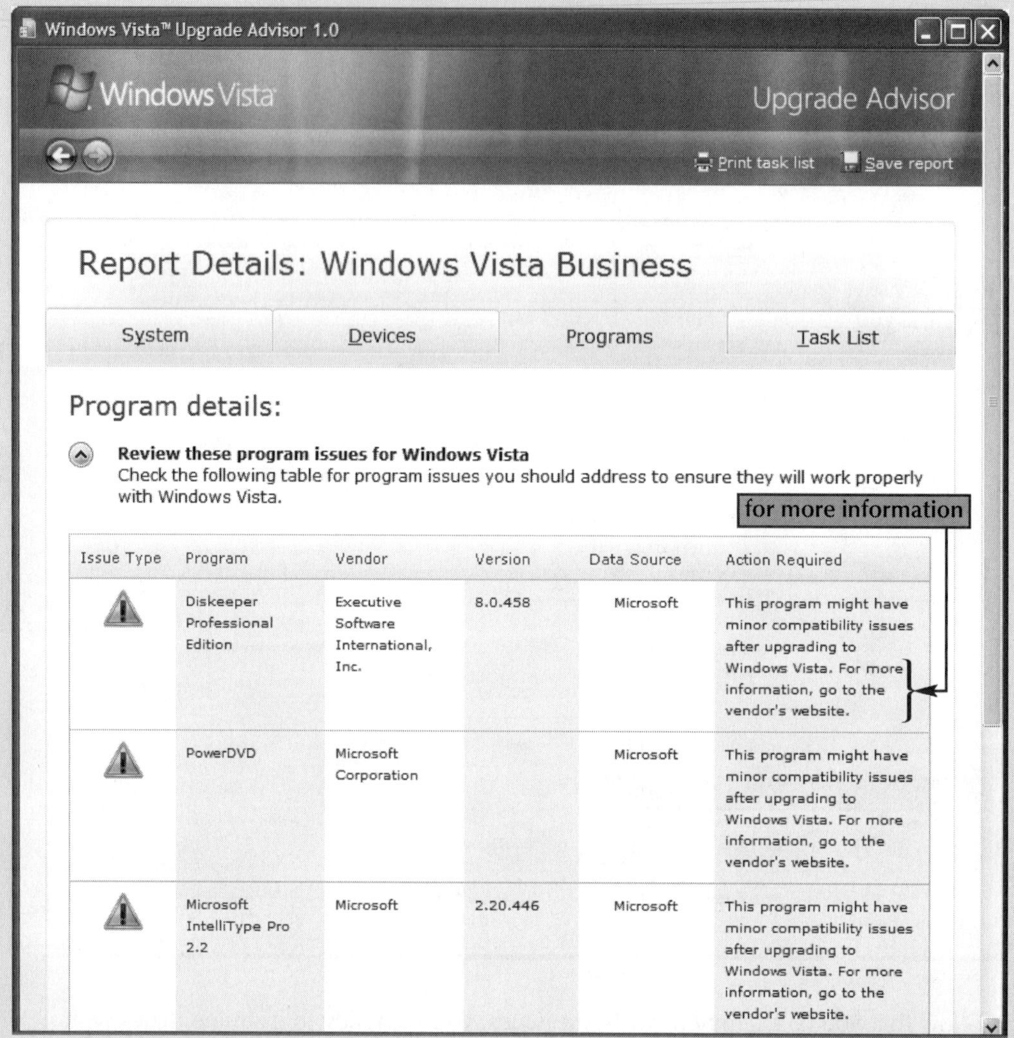

2. Scroll to the top of the Windows Vista Upgrade Advisor window (if necessary), click the **Task List** tab, and examine the recommendation for your computer. As shown for the computer used in Figure 11-22, the Task List notes that Windows Vista Business Edition is the recommended upgrade version for this computer. It also provides specs for the computer. Then, the Task List identifies the actions you need to complete before installing Windows Vista. Your recommendation may differ.

Figure 11-22

Recommended edition and computer specs

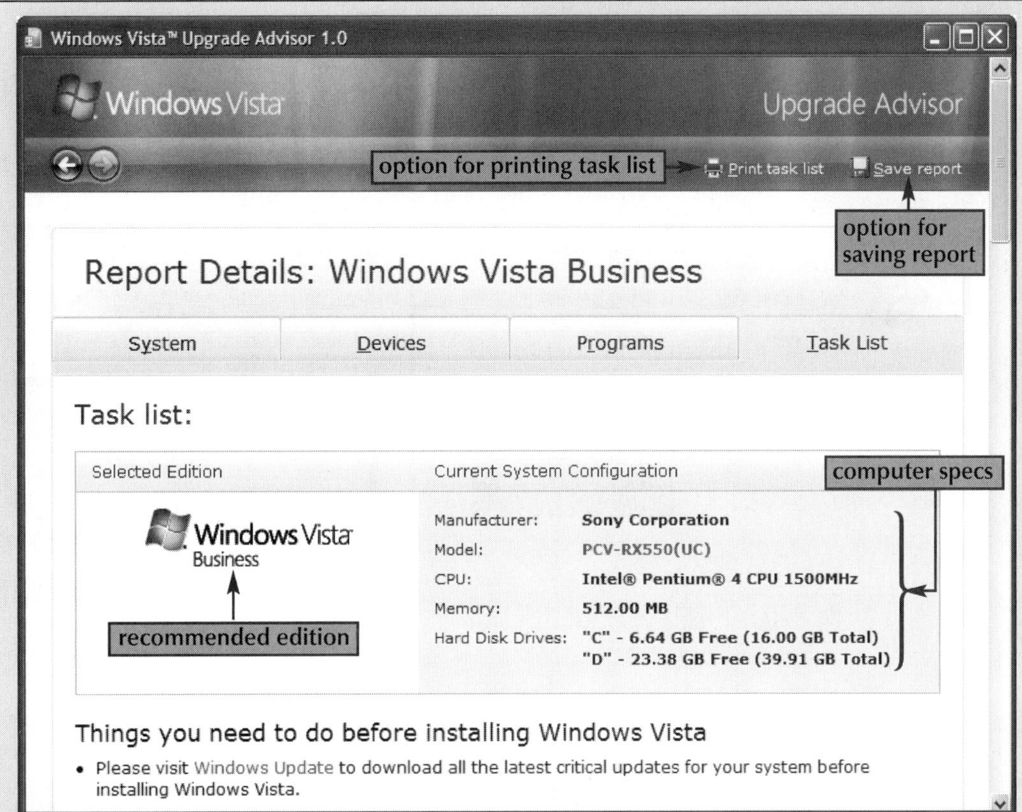

3. Adjust your view (if necessary) so that you can see the Task List. Next, the Task List may identify things you need to do before installing Windows. As shown in the computer used for Figure 11-23, the Task List reminds you of the lack of available hard disk storage on drive C for installing Windows Vista. This is the only system issue that must be resolved on this computer before installing Windows Vista. Then, it notes what you need to do after installing Windows Vista. This list includes all the other system, device, and program problems that you previously examined. For this computer, the Windows Vista Upgrade Advisor recommends replacing the video display adapter, increasing the amount of RAM, and resolving minor compatibility issues with software. Your Task List recommendations may differ.

Figure 11-23 Viewing task(s) required before installing Windows Vista

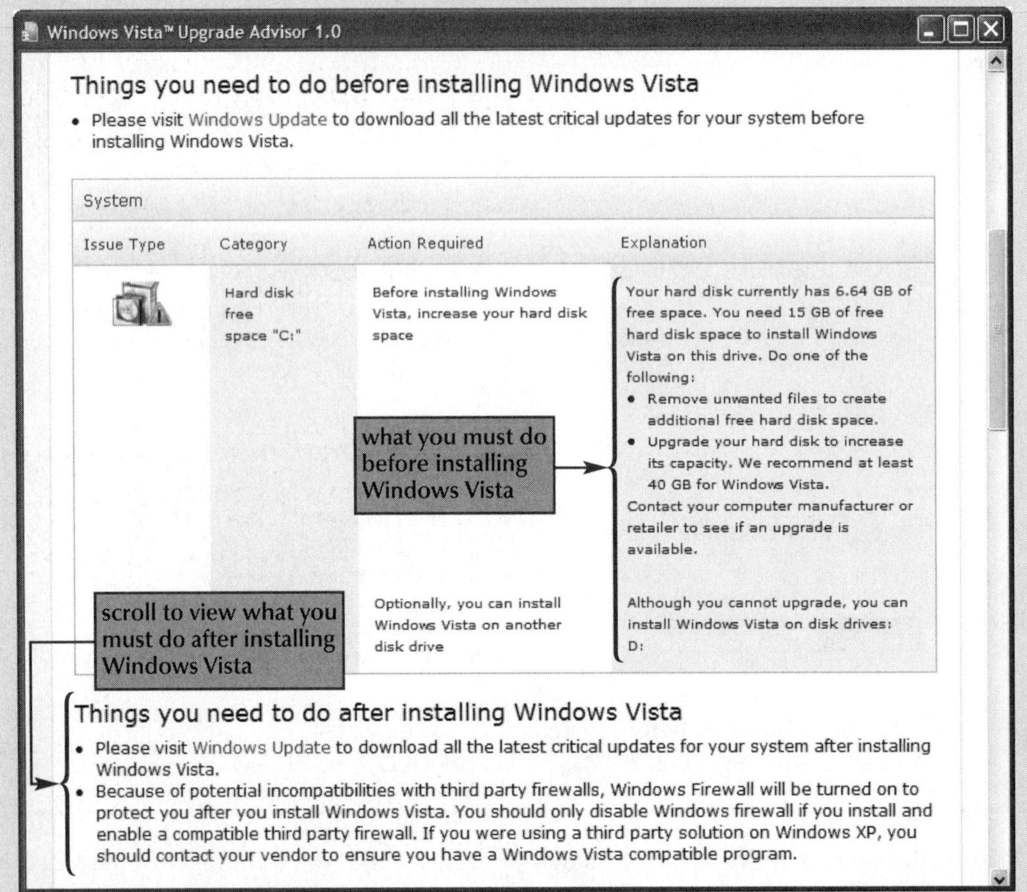

4. Close the Windows Vista Upgrade Advisor window.

If the user of this computer had not run the Windows Vista Upgrade Advisor, but instead had purchased Windows Vista Business (for example), that user would have immediately discovered that drive C did not have enough storage space for installing Windows Vista. That user would also discover that the video display adapter did not support Windows Aero, requiring a purchase of a new video display adapter. In fact, that video card had only 32 MB of graphics memory, the minimum required for Windows Vista Home Basic. Furthermore, that user might discover that the copy of Windows Vista cannot be returned after opening the software package. Also, if that user encountered problems during the upgrade, the computer system might be unusable, and that user might even lose personal files. Rather than upgrading, the user might have decided to purchase a new computer system with hardware that supported Windows Vista. It is far better to know of potential problems, and if possible, resolve those problems before purchasing a product that may not work on your computer and that may not install properly.

When the same Windows Vista Upgrade Advisor checked another computer which already had Windows Vista Ultimate installed on the computer, it reported no issues and recommended Windows Vista Ultimate for this computer. See Figure 11-24 and Figure 11-25. If that computer had another edition of Windows Vista installed on it, such as Windows Vista Home Basic or Windows Vista Home Premium, the Windows Vista Upgrade Advisor might recommend upgrading to Windows Vista Business or Windows Vista Ultimate. If you use the Windows Vista Upgrade Advisor to check a computer with Windows Vista Ultimate installed on it (or any other edition of Windows Vista), you can verify whether there are compatibility problems or issues that you might need to resolve.

Recommended Windows Vista edition **Figure 11-24**

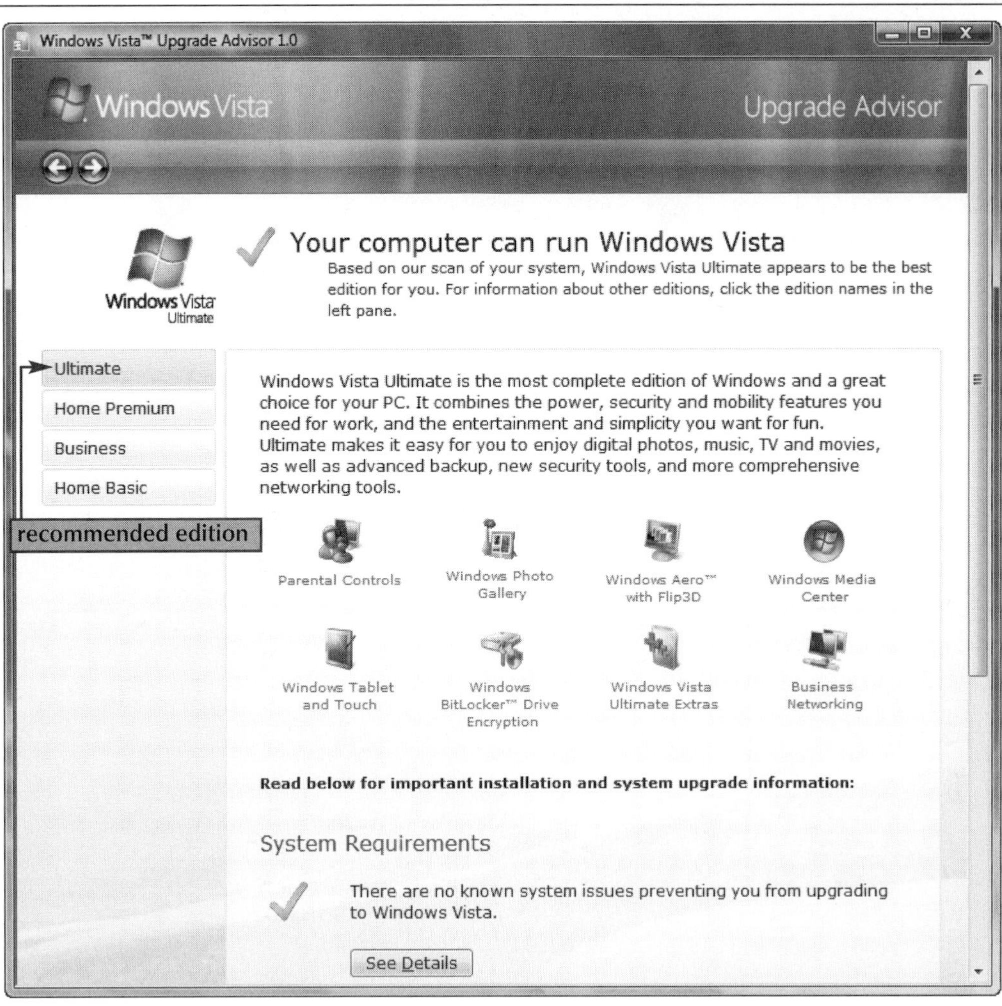

Figure 11-25 Upgrade Advisor's findings

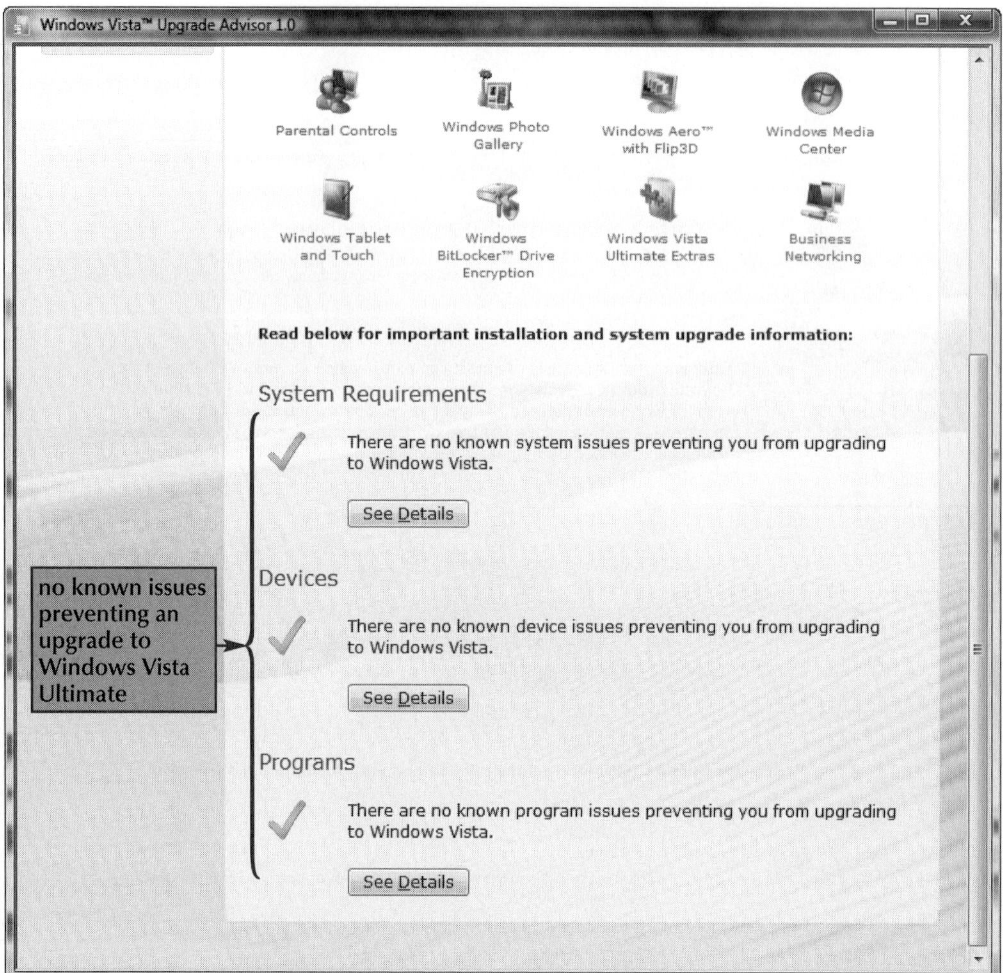

InSight | Saving Time and Money Before Upgrading Windows

Whenever Microsoft releases a new version of the Windows operating system, check its Web site for an Upgrade Advisor because it saves you valuable time and money by identifying problems that would otherwise interfere with an upgrade to a new version or edition of Windows and by recommending ways to correct those problems so that an upgrade goes as smoothly as possible. If an Upgrade Advisor recommends that you upgrade your hardware device drivers, check the manufacturer's Web site for newer device drivers and install them on your computer. Then, use the Upgrade Advisor again to make sure that the new device drivers have resolved the problems that prevent you from upgrading to a newer version or newer edition of Windows.

Evaluating a Computer with the Windows Vista Upgrade Advisor | Reference Window

- Attach any devices that you regularly use, such as a printer or scanner, to your computer system before you open the Windows Vista Upgrade Advisor.
- Open the Start menu, point to All Programs, and then click Windows Vista Upgrade Advisor.
- Click the Start Scan button, and after the scan is complete, click the See Details button and examine the information on the recommended upgrade of Windows Vista.
- Under System Requirements, click the first See Details button, and then examine the information on system issues.
- Scroll to the top of the Windows Vista Upgrade Advisor window (if necessary), click the Devices tab, and examine the information on device issues.
- Scroll to the top of the Windows Vista Upgrade Advisor window (if necessary), click the Programs tab, and examine the information on program issues.
- Scroll to the top of the Windows Vista Upgrade Advisor window (if necessary), and then click the Task List tab.
- Check the Task List for tasks that must be performed before upgrading to a new version or edition of Windows and also for tasks that must be performed after upgrading.
- Click the Save report button on the command bar to save a copy of the information compiled by the Windows Vista Upgrade Advisor. Click the Print task list button on the command bar to print a copy of the Task List.
- Close the Windows Vista Upgrade Advisor window.

Next, you can complete the upgrade preparation.

Completing the Upgrade Preparation

After examining Microsoft's Web site and checking product features, system requirements, upgrade paths, and hardware and software compatibility, you're ready to make a decision about upgrading your computer. Before installing that operating system upgrade, you should also perform the following important steps:

- **Document hardware, software, and network settings** Before installing an operating system upgrade, you should compile important information about your computer's hardware and software settings. You can use Device Manager (covered in Tutorial 12) to document hardware configuration settings on your computer and the System Information Utility (covered in Tutorial 8) to document hardware, software, and system settings. If your computer is part of a network, you should know your computer name, your workgroup or domain name, and your IP address unless it is automatically assigned. An **IP address** is a unique 32-bit address that identifies a computer on a network or the Internet. You can use the Network and Discovery Center or the IPCONFIG command-line utility to obtain your IP address.
- **Check the available storage space on your hard disk** Make sure you have enough storage space on the drive where you intend to install Windows Vista. As noted earlier, the Windows Vista Home Basic, Home Premium, Business, and Ultimate Editions require 15 GB of storage space. Also, make sure that this drive contains enough available storage space for installing periodic service pack upgrades and other important updates, which all increase the amount of disk space used by Windows Vista. Take into account the storage space required for the virtual memory paging file, the Internet cache, printer spool files, and temporary files as well as updates to all your other software.

Tip

To obtain your Windows edition, computer name, and workgroup or domain name, you right-click the Computer icon and select Properties.

To free storage space, you can perform the following tasks:

- **Empty the Internet cache** Use your Web browser to empty the contents of the folder used to cache files downloaded from the Internet and World Wide Web. You can also use the Disk Cleanup Wizard to help you find these and other files, such as temporary files.
- **Archive document files** If your computer contains important document files that you no longer use but want to keep in case you need them in the future, consider archiving them. Make sure you have backup copies of these files, and then move them off your hard disk onto a permanent storage medium, such as a DVD. If you want to keep them on your hard disk, you can create and store them in a Compressed (zipped) Folder so that they require less storage space.
- **Uninstall unneeded software applications and utilities** Examine the software installed on your computer and decide whether you still need those applications, utilities, and games. If not, uninstall them.

- **Scan for computer viruses and other types of malicious software** Even if you've installed antivirus software and antispyware to monitor your computer for computer viruses and other types of malicious software, Microsoft recommends that you download updates to your antivirus software, and then perform a full scan of your computer with your antivirus software prior to installing a new operating system.
- **Back up important files on your hard disk** Use the backup software in your version of Windows to back up all your important files. As you discovered in Tutorial 10, you can use the Backup and Restore Center to perform a Complete PC Backup (if your edition of Windows Vista supports this feature), and you can back up your personal user files. You can also purchase, install, and use backup software that allows you to back up your entire computer system as well as individual folders and files.
- **Check the hard disk for errors** Before you install or upgrade a new operating system, application, or utility, use a disk analysis and repair utility, such as the Error-Checking Tool or the command-line Check Disk utility that you examined in Tutorial 6 to verify the integrity of the file system, and if necessary, repair errors in the file system.
- **Optimize hard disk storage space** If necessary, use Disk Defragmenter in your version of Windows or a third party utility to optimize the storage space on your hard disk. After upgrading Windows, it's a good idea to use the Disk Defragmenter again to optimize the hard disk. Although the Disk Defragmenter under Windows Vista is scheduled to defragment the hard disk once a week, you can initiate a manual defragmentation, as you discovered in Tutorial 6.
- **Reboot your computer** Prior to installing or upgrading an operating system or major software products (such as Microsoft Office), close all open applications, utilities, and windows, and then reboot your computer to clear memory.
- **Turn off background programs** Programs, such as antivirus software or a screen saver that operates in the background, can interfere with the installation of an operating system or a software application. Since one of the functions of an antivirus program is to alert you to attempts to modify or replace system files or the contents of the boot sector, it might interfere with the installation of an operating system as well as other types of software products that update system files. If your antivirus software places an icon in the system tray, you can right-click this icon and close the program. Remember, however, to re-enable your antivirus software after you install an operating system upgrade and after you install other software.

Then, you're finally ready to install the operating system upgrade. Although it takes time to prepare your computer for an operating system upgrade, it's far more time-consuming to rebuild your computer from scratch. Follow the preceding steps, examine the information Microsoft posts at its Web site on upgrading to Windows Vista, review the information in the Windows Vista Resource Kit on deploying and installing Windows Vista (if necessary), and examine your computer's hardware and software documentation to ensure a reliable and problem-free installation of Windows Vista.

Keep the following rule of thumb in mind: *The more carefully you prepare for an installation of a new operating system, the less likely you will encounter problems during the installation.*

Installing Windows Vista

Once you've assured yourself that your computer is ready for Windows Vista or for an upgrade to another edition of Windows Vista, the simplest way to install Windows Vista is to insert the Windows Vista DVD in your DVD drive. An autorun.inf ("inf" for Setup Information file) on the DVD opens the Setup program for installing Windows Vista. Figure 11-26 shows the contents of the Autorun.inf file, a simple text file. [autorun] is a section name, followed by two keys, or entries (similar to the one you created in Tutorial 4 to specify a custom icon for your flash drive). The open key specifies the program to run (in this case, setup.exe), and the icon key specifies the location of the icon in the program file (0 for the first icon in the file). If a path is not included with the open key, Windows assumes the program is in the top-level folder (or root directory) of the disk.

Windows Vista autorun.inf file | Figure 11-26

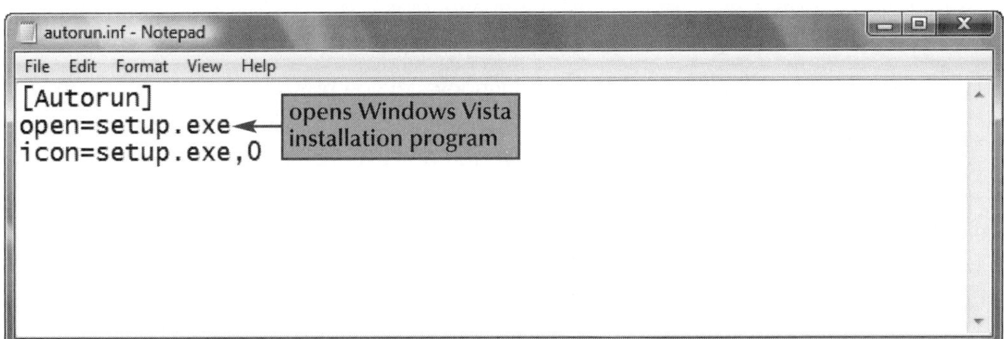

After the Windows Vista Setup program starts from the Windows Vista DVD, you can use the "Check compatibility online" link to go to Microsoft's Web site for downloading the Windows Vista Upgrade Advisor. See Figure 11-27. The "What to know before installing Windows" link displays Help information on installing Windows Vista. The "Transfer files and settings from another computer" link opens Windows Easy Transfer, which you will examine later in this tutorial.

Figure 11-27 Windows Vista Setup program

When you choose the option for installing Windows Vista, the Setup program takes you through the following steps:

1. **Obtain updates online** In the first Install Windows dialog box, Setup recommends that you go online to get the most recent Windows updates so that it can install those updates as part of installing Windows Vista. You do have the option of not downloading updates; however, Setup notes that the Windows Vista installation might fail and that your computer could be more vulnerable to security threats. (However, on the Windows Vista Ultimate computer used for this book, no problems were encountered by downloading updates after installing Windows Vista Ultimate.) At this point, you can also read Microsoft's privacy statement. Setup also informs you that it will first collect information about your computer before it installs Windows Vista.
2. **Provide Product ID** After you advance to the next step, you are prompted for your Product Key so that Setup can activate Windows Vista after it is installed. You can find the sticker with the Product Key on the back of the plastic DVD holder within the product package. It notes that you can enter the Product Key without typing the dashes (they are automatically added). The "Automatically activate Windows when I'm online" check box is already enabled so that this essential step is performed after you install Windows Vista. There is also a link for viewing information about activation.
3. **Agree to the License Agreement** You must accept the conditions of the License Agreement before you can continue. This contract is a legally binding agreement, and you should read and understand all its components before you accept the agreement.

4. **Choose the type of installation** You are prompted for the type of installation you want to perform—Upgrade or Custom (Advanced). Setup notes that the Upgrade option keeps your existing settings and applications and recommends that you back up your files before installing Windows Vista. If you choose Custom (Advanced), Setup notes that it will perform a clean install, prompt you where to install Windows, and ask if you want to make changes to disks and partitions during the installation. Setup further notes that this option does not keep your files, settings, and programs. Recall that if your current version of Windows supports an upgrade to Windows Vista, you should choose the Upgrade option. If your computer contains a version of Windows that does not support an upgrade to Windows Vista, you must perform a clean install of Windows Vista. (Even if your current version of Windows supports an upgrade, you can still perform a clean install.) If you choose the option for a clean install, Setup will display a list of disks and partitions on your computer so that you can select the partition where you want to install Windows Vista. If Windows Vista does not detect any disks, you can choose the option for loading drivers for your hard disk drive. Once you select a partition, you have the option of formatting the partition; however, Setup warns you that this option erases everything on the partition.
5. **Review the compatibility report** Next, Setup warns you of any compatibility problems and identifies them. It may also note that these problems do not prevent the upgrade, but some application and devices might not work after the upgrade.
6. **Start upgrading Windows** Setup starts upgrading your computer to Windows Vista by copying Windows files, gathering files, expanding files, installing features and updates, and completing the upgrade. Setup reboots the computer several times as it completes the installation of Windows Vista.
7. **Set up Windows** After the installation, you are prompted to choose a user name and picture for your user account. Setup also notes that the first user account is a Computer Administrator account. You enter a user name, specify a password and verify it, specify a password hint, and choose a picture for your user account.
8. **Enter the computer name and desktop background** Next, you enter a name for your computer and select desktop wallpaper.
9. **Select Windows updates** Here you specify how you want to handle Windows updates.
10. **Adjust time and date settings** Review and, if necessary adjust, your date, time, and time zone settings.
11. **Provide computer location** Next, you specify network settings. Setup notes that it will automatically apply the correct settings to your network; however, you should verify that the option Setup selects is not only appropriate but the one you want to use. The options are Home, Work, or Public Location. It notes that if you choose Home or Work, your network is discoverable, and you can see other computers and devices on the network. Setup recommends Public Location for a computer in a public location, such as an airport or coffee shop, and for a computer that is directly connected to the Internet. Setup notes that discovery of other computers and devices on your network are limited with this option.
12. **Review the evaluation of your computer's performance** After thanking you, Setup checks your computer's performance, and then it reboots your computer.

Tip

IT administrators should refer to the 1,527-page Microsoft Windows Vista Resource Kit, which includes extensive information on deploying and installing Windows Vista (including customizing and automating installations).

13. **Log on your user account** After the reboot, Windows Vista displays the Welcome screen with your user account name and picture so that you can log on under your user account. Then, Windows Vista prepares your desktop and opens the Welcome Center where you can set up your Internet connection, transfer files and settings from another computer, view system settings, or view Microsoft offers, to name a few options.

If you opted for a clean install, you then must reinstall your software and restore your personal files from a backup.

Using Windows Easy Transfer

When Kai upgraded her computer, a computer tech that performed the upgrade used Windows Easy Transfer to transfer her user account, user settings, and files from her old computer to her new computer. That not only saved Kai valuable time and effort, but she was ready to work on her new computer within a short period of time, plus her new computer was set up in the same way as her old computer.

If your computer uses Windows XP or Windows Vista, you can use Windows Easy Transfer to copy all your user files (including favorites) and settings as well as those of all other users on the same computer to another computer. User and computer settings include Start menu and taskbar settings, desktop settings, display and screen saver settings, fonts, mouse and keyboard settings, accessibility settings, Internet connection settings, and network settings. During the Windows Easy Transfer process, you can check and specify which settings are copied to the new computer because not all the settings might be applicable. For example, do you want to copy Start menu program shortcuts from an older computer to a newer computer that does not contain the same installed software (and versions of that software) found on your older computer? As part of this transfer process, Windows Easy Transfer copies everything in the Documents, Pictures, and Shared Documents folders, and you can include other folders as well. You can also copy all your e-mail messages, contacts, and e-mail settings to your new computer as well as program settings and Internet settings; however, you have to install the programs on your new computer first. If your older computer uses Windows 2000 Professional, you can only copy your files.

You can use one of the following methods to make the transfer:

- **Easy Transfer Cable** The simplest way to transfer files and settings from one computer to another is to use an Easy Transfer Cable, which you can purchase online or at a local computer or electronics store. An Easy Transfer Cable is a special type of USB cable, so you need to use USB ports for the transfer; also, you cannot use a standard type of USB cable. You can then transfer files and settings from your old computer to your new computer over the Easy Transfer Cable by using Windows Easy Transfer on your new computer.
- **Networked connection** If your new and older computers are on the same network, you can transfer files and settings over the network connection by using Windows Easy Transfer on the new computer.
- **Removable media** You can use removable media, such as writeable DVDs, writeable CDs, a flash drive, or an external hard disk drive to transfer files and settings from computer to computer.

If you have an Easy Transfer Cable or a network connection between your old computer and your new computer, you can start Windows Easy Transfer on your new computer. If you do not have an Easy Transfer Cable or network connection, you must copy Windows Easy Transfer from your new Windows Vista computer to removable media (such as a flash drive), and then run Windows Easy Transfer from that removable media on your old computer. The steps for copying Windows Easy Transfer to removable media are as follows:

1. Open Accessories from the All Programs menu, then open System Tools, select Windows Easy Transfer, and provide Administrator credentials. After you open Windows Easy Transfer, it notes that no information is deleted from your old computer. See Figure 11-28. It also notes that neither computer is available during the transfer. Then, it itemizes what it will transfer, namely, user accounts, folders and files (including music, pictures, and video); program settings; Internet settings and favorites; and e-mail settings, contacts, and messages. You can click the "Which versions of Windows work with Windows Easy Transfer" link to determine whether your Windows version supports Windows Easy Transfer.

Using Windows Easy Transfer **Figure 11-28**

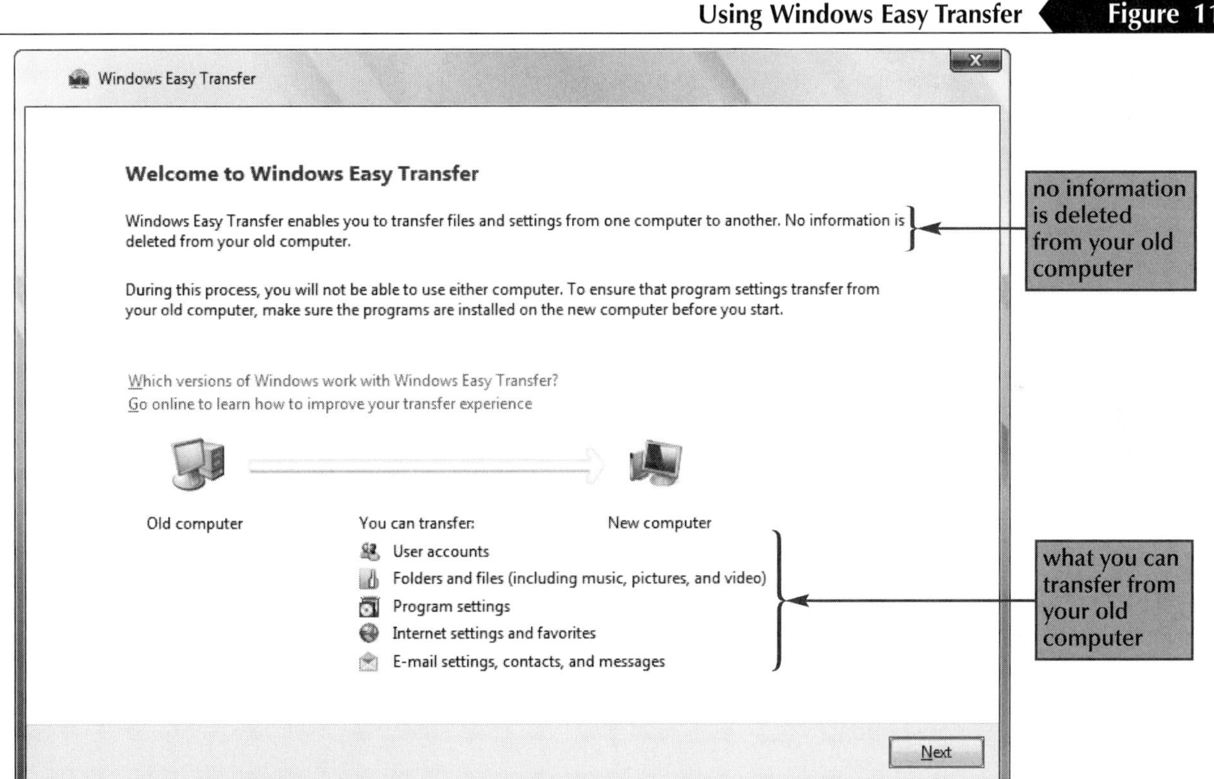

2. Windows Easy Transfer asks if you want to start a new transfer or continue a transfer in progress. See Figure 11-29. You would choose "Start a new transfer."

Figure 11-29 Options for initiating a new transfer or continuing a previous transfer

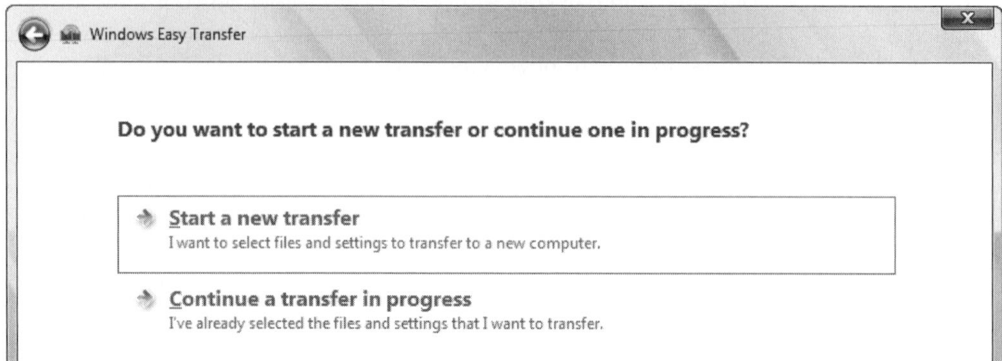

3. Windows Easy Transfer asks whether the computer you are using is your new one or your old one. It notes that if you want to transfer files from the computer you are currently using to a new computer, you choose "My old computer." If you want to transfer files from your old computer to the computer you are currently using, you choose "My new computer." See Figure 11-30. To copy Windows Easy Transfer to a removable device so that you can run it on your old computer, you choose "My new computer."

Figure 11-30 Identify the computer you are using

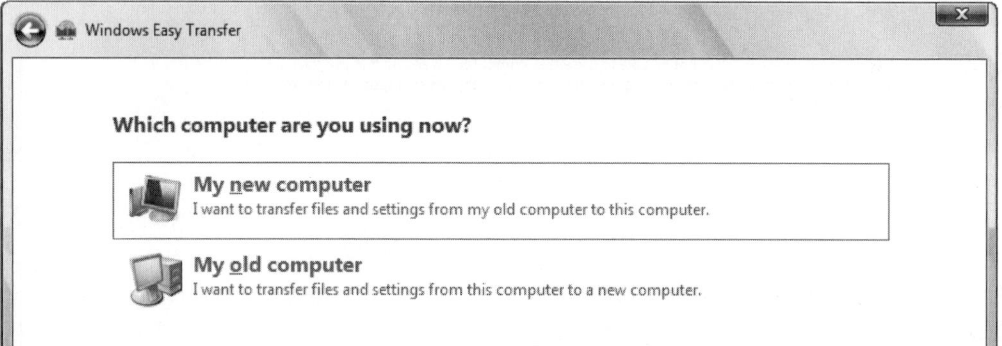

4. Windows Easy Transfer asks if you have an Easy Transfer Cable. See Figure 11-31. If you don't have this type of cable and want to copy Windows Easy Transfer to removable media so that you can install it on your older computer, choose "No, show me more options."

Figure 11-31 Option for using an Easy Transfer Cable or another transfer option

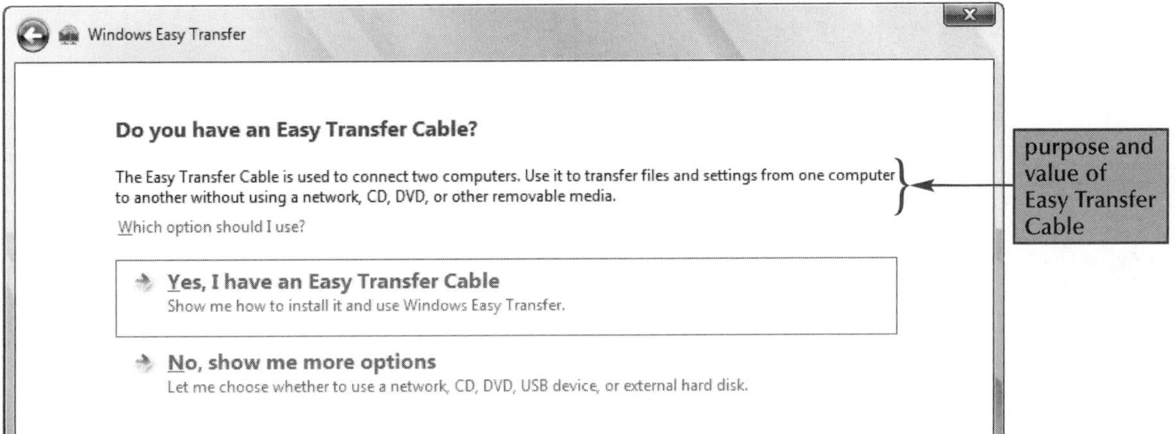

5. Windows Easy Transfer asks if Windows Easy Transfer is installed on your old computer, as shown in Figure 11-32. Here you select the option "No, I need to install it now."

Figure 11-32 Options for using Windows Easy Transfer on your old computer

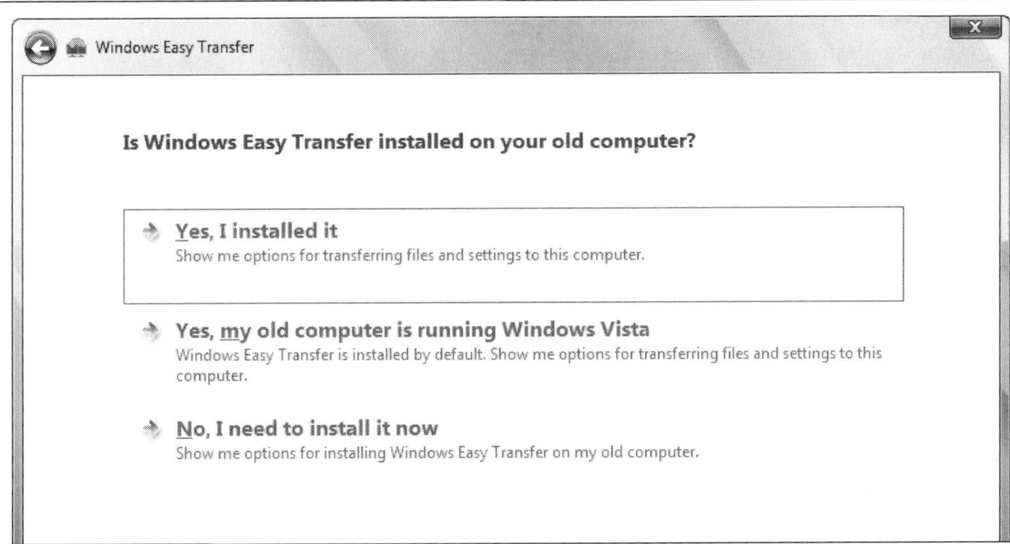

6. Windows Easy Transfer next asks you to choose how you want to install Windows Easy Transfer on your old computer. See Figure 11-33. Your options are CD, USB flash drive, external hard disk or network shared folder, or Windows installation disc or Windows Easy Transfer CD. Since a flash drive is the easiest to use for this purpose, you would choose USB flash drive.

Figure 11-33 Choose media for installing Windows Easy Transfer

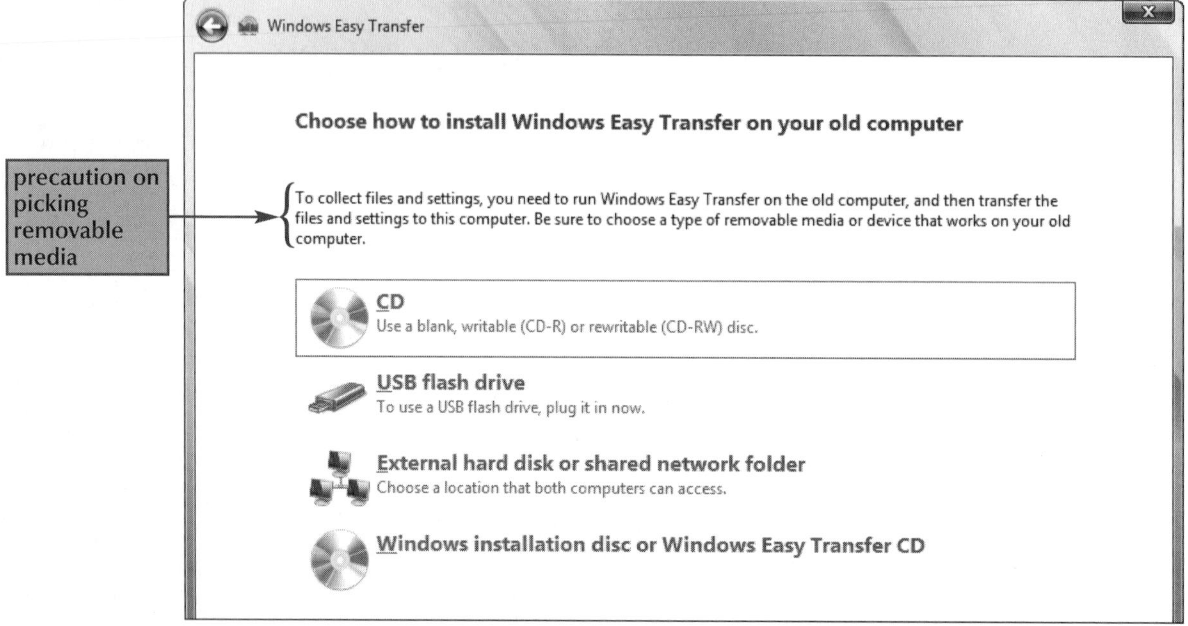

7. After you select the media type and advance to the next step, Windows Easy Transfer copies the Windows Easy Transfer software to your flash drive. Then, Windows Easy Transfer instructs you to remove the media or device and attach it to your older computer. Figure 11-34. It informs you that Windows should detect the device and ask you whether you want to run Windows Easy Transfer on the old computer.

Figure 11-34 Ways to run Windows Easy Transfer on your old computer

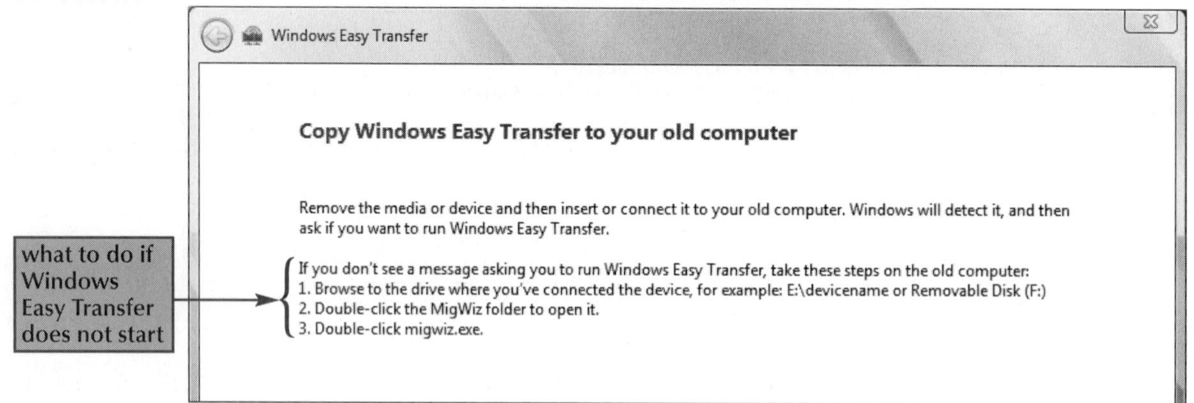

8. Use the Safely Remove Hardware icon in the notification area to select the flash drive with the Windows Easy Transfer software.

Now, you're ready to copy the files and settings that you want to use on your new computer from your older computer. The steps are as follows:

1. You attach your flash drive to your old computer, and in the Removable Disk dialog box, you select the option "Run Windows Easy Transfer using the program provided on the device." In Figure 11-35, the flash drive was attached to a computer with Windows XP Professional. If Windows on your old computer does not prompt you to run Windows Easy Transfer from the flash drive, you open a window onto the flash drive, open the MigWiz folder, and then click (or double-click) migwiz.exe.

Option for running Windows Easy Transfer on a Windows XP Professional computer **Figure 11-35**

2. Windows Easy Transfer starts from your flash drive and asks you to choose how you want to transfer files and settings to your new computer. You can use an Easy Transfer Cable (the recommended option), transfer directly using a network connection, or use removable media, such as a CD, DVD, external hard disk, or other type of removable media. See Figure 11-36. Assume you plan on using an external hard disk.

Tip

Whatever type of media you choose, make sure it will hold a backup of all your user files and settings.

Ways to transfer files and settings **Figure 11-36**

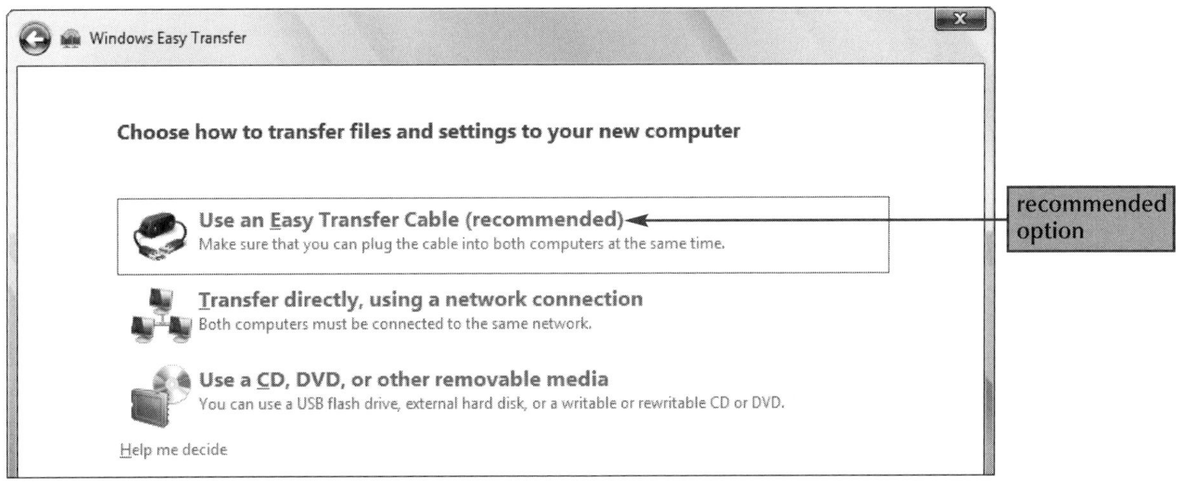

3. If you choose the option for using removable media, you are prompted for the type of removable media, namely CD or DVD, flash drive, or an external hard disk drive or network connection. See Figure 11-37. Windows Easy Transfer also reminds you that you want to make sure that your choice works on both computers.

Figure 11-37 **Pick your transfer option**

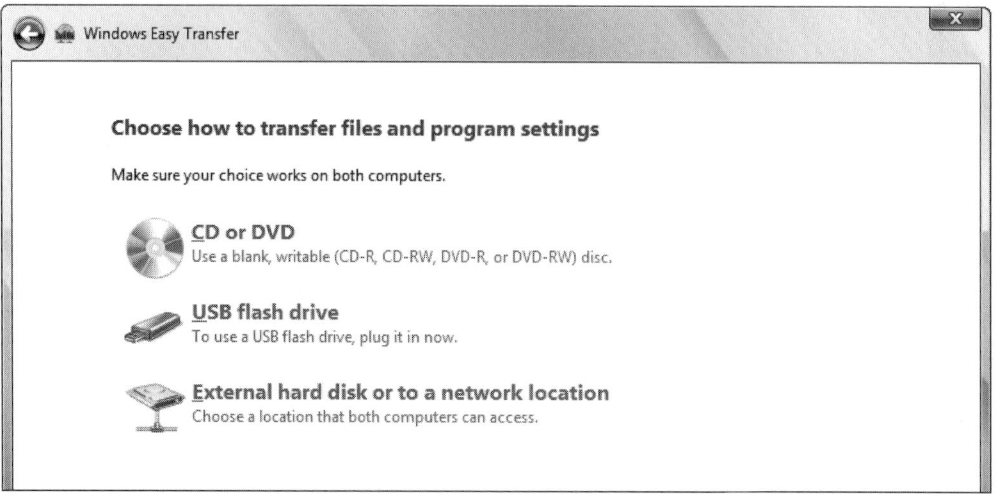

4. If you choose the option for using an external hard disk drive or a network connection, Windows Easy Transfer prompts for the network connection in the next dialog box. See Figure 11-38. You can browse and locate the external hard disk drive or network location. Also, note that your files and settings are copied to a file named SaveData.MIG. Windows Easy Transfer also recommends that you create and confirm a password.

Figure 11-38 **Specifying the path or location for a network location**

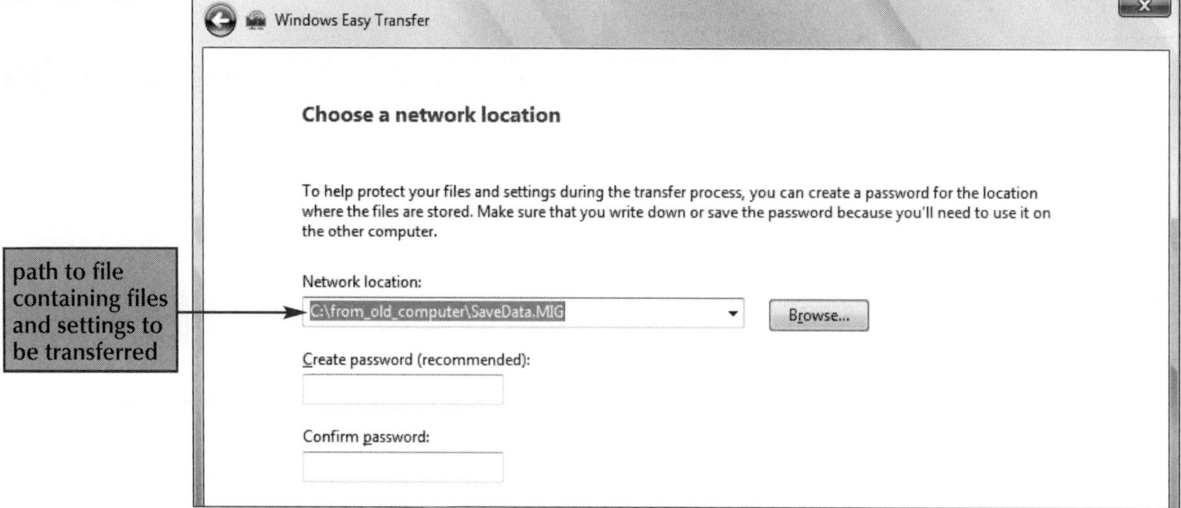

5. After you select the location and advance to the next step, Windows Easy Transfer asks what you want to transfer to your computer. See Figure 11-39. You can transfer all user accounts, files, and settings or just your user account, files, and settings.

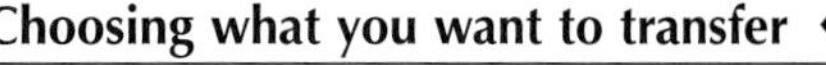

Choosing what you want to transfer **Figure 11-39**

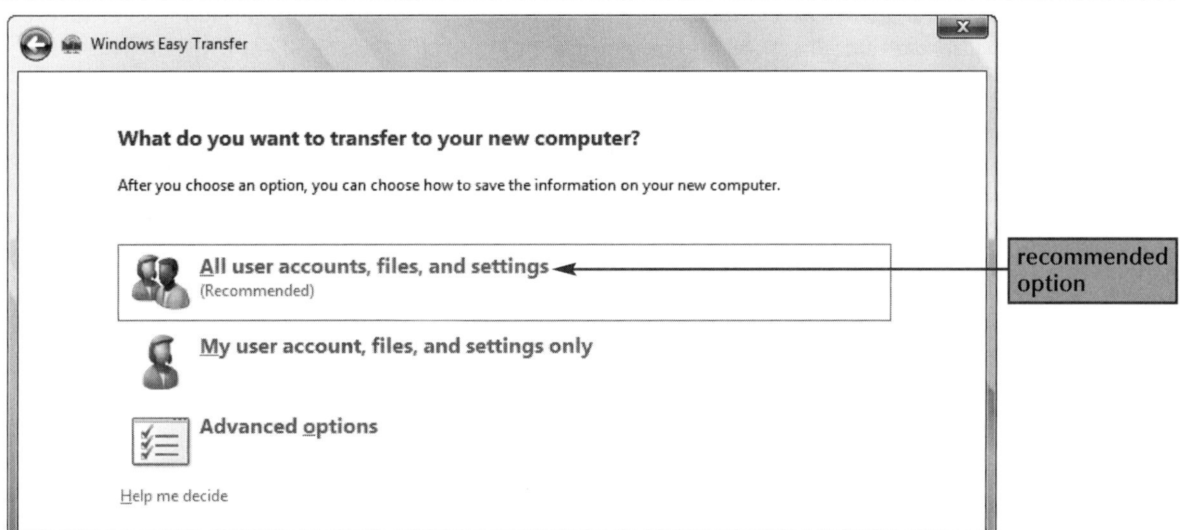

6. If you choose Advanced options, Windows Easy Transfer checks to see what can be transferred and displays a folder structure that identifies the files and settings to transfer. See Figure 11-40. At the top of the folder structure is Kai's user account folder. Kai's files and settings are organized into three groups—Application Settings, Documents, and Windows Settings.

Option for reviewing files and settings selected for the transfer **Figure 11-40**

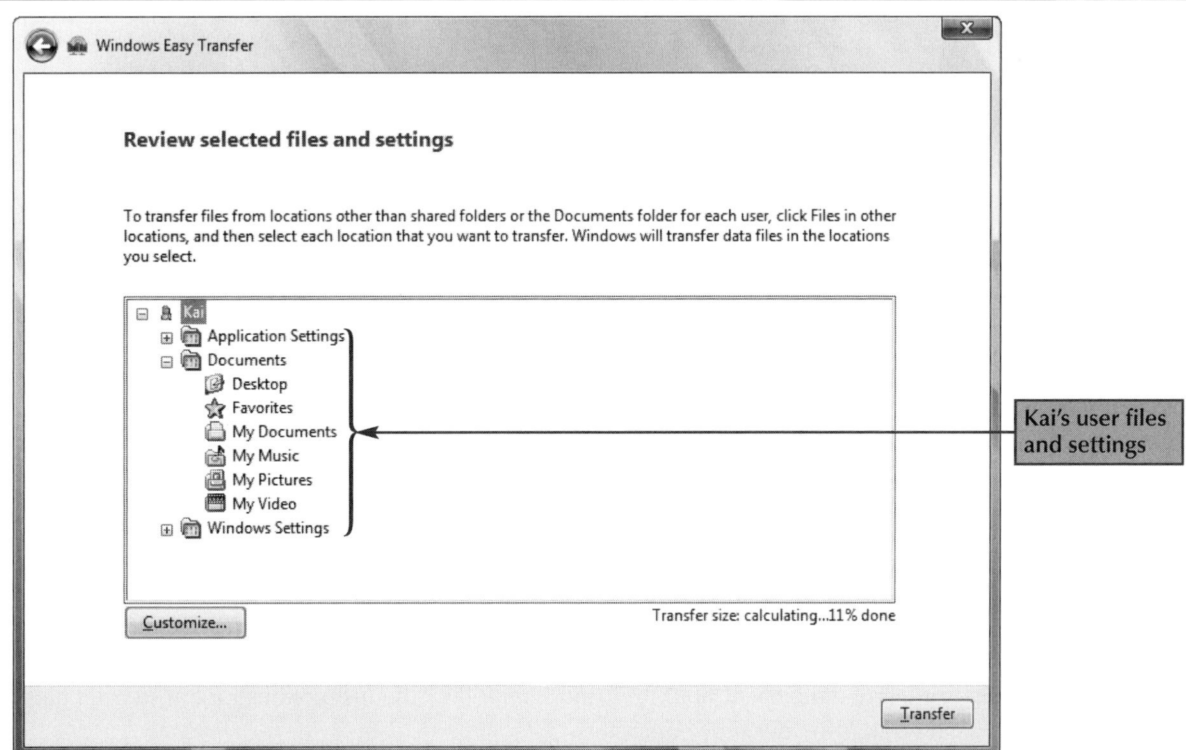

If Kai had chosen all user accounts, files, and settings, and assuming the computer included other user accounts, a folder would appear at the top of the folder structure transferring all system and program settings for all users. See Figure 11-41. Those settings are organized into three groups—Application Settings, Shared Folders, and Windows Settings. The folder structure then includes a folder for each user, and within each user's folder, includes folders for transferring that user's Application Settings, Documents, and Windows Settings. At the bottom of this folder structure is a folder for choosing "Files in other locations," such as an external hard disk drive. You want to examine that folder to make sure that Windows Easy Transfer does not transfer anything you do not need (such as backups from an external hard disk drive). Under the folder structure box are options for adding files, adding folders, selecting drives, and excluding folders so that you can further fine-tune your selection. Note also that the transfer size of 86.6 GB on the computer used for this figure means that the transfer will require time for the transfer and enough storage space or media to complete the transfer.

Figure 11-41 **Options for reviewing all user files and settings selected for the transfer**

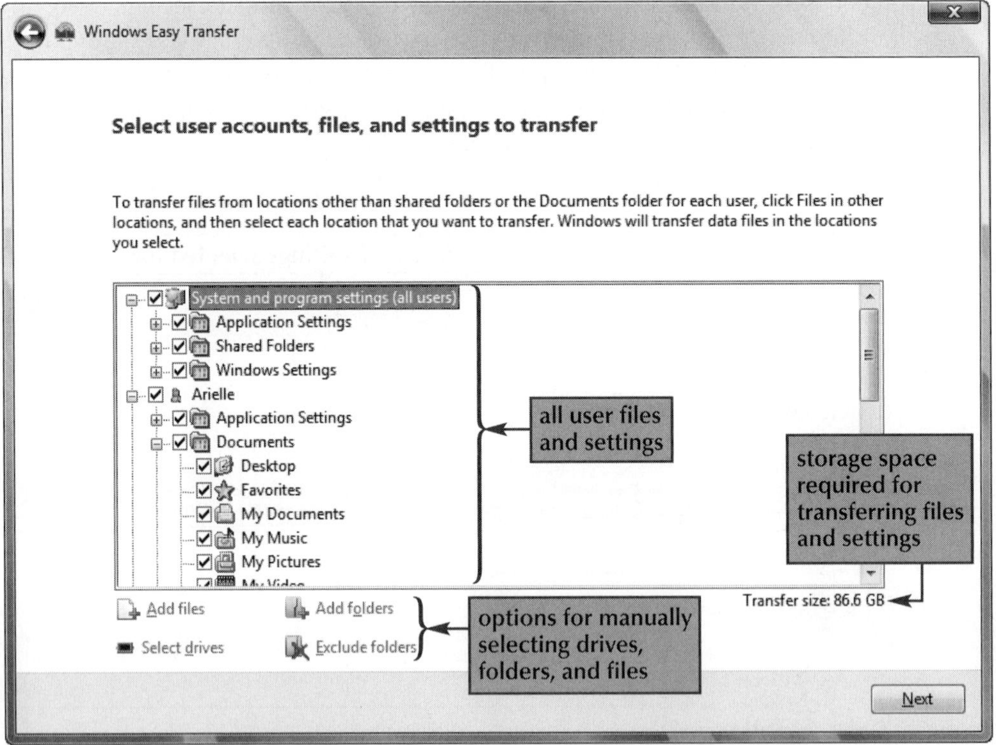

7. Windows Easy Transfer collects your files and settings and copies them from the old computer. After that process, which can take time, Windows Easy Transfer informs you that you are ready to transfer your files and settings to your new computer. See Figure 11-42. Windows Easy Transfer recommends that you open the location where you copied files and settings from your old computer, click (or double-click) the location (the file SaveData.MIG), and then follow the instructions for transferring files and settings to your new computer.

How to transfer files and settings to the new computer **Figure 11-42**

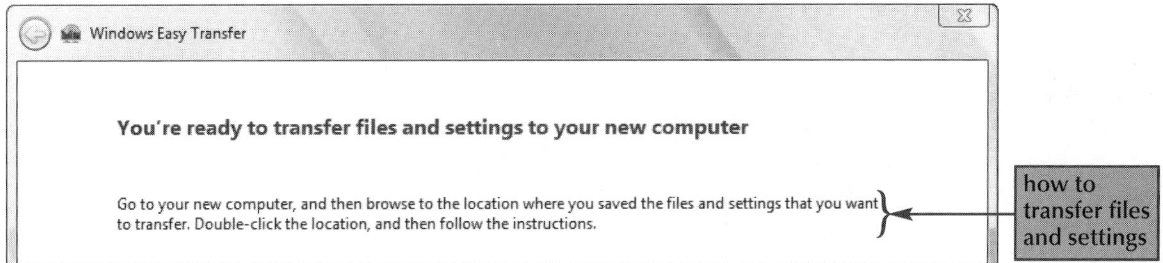

Now, you're ready to complete the last phase in which you transfer files and settings from your old computer to your new computer. Next, you perform these steps:

1. If you had used an external hard disk drive, you would need to detach it from your old computer, attach it to your new computer, and then open a window onto that drive.
2. Next, you open the folder that contains the files and settings you copied from your older computer and click (or double-click) the file named SaveData.MIG.
3. Windows Easy Transfer opens and asks you to type a new user name to create a new user account on the new computer or select a user name from a list of user names on the new computer. See Figure 11-43. It shows you the name of the user account on the old computer (in this example, Kai) and matches that with the same user name on the new computer (Kai). In a footnote, Windows Easy Transfer notes that if you create a new user account, the password for the older user account is not transferred to the new computer; however, you can create a new password for that account after you log on your computer.

Specifying the user account on the new computer **Figure 11-43**

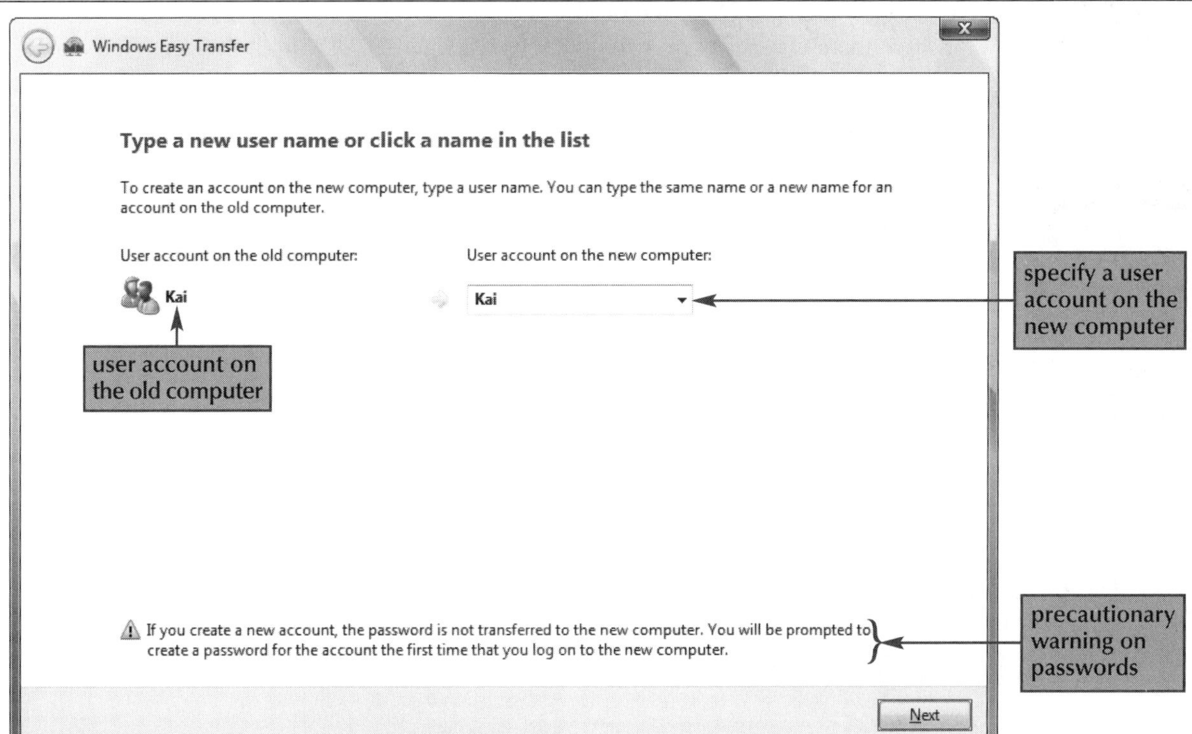

4. Next, Windows Easy Transfer asks you to review your selected files and settings, as shown in Figure 11-44.

Figure 11-44 Options for reviewing files and settings to transfer to the new computer

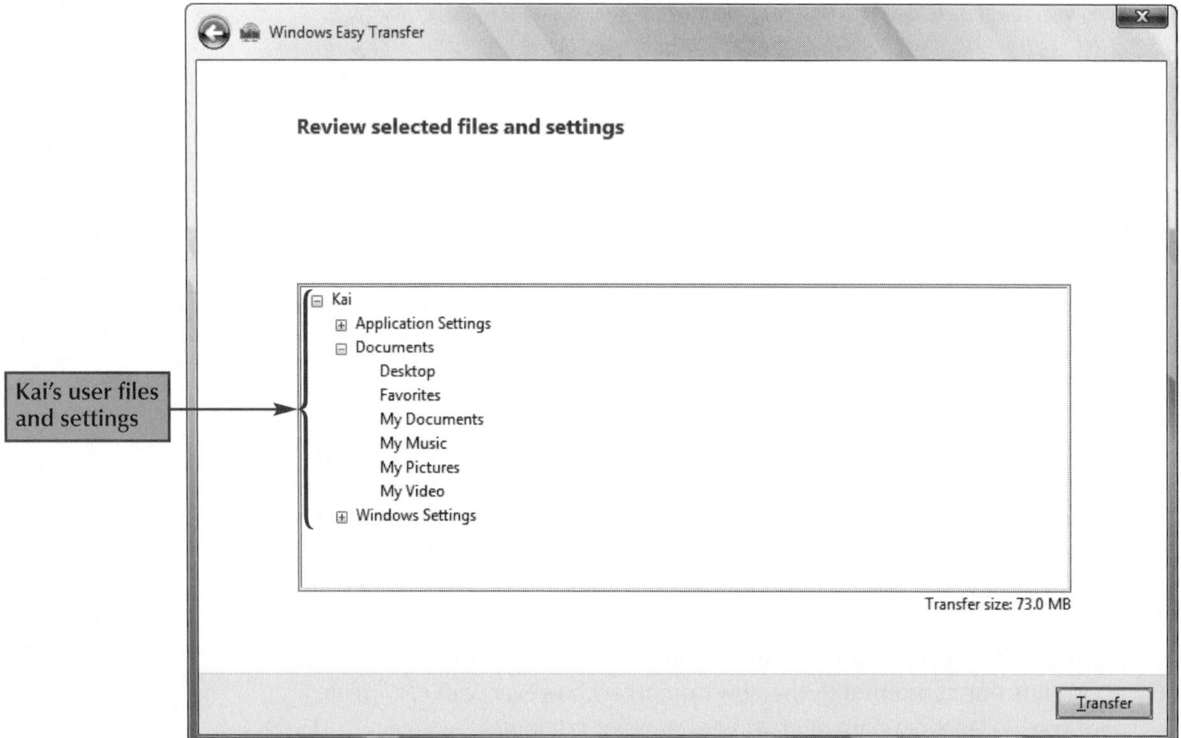

5. After you click Transfer, the files and settings from your old computer are copied to your new computer. Once the process completes, Windows Easy Transfer informs you that the transfer is complete, as shown in Figure 11-45. In the Transfer summary, it shows the number of user accounts, files, folders, program settings, and system settings that were transferred.

Figure 11-45 Summary of what was transferred to the new computer

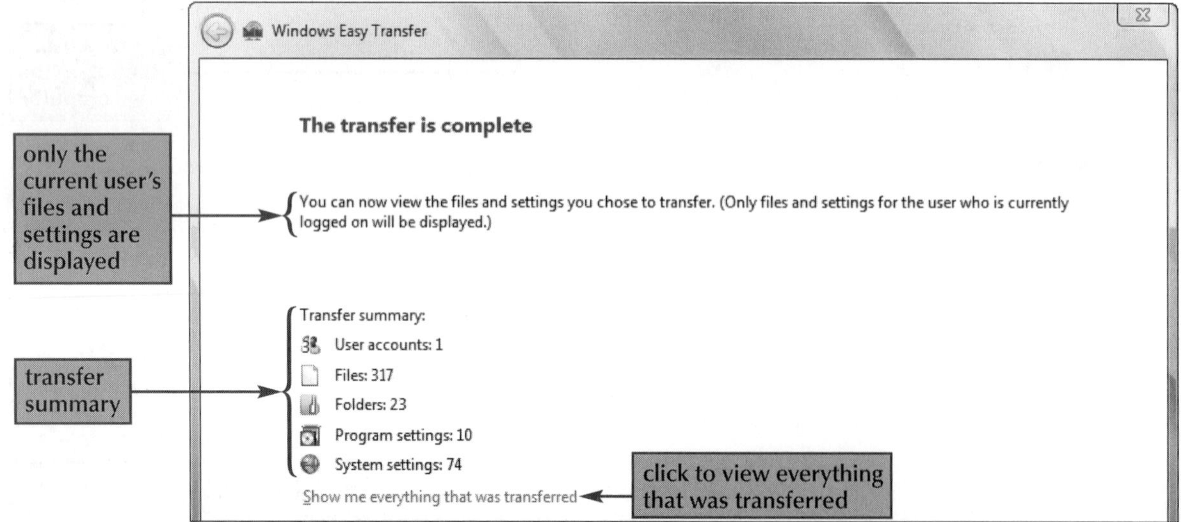

6. After you click the Close button, you are prompted to restart your computer with the new settings.

Windows Easy Transfer guides you through the steps to complete this process, no matter which options you select. However, if you are transferring files and settings from an older computer without Windows Easy Transfer, and if you do not have an Easy Transfer Cable or a network connection that you can use, you need to copy Windows Easy Transfer to a removable device so that you can run it on that computer.

Although the time that it takes to back up a user account can be substantial, Windows Easy Transfer simplifies the process of gathering all your user settings and files and copying those to your new computer so that it is ready for you to use. You do not need to reconfigure the new computer unless you want to specify even newer user settings.

Session 11.1 Quick Check | Review

1. When evaluating whether a new operating system or software product will work on your computer, you want to examine its ________________ requirements.
2. Name four important computer components that determine whether you can upgrade your computer to Windows Vista.
3. The ________________ identifies whether you can upgrade your current version or edition of Windows to a newer version or edition or whether you must perform a clean install.
4. What program can you use to identify hardware, software, and other compatibility problems before upgrading your computer to Windows Vista or to a new edition of Windows Vista?
5. What type of file extension do you find on a Setup Information File?
6. What program can you use to copy files and settings from an older computer with a previous version of Windows to a newer computer that contains Windows Vista?

Session 11.2

Turning Windows Features On or Off

Windows Vista takes a new approach to handling the installation of Windows components. Under Windows Vista, you do not uninstall a Windows feature, instead you turn off the Windows feature. The component remains installed on your computer, so you can always turn the feature back on later. That means all the components are installed when you install Windows Vista.

One useful Windows feature is Windows Fax and Scan. This feature enables you to send and receive faxes using your computer. You can also fax or e-mail documents that you scan and forward faxes as e-mail attachments. Windows Fax and Scan is available in Windows Vista Business and Windows Vista Ultimate, but it is not available in Windows Vista Home Basic or Windows Vista Home Premium.

In the next set of steps, you are going to examine the process for turning on and off Windows Fax and Scan. For this feature to work, you must restart your computer after you turn it on and when you turn it off. If you are working in your college's computer lab, and if it does not permit you to modify software, do not keystroke the following steps, but rather read the steps and examine the figures so that you are familiar with how to turn Windows features on and off. Also, in some computer labs, any settings you specified are no longer applicable as the computer rebuilds itself during the next boot.

Also, to complete the following tutorial steps, you need to provide Administrator credentials. If you are not logged on under an Administrator account, if you do not know the password for an Administrator account, or if your college's computer lab does not permit you to modify Windows components, do not keystroke the following steps, but instead read the steps and examine the figures so that you are familiar with the use of this new Windows Vista feature.

If you are using Windows Vista Basic or Windows Vista Home Premium, read the steps and examine the figures so that you are familiar with the process of turning Windows features on and off, but do not keystroke the steps, because these editions of Windows Vista do not contain Windows Fax and Scan.

To turn a Windows feature on and then off:

Tip

Under Print Services, you can turn on an Internet Printing Client option so you can connect to and print to a Web print server.

1. From the Start menu, open Control Panel, click the **Programs** link, click the **Turn windows features on or off** link, provide Administrator credentials, and then resize the Windows Features window so that you can see the complete list of Windows features available on your computer. In the Windows Features window, Windows Vista explains how to turn on or off a Windows feature. See Figure 11-46. The Windows Features dialog box lists Windows features or Windows components in alphabetical order by name. Features that are enabled have a check mark in the check box, and features that are not enabled do not have a check mark in the check box. Check boxes with a blue fill indicate that one or more components or features within that category are enabled and others are not enabled.

Figure 11-46 Viewing the availability of Windows Features

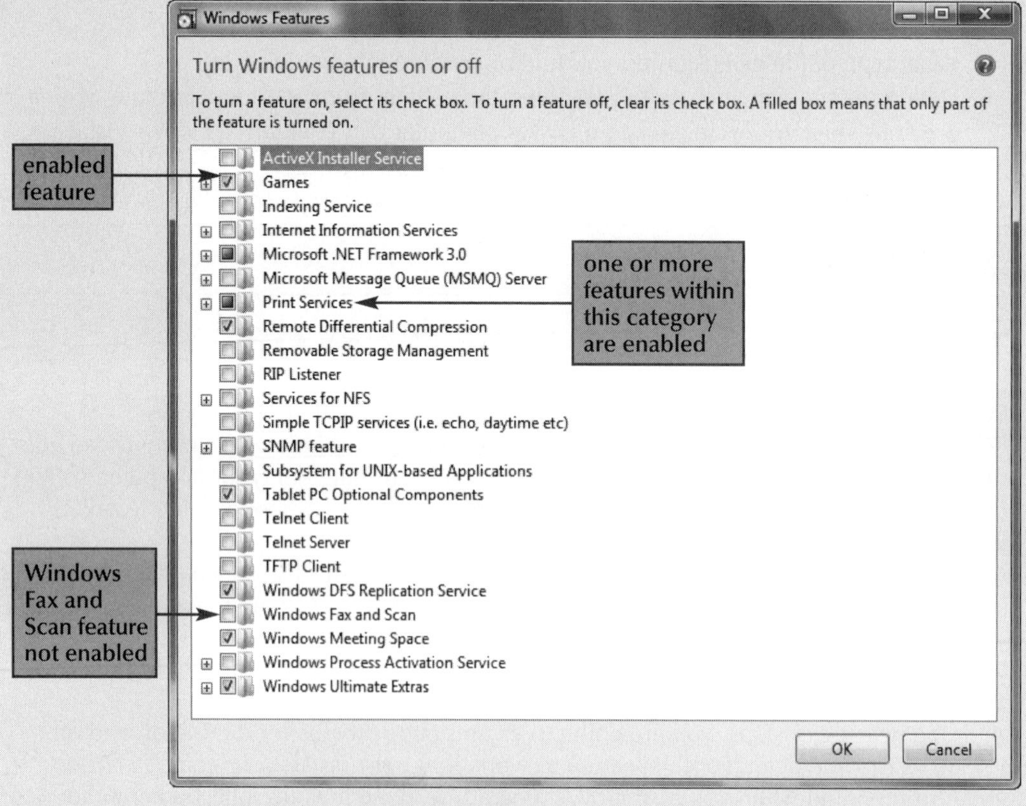

2. If you want to enable the Windows Fax and Scan feature, and if it is not already enabled, click the **Windows Fax and Scan** check box, and then click the **OK** button. A Microsoft Windows dialog box asks you to wait while the features are configured and notes that it might take several minutes. After the process is complete, the Microsoft Windows dialog box informs you that you must restart your computer to apply these changes. It also recommends that you save any open files and close all programs before restarting.

3. If you enabled Windows Fax and Scan, click the **Restart Now** button in the Microsoft Windows dialog box. Windows Vista restarts your computer and applies your change. Windows Fax and Scan is now available on your All Programs menu.

4. After logging on your computer, open the **All Programs** menu, and then click **Windows Fax and Scan**. After you open Windows Fax and Scan for the first time, the Welcome message explains how to use Windows Fax and Scan. See Figure 11-47.

Figure 11-47 Windows Fax and Scan window

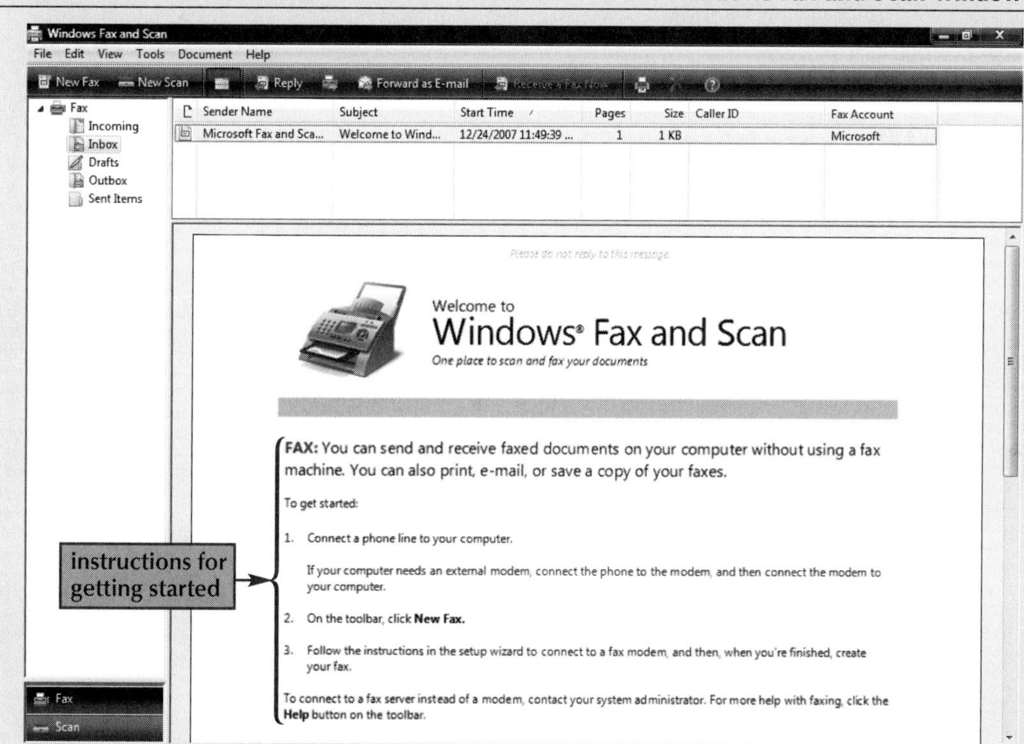

5. Close the Windows Fax and Scan window.

6. If you want to turn off the Windows Fax and Scan feature, click the **Control Panel\Programs** button (or if you closed the Programs window, open it again from the Control Panel), click the **Turn Windows features on or off** link, and then provide Administrator credentials.

7. In the Windows Feature window, locate and click the **Windows Fax and Scan** check box (to remove the check mark), click the **OK** button, and after Windows Vista applies these changes to your computer, click the **Restart Now** button in the Microsoft Windows dialog box. Windows Vista closes the Windows Features window. Windows Fax and Scan is no longer available on your All Programs menu.

You should examine each category of Windows Vista components to determine whether you need to turn on any additional components that might prove useful to you or turn off components that you do not need and do not use.

Reference Window | **Turning Windows Features On and Off**

- From the Start menu, open Control Panel, click the Programs link, click the Turn windows features on or off link, provide Administrator credentials, and then resize the Windows Feature window so that you can see the complete list of Windows features available on your computer.
- If you want to turn a feature on or off, click that feature's check box, and then click the OK button.
- After Windows Vista configures the feature and prompts you to restart your computer, click the Restart Now button.

Next, you can turn your attention to installing software, such as the applications you use regularly.

Installing Software

Kai not only relies on the applications included in Microsoft Office, but she also uses other applications, such as project management software. As she has discovered from installing software on her home computer, acquiring and installing software is easier than ever thanks to the Internet. If she discovers she needs a specific type of software product, she gets on the Internet and searches for reviews in online technical magazines and then evaluates different products. Once she's decided on which product to use, she downloads the software she needs from the vendor's Web site, installs the software, and within minutes she is using that software.

Currently, software products, such as Microsoft Office 2007, are designed for use under a 32-bit Windows operating system, such as the 32-bit editions of Windows Vista and Windows XP (as well as Windows 2000, Windows ME, Windows 98, and Windows 95). These types of applications are referred to as **Win32 applications** (or more generally **32-bit applications**), and they include an Uninstall program so that a user can remove the software from a computer. As noted earlier, a 32-bit operating system is designed for 32-bit processors that handle 32 bits of data at a time and that support up to 2^{32}, or 4 GB, of RAM.

With earlier versions of the Windows operating systems, individuals also installed and used two other types of applications:

- **Win16 applications** These types of applications were originally developed for use in **16-bit Windows operating environments**, such as Windows 3.1, where MS-DOS, a 16-bit operating system, was installed. A 16-bit operating system was designed for 16-bit processors that handled 16 bits of data at a time and that, in theory, supported up to 2^{16} or 64 KB of RAM, but in practice, supported up to 2^{20}, or 1 MB, of RAM (due to the way the early 16-bit processors were designed).
- **DOS applications** Like Win16 applications, DOS applications were developed for 16-bit operating environments where MS-DOS or PC-DOS was installed as the operating system.

Support for Win16 applications and DOS applications under the Windows operating systems varies, especially in the case of DOS applications. However, by now, most people use more reliable and readily-obtainable Win32 applications.

Today, software developers are also releasing Win64 versions of their software products (called **Win64 applications**, or more generally, **64-bit applications**) for newer types of 64-bit Windows operating systems, such as the 64-bit editions of Windows Vista and Windows XP. Although these Windows 64-bit operating systems support the use of both Win32 and Win64 applications, they require 64-bit device drivers, and the latter has affected the adoption and use of 64-bit editions of Windows because 64-bit device drivers have not always been available. As noted earlier, a 64-bit operating system is designed for 64-bit processors that handle 64 bits of data at a time and that, in theory (but not in practice), support up to 2^{64}, or 16 EB (exabytes) (or 16 billion gigabytes), of RAM.

Before you purchase software, you should verify that it will work with Windows Vista. You can check the software vendor's Web site or use Microsoft's Windows Marketplace Web site (*www.windowsmarketplace.com*) to determine whether it is compatible with Windows Vista. If a software product that you install does not function properly under Windows Vista, you might be able to use Windows Vista's Program Compatibility Wizard to determine the best settings for use with that software under Windows Vista. You will examine the Program Compatibility Wizard later in this section of the tutorial.

Preparing for a Software Installation or Upgrade

Kai has discovered that the guidelines that apply for preparing for an operating system upgrade are also useful when installing new software products on her computer.

Before you install an application, utility, game, Web browser, or e-mail software under Windows Vista, you should prepare your computer system, using the guidelines described earlier for installing or upgrading an operating system. You should make sure that you have a recent backup of your document files before installing a new software product or a major upgrade to an existing software product. You should also use the Error-Checking Tool or the command-line Check Disk utility to check for and repair file system problems. Although Disk Defragmenter automatically defragments your hard disk under Windows Vista, you can manually optimize storage space on your hard disk with Disk Defragmenter before installing a new software product.

When you install a Win32 application, the Setup program performs the following types of operations:

- **Installs the application** The Setup program creates a folder for the application on the hard disk drive and creates any subfolders needed for installing the product's program files and supporting files. When you install a Win32 application, you can use the default path and folder name that the Setup program proposes, or you can choose your own folder name. Most Setup programs install software in a folder under the Program Files folder (as recommended by Microsoft). For example, you installed the Windows Vista Upgrade Advisor, a Win32 application, earlier. The software for this program installed in the Microsoft Windows Vista Upgrade Advisor folder under the Program Files folder. If the Setup program indicates that it will install the software product elsewhere, you can override this option and designate the Program Files folder.
- **Updates the Registry** The Setup program copies software settings and other information, such as the full path for program files and registration information, to the Windows Registry.
- **Creates a group folder and shortcuts** The Setup program either adds a group folder or a program shortcut to the All Programs menu. After a Setup program creates a group folder for the software product, such as Microsoft Office, it creates shortcuts to the programs included with the software product. It may also create shortcuts to an Uninstall program and to Help and Readme files that contain information and last-minute documentation on using the software product.

- **Installs an Uninstall program** As required by Microsoft, Win32 applications include an Uninstall program that allows Windows Vista or you to remove that application from your computer system. In fact, as just noted, the Uninstall program might be one of the options in the application's group folder on the Start or All Programs menu. In contrast, Win16 and MS-DOS applications typically do not include an Uninstall program or option.

You can install a Win32 application in one of the following ways:

Tip

The installation program for many software products is typically named Setup.exe.

- **Use a software product's DVD or CD** If you purchase a software product in a store, you can easily install the software by using the product's DVD or CD. As soon as you insert the DVD or CD in your computer, Windows Vista starts the installation program, and you can then install the software product. If the installation program doesn't start, you can open a window on the DVD or CD, and then locate and click (or double-click) Setup.exe to start the installation of the software product.
- **Use a self-extracting executable file** When you download a program from a Web site, the downloaded program might be stored in a self-extracting executable file with the "exe" file extension. A **self-extracting executable file** is a file that contains one or more files stored in a compressed format, plus a program for extracting the contents of the self-extracting executable file itself. When you click (or double-click) the self-extracting executable file, a program within the downloaded file extracts the contents of this downloaded file and then starts the Setup program for installing the software product.
- **Use a Compressed (zipped) Folder** If the program you download is stored in a file with the "zip" file extension, it contains one or more files stored in a compressed format. The Zip file format is commonly used for compressing files for downloading from the Internet or a Web site or for compressing files that are then included as an attachment to an e-mail message (though not all e-mail software allows these types of attachments for security reasons). Since Windows Vista treats a file with the "zip" file extension as a Compressed (zipped) Folder, you can open the Compressed (zipped) Folder like any other folder, and then extract the files.
- **Use a Microsoft Installer file** Certain programs that you download from the Internet, such as the Windows Vista Upgrade Advisor you installed earlier, are stored in a file with the "msi" file extension (for Microsoft Installer or Windows Installer Package). You can click (or double-click) the file icon to start Windows Installer on your computer, and it will monitor the installation of the software product.

Downloading software from Web sites is becoming increasingly more common. In fact, in most cases, you can obtain and install software by downloading self-extracting executable files.

Viewing Installed Software

Earlier, you installed the Windows Vista Upgrade Advisor, so you are already familiar with the process for installing a Win32 application. The process for installing other software is very similar to that shown for the Windows Vista Upgrade Advisor. However, if you are installing an office suite like Microsoft Office, you are installing multiple applications, and therefore, you can choose which components within each application to install as well as decide which shared components you want to install. **Shared components** consist of components of program code used by two or more programs.

Before you install a software product on your computer, you should make sure that Windows Vista supports that software product. You can check the Web site of the company that makes the software you want to download to determine which versions and editions of Windows support that product, and if it is supported by more than one version or edition of Windows, to make sure that you download the correct version or edition.

After you install software on your computer, you can view, uninstall, change, or repair software already installed on your computer system.

Kai recommends you check the software installed on your computer. If you find you do not need or use certain software, you can uninstall it from your computer.

To view installed applications:

1. From the Start menu, open the **Control Panel**, click the **Programs** link, and in the Programs window, click the **Programs and Features** link, switch to Details view (if necessary), and then press the **Ctrl** and **+** keys to adjust column widths for a best fit. In the Programs and Features window, Windows Vista displays a list of installed software on your computer. See Figure 11-48. Your list of installed software will differ. Windows Vista not only shows the full name of each installed program, but also displays the name of the Publisher (or the company that developed the software), the installation date, and the disk storage space required for the software. At the top of the window, Windows Vista informs you that if you want to uninstall a program, you first select the program from the list, and then choose the option for uninstalling, repairing, or changing the software product. After you select an installed program, Windows Vista displays one or more of the following buttons on the command bar: Uninstall, Change, Repair, or Uninstall/Change. For example, if you choose Windows Vista Upgrade Advisor (not visible in the figure), the command bar contains Uninstall, Change, and Repair buttons. The Change button provides you with two or more options. For example, if you choose the Windows Vista Upgrade Advisor and select Change, the Windows Vista Upgrade Advisor Setup Wizard will display two options, one for repairing the installation of this software and another for removing the software. See Figure 11-49. In the Details Pane at the bottom of this list of installed programs, Windows Vista reports on the total number of installed programs and the total amount of storage space that these installed programs require on the hard disk drive. Although not visible in the figure, there are 33 installed programs on the computer used for this figure, and they require a total of 1.73 GB of storage space on disk.

   Trouble? If Windows Vista does not display the Publisher, Installed On, and Size columns, right-click a Column header, and select the option for displaying these column headings.

Tip

If you right-click an installed program, the shortcut menu shows options for uninstalling, changing, or repairing the program.

Figure 11-48 Viewing software installed on a computer

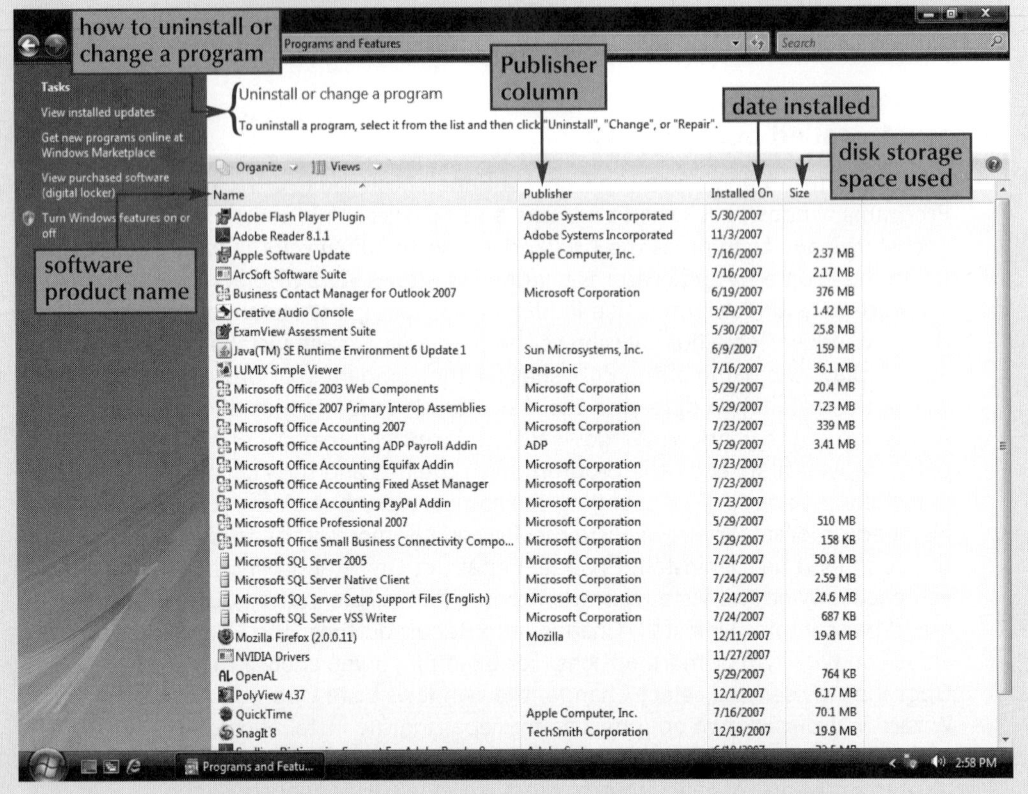

Figure 11-49 Options for repairing or uninstalling a Win32 application

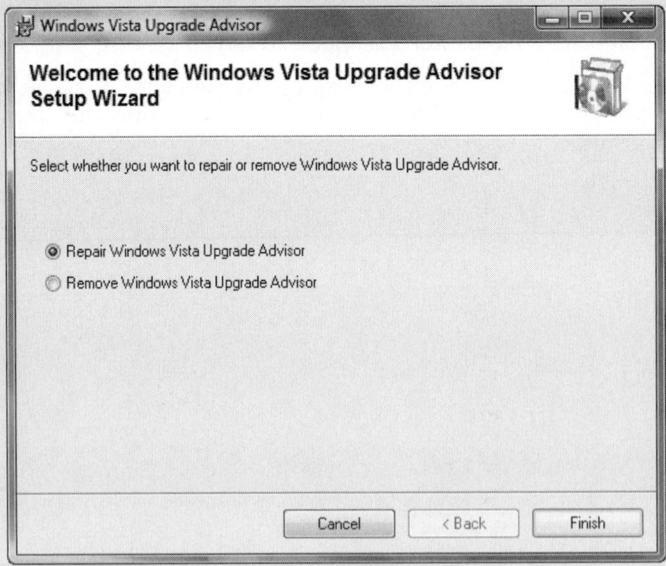

2. Click the **Publisher** column button, and if necessary, scroll to the top of the list of installed programs. Windows Vista lists the installed programs in alphabetical order by Publisher.

3. Click the **Installed On** column button. Windows Vista lists the installed programs in order from the most recently installed. You can use this option to quickly locate recently installed software that you might want to change or remove.

4. Click the **Installed On** column button again. Windows Vista lists the installed programs in order from the oldest installed program.
5. Click the **Size** column button. Windows Vista lists the installed programs in order based on the amount of disk storage space required for the installed program, starting with the one that requires the most disk storage space. You can use this option to quickly identify software that requires a lot of storage space on your hard disk drive, and then decide whether you need to retain the software.
6. Click the **Name** column button. Windows Vista restores the original list of program names.
7. Close the Programs and Features window.

Although it's easy to identify which software is installed on your computer by using the All Programs menu, the Programs and Features window provides more detail on the installed software and may include options (such as plug-ins, video display adapter drivers, software dictionaries, and even utilities) not shown on the All Programs menu.

Reviewing Installed Software | InSight

You should periodically review the software on your computer by using the Programs and Features window to identify software that you never use. Then, you can uninstall it from your computer system to free up valuable disk storage space. However, before you uninstall it, verify that you have the original installation DVDs or CDs for that software so that you can reinstall it if you find that you need it later. Likewise, if you download software from a Web site, store the downloaded file in your user account's Downloads folder so that you can easily reinstall it later. Another option is to download the software again from the Internet and, at the same time, determine whether there is a newer version with improved features.

Viewing Installed Software | Reference Window

- From the Start menu, open the Control Panel, click the Programs link, and in the Programs window, click the Programs and Features link, switch to Details view (if necessary), and then use the Ctrl and + keys to adjust column widths for a best fit.
- Examine the information on the installed software in the Programs and Features window.
- To sort the list of installed software, click the Publisher, Installed On, Size, or Name column button for an ascending sort. Click a column button a second time for a descending sort.

Next, you use the Program Compatibility Wizard to specify new settings for a program that does not run properly.

Using the Program Compatibility Wizard

After upgrading to Windows Vista, Kai encountered problems with a few programs on her computer. At the suggestion of her IT staff, she decided to use the Program Compatibility Wizard to determine whether she could resolve the problems.

You can use the Program Compatibility Wizard to specify new settings for running a program that does not run properly. If the program worked with an earlier version of Windows, you can specify that Windows Vista simulate the conditions under which that program would have run in the earlier version of Windows.

Kai suggests that you test the Program Compatibility Wizard on the Windows Vista Upgrade Advisor so that you are familiar with the use of this feature.

To use the Program Compatibility Wizard:

1. From the Start menu, click **Control Panel**, click the **Programs** link, and then click the **Use an older program with this version of Windows** link. Windows Vista opens the Program Compatibility Wizard in a "Start Application in Compatibility Mode" dialog box. See Figure 11-50. The Program Compatibility Wizard notes that if you are experiencing problems with a program that worked correctly with an earlier version of Windows, the Program Compatibility Wizard helps you select and test compatibility settings so that the program works properly under Windows Vista. The Caution emphasizes that you should not use this wizard for older antivirus software, backup programs, and system utilities. The same precaution applies to disk utilities, firewall software, and software for burning CDs. When you upgrade to Windows Vista, you also have to upgrade these types of software products.

Figure 11-50 Program Compatibility Wizard

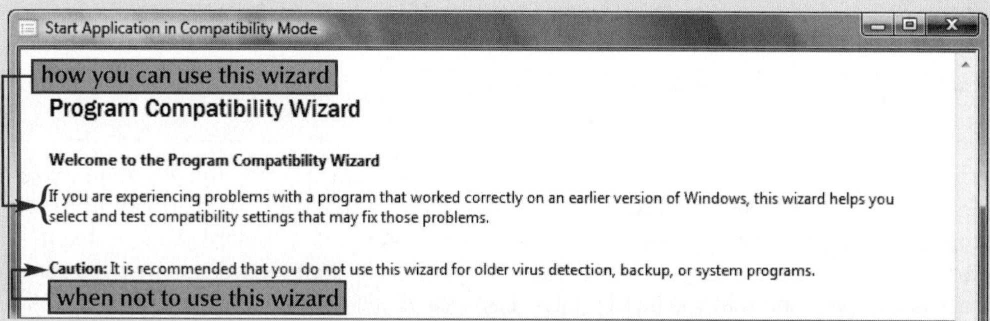

2. Click the **Next** button. The Program Compatibility Wizard asks you how you want to locate the program that you would like to run with compatibility settings. See Figure 11-51. You can choose the program from a list of programs on your computer that the wizard compiles, specify that it use a program in your CD drive, or locate the program manually. If you choose the last option, you can specify the path to that program or browse for that program in the next step.

Figure 11-51 Options for locating a program with compatibility problems

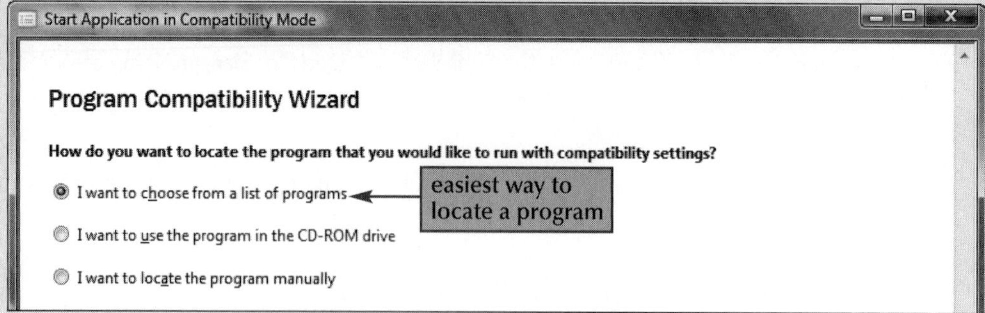

3. With the "I want to choose from a list of programs" option already selected, click the **Next** button. The Program Compatibility Wizard scans your computer for programs, and then displays a list of programs from which you can choose. See Figure 11-52.

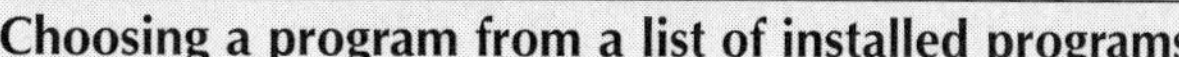

Figure 11-52 Choosing a program from a list of installed programs

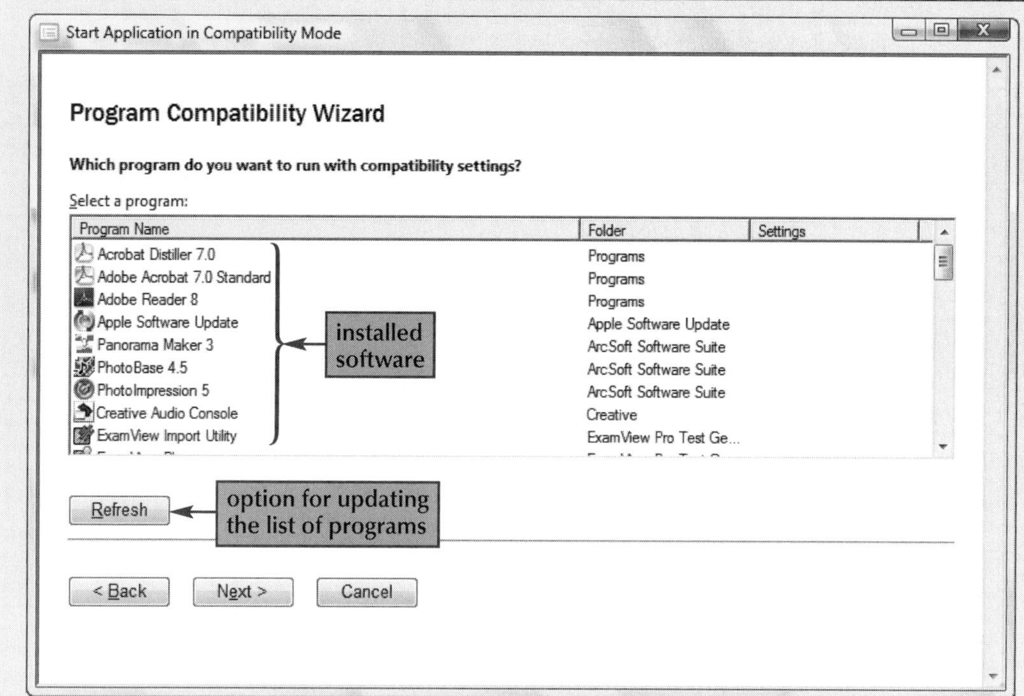

4. In the Select a program box, locate and click **Windows Vista Upgrade Advisor**, and then click the **Next** button. Now, you select a compatibility mode by choosing the operating system recommended for this program or by choosing the operating system under which this program functioned properly. See Figure 11-53. You can choose Microsoft Windows 95, Microsoft Windows NT 4.0 Service Pack 5 (only), Microsoft Windows 98/Windows ME, Microsoft Windows 2000, or Microsoft Windows XP Service Pack 2. So that you can examine compatibility settings, assume you know that this program works under Microsoft Windows XP Service Pack 2.

Figure 11-53 Compatibility Mode options

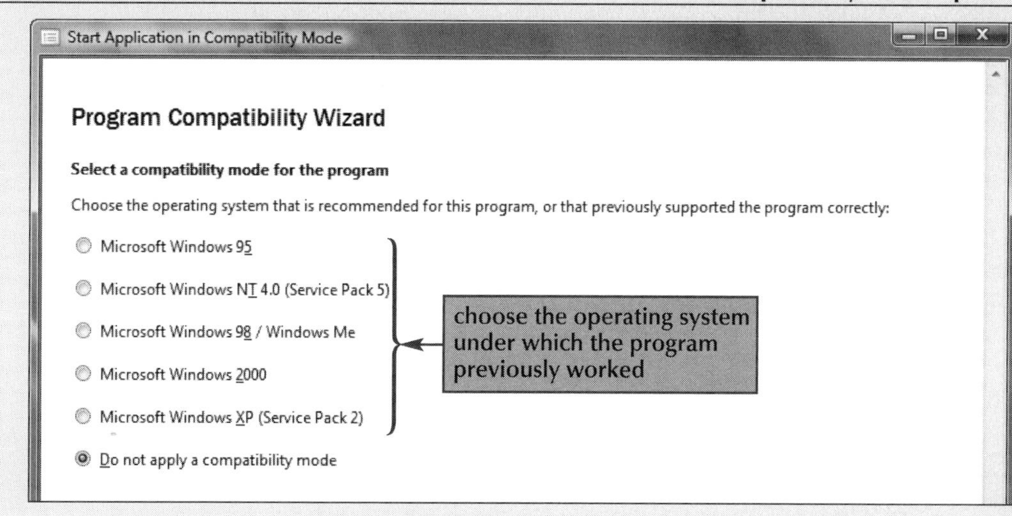

5. Click the **Microsoft Windows XP (Service Pack 2)** option button, and then click the **Next** button. Now, you select any display settings recommended for the program or any settings that worked previously with the program under an earlier version of Windows. See Figure 11-54.

Figure 11-54 **Options for adjusting program display settings**

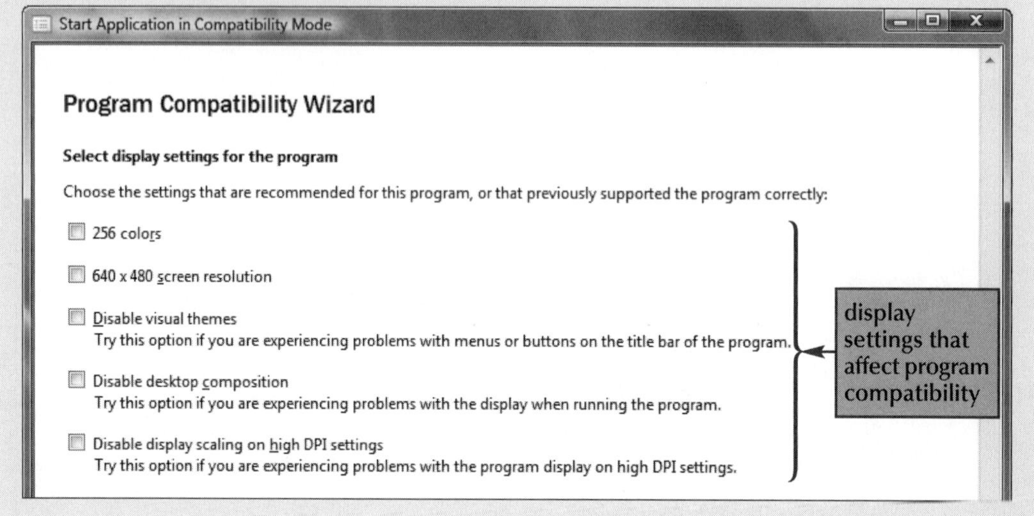

The following bulleted list describes each of these options:

- **256 colors** You try this option if you think that an older program might have been designed for a low color setting.
- **640 x 480 screen resolution** Again, older programs might be designed to run at a low resolution. Microsoft recommends that you try this option if the graphical user interface appears jagged or is rendered improperly. If you choose this option, the program appears in a smaller-sized window on the desktop.
- **Disable visual themes** This option disables the use of themes on your computer. The Program Compatibility Wizard notes that you should try this setting if you are experiencing problems with menus or buttons on the program's title bar.
- **Disable desktop composition** This option turns off transparency and other advanced display features. The Program Compatibility Wizard recommends that you try this option if you are experiencing problems with the display when running the program.
- **Disable display scaling on high DPI settings** This option turns off the automatic resizing of windows after you switch to a high DPI (dots per inch) setting that increases both the size of fonts and objects in the graphical user interface. The Program Compatibility Wizard recommends that you try this option if you are experiencing problems with the program display on high DPI settings.

If you are not sure which, if any, settings are the ones required for the program, you can advance to the next step and test the program with the compatibility mode for an earlier version of Windows. If the program still does not work properly, you can choose one display setting at a time until you locate the setting (or settings) needed by the program to work properly under Windows Vista.

Now, you can continue with the Program Compatibility Wizard.

To examine additional settings:

1. Click the **Next** button. The Program Compatibility Wizard notes that some programs require Administrator privileges to run properly. See Figure 11-55. It also notes that this option applies primarily to program installers and system utilities and to older programs designed for Windows 98 or earlier versions of Windows. Also, programs designed for earlier Windows versions assume they have Administrator privileges, and they attempt to modify system settings by writing to system folders or the Windows Registry. To guarantee the security of your computer, Windows Vista does not allow programs to perform these operations. That means that software developers must upgrade their software so that the software works properly with Standard User privileges and with User Account Control. If you enable Administrator privileges for a program here, you are side-stepping the additional security and protection in Windows Vista. Rather than compromise the security of your computer, you need to upgrade your software.

Figure 11-55 Option for running a program as an Administrator

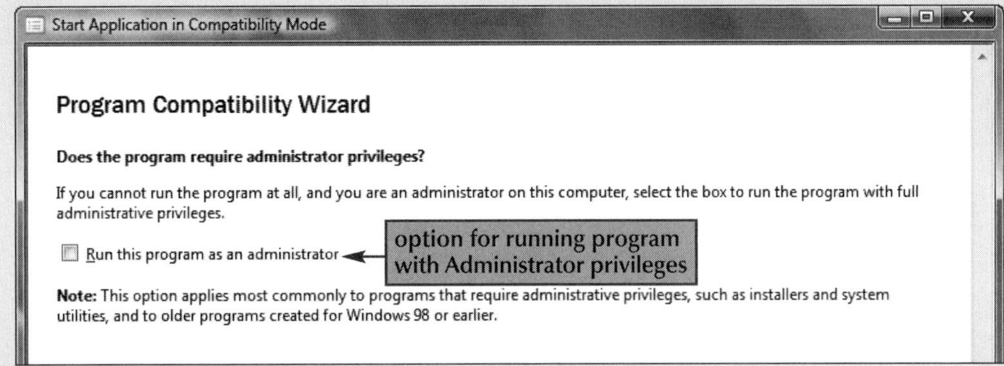

2. Click the **Next** button. The Program Compatibility Wizard now summarizes your compatibility settings and explains how to test these settings with the program you specified earlier. See Figure 11-56.

Figure 11-56 Compatibility settings selected for a program

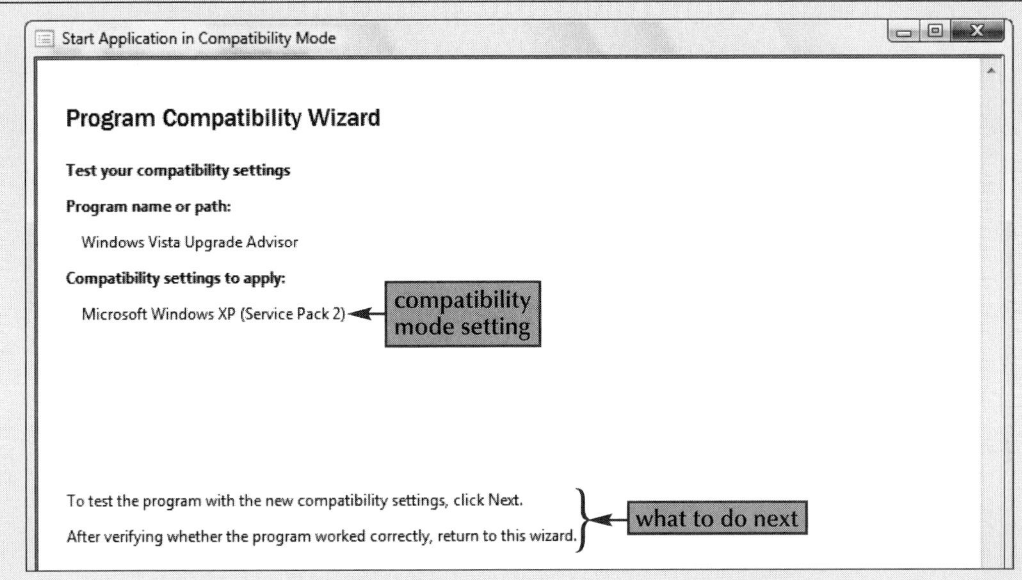

3. Click the **Next** button. The Program Compatibility Wizard opens the program so that you can use and test the program with the new compatibility mode and compatibility settings.
4. Close the Windows Vista Upgrade Advisor window. In the Start Application in Compatibility Mode window, the Program Compatibility Wizard asks you if the program works correctly. See Figure 11-57. If so, you can set this program so that it always uses the compatibility settings you selected. If not, you can try different compatibility settings, or you can indicate that you are finished trying compatibility settings.

Figure 11-57 **Options for applying or changing compatibility settings**

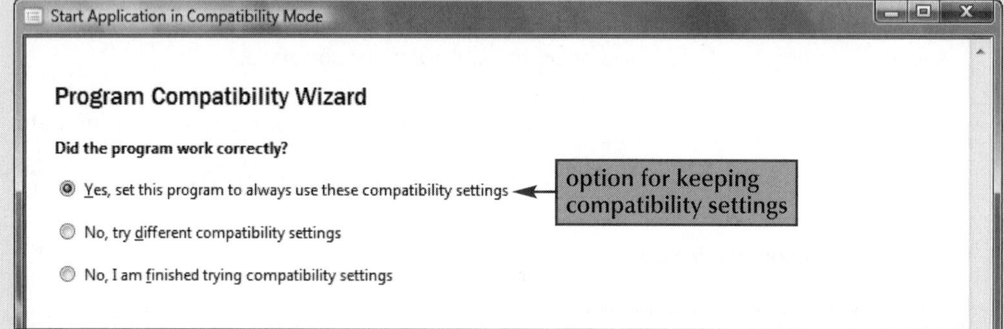

5. Click the **No, I am finished trying compatibility settings** option button, and then click the **Next** button. The Program Compatibility Wizard notes that it has created temporary files that contain information about the compatibility settings you tested and whether those settings corrected the problem. You have the option of sending the information to Microsoft so that it can improve its support for programs.
6. Click the **No** option button, and then click the **Next** button. The Program Compatibility Wizard notes that it did not change compatibility settings for any program. It also notes that if you need to readjust or remove compatibility settings, you should run this wizard again.
7. Click the **Finish** button. The Program Compatibility Wizard closes.
8. Close the Programs window.

Using the Program Compatibility Wizard | Reference Window

- From the Start menu, click Control Panel, click the Programs link, and then click the "Use an older program with this version of Windows" link.
- Read the information on the use of the Program Compatibility Wizard, as well as the precautionary warning, and then click the Next button in the "Start Application in Compatibility Mode" dialog box.
- To specify the location of the program exhibiting compatibility problems with Windows Vista, click the option button for "I want to choose from a list of programs," "I want to use the program in the CD-ROM drive," or "I want to locate the program manually," and then click the Next button.
- If necessary, select the program from a list of programs installed on your computer, from your CD-ROM drive, or by manually browsing and locating the program, and then click the Next button.
- Select a compatibility mode for the program (by choosing the operating system recommended for this program or the operating system under which this program functioned properly), and then click the Next button.
- Select one or more display settings required of the program, and then click the Next button.
- If necessary, click the "Run this program as an administrator" check box if the program requires Administrator privileges, and then click the Next button.
- Verify your compatibility mode settings, and then click the Next button.
- After the Program Compatibility Wizard opens the program, test the program to make sure it is working properly, and then close the program and return to the Program Compatibility Wizard.
- When asked whether the program worked properly, select the option button for "Yes, set this program to always use these compatibility settings," "No, try different compatibility settings," or "No, I am finished trying compatibility settings," and then click the Next button.
- Finally, indicate whether you want to send the compatibility data to Microsoft.

You can also use an alternate approach to specify compatibility settings. First, you open the folder that contains the program for which you want to specify compatibility settings, then you right-click the program file and choose Properties. After the Properties dialog box for that program opens, you select the Compatibility property sheet where you can specify compatibility mode and display settings. See Figure 11-58. You have access to the same settings; however, if you click the check box for Compatibility mode, you will discover that the drop-down Compatibility mode list also includes Windows 2003 Server Service Pack 1, an option not available with the Program Compatibility Wizard. Also, the "Show settings for all users" button allows you to specify program compatibility settings for all users. The settings you choose become a property of this object on your computer, and Windows Vista uses these settings when you open the program. To test these settings, you must open and work with the program.

Figure 11-58 **Compatibility property sheet for a program**

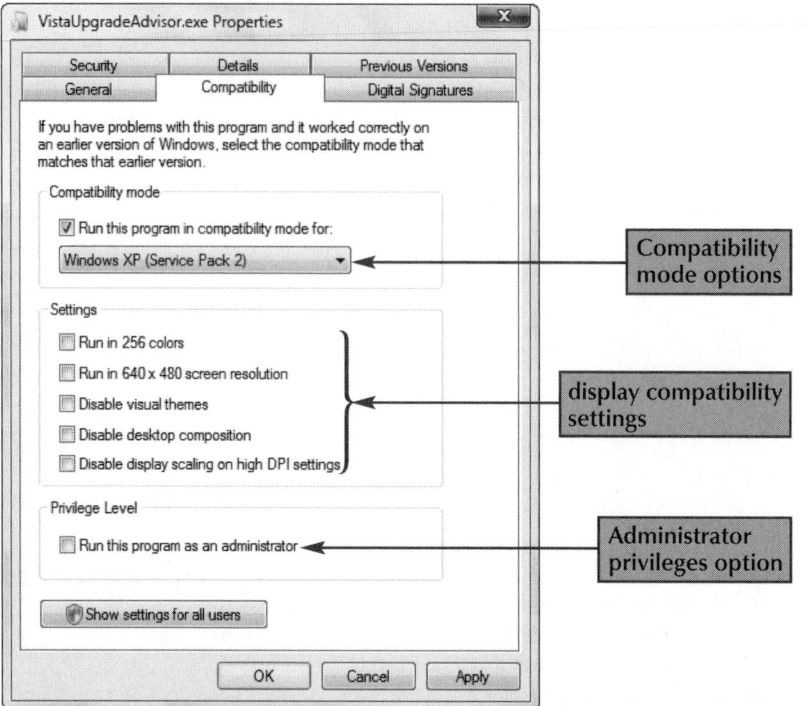

If the Program Compatibility Wizard does not correct the problem, check the Web site of the manufacturer of the software to determine if there is an update that enables the program to work properly under Windows Vista or upgrade to a program that does work under Windows Vista.

Windows Vista also has a Program Compatibility Assistant, which is different from the Program Compatibility Wizard. Windows Vista runs the Program Compatibility Assistant automatically when it detects a problem with a program. (There is no manual option for running the Program Compatibility Assistant.) The Program Compatibility Assistant adjusts compatibility settings for a program based on known compatibility issues for the program in question. Also, the Program Compatibility Assistant can resolve conflicts a program might encounter with User Account Control. If the Program Compatibility Assistant detects a serious compatibility problem, it might warn you, or it might completely block the program from running. Your next step is to check the vendor's Web site for information on this problem or, better yet, for an upgrade that resolves the problem.

Uninstalling Software

If you no longer need a program, you can uninstall it from your computer, using the Programs and Features window. Likewise, if you are experiencing a problem with a program, you open the Programs and Features window, and then choose the option for repairing the problem. If the problem still remains, you can uninstall the software, and then reinstall it.

Now that she's checked her laptop for compatibility with Windows Vista, Kai wants to uninstall the Windows Vista Upgrade Advisor.

If you want to uninstall the Windows Vista Upgrade Advisor, complete the following steps. If you do not want to uninstall the Windows Vista Upgrade Advisor, read the following steps and examine the figures, but do not keystroke the steps.

To uninstall a program:

1. From the Start menu, click **Control Panel**, and then click the **Uninstall a program** link under Programs.
2. In the Programs and Features window, locate and point to **Windows Vista Upgrade Advisor**, and then click the **Uninstall** button on the command bar at the top of the Programs and Features window. Windows Vista displays a Programs and Features dialog box and asks if you are sure you want to uninstall the Windows Vista Upgrade Advisor.
3. Click the **Yes** button, and after Windows Installer prepares to remove the Windows Vista Upgrade Advisor, provide Administrator credentials. Windows Installer then uninstalls the Windows Vista Upgrade Advisor, and the program no longer appears in the list of installed programs. That program also no longer appears on the Programs Menu.
4. Close the Programs and Features window.

In the case of the Windows Vista Upgrade Advisor program, you could have also opened the folder with the downloaded program and clicked (or double-clicked) that program to open the Windows Vista Upgrade Advisor Setup Wizard dialog box, as shown in the earlier Figure 11-49. Then, you could select either the option to repair the installation of this program or the option to completely remove it from your computer.

Uninstalling Software | Reference Window

- From the Start menu, click Control Panel, and then click the "Uninstall a program" link under Programs.
- Locate and select the program you want to uninstall, and then click the Uninstall button on the command bar (or right-click the program and click Uninstall).
- Close the Programs and Features window.

Next, you can add and remove Microsoft Office components.

Adding and Removing Microsoft Office Components

People who use the Microsoft Office suite often find that they do not have access to all the features and components included in the software suite because they choose the default install option. Or perhaps someone else installed the software on their behalf and therefore did not do a full install because they decided that the individual did not need certain features. As a result, those Microsoft Office users discover that they do not always have access to the features they need. However, you can open the Setup installation program for Microsoft Office, examine what's installed, and add or remove individual components.

When installing software on her laptop, Kai always makes a point of performing a full install or choosing the option that permits her to pick and choose which program components to install. That way her laptop is set up with everything she needs. She suggests that you do the same on your office laptop.

In the next section of the tutorial, you are going to open Microsoft Office Setup and examine installed components. You will need your Microsoft Office CD. If you do not have a Microsoft Office CD, or if you are working on a computer in a computer lab which does not permit you to install or remove software, do not keystroke the following steps, but rather read the steps and examine the figures so that you are familiar with how to add and remove program components within an installed application. The following steps illustrate the use of Microsoft Office Professional 2007. If you have a different version, you will notice differences in the availability of features.

To complete the following tutorial steps, you need to provide Administrator credentials. If you are not logged on under an Administrator account, if you do not know the password for an Administrator account, or if your college's computer lab does not permit you to modify installed software, do not keystroke the following steps, but instead read the steps and examine the figures so that you are familiar with the use of this new Windows Vista feature.

To examine installable Microsoft Office components:

Tip

You can also open Programs and Features from the Control Panel, select Microsoft Office in the list of installed programs, and then click the Change button.

1. Insert your Microsoft Office CD into your DVD or CD drive, close that drive, and in the AutoPlay dialog box, click **Run SETUP.EXE**, and then provide Administrator credentials. As shown in Figure 11-59, the Microsoft Office Professional 2007 dialog box displays options for adding or removing features, for repairing Office, and for removing (or uninstalling) Office.

   Trouble? If the Setup program does not open, open a window onto the CD drive (if necessary), click Setup.exe, and then provide Administrator credentials.

Figure 11-59 Modifying a Microsoft Office installation

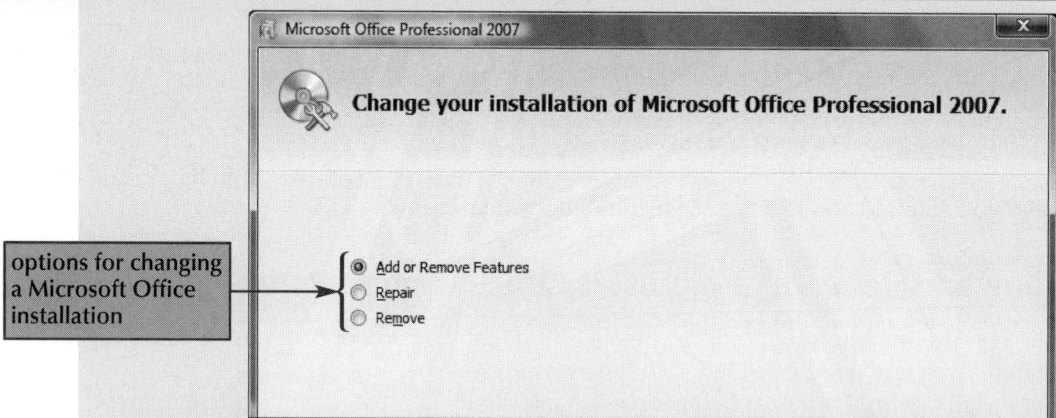

2. Click the Add or Remove Features option button (if necessary), and then click the **Continue button**. You can now choose Installation Options for your version of Office. See Figure 11-60. Note that the features are divided into categories for each application and include Office Shared Features and Office Tools. Your Microsoft Office options may differ. If a component has a white list button to its left, that means all the components within that category are installed. If a component has a gray list button to its left, that means that only some of the components within that category are installed. Notice that this installation of Microsoft Office requires 1,513 MB (or approximately 1.5 GB).

Figure 11-60 Examining options for installing Microsoft Office components

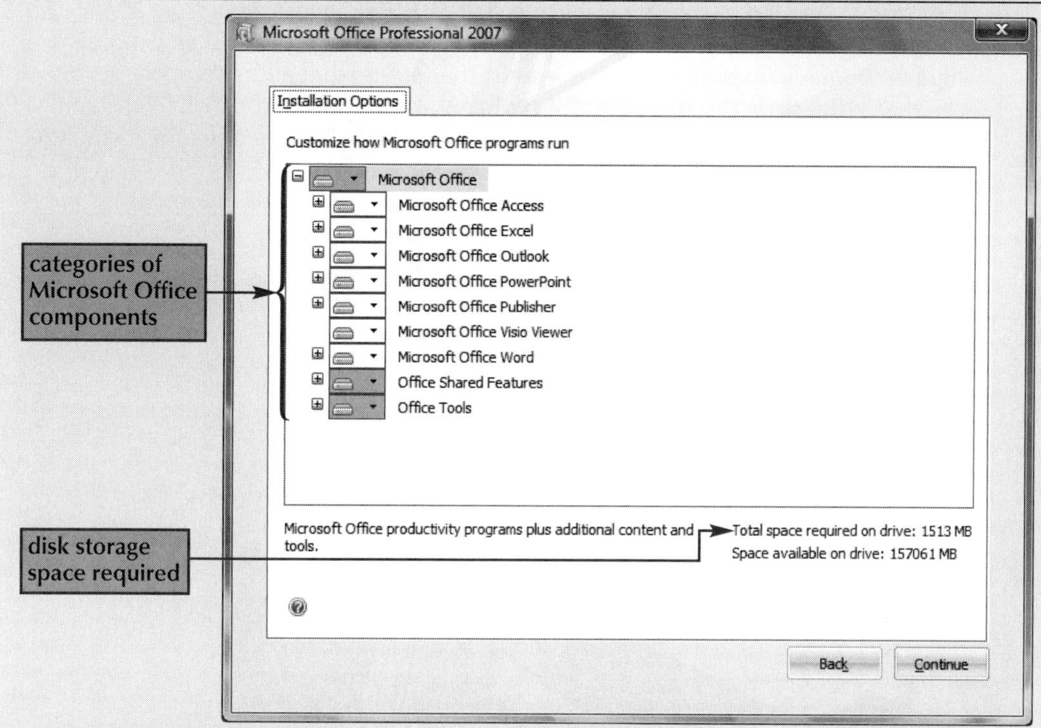

3. Click the **Expand View** button ⊞ to the left of the Office Tools category. Setup displays the tools provided with this version of Office. See Figure 11-61. Yours may differ.

Figure 11-61 Viewing Office Tools

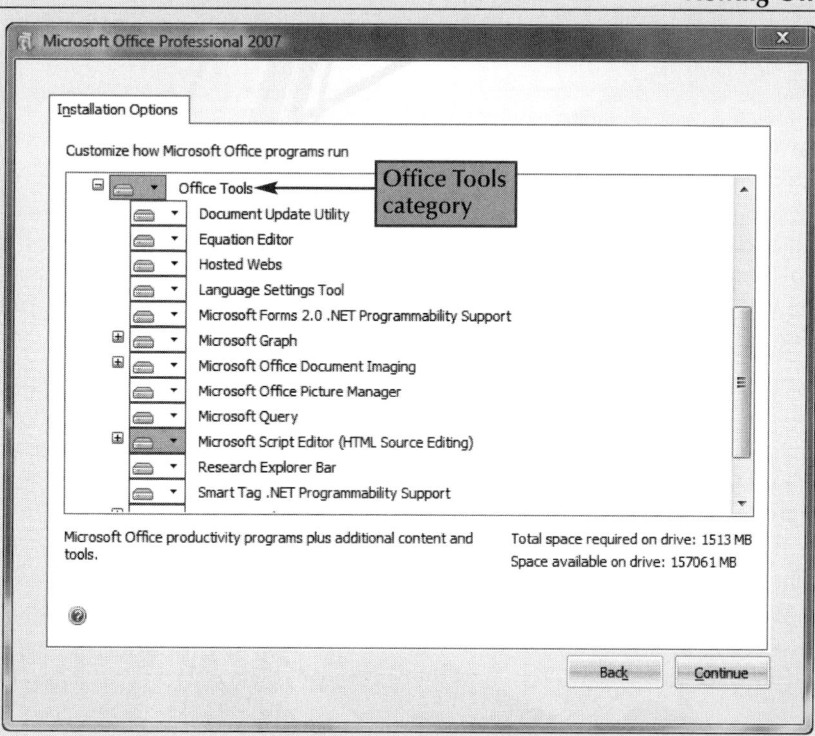

4. Click the **Microsoft Office Document Imaging** button. As shown in Figure 11-62, Setup displays a menu that allows you to choose whether you want to install that component, and if so, how you want to install it. If you choose "Run from My Computer," Setup installs the component on your hard disk drive. If you choose "Run all from My Computer," Setup installs the feature and all its components on your hard disk drive. If you choose "Installed on First Use," Setup installs the component when first needed. If you choose "Not Available," Setup does not install the component, or it removes the component.

Figure 11-62 Viewing options for installing Microsoft Office Document Imaging

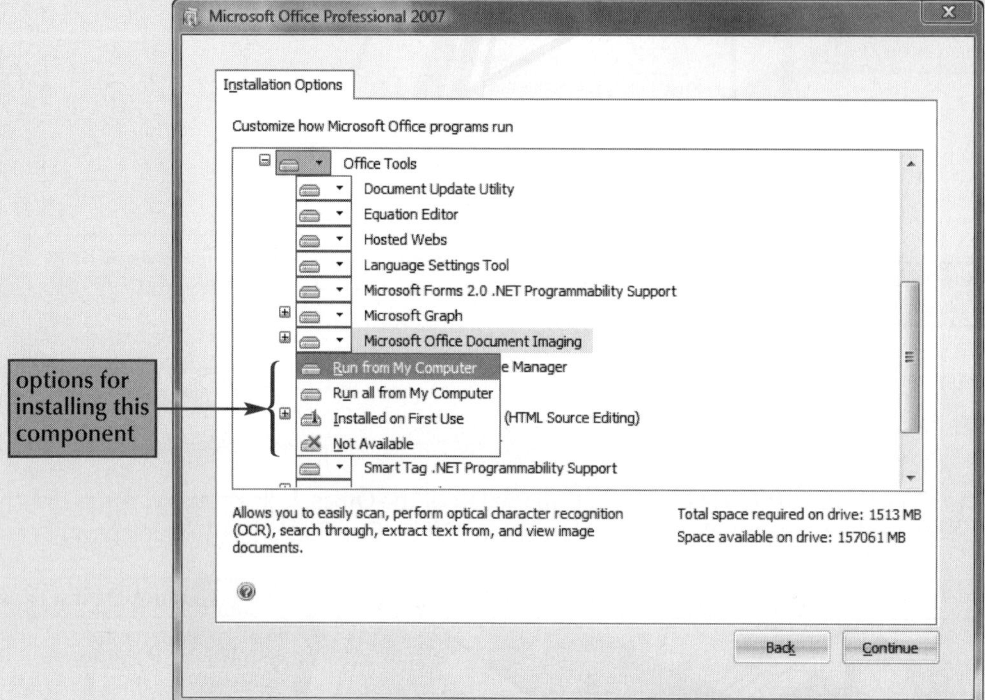

5. If hard disk storage space is limited on your computer, or if you prefer to keep as much of your hard disk as free as possible, you can review these options to determine which ones you actually need. Then, only install the ones that you will be using and save disk space by not installing components you'll never use. If you have plenty of hard disk storage space, and if you want to install components on your computer, or if you want to remove components, you can review these options and decide which ones to install and which to uninstall.

6. If you make changes to the selections for your version of Microsoft Office and want to keep those changes, click the **Continue** button. Then, Setup will configure your installed version of Microsoft Office and make the changes you specified, and then it will inform you that the configuration of your version of Microsoft Office was completed successfully so that you can close the Setup installation program. After the installation is complete, the Microsoft Office XP dialog box opens to verify that the installation of this software product was successful.

   Trouble? If you do not want to make any changes to your installed version of Microsoft Office, click the Close button in the Microsoft Office dialog box, verify that you want to cancel Setup, and then close the Microsoft Office dialog box.

If your computer comes with installed software, or if you or someone else opted for a standard, typical, or default installation of a software product on your computer, you might want to open the Setup program for that software product, examine the list of installed and uninstalled components, and change options so that you have the tools you need for your work.

Adding or Removing Microsoft Office Components | Reference Window

- Insert your Microsoft Office CD into your DVD or CD drive, and then click Run SETUP.EXE in the AutoPlay dialog box. If the Setup program does not open, or if you do not see an AutoPlay dialog box with an option for running Setup, open a window onto the CD drive (if necessary), and then click Setup.exe.
- In the Microsoft Office dialog box, choose Add or Remove Features, Repair, or Remove, and then click the Continue button.
- If you choose "Add or Remove Features," click the Expand View button to expand a category to see which options are installed under that category. Click the list button to the left of each category of options or to the left of a specific component to choose "Run from My Computer," "Run all from My Computer," "Installed on First Use," or "Not Available." Then, click the Continue button to install and uninstall options you've selected. Then, close the Microsoft Office dialog box after the configuration changes are made.
- If you want to exit Setup at any time without making changes, click the Close button and verify that you want to cancel Setup. Then, close the Microsoft Office dialog box.

Another way to configure the software on your computer is to set program defaults, which you'll do next.

Setting Program Defaults

During the installation of software on a computer, the installation program specifies default settings and file types for the software product. When you initiate a certain type of activity, such as browsing the Web, watching video, or playing music, Windows Vista opens a specific program to handle the operation. However, you might have several different programs that you use for the same purpose. For example, you might use both Windows Internet Explorer and Mozilla Firefox to browse the Web, and you might use Windows Media Player and QuickTime Player to watch videos or listen to music. In each case, you might prefer to use one of two or more programs for a specific activity.

When you install or set up software for use on your computer, the installation program or software might prompt you whether you want to make that program the default program for a specific activity and might also prompt you to specify which file types that software product uses. As shown in Figure 11-63, Windows Media Player 11 prompts the user for both of these types of settings when first used. In other cases, the installation program installs itself as the default program for a specific type of activity or for use with specific file types without asking you, or worse yet, provides you with no other option than to use that program as the default program with its file type settings. Then, you discover that the program that Windows opens is not the one that you want to use for a specific activity (at least most of the time). However, under Windows Vista, you can change program defaults and settings and specify how you want Windows Vista to handle programs by choosing Default Programs on the Start Menu.

Figure 11-63 Options for choosing Windows Media Player default settings

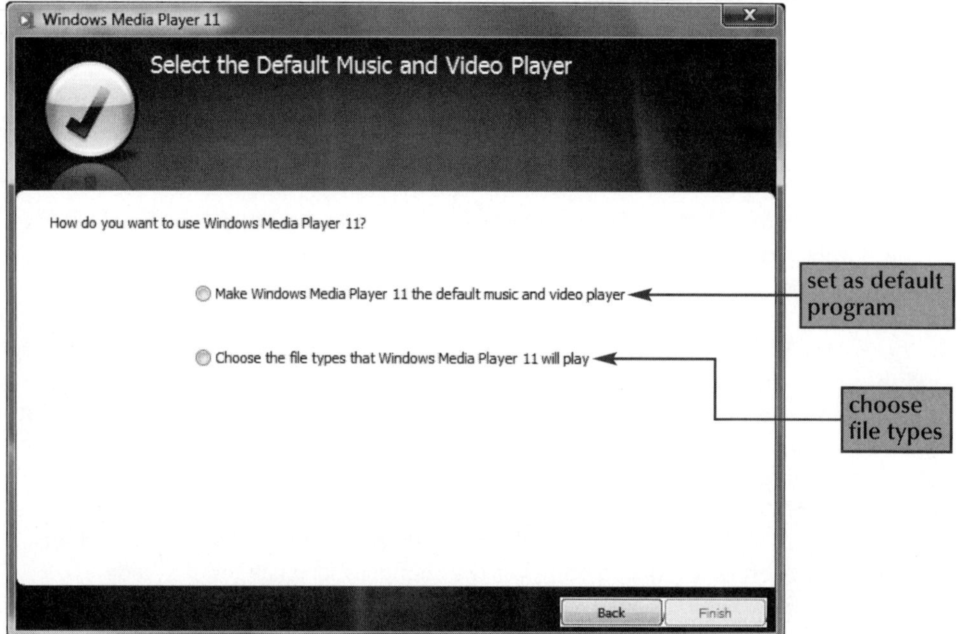

You can specify default programs and settings in four ways:

- **Set your default programs** You can use this option to make a specific program the default for all file types and protocols. For example, you might want to specify Mozilla Firefox as your default Web browser.
- **Associate a file type or protocol with a program** You can specify which program is associated with a specific file extension. For example, you might want to specify that all MP3 music files open in a specific media player.
- **Change AutoPlay settings** You can specify default settings or different types of media and media devices. For example, you might want to specify how Windows Vista handles DVD movies.
- **Set program access and computer defaults** You can use this option to specify the default Web browser, e-mail program, media player, instant messaging program, and virtual machine for Java. For example, you might want to specify Microsoft programs for all of these activities. **Java** is a hardware-independent Web programming language for creating interactive or animated content on Web pages. When you visit a Web site that has interactive or animated content, Java programs are downloaded so that you can view and use that content. However, for these Java programs to run on your computer, Windows Vista must use a virtual machine (VM) environment to translate Java program code into processor-specific instructions. A **virtual machine** is a software product (like Microsoft's Virtual PC) that simulates an actual computer and therefore provides a working environment in which you can install and use other operating systems and applications.

Kai wants to check the default settings used by her Web browser so that she can verify that Windows Vista uses the program and settings she prefers.

You must provide Administrator credentials to use "Set program access and computer defaults" in the following steps. If you are not logged on under an Administrator account or do not know the password for an Administrator account, do not keystroke the following steps, but rather read the steps and examine the figures so that you are familiar with this feature. If you are working in your college computer lab, make sure you have permission to examine default computer and program settings.

To check and specify program access and computer defaults:

1. From the Start menu, click **Default Programs**. In the Default Programs window, you can specify default settings using the four options previously described. See Figure 11-64.

Figure 11-64 Options for specifying default program and computer settings

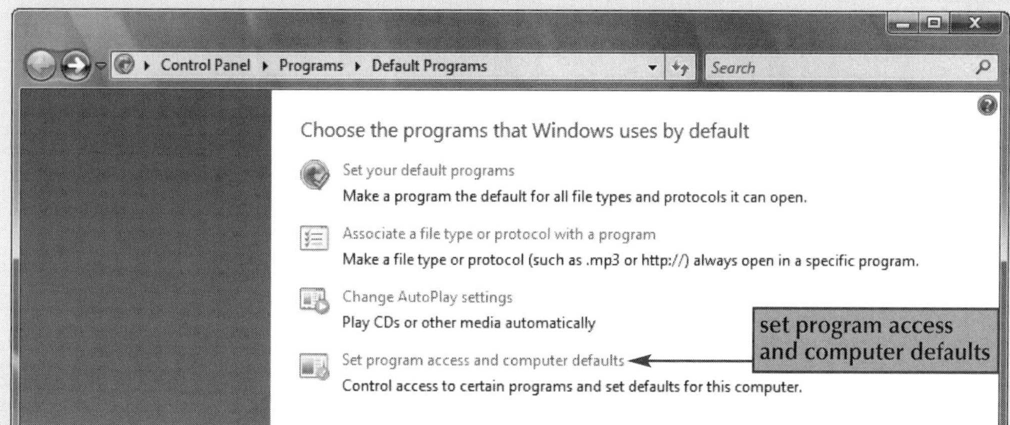

2. Click the **Set program access and computer defaults** link and provide Administrator credentials. In the Set Program Access and Computer Defaults window, Windows Vista notes that a program configuration specifies default programs for certain activities, such as Web browsing, and determines which programs are accessible from the Start menu, desktop, or other locations. See Figure 11-65.

Figure 11-65 Program configuration options

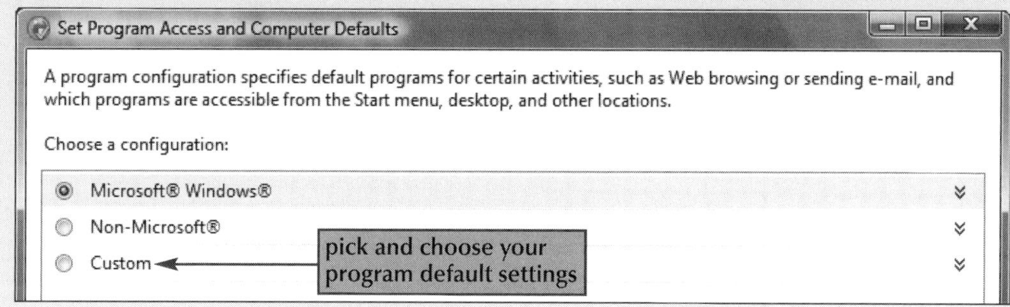

3. Click the **Expand View** button to the right of Microsoft® Windows®. Note that this option sets Microsoft Windows programs as defaults and enables or removes access to the programs listed. If you choose this option, Windows Vista uses Internet Explorer as your default Web browser, Windows Mail as your default e-mail program, Windows Media Player as your default media player, your current instant messaging program (whatever it may be), and your current virtual machine (whatever it may be) for Java. Notice also that this option enables access to these programs on the Start menu or All Programs menu, and the Media player default setting enables access to the Windows Media Center (in the edition of Windows Vista used on this computer) as well as Windows Media Player.

4. Click the Microsoft® Windows® **Collapse View** button , and then click the Non-Microsoft **Expand View** button . Notice that this category of options removes access to Internet Explorer, Windows Mail, and Windows Media Player (as well as Windows Media Center for this computer's edition of Windows Vista). That means these programs are no longer displayed on the Start menu or All Programs menu (but they are still installed on the computer).

5. Click the Non-Microsoft **Collapse View** button , and then click the Custom **Expand View** button . The Custom category of options allows you to pick and choose which program you want to use for most of these categories and whether you also want to enable access to one or more other programs by displaying them on the Start menu and All Programs menu. See Figure 11-66. Note that, for example, this option uses your current Web browser; in other words, the one that you specified as the default program you want to use. You can select Internet Explorer, or you can just enable access to Internet Explorer so that it appears as an option on the Start menu and All Programs menu.

Figure 11-66 Options for picking and choosing default programs

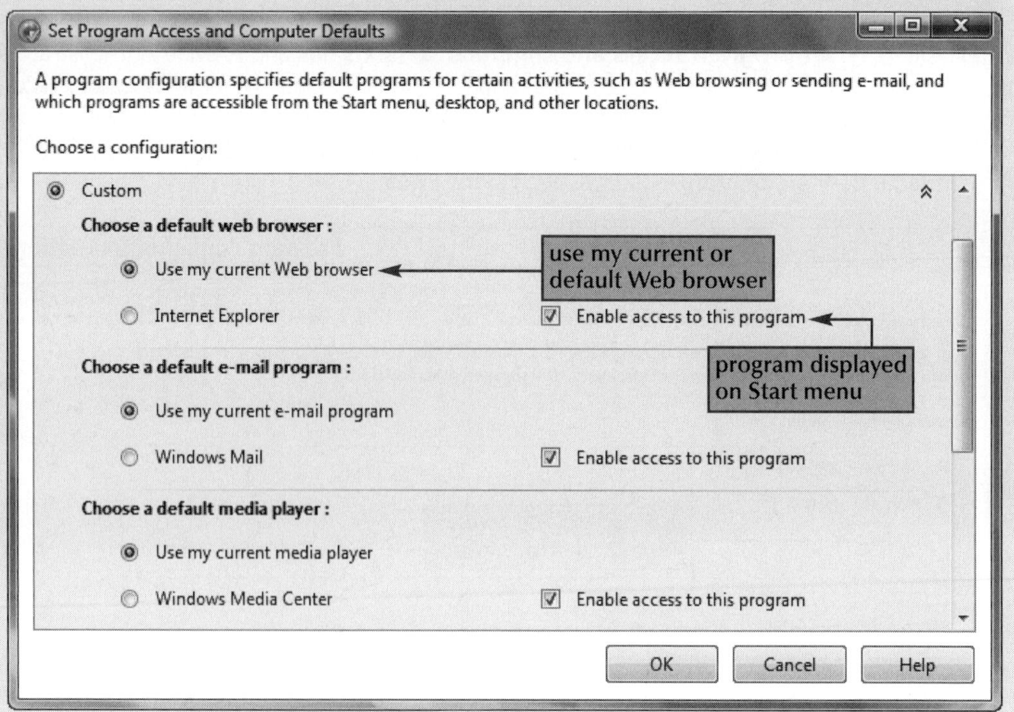

6. If you are working on your own computer, and if you have made changes that you want to continue to use on your computer, click the **OK** button, and then Windows Vista will display an Applying Settings dialog box as it applies the new settings you specified. If you do not want to change the default settings for your computer, or if you are working in a college computer lab, click the **Cancel** button to close the Set Program Access and Computer Defaults window without making any changes to the computer you are using.
7. Keep the Default Programs window open for the next set of tutorial steps.

This feature allows you to identify quickly the default programs that you want to use for the most common types of operations you perform on your computer in one step. You can also set a specific program as the default program for all file types and protocols it can open.

To set default programs:

1. In the Set Default Programs window, click the **Set your default programs** link, and in the Programs box, click **Internet Explorer**. Windows Vista displays information about Internet Explorer, identifies how many defaults are currently set for this program (in this case, 3 out of 9 defaults), and allows you to set this program as the default for all file types and protocols it can open or pick and choose which file types and protocols it opens by default. See Figure 11-67.

Figure 11-67 Options for choosing default program settings

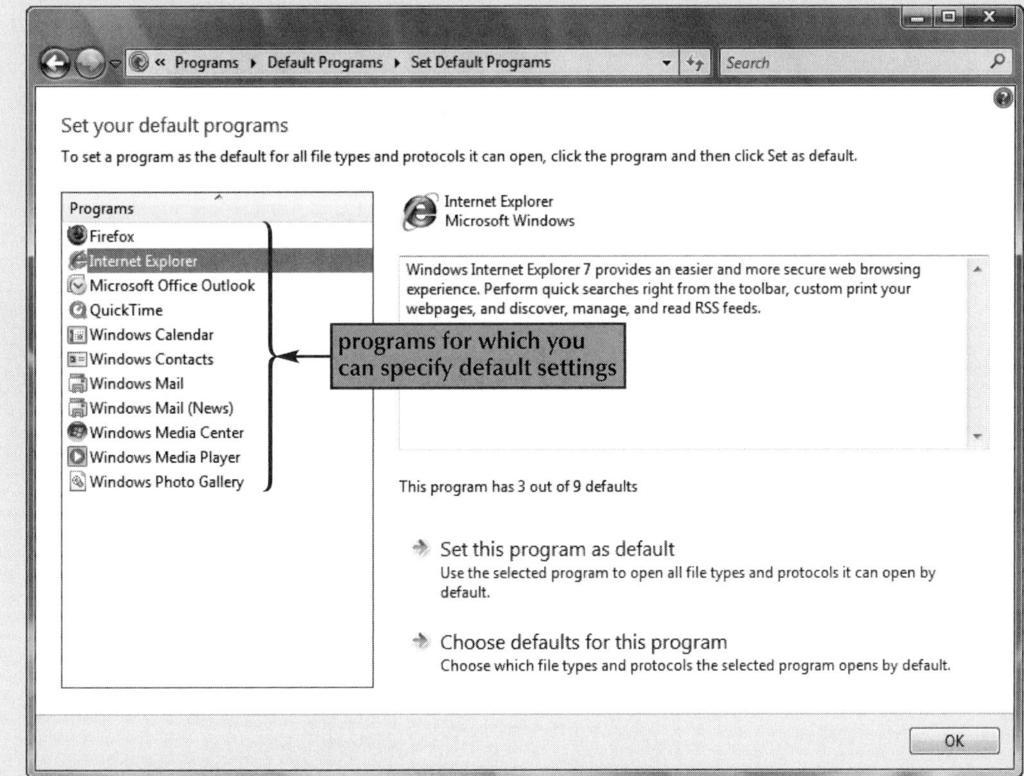

2. Click **Choose defaults for this program**. In the Set Program Associations window, you can specify which file extensions open with this program, which protocols it opens, and whether it is listed as the default program for the Internet link in the pinned items list on the Start menu (the last option listed). On the computer used for Figure 11-68 (which has both Windows Internet Explorer and Mozilla Firefox), Internet Explorer is set as the default program for opening the "mht," "mhtml," and "url" file extensions, but not the "htm" and "html" file extensions. If, for example, you click an Internet shortcut on your desktop, Windows Vista opens Internet Explorer, and then locates and displays the Web page for a specific Web site. If you remove the check mark from the ".url" check box, Windows Vista will locate and display a Web page for an Internet shortcut using your default Web browser, or you can back up one step, select Mozilla Firefox, and then specify that Windows Vista open all Internet shortcuts using Firefox. You can specify whether Windows Vista uses Internet Explorer for "ftp" (File Transfer Protocol) Web sites to upload and download files, "http" (HyperText Transport Protocol) for World Wide Web sites, and "https" for secure World Wide Web sites.

Figure 11-68 Viewing Internet Explorer default settings

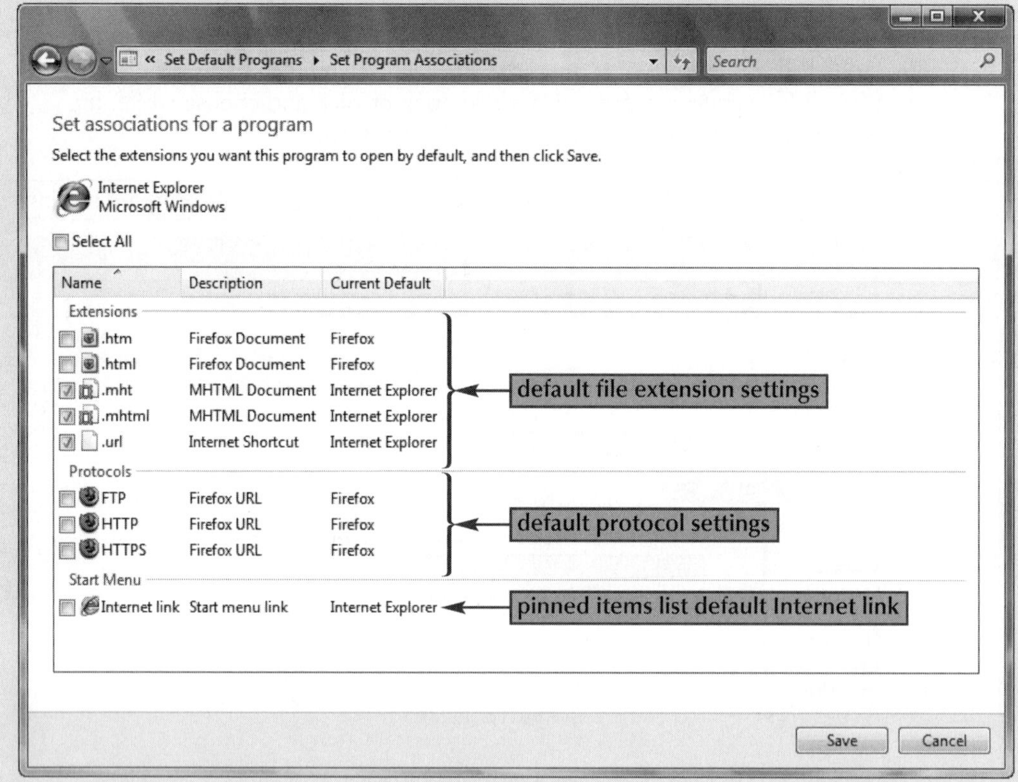

3. If you are working on your own computer, and if you have made changes that you want to continue to use on your computer, click the **Save** button. If you do not want to change the default settings for your computer, or if you are working in a college computer lab, click the **Cancel** button.

4. Click the **OK** button to close the Set Default Programs window.

5. Keep the Default Programs window open for the next set of tutorial steps.

This option for setting defaults for using file types and protocols is useful when you want to customize the use of commonly used programs on your computer. You can also associate a file type or protocol with a specific program. For example, you might want to specify which program opens different types of file formats (such as Bitmap Image, JPEG, GIF, and PNG) for files that contain images or pictures so that you can use a specific program to perform a specific type of operation on a specific type of image. If you are designing Web pages, you might want to be able to open each of the different image types that you will put on that Web page with Internet Explorer so that you can view how an image appears under that Web browser.

To associate a file type or protocol with a specific program:

1. In the Default Programs window, click the **Associate a file type or protocol with a program** link. Windows Vista displays a list of all file extensions on your computer, provides a description or name for each file type, and identifies the program currently assigned as the default program for opening that file type. However, certain file extensions and protocols might not be defined yet. See Figure 11-69.

Tip

If you want to view file extensions and protocols by program, click the Current Default column header button.

Figure 11-69 Program associations for different file types

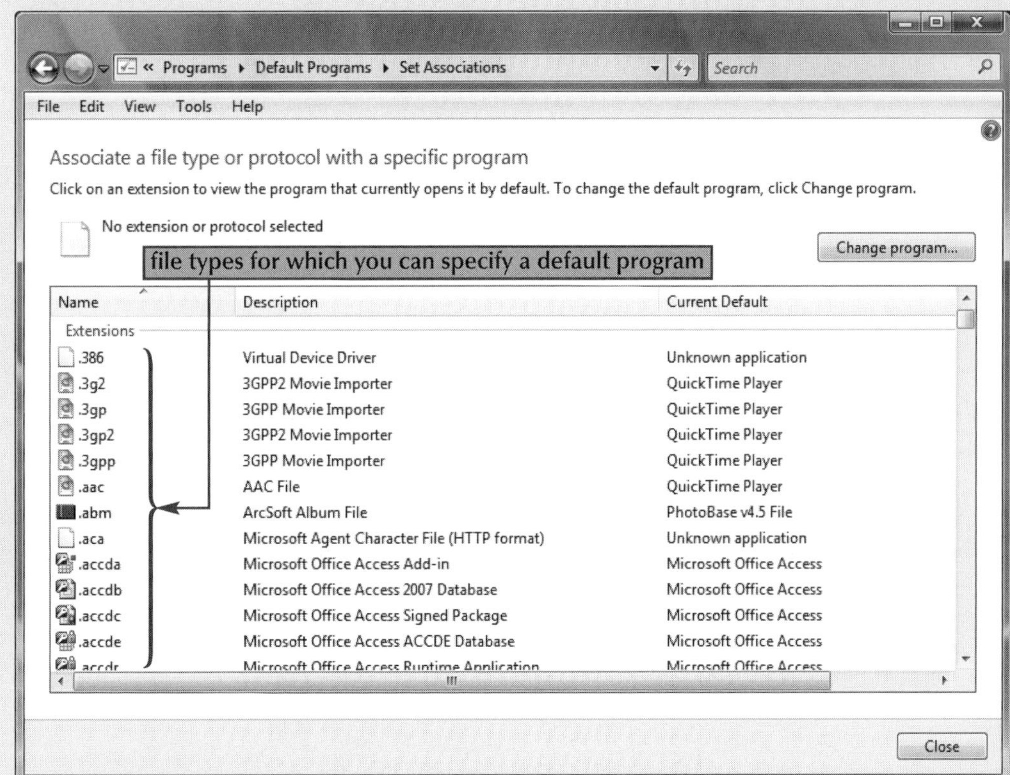

2. Locate the "bmp" file extension (or file type) and note that, by default, this file type opens in Windows Photo Gallery. If you locate the "gif," "jpg," and "png" file extensions, you will discover that files with GIF images open with Internet Explorer, JPEG Images open with Windows Photo Gallery, and PNG Images open with Windows Photo Gallery. If you prefer to open these file types in another program, you can change the default file type by selecting the file extension, and then clicking the Change program button.

3. Under name, click the **.bmp** file extension, and then click the **Change program button**. Windows Vista displays an Open With dialog box and displays a list of recommended programs (and perhaps other programs) which you can use to open this specific file type. On the computer used for Figure 11-70, the user can change the file association from Windows Photo Gallery to either Microsoft Office Picture Manager or Paint, or the user can use the Browse button to locate another graphics program (or a Web browser) for viewing or working with this file format. If you browse for another program, Windows Vista lists installed software programs under "Other Programs."

Figure 11-70 **Choosing a different program for opening a file type**

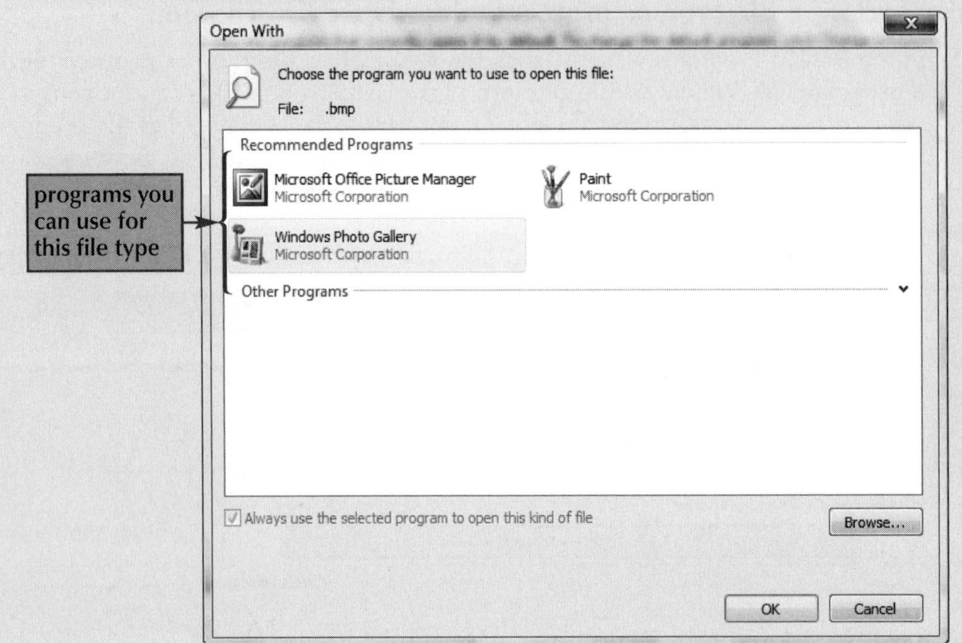

4. Click **Cancel** to close the Open With dialog box, click **Close** in the Set Associations window, and then close the Default Programs window.

This ability to modify individual file extensions and protocols provides the greatest control for customizing the use of programs on your computer by enabling you to pick and choose which program opens which file type. You can combine the use of these three different ways for specifying program defaults and settings to meet your specific needs.

Specifying Program Defaults and Settings | Reference Window

- From the Start menu, click Default Programs.
- To specify defaults for certain programs and specify computer defaults, click the "Set program access and computer defaults" link, provide Administrator credentials, and choose a computer configuration. If you choose Custom, you can further customize defaults by program type and enable access to alternate programs on the Start Menu and All Programs menu. Click OK to save your computer configuration.
- To specify defaults by program, click the "Set your default programs" link, select a program in the Programs list box, click "Set this program as default" to use this program for all file types and protocols that it can open, or click "Choose defaults for this program" to specify which file extensions and protocols this program will open and, in certain cases, to also specify whether the program appears in the pinned items list on the Start menu. Save your settings and close the Set Default Programs window.
- To specify a program for each file type or protocol on your computer, click the "Associate a file type or protocol with a program" link, locate and select a file extension, click the Change program button, choose a recommended program or browse to locate a program that's not listed in the Open With dialog box, click OK to save your changes, and then click Close to close the Set Associations dialog box.
- Close the Default Programs window.

Restoring Your Computer

If you are working in a computer lab, or if you want to restore your desktop computer to the settings that existed prior to working on this tutorial, complete the following steps.

To restore your computer:

1. To restore double-click activation, click the **Computer** icon on the desktop, click the **Organize** button on the command bar, click **Folder and Search Options**, and on the General property sheet in the Folder Options dialog box, click the **Double-click to open an item (single-click to select)** option button, click the **OK** button to close the Folder and Options dialog box, and then close the Computer window.
2. To remove the Computer icon from the desktop, open the Start menu, right-click **Computer**, and then click **Show on Desktop**.

Kai appreciates that you've learned the importance of updating the Windows Vista operating system, Microsoft Office, project management software, and the other software products you use every day.

Review | Session 11.2 Quick Check

1. Win32 applications are applications designed for a _______________ operating system.
2. True or False. Windows 64-bit operating systems do not support the use of Win32 applications.
3. What is a self-extracting executable file?
4. What Windows Vista feature can you use to adjust program settings for a program that does not function properly, or at all, under Windows Vista?
5. True or False. You can specify a default computer configuration for specific programs, default settings for specific programs, and default programs for specific file extensions.
6. The _______________ can resolve conflicts that a program encounters with User Account Control.

Review | Tutorial Summary

In this tutorial, you examined how to prepare for an operating system upgrade or a clean install of an operating system. You downloaded, installed, and used the Windows Vista Upgrade Advisor to evaluate the feasibility of upgrading a computer to Windows Vista. You looked at the steps for installing Windows Vista, and you examined how to use Windows Easy Transfer to copy files and settings from an older computer to a new computer with Windows Vista. You viewed a list of installed Windows features, and then turned Windows Fax and Scan on and off. You used the Program Compatibility Wizard to adjust program compatibility settings so that the program works properly under Windows Vista. You uninstalled the Windows Vista Upgrade Advisor, and then examined the options for installing and uninstalling Microsoft Office components. And finally, you examined the different ways in which you can specify program defaults and settings.

Key Terms

16-bit operating environment
32-bit application
64-bit application
clean install
full version
IP address
Java
self-extracting executable
shared components
upgrade copy
upgrade in-place
upgrade path
virtual machine
Win16 application
Win32 application
Win64 application

Practice | Review Assignments

Practice the skills you learned in the tutorial.

There are no Data Files needed for the Review Assignments.

Now that Kai has upgraded her laptop to Windows Vista Ultimate, she's ready to upgrade the software on her home computer so that it is similar to her office computer and her laptop. When the need arises, she can then work at home and have access to the same features she has on her office computer. Since the Windows Vista Home Premium Edition is currently installed on her home computer, her first step in upgrading her home computer is to determine whether she can upgrade and, if so, which Windows Vista edition is the best possible edition. Kai also wants to make sure that the Windows Vista edition she upgrades to supports Windows Media Center, Windows Complete PC Backup and Restore, and Windows Sideshow.

Some of the following steps require Administrator credentials. As you complete each step in these Review Assignments, use a word processing application, such as Microsoft Word or WordPad, to record your answers to questions so that you can submit them to your instructor. Also, if you change any settings on the computer you are using, note the original settings so that you can restore them later. Complete the following:

1. Kai's first step is to review the information on Windows Vista at Microsoft's Web site.
   a. Open your Web browser and go to Microsoft's Web site: **www.microsoft.com**
   b. Search for information about Windows Vista editions using the following search criteria, and then locate the Web page that has information on: **Windows Vista Compare Editions**
   c. Which edition or editions of Windows Vista support Windows Media Center, Windows Complete PC Backup and Restore, and Windows Sideshow? Which edition provides support for all three features?
2. Next, Kai wants to review system requirements for Windows Vista Ultimate:
   a. Search using the following search criteria, and then locate the Web page that contains information on: **Windows Vista recommended system requirements**
   b. How much RAM and graphics memory must her computer have in order to upgrade to Windows Vista Ultimate?
   c. What system requirements must her computer meet in order to support Windows Aero?
3. Kai has a second, older computer with Windows XP Professional on her home network, and she wants to know what editions of Windows Vista she can use to upgrade that computer.
   a. Choose the "Buy or Upgrade" option, or search using the following search criteria, and then locate the Web page that contains information on: **Windows Vista upgrade paths from previous versions**
   b. If Kai wants to perform an upgrade-in-place on her Windows XP Professional computer, what edition or editions can she upgrade to?
4. What Microsoft tool can Kai use to check her two home computers for compatibility with Windows Vista, and what types of information does it provide on Windows Vista compatibility?
5. Outline the steps that Kai should take prior to installing Windows Vista on these two computers. Include any steps Kai should take to improve the chances of a successful installation or upgrade and, if necessary, to restore her computers to their original state.
6. If Kai decides to replace her older Windows XP Professional computer with a new computer, can she transfer her files and computer settings from that computer to her new computer, and if so, how, and what type of media can she use?

7. After upgrading her home computers, explain how Kai would examine and choose only those Windows features that she needs on each of her two computers.
8. Kai had a couple of Win16 applications that she used on the older of her two home computers. Can she use those applications under Windows Vista, and if so, how? Would you recommend that she upgrade those applications, and if so, what type of applications should she acquire?
9. Kai also wants to check her installed version of Microsoft Office to make sure all the features she needs are installed and to also remove features she does not need. How can she perform this task?
10. Examine the installed software on your computer. How many programs are installed on your computer, and how much disk storage space do they use? List the names and publishers of the three applications that require the most space on your hard disk, and list their sizes. Describe how you would remove an application or program that you no longer need from your computer.
11. Describe how Kai can use Windows Vista to set her computer's configuration so that she can use another software product as her default Web browser and e-mail program.
12. Explain how Kai can modify default program settings for Internet Explorer and her other Web browser so that they work with specific files and protocols.
13. Describe how Kai can modify her program settings so that files with graphic images automatically open in a specific program installed on her computer. Assume she works with GIF, JPEG, PNG, and Bitmap Image files.
14. If necessary, restore any default settings on the computer you used for the Review Assignments.
15. Submit your answers to the review assignments to your instructor, either in printed or electronic form, as requested.

Apply | Case Problem 1

Use the skills you learned to evaluate a proposed Windows Vista upgrade.

There are no Data Files needed for this Case Problem.

Reflection Recording, Ltd. Alaric Richardson works as a Marketing Associate for Reflection Recording, Ltd. He depends on the use of his company laptop when traveling on business, when meeting with clients, and when working at home on special projects. Before he upgrades his laptop from Windows Vista Business Edition to Windows Vista Ultimate Edition, he wants to make sure that the upgrade goes smoothly and that his computer meets the requirements for using Windows Vista Ultimate. He asks you to identify the approach he should use for this upgrade.

As you complete each step in this case, use a Word processing application, such as Microsoft Word or WordPad, to record your answers to questions so that you can submit them to your instructor. Also, if you change any settings on the computer you are using, note what the original settings were so that you can restore them later. Complete the following:

1. Open the System window and view properties of your computer so that you can document your computer system for a possible upgrade. Identify your Windows version and edition, your Windows Experience Index rating, your processor and its clock speed, the amount of system memory (or RAM), the System type (i.e., 32-bit or 64-bit operating system), your computer name, and your workgroup name (if applicable).

2. Open a Computer window. What is the storage capacity of your hard disk(s)? If you have multiple drives, identify each drive by name and list each drive's storage capacity. How much storage space is used on each drive? How much storage space is available on each drive? What percent of the volume's storage space is available? What file system is used on each drive? What drive is Windows Vista installed on?
3. Open a window onto drive C and view the properties of the Windows folder. What is the total size on disk required for the contents of the Windows folder? View properties of the Program Files folder. What is the total size on disk for the contents of the Program Files folder? Close the drive C window.
4. View a list of the installed software on your computer. What type of applications do you use on your computer (Win32, Win64, or Win16 applications)? How many programs are installed on your computer, and how much disk storage capacity do all these programs require? Sort the list of installed software by size. What five programs require the most amount of disk storage space? Sort the list of installed software by Installed On date. What were the last five programs installed on your computer?
5. If Microsoft Office is installed on your computer, what version of Microsoft Office do you use? How much storage space does Microsoft Office require?
6. Visit the Microsoft Web site and locate information on features available in different editions of Windows Vista. Identify which of the following features you can use in your edition of Windows Vista: Windows DVD Maker, Windows Media Center, Windows Movie Maker in High Definition, Windows SideShow, Windows Mobility Center, Windows Meeting Space, and Windows Aero.
7. What edition or editions of Windows Vista, if any, can you upgrade to? Would you have to purchase an upgrade copy or a full version of Windows Vista? Would you need to upgrade the hardware on your computer, and if so, what would you need to do? Would you need or prefer to perform a clean install or an upgrade-in-place? From your perspective, what advantages do each of these types of upgrades offer, and what disadvantages do each of these types of upgrades pose?
8. Before upgrading your computer to a new edition of Windows Vista, what Microsoft tool could you use to determine the compatibility of hardware and software on your computer?
9. What precautions would you take before installing a new edition of Windows Vista or a new version of the Windows operating system?
10. What precautions would you take before installing a new edition of a major software application like Microsoft Office?
11. Submit your paper to your instructor, either in printed or electronic form, as requested.

Apply | Case Problem 2

Use the skills you learned to evaluate upgrading a computer to a new edition of Windows Vista.

There are no Data Files needed for this Case Problem.

McDaniel & Atkins Financial Services Leah McDaniel owns and manages McDaniel & Atkins Financial Services. As a member of her IT Department, you are going to assist in the process of evaluating the company's desktop computers and laptops for an upgrade to Windows Vista Ultimate so that all staff members have access to all the features available in Windows Vista.

This Case Problem requires that you download and install the Windows Vista Upgrade Advisor and any additional software needed to support the use of the Windows Vista Upgrade Advisor on the computer you are using for this Case Problem. Also, you must provide Administrator credentials to install the Windows Vista Upgrade Advisor.

As you complete each step in this Case Problem, use a word processing application, such as Microsoft Word or WordPad, to record your answers to questions so that you can submit them to your instructor. Also, if you change any settings on the computer you are using, note what the original settings were so that you can restore them later. Complete the following:

1. From the Microsoft Web site and its Downloads Web site, locate the most recent version of the Windows Vista Upgrade Advisor and download it to your computer. Save the downloaded file in a subfolder within your user account's Downloads folder.
2. Open the folder that contains the program you downloaded. What is the name of the file that you downloaded? What is its file extension and file type? How do you install this type of file on a computer?
3. Install the Windows Vista Upgrade Advisor. Identify the names of any additional Microsoft software you have to download to use the Windows Vista Upgrade Advisor.
4. Run the Windows Vista Upgrade Advisor. What edition of Windows Vista does it recommend for the computer you are using? In the summary of its findings, what does the Windows Vista Upgrade Advisor report for System, Devices, and Programs?
5. View report details. What are the most significant computer, hardware, and software compatibility problems (if any), and what does it recommend you do to resolve each problem?
6. Choose the option for saving the Task List report as a Web archive (a type of Web page).
7. Uninstall Windows Vista Upgrade Advisor from your computer. Provide a brief overview of how you uninstalled this software.
8. Submit your answers to the questions in this case problem and your Windows Vista Upgrade Advisor Web archive report to your instructor, either in printed or electronic form, as requested.

Research | Case Problem 3

Work with the skills you've learned and use the Internet to prepare for a Microsoft Office upgrade.

There are no Data Files needed for this Case Problem.

Estuary Restoration Foundation Jarrod Terrell and Ian Douglas are codirectors of an American foundation for restoring estuaries. Thanks to the generosity of several prominent donors, their foundation now has two state-of-the-art Windows Vista computer systems that the foundation will use to track the status of restoration projects and funding. Jarrod asks you to evaluate the different editions of Microsoft Office and prepare their computers for an Office upgrade. He also reminds you that they will need an Office suite that contains Microsoft Access, Microsoft PowerPoint, and Microsoft Outlook.

As you complete each step in this Case Problem, use a word processing application, such as Microsoft Word or WordPad, to record your answers to questions so that you can submit them to your instructor. Also, if you change any settings on the computer you are using, note what the original settings were so that you can restore them later.

To complete this case problem, you must use Windows Internet Explorer, and you must enable cookies on your computer. Complete the following:

1. Open your Web browser and visit the Microsoft Office Online Web site: http://office.microsoft.com.
2. Choose the option for viewing information about products, and then choose the option for comparing Office suites for the current version of Microsoft Office. List the names of the current suites of Microsoft Office.
3. What Office suites contain Microsoft Word, Microsoft Excel, Microsoft PowerPoint, and Microsoft Access? Which Office suites also contain Outlook?
4. Which Office suit would you choose if you wanted Microsoft Word, Microsoft Excel, Microsoft PowerPoint, and Microsoft Outlook?
5. Choose the link for viewing details for the Microsoft Office Small Business Suite, and then choose the link for viewing system requirements of this Office suite. What are the processor, memory, hard disk drive, display, and operating system requirements of this Office suite?
6. Choose the option for viewing information about pricing and upgrades for the Microsoft Office Small Business Suite. What do the full version and the upgrade copy cost? What installed products would qualify for an upgrade?
7. If you have a version of Microsoft Office installed on the computer you are using, choose the link to check for free updates, and then check your computer for Microsoft updates. What updates (if any) are available for your Microsoft Office suite? What is the estimated disk space required for installing those updates?
8. Outline the steps you would follow to upgrade your computer to a newer Microsoft Office suite.
9. Submit your answers to the questions in this case problem to your instructor, either in printed or electronic form, as requested.

Challenge | Case Problem 4

Use the skills you learned in the tutorial to specify default program settings for a Web page design company.

There are no Data Files needed for this Case Problem.

Web Arts Design, Inc. Devon Flynn designs Web pages for her company Web Arts Design, Inc. She wants to check program default settings for her computer and make any adjustments that simplify her use of her computer plus permit her to use those programs she prefers. Since she has not yet worked with these settings, she asks you to assist her in this process and point out any options of particular benefit to her line of work.

To complete this case problem, you will need to provide Administrator credentials to view and make changes to program access settings and computer defaults.

As you complete each step in this case, use a Word processing application, such as Microsoft Word or WordPad, to record and print your answers to questions so that you can submit them to your instructor. Also, if you change any settings on the computer you are using, note what the original settings were so that you can restore them later.

1. Choose the option for examining Program Defaults from the Start menu, and then choose the option for setting program access and computer defaults. Is the computer you are using set for a Microsoft, Non-Microsoft, or Custom computer configuration? What are this computer's default Web browser, e-mail program, and media player settings? Under what circumstances might you use a Custom computer configuration, and what benefits would you derive? Close the Set Program Access and Computer Defaults without making changes to the computer you are using.
2. Choose the option to set default program settings. What Web browser(s) are installed on your computer? Select Internet Explorer, and then select the option for choosing defaults for this program. What is the default program for files with the "htm," "html," and "url" file extension? What protocols are set for Internet Explorer? What Web browser is specified as the Internet link on the pinned items list?

EXPLORE

3. If you want to specify another Web browser as the default for all extensions, protocols, and Internet link, how would you make this change?

EXPLORE

4. In the Set Default Programs window, choose Windows Photo Gallery, and then select the option for choosing defaults for this program. What file extensions are set as defaults for Windows Photo Gallery? Return to the Default Programs window without making any changes to default file extensions for Window Photo Gallery.
5. Return to the Default Programs window and choose the option for associating a file type or protocol with a program. What is the description for each of the following file extensions, and what program on your computer is associated with each of these file extensions?
   a. docx (or doc)
   b. eml
   c. gadget
   d. htm
   e. html
   f. jpg
   g. mig
   h. msi
   i. pdf
   j. png
   k. txt
   l. url
   m. vbs
   n. xps
   o. MAILTO

EXPLORE

6. If you wanted to change the program associated with a file extension, how would you do it?
7. Close the Set Associations window without making any changes to extension and protocol settings on the computer you are using.
8. Submit your answers to the questions in this case problem to your instructor, either in printed or electronic form, as requested.

Review | Quick Check Answers

Session 11.1

1. system (requirements)
2. processor, system memory, hard disk storage space, and graphics memory
3. upgrade path
4. Windows Vista Upgrade Advisor
5. inf
6. Windows Easy Transfer

Session 11.2

1. 32-bit
2. False
3. A self-extracting executable file is a file that contains one or more files stored in a compressed format, plus a program for extracting the contents of the self-extracting executable file itself.
4. Program Compatibility Wizard
5. True
6. Program Compatibility Assistant

Ending Data Files

There are no ending Data Files needed for this tutorial.

Tutorial 12

Objectives

Session 12.1
- Learn about Plug and Play hardware
- Examine Windows Vista support for newer types of hardware
- Examine the importance of hardware resource assignments
- Open Device Manager
- Troubleshoot hardware problems
- Use System Information

Session 12.2
- Check your computer name and workgroup or domain name
- View networked computers in the same workgroup
- Open the new Network and Sharing Center
- Compare three ways to share folders on a network
- Create a mapped drive

Managing Hardware and Networks

Troubleshooting Hardware and Setting Up Workgroups

Case | Alexander Medical Research Institute

The Alexander Medical Research Institute in Atlanta uses specialists in different disciplines to tackle the most pressing medical problems today. Remy Besson, a technical support specialist, evaluates new software and hardware technologies for use by research and administrative staff. In addition to setting up, configuring, customizing, and troubleshooting computers, he advises staff on how to set up home computer networks that connect to the Institute's network so that they have access to the resources they need any time of the day.

In this tutorial, you will compare Plug and Play and legacy hardware and discover the advantages that Plug and Play computer systems offer. You will also survey Windows Vista support for newer types of hardware devices. After learning about the importance of hardware resource assignments, you will open Device Manager and examine your computer's hardware configuration. Next, you look at the process for checking your computer name and workgroup or domain name and view networked computers in the same workgroup. You open the new Network and Sharing Center to view network settings, compare three different ways to share folders on a network, and create a mapped drive to a shared network folder.

Starting Data Files

There are no starting Data Files needed for this tutorial.

Session 12.1

Comparing Types of Hardware Devices

The Director of the Alexander Medical Research Institute asked Remy to supervise a group of technical staff and managers in identifying and implementing new hardware technologies. Remy's 15 years of experience in the computer industry has helped him realize the importance of choosing hardware technologies that are reliable, stable, easy to install and use, and designed to meet the future needs of his company.

One of the major problems computer users faced in the past was the overly complex process for installing and configuring new hardware devices. To reduce the problems and support costs that often resulted from installing new components, hardware manufacturers now design their devices using a set of standards called **Plug and Play (PnP)** so that the Windows operating system can detect a hardware device, install device drivers for that device, and configure the device during booting or when the device is attached to the computer. The goal of Plug and Play is simple: You plug in the device, Windows detects and installs support for the device, and you are ready to "play." Hardware devices that do not support Plug and Play are called **non-Plug and Play** or **legacy devices**. They require manual installation and configuration and often extensive troubleshooting. Fortunately, Plug and Play hardware is the standard today.

Each time you boot your computer or attach a hardware device to your computer, Windows Vista checks for any new hardware. If Windows Vista detects a new hardware component that supports Plug and Play, it installs and loads the device drivers for that component, and then configures the device to work properly. If Windows Vista does not have a device driver for that Plug and Play component, it prompts you to insert a disk with the software that includes the device driver(s).

A *bona fide* Plug and Play computer system has the following features:

- **ACPI BIOS** Windows Vista requires that a computer have an **Advanced Configuration and Power Interface BIOS (ACPI BIOS)**. In addition to performing the operations you examined in Tutorial 1, namely, performing a Power-On Self-Test and locating and loading the operating system from disk, an ACPI BIOS or the earlier Plug and Play BIOS identifies and activates hardware devices, determines their resource requirements, creates a nonconflicting hardware configuration, loads device drivers, passes configuration information to the operating system, and notifies it of any configuration changes. An ACPI BIOS also determines the power management capabilities of hardware devices. The Windows Vista operating system, not the BIOS, is now responsible for configuring a computer system and managing power to devices and the computer itself.
- **Plug and Play hardware devices and device drivers** For a hardware device to be automatically detected and configured with the proper device drivers, it must be a Plug and Play device. Plug and Play hardware devices have a Plug and Play ID that uniquely identifies the hardware device. Today, a wide range of devices fully support Plug and Play, so there's no need to use legacy devices. Windows Vista can also use a Plug and Play driver for a legacy device and thereby improve Windows Vista support for the device.
- **Plug and Play operating system** Like its predecessors, Windows Vista is a Plug and Play operating system. Windows Vista stores configuration information on Plug and Play devices in the Registry. When you install a new Plug and Play device, it checks the resources used by other Plug and Play devices in the Registry and configures the new device without introducing conflicts between hardware devices.

Windows Vista also uses **Universal Plug and Play (UPnP)** to detect and configure wired and wireless devices in a networking environment, consumer electronics equipment (such as home entertainment systems and appliances connected to a Windows Vista computer), and Internet gateways. A **gateway** consists of hardware and software that provide an access point to another network. UPnP relies on Internet and Web protocols (TCP/IP, HTTP, and XML) to enable devices to configure themselves, announce themselves on the network, discover or locate other devices on the network, communicate directly with other devices, and direct the operation of other devices. **TCP/IP (Transmission Control Protocol/Internet Protocol)** is a standard protocol for transferring data in packets with a source and destination address over the Internet or a private network. A **packet** consists of a set of data (such as part of a file), as well as a source address and destination address, sent from one location to another over the Internet or other network. HTTP (Hypertext Transfer Protocol) is a standard protocol for transferring files from a Web server to your browser so that you can view the contents of a Web page over the World Wide Web. Recall from Tutorial 10 that XML (Extensible Markup Language), like HTML (Hypertext Markup Language), describes the layout of a Web page and your ability to interact with that content, but unlike HTML, XML can also describe data to support the transfer and sharing of information.

Examining Windows Vista's Increased Hardware Support

For the Alexander Medical Research Institute, the increased support that Windows Vista provides for new hardware technologies is one of its most important features.

In addition to supporting many of the hardware technologies introduced in earlier versions of Windows, Windows Vista provides enhanced support for the following technologies:

- **Human Interface Devices (HID)** A broad category of hardware devices, **Human Interface Devices (HID)**, includes devices for interacting with and controlling computers. HIDs include not only the standard types of devices that people use on their computers, such as the keyboard, mouse, trackball, joystick, and wireless pointing devices for presentations, they also include devices used to control home entertainment systems, smart appliances, and virtual reality simulations (for example, head-mounted displays).
- **Multimonitor Support** Windows Vista supports the simultaneous use of two or more monitors. **DualView** is another term used to describe the use of two monitors. If you have a video display adapter card that provides connections for two monitors, you can set up those monitors to display images in one of three ways:
    - **Mirrored** This default setting displays the same image on two monitors. This display option is useful if you want to display the same image on both a desktop computer or laptop and an overhead projector in a conference room, lecture hall, or classroom.
    - **Extended** This display setting extends the desktop across two monitors. You can drag a window from one monitor to another monitor (across virtual space). With this option, you can view different documents in different applications on different monitors (such as a Microsoft Word document on one monitor and your e-mail Inbox on the other monitor), and view the same document over multiple monitors (such as a wide Microsoft Office Excel spreadsheet).
    - **External Display Only** This display option displays the desktop on an overhead projector (for example) and is useful when you have a laptop connected to an overhead projector for playback of a video and at the same time want to conserve battery power on the laptop.

Besides using different desktop settings on each monitor, you can designate which monitor is the primary monitor (for booting), set the orientation of the monitors as right to left or top to bottom, and drag and drop objects across virtual space from one monitor to the next. For monitors and projects that support the new Extended Display Identification Data (EDID), Windows Vista can detect the monitor and apply the most appropriate video display settings. You can also customize each monitor's display settings. **Extended Display Identification Data (EDID)** is a standard video data format that contains information about the capabilities of a monitor, such as the screen resolution and color depth. If a monitor does not support EDID, then you can manually adjust settings of each monitor using the Control Panel. To use multiple monitors, all video display graphic adapters must use the same type of display driver, preferably the new Windows Vista Display Driver Model (WDDM).

- **Universal Serial Bus (USB)** The **Universal Serial Bus (USB)** is an external, bidirectional, Plug and Play bus for connecting up to 127 high-speed serial devices via one port on your computer; however, there is a practical limitation in terms of providing power to multiple devices. A **bus** is a path for transferring data between computer components. In the past, each type of device required a separate port, which meant that you had to install device drivers for each device and then figure out how to assign resources to each device; to complicate matters, resources were limited. With USB and IEEE 1394 devices (covered in the next bullet), you no longer need to deal with limited resources, such as IRQ settings, DMA channels, and I/O addresses (covered later in the tutorial). For certain types of devices, such as mouse or keyboard, you do not need extra power cables because the USB connection provides power to those devices.

  The initial first-generation USB bus, identified as USB 1.x (USB 1.0 and USB 1.1) supports two data speeds: **Full-Speed** at 12 Mbps (12 Megabits per second or 12 million bits per second) for devices that require large amounts of bandwidth, such as devices that process video and audio, and **Low-Speed** at 1.5 Mbps (1.5 Megabits per second or 1.5 million bits per second) for devices such as keyboards and mice. **Bandwidth** refers to the amount of data that can be transmitted over a device in a fixed amount of time; digital devices measure bandwidth in bytes per second or bits per second. Today's second-generation USB devices (USB 2.0) support a data transfer rate of 480 Mbps (480 Megabits per second or 480 million bits per second) called **Hi-Speed**.

  USB also supports Plug and Play, power management, and **hot swapping** (also called **hot plugging** or **hot insertion and removal**), which means that you can connect or disconnect a USB device while the computer is still running. You do not need to power down your computer before adding or removing the USB device, though it is a good idea to check your hardware manual to verify its ability to support hot swapping. Also, you should always use the Safely Remove Hardware icon in the notification area of the taskbar before detaching a device to guarantee that you do not lose data or damage the device.

  If you want to take advantage of the newest types of hardware technologies, or if you want to upgrade the hardware on your computer, purchase USB devices for easy installation, automatic configuration, speed, and support for a greater number of devices.

- **IEEE 1394** First-generation **IEEE 1394** (for Institute of Electrical and Electronics Engineers) is another high-speed Plug and Play bus with data transfer rates of 100, 200, and 400 Mbps (Megabits per second or millions of bits per second). Second-generation **IEEE 1394b** supports data transfer rates of 800 Mbps to 3.2 Gbps (Gigabits per second). Apple originally developed this technology and called it **FireWire**; however, this technology is now available on the PC. IEEE 1394 supports the connection of up to 63 devices via one bus. IEEE 1394 supports high-bandwidth devices and thereby plays an important role in digital imaging and video teleconferencing, and as a bridge for connecting consumer electronics to computers. Like USB, IEEE 1394 supports Plug and Play, power management, and hot swapping.

Although you might wonder how to use and benefit from these new technologies, consider that CD drives were novelties when they were first introduced. Within a few years after their appearance in the marketplace, CD drives were standard components on new computers and became the primary medium for installing software. Now, DVD drives are replacing CD drives and are included with new computers. Within a few years even newer hardware technologies will become indispensable to the way you work and play.

Understanding Hardware Resource Assignments

Windows Vista can allocate four types of resources to hardware devices that require them:

- **Interrupt request (IRQ) resources** An interrupt is a signal transmitted by hardware or software to the processor or operating system for some type of service. Hardware devices and software constantly interrupt the processor and operating system with requests for specific services. An **interrupt request** might require the processor to perform a function, handle an error condition, or move data. For example, when you press a key on the keyboard, you generate a **hardware interrupt**, and the operating system interprets the scan code generated by the keystroke. When you issue a command to save a document, the software application you are using generates a **software interrupt** for recording the contents of the file on disk. An interrupt request from a hardware device is transmitted to the processor via an IRQ hardware line. Typically, each hardware device that requires an IRQ line is assigned its own line. In the past, the number of available IRQs was a limiting factor in adding new hardware to a computer. That's why it's becoming increasingly important to purchase computers with USB and IEEE 1394 ports and devices because they bypass this limitation by supporting more than one device on the same port.
- **Input/Output (I/O) resources** Each hardware device that handles I/O, such as ports and disk drives, must have a unique address in memory, a resource called **Input/Output (I/O) resources** or an **I/O address**. This I/O address uniquely identifies a hardware device and serves as a channel for communicating with the device.
- **Direct Memory Access (DMA) resources** A channel you use to transfer data between two devices without the intervention of the processor is called a **Direct Memory Access channel** and the resources for this channel are called **Direct Memory Access resources**. For example, by using a DMA channel, your computer can transfer data from a hard disk drive into system memory without the processor. If the processor handles the data transfer, the overall process is much slower than a direct transfer to memory. DMA channels are obviously important in the transfer of video, audio, and graphics data.

- **Memory resources** Specific regions of memory allocated to a hardware device are called **memory resources**. For example, one or more regions of memory might be designated for the video display adapter that generates the image you see on the monitor. These memory resources are identified as a range of memory addresses assigned to a device.

Windows Vista assigns hardware resources to hardware devices during booting or when the device is attached to the computer. Next, you are going to view an important Windows tool for managing hardware—Device Manager.

Using Device Manager

Device Manager provides an important source of information about the hardware components on a computer and shows the configuration settings that Windows Vista uses for both Plug and Play and legacy devices. After you open Device Manager, it displays a **hardware tree** that identifies the classes of hardware (such as video display adapters) installed on your computer. You can use Device Manager to document hardware settings, verify the installation of a hardware device, check for hardware conflicts, troubleshoot hardware problems, change the configuration of a hardware device, and update device drivers for a hardware device.

Changing a configuration setting in Device Manager might create a conflict with another hardware device. A **hardware conflict**, **device conflict**, or **resource conflict** occurs when two hardware devices attempt to share the same resource. When a hardware conflict exists, one or both devices might not work properly, or at all. Worse yet, the computer might become unstable or not function at all. Before you examine or make changes to the hardware configuration settings in Device Manager, you should document the current hardware configuration settings that you intend to change and make sure that you understand how changes to your computer's configuration will affect your computer's operation.

Remy depends on Device Manager to provide him with important information about the hardware configuration of an employee's computer. Also, if an employee experiences a problem with a hardware device, the first tool Remy turns to is Device Manager. To illustrate how Device Manager is automatically updated when you make hardware changes to a computer, Remy asks you to remove your flash drive, open Device Manager, and then reattach the flash drive.

The instructions in the tutorial steps request that you view, but not change, hardware configuration settings in Device Manager. Only users with expert knowledge of computer hardware and hardware configuration settings should change resource settings for hardware devices. Also, you must provide Administrator credentials before you can examine or make changes to resource settings in Device Manager.

To open Device Manager and view information about hardware devices:

1. If necessary, display the Computer icon on the desktop, switch your computer to single-click activation (or Web style), and activate the option for displaying file extensions.
2. If your flash drive is already attached to the computer you are using, save, and then close your open files and applications, click the **Safely Remove Hardware** icon in the notification area of the taskbar, select the option for removing your flash drive, and after Windows Vista displays a Safe to Remove Hardware dialog box informing you that you can now safely remove the device, click the **OK** button, and then remove your flash drive.

3. Right-click the **Computer** desktop icon, and then click **Properties** on the shortcut menu. Windows Vista opens the System window.
4. Under Tasks, click the **Device Manager** link. Windows Vista switches to Secure Desktop Mode and displays a User Account Control dialog box.
5. In the User Account Control dialog box, click the **Continue** button if you are logged on under an Administrator account. If you are logged on under a Standard User account, enter the **password** for an Administrator account, and then click the **OK** button. Windows Vista opens Device Manager.
6. If necessary, adjust the height of the Device Manager window to display all the information in it. Windows Vista displays a hardware tree that identifies categories of hardware components installed on your computer, as shown in Figure 12-1. This view is referred to as "Devices by type." Each device type category contains one or more hardware devices. Hardware devices include the computer itself, peripherals (external hardware devices), adapters and controllers connected to the system board, ports, and components on the system board itself. Some of your hardware categories will differ.

   Trouble? If Device Manager does not display devices by type, click View on the menu bar, and then click "Devices by type."

Figure 12-1 Viewing hardware tree categories in Device Manager

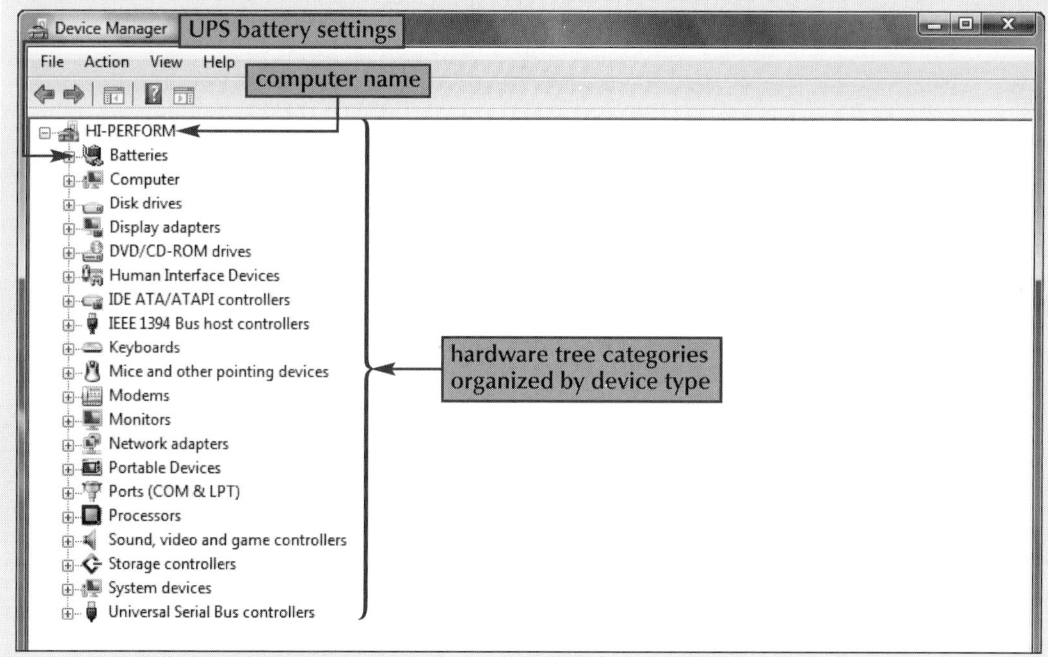

7. Keep the Device Manager window open for the next set of tutorial steps.

After you open Device Manager, you can view properties of a hardware device and determine whether the device is working properly. For example, the video display adapter is not only a standard hardware component, but also takes on added importance in Windows Vista by providing support for Windows Aero. If you are having a problem with Windows Aero features, you can examine Windows Aero display settings and also examine the video display adapter properties in Device Manager.

Remy asks you to examine properties of your video display adapter.

Tip

You can also double-click a device type category to expand the category.

To view properties of the display adapter:

1. Click the **Expand View** button ⊞ to the left of the Display adapters category. Windows Vista expands the category to show the type of display adapter used on your computer. On the computer used for Figure 12-2, Device Manager identifies the display adapter as an NVIDIA GeForce 7900 GTX display adapter. Your display adapter will differ.

Figure 12-2 Viewing the Display adapters category

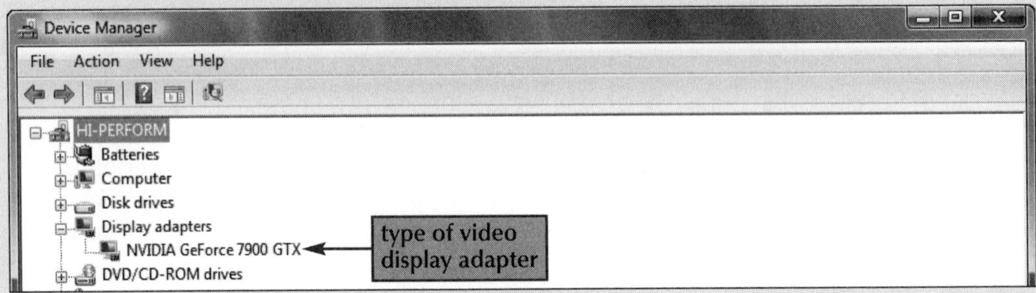

Tip

You can also right-click the device, and then click Properties, or click the device, and then click the Properties button on the Device Manager toolbar.

2. Double-click your **display adapter type**. Device Manager opens a Properties dialog box for your display adapter type. On the computer used for Figure 12-3, Device Manager opens an NVIDIA GeForce 7900 GTX Properties dialog box. Each hardware device has one or more property sheets. The General property sheet, common to all hardware devices, identifies the device type, the manufacturer (if known), and the location of the device. The most important information on this property sheet is shown in the Device status box. If there are no problems with the hardware device, Device Manager reports that "This device is working properly." If there is a hardware problem or conflict, Device Manager briefly describes the problem, displays a problem code, and suggests a solution. Microsoft technical support uses the problem code to troubleshoot your hardware problem.

Figure 12-3 Viewing properties of a video display adapter

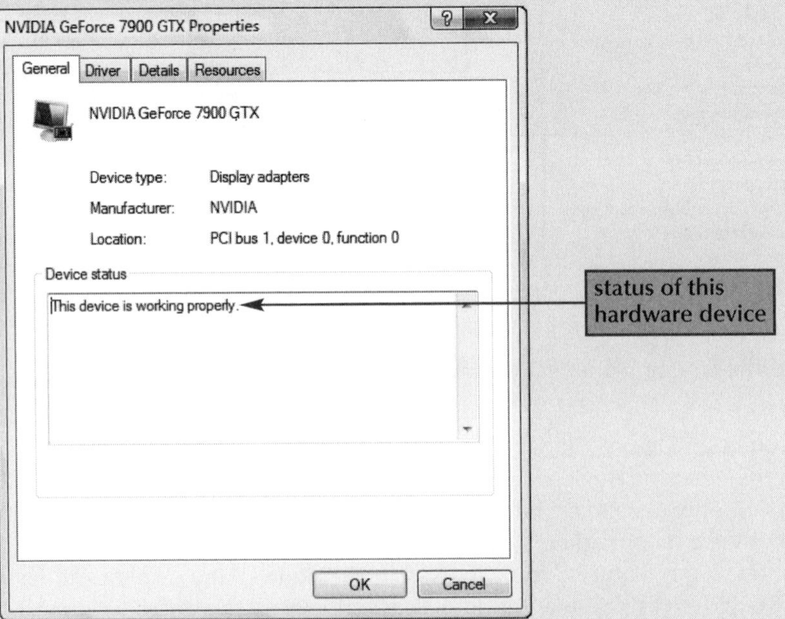

3. Click the **Driver** tab. Device Manager provides information about the driver used for this device, including the driver version and whether the driver is digitally signed and therefore certified for use with Windows Vista. See Figure 12-4. Your details will differ. You can click the Driver Details button to view information about the device drivers for this hardware device. The Update Driver button opens the Update Driver Software dialog box, which then steps you through the process of checking online for an update to the device driver. If you install a new driver, and then discover that it doesn't work or that it creates a problem on your computer, you can click the Roll Back Driver button to restore the previously used device driver. This option is easier than using System Restore and it makes fewer changes to your computer system than a restore point. You can click the Uninstall button to remove the hardware device and the Disable button to disable the device.

Figure 12-4 Viewing the Driver property sheet for a video display adapter

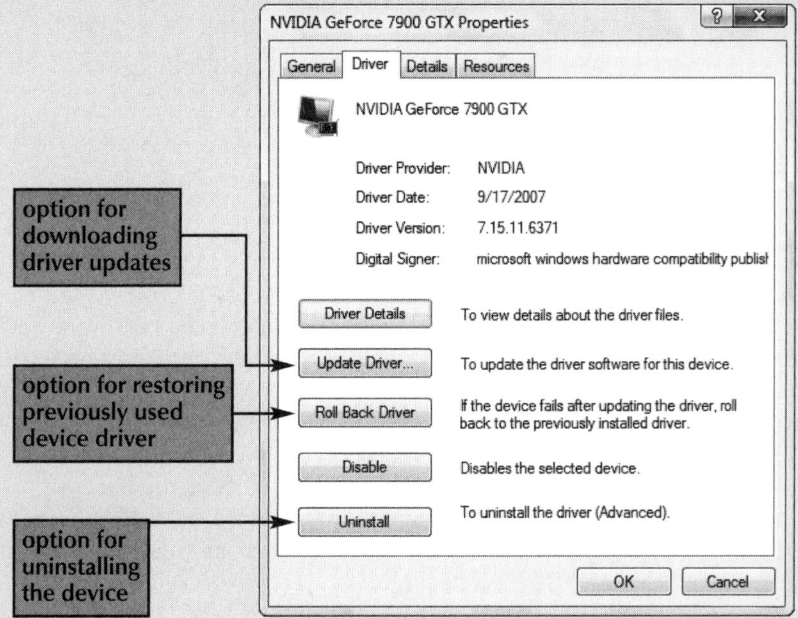

4. Click the **Driver Details** button. In the Driver File Details dialog box, Windows Vista displays the name of the driver files used for this hardware device. On the computer used for Figure 12-5, Device Manager lists 39 driver files for the video display adapter. If you select a driver file in the Driver files box, Device Manager provides information on the provider, file version, copyright, and digital signer (if known). The digital signer is "Microsoft Windows Hardware Compatibility," indicating that the drivers were tested for compatibility with Windows Vista. Your details will differ.

Figure 12-5 **Viewing details on driver files for a video display adapter**

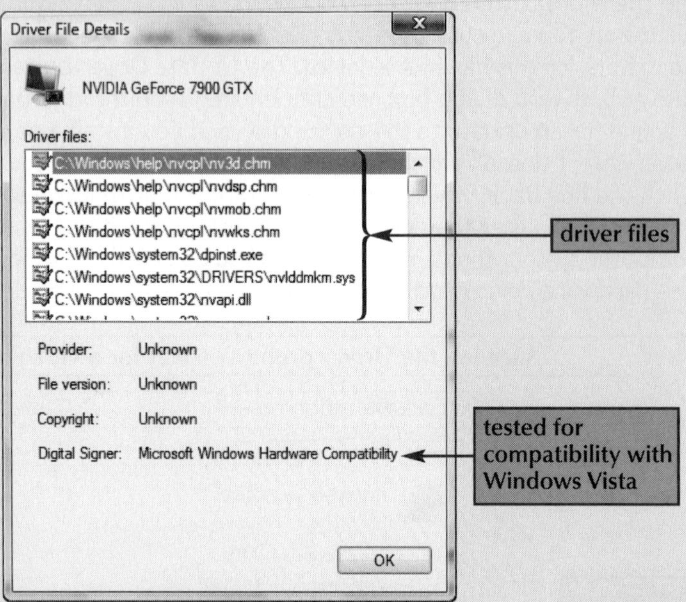

5. Click the **OK** button to close the Driver File Details dialog box, and then click the **Resources** tab. Under Resource settings on the Resources property sheet, Windows Vista lists the types of resources assigned to a specific hardware device. On the computer used for Figure 12-6 Device Manager lists eight resource settings used by this video display adapter—1 IRQ, 4 Memory Ranges, and 3 I/O Ranges (although not all are visible in the figure). Your settings may differ. A check mark in the "Use automatic settings" check box indicates that Windows Vista automatically assigns resource settings to this hardware device, which is the best approach for configuring a hardware device. If you configure a device manually, you create a forced configuration, and Windows Vista must always use the setting you specify. That provides Windows Vista less flexibility for adjusting device resources and configurations when you install a new hardware device. The most important information in the Resources property sheet is in the Conflicting device list box. Device Manager either reports no conflicts with other hardware devices, or it identifies the devices and the resource or resources involved in the hardware conflict.

Figure 12-6 Viewing hardware resources for the video display adapter

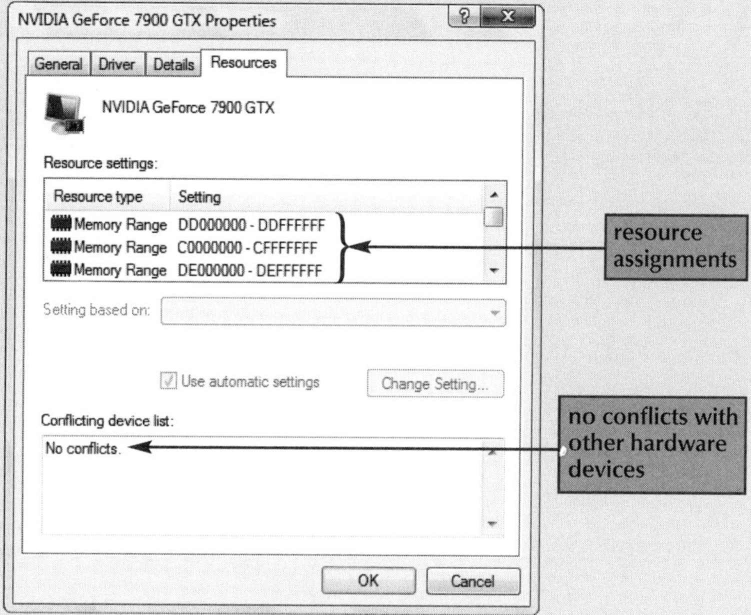

6. Click the **Cancel** button to close the Properties dialog box for your video display adapter without inadvertently making changes to your hardware configuration settings.
7. Click the **Collapse View** button ⊟ to the left of the Display adapters category.
8. Keep the Device Manager window open for the next set of tutorial steps.

Remy notes that some hardware devices, such as the mouse and keyboard, might have a Power Management property sheet where you can specify whether the device wakes up a computer from a sleep state. You decide to examine that property sheet.

To examine the mouse's Power Management property sheet:

1. Click the **Expand View** button ⊞ to the left of the Mice and other pointing devices category, double-click your **mouse device**, and then click the **Power Management** tab. On the Power Management property sheet for the computer used for Figure 12-7, Device Manager shows that you can set the HID-compliant mouse device on this computer to wake the computer from a sleep state. As noted earlier, HID stands for Human Interface Device (a broad category of input devices). For other hardware devices, such as a network adapter, there may be an option on the Power Management property sheet for Windows Vista to turn off the hardware device in order to save power.

   Trouble? If your mouse Properties dialog box does not have a Power Management property sheet, read the steps in this section and examine the figure, but do not keystroke the steps.

Figure 12-7 Viewing power management options for a mouse

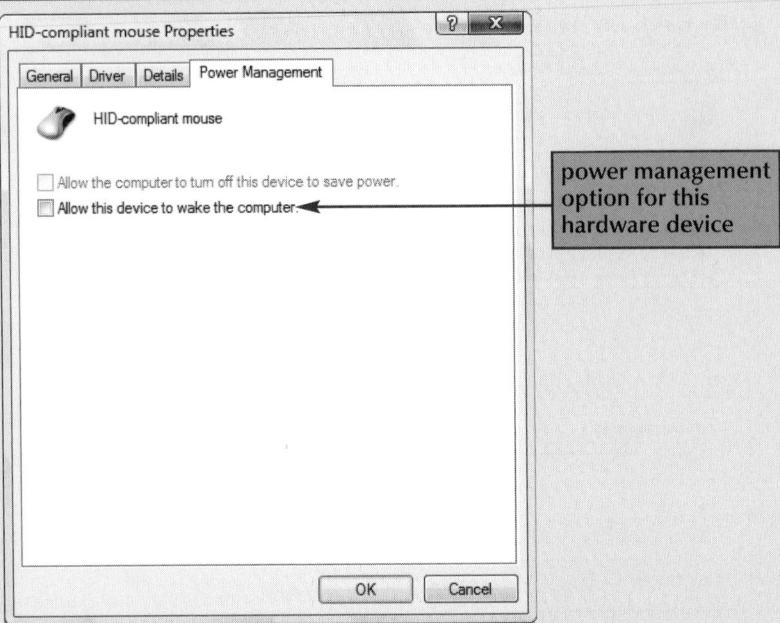

2. Click the **Cancel** button to close the Properties dialog box for your mouse without inadvertently making changes to your mouse hardware configuration settings.
3. Click the **Collapse View** button ⊟ to the left of the Mice and other pointing devices category.
4. Keep the Device Manager window open for the next set of tutorial steps.

You can also examine write-caching policies for a flash drive. **Write caching** refers to the process of holding changed data in the system cache and then writing it to disk not immediately, but shortly thereafter. Write caching improves the performance of your computer ever so slightly by writing data to disk at periodic intervals.

Remy asks you to view the devices in the Disk drives category, and then attach your flash drive and watch Device Manager update the list of devices in the Disk drives category. He also asks you to examine your flash drive's write-caching properties.

To examine the Disk drives category:

1. Click the **Expand View** button ⊞ to the left of the Disk drives category. Windows Vista expands the category to show the type of disk drives used on your computer. On the computer used for Figure 12-8, Device Manager identifies six disk drives. The Seagate FreeAgentDesktop USB Device is an external hard disk drive used for backups. The four TEAC USB devices are media card readers for four different types of memory cards. The WDC SCSI Disk Device is a Western Digital hard disk drive that is misidentified as a SCSI Disk Device. It is actually a SATA (Serial ATA) device. Small Computer Systems Interface (SCSI, pronounced "skuzzy"), is an older, high-speed interface that enables a computer to transmit data to and from a hardware device. You can attach from 7 to 15 devices to a SCSI port. On the other hand, SATA (Serial ATA or Serial Advanced Technology Attachment) is a newer, high-speed interface for hard disk drives that is recommended for Windows Vista computers. Your drives may differ.

Figure 12-8 **Viewing disk drives in Device Manager**

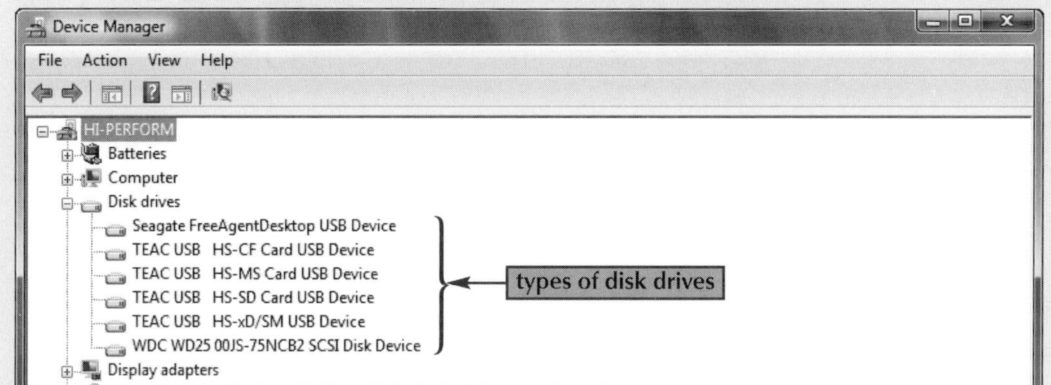

2. Read this step first, and then perform the operations. Attach your flash drive to the computer you are using and watch for changes in Device Manager. Device Manager updates the hardware tree and includes your flash drive in the Disk drives category. On the computer used for Figure 12-9, Device Manager identifies the flash drive as a PNY USB 2.0 FD USB Device. Windows might identify your flash drive as another model or as a Generic USB Flash Disk USB Device.

   Trouble? If Windows Vista opens a window for your flash drive, close that window.

Figure 12-9 **Device Manager updated to include flash drive**

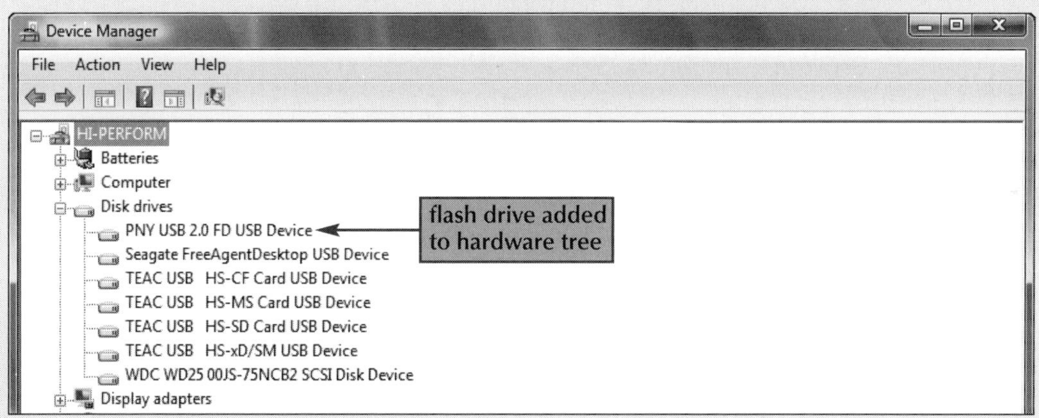

3. Under the Disk drives category, double-click your **flash drive**. Device Manager opens a Properties dialog box for your flash drive. On the General property sheet, Device Manager identifies the Device type, manufacturer (if known), and location. Device Manager should also report that the device is working properly.

4. Click the **Policies** tab. Device Manager reports on the setting for Write caching and Safe Removal. As shown on the Policies property sheet in Figure 12-10, the "Optimize for quick removal" setting disables write caching on the flash drive, and you can remove the flash drive without using the Safely Remove Hardware icon. The "Optimize for performance" setting enables write caching to improve disk (and system) performance. If you enable the Optimize for performance setting, and then remove a flash drive without first using Safely Remove Hardware, then data still stored in the system cache, but not yet written to disk, is lost. Likewise, you can lose data with write caching enabled if a power outage or hardware failure occurs. That's one reason you should always use the Safely Remove Hardware icon before removing a flash drive because Windows Vista writes the remainder of the changes to a document to disk before informing you that it's safe to remove your flash drive. Another reason for using the Safely Remove Hardware icon is to reduce the chance of damage to your flash drive.

Figure 12-10 Reviewing write caching policies

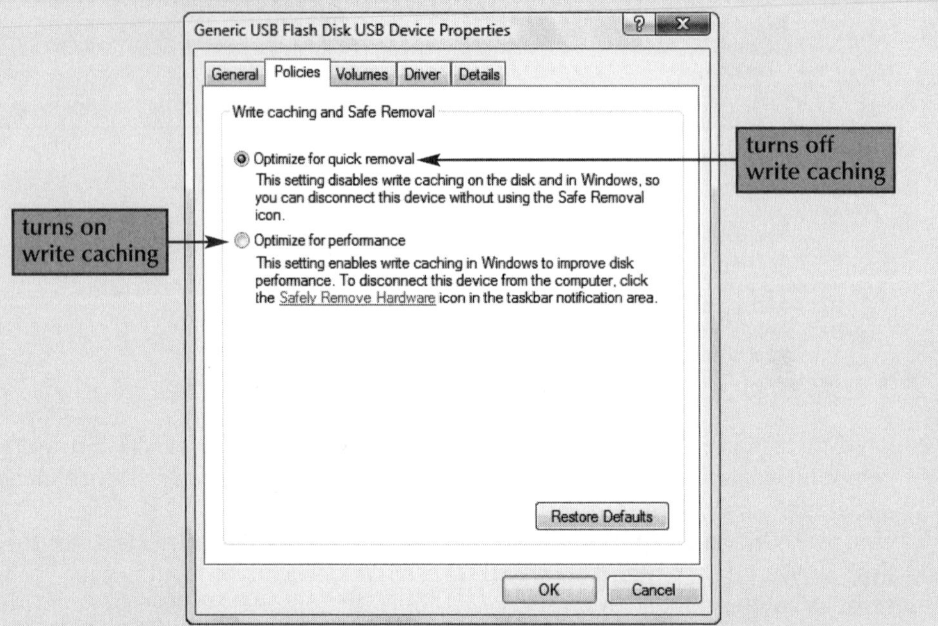

5. Click the **Driver** tab, and then click the **Driver Details** button. On the computer used for Figure 12-11, the flash drive has two driver files. Note that both driver files have a "sys" file extension—typical of files with device drivers. If Windows Vista highlights the first driver file, it also shows information on the driver's Provider, File version, Copyright, and Digital Signer.

Figure 12-11 Viewing drivers for a newly attached flash drive

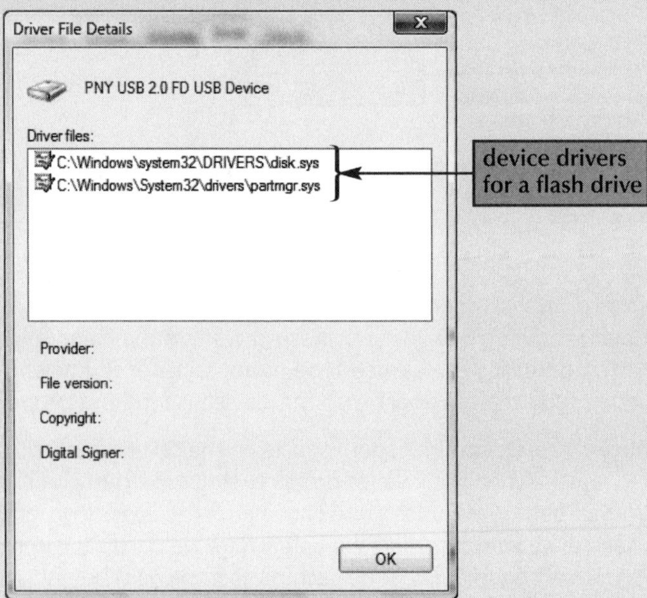

6. Click the **OK** button to close the Driver Details dialog box, and then click the **Cancel** button to close the Properties dialog box for your flash drive without inadvertently making any changes to hardware configuration settings for your flash drive.

7. Do not remove your flash drive, but do keep the Device Manager window open for the next set of tutorial steps.

Now, watch how Device Manager dynamically updates the hardware tree when you remove a flash drive.

To examine changes to the hardware tree when removing a flash drive:

1. Click the **Safely Remove Hardware** icon in the notification area of the taskbar, click the option for removing your flash drive, click the **OK** button in the Safe to Remove Hardware dialog box, *but do not remove your flash drive yet*. Device Manager updates the hardware tree and removes the flash drive from the Disk drives category.

   Trouble? If Windows Vista does not display a Safe to Remove Hardware dialog box, you may not be able to perform all the steps. Instead, continue to read the steps and then perform the next step that matches what you see on your computer.

2. If necessary, adjust your view of the hardware tree so that you can see the Universal Serial Bus controllers category. Notice that one of the listings for USB Mass Storage Device displays an error icon overlaying part of the icon for the hardware device to indicate a problem with the hardware device. See Figure 12-12.

Figure 12-12 Device Manager reports a device problem

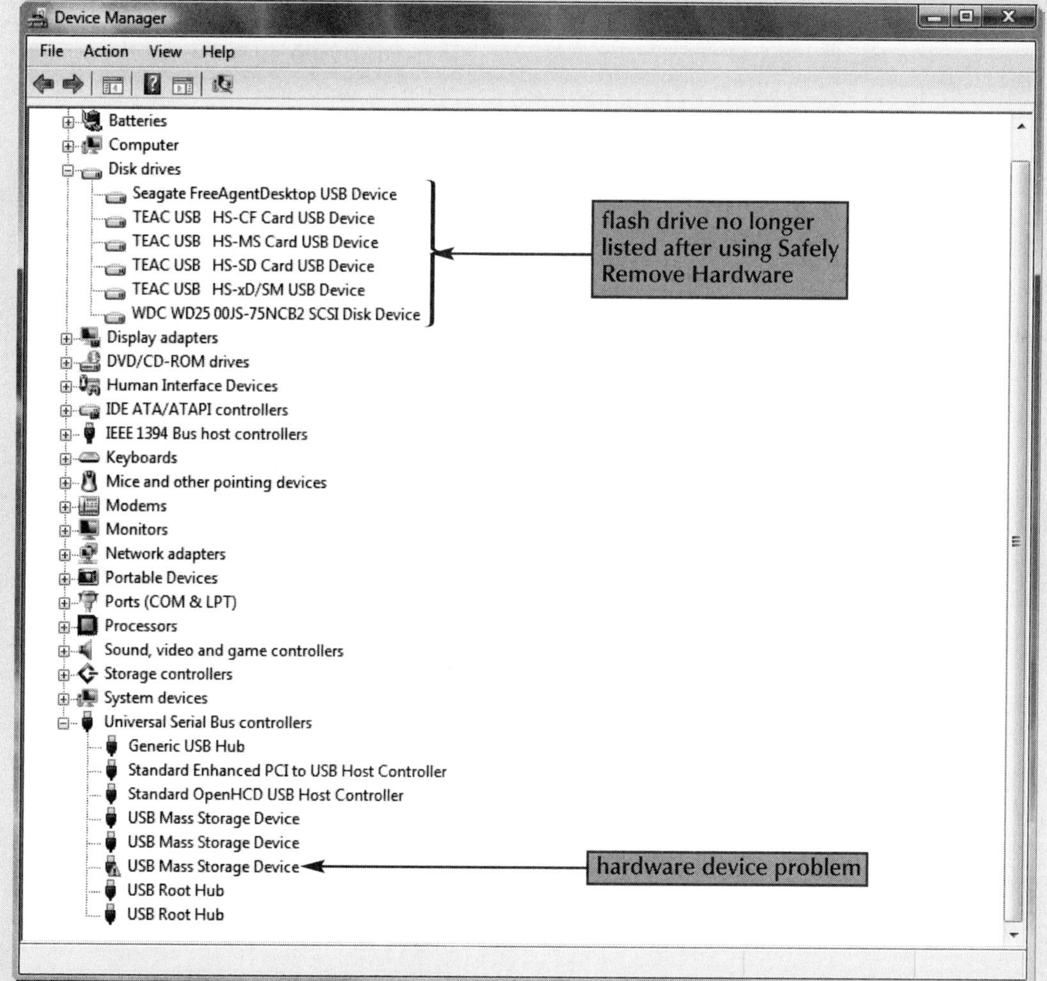

3. Double-click the **USB Mass Storage Device with the error** icon. In the Device status box on the General property sheet, Device Manager informs you that "Windows cannot use this hardware device because it has been prepared for 'safe removal,' but it has not been removed from the computer. (Code 47)". See Figure 12-13. Device Manager then informs you that you can fix this problem by unplugging the device from your computer and then plugging it in again. You can also use the "Check for solutions" button to send data about this device to Microsoft to find out if there is a solution available. In this case, the solution is clear.

Figure 12-13 **Viewing the status of a device with a hardware problem**

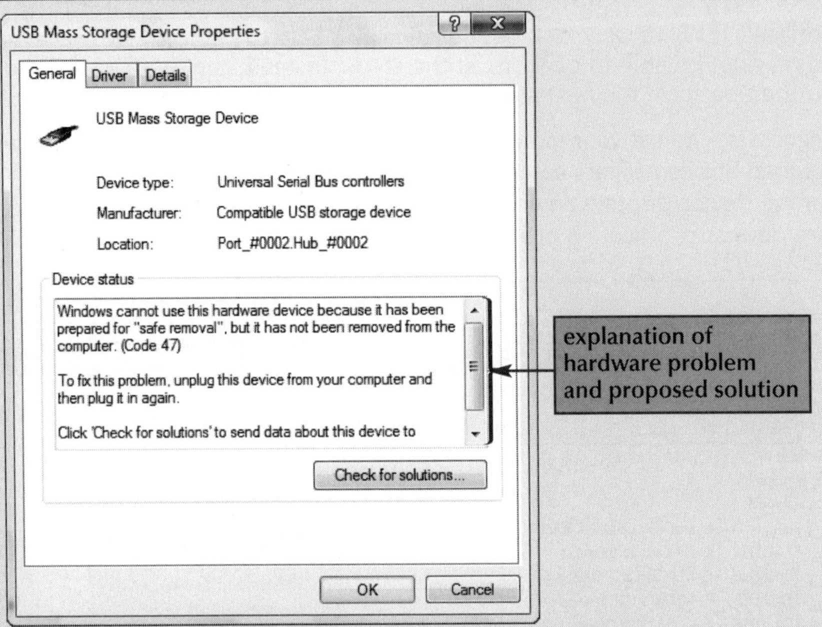

4. Leave the USB Mass Storage Device dialog box open, but remove the flash drive from your computer. Device Manager updates the information in this dialog box and informs you that "Currently, this hardware device is not connected to the computer. (Code 45)". See Figure 12-14. To correct this problem, it suggests that you reconnect this hardware device to your computer. Notice also that Windows Vista removed the USB Mass Storage Device listing with the error icon from the hardware tree.

Figure 12-14 Viewing the updated status of a device with a hardware problem

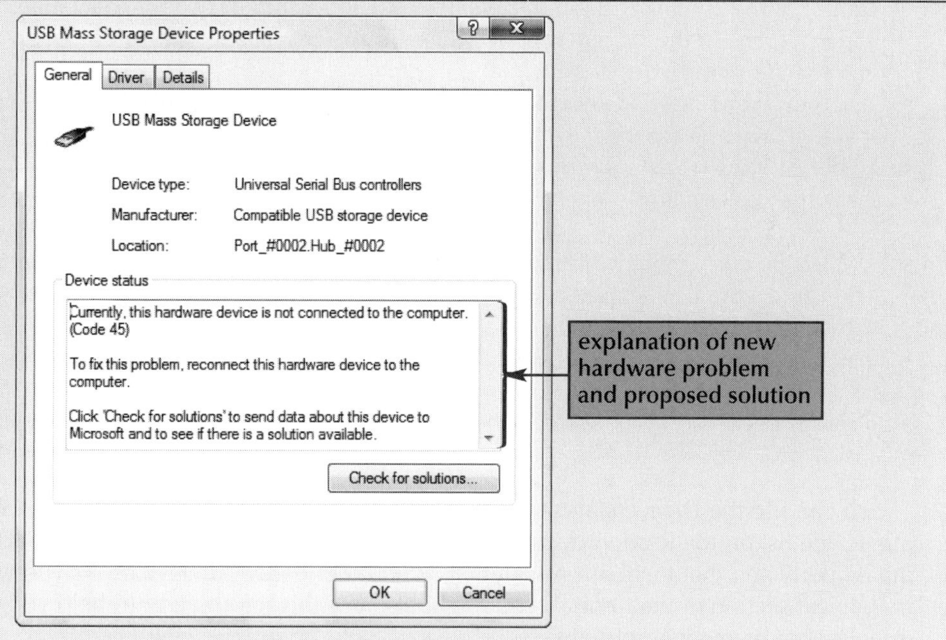

5. Click the **OK** button to close the USB Mass Storage Device dialog box.
6. Close the Device Manager window and then the System window.

Each **USB Host Controller** listed under the Serial Bus controllers category consists of one or more computer chips that identify a USB hardware device and its bandwidth requirements. The USB Host Controller also mediates the transfer of data to and from USB devices. An **Enhanced Host Controller Interface (EHCI)** is one that supports the use of second-generation Hi-Speed USB 2.0 devices with data transfer rates of 480 Mbps. This type of host controller also supports the use of first-generation Low-Speed and Full-Speed USB 1.x devices with data transfer rates of 1.5 and 12 Mbps. If you see "Enhanced" in a Host Controller name, then you know that your computer supports the use of USB 2.0 devices. The **Universal Host Controller Interface (UHCI)** and the **Open Host Controller Interface (OHCI)** support the use of first-generation USB 1.x devices with data transfer rates of 1.5 and 12 Mbps.

The **USB Root Hub** detects the attachment or removal of a USB device, manages power to USB devices, and handles the distribution of signals to USB devices attached to the same USB Root Hub. Each USB Root Hub contains one or more USB ports for attaching USB devices to your computer. If you examine properties of a USB Root Hub, the Power property sheet shows the number of attached devices, their power usage, and the number of available ports. The USB Root Hub's Advanced property sheet shows whether it is operating at Hi-Speed (480 Mbps) or Full-Speed (12 Mbps).

Reference Window | Viewing Device Properties

- Right-click the Computer desktop icon, or right-click Computer on the Start menu, click Properties, and in the System window, click the Device Manager link under Tasks, and then provide Administrator credentials.
- Click the Expand View box next to the hardware device type category that contains the device you want to examine.
- Double-click the hardware device name to view its properties.
- Check the Device status section on the General property sheet to determine if the device is working properly.
- Click the Resources tab (if available) to view information on a device's resource settings and examine the Conflicting device list to determine if there are any hardware conflicts with other devices.
- Click the Drivers tab and use the Roll Back Driver button if you want to restore the previously used device driver.
- Close the device's Properties dialog box, and then close the Device Manager window.

You can use the Device status section on the General property sheet and the Conflicting device list on the Resources property sheet to verify that a hardware device is working properly and that there are no conflicts with other hardware devices. As you will see in the next section of the tutorial, you might also use this information to help you troubleshoot hardware problems.

As you will see later when you examine how to troubleshoot hardware conflicts, resources are a precious commodity, and Windows Vista attempts to assign resources without creating hardware conflicts. In the past, the limited number of IRQs has been the primary source of problems for PC users who wanted to add more hardware devices than their computer could support. As noted earlier, newer hardware technologies and Windows Vista's support for those newer hardware technologies overcomes these limitations.

Another valuable use of Device Manager is to identify the exact models of the hardware devices on your computer (information that you might find difficult to locate using other techniques).

Troubleshooting Hardware Problems

Remy relies on Device Manager to help him troubleshoot hardware configuration problems and reconfigure devices so they do not conflict with each other. At your next meeting with him, he describes how to recognize and troubleshoot hardware conflicts with Device Manager.

If there is a problem with the configuration of a hardware device, Windows Vista expands that portion of the hardware tree category where the problem occurs, shows the configured hardware devices within the category, and then displays an error icon over the hardware device icon to identify a problem.

Device Manager detects three types of hardware problems:

- **Disabled device** If a device is disabled for some reason, Windows Vista displays an icon with a black arrow pointing down against a white background in a circle overlaying part of the icon for the hardware device to indicate that the hardware device has been disabled for some reason. On the computer used for Figure 12-15, Windows Vista detected the presence of the DVD drive; however, it is not included in the configuration of the computer because it is disabled.

Figure 12-15 Device Manager reports a problem with a disabled device

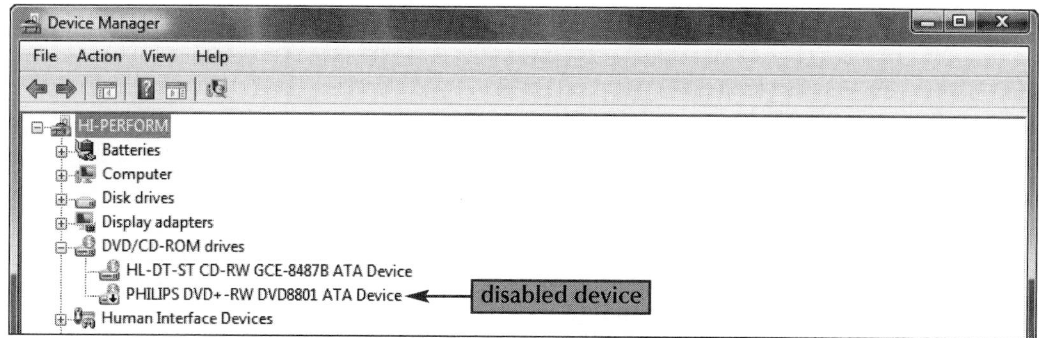

To correct this problem, open Device Manager, double-click the disabled hardware device, and then check the Device status section on the General property sheet for information about the problem. See Figure 12-16. Windows Vista reports that the device is disabled and includes a hardware code (Code 22) for Microsoft support technicians to use in troubleshooting the problem. If you see a "Check for solutions" button, then you can click that button to send a Windows Error Report to Microsoft. If a device is disabled, then Windows Vista does not load the device drivers for the hardware device.

Figure 12-16 Viewing the status of a disabled device

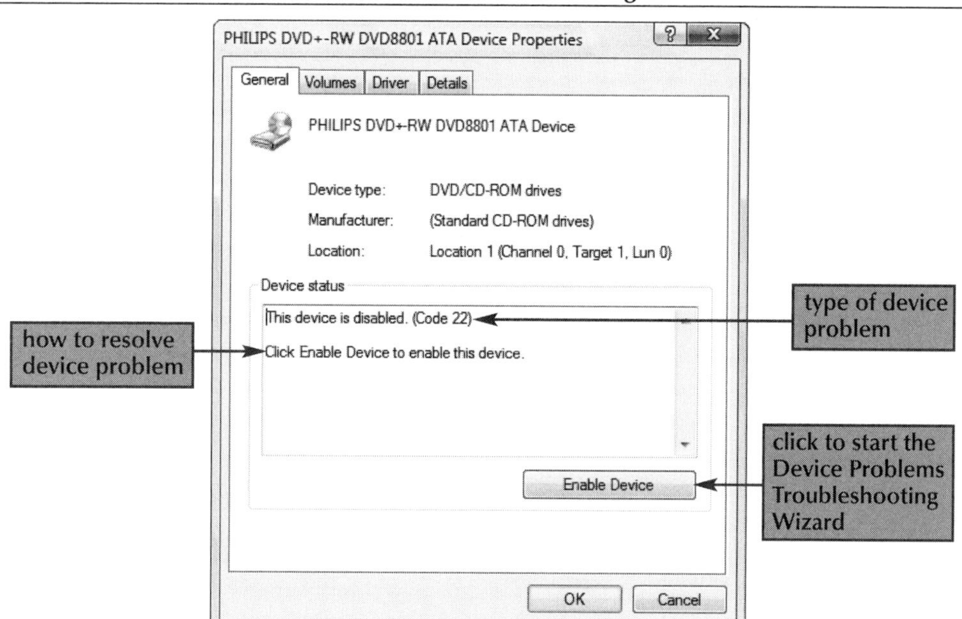

Windows Vista instructs you to click the Enable Device button if you want to include the device as part of the system's configuration. If you click the Enable Device button, Windows Vista opens the Device Problems Troubleshooting Wizard and explains why a device might be disabled. As shown in Figure 12-17, the device might not be working properly, or it might be causing a resource conflict.

Figure 12-17 Using the Device Problems Troubleshooting Wizard

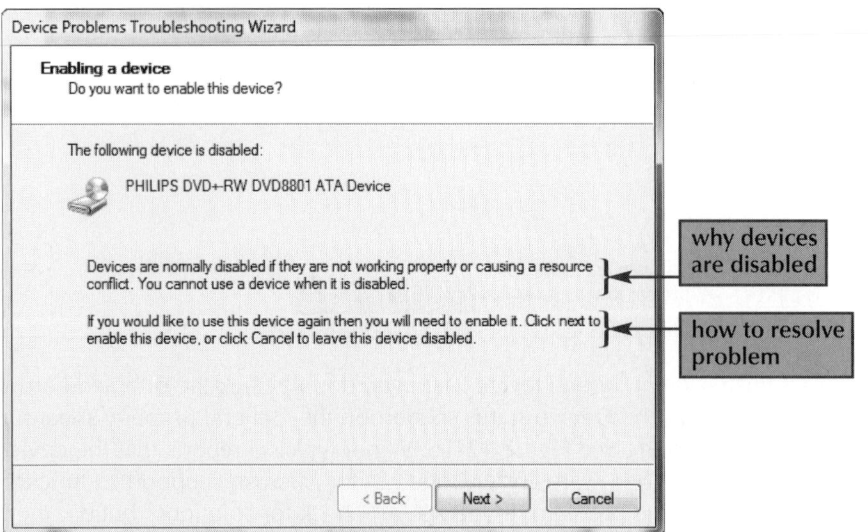

If you click the Next button, the Device Problems Troubleshooting Wizard tells you that it successfully enabled the device, as shown in Figure 12-18.

Figure 12-18 Device successfully enabled

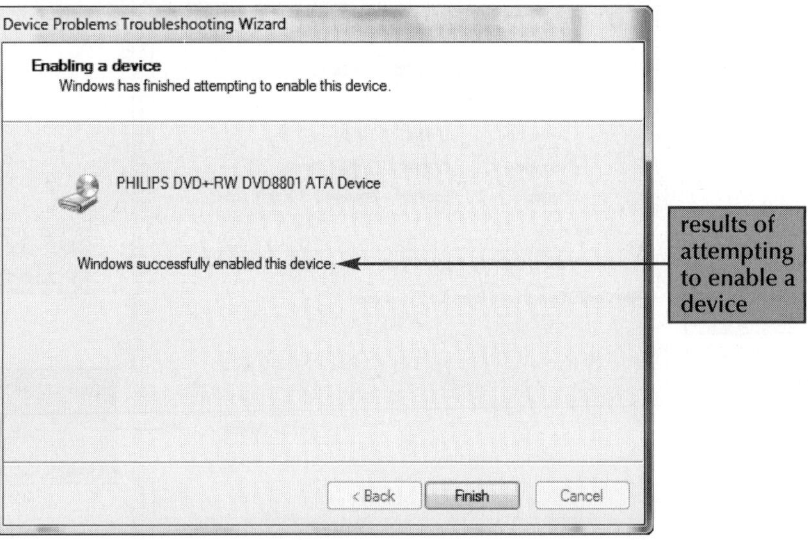

Tip

You can also right-click a disabled device in the Device Manager hardware tree, and then click Enable.

After you click the Finish button, Windows Vista closes the Device Problems Troubleshooting Wizard and returns you to the Properties dialog box for the hardware device. After you close the hardware device's Properties dialog box, Windows Vista updates Device Manager and removes the error icon that indicated a problem with the device. See Figure 12-19.

Figure 12-19 DVD device no longer disabled

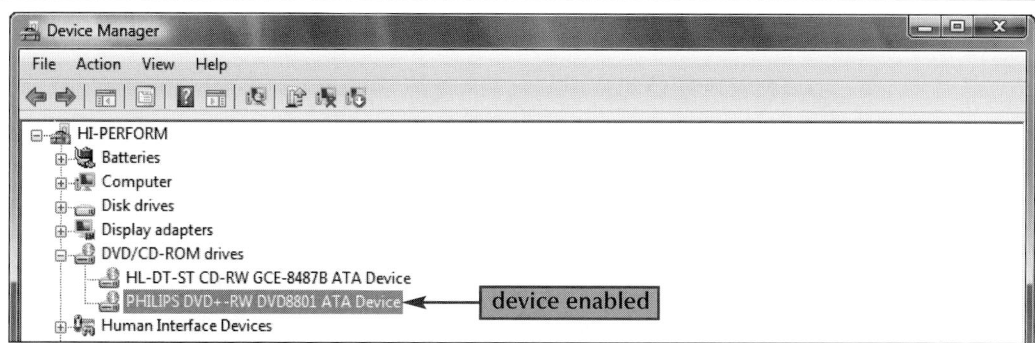

- **Resource conflict** Thanks to the widespread use of USB and IEEE 1394 hardware devices, a far less frequent type of problem that you might encounter is a **resource conflict**—one in which two hardware devices use the same resource, such as the same IRQ or I/O address. If there is a resource conflict, then Device Manager displays an error icon with a black exclamation mark against the background of a yellow triangle over the hardware device icon to identify the problem. If you then check the Conflicting device list on the Resources property sheet for that device, Device Manager identifies the names of the devices and the resources that are causing the conflict. As noted earlier, a check mark in the "Use automatic settings" check box on the Resources property sheet means that Windows Vista chooses resource settings for the hardware device. If you remove the check mark, you can manually configure the device by choosing another combination of resource settings from the "Setting based on" list box. The configuration settings for a hardware device will include "Current configuration" and will also include one or more other configurations identified by names, such as "Basic configuration 0000," "Basic configuration 0001," and "Basic configuration 0002." An example of these settings is shown in Figure 12-20 for Communications Port (COM1). These basic configurations are combinations of resource settings that work for this particular hardware device. Other devices will have different combinations of configuration settings. Choosing another combination of configuration settings might resolve the conflict. After you select another combination of configuration settings, Device Manager updates the Conflicting device list and might report that the new configuration creates no conflicts. If you manually configure resources for a hardware device, you are creating a **forced hardware configuration**, and Windows Vista has less flexibility in assigning resources to other devices that you might later add to your computer. Furthermore, this option is not available for most devices and is not recommended because it may affect the performance of your computer.

Figure 12-20 Viewing configuration options for a hardware device

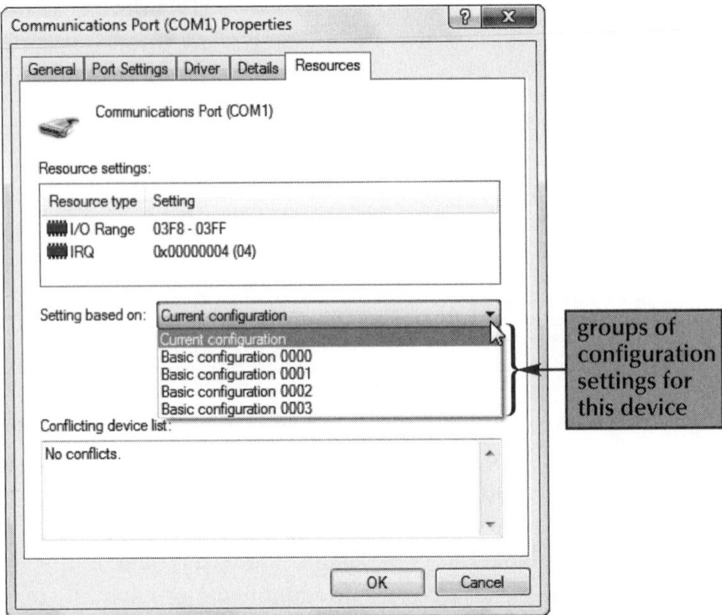

- **Unknown device** Windows Vista might detect a hardware device but identify it as an **Unknown device** and place it in an Other Devices category. The Other Devices icon also includes an icon containing a white circle with a blue question mark, as shown in Figure 12-21. In this example, Windows Vista displays a warning icon with a black exclamation mark against a yellow background overlaying part of the icon for the hardware device. Windows Vista identified the hardware device as an EPSON Scanner because it's a Plug and Play device, but placed it in an Other devices category. Windows Vista also displays a Found New Hardware dialog box informing you of the nature of the problem and providing you with three options. The Found New Hardware Wizard can guide you through the process of locating and installing driver software (the recommended option), it can ask you again later when you attach the device or log on, or you can choose to not display this message again (in which case, the device will not function). If Windows Vista detects a device, but does not have the proper device drivers, you can resolve this problem by identifying the device using whatever information Windows Vista provides and by then installing updated device drivers and updated software for the hardware device. That might mean that you have to go to the manufacturer's Web site and specifically locate Windows Vista device drivers for the exact model of the hardware device that you have.

Found New Hardware Wizard dialog box

Figure 12-21

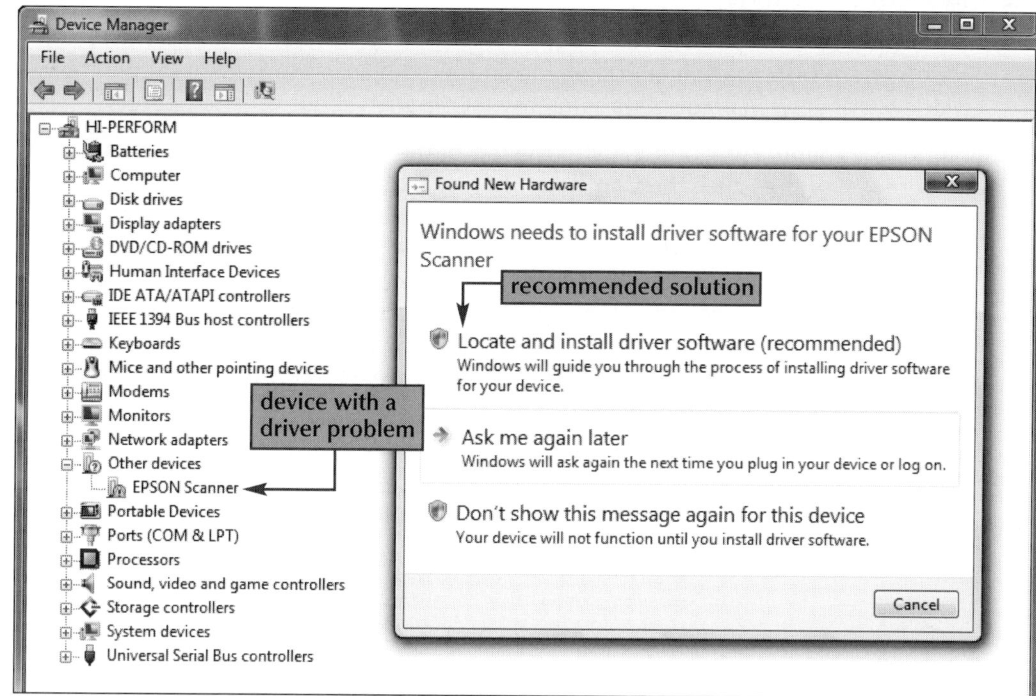

Tip

You can also use the Windows Vista Upgrade Advisor to check for hardware problems before and after upgrading to Windows Vista.

Make sure the computer contains hardware devices that are supported by Windows Vista. You might have to do some research and determine whether Windows Vista supports the hardware devices you want to use in that computer, but the effort saves you time later and reduces troubleshooting problems.

Checking Device Manager on a New Computer | InSight

You can use Device Manager in yet another way. Before you buy a computer on display in a store, open Device Manager on the computer and check the hardware configuration. If Windows Vista reports a hardware conflict, don't buy that computer. If you do purchase it, you might find it difficult to resolve the problem, or your computer might not perform optimally. If you purchase a computer online, check Device Manager immediately after you receive the computer while the computer is under warranty. You may be able to return the computer within a short time period for a full refund.

Using System Information

You can use System Information to verify and supplement the information shown in Device Manager. You might be able to pick up additional clues that help you troubleshoot problems on your computer or enhance your understanding of its configuration.

In addition to Device Manager, Remy suggests you use the System Information utility to provide more detailed information on hardware devices in your computer.

To use System Information to view information on hardware configuration settings:

Tip

You can also press the Windows logo key, type MSINFO32 in the Search box, and then press the Enter key.

1. On the Start menu, point to **All Programs**, click **Accessories**, click **System Tools**, click **System Information**, and then maximize or enlarge the System Information window. Windows Vista displays summary information about your computer.
2. Click the **Expand View** button ⊞ to the left of the Hardware Resources node (or category), and then click the **Conflicts/Sharing** category. System Information shows which devices share specific types of resources or conflict with other devices. Note that on the computer used for Figure 12-22, devices share I/O ports, memory addresses, and IRQs. Your computer's configuration will differ. The sharing of resources does not necessarily indicate a problem because Windows can dynamically assign and reassign device resources. If Device Manager does indicate a problem with a device, and if that device shares a resource with another device, the resource sharing might be the source of the problem.

Figure 12-22 Viewing shared resources in System Information

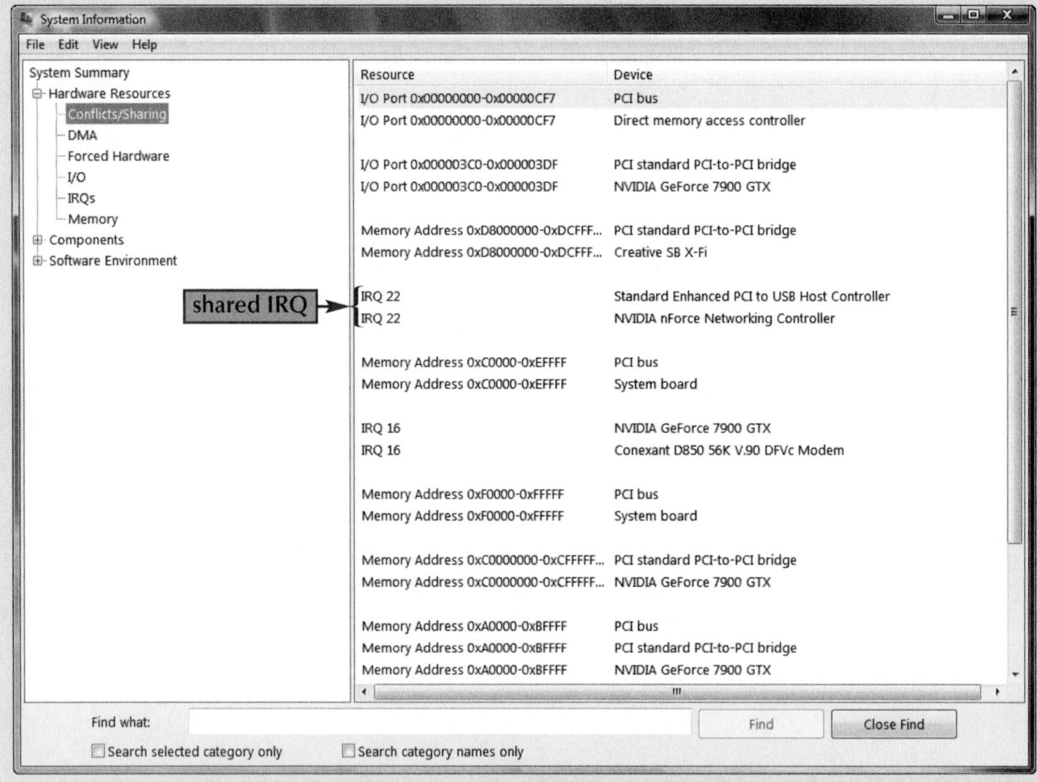

3. Click the **Forced Hardware** category. Here, System Information lists manually configured devices (if any) that require specific resources to function. When you manually configure a device, even a Plug and Play device, you assign specific resources to it; as a result, Windows Vista has less flexibility in finding the right mix of resource assignments that work for all your other hardware devices and newer devices that you add later. If you need to troubleshoot resource conflicts on a computer, you can check this category to quickly find out which devices are manually configured.
4. Click the **DMA** category to display the DMA channels assigned to devices and view their status. See Figure 12-23. If Windows Vista reports a problem in the Status column, you can use Device Manager to locate and troubleshoot the problem.

Figure 12-23 Viewing DMA resource assignments

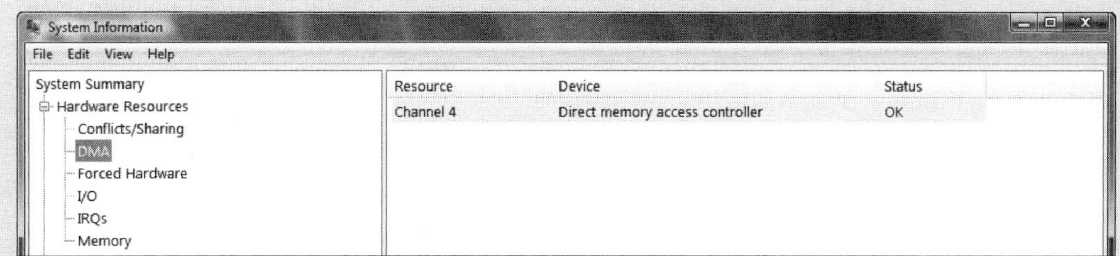

5. Click the **I/O** category to display the I/O resources assigned to devices and view their status. On the computer used for Figure 12-24, all I/O resource assignments are listed as "OK." Your I/O resource assignments may differ. Again, if there is a sharing conflict, you turn to Device Manager.

Figure 12-24 Viewing I/O resource assignments

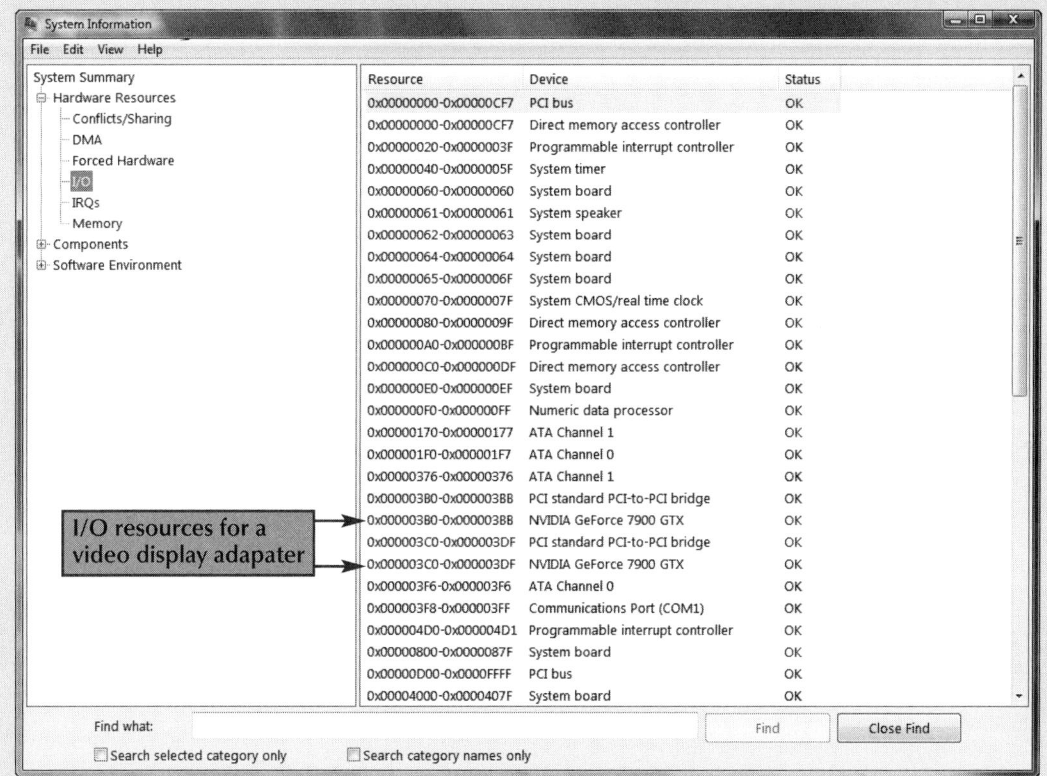

6. Click the **IRQs** category to display the IRQ resource assignments and view their status. See Figure 12-25. The first 24 IRQs (from IRQ 0 through IRQ 23) are assigned to hardware devices on your computer that need an IRQ. In some cases, Windows Vista might be able to assign IRQs dynamically; in other words, on an as-needed basis.

Figure 12-25 **Viewing IRQ resource assignments**

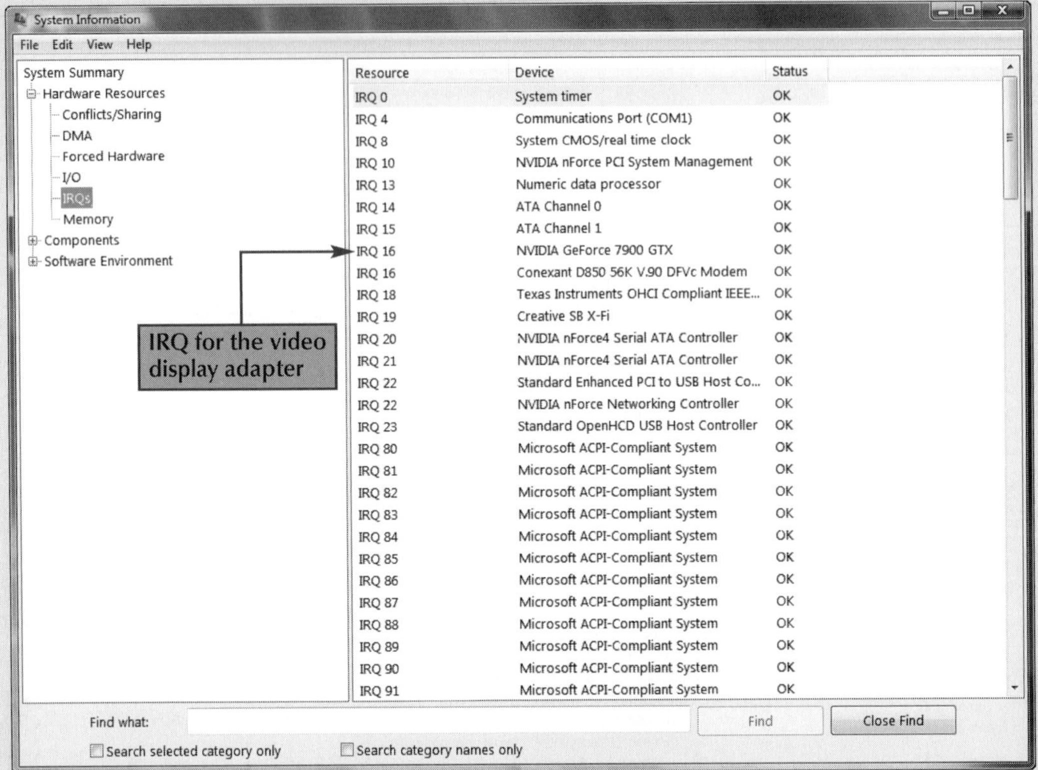

7. Click the **Memory** category to display the memory resources assigned to devices and view their status. See Figure 12-26. If two devices are configured to use the same memory address range, you would use Device Manager to identify and troubleshoot the problem.

Figure 12-26 Viewing Memory resource assignments

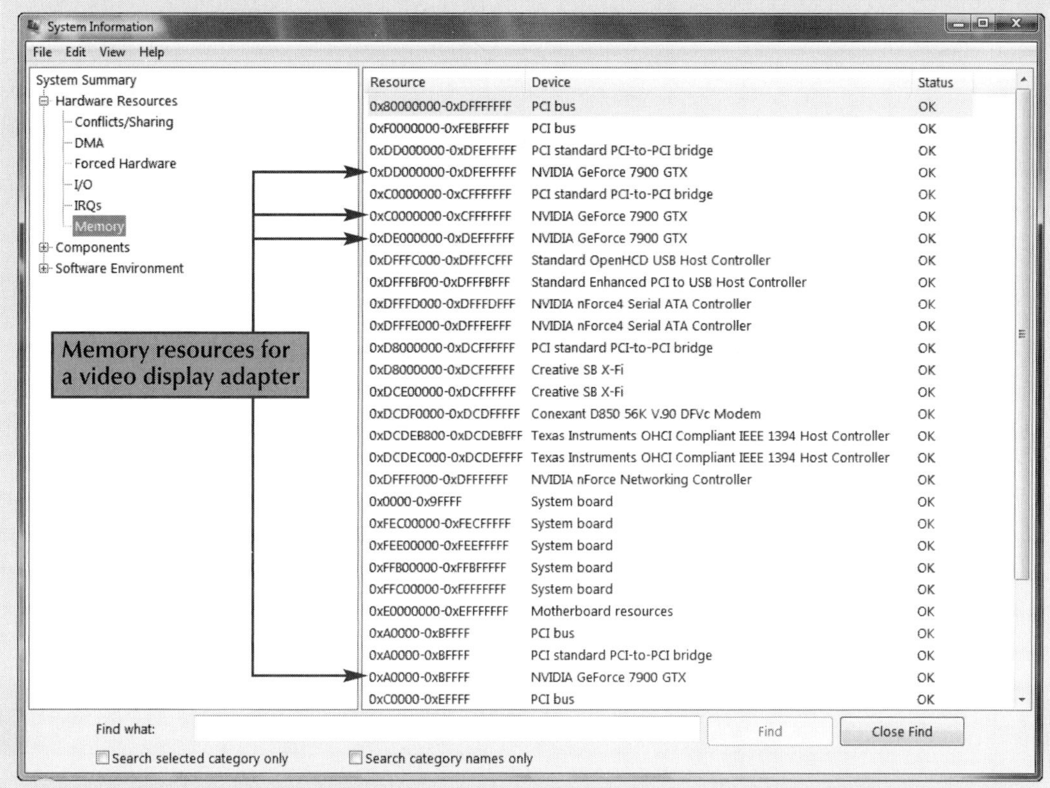

8. Click the **Expand View** button ⊞ to the left of the Components category, and then click **Problem Devices**. System Information provides information on any devices that are not properly configured and identifies the problem in the Error Code column (such as "The device is disabled."). If a problem exists, you would attempt to resolve it with Device Manager.
9. Close the System Information window.

As noted in Tutorial 8, you can use the File menu to print all of the system data (which might be extensive), a selected category and its subcategories, or even a range of pages of the system data. You can also save system data for the entire system or for a category to a text file.

Although Device Manager is the tool you are most likely to use when troubleshooting hardware, System Information can provide more details about your computer configuration and verify the status of resource assignments.

Reference Window | Using System Information to Identify Hardware Problems

- On the Start menu, point to All Programs, click Accessories, click System Tools, and then click System Information. (Or press the Windows Logo key, type MSINFO32 in the Search box, and then press the Enter key.)
- Click the Expand View button to the left of the Hardware Resources category, and then click Conflicts/Sharing to examine information on shared resources and potential resource conflicts.
- Using the same approach, examine the DMA, I/O, IRQs, and Memory categories to view resource assignments and verify the status of those assignments.
- Click the Expand View button to the left of the Components category, and then click Problem Devices to examine information on forced hardware configuration problems identified by Windows Vista.
- If you discover a problem, use Device Manager to locate and troubleshoot that problem, and consider the possible need for an updated device driver.
- Close the System Information window.

System Information not only provides a broad spectrum of information about your computer system, but it also identifies shared devices, hardware conflicts, forced hardware configurations, and problem devices. When troubleshooting a hardware problem, you can use both Device Manager and the System Information utility to provide the data you need to analyze and resolve the problem.

Review | Session 12.1 Quick Check

1. Windows Vista can automatically detect and configure a(n) ________________ hardware device.
2. ________________ is an external, bidirectional, Plug and Play bus for connecting up to 127 high speed serial devices via one port on your computer while ________________ supports up to 63 devices via one bus.
3. ________________ refers to the amount of data that can be transmitted over a device in a fixed amount of time.
4. You can use ________________ to document hardware settings, verify the installation of a hardware device, check for hardware conflicts, troubleshoot hardware problems, change the configuration of a hardware device, and update device drivers for a hardware device.
5. What is a resource conflict?
6. To restore the previously used device driver for a hardware device, you use the ________________ .

Session 12.2

Evaluating Windows Vista's Networking Capabilities

Over the last several months, the Alexander Medical Research Institute hired additional research staff to keep up with its rapid growth. Remy and his staff set up the researchers' new computers on the company's network so that they can access the company resources they need for their jobs.

In a business environment, networks are required so that users can access important applications and documents, hardware devices (such as printers), and resources on the World Wide Web via their company's Internet connection. Now, more people set up small networks at home so that everyone who uses one of the computers in the home computer network can access a shared Internet connection as well as shared hardware and files.

If you are connected to a network, it is either a server-based network or a peer-to-peer network. In a server-based network, the **server** is the computer that manages the network and provides shared resources to network users within a domain. A **domain** consists of a group of networked computers that share a common directory database and security policy as well as network resources. Your user account gives you access to all of the domain resources, such as printers, for which you also have permissions. Workplace computers are typically part of a domain, and one or more computers function as servers.

In contrast, a **peer-to-peer network**, or **workgroup**, is a network in which each computer is an equal; no server manages network resources and provides network users access to those resources. Instead, computers communicate directly with each other, and each user decides which resources to share with other users on the same network. Also, each computer has a user account for each user who uses that computer. Peer-to-peer networks are typically home or small office networks with less than 10 to 20 computers and include shared devices, such as printers and scanners.

The remainder of this tutorial focuses on peer-to-peer networks, or workgroups, supported by Windows Vista.

Setting Up Your First Network | InSight

Although Windows Vista provides tools for detecting and configuring networked computers, setting up a new network takes careful planning and preparation so that you can purchase and install the hardware you need for your particular network. For assistance with this process, you can draw on information in the Help and Support Center. By examining information on the following Help topics, you can broaden your understanding of networks and determine how best to proceed:

- What you need to set up a home network
- Setting up a home network
- File sharing essentials
- Making your network more secure
- Wireless networking: frequently asked questions
- How do hubs, switches, routers, and access points differ?
- What are the different wireless network security methods?
- Understanding offline files

Viewing Your Computer's Name

Each computer in a workgroup has a name that uniquely identifies the computer on the network. The computer name is important because it determines how Windows Vista identifies a computer when you are viewing network connections and therefore makes it easier for you to locate a specific computer on a network and access resources you need on that networked computer. If you have a peer-to-peer network at home, each computer should use the same workgroup name so that you can easily access other computers on your home network.

If you are working on your own computer and do not have a network, read the steps in the second session of this tutorial and examine the figures, but do not keystroke the steps. If you are working in a computer lab where computers are typically part of a domain, you may not be able to complete some or all of the tutorial steps because of network restrictions. If that's the case, read the steps in this session of the tutorial and examine the figures, but do not keystroke the steps.

To check your computer name, domain, and workgroup settings:

Tip

The default workgroup name is WORKGROUP.

1. Right-click **Computer** (on the desktop or Start menu), and then click **Properties**. Windows Vista opens the System window, and under "Computer name, domain, and workgroup settings," displays the computer's name and any description you've provided for the computer as well as the workgroup name. On the computer used for Figure 12-27, the computer name is HI-PERFORM. The workgroup name for this computer is ALAN TURING.

Figure 12-27 Viewing a computer's network settings in the System window

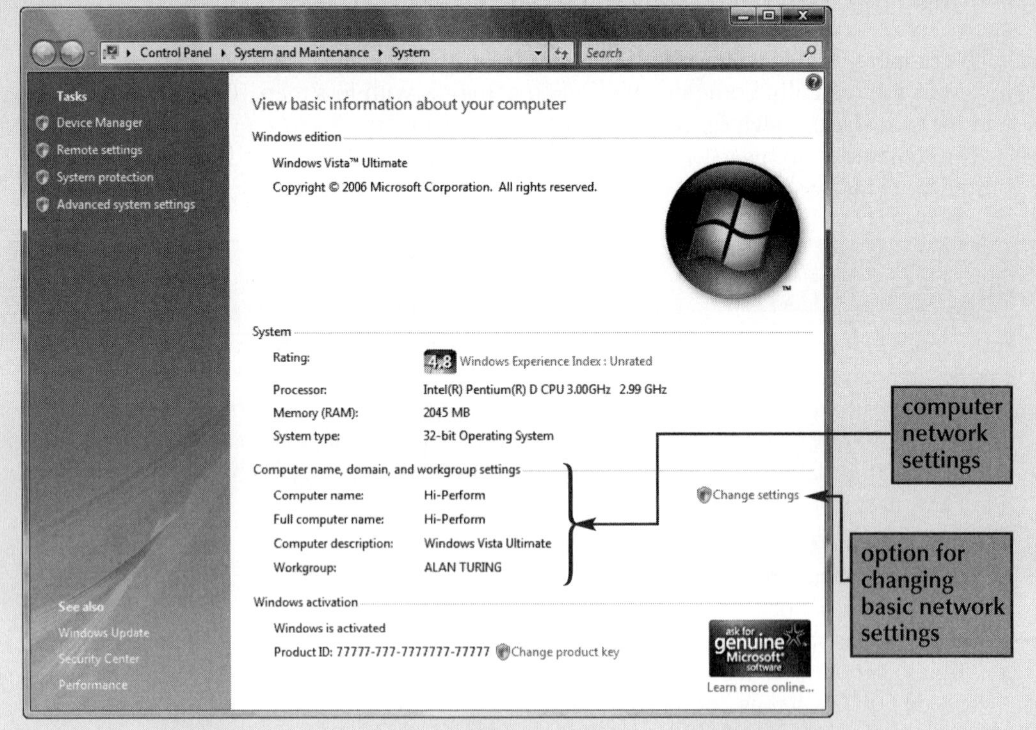

2. Click the **Change settings** link under the Computer name, domain, and workgroup settings section, and then provide Administrator credentials. Windows Vista opens the System Properties dialog box, as shown in Figure 12-28, and then explains that it uses the information you see on this property sheet to identify your computer on a network. You can also specify a friendly computer description to more easily identify your computer, such as the examples shown on this property sheet. If available in your edition of Windows Vista, you can use the Network ID button to start the Join a Domain or Workgroup Wizard and specify whether your computer is part of a business network that you use to connect to other computers at work or whether it is part of a small home computer network.

Figure 12-28 Viewing computer network settings in the System Properties dialog box

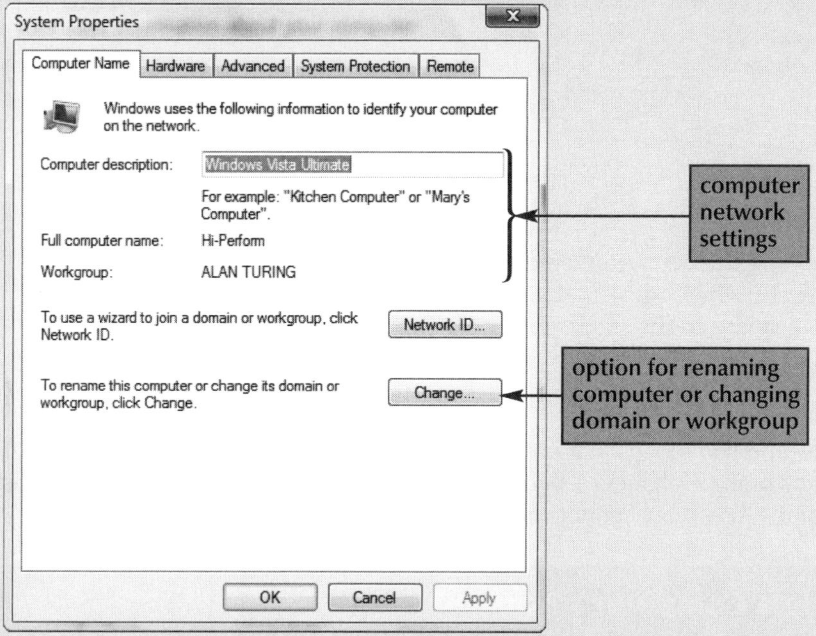

3. Click the **Change** button on the Computer Name property sheet. Windows Vista opens the Computer Name/Domain Changes dialog box. See Figure 12-29. You can change the name of your computer and identify the domain or workgroup in which you already have an account.

   Trouble? The dialog box name in your edition of Windows Vista may be "Computer Name Change."

Figure 12-29 Computer Name/Domain Changes dialog box

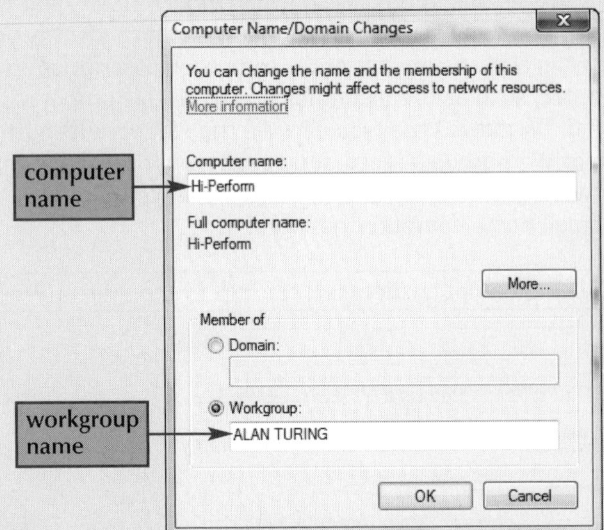

4. Click the **Cancel** button on the Computer Name/Domain Changes dialog box, and then click the **Cancel** button on the System Properties dialog box without making any changes to the settings of the computer you are using.
5. Close the System window.

Microsoft recommends that computer names be 15 characters or less and that you use only letters of the alphabet (A through Z), numbers (0 through 9), and hyphens in a computer name. Also, you cannot use the following symbols: < > ; : " * + = \ | ?

Reference Window | Viewing a Computer's Name

- Right-click Computer (on the desktop or Start menu), and then click Properties.
- Click the Change settings link under the Computer name, domain, and workgroup settings section, and then provide Administrator credentials.
- If necessary, enter a description of your computer in the Computer description box on the Computer Name property sheet.
- To start the Join a Domain or Workgroup Wizard, click the Network ID button (if available in your Windows edition), and then specify whether your computer is part of a business network that you use to connect to other computers at work or whether it is part of a small home computer network.
- To change the computer name or workgroup name, or specify a domain name, click the Change button on the Computer Name property sheet. To specify a new computer name, enter a name in the Computer name box. To specify a workgroup name, click the Workgroup option button (if necessary) and type a name in the Workgroup text box. To specify a domain name, click the Domain option button, and then type a domain name in the Domain text box.
- Click the OK button to close the Computer Name/Domain Changes dialog box and save changes to your network settings, or click the Cancel button to close the Computer Name/Domain Changes dialog box without changing your network settings.
- Click the OK button to close the System Properties dialog box and save changes to your network settings, or click the Cancel button to close the System Properties dialog box without changing your network settings.
- Close the System window.

If you make changes in the System Properties or Computer Name/Domain Changes dialog boxes or use the Join a Domain or Workgroup Wizard, those changes affect your access to network resources, and you must restart your computer so that Windows Vista can apply the changes.

Using Network Explorer to View Resources

You can use Network Explorer to browse resources on your local network, including computers on the network and shared resources, such as printers.

If you are working on a domain instead of a workgroup, then you can adapt the techniques in the following steps for your domain. If you encounter problems while working in a computer lab or just need assistance, ask your technical support staff for help.

To open Network Explorer and browse your workgroup:

1. Click **Network** on the Start menu. Windows Vista opens the Network window and shows computers in the same workgroup. On the computer used for Figure 12-30, the computer network consists of two computers—one identified as HI-PERFORM (a computer with Windows Vista Ultimate) and the other as HI-TECH (a computer with Windows XP Professional). These two computers are part of the same workgroup on a peer-to-peer network. Your networked computers will differ.

   Trouble? If Windows display the message, "Network discovery and file sharing are turned off, Network computers and devices are not visible. Click to change...", then click to change your current settings before continuing with this section of the tutorial.

   Trouble? If Network Explorer does not display other networked computers in your workgroup, the version of Windows used on one of the networked computers arbitrarily changed your workgroup name. Check the workgroup name on each networked computer, and if Windows changed the workgroup name, change the workgroup so that it matches the workgroup name used by other computers on the network, and then reboot each computer and log on a user account.

Tip

You can add a network printer or wireless device using options on the command bar in this window.

Figure 12-30 Viewing networked computers in the Network window

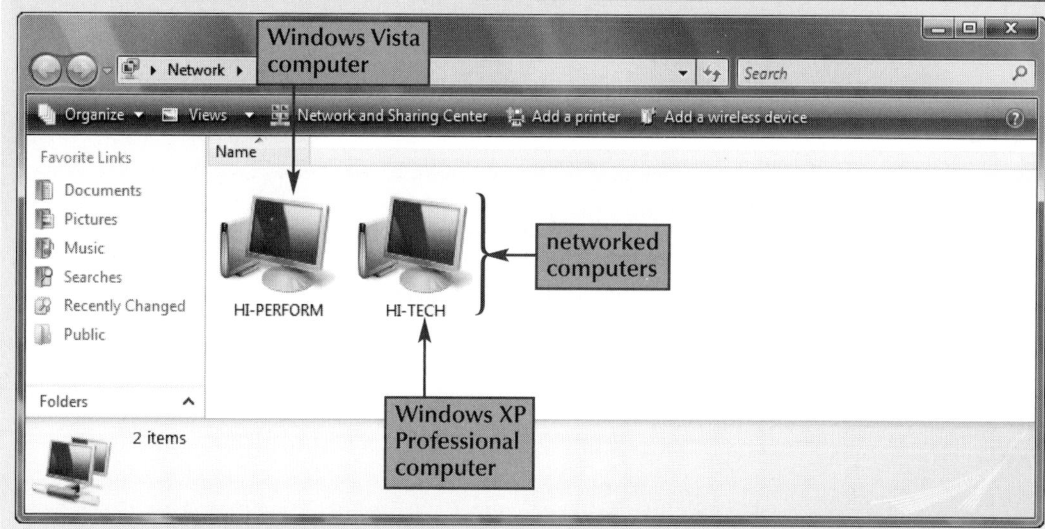

2. Click a **networked computer** icon, and if necessary, provide the user name and password for a user account on that computer in the Connect to dialog box. Windows Vista opens a window onto that networked computer and shows the shared devices on that networked computer. On the computer used for Figure 12-31, Windows Vista shows a shared Alexander Medical Research Institute folder, a shared LaserJet printer, and the Printers folder for a Windows XP Professional computer named HI-TECH. Your shared network resources will differ. You can open a shared folder (such as the Alexander Medical Research Institute folder) from another computer in the same workgroup and access any shared files in that folder. You can also print to a shared printer on another computer in the same network by first opening the Print dialog box in the program you are using and then by choosing the shared printer from a printer name list box. The printer name list box may show a friendly name for the networked printer, or it may show the UNC path for the networked printer. If possible, record the **UNC (Universal Naming Convention)** path, which identifies the location of a computer or a shared resource on a network. When identifying a computer, the UNC path consists of two backslashes followed by the computer name. Unlike URLs, which use forward slashes, the UNC path uses backslashes. For example, if you see a network printer listed as \\HI-TECH\LaserJet, then you know that this printer is located on the networked computer named HI-TECH.

Figure 12-31 Viewing shared network resources on another computer

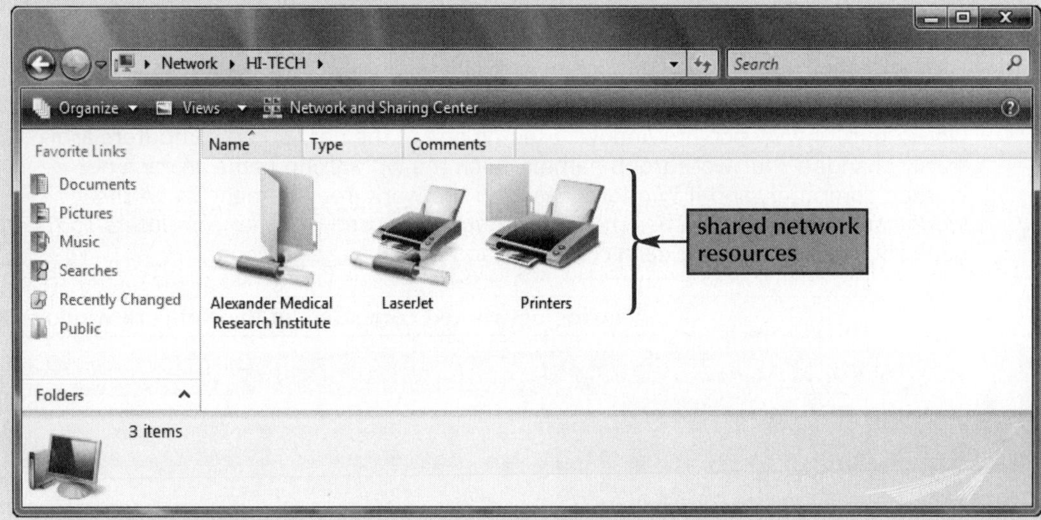

3. Click the **icon** on the left side of the Address Bar. Windows Vista displays the UNC path for the networked computer. On the computer used for Figure 12-32, the UNC path is \\HI-TECH. Your network path is different.

Figure 12-32 Viewing the UNC path for a shared network folder

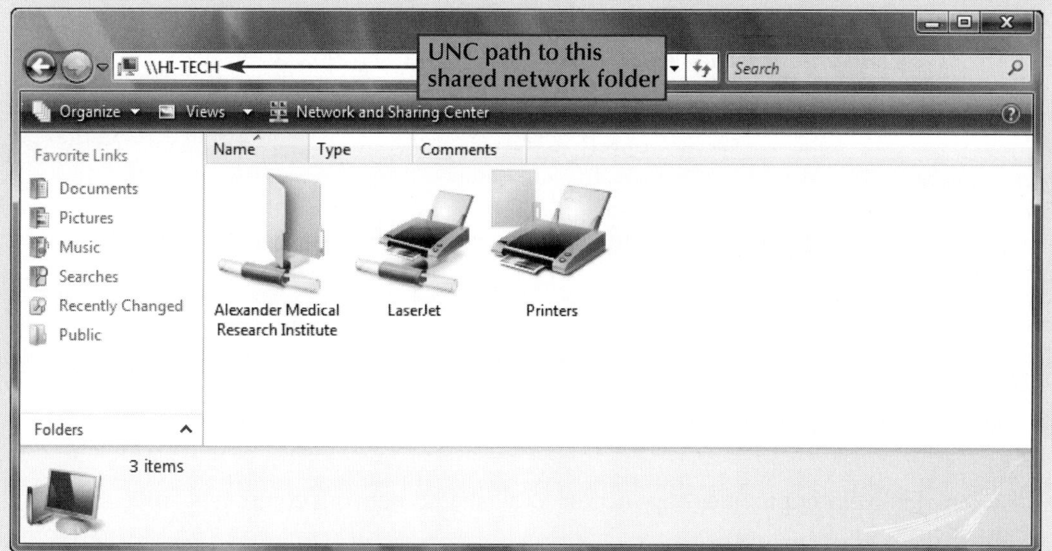

4. Click a **networked folder** icon. Windows Vista opens the network folder and displays its contents. On the computer used for Figure 12-33, Windows Vista displays two subfolders—Interdisciplinary Resources and Research Projects—on the networked computer. Because the parent folder of these subfolders is shared, these folders are also shared. Your network folders will differ. The UNC path for this network folder is \\HI-TECH\Alexander Medical Institute. Your network path is different.

Figure 12-33 Viewing shared subfolders on another networked computer

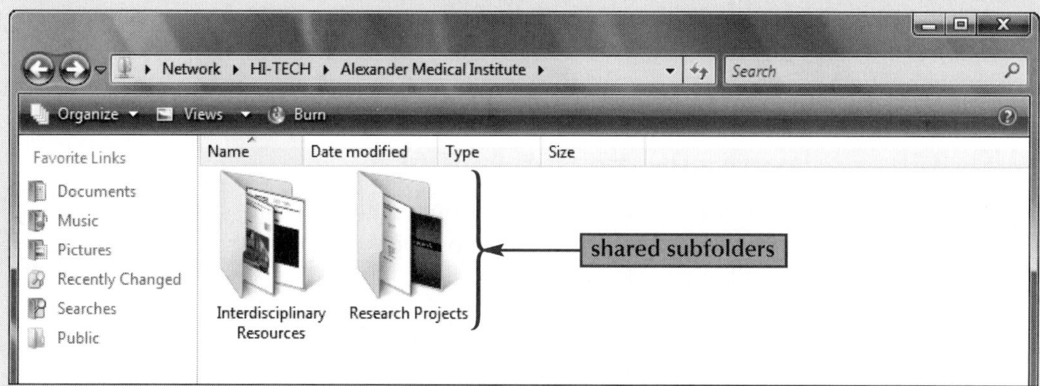

5. Click a **folder** icon. Windows Vista opens the folder and display files on another network computer that you can access. On the computer used for Figure 12-34, Windows Vista displays two files—a Medical Personnel Directory and a Pilot Project Proposal file—in the Interdisciplinary Resources folder. Because the parent folder of the subfolder containing these files is shared, these files are also shared. The UNC path for this folder is \\HI-TECH\Alexander Medical Institute\Interdisciplinary Resources. The UNC path for the Medical Personnel Directory file is \\HI-TECH\Alexander Medical Institute\Interdisciplinary Resources\Medical Personnel Directory.doc. Your network paths are different.

Figure 12-34 Viewing shared files on another networked computer

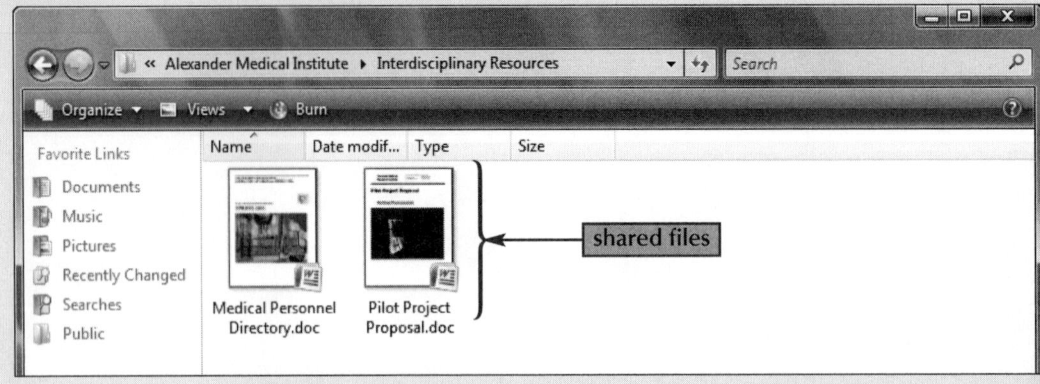

6. Close the open network window.

Network Explorer provides easy access to all shared network computers, folders, files, and devices.

Reference Window | Viewing Computers and Shared Resources in a Workgroup

- From the Start menu, click Network to view networked computers.
- To view shared resources of a networked computer, click the networked computer icon, and then browse and examine shared folders and files as well as shared hardware.
- To view the UNC path, click the icon on the left side of the Address Bar.
- When finished browsing network resources, close the current window.

While Network Explorer displays an overview of a network and its computers and resources, the Network and Sharing Center displays your network settings, which you'll examine next.

Using the Network and Sharing Center

The **Network and Sharing Center** displays your current network settings and a simple network map that visually illustrates the setup of your network. From the Network and Sharing Center, you can change network settings, view a full network map, and access other tools for displaying other network settings and for troubleshooting networks.

Remy uses the Network and Sharing Center to verify that network settings on new computers are correct and, when necessary, to resolve problems. He asks you to check the Network and Sharing Center on an employee's computer who recently reported a network problem.

To open the Network and Sharing Center:

Tip

You can use the Customize link to specify a Private or Public network.

1. Click **Network** on the Start menu, and in the Network window, click the **Network and Sharing Center** button on the command bar. Windows Vista opens a Network and Sharing Center window. At the top of the window, Windows Vista displays a simple map of your network. See Figure 12-35. If you click the "View full map" link, then Windows Vista displays a more detailed diagram of your network setup, including the names of each PC on the network and how they connect with each other and the Internet. It might also show other devices that it discovered that cannot be placed on the simple network map.

Figure 12-35 Network and Sharing Center

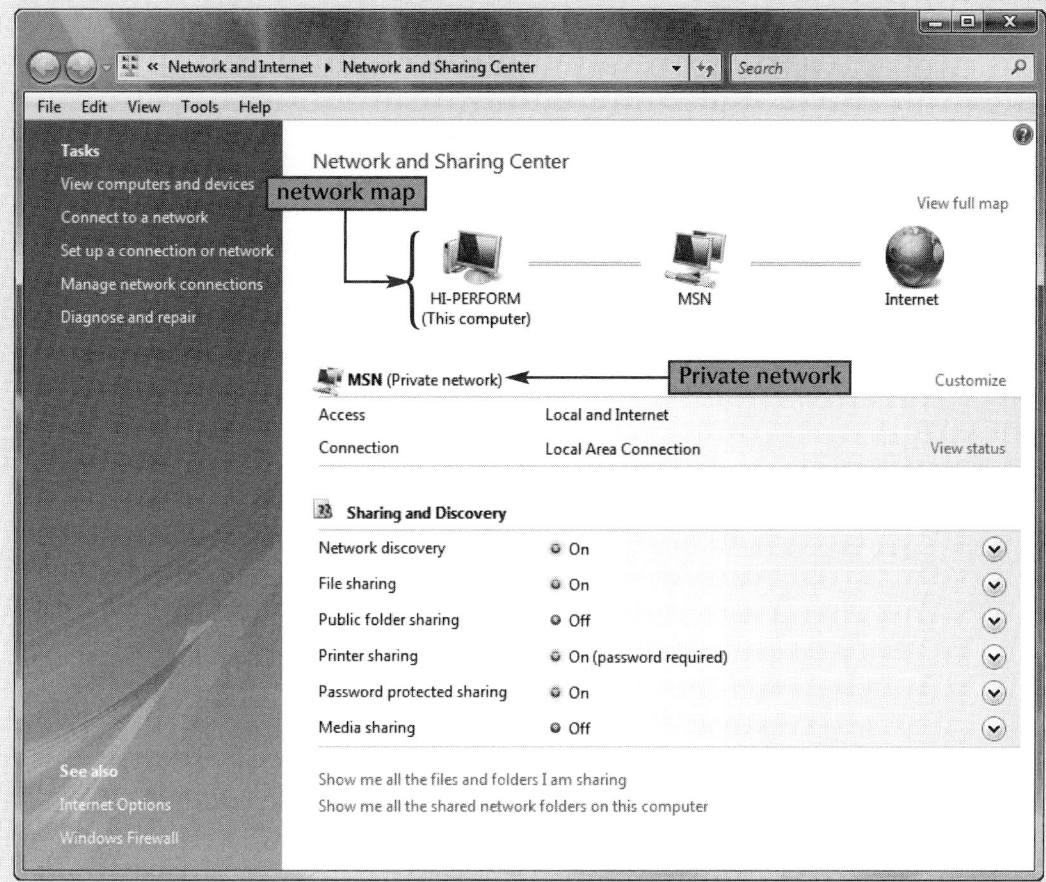

2. Keep the Network and Sharing Center window open as you examine this new Windows Vista feature.

Under "Sharing and Discovery," Windows Vista shows your current network settings:

- **Network discovery** This setting determines whether your computer can detect other computers and devices on the same network and whether those other computers can detect your computer. Network discovery works more quickly if all computers on the network are in the same workgroup.
- **File sharing** If **file sharing** is enabled, users on other computers connected to the same network as your computer can access any files or printers that you choose to share.
- **Public folder sharing** If this setting is enabled, users on other computers connected to the same network as your computer can access the Public folder and its contents. You can also specify whether those people can only open files or whether they can open, change, and create files.
- **Printer sharing** If printer sharing is enabled, users on other computers connected to the same network as your computer can connect to and use printers connected to your computer.
- **Password-protected sharing** When this setting is enabled, only people who have user accounts and a password on the same computer can access shared files, shared printers, and the Public folder.

- **Media sharing** When media sharing is enabled, users and devices on the same network can access shared music, picture, and video files on your computer, and your computer can find and access the same types of shared files on the network.

From the Network and Sharing Center, you can view shared network folders and files.

To view shared network folders and files:

1. Click the **Show me all the files and folders I am sharing** link. Windows Vista opens a Shared by Me folder (under Searches) to show you shared folders and files. On the computer used for Figure 12-36, Windows Vista shows one shared folder. Notice that shared folders have an icon of two people at the bottom left of the folder icon. Your shared files and folders will differ.

Figure 12-36 **Viewing all shared folders and files on the currently used computer**

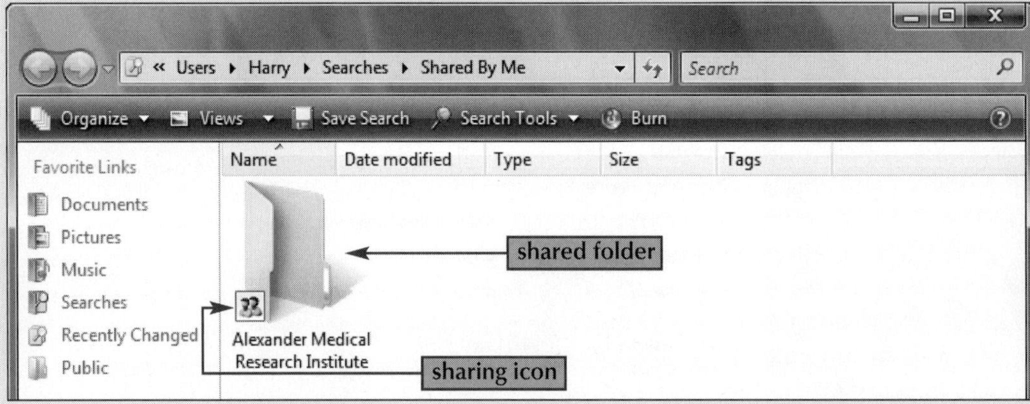

2. Close the Shared by Me folder window, and if necessary, click the Network and Sharing Center task button to bring this window to the foreground.
3. Click the **Show me all the shared network folders on this computer** link. Windows Vista opens a window with your computer name and shows shared folders and printers. On the computer used for Figure 12-37, Windows Vista shows a shared Alexander Medical Research Institute folder and two shared printers as well as a shared Printers folder.

Figure 12-37

Viewing all shared resources on the currently used computer

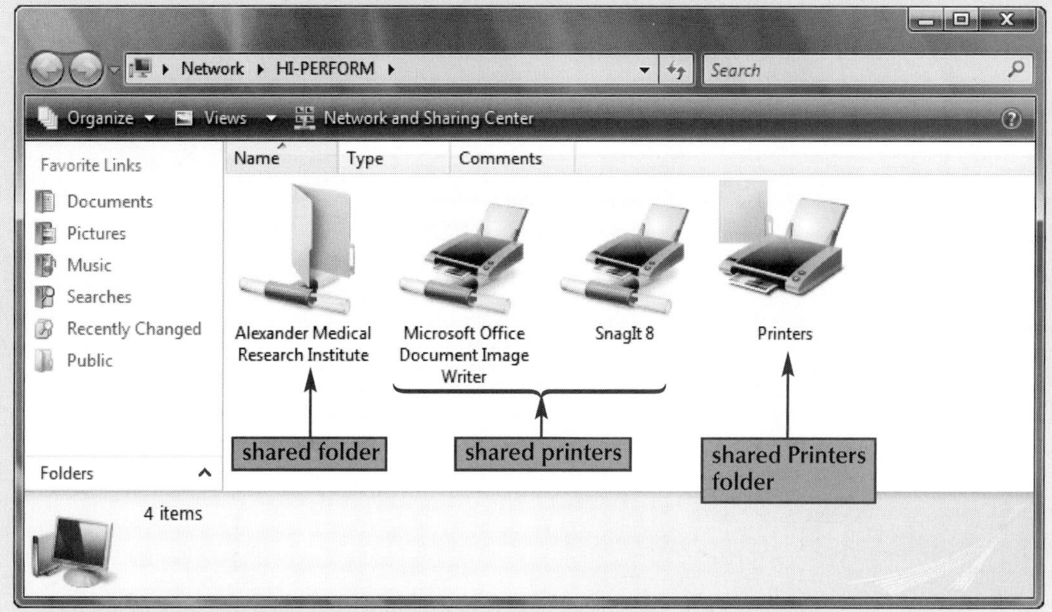

4. Close the folder window with a view of network shared folders, and if necessary, click the Network and Sharing Center taskbar button to bring this window to the foreground.

5. In the Network and Sharing Center window, click the **Manage network connections** link under Tasks in the Network and Sharing Center window. Windows Vista opens a Network Connections folder and displays a list of your computer's network connections.

6. Click **Local Area Connection**. Windows Vista then opens a Local Area Connection Status dialog box, which contains information about your current connection, including the status of IPv6 and IPv4 (described in the following bulleted list), the speed of your connection, and the number of bytes sent and received.

   Trouble? If Windows Vista opens a Properties dialog box instead of a Local Area Connection Status dialog box, continue with Step 7 and read the explanatory text in Step 7.

   Trouble? If Windows Vista opens a Local Area Connection Properties dialog box and prompts for Administrator credentials, provide those Administrator credentials and continue with Step 7.

7. Click the **Properties** button in the Local Area Connection Status dialog box and provide Administrator credentials. Windows Vista opens the Local Area Connection Properties dialog box and displays information about your network settings, as shown in Figure 12-38. In the Connect using box, Windows Vista identifies your network interface card (NIC).

Figure 12-38 Local Area Connection Properties dialog box

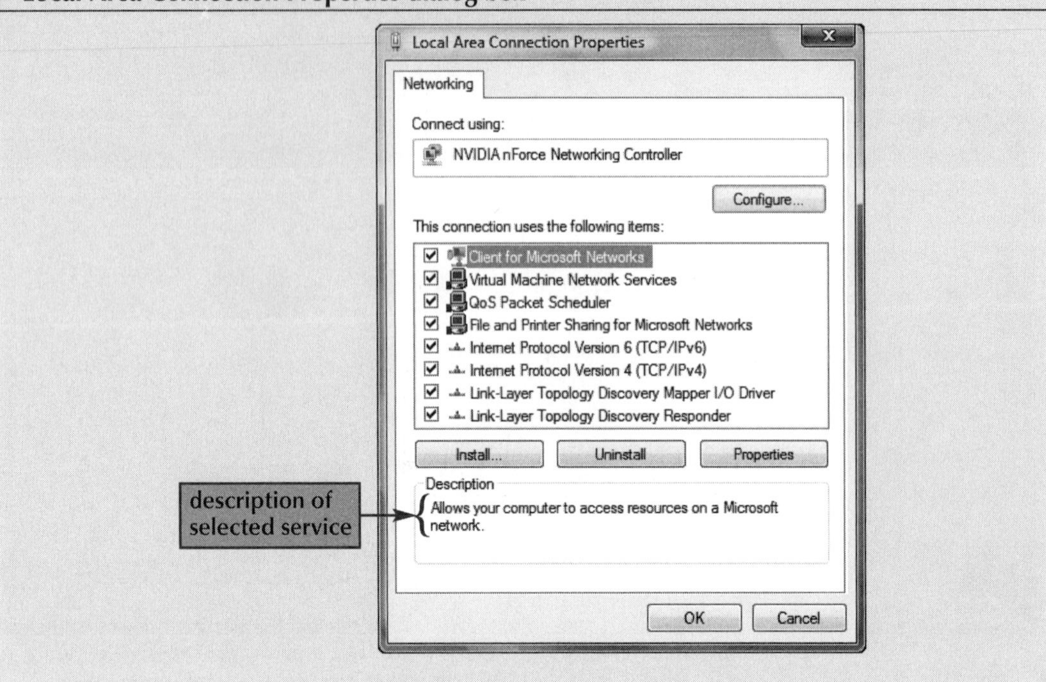

Under "This connection uses the following items," Windows Vista lists the services used by this connection:

- **Client for Microsoft Networks** (a required networking component) is **client software** for accessing resources on a Microsoft network. A **client** is a computer or a program that connects to, or requests services of, another computer or program.
- **Virtual Machine Network Services** provides networking access to, and communication with, a host operating system for a virtual PC environment. The Windows XP Professional and MS-DOS 6.22 operating systems are running under a virtual environment on this computer using Microsoft's Virtual PC software.
- **QoS (Quality of Service) Packet Scheduler** provides for the efficient flow of data on a network by handling the scheduling of packets of data over a network.
- **File and Printer Sharing for Microsoft Networks** is **service software** that enables users of other computers within the same network to access your files and printer.
- **Internet Protocol Version 6 (TCP/IPv6)** and **Internet Protocol 4 (TCP/IPv4)** are a set of protocols for the transmission of data over the Internet as well as business and home networks. One important feature of the newer Internet Protocol Version 6 (TCP/IPv6) over TCP/IPv4 is that it increases the number of bits used for network addresses from 32 bits to 128 bits, thus providing support for more Internet and network addresses necessary for the inevitable growth of the Internet and also providing enhanced security.
- **Link-Layer Topology Discovery (LLTD) Mapper I/O Driver** and **Link-Layer Topology Discovery (LTTD) Responder** are two network components that discover computers on a network and determine the network topology (or layout) so that Windows Vista can display a network map.

Next, return to the Network and Sharing Center and examine other network options.

To examine other Network and Sharing Center options:

1. Click the **Cancel** button in the Local Area Connection Properties dialog box, click the **Close** button in the Local Area Connection Status dialog box (if necessary), close the **Network Connections** window, and if necessary, click the **Network and Sharing Center** taskbar button to bring this window to the foreground.
2. Keep the Network and Sharing Center window open for the following explanation and for the next section of the tutorial.

Under Tasks in the Network and Sharing Center, you can also connect to a network (such as the Internet) using an already configured network connection, set up a connection or network, and diagnose and repair network problems. You can use the "Set up a connection or network" link to set up an Internet connection using a wireless, broadband, or dial-up connection; set up a wireless router or access point; set up a dial-up connection; and connect to a workplace using a VPN (Virtual Private Network) or dial-up connection. A **broadband connection** is a high-speed connection, such as DSL (Digital Subscriber Line) or cable. A **router** (wired or wireless) routes traffic between networks and over Internet connections and typically includes built-in security (such as a firewall). An **access point** (or wireless router) provides a mechanism for transmitting and receiving data over a wireless connection. A **Virtual Private Network (VPN)** connection allows authorized users to connect to a larger network, such as a business network, through the Internet. The VPN consists of the public and private networks used to make the connection. You can use the "Diagnose and repair" link to open Windows Network Diagnostics and troubleshoot a problem with your network. If the Network and Sharing Center displays a red X icon on the network map, you can click that icon to start Windows Network Diagnostics.

Using the Network and Sharing Center | Reference Window

- To open the Network and Sharing Center, click Network on the Start menu.
- Click the Network and Sharing Center button on the Network window's command bar.
- To view shared resources on the computer you are using, click the "Show me all the files and folders I am sharing" link, examine the shared resources, and then close the Shared by Me folder window.
- To view shared network computers on the computer you are using, click the "Show me all the shared network folders on this computer" link, examine the shared resources, and then close the window.
- To view network connections, click the "Manage network connections" link under Tasks. To view the status of your local area connection, click the Local Area Connection icon. To view properties of your local area connection, click the Properties button in the Local Area Connection Status dialog box. When finished examining the status and properties of your local area connection, close the Local Area Connection Properties dialog box, close the Local Area Connection Status dialog box, and then close the Network window.
- Close the Network and Sharing Center window.

One advantage of working on a network is that you can share folders and files, which Remy suggests you do next.

Sharing Folders

You can use the File Sharing Wizard to share your folders and files on a network so that other network users can access and use those folders and files. The object that you make available to other users on a network is called a **share**. When you share folders or files, you are granting permission for everyone or for specific designated users and groups to access and use those folders and files in a specific way. A **permission** is therefore a setting that determines who can access a network resource and how they can use it. For example, you might grant one or more users permission to read a document, but not permission to change that document. Once shared, anyone who has access to the computer network also has access to the shared folder or file using whatever permission level you specified. You can also share hardware, such as network printers.

Remy asks you to create an Alexander Medical Research Institute folder on a new computer, and then compare two different approaches for sharing folders. He also notes that if you turn on sharing for a folder, then all files you place in that folder are also shared.

To use the File Sharing Wizard:

1. Open the **Documents** folder, click **Public** in the Navigation Pane, and then click the **Public Documents** folder icon.
2. Right-click the **white background** of the Public Documents window, point to **New**, click **Folder**, type **Alexander Medical Research Institute**, and then press the **Enter** key.
3. Right-click the **Alexander Medical Research Institute** folder, click **Properties**, and in the Alexander Medical Research Institute Properties dialog box, click the **Sharing** tab. On the computer used for Figure 12-39, Windows Vista notes that the folder is "Not Shared."

Figure 12-39 Sharing property sheet for a folder

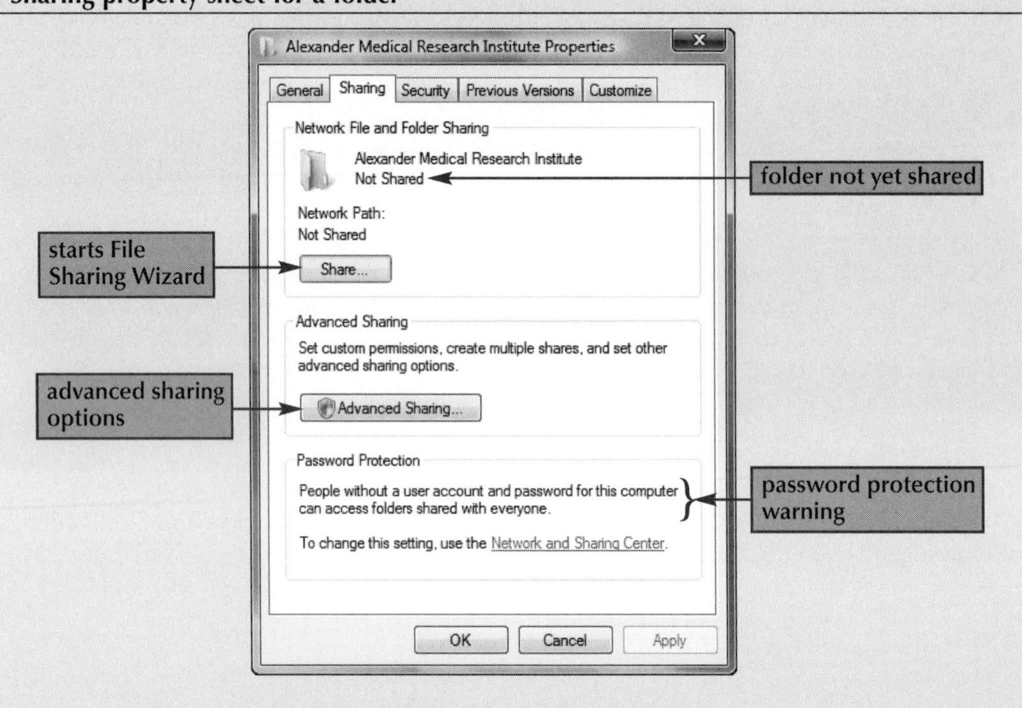

4. To start the File Sharing Wizard, click the **Share** button. The File Sharing dialog box shows the owner of this folder; in this example, Remy. See Figure 12-40. Your owner name will differ. You can type the name of the user or group with whom you want to share the folder or file, or you can choose the user or a group from a drop-down list.

Choosing a user or group to share a folder with **Figure 12-40**

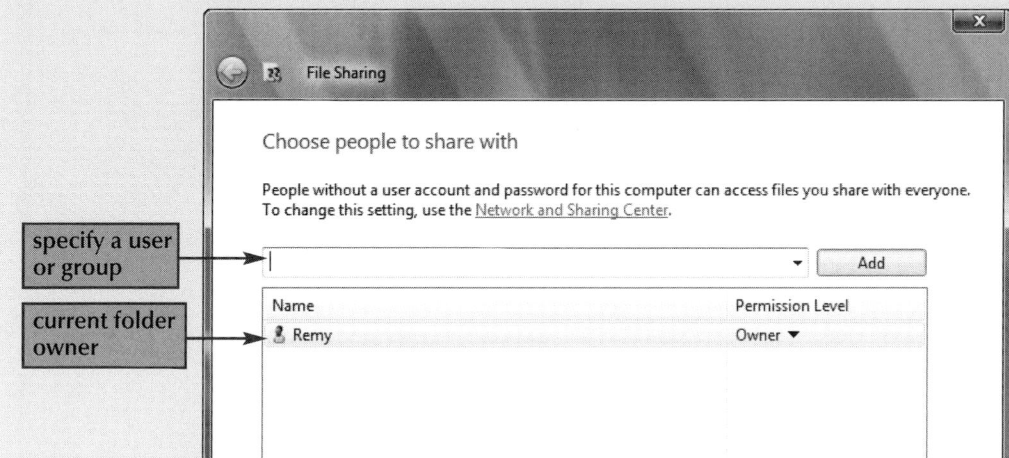

5. Click the list arrow button, and then click another user name or click **Everyone (All users in this list)**. If you choose Everyone, the folder is shared with all users on the same computer. However, under Password Protection in the earlier Figure 12-39, Windows Vista warns you that people without a user account and password for this computer can access folders shared with everyone.

6. Click the **Add** button. Windows Vista lists the user or group under Name and assigns the user or group the Reader permission level. See Figure 12-41. Reader, the default permission level, indicates that a user or group can open a folder (or file).

Figure 12-41 Users sharing the same folder

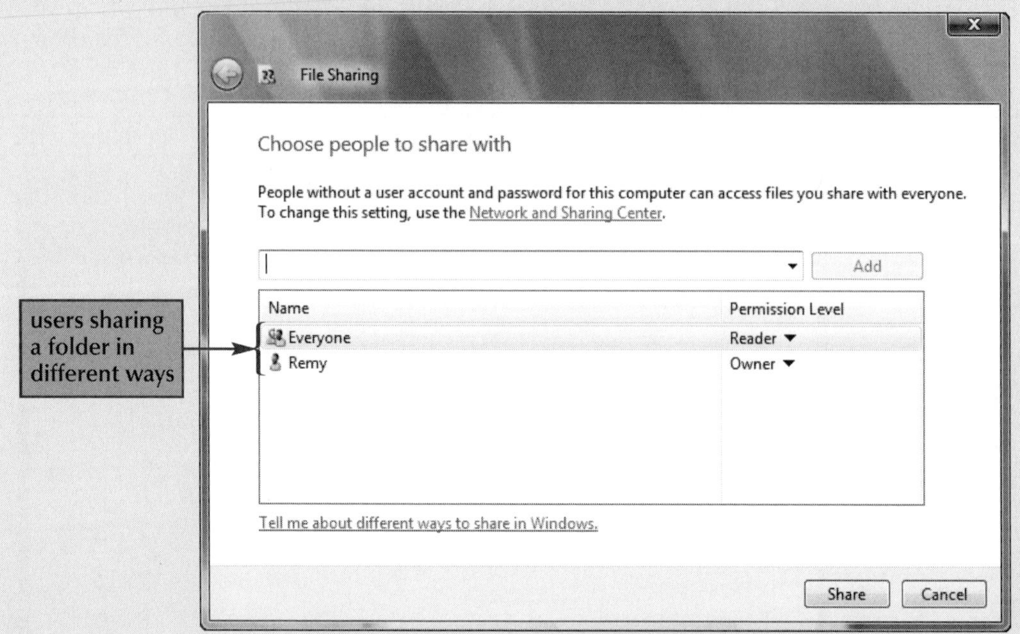

Tip

Contributor is not an option if you are specifying a permission level for a file.

7. Under Permission Level, click the **Reader** drop-down list arrow. From this list, you can choose Contributor, Co-owner, or Remove. See Figure 12-42. Co-owner allows the user or group the same full control as the owner of the file. Contributor applies to folders only and permits a user to read existing files and create new files in the folder, but the user cannot modify files created by other users.

Figure 12-42 Viewing permission levels for a group

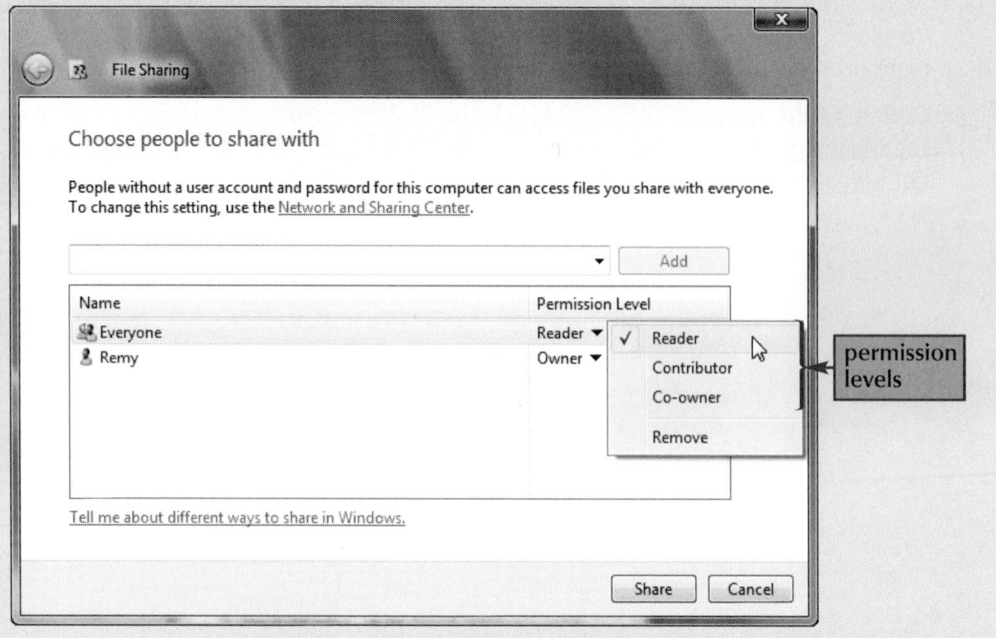

8. Click **Reader** (the default option), click the **Share** button, and if necessary, provide Administrator credentials. As shown in Figure 12-43, the File Sharing Wizard reports that the folder (or file) is shared and shows the UNC path to the folder (or file); in this case, **\\HI-PERFORM\Users\Public\Documents\Alexander Medical Research Institute** (your UNC path will differ).

Figure 12-43 **File sharing operation completed**

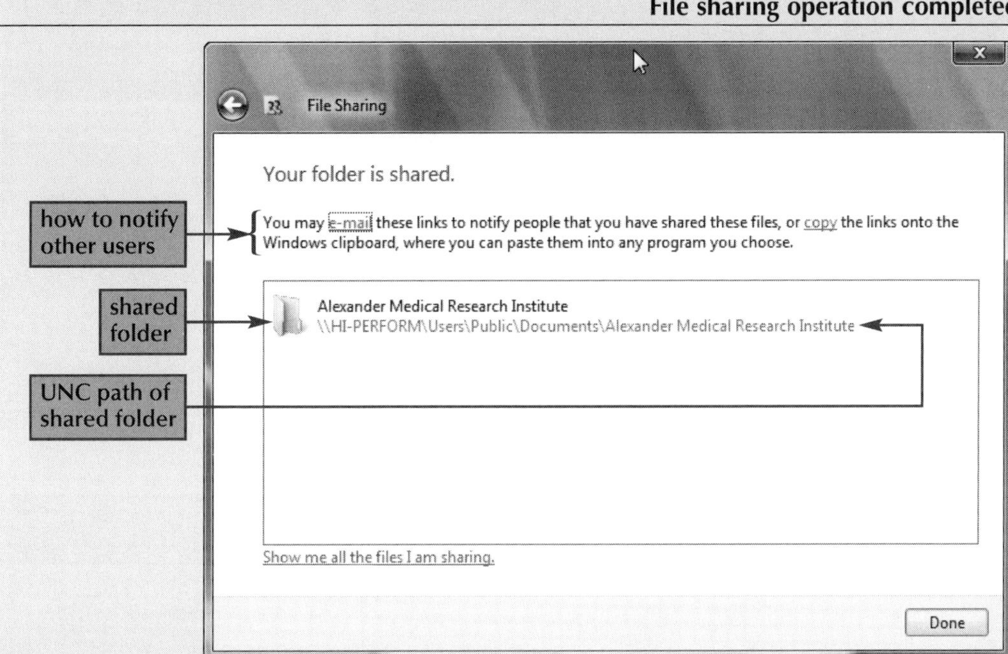

Tip

After you share a folder or file, notify other users of the availability of the shared resource.

9. Click the **Done** button. On the Sharing property sheet, Windows Vista now notes that the folder (or file) is "Shared," and it also shows the UNC path (or, at least, part of the path in this example). See Figure 12-44.

Figure 12-44 **Viewing properties of a shared network folder**

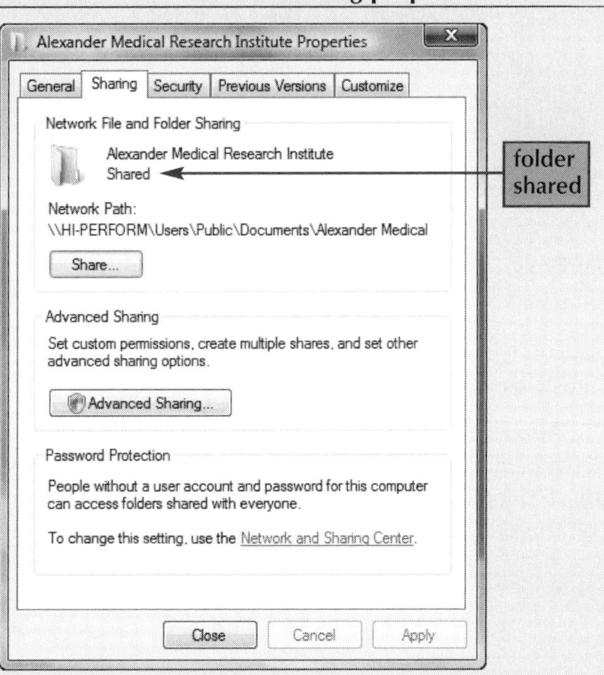

10. Close the Alexander Medical Research Institute Properties dialog box. In the Public Documents folder window, Windows Vista now displays a sharing icon as part of the folder icon. See Figure 12-45.

Figure 12-45 Shared folder with sharing icon

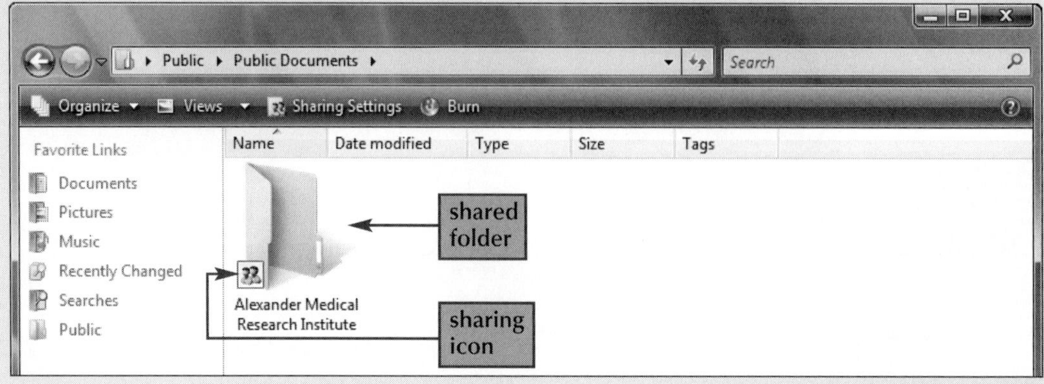

All of the files stored in the Alexander Medical Research Institute folder will be shared so that everyone who uses the computer can open the files.

Reference Window | Using the File Sharing Wizard

- Right-click the folder icon of the folder you want to share, click Properties, and in the folder Properties dialog box, click the Sharing tab.
- To start the File Sharing Wizard, click the Share button.
- In the File Sharing dialog box, click the drop-down list arrow, click the user or group with which you want to share the folder, and then click the Add button.
- Under Permission Level, click the Reader drop-down list arrow for the user or group you just added, and then choose Reader to specify that a user or group can open the folder; click Contributor to specify that a user or group can read existing files and create new files (but cannot modify existing files), or click Co-owner to specify that a user or group have the same full control as the owner.
- Click the Share button, provide Administrator credentials, and then click the Done button.
- Close the folder's Properties dialog box.

Later, if you change your mind about sharing a folder or file, you can turn off sharing of the folder.

To turn off sharing on a folder:

1. Right-click the **Alexander Medical Research Institute** folder, and then click **Share**. As shown in Figure 12-46, you can change sharing permissions and choose to add or remove people or permissions. You can also stop sharing and remove permissions for all the people you've added to your sharing list.

Viewing file sharing options **Figure 12-46**

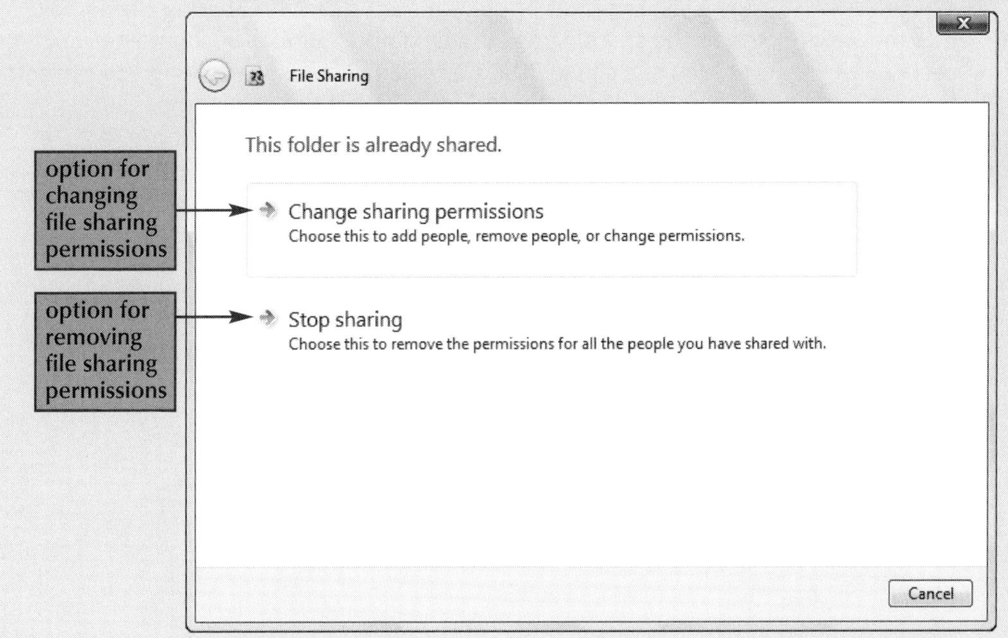

2. Click **Stop sharing**. In the next File Sharing dialog box, Windows Vista informs you that you have stopped sharing the selected folder.
3. Click the **Done** button.
4. Right-click the **folder** and then click **Share**. Your user account is the only one listed in the File Sharing dialog box. When you stopped sharing, you removed Everyone from your sharing list.
5. Click the **Cancel** button to close the File Sharing dialog box. Notice that the sharing icon is removed from the Alexander Medical Research Institute folder, indicating the folder is no longer shared.

Now, others on the computer cannot open the Alexander Medical Research Institute folder or its files.

Turning Off Sharing of a Folder | Reference Window

- Right-click the shared folder, and then click Share.
- In the File Sharing dialog box, click Stop sharing, and then click the Done button.

You can also use Advanced Sharing to share a folder or file. To use Advanced Sharing, you must specify Administrator credentials.

To use Advanced Sharing:

1. Right-click the **Alexander Medical Research Institute** folder, click **Properties**, and then click the **Sharing** tab. Under Advanced Sharing, Windows Vista notes that you can set custom permissions, create multiple shares, and set other advanced sharing options.

2. Click the **Advanced Sharing** button, provide Administrator credentials, and in the Advanced Sharing dialog box, click the **Share this folder** check box. As shown in Figure 12-47, Windows Vista enables options in the Advancing Sharing dialog box, lists the folder name as the share name, and limits the number of simultaneous users to 10. However, you can change the share name if you prefer, and you can set the number of users who can access this folder or file at the same time.

Figure 12-47 Enabling sharing and specifying a share name

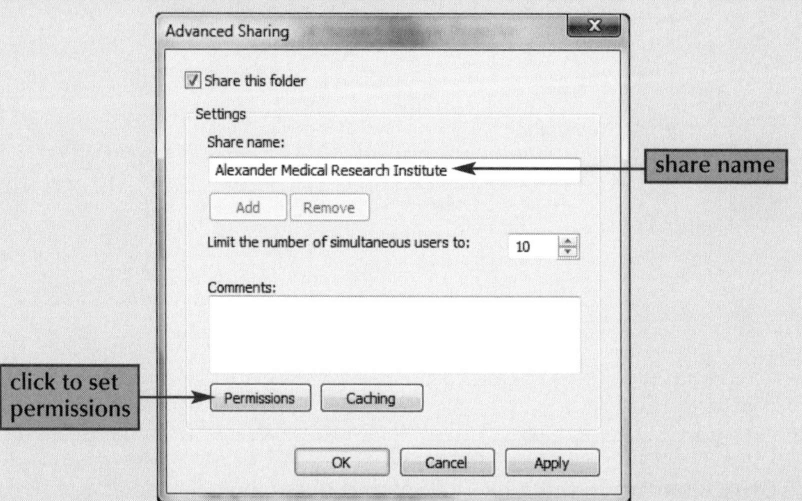

3. Click the **Permissions** button. Windows Vista shows the permission assigned to the user or group, namely the Read (the default permission) permission for the Everyone group. See Figure 12-48. You can now allow or deny a permission. You can specify Full Control (equivalent to the owner) or Change (so that users can modify the file). You can also use the Add button to add users or groups and the Remove button to remove users or groups. Remember that if you grant access to the Everyone group, anyone who accesses the computer from a domain or workgroup has access to the folder at the permission level you specified.

Figure 12-48 Viewing permissions for a shared folder

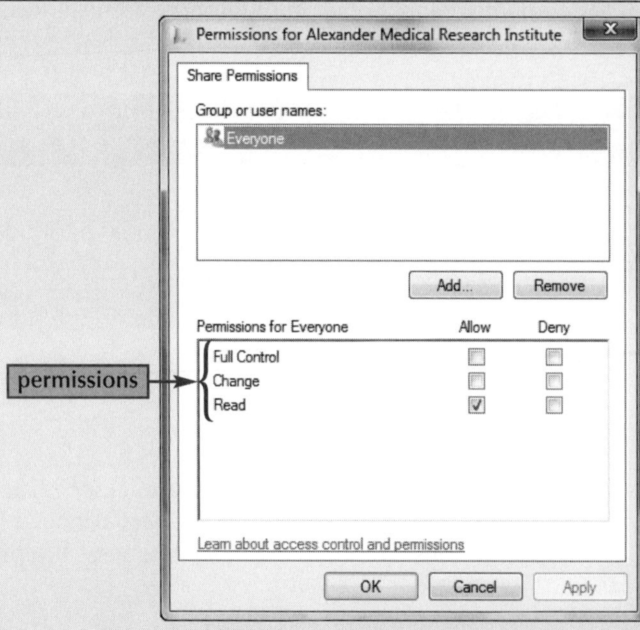

4. In the Permissions for Alexander Medical Research Institute dialog box, click the **OK** button to keep the default Read permission for Everyone.

5. In the Advanced Sharing dialog box, click the **Caching** button. In the Offline Settings dialog box, you can specify whether users can access folders and files when they are working offline, and how. See Figure 12-49. You can also specify that Offline Files include only the folders and files that the users designate as such, or you can specify all files and programs from the share opened by the user are available in Offline Files. You can also specify that files or programs from the share are not available offline. Any Offline Files are copies of files on the network. One advantage of Offline Files is that you can work with files even when not connected to the network (such as when you are traveling or working at home). Once you reconnect to that network, Windows Vista will automatically update the files on the network (or vice versa), or you can use the Sync center to synchronize files (covered in Tutorial 10).

Specifying Offline Settings **Figure 12-49**

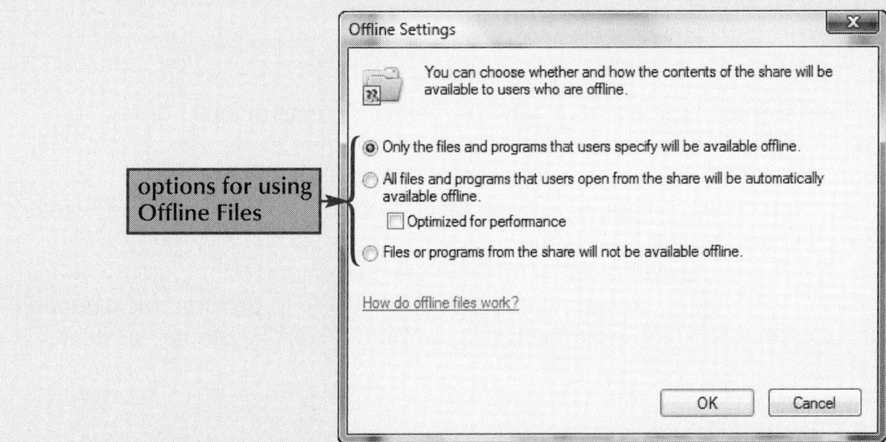

6. Click the **OK** button in the Offline Settings dialog box, click the **OK** button in the Advanced Sharing dialog box, and then click the **OK** button in the Alexander Medical Research Institute Properties dialog box. As you can tell from the Alexander Medical Research Institute folder, you have now shared the folder.

To make files available offline, you need to enable Offline Files by opening the Control Panel, then Network and Internet, and finally, Offline Files. On the General property sheet in the Offline Files dialog box, you click the Enable Offline Files button. You can also view Offline Files from that property sheet. When you decide to make a file available offline, you right-click the file, and then you click "Always Available Offline." To access Offline Files, you can click "View offline files" button on the General property sheet of the Offline Files dialog box. Also, if you are using a shared network folder and want to work with a file offline, you can select the file, and then click the "Work Offline" button on the command bar.

You can also use the Public folder to share files. If you place files in the Public folder, then different users on the same computer can share files, but by default, the Public folder is not shared on a network. To share the Public folder on a network, you open the Network and Sharing Center, expand the Public folder sharing section, and then turn on sharing in one of two ways: "Turn on sharing so anyone with network access can open files," or "Turn on sharing so anyone with network access can open, change, and create files."

Reference Window | Using Advanced Sharing to Share a Folder

- Right-click the folder you want to share, click Properties, and in the folder Properties dialog box, click the Sharing tab.
- Click the Advanced Sharing button, and in the Advanced Sharing dialog box, click the Share this folder check box.
- To specify permissions, click the Permissions button, adjust permissions for the group or user, click the Add button to add new users (and then adjust their permissions), and then click the OK button.
- In the Advanced Sharing dialog box, click the Caching button, choosing the caching option that you want to use, and then click the OK button.
- Click the OK button in the Advanced Sharing dialog box, and then click the OK button in the folder's Properties dialog box to apply your share settings.

Sharing of folders on a network enables selected users or all users to access and work with the same files and thereby improves productivity.

Creating a Mapped Drive

To simplify access to shared folders on a network, you can create mapped drives. A **mapped drive** is a shared network folder that is assigned a drive name. The drive name acts as a shortcut to the shared network folder from a Computer window.

Remy suggests you create a mapped drive to the shared Alexander Medical Research Institute folder on the network.

In the following steps, you will create a mapped drive on another computer in your network. If you are working in a computer lab and are not able to perform this operation, then read the following steps and examine the figures, but do not keystroke the steps.

To create a mapped drive:

1. From the Start menu, click **Network**, and in the Network window, click the **icon** of a computer on your network. Windows Vista displays shared folders and devices on that networked computer.

   Trouble? Widows Vista may prompt you for Administrator credentials to access another computer on your network. If that occurs and if you do not know the Administrator password, then click the icon for the computer you are currently using.

2. Right-click a **shared network** folder icon, and then click **Map Network Drive**. Windows Vista opens a Map Network Drive dialog box, as shown in Figure 12-50. In the Map Network Drive dialog box, you can select a drive name to map to the shared folder from the Drive list box. Drive names are listed and used in reverse alphabetical order. The folder list box shows the UNC path to the shared folder; in this case, \\HI-TECH\Alexander Medical Research Institute. The general format that you use in a UNC path is **\\server\share**" in which server is the name of the networked computer, and share is the name of the shared folder or device. You also have the options of reconnecting to the mapped drive at logon, connecting under a different user name (and password), and connecting to a Web site where you store documents and pictures. The "different user name" link opens a Connect As dialog box that prompts you for another user's name and password. The "Connect to a Web site that you can use to store your documents and pictures" link opens the Add Network Location Wizard to help you sign up for a service that offers online storage space. You can also use the Add Network Location Wizard to create a shortcut to a Web site, FTP site, or another network location. An FTP (for File Transfer Protocol) site is a Web site for uploading or downloading files.

Figure 12-50 Mapping a drive

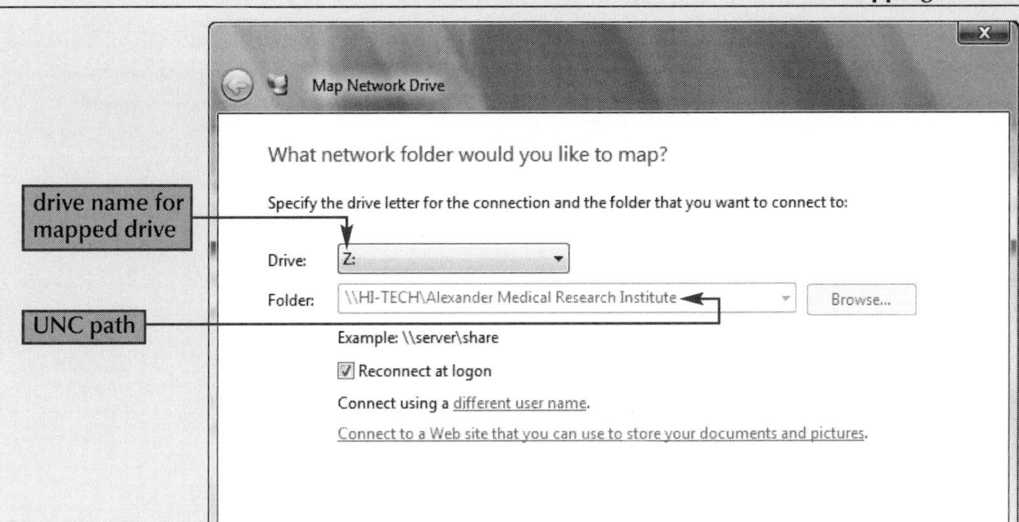

3. Click the **Finish** button. Windows Vista opens a window onto the mapped drive. See Figure 12-51. If you examine the Address Bar, you will notice that the mapped drive is accessible from the Computer window. Your shared folder name and path will differ.

Figure 12-51 Viewing the contents of a mapped drive

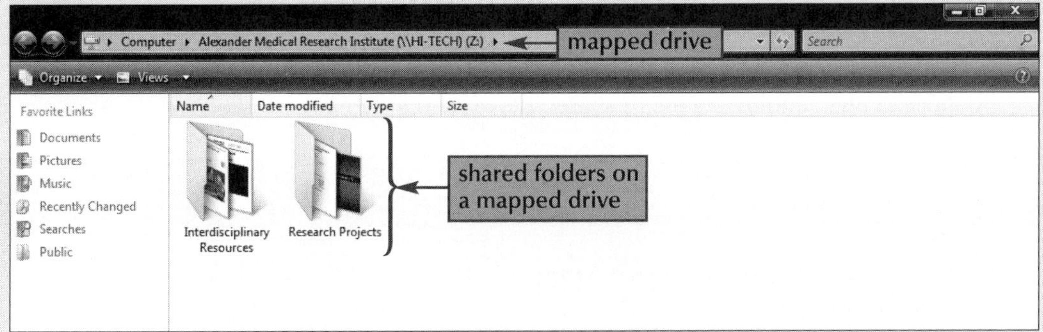

4. Click **Computer** in the Address Bar. Under Network Location, Windows Vista displays a new drive Z, named after the shared network folder in the Computer window on your local computer. See Figure 12-52. As part of the drive's friendly name, Windows Vista also shows the UNC path to the networked computer that contains the shared folder (in this case, \\HI-TECH, a Windows XP Professional computer).

Trouble? If you cannot see Computer in the Address Bar, click the Location button (the double arrow), and then click Computer.

Figure 12-52 Viewing a mapped drive in the Computer window

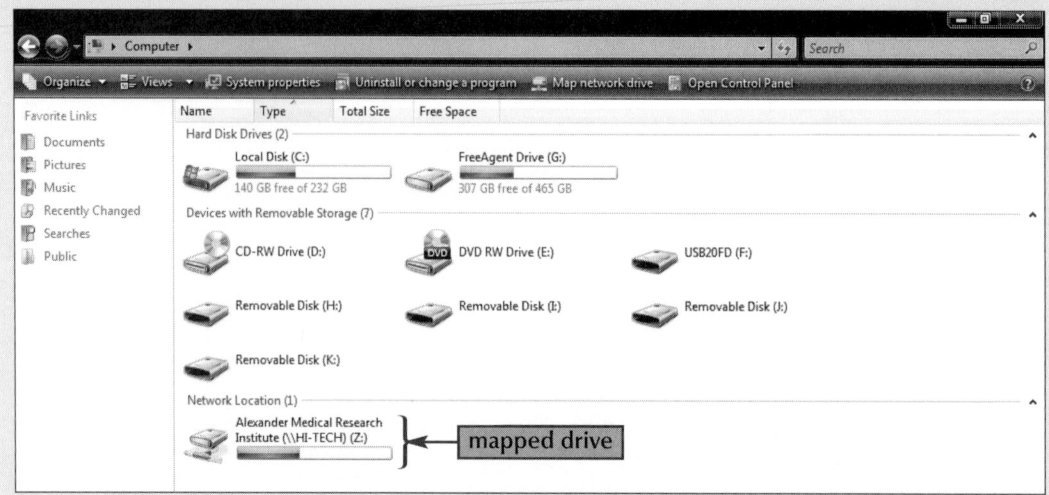

5. Keep the Computer window open for the next set of steps.

Like regular shortcuts, mapped drives provide quick access to shared folders on a network. Furthermore, you can create desktop shortcuts to the mapped drives.

You can also remove a drive name to a mapped drive.

To disconnect a mapped drive:

1. In the Computer window, right-click the **mapped drive**, and then click **Disconnect**. Windows Vista no longer displays the mapped drive in the Computer window.
2. Close the Computer window.

Mapped drives simplify access to shared networked folders.

Reference Window | Creating and Removing a Mapped Drive

- From the Start menu, click Network, and in the Network window, click the icon of a computer on your network.
- Right-click a shared network folder, and then click Map Network Drive. To specify a drive name other than the drive name shown on the Drive button, click the Drive button, click the drive name you want to use, and then click the Finish button.
- To access a mapped drive, open a Computer window, and then click the mapped drive.
- To disconnect a mapped drive, open a Computer window, right-click the mapped drive, click Disconnect, and then close the Computer window.

Now that you are finished working with network resources, Remy suggests that you restore your computer to its initial state.

Restoring Your Computer

If you are working in a computer lab, or if you want to restore your desktop computer to the settings that existed prior to working on this tutorial, complete the following steps.

To restore your computer:

1. To remove the shared network folder that you created earlier in the tutorial, open the **Public Documents** folder, right-click the **Alexander Medical Research Institute** shared folder, click **Delete**, and in the Delete Folder dialog box, click the **Yes** button. In a Sharing dialog box, you are warned that if you delete the folder, it will no longer be shared.
2. Click the **Continue** button, and then provide Administrator credentials.
3. Close the Public Documents window.
4. To restore double-click activation, click the **Computer** icon on the desktop, click the **Organize** button on the command bar, click **Folder and Search Options**, and on the General property sheet in the Folder Options dialog box, click the **Double-click to open an item (single-click to select)** option button; click the **OK** button to close the Folder Options dialog box, and then close the Computer window.
5. To remove the Computer icon from the desktop, open the **Start** menu, right-click **Computer**, and then click **Show on Desktop**.

After your thorough tour of the network tools in Windows Vista, you are now ready to assist Remy in setting up, configuring, customizing, and troubleshooting computers at the Alexander Medical Research Institute and help users connect to the Institute's network so that they have access to the resources they need.

Session 12.2 Quick Check | Review

1. What is a peer-to-peer network, or workgroup?
2. The ________________ identifies the location of a networked computer as well as shared resources on a network.
3. If ________________ is enabled, then your computer can detect other computers and devices on the same network, and those other computers can also detect your computer.
4. Explain what the following notation means: \\HI-TECH\Alexander Medical Research Institute
5. True or False. One advantage of Offline Files is that you can work with files even when not connected to a network (such as when you are traveling or working at home).
6. A(n) ________________ is a shared network folder that is assigned a drive name.

Review | Tutorial Summary

In this tutorial, you examined the difference between Plug and Play and legacy hardware devices, components of a *bona fide* Plug and Play computer system, and Windows Vista support for newer types of hardware technologies. You learned about the four different types of resource assignments Windows Vista allocates to hardware devices, and you opened Device Manager and examined hardware configuration settings and resource assignments for hardware devices. You learned how to identify and troubleshoot disabled devices, resource conflicts, and unknown devices with Device Manager. You compared the information provided by System Information with that provided by Device Manager, and you used System Information to identify hardware problems. You examined the difference between a server-based network and a peer-to-peer network. You viewed your computer's name and your computer's workgroup or domain name. You used Network Explorer to view computers in a workgroup, and then you opened the Network and Sharing Center and examined network settings, shared network folders and files, the status of your local area connection, and local connection properties. You used the File Sharing Wizard and Advanced Sharing to share a folder and specify share permissions. You also turned off sharing of a folder. Finally, you created a mapped drive and assigned a drive name to a networked folder, and you disconnected a mapped drive.

Key Terms

access point
Advanced Configuration and Power Interface BIOS (ACPI BIOS)
bandwidth
broadband connection
bus
client
client software
device conflict
Direct Memory Access (DMA)
Direct Memory Access channel
Direct Memory Access resources
domain
DualView
Enhanced Host Controller Interface (EHCI)
Extended Display Identification Data (EDID)
file sharing
File Transfer Protocol (FTP)
FireWire
forced hardware configuration
Full-Speed USB
gateway
hardware conflict
hardware interrupt
hardware tree
Hi-Speed USB
hot insertion and removal
hot plugging
hot swapping
Human Interface Device (HID)
IEEE 1394
IEEE 1394b
Input/Output (I/O) resources
I/O address
interrupt request resource
IRQ (interrupt request)
legacy devices
Low-Speed USB
mapped drive
memory resources
Network and Sharing Center
non-Plug and Play devices
Open Host Controller Interface (OHCI)
packet
peer-to-peer network
permission
Plug and Play (PnP)
Plug and Play devices
resource conflict
router
server
service software
share
software interrupt
TCP/IP (Transmission Control Protocol/Internet Protocol)
UNC (Universal Naming Convention) path
Universal Host Controller Interface (UHCI)
Universal Plug and Play (UPnP)
unknown device
USB (Universal Serial Bus)
USB Host Controller
USB Root Hub
Virtual Private Network (VPN)
workgroup
write caching

Practice | Review Assignments

Practice the skills you learned in the tutorial.

There are no Data Files needed for the Review Assignments.

Remy asks you to assist him with documenting hardware and network settings on a new set of computers designed for use in a new research group at Alexander Medical Research Institute.

As you complete each step in these Review Assignments, record your answers so you can submit them to your instructor. Use a word processing application, such as Word or WordPad, to prepare your answers to these questions. To save time in reporting or recording information, use the Alt and Print Screen keys to capture images of property sheets and print them with WordPad. Also, if you change any settings on the computer you are using, note the original settings so you can restore them later.

To open Device Manager, you must provide Administrator credentials. To complete some of the network steps, the computer you are using must be connected to a workgroup or domain, and you may need to provide Administrator credentials. Complete the following:

1. Open Device Manager. Does Device Manager identify any hardware problems, and if so, what types of hardware problems are they? How does Device Manager identify hardware problems?
2. Examine the Computer category. How does Device Manager identify your computer?
3. Examine hardware in the Disk drives category, and then list the names of your disk drives. Which drive is your hard disk drive? View properties of your hard disk drive. What policies does your hard disk drive use for write caching and Safe Removal? Close the Properties dialog box for your hard disk drive.
4. Expand the Network adapters category. How does Device Manager identify your network adapter? View properties of your network adapter. What resource settings are assigned to your network adapter? Are there any device conflicts? What power management options are available for your network adapter? Close the Properties dialog box for your network adapter.
5. Expand the Processors category. What type of processor or processors does your computer have?
6. Expand the Universal Serial Bus controllers category. Does your computer support USB 2.0 and USB 1.x? Explain how you arrived at this conclusion using information in Device Manager. Close Device Manager.
7. Open System Information, expand the Hardware Resources category, and then select the IRQs category. What IRQ is assigned to your video display adapter and network adapter? Are either or both of the IRQs shared and, if so, by what devices?
8. If you want to determine if your computer uses any forced resource assignments, where would you look in System Information? If you wanted to determine if there were any hardware problems, where would you look in System Information?
9. Open the Components category and select Display. How much adapter RAM does your video display adapter have? Close the System Information window.
10. Open the System window. What is your computer's name? Is the computer you are using part of a workgroup or a domain? What is the workgroup or domain name? Close the System window.
11. Open a Network window. What computers does Windows Vista identify? Open a window onto one or more networked computers and identify what types of shared resources (if any) are available, and then close the window.

12. Open the Network and Sharing Center. Draw a diagram of your computer network using the network map provided by Windows Vista. How does Windows Vista identify your network? List the Network Sharing and Discovery settings for your computer network.
13. Use the link provided in the Network and Sharing Center to view all the shared network folders on your computer. What are the names of (up to five) shared network folders (or network hardware devices)? Close the networked computer window.
14. Use the link provided in the Network and Sharing Center to view all the files and folders you are sharing. What are the names of (up to five) shared files and folders? Close the Shared by Me window, and then close the Network and Sharing Center.
15. Describe one way in which you can share a folder or file. How can you remove sharing from a folder?
16. Open a Computer window. Are there any mapped drives, and if so, what is the drive name, and what is the UNC path for one of the mapped drives? What process can you use to create a mapped drive? Close the Computer window.
17. Submit your document to your instructor, either in printed or electronic form, as requested.

Apply | Case Problem 1

Use the skills you learned in the tutorial to identify a hardware configuration problem.

There are no Data Files needed for this Case Problem.

WTI Insurers, Inc. Eunice Lyons works as technical support specialist and troubleshooter for WTI Insurers, Inc. During an interview for a position as her assistant, she asks you to identify and describe how you would resolve a hardware configuration problem. To assist you with this task, she hands you a printed copy of the Device Manager hardware tree shown in Figure 12-53.

Figure 12-53

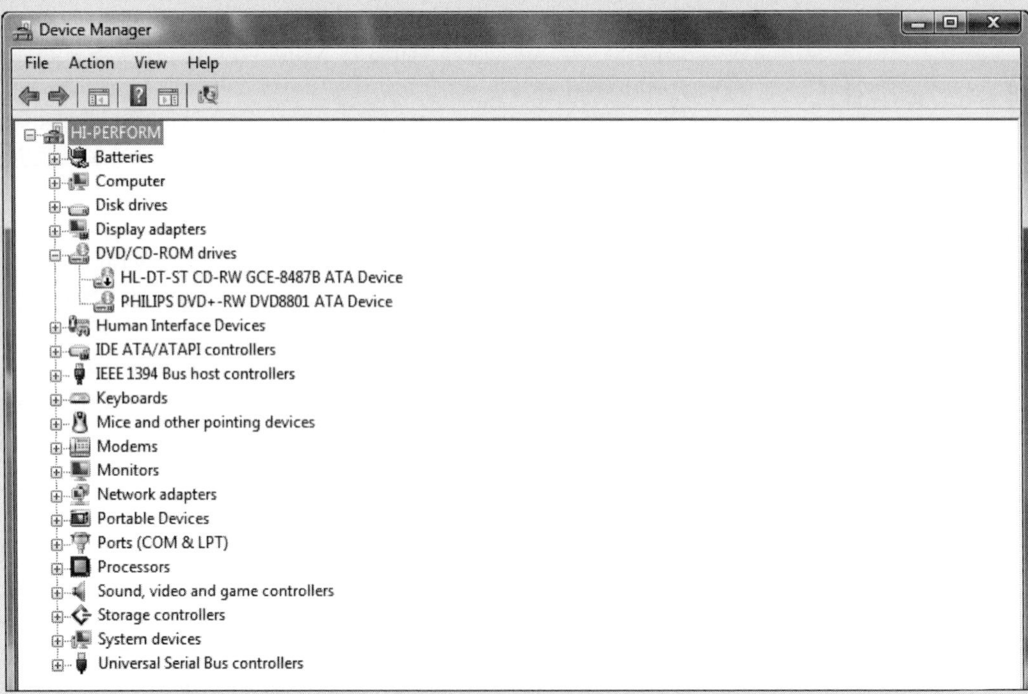

As you complete each step in this case, record your answers so you can submit them to your instructor. Use a word processing application, such as Word or WordPad, to prepare and then print your answers to these questions. Also, if you change any settings on the computer you are using, note the original settings so you can restore them later.

1. Which device does Device Manager identify as the one with a problem?
2. What type of hardware configuration problem is this?
3. Describe how you would find out more information about this problem using Device Manager.
4. How would you correct this problem using the information provided and tools found in Device Manager?
5. Submit your document to your instructor, either in printed or electronic form, as requested.

Apply | Case Problem 2

Use the skills you learned in the tutorial to troubleshoot a hardware problem.

There are no Data Files needed for this Case Problem.

Safety First Chimney Services Ruben Dickson operates his own chimney services company and keeps track of all his clients, billing, financial information, taxes, and other business information on a networked computer in his office. Recently, he encountered a problem with one of the hardware devices on his computer, and he asks you to help him identify and troubleshoot the problem. You start by examining a printout of the Device Manager hardware tree from his computer. See Figure 12-54.

Figure 12-54

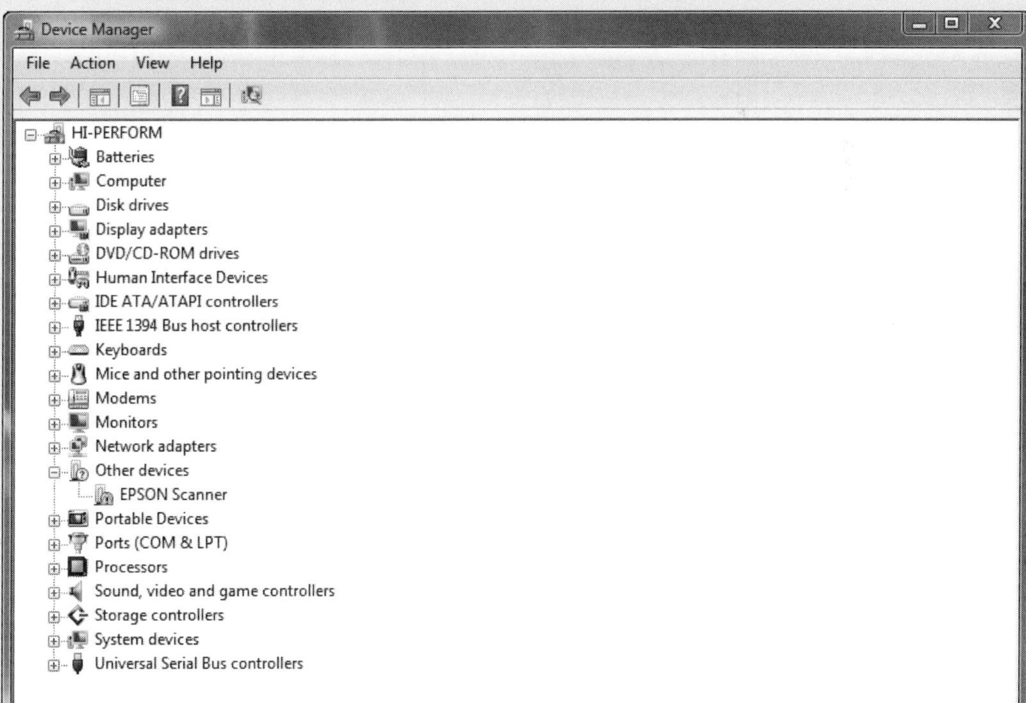

As you complete each step in this case, record your answers so you can submit them to your instructor. Use a word processing application, such as Word or WordPad, to prepare your answers to these questions. Also, if you change any settings on the computer you are using, note the original settings so you can restore them later.

1. Which device does Device Manager identify as the one with a problem?
2. What type of hardware configuration problem is this?
3. How can you use Device Manager to obtain information about this problem?
4. How can you use System Information to obtain information about this problem? (EXPLORE)
5. What is the most likely cause of this problem, and what approaches can you use to resolve this problem?
6. Submit your document to your instructor, either in printed or electronic form, as requested.

Apply | Case Problem 3

Use the skills you learned in the tutorial to troubleshoot a hardware installation problem.

There are no Data Files needed for this Case Problem.

Specialists To Go Antwan Bourdon works for a temporary employment agency that places network specialists and technical support personnel on temporary assignments for businesses in the greater Chicago metropolitan area. As he starts his next temporary job assignment, Device Manager reports a hardware problem when he attempts to install an ink-jet printer on a computer for his client, as shown in Figure 12-55. He asks you to help him figure out the best approach to take in resolving this problem.

Figure 12-55

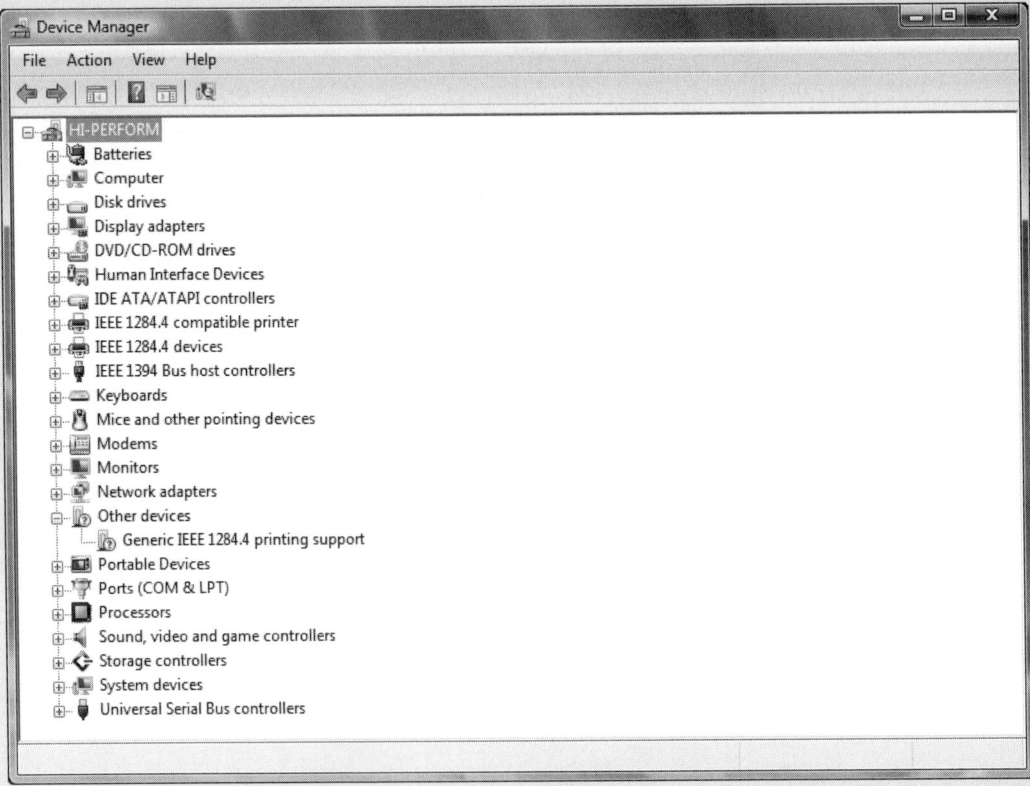

As you complete each step in this case, record your answers so you can submit them to your instructor. Use a word processing application, such as Word or WordPad, to prepare your answers to these questions. Also, if you change any settings on the computer you are using, note the original settings so you can restore them later.

1. Which device does Device Manager identify as the one with a problem?
2. What type of hardware configuration problem is this?
3. EXPLORE What would be your first guess as to the cause of this problem?
4. After examining the General property sheet for this device, you discover that Windows Vista reports that the device is working; however, you are unable to print with this device. When you examine the Drivers property sheet, Windows Vista notes that the Driver Provider is unknown, the Driver Date and Driver Version are not available, and that the driver is not digitally signed. When you open the Driver File Details dialog box, Windows Vista reports that no driver files are required or have been loaded for this device. You also discover that System Information does not report any problems with hardware devices. Does this additional information confirm your initial conclusion? Explain.
5. EXPLORE How would you correct this problem using the information provided and tools found in Device Manager?
6. Submit your document to your instructor, either in printed or electronic form, as requested.

Challenge | Case Problem 4

Use the skills you learned in the tutorial to set up a small business network.

There are no Data Files needed for this Case Problem.

Mark West Modeling Company Rex Soliz is the IT specialist for Mark West Modeling Company in New York City. He is in the process of setting up a small business workgroup for his employer, and he enlists your help so that he can complete the task today.

To complete this Case Problem, you must be working on a networked computer that is part of a workgroup. As you complete each step in this case, record your answers so you can submit them to your instructor. Use a word processing application, such as Word or WordPad, to prepare your answers to these questions. Also, if you change any settings on the computer you are using, note the original settings so you can restore them later.

1. Locate and list the Computer Name, Computer Description, and Workgroup Name for your computer.
2. When you are ready to set up the other computers on the same network, what should you do so that each computer can access network resources on other computers in the same workgroup?
3. What are the names of the computers in your workgroup, and what operating system is installed on each computer?
4. EXPLORE Draw a diagrammatic representation of the makeup of this workgroup and indicate how each computer is connected to each other and to the Internet. Include any networked printers in your diagram.
5. EXPLORE Is your network a Public or a Private network? What are the advantages of each type of network location? (*Hint*: Try the Customize link in the Network and Sharing Center.)

EXPLORE

6. Examine the options for each of the Sharing and Discovery settings in the Network and Sharing Center. (*Hint*: Expand each of the Sharing and Discovery settings.) What are your current Sharing and Discovery settings, and how do those settings affect the use of your computer in your workgroup?
7. Create, and then share a folder named "Mark West Modeling Company" in your Public Documents folder. Then, describe the process that you used. What is the UNC path to this shared folder?
8. Remove sharing from this folder, and then describe the process that you used.
9. Create a "Mark West Modeling Company" folder on another computer in the same workgroup, and then share the folder.
10. Create a mapped drive to the shared "Mark West Modeling Company" folder on that other computer in the same workgroup. Describe how you created the mapped drive, and then open a Computer window and identify its UNC path and drive name.
11. Remove the mapped drive, and then describe the process that you used.
12. Submit your document to your instructor, either in printed or electronic form, as requested.

Review | Quick Check Answers

Session 12.1

1. Plug and Play
2. USB, IEEE 1394 (or IEEE 1394b)
3. Bandwidth
4. Device Manager
5. A resource conflict occurs when two hardware devices attempt to share the same resource.
6. Roll Back Driver button

Session 12.2

1. A peer-to-peer network, or workgroup, is a network in which each computer is an equal; there is no server that manages network resources and provides network users access to those resources. Instead, computers communicate directly with each other, and each user decides which resources to share with other users on the same network.
2. UNC (Universal Naming Convention) path
3. network discovery
4. \\HI-TECH\Alexander Medical Research Institute is the UNC path for a shared folder named "Alexander Medical Research Institute" located on a network computer named "HI-TECH."
5. True
6. mapped drive

Ending Data Files

There are no ending Data Files needed for this tutorial.

Tutorial 13

Objectives

Session 13.1
- Learn about the importance of command-line skills
- Use internal and external commands
- Obtain Help on the use of a command
- Customize a command-line window
- Display a command reference list

Session 13.2
- Display a directory tree
- Change directories and view directory listings
- Create a directory and copy files
- Use wildcards
- Create a batch program

Using the Windows Command-Line Environment

Complementing GUI Skills with Command-Line Skills

Case | Assets First Credit Union

As the IT Administrator for Assets First Credit Union in Appleton, Wisconsin, Eve Larsen manages the credit union's computer network. Like other skilled computer professionals, she relies on the use of Windows Vista's command-line environment to configure and troubleshoot problems as well as perform operations not possible from the graphical user interface. Eve recently hired you as a network technician to assist her with managing and troubleshooting the credit union's network.

Starting Data Files

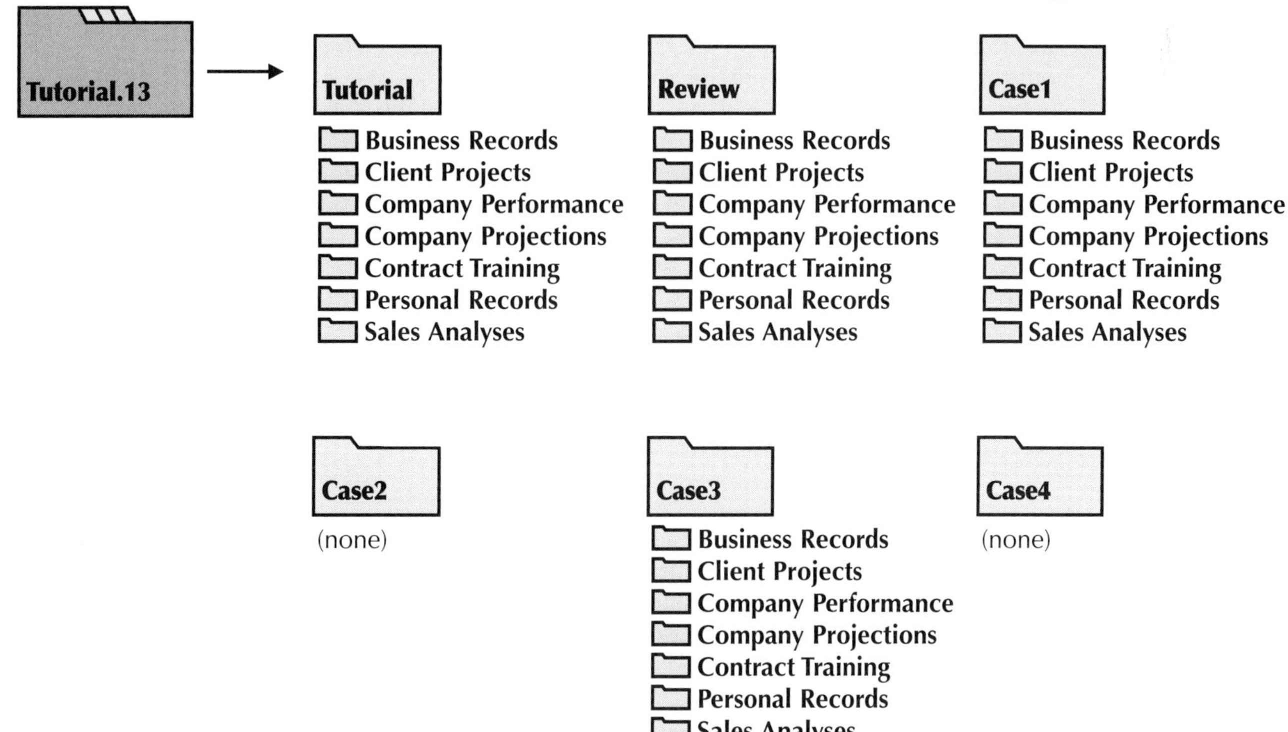

Session 13.1

Understanding the Importance of Command-Line Skills

After the introduction of the Windows operating system, there has been a gradual, but dramatic, shift from working in a command-line environment, as typified by DOS, to operating systems like Windows that rely primarily on a graphical user interface. However, command-line skills are still essential today, especially for those who manage networks and for those who provide technical support and troubleshooting. Furthermore, concepts and features incorporated into DOS are important for understanding the Windows operating system and how it works. For example, when working with DOS, you had to know how to navigate a computer system by specifying the MS-DOS path to drives and directories (or folders). DOS also relied on the path for locating and loading applications and other programs stored in different directories. Likewise, Windows Vista and all previous versions of the Windows operating system rely on the path to locate and load applications and other programs. However, instead of navigating your computer in a command-line environment by specifying the path of each and every location you want to use, you now click icons to select and open folders and subfolders.

If you are a network administrator, specialist, technician, or troubleshooter, you must know command-line skills and concepts because you will need to use them to set up, configure, and troubleshoot a network. These same skills and concepts are also important if you need to troubleshoot operating system, hardware, and software problems on a client's, employee's, or friend's computer, or even your own computer. If you experience a serious problem with starting Windows Vista, you can use the Safe Mode with Command Prompt option on the Advanced Boot Options menu to boot your computer and troubleshoot a problem in a command-line environment. If you contact technical support to help you with a problem, that person might guide you through the process of working with commands from a command-line environment to resolve the problem. If you need to perform a task not possible in the graphical user interface, you turn to a command-line environment.

To acquire professional certifications in certain specialties, such as networking, you have to prove competency in the use of command-line skills. At many colleges, a command-line class is a requirement for networking courses that lead to certification in a specific area and that provide skills for a particular type of job. Other professions, such as trainers, also benefit from command-line skills, as those skills may prove valuable when trying to resolve a problem or when trying to illustrate a concept or feature. Also, as you will discover in this tutorial, you can perform operations in a command-line window far faster than in the graphical user interface.

Setting Up Your Computer

To complete this section of the tutorial, you must display the Computer icon on the desktop, switch your computer to single-click activation, and display Run on the Start menu.

To set up your computer:

1. If necessary, display the Computer icon on the desktop, open a Computer window, enable single-click activation, and then close the Computer window.

2. Check your Start menu, and if the Run option is not displayed on the Start menu, right-click the **Start** button, click **Properties**, click the **Customize** button to the right of the Start menu style option button on the Start Menu tab in the Taskbar and Start Menu Properties dialog box, locate and click the **Run command** check box in the Customize Start Menu dialog box, click the **OK** button to close the Customize Start Menu dialog box, and then click the **OK** button to close the Taskbar and Start Menu Properties dialog box.

Now, you are ready to examine the command-line environment.

Conventions for Working in a Command-Line Environment

Since the process for working in a command-line environment is different from that used when working in a graphical user interface, and since this process relies on the precise use and approach for entering commands, the following conventions are used for this tutorial only:

- Commands you type in tutorial steps are displayed in lowercase and in boldface. In most cases, you can use uppercase, lowercase, or mixed case when entering commands.
- Punctuation (such as commas, semi-colons, or periods) is not used after commands (even though it might be grammatically correct) because you might conclude that the punctuation is part of the command, and then enter it with the command. That creates an error condition, and Windows Vista displays an error message.
- If a command contains multiple parts, each part may be separated from the part that preceded it and the part that follows it by two spaces or by an extra wide space, so that you know that you should use a space and so that you do not inadvertently run two parts of a command together and encounter a problem.
- Certain commands are displayed in a monospaced font (where each character takes up the same amount of space) rather than a proportional font (where each character takes up only the space it needs) so that you can more easily identify hard-to-distinguish characters or symbols in a command.
- Commands that include the number 0 or 1 are identified as such (namely, zero or the number one) so that you do not interpret the 0 or 1 as the uppercase letter "O" or the lowercase letter "L" (which look similar).
- Commands listed in Reference Windows, which summarize steps, are displayed in all uppercase. In the tutorial steps, commands are shown in lowercase and boldface, which helps you spot and distinguish the command from the surrounding text; however, this is not the case in the Reference Windows, so uppercase serves the same purpose.
- Commands and switches (optional parameters described in more detail later) are displayed in uppercase in explanatory text so that they are consistent with how they are presented when viewing Help on a command. When entering the actual command with the switch, you typically use lowercase because it's easier than typing in uppercase.

Although you might have some flexibility in entering commands in some cases, such as whether you include a space between a command and a switch, it is good practice to be consistent in the way you work to reduce the chances of accidentally entering a command in a format that results in an error condition.

When entering commands from the keyboard, it's not uncommon to press the wrong key or keys and make mistakes. If you inadvertently mistype a command in the Command Prompt window, you might see the following type of message:

'*Command*' is not recognized as an internal or external command, operable program or batch file

In this error message, *Command* (in italics) is the actual command you typed. If this occurs, you enter the command again with the correct spelling and spacing. If you type the command itself correctly, but make a mistake with the use of an optional parameter, such as a switch, the type of error message that you see will differ.

Opening a Command Prompt Window

In Tutorial 6, you examined how to use the command-line Check Disk utility and command-line DEFRAG utility from a Command Prompt window. In Tutorial 8, you learned how to boot your computer to a command prompt with the Advanced Boot Options menu. Therefore, you are already familiar with the use of specific Windows Vista features that require a command-line environment.

To work in a command-line environment under Windows Vista, you open a Command Prompt window in one of the following ways:

- **Accessories menu** You can choose Command Prompt on the Accessories menu. If you right-click Command Prompt on the Accessories menu, you can choose the "Run as administrator" option to work in a command-line window with commands that require Administrator privileges.
- **Start menu** You can choose Run on the Start menu, type cmd (a command), and then click the OK button. However, you first have to enable the option for displaying the Run command on the Start menu.
- **Search** If you press the Windows Logo key, you can type command in the Search box, and then click Command Prompt in the Search results. You can also type cmd (a command) in the Search box, and then press the Enter key or click cmd.exe in the Search results.
- **Folder shortcut menu** If you hold down the Shift key while you right-click a folder, Windows Vista may display the option "Open Command Window Here" on the shortcut menu. When available, this option opens a Command Prompt window so that you can work with the contents of the folder.

In each of these cases, Windows Vista uses the cmd.exe program in the System32 directory to open a Command Prompt window. A **directory** is the command-line term for a folder. Cmd.exe is the Windows command interpreter. A **command interpreter** is a program that interprets commands entered at the command prompt, locates the appropriate program in memory or on disk, loads the program (if necessary), and then executes the program. The Windows command interpreter also displays the command prompt `C:\>` so that you can enter commands. The **command prompt**, or **operating system prompt**, is the notation used in a command-line window to identify the path, drive, and directory currently in use. The command prompt therefore provides you with a reference point for working in the directory structure of a drive.

After your initial orientation, you and Eve agree to spend a couple of hours each afternoon during your first week of work to review the basics of working with Windows Vista's command-line environment. Eve wants to start by showing you how to open a command-line session, enter and use some basic Windows Vista commands, navigate the directory structure of your computer, and customize system settings.

In the following steps, you are going to examine two approaches for opening a command-line session.

To open a Command Prompt window:

1. On the Start menu, point to **All Programs**, click **Accessories**, and then click **Command Prompt**. Windows Vista opens a Command Prompt window on the desktop and displays a command prompt (or operating system prompt) that identifies the default drive (in this case, drive C) and the path to your user account directory. See Figure 13-1. Note that "Command Prompt" appears on the title bar of the window. On Eve's computer, the command prompt in the Command Prompt window shows the path to the directory for Eve's user account. After this path, the Windows command interpreter displays a greater than symbol (>) to separate the path from any command that you enter. Note that the Command Prompt window also identifies the operating system (Microsoft Windows), and the version of Windows (Version 6.0.6000, the original version of Windows Vista on the computer used for this figure). Your version may differ. When you work in the graphical user interface, you use the terms "folder" and "subfolder" to describe the file system components for organizing and tracking files. However, when working in a command-line environment, you use the comparable terms "directory" and "subdirectory" instead.

Figure 13-1 Command Prompt window

2. Type **exit** and then press the **Enter** key. Windows Vista closes the Command Prompt window. After you enter a command at the command prompt, you must press the **Enter** key; otherwise, nothing will happen. The **Enter** key signals the operating system to execute the command you typed.

Tip

When entering commands in a Command Prompt window, you can use uppercase, lowercase, or mixed case.

You must also be familiar with the difference between the concept of the current directory and the default directory when working in a command-line window. The **current directory** is the directory currently in use. The Windows command interpreter displays the path to the current directory in the command prompt. If you change to another directory, that directory becomes the current directory. If you change to another drive, the Windows command interpreter switches to a specific directory on that drive, and that directory becomes the current directory. The **default drive** and the **default directory** are the drive and directory used by the Windows command interpreter when you first open a Command Prompt window.

Next, open a Command Prompt window using the Run command.

To open a Command Prompt window:

1. On the Start menu, click **Run**, type **cmd** in the Open text box, and press the **Enter** key (as you would in a command-line environment). Windows Vista opens a command-line window, but instead of displaying the label "Command Prompt" in the title bar, it displays the path to the program that it opened, namely, cmd.exe from the system32 directory. See Figure 13-2.

Figure 13-2 **Command-line window**

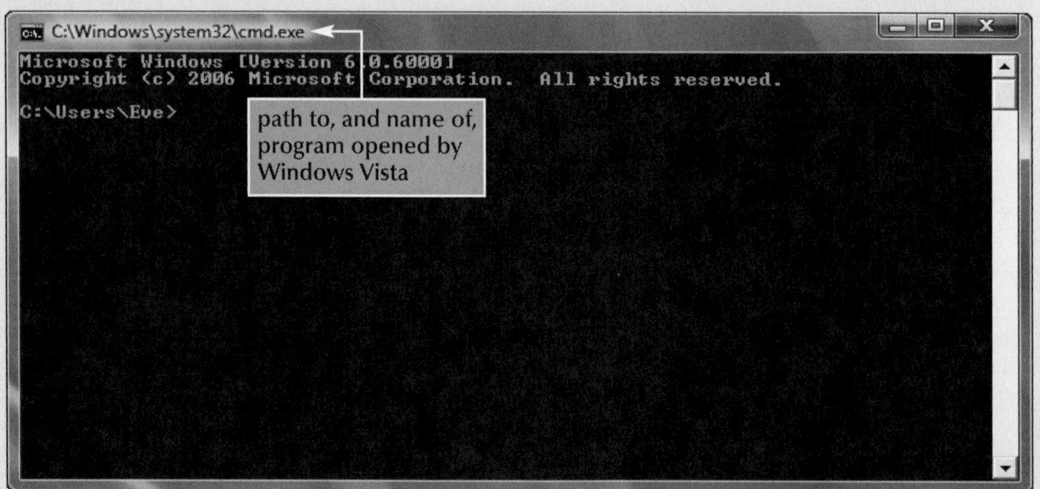

2. Type **exit** and press the **Enter** key to close the command-line window.

The commands in this tutorial do not require Administrator privileges. However, if you are working with certain commands, such as CHKDSK and DEFRAG that require Administrator privileges, you can open a command-line window with Administrator credentials using either Run or the Search box on the Start menu by using the following command:

```
runas /user:<Administrator account name> cmd
```

The first part of the command is the RUNAS ("Run As") command. The second part of the command specifies the name of the user account that you want to use. The third part of the command is "cmd" for opening a Command Prompt window. When you type this command, you replace <Administrator account name> with the name of an Administrator account. For example, when Eve wants to work in a command-line window with Administrator credentials, she enters the following command:

```
runas /user:Eve cmd
```

As shown in Figure 13-3, Windows Vista then opens a command-line window with "C:\Windows\system32\runas.exe" displayed in the title bar, and then displays a prompt for the password for this account.

Figure 13-3 RUN AS program prompts for Administrator account password

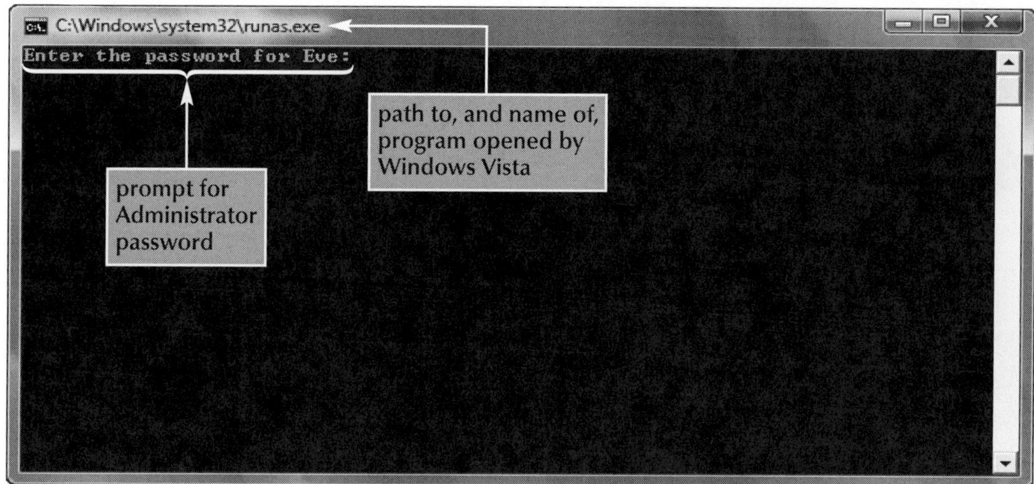

As Eve types her password, Windows Vista does not display any characters. After she finishes typing the password, she presses the Enter key, and then Windows Vista updates the command-line window. See Figure 13-4. Note that Windows Vista displays "cmd (running as HI-PERFORM\Eve)" on the title bar; HI-PERFORM is the name of the computer used for this figure.

Figure 13-4 Command-line window opened under an Administrator account

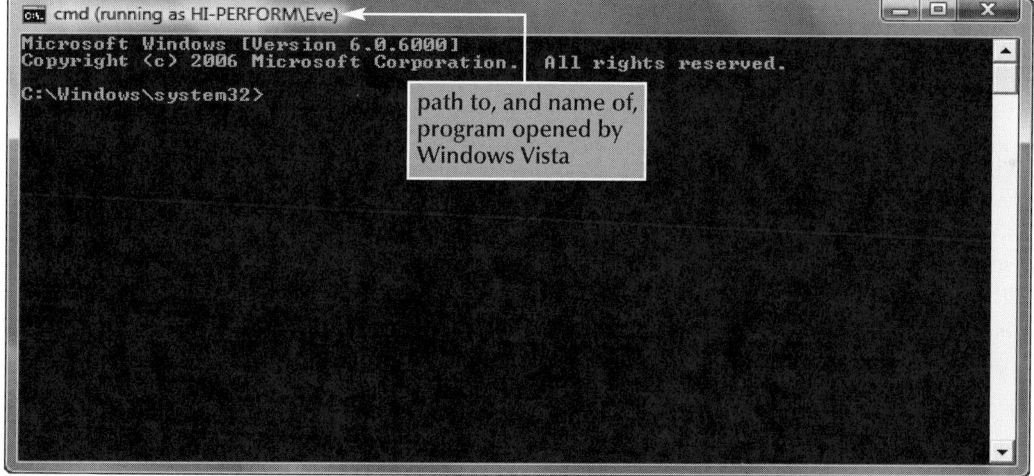

Eve can also enter the command as follows:

```
runas /user:HI-PERFORM\Eve cmd
```

In this case, she specifies the computer name HI-PERFORM.

`/user:<user account name>` is an example of a more complex switch. A **switch** is an optional parameter that you use with a command to change the way in which the command works. Most switches are preceded by a forward slash (/); however, a few, such as the DEFRAG command-line switches you examined in Tutorial 6, are preceded with a hyphen (-). `<user account name>` is a required component of the user switch (as indicated by the use of angular brackets).

Reference Window | Opening and Closing a Command Prompt Window

- On the Start menu, point to All Programs, click Accessories, and then click Command Prompt. (Or on the Start menu, click Run, type CMD (case does not matter) in the Open text box, and then press the Enter key. However, you must first enable the option for displaying Run on the Start menu.)
- To close the Command Prompt window, type EXIT and then press the Enter key.

As you can see, using Run or Search on the Start menu is a faster way to open a Command Prompt window. When you use the Run option, you are, in effect, working in a miniature command-line window. As a power user, one of the first things you will want to do when setting up a computer is to include Run on the Start menu.

Using Internal and External Commands

Once you open a Command Prompt window, you can enter commands at the command prompt to perform specific operations. These commands fall into two groups: internal commands and external commands. Internal commands are usually commands for common and important types of operations, such as creating a directory (or folder). The program code for an **internal command** is stored in the file cmd.exe.

When you open a Command Prompt window, Windows Vista loads the program code contained in the file cmd.exe into memory. Then, cmd.exe performs specific operations, such as displaying a **text user interface (TUI)** with a command prompt and interpreting commands that you enter. Once cmd.exe loads into memory, you can access the program code for any of the internal commands it contains within itself. Since the operating system does not have to go back to disk to locate and load the program code for an internal command (it's already in memory), internal commands execute more quickly. **Execute** means that the instructions in the program are processed. Figure 13-5 lists examples of internal commands and their usage. Commands are shown in uppercase; however, as noted earlier, you can use lowercase when you enter a command. Items shown in italics within square brackets, such as [*drive:*] and [*path*], are optional **parameters** or items of data that you can use with the command. If you do not specify the drive and path for those commands that use them, Windows Vista uses the current drive and directory. Items shown in italics without square brackets, such as *drive:* and *filename* are required parameters; you must enter them. The EXIT command, which you used in the previous section's tutorial steps, is an example of an internal command.

Internal commands **Figure 13-5**

Internal Command	Use
ASSOC	Displays associations for specific file types and changes associations for file types
CD [*drive:*]*path* CHDIR [*drive:*]*path*	Changes from the current directory to another directory
CD \ CHDIR \	Changes from the current directory to the root directory
CD .. CHDIR ..	Changes to the parent directory of the current subdirectory
CLS	Clears the Command Prompt or command-line window
COLOR [*attr*]	Sets foreground and background colors
command /?	Displays Help information on the command you specify
COPY *directory1 directory2*	Copies all the files in the source directory (*directory1*) to another directory (*directory2*)
COPY *filename directory*	Copies a file to another directory (using the same filename)
COPY *filename drive:*	Copies a file to another drive (using the same filename)
COPY *filename1 filename2*	Copies a file in the current directory and creates a new file with a new name in the same directory
DATE	Displays or sets the system date
DEL [*drive:*][*path*]*filespec* [/*p*] ERASE [*drive:*][*path*]*filespec* [/*p*]	Deletes a file, or a group of files (if wildcards are used), with an option to prompt for verification (/p)
DIR	Displays a directory listing of the current subdirectory on the current drive
DIR *directory*	Displays a directory listing for a specific directory
DIR *drive:*	Displays a directory listing of the current directory on a specific drive
DIR *filespec*	Displays a directory listing for a specific group of files (if wildcards are used) or for a single file
EXIT	Closes the Command Prompt window
MD [*drive:*]*path* MKDIR [*drive:*]*path*	Creates a directory
MOVE [*drive:*][*path*]*filespec destination*	Moves one or more files to another drive, directory, or drive and directory
MOVE *directory1 directory2*	Renames a directory
PATH	Displays the Windows path
PATH [*drive:*]*path1*;[*drive:*]*path2*;...	Changes the current Windows path to a new path that includes the paths of directories listed after the Path command
PROMPT PG	Displays the full path in the command prompt, followed by a greater-than symbol
PROMPT [*metastring*]	Customizes the appearance of the command prompt
RD [*drive:*]*path* [/*s*] RMDIR [*drive:*]*path* [/*s*]	Removes a directory and all its contents when used with the Subdirectory switch (/s)
REN [*drive:*][*path*]*filename1 filename2* RENAME [*drive:*][*path*]*filename1 file-name2*	Changes the name of a file, or if wildcards are used with a file specification, changes the name of a group of files
SET	Displays, sets, or removes environment variables and their settings
START *filespec*	Opens a file and its associated Windows application from a command prompt
START *program*	Opens a Windows application from a command prompt
TIME	Displays or sets the system time
TITLE [*text*]	Changes the text displayed in the title bar of a Command Prompt or command-line window
TYPE [*drive:*][*path*]*filename*	Displays the contents of a text file
VER	Displays the Windows version
VERIFY [*ON*] or [*OFF*]	Instructs Cmd.exe whether to verify that files are correctly written to disk, or displays the current verify setting
VOL [*drive:*]	Displays the volume label for a drive

In contrast to internal commands, the program code for an **external command** resides in a specific file on disk. When you enter an external command in a command-line environment, the command you type is actually the first part of the filename—the part before the file extension. The operating system locates the file on disk, and then loads the program into memory so that it can perform its intended function. As you discovered in Tutorial 8, Windows Vista looks for files that have the name you specify and that have a specific file extension, such as "com," "exe," and "bat". Figure 13-6 lists examples of some external commands and their usage. The external commands are stored in the System32 directory under the Windows directory. The command CMD that you used in the previous section's tutorial steps is an example of an external command.

Figure 13-6 **External commands**

External Command	Use
ATTRIB [*drive*:][*path*][*filename*]	Displays file attributes
ATTRIB *filespec* ±[*attribute*]	Assigns or removes a file attribute
CHKDSK [*drive*:] [/*f*]	Examines the status of a disk, checks for errors, produces a report on disk space usage, and when used with /F, fixes file system errors on the disk
CHKNTFS *volume*	Displays or modifies the checking of a disk during booting
CMD	Runs the Windows command interpreter and opens a Command Prompt or command-line window
<*command*> /?	Displays Help information on a command you specify
COMP *filename1 filename2*	Compares the contents of two files
COMPACT [*filename*]	Displays or changes the compression of a file on an NTFS volume
CONVERT *volume*	Converts a FAT volume to an NTFS volume
DEFRAG *volume* [/*a*]	Defragments a volume, or when used with the /A switch, produces a fragmentation analysis of a volume
DOSKEY	Edits and recalls commands entered at the command prompt
DRIVERQUERY	Displays a list of installed device drivers
EXPAND *source destination*	Expands (and extracts) one or more compressed files
FC *filename1 filename2*	Compares two files and displays information on differences between the files
FIND "string" *filespec*	Searches for a text string (set of characters) in a file or group of files
FINDSTR [*strings*] [*filespec*]	Searches for strings in files
FORMAT *drive*:	Formats a disk in a drive to the maximum capacity of that drive
FTYPE	Displays or modifies file types
HELP [*command*]	Displays Help information on one or more commands
IPCONFIG [/all]	Displays the IP address, subnet mask, and default gateway for each network adapter bound to TCP/IP, and displays full configuration information with the All switch (/all)
LABEL [*drive*:]	Displays, creates, changes, or removes a disk's volume label
MMC	Opens Microsoft Management Console from a Command Prompt window
MODE	Configures system devices, including serial and parallel ports, the video display, and keyboard; and redirects output from a parallel port to a serial port
MORE	Produces paged output when used with another command and the pipe operator (I)

External commands (continued)

Figure 13-6

External Command	Use
PRINT *filespec*	Prints a text file
RECOVER *drive*	Recovers data from defective sectors on a disk
REPLACE *source destination*	Replaces (or updates) files, and adds new files
SCHTASKS	Lists, creates, deletes, changes, runs, and ends scheduled tasks
SORT	Sorts output when used with another command and the pipe operator (|)
SUBST *drive*: [*drive*:]*path*	Creates a virtual drive by assigning a drive name to a directory
SUBST *drive*: /d	Removes a virtual drive
SYSTEMINFO	Compiles information about the configuration of a computer system
TASKKILL	Ends one or more processes using the Process ID (PID) or image name
TASKLIST	Displays a list of currently running processes on a computer
TREE [*drive*:][*path*]	Graphically displays the directory structure of a drive or path
XCOPY *source destination* [/s]	Copies all the files in a directory, or a group of files, or a single file, to another disk and, when used with the Subdirectory switch (/s), also copies the subdirectory structure to that disk

To use internal and external commands, you must not only know what commands are available, but you also must know the syntax for entering each command. **Syntax** (pronounced "sin tax") refers to the proper format for entering a command, including how to spell the command (some are abbreviated, such as CHKDSK for "Check Disk"), how to use required parameters (such as specifying a drive), and optional parameters (such as a switch), as well as the spacing between the command, required parameters, and optional parameters. As you will discover in this tutorial, the command-line interface is syntax sensitive. You must type the command exactly as specified, or the command interpreter will display an error message. Even the use of spaces (by pressing the Spacebar) count when entering commands; if you forget a required space, the command interpreter will display an error message.

To locate Help information about the use of the internal and external commands shown in Figure 13-5 and Figure 13-6, you can use the Help switch (/?) or the HELP command (both of which you will examine in the next two sections) to extract Help information from the program code for a command.

Using Help to Specify Console Colors

The default background color for the console (the command-line window) is black, and the default foreground color is white. In other words, when working in a command-line window, Windows Vista displays white text against a black background. The term **console** refers to the keyboard and monitor, which are used for input and output. Although it is possible to use a mouse in a Command Prompt window, you primarily use the keyboard.

In Windows Vista (and previous versions of Windows), you can use the COLOR command, an internal command, to change the background and foreground colors so that it is easier to work in a command-line window.

Eve suggests that you use the COLOR command to customize the Command Prompt window to best suit your needs. She also recommends that you use the Help switch (**/?**) to view options available for this command.

To view Help information on the use of the internal COLOR command:

1. On the Start menu, click **Command Prompt** in the recently used programs list, or if you do not see Command Prompt in the recently used programs list, point to the **All Programs** menu, click **Accessories**, and then click **Command Prompt**.
2. Point to the title bar of the Command Prompt window, hold down the left mouse button and drag the Command Prompt window to the top of the desktop, point to the bottom border of the Command Prompt, and when the mouse pointer changes to a double-head white arrow ⇳, drag the window border down to fill as much of the desktop above the taskbar as possible. (*Note:* Since the command-line window is an object, you can right-click the command-line window's title bar, and then select Properties to specify custom settings for the command-line window.)

   Trouble? If you maximized the window, the lower part of the window might be hidden behind the taskbar, making it difficult to view the window's contents at times. Click the Restore Down button on the Command Prompt window title bar, and then manually resize the window.

Tip

You can display the same Help information by typing HELP followed by a space and the command.

3. Type **color /?** and then press the **Enter** key. Windows Vista displays Help information on the use of the COLOR command. See Figure 13-7. After completing the command, the Windows command interpreter redisplays the command prompt so that you can enter another command.

Figure 13-7 **Viewing Help information on the COLOR command**

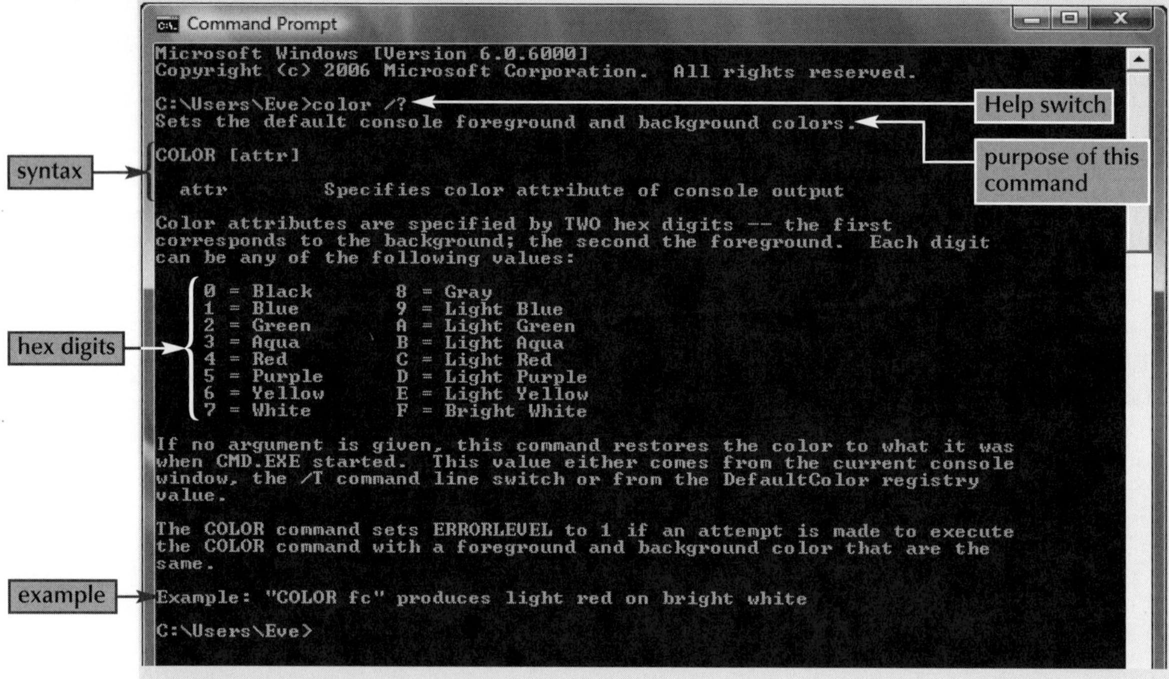

4. Keep the Command Prompt window open for the next set of tutorial steps.

The COLOR program explains the purpose of the COLOR command. As noted, you can use this command to change the default console foreground and background colors. Then, the Help information shows the syntax for the COLOR command: COLOR [attr]

That means that you type the command COLOR (using uppercase, lowercase, or mixed case) with or without the optional parameter [attr], which specifies the color attribute of the console output. If you use the optional parameter and specify a color attribute, you must include a space between the command and the optional parameter.

As shown in the Help explanation for the use of this command, you use two hex digits to specify the color attribute. A **hex digit** is one of the 16 digits used in the hexadecimal number system (0 through 9 *and* A through F). As you can see, a digit can be a number as well as a letter of the alphabet. The first hex digit is the color attribute for the background color, and the second hex digit is the color attribute for the foreground color. (This is logically backwards from the way in which individuals think of a user interface and even how they work in a text user interface. They typically think of text first and background next rather than vice-versa.) Help also lists the hex digits and their corresponding color assignments.

If you use the COLOR command without the optional color attribute parameter (also called an **argument**), the command restores the default background and foreground colors that were used when you first opened the Command Prompt window. As noted, the default settings it uses can derive from three sources—the current console window, the use of the /T switch with the CMD command, or from a setting stored in the Registry under the DefaultColor Registry value entry (covered in Tutorial 14).

The Help information also includes an example. If you enter the command "COLOR fc" without the quotation marks, the COLOR command changes the foreground and background colors so that text is displayed in light red (the color attribute "c") against a bright white background (the color attribute "f"). The default console colors (white text on a black background) would be represented by the color attribute "07" without the quotation marks.

The Help switch works with almost every command. Like any other switch, it modifies the way in which the command works.

Using the Help Switch to Display Help for a Command | Reference Window

- From the All Programs menu, click Accessories, and then click Command Prompt.
- Type the command for which you want to view Help information, press the Spacebar, type /? (the Help switch), and then press the Enter key.

Eve recommends that you first try black text against a bright white background, and then try bright white text against a light blue background.

To change the console colors:

1. Type **color f0** (the letter "f" followed by a zero), and then press the **Enter** key. The COLOR command applies the new color attributes. See Figure 13-8. If you are working in a Command Prompt window, and if that image is projected onto a screen by an overhead projector, this color attribute makes it easier for everyone in the audience to see what you are doing in the Command Prompt window.

Figure 13-8 **Console colors changed**

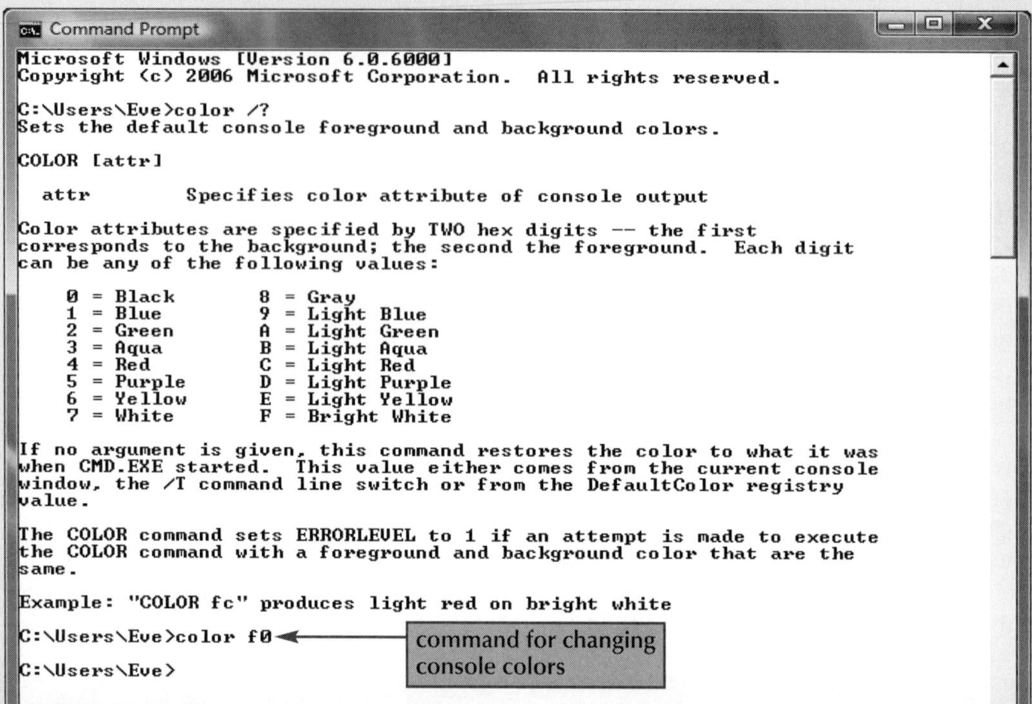

```
Microsoft Windows [Version 6.0.6000]
Copyright (c) 2006 Microsoft Corporation.  All rights reserved.

C:\Users\Eve>color /?
Sets the default console foreground and background colors.

COLOR [attr]

  attr        Specifies color attribute of console output

Color attributes are specified by TWO hex digits -- the first
corresponds to the background; the second the foreground.  Each digit
can be any of the following values:

    0 = Black       8 = Gray
    1 = Blue        9 = Light Blue
    2 = Green       A = Light Green
    3 = Aqua        B = Light Aqua
    4 = Red         C = Light Red
    5 = Purple      D = Light Purple
    6 = Yellow      E = Light Yellow
    7 = White       F = Bright White

If no argument is given, this command restores the color to what it was
when CMD.EXE started.  This value either comes from the current console
window, the /T command line switch or from the DefaultColor registry
value.

The COLOR command sets ERRORLEVEL to 1 if an attempt is made to execute
the COLOR command with a foreground and background color that are the
same.

Example: "COLOR fc" produces light red on bright white

C:\Users\Eve>color f0

C:\Users\Eve>
```


2. Type **color 9f** and then press the **Enter** key. The COLOR command changes the foreground color to bright white and the background color to blue (called light blue in the Help information for the COLOR command). If you are working on your own computer in a Command Prompt window for an extended period of time, this combination of colors is easier on the eyes than the default colors.

   Trouble? If you find the background color too bright, try another background color.

3. Keep the Command Prompt window open for the next set of tutorial steps.

You can change the console colors at any point. If you close the Command Prompt window and then later open it again, Windows Vista reverts back to the default console colors. In Tutorial 14, you will examine how to change the Windows Registry so that Windows Vista always uses console colors of your own choosing.

Reference Window | Changing Console Colors

- From the All Programs menu, click Accessories, and then click Command Prompt.
- Type COLOR /? and press the Enter key to display Help information on the use of the COLOR command, including the hex digits that you use to specify the background and foreground colors.
- To change the console colors, type COLOR followed by a space, and then the two hex digit code for the color attribute that you want to use, and then press the Enter key. For example, if you want to use white text on a blue background, you would type COLOR 9f and then press the Enter key.

When working in a Command Prompt window, you can recall previously entered commands by using the Up Arrow key, and you can use the F7 function key to display a command history. The **command history** is an area of memory that stores commands you previously entered.

To recall previously entered commands, and to view a command history:

1. Press the **Up Arrow** key once. Windows Vista recalls the previously used command: color 9f
2. Press the **Up Arrow** key again. Windows Vista recalls the command used before the color 9f command, namely: color f0
3. Press the **Enter** key. The COLOR command changes the console colors.
4. Press the **F7** function key. Windows Vista displays a command history. See Figure 13-9.

Tip

You can also use the F3 key to recall the last command.

Figure 13-9 Viewing the command history

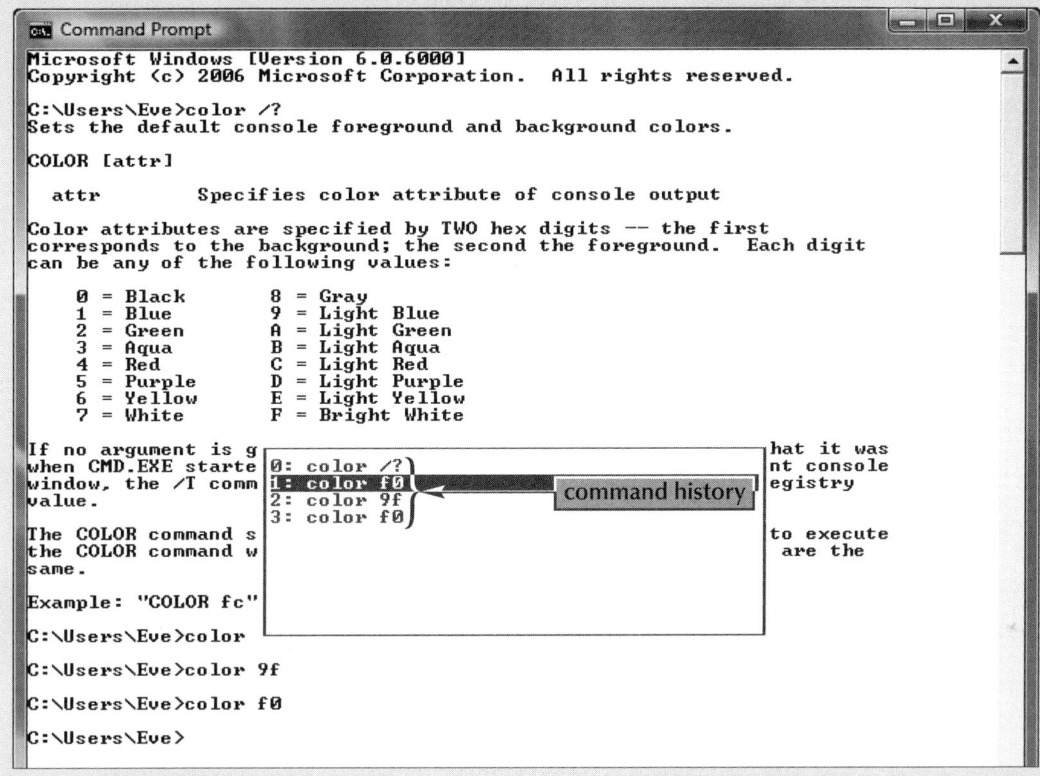

5. Press the **Down Arrow** key to select the **color 9f** command, and then press the **Enter** key. Windows Vista uses the previously entered command that you selected from the command history, and the COLOR command changes the console colors to white text against a blue background.
6. Press the **F7** function key again, press the **Down Arrow** key to select the **color f0** command, and then press the **Enter** key. The COLOR command changes the console colors again to black text against a white background. The remainder of this tutorial uses this color option for all figures so that it is easier to see the contents of the Command Prompt window.
7. Keep the Command Prompt window open for the next section of the tutorial.

You can use the Up Arrow key and Down Arrow key to scroll through the commands in the command history. You can also use the Alt+F7 keys to clear the command history and the Esc key to close the command history.

Another advantage of using the command history is that you can recall complex commands and then edit them without having to retype the entire command. When you close the Command Prompt window, all of the commands stored in the command history are erased.

Under DOS, you had to use the DOSKEY command, an external command, if you wanted to recall and edit previously entered commands and use a command history; however, under Windows Vista, these features are available as soon as you open a Command Prompt window. The DOSKEY command is also available under Windows Vista so that you can access more advanced features, such as the ability to set the size of the **buffer** (or area of memory) used for the command history.

InSight | Editing a Command Line

As you have just seen, when you work in a Command Prompt window, you have access to features that simplify selecting and entering commands. After you enter or recall a command, you can also edit the command. If you make a mistake, or if you want to change the parameters of a command, and if you have not pressed the Enter key, you can use Left Arrow key and Right Arrow key to move one character to the left or right on the command line. If you then type a character, it's inserted where you type it because **insert mode** is the default mode when editing a command line. If you want to type over one or more characters, you first press the Insert key to switch to **overtype mode**, and then start typing. The Insert key is a toggle key, so you can press the Insert key again to switch back to insert mode. A **toggle key** alternates between two related uses each time you press the key. You can use the Delete key to delete part of a command, one character at a time. You can also press the Home key to move the blinking cursor to the beginning of a command line, and the End key to move the blinking cursor to the end of the command line. If you recall a command, and then decide you do not want to use it, you press the Esc key to clear the command-line. You can also use the Esc key to clear a command that you've just typed before you press the Enter key.

Reference Window | Recalling Commands from the Command History

- To recall the previously entered command in a Command Prompt window, press the Up Arrow key or press the F3 key.
- To display the command history, press the F7 function key, use the Up Arrow key or Down Arrow key to select the command you want to use, and then press the Enter key.

Now, you and Eve turn your attention to external commands.

Using External Commands

When you opened a command-line window earlier by typing CMD in the Run box, you used an external command, and Windows Vista had to locate the file CMD.EXE in the System32 folder, and then load the program into memory before you could use it. That process is slower than using an internal command, but external commands are typically ones that you do not use as frequently. Furthermore, to locate an external command, Windows Vista must use the list of directories (or folders) specified in the path.

You can use the LABEL command, another external command, to assign a volume label to a drive, such as a flash drive. A **volume label** is an electronic label assigned to a drive. You can use volume labels to more easily distinguish one drive for another.

Before you use the LABEL command or any other command, you can use the Clear Screen (CLS) command, an internal command, to clear the Command Prompt window of the output of any previous commands. Before each step in each section of the tutorial, you will be asked to use this command so that you can clear the Command Prompt window and focus on the output of the next command. That will also make it easier for you to compare your output with that shown in the figures.

Eve points out that you can use the LABEL command to assign a custom volume label to your flash drive. She suggests that you use the HELP command first to display information on how to use this external command.

To view Help information on how to assign a volume label to a drive:

1. Type **cls** and then press the **Enter** key. The Clear Screen command (CLS) clears the window of any output and displays the command prompt in the upper-left corner of the window. Although you do not need to enter this command before you enter another command, this command does allow you to focus on the current command and its output, without having to view output of the previous command or commands.
2. Type **help label** and then press the **Enter** key. The HELP command displays Help information on the LABEL command. See Figure 13-10.

Tip

You can also obtain Help on this command by entering: LABEL /?

Figure 13-10 Viewing Help information on the LABEL command

```
Command Prompt

C:\Users\Eve>help label
Creates, changes, or deletes the volume label of a disk.

LABEL [drive:][label]
LABEL [/MP] [volume] [label]

  drive:          Specifies the drive letter of a drive.
  label           Specifies the label of the volume.
  /MP             Specifies that the volume should be treated as a
                  mount point or volume name.
  volume          Specifies the drive letter (followed by a colon),
                  mount point, or volume name.  If volume name is specified,
                  the /MP flag is unnecessary.

C:\Users\Eve>
```

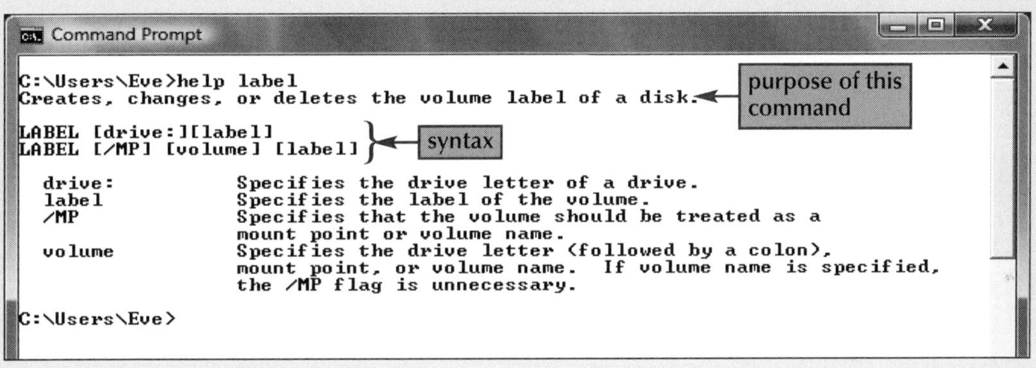

The Help information explains that the Label program creates, changes, or deletes the volume label of a disk (drive). Then, the Help information displays two different ways for entering and using this command. With the first option, LABEL [drive:][label], you type the command LABEL with or without a drive name and with or without a volume label. As noted earlier, the parameters included within square brackets are optional parameters that change the way the command works. You can use this command option in one of four ways:

- If you type LABEL and press the Enter key, the program assumes you want to create, change, or delete the volume label for the default drive, i.e., the current drive, and prompts you for the volume label. When you open a Command Prompt, Windows Vista automatically uses drive C, and that drive is now the default drive (however, you can also change the default drive).
- If you type LABEL followed by a space and then a drive name, the program prompts you to create, change, or delete the volume label for the drive you specified.
- If you type LABEL followed by a space and a volume label, the program assigns the volume label you specified to the current drive (i.e., the default drive).
- If you type LABEL followed by a space, the drive name, and a volume label (with or without a preceding space), the program assigns the volume label you specify to the drive you designated.

Now that you understand the syntax of this command, you're ready to assign a volume label to your flash drive. However, you are also going to first use the internal VOL command to display the volume name of your flash drive.

To complete the next set of tutorial steps, you must know the drive name for the flash drive. The following steps use drive F: because it's the flash drive name on the computer used in the figures; however, you will use your flash drive name when entering commands. In the following steps, drive name refers to the drive letter followed by the colon.

To clear the screen and then assign a volume label to your flash drive:

1. Attach your flash drive to the computer you are using and close any dialog boxes or windows that open.
2. If you do not know the drive name for your flash drive, open a Computer window, find the drive name of the flash drive, and then close the Computer window.
3. Return to the Command Prompt window, type **cls** and then press the **Enter** key to clear the screen.
4. Type **vol** at the command prompt, press the **Spacebar**, and then type the **drive name** of your flash drive. For example, if your flash drive has the drive name F: then you type: **VOL F:**
5. Press the **Enter** key. The Volume program displays the volume label for your flash drive (if any), and then displays its serial number. The flash drive used for Figure 13-11 does not have a volume label. Yours may differ.

Figure 13-11 Checking a flash drive's volume label

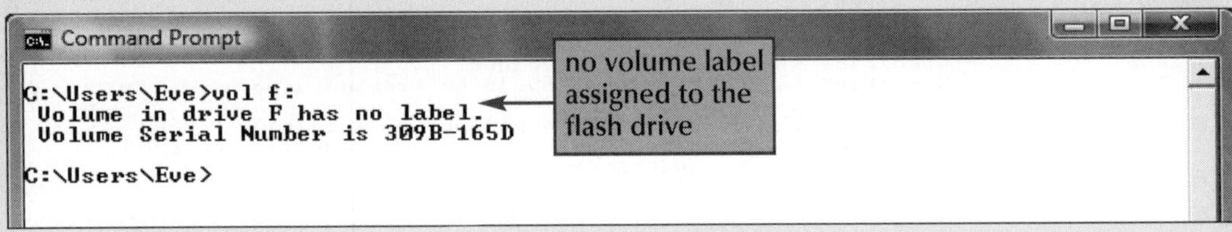

6. Type **label** at the command prompt, press the **Spacebar**, and then type the **drive name** of your flash drive. For example, if your flash drive has the drive name F: then you type: **LABEL F:**
7. Press the **Enter** key. The program displays the current volume label of your flash drive (if any), identifies its serial number, and then prompts for a volume label. See Figure 13-12. You can use up to 11 characters for the volume label on a FAT volume. If you do not want a volume label, you just press the **Enter** key (for none).

Figure 13-12 Using the LABEL command to assign a volume label

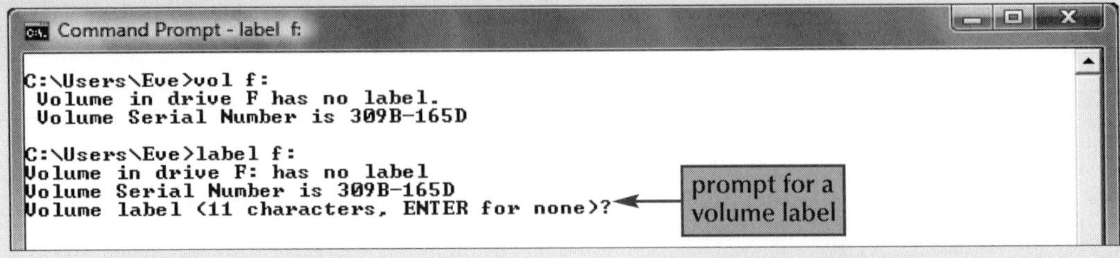

8. Type **classes** and then press the **Enter** key. The LABEL program assigns CLASSES (all uppercase) as the volume label for your flash drive.

9. Press the **Up Arrow** key *twice* to recall the `VOL F:` command that you entered previously, and then press the **Enter** key. The program displays the newly assigned volume label for your flash drive. See Figure 13-13.

Figure 13-13 Viewing a newly assigned volume label

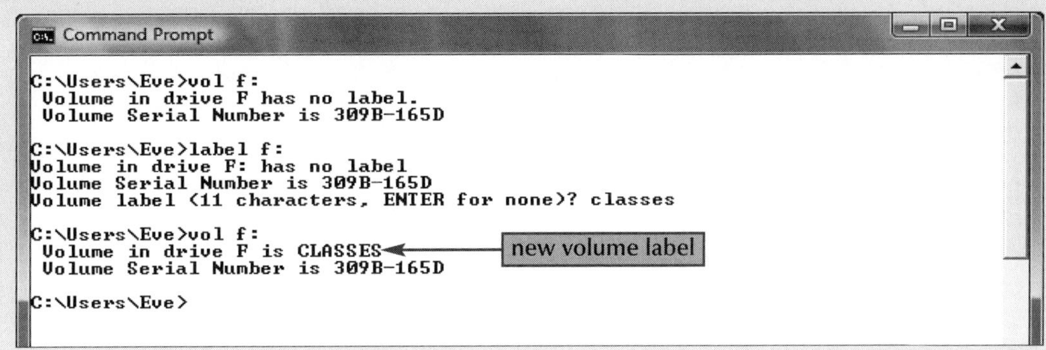

10. Keep the Command Prompt window open for the next set of tutorial steps.

You may want to assign your last name, or perhaps your first initial and last name, as a volume label for your flash drive. If you accidentally leave the flash drive in a computer lab, the lab staff and you can quickly verify that the flash drive belongs to you by examining the volume label.

In the next set of steps, you restore the original volume label for your flash drive, remove the volume label, assign a volume label of your own choosing, or keep the same volume label. (If you read but do not keystroke the following steps, your flash drive volume name will remain unchanged.)

To restore, specify, keep, or remove the volume label on your flash drive:

1. Use the **Down Arrow** key to recall the LABEL command with your flash drive name, and then press the **Enter** key.
2. To restore the original volume label or specify a different volume label for your flash drive, type the **volume label** you want to use, and then press the **Enter** key. To keep the same volume label, type the volume label again, and then press the Enter key. To remove the volume label, press the **Enter** key, and when prompted to delete the current volume label, type **Y** (case does not matter) for Yes.
3. To verify the operation, use the **Up Arrow** key to recall the last `VOL F:` command, and then press the **Enter** key.
4. Keep the Command Prompt window open for the next section of the tutorial.

You may also want to assign a custom volume name to your hard disk drive so that you can more quickly identify the drive when you open a Computer window.

Reference Window | **Checking, Assigning and Removing a Volume Label for a Flash Drive**

- If necessary, attach your flash drive to your computer, and then close any dialog boxes or windows that open.
- If you do not know the drive name for your flash drive, open a Computer window, locate its drive name, and then close the Computer window.
- Open the All Programs menu, click Accessories, and then click Command Prompt.
- Type LABEL followed by a space, type the drive name for your flash drive, and then press the Enter key.
- When prompted, type a volume label, and then press the Enter key.
- To verify the volume name, type VOL followed by a space, type the drive name for your flash drive, and then press the Enter key.
- To remove a volume name from your flash drive, type LABEL followed by a space, type the drive name for your flash drive, press the Enter key, and when prompted for a volume name, press the Enter key again, type Y for Yes to the prompt for deleting the volume label, and then press the Enter key.

Eve mentions that you can also display a list of available commands whenever you need help locating a command.

Displaying a Command Reference List

If you want to locate a specific command or just find out what types of commands are available, you can display a list of commands from the Command Prompt window by using the external HELP command.

To view the commands for which Help is available, Eve suggests you use the HELP command by itself.

To display a command reference list:

1. Type **cls** and press the **Enter** key to clear the screen.
2. Type **help** and then press the **Enter** key. The Help program lists commands in alphabetical order and provides a brief description of the use of each command. Notice that for the VOL command, HELP explains that this command "displays a disk volume label and serial number." Because the window is not large enough to display all the commands in this command reference list, the first commands that were displayed scrolled off screen.
3. Press the **Up Arrow** key to recall the HELP command you previously entered, press the **Spacebar**, type **|** (a vertical bar found as the uppercase character on the key with the backslash character), press the **Spacebar** again, type **more** and then press the **Enter** key. Your final command should be: **HELP | MORE**

   In the Command Prompt window, you can now see the first page of commands, followed by a More prompt at the bottom of the window. See Figure 13-14.

   Trouble? Although the vertical bar appears as a single vertical bar in a document, it appears as a vertical bar with two separate smaller bars in a Command Prompt window. The key on your keyboard might show a single vertical bar or two separate smaller vertical bars.

Figure 13-14 Command reference list

This last command relies on some important concepts and provides insight into the use of other command-line techniques. The command was:

```
HELP | MORE
```

The vertical bar is called the **pipe operator**, and it pipes (or redirects) the output of the HELP command to the MORE filter. When you **pipe** output, you are using the output of one command (i.e., HELP) as the input for another command (i.e., MORE). In this case, the HELP command outputs a list of commands for which Help information is available, along with a brief description of the use of each command. Rather than displaying the output in the Command Prompt window, that output is then passed to the MORE filter by the pipe operator. The MORE filter then produces **paged output**; in other words, it displays one window (i.e., one page) of output at a time. After each page of output, the MORE filter displays the prompt "-- More --" so that you know there is more output to view.

The MORE command (an external command) is called a **filter** because it modifies the output of another command. The entire command is called a **pipeline**. These techniques enable you to modify the use of one command with another command so that it is easier to work within a command-line environment. Some commands (one of which you will examine later) include a Pause or Page switch (/P) for producing paged output, so in those instances, you do not need to use this technique with those commands.

InSight | **Understanding Computer Pages**

When most people use the word "page," they are thinking of an 8½ × 11-inch sheet of paper. Even though monitors typically display only one-third to one-half of the viewable area found on a sheet of paper, the viewable area within a window on the screen is still called a page. However, it is a logical page, not a physical page. When you press the Page Down key, for example, you advance a distance equal to the visible screen or window and view the next logical page within the document.

Next, you'll view the rest of the command reference list.

To view the remainder of the output:

1. Press the **Spacebar** repeatedly so that the MORE filter displays the remainder of the output, type **cls** and then press the **Enter** key.
2. Keep the Command Prompt window open for the next section of the tutorial.

Tip

If you press the Enter key, you advance through the remainder of the command list, one command at a time.

You can use the pipe operator with other commands that produce more than one screen (or one page) of output. Also, if you are using the Help switch with a command, and if the Help information exceeds more than the length of a window, you can recall the command and use the pipe operator and MORE filter to produce paged output.

Reference Window | **Displaying a Command Reference List**

- From the All Programs menu, click Accessories, and then click Command Prompt.
- To display a list of commands for which Help is available, type `HELP | MORE` and press the Enter key. After you examine the first page of output, press the Spacebar to view each of the next pages until the Windows command interpreter displays a command prompt.
- If you want to view Help information on a specific command, type the command, press the Spacebar, type /? and then press the Enter key. Or type HELP followed by a space, type the command for which you want help, and then press the Enter key.

Although you cannot use the HELP command with commands other than those shown in the command reference list that it produces, you can use the Help switch (/?) with almost all commands. You can even display Help on the HELP command by entering: HELP HELP

Unfortunately, this command reference list does not include all the commands available within Windows Vista's command-line environment, but only the commands previously used with the DOS operating system. You can, however, use Help and Support to locate online information at the Microsoft Web site about the use of all available commands.

Using the SystemInfo Command

SystemInfo, an external command, displays configuration information about a computer and its operating system.

So that you are familiar with how to check employee's computers for information about the configuration of that system and its operating system, Eve suggests that you use the SYSTEMINFO command to check her computer system, and then pipe the output of the SYSTEMINFO command to the MORE filter.

To view system information about a computer:

1. If necessary, clear the screen.
2. Type **systeminfo | more** and then press the **Enter** key. The SYSTEMINFO command compiles information for your computer, and then the MORE filter displays the first page of output. See Figure 13-15. The details of your output will differ.

System configuration information — **Figure 13-15**

```
Host Name:                 HI-PERFORM
OS Name:                   Microsoftr Windows VistaT Ultimate
OS Version:                6.0.6000 N/A Build 6000
OS Manufacturer:           Microsoft Corporation
OS Configuration:          Standalone Workstation
OS Build Type:             Multiprocessor Free
Registered Owner:          Eve
Registered Organization:
Product ID:                77777-777-7777777-77777
Original Install Date:     5/29/2007, 11:05:03 AM
System Boot Time:          12/29/2007, 8:24:59 AM
System Manufacturer:       Dell Inc.
System Model:              Dell DXG051
System Type:               X86-based PC
Processor(s):              1 Processor(s) Installed.
                           [01]: x64 Family 15 Model 6 Stepping 4 GenuineIntel ~
2992 Mhz
BIOS Version:              Dell Inc.                    A09, 5/2/2006
Windows Directory:         C:\Windows
System Directory:          C:\Windows\system32
Boot Device:               \Device\HarddiskVolume2
System Locale:             en-us;English (United States)
Input Locale:              en-us;English (United States)
Time Zone:                 (GMT-08:00) Pacific Time (US & Canada)
Total Physical Memory:     2,045 MB
Available Physical Memory: 1,203 MB
Page File: Max Size:       4,305 MB
Page File: Available:      3,439 MB
Page File: In Use:         866 MB
Page File Location(s):     C:\pagefile.sys
Domain:                    ALAN TURING
Logon Server:              \\HI-PERFORM
Hotfix(s):                 57 Hotfix(s) Installed.
                           [01]: {AC76BA86-7AD7-0000-2550-7A8C40000000} -
                           [02]: {7485C1F2-1391-46D4-B7A0-4AA27C6959CF} - Micros
oft Office Accounting Equifax Addin
                           [03]: {7485C1F2-1391-46D4-B7A0-4AA27C6959CF} - Micros
oft Office Accounting Fixed Asset Manager
                           [04]: {7485C1F2-1391-46D4-B7A0-4AA27C6959CF} - Micros
oft Office Accounting PayPal Addin
                           [05]: 933246
                           [06]: KB931133 Windows DreamScene Content
                           [07]: 929327
                           [08]: 932926
                           [09]: KB905866
                           [10]: KB925902
                           [11]: KB929399
                           [12]: KB929735
                           [13]: KB930178
                           [14]: KB930857
                           [15]: KB931099
                           [16]: KB931573
                           [17]: KB932471
                           [18]: KB932818
                           [19]: KB933579
                           [20]: KB933729
-- More --
```

hot fixes

More prompt

The Host Name identifies the name of the computer you are examining. The OS Name and OS Version identify the edition and version of Windows Vista used on a computer. The OS configuration identifies the computer used for Figure 13-15 as a standalone workstation. Another piece of information that might prove helpful in analyzing a computer is the Original Install Date, especially if you are checking dates and times on system files while troubleshooting a problem. System Model identifies the specific model of your computer. You can use the System Type to identify whether a 32-bit or 64-bit version of Windows Vista is installed on a computer. Processor(s) identifies the number of processors and provides you with the exact operating speed of your computer (though it may wrap around to the beginning of the next line).

The SYSTEMINFO command identifies the paths for the Windows Directory, System Directory, and Boot Device. It provides information on memory usage, including the total RAM (Total Physical Memory) and details on page file settings and location. Hotfix(s) identifies how many updates, or **hot fixes**, have been applied to this computer, and more importantly, it identifies the Microsoft Knowledge Base Article Number that identifies each hot fix. If you have a question about an update, you can use Microsoft's Knowledge Base to locate the article by the Article ID number, and then examine information about the hot fix. The SystemInfo utility also provides information about your network card.

To view the remainder of the output:

1. Press the **Spacebar**. The MORE filter displays the remainder of the output.
2. Keep the Command Prompt window open for the next section of the tutorial.

Instead of using the MORE filter with this command, you could also have adjusted your view by using the mouse and the vertical bar in the Command Prompt window. However, the mouse may not always be available, or if you are skilled in the use of a command-line environment, you may prefer to use the keyboard.

You can also record this information in a file on disk by using the **output redirection operator (>)** to redirect the output to a file using the following syntax:

```
systeminfo >  [drive:][path]filename
```

For example, you might enter the command: SYSTEMINFO > F:\ComputerInfo.txt

In this example the SYSTEMINFO command analyzes your computer and compiles information but does not display the information on the screen. Instead, that output is redirected to a simple text file named ComputerInfo.txt in the top-level folder of drive F (a flash drive). You can open the file in Notepad, WordPad, or Microsoft Word, and then view and print the information.

So that you can show Eve the system information on this new computer, you decide to send the output to a file on your flash drive.

To redirect the output of the SYSTEMINFO command to a file:

1. If necessary, attach your flash drive and close any windows or dialog boxes that open.
2. Open the Computer window, locate the drive name for your flash drive, and then close the Computer window.
3. Click the **title bar** of the Command Prompt window, clear the screen, type **systeminfo >** followed by your **flash drive name** (for example, F:), type a **backslash** (\ ), type **ComputerInfo.txt** and then press the **Enter** key. For example, if your flash drive name is F: you would type systeminfo > f:\ComputerInfo.txt and then press the Enter key. Notice that the output of the SYSTEMINFO command does not appear on the screen; however, the command does display messages to indicate what type of data it is compiling. After the operation is complete, the Windows command interpreter redisplays the command prompt.
4. To open the file from the command-line window, type **notepad f:\ComputerInfo.txt** (substituting your flash drive's name for f: if it is different). Windows Vista opens the file created by redirecting SYSTEMINFO's output to a text file.
5. Close the ComputerInfo.txt file.

As you've just discovered, you can open Windows programs from a command-line window if you know the name of the program file.

Displaying System Information | Reference Window

- From the All Programs menu, click Accessories, and then click Command Prompt.
- Type SYSTEMINFO | MORE and then press the Enter key.
- After examining the first page of output, press the Spacebar to view each of the next pages.
- To record the output of this command in a file, type SYSTEMINFO > f:\ComputerInfo.txt (using the drive name and filename of your own choice), and then press the Enter key.
- To view the output of this command redirected to a file, type notepad followed by the filename, and then press the Enter key.

If you want to examine other ways in which to use the SYSTEMINFO command, you can use the Help switch with this command.

Session 13.1 Quick Check | Review

1. A(n) ________________ is a program that interprets commands entered at the command prompt, locates the appropriate program in memory or on disk, loads the program, and then executes the program.
2. Briefly describe the difference between an internal and external command.
3. What is a switch?
4. Commands are stored in a(n) ________________ so that you can recall previously used commands.
5. True or False. When you pipe output, you are using the output of one command as the input for another command.
6. What is a filter?

Session 13.2

Copying the Data Files

To complete this section of the tutorial, you must copy the Data Files to the Public Documents folder.

To copy the Data Files to your Public Documents folder:

1. Make sure you have a copy of the Windows Vista for Power User Data Files for Tutorial 13.

   Trouble? If you don't have the starting Data Files, you need to get them before you can proceed. Your instructor will either give you the Data Files or ask you to obtain them from a specified location (such as a network drive). In either case, make a backup copy of the Data Files before you start so that you will have the original files available in case you need to start over. If you have any questions about the Data Files, see your instructor or technical support person for assistance.

2. Close all open windows.

3. Open a window onto the Documents subfolder, your flash drive folder, or the network folder that contains a copy of the Tutorial.13 Data Files file, point to the **Tutorial** folder icon, click the **Organize** button on the command bar, and then click **Copy**.
4. On the Start menu, open **Documents**, click **Public** under Favorite Links in the Navigation Pane, click **Public Documents**, click the **Organize** button on the command bar, and then click **Paste**. Windows Vista copies the Tutorial folder from the Tutorial.13 folder to the Public Documents folder.
5. Select the **Tutorial** folder icon, press the **F2** key (the Rename key), type **Assets First** and then press the **Enter** key.
6. Close the Public Documents folder window and the folder window that contains the original copy of the Tutorial.13 Data Files.

Now, you can view techniques for examining the directory structure of a disk.

Working with Directories and Files

To effectively work with directories and files in a command-line environment, you must understand the directory structure of your computer and know how to navigate from the directory structure of a disk using a path. Once you open a directory, you can view information about the files included in that directory. Windows Vista includes internal and external commands that provide you with the information you need.

Displaying a Directory Tree

When you work in the Windows Vista graphical user interface, you use Windows Explorer (different from Internet Explorer) to view the folders at any folder level within the hierarchy of your computer system and also to navigate from one folder level to another or one drive to another. If you want to view the directory structure in a command-line environment, you use the TREE command, an external command. The TREE command (without any parameters) displays the directory structure of the current directory and its subdirectories.

Eve encourages you to examine the directory structure of your user account.

To view a directory tree for the current directory:

1. From the All Programs menu, click **Accessories**, click **Command Prompt**, and then clear the screen.
2. Type **tree** and then press the **Enter** key. The TREE command produces a diagrammatic view of the directory structure under your user account directory. See Figure 13-16. At this point, your user account directory is the current directory. Your directory structure will differ.

Displaying a directory tree **Figure 13-16**

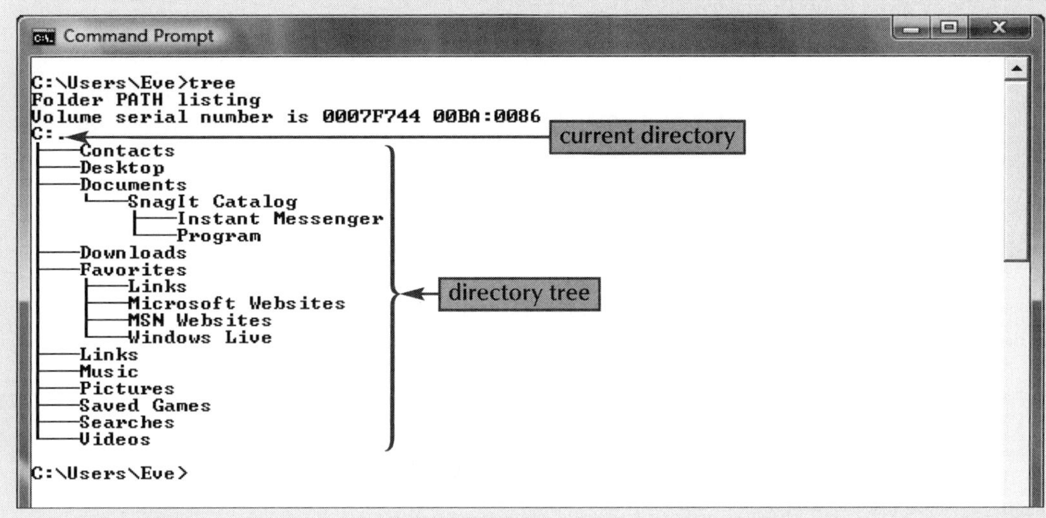

As shown in this figure, the TREE command identifies the output as a Folder PATH listing. Under the serial number, the notation `C:.` (pronounced "C colon dot") marks the top of the directory tree, and the period (called a "dot") after C: is a special notation used to denote the current directory. So, you interpret `C:.` as meaning the current directory on drive C. Your Contacts, Desktop, Documents, Downloads, Favorites, Links, Music, Pictures, Saved Games, Searches, and Videos are subdirectories under your user account directory. The Documents and Favorites directories also have subdirectories.

Understanding Directory References | InSight

After you open a Computer window and then select a drive, you are in the top-level folder, top-level directory, or **root directory** of that drive. Within the top-level folder, you have subfolders or subdirectories. For example, under the top-level folder of drive C, you have the Windows and Program Files subfolders or subdirectories. If you open a subfolder or subdirectory (like the Windows subdirectory) to work with its contents, you refer to that subfolder or subdirectory as a directory, and you refer to its subfolders as subdirectories. If you then refer to the folder or directory above the current directory, that folder or directory is called the **parent folder** or **parent directory**. Thus, how you use the terms "directory" or "subdirectory" depends on where you are located in the folder or directory structure of a disk at any given time.

To view a directory tree of the current drive:

1. Clear the screen.
2. Type **tree \ | more** and press the **Enter** key. The TREE program displays the first part of the directory tree for drive C. The notation `C:\` at the top of the directory tree indicates that the directory tree starts with the top-level directory (represented by the backslash symbol), or root directory, of drive C. In the command you entered, you used the backslash to instruct the TREE command to display the directory structure starting not from where you are currently located, but at the top-level directory, or root directory, instead. Since you did not specify the drive, the TREE program displays a view of the directory structure of the current drive (i.e., the default drive).

3. Press the **Spacebar**. The MORE filter displays the next page of output produced by the Tree program. Because the directory structure of a hard disk drive is extensive, your output could comprise many pages.
4. Press the **Ctrl+C** keys. The Windows command interpreter interrupts the output of the TREE program, displays ^C after the output (for Ctrl+C), and then displays a command prompt. This command will cancel any command you enter and is particularly useful in cases where the output of a command is extensive or when a command-line program is taking too long to complete.
5. Keep the Command Prompt window open for the next section of the tutorial.

Tip

You can also use the Ctrl+Break keys to cancel a command.

The Ctrl+C key combination is called the **interrupt command** or Cancel command because you use it to interrupt and cancel a command operation.

Reference Window | Displaying a Directory Tree

- From the All Programs menu, click Accessories, and then click Command Prompt.
- If you want to display a directory tree for the current directory, type TREE and then press the Enter key.
- If you want the directory tree to start with another directory, or on another drive, type TREE, press the Spacebar, type the drive name (if needed), the path, press the Spacebar, type | (a vertical bar for the pipe operator), press the Spacebar, type MORE, and then press the Enter key.
- If you want the directory tree to start from the top-level directory of the current drive, type TREE and then press the Spacebar followed by the drive name and a backslash symbol for the root directory, for example: TREE \ or TREE C:\

If you view the directory structure using the TREE command, and then decide that you want to save that directory tree in a file on disk, you use the output redirection operator (>) to redirect the output to a file using the following syntax:

```
TREE  >  [drive:][path]filename /A
```

For example, you might enter the command: TREE > F:\Eve.txt /A

In this example the TREE command produces a directory tree but does not display it on the screen. Instead, that output is redirected to a simple text file named Eve.txt on drive F (a flash drive). The ASCII switch (/A) converts the vertical and horizontal lines in the directory tree to plus and minus signs, as well as vertical bars and backslashes, to simulate the appearance of vertical and horizontal bars in the text file. **ASCII** stands for **American Standard Code for Information Interchange**, and it refers to the use of a set of computer codes to represent letters of the alphabet (uppercase and lowercase), numbers, symbols, and certain simple graphic symbols. ASCII files are simple text files.

You can also view a directory tree of your entire hard disk drive; however, that directory tree is extensive and exceeds one page of output on the screen. However, you can pipe that output to the MORE filter so that you can examine the directory tree of your entire hard disk drive, one window (or page) at a time.

Changing to the Root Directory

To navigate from directory to directory in a command-line environment, you use the Change Directory (CD) command, an internal command. When you use this command, you also include the path to the directory to which you want to switch. If you want to switch to the root directory of the current drive, you specify the path for that directory, which, as noted earlier, is represented by a backslash (\ ).

Eve asks you to change to the root directory, and then examine the contents of that directory.

To change to the root directory:

1. Clear the screen. From the path shown in the command prompt, you can tell that you are currently in the directory for your user account and that you are on drive C.
2. Type **cd ** (a backslash symbol), and then press the **Enter** key. As shown by the path in the command prompt, you just changed from the directory for your user account to the root directory of drive C. See Figure 13-17. No matter where you are located in the directory structure of the disk, this command switches you to the root directory.

Figure 13-17 Changing to the root directory

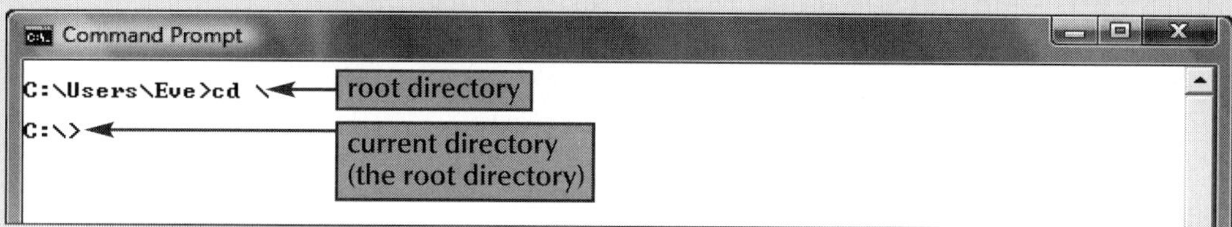

3. Keep the Command Prompt window open for the next section of the tutorial.

   Later, you will examine other ways in which to use the CD command to change directories.

Changing to the Root Directory | Reference Window

- From the All Programs menu, click Accessories, and then click Command Prompt.
- From any subdirectory, type CD **** and then press the Enter key.

Once you switch to another directory, you usually want to know what's stored in that directory.

Viewing the Contents of a Directory

You can use the Directory command (DIR), an internal command, to display a list of subdirectories and files within a directory, along with information about the contents of the directory. In fact, the Directory command is one of the most commonly used commands, and when used with switches, it is also a very versatile command.

Eve points out to you that you should become familiar with the contents of the root directory and also with the different ways in which you can use the Directory command to view information about files on a disk.

To view the contents of the current directory:

1. Clear the screen.
2. At the command prompt, type **dir** and then press the **Enter** key. The Directory command displays the contents of the current directory—the root directory of the current drive (drive C). See Figure 13-18. At the end of the directory listing, the Directory command reports that there are two files and four directories in the root directory. The contents of your root directory may differ from that shown in this figure. Note that the DIR command does not display the contents of each subdirectory under the root directory.

Figure 13-18 **Viewing a directory listing**

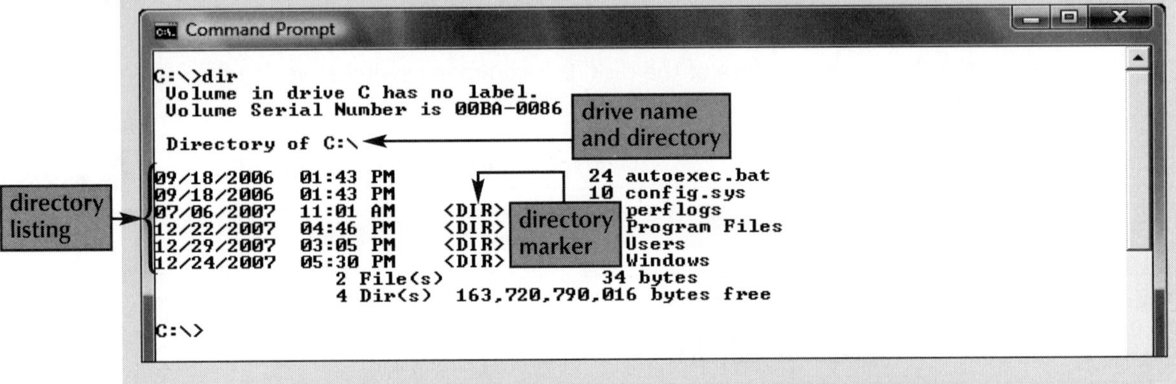

The first two columns of this **directory listing** show the date and time that each subdirectory or file was last modified, the third column identifies subdirectories with the use of the **directory marker** `<DIR>`, the fourth column displays file sizes in bytes (but not subdirectory sizes), and the fifth column displays the name of the subdirectory or file. On the NTFS volume of the computer used for this figure, the DIR command displays filenames first in alphabetical order, and then it displays folder names in alphabetical order. The DIR command also reports on the total amount of space used by files and the amount of available space on the drive. The two files config.sys and autoexec.bat are DOS startup configuration files kept for backward compatibility with older programs.

The Directory listing does not show hidden directories and hidden files. To view all subdirectories and files within a directory, you use the Attribute switch (/A) with the Directory command. The Attribute switch (/A) instructs the Directory command to list all subdirectories and files, no matter what attributes are assigned to the subdirectories and files. If it makes it easier to remember, you can think of /A as meaning "all files."

To view all subdirectories and files within the root directory:

1. Clear the screen.
2. Type **dir /a** and then press the **Enter** key. The Directory command displays a directory listing that now includes hidden directories and files in the directory listing. See Figure 13-19. As shown for the NTFS volume on the computer used for this figure, the DIR command did not group directories together and list them after files (as occurred when you did not use the Attribute switch). However, it did list folders and files in alphabetical order. Note also that the amount of storage space used by files is significantly greater now that the directory listing includes hidden files. The contents of your root directory may differ from that shown in this figure.

Figure 13-19

Using the Attribute switch to view all files and directories

Command Prompt

```
C:\>dir /a
 Volume in drive C has no label.
 Volume Serial Number is 00BA-0086

 Directory of C:\

12/29/2007  03:06 PM    <DIR>          $Recycle.Bin
09/18/2006  01:43 PM                24 autoexec.bat
07/29/2007  11:05 AM            21,504 BCD Backup.txt.LOG
07/29/2007  11:05 AM                 0 BCD Backup.txt.LOG1
07/29/2007  11:05 AM                 0 BCD Backup.txt.LOG2
05/29/2007  10:54 AM    <DIR>          Boot
11/02/2006  01:53 AM           438,840 bootmgr
05/29/2007  10:54 AM             8,192 BOOTSECT.BAK
09/18/2006  01:43 PM                10 config.sys
11/02/2006  05:00 AM    <JUNCTION>     Documents and Settings [C:\Users]
12/29/2007  08:25 AM     2,144,903,168 hiberfil.sys
10/13/2007  10:40 AM                 0 IO.SYS
10/13/2007  10:40 AM                 0 MSDOS.SYS
05/29/2007  03:16 PM    <DIR>          MSOCache
12/29/2007  08:25 AM     2,458,828,800 pagefile.sys
07/06/2007  11:01 AM    <DIR>          perflogs
12/22/2007  04:46 PM    <DIR>          Program Files
12/21/2007  12:29 PM    <DIR>          ProgramData
12/29/2007  01:00 PM    <DIR>          System Volume Information
12/29/2007  03:05 PM    <DIR>          Users
12/24/2007  05:30 PM    <DIR>          Windows
              11 File(s)  4,604,200,538 bytes
              10 Dir(s)  163,719,065,600 bytes free

C:\>
```

Attribute switch

alphabetical list of all files, directories, and junctions

On the computer used for Figure 13-19, the Directory command reports that there are 11 files (9 of which are hidden files) and 10 directories (6 of which are hidden directories) in the root directory. The largest file is the virtual memory paging file with the filename pagefile.sys. As you learned in Tutorial 9, Windows Vista uses this file as supplemental RAM. As shown for this computer, if hibernation is enabled on your computer, you will also see a hibernation file (which you examined in Tutorial 2) named hiberfil.sys with a file size close to the amount of installed RAM on your computer. The hidden file bootmgr is the Windows Boot Manager file that you examined in Tutorial 8, and the hidden Boot directory is the folder that contains boot configuration data and files that you also examined in Tutorial 8. Windows Vista displays `<JUNCTION>` for the hidden Documents and Settings directory because it is an NTFS pointer to the C:\Users directory, which contains the directories for each user account. Junctions provide backward compatibility with programs designed before the introduction of Windows Vista so that they can work with the new folder names and paths found in Windows Vista. In Windows XP, the Documents and Settings folder stored user accounts; however, under Windows Vista, that folder no longer exists, and instead, user accounts are found in the Users folder. Junctions, therefore, redirect programs designed for Windows XP to the corresponding Windows Vista folders.

The Program Files subdirectory contains directories for operating system components (such as Internet Explorer) and directories for different software products installed on your computer. The hidden Recycled folder contains the deleted files stored in the Recycle Bin. The Windows directory contains the bulk of the installed software for the operating system.

You can also use another switch, the Sort Order switch (/O), to list subdirectories first in alphabetical order by directory name, followed by files in alphabetical order by filename. Note that the "O" in the Sort Order switch (/O) is the uppercase letter "O", not the number 0 (zero).

To view subdirectories and files in the root directory in alphabetical order:

1. Clear the screen.
2. Type **dir /a /o** and then press the **Enter** key. The DIR command displays a directory listing in alphabetical order, first by directory, and then by files. See Figure 13-20. Note the name of your Windows directory because you will need to know that name in the next set of tutorial steps.

Tip

The order in which you list switches with this command does not affect the output.

Figure 13-20 Viewing a directory with the Attribute and Sort Order switches

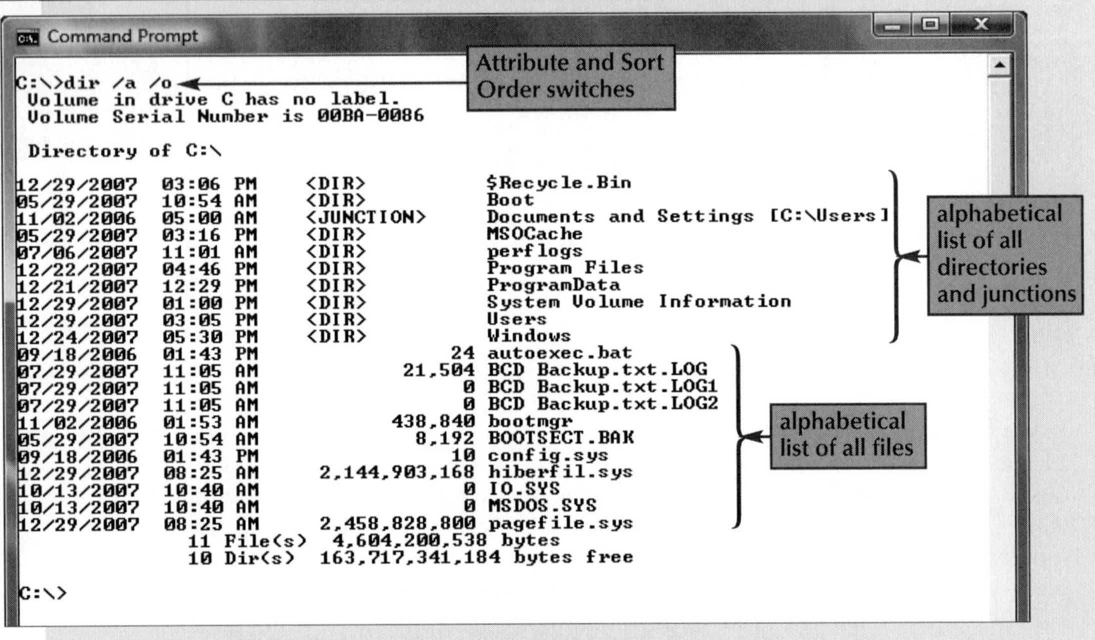

```
C:\>dir /a /o
 Volume in drive C has no label.
 Volume Serial Number is 00BA-0086

 Directory of C:\

12/29/2007  03:06 PM    <DIR>          $Recycle.Bin
05/29/2007  10:54 AM    <DIR>          Boot
11/02/2006  05:00 AM    <JUNCTION>     Documents and Settings [C:\Users]
05/29/2007  03:16 PM    <DIR>          MSOCache
07/06/2007  11:01 AM    <DIR>          perflogs
12/22/2007  04:46 PM    <DIR>          Program Files
12/21/2007  12:29 PM    <DIR>          ProgramData
12/29/2007  01:00 PM    <DIR>          System Volume Information
12/29/2007  03:05 PM    <DIR>          Users
12/24/2007  05:30 PM    <DIR>          Windows
09/18/2006  01:43 PM                24 autoexec.bat
07/29/2007  11:05 AM            21,504 BCD Backup.txt.LOG
07/29/2007  11:05 AM                 0 BCD Backup.txt.LOG1
07/29/2007  11:05 AM                 0 BCD Backup.txt.LOG2
11/02/2006  01:53 AM           438,840 bootmgr
05/29/2007  10:54 AM             8,192 BOOTSECT.BAK
09/18/2006  01:43 PM                10 config.sys
12/29/2007  08:25 AM     2,144,903,168 hiberfil.sys
10/13/2007  10:40 AM                 0 IO.SYS
10/13/2007  10:40 AM                 0 MSDOS.SYS
12/29/2007  08:25 AM     2,458,828,800 pagefile.sys
              11 File(s)  4,604,200,538 bytes
              10 Dir(s)  163,717,341,184 bytes free

C:\>
```


Eve suggests that you examine the Windows folder next, and since the Windows folder contains many different directories and files, she also suggests that you use the Page or Pause switch (/P) to display one screen of output at a time.

To view a directory listing of the Windows folder:

1. Clear the screen.
2. Type **dir windows /a /o /p** (replacing "windows" with the name of your Windows directory if it is different), and then press the **Enter** key. You are not viewing the contents of the root directory. Instead, since you specified the path to the Windows directory, you are now viewing its contents. See Figure 13-21. You also specified the Page switch, so the Directory command produces paged output, and then displays the prompt "Press any key to continue..." The contents of your Windows directory will differ. Since this command has its own switch for producing paged output, you do not need to use the pipe operator and the MORE filter (though they work).

Figure 13-21 Using the Page switch to produce paged output of the Windows directory

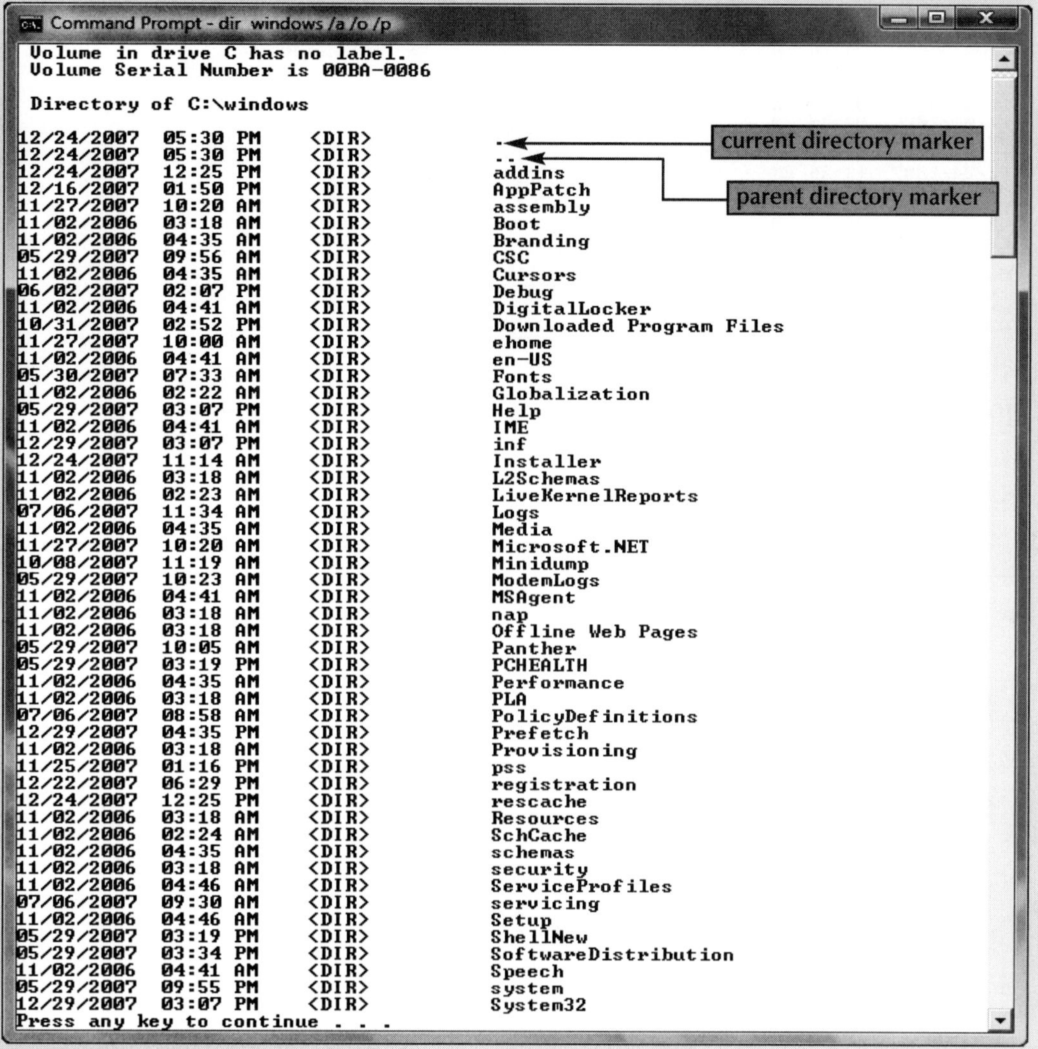

```
Command Prompt - dir windows /a /o /p
 Volume in drive C has no label.
 Volume Serial Number is 00BA-0086

 Directory of C:\windows

12/24/2007  05:30 PM    <DIR>          .
12/24/2007  05:30 PM    <DIR>          ..
12/24/2007  12:25 PM    <DIR>          addins
12/16/2007  01:50 PM    <DIR>          AppPatch
11/27/2007  10:20 AM    <DIR>          assembly
11/02/2006  03:18 AM    <DIR>          Boot
11/02/2006  04:35 AM    <DIR>          Branding
05/29/2007  09:56 AM    <DIR>          CSC
11/02/2006  04:35 AM    <DIR>          Cursors
06/02/2007  02:07 PM    <DIR>          Debug
11/02/2006  04:41 AM    <DIR>          DigitalLocker
10/31/2007  02:52 PM    <DIR>          Downloaded Program Files
11/27/2007  10:00 AM    <DIR>          ehome
11/02/2006  04:41 AM    <DIR>          en-US
05/30/2007  07:33 AM    <DIR>          Fonts
11/02/2006  02:22 AM    <DIR>          Globalization
05/29/2007  03:07 PM    <DIR>          Help
11/02/2006  04:41 AM    <DIR>          IME
12/29/2007  03:07 PM    <DIR>          inf
12/24/2007  11:14 AM    <DIR>          Installer
11/02/2006  03:18 AM    <DIR>          L2Schemas
11/02/2006  02:23 AM    <DIR>          LiveKernelReports
07/06/2007  11:34 AM    <DIR>          Logs
11/02/2006  04:35 AM    <DIR>          Media
11/27/2007  10:20 AM    <DIR>          Microsoft.NET
10/08/2007  11:19 AM    <DIR>          Minidump
05/29/2007  10:23 AM    <DIR>          ModemLogs
11/02/2006  04:41 AM    <DIR>          MSAgent
11/02/2006  03:18 AM    <DIR>          nap
11/02/2006  03:18 AM    <DIR>          Offline Web Pages
05/29/2007  10:05 AM    <DIR>          Panther
05/29/2007  03:19 PM    <DIR>          PCHEALTH
11/02/2006  04:35 AM    <DIR>          Performance
11/02/2006  03:18 AM    <DIR>          PLA
07/06/2007  08:58 AM    <DIR>          PolicyDefinitions
12/29/2007  04:35 PM    <DIR>          Prefetch
11/02/2006  03:18 AM    <DIR>          Provisioning
11/25/2007  01:16 PM    <DIR>          pss
12/22/2007  06:29 PM    <DIR>          registration
12/24/2007  12:25 PM    <DIR>          rescache
11/02/2006  03:18 AM    <DIR>          Resources
11/02/2006  02:24 AM    <DIR>          SchCache
11/02/2006  04:35 AM    <DIR>          schemas
11/02/2006  03:18 AM    <DIR>          security
11/02/2006  04:46 AM    <DIR>          ServiceProfiles
07/06/2007  09:30 AM    <DIR>          servicing
11/02/2006  04:46 AM    <DIR>          Setup
05/29/2007  03:19 PM    <DIR>          ShellNew
05/29/2007  03:34 PM    <DIR>          SoftwareDistribution
11/02/2006  04:41 AM    <DIR>          Speech
05/29/2007  09:55 PM    <DIR>          system
12/29/2007  03:07 PM    <DIR>          System32
Press any key to continue . . .
```


The single period (called "dot") in the column to the right of the first directory marker (<DIR>) refers to the current directory—the one you are viewing (in this case, Windows). The two periods (called "dot dot") to the right of the second directory marker refer to the parent directory of the current directory. In this case, the parent directory of the Windows subdirectory is the root directory of drive C—in other words, C:\. Windows Vista (and DOS) both use these directory markers to keep track of where they are in the directory structure of a disk and to navigate the directory structure. Every subdirectory has a "dot" and a "dot dot" entry.

To view the next page of the directory listing:

1. Press the **Spacebar**. The next part of the directory listing for the computer used for this figure shows some of the names of files stored in the Windows folder, listed in alphabetical order. See Figure 13-22. The contents of your Windows directory may differ.

Figure 13-22 Viewing the next screen of paged output

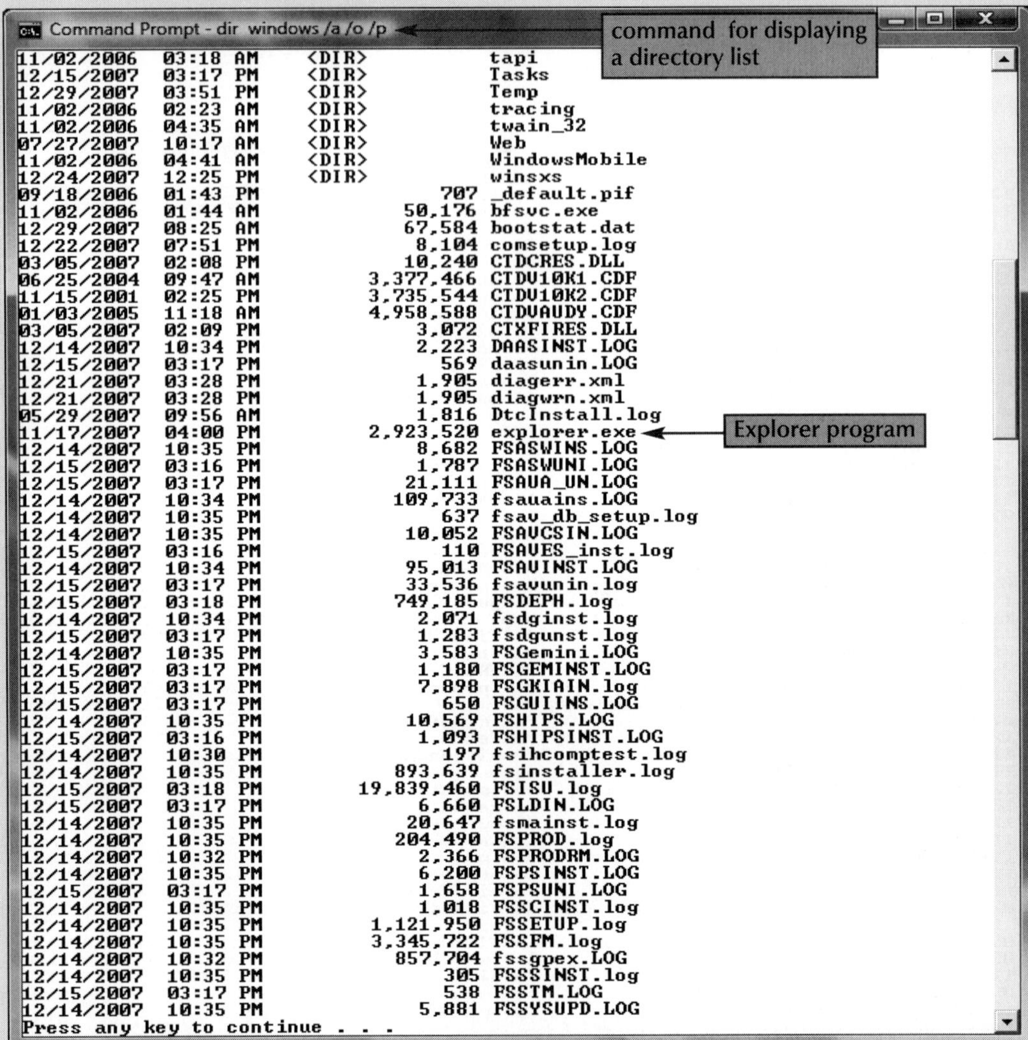

2. Keep pressing the **Spacebar** to view the remainder of the output.

3. At the next command prompt, clear the screen.

4. Type **cd windows** (replacing "windows" with the name of your Windows directory if it is different), and then press the **Enter** key. The Change Directory command switches to the Windows directory. See Figure 13-23. The Windows command interpreter updates the command prompt to show the path to the current directory—now the Windows directory.

Tip

If you type CD and press the Enter key, the CD command displays the path of the current directory.

Figure 13-23 Changing directories

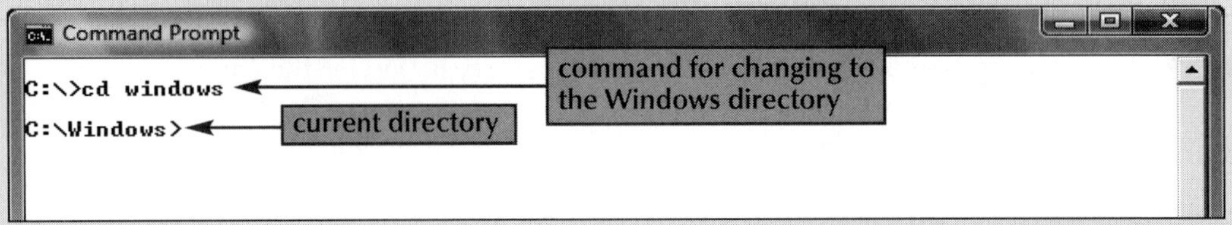

Command Prompt

```
C:\>cd windows
C:\Windows>
```

command for changing to the Windows directory

current directory

5. Type **dir /ad /o /p** and then press the **Enter** key. The DIR command displays only the subdirectories under the Windows directory. See Figure 13-24. By adding the "d" parameter for "directory" to the Attribute switch (**/**A), you changed the way in which it operates and specified that the DIR command only show directories. You can use this technique to view and concentrate on subdirectories within a directory.

Displaying an alphabetical list of only directories | **Figure 13-24**

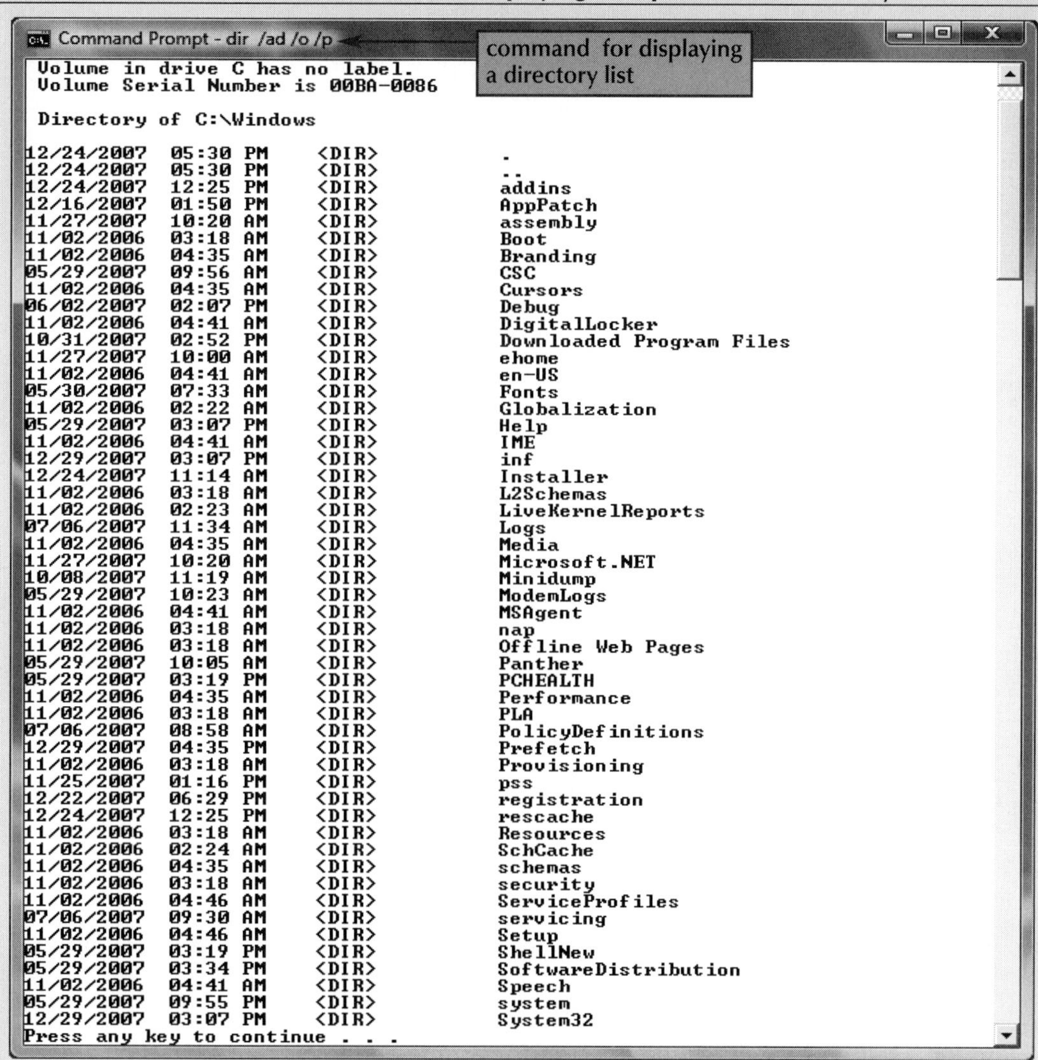

6. Press the **Spacebar** to view the remainder of the directory listing, and then clear the screen.

7. Type **dir /a-d /o /p** and then press the **Enter** key. The Directory command now displays only the files in the Windows directory. See Figure 13-25. If you place a minus sign before a parameter in a switch, you reverse its effect. **/**a-d instructs the DIR command to exclude directories. By modifying the Attribute switch again, you changed the way in which the DIR command operates. You can use this technique to view and concentrate on files within a directory.

Tip

If you recall the previous command with F3, you can type a hyphen between "a" and "d", and then press the Enter key.

Figure 13-25 Displaying an alphabetical listing of only files

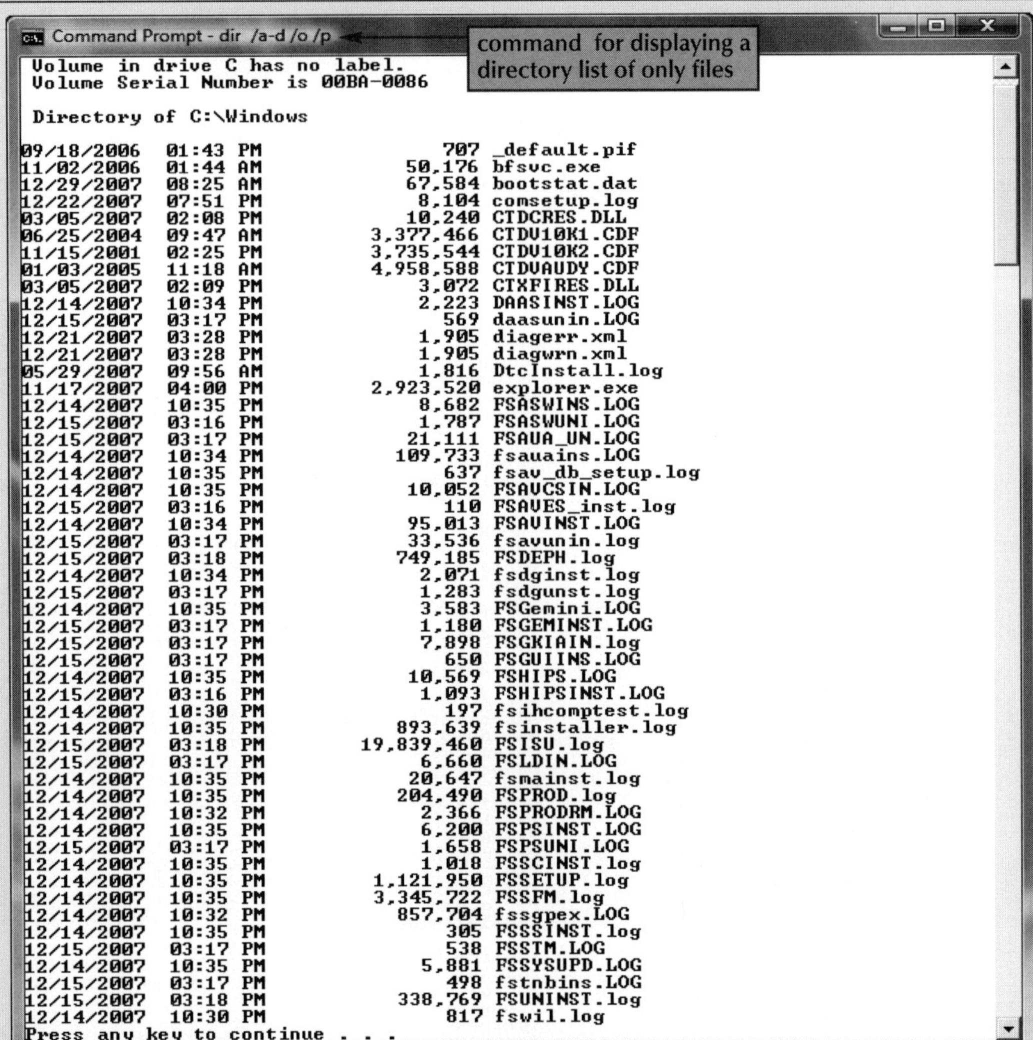

8. Use the **Spacebar** to view the remainder of the directory listing and return to the command prompt.

9. Keep the Command Prompt window open for the next section of the tutorial.

When using the Directory command, you can specify the path to the directory you want to examine, or if you prefer, you can use the Change Directory command to first switch to that directory using its path, and then use the Directory command to view its contents.

Changing Directories | Reference Window

- From the All Programs menu, click Accessories, and then click Command Prompt.
- Type CD, press the Spacebar, type the path and name of the directory or subdirectory that you want to switch to, and then press the Enter key.
- If you want to change to the root directory, no matter where you are located, type CD \ and then press the Enter key.

Since the Directory command has an extensive list of switches, and since the switches can be combined and used in different ways, you can use the Help switch (/?) with the Directory command to learn and refresh your memory about the types and uses of the DIR command's switches.

Displaying a Directory Listing | Reference Window

- From the All Programs menu, click Accessories, and then click Command Prompt.
- If you want to view Help information on the Directory command and its switches, type DIR /? and then press the Enter key.
- If you want to view a directory listing of the current directory, type DIR and then press the Enter key. Type DIR /A and press the Enter key to view a directory listing of all directories and files, no matter what attributes are assigned to them. Type DIR /O /P and press the Enter key to display a list of directories and files in alphabetical order with directories grouped first followed by files, one screen at a time. Type DIR /A /O /P and press the Enter key to display a directory listing of all directories files (including hidden and system files) in alphabetical order with directories grouped first, followed by files, one screen at a time. Type DIR /AD /O /P and press the Enter key to view an alphabetical directory listing of only directories (including hidden directories), one screen at a time. Type DIR /A-D /O /P and press the Enter key to view an alphabetical directory listing of just files, one screen at a time.

As you can tell, the DIR command is quite versatile, and also quite important, because it provides you with the information you need about the contents of a disk and directory.

Viewing File Attributes

Another important command is the Attribute command (ATTRIB), an external command that lists attributes assigned to files by the operating system (or by you or someone else). You can also use this command to change file attributes. For example, if you need to edit a file assigned the Read-Only attribute, you must first turn off the Read-Only attribute so that you can make changes to the file, and then save the changes. Then you can turn on the Read-Only attribute again to protect the file from further modification.

Eve suggests that you return to the root directory and examine the attributes of the files, most of which are system files. Eve also suggests you use another variation of the Change Directory command to return to the root directory.

To change to the root directory and then view attributes of directories and files:

1. Clear the screen.
2. Type **cd ..** (dot dot) and then press the **Enter** key. The Change Directory command switches to the parent directory of the current directory, as shown in the command prompt (C:\). See Figure 13-26. The current directory is the Windows directory, and its parent directory is the root directory. This command allows you to step up one directory level in the directory structure of a disk. Since you were one directory below the root directory, it has the same effect as the CD \ command. If you were working in the C:\Windows\system32 directory instead, this command would take you up one level in the directory structure to the C:\Windows directory (the parent directory of the system32 directory).

Figure 13-26 Stepping up one directory level

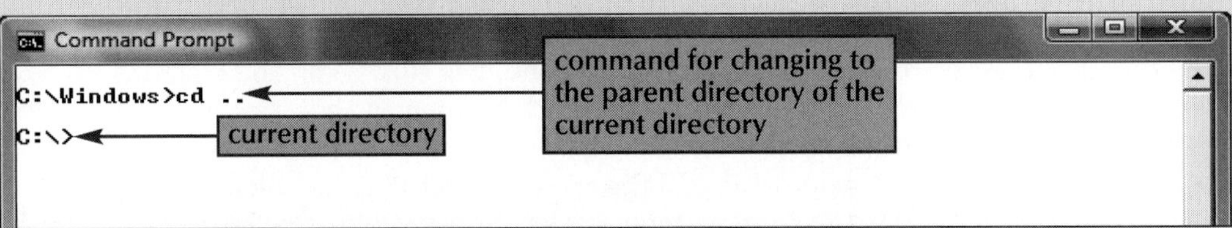

3. Clear the screen, type **attrib** and then press the **Enter** key. The Attribute command lists the attributes of all the files in the root directory. On the computer used for Figure 13-27, all of the files are assigned the Archive attribute (identified by the code "A"), indicating that they have been modified, but not yet backed up. Bootmgr, hiberfil.sys, IO.SYS, MSDOS.SYS, and pagefile.sys are assigned the System attribute (identified by the code "S"), indicating that they are operating system files. Bootmgr, hiberfil.sys, IO.SYS, MSDOS.SYS, and pagefile.sys are also assigned the Hidden attribute (identified by the code "H"), indicating that they are hidden files and therefore are not displayed in a directory listing unless you specify otherwise. Bootmgr, IO.SYS, and MSDOS.SYS are assigned the Read-Only attribute (identified by the code "R"), indicating that you cannot modify or delete the files. Since Windows Vista needs to write to pagefile.sys to use virtual memory and to write to hiberfil.sys before a computer switches to hibernation, these files cannot be Read-Only. As you can tell from this view of file attributes, a file might be assigned more than one attribute.

Figure 13-27 Viewing file attributes

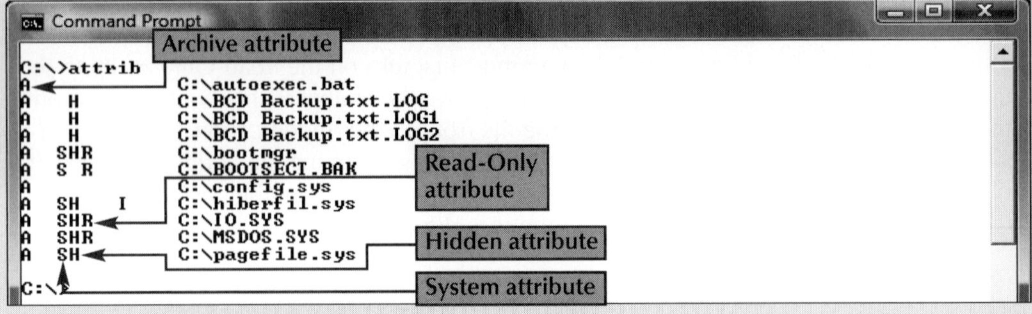

4. Type **attrib /?** and then press the **Enter** key. The Help information shows how to turn on and turn off an attribute. See Figure 13-28. Note that you can also use the Subdirectory switch (**/S**) to view information or change attributes of files in the current directory as well as all subdirectories under the current directory. When used with the Subdirectory switch (/S), the Directory switch (**/D**) also displays attributes of subdirectories.

Viewing Help on the Attribute command **Figure 13-28**

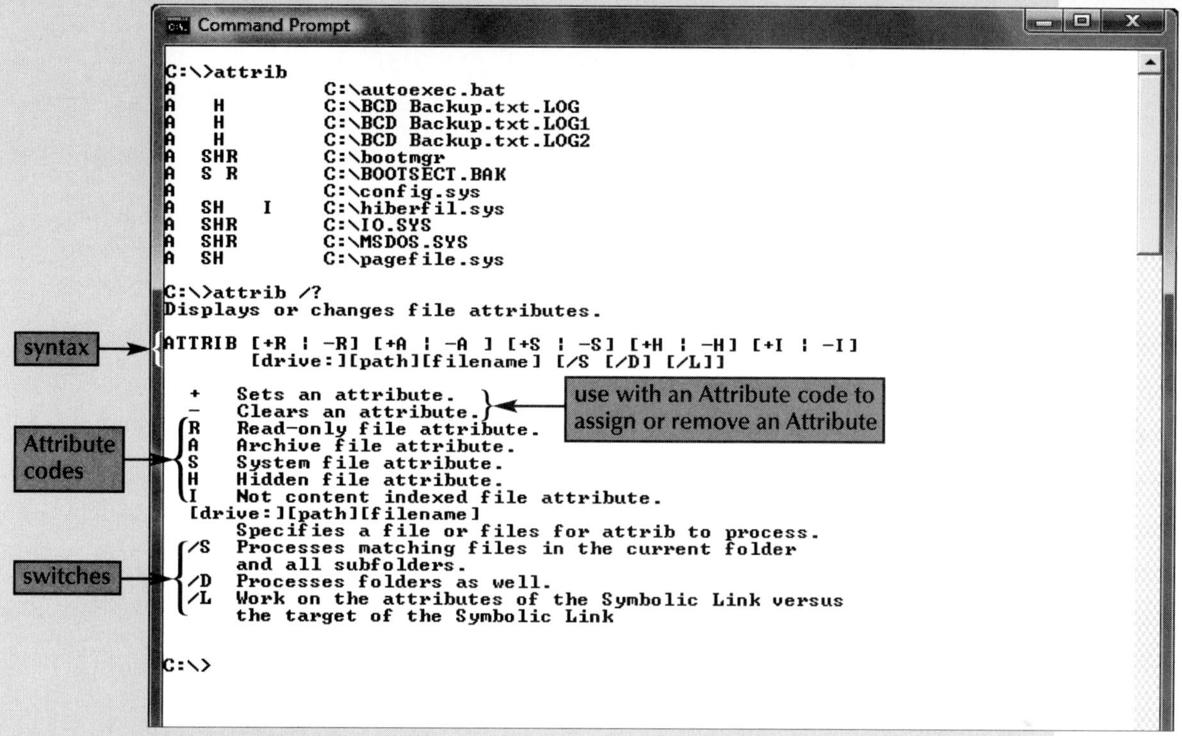
Command Prompt
C:\>attrib
A C:\autoexec.bat
A H C:\BCD Backup.txt.LOG
A H C:\BCD Backup.txt.LOG1
A H C:\BCD Backup.txt.LOG2
A SHR C:\bootmgr
A S R C:\BOOTSECT.BAK
A C:\config.sys
A SH I C:\hiberfil.sys
A SHR C:\IO.SYS
A SHR C:\MSDOS.SYS
A SH C:\pagefile.sys
C:\>attrib /?
Displays or changes file attributes.
ATTRIB [+R | -R] [+A | -A] [+S | -S] [+H | -H] [+I | -I]
[drive:][path][filename] [/S [/D] [/L]]
+ Sets an attribute.
- Clears an attribute.
R Read-only file attribute.
A Archive file attribute.
S System file attribute.
H Hidden file attribute.
I Not content indexed file attribute.
[drive:][path][filename]
Specifies a file or files for attrib to process.
/S Processes matching files in the current folder and all subfolders.
/D Processes folders as well.
/L Work on the attributes of the Symbolic Link versus the target of the Symbolic Link
C:\>
syntax
Attribute codes
switches
use with an Attribute code to assign or remove an Attribute

5. Leave the Command Prompt window open for the next section of the tutorial.

To use the Attribute command to change attributes, you type ATTRIB followed by a space and the filename, and then you specify which attributes you want to turn on or off. If you place a plus sign before the code for an attribute, you enable or turn on that attribute. For example, if you want to hide a file named passwords.docx so that it is not displayed in a directory listing (or in a folder), you enter this command:

```
attrib passwords.docx +h
```

If you want to hide and make the file Read-Only, you enter this command:

```
attrib passwords.docx +h +r
```

If you place a minus sign (or hyphen) before the code for an attribute, you remove or turn off that attribute. For example, if you want to display the hidden file passwords.docx so that it is displayed in a directory listing or in a folder, you enter this command:

```
attrib passwords.docx -h
```

Reference Window | Changing to the Parent Directory

- From the All Programs menu, click Accessories, and then click Command Prompt.
- Type CD .. (dot dot) and then press the Enter key.

Reference Window | Viewing File Attributes

- From the All Programs menu, click Accessories, and then click Command Prompt.
- If you want to view Help information on the Attribute command, type ATTRIB /? and then press the Enter key.
- If you want to view attributes of files within a directory, change to that directory first (just to make it simpler), type ATTRIB and then press the Enter key.

The Attribute command is often used with the Directory command when troubleshooting problems in a command-line environment. You use the Directory command first to view the contents of a directory with or without the Attribute switch. Then, you use the Attribute command to display attributes of one or more files.

Creating a Directory

You can use the Make Directory (MD) command, an internal command, to create directories on a disk. When you use the Make Directory command, you specify the name of the directory you want to create. If you want to create the directory on another drive, you must also specify the drive name as part of the path with the new directory name.

If you are entering a command in the Command Prompt window and also need to include a reference to a directory name that contains one or more spaces or a path that contains spaces in directory and filenames, you enclose the directory name, filename, or path within quotation marks. Otherwise, Windows Vista might interpret the spaces as delimiters like the backslash (\ ) in a path and assume that each space separates two different parameters within the command. For example, if you want to create a directory called Performance Measurements on drive F (for example, your flash drive), and assuming you are already at the root directory of that drive, you enter this command:
MD "Performance Measurements"

If you do not use the quotation marks, the Make Directory command creates two directories—one called Performance and the other called Measurements. It does not create a directory named Performance Measurements.

If you want to create that same subdirectory on a flash drive in drive F from drive C, you enter one of the following commands:

```
MD "F:\Performance Measurements"
MD F:\"Performance Measurements"
```

If you do not use quotation marks in this example, the Make Directory command creates a directory on drive F called Performance and another directory *on drive C* called Measurements. (That also gives away the fact that you can use the Make Directory command to create multiple directories at the same time.) For certain other commands, such as the Change Directory (CD) command, which you examined earlier, you may or may not need to use quotation marks around subdirectory names or filenames with one or more spaces.

If a directory name or filename does not contain spaces, you do not need to use quotation marks even if the name is longer than eight characters. For example, to create a directory named Performance on drive F, and assuming you were already at the root directory of drive F, you enter this command: MD Performance

After asking Eve how to back up some important files on your computer and store the backups on your flash drive, she recommends that one simple way is to copy the files individually or as a group. However, she notes that you first need to create a directory on your flash drive for the files you copy. If you switch to the subdirectory under the Public Documents directory that contains the files you want to copy, you can copy the files from that directory.

To create a subdirectory on a flash drive:

1. If necessary, attach your flash drive to the computer you are using, and then close any dialog boxes or windows that open.
2. If necessary, open a Computer window, locate the drive name for your flash drive, and then close the Computer window.
3. Clear the screen, type **cd "\users\public\documents\assets first\business records"** and then press the **Enter** key. You switch from the root directory to the Business Records directory. See Figure 13-29. By specifying the path to the Business Records, you can change to that directory in one step. If you are already in the root directory, you do not need the first backslash symbol in the path because the Change Directory command assumes that you want to switch to a directory relative to the one where you are located, i.e., to a subdirectory under the current directory. However, the advantage of using the first backslash symbol in the path is that you can change to the Documents folder from *any* other directory on drive C. You do not need to be in the root directory first.

   Trouble? If the Windows command interpreter displays the message "The system cannot find the path specified," you mistyped the path. Repeat this step again and verify that you typed the path correctly.

Figure 13-29 Changing to a new directory using a path

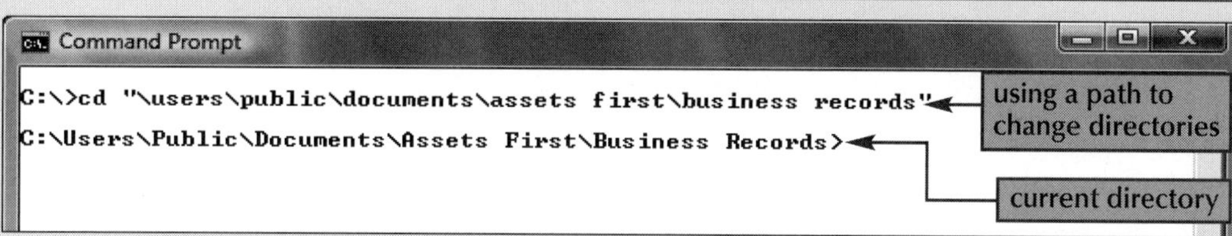

4. To create a directory on your flash drive from drive C, and assuming your flash drive name is F: (if not, replace F: in the command with your flash drive name), type **md "f:\Assets First"** (you *must* type the quotation marks because of the space in the directory name, and if you want the directory name to use mixed case, with uppercase characters for the first character in each word, you must type it as shown because Windows Vista is case aware), and then press the **Enter** key. After you create a directory, the directory is empty (except for the dot and "dot dot" directory markers). You can then create subdirectories in that directory and add files to that directory.
5. Type **dir** followed by a **space** and the **drive name** for your flash drive, and then press the **Enter** key. For example, if your flash drive is assigned the drive name F:, you enter this command: **DIR F:** As shown for the flash drive assigned the drive name F: in Figure 13-30, the Make Directory command created a directory named Assets First.

Figure 13-30 Viewing a directory on your flash drive

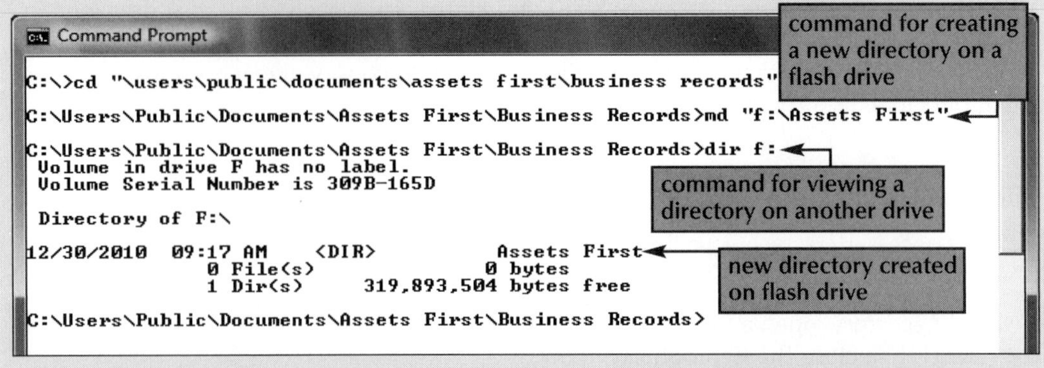

6. Keep the Command Prompt window open for the next section of the tutorial.

Since drive names are device names, and since device names are **reserved names** that cannot be used as filenames, you cannot create a directory or file that has the same name as a device. Also, you cannot use the colon in a directory or filename.

Reference Window | Creating a Directory

- From the All Programs menu, click Accessories, and then click Command Prompt.
- Type MD, press the Spacebar, type the drive name and path, along with the name of the new directory you want to create, and then press the Enter key. If you are using a directory name that includes one or more spaces, include the drive name and path of the new directory within quotation marks. If you are working from another drive and directory, you must type the drive name, as well as the path to, and name of, the new subdirectory you want to create.
- To verify that the directory is created properly, type DIR and the drive name, as well as path (if needed), to the location of the new directory.

If you want to remove a directory, you can use the Remove Directory (RD) command. The syntax is similar to that of the Make Directory (MD) command. For example, to remove a directory on your flash drive named Performance, you enter this command:
rd performance

If the directory that you want to use contains other subdirectories and/or files, you must use the Subdirectory (/S) switch with the Remove Directory (RD) command, and then verify that you want to remove the directory and all its contents.

If you want to delete a file rather than a directory, you use the DEL or ERASE command, and then specify the name of the file you want to delete. If you want the command to prompt you before deleting a file, you include the Prompt for Verification switch (/P) in the command.

Copying Files

You can use the COPY command, an internal command, to copy files from one location to another. The general syntax for the COPY command is as follows:

```
COPY source destination
```

The **source** is the directory, files, or file you want to copy. If you want to copy files from another drive, you have to also specify the name of the drive that contains the files you want to copy. The **destination** is the drive or directory where you want to copy the files. When you use this command, you can specify the path of the source and destination so that Windows Vista knows exactly what to copy and where to copy it to. After a copy operation, you have two identical copies of the same file in two different locations.

Next, Eve shows you how to use the COPY command to copy a single file to the directory on your flash drive.

To copy files:

1. Clear the screen, type **DIR** and then press the **Enter** key. The file that you want to copy is "Balance Sheet.xlsx." If your flash drive is not drive F, replace F: in the command in the next step with the correct drive name.
2. Type **copy "Balance Sheet.xlsx" "F:\Assets First"** and then press the **Enter** key. Because of the long path in the command prompt for the current directory, your command will wrap around to the next line in the window, but it will still work. If the operation is successful, you will see the message "1 file(s) copied," as shown in Figure 13-31.

   Trouble? If you see the message "The system cannot find the file specified," use the F3 key or Up Arrow key to recall the command you just entered, check to make sure your command is entered correctly, edit the command (if necessary), and then try this step again. Also, make sure you use the correct drive name.

   Trouble? If you see a "Windows - No Disk" dialog box, you entered the incorrect drive name. In the Command Prompt window, you will also see the message "The device is not ready. 0 file(s) copied." Click Cancel in the "Windows - No Disk" dialog box and enter the command again using the correct (and a valid) drive name.

Figure 13-31 Copying a file to a directory on your flash drive

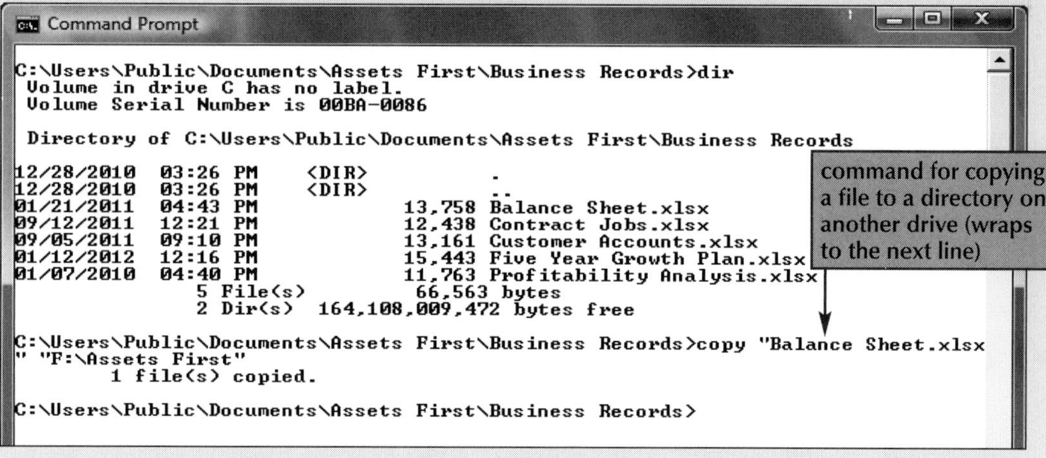

3. Leave the Command Prompt window open for the next section of the tutorial.

If you specify a directory as the source, the COPY command copies the contents of the directory (but not the directory itself) to whatever destination you specify.

If you specify a path with a command, but do not specify a drive name in the path, the command uses the current drive. If you don't specify a directory name in a path with a command, the command assumes you want to use the current directory.

Reference Window | Copying a File to a Flash Drive

- Attach the flash drive to your computer and close any dialog boxes or windows that open.
- From the All Programs menu, click Accessories, and then click Command Prompt.
- Use the CD command, followed by a space and the path of the directory that contains the files you want to copy to change to that directory.
- Type COPY, press the Spacebar, type the name of the file you want to copy, press the Spacebar, type the path of the drive and directory where you want to copy the files to, and then press the Enter key. If you are using directory names or filenames with one or more spaces, enclose the source and, if necessary, the destination, within quotation marks.
- To verify the copy operation, type DIR, press the Spacebar, type the path of the drive and directory that contains the copied files, and then press the Enter key.

The COPY command only copies files within a single subdirectory. If you need to copy files in several directories at once and create the same directory structure on a target disk, you would use the XCOPY command (for Extended Copy), an external command.

Changing Drives

Another simple, but important, operation is changing from one drive to another drive. To perform this operation, you just type the drive name after the command prompt and press the Enter key. A drive name always consists of a letter of the alphabet followed by a colon. Therefore, you must use the colon when typing a drive name.

Eve suggests you switch to your flash drive, and then open the Assets First directory.

To change drives and open a directory:

1. Clear the screen, type **F:** (or the drive name for your flash drive if it is different), and then press the **Enter** key. Windows Vista changes to your flash drive and updates the command prompt. See Figure 13-32.

Figure 13-32 Changing from drive C to a flash drive

2. Type **cd Assets First** (you do not always need to use quotation marks with the Change Directory command, though they work as well), and then press the **Enter** key. Windows Vista changes to the Assets First directory on your flash drive and updates the command prompt to show your exact location. See Figure 13-33.

Figure 13-33 Changing directories on a flash drive

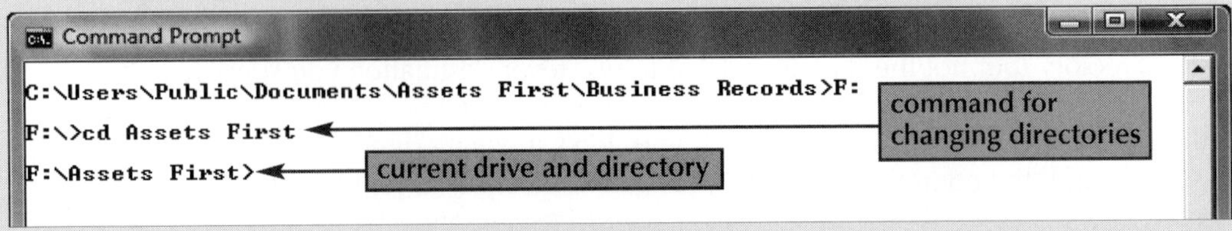

3. Type **dir** and then press the **Enter** key. Windows Vista displays the file copied to the Assets First directory on your flash drive. See Figure 13-34. Unlike earlier, when you specified the path to this directory, you did not need to specify the drive name or directory name, because you have already switched to this drive and subdirectory before, using the Directory command.

Figure 13-34 **Viewing the contents of a new directory**

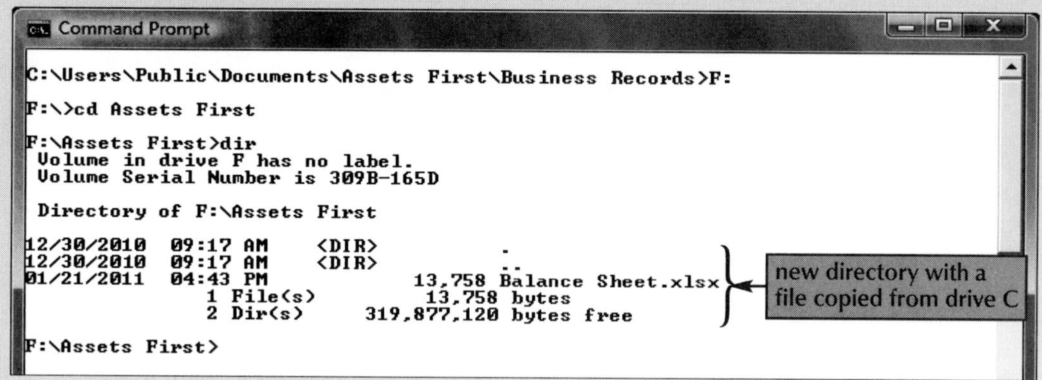

4. Type **C:** and then press the **Enter** key. You switch to the last directory that you were using on drive C.

5. Keep the Command Prompt window open for the next section of the tutorial.

You cannot use the Change Directory (CD) command to change from one drive to another. For example, assume the current drive is drive C. If you type CD F: and press the Enter key, Windows Vista does not change to drive F. Instead, you remain on drive C. However, the Change Directory program does display under the command prompt which directory is the current directory on drive F. You can also use this command to change to another directory on another drive and make it the current directory on that drive without actually switching to that drive. Then, if you want to copy files to the current directory on the other drive, you do not need to specify the directory's path (you just specify the drive name) as the target. For example, assume you are in the Public Documents folder on drive C and want to copy a file named Conference Highlights.docx from that folder to a directory named Meeting Agenda on drive F (your flash drive). First, you enter the following command to change to the Meeting Agenda directory on drive F:

```
CD "F:\Meeting Agenda"
```

(The quotation marks are not needed; however, they always guarantee that the command works as you expect.)

Then, you enter the following command to copy Conference Highlights.docx to the Meeting Agenda folder:

```
COPY "Conference Highlights.docx" F:
```

Note in the last command that you did not specify the path to the Meeting Agenda folder because you had already specified that as the default directory on your flash drive (in this example, drive F). If you had not performed that step, the Windows command interpreter would copy the file to the root directory of drive F (namely, `F:\`).

Now, if you enter the drive name for your flash drive, the Windows command interpreter switches you to the Meeting Agenda folder on drive F because it's the default directory established by the earlier CD command.

Once you become more familiar with the nuances of how the Windows command interpreter uses default drives and directories, you can become more efficient and productive.

Reference Window | Changing Drives

- From the All Programs menu, click Accessories, and then click Command Prompt.
- If you need to change to another drive, type the drive name (including the colon) at the command prompt, and then press the Enter key.

Next, you'll use wildcards to perform operations on multiple files at the same time.

Using Wildcards in File Specifications

When you perform certain types of operations, such as copying multiple files, you can streamline the process with the use of wildcards if the filenames have some feature in common, such as the same set of characters at the beginning of the filename or the same file extension, when you enter a file specification in a command. A **file specification** is a notation for selecting one or more files in a command operation.

A **wildcard** is a symbol used in a file specification to select a group of files. There are two wildcards. The **asterisk wildcard (*)** substitutes for all or part of a filename. The **question mark wildcard (?)** substitutes for a single character in a filename.

The asterisk wildcard is more commonly used because it makes it easier to select files using some common pattern in the filename. For example, if you want to copy all your Microsoft Word files in a folder to your flash drive (and assuming your flash drive name is F:), you enter the following command:

```
COPY *.DOCX F:
```

In this command, the file specification for the source is "*.DOCX". The asterisk wildcard before the period in the file extension substitutes for any filename, so the COPY command selects all files regardless of their filename. However, because you also specified that the file extension must be "docx", the COPY command only copies files with this extension. The net effect is that the COPY command copies all Microsoft Office Word 2007 documents regardless of their filename. Using this approach, you can copy them as a group, rather than having to copy each Microsoft Word file separately by specifying each filename. Using this wildcard, you can save yourself considerable time and effort.

Let's look at another example where you might use the asterisk wildcard. Assume you have a set of budget files for different fiscal years, such as budget reports and financial projections, each with different file extensions, and all the files are stored in the same directory. Also, assume you anticipated the day when you would need to copy all the files for a given fiscal year, and you named the files accordingly by using FY2010 as the first set of characters in each filename. To copy all the files for a specific fiscal year by using the asterisk wildcard, you enter the following command:

```
COPY FY2010* F:
```

This COPY command uses the file specification for the source, namely FY2010*, to select all files that have the *same* first six characters in the filename, no matter what the remainder of the filename is, and no matter what the file extension is. The COPY command then, for example, copies the files named "FY2010 Budget Report.docx", "FY2010 Company Budget.xlsx", and "FY2010 Company Budget Presentation.ppsx" to your flash drive in one step.

If you only want to copy Microsoft Excel files with filenames that start with FY2010 and not copy other files, such as Microsoft Word files, that start with the same six characters but have a different file extension, you can use the following variation of this command:

```
COPY FY2010*.XLSX F:
```

In this instance, you are specifying that the first six characters of a filename must be FY2010, and the file extension must be XLSX (for Microsoft Office Excel 2007 files). The asterisk wildcard means that any combination of characters can follow FY2010 and precede the period and the file extension.

If you want to copy all the files in a directory, such as the Company Projections directory to your flash drive, and assuming you had already switched to the Company Projections directory first, you enter the command:

```
COPY *.* F:
```

In this command, the file specification for the source is "*.*" (pronounced "star dot star"). The asterisk wildcard before the period selects all files, no matter what the main part of the filename is, and the asterisk wildcard after the period selects all files, no matter what the file extension is. In other words, the file specification (*.*) selects all files.

If you are already in the directory that contains the files you want to copy, you can also use this command:

```
COPY . F:
```

This file specification for the source is represented by a dot (i.e., a period), the directory marker for the current directory, and the COPY command therefore copies all files in the current directory. This power user's technique simplifies the process for copying all files in a directory.

Although the asterisk wildcard is commonly used because of its ability to easily select groups of files, you might also need to use the question mark wildcard in a file specification. For example, assume you have five versions of your resume stored in files with the filenames Resume #1.docx, Resume #2.docx, Resume #3.docx, Resume #4.docx, and Resume #5.docx. To copy these files to your flash drive, you might use the following command:

```
COPY "Resume #?.docx" F:
```

In this example, the question mark wildcard substitutes for a single character at the ninth position in each filename, and therefore, the COPY command copies Resume #1.docx, Resume #2.docx, Resume #3.docx, Resume #4.docx, and Resume #5.docx. If you also had a variation of Resume #1.docx named Resume #1A.docx, the Copy command does not copy that file because it does not meet the file specification (it has the letter "A" after the number represented by the wildcard). However, you could use the following command to perform the same operation without using quotation marks and without specifying the file extension:

```
COPY Resume* F:
```

Here's another example of when you might want to use the question mark wildcard. Assume you have created budget documents over the years and named the files so that the first six characters identified the fiscal year. For example, you might have files named FY2010 Budget.xlsx, FY2011 Budget.xlsx, and FY 2012 Budget.xlsx. To copy all these files in one step, you could replace the sixth character in the filename with the question mark wildcard and use this file specification:

```
COPY "FY201? Budget.xlsx" F:
```

This wildcard specification selects all Microsoft Office Excel 2007 files with the "xlsx" file extension that have the same characters in the first through fifth positions and the seventh through thirteenth positions in the filename (including the blank space) and have any character at the sixth position in the filename. Also, the quotation marks are required.

Now that Eve has shown you how to copy files to your flash drive in a command-line environment, you want to copy all the files in the Company Projections directory. Before you change to the Company Projections directory, you want to make sure you are located in the correct starting directory, which should be the Business Records directory. In this case, Business Records and Company Projections are referred to as **parallel directories** because they are under the same subdirectory and are therefore located at the same level in the directory tree.

To copy files using a wildcard:

1. If the command prompt does not contain the path C:\Users\Public\Documents\Assets First\Business Records, type **CD C:\Users\Public\Documents\Assets First\Business Records** and then press the **Enter** key.

2. Clear the screen and type **cd ..\company projections** and then press the **Enter** key. The current directory is now the Company Projections directory. See Figure 13-35. In this command, the ". ." (dot dot) instructs the Change Directory program to first switch to the parent of the current directory (in other words, to Assets First), and then switch to the Company Projections directory (under the Assets First directory).

   Trouble? If the Windows command interpreter displays the message "The system cannot find the path specified," repeat the first step and verify that you are in the correct subdirectory, and then complete the second step.

Tip

You could also type CD . . to step up one directory, and then type CD Company Projections to step down one directory.

Figure 13-35 Changing to a parallel directory

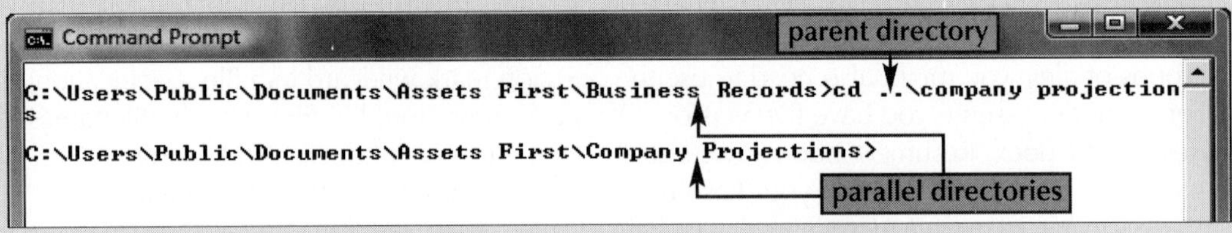

3. Clear the screen and type **copy *.* "F:\Assets First"** (replacing F: with the drive name of your flash drive, if necessary), and then press the **Enter** key. The COPY command uses wildcards to copy three files that match the file specification for the source to the Assets First directory on your flash drive (in other words, all the files in the Company Projections folder). See Figure 13-36.

Figure 13-36 Copying files to a flash drive

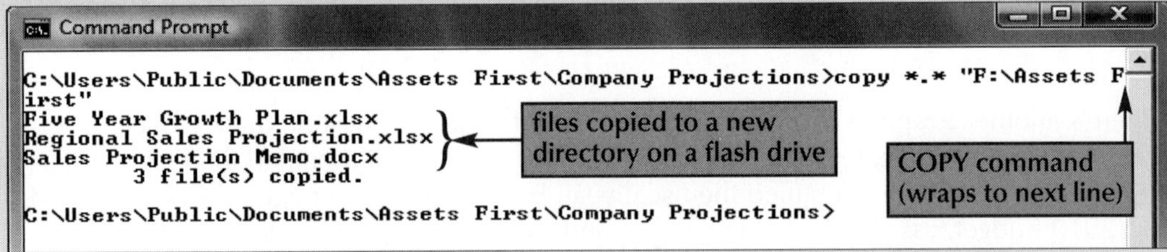

4. To verify that the copy operation worked properly, type **dir "F:\Assets First"** (replacing F: with the drive name of your flash drive, if necessary), and then press the **Enter** key. The Assets First directory on your flash drive now has four files. See Figure 13-37.

Verifying copied files **Figure 13-37**

```
C:\Users\Public\Documents\Assets First\Company Projections>copy *.* "F:\Assets F
irst"
Five Year Growth Plan.xlsx
Regional Sales Projection.xlsx
Sales Projection Memo.docx
        3 file(s) copied.

C:\Users\Public\Documents\Assets First\Company Projections>dir "F:\Assets First"

 Volume in drive F has no label.
 Volume Serial Number is 309B-165D

 Directory of F:\Assets First

12/30/2010  09:17 AM    <DIR>          .
12/30/2010  09:17 AM    <DIR>          ..
01/21/2011  04:43 PM            13,758 Balance Sheet.xlsx
01/12/2012  12:16 PM            15,443 Five Year Growth Plan.xlsx
10/21/2011  08:44 AM            21,013 Regional Sales Projection.xlsx
01/11/2012  05:46 PM            16,892 Sales Projection Memo.docx
               4 File(s)          67,106 bytes
               2 Dir(s)    319,815,680 bytes free

C:\Users\Public\Documents\Assets First\Company Projections>
```

viewing a directory listing of the copied files

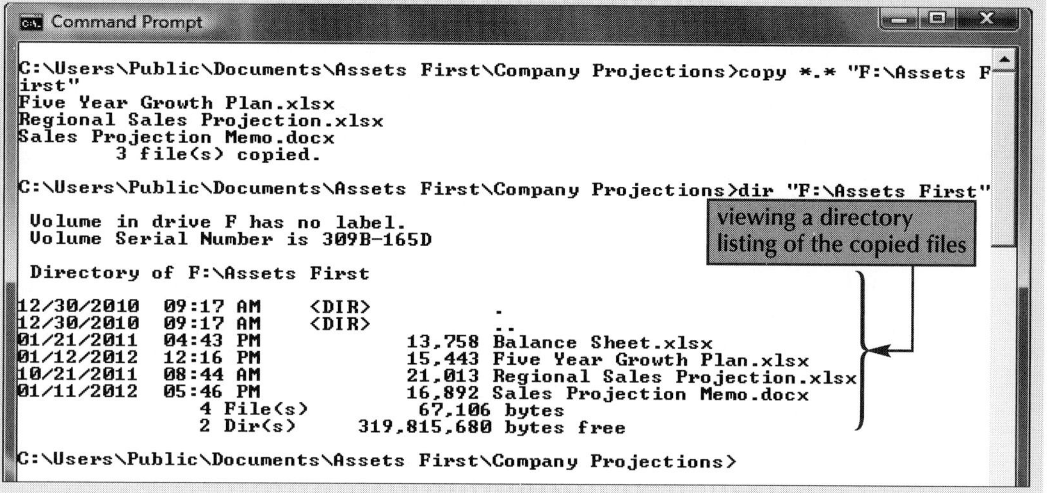

5. Keep the Command Prompt window open for the next section of the tutorial.

You can also combine the use of the asterisk and question mark wildcards in the same file specification, and you can use the two wildcards more than once in a file specification. For example, the following command copies all budget files that contain FY20 as the first four characters in the filename, any character in the fifth and sixth position of the filename, a space in the seventh position of the filename, the word Budget for the eighth through thirteenth characters, and any file extension:

```
COPY "FY20?? Budget.*" F:
```

You can also use wildcards in file specifications with directory names. For example, if you want to change to a directory named Company Projections under the current directory, you can type CD Company* and then press the Enter key. This file specification works as long as no other directory name starts with the word "Company". Depending on the names of the directories located under the current directory, you might also be able to use CD C* or CD Co* or CD Com* or CD Comp*. In other words, you need to use only enough characters in a file specification to distinguish one directory from all others with similar names.

Many commands permit the use of a file specification with or without wildcards to select one or more files for an operation. A file specification can therefore refer to a specific directory or file, a group of directories, or a group of files selected with the use of wildcards. By using some forethought when naming folders files, you can switch directories and copy files more easily with the use of wildcards.

Reference Window | Copying Files Using Wildcards

- From the All Programs menu, click Accessories, and then click Command Prompt.
- Use the Change Directory (CD) command to change to the directory that contains the files you want to copy.
- If you want to copy all the files in a directory to a flash drive (for example), type COPY *.* F: (where F: is the drive name for the flash drive), and then press the Enter key (or type COPY . F: and then press the Enter key).
- If you want to copy all files with a certain file extension, such as "docx", to a flash drive, type COPY *.DOCX F: (where F: is the drive name for the flash drive), and then press the Enter key.
- If you want to copy all files that begin with the same set of characters in the filename, such as "Resume", to your flash drive, type COPY RESUME* F: (where F: is the drive name for the flash drive), and then press the Enter key. If the source filenames contain one or more spaces, include the file specification for the source within quotation marks.
- If you want to copy files with identical filenames, except for one character, such as Resume #1.docx, Resume #2.docx, etc., type COPY "RESUME #?.DOCX" F: (where F: is the drive name for the flash drive), and then press the Enter key. If the source filenames contain one or more spaces, include the file specification for the source within quotation marks.

Another advantage of the asterisk wildcard is that you do not have to specify quotation marks around the main part of the filename in a file specification if the filename contains spaces.

InSight | Careful Use of Wildcard Specifications

You have to be careful with the use of wildcards because you might end up selecting far more files than you would have otherwise expected for an operation, such as a copy or delete operation. A safe strategy is to test wildcard file specifications first by using them with the DIR command. This approach selects the files based on the wildcard file specification you use (but makes no changes to the files), and you can then check to make sure the correct set of files is selected before then using that same wildcard file specification with another command, such as one for deleting all files using that wildcard specification. Also, files you delete in a command-line window are not placed in the Recycle Bin, so you cannot undelete them with Windows Vista.

You can even use wildcards as you perform operations in the Windows graphical user interface. For example, suppose you downloaded a self-extracting executable file with the "exe" file extension from the Internet and now want to extract its contents into the current directory. After you click (or double-click) the downloaded file icon, you are prompted for the path to the folder where you want to store the extracted files. If you want to store the extracted files in the current folder, type a dot (or period) to denote the current directory, and then click the OK button. This power user technique also works if the self-extracting executable file displays a proposed path. You type a period to replace the path. This technique also allows you to save the original downloaded self-extracting executable file with the extracted files in case you need to re-extract the downloaded file again.

Viewing the Windows Environment

In Tutorial 8, you examined environment variables and their settings. You can also check settings for environment variables while working in a command-line environment. One particularly important setting for working in a command-line environment is the one for the PATH environment variable. Windows Vista uses this setting, called the **Windows path**, to locate the program files for external commands.

Eve emphasizes the importance of the Windows environment and path to you so that you can more effectively troubleshoot problems and customize your use of the command-line environment. Eve also notes that you can create new environment variables to simplify the use of commands in a command-line environment. She recommends that you examine the Windows environment with the SET command and that you customize the use of the DIR command by creating a new environment variable.

To view the contents of the Windows environment:

1. Clear the screen, type **set** and then press the **Enter** key. The SET command, an internal command, displays the contents of the Windows environment (which used to be called the DOS environment). See Figure 13-38. The environment variable names are listed in alphabetical order. Some of your settings will differ.

Figure 13-38 Viewing environment variables and their settings

```
Command Prompt

C:\Users\Public\Documents\Assets First\Company Projections>set
ALLUSERSPROFILE=C:\ProgramData
APPDATA=C:\Users\Eve\AppData\Roaming
CLASSPATH=.;C:\Program Files\Java\jre1.6.0_01\lib\ext\QTJava.zip
CommonProgramFiles=C:\Program Files\Common Files
COMPUTERNAME=HI-PERFORM
ComSpec=C:\Windows\system32\cmd.exe
FP_NO_HOST_CHECK=NO
HOMEDRIVE=C:
HOMEPATH=\Users\Eve
LOCALAPPDATA=C:\Users\Eve\AppData\Local
LOGONSERVER=\\HI-PERFORM
NUMBER_OF_PROCESSORS=2
OS=Windows_NT
Path=C:\Windows\system32;C:\Windows;C:\Windows\System32\Wbem;c:\Program Files\Mi
crosoft SQL Server\90\Tools\binn\;C:\Program Files\QuickTime\QTSystem\
PATHEXT=.COM;.EXE;.BAT;.CMD;.VBS;.VBE;.JS;.JSE;.WSF;.WSH;.MSC
PROCESSOR_ARCHITECTURE=x86
PROCESSOR_IDENTIFIER=x86 Family 15 Model 6 Stepping 4, GenuineIntel
PROCESSOR_LEVEL=15
PROCESSOR_REVISION=0604
ProgramData=C:\ProgramData
ProgramFiles=C:\Program Files
PROMPT=$P$G
PUBLIC=C:\Users\Public
QTJAVA=C:\Program Files\Java\jre1.6.0_01\lib\ext\QTJava.zip
SESSIONNAME=Console
SystemDrive=C:
SystemRoot=C:\Windows
TEMP=C:\Users\Eve\AppData\Local\Temp
TMP=C:\Users\Eve\AppData\Local\Temp
USERDOMAIN=Hi-Perform
USERNAME=Eve
USERPROFILE=C:\Users\Eve
windir=C:\Windows

C:\Users\Public\Documents\Assets First\Company Projections>
```

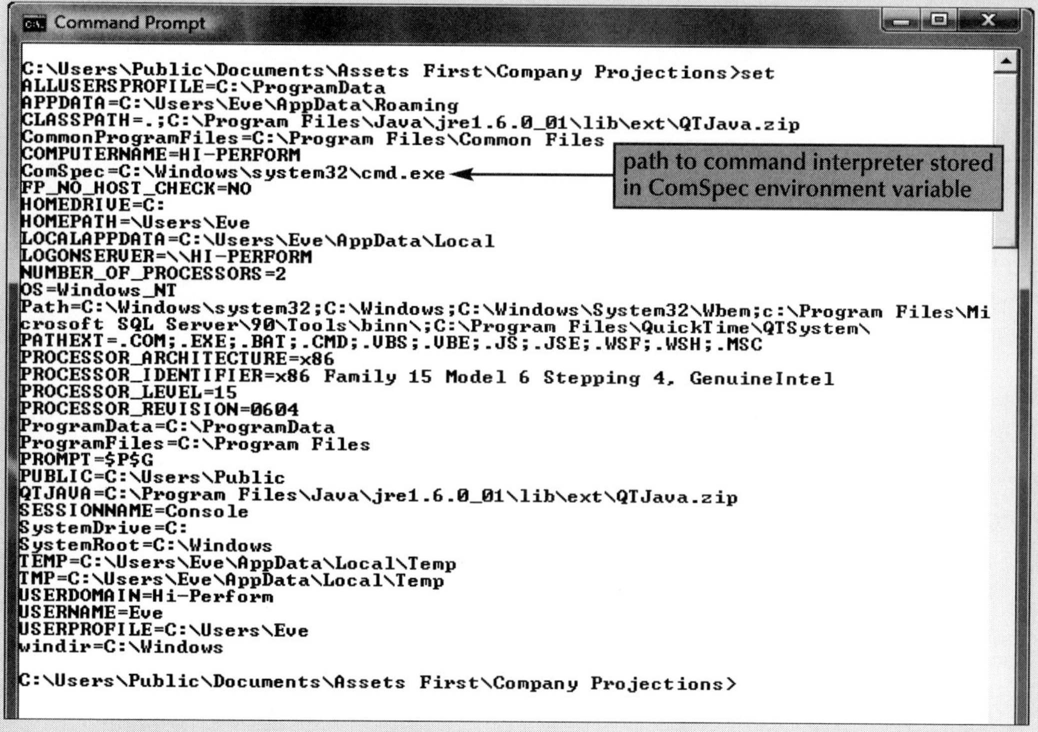

2. Locate the setting for the ComSpec environment variable.

As you learned in Tutorial 8, the setting for the ComSpec environment variable is the path of the program for opening a Command Prompt window. If Windows Vista needs to find cmd.exe so that it can load it from disk, it checks the Windows environment for the ComSpec environment variable to determine the location and name of this program.

The PROMPT environment variable determines how the command prompt appears in a command-line window. PG, the setting for the PROMPT environment variable, is called a **metastring** or code that specifies how the Windows command interpreter (cmd.exe) displays the command prompt. $P (for "path") instructs the command interpreter to display the path of the current drive and directory (in this case, C:\Users\Public\Documents\Assets First\Company Projections) at the beginning of the command prompt. $G (for "greater than") instructs the command interpreter to next display the greater than symbol (>) after the path. As noted earlier, the greater than symbol (>) separates the path of the current drive and directory from the command you type. You can actually use the PROMPT command (and the Help switch) to design your own custom command prompts.

Notice that the SystemRoot environment variable is assigned the path to your Windows Vista directory, and the SystemDrive environment variable stores the setting for the drive where Windows Vista is installed.

As noted in Tutorial 8, the Path environment variable lists the names of directories for Windows Vista to search if it needs to locate a program file. If you want to view just the setting for just the Path environment variable, you can use the PATH command. You can also copy paths from the command-line environment to the Address Bar in a folder window (for example), and you can copy paths from the Address Bar in a folder window and paste them in as part of a command in a command-line window.

To view only the path:

1. Clear the screen, type **path** and then press the **Enter** key. The PATH command, an internal command, displays the Windows path. See Figure 13-39. If the path is too long to fit within the width of the window, it wraps around to the next line.

Figure 13-39 **Viewing the path**

2. Type **path /?** and then press the **Enter** key. The PATH command displays Help information on the use of itself. See Figure 13-40. Note that this command displays or sets a search path for executable files.

Figure 13-40 **Viewing Help on the Path command**

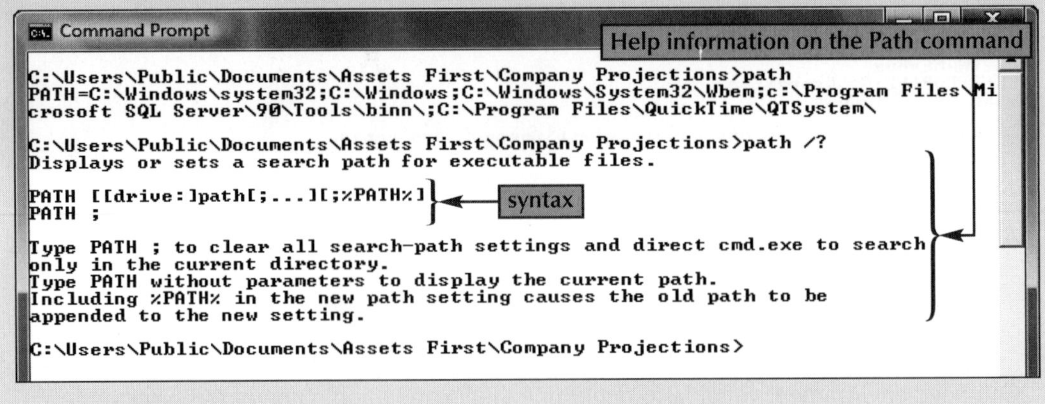

If you want to change the path to include additional directories, to change the order of directories, or to exclude directories, you can type the PATH command followed by the sequence of directories you want to use. For each directory, you specify the path (including the drive) so you clearly identify where to search for executable files. You separate each directory path from the previous one by a semicolon. You do not include a space after the semicolon. If you want to remove the path setting for the Window path, you type the PATH command followed by a space and then a semicolon. That limits the command interpreter to program files stored in the current directory.

Viewing Settings for Environment Variables

| Reference Window

- From the All Programs menu, click Accessories, and then click Command Prompt.
- To view all environment variables and their settings, type SET and then press the Enter key.
- To view settings for the PATH environment variable, type PATH and then press the Enter key.

You can also add settings to the Windows environment. For example, when you first used the DIR command without any switches, it grouped and displayed directories and files in alphabetical order. You used the Attribute switch (/A) to list all files, including hidden system files. You also used the Page or Pause switch (/P) to display the directory listing, one screen at a time. If you frequently use certain switches for the DIR command, such as the Attribute, Sort Order, and Page switches, you can assign them to the DIRCMD environment variable in the Windows environment. Then, when you use the DIR command, you do not have to type the same switches every time you use the command.

Eve encourages you to try this power user's technique from the root directory of drive C.

To assign switches to the DIRCMD environment variable:

1. Type **cd ** and then press the **Enter** key. You switch to the root directory of drive C.
2. Clear the screen, type **set** and then press the **Enter** key. Note that no DIRCMD environment variable is listed in the Windows environment (unless, of course, you or someone else has already added it). If there is a DIRCMD environment variable, make a note of its setting so that you can restore it later.
3. Clear the screen, type **dir \windows** (replacing "windows" with the name of your Windows directory, if necessary), and then press the **Enter** key. Note that although the directory listing is in alphabetical order (on an NTFS volume only), directories and files are not grouped together, hidden files are not displayed, and the directory listing does not pause after one screen.
4. Clear the screen, type **set DIRCMD=/a /o /p** (do not include a space between the DIRCMD and the equal sign or between the equal sign and the first switch), and then press the **Enter** key. Although case does not matter when you type DIRCMD, it is easier to spot when viewing environment variables and their settings. By including the Sort Order switch (/O), you are also guaranteeing that folders and files on FAT volumes are listed in alphabetical order.
5. Type **set** and then press the **Enter** key. The SET command in the previous step created a new environment variable called DIRCMD and assigned the Directory command's **/**a, **/**o, and **/**p switches to that variable. See Figure 13-41.

Figure 13-41 Viewing a new environment variable in the Windows environment

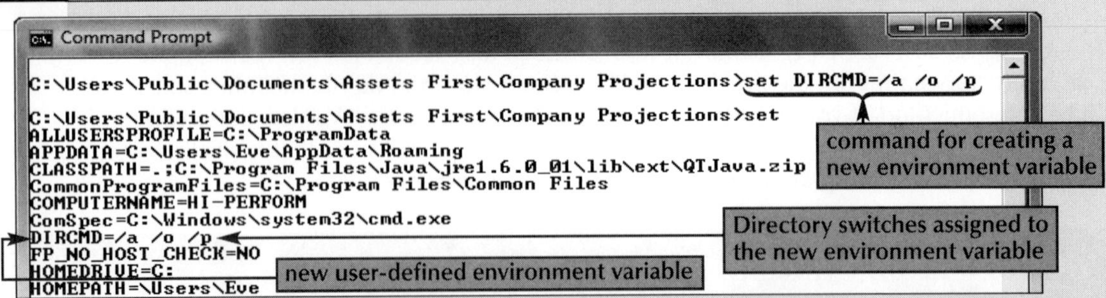

6. Clear the screen, type (or recall from the command history) **dir \windows** (replacing "windows" with the name of your Windows directory, if necessary), press the **Enter** key, and after the first page of output, press the **Spacebar** to view the next page of output. Note that the directory listing is now in alphabetical order, first by directory name, and then by filename; directories are grouped together; files are grouped together; hidden folders and files are displayed; and the directory listing pauses after each screen. You did not have to type the three switches to produce this type of directory listing; instead, the Directory command automatically used the switches you assigned to the DIRCMD environment variable.

   Trouble? If your directory listing does not include hidden folders and files, repeat Step 4, making sure you do not include a space before or after the equal sign (=) in the SET command. Then, try this step again.

7. If necessary, use the **Spacebar** to view the remainder of the directory listing.
8. To close the Command Prompt window, type **exit** and then press the **Enter** key. When you next open a Command Prompt window, you will need to specify a setting for the DIRCMD environment variable again because it is only retained for the current Command Prompt session.

If you want to update the settings stored in the Windows environment for the DIRCMD variable, just use the SET command to assign a new set of switches to the DIRCMD environment variable (it will automatically overwrite the existing setting). If you want to remove this environment variable and its setting from the Windows environment, just type SET DIRCMD= followed by nothing (not even a space), and then press the Enter key. By assigning "nothing" to the environment variable, you remove it from the Windows environment. If you press the Spacebar after the equals sign, you assign a space to the DIRCMD environment variable.

Reference Window | Creating a DIRCMD Environment Variable

- From the All Programs menu, click Accessories, and then click Command Prompt.
- To assign switches to the DIRCMD environment variable, such as the switches /a /o /p (for example), type SET DIRCMD=/A /O /P (with no spaces before or after the equal sign), and then press the Enter key.
- To verify the new setting for the DIRCMD environment variable, type SET and then press the Enter key.
- To remove the DIRCMD environment variable from the Windows environment, type SET DIRCMD= followed by nothing (not even a space), and then press the Enter key.

When you work in a command-line environment, you might need to execute specific programs to troubleshoot a problem. You can switch to the directory that contains those additional programs, or you can change the setting for the PATH environment variable to include that directory. That's why you should know how to check the settings in the Windows environment so that you can verify, modify, or replace those settings. Without the correct path, Windows Vista (like DOS) cannot find and load programs—unless you are in the directory where the program is stored or unless the directory is included in the Windows path. You can speed up a search for a program by listing the directories in the order you want Windows Vista to search them (for example, the most frequently used, or most important, directory is listed first, and then the less frequently used, or the least important, directory is listed last). If you close the Command Prompt window, and then open it later, you will find that Windows Vista uses the original path setting (not the one you specified for the last command-line session).

Before you change the path, you can record the current path in a file on disk by using the output redirection operator (**>**). You just enter the following command:

PATH > OriginalPath.bat

The new file, OriginalPath.bat, is a batch file (also called a script) that you can then use later to restore the original path during the same command-line session. To use this batch file, all you have to do is type the command OriginalPath and press the Enter key. (In essence, you've created a simple program.) Another advantage of storing a new path in a batch file like this one is that you can automatically restore the path or specify an alternate path every time you open a Command Prompt window. Just make sure that you store the batch file in the directory opened by the Command Prompt or in one of the directories in the Windows path.

A **batch program** or **batch file** is therefore a user-defined program file with the "bat" file extension that contains a list of executable commands that the Windows command interpreter can process one right after the other. Simple batch programs allow users to automate common types of operations. Since batch programs are text files, you can open them or create them with simple text editors like Notepad. In the next section of the tutorial, you will create a simple batch file.

Creating a Batch Program

Since you periodically need to update information about a computer system using the SYSTEMINFO command, Eve recommends that you create a simple batch program to automate this operation.

When you create a batch program, you list each command on a different line. When you execute a batch program, the Windows command interpreter processes each command on a line-by-line basis, one at a time. So the order in which you list commands is important. Furthermore, it reflects the logic you used in creating the batch program.

When the command interpreter executes a batch program, it displays each command in the command-line window as it processes the command. To hide the display of these commands so that they are not echoed (or repeated) in the command-line window, you enter the ECHO OFF command on the first line in the batch program file. On the second line, you enter CLS to clear the command-line window of any previous output from commands you've entered. Then, you list the command or commands, such as SYSTEMINFO, that you want the batch program to execute and perform a specific type of operation. As described earlier in the tutorial, you can use the following SYSTEMINFO command to compile information on the configuration of your computer system, and you can redirect that output to a file on disk, as follows:

```
SYSTEMINFO > F:\SystemReport.txt
```

After you create your batch program with Notepad, you save it with the "bat" file extension to designate it as a batch program that the Windows command interpreter can open and execute. As you will recall from examining the PATHEXT environment variable in Tutorial 8, the third file extension used by Windows Vista and the Windows command interpreter to locate program files in a directory is the "bat" file extension.

Your first step is to create your batch program with Notepad.

To create a batch program with Notepad:

1. From the All Programs menu, click **Accessories**, and then click **Notepad**.
2. After Windows Vista opens Notepad, enter the commands shown in Figure 13-42. Make sure you replace F: with the drive name of your flash drive in the SYSTEMINFO command. The commands shown in this figure are entered in uppercase to make them easier to read, but you can use lowercase if you prefer. Also, the last ECHO command displays a message in the command-line window to let you know that the SYSTEMINFO program has completed compiling the report with configuration information about your computer.

Figure 13-42 Creating a batch file with Notepad

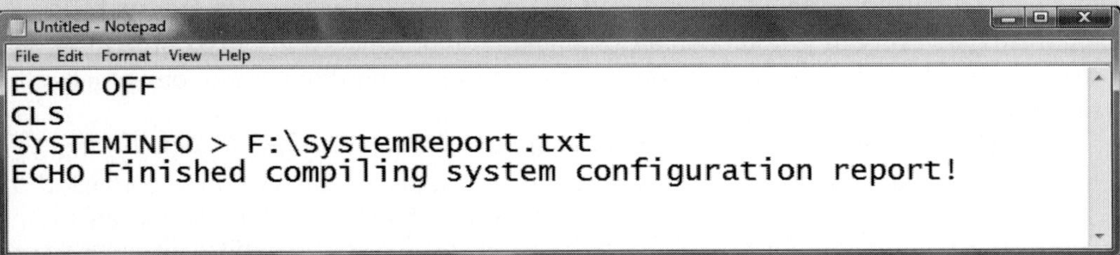

3. Check your batch program file using Figure 13-42 to make sure you have included every line in the order shown and that you have correctly spelled each command and used the proper syntax.
4. To save your batch program, click **File** on the menu bar, click **Save**, click the **Browse folders** button to expand the Save As dialog box (if not already expanded), click **Computer** under Favorite Links, locate and click your **flash drive** icon, click the **Save as type** button, click **All Files (*.*)**, click inside the File name box, type **SysInfoReport.bat** and then click the **Save** button.
5. Close the Notepad window.

Now that you've created your batch program, you're ready to test it. To run your program, all you have to do is type the main part of the filename—just as you would enter a command. You do not need to type the file extension because it's specified as a program file in the PATHEXT setting.

To test your batch program:

1. Open a Command Prompt window from the Start menu's recently opened programs list or from the Accessories menu on the All Programs menu.
2. Type the **drive name** for your flash drive, and then press the **Enter** key. For example, if your flash drive is drive F, you type F: and then press the Enter key. The Windows command interpreter switches you to your flash drive.

3. Type **SysInfoReport** (case does not matter, but uppercase characters can make a filename easier to read), and then press the **Enter** key. Notice that the Windows command interpreter displays the name of your batch program in the title bar. Your batch program then turns off the echoing of commands (so, for example, you do not see the SYSTEMINFO command displayed in the window) and clears the command-line window of any previous output. However, you do see messages that identify what type of information SYSTEMINFO is compiling at any given time. After SYSTEMINFO completes the process of compiling the information, the batch program displays the message "Finished compiling system information report!" in the command-line window. Then, the Windows command interpreter redisplays the command prompt.

   Trouble? If the Windows command interpreter displays an error message, or if the batch program does not perform correctly or does not perform all the operations specified in the batch program, open the batch program in Notepad, correct the problem, save your changes, and then test the batch program again.

4. Type **dir /o** and then press the **Enter** key. Your new report is displayed in the directory listing along with your batch program.

5. Close the Command Prompt window.

Each time you use this batch program, it will overwrite your previous copy of this file (except of course, the first time, when it creates the first copy of this file). If you want a running history of your computer's configuration retained in this file, you can use the **append output redirection operator** (>>) to tack each new system information report to the bottom of the existing file. The command is as follows:

```
SYSTEMINFO >> F:\SystemReport.txt
```

Batch programs are simple and powerful ways to automate routine or specialized types of tasks that you perform on your computer. If you routinely perform multiple tasks, you combine them in one file and perform all the tasks at the same time, one right after another.

Creating a Batch Program

| Reference Window

- From the All Programs menu, click Accessories, and then click Notepad.
- Enter the commands for your batch program, each on a different line (case does not matter). For the first line, you can enter the ECHO OFF command to turn off the display of commands in the batch program. On the second line, you can enter the CLS command to clear the command-line window of any previous output. Then, list the commands that constitute the main part of the batch program and that perform the operations you want.
- To save your batch program, click File on the menu bar, click Save, click the Browse folders button to expand the Save As dialog box (if not already expanded), click Computer under Favorite Links, locate and open the drive and folder where you want to save the batch program, click the Save as type button, click All Files (*.*), click inside the File name box, type a name for your batch program and add the "bat" file extension to the end of the filename, click the Save button, and then close the Notepad window.
- To test your batch program, open a Command Prompt window, switch to the drive and folder where you save the batch program (or work from any directory if you saved the batch program in a folder in your Windows path), and then type the filename you used for the batch program.
- After you test your batch program, close the Command Prompt window.

Once you create a batch program, you can create a desktop shortcut to the batch program so that you can run the batch program from the desktop, just as you would any other program you use. After you click the desktop shortcut, Windows Vista opens a command-line window, executes your batch program, and then closes the command-line window after it processes the entire batch program.

Restoring Your Computer

To restore your computer:

1. Open the **Public Documents** folder, delete the **Assets First** folder, and then close the Public Documents folder.
2. Open a window onto your flash drive and delete the **Assets First** folder. If requested by your instructor, submit copies of the ComputerInfo.txt, SystemReport.txt, and SysInfoReport.bat files, either in printed or electronic form. Then, if you no longer need the ComputerInfo.txt file, the SystemReport.txt file, and SysInfoReport.bat file (your batch program), select and delete these files as well.
3. If you want to turn off single-click activation, click the **Computer** icon on the desktop, click the **Organize** button on the command bar, click **Folder and Search Options**, and under "Click items as follows" on the General property sheet in the Folder Options dialog box, click the **Double-click to open an item (single-click to select)** option button, click the **OK** button to close the Folder and Options dialog box, and then close the Computer window.
4. If you want to remove Run from the Start menu, right-click the **Start** button, click **Properties**, click the **Customize** button to the left of the Start menu option button in the Taskbar and Start Menu Properties dialog box, locate and click the **Run command** check box in the Customize Start Menu dialog box, click the **OK** button to close the Customize Start Menu dialog box, and then click the **OK** button to close the Taskbar and Start Menu Properties dialog box.
5. If you want to remove the Computer icon from the desktop, open the **Start** menu, right-click **Computer**, click **Show on Desktop**, and then close the Start menu.

Eve is now confident you can work from the command line to help her manage and troubleshoot the credit union's network.

Review | Session 13.2 Quick Check

1. To refer to the root directory of drive C in a command, you type a(n) ________________ .
2. . (dot) refers to the ________________ .
3. . . (dot dot) refers to the ________________ .
4. When you perform a copy operation, you specify the ________________ and ________________ .
5. To change from drive C to drive F, you type ________________ .
6. A(n) ________________ is a symbol used in a file specification to select a group of files.

Tutorial Summary | Review

In this tutorial you learned the importance of command-line skills and the command-line environment. You opened a Command Prompt window, examined the difference between internal and external commands, used an internal command to customize the Command Prompt window, used the Help switch to obtain command-specific Help information, recalled commands from the command history, used an external command to assign a volume label to a drive, and displayed a command reference list. You also used the SYSTEMINFO command to view information about your computer system. You displayed a directory tree, learned how to change to the root directory, viewed the contents of a directory, changed directories, viewed file attributes, and created a directory. You copied a file from one directory to another directory and from drive to drive, changed drives, and used a wildcard to copy a group of files. You viewed the Windows environment, and then created and used an environment variable for the Directory command. Finally, you created and tested a simple batch program.

Key Terms

*
.
..
?
\
American Standard Code for Information Interchange (ASCII)
append output redirection operator
argument
asterisk wildcard (*)
batch file
batch program
buffer
command history
command interpreter
command prompt
console
current directory
default directory
default drive
destination
directory
directory listing
directory marker
execute
external command
file specification
filter
hex digit
hot fixes
insert mode
internal command
interrupt command
metastring
operating system prompt
output redirection operator
overtype mode
paged output
parallel directory
parameter
parent directory
parent folder
pipe
pipe operator
pipeline
question mark wildcard (?)
reserved names
root directory
source
switch
syntax
text user interface (TUI)
toggle key
volume label
wildcard
Windows path

Practice | Review Assignments

Practice the skills you learned in the tutorial.

For a list of Data Files in the Review folder, see page 821.

Eve recommends that you practice using the commands and features that the two of you examined, and then use the SYSTEMINFO command to document your computer system's settings. She also recommends that you try different variations of these commands and features.

As you complete each step in this Review Assignment, record your answers to questions so that you can submit them to your instructor. Use a word processing application, such as Word or WordPad, to prepare your answers to these questions. Also, if you change any settings on the computer you are using, note the original settings so that you can restore them later. Complete the following:

1. If necessary, attach your flash drive to your computer and close any dialog boxes or windows that open.
2. Display the Run command on the Start menu.
3. What is the drive name for your flash drive?
4. Copy the Review folder from the Tutorial.13 folder provided with your Data Files to the Public Documents folder, and then change the name of the Review folder to Assets First.
5. Use Run from the Start menu to open a Command Prompt window, and then resize the command-line window so that you can see the output of commands. What is the path of the program that Windows Vista uses to open this Command Prompt window? What is the current drive? What is the path to the current directory?
6. Use the HELP command to display Help information about the COLOR command. What command did you enter? Change the console colors so that the command-line window uses a light aqua background and a blue foreground. What command did you enter? If you want to return to the default console colors without specifying hex digits for the color attribute, what command would you enter? Use the COLOR command to specify background and foreground colors of your own choosing.
7. View Help information on the VOL command. What command did you enter? What does the VOL command do? What is the syntax of the VOL command? Which parts of the command are required and optional?
8. Use the VOL command to view the volume label for your flash drive. What command did you enter? What is the volume label for your flash drive (if any)?
9. Use the LABEL command to assign a volume label to your flash drive. What command did you enter, and what volume label did you specify?
10. Verify the volume label for your flash drive. What command did you use? What is the volume name now?
11. Use the LABEL command to restore your flash drive's original volume label or to remove the new volume label without specifying another volume name. What command did you enter? Verify the change.
12. Clear the screen, and then display a command reference list, one page at a time. What commands did you enter? What is the function of the DOSKEY command? View the next page of output. What is the function of the SYSTEMINFO command? If necessary, view the remainder of the command reference list and return to the command prompt.

13. Clear the screen and use the SYSTEMINFO command to display information about your computer, one page at a time. What command did you enter? What are the OS Name, OS Version, OS Configuration, System Model, System Type, Processor(s) clock speed, Windows Directory, System Directory, Boot Device, Total Physical Memory, and Page File Location(s) for your computer? View the remainder of the output of this command.
14. Clear the screen and enter the following command: TREE C:\ | MORE
Explain what happens. Where does the directory tree start? Interrupt the TREE command and return to the command prompt. What command did you use to interrupt this command?
15. Clear the screen, and then change to the root directory. What commands did you enter?
16. Change to the Assets First directory under the Public Documents directory. What command did you enter? What does the command prompt display?
17. Display a directory listing of the Assets First directory. What subdirectories are contained in the Assets First directory? How are the subdirectories listed? What do the **.** (dot) and **..** (dot dot) entries in the directory listing refer to?
18. Display a directory tree of the Assets First directory. What command did you enter? What are the subdirectories under Contract Training?
19. Change to the Business Records directory. What command did you enter?
20. Display a directory listing of the files in the Business Records directory. What command did you enter? If this directory listing displayed more than one page of output, what command would you use to display only one screen at a time? If this directory listing contained both subdirectories and files, what command would you use to display a list of subdirectories only, and what command would you use to display a list of files only?
21. View attributes of the files in this directory. What command did you use? What attributes are assigned to the files?
22. Create a directory named Business Records on your flash drive, and then verify the operation by displaying the contents of your flash drive. What commands did you use?
23. Copy all the files in the Business Records directory under Public Documents to the Business Records directory on your flash drive, and then verify the operation. What commands did you use?
24. Switch to the parent directory of the Business Records subdirectory. What command did you enter?
25. Switch to the Client Projects subdirectory. What command did you enter?
26. Copy the Break-Even Analysis.xlsx file to the Business Records directory on your flash drive. What command did you enter?
27. Change to the flash drive. What command did you use?
28. Display a directory listing of the Business Records subdirectory. What command did you use?
29. Change to the hard disk drive, and then change to the root directory. What commands did you use?
30. View the contents of the Windows environment. What command did you use? What are your HOMEDRIVE and HOMEPATH settings?
31. Add the DIRCMD environment variable to the Windows environment and specify that it use the Page, Sort Order, and Attribute switches for the Directory command. What command did you use to perform this operation?

32. Display a directory listing for the root directory. What command did you use? Describe how the Directory command listed directories and files in the root directory.
33. Switch to your flash drive, and then create a simple batch file named OriginalPath.bat that stores the current path in the batch file. Describe how you created the batch file and what happens when you test the batch file.
34. Close the command-line window, delete the Assets First folder under the Public Documents folder, delete the Business Records folder on your flash drive, and then restore any other settings you changed.
35. Submit the results of the preceding steps to your instructor, including your batch program, either in printed or electronic form, as requested.

Apply | Case Problem 1

Use the skills you learned in the tutorial to check directory listings at a realty company.

For a list of Data Files in the Case1 folder, see page 821.

J&B Realty, Inc. J&B Realty is a large firm that provides a variety of realty services to its clients in the greater New York City metropolitan area. As J&B Realty's network administrator, Alessandro Bolzoni uses his command-line skills to quickly locate and compile files for use by other employees in the firm and to examine directory information about installed software files and operating system files. He wants you to become familiar with the use of the various Directory command switches, as well as wildcards, so that you can assist him with troubleshooting.

As you complete each step in this case problem, record your answers to questions so that you can submit them to your instructor. Use a word processing application, such as Word or WordPad, to prepare your answers to these questions. Also, if you change any settings on the computer you are using, note the original settings so that you can restore them later. Complete the following:

1. Copy the Case1 folder from the Tutorial.13 folder provided with your Tutorial 13 Data Files to the Public Documents folder, and then change the name of the Case1 folder to J&B Realty.
2. Open a Command Prompt window, and then change to the root directory of drive C. What command did you use for this operation? What path is shown in the command prompt?
3. Use the HELP command to display Help information on the use of the Directory command. What command did you enter? What are the purposes of the /B, /W, and /D switches?
4. **EXPLORE** Use the Directory command with the /B, /W, and /D switches to display the contents of the root directory. What command did you enter with each switch? Describe the appearance and contents of each directory listing. In what way(s) are the /W and /D switches similar and dissimilar?
5. Switch to the J&B Realty subdirectory under the Public Documents folder. What command did you use for this operation? What path is shown in the command prompt?
6. View Help on the Directory command again. What is the purpose of the /S and /X switches?
7. **EXPLORE** Use the Directory command with the /S switch and then with just the /X switch. Describe how these switches alter the output of the Directory command. What advantage do these switches have over the other switches you've examined?

8. Change to the Business Records subdirectory. What command can you use to display a list of only those files that start with the letter "C" at the beginning of the filename?
9. Switch to the Company Projections subdirectory. What command did you use?
10. What command can you use to display a list of only those files that have a "docx" file extension?
11. How can you customize the Windows environment so that the Directory command always lists short filenames (or 8.3 filenames) along with long filenames?
12. Close the Command Prompt window, delete the J&B Realty folder in the Public Documents folder, and restore any other settings that you changed for this case problem.
13. Submit the results of the preceding steps to your instructor, either in printed or electronic form, as requested.

Challenge | Case Problem 2

Expand your command-line skills to prepare a workshop on environment variables.

There are no Data Files needed for this Case Problem.

Brockmann Computer Outlet Ursula Friedländer works as a network technician at Brockmann Computer Outlet in Indianapolis, Indiana. Ursula relies on her command-line skills to quickly compile information about a computer so that she can effectively troubleshoot problems encountered by customers. At the request of her supervisor, she presents a workshop for co-workers where she demonstrates power user tips for working in a command-line environment.

As you complete each step in this case problem, record your answers to questions so that you can submit them to your instructor. Use a word processing application, such as Word or WordPad, to prepare your answers to these questions. Also, if you change any settings on the computer you are using, note the original settings so that you can restore them later. Complete the following:

1. Open a Command Prompt window and change to the root directory in one step. What command did you use? What is the path of the current directory?
2. Display the contents of the Windows environment. What command did you use? What setting is assigned to the OS and NUMBER_OF_PROCESSORS environment variables?
3. **EXPLORE** Enter the follow command: SET USERPROFILE

   What setting is stored in this environment variable? Why might you prefer to use this variation of the SET command?
4. **EXPLORE** Enter the following command: CD %USERPROFILE%

   (Case does not matter, but you must type the percentage symbols.) What directory did the Change Directory command switch to? Explain why this happened.
5. Use the SET command with each of the following variables: SystemRoot, HOMEPATH, ProgramFiles, and TEMP. What setting is stored in each environment variable?
6. Try the Change Directory command with the SystemRoot, HOMEPATH, ProgramFiles, and TEMP environment variables. (*Hint*: Remember to use the percentage symbols around the variable name.) List each command you entered and what directory you switched to.
7. Are there any advantages to using these environment variables over specifying the path? Explain.

EXPLORE

8. Use the SET command to create a new environment variable named PublicDocs and assign the path (with the drive name) to the Public Documents directory to this environment variable. What command did you enter?
9. Change to your Public Documents subdirectory using the PublicDocs environment variable. What command did you enter to change to the Public Documents subdirectory? What advantage does this new type of environment variable offer?

EXPLORE

10. To restore your computer, remove the PublicDocs environment variable from the Windows environment, and then verify this operation. What commands did you use?
11. Close the Command Prompt window and restore any other settings that you changed for this case problem.
12. Submit the results of the preceding steps to your instructor, either in printed or electronic form, as requested.

Challenge | Case Problem 3

Expand your command-line skills to examine computer settings for a land survey company.

For a list of Data Files in the Case3 folder, see page 821.

Lyang Surveying Daeshim Lyang works as a computer troubleshooting specialist for his father's land surveying firm. He is particularly adept at using the command-line environment while working on projects for his father's employees. When setting up and configuring a computer, Daeshim checks and customizes computer system settings. He asks you to assist him by documenting the directory structure and settings on a new computer.

As you complete each step in this case problem, record your answers to questions so that you can submit them to your instructor. Use a word processing application, such as Word or WordPad, to prepare your answers to these questions. Also, if you change any settings on the computer you are using, note the original settings so that you can restore them later. Complete the following:

1. Copy the Case3 folder from the Tutorial.13 folder provided with your Tutorial 13 Data Files to the Public Documents folder, and then change the name of the Case3 folder to Lyang Surveying.
2. Attach your flash drive to the computer you are using and close any dialog boxes or windows that open.
3. Open a Command Prompt window, and then create a directory named Documentation on your flash drive. What command did you use?
4. Display a directory listing for your flash drive and verify that you created the Documentation directory. What command did you use?
5. Display an alphabetical listing of *all* directories and files in the root directory of drive C in alphabetical order, one page at a time. What command did you use?

EXPLORE

6. Recall the previous command from the command history, remove the switch for displaying directories and files one screen at a time, and then modify the command so that it redirects its output to a file named **DriveCRootDir.txt** in the Documentation directory on your flash drive. What command did you use?
7. To verify that you created this file, display a directory listing for the Documentation directory on your flash drive. What command did you use?
8. Change to the root directory of drive C and display a list of attributes assigned to all files in the root directory. What commands did you use?

EXPLORE 9. Recall the previous command from the command history, and then modify it so that the command redirects the output to a file named **DriveCRootAttributes.txt** in the Documentation directory on your flash drive. What command did you use? Recall from the command history the command that you used to view a directory listing of the Documentation subdirectory on your flash drive, and then use the command to verify that you created the DriveCRootAttributes.txt file.

10. Display an alphabetical listing of *all* directories and files in the Windows directory in alphabetical order, first by directory name, then by filename. What command did you use?

EXPLORE 11. Recall the previous command from the command history, and then modify the command so that it redirects its output to a file named **WinDir.txt** in the Documentation subdirectory on your flash drive. What command did you use? Recall from the command history the command that you used to view a directory listing of the Documentation subdirectory on your flash drive, and then use the command to verify that you created the WinDir.txt file.

12. Change to the Lyang Surveying subdirectory under the Public Documents directory.

13. Display a directory tree (not a directory listing) of this directory and its subdirectories. What command did you use?

EXPLORE 14. Display Help information on the use of the TREE command. What command did you use? What does the /F (for Filename) switch do? (*Note*: The ASCII switch (/A) replaces the graphical lines in a directory tree with text characters.)

EXPLORE 15. Use the TREE command with the Filename switch (/F) and the ASCII Switch (/A) to display a directory tree of the current directory and its subdirectories. What command did you use? How does the directory tree differ?

EXPLORE 16. Recall the previous command from the command history, and then modify it so that the command uses only the ASCII switch (/A) and so that it redirects the output to a file named **LyangSurveying.txt** in the Documentation directory on your flash drive. What command did you use? Recall from the command history the command that you used to view a directory listing of the Documentation directory on your flash drive, and then use the command to verify that you created the LyangSurveying.txt file.

EXPLORE 17. Do not enter a command, but instead enter the path to the LyangSurveying.txt file on your flash drive. What command path did you enter at the command prompt? Describe what happens and what the TREE command produced in Step 16.

18. Close any open windows, including the Command Prompt window, delete the Lyang Surveying folder in the Public Documents folder, and restore any other settings that you changed for this case problem.

19. Submit the results of the preceding steps to your instructor, including the files in the Documentation folder on your flash drive, either in printed or electronic form, as requested. Then, delete the Documentation folder on your flash drive.

Create | Case Problem 4

Use the skills you learned in the tutorial to create a simple batch file.

For a list of Data Files in the Case4 folder, see page 821.

Golden Gate Wireless Consuelo Orozco works as a network specialist for Golden Gate Wireless on the West Coast and assists staff members in setting up, configuring, customizing, and troubleshooting wireless networks for clients. Since you frequently use the command-line environment and your flash drive to document problems and information about company computers that you troubleshoot, Consuelo recommends that you create a simple batch file on your flash drive to automate routine operations you perform.

Complete the following steps:

1. Open Notepad and create a batch program that performs the following operations in the following order:
   - Turns off the display (or echo) of commands in the batch file when you execute the batch file.
   - Clears the screen.
   - Changes to your flash drive.
   - Uses the SYSTEMINFO command to document configuration information about a computer and store the results in a file named SysInfoAnalysis.txt on your flash drive.
   - Opens the SysInfoAnalysis.txt file so that you can examine the information and add any additional notes as you document and troubleshoot a computer. (*Hint*: To open a file from the command prompt, you type the full filename of the file, and Windows Vista opens the program associated with the file's extension. If you prefer, you can also use the path to this file.)
2. After you create the batch program, save it in the Public Documents folder under the filename AnalyzeComputer.bat, and then close Notepad.
3. Open a command prompt window, change to the Public Documents folder, and then execute your batch file. After your batch file opens the SysInfoAnalysis.txt file, examine the file, and then close Notepad. If the batch file does not operate correctly, open the batch file with Notepad, correct any problems, save your changes, close Notepad, and then test the batch file again.
4. Close the Command Prompt window, and then copy the AnalyzeComputer.bat file from the Public Documents folder to your flash drive.
5. Submit your batch file and the SysInfoAnalysis.txt file to your instructor, either in printed or electronic form, as requested.

Review | Quick Check Answers

Session 13.1

1. command interpreter
2. An internal command's program code is stored in the file cmd.exe and loaded into memory when a Command Prompt window is opened. In contrast, an external command's program code resides in a specific file on disk that must be opened and then loaded in order to use the program.
3. A switch is an optional parameter that you use with a command to change the way in which the command works.
4. command history
5. True
6. A filter is a program that modifies the output of another program.

Session 13.2

1. \
2. current directory
3. parent directory
4. source and destination
5. F:
6. wildcard

Ending Data Files

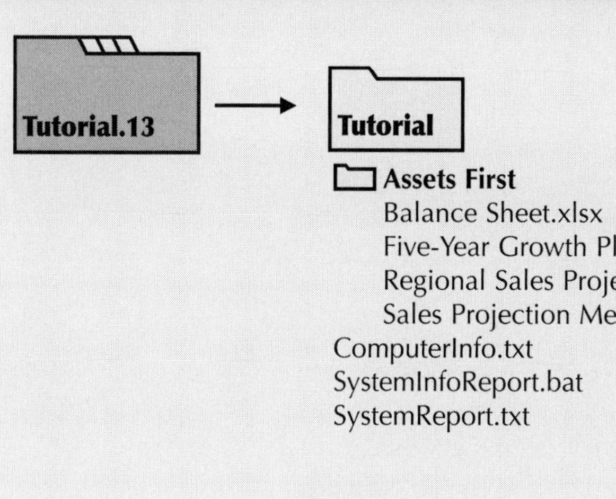

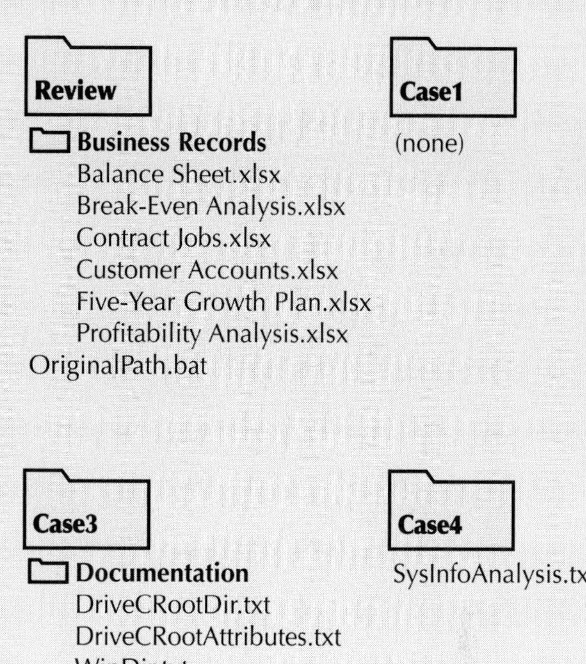

Tutorial 14

Objectives

Session 14.1
- Learn about the role and importance of the Registry
- Create a restore point prior to using the Registry
- Open and examine the Registry with the Registry Editor
- Export Registry settings to a registration file

Session 14.2
- Examine the structure and organization of the Registry
- Trace information on registered file types
- View information on Class Identifiers
- Examine how to edit and add a new Registry entry

Exploring the Windows Registry

Customizing Desktops with the Windows Registry

Case | Mobile Software Center, Inc.

Mobile Software Center, Inc., which develops software for mobile devices, is experiencing a phenomenal growth due to the increasing popularity and dependence on mobile devices. Ian Caplinger works as one of the company's programmers. Ian modifies the Windows Vista Registry to customize and streamline the use of his computer so that he is more efficient and productive, and he also uses the Windows Vista Registry Editor to troubleshoot system configuration problems and remove malicious software.

In the first section of the tutorial, you will examine the role and importance of the Windows Registry. You will create a restore point prior to opening the windows Registry. Then, you will export Registry settings so that you have a backup of the Registry. You will also examine the structure of the Registry, trace information on registered file type, examine Class Identifiers, and look at how to edit the Registry and add new Registry settings.

Starting Data Files

There are no starting Data Files needed for this tutorial.

Session 14.1

Understanding the Role of the Windows Registry

Windows Vista stores your computer's hardware, software, security, network, system performance, and user settings (or user profiles) in a database known as the **Registry**.

When you perform a normal boot of your computer, Windows Vista processes the information in the Registry to properly configure your computer. For example, the Registry contains information on hardware devices and resources (such as IRQs, I/O addresses, and DMA channels) assigned to both Plug and Play and legacy devices. During booting, Windows Vista uses the Registry to load the appropriate device drivers, reconfigure hardware devices (if necessary), and update the Registry. Windows Vista also loads services and startup programs and configures your computer for one or more users and for applications.

When you log on your computer, Windows Vista uses your **user profile** (or user account settings) in the Registry to customize your display of the desktop. Windows Vista updates the contents of the Registry when you change settings on your computer, such as when you customize your desktop with the Display Properties dialog box, when you install Plug and Play devices, when you install or remove software, when you change settings using the Control Panel and Device Manager, and when you define user accounts and groups. When you install software, the Setup program adds information about the application to the Windows Vista Registry, including, for example, which file types (and therefore which file extensions) it supports. For example, if you click (or double-click) a file icon in a folder window, Windows Vista uses the Registry to locate the application associated with the file extension of the file that you selected. Then, it loads that application and opens the document in the file. Using file associations with the Registry allows you to work in a document-oriented, or docucentric, environment. The Registry is constantly changing and gradually increases in size as it tracks all system and user settings.

Microsoft recommends that you use tools, such as the Control Panel, Device Manager, and property sheets, to make configuration changes whenever possible rather than opening and editing the Registry. If you open the Registry and make a mistake while you are changing a Registry setting, you might not even be able to use your computer, or you might introduce errors that affect the hardware and software configuration of your computer so that you cannot boot it. Windows Vista does not warn you if the change you made is incorrect, either at the time you make that change, or when you close the Registry. Instead, Windows Vista applies the change immediately. *Furthermore, there is no Undo feature, so any changes you make are final.*

The Windows Vista Registry database consists of a set of files named Default, Sam, Security, Software, System, and Components. Each of these files and its associated log file (Default.log, Sam.log, Security.log, Software.log, System.log, and Components.log), is called a **hive**. Each log file has a list of changes made to the keys and values of a hive. Files with the "sav" file extension (Default.sav, Sam.sav, Security.sav, Software.sav, System.sav, and Components.sav) are backup copies of Registry files. All of these hives are stored in the %SystemRoot%\system32\config folder, where %SystemRoot% is the path to your Windows folder. Since the log files are hidden files, you have to specify that Windows Vista display hidden files and folders. Figure 14-1 lists the names of hives and the types of information stored in each hive. The BCD00000000 hive contains Boot Configuration Data settings. You examined the importance of Boot Configuration Data (BCD) in Tutorial 8. The Components and BCD00000000 hives are new to Windows Vista and are not found in earlier versions of the Windows desktop operating system.

Figure 14-1 Registry files

Registry Files	Contents
BCD00000000	Boot Configuration Data settings
Components	Windows Vista components settings
Default	Default system settings
SAM (Security Account Manager)	Information on user and group accounts
Security	Security information, such as user rights, password policy, and local group membership
Software	Software configuration settings
System	Hardware and startup configuration settings

Figure 14-2 shows the hives on Ian's computer arranged in order by Date modified. Note that on the computer used for this figure, the hives and supporting files are stored in the config folder. The path to that folder is C:\windows\system32\config. The RegBack folder contains backup copies of the Registry files for the current day, the previous day the computer was booted, and the date when Windows Vista was installed.

Figure 14-2 Viewing the contents of the Config folder

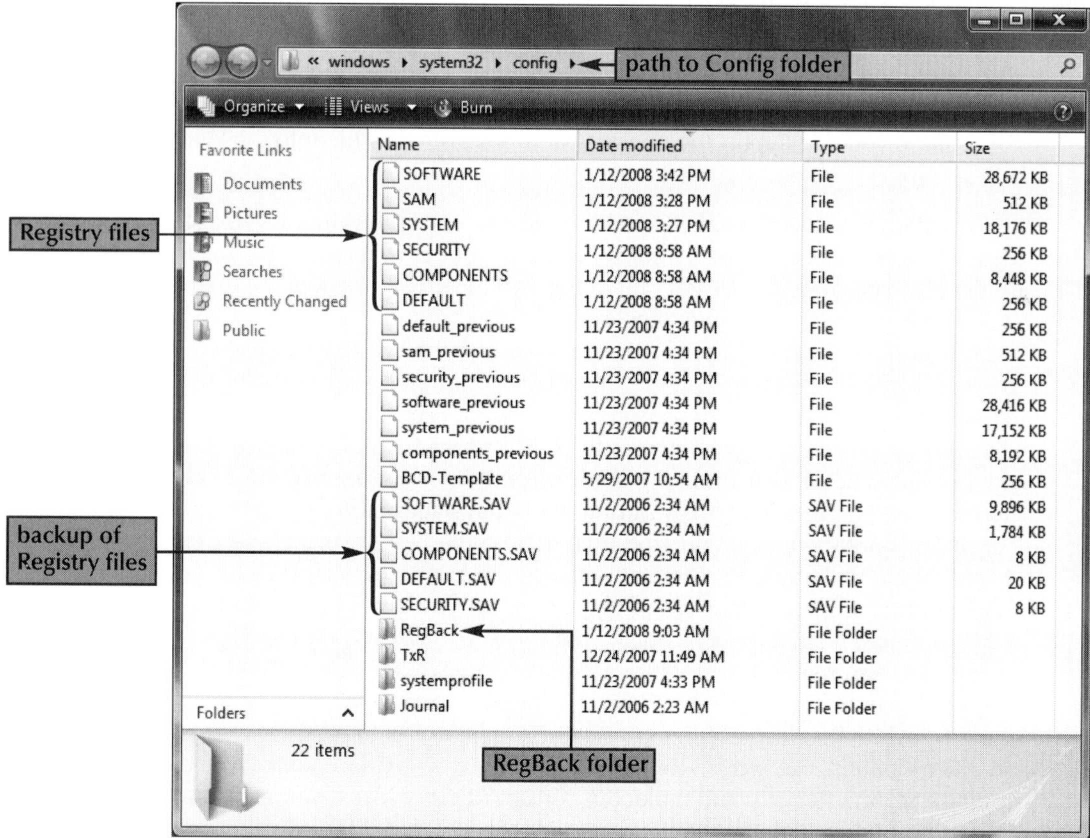

Although you generally make changes to your computer's hardware configuration and installed software, as well as user settings and preferences, using Windows tools, such as the Control Panel, Device Manager, and property sheets, you may need to open the Registry to view, change, add, or troubleshoot settings. Therefore, it's important to become familiar with the structure of the Registry and its use.

Backing Up the Windows Registry

Ian emphasizes to you the importance of backing up the Windows Registry before making any changes to the Registry. Since the Windows Registry is critical to the booting and functioning of your computer, the backup strategies that you develop for your computer system should also take into account the Registry. You can back up the Registry in several ways:

- **Use Complete PC Backup** As you discovered in Tutorial 10, you can use Complete PC Backup in Windows Vista Ultimate, Windows Vista Business, or Windows Vista Enterprise to back up your entire computer system. Since your computer's configuration and content are constantly changing as the result of Windows updates and other changes you make to your computer, you need to make and keep as recent a Complete PC Backup as is feasible. If you need to restore your computer from a Complete PC Backup, then you must boot from your Windows DVD and open the System Recovery Tools because a complete restore of your computer overwrites everything on the system volume.
- **Use System Protection** As you discovered in Tutorial 8, you can use System Protection to create a restore point for a fixed point in time, and then you can use System Restore to roll back your computer to that point should a problem arise later. *Before you make a change to the Windows Registry, you should always create a manual restore point because System Protection does not automatically create a restore point prior to making changes to the Registry.*
- **Export the Registry** You can also open the **Registry Editor**, a utility for viewing the contents of, and making changes to, the Registry, and then **export** (or transfer) a copy of the Registry to a **registration file** (with the "reg" file extension) on disk. If you have a problem, you can import the contents of this registration file into the Windows Registry if you need to restore the Registry.

As noted, Windows Vista keeps additional copies of the Windows Registry from the date when you first installed Windows Vista on your computer. One copy is in the config folder (C:\windows\system32\config), and the other is in the RegBack folder (C:\windows\system32\config\RegBack).

As you discovered in Tutorial 8, you can restore the Windows Registry using the Last Known Good Configuration on the Advanced Boot Options menu. Whenever Windows Vista successfully loads all its startup drivers and a user logs onto a computer, it copies those startup settings, now known as the Last Known Good Configuration, to the Registry. If a problem occurs after installing a new device driver or application, you can reboot your computer, press the F8 key during the initial stages of booting to display the Advanced Boot Options menu, and then choose the Last Known Good Configuration from that menu. However, when you choose the Last Known Good Configuration, you lose all of your other configuration changes since you last successfully booted your computer, and you might need to update your computer system afterwards.

You can also repair or restore the Windows Registry by booting from your Windows Vista DVD and choosing the option to repair your computer. Then, Windows Vista displays a System Recovery Options dialog box (covered in Tutorial 8) with various troubleshooting options. The Startup Repair option will try to repair damage to the Registry by rolling back the Registry and replacing corrupt Registry hives with a backup copy. Startup Repair can also initiate System Restore (covered in Tutorial 8), or you can choose System Restore from the System Recovery Options dialog box and roll back your computer (and the Registry) to an earlier functioning state. If your edition of Windows Vista supports Complete PC Backup (covered in Tutorial 10), then you can restore your system volume and the Registry from a recent backup.

Since your Windows Vista settings change over time (as you upgrade Windows Vista, install new hardware and software, and reconfigure your system), you must make sure you perform regular backups of the Windows Registry.

Using a Consistent Strategy for Working with the Registry | InSight

It is a good idea to develop a consistent strategy for working with the Windows Registry, including backing up the Registry, repeatedly verifying changes that you make before you commit those changes, and documenting any changes made to the Registry so that you can effectively troubleshoot problems that might arise later.

Setting Up Your Computer

To complete this tutorial, you must display the Computer icon on the desktop, switch your computer to single-click activation, and display the Run command on the Start menu. In the following steps, you will check, and if necessary, change these settings.

To set up your computer:

1. If you need to display a Computer icon on the desktop, open the **Start** menu, right-click **Computer**, click **Show on Desktop**, and then close the Start menu.
2. If you need to enable single-click activation, double-click the **Computer** icon on the desktop, click the **Organize** button on the command bar, click **Folder and Search Options**, and under "Click items as follows" on the General property sheet in the Folder Options dialog box, click the **Single-click to open an item (point to select)** option button, click the **Underline icon titles only when I point at them** option button, click the **OK** button to close the Folder Options dialog box, and then close the Computer window.
3. If the Run option does not appear on your Start menu, right-click the **Start** button, click **Properties**, click the **Customize** button to the right of the Start menu option button, locate and click the **Run command** check box, click the **OK** button to close the Customize Start Menu dialog box, and then click the **OK** button in the Taskbar and Start Menu Properties dialog box.

Now, you're ready to create a restore point before you open the Windows Registry.

Creating a Restore Point for the Windows Registry

Even though Windows Vista automatically creates restore points on a periodic basis or when you make significant changes to your system, you should *always* create a restore point before opening and working with the Registry. If you have not made a recent backup copy of your computer and your document files, this is the time to do it. Make these backups before you proceed with the remainder of this tutorial.

Next, Ian recommends that you manually create a restore point before you examine the Windows Registry.

To open System Protection in the following steps, you must provide Administrator credentials.

Do not skip the following steps as they are an important part of working with the Registry.

To create a restore point:

1. Right-click the **Computer** desktop icon, click **Properties**, and in the System window, click the **System protection** link under Tasks. Windows Vista switches to Secure Desktop Mode and displays a User Account Control dialog box.
2. If you are logged on under an Administrator account, click the **Continue** button. If you are not logged on under an Administrator account, enter the **password** for an Administrator account, and then click the **OK** button. Windows Vista displays the System Protection property sheet in the System Properties dialog box. Before you can continue, you have to wait while System Protection searches for your existing restore points.
3. Click the **Create** button, type **Windows Registry Manual Restore Point** in the next System Protection dialog box, click the **Create** button in this same dialog box, wait for System Protection to create a restore point, and then click the **OK** button in the System Protection dialog box.
4. Click the **OK** button to close the System Properties dialog box, and then close the System window.
5. You have successfully created a manual restore point.

Tip

You can also use the Windows Logo + Break keys to open a System window.

Tip

When creating Registry restore points on your computer, use a description that identifies more clearly the purpose of the restore point.

Opening the Windows Registry

If you want to view the contents of the Registry or make changes to the Registry, either to customize your computer or troubleshoot problems, you use the Windows Vista tool called the Registry Editor.

Since there is no option on the Start menu for opening the Registry Editor, you can either create a desktop shortcut to the Registry Editor (C:\Windows\regedit.exe) or use the Run option on the Start menu to enter the command for opening the Registry Editor. After the Registry Editor opens, the Registry Editor displays a **Registry tree** in the Navigation Pane. The Registry Editor organizes settings in the Windows Registry by **keys**, each of which is represented by a folder icon in the Registry tree. Each key may have one or more **subkeys** (also represented by folder icons). When you work directly with a subkey, you refer to it as a key.

After you open the Registry, you export Registry settings to a file on disk so that you have an additional, alternate backup. You can then examine the structure and contents of the Registry, and if necessary, add new settings or modify existing settings in the Registry. *Remember that all accidental or deliberate edits are final and that the Registry Editor and Windows Vista do not ask for verification.*

Exporting Registry Settings

If you open the Registry Editor and then export Registry settings, the Registry Editor creates a registration file with the "reg" file extension that contains a copy of all or part of the Registry's settings. This type of backup is the easiest and fastest to make. If necessary, you can restore the Registry or a part of the Registry from a registration file.

Safeguards for Working with the Registry | InSight

The Registry Editor is designed for the more advanced user, not a casual or inexperienced user. You must exercise *caution* as you use the Registry Editor, closely follow any instructions you might have for navigating, viewing, and modifying the Registry, double check and perhaps even triple check changes you make, and be prepared to restore your computer and its Registry if you run into a problem. The well-known adage "Measure twice, cut once" especially applies to the use of the Registry. If you want to create or modify a Registry setting, check your new setting at least twice before you apply it. If you want to delete a Registry setting, check at least twice to make sure you have selected the correct setting before you delete it.

Ian recommends that you start by opening the Registry with the Registry Editor, and then export Registry settings to a registration file on disk so that you have a backup of the Registry.

If your computer lab does not permit you to use the Registry Editor, or if you prefer not to use it on your computer until you better understand how it works, then read the remainder of the steps in this tutorial and examine the figures, but do not keystroke the steps.

In the next set of steps, you are going to open and export the Registry to a file on disk. *Do not skip the following steps as they are an important part of working with the Registry.*

To open the Registry Editor:

1. From the Start menu, click **Run**, type **regedit** and then press the **Enter** key. The Registry Editor displays the Registry tree in the Navigation Pane. See Figure 14-3. As you can tell, even though the Registry consists of separate files, the Registry Editor combines the contents of those files into a single, unified view.

   Trouble? If Windows Vista switches to Secure Desktop Mode and prompts for Administrator credentials, click the Continue button in the User Account Control dialog box.

Figure 14-3 Viewing the Registry tree

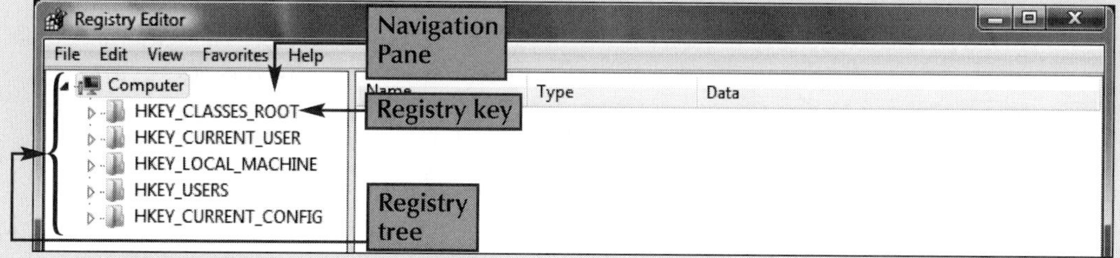

2. If Computer is not already selected in the Navigation Pane on the left side of the window, click **Computer**. By selecting Computer first, you are guaranteeing that the Registry Editor will export all the Registry settings to a registration file.

3. Click **File** on the menu bar, and then click **Export**. Windows Vista opens the Export Registry File dialog box, and if necessary, click your **user account name** in the Places Bar on the left side of the dialog box, and then click your **Documents** folder icon. See Figure 14-4. The Save as type box identifies the file type as Registration Files (*.reg). Under Export range, the Registry Editor is set to export the entire range, not just a selected branch.

Tip

If you select a specific key, the Registry Editor exports only that portion of the Registry that falls under the key.

Figure 14-4 Exploring Registry settings

> **Tip**
>
> You can also export all or part of the Registry to a text file, Registry hive file, or Win9x/NT4 registration file.

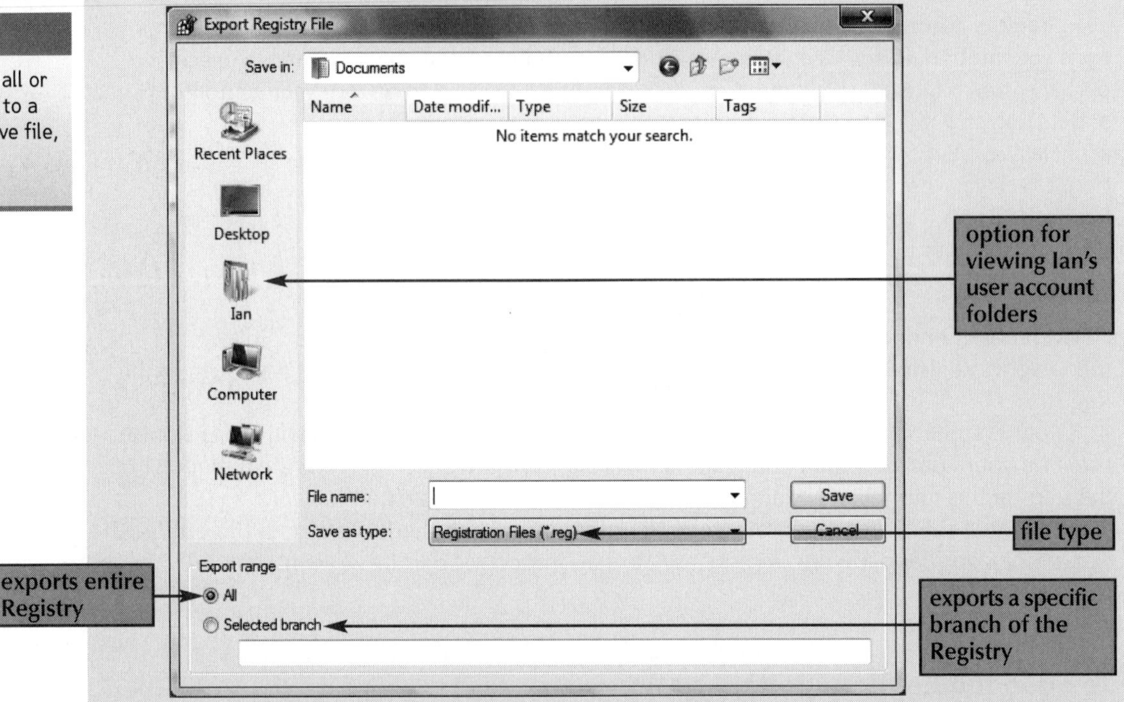

4. Click the **Create New Folder** button, type **Registry Backup** and then press the **Enter** key to open the new Registry Backup folder.

> **Tip**
>
> If you are exporting the Registry to your flash drive, make sure you have enough storage space on the flash drive for the registration file.

5. In the File name box, type **Registry Backup (yyyy-mm-dd)** replacing "yyyy" with four digits for the current year, "mm" with two digits for the current month, and "dd" with two digits for the current day, click the **Save** button, and be patient while the Registry Editor exports all the Registry settings to a registration file on disk.
6. From the Start menu, open the **Documents** folder (or the drive and folder where you exported Registry settings), open the **Registry Backup** folder, click the **Views button arrow** on the command bar and click **Details** (if necessary), click the **background window**, and then press the **Ctrl** and **+** keys (using the plus sign on the numeric keypad) to adjust all columns for a best fit. On the computer used for this figure, the registration file is 126,808 KB (or approximately 128 MB). See Figure 14-5. If you instead exported the Registry on the computer used for the figures in this tutorial to a text file, then you would discover that the file is just under 85,000 pages long.

Figure 14-5 Viewing the registration file

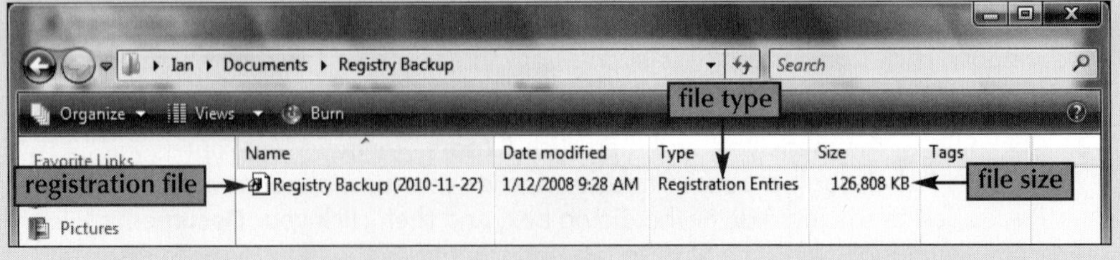

7. Close the Registry Backup folder window.

8. If you are going to continue with the tutorial, leave the Registry Editor window open for the next section of the tutorial; otherwise, if you are going to continue the tutorial later, close the Registry Editor window. You should never leave the Registry Editor open and unattended when you are working in a public location, such as a college computer lab.

You have just successfully created a backup of the Registry by exporting Registry settings.

Exporting Registry Settings | Reference Window

- From the Start menu, select Run, type REGEDIT in the Open text box, press the Enter key (or click the OK button) and, if prompted, provide Administrator credentials.
- Click Computer in the Registry tree in the Navigation Pane.
- Click File on the menu bar, and then click Export.
- In the Export Registry File dialog box, locate the drive and folder where you want to store the exported Registry settings, then in the File name box, type a name for your registration file and click the OK button.
- Close the Registry Editor.

If you need to restore the Registry from this registration file, you open the Registry and use the Import command on the File menu. In the Import Registry File dialog box, you select the registration file to import. The Import Registry File dialog box then shows a progress indicator. If the Registry Editor cannot import all of the data to the Registry, it will display a Registry Editor dialog box explaining that some keys are open by the system or by other processes. You can also open the folder that contains the registration file, and then click (or double-click) it to restore the Registry (because of the association of the "reg" file extension with the Registry Editor). To perform this operation, you must provide Administrator credentials, and then Windows Vista warns you in a Registry Editor dialog box that adding information can unintentionally change or delete values and thereby cause components to stop working properly. Windows Vista points out that, if you do not trust this source, then do not add the information in the registration file to the Registry.

Like other types of backups, you have to periodically make new backups of the Registry because the Registry is constantly changing. If you restore the Registry from a registration file that is not recent, then any configuration changes made since the date when you exported settings to a registration file are no longer in the Registry.

Session 14.1 Quick Check | Review

1. Windows Vista stores your computer's hardware, software, security, network, system performance, and user settings (or user profiles) in a database known as the ________________ .
2. A(n) ________________ consists of a set of Windows Registry files named Default, Sam, Security, Software, or System and its associated log files.
3. The Windows Registry is stored in the ________________ , and backups are stored in the ________________ and ________________ folders.
4. To restore the Windows Registry using the Advanced Boot Options menu, you select ________________ .

5. A group of related settings stored in the Windows Registry is called a(n) ________________ .

6. What type of file does the Registry Editor automatically create when you export the Windows Registry?

Session 14.2

Examining the Structure of the Registry

Tip

You cannot delete or rename a root key.

The Registry consists of five major keys called **root keys**, each of which starts with HKEY. The "H" in HKEY stands for "Handle," meaning each key is a handle for a specific group of settings. Within each key are sets of subkeys that contain groups of related settings. Under each subkey, there may be additional keys that break down the settings into smaller groups. In other words, Registry keys and settings are organized using a hierarchical approach.

Before you examine specific keys, Ian suggests that you first examine the major Registry keys at the top of the Registry tree structure.

To view the contents of the main Registry keys:

1. If you closed the Registry Editor after the first session, then open the Registry Editor and maximize the Registry Editor window.
2. Click the **Expand View** indicator ▷ to the left of the HKEY_CLASSES_ROOT key (commonly abbreviated as HKCR). As you can immediately tell from the Navigation Pane, this key contains subkeys for each registered file type and therefore identifies the programs associated with each file type. See Figure 14-6. Your keys will differ from those shown in the figure because the types of subkeys found under this key depend on what file types are available on your computer system, and that, in turn, depends in part on the type of software installed on your computer. This key also contains information on Windows objects, such as Computer and the Recycle Bin.

Figure 14-6 Viewing subkeys in the HKEY_CLASSES_ROOT key

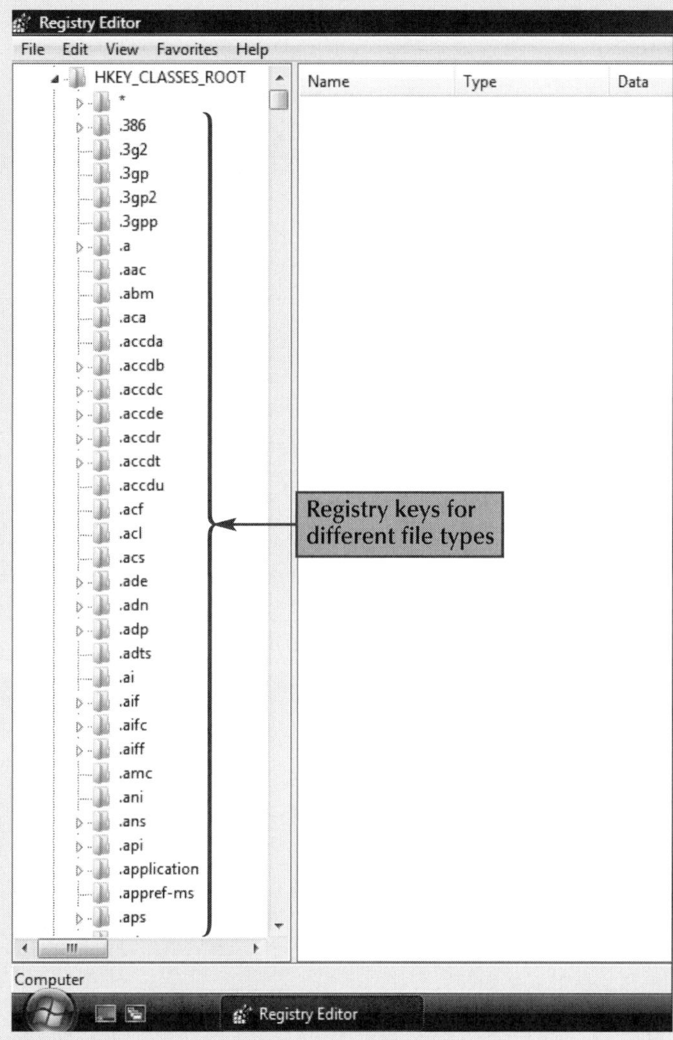

3. Click the **Collapse View** indicator ◢ to the left of the HKEY_CLASSES_ROOT key.

4. Click the **Expand View** indicator ▷ to the left of the HKEY_CURRENT_USER folder icon, and then click the **Expand View** indicator ▷ to the left of the Control Panel key. The HKEY_CURRENT_USER key (commonly abbreviated as HKCU) and its subkeys, such as Control Panel and Mouse, contain settings for the current user logged onto the computer. See Figure 14-7. The information for a specific user is derived from the HKEY_USERS key. Each user logged on the same computer system has access to his or her personal settings via the HKEY_CURRENT_USER key.

Tip

System Configuration uses Registry key abbreviations (such as HKLM and HKCU) to identify where startup programs load from during booting.

Figure 14-7 Viewing subkeys in the HKEY_CURRENT_USER key

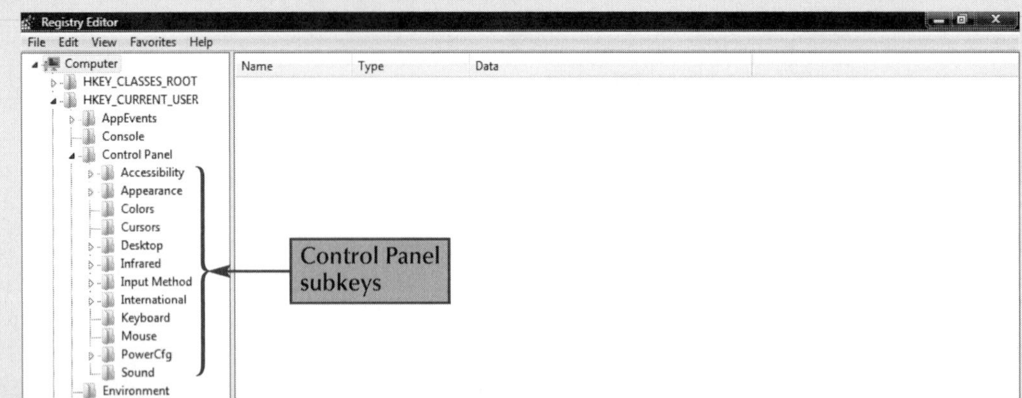

5. Click the **Collapse View** indicator to the left of the HKEY_CURRENT_USER folder icon, and then click the **Expand View** indicator to the left of the HKEY_LOCAL_MACHINE folder icon. The HKEY_LOCAL_MACHINE key (commonly abbreviated HKLM) contains hardware and operating system configuration settings for the local computer system. See Figure 14-8. Notice that there are keys for the Registry hives.

Figure 14-8 Viewing subkeys under the HKEY_LOCAL_MACHINE key

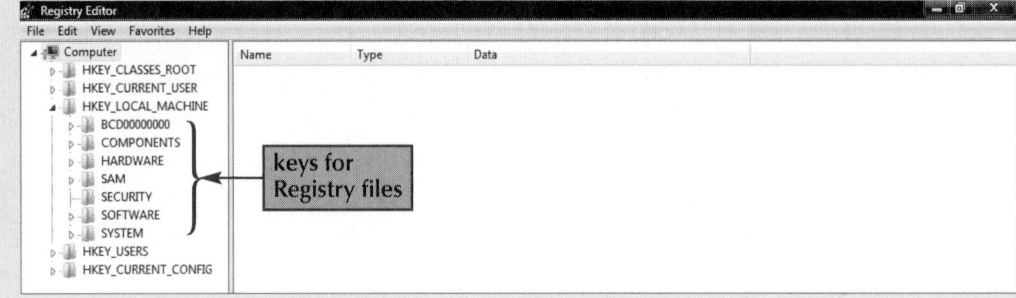

6. Click the **Collapse View** indicator to the left of the HKEY_LOCAL_MACHINE folder icon.

7. Keep the Registry Editor window open for the next section of the tutorial.

The HKEY_USERS key (also abbreviated as HKU) contains user profile settings for all users as well as a default profile. The HKEY_CURRENT_USER key is a subkey of HKEY_USERS.

The HKEY_CURRENT_CONFIG key (also abbreviated as HKCC) contains configuration settings for the currently used hardware profile for the local computer at system startup. The settings determine which device drivers to load and the final display resolution.

Tracing Registered File Types

By examining information on registered files in the Windows Registry, you can gain a better understanding of the organization of the Registry and how to work with the Registry, and you can also improve your understanding of how Windows Vista functions by drawing on information in the Registry.

When you select a key in the Registry Editor, Windows Vista displays the value entries associated with that key. Each **value entry** is a Windows Registry setting that contains three parts: a **value name**, **value data type**, and the actual **value data** (or setting). For example, in the next set of steps you examine the .bmp Registry key. The first value entry in the .bmp key has the name (Default), and the value for the (Default) value entry is Paint.Picture (all one word). Its data type is REG_SZ, which identifies the value (Paint.Picture) as a fixed-length text string. A **string** is a nonnumeric value that contains a set of characters that are treated exactly as they are typed or shown; in this case, .bmp (with the period). A string can contain digits, but they are treated as text, not numeric values.

Ian suggests that you next view information on file associations and registered file types so that you become familiar with the process of navigating around the Registry.

To view information on registered file types:

1. Click the **Expand View** indicator ▷ to the left of the HKEY_CLASSES_ROOT key in the Navigation Pane.
2. Scroll down the Navigation Pane to locate and double-click the **.bmp** key, and then adjust your view of the Registry tree so that the **.bmp** key is near the top of the Navigation Pane. Not only do you select this key and see its associated value entries or settings in the Topic Pane on the right, but the Registry Editor also expands this part of the Registry tree in the Navigation Pane and displays the subkeys located below the .bmp key. See Figure 14-9. The settings shown in the Topic Pane on the right are the value entries. As noted earlier, the value for the (Default) value entry is Paint.Picture, and its data type is REG_SZ (a String Value). This value entry points to another key—a class definition key—by the same name (Paint.Picture). The Paint.Picture Class-Definition key contains additional information about this file association. Notice also that the path to the current key, shown on the status bar, is Computer\HKEY_CLASSES_ROOT\.bmp. Like UNC paths, this type of notation uses backslashes (\ ) rather than regular (or forward) slashes (/).

   Trouble? If the Navigation Pane is not wide enough to display the full names of subkeys, point to the split bar (or vertical bar) separating both panes, and when the pointer changes to ↔, drag the split bar to the right and adjust your view onto both panes.

Tip

You can click View on the menu bar, and then click Split to adjust the width of the Navigation and Topic Panes.

Figure 14-9 Viewing value entries for the .bmp key

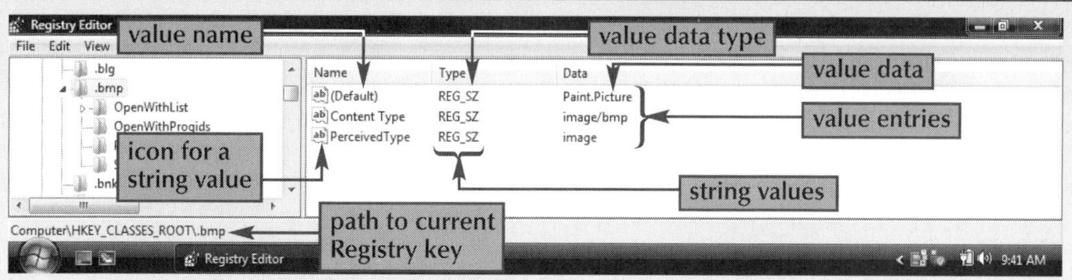

3. In the Navigation Pane, click the **ShellNew** subkey below the .bmp key. The Registry Editor shows three value entries for the ShellNew subkey—a (Default) value entry, ItemName, and a NullFile value entry (explained in the next paragraph). See Figure 14-10.

Figure 14-10 Viewing the ShellNew's value entries

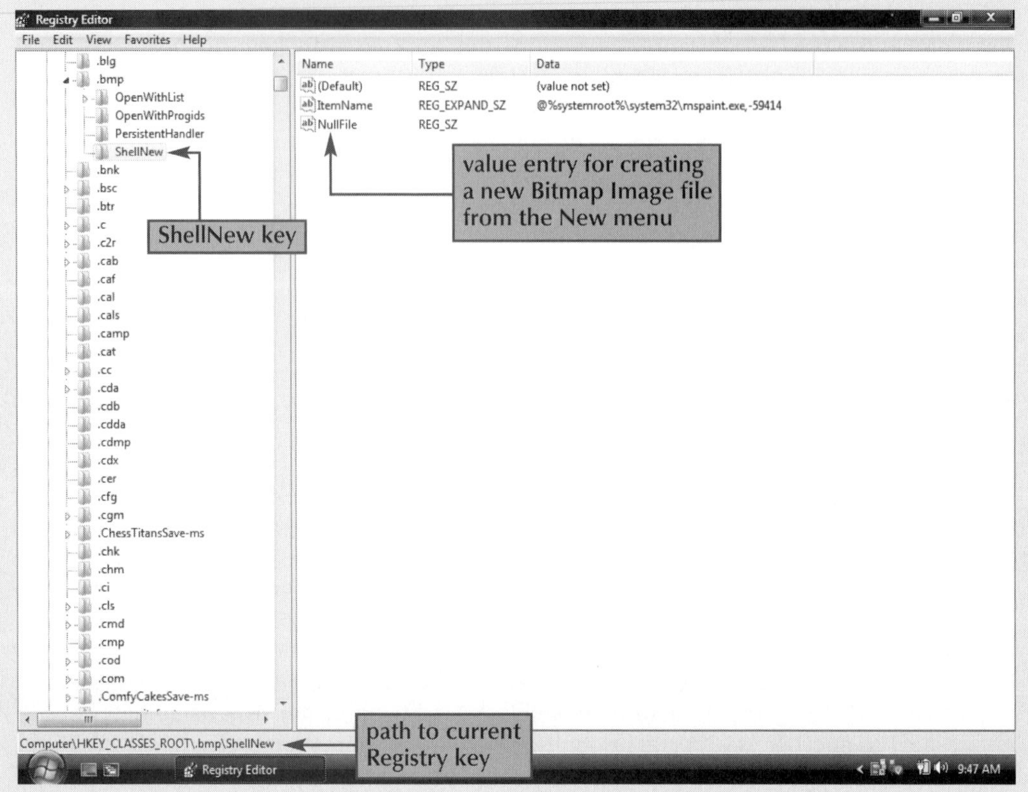

When you right-click the desktop or the background of a folder window, point to New on the folder's shortcut menu, and then click Bitmap Image, Windows Vista uses the information in the .bmp key's ShellNew subkey to create a new, empty Bitmap Image file that has no associated template (called a NullFile or null file). A **null file** is a file that is zero bytes in size. You can then open the file and create a new document using the application associated with this registered file type. Each menu option on the New menu has a corresponding ShellNew key in the Registry below that registered file type.

InSight | Understanding the Concept of a Shell

In the Windows Vista operating system, the term **shell** refers to the software (Windows Explorer) that provides a graphical user interface for interacting with the operating system. In a command-line environment, the command interpreter (Cmd.exe) is the shell that provides a text user interface for interacting with the Windows operating system. The shell separates the user from the core operating system services referred to as the **kernel**. That also means that a shell is the "outermost layer," and the kernel is the "innermost layer."

Next, you and Ian decide to locate the Paint.Picture key. Although you could scroll through the Registry, it is faster to use Find to search for the key because of the extensive amount of information stored in the Registry.

To locate Paint.Picture:

1. Click **Edit** on the menu bar, and then click **Find**. In the Find dialog box, you can enter a search string and specify what components of the Registry to examine during the search—keys, values, and/or data. See Figure 14-11. You can also specify that any matches found by the Registry Editor are ones that match your whole search string.

Figure 14-11 Using the Find option

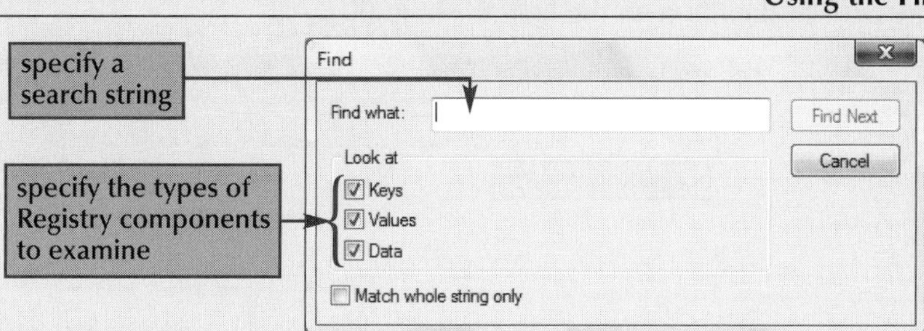

2. Type **Paint.Picture** (with the period between "Paint" and "Picture" and with no spaces) in the Find what box, make sure the Keys check box has a check mark, click the **Values** and **Data** check boxes to remove their check marks (if necessary), click the **Match whole string only** check box to insert a check mark (if necessary), and then click the **Find Next** button. By limiting the search to just the keys and by specifying whole strings only, you speed up your search for this key.

> **Tip**
> You can press the F3 key (the Find Next key) to continue the search with the same search string.

3. After the Registry Editor finds the Paint.Picture key, adjust your view so that the Paint.Picture key appears near the top of the Navigation Pane, double-click the **Paint.Picture folder icon** to expand this key, click **(Default)** in the Topic Pane, and press the **Ctrl** and **+** keys (using the plus sign on the numeric keypad) to adjust column widths for a best fit. The (Default) value entry for this key identifies this object as a Bitmap Image (a REG_SZ data type or String Value). See Figure 14-12. When you switch to Details view in a folder window, and then sort the files in the folder by file type (by clicking the Type column button), Windows Vista uses this Registry setting to identify the file type and to group related file types together using this description. If you right-click a Bitmap Image file, and then choose the option to view its properties, Windows Vista uses the (Default) value from this Registry key to identify the file type as a Bitmap Image on the property sheet. Notice also that the path on the Status Bar to this key is Computer\HKEY_CLASSES_ROOT\Paint.Picture.

Figure 14-12 Viewing Paint.Picture key value entries

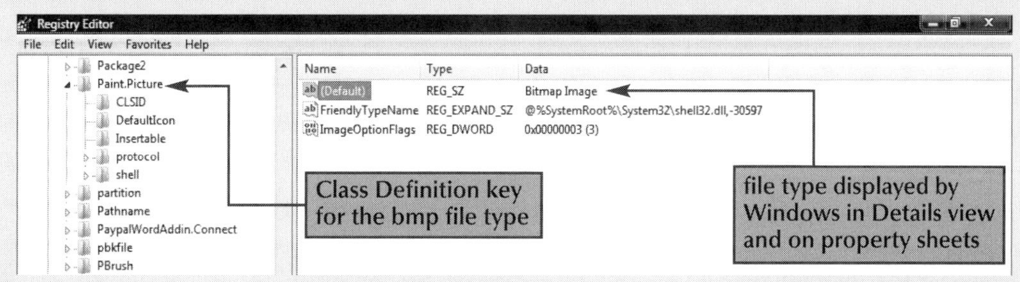

4. Under the Paint.Picture key in the Navigation Pane, click the **DefaultIcon** subkey. The (Default) value in the Topic Pane shows the path to the program file that is associated with this file type, namely %systemroot%\system32\imageres.dll. On the computer used for Figure 14-13, the icon for the "bmp" file type is drawn from a dynamic link library file named imageres.dll. If Windows Vista is installed on drive C in a folder named Windows, then the path to the file with the icon is C:\Windows\System32\imageres.dll.

Figure 14-13 **Viewing the path to the file with the icon for bmp files**

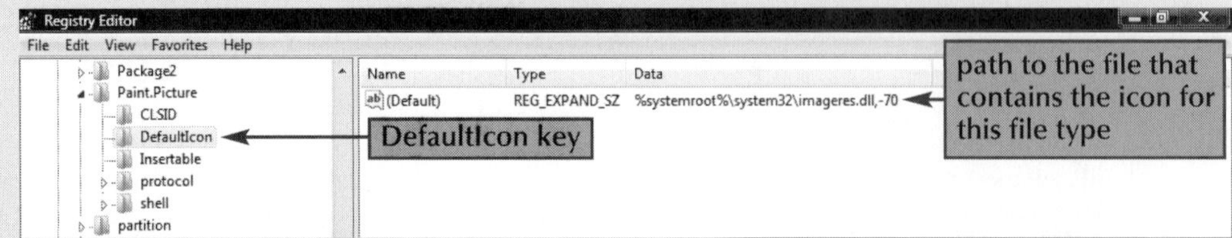

5. In the Navigation Pane, double-click the **shell** subkey under the Paint.Picture key, double-click the **edit** subkey under the shell key, and then click the **command** subkey under the edit key. Below the shell key in the Navigation Pane, the Registry Editor lists subkeys that represent different actions you can perform on this type of object: edit, open, and printto. See Figure 14-14. These actions are displayed on a shortcut menu for a Bitmap Image file as Preview (the default action), Edit, and Print.

Figure 14-14 **Viewing the program path for editing bmp files**

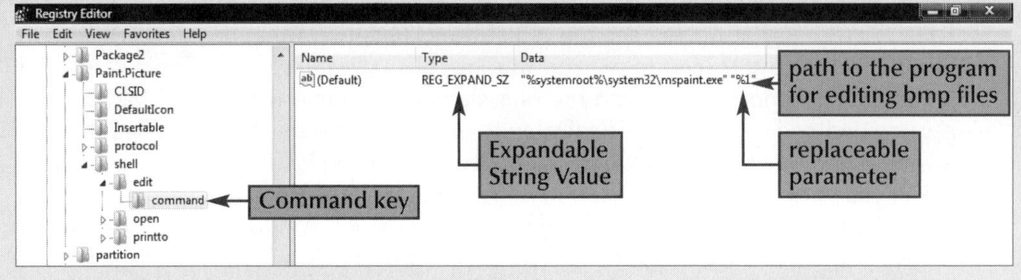

REG_EXPAND_SZ is an **Expandable String Value** or **variable-length string** value because it contains a variable (in this case, an environment variable) that is converted into the actual value when a program or service uses this Registry entry. Like a String Value, an Expandable String Value stores a string value; however, the value is expanded once the string is referenced and used.

On the computer used for this figure, the value for the Edit command is:

```
"%systemroot%\system32\mspaint.exe" "%1"
```

Your path might differ. This (Default) value contains the environment variable systemroot as a replaceable parameter. If Windows Vista is installed in the Windows folder on drive C, Windows Vista expands this string to include the path to the Windows folder in the path to the Paint program, namely: "C:\Windows\system32\mspaint.exe"

The %1 after the path to the program file is another replaceable parameter. When you right-click a Bitmap Image file, and then click Edit on the shortcut menu, Windows Vista replaces %1 with the filename of the Bitmap Image file, and then opens that file. For example, if you right-click a Bitmap Image file named Hot Air Balloons.bmp and choose Edit on the shortcut menu, the Edit command is converted to:

```
"C:\Windows\system32\mspaint.exe" "Hot Air Balloons.bmp"
```

Windows Vista then opens the Paint program so that you can edit the image in this file.

The quotation marks are included around the path to the program in the event the value for the systemroot environment variable is a long folder name with one or more spaces. Likewise, the replaceable parameter %1 is enclosed within quotation marks in case the file in question has a long filename with one or more spaces.

Next, examine the printto action.

To continue your examination of the Paint.Picture key:

1. In the Navigation Pane, double-click the **printto** subkey folder icon, click the **command** subkey folder icon under the open subkey, click the **(Default)** value entry in the Topic Pane, and then press the **Ctrl** and **+** keys (using the plus sign on the numeric keypad) to adjust the columns for a best fit. The (Default) value is "%systemroot%\system32\mspaint.exe" /pt "%1" "%2" "%3" "%4". The "pt" in the /pt switch stands for "PrintTo." See Figure 14-15. Your path might differ. This command is similar to the one for opening a Bitmap Image file, except the /pt switch instructs the Paint program to print the contents of the file (rather than open it). Each of the replaceable parameters after the path to the program represent multiple files that can be printed one right after the other.

Figure 14-15 Viewing the command for printing bmp files

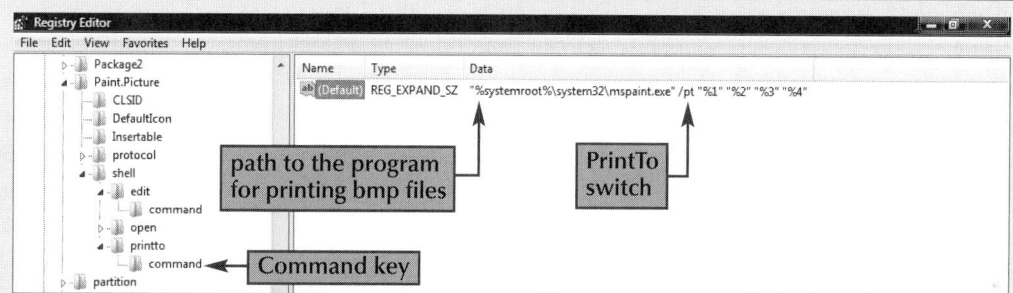

2. Under the Paint.Picture key in the Navigation Pane, click the **CLSID** (for Class ID, or Class Identifier) subkey. The Registry Editor shows the CLSID for Paint.Picture, namely {D3E34B21-9D75-101A-8C3D-00AA001A1652}. See Figure 14-16.

Figure 14-16 Viewing the CLSID for Paint.Picture

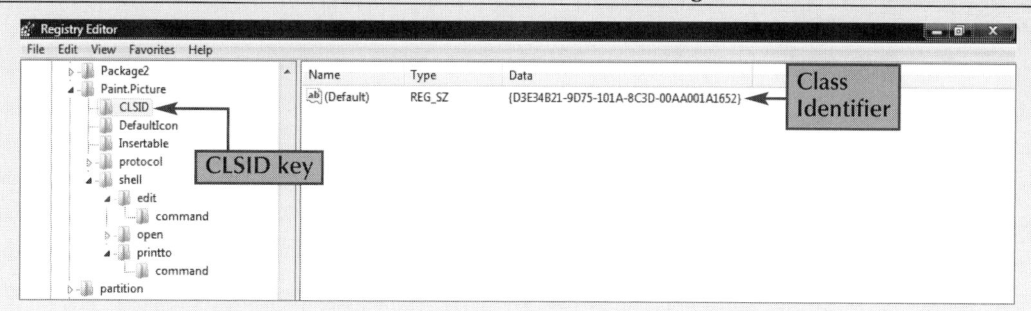

The **CLSID** (or **Class Identifier**) is a globally unique identifier (or unique code) that identifies a component as a COM class object in Windows Vista. The **Component Object Model (COM)** is a platform-independent approach to creating software components that can interact with each other. A **component** is an object that consists of program code and data as well as a set of services.

You can use the same strategy and approach to locate similar types of information on other types of registered files.

Reference Window | Tracing Information on Registered File Types

- From the Start menu, select Run, type REGEDIT in the Open box, and then click OK.
- Use Find on the Edit menu to locate the key for the file extension of a specific type of file (such as .bmp), and then view the (Default) value in the Topic Pane.
- Use Find on the Edit menu to locate the key with the same name as the (Default) value, and then double-click that key to view its subkeys. Double-click the shell key to view actions for this file type. Double-click an action subkey (such as edit, open, and printto), and then click the command key to view the command for executing the specific action.
- Close the Registry Editor.

By examining information on registered files in the Windows Registry, you can get a better idea or "picture" of how Windows Vista handles routine operations that you perform every day.

Using CLSIDs

Windows Vista also assigns CLSIDs, or Class Identifiers, to system objects, such as Computer and the Recycle Bin. You can find the CLSIDs for these objects in the Registry's HKEY_CLASSES_ROOT key. If you need to view or change properties of these objects, you need to know how to work with CLSIDs in the Registry. In some cases, the only way to change a property of a system object might be via the Registry.

To search for an object's CLSID, you can search for the object name (such as Recycle Bin). However, in some cases, you might need to know the hexadecimal code for the object to locate its CLSID key. After the next set of tutorial steps is a figure with a list of the CLSIDs for system components, such as the Recycle Bin.

So that you are familiar with the use of CLSIDs, Ian wants you to locate the CLSID for the Recycle Bin.

To locate the CLSID key for the Recycle Bin:

1. Press the **Home** key to move to the top of the Registry tree, and make sure **Computer** is selected in the Navigation Pane. Your search will start from this point in the Registry.

   Trouble? If you changed the focus from the Navigation Pane to the Topic Pane (perhaps by clicking the background of the Topic Pane), you will have to click a key in the Navigation Pane, and then press the Home key.

2. Click **Edit** on the menu bar, click **Find**, type **645FF** (case does not matter) in the Find what text box, make sure the Keys check box has a check mark, make sure the Values and Data check boxes do not have a check mark, click the **Match whole string only** check box to remove the check mark, click the **Find Next** button, and then be patient while the Registry Editor locates the CLSID key for the Recycle Bin.

3. Adjust your view in the Navigation Pane so that the {645FF040-5081-101B-9F08-00AA002F954E} key is near the top of the Navigation Pane, click the **(Default)** value entry in the Topic Pane, and then press the **Ctrl** and **+** keys (using the plus sign key on the numeric keypad). In the Topic Pane, the Registry Editor identifies this key as the CLSID for the Recycle Bin (see the (Default) value). See Figure 14-17. The status bar shows that the path to the Recycle Bin CLSID key is the following:

   ```
   Computer\HKEY_CLASSES_ROOT\CLSID\ {645FF040-5081-101B-9F08-00AA002F954E}
   ```

Figure 14-17

Viewing value entries for the Recycle Bin CLSID

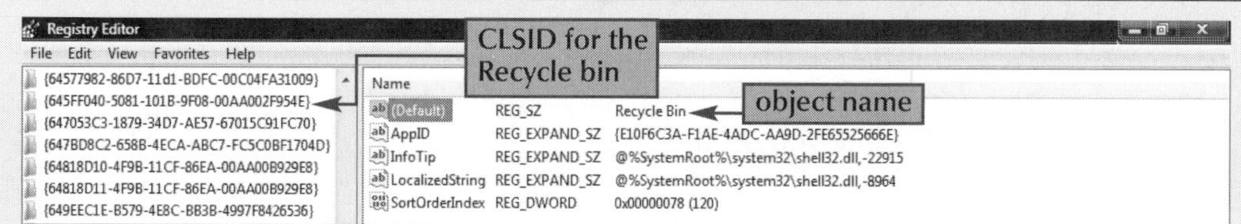

4. Double-click the **{645FF040-5081-101B-9F08-00AA002F954E}** key in the Navigation Pane, and then click the **DefaultIcon** subkey in the Navigation Pane. The Empty value entry identifies the full path and name of the file that contains the icon that Windows Vista uses for the Recycle Bin when it is empty. It also identifies the location of the icon within that program file. See Figure 14-18. As noted previously, SystemRoot is an environment variable that represents the path of the Windows folder (C:\Windows on this computer) determined during booting. The full path on this computer for the file that contains the icon for an empty Recycle Bin is therefore: C:\Windows\system32\imageres.dll

Figure 14-18

Examining Recycle Bin icon locations

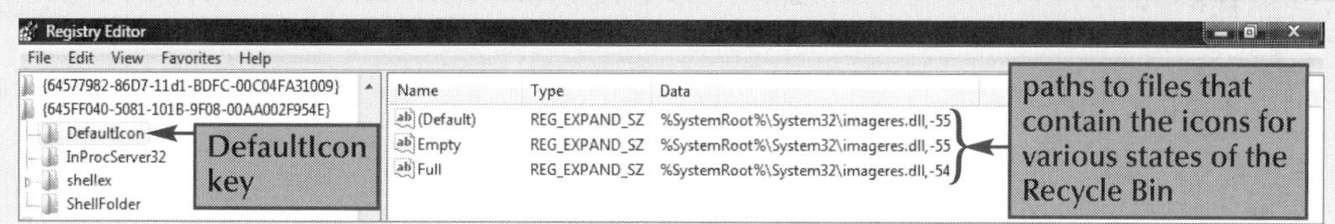

The Full value entry identifies the full path and name of the file that contains the icon Windows Vista uses for the Recycle Bin when it contains deleted files. This icon is also derived from the same dynamic link library, imageres.dll, but the icon number after the path is different. The (Default) value entry identifies the full path and name of the file that contains the icon Windows Vista uses to represent the default status of the Recycle Bin; in this case, empty on the computer used for this figure.

5. To close the Registry Editor, click **File** on the menu bar, and then click **Exit**.

Although you have just examined only a very small amount of the information stored in the Registry, the information that you did examine shows how Windows Vista uses Registry settings to support your use of registered file types.

Locating Information on CLSIDs | Reference Window

- From the Start menu, select Run, type REGEDIT in the Open box, and then click the OK button.
- Click Edit on the menu bar, click Find, type part of the CLSID for the object you want to find (you might be able to search by object name, such as Recycle Bin, or you might have to know the CLSID), add a check mark to the Keys check box, remove the check marks from the Values, Data, and "Match whole string only" check boxes, and then click the Find Next button.

Figure 14-19 lists the CLSIDs for objects commonly found on a Windows Vista computer. These same CLSIDs are used in previous versions of Windows. You can use these CLSIDs to locate the key in the Registry for an object so that you can customize your computer or correct an error condition. Although you could search for objects by name, not all objects are identified by name, so you might have to examine different CLSIDs until you find the one you need.

Figure 14-19 **CLSIDs for system objects**

OBJECT	CLASSID
ActiveDesktop	{75048700-EF1F-11D0-9888-006097DEACF9}
Briefcase	{85BBD920-42A0-1069-A2E4-08002B30309D}
CompressedFolder	{E88DCCE0-B7B3-11d1-A9F0-00AA0060FA31}
Computer	{20D04FE0-3AEA-1069-A2D8-08002B30309D}
Computers and Devices	{F02C1A0D-BE21-4350-88B0-7367FC96EF3C}
Control Panel	{21EC2020-3AEA-1069-A2DD-08002B30309D}
Desktop	{00021400-0000-0000-C000-000000000046}
File Open Dialog	{DC1C5A9C-E88A-4dde-A5A1-60F82A20AEF7}
File Save Dialog	{C0B4E2F3-BA21-4773-8DBA-335EC946EB8B}
Folder	{C96401CC-0E17-11D3-885B-00C04F72C717}
Help and Support	{2559a1f1-21d7-11d4-bdaf-00c04f60b9f0}
History	{FF393560-C2A7-11CF-BFF4-444553540000}
Installed Updates	{d450a8a1-9568-45c7-9c0e-b4f9fb4537bd}
Internet Shortcut	{FBF23B40-E3F0-101B-8488-00AA003E56F8}
Network	{208D2C60-3AEA-1069-A2D7-08002B30309D}
Network Map	{E7DE9B1A-7533-4556-9484-B26FB486475E}
Printers	{2227A280-3AEA-1069-A2DE-08002B30309D}
Problem Reports and Solutions	{FCFEECAE-EE1B-4849-AE50-685DCF7717EC}
Recycle Bin	{645FF040-5081-101B-9F08-00AA002F954E}
Scanners and Cameras	{E211B736-43FD-11D1-9EFB-0000F8757FCD}
Security Center	{E9495B87-D950-4ab5-87A5-FF6D70BF3E90}
Shortcut	{00021401-0000-0000-C000-000000000046}
Start Menu	{4622AD11-FF23-11d0-8D34-00A0C90F2719}
Taskbar and Start Menu	{0DF44EAA-FF21-4412-828E-260A8728E7F1}
System Configuration Utility	{D1F60CCB-8329-406E-976F-660B1BDF0D97}
The Internet	{3DC7A020-0ACD-11CF-A9BB-00AA004AE837}
Windows Defender	{D8559EB9-20C0-410E-BEDA-7ED416AECC2A}

As you select and examine keys for registered file types and objects, you will discover that you are already familiar with some or many of the settings because you access and work with these settings, using Windows Vista tools, property sheets, and dialog boxes.

Editing the Registry

Computer trade magazines, professional and personal Web sites, and even Microsoft's Knowledge Base abound with tips and information that allow you to customize your computer, improve its performance, increase security, improve network connectivity, enhance hardware and software support, and troubleshoot problems by making changes to the Registry. In every instance, these sources for Registry tips also warn you to be especially cautious when you make changes to the Windows Registry as errors might result in an unstable system or prevent you from even booting your computer. However, in certain cases, you might want or need to make changes to your computer system that require you to edit the Registry because you have no other option for making that change.

For example, when you create a shortcut, Windows Vista automatically appends the text "- Shortcut" to the end of the shortcut name. If you don't want this label at the end of a shortcut name, or if you want a shorter name for a shortcut, then you have to rename the shortcut. While this identifier might be useful to some users in distinguishing a shortcut from an actual object (such as a folder or file), desktop shortcuts have an arrow icon as part of the icon to identify the object as a shortcut. So "- Shortcut" is redundant and unneeded. A simple change in a setting in the Windows Registry will remove this appended text from new shortcut names (but not existing shortcut names). If you prefer not to change Registry settings manually, you might be able to locate and download a utility (such as TweakVI designed for Windows Vista) that makes the corresponding change in the Windows Registry. However, make sure the utility is designed for use with Windows Vista.

To make this change, you first have to locate the correct subkey in the Registry and edit the existing setting of that value entry. In some cases, you might also need to log off your computer and then log back on your computer, or restart your computer.

Since you are now familiar with Windows Vista, Ian encourages you to modify the Registry and remove the text Windows Vista appends to the end of new shortcuts. At your request, Ian guides you through this process.

Since changes to the Registry can adversely affect the performance of a computer, the next section of the tutorial will *not* include hands-on steps, but rather will describe the process for making this change and illustrate it with figures. If you are working in a computer lab, your technical support staff may limit access to the Registry Editor and Registry so that someone cannot accidentally or deliberately modify configuration settings that, in turn, might adversely affect the performance of that computer and the network. Also, some computer labs may be configured so that your computer's settings are restored to their previous state after you log off and then log back on (or reboot the computer), thereby eliminating any changes you might have made which would otherwise affect other users. Ask your instructor or technical support whether you might be able to test the type of changes described in the remainder of this section of the tutorial on computers in your college lab.

Before you attempt to make this change on your own computer, you might want to read the following section so that you are familiar with the process for changing a setting in the Registry before you actually attempt it. Make sure you have the necessary backups you might need if you need to restore your computer, including recent backups of the Registry. *Even Microsoft explicitly states that it cannot guarantee that changes you make with the Registry Editor can be resolved if a problem occurs.*

Locating the Correct Registry Key

After opening the Registry, the first step is to locate the correct key. Before you can edit the Registry, you must know the path to, and name of, the key. You also have to know the name of the value stored in the Registry, and if it's not present, you need to know how to add it to the Registry. You obviously also have to know the setting that you are going to assign to this value. As noted earlier, articles in computer magazines, Web sites that specialize in Registry tips, and reference books on Windows Vista, as well as Microsoft's Online Support Web site, will provide you with step-by-step details on how to make a change to the Registry so that you can customize or troubleshoot your computer. Also, as previously noted, these sources for Registry tips will also always include a disclaimer warning you that making changes to the Registry might adversely affect the performance of your computer. *So any changes you make are at your own risk.* As is the case with researching information on startup programs (covered in Tutorials 7 and 8) and Browser Helper Objects (covered in Tutorials 6 and 7), you should not depend on just one source, but rather examine multiple sources of information and compare your findings before you make changes to the Registry.

The Registry path to the correct Explorer key for modifying how Windows Vista names new shortcuts is as follows:

```
Computer\HKEY_CURRENT_USER\Software\Microsoft\Windows\CurrentVersion\Explorer
```

To locate this key, you can open each key and subkey in the Registry path (a slow process). If your user account is a new one, and if you have never created a shortcut, then you would use this approach because the Registry does not yet contain the link key with the setting for specifying the way in which to name shortcuts. After you locate this key, you have to create a new Registry Binary Value named link (described in the next part of the tutorial for a different example).

As an alternative, you can use the Find feature to search for the Explorer key (also using the "Match whole string only" option); however, although this approach is quicker than the previous option, "Explorer" is a common term found in many Registry keys. Another option is to search for the "link" value name because it contains the setting you want to modify. This approach should enable you to go directly to the setting you want to change in one step. If you use this approach for searching for the link value entry, you start at the top of the Registry tree and instruct the Registry Editor to look at only values (not keys or data) and to match whole strings only.

Once you locate the link key, you check the path on the Status Bar at the bottom of the Registry Editor window to verify that you have found the correct key. Figure 14-20 shows the Explorer key, its current value entries, and the path to the Explorer key on the Status Bar. This key may contain a number of settings that you can customize. Your list may differ from that shown for the computer used for this figure.

Tip

If you do not see the Status Bar, click View on the menu bar, and then click Status Bar.

Figure 14-20 **Viewing the Registry entry that affects the naming of shortcuts**

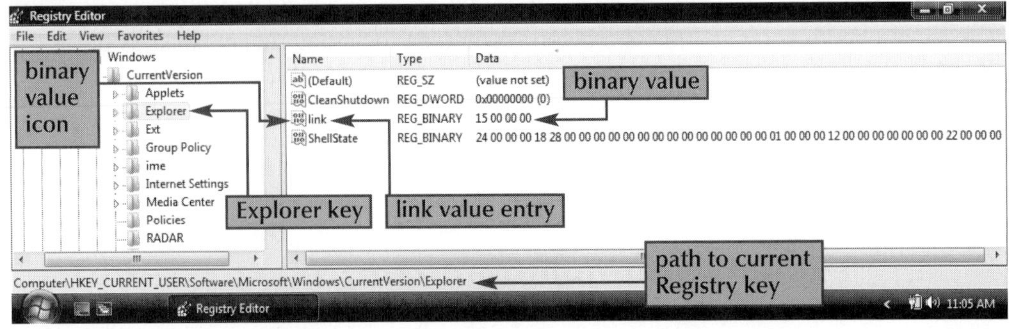

The value entry for controlling the way in which Windows Vista names new shortcuts is called link, and its data type is REG_BINARY, which identifies the setting as a binary value. **Binary values** are numeric values displayed in a hexadecimal format or **hexadecimal code** (a base-16 number system that uses the digits 0 through 9 and the uppercase and lowercase letters A through F to encode data). Under the Data column, you can see a part of the binary value, in this case 15 00 00 00. (The default setting is 0000 1e 00 00 00.) Your binary value may differ.

The next step is to export the Explorer key to a registration file on disk so that, if a problem occurs, you can double-click that registration file to restore the previous settings for this key. You first select the Explorer key in the Navigation Pane. Then you click File on the menu bar, and select Export. Next, you select (or create) the folder where you want to store the registration file. After that, you enter a name for the registration file and save it to disk. You might, for example, use the filename CurrentVersionExplorerSubkey.reg. This operation saves not just the link setting but all the settings in the Explorer key and all of its subkeys.

Editing a Registry Value

You can edit the link setting in one of three ways:

- You can double-click the value entry's name in the Topic Pane.
- You can single-click the value entry's name in the Topic Pane, and from the Edit menu, select Modify.
- You can right-click the value entry name in the Topic Pane, and then click Modify.

The Registry Editor then displays an Edit Binary Value dialog box, as shown in Figure 14-21.

Editing a binary value **Figure 14-21**

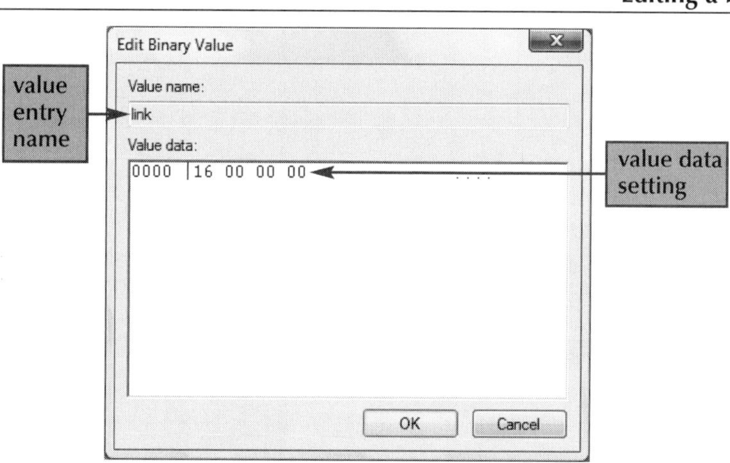

This dialog box shows the value name (link), the value data; in this case, 0000 16 00 00 00. You double-click 16 (or whatever hexadecimal value follows 0000), as shown in Figure 14-22 and type 00 (*two zeroes, not an uppercase "o"*), as shown in Figure 14-23, and then click OK.

Figure 14-22 Selecting the value to change

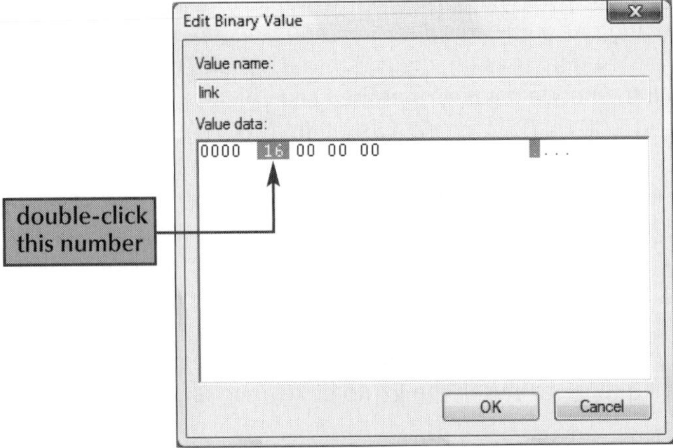

Figure 14-23 Modified value entry data

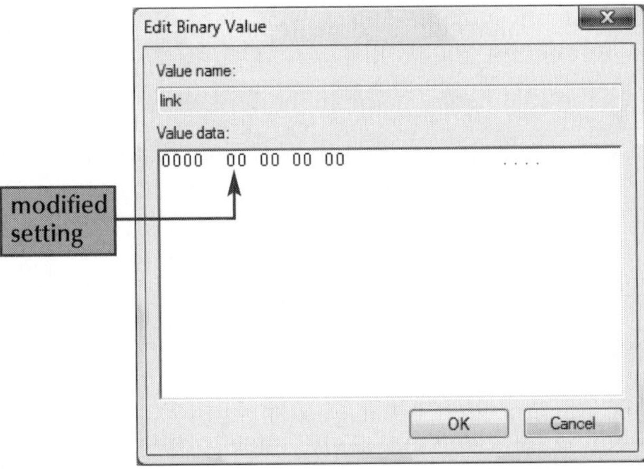

Figure 14-24 shows the new setting for the link value entry.

Figure 14-24 Viewing the new setting for naming shortcuts

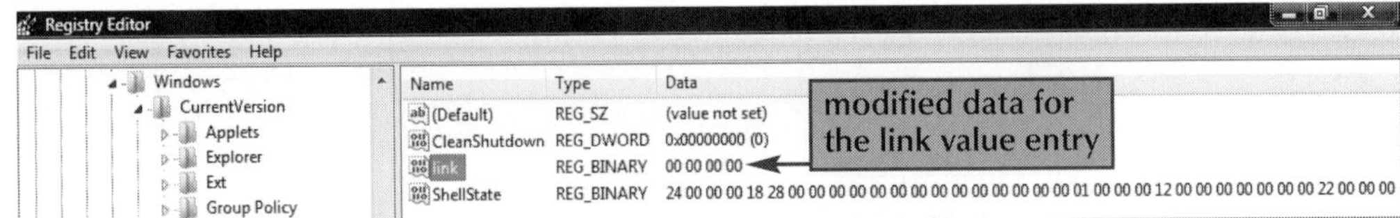

Before you log off and then log back on your computer (or restart your computer), you can bookmark this location in the Registry in case you need to return to it later.

Adding a Registry Key Location to the Favorites Menu

If you want to quickly return to a specific key in the Registry, you can use the Favorites menu to bookmark that Registry key. First, you select the key that you want to bookmark (for example, the Explorer subkey with the link value entry and setting). Then, you open the Favorites menu and choose the "Add to Favorites" option. The Registry Editor then displays an Add to Favorites dialog box and prompts you for the Favorite name you want to use for this Registry key. As shown in Figure 14-25, after you click the OK button in the Add to Favorites dialog box, the Favorites menu now identifies this Registry location as "Explorer."

Viewing the Explorer key bookmark

Figure 14-25

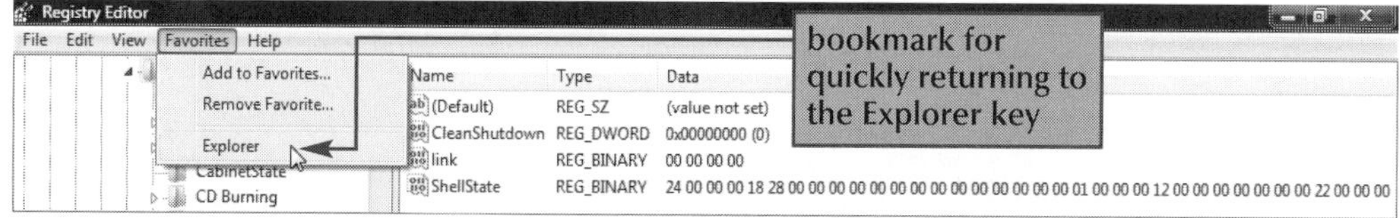

To return to this same Registry key, you open the Registry Editor, and from the Favorites menu, click the bookmark. You can use the "Remove Favorite" option on the Favorites menu to remove a bookmark that you no longer need. Then, in the Remove Favorites dialog box, you can select the bookmark that you want to remove.

After you make a change to the link Registry setting and bookmark the key, you close the Registry Editor window. Finally, you log off and then log back on your computer. Now, any new shortcut you create no longer has "- Shortcut" appended to the end of the shortcut name. This change does not affect other user accounts on the same computer.

To reverse this change, you repeat the same steps described previously for changing the link setting, and then restore the original setting for the link value setting, or you can use the registration backup file you created to restore the previous Registry settings.

Adding a New Value Entry to a Registry Subkey

Windows Vista displays balloon tips that are designed to be helpful and to provide you with information that you might need to know (such as the completion of a backup). However, those balloon tips interfere with the productivity of experienced and power users. Likewise, though these balloon tips might be initially useful to a novice, after a while even a novice knows how to work with basic Windows Vista features and is aware of the status of those features (or checks them periodically).

You can create a new Registry key named EnableBalloonTips so that Windows Vista does not display balloon tips. The path to the key for adding this new Registry setting is:

```
Computer\HKEY_CURRENT_USER\Software\Microsoft\Windows\CurrentVersion\Explorer\Advanced
```

To locate this key, you can use the Find option on the Edit menu to search for Advanced and choose the options to search for keys and matching whole strings only. After you locate the Advanced key, check the path on the Status Bar to make sure it matches the path shown above (or shown in whatever reference you use). If you have a bookmark to the Explorer key, you can select it from the Favorites menu, double-click the Explorer key, and then select the Advanced subkey.

As you can see from Figure 14-26, the EnableBalloonTips value entry is not present in this Registry key, so you have to add a new key and, in the process, specify a setting for the value entry.

Figure 14-26 **Viewing value entries for the Advanced key**

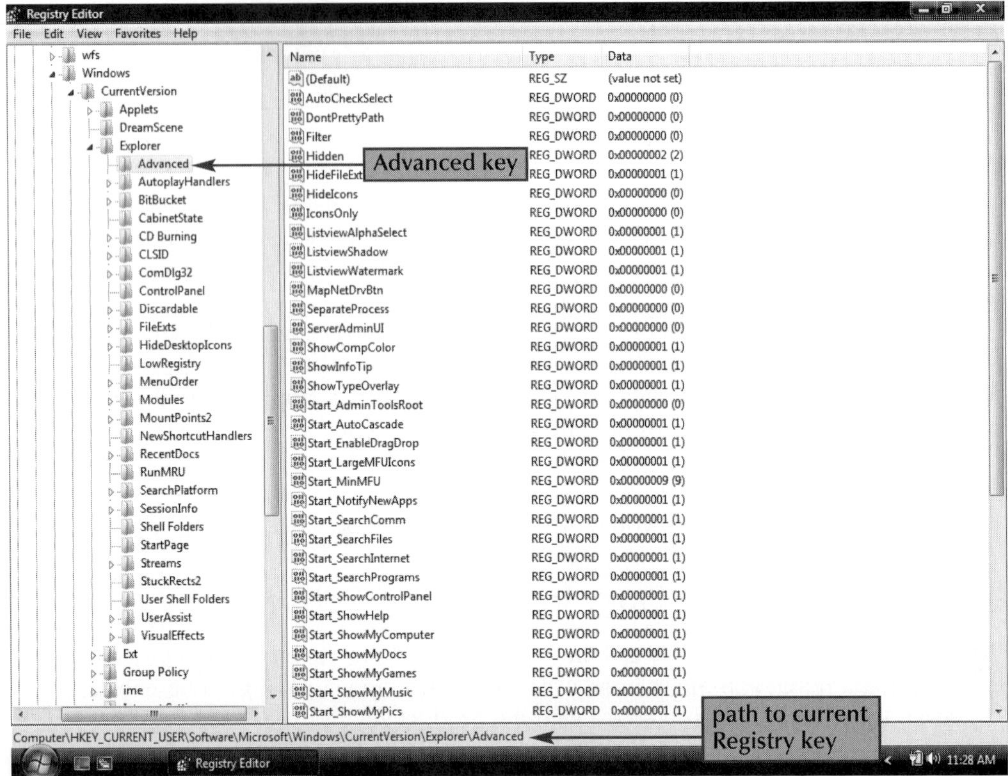

From the Edit menu, you choose New, and choose the data type for the new value entry. You can add one of six types of values: a String Value, a Binary Value, a DWORD (32-bit) Value, a QWORD (64-bit) Value, a Multi-String Value, or an Expandable String Value. See Figure 14-27.

Figure 14-27 **Options for adding new types of value entries**

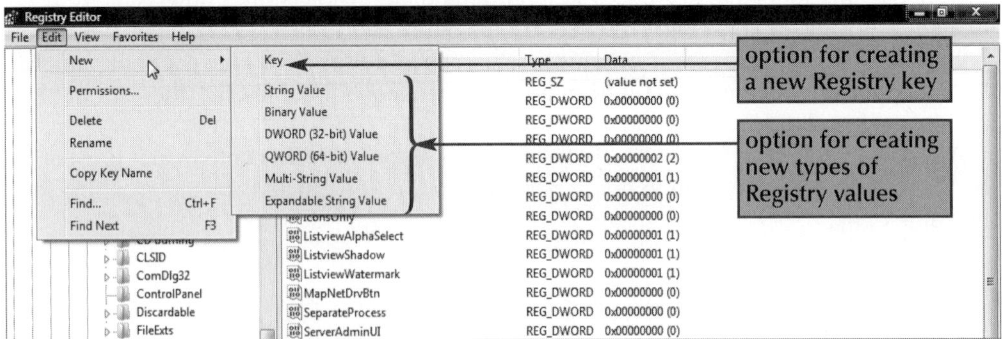

You are already familiar with REG_SZ (a String Value), REG_EXPAND_SZ (Expandable String Value), and REG_BINARY (a binary value). Another type of string value is REG_MULTI_SZ (a **Multi-String Value**) used to store lists or multiple values. A **DWORD** value, identified by the REG_DWORD data type, is a four-byte number (or 32-bit number) displayed in binary, hexadecimal, or decimal format. For example, the DWORD value 0x00000000 (0) for the SuperHidden value entry under the Advanced key indicates that Windows Vista does not display file extensions for certain types of files, such as desktop shortcuts and Internet shortcuts. The value in parentheses is the decimal equivalent (the standard base-10 number system) of the DWORD value.

EnableBalloonTips requires a DWORD value, so from the Edit menu, you point to New, and then click DWORD (32-bit) Value. After you select DWORD (32-bit) Value, the Registry Editor inserts a new DWORD value, assigns it the name "New Value #1", and waits for you to specify a new name, as shown in Figure 14-28. The value in parentheses (0) for the DWORD value 0x00000000 (0) is the decimal equivalent of the value assigned to EnableBalloonTips. This default setting 0 (for "disabled") instructs Windows Vista to not display balloon tips. If you change this value to 1 (for "enabled"), you are instructing Windows Vista to display balloon tips.

Figure 14-28 Option for naming new DWORD value

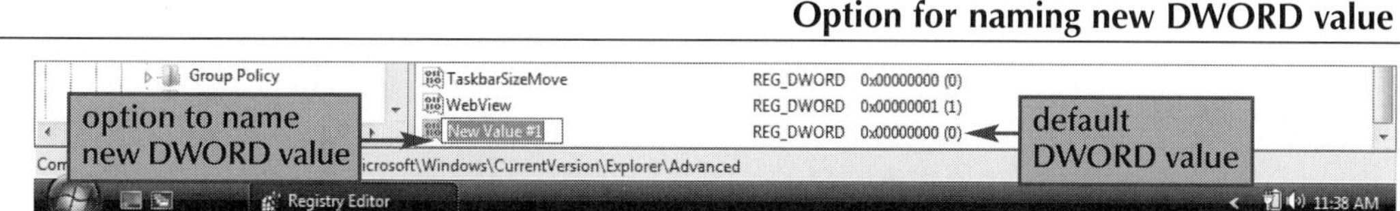

Next, you type EnableBalloonTips and press the Enter key, as shown in Figure 14-29.

Figure 14-29 Name assigned to new DWORD value

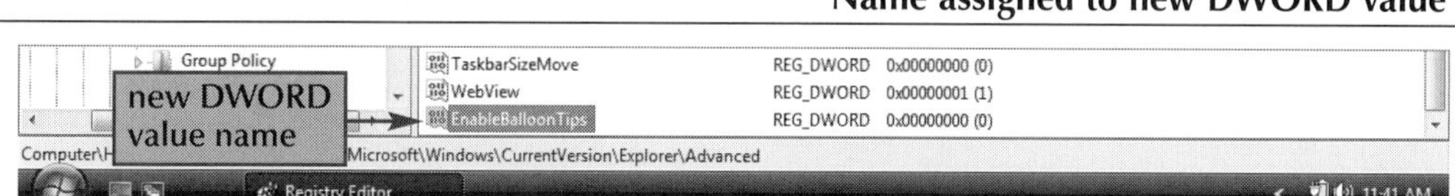

The Registry Editor then updates the value entry's name. The next time you log on your computer, Windows Vista will not display balloon tips.

If you later want to change the setting for the EnableBalloonTips value entry for a new user, you can open the Registry, search for and locate the EnableBalloonTips value entry name, and then double-click the value entry's name; or single-click the value entry's name, select the Edit menu, and then select Modify; or right-click the value entry name and select Modify. The Registry Editor then displays an Edit DWORD (32-bit) Value, as shown in Figure 14-30. The dialog box shows the value entry's name (EnableBalloonTips), the value data (0), and the base (how you want to represent the value).

Figure 14-30 Editing the new DWORD value

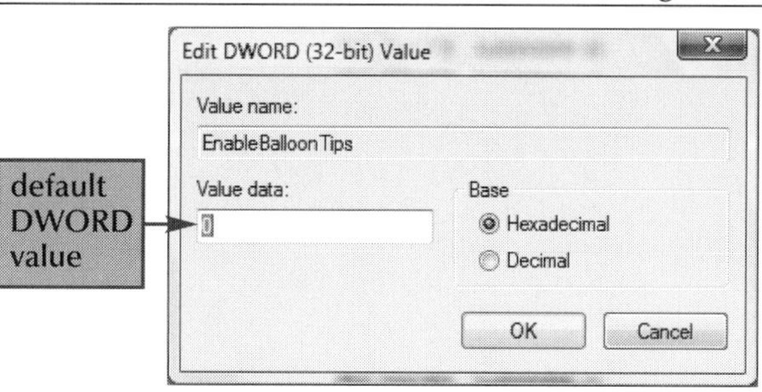

The value data 0 is already highlighted, so all you need to do is to type 1 (*the number one, not a lowercase "L"*) to replace the current value, as shown in Figure 14-31.

Figure 14-31 **New DWORD value for the EnableBalloonTips value entry**

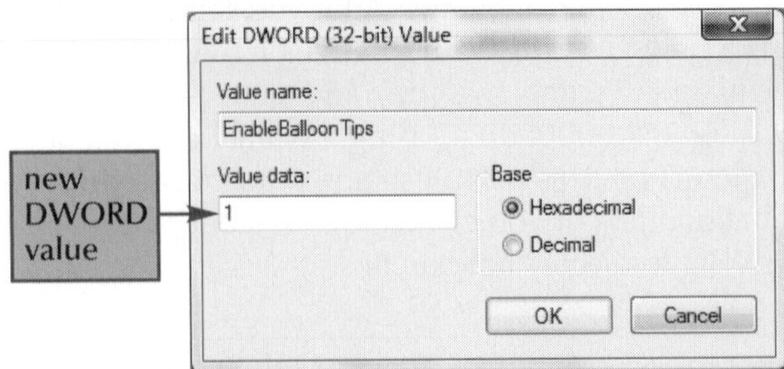

After you click the OK button, the Registry Editor shows the updated DWORD value in the Topic Pane. See Figure 14-32.

Figure 14-32 **New DWORD value for controlling the display of balloon tips**

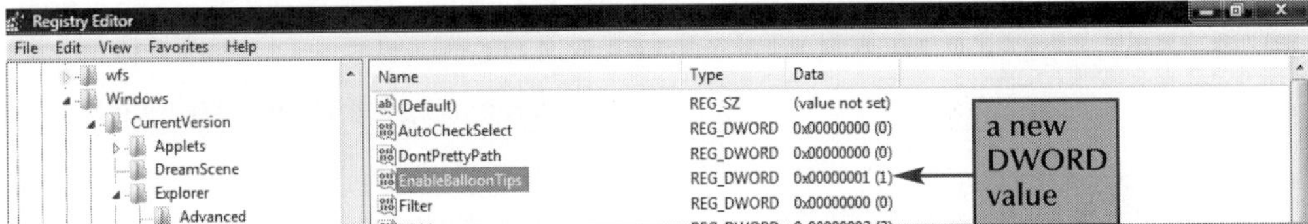

This change applies only to the current user's account; it does not apply to other accounts on the same computer.

If you need to delete a Registry value entry or key, you can first export the Registry key to a registration file on disk. If you later discover that you need to restore that key, you can just double-click the registration file you created and restore the Registry key to the Windows Registry. Then, to delete the Registry value entry or key, you select the value entry or key, and from the Edit menu, choose Delete. Or you can right-click the value entry or key and choose Delete from the shortcut menu. If you choose the option for deleting a value entry, the Registry Editor will display a Confirm Value Delete dialog box and inform you that deleting certain registry values could cause system instability and will then ask if you want to permanently delete the value. If you choose the option for deleting a Registry key, the Registry Editor will display a Confirm Key Delete dialog box and ask you if you are sure you want to permanently delete the key and all of its subkeys.

Customizing the Command Prompt Window Using the Registry | InSight

You can also use the Registry to customize a command-line environment. For example, in Tutorial 13 you used the Color command to set the background and foreground colors. However, if you close a Command Prompt window and then open it later, Windows Vista reverts back to the default background and foreground colors. If you want to change the console colors permanently, you can open the Windows Registry and locate the Command Processor key, using the following Registry path:

```
Computer\HKEY_CURRENT_USER\Software\Microsoft\Command Processor
```

After you locate this key, you export the Registry settings for this key. Then, you double-click the DefaultColor value entry, and in the Edit DWORD (32-bit) Value dialog box, verify that you are using the correct value name (DefaultColor), type the hex digits for the color attribute that you want to use (for example, 1f for a bright white foreground color for text and a dark blue background color), and then press Enter (or click OK). You can display Help on the COLOR command in a Command Prompt window to locate the hex code that you then want to use in the Command Processor key. Continuing with this example, the data for the DefaultColor value entry then changes from 0x00000000 (0) to 0x0000001f (31), and Windows Vista immediately applies the change to your computer system. Now, each time you open a Command Prompt window, Windows Vista will use the background and foreground colors you specified with the DefaultColor value entry.

Restoring Your Computer

If you are working in a computer lab, or if you want to restore your computer, you need to delete the folder that contains the registration file you created earlier in the tutorial. If you decide that you want to keep the registration file, then you can skip the last step in this section.

To restore your computer:

1. To remove the Run option from your Start menu, right-click the **Start** button, click **Properties**, click the **Customize** button to the right of the Start menu option button, locate and click the **Run command** check box, click the **OK** button to close the Customize Start Menu dialog box, and then click the **OK** button in the Taskbar and Start Menu Properties dialog box.
2. To restore double-click activation, click the **Computer** icon on the desktop, click the **Organize** button on the command bar, click **Folder and Search Options**, and on the General property sheet in the Folder Options dialog box, click the **Double-click to open an item option button (single-click to select)**, click the **OK** button to close the Folder Options dialog box, and then close the Computer window.
3. To remove the Computer icon from the desktop, open the **Start menu**, right-click **Computer**, and then click **Show on Desktop**.
4. If you do not want to keep, or no longer need, the registration file you created at the beginning of this tutorial, open the Documents folder (or the folder that contains the registration file), and then select and delete the Registry Backup folder.

Ian is confident you can now work with the Windows Vista Registry to customize and streamline computers and to become more productive at Mobile Software Center, Inc.

Review | Session 14.2 Quick Check

1. What three components are included in a Registry value entry?
2. A(n) ________________ is a nonnumeric value which contains a set of characters that are treated exactly as they are typed or shown.
3. In the Windows Vista operating system, the term ________________ refers to the software (Windows Explorer) that provides a graphical user interface for interacting with the operating system.
4. systemroot is an example of a(n) ________________ .
5. "%1" is an example of a(n) ________________ .
6. A(n) ________________ value is a four-byte number (or 32-bit number) displayed in binary, hexadecimal, or decimal format.

Review | Tutorial Summary

In this tutorial, you learned about the role and the importance of the Windows Registry and methods for backing up the Registry. Before opening the Registry, you created a restore point. After you opened the Registry, you exported all of the Registry settings to a registration file on disk. Then, you examined the structure, terminology, organization, and function of the Registry. You traced information on a registered file type, viewed information on Class Identifiers, and examined the process for editing and adding a new Registry entry.

Key Terms

Binary value
CLSID (Class Identifier)
component
Component Object Model (COM)
DWORD
Expandable String Value
export
hexadecimal code
hive
kernel
key
Multi-String Value
null file
registration file
Registry
Registry Editor
Registry tree
root keys
shell
string
subkey
user profile
value data
value data type
value entry
value name
variable-length string value

Practice | Review Assignments

Practice the skills you learned in the tutorial.

There are no Data Files needed for the Review Assignments.

During your first week on the job, Ian mentions that staff members frequently work with files with the "rtf" file extension. Since Microsoft Word is the most commonly used word processing application at Mobile Software Center for opening files with the "doc" and "rtf" file extensions, Ian recommends that you open the Registry and examine information on the "rtf" file association, using the same approach that you used earlier for "bmp" file extensions.

To complete this case problem, you must provide Administrator credentials to create a restore point and you may need to provide Administrator credentials to open the Registry Editor.

As you complete each step in the Review Assignments, record your answers to questions so that you can submit them to your instructor. Use a word processing application, such as Word or WordPad, to prepare your answers to these questions. Also, if you change any settings on the computer you are using, note the original settings so that you can restore them later. Complete the following:

1. If necessary, display the Computer icon on the desktop, enable single-click activation, and display the Run command on the Start menu.
2. Use System Protection to create a restore point named **Registry Restore Point**, and then close the System Properties dialog box and System window.
3. Use Run on the Start menu to open the Registry Editor. If Computer is not selected in the Registry Tree pane, select a key in the Navigation Pane and press the Home key.
4. Export all of the Registry settings to a file named **Review Assignments Registry Backup** in a folder named **Registry Backup** within the Documents or Public Documents folder. Examine the registration file in the Registry Backup folder. What is its file size? Close the Registry Backup folder window.
5. What Registry key contains information on file types and file associations?
6. In the Registry Editor window, search for the following key: .rtf
7. What is the path to the .rtf key? What is the (Default) value entry data setting for this file type? Is this setting a string, binary, or DWORD value?
8. Use Find to locate the subkey *under* the HKEY_CLASSES_ROOT key (*not* the subkey under the .rtf key) that contains the same name as the (Default) value entry data for the .rtf key. What is the (Default) setting that Windows uses to identify files of this type in Details view?
9. Expand this subkey and choose the DefaultIcon subkey. What is the name of the program file from which Windows Vista extracts the icon for this file type?
10. Open the shell subkey. What types of actions or operations can you perform on the .rtf file type?
11. Open the key for creating a new document of this file type, and then examine the (Default) value entry. What is the command for creating a new document of this file type?
12. Search for the CLSID key for a CompressedFolder. (*Hint*: Check Figure 14-19 for the first 8 hexadecimal digits in the CLSID for this object, and then use those hexadecimal digits to search for this key.) What is the value data or setting for the (Default) value entry?

13. Expand this key and select the DefaultIcon subkey. What is the path to the file that contains the icon that Windows Vista uses for a CompressedFolder? What is the data type? Explain why Windows Vista uses this data type for this (Default) value entry.
14. Locate and open the following key:

    `Computer\HKEY_CURRENT_USER\Software\Microsoft\Windows\CurrentVersion\Themes\LastTheme`

15. What is the path to the last Wallpaper image used by Windows Vista? If you change the desktop background wallpaper image, log off your computer, log back on your computer, and examine the Wallpaper value entry, what change (if any) would you expect in the Wallpaper value entry setting?
16. Close the Registry Editor, and then close the System window.
17. If you do not want to keep, or no longer need, the registration file you created at the beginning of this Review Assignment, open the Documents folder (or the folder that contains the registration file), and then select and delete the Registry Backup folder.
18. Submit the results of the preceding steps to your instructor, either in printed or electronic form, as requested.

Apply | Case Problem 1

Use the skills you learned in the tutorial to document registered files for a satellite and cable company.

There are no Data Files needed for this Case Problem.

Internet Bypass, Inc. Rosalyn McCullough works part-time as a computer and network troubleshooter for Internet Bypass, Inc., a satellite and cable company in Omaha, Nebraska. She also teaches part-time at nearby Locey Community College. For her next class, she wants to prepare a handout that lists different file types and the friendly name that Windows Vista displays for the file type in folders and on property sheets. Since she is quite busy with several tasks, she asks you to help her prepare this handout and provides you with a list of the file types. See Figure 14-33.

Figure 14-33

Class Definition	Data Value (Description of File Type)
anifile	
batfile	Windows Batch File
chkfile	
cmdfile	
comfile	
CompressedFolder	
cplfile	
Directory	
dllfile	
drvfile	
exefile	
fonfile	
giffile	
hlpfile	
icofile	
inffile	
inifile	
lnkfile	
piffile	
RDP.File	
regfile	
rtffile	
scrfile	
SHCmdFile	
sysfile	
txtfile	
VBS	
zapfile	

To complete this case problem, you must provide Administrator credentials to create a restore point and you may need to provide Administrator credentials to open the Registry Editor.

As you complete each step in this case, record your answers to questions so that you can submit them to your instructor. Use a word processing application, such as Word or WordPad, to prepare your answers to these questions. Also, if you change any settings on the computer you are using, note the original settings so that you can restore them later. Complete the following:

1. Use System Protection to create a restore point. Why should you perform this operation before using the Windows Registry? How might you use this restore point if you run into a problem after changing the Windows Registry?
2. Open the Registry Editor and export the contents of the Registry to a registration file on disk. If you want to make sure that the registration file contains a copy of all Registry settings, what must you first select before exporting Registry settings? Why should you perform this operation before using the Registry?

EXPLORE

3. Using the information in the HKEY_CLASSES_ROOT key, prepare a table similar to that shown in Figure 14-33 to identify the friendly name for each of the file types in this figure. For example, the (Default) value entry for the Class-Definition "batfile" is "Windows Batch File." (*Hint*: Use the Find feature to quickly locate keys.) If your Registry does not contain a file type listed in Figure 14-33, then record N/A for Not Available.
4. Close the Registry Editor.
5. Name at least three other places where you have seen some of the descriptions for these different file types.
6. If you do not want to keep, or no longer need, the registration file you created at the beginning of this case problem, open the Documents folder (or the drive and folder that contains the registration file), and then select and delete the registration file.
7. Submit the results of the preceding steps to your instructor, either in printed or electronic form, as requested.

Apply | Case Problem 2

Use the skills you learned in the tutorial to identify startup programs for a retail computer store.

There are no Data Files needed for this Case Problem.

Computer Tech Center, Inc. Renaldo Urquidez works as a computer specialist for a large retail store that sells computers and electronic equipment, and he troubleshoots problems that customers encounter with new computers that they purchase from the Computer Tech Center.

To complete this case problem, you must provide Administrator credentials to create a restore point and you may need to provide Administrator credentials to open the Registry Editor.

As you complete each step in this case, record your answers to questions so that you can submit them to your instructor. Use a word processing application, such as Word or WordPad, to prepare your answers to these questions. Also, if you change any settings on the computer you are using, note the original settings so that you can restore them later. Complete the following:

1. Use System Protection to create a restore point. Why should you perform this operation before using the Windows Registry? How might you use this restore point if you run into a problem after changing the Windows Registry?
2. Open the Registry Editor and export the contents of the Registry to a registration file on disk. If you want to make sure that the registration file contains a copy of all Registry settings, what must you first select before exporting Registry settings? Why should you perform this operation before using the Registry?
3. Open the Registry Editor, and then locate and select the following key:
   `Computer\HKEY_CURRENT_USER\Software\Microsoft\Windows\CurrentVersion\Run`
4. With the Run key selected, export the contents of this one Registry key to a registration file on disk. If you had intended to make changes to one or more of the settings in this Registry key, why would you export Registry settings first? If you encountered a problem, how would you restore the original Registry settings?
5. List the name, type, and data for each setting stored under the Run Registry key. Using this information, what programs does Windows Vista automatically load and run at startup? If you cannot determine the purpose of a specific program, use a search engine to locate information on the program.

6. Open Task Manager, and then sort the program filenames on the Processes sheet in alphabetical order. Which of the startup programs that you identified in Step 5 are listed as processes?
7. Close Windows Task Manager, and then close the Registry Editor.
8. If you do not want to keep, or no longer need, the registration files you created in this case problem, open the Documents folder (or the drive and folder that contains the registration files), and then select and delete the registration files.
9. Submit the results of the preceding steps to your instructor, either in printed or electronic form, as requested.

Research | Case Problem 3

Use the skills you learned in the tutorial to locate information on using Registry tips at a graphics services firm.

There are no Data Files needed for this Case Problem.

Cutting Edge Graphics Services, Inc. Talisha Vannoy works as a Help Desk technician for a large graphics services company in St. Louis, Missouri. She relies on Registry tips to customize, troubleshoot, and enhance the performance of employee computers. She asks you to use a search engine to locate information on Windows Vista Registry tips that she might be able to apply to employees' computers.

As you complete each step in this case, record your answers to questions so that you can submit them to your instructor. Use a word processing application, such as Word or WordPad, to prepare your answers to these questions. Also, if you change any settings on the computer you are using, note the original settings so that you can restore them later. Complete the following:

1. Use a search engine to search for Windows Vista Registry tweaks. Examine information on Registry tips at what you feel are three to five reputable Web sites. What Registry tips did you locate that you might find useful for your own computer?
2. Select a Windows Vista Registry tip of interest to you and provide the following information on how to implement the Registry tip:
   - Describe how the Registry tip can change the way in which Windows Vista works.
   - Identify the path of the Registry key where you would make the change.
   - Describe how you make the change to a Registry value entry. Include in your description the value entry name, the value entry data type, and the value entry data.
   - Explain whether the changes take effect immediately, whether you need to log off and then log back on your computer, or whether you need to restart your computer.
   - Explain how you can restore the original Registry setting.
3. Explain what precautions you would take before making a change to the Windows Registry.
4. Can you make this change using tools available in Windows Vista, and if so, how?
5. List the URL of the Web site from which you derived information on the Registry tip.
6. Submit the results of the preceding steps to your instructor, either in printed or electronic form, as requested.

Apply | Case Problem 4

Use the skills you learned in the tutorial to search the Registry for information.

There are no Data Files needed for this Case Problem.

Everhardt Computer Recycling Center Wardell Weldin works as a computer specialist for a computer recycling company in Detroit. After individuals donate used computers to the recycling center, Wardell examines the computers for any personal or product registration information, as well as personal folders and files that may remain on the computer, before he sets up the computer for reuse by another customer. He enlists your help to check a newly donated computer.

To complete this case problem, you must provide Administrator credentials to create a restore point and you may need to provide Administrator credentials to open the Registry Editor.

As you complete each step in this case, record your answers to questions so that you can submit them to your instructor. Use a word processing application, such as Word or WordPad, to prepare your answers to these questions. Also, if you change any settings on the computer you are using, note the original settings so that you can restore them later. Complete the following:

1. Use System Protection to create a restore point. Why should you perform this operation before using the Windows Registry? How might you use this restore point if you run into a problem after changing the Windows Registry?
2. Open the Registry Editor and export the contents of the Registry to a registration file on disk. If you want to make sure that the registration file contains a copy of all Registry settings, what must you first select before exporting Registry settings? Why should you perform this operation before using the Registry?
3. Make sure Computer is selected in the Registry Tree pane, and then use Find to search for the value entry RegisteredOwner (one word with no spaces) under the Windows NT key. To save time, specify that you only want to search for Values. What is the path to the subkey that contains this value entry? What is the data type for the RegisteredOwner value entry? Who is listed as the RegisteredOwner?
4. Examine the other settings in this subkey and list the settings for the CurrentBuildNumber, CurrentType, CurrentVersion, EditionID, InstallDate, ProductName, RegisteredOrganization (if any), and SoftwareType value entries.
5. If your name or the registered organization were incorrectly spelled, could you correct that information here, and if so, how would you make this change?
6. Return to Computer at the top of the Navigation Pane.
7. Use Find to search for your last name, and to save time, specify that you only want to search for Data. After Find locates the first instance of where your name is used, use the F3 key to continue the search from that point. List the key and the types of information (including the value entry) that identify you by name. Because the amount of information might be extensive, limit your list to no more than 5 items. If the name of the software product is not obvious from the name of the key, then use the other value entries under that key to identify the software product.
8. List at least three other types of personal information you might search the Registry for.
9. Close the Registry Editor.
10. If you do not want to keep, or no longer need, the registration file you created at the beginning of this case problem, open the Documents folder (or the folder that contains the registration file), and then select and delete the registration file.
11. Submit the results of the preceding steps to your instructor, either in printed or electronic form, as requested.

Review | Quick Check Answers

Session 14.1

1. Registry
2. hive
3. Config, Config and RegBack
4. Last Known Good Configuration
5. key
6. registration file

Session 14.2

1. value name, value data type, and value data
2. string
3. shell
4. environment variable
5. replaceable parameter
6. DWORD

Ending Data Files

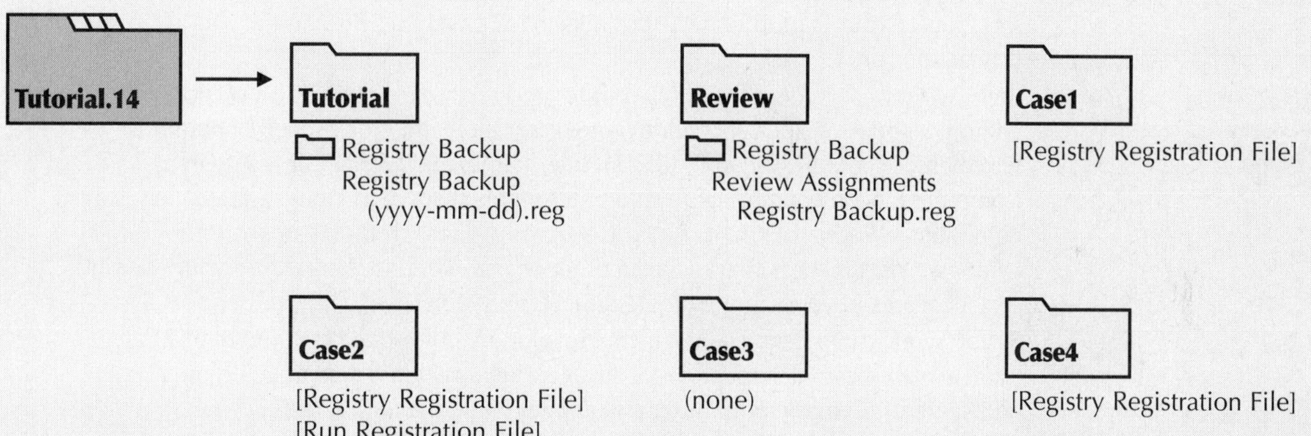

Reality Check

It's time for your quarterly system tune-up! Complete the following steps to document, customize, check, evaluate, update, and optimize the performance of your computer. To complete some of the following steps, you will need to log on under an Administrator account or provide Administrator credentials.

Note: Please be sure *not* to include any personal information of a sensitive nature in the documents you create to be submitted to your instructor for this exercise. Later on, you can update your computer with such information for your personal use.

1. Use System Protection to create a manual restore point for your computer.
2. Open the Registry Editor and export the contents of the Registry to a registration file on backup media. Use the Backup and Restore Center to perform a Complete PC Backup (if available in your edition of Windows Vista) or to perform a back up of your document files.
3. Evaluate your existing desktop and Quick Launch toolbar shortcuts and decide whether you want to retain, delete, or archive those shortcuts. Use Search Explorer to locate programs, folders, and files that you frequently access, and then create and customize desktop or Quick Launch toolbar shortcuts to those programs, folders, and files. For shortcuts that you want Windows to open at startup, copy or move the shortcuts to your Startup folder. Add links to frequently used folders to the Navigation Pane.
4. View system properties for your computer and record your Windows version and edition, Windows Experience Index, processor type and clock speed, amount of system memory (RAM), system type, computer name, and workgroup name in a Computer Documentation table similar to the one shown in Figure 14-34. View your computer's Windows Experience Index subscores, refresh those subscores if Windows Vista records that it detected new hardware, and then record your computer's subscores in your Computer Documentation table.
5. Record your computer's color scheme, resolution, color depth setting, refresh rate, total available graphics memory, dedicated video memory, system video memory, and shared system memory in your Computer Documentation table.
6. Open the Disk Management Administrative tool and record in your Computer Documentation table the disk number, disk layout, disk type, partition style, device type, total capacity, file system, and status for your hard disk drive. View properties of your hard disk drive and record the name (manufacturer and disk device type) in your Computer Documentation table.
7. Create a system health report. Check the Diagnostics section and Basic System Checks and examine, review, and troubleshoot any problems reported by Reliability and Performance Monitor. Under Resource Overview, record your CPU, Network, Disk, and Memory Utilization settings in your Computer Documentation table. Under Hardware Configuration, check the System section and document your Page size. Check the Physical Disk section and document Bytes/Sector, Sectors/Track, Tracks/Cylinder, Cylinders , and number of Partitions. Under Report Statistics, document your Windows Build and number of processors.
8. View performance information using Task Manager and record the following information in your Computer Documentation table: Cached physical memory, and page file usage and maximum size.

9. Open Device Manager and record the following hardware configuration information in your Computer Documentation table: Type of computer, display adapter, DVD and CD drive manufacturer and type (if present), monitor, network adapter, and sound, video and game controllers. If Device Manager identifies hardware configuration problems, examine information on those hardware problems, locate Help information on the problem, and implement a strategy for troubleshooting the hardware problems.
10. Open System Information and record the Windows Version number and System Model in your Computer Documentation table. Check the Hardware Resources' Conflicts/Sharing and Forced Hardware categories and the Components' Hardware Problems categories for hardware configuration problems and, if necessary, troubleshoot those hardware problems.
11. Open the Network and Sharing Center and record the following network settings in your Computer Documentation table: Type of network, Access, Connection, Network discovery, File sharing, Public folder sharing, Printer sharing, Password protected sharing, and Media sharing. Also open a Computer window and document the drive names, UNC paths, and friendly names of mapped drives.
12. Open the Windows Security Center and check the status of your firewall, Automatic updating, Malware protection, and Other security settings. If necessary, update your antivirus and antispyware software. If Windows Defender is installed on your computer, perform a quick scan of your computer.
13. Open a Command Prompt window and use the SYSTEMINFO command to produce a system report and redirect the output to a file named SystemInfoReport.txt on your flash drive.
14. Use the Disk Cleanup Wizard to remove unnecessary files that it recommends are safe to remove. Use the Error-Checking Tool to perform a read-only, diagnostic check of your hard disk drive for file system errors and, if it reports errors, use that tool to fix those errors at the next boot. Use the command-line DEFRAG utility to produce a defragmentation analysis of your hard disk and redirect the output to a file named DefragAnalysis.txt on your flash drive. Examine the defragmentation analysis report and, if necessary, perform a manual defragmentation of your hard disk.
15. Use the Control Panel to view and evaluate the software installed on your computer. If necessary, check for updates for your installed software. Examine and evaluate Windows features and decide whether you want to enable or disable specific features. If necessary, use Windows Update to check for and install updates to Windows Vista and other Microsoft software on your computer.
16. Use System Configuration to verify that your Windows Vista edition does not load any unnecessary startup programs or malicious software from the Windows Registry. Evaluate the purpose and need for any new startup items since your last review of startup programs with this utility.
17. If requested by your instructor, submit your Computer Documentation table, SystemInfoReport.txt file, and DefragAnalysis.txt file either in printed or electronic form.

Figure 14-34 **Computer Documentation**

System Information	Setting on Your Computer
System Properties:	
Windows Version and Edition	
Windows Experience Index	
Processor Type and Clock Speed	
System Memory (RAM)	
System Type	
Computer Name	
Workgroup Name	
Windows Experience Index Subscores:	
Processor	
Memory (RAM)	
Graphics	
Gaming Graphics	
Primary Hard Disk	
Video Display Adapter Settings:	
Color Scheme	
Resolution	
Color Depth	
Refresh Rate	
Total Available Graphics Memory	
Dedicated Video Memory	
System Video Memory	
Shared System Memory	
Hard Disk Drive:	
Disk Number	
Disk Layout	
Disk Type	
Partition Style	
Device Type	
Total Capacity	
File System	
Status	
Properties: Manufacturer & Disk Device Type	
System Health Report:	
Resource Overview:	
CPU Utilization	
Network Utilization	
Disk Utilization	
Memory Utilization	
Hardware Configuration, System:	
Page Size (Bytes)	
Physical Disk:	
Bytes/Sector	
Sectors/Track	
Tracks/Cylinder	
Cylinders	
Partitions	
Report Statistics:	
Windows Build	
Processors	

Figure 14-34 Computer documentation (continued)

System Information	Setting on Your Computer
Task Manager: Cached Physical Memory Page File Usage and Maximum Size	
Device Manager: Computer (Type): Display Adapter DVD Manufacturer and Type CD Manufacturer and Type Monitor Network Adapter Sound, Video and Game Controllers	
System Information: Windows Version Number System Model	
Network and Sharing Center: Type of Network Access Connection Network discovery File sharing Public folder sharing Printer sharing Password protected sharing Media sharing	
Mapped Drives: Drive Name UNC Path Friendly Name	

Glossary/Index

Note: Boldface entries include definitions.

Special Characters

A

B

backup drive The drive that contains the media for storing backups. WIN 623

backup sets The folders on your backup media that contains the backups of the folders and files on your hard disk. WIN 620, WIN 623, WIN 634

backup software Software that copies folders and files from your hard disk drive or that copies everything on a hard disk to a disk or another hard disk drive. WIN 219

backup strategy A process and schedule for efficiently backing up important files on your computer. WIN 618–622

backup utility A program to back up files onto some type of permanent, high-capacity storage medium, such as an external hard disk. WIN 617

backup Zip files The Compressed (zipped) Folders on your backup media that contain a set of backed-up folders and files. WIN 636–637

backward compatibility The ability of an operating system to handle hardware and software designed for earlier types of computers, microprocessors, and operating systems. WIN 11
    software, testing, WIN 731–738

bad cluster A cluster on a hard disk that contains one or more defective sectors. WIN 286

bad sectors, cleaning up, WIN 343

bandwidth The amount of data that can be transmitted over a device in a fixed amount of time (measured in bits per second, or bytes per second). WIN 764

base score A Windows Experience Index rating that measures the overall capability and performance of your computer hardware and software. WIN 53, WIN 54

basic disk A physical disk that Windows Vista can access. WIN 303

Basic Input/Output System (BIOS) A special type of computer chip on the motherboard that performs a series of important startup operations to make sure that your computer hardware is working and to load the operating system. WIN 2
    and boot sequence, WIN 507
    using your computer's, WIN 500–511

batch file A user-defined program file with the file extension "bat" that contains a list of executable commands that the Windows Vista command interpreter can process one right after the other. Batch programs are often used to automate common types of operations. WIN 875

batch program. *See* batch file.

BHO. *See* Browser Helper Object

binary digit (bit) A number (0 or 1) used in the binary numbering system. WIN 57

binary value A Registry value or setting, identified by the REG_BINARY data type, which consists of a hexadecimal code (a base-16 number system that uses the digits 0 through 9 and the uppercase and lowercase letters A through F to encode data). WIN 911

BIOS (Basic Input/Output System) A computer chip that contains embedded software with important system settings that are retained after you power off your computer and that are used during the next boot to help configure your computer. WIN 2

BIOS Setup Utility A computer's built-in utility for viewing and changing BIOS settings. WIN 500–511

bit. *See* binary digit.

BitLocker Drive Encryption A Windows Vista Ultimate Edition and Enterprise Edition feature for increasing the security of a computer by encrypting the boot volume. WIN 323–324

Bitmap Image (BMP) A graphic file format for bitmapped graphics. Bitmap Images contain hundreds of thousands or millions of pixels in an uncompressed format and therefore are relatively large files; however, they accurately represent the image contained in the file. WIN 89–90

bitmapped graphic An image represented by a pattern of pixels, or picture elements. WIN 89–90

blocking cookies, WIN 448–453

Blue Screen of Death (BSOD) A fatal error from which a computer cannot recover and which therefore requires a reboot. WIN 510

bookmark An Internet shortcut. WIN 251
    for a Registry key, WIN 913

Boolean filter A word or phrase used with a logical operator, a comparison operator (or relational operator), or symbols (such as quotation marks or parentheses) to specify one or more criteria for a search. WIN 182–187

Boot Configuration Data (BCD) A Windows Vista database file that contains boot configuration settings and information about the location of boot files which, in turn, determines how the Windows operating system loads from disk. WIN 506

boot loader, WIN 507

boot partition The partition that contains the Windows Vista operating system files. WIN 507

boot record A hidden table in the system area of a disk that contains information about the version of the operating system used to format a disk and the physical characteristics of the disk, such as the number of bytes per sector, sectors per cluster, maximum number of files per disk, total number of sectors, and sectors per track. WIN 287, WIN 291–292

boot sector. *See* boot record

boot sequence The boot order for a computer, which consists of a list of devices that the BIOS examines during booting in order to locate the operating system. WIN 502

boot volume and system volumes, WIN 284

booting To power on a computer system and load the operating system into memory so that it can configure the computer system and manage the basic processes of the computer, including providing support for applications. WIN 2
    examining your computer's sequence, WIN 504
    Windows Vista boot process, WIN 506–508
    your computer in Safe Mode, WIN 511–516

bootstrap loader A program in the boot record that locates and loads the operating system or that displays an "Invalid system disk" error message, or comparable error message, if your computer attempts to boot from a non-bootable disk. WIN 292

bot or **botnet** A home network infected with malware and controlled remotely by a single user in order to overwhelm a Web site with traffic and thereby shut down the Web site. WIN 402

Briefcase A special type of Windows Vista folder that contains a copy of files stored on another computer and that is capable of synchronizing and updating the two sets of files after changes are made to one or both sets of files. WIN 658–667

broadband connection A high-speed Internet connection, such as DSL (Digital Subscriber Line) or cable. WIN 801

Browser Helper Object (BHO) A small program that works with your Web browser so that you can view specific types of Web content or that provides additional features in your Web browser. WIN 342

browser hijacker Malicious software that changes your Web browser's home page to the Web site of the maker of the hijacker software or to another Web site, hijacks your computer and takes it to that Web site without your permission, and prevents you from navigating to other Web sites and from changing your Web browser settings back to what you originally specified. WIN 401

browsing history A list of Web sites that you've visited. WIN 459–461

buffer An area of memory for storing data. WIN 836

bus The electronic pathways or channels on the motherboard for transmitting data using address and data lines between two or more devices. WIN 764

byte (1) The storage space required on disk or in memory for one character; (2) A combination of eight bits, used to encode common characters, including letters of the alphabet, numbers, and symbols. WIN 46

C

ToolTips for shortcuts, WIN 244
Windows Sidebar gadgets, WIN 29–30
Windows Vista generally, WIN 69

cylinder A combination of tracks on different sides of the same platter and on different platters on a hard disk that are treated as a logical unit for recording data on a hard disk. WIN 285

D

daily backup A type of backup that includes selected files that have been created or modified the day you perform the backup and that does not affect other types of backups that you perform during a backup cycle. Backup utilities do *not* change the Archive bit of the backed-up files after the daily backup is complete. WIN 623

data redundancy The process of duplicating data on a volume different from the original volume. WIN 304

data stream A set of data stored within a file. WIN 290

Date and Time dialog box, WIN 421

DDoS. *See* Distributed Denial of Service

decrypting folders and files, WIN 319–323

dedicated graphics memory The memory available on the video display card or a portion of system memory dedicated exclusively for use by the Windows Vista graphics subsystem. WIN 57

default action The action a program takes until you specify another action. WIN 10, WIN 178

default directory The directory used by the Windows command interpreter when you first open a Command Prompt window. WIN 825

default drive The drive used by the Windows command interpreter when you first open a Command Prompt window. WIN 825

default setting The setting or reference point a program uses until you specify another setting or reference point. WIN 21

definition version The most recent update that contains files which Windows Defender uses to detect harmful or potentially unwanted software and thereby prevent the installation or use of that unwanted software. WIN 408

Defrag A command-line disk-optimization tool for (1) reducing file fragmentation by reorganizing the clusters assigned to each file so that they are located in contiguous clusters and by also rearranging files so that they are stored in contiguous clusters, and for (2) reducing free space fragmentation by removing free space (or unused space) between files. *See* Disk Defragmenter, Analysis switch (-A or /A), and Verbose switch (-V or /V). WIN 365–369

delimiter (1) The backslash symbol (\ ), which separates one folder or directory name from another folder or directory name, or a folder or directory name from a filename, in the full path; (2) A period in a filename that separates the main part of the filename from the file extension. WIN 44, WIN 165

demos, Windows Vista, WIN 6, WIN 36, WIN 41

Denial of Service (DoS) A situation in which users of a Web site are denied access to one or more services at the Web site as the result of an attack that exploits a weakness in the software at the Web site, or that sends more traffic to the Web site than can be handled. WIN 402

desktop
changing background, WIN 89–93
color themes, WIN 70–76
exploring Windows Vista, WIN 20
placing icons on, WIN 33
shortcuts, WIN 212, WIN 219, WIN 241

desktop background The background of the graphical user interface on which Windows displays icons, the taskbar, menus, windows, and dialog boxes. WIN 20, WIN 89–93

desktop composition The Windows Vista window-management technology for updating your view of the desktop and open windows and for supporting the use of Windows Aero. Desktop composition must be enabled to view translucent window borders, Live Taskbar Thumbnails, Windows Flip, and Windows Flip 3D. WIN 87

desktop toolbar A toolbar created on the desktop from the contents of a folder (subfolders, files, and shortcuts). WIN 104–106

Desktop Window Manager (DWM) The Windows Vista component that manages Windows Aero. WIN 25–26

destination The drive or subdirectory you want to copy folders or files to. WIN 863

Details Pane A pane that appears at the bottom of a folder window and that Windows Vista uses to display information about the object selected in the window. WIN 47, WIN 152

device A hardware component in a computer system, such as a keyboard, mouse, system unit, monitor (or video display unit), disk drive, or printer. WIN 2, WIN 764, WIN 778–783. *See also specific device*

device conflict A problem that results when two hardware devices attempt to share the same resource, such as the same IRQ (interrupt request line). WIN 766

device driver A file with program code that enables the operating system to communicate with, manage, and control the operation of a hardware or software component. WIN 3

Device Independent Bitmap (DIB) A device-independent, bitmap image format used by Windows to render images on the screen and printer. The colors in the file are represented in a format that is independent of the output device (monitor or printer). The device driver for the monitor translates the DIB color format into colors that the monitor can display. WIN 89–90

Device Manager A Windows component for (1) examining information on hardware components, connections, and resources, (2) viewing the current operating status of hardware devices, (3) viewing hardware properties, drivers and driver details, resource settings, power management settings, and configuration settings; (4) identifying, changing, and troubleshooting hardware problems, including disabled devices, resource conflicts, and unknown devices, (5) rolling back device drivers, and (6) uninstalling hardware. WIN 766–778

Device Problems Troubleshooting Wizard, WIN 779–780

diacritics Accents that you can use to index and to select similarly-spelled words, such as jalapeño or jalapeno, when performing a search. WIN 193

Diagnostic Mode A mode in which the Check Disk utility examines a disk for errors and reports on any errors that it finds, but does not correct the errors. Instead, it identifies what it would do if you decide to correct the file system errors. WIN 343

dialog box A component of the graphical user interface that displays information, lists object properties and settings, and provides options from which to choose as you complete a command operation. WIN 10

differential backup A type of backup performed during a backup cycle that includes all new or modified files since the last normal or last full backup. Backup utilities do *not* turn off the Archive bit of backed-up files after the differential backup is complete. WIN 618, WIN 619–620

digital signature An encoded tag that verifies the authenticity of the originating party by binding information about that party to the file. WIN 445

DIR The Directory command, an internal command used in a command-line window to display a list of subdirectories and files within a directory, along with information about the contents of the directory in a command-line window. *See* Attrib switch (/A), Page switch or Pause switch (/A), and Sort Order switch (/O). WIN 849–857

DIRCMD A user-defined environment variable that stores default switches for use with the DIR command. WIN 873–875

Direct Memory Access (DMA), or **Direct Memory Access channel** A channel used to transfer data between two devices without the intervention of the processor. WIN 765

Direct Memory Access resources The resources for a DMA channel. WIN 765

directory The command-line or DOS term for a folder. WIN 43, WIN 195, WIN 286

directory listing A list of information about the names of subdirectories and files on a disk, produced by the Directory (DIR) command in a command-line environment, and including the name of each subdirectory and file, the file extension of each file, the file size, and the date and time of each subdirectory and time. WIN 850–857

directory marker The <DIR> notation in a directory listing that identifies the file as a directory (or subdirectory). WIN 850

directory space The storage space available in a directory table for tracking information about files on a disk. WIN 294

directory table A table or file in the system area of a FAT volume that keeps track of the folders and files stored in the top-level folder or root directory of that volume. WIN 293

DirectX A Windows technology that enables games and programs to use the capabilities of your computer's multimedia hardware devices. WIN 57

Disable automatic restart on system failure A Windows Vista boot option for preventing Windows Vista from repeatedly restarting after encountering a serious boot error, such as a Stop error. WIN 510

Disable Driver Signature Enforcement A Windows Vista boot option for installing device drivers that do not contain the proper driver signatures. WIN 511

disk A physical storage device, such as a hard disk, DVD, CD, or USB flash drive. WIN 284. *See also* hard disks

Disk Cleanup Wizard A tool for locating and removing temporary internet files, downloaded program files, offline Web pages, the hibernation file, debug dump files, deleted folders and files in the Recycle Bin, setup log files, system error memory dump and minidump files, and temporary files. WIN 334–341, WIN 375–388, WIN 462, WIN 616

Disk Defragmenter A disk-optimization tool for (1) reducing file fragmentation by reorganizing the clusters assigned to each file so that they are located in contiguous clusters and by also rearranging files so that they are stored in contiguous clusters, and for (2) reducing free space fragmentation by removing free space (or unused space) between files. *See* Defrag. WIN 363–365, WIN 546, WIN 616

Disk Management An Administrative snap-in or system utility for viewing information on, and for managing, disks, partitions, volumes, and drives. WIN 303–307

disk quotas A Windows Vista feature that enables Administrators to control, allocate, and track the usage of storage space on a disk by user account. WIN 369–375

Distributed Denial of Service (DDoS) A type of attack that relies on the use of hundreds or thousands of interconnected home computers infected with malware and controlled remotely by a single user to overwhelm a Web site with traffic and thereby shut down the Web site. WIN 402

document-oriented approach An operating mode in which you locate and open the document you want to use, and then the operating system opens the application that originally produced the document or the application currently associated with that type of file. WIN 10

document window The window within an application window where you work on a single document. WIN 10

domain A group of computers on a network that share a common directory database. WIN 290, WIN 789

domain controller A computer that uses Active Directory to manage access to a network—including logging on and authenticating users and providing access to the directory and shared resources. WIN 483

DOS (Disk Operating System) (1) The Microsoft command-line operating system introduced and used on the first IBM PC; (2) A generic name for three related operating systems: MS-DOS, PC-DOS, and IBM-DOS. WIN 7–9

dots per inch (DPI) (1) A display setting (called DPI Scaling) used to increase the size of desktop icons and the content of windows and dialog boxes as well as the text of icon titles and menus; (2) A measurement of the resolution of a printer. WIN 117–120

Downloaded program files ActiveX controls and Java applets that Windows Internet Explorer automatically downloads and stores in the Downloaded Program Files folder under the Windows folder. WIN 334, WIN 339, WIN 462, WIN 547

DPI Scaling The process of adjusting the number of dots per inch for the video display so that the content of windows and dialog boxes as well as the text of icon titles and menus is displayed at a specific size. WIN 117–120

drive A name (such as C: and A:) assigned by the operating system to all or part of the storage space on a physical disk, such as a hard disk, CD-ROM, USB flash drive, or a virtual hard disk. WIN 284

drive name A device name that consists of a letter of the alphabet and a colon (such as C: for drive C) and that is assigned to a disk drive by the operating system. WIN 43

dual-core processor A processor with two execution cores that can process two sets of instructions from the same program or two different programs simultaneously. WIN 53

DualView A term used to describe the simultaneous use of two monitors. WIN 763

DWM. *See* Desktop Window Manager

DWORD A Registry value, identified by the REG_DWORD data type, which consists of a four-byte number displayed in binary, hexadecimal, or decimal format; for example, the DWORD value 0x000000001 (1) is a DWORD for the WebView value entry. WIN 914–916

dynamic disk A physical disk that only Windows Vista, Windows XP and Windows 2000 can access, and that provides additional features not supported on basic disks, such as volumes that scan multiple disks. WIN 303

dynamic library file A dynamic link library file with a "dll" file extension that contains executable program code and that provides support to one or more programs. WIN 227

dynamic volume A volume that uses a relational database to keep track of information about volumes. WIN 288

E

Easy Transfer Cable A special type of USB cable for transferring user files and settings from an older computer with a previous Windows version to a newer computer with a different Windows version or edition. WIN 712–715, WIN 717

ECHO OFF command, WIN 875

EDID. *See* Extended Display Identification Data

editing
- command line, WIN 834–836
- Registry, WIN 909, WIN 911–912

edition A different version of the same Windows operating system. WIN 16, WIN 18–19

EFS. *See* Encrypting File Service

EHCI. *See* Enhanced Host Controller Interface

e-mail
- attachments, cautions about opening, WIN 404–406
- backing up, WIN 631
- spam, WIN 406

e-mail shortcut A shortcut that uses the mailto: URL to create a Microsoft Office Outlook or Windows Mail email message with or without predefined email addresses in the To, CC, and BCC fields, predefined subject in the Subject field, and predefined text in the body of the email message. WIN 212, WIN 257–266

Enable Boot Logging A Windows Vista boot option for performing a full boot and logging all startup operations to an NT Boot Log file named Ntbtlog.txt. WIN 508

Enable low-resolution video (640×480) A Windows Vista boot option for booting a computer at low resolution and a lower refresh rate to troubleshoot a problem with video display settings or the video display driver. WIN 509

encoding, URL, WIN 261

Encrypt attribute An attribute available on an NTFS volume that, when enabled, prevents access to a folder or file by any person other the user who encrypted the folder or file (and, of course, the Administrator). WIN 288

encrypting folders and files, WIN 319–323

Encrypting File Service (EFS) A service for encrypting and decrypting folders and files on NTFS volumes. WIN 319

encryption A way to encode folders and files on an NTFS volume so that only the original user can access that data. WIN 319
- BitLocker Drive Encryption, WIN 323–324
- file and folder settings, WIN 193
- of files, folders, WIN 291

encryption key A code that Windows Vista uses to encrypt and decrypt files. WIN 322

end-of-file (EOF) The code in the File Allocation Table that identifies a cluster as the last cluster in use by a specific file. WIN 292

Enhanced Host Controller Interface (EHCI) A host controller that supports the use of second-generation Hi-Speed USB 2.0 devices with data transfer rates of 480 Mbps. WIN 777

environment variable A setting stored in the Windows environment that contains information about the computer system (such as the name of the operating system), and that is assigned to a symbolic name (such as "OS"). WIN 232
- viewing settings for, WIN 527–528, WIN 873–875

EOF. *See* end-of-file

Error-Checking Tool A GUI tool for (1) examining a disk for file system errors and repairing those errors where possible, (2) checking the integrity of sectors on a disk, and (3) moving data in defective sectors to good sectors. *See* Check Disk. WIN 342–350
- using on FAT volumes, flash drives, WIN 350–355
- vs. Check Disk utility, WIN 358

errors
- and DOS CHKDSK command, WIN 8
- resolving system, WIN 5
- Stop Error, WIN 510

event A significant occurrence in the system or an application that requires Windows Vista to notify users of the event and to log the event. WIN 378
- monitoring with Event Viewer, WIN 483–491

event log A file that lists operating system events. WIN 483

Event Viewer A Windows Vista troubleshooting tool that provides detailed information about every event that occurs on a computer. WIN 483–491

exception A rule for a program or service that permits the program or service to communicate through a firewall. WIN 426, WIN 428–429

executable file A file with the file extension "exe" that contains program code which Windows Vista can load into memory and run. WIN 142, WIN 231

execute To run, carry out, or process instructions in a program. WIN 11, WIN 828

execution core A processor core which is equivalent to a separate processor and can process a set of instructions. WIN 56

exFAT. *See* Extended FAT

EXIT An internal command for closing a command-line window. WIN 829–830

expandable string value A type of Registry string value that contains a reference to a variable value, such as %SystemRoot%—the environment variable for the path to the Windows folder. WIN 904

explicit consent A situation in which you specifically agree that a Web site can use information it collects about you to contact you. WIN 449

Explorer. *See* Search Explorer

export To transfer data to a file or another program. WIN 892
- Registry settings, WIN 894–897

Extended Display Identification Data (EDID) A standard video data format that contains information about the capabilities of a monitor, such as the screen resolution and color depth. WIN 764

extended FAT (exFAT) A new file system designed for mobile devices. WIN 297

extended partition A partition on a disk that does not contain operating system files, but which can be divided into additional logical drives. WIN 286, WIN 303

Extensible Markup Language. *See* XML

extension. *See* file extension

external command A command whose program code is stored in a file on disk; the operating system must locate and then load the program code in the file to perform the operation. WIN 830–831, WIN 836–840

F

G

H

I

IBM PC operating systems, WIN 7

icon An image or picture displayed on the screen to represent hardware and software resources (such as drives, disks, applications, and files) as well as system tools on your computer that you can open and use. WIN 9

- changing desktop, WIN 21–23, WIN 33, WIN 95
- changing for shortcuts, WIN 225–227
- customizing drive, WIN 247–251, WIN 247–251
- customizing GUI, WIN 79
- customizing taskbar and notification area, WIN 98–99

icon title A label that describes the purpose of an icon. WIN 9–10

IEEE 1394 A high-speed Plug and Play bus with data transfer rates of 100, 200, and 400 Mbps (Megabits per second or millions of bits per second). WIN 765

IEEE 1394b A second-generation high-speed Plug and Play bus with data transfer rates of 800 Mbps to 3.2 Gbps (Gigabits per second); equivalent to FireWire. WIN 765

implicit consent A situation in which you have not informed a Web site that you do not want it to use information it collects about you to contact you; in other words, you have not opted out. WIN 449

Import Registry File dialog box, WIN 897

incremental backup A type of backup performed during a backup cycle that includes only those files that you created or changed since your last normal backup or last incremental backup. Backup utilities turn off the Archive bit of all backed-up files after the incremental backup is complete. WIN 620–622

index A file that contains a collection of information about the folders and files on your computer. WIN 174

- verification, WIN 344

indexes. *See* NTFS directories

Indexed Location dialog box, WIN 192

indexing settings, WIN 190–197

.inf files, WIN 251

input Data that you provide to a program. WIN 4

Input/Output (I/O) resources *See* I/O address. WIN 765

insert mode A mode in which you insert a character in the existing text at the point where you type it. WIN 836

installing

- operating system upgrade, WIN 680–709
- software, WIN 726–738
- Windows Vista, WIN 709–723

instance An option for sampling a performance counter in a different way; for example, under the Process performance object, you can monitor the % Processor Time (a performance counter) used by all programs, or by one specific program (the latter two of which are examples of instances). WIN 566

Instant Search A Windows Vista feature for quickly locating programs, folders, and files on your computer. WIN 31–32, WIN 174–190

internal command A command whose program code is contained in the file Cmd.exe and therefore is available once Cmd.exe loads into memory. The program code for an internal command does not load from a file on disk. WIN 828–829

Internet A Windows Internet Explorer security zone that includes Web sites not found in the Local intranet, Trusted sites, and Restricted sites security zones. WIN 6, WIN 12–13

Internet cache The Temporary Internet Files folder used to store downloaded copies of Web pages and Web page content (such as video, music, and animation) from each Web site you visit. WIN 334, WIN 341, WIN 547

Internet Explorer. *See* Windows Internet Explorer

Internet Protocol 4 (TCP/IPv4), WIN 800

Internet shortcut A shortcut that uses a URL to locate a Web site or Web page. WIN 212, WIN 251–257

Internet worm An independently functioning program that adversely affects the performance of a computer and may compromise its security and that reproduces and spreads across networks producing network congestion. WIN 400

interrupt command The Ctrl+C key combination or Cancel command, which you use to interrupt and cancel a command operation in a command-line window. WIN 848

interrupt request resource An IRQ assigned to a hardware device. *See* IRQ

intranet A private network that relies on the use of Internet technologies and protocols and that is limited to a specific group of people, such as employees within a company. WIN 445

invalid page fault An error condition that occurs when Windows Vista is not able to find data in the paging file. WIN 571

IP address A unique 32-bit address that identifies a computer on a network or the Internet. WIN 707

IRQ (interrupt request) A hardware line used for transmitting signals from a hardware device to the processor. WIN 765

J

jaggies A stairstep effect that occurs when rendering diagonal and curved lines on a video display device. WIN 81, WIN 83

Java A hardware-independent Web programming language for creating interactive or animated content on Web pages. WIN 744

Java applet A small program, such as an animated counter, that is written in the Java programming language and that is downloaded from a Web site and run locally on your computer. WIN 334

Joint Photographic Experts Group (JPG or **JPEG)** A graphics file format that achieves higher compression ratios of 10:1 or 20:1 by removing some of the detail in an image (changes that the human eye cannot detect). WIN 89–90

K

kernel That portion of the Windows Vista operating system that resides in memory at all times and that provides services for applications. WIN 902

kernel memory Memory used by the core components of the operating system and by device drivers. WIN 550

key (1) The length of a variable value applied by an algorithm to a string or block of unencrypted text during the process of encrypting data; (2) A group of related Registry settings, such as the .bmp key, that contains information on the Bitmap Image file type. WIN 894

keyboard shortcut A key or combination of keys used to accomplish a task that you might otherwise accomplish with a mouse. WIN 23

- creating for desktop shortcuts, WIN 219

keylogger Malicious software that can monitor your computer, record keys that you press, and send the information it compiles via e-mail to a third party. That information may include passwords, PINs, a social security number, and credit card numbers. It can also track and report your Web browsing habits, and it can become active when you connect to a secure Web site, such as an online banking Web site. WIN 401

keyword A descriptive word you use when searching for files or other information. WIN 36, WIN 39–41

L

LABEL An external command used in a command-line window to display, create, change, or delete the volume label of a disk (drive). WIN 10

M

N

O

Offline File A folder on your local computer that acts as a temporary storage location for copies of network files and that provides you with faster access to the files as well as access to the files when your computer is not connected to the network. WIN 809

Offline Web Pages Web pages stored on your computer so that you can view them without being connected to the Internet. WIN 335

OHCI. *See* Open Host Controller Interface

one-way sync partnership A sync relationship in which the Sync Center copies files from what you designate as a primary location (such as your hard disk) to a secondary location (such as a flash drive or mobile device). It never copies files from the secondary location to the primary location. WIN 668

Online Help Help information provided at a Web site by the manufacturer of the software you are using on your computer. WIN 6

online privacy Privacy you have (or the lack thereof) while using the Internet. WIN 448

online profiling A description of your interests developed from the Web sites that you visit, and then used to develop more effective marketing strategies that promote products you are likely to find interesting and that display that information in customized banner advertising. WIN 448

opacity The level of transparency of an object, such as a Windows Sidebar gadget. WIN 29

Open Host Controller Interface (OHCI) A host controller that supports the use of first-generation USB 1.x devices with data transfer rates of 1.5 and 12 Mbps. WIN 777

opening
- Computer window, WIN 45
- Registry Editor, WIN 895
- user accounts, WIN 421–422

operating environment A software product that performs the same functions as an operating system, except for configuring and customizing a computer system and handling the storage and retrieval of data in files on a disk. WIN 9

operating system (OS) A software product that manages the basic processes that occur within a computer, coordinates the interaction of hardware and software so that each component works together, and provides support for the use of other software, such as application software. WIN 2
- failures, information about, WIN 476
- PC types of, WIN 7–17
- Plug and Play, WIN 762
- preparing for upgrade, WIN 680–709
- Windows Vista, WIN 18–23

operating system prompt A set of characters displayed in a command-line environment to provide an interface for interacting with the computer. WIN 7, WIN 824

OR A Boolean filter that combines two criteria and requires that any folders or files listed in the search results meet at least one of the two conditions. WIN 183, WIN 185

organizing
- files and folders for backup, WIN 617–618
- files and folders generally, WIN 138–140
- files in groups and stacks, WIN 167–173
- your personal folders, WIN 140–142

orphaned file A file that has a valid file record segment in the Master File Table, but which is not listed in any directory. WIN 344

OS. *See* operating system

Outlook (Microsoft), WIN 258

output The results produced by a program. WIN 4
- pipe, paged, WIN 841

output redirection operator (>) An operator that redirects output to another device, such as a port or a txt file, rather than to the monitor. WIN 844–845

overtype mode A typing mode in which you type over one or more existing characters. WIN 836

P

packet A set of data (such as part of a file), as well as a source address and destination address, sent from one location to another over the Internet or other network. WIN 763

packet sniffer Software that enables a third party to eavesdrop on computer transmissions, collect user names and passwords, convert Internet transmissions into readable data, and identify weaknesses in a computer's security. WIN 402

page (1) A segment of memory 4 KB (or 4,096 bytes) in size that can be swapped to a paging file on disk by Windows Vista; (2) Output displayed on the monitor or within a window (a logical concept rather than a physical concept). WIN 544

Page switch, or **Pause switch (/P)** A DIR command switch that displays one screen of output at a time. WIN 852, WIN 873

paged kernel memory Memory used by the operating system that can be paged, or swapped, to disk so that other programs can use that memory. WIN 551

paged output Output displayed one window or one screen at a time (hence, a page). WIN 841, WIN 842

paging To swap pages to and from the paging file on disk. WIN 544

paging file A hidden system file (Pagefile.sys) created on a hard disk by Windows Vista for use as supplemental RAM (also called virtual memory). WIN 544, WIN 547–550, WIN 597

palette (or color palette) A set of colors used by either an application or by the operating system. WIN 90

Parallel Advanced Technology Attachment. *See* PATA

parallel directory A directory located under the same subdirectory as another directory and therefore located at the same level in the directory tree. WIN 868

parameter An optional or required item of data for a command in a command-line environment, WIN 8, WIN 828

parent directory The directory located one level above the current directory. WIN 847

parent folder The folder located one level above the current folder. WIN 847

parentheses () A Boolean filter used in a search condition to locate all words enclosed within the parentheses; however, the words can be arranged in any order. WIN 184

parity A calculated value derived from a data (or an error-checking) feature that enables the operating system to reconstruct lost data if a physical hard disk, or a portion of a physical hard disk, fails. WIN 304

partition (1) All or part of a physical hard disk that is set aside for a drive or set of logical drives; (2) A subdivision of a physical disk that functions as if it were a separate physical disk; (3) To subdivide a hard disk into one or more logical drives, either for storing different types of files or for installing different operating systems. WIN 4, WIN 286
- active and extended, WIN 303

password, WIN 19–20
- creating strong, WIN 424–425
- power option settings, WIN 125
- for user accounts, WIN 6

password reset disk A disk you create in case you forget the password to your user account. WIN 421–424

Password-protected sharing A network setting that determines whether other people who have user accounts and a password on the same computer can access shared files, shared printers, and the Public folder. WIN 797

PATA (Parallel ATA or **Parallel Advanced Technology Attachment)** An older bus technology for connecting a hard disk drive to a computer. WIN 505

patch Program code that is inserted into an executable program. WIN 338

path (1) The notation used to identify the location of a folder or file. For example, C:\Windows is the path for the Windows folder on drive C, and C:\Windows\Explorer.exe is the path for the Explorer program file; (2) An internal command used in a command-line window to display the settings for the PATH environment variable; (3) An environment variable that contains the sequence of directories (or folders) that Windows Vista searches to locate and load a program from disk. WIN 164–167, WIN 210–213
    automatically updating shortcut, WIN 235–238
    environmental variable, System Information, WIN 528
    UNC, WIN 210
    upgrade, WIN 681, WIN 686
    Windows, WIN 874

PATHEXT An environment variable that contains a set of file extensions used by Windows to locate a program file (in conjunction with the path in the PATH environment variable). WIN 876

PC operating systems, WIN 7–17

PDF (Portable Document Format) A file that contains an image of the contents of another file so that you can view and print that file. WIN 342

peer-to-peer network A simple type of network in which each computer is equal and can access other computers to which they are connected and share hardware, such as the same printer(s), hard disk drives, removable storage devices (such as CD, DVD, and external hard disk drives) as well as software, folders, and files. (This type of network does not rely on a server to manage network resources and provide network users access to those resources). WIN 789

percentage sign (%) in URL encoding, WIN 261

performance
    balancing speed and storage space, WIN 337
    evaluating computer, WIN 53–55
    evaluating with Performance Monitor, WIN 566–592
    evaluating with Resource Overview, WIN 555–559
    optimizing system, WIN 5
    RAM and, WIN 544–547
    viewing system, WIN 550–555

performance counter An item of data associated with a performance object, such as Available Bytes for the Memory performance object. WIN 566, WIN 579, WIN 595, WIN 597

Performance Monitor An administrative tool that uses performance counters to monitor and evaluate the performance of a computer, evaluate the use of resources (such as memory), and identify bottlenecks and other problems that affect the use and performance of a computer. WIN 566–597

performance object A logical collection of performance counters associated with a resource or service that you can monitor, such as memory. WIN 566

permission A rule that determines which users can access an object and how they can access that object. WIN 289, WIN 802, WIN 804

persistent cookie A cookie that remains on your computer and that can be read by the Web site that created it when you next visit that Web site. WIN 449

personalized menu A menu that displays only the most commonly used menu options or menu options that were previously used. WIN 97

pharming (pronounced "farming") A type of hoax that relies on e-mail messages that inform you to immediately update account information in an attempt to trick you into disclosing personal and financial information. Pharming may use malicious software or tamper electronically with a URL to redirect your Web browser to a Web site that appears identical or very similar to that of a company with which you do business. WIN 402, WIN 406

phishing (pronounced "fishing") A type of hoax in which you receive an e-mail message that appears to be sent from a reputable company with which you do business (such as an ISP or bank) in an attempt to trick you into disclosing personal and financial information. WIN 402, WIN 406

Phishing Filter A Windows Internet Explorer component for checking Web sites for phishing activities. WIN 459–461

Pictures folder, WIN 139

pinned items list An area located in the upper-left corner of the Start menu that contains a list of programs that always remain on the Start menu. WIN 30, WIN 94
    pinning programs to Start menu, WIN 239–240

pipe operator A symbol (|) used between two commands in a command-line environment to indicate that the output of the first command is to be used as the input for the second command. WIN 841

pipeline A command that uses a pipe operator in a command-line environment to transfer the output of one command so that it becomes the input for another command. WIN 841

piping To use the output of one command in a command-line environment as the input for another command. WIN 841

pixel One or more dots, or points, that are treated as one unit on the monitor. WIN 57
    and font display, WIN 81–84
    resolution and aspect ratio, WIN 109

pixel shader Software that renders (or generates) graphics effects on a pixel-by-pixel basis. WIN 57

Plain Text file format, WIN 406

platter A disk within a hard disk drive that provides all or part of the storage capacity of the entire hard disk drive. WIN 285

Plug and Play (PnP) A set of specifications for designing hardware so that an operating system can automatically detect and configure the device either during booting or (in some cases) when the computer is already on, with little or no intervention on your part. WIN 12, WIN 762

pointer The cluster number of the next available cluster for a folder or file. WIN 292, WIN 351

Pop-up Blocker A Windows Internet Explorer component for managing pop-up windows. WIN 453–456

pop-up window A window used to display advertising from Web sites that you visit. WIN 453–456

Portable Network Graphics (PNG) A graphics file format similar to the GIF file format, but which achieves a slightly greater compression, and which may eventually replace the GIF file format since it improves on GIF in several ways, and is patent-free, therefore requiring no license for its use. WIN 90

POST (Power-On Self-Test) settings, WIN 502

power management The management of device power usage by the operating system. WIN 5
    examining mouse's property sheet, WIN 771–772
    using, changing settings, WIN 120–126, WIN 502

power plan A combination of settings used by Windows Vista to manage power usage on a computer. WIN 121–124

PnP. *See* Plug and Play

preview handler A component of the Windows Vista operating system that displays the contents of certain types of files in the Preview Pane. WIN 155

Preview pane, WIN 152

previewing files, WIN 152–153

Previous Versions Shadow copies and backup copies of previous versions of folders and files. WIN 613

primary partition A partition on a basic disk (a physical disk) that contains the boot files for loading the operating system and that is therefore designated as the active partition. WIN 286

print queue A list of all print jobs or documents that are scheduled to print, along with information about each print job, such as the document name, the status of the document, the owner (or username of the person who submitted the print job), the number of pages that have printed and the total number of pages, the document size (in kilobytes), the time and date the print job was submitted, and the port used by the printer. WIN 4

Printer sharing A network setting that determines whether users on other computers connected to the same network as your computer can connect to and use printers connected to your computer. WIN 797, WIN 800

process An executable program, such as Microsoft Office Word or Task Manager itself; a service, such as the Print Spooler service, which handles the printing of files in the background; or a subsystem, such as the one for Windows Vista applications. WIN 11, WIN 414

processor core The equivalent of a separate processor that can process a set of instructions. WIN 56

Program Compatibility Wizard A tool for identifying, selecting, applying, and testing compatibility mode settings and for resolving compatibility mode problems for certain types of programs so that they function properly under Windows Vista. WIN 731–738

Program Defaults A Start menu option for (1) viewing, changing or specifying default file types and protocols for a program, (2) associating a file type or protocol with a program, (3) changing AutoPlay settings, and (4) setting program access to certain programs as well as computer default settings. WIN 743–751

Programs and Features A Control Panel component for viewing, organizing, uninstalling, repairing, and changing installed software as well as viewing installed updates and turning Windows features on and off. WIN 719, WIN 731, WIN 738, WIN 739

property A characteristic or setting of an object. WIN 10–11, WIN 52

property sheet A group of related settings displayed on a sheet in a dialog box. WIN 34

Protected Mode A feature of Windows Internet Explorer for operating with limited privileges and for preventing changes to Windows Registry settings and to files in system and user folders. This feature protects your computer from Web sites that attempt to install malicious software on your computer and from hackers or intruders who attempt to make changes to your computer system. WIN 446

protocol The set of rules and conventions for transmitting data over a network. WIN 445

Public folder sharing A network setting that determines whether users on other computers connected to the same network as your computer can access the Public folder and its contents. WIN 797

Q

QoS (Quality of Service) Packet Scheduler A network component that provides for the efficient flow of data on a network by handling the scheduling of packets of data over a network. WIN 800

quarantine To move a program to another location and prevent it from becoming active again (usually by changing the file extension). WIN 407, WIN 413–414

question mark wildcard (?) A symbol used as part of a file specification to substitute for a single character in the filename or file extension. WIN 257, WIN 866–871

Quick Launch toolbar A taskbar toolbar that contains a Show Desktop button and Switch between windows button that that may also include desktop or Internet shortcuts. WIN 98, WIN 102–104

quick scan A fast scan that examines specific components, such as memory and the Windows Registry, to check for infection by malicious software. WIN 407–411

quotes, or quotation marks ("") A Boolean filter used in a search condition to find an exact match for the words or a phrase enclosed within the quotation marks. WIN 183–184

R

RAID-5 volume A fault-tolerant volume that stores data and parity information in stripes across three or more physical hard disks. WIN 304

Random-Access Memory (RAM) (1) The predominant type of memory within a computer; (2) temporary, or volatile, computer memory used to store programs, input, processing, and output; (3) work space for using software and documents. WIN 2

Read-Only An attribute assigned to a file by the operating system to indicate that you can read from, but not write to, the file. WIN 288

Read-Only Mode A diagnostic mode of operation in which the command-line Check Disk utility checks a drive and, if it finds errors, reports the presence of these errors and identifies how it would correct the problem. WIN 343

ReadyDrive A Windows Vista technology that works with hybrid hard disks which contain built-in flash memory where ReadyDrive caches data. WIN 602

real-time protection A Windows Defender operating mode for constantly monitoring a computer for potentially unwanted software. WIN 408

Really Simple Syndication (RSS) Feed A automated approach to receiving updated news or headlines from Web sites onto your desktop. WIN 27, WIN 342

recently opened programs list An area of the Start menu where Windows Vista lists your most recently used programs so that you can quickly open a program you recently used. WIN 30

record A row of file information organized into columns. WIN 287

recovery partition A hidden hard disk partition that contains software for recovering and restoring your computer. WIN 651

Redundant Array of Independent Disks (RAID) The use of use of multiple hard disks to store data in order to improve performance or reliability. WIN 304

refresh rate The number of times that the image on the screen is redrawn by the video card (and thereby refreshed). WIN 114–116

S

Superfetch A Windows Vista technology that monitors the programs you use, the frequency with which you use those programs, and the dates and times you use those programs over a period of time in order to determine how you use your computer. Then, it preloads those programs at the appropriate time so that they are available when you need them. WIN 602

switch An optional parameter or item of data that is used with a command to modify the way in which a program operates. WIN 8, WIN 357, WIN 823, WIN 827

symbols, reserved. *See* reserved symbols

Sync Center A Windows Vista feature for synchronizing (or updating) one or more files if you make changes to files in one location. WIN 668

sync conflict A conflict that occurs when you are synchronizing two files, both of which you had previously changed separately. WIN 668

sync partnership A process for synchronizing two copies of the same file in two separate locations based on the type of relationship between the two copies of the same file. WIN 668

syntax The proper format for entering a command, including how to spell the command, how to use required parameters (such as a drive) and optional parameters (such as a switch), and the spacing between the command, required parameters, and options parameters. WIN 8, WIN 831

system area The area of a disk that contains the boot sector, File Allocation Tables, and directory table on a FAT volume. WIN 291

System attribute An attribute assigned by the operating system to a folder or file to identify the folder or file as an operating system folder or file. WIN 288

system cache The amount of RAM used to store pages of open files. WIN 551

system checkpoint A point in time when the Windows Vista System Protection feature saves changes to system files, device drivers, and system settings on your computer system so that if you run into a problem later, you can roll back the computer system and restore it to an earlier working state. WIN 492

System Configuration, using, WIN 519–525

System Diagnostics Report A system health report that provides detailed information on the use of hardware resources, system response times, processes, system information, and configuration data and that identifies ways to maximize system performance. WIN 595–597

system drivers, WIN 530

System error minidump files, WIN 335

System Information A tool for compiling information on hardware resources, hardware components, and your computer's software environment. WIN 525–531
    viewing hardware information with, WIN 782–789

system memory Random access memory (RAM), the predominant type of memory within a computer, used to store currently used programs, documents, and data, and thereby provide a temporary workspace. WIN 2, WIN 685

System Protection The Windows component that creates and saves restore points so that you can roll back your computer with System Restore and restore it to an earlier working state. WIN 491–500, WIN 892

system resources, managing, WIN 5

System Restore The Windows component for rolling back a computer to an earlier working state by using a restore point or for undoing a restoration. WIN 15

System Stability Index The reliability rating produced by Reliability Monitor to measure the current performance of your computer. WIN 476–482

SYSTEMINFO An external command that displays configuration information about a computer and its operating system in a command-line window. WIN 842–844

SystemRoot An environment variable that contains the path to the Windows folder on a computer. WIN 211, WIN 233, WIN 376, WIN 528, WIN 872, WIN 890

T

tag A word or phrase that you assign as a property to a folder or file to help you organize and locate folders and files. WIN 174
    combining with Boolean filters in searches, WIN 186–187
    searching for, WIN 180–182

Task Manager A program that provides information on currently-running applications, processes, and services; monitors memory and CPU usage and provides performance information; monitors the status of a network and the users on a computer; and enables the user to identify and shut down non-responding programs. WIN 550–555

Task Scheduler A Windows Vista tool for (1) viewing, creating, editing, and customizing scheduled tasks that automate routine and important operations on a computer, (2) viewing a list of events (or the history of) a scheduled task, and (3) viewing properties of a scheduled task. WIN 375–388

task-switching The ability to switch from one open task, or process, in one window to another task in another window. WIN 11

Taskbar The Windows GUI component that displays the Start button, the Quick Launch toolbar, the notification area, and buttons for open folder windows, open applications, and open documents. WIN 76–78, WIN 98–102

taskbar grouping A Windows Vista feature that provides access to all open documents of a certain type (such as Word documents) grouped on one taskbar button. WIN 98

TCP/IP (Transmission Control Protocol/Internet Protocol) A set of networking protocols that determine how computers communicate, how they connect to networks, and how they route data. WIN 763, WIN 800

Temporary files Files created by the operating system and applications for processing data and performing some type of operation. Once the operation is completed, these temporary files are deleted. WIN 335

Temporary Internet Files Web pages and content on Web pages that Windows Internet Explorer downloads and stores in the Temporary Internet Files folder for your user account. WIN 334

text mode A simple and fast video display mode for displaying text, including letters, numbers, symbols, and a small set of graphics characters, usually using white characters on a black background. WIN 9

text user interface (TUI) A command-line interface that displays a command prompt and interprets commands that you enter from the keyboard. WIN 9

texture The detail applied to the surface of three-dimensional graphics. WIN 53

theme A set of visual elements that are designed to provide a unified look for your desktop and user interface. WIN 70–76

third-party Web site A Web site that provides content (such as banner advertising and images) to the Web site you're visiting. WIN 449

thread A segment or unit of program code within an application that Windows can execute at the same time it is executing the same segment or another segment of program code within the same program. WIN 11, WIN 551

timer bar The red vertical bar in the Performance Monitor pane that slowly moves to the right as values are sampled, plotted on the graph, and added to the value bar. WIN 568

toggle Using an option or key to switch between two related uses. WIN 33

toggle key A key that alternates between two related uses each time you press the key. WIN 836

toolbars
    creating desktop, WIN 104–106
    creating folder, WIN 107

U

W

wallpaper A graphic image that appears on, or overlays, the desktop. WIN 20, WIN 92

warm boot A type of boot in which you press your computer's Reset button on the front of the system, or simultaneously press the Ctrl+Alt+Del keys to restart your computer and, in the process, skip the Power-On Self Test (POST). WIN 2

Web bug HTML code that uses links on a Web page, in a document, or in an e-mail message to reference a Web site that in turn monitors your use of the Web page, document, or e-mail message in order to develop a profile of your interests, track copyrighted documents, or track the flow of e-mail from one person to another. WIN 401

Web Style (1) A Windows Vista setting that allows you to work on your local computer in the same way that you work on the Web and that treats objects on your local computer like hyperlinks on a Web page. WIN 34

wildcard A symbol used in a file specification to select a group of files. WIN 190, WIN 866

Win16 application *See* 16-bit application.

Win32 application *See* 32-bit application. WIN 726

Win64 application *See* 64-bit application. WIN 727

window A work area on the screen defined by borders and designed to organize your view of applications, documents, drives, folders, and files. WIN 10

Windows 9x product line A Microsoft product line that included Windows 95, Windows 98, and Windows ME and that provided home users easy access to the Internet and multimedia content on their computer. WIN 16

Windows Aero (1) A user interface enhancement available in certain Windows Vista editions that operate on higher performance computers with specific hardware capabilities and that includes object translucency, smooth scaling of icons, glowing effects when you point to a window's or dialog box's resizing buttons, and smooth visual refreshing (updating your view) of the Windows desktop, Live Taskbar Thumbnails, Windows Flip, and Windows Flip 3D; (2) a color scheme in certain editions of Windows Vista. WIN 23, WIN 71

Windows Boot Loader The program that loads the Windows Vista operating system and basic hardware device drivers. WIN 507

Windows Boot Manager The program that starts the process of loading the Windows Vista operating system by examining the Boot Configuration Data to determine what operating systems are installed on the computer. WIN 507

Windows Defender An antispyware program for detecting and removing spyware on computers used by small office and home users. WIN 407–419

Windows demo A Help and Support video clip that explains a feature or shows you how to complete an operation. WIN 41

Windows Display Driver Model (WDDM) Specifications for a new type of video display adapter device driver required by Windows Vista to deliver high-performance and high-quality graphics and video and which supports the use of Windows Aero. WIN 57, WIN 121, WIN 685

Windows Easy Transfer A Windows tool for simplifying the task of transferring user files and settings from an older computer with a previous Windows version to a new computer with a different Windows version or edition. WIN 712–723

Windows environment An area of memory that stores environment variables and their settings which Windows Vista, applications, and utilities check. WIN 232, WIN 528

Windows Experience Index A rating that measures the overall capability and performance of your computer hardware and software. WIN 53–55

Windows Flip A Windows Aero feature that displays a pane with thumbnails of open windows when you press Alt+Tab so that you can pick the window in which you want to work. WIN 23–24

Windows Flip 3D A Windows Aero feature that stacks all open windows at a 3D angle on the desktop so that you can see more of the content of open windows and select the window in which you want to work. WIN 24–25

Windows Memory Diagnostic Tool A startup repair tool for performing a thorough check of the RAM on a computer. WIN 531

Windows NT product line A Microsoft product line that includes the Windows NT Workstation 4.0, Windows 2000 Professional, Windows XP, and Windows Vista operating systems used by businesses and more advanced users. WIN 16

Windows path A setting Windows Vista uses to locate the program files for external commands. WIN 874

Windows ReadyBoost A Windows Vista feature that uses some of the high-speed storage space on a flash drive to boost the performance of your computer by storing cached data on the flash drive. WIN 600–602

Windows Recovery Environment (WinRE) A special Windows Vista environment for troubleshooting computer startup problems, such as a Windows Vista boot failure. WIN 530–532

Windows Resume Loader The program that reads the hibernation file and restores Windows Vista to its previous state before Windows Vista switched to hibernation. WIN 507

Windows Security Center A Control Panel component that provides information on the status of your computer's firewall, Automatic updating, malware protection, and other security settings. WIN 439–444

X

Z

Task Reference

TASK	PAGE #	RECOMMENDED METHOD
Administrative Tools, add to the Start menu	548	Right-click [Start button], click Properties, click Customize, under System administrative tools, click Display on the All Programs menu and the Start menu, click OK twice
Advanced Boot Options menu, display	512	Boot or restart computer, press the F8 key before you see Windows logo
Advanced sharing, use to share folder	810	*See* Reference Window "Using Advanced Sharing to Share a Folder"
Application, create shortcut to	233	*See* Reference Window "Creating a Shortcut to an Application"
Attribute command, use	860	*See* Reference Window "Viewing File Attributes"
Back up files and folders	634	*See* Reference Window "Backing Up Files and Folders"
Back up to previous window	313	Press Backspace key
Background, choose desktop	93	*See* Reference Window "Choosing Desktop Backgrounds"
Batch program, create	877	*See* Reference Window "Creating a Batch Program"
Boot sequence, change	506	*See* Reference Window "Changing the Boot Sequence"
Briefcase action, change	663	Right-click the Update Briefcase action arrow, click Replace or Skip
Briefcase, copy folders and files to	661	*See* Reference Window "Copying Folders and Files to a Briefcase on a Flash Drive"
Briefcase, create	660	Right-click desktop or folder window background, point to New, click Briefcase
Briefcase, modify file in	662	*See* Reference Window "Modifying a File in a Briefcase"
Briefcase, update files in	667	*See* Reference Window "Updating Files in a Briefcase"
Capture image of a dialog box or active window	475	Press Alt+Print Screen keys
Cancel command, use command-line	848	Press Ctrl+C to interrupt or cancel a command
Change Directory command, use	857	*See* Reference Window "Changing Directories"
Check Disk utility, use command-line	358	*See* Reference Window "Using the Check Disk Utility in a Command Prompt Window"
Classic menu bar, display or hide	50	Press Alt (or press F10)
Clear Command Prompt window or screen	837	Type CLS and press the Enter key
CLSIDs, locate information on	907	*See* Reference Window "Locating Information on CLSIDs"
Collection of drives, folders, files, or shortcuts, select	217	Press and hold down the Ctrl key while you point to and select each object in Web style
Color command, use	834	*See* Reference Window "Changing Console Colors"
Color depth setting, change	114	*See* Reference Window "Changing the Color Depth Setting"
Color scheme, choose	75	*See* Reference Window "Choosing a Theme and Color Scheme"
Colors, adjust for Start menu, taskbar, and window frame	78	*See* Reference Window "Adjusting Window Frame, Start Menu, and Taskbar Colors"
Column widths in a window or dialog box, adjust for best fit	522	Click background of window or dialog box, press Ctrl key and + key on numeric keypad
Command, cancel or interrupt a command-line	848	Press Ctrl+C

TASK	PAGE #	RECOMMENDED METHOD
Command, recall the previous	855	Press F3 key
Command history, display	836	*See* Reference Window "Recalling Commands from the Command History"
Command in a Command Prompt window, repeat or recall	836	*See* Reference Window "Recalling Commands from the Command History"
Command Prompt window, close	828	*See* Reference Window "Opening and Closing a Command Prompt Window"
Command Prompt window, open	828	*See* Reference Window "Opening and Closing a Command Prompt Window"
Command reference list, display	842	*See* Reference Window "Displaying a Command Reference List"
Compatibility settings, specify program	732	Right-click program file, click Properties, click Compatibility tab, change compatibility settings, click OK
Complete PC Backup, perform	649	*See* Reference Window "Performing a Complete PC Backup"
Compress folder and its contents	315	*See* Reference Window "Compressing and Uncompressing a Folder"
Compressed (zipped) Folder, create and extract	317	*See* Reference Window "Creating and Extracting a Compressed (Zipped) Folder"
Computer icon, display on desktop	33	Click , right-click Computer, click Show on Desktop
Computer name, view	792	*See* Reference Window " Viewing a Computer's Name"
Computer, navigate	51	*See* Reference Window "Navigating Your Computer"
Computer, view information about	531	*See* Reference Window "Using System Information"
Computer, view properties of	52	Click , right-click Computer, click Properties
Computers, view in workgroup	792	*See* Reference Window "Viewing Computers and Shared Resources in a Workgroup"
Computer window, use keyboard to open	45	Press Windows Logo+E keys
Console colors, change the Command Prompt window's	834	*See* Reference Window "Changing Console Colors"
Copy command, use	864	*See* Reference Window "Copying a File to a Flash Drive"
Decrypt folder and its contents	322	*See* Reference Window "Encrypting and Decrypting a Folder"
Defaults, set program	751	*See* Reference Window "Specifying Program Defaults and Settings"
Demos, locate and view for Windows Vista	41	*See* Reference Window "Locating and Viewing Windows Vista Demos"
Desktop, display and minimize all windows	26	Click on Quick Launch toolbar
Desktop background, choose	93	*See* Reference Window "Choosing Desktop Backgrounds"
Desktop icon, change and restore size	23	*See* Reference Window "Changing and Restoring Desktop Icon Sizes"
Details view, change to	177	Click Views button arrow, click Details
Device properties, view	778	*See* Reference Window "Viewing Device Properties"
DIRCMD environment variable, create	874	*See* Reference Window "Creating a DIRCMD Environment Variable"
Directories, change	857	*See* Reference Window "Changing Directories"

TASK	PAGE #	RECOMMENDED METHOD
Directory, display the path to the current	854	Type CD at the command prompt and press Enter
Directory command switches, use	857	*See* Reference Window "Displaying a Directory Listing"
Directory command, use	857	*See* Reference Window "Displaying a Directory Listing"
Directory listing, display	857	*See* Reference Window "Displaying a Directory Listing"
Directory tree, display	848	*See* Reference Window "Displaying a Directory Tree"
Disk Cleanup Wizard, run	341	*See* Reference Window "Using the Disk Cleanup Wizard"
Disk Defragmenter, use	365	*See* Reference Window "Opening Disk Defragmenter"
Disk Management snap-in tool, open	305	*See* Reference Window "Using the Disk Management Snap-In Tool"
Disk quotas, set	375	*See* Reference Window "Setting Disk Quotas"
Disk, defragment	365	*See* Reference Window "Opening Disk Defragmenter"
Display effects, choose special	89	*See* Reference Window "Choosing Special Display Effects"
Document, open in another application	662	Right-click file icon, point to Open With, click program
Documents shortcut, add to the Quick Launch toolbar	104	*See* Reference Window "Adding a Documents Shortcut to the Quick Launch Toolbar"
DPI setting, check	120	*See* Reference Window "Checking the DPI Setting"
Drive, create shortcut to	217	*See* Reference Window "Creating a Shortcut to a Flash Drive"
Drive, scan with Windows Defender	411	*See* Reference Window "Using Windows Defender to Scan a Drive"
Drives, change	866	*See* Reference Window "Changing Drives"
E-mail shortcut, create	266	*See* Reference Window "Creating E-mail Shortcuts"
Encrypt folder and its contents	322	*See* Reference Window "Encrypting and Decrypting a Folder"
Environment variables, view settings for	873	*See* Reference Window "Viewing Settings for Environment Variables"
Error-checking tool, use	350	*See* Reference Window "Using the Error-Checking Tool to Check the File System on a Hard Disk Drive"
Event Viewer, use	491	*See* Reference Window "Using Event Viewer"
Extract files from Compressed (zipped) Folder	317	*See* Reference Window "Creating and Extracting a Compressed (Zipped) Folder"
File attributes, view	860	*See* Reference Window "Viewing File Attributes"
File properties, view	163	*See* Reference Window "Viewing Properties of Files"
File property, search by	180	*See* Reference Window "Searching Using a File Property, File Type, or Tags"
File Sharing Wizard, use	806	*See* Reference Window "Using the File Sharing Wizard"
File system, identify drive's	303	*See* Reference Window "Identifying a Drive's File System"
File tag, assign	181	*See* Reference Window "Assigning a Tag or Tags to a File"
File tag, search by	180	*See* Reference Window "Searching Using a File Property, File Type, or Tags"
File type, search by	180	*See* Reference Window "Searching Using a File Property, File Type, or Tags"
File, copy to folder using Send To menu	314	Right-click file, point to Send To, click drive or folder

TASK	PAGE #	RECOMMENDED METHOD
File, create a shortcut to	228	Right-click file, point to Send To, click Desktop (create shortcut)
Files and folders, back up	634	*See* Reference Window "Backing Up Files and Folders"
Files and folders, restore	644	*See* Reference Window "Restoring Files and Folders"
Files, copy	144	Select files, hold down Ctrl key as you drag the files to a location
Files, organize by groups and stacks	173	*See* Reference Window "Organizing Files by Groups and Stacks"
Files, use wildcards to copy	870	*See* Reference Window "Copying Files Using Wildcards"
Files, use Search Explorer to search for	190	*See* Reference Window "Using the Search Explorer"
Flash drive icon, customize	251	*See* Reference Window "Customizing a Flash Drive Icon"
Flash drive, check, assign, and remove volume label for	840	*See* Reference Window "Checking, Assigning, and Removing a Volume Label for a Flash Drive"
Flash drive, create shortcut to	217	*See* Reference Window "Creating a Shortcut to a Flash Drive"
Flip, use Windows	23	Press Alt+Tab
Flip 3D, activate Windows	24	Click [icon] on Quick Launch toolbar
Folder properties, view	164	*See* Reference Window "Viewing Properties of Folders"
Folder sharing, turn off	807	*See* Reference Window "Turning Off Sharing of a Folder"
Folder shortcut, create	222	Right-click folder, point to Send To, click Desktop (create shortcut)
Folder toolbar, create	107	*See* Reference Window "Creating a Folder Toolbar"
Folder, compress	313	*See* Reference Window "Compressing and Uncompressing a Folder"
Folder, copy	144	Select folder, hold down Ctrl key as you drag the folder to a location
Folder, create a shortcut to a	227	*See* Reference Window "Creating a Shortcut to a Folder and Customizing the Shortcut Icon"
Folder, decrypt	322	*See* Reference Window "Encrypting and Decrypting a Folder"
Folder, encrypt	322	*See* Reference Window "Encrypting and Decrypting a Folder"
Folder, select everything in	160	Press Ctrl+A
Folder, uncompress	313	*See* Reference Window "Compressing and Uncompressing a Folder"
Folders and files, back up	634	*See* Reference Window "Backing Up Files and Folders"
Folders and files, restore	644	*See* Reference Window "Restoring Files and Folders"
Fragmentation, analyze a disk for	369	*See* Reference Window "Producing a Fragmentation Analysis Report Using the Command-Line Defrag Utility"
Gadget, add to Windows Sidebar	29	*See* Reference Window "Adding Gadgets to the Windows Sidebar"
Group files	173	*See* Reference Window "Organizing Files by Groups and Stacks"
Hardware problems, use System Information to identify	788	*See* Reference Window "Using System Information to Identify Hardware Problems"
Help and Support Center, use	39	*See* Reference Window "Browsing Windows Help and Support"
Help and Support, browse	39	*See* Reference Window "Browsing Windows Help and Support"
Help and Support, search	40	*See* Reference Window "Searching Windows Help and Support"

TASK	PAGE #	RECOMMENDED METHOD
Help command, use	842	*See* Reference Window "Displaying a Command Reference List"
Help for a command, display	833	*See* Reference Window "Using the Help Switch to Display Help for a Command"
Help switch, use	833	*See* Reference Window "Using the Help Switch to Display Help for a Command"
Help, search	40	*See* Reference Window "Searching Windows Help and Support"
Icon, desktop, change and restore size of	23	*See* Reference Window "Changing and Restoring Desktop Icon Sizes"
Icon, customize flash drive	251	*See* Reference Window "Customizing a Flash Drive Icon"
Index settings, examine	195	*See* Reference Window "Examining Search and Index Settings"
Installed software, view	731	*See* Reference Window "Viewing Installed Software"
Internet Explorer security settings, check and change	463	*See* Reference Window "Checking Internet Explorer Security and Privacy Settings"
Internet Explorer without add-ons, open	456	Open All Programs menu, click Accessories, click System Tools, click Internet Explorer (No Add-ons)
Internet shortcut, create	257	*See* Reference Window "Creating an Internet Shortcut on the Desktop"
Interrupt command, use command-line	848	Press Ctrl+C to interrupt or cancel a command
Links, add and remove in Navigation pane	247	*See* Reference Window "Adding and Removing Links in the Navigation Pane"
Live Taskbar Thumbnail, display	25	Point to taskbar button
Local reboot, performing	519	*See* Reference Window "Using Task Manager to Shut Down a Nonresponding Program"
Make Directory command, use	862	*See* Reference Window "Creating a Directory"
Mapped drive, create and remove	812	*See* Reference Window "Creating and Removing a Mapped Drive"
Memory usage, evaluate	559	*See* Reference Window "Using Resource Overview to Evaluate Memory Usage and System Performance"
Microsoft Office components, adding or removing	743	*See* Reference Window "Adding or Removing Microsoft Office Components"
Name of computer, view	792	*See* Reference Window "Viewing a Computer's Name"
Navigation Pane, add and remove links in	247	*See* Reference Window "Adding and Removing Links in the Navigation Pane"
Navigation pane, use	51	*See* Reference Window "Navigating Your Computer"
Network and Sharing Center, use	801	*See* Reference Window "Using the Network and Sharing Center"
Nonresponding program, shut down	519	*See* Reference Window "Using Task Manager to Shut Down a Nonresponding Program"
Notification area, customize	102	*See* Reference Window "Customizing the Taskbar and Notification Area"
Office components, add or remove	743	*See* Reference Window "Adding or Removing Microsoft Office Components"
Paging file, locate and examine	549	*See* Reference Window "Locating and Examining the Paging File"

TASK	PAGE #	RECOMMENDED METHOD
Parent directory, change to the	860	*See* Reference Window "Changing to the Parent Directory"
Password Reset Disk, create	424	*See* Reference Window "Creating a Password Reset Disk"
Path command, use	873	*See* Reference Window "Viewing Settings for Environment Variables"
Performance options for applications, view and change	600	*See* Reference Window "Viewing Virtual Memory Settings"
Performance, use Resource Overview to monitor	559	*See* Reference Window "Using Resource Overview to Evaluate Memory Usage and System Performance"
Performance, using Windows Task Manager to monitor	555	*See* Reference Window "Using Task Manager to Monitor System Performance"
Pinned items list, remove item from	240	*See* Reference Window "Pinning and Unpinning Programs on the Start Menu"
Power management settings, checking	126	*See* Reference Window "Checking Power Management Settings"
Privacy settings, check and change	463	*See* Reference Window "Checking Internet Explorer Security and Privacy Settings"
Program compatibility settings, specify	732	Right-click program file, click Properties, click Compatibility tab, change compatibility settings, click OK
Program Compatibility Wizard, specify program compatibility settings with	737	*See* Reference Window "Using the Program Compatibility Wizard to Specify Program Compatibility Settings"
Program defaults and settings, specify	751	*See* Reference Window "Specifying Program Defaults and Settings"
Program, pin and unpin from Start menu	240	*See* Reference Window "Pinning and Unpinning Programs on the Start Menu"
Properties of devices, view	778	*See* Reference Window "Viewing Device Properties"
Properties of folders, view	164	*See* Reference Window "Viewing Properties of Folders"
Properties of folders or files, view	309	Select folder or file, press Alt+Enter
Quick Launch toolbar, display	102	Right-click taskbar, point to Toolbars, click Quick Launch
RAM in your computer, find total amount of	52	Click , right-click Computer, click Properties
Registered file types, view information on	906	*See* Reference Window "Tracing Information on Registered File Types"
Registry Editor, open	897	*See* Reference Window "Exporting Registry Settings"
Registry search, continue	903	Press the F3 key
Registry settings, export	897	*See* Reference Window "Exporting Registry Settings"
Reliability Monitor, use	483	*See* Reference Window "Using Reliability Monitor"
Rename folder or file	214	Select folder or file, press F2, type new name, press Enter
Resolution, change the screen	112	*See* Reference Window "Changing the Resolution"
Resource assignments, view	788	*See* Reference Window "Using System Information to Identify Hardware Problems"
Resource Overview, use to evaluate memory usage and system performance	559	*See* Reference Window "Using Resource Overview to Evaluate Memory Usage and System Performance"
Restore point, create manual	496	*See* Reference Window "Creating a Manual Restore Point"

TASK	PAGE #	RECOMMENDED METHOD
Restore point, undo	497	Click [Start button], right-click Computer, click Properties, click System Restore, click Undo System Restore, click Next, click Finish
Root directory, change to	849	*See* Reference Window "Changing to the Root Directory"
Safe mode, boot in	516	*See* Reference Window "Booting in Safe Mode"
Scan drive with Windows Defender	411	*See* Reference Window "Using Windows Defender to Scan a Drive"
Scan history, view	414	*See* Reference Window "Viewing Your Scan History"
Scheduled task, create	385	*See* Reference Window "Creating a Scheduled Task"
Scheduled task, delete	388	*See* Reference Window "Deleting a Scheduled Task"
Scheduled task, view and change settings for a	388	*See* Reference Window "Checking Settings for a Scheduled Task"
Screen, clear Command Prompt window	837	Type CLS and press the Enter key
Search Explorer, open	187	Press Windows Logo+F keys
Search Explorer, use	190	*See* Reference Window "Using the Search Explorer"
Search options, customize	196	*See* Reference Window "Customizing Search Options"
Search settings, examine	195	*See* Reference Window "Examining Search and Index Settings"
Set command, use	873	*See* Reference Window "Viewing Settings for Environment Variables"
Share folder, turn off	807	*See* Reference Window "Turning Off Sharing of a Folder"
Share folder, use advanced sharing	810	*See* Reference Window "Using Advanced Sharing to Share a Folder"
Shared resources, view workgroup	796	*See* Reference Window "Viewing Computers and Shared Resources in a Workgroup"
Shortcut icon, customize	227	*See* Reference Window "Creating a Shortcut to a Folder and Customizing the Shortcut Icon"
Shortcut properties, view	222	*See* Reference Window "Viewing Properties of a Shortcut"
Shortcut, add to Start menu	241	*See* Reference Window "Adding a Desktop Shortcut to the Start Menu"
Shortcut, add to startup folder	268	*See* Reference Window "Adding Shortcuts to Your Startup Folder"
Shortcut, create application	233	*See* Reference Window "Creating a Shortcut to an Application"
Shortcut, create e-mail	266	*See* Reference Window "Creating E-mail Shortcuts"
Shortcut, create from existing	235	*See* Reference Window "Creating a New Shortcut from an Existing Shortcut"
Shortcut, rename	223	Select a shortcut, press F2, type or edit name, press Enter
Shortcut, view properties of	222	*See* Reference Window "Viewing Properties of a Shortcut"
Shut Down Windows dialog box, open	60	Press Alt+F4
Sidebar, display Windows	26	Click [Sidebar icon] in notification area
Sidebar, add gadget to	29	*See* Reference Window "Adding Gadgets to the Windows Sidebar"
Single-click activation, enable	36	*See* Reference Window "Enabling Single-Click Activation"
Software Explorer, use	417	*See* Reference Window "Using Software Explorer"

TASK	PAGE #	RECOMMENDED METHOD
Software, uninstall	739	*See* Reference Window "Uninstalling Software"
Software, view installed	731	*See* Reference Window "Viewing Installed Software"
Special display effects, choose	89	*See* Reference Window "Choosing Special Display Effects"
Stack files	173	*See* Reference Window "Organizing Files by Groups and Stacks"
Start menu color, adjust	78	*See* Reference Window "Adjusting Window Frame, Start Menu, and Taskbar Colors"
Start menu, add Administrative Tools to	548	Right-click [Start button], click Properties, click Customize, under System administrative tools, click Display on the All Programs menu and the Start menu, click OK
Start menu, add desktop shortcut to	241	*See* Reference Window "Adding a Desktop Shortcut to the Start Menu"
Start menu, customize	98	*See* Reference Window "Customizing the Start Menu"
Start menu, use keyboard to open or close	33	Press Windows Logo key
Startup folder, add shortcuts to	268	*See* Reference Window "Adding Shortcuts to Your Startup Folder"
Startup, customize with shortcuts	268	*See* Reference Window "Adding Shortcuts to Your Startup Folder"
Subdirectory, view contents of	857	*See* Reference Window "Displaying a Directory Listing"
System Configuration, use	525	*See* Reference Window "Using System Configuration"
System Health report, create	565	*See* Reference Window "Creating a System Health Report"
System information, display	845	*See* Reference Window "Displaying System Information"
System Information, use	531	*See* Reference Window "Using System Information"
System Information, use to identify hardware problems	788	*See* Reference Window "Using System Information to Identify Hardware Problems"
System performance, evaluate with Resource Overview	559	*See* Reference Window "Using Resource Overview to Evaluate Memory Usage and System Performance"
System Protection settings, check	494	*See* Reference Window "Checking System Protection Settings"
System window, open	86	Press Windows Logo+Break keys
SystemInfo command, use	845	*See* Reference Window "Displaying System Information"
Tag, assign to file	181	*See* Reference Window "Assigning a Tag or Tags to a File"
Tag, search files by	180	*See* Reference Window "Searching Using a File Property, File Type, or Tags"
Taskbar color, adjust	78	*See* Reference Window "Adjusting Window Frame, Start Menu, and Taskbar Colors"
Taskbar, customize	102	*See* Reference Window "Customizing the Taskbar and Notification Area"
Task Manager, open	517	Press Ctrl+Alt+Del, click Start Task Manager
Task Manager, open	550	Press Ctrl+Shift+Esc
Task Manager, use	555	*See* Reference Window "Using Task Manager to Monitor System Performance"
Theme, choose desktop	75	*See* Reference Window "Choosing a Theme and Color Scheme"
Toolbar, create folder	107	*See* Reference Window "Creating a Folder Toolbar"
Tree command, use	848	*See* Reference Window "Displaying a Directory Tree"

TASK	PAGE #	RECOMMENDED METHOD
Uncompress folder and its contents	313	*See* Reference Window "Compressing and Uncompressing a Folder "
Undo task	247	Press Ctrl+Z
Unpin program from Start menu	240	*See* Reference Window "Pinning and Unpinning Programs on the Start Menu"
Upgrade Advisor, evaluate a computer with	707	*See* Reference Window "Evaluating a Computer with the Windows Vista Upgrade Advisor"
Upgrade Advisor, install	693	*See* Reference Window "Installing the Windows Vista Upgrade Advisor"
User interface elements, customize	81	*See* Reference Window "Customizing Elements of the User Interface"
Video display settings, check	117	*See* Reference Window "Checking Video Display Settings"
Volume label (flash drive), check, assign, and remove	840	*See* Reference Window "Checking, Assigning and Removing a Volume Label for a Flash Drive"
Wallpaper, choose background	93	*See* Reference Window "Choosing Desktop Backgrounds"
Web style, change to	36	*See* Reference Window "Enabling Single-Click Activation"
Wildcards, use	870	*See* Reference Window "Copying Files Using Wildcards"
Window frame color, adjust	78	*See* Reference Window "Adjusting Window Frame, Start Menu, and Taskbar Colors"
Windows, minimize all	26	Click [icon] on Quick Launch toolbar
Windows Defender settings, examine	419	*See* Reference Window "Examining Windows Defender Settings"
Windows Defender, use to scan drive	411	*See* Reference Window "Using Windows Defender to Scan a Drive"
Windows edition, find	52	Click [icon], right-click Computer, click Properties
Windows environment, view	873	*See* Reference Window "Viewing Settings for Environment Variables"
Windows features, turn on and off	726	*See* Reference Window "Turning Windows Features On and Off"
Windows Firewall, view and change settings	430	*See* Reference Window "Viewing and Changing Windows Firewall Settings"
Windows Help and Support, browse	39	*See* Reference Window "Browsing Windows Help and Support"
Windows Help and Support, search	40	*See* Reference Window "Searching Windows Help and Support"
Windows Sidebar, display	26	Click [icon] in notification area
Windows Sidebar, add gadget to	29	*See* Reference Window "Adding Gadgets to the Windows Sidebar"
Windows Update history and settings, check	439	*See* Reference Window "Checking Your Windows Update History and Settings"
Windows Update, use	435	*See* Reference Window "Using Windows Update"
Windows Vista Upgrade Advisor, evaluate computer with	707	*See* Reference Window "Evaluating a Computer with the Windows Vista Upgrade Advisor"
Windows Vista Upgrade Advisor, install	693	*See* Reference Window "Installing the Windows Vista Upgrade Advisor"
Workgroup, view computers and shared resources in	796	*See* Reference Window "Viewing Computers and Shared Resources in a Workgroup"